Military Register of Custer's Last Command

Military Register of Custer's Last Command

by
Roger L. Williams

UNIVERSITY OF OKLAHOMA PRESS
Norman

Page 5 illustration: from photograph of author's mother during family vacation to Custer Battlefield, 1952.

Page 27 illustration: white marble markers and monument on site of Custer's last stand. Detail of photograph by Christian Barthelmess, ca. 1896. Courtesy of Montana Historical Society (Robert C. Morrison Collection).

Library of Congress Cataloging-in-Publication Data

Williams, Roger L., 1937–
 Military register of Custer's last command / by Roger L. Williams.
  p. cm. — (Hidden springs of Custeriana ; 14)
 Includes bibliographical references.
 ISBN 978-0-87062-368-4
 ISBN 978-0-8061-4274-6 (paper)
 1. Little Bighorn, Battle of the, Mont., 1876. 2. United States. Army. Cavalry, 7th—Registers. 3. Little Bighorn, Battle of the, Mont., 1876—Casualties. 4. Soldiers—Montana—Registers. 5. Indian scouts—Montana—Registers. 6. Civilians in war—Montana—Registers. 7. Registers of births, etc.—Montana. I. Title. II. Series.

E83.876.W486 2009
973.8'2—dc22

2009009872

The paper in this book meets the guidelines for permanence and durability of the Committee on Production Guidelines for Book Longevity of the Council on Library Resources, Inc. ∞

Originally published by the Arthur H. Clark Company copyright © 2009 by Roger L. Williams. Paperback edition published 2012 by the University of Oklahoma Press, Norman, Publishing Division of the University. Manufactured in the U.S.A.

All rights reserved. No part of this publication may be reproduced, stored in a retrieval system, or transmitted, in any form or by any means, electronic, mechanical, photocopying, recording, or otherwise—except as permitted under Section 107 or 108 of the United States Copyright Act—without the prior permission of the University of Oklahoma Press.

To my parents,
whose encouragement,
unpronounced,
contributed nobly
to the foundation
of this book

And let us not grow weary in well doing; for in due season we shall reap, if we faint not.

Galatians 6:9

Contents

Preface	9
Acknowledgments	13
Introduction	15
Abbreviations	23
Sketches A–Z	27
Indian Scouts	323
Addendum	345
Appendix A	
Table A.1. Tabulation of Enlisted Men	348
7th Cavalry Rosters, June 1876	349
Roster of Lt. Varnum's Detachment of Indian Scouts	363
Wounded June 25–26, 1876	365
List of Civilians	366
Appendix B: Recapitulations of Enlisted Men and Horses	367
Appendix C: Research Notes and Minutiae	387
Appendix D: Rates of Pay in the U.S. Cavalry, 1876	397
Bibliography	399

Preface

The idea for this book originated in the summer of 1962, during a visit to what was then called the Custer Battlefield National Monument. The seeds, however, had been sown more than fourteen summers earlier on the South Side of Chicago, beginning one morning at the old Perkins Bass Public School, during library class. As I sat browsing through a large volume of *The World Book Encyclopedia*,[1] my gaze was drawn suddenly to a small photo of white markers scattered on a grassy hillside, described as the scene of "Custer's last stand." The caption's statement that General Custer's entire command of 208 men was killed in twenty minutes struck me as incredible and stirred my near-dormant intellect to learn more about the battle.

Pointing to the reference, I queried our ever helpful library teacher, Mrs. Forsyth, who promptly produced a copy of *Custer, Fighter of the Plains*,[2] a popular children's book enhanced with excellent illustrations. The artistic renderings were so impressive that I soon acquired my own copy of the book, which proved the genesis of an extensive library on the subject of the Battle of the Little Big Horn.

At about that same time, another seed was sown when a large, brightly colored picture appeared in the window of the corner tavern I passed each school day. Upon a closer perusal I was awed by the famous Anheuser-Busch painting *Custer's Last Fight*, longtime fixture in dramshops across America. The huge framed lithograph stood aglow in rays of morning sunlight, and the eye level for the ten-year-old face that pressed to the glass, virtually absorbing the near-panoramic battle scene.[3]

My rapture must have been fully recounted, for a few weeks later, upon hurrying home for the noontime snack awaiting, I was greeted by the biggest surprise of my young life. As I bounded from the front door to the kitchen, zipping past the dining-room archway on the right, I glimpsed a large object on the far wall, directly above my small desk in the corner of the room. Taking a step back to peer in, lo and behold,

---

1. *World Book Encyclopedia*, vol. 3 (C) (Chicago: Quarrie, 1946).
2. Garst, *Custer, Fighter of the Plains*, illustrated by Harve Stein.
3. For a history of the popular painting, see Carroll, "Anheuser Busch and Custer's Last Stand"; Russell, "906 Custer's Last Fight Pictures"; Graham, *The Story of the Little Big Horn*, xi.

Preface

'twas an exact replica of the Custer battle lithograph, delivered just that morning from the Budweiser Company.

From that day, time at my desk was often spent staring upward, studying every detail of the grand painting, and because so few soldiers were depicted, I wondered about scenes on other parts of the field, and how many soldiers there were. To find the answer I went to the neighborhood libraries, only to learn the same number rarely appeared twice. Bewildered by the inconsistency, I decided greater resources were needed, and—after convincing my brother Dick, two years my elder (to the day), to accompany me—I ventured downtown early on Saturday to the largest public library in the city. The exercise was repeated a week later to the renowned Newberry Library on the near northside. Each time my disappointment was tempered by the thrill of the long trolley-car ride home, my other fancy in those days (my brother's too) ever since our dad became a motorman on the cars.

As my "Custer project" slowly took root, inspiration most timely was provided by the movie mills of Hollywood. In the course of three years, Argosy Pictures produced a trilogy of classic films of the U.S. Cavalry: *Fort Apache, She Wore a Yellow Ribbon,* and *Rio Grande,* all in rugged outdoor style by the legendary director John Ford.

She Wore a Yellow Ribbon, with its appealing title song, was released in the autumn of 1949, not long after my family had begun a year-long sojourn in Denver, Colorado. Actually, the first few months were spent in suburban Englewood, where I soon boarded a yellow No. 3 trolley bound for the Civic Center and the main public library of the Mile High City. My expectation that a "western" library would have more on my favorite subject was fully met when rosters of Custer's entire 7th Cavalry regiment (the first ever published) were found in a small hardcover book of little more than a hundred pages: *Keogh, Comanche and Custer*, the author none other than Edward S. Luce, then superintendent of Custer Battlefield.[4]

Eager for my own copy of the "official" rosters, I resorted to the neatest method, the family typewriter, and within a few days successfully pecked duplicates of every page bearing the names of Custer's 7th Cavalrymen. To my dismay, analysis of the rosters showed that 630 enlisted men participated in the battle, whereas the combined total of the regiment's four detachments on the day of the fight, cited in numerous writings, indicated fewer than 580 (with nearly half the difference, glaringly, in B Troop alone).[5]

---

4. Luce was superintendent of Custer Battlefield from 1941 to 1956. Although his rosters contain some errors, the book is a valuable contribution to the study of the battle. Updated rosters were published by Chandler in *Of Garry Owen in Glory*, 429–39.

5. Captain McDougall several times said his troop had about forty-five men at the battle. However, the first published rosters showed Company B with sixty-six men, not listing anyone left at Powder River. A review of the muster roll at the National Archives found nineteen B men detached at the supply camp.

Preface

The disparities loomed larger than ever, and when my letters to Custer Battlefield inquiring for the correct numbers yielded no definitive answer, I resolved to someday unravel the tangle of statistical minutiae. But as more youthful pursuits arose, even before my first trip to the battlefield in 1952, the urgency of my quest diminished.

Several years passed before I again set foot in the downtown library, curious to learn of any new "Custer books." Foremost among the new works was *The Custer Myth*, an impressive tome compiled by Col. William A. Graham, which included a list of the names on the famous "Reno Petition." A linchpin in this study, the document was signed by most of the surviving enlisted men on July 4, 1876, calling for the promotion of Major Reno and Captain Benteen. Graham's statement that the 235 signers represented approximately 80 percent of the survivors of Major Reno's command renewed my faith that the total number must be written somewhere.[6]

The notion called out especially from Graham's references to Walter Camp (first historian of the battle), who during the early 1900s interviewed many of the actual participants. His papers, I reasoned, likely held the answers to many questions about the fight. But alas, to my great disappointment in the years following this revelation, nary a word did I find of the whereabouts of the Camp material, or whether it even still existed, only vague rumors.

Then in November 1968, my prayers were answered when I learned the famous "Camp Notes" were at the Lilly Library of Indiana University. Within a fortnight I drove in darkness the two hundred plus miles from Chicago to Bloomington, timing my arrival with the opening of the library doors early the next morning. The entire day was spent intently examining the notes, all handwritten in pencil, many on mere pieces and scraps of paper of every description, and all contained in over eighty small, formerly white envelopes. Fortunately, the handwriting became quite legible.

I was astonished to learn that many of Camp's concerns mirrored my own, particularly with regard to the number of troopers in Companies E and F and whether or not Pvt. Hobart Ryder was on the steamer *Far West* at the time of the battle. The former question I had pondered many times during the previous eighteen years, while the latter had emerged more recently from a review of the field orders of the Department of Dakota.

During the next twenty-three years, other large caches of Camp's research material came to light, scattered across the land, and each time I went forth—to Brigham Young University in 1971, Denver Public Library in 1975, Custer battlefield in 1986, and again the Denver library in 1991.

Smaller portions of Camp correspondence and memoranda I found in various other collections, notably the General Godfrey Papers at the Library of Congress, the General William Carey Brown Papers at the University of Colorado, and the Robert

---

6. Graham, *The Custer Myth*, 283–85. The list of names is also the subject of Gray, "The Reno Petition."

Preface

S. Ellison Collections at Indiana and Brigham Young universities, also a few letters in the Elizabeth Custer collection at the battlefield and in the papers of Col. Charles F. Bates at Yale University.[7]

Some of Camp's earliest correspondence (1908–10) to the adjutant general in Washington, I found at the National Archives. Camp indicated he had been studying the Custer battle since 1903 with a view to writing a complete history of the campaign, and had spoken to several officers of the 7th Cavalry retired. By early 1910 he was permitted to review the regimental muster rolls at the office of the auditor of the army, and at Fort Riley, also the monthly troop reports at the latter place. He requested, if not contrary to regulations, to be furnished the addresses of certain enlisted men formerly of the 7th Cavalry in 1876 and, if deceased, the dates of same. The majority of the names Camp listed were survivors of the five troops that fell with Custer.[8]

Camp declared in 1909 that his study of the Little Big Horn campaign had begun fifteen years earlier in leisure time, not as a business enterprise. He became more actively engaged by 1903 and, during the next eleven years, traveled by team and on horseback over a large part of Montana, North Dakota, South Dakota, and Wyoming.[9]

In 1918 he related that his history studies in the West since 1903 had cost him each year $150 to $200 for railroad fares, stage fares, livery hire, and other travel expenses—all he could afford from his salary. He recalled in 1921 that he had traveled all over the plains for the past twenty-one years and had devoted nineteen summer vacations following his historical interests.[10]

Truly, the pioneering efforts of Walter Camp made this present work possible, representing more than one lifetime of research to learn who was where, when, and why, on June 25, 1876. And just as Camp told General Godfrey in 1919, I too can say: "I am much fascinated by that sort of study, and am glad I did not yield to the temptation to 'rush into print' years ago . . . for I have learned a 'heap' by keeping persistently at the thing."[11]

I might add, though, that determining with certainty the exact status of many troopers, in the absence of pertinent records no longer extant, has proven an insurmountable task. The following pages bear testimony of that lesson learned and are now that book envisioned, and so earnestly sought, long ago.

Roger Lester Williams

---

7. For a history of the Walter Camp material, see Liddic and Harbaugh, *Camp on Custer*, 13–28; and Hardorff, *Camp, Custer, and the Little Big Horn*, 11–33.

8. RG 94, Entry 25, file 510468 R & P 1898 (Custer Massacre).

9. Camp to James Flanagan, Sept. 28, 1909; Camp to Elizabeth B. Custer, Dec. 18, 1912; Camp to Peter Thompson, July 7, 1914, WMC-LBHB.

10. Camp to Elizabeth B. Custer, Oct. 31, 1917, WMC-LBHB. Camp to Gen. Anson Mills, Apr. 14, 1918; Camp to H. H. Larned, Aug. 16, 1921, WMC-BYU.

11. Camp to Godfrey, Nov. 13, 1919, Godfrey Papers, LOC. Walter Camp was editor of *The Railway Review* in Chicago from 1897 until his death, August 3, 1925, at age fifty-eight.

Acknowledgments

During the many years spent gathering material for this work, I amassed a huge debt of gratitude to many individuals, beginning with the distinguished Custer battle authority Dr. Kenneth Hammer, who pointed me in the right direction. As a result of that kindness, foremost appreciation is due the staff of the Military Reference Branch of our National Archives: Bill Lind, Mike Meier, and Mike Pilgrim; also Tod Butler, Stuart L. Butler, Bob Matchette, DeAnne Blanton, Gary Morgan, Mike Musick; and away back in the very beginning, to Milton Chamberlain, Sara Jackson, and Elmer O. Parker. Thanks also to Bill Sherman of the Judicial Branch of the Archives for his vast knowledge of military fiscal records; and to John Vandereedt out at Archives II for his valuable assistance upon my discovery in 2005 of the pay accounts of Major William Smith, paymaster for the 7th Cavalry in 1876.[1]

Likewise I am indebted to the staff of Little Big Horn Battlefield, particularly Neil Mangum, former Chief Historian and Superintendent, for many courtesies extended, and to his successors Doug McChristian and John Doerner. Also to Miss Kitty Deernose, Museum Curator, for her diligence and ingenuity assembling important primary documents.

I am grateful to Carl Katafiasz of the Monroe County Library System and to George Miles of the Beinecke Library of Yale University for their resourcefulness with important papers; and to various staff members of the state historical societies of Minnesota, Montana, and Dakota (North and South).

And, the truth be known, there would have been no satisfactory conclusion to this project were it not for a cadre of private researchers and genealogists, the majority in the Washington, D.C., area, whose frequent visits on my behalf to the National Archives brought to light many primary records containing important details and dates that might otherwise have been excluded from this work. Thank you, John Bowen, Sharon Crandall, Dan Fantore, Norma Gransee, Charles S. Mason, Jr., Susan N. Molye, Ellen Rafferty, Ed Schott, Pamela Taylor, Marilyn Vineyard, and Noelle Yetter. Particular

---

1. RG 217 (UD), Entry 530, Records of the Accounting Officers of the Department of the Treasury, NARA. Hereafter records in the National Archives are cited by record group (RG) number, followed by the entry number in the inventory describing the content of that series. The bibliography includes a brief description of material cited from the National Archives.

Acknowledgments

thanks are due Sharon Hodges and Alice Evans for their untiring efforts to seek out desired materials.

I am also grateful to Adrienne Stepanek, genealogist extraordinaire of Williston, North Dakota; and the same may be said of Christine Dierks of Pierre, South Dakota, and of Lilah Morton Pengra in Buffalo Gap, South Dakota.

In addition I must acknowledge assistance from Vernon Ashley, Rosalind L. Ashmun, Arlene Baker, Bill Boyes, Eileen Chandler, Paul Connor, Sr., Elizabeth Blair Douglas, Charles G. duBois, Robert J. Ege, Chad Flake, Lawrence A. Frost, Eleanor M. Gehres, Dr. John S. Gray, Ann B. Hambrecht, Patricia Hammer, Faye Hilton, Marian Pries Hintermeister, Adrain Krusee, Elfrieda Lang, A. Dean Larsen, Shirley Leckie, Bruce Liddic, Robert B. MacLaine, Sr., John S. Manion, A. D. Mastrogiuseppe, Chuck Merkel, Brian Pohanka, Margaret Rose, Dennis Rowley, Dennis Sanders, Bill Shemorry, John J. Slonaker, John Trowbridge, Rev. Garford F. Williams, and to Fritz Stein (son of nationally acclaimed illustrator Harve Stein).

To those omitted here—and there are many—I offer my sincerest apology and, due to the long duration of this complex project, the plea of a now aged memory.

Introduction

This annotated study of the last command of General George A. Custer is the culmination of decades of research to learn the battle strength of the 7th Cavalry on June 25, 1876. The data, culled largely from official military records deposited in the National Archives in Washington, D.C., is complemented by the pioneering work of Walter Mason Camp, first historian of the Custer battle.

Primary source material presented herein includes an outline of the military career of each 7th Cavalryman on the regimental roll in June 1876, with several newly discovered names; the date and place each man joined the regiment; all known pension file numbers; personal file numbers of each commissioned officer; new details from the career of General Custer; new information on the African American interpreter Isaiah Dorman, the veterinary surgeon Charles A. Stein, and numerous other individuals with the command, including the somewhat enigmatic citizen packers employed with the expedition.

Great care has also been taken to provide details for many of the men during the popular and more studied campaigns of the regiment, with further amplification devoted to the whereabouts of each trooper in June 1876.

The appendices, too, contain ample fresh data, featuring a tabulation of enlisted men at the time of the action at the Little Big Horn; tables of statistics for each troop, transcribed from regimental and troop returns and muster rolls, with notes added relating to each unit; and a table of pay rates in the cavalry service in 1876. In early 1881, the term "Troop," used unofficially for many years prior, replaced "Company" on the Returns and Muster Rolls of the 7th Cavalry.

In the regimental rosters reproduced here, an asterisk before a man's name indicates that evidence affirms, or nearly so, that he did not participate in the battle. A sword (†) after a name means that the soldier's signature appears on the "Reno Petition," the document calling for the promotion of Major Reno and Captain Benteen and signed by most of the surviving enlisted men on July 4, 1876.[1] The names on the petition were published in Col. William A. Graham's *The Custer Myth*, and Graham's statement that

---

1. The petition was believed to have originated at Major Reno's headquarters, whence it was circulated by the chief trumpeter and signed by most of the men rather than give offense by their refusing. Taylor, *With Custer on the Little Big Horn*, 119. See also duBois, "The Case of the Perfidious Petition," in *Kick the Dead Lion*, 47–59.

The petition's six pages of penciled signatures became file 3984 ACP 1876, in RG 94, Entry 297, at the National Archives, and were subsequently transferred to the Treasury Room (TR-126), repository of fragile and important documents.

Introduction

the 235 signers were about 80 percent of the survivors of Major Reno's command sparked the renewal of my quest to learn the actual total.[2] However, that number remained elusive until the publication of the little-known field diary of General Terry. Therein, on a page crowded with text near the back of the small journal, beneath a list of 7th Cavalry officers living and killed, Terry added, "Remaining men wounded and unwounded 329 Wounded about 40."[3] I recalled the number from a newspaper dispatch of 1876, but owing to the presumption that such details in the press were often unreliable, I had given it little credence.[4]

I also recalled, from the myriad of newspaper columns reporting on the campaign, a letter dated June 29, 1876, Mouth of Little Horn River, and allegedly bearing the signature of Lieut. John Carland, Co. B, 6th Inf. (on steamer *Far West*), relating, "Out of the whole regiment only 328 men are left and forty of them are badly wounded."[5]

General Terry reiterated his number elsewhere in his journal, probably about mid-July, when he tallied the strength of each regiment then represented, or soon to be, with his command.[6] The 7th Cavalry he numbered at 275, apparently all that remained after the transfer of the 40 seriously wounded men to Fort Lincoln on July 3, and reflecting the anticipated early discharge of another dozen battle survivors (13 if including Hunter of Company F), whose term of service expired by the 15th of September.[7]

---

2. Graham, *The Custer Myth*, 283–85. See also Gray, "The Reno Petition."
3. Koury, *The Field Diary of General Alfred H. Terry*, 35. The original Terry journal is in the Manuscript Division of the Library of Congress.
4. Dispatch, "Sioux Expedition, Mouth of the Big Horn, July 1, Via Bismarck, D. T., July 6, 1876." *Saint Paul Dispatch*, July 7, 1876; *St. Paul and Minneapolis Pioneer Press and Tribune*, July 7, 1876; *New York Herald*, July 8, 1876.
5. *New York Herald*, July 14, 1876; *Detroit Free Press*, July 14, 1876, reprinted as "The Massacre of Custer, Description of a Michigan Soldier Who Saw the Field of Battle," *Big Horn-Yellowstone Journal*, Vol. 1, No. 4, Autumn 1992. The author of the letter was actually Willis Ward Carland (son of Lieutenant Carland), employed as a herder in the subsistence department of the expedition, who said he was in charge of five or six steers on the boat at the mouth of the Little Big Horn. Willis claimed: "In July '76 I wrote a romantic falsehood to a little newspaper in Michigan describing [General] Terry standing over the body [of] dead Custer tears coursing down his cheeks as he said, 'The flower of the Army is gone at last'—drivel like that. I signed my own name. The New York Herald copied it, but probably examining the blue book found father's name, as in the Herald reproduction it appeared as from John Carland. A month or so, copy of Herald came to one of the officers and father saw it, suspecting me." Willis W. Carland to William J. Ghent, nd.

It is interesting to speculate whether young Carland took the liberty to subtract from the count of 329 survivors the one wounded man, Corporal King, who died on the boat before the departure to Fort Lincoln. The Ghent Papers at the Library of Congress include several letters from Carland, most dated 1934.

6. On July 15, General Terry received dispatches from Gen. Sheridan informing him that six companies of the 5th Infantry and six companies of the 22d Infantry would soon join his command. (Terry's count for these two regiments reflect an average of forty men per company.) Presumably he used the same formula for Major Moore's command at Powder River, which he tallied at 470 men (five companies of infantry, plus 130 men of the 7th Cavalry and 140 citizen employees of the quartermaster department). Stewart and Stewart, *The Field Diary of Lt. Edward Settle Godfrey*, 24 (hereafter cited as Godfrey Diary). Koury, *The Field Diary of General Alfred H. Terry*, 28, 34–35.
7. Special Field Order No. 37, Hq Dept. of Dakota, In the Field, Aug. 5, 1876, directed the discharge of sixteen 7th Cavalrymen under the provisions of General Order No. 24, Adjutant General's Office, 1859. (See "Sketches," Wm. G. Abrams, note 7.

Introduction

Of course, the mystery would not exist but for the failure of Companies E and F to name anyone left at the Powder River supply camp. Walter Camp, whose name appears throughout this volume, expended considerable energy investigating the issue after the adjutant general informed him in 1910 that no detachment rolls or separate returns were furnished that office in the case of Companies E and F, and no records were found among the discontinued commands pertaining to the supply camp at Powder River.[8]

The strength of the 7th Cavalry at the Little Big Horn has often been debated. The number of enlisted men is generally believed to have been 585, though no reference thereto has ever included the source of that information.[9] During more than two score and ten plus years of pertinacious research into the many issues of the battle, I have learned the number first appeared in a lengthy dispatch dated "Custer's Battle Field, Little Horn, June 28, Via Bismarck, D. T., July 6, 1876," which states, "There were in Custer's regiment when he went into battle 585 men and twenty-six officers."[10]

Also, a piece of Indian parchment found on the battlefield by Billy Logan, son of Capt. Will Logan, Co. A, 7th Inf. (with Colonel Gibbon's command), was allegedly used by Logan's company clerk to list the battle statistics of the 7th Cavalry, including the number of enlisted men going into action—585. A related statement furnished the *Bozeman Times* described the parchment as a finely finished piece of elk skin and a specimen of the art and ingenuity of the Sioux, equal to the best of English manufacture.[11]

Pvt. Geant recorded July 16 at the camp at mouth of Big Horn River that twenty men whose time expired within the 15th of August were discharged and departed on the steamer *Josephine*. Journal of Pvt. Eugene Geant, Co. H, 7th Inf. (copy in Walter Camp notes, env. 122, BYU). SFO 27, DD, July 14, 1876, designated ten 7th Infantrymen to be discharged in accord with GO 24, AGO, 1859. Nine others were discharged in SFO 35, DD, Aug. 2, 1876.

8. Fred C. Ainsworth, Adjutant General, to Walter Camp, Mar. 17, 1910, WMC-LBHB.

9. *Contributions to the Historical Society of Montana*, Vol. 2 (1896), 225; Hanson, *The Conquest of the Missouri*, 265; Wheeler, *Buffalo Days*, 172; Stewart, *Custer's Luck*, 245.

10. *New York Herald*, July 8, 1876. Though unsigned, the dispatch has been credited to Major Brisbin, 2d Cav. Clement Lounsberry, editor of the *Bismarck Tribune*, said Brisbin forwarded to him the manuscript found in Mark Kellogg's haversack, written up to an hour before Custer's fatal charge, and for two days after the arrival of the steamer *Far West*, every word of news that went out over the telegraph line from Bismarck was from his pen or under Brisbin's direction. Brisbin's copious notes made on the battlefield were also put on the wires. Lounsberry interviewed Captain Smith (of General Terry's staff), Dr. Porter, Grant Marsh, and others who came down on the *Far West*, and obtained full lists of the dead and wounded. The mass of matter made fourteen columns in the *New York Herald*, which is said to have paid in telegraph tolls the sum of $3,000. Major Brisbin received $500, the daughters of Mark Kellogg $2,000, and Lounsberry a liberal compensation. C. A. Lounsberry, ed., "The Custers at Home," *The Record* (Fargo, N.D.), Vol. 1, No. 4, August 1895. Walter Camp to Lounsberry, Sept. 19, 1911, and Lounsberry to Camp, Oct. 16, 1911, WMC-BYU.

Gen. Owen J. Sweet, whom Brisbin assisted in placing the marble markers on the battlefield in 1890, said Brisbin gathered up the notes and data found near the remains of Mark Kellogg (in 1876) and made the first reports of the fight to the press. Sweet to Walter Camp, Nov. 24, 1912, WMC-LBHB. See Knight, *Following the Indian Wars*, 214–16; Barnard, *I Go with Custer*, 132–33. Also see note accompanying Walter Camp interview with William R. Logan[, Jr.], n.d., WMC-BYU.

11. *Bozeman Times*, July 27, 1876. William R. Logan [Jr.], age seventeen, was employed with Col. Gibbon's column, April 21, 1876, as a messenger at $50 pay (job). RG 92, Entry 238, Supplemental Report, 1876/240, Lieutenant Jacobs, 7th Inf., acting assistant quartermaster. Billy Logan also served as mail carrier for the command. Johnson,

Introduction

The number 585 likely represents only men present with their troop (excluding Sharrow and Voss) and is consistent with the 717 enlisted men known to have departed with the regiment from Fort Lincoln, and with the report of Dr. Elbert J. Clark that there were "about one hundred and thirty cavalrymen (detachment of the 7th Cavalry)" at the supply camp on Powder River.[12]

Lieut. Winfield S. Edgerly said the regiment numbered "less than six hundred men" when it left the Yellowstone,[13] while Lieut. Charles A. Varnum said General Custer started up the Rosebud with the entire regiment, numbering about 605 strong, plus his detachment of 36 scouts, guides, and interpreters.[14] Major James S. Brisbin, who commanded the battalion of 2d Cavalry with Colonel Gibbon's command, wrote to Captain Godfrey on Jan. 1, 1892, "From mouth of the Rosebud, [General] Terry . . . turned his wild man loose, with the lives of 650 precious men in his hands."[15]

Thus, adding the number killed in action to the count reported saved with Reno demonstrates that the enlisted strength of the regiment upon starting up the Rosebud June 22 was probably no more than 566, while about 20 others likely remained behind with General Terry or on the steamer *Far West*.

Sgt. James E. Wilson of the Engineers, who was on the *Far West* from June 24 to 29, reported the boat's escort consisted of Co. B, 6th Infantry (38 enlisted men), commanded by Capt. Stephen Baker and Lt. John Carland, to which were attached some soldiers left in charge of property belonging to the absent portion of the command. A few sick men in the care of Hospital Steward Dale occupied the rear portion of the cabin-deck. These, with 1st Class Pvt. Culligan of the engineer detachment, made up the total commissioned and enlisted on board; the whole force, including armed civilians, did not exceed 60 men.[16]

"With Gibbon against the Sioux in 1876: The Field Diary of Lieut. William L. English," (7th Inf.), *The English Westerners' Brand Book*, Vol. 9, No. 1, Oct. 1966.

Logan served as the first superintendent of Glacier National Park from 1910 until his death two years later. An undated story purportedly related by Logan is found in Coburn, "The Battle of the Little Big Horn." Capt. William Logan, 7th Inf., was killed Aug. 9, 1877, in action with Nez Perce Indians at Big Hole Pass, Montana.

A facsimile of the data on the Logan parchment was published with the journal of Lieut. James H. Bradley, 7th Inf., who commanded the detachment of Indian scouts with Colonel Gibbon's command. *Contributions to the Historical Society of Montana*, Vol. 2 (1896), reprinted in Stewart, *The March of the Montana Column*, 164.

The same numbers were reported in the *Saint Paul and Minneapolis Pioneer-Press and Tribune*, Aug. 13, 1876.

12. RG 94, Entry 561, Monthly Report of Dr. Elbert J. Clark, Acting Assistant Surgeon, July 31, 1876. Dr. Clark had charge of the field hospital at Powder River from June 15 to July 21.

13. Article written by Edgerly at Fort Clark, Texas, between 1892 and 1895. In an unpublished reply to an article by Col. Robert P. Hughes (of Gen. Terry's staff) published in the *Journal of the Military Service Institution*, Jan. 1896, General Miles referred to the Edgerly paper as having been "read before the officers at Fort Clark." Mrs. Edgerly loaned the manuscript to Col. Charles Francis Bates in 1933, and three typescript copies were made—one each to Colonel Bates, William J. Ghent, and Dr. Francis R. Hagner.

14. Letter from Lieutenant Varnum to his parents, July 4, 1876, published in the Lowell, Mass., *Weekly Journal*, August, 1876. See Graham, *The Custer Myth*, 342.

15. Brininstool, *Troopers with Custer*, 280.

16. Report to Chief Engineer, Department of Dakota, Jan. 3, 1877, in *Annual Report of the Secretary of War, 1877*, Appendix PP

Introduction

Format of Entries in the Register

All names are arranged alphabetically, followed by rank and unit; date and/or place of birth; personal memoranda and Civil War service, if known; enlistment date, place, and term; age; occupation; physical description; chronological outline of military career; and subsequent data if available. For those 7th Cavalrymen with naval service, records of ships [in brackets] are from the *Dictionary of American Naval Fighting Ships*, an eight-volume series published by the Navy Department between 1959 and 1981. Names of Indian scouts in bold print are from official records, primarily the detachment muster roll of Lieutenant Varnum, April 30–June 30, 1876;[17] other Indian scout names and translations are from the interviews conducted by Walter Camp and by Dr. Orin G. Libby.[18]

Immediately following many sketches, in smaller print, is pension file information for that soldier: date of claim, or filing/class/application (claim) number/certificate number (if claim approved); important information appertaining thereto; and subsequent claims.

Following the sketch of each commissioned officer [in brackets] is his personal file number, which in several cases precedes his pension file data. "XC" file numbers are from the project started in 1934 by the Veterans Administration for flat filing all active claim files. The new series was originally established for the filing of World War I compensation claims but was expanded to include active claim files from the Mexican War, Indian wars, and Navy series and certain blocks of both active and inactive files in the Civil War and later series. The claims were designated by the letters *C* and *XC*, the *X* added upon death of the claimant.

A Word about Pensions

The first United States Congress, recognizing an obligation to give financial aid to Revolutionary War veterans and their dependents, passed an act on September 29, 1789, providing for the payment of military pensions. This was only the first of a long series of pension laws. The act of July 14, 1862, allowed for pension claims based on death or disability incurred while in military service after March 4, 1861. Pertaining to the army and navy, including regulars, volunteers, and militia, and to the Marine Corps, it applied

---

17. RG 94, Entry 53, Muster Rolls of Regular Army Organizations, 1784-1912. RG 393, Part V, Fort A. Lincoln, D. T., Detachment of Indian Scouts Descriptive Book, 1876–1878.

18. Hammer, *Custer in '76,* 155–94; Liddic and Harbaugh, *Camp on Custer,* 127–32; Hardorff, *Camp, Custer, and the Little Big Horn,* 49–60.

The interviews by Dr. Libby were published as volume 6 of the North Dakota Historical Collections, entitled *The Arikara Narrative of the Campaign against the Hostile Dakotas, June 1876*. Walter Camp told General Godfrey that Libby got the idea to interview the scouts after he (Camp) had visited five years in succession and interviewed nine of the eleven 'Ree scouts. Camp to Godfrey, Jan. 14, 1918, Godfrey Papers, LOC.

not only to the Civil War but to all future wars in which the United States became engaged. The system of benefits provided by this act came to be known as the general law pension system and was the only pension system in effect for Civil War survivors and their dependents until passage of the act of June 27, 1890. According to the 1890 law, a Civil War veteran could apply for a pension upon submission of proof of ninety or more days of service and an honorable discharge, together with a statement of disability. The origin of the disability did not affect the claim except when caused by vicious habits. Under this law the widow and dependent children of a veteran with ninety or more days of service and an honorable discharge were entitled to a pension regardless of the cause of the veteran's death. Later acts provided greater benefits for Civil War veterans and their widows and dependents.

The act approved July 27, 1892, provided that pensions should be paid to surviving officers and enlisted men who had been in the army or naval service for thirty days or longer in certain Indian wars between the years 1832 and 1842 and had been honorably discharged. The act also authorized pensions for the surviving widows of such men. This act was the first to grant ordinary service pensions for veterans of any of the Indian wars, though provisions had been made under earlier acts for the pensioning of persons disabled during such service and for the widows and orphans of those killed in such wars. The provisions of this act were extended to cover veterans of specified Indian wars between the years 1817 and 1858 by an act approved June 27, 1902; veterans (survivors) of certain Indian wars between 1859 and 1891 by an act approved March 4, 1917; and finally, those who had served in any Indian war or campaign between January 1, 1817, and December 31, 1898, by an act approved March 3, 1927.[19]

Benefits for veterans were for many years administered by the Bureau of Pensions of the Department of the Interior. In September 1914, Congress created the Bureau of War Risk Insurance, under the jurisdiction of the Treasury Department, which originally had nothing to do with veterans benefits but instead insured U.S. ships and cargoes against the risks of mines, submarines, and other warships.

When the United States entered World War I in 1917, Congress added new veterans benefits, including disability compensation, insurance for servicemen, a family allotment program, and vocational rehabilitation for the disabled. All but the last were administered by the Bureau of War Risk Insurance. Another agency, the Public Health Service, provided physical examinations to veterans who applied for compensation, vocational rehabilitation, or medical and hospital care.

The divided responsibility proved unwieldy, however, and in 1921 a presidential study commission prompted Congress to establish the United States Veterans' Bureau,

---

19. *Preliminary Inventory of Pension Case Files of the Bureau of Pensions and the Veterans Administration, 1861–1942* (NM-17), 1963 (RG 15), National Archives microfilm publication T288, General Index to Pension Files, 1861–1934. Hereafter microfilm in the National Archives is cited by the M or T publication number. The bibliography includes a description of microfilm cited from the National Archives.

Introduction

which took over the functions of the Bureau of War Risk Insurance, as well as responsibility for vocational education and the functions of the Public Health Service having to do with physical examination and care and treatment of veterans. Public Health Service hospitals serving veterans were transferred to the Veterans' Bureau in 1922.

The reorganization resolved some of the problems but left three agencies administering veterans benefits—the Veterans' Bureau, the Bureau of Pensions in the Interior Department, and the National Homes for Disabled Volunteer Soldiers. Thus, on July 21, 1930, President Herbert Hoover signed Executive Order 5398, establishing the Veterans Administration and finally consolidating under a single agency the responsibility for the various veterans programs passed by Congress over the years.[20]

Longevity Retirement of Enlisted Men

The Regular Army offered no incentive for ambitious soldiers until an act of Congress on February 14, 1885, approved the creation of a retired list for enlisted personnel. Once an enlisted man had served as such for thirty years in the army or Marine Corps, as either a private or noncommissioned officer, or both, he could apply to be placed on the retired list and thereafter receive 75 percent of the pay and allowances of the rank upon which he was retired.[21]

A proviso was added on September 30, 1890: "That if said enlisted man had war service with the Army in the field, or in the Navy or Marine Corps in active service, either as volunteer or regular, during the war of the rebellion, such war service shall be computed as double time in computing the thirty years necessary to entitle him to be retired" (51st Congress, 1st session, chap. 1125).[22]

In 1891, Secretary of War Stephen B. Elkins recommended that the law be amended to permit enlisted men to retire after twenty-five years' service and to allow men who served twenty years to seek, upon discharge, entry to the Soldier's Home or obtain from it outdoor relief, if they were incapacitated. Elkins spoke eloquently on behalf of the amendment:

> With years and duty the soldier who has rendered honorable service deserves well of the Republic. He has borne his life in his hands, an offering for the public good. His comrades have filled unnoticed graves from everglade to canon. Exposure and hardship have bronzed his face and stiffened his limbs, and the friends of his youth are in other paths, with other interests. He has had human frailties, but he has also had

---

20. *VA History in Brief: What It Is, Was, and Does,* VA Pamphlet 06-83-1, May 1986. See also Greene, *Indian Wars Veteran Organizations.*
21. GO 18, HQA, AGO, Feb. 27, 1885. See also Rickey, *Forty Miles a Day on Beans and Hay,* 337.
22. *Statutes at Large of the United States of America, From December, 1889, to March, 1891,* Vol. 26, p. 504.

manly devotion, and the raw boy who, half in ignorance, swore to obey the orders of the officers appointed over him, has become the faithful soldier through whom and his fellows alone have those officers been able to discharge their own duties, and upon whom, as on a strong arm, the physical security of the nation has rested.

The enlisted soldier rarely has a pen or a voice given to his public praise; yet, man for man, the regular troops of the United States have no equal in intelligent valor and soldierly devotion.

When physical infirmity overtakes these men, as it generally does after ten or fifteen years, there should be appropriate provision for them. They are neither saints nor demi-gods. They are men, often rough in body, ignorant of books, and sometimes deficient in the minor morals, but strong in the sturdy virtues of obedience, truthfulness, fidelity. Prevented from forming family ties, they are friendless in the social world, and with a long training that has eliminated all personal responsibility beyond that of submission to authority, they are so guileless and as helpless as children in the sharp competition of civil life.

The retired list after 30 years is a well-merited boon, but the limit should be lowered to 25, certainly for service below that of the noncommissioned officer. Not one man in ten thousand can carry a musket more than 25 years. And a corps of watchman in garrison and over the public civil buildings might well be opened to the retired enlisted soldier.[23]

Legislation to change the retirement system for enlisted men was not enacted until the mid-twentieth century. By 1945, enlisted personnel of all branches became eligible for retirement, with half-pay, upon completing twenty years of active service, the same benefit as that received by the officer corps. The percentage formula for military retired pay has undergone periodic revision and remains an object of congressional review to the present day.

---

23. "Report of the Secretary of War," *Executive Documents of the House of Representatives for the First Session of the Fifty-second Congress,* 1891–92, pp. 84–85. Rickey, *Forty Miles a Day on Beans and Hay,* 341.

Abbreviations

Abbreviations within this work contain some variations in the use of periods, apostrophes, and capitalization.

aag	assistant adjutant general	b.	born
AAS	acting assistant surgeon	bal	balance
abs	absent, absence	battn	battalion
ac.	acute	batt'y	battery
accdt	accident, accidental	bd	board
accomp	accompany, accompanied	Benj.	Benjamin
acc't	on account of	bks	barracks
ACP	Acceptance, Commission, and Personal	bldg	building
		blk	black
ACS	acting commissary of subsistence	blks	blacksmith
actg	acting	brig	brigade
adc	aide-de-camp	brig-gen	brigadier-general
addl	additional	brkft	breakfast
adjt	adjutant	brn	brown
adm	admit, admitted	bro	brother
agcy	agency	bronc	bronchitis
AGO	Adjutant General's Office	bro't	brought
aig	assistant inspector general	bvt	brevet
Ala.	Alabama	BYU	Brigham Young University
amm'n	ammunition	Calif.	California
amp'd	amputated	campn	campaign
appd	applied	Cant'mt	Cantonment
apph	apprehended, apprehension	capt	captain
appmt	appointment	cav	cavalry
appn	application	CB	Commission Branch
appt	appointed	CBHMA	Custer Battlefield and Historical Museum Association
appv	approved		
aqm	assistant quartermaster	cert	certificate
AR	Army Regulations	ch.	child, children
Ariz.	Arizona	char	character
arr	arrive, arrived	Chas.	Charles
ars'l	arsenal	chf	chief
artf'r	artificer	chg	charge, charged
art'y	artillery	chr.	chronic
assd	assigned	cl.	class
asst	assistant	clmt	claimant
AT	Arizona Territory	cm	court martial
attd	attached	CN	A part of Indian Territory (Oklahoma) established as independent nations by the Five Civilized Tribes: Cherokee, Creek, Choctaw, Chickasaw, and Seminoles
attdt	attendant		
atty	attorney		
auth	authority		
awl	absent with leave		
awol	absent without leave		

Abbreviations

Co.	County	disappv	disapproved
co	company	disch	discharge, discharged
col	colonel	dishon	dishonorable
col'd	colored	dismtd	dismounted
Coll.	Collection	disp'n	disposition
Colo.	Colorado	dist	distinguished
comd	command, commanded	distr	district
comdg	commanding	div	division
comdr	commander	dk	dark
comd't	commandant	DM	Department of the Missouri
com'n	commission, commissioned	DPL	Denver Public Library
comp	complexion	drg	dragoon
comp'd	compound	ds	detached service
comp'n	competition	DT	Dakota Territory
com'r	commissioner	dur	during
comsy	commissary	ed	extra duty
cond	conduct	educ	educated
cond'n	condition	Edw.	Edward
conft	confinement	endmt	endorsement
Conn.	Connecticut	engr	engineer
consid'n	consideration	enl	enlisted, enlist
consol	consolidate, consolidated	enlmt	enlistment
consol'n	consolidation	enr	enrolled
conspic	conspicuous	env	envelope
const.	constitution, constitutional	E'town	Elizabethtown, Kentucky
constip'n	constipation	exam'n	examination
cont'd	continued	expir	expiration
cont'n	contusion	exp'n	expedition
contr	contract, contracted	eve	evening
cpl	corporal	ext'd	extended
DA	Department of Arizona	ext'n	extension
Dak.	Dakota	far'r	farrier
Dan'l	Daniel	fl.	flesh
D.C.	District of Columbia	for'd	forward, forwarded
DD	Department of Dakota	forf	forfeit
dd	daily duty	Fr.	French
DE	Department of the East	frac.	fracture
def't	defendant	fraud't	fraudulent
deg	degree	Fred'k	Frederick
del	delivered	Ft	Fort
Del.	Delaware	furl	furlough
dep	depart, departed, departure, departing	furn	furnish, furnished
		gal	gallant, gallantry
dept	department	gar cm	garrison court martial
des	deserted	gd	guard
desig	designate, designated	gen	general
des'n	desertion	Geo.	George
desp	despatch, despatched	GO	General Order
des'r	deserter	gov'r	governor
detmt	detachment	govt	government
DG	Department of the Gulf	grad	graduate, graduated
diag	diagnosis	grd	grounds
diar	diarrhea	gsw	gunshot wound
dis	disability	hon	honorable, honorably

Abbreviations

hosp	hospital	Miss.	Mississippi
hq	headquarters	Mo.	Missouri
hqa	headquarters army	mo	month, months
Ill.	Illinois	m.o.	muster out
incl	include, included, including	morn	morning
incr	increase	msgr	messenger
Ind.	Indiana	MT	Montana Territory [later Montana]
ind	indian		
indpt	independent	mtd	mounted
Ind. Surv.	Indian [War] Survivor	Mtn	Mountain
Ind. Wid.	Indian [War] Widow	mus'n	musician
inf	infantry	natl	national
infl.	inflamed, inflammation	NBS	Northern Boundary Survey (49th Parallel north latitude) locating the line separating the United States and Canada
inq	inquire, inquired, inquiry		
inst	instant (current month)		
instr	instruct, instructor		
instr'n	instruction	ncs	non-commissioned staff
intm.	intermittent	N.Dak.	North Dakota
intrpr	interpreter	N.H.	New Hampshire
inv	invalid	NM	New Mexico
Isl	Island, Isle	NPRR	Northern Pacific Rail Road
IT	Indian Territory	N.Y.	New York
IU	Indiana University	NYC	New York City
Jas.	James	NYH	New York Harbor
Jeff'n	Jefferson	Okla.	Oklahoma
Jno.	John	opr	operator
Jos.	Joseph	ordn	ordnance
kit'n	kitchen	Ore.	Oregon
Kans.	Kansas	org	organize, organized
Ky.	Kentucky	org'n	organization
l.	left	orig'l	original
LBH	Little Big Horn	P.A.	Pension Agent (Agency) or attorney
LBHA	Little Big Horn Associates		
LBHB	Little Big Horn Battlefield	Pa.	Pennsylvania
lt	light	par	paragraph
Lt	Lieutenant	Pat'k	Patrick
Lt-col	lieutenant-colonel	pens'r	pensioner
1Lt	1st Lieutenant	perm'n	permission
2Lt	2d Lieutenant	Phil'a	Philadelphia
L'worth	Leavenworth	PI	Philippine Islands
M	microcopy (microfilm)	P.O.	Post Office
m.	married	pr.	primary
maj	major	PRD	Principal Record Division
maj-gen	major-general	prep	prepare, preparation
max	maximum	pres	present, presented
Mass.	Massachusetts	pres't	president
MDM	Military Division of the Missouri	prin	principal
mech	mechanic	pris'r	prisoner
med	medical	prof	professor
Mich.	Michigan	prom	promoted
Mich'l	Michael	prom'n	promotion
mil	military	prop	property
Minn.	Minnesota	prov	provost

25

Abbreviations

prov'n	provision	sqdn	squadron
Pt	Point	SO	Special Order
pty	party	sol.	soldier, soldiers
pub	public	spl	special
pvt	private	St	Saint
qm	quartermaster	sta	station
qmd	quartermaster department	stew'd	steward
qm-sgt	quartermaster sergeant	str	steamer, steamboat
qrs	quarters	stric.	stricture
r.	right	subs	subsistence
rct	recruit	supt	superintendent
rctg	recruiting	surd	surrender, surrendered
rec	record	surg	surgeon
rec's	records	surv	survivor
recd	received	syph.	syphilis, syphilitic
recom	recommend, recommended	Switz	Switzerland
recom'n	recommendation	td	temporary duty
redesig	redesignated	tel	telegraph, telegram
reenl	reenlisted, reenlist	tert.	tertian [fever, recurring approximate 48 hour intervals]
reenlmt	reenlistment		
reg	regular	Tex.	Texas
Regs	Regulations	tho'	though
regt	regiment	Thos.	Thomas
regtl	regimental	tho't	thought
rej	rejected	thro'	through
rel	release, released	TNA	The National Archives (Great Britain)
rem'd	remitted		
remit	remittent	tr	transfer, transferred
req	request, requested	transp	transportation
res	reside, resident	trump'r	trumpeter
resd	resign, resigned	Ty	Territory
ret	return, returned	univ	university
retd	retired	USA	United States Army
rheum.	rheumatism	USMA	United States Military Academy
Rich'd	Richard		
Robt.	Robert	UT	Utah Territory
R & P	Record & Pension Office	Va.	Virginia
rqm	regimental quartermaster	vet	veteran
R.S.	Revised Statutes	vet'y	veterinary
sad'r	saddler	vol	volunteer
sad-sgt	saddler-sergeant	wag	wagoner
Sam'l	Samuel	Wash'n	Washington
sd	special duty	wd.	wound, wounded
S.Dak.	South Dakota	Wid	Widow
sec	section	Wis.	Wisconsin
sen	sentence, sentenced	wk	week, weeks
serv	service	Wm.	William
sgt	sergeant	WMC	Walter Mason Camp
sgt-maj	sergeant-major	WT	Washington Territory
1sgt	first sergeant	Wyo.	Wyoming
sim.	simple	xclt	excellent
sl.	slight		

A

Abbotts, Harry. Pvt co E; b. New York N.Y.; enl 8 Oct 1875 Louisville Ky. for 5 yrs; age 22; bricklayer; hazel eyes, dk hair, dk comp, 5' 9 1/4" high; join co E 29 Oct 1875 Ft Totten DT; sick hosp 24 Nov to 1 Dec 1875 (frostbite, fingers both hands); sick qrs Ft Lincoln DT 19–21 Apr 1876 (constip'n); sick 3 May (no diag); sick qrs 4–5 May (no diag);[1] ed hosp attdt with Dr. DeWolf 6 May; ed hosp attdt June 1876; [at LBH orderly to Dr. DeWolf says Pandtle; not sure says Berwald];[2] sick 30 May 1877 (no diag); sick camp on Cedar Creek MT 8 July 1877 (stric.) & tr to Yellowstone River for first boat; sick Ft Buford DT from 16 July; tr on str *Big Horn* 19 Oct [with pvt Van Pelt] to Ft Lincoln; disch 3 Dec 1877 at Ft Lincoln on surg cert dis (stric. urethra, treated at intervals past 10 mos; not contr line of duty) a pvt char good; res Parkersburg W.Va.

Abos, Jas. A. Pvt co B; b. Albany N.Y.; enl 10 Dec 1874 New York N.Y. for 5 yrs (upon consent of guardian); age 17 5/12; hostler; grey eyes, brn hair, fair comp, 5' 8 1/4" high; join co B 10 Feb 1875 Shreveport La.; dd co teamster from Aug 1875; des 29 Mar 1876 at Shreveport (with pvt Lewis who took Abos's money & left him at Dallas Tex.); surd 6 Apr 1876 Ft Richardson Tex; sen gen cm 5 June 1876 to dishon disch & 2 yrs conft mil prison Ft L'worth Kans.; disch remitted & conft reduced to one yr (clemency acc't youth of sol., short time abs, vol'y surd & xclt cond); escaped 12 Feb 1877 while working outside prison.

Abrams, Wm. G. Pvt co L; b. 1 Dec 1839 Baltimore Md.;[3] enr as vol substitute [for Wm. Sheldon] for sufficient sum paid 30 Sep 1863 Hartford Conn. a pvt co A 14 Conn. inf for 3 yrs; gsw l. thigh (fl. wd.) 14 Oct 1863 in action near Bristow Sta Va.; duty 5 May 1864; claimed to be rebel des'r & req serv not in front of rebel armies; sent to Ft Ridgely Minn. June 1864 with unattd & drafted men (reenl rebels) desig detmt 1 Conn. cav; redesig 1st indpt co US vols 6 Apr 1865; tr to Ft Snelling Minn. 18 Aug 1865 thence to Hartford Conn. for m.o.; found on rolls of 14 Conn. inf as des from hosp Nov 1864 but upon investigation chg of des'n removed, having been erroneously preferred; m.o. vol serv 18 Oct 1865 to date (with co) 31 May 1865;[4] enl reg army 29 Aug 1866 Troy N.Y. for 5 yrs; age 28; laborer; blk eyes, dk hair, dk comp, 5' 10" high; join co L 7 cav 29 Sep 1866 Ft Riley Kans.; cpl 20 Oct 1866; des 14 Jan 1867 Ft Morgan Colo. Ty; surd 25 Jan at Ft Morgan;[5] in arrest to 4 Sep 1867 when returned to duty a pvt;[6] ed post blks to Jan 1868; ed qmd mech Feb to Apr 1868; cpl 15 May 1868; sgt 1 Aug 1868; ds div hq Chicago Ill. Apr & May 1869 chg of orderlies; 1sgt 1 Nov 1870; sgt 22 Jan 1871; disch 29 Aug 1871 Winnsboro S.C. expir of serv a sgt & reenl 3 days later in co L for 5 yrs; wag 8 Sep 1871; ed qmd teamster 12–26 Apr 1873; ed qmd Oct 1873 to Jan 1874; dd qmd teamster Feb to Apr 1874; dd qmd teamster Aug 1874 (Black Hills Exp'n); pvt 12 Apr 1875; ed qmd teamster Aug 1875 to Mar 1876; disch 5 Aug 1876 mouth of Rosebud Creek MT (in time to go down river by first boat) per GO 24 AGO 1859 a pvt;[7] arr Ft Lincoln DT 10 Aug 1876 on str *Durfee*; died 28 May 1901 Sioux City Iowa.

Pension: 14 Aug 1891 / Inv / 1046841 / 906976. widow / 742946; submitted for spl exam'n 8 July 1903; rej 8 Dec 1905 after exhaustive spl exam'n [20 spl reports] failed to show clmt as legal Wid of sol., nor evidence of death or divorce of former wife.

Ackerman, Chas. Pvt co K; b. 5 Sep 1848 Baden Germany; enl 9 Sep 1875 St Louis

Mo. for 5 yrs; age 27; cook; hazel eyes, brn hair, fair comp, 5' 8" high; join co K 27 Apr 1876 St Paul Minn.; cook for Lt Godfrey Aug 1876 [Burkhardt disch];[8] dd co cook Oct 1876; dd co cook Oct 1877; dd co cook June to Aug 1878; disch 8 Sep 1880 Ft Totten DT expir of serv a pvt char xclt & reenl in co K for 5 yrs; dd co clerk June to Aug 1881; cpl 23 Sep 1881; dd actg co qm sgt Oct 1881 to June 1882; dd co clerk Oct 1882; sgt 1 Nov 1882; dd chg co mess Dec 1882; actg 1sgt Oct 1883; disch 8 Sep 1885 Ft Meade DT expir of serv a sgt; died 6 Apr 1930 St Paul Minn.
Pension: 4 Mar 1917 / Ind. Surv. / 15391 / 7944.

Ackison, David. Pvt co E; b. Troy N.Y.; enl 1 Oct 1873 Pittsburgh Pa. for 5 yrs; age 21 9/12; railroader; grey eyes, brn hair, fair comp, 5' 6" high; join co E 18 Oct 1873 Ft Lincoln DT; sick (neuralgia & consumption) 13 June to 5 Sep 1874 at Ft Lincoln;[9] sick on str *Far West* 22 June 1876 (constip'n) & tr with wd to Ft Lincoln 3 July;[10] duty 28 Sep 1876; disch 1 Oct 1878 Camp Ruhlen DT expir of serv & reenl in co E for 5 yrs; sick Nov 1881 to Mar 1882 (eczema); dd prov gd Aug 1882; disch 30 Sep 1883 Ft Meade DT expir of serv a pvt char good; reenl in co E 10 Oct 1883 at Ft Meade for 5 yrs; on furl 4 mos 5 Nov 1883 Deadwood DT; disch 20 Aug 1885 at Ft Meade on surg cert dis a pvt char good; (eczema of face last 5 yrs resists all treatment, cause unknown; very aggravated & offensive eruption on face extending to ears, breaking out in ulcerated sores, repulsive to men at mess table & in ranks; on furl 6 mos to visit "Hot Springs" proved no benefit; degree of dis 1/4); res Sturgis DT.

Adams, Geo. E. Pvt co L; b. Minersville Pa.; enl 26 Mar 1866 St Louis Mo. for 3 yrs; age 19 8/12; laborer; blue eyes, sandy hair, ruddy comp, 5' 7 1/2" high; join co H 3 battn 13 inf 29 Mar 1866 Jeff'n Bks Mo.; [co tr to Ft Rice DT]; dd qmd teamster June 1866; (battn redesig 31 inf regt Sep 1866); dd with mtd detmt Oct 1866 to Feb 1867; ed qmd teamster June 1868 to Mar 1869; disch 26 Mar 1869 Ft Stevenson DT upon expir of serv & reenl in same co for 3 yrs; wag 1 Apr 1869; (co H 31 inf consol with co F 22 inf May 1869); disch 25 July 1869 at Ft Stevenson per AGO (enlmts ext'd to 5 yrs 3 Mar 1869 & upon refusing to sign paper for ext'n sol. could not be legally held); reenl 18 Oct 1869 Ft Randall DT for 5 yrs in co D 22 inf; ed qmd laborer Feb to Nov 1871; ed qmd teamster June 1872; [co with Yellowstone Exp'n July to Oct 1872 escort NPRR surveyors]; ed qmd teamster Oct 1872; disch 19 Dec 1872 at Ft Randall on surg cert dis (r. index finger shot away while on gd duty, unfit for duty last 60 days) a pvt; enl in co L 7 cav 27 Jan 1874 Ft Lincoln DT for 5 yrs; dd hq Black Hills Exp'n Aug 1874 with engrs; dd qmd teamster Sep 1874 to Jan 1875; in conft Feb 1875; sen gen cm 7 June 1875 forf $10 pay per mo for 3 mos & conft same period; dd post woodcutter Jan 1876; killed with Custer column 25 June 1876.

Adams, Jacob. Pvt co H; b. 12 July 1851 near Canton Ohio; enl in co H 13 Apr 1873 Yankton DT for 5 yrs; age 21; farmer; blue eyes, brn hair, fair comp, 5' 8" high; ed qmd teamster Oct 1873; dd subs dept herder Oct & Nov 1875; with pack train June 1876; dd bldg stable guardhouse Feb 1877; ed qmd teamster Feb 1878; disch 13 Apr 1878 Ft Rice DT expir of serv a pvt char xclt; died 13 May 1934 Vincennes Ind.
Pension: 7 May 1885 / Inv / 539334 / 359286. (XC-895,426).

Akers, Jas. Cpl co G; b. Kings Co Ireland; enl 4 Dec 1874 Boston Mass. for 5 yrs; age 23; plasterer; hazel eyes, auburn hair, fair comp, 5' 6" high; join co G 10 Feb 1875 Shreveport La.; dd clerk distr hq at Shreveport June 1875 to Mar 1876; cpl 3 May 1876; sgt 9 July 1876; sick qrs 29 Sep to 23 Oct 1876 (ac. rheum.); dd chg co kit'n Dec 1876; dd actg co qm sgt Feb 1877; ds Ft Lincoln 14 Oct 1877; cited by capt Benteen for conspic gal in two mtd chgs against Nez Perce inds at Canon Creek MT 13 Sep 1877; disch 12 Jan 1878 Ft Lincoln DT on surg cert dis a sgt char good (chr. rheum. knees & ankles; on sick report last 4 mos & sent home for med treatment); said he contr rheum. at LBH 25 June 1876 & unable to perform duty for 3 mos; cond'n aggravated dur battle at Canon Creek MT 13 Sep 1877; died 3 Aug 1881 sol. Home Wash'n D.C.; (pythisis pulmonalis).
Pension: 4 Feb 1878 / Inv / 247294 / 151287.

Alberts, Jas. H. Pvt co D; b. Woodstock Ill.; enl 24 Sep 1875 St Louis Mo. for 5 yrs; age 28; farmer; blue eyes, brn hair, fair comp, 5' 5 3/4" high; join co D 21 Oct 1875 Ft Lincoln DT; cpl 1 Feb 1877; (recom by Lt Edgerly for medal of honor for conspic gal at LBH but name not on revised list);[11] sgt 24 June 1877; killed 30 Sep 1877 Snake Creek MT (Bear's Paw Mtns) in action with Nez Perce inds.

Alcott, Sam'l. Sgt co A; b. Allegheny Pa.; enl 10 Jan 1872 Troy N.Y. for 5 yrs; age 21; file cutter; brn eyes, blk hair, dk comp, 5' 6" high; join co A 11 Feb 1872 E'town Ky.; cpl 6 May 1873; sgt 29 Jan 1875; dd chg co kit'n Dec 1874 to May 1875; dd actg co qm sgt Oct 1875 to Nov 1876; ds camp Powder River MT chg co prop 15 June 1876; disch 10 Jan 1877 Ft Rice DT expir of serv a sgt char xclt; died 24 Mar 1926 Toronto Canada.[12] Pension: 27 June 1927 / Wid / 1584307 / A-2-9-28. (XC-2,999,524).

Alexander, Wm. Citizen packer, qmd; b. 8 Apr 1838 Armagh Ireland; enl 10 July 1860 New York N.Y. for 5 yrs; age 22; shoemaker; blue eyes, lt hair, fair comp, 5' 9" high; join co F 7 inf 18 Oct 1860 Ft Craig NM; tr to co A 5 inf 2 June 1864 Ft Marcy NM;[13] disch 10 July 1865 Ft Larned Kans. expir of serv a pvt; [m. June 1872 Woodbury Minn. to Mary Sloan; divorced May 1874];[14] hired Apr 1876 St Paul Minn. by Lt Gibbs 6 inf actg aqm to pack supplies on pub animals of exp'n; rate of pay $50 mo & entitled to one ration per day & transp back to St Paul if hon disch; tr to Lt Nowlan at Ft Lincoln DT 17 Apr 1876 with pay to commence from that date; drove pack mules alongside wagon train dur march to Powder River;[15] disch 23 Sep 1876 due $138.33 pay from 1 July;[16] employed as outrider for Northwestern Stage co & recd gsw r. arm 7 May 1878 in fracas at ranch of sta owner at Sturgis City; arm amp'd above elbow by Dr. Porter at Bismarck, mortification having set in;[17] died 6 Feb 1922 Sol. Home Wash'n D.C.[18] Pension: 15 July 1890 / Inv / 811584 / 612656.

Allan, Fred E. Pvt co C; b. Milton England; enl 3 Oct 1873 Boston Mass. for 5 yrs; age 25; watchmaker; brn eyes, blk hair, dk comp, 5' 8 1/2" high; join co C 21 Oct 1873 Ft Rice DT; ed subs dept Sep 1874 to Oct 1875; ed subs dept 5 Jan to 13 May 1876; killed with Custer column 25 June 1876.

Aller, Chas. Pvt co A; b. Prussia Germany; enl 9 Dec 1874 New York N.Y. for 5 yrs; age 27; cooper; blue eyes, brn hair, fair comp, 5' 7 3/4" high; join co A 6 Feb 1875 Livingston Ala; dd co cook June 1875; dd qmd teamster Oct 1875 to Mar 1876; des 24 Apr 1877 camp near Ft Lincoln DT; surd 15 Sep 1877 Ft Sanders Wyo. Ty; escaped from conft at Ft Sanders 23 Oct 1877.[19]

Anderson, Chas. L. Pvt co C; b. Albion N.Y.; enl 15 Sep 1875 Boston Mass. for 5 yrs; age 29; sailor; grey eyes, dk hair, dk comp, 5' 8 1/4" high; join co C 21 Oct 1875 Ft Lincoln DT; dd qmd Dec 1875; dd post hq Feb to May 1876; des 20 June 1876 camp mouth of Powder River MT.[20]

Anderson, Geo. Pvt co K; b. 14 June 1842 St Catherines Canada; enl 3 Sep 1866 Cincinnati Ohio for 5 yrs; age 24; teamster; blue eyes, lt hair, lt comp, 5' 5 1/2" high; join co K 30 Sep 1866 Ft Riley Kans.; ed qmd teamster Dec 1867 to Feb 1868; ds hq detmt Ft Hays Kans. 4 Aug 1870; (tr to co B 9 Aug 1870); ds Ft L'worth Kans. 19 Oct 1870; ed qmd laborer Oct 1870 to Jan 1871; ds regtl hq Louisville Ky. 18 Jan to 3 Sep 1871 when disch by expir of serv a pvt; reenl for co K 16 Sep 1871 at Louisville for 5 yrs; ds regtl hq to Nov 1871; ed qmd teamster 12–26 Apr 1873; sen gen cm 2 July 1873 forf $10 pay per mo for 2 mos; dd qmd 21 Aug to 11 Sep 1873; ds Ft Rice DT 29 Sep 1874 with co prop awaiting transp to Dept of the Gulf; dd qmd Jan to Apr 1875; ds Ft Lincoln DT 17 May 1876 chg co prop; dd post qmd laborer 24 May 1876; sent with Lt Garlington on str *Josephine* 24 July to join co in field; ret to Ft Lincoln 10 Aug on str *Durfee*; disch 16 Sep 1876 at Ft Lincoln by expir of serv a pvt char xclt; reenl 6 Dec 1878 Ft Meade DT for 5 yrs in co C 7 cav; dd qmd teamster Feb 1879; dd regtl hq Apr & May 1879; sick hosp 25 July to 5 Sep 1879 at Ft Meade when disch on surg cert dis (granular conjunctivitis both

eyes contr dur winter campn Nov 1868); died 19 Sep 1912 Minneapolis Minn.
Pension: 22 Nov 1880 / Inv / 411996 / 184717. Wid / 1011237. (Abandoned).

Andrews, Wm. Pvt co L; b. Prussia Germany; enl 19 Dec 1865 New York N.Y. for 3 yrs; age 22; farmer; blue eyes, brn hair, fair comp, 5' 6 1/4" high; join co H 5 cav 5 Jan 1866 Wash'n D.C.; dd co teamster June 1866; co wag Dec 1867 to Dec 1868; disch 19 Dec 1868 Ft Wallace Kans. expir of serv a pvt; reenl 21 May 1869 Ft L'worth Kans. for 5 yrs in co L 7 cav; dd co cook July 1872; disch 21 May 1874 Ft Lincoln DT expir of serv a pvt; reenl same day in co L for 5 yrs & on furl 30 days at Ft L'worth [see sgt Smith & pvt O'Connell]; killed with Custer column 25 June 1876.

Armstrong, Jno. E. Pvt co A; b. 4 Nov 1836 Phil'a Pa.; enr 12 Apr 1865 a pvt co F 215 Pa. inf for one yr; age 28; plumber; blue eyes, brn hair, lt comp, 5' 8 1/4" high; m.o. vol serv 31 July 1865 Ft Delaware (Phil'a) a pvt; enl reg army 25 Aug 1865 at Phil'a for 3 yrs; join co G 6 cav 8 Sep 1865 camp near Frederick Md; sad'r 27 Jan 1866; pvt 20 Oct 1866; ds hq 5th mil distr New Orleans La. Apr to July 1867; sad'r July 1867; pvt 15 Mar 1868; disch 25 Aug 1868 at New Orleans expir of serv a pvt; reenl 7 July 1869 at Phil'a for 5 yrs; join co C 1 cav 18 Dec 1869 Camp Crittenden AT; sad'r Apr to July 1870; sad'r 1 Mar 1872; pvt 16 Nov 1872 & in confT to Mar 1873; sen gen cm 21 Jan 1873 forf $8 pay per mo for 3 mos & confT same period; sad'r 1 May 1873; disch 7 July 1874 Camp McDermit Nevada expir of serv a sad'r; reenl 2 Apr 1875 at Phil'a for 5 yrs; join co A 7 cav 21 Oct 1875 Ft Lincoln DT; killed dur retreat from valley fight 25 June 1876 [near Isaiah].[21]
Pension: 5 Apr 1880 / Father / 262686 / 225435.

Arndt, Otto. Pvt band; b. 25 Jan 1844 Bavaria Germany; enl 22 Apr 1867 New York N.Y. for 3 yrs; age 23; barber; grey eyes, dk hair, fair comp, 5' 7 1/2" high; assd to co B 37 inf; tr to co E Mar 1869; tr to co A 3 inf 14 Oct 1869 (dur reorganization of inf regts);[22] disch 22 Apr 1870 Ft Dodge Kans. expir of serv a pvt; reenl 19 May 1870 Ft L'worth Kans. for 5 yrs in band 7 cav; des 12 Mar 1871 at Ft L'worth; enl as Max Cernow 28 Sep 1871 Chicago Ill. for 5 yrs; assd to band 15 inf; surd as des'r 12 Oct 1873 under GO 102 AGO 1873;[23] ds Ft Snelling Minn. to 14 July 1874 when restored to duty without trial & tr to 7 cav to serve bal of orig'l enlmt; ds camp Powder River MT 14 June 1876; ds str *Josephine* 6 Aug 1876 to Ft Lincoln with band; disch 21 Dec 1877 at Ft Lincoln expir of serv a pvt char xclt; reenl 12 Jan 1878 Ft Hamilton N.Y. for 5 yrs in band 3 art'y & served continuously with same unit till 23 Jan 1900 when retd a prin mus'n; died 6 Feb 1917 Presidio San Francisco Calif.
Pension: 15 Feb 1917 / Wid / 1093904. Rej on grd sol.'s death from cerebral apoplexy not due to mil serv. (Claim appv under act 4 Mar 1917); Ind. Wid / 11853 / 8538. (XC-2,664,904).

Arnold, Herbert H. Pvt co C; b. 19 May 1853 Rocky Hill Conn.; enl 30 Oct 1872 Springfield Mass. for 5 yrs; age 21; burnisher; grey eyes, brn hair, ruddy comp, 5' 7 1/2" high; join co C 9 Dec 1872 Charlotte NC; dd co baker Dec 1874 to May 1875; dd qmd Dec 1875 to Mar 1876; dd co gardener Apr 1876; ds Ft Lincoln chg co prop 5 May 1876; ed qmd teamster 16 Oct 1876; cpl 2 Jan 1877 to date 1 Dec 1876; dd chg co cook house Apr 1877; disch 16 June 1877 Ft Totten DT per SO 72 Dept of Dak. 1877 a cpl;[24] died 6 Apr 1929 Meriden Conn.
Pension: 20 Apr 1917 / Ind. Surv./ 11282 / 7462. Ind. Wid / 1639951 / A-12-5-29.

Ascough, Jno. B. Pvt co D; b. Phil'a Pa.; enr 1 Sep 1861 a pvt co C 23 Pa. inf for 3 yrs; gsw l. shoulder 1 June 1864 action at Cold Harbor Va. & in hosp to 12 June thence sick hosp to 24 Aug 1864 (syph.); m.o. with co 8 Sep 1864 at Phil'a; enl reg army 3 Sep 1872 at Phil'a for 5 yrs; age 28; shoemaker; brn eyes, dk hair, ruddy comp, 5' 9 1/4" high; join co D 8 Dec 1872 Opelika Ala; blks 1 Jan 1873; pvt 1 June 1875; in confT Dec 1875; ed qmd blks 3 Oct to 10 Nov 1876; cpl 15 Nov 1876; disch 23 June 1877 camp near Tongue River MT per SO 70 Dept of Dak. 1877 a cpl;[25] reenl 12 Feb 1879 Ft Lincoln DT for 5 yrs; assd to co L 7 cav 4 Mar 1879; far'r 11

May 1879; blks 1 Oct 1879; ed tel line repairer June 1880; wag 1 June 1881; cpl 7 Sep 1881; pvt 21 Sep 1881; awol Oct 1881; in conft Nov 1881 to Jan 1882; disch 30 Jan 1882 at Ft Lincoln per SO 16 AGO 1882 (by way of favor; father near death & leaving estate) a pvt char fair.[26]
Pension: 28 July 1891 / Inv / 883841 / 721330. Dropped from roll 31 May 1907, failure to claim; last paid to 4 Dec 1903.

Assadaly, Antony. Pvt co L; b. Prussia Germany; enr 6 Aug 1861 Lewistown Pa. a pvt co C 1 Pa. cav for 3 yrs; wd 12 Dec 1862 battle of Fredericksburg; duty Feb 1863; cpl 25 Nov 1863; gsw l. hip 15 May 1864 battle at Old Church Va.; disch 22 Sep 1864 Satterlee hosp Phil'a Pa. on surg cert (dis 1/2) & expir of serv a cpl; enl reg army 23 June 1865 at Phil'a for 3 yrs; age 23; soldier; blue eyes, brn hair, fair comp, 5' 3" high; join co I 3 cav 28 July 1865 Little Rock Ark; disch 22 June 1868 Ft Sumner NM expir of serv a pvt; enl in 7 cav 21 July 1868 Ft L'worth Kans. for 5 yrs; join co F 28 July 1868; dd co cook May 1869; ds dept hq in field July 1869; dd chg co prop Oct 1869; dd regtl hq Mar & Apr 1870; ds regtl hq Ft L'worth May 1870 to June 1871; ds regtl hq Louisville Ky. July to Nov 1871; ds regtl hq St Paul Minn. from Apr 1873; disch 21 July 1873 at St Paul by expir of serv & reenl for 5 yrs in co L; ds regtl hq to Dec 1873; in conft Ft Snelling Minn. 26 Dec 1873; sen gen cm 13 Feb 1874 forf $10 pay per mo for 3 mos (damaged one pub horse); ds Ft Snelling to 10 May 1874 when tr to Ft Lincoln DT; dd qmd teamster Jan to Aug 1875; killed with Custer column 25 June 1876.

Atchison, Thos. Pvt co F; b. Antrim Co. Ireland; enr 14 Apr 1863 Phil'a Pa. a pvt co D 2 Pa. art'y for 3 yrs; age 28; brick moulder; hazel eyes, brn hair, fair comp, 5' 5 1/2" high; cpl 3 Sep 1863; sgt 1 Sep 1864; m.o. vol serv 29 Jan 1866 City Point Va.; enl reg army 21 Aug 1866 at Phil'a for 5 yrs; join co F 7 cav 10 Sep 1866 Ft Riley Kans.; cpl 17 Sep 1866; pvt 17 Dec 1866; in conft Dec 1866; cpl 1 May 1867; pvt 22 Jan 1868; ds orderly to gen Sheridan Apr & May 1868; cpl May 1869; sgt 10 May 1871; ds Taylor Bks (Louisville) Ky. 22 July 1871; disch 21 Aug 1871 Meridian Miss upon expir of serv a sgt & reenl in co F for 5 yrs; on furl 25 Aug to Oct 1871 at Phil'a; ds herding co horses Aug & Sep 1872; pvt 1 Oct 1873; sick 11 Dec 1875 to 18 Jan 1876 (ac. rheum.); killed with Custer column 25 June 1876.

Avery, Chas. E. Pvt co H; b. Peterboro N.H.; enl 30 Oct 1872 Lowell Mass. for 5 yrs; age 21; laborer; blue eyes, dk hair, dk comp, 5' 8" high; join co H 3 Dec 1872 Nashville Tenn; unfit for duty with Yellowstone Exp'n 21 July 1873 (consumption) & tr by boat to hosp Ft Lincoln DT; duty 21 Aug 1873; in conft Ft Rice DT 28 Apr 1876; in conft Ft Lincoln 17 May 1876; sent with Lt Garlington on str *Josephine* 24 July to join co in field; disch 24 June 1877 camp on Sunday Creek MT per SO 70 Dept of Dak. 1877 a pvt.[27]

Notes—A

1. RG 94, Entry 529.

2. SO 34, Hq 7th Cavalry, May 6, 1876, RG 391, Entry 859; Chris Pendle (Pandtle) said Abbotts was orderly to Dr. DeWolf when company left Fort Totten (March 10). Pendle to Walter Camp, July 14, 1919, WMC-BYU; Berwald interview, nd, WMC-BYU.

Lt. Varnum said that, during the retreat from the valley fight, DeWolf was followed by his orderly, who joined the column when DeWolf was killed, Carroll, *Custer's Chief of Scouts,* 67, 91; hospital steward Alfred W. Dale said one of the two men detailed from 7th Cavalry was with Reno's battalion, Dale to Walter Camp, Jan. 7, 1911, WMC-BYU.

3. Abrams claimed to be a native of Pacolet, Spartanburg County, South Carolina, and related that he left home about 1860 and came north to avoid working on his father's large farm. His father's name was William, and his mother, Artemesia; he had three sisters and his brother George was in the rebel army. When 7th Cavalry was in South Carolina, he never went near his former home nor hunted up relatives.

William J. Logue thought Abrams was from Kentucky or Tennessee because he spoke with a southern dialect and southern nature. J. W. Obenchan, son-in-law of Mrs. Abrams, said Abrams claimed he was from down South and spoke just like a southerner.

The 1880 Dakota and 1900 Iowa federal censuses report Abrams was born in South Carolina. R. McMorris, one of several special examiners investigating Mrs. Abrams's claim for pension, inquired at Spartanburg in 1904 and personally searched tax books and mortgage and deed books, but found no trace of Abrams's relatives. The postmaster at Pacolet was unable to find any trace of parties inquired for. Henry A. Hazard, another special examiner, called on all 23 Abramses listed in the Baltimore City Directory of 1905, but none knew anything of William G. Abrams or his relatives. When Abrams was admitted to Claremont Hospital in April 1864, his age was given as 24 and nearest relative residing in Baltimore was Jefferson Abrams.

4. SO 237, Hq DE, Oct. 14, 1865, RG 393, Part I, Entry 1409; RG 393, Part IV, Entries 1068, 1070, 1071; RG 393, Part V, Fort Ridgely, Minn., NA, M535, Roll 1, and M617, Rolls 1010 and 1196.

5. Abrams was 1 of 29 men of Company L who deserted January 14 at Fort Morgan. (Joseph Kretchmer was the only other deserter of this group still with the regiment in 1876.) The incident was described or mentioned in three different accounts, Lt. Bell in "Reminiscences," *Journal of the United States Cavalry Association*; E. B. Custer in *Tenting on the Plains* (1915), 395; and Frost in *The Court Martial of General George Armstrong Custer*, 201–202, 244.

General Godfrey said the affair was the high tide of desertions and was orchestrated by the first sergeant, who turned the troop out after tattoo for detached service and after a hard and rapid march of about 30 miles, told them they were all deserters, and they could do what they pleased—that it was every fellow for himself. Nearly all were afraid to return for fear of the consequences, but some did return. *Fort Riley (Kans.) Guidon*, July 25, 1908.

6. SO 195, Hq DM, Sept. 4, 1867, RG 393, Part I, Entry 2625.

7. GO 24, AGO, 1859, RG 94, Entry 44, authorized early discharge up to three months to allow soldiers at remote stations to avail themselves of infrequent transportation opportunities to the settlements, whenever there was reasonable certainty they would otherwise be detained beyond their term of service. John Burkman said Abrams was not at the Little Big Horn because if his memory served him right, Abrams was discharged at Fort Lincoln and stayed at Bismarck. Walter Camp to Burkman, Nov. 20, 1908, with roster of Company L and remarks added by Burkman after each name, LBHB Coll., M Roll 9 frame 0774; also Camp to Burkman, Dec. 5, 1908, WMC-LBHB.

Abrams's widow, in affidavit, Aug. 1, 1903, declared that her husband's comrades in Custer's command were all killed or missing except those in the wagon train (of which detail he was one) at the battle of the Little Big Horn, Pension File, RG 15.

8. Godfrey, *Diary*, 31.

9. RG 94, Entry 529

10. Company Return, June 30, 1876, LBHB Coll, Rolls 12 and 15; Ackison said he took sick on June 20 and was left on the steamboat when the regiment rode up the Rosebud. Ackison to Mrs. Maria Dresser (mother of Sgt. Ogden), Aug. 9, 1876, LBHB.

The fallibility of memory was clearly demonstrated when Bromwell said Ackison was at Powder River for sure, and Berwald said Ackison was at the Little Big Horn in the kitchen, WMC, rosters, IU; also Lange recalled that Ackison was at the Little Big Horn and was wounded slightly in the back, Lange interview, nd, WMC-BYU.

11. RG 94, Entry 409, file 10818 A (EB) AGO 1878, Capt Godfrey to Regimental Adjutant, May 7, 1877.

12. *Toronto (Can.) Daily Star*, Mar. 25, 1926; Alcott's sister was married to the brother of William O. Taylor, Taylor to Walter Camp, July 20, 1922, WMC-BYU.

13. SO 150, AGO, 1864, RG 94, Entry 44, ordered the three companies of 7th Infantry serving in New Mexico to be broken up and the enlisted men transferred to the 5th Infantry.

14. At the time divorce proceedings were initiated on Mar. 26, 1874, Plaintiff was 18 years old, whereas Defendant was said to be 33 years of age. Divorce granted on May 4, 1874, because of the defendant's alleged drunkenness, physical and verbal abuse of plaintiff, and non-support and was ordered to pay $9 per month child support until said child, Stella Edna, should attain age 18. Records of 2nd Judicial District Court, Ramsey County, Minnesota Historical Society.

15. Narrative of Lt. Godfrey, in Graham, *The Custer Myth*, 127.

16. Letter received from Cochran & Walsh, St. Paul, Minn., Oct. 25, 1876, seeking to collect amount paid by Capt. Nowlan to William Alexander for service as packer, RG 393, Part V, Fort Abraham Lincoln, DT.

17. *Bismarck (N.Dak.) Tribune*, May 10, 1878. Alexander, it was said, indulged too freely in fluid extracts, and while playing "Big Indian" at Sturgis City, he was roughly but justly dealt with by (Mr.) Mitchell. Alexander had driven Mitchell into the house and abused his wife and fired two shots at Mitchell, who then put a couple holes in Alexander for keepsakes. Alexander's version was that he was with a group taking horses out on the stage road and was sent ahead to water some of the horses at the ranch at Sturgis. There he had words about a pail with a man under the influence of liquor, and when the man pointed a Winchester at him to drive him away, the gun went off. The man claimed he did not know the gun was loaded. (Affidavits in pension file, RG 15, from Alexander and two witnesses, Dan Baker and George L. Simons, members of Alexander's group).

18. Walter Camp was informed in a letter from Henry Jones, April 11, 1913, that William Alexander was at the Soldier's home claiming to have been with the packers (packing for headquarters officers). Camp verified Alexander's claim to have been on Reno Hill, Camp to Jones, May 5, 1913, WMC-DPL; but elsewhere Camp said, "I doubt whether Alexander was along on the expedition at all," Miscellaneous Notes re: pack train, box 5, env 17, WMC-BYU.

The St. Paul City Directory of 1875 lists William Alexander, cook, boards at Cosmopolitan Hotel; the federal census of Boreman County, DT, June 1880, also lists Alexander as a cook, age 36, born in Ireland, single, resident Fort Rice.

19. Hardy declared Aller, "Dead, killed as a deserter," WMC, rosters, IU.

20. Private Henry Hammond, Company I, 6th Infantry, also deserted June 20, taking his gun and a small boat belonging to Lt. Walker. He surrendered at Fort Buford, July 2, Samuel L. Meddaugh, Diary, May 14–Sept. 15, 1876, (hereafter cited as Meddaugh Diary), typescript copy at The Newberry Library, Chicago.

Private Wilmot Sanford, Company D, 6th Infantry, recorded that three soldiers and a citizen deserted the night of June 19, Hill and Innis, eds., "The Fort Buford Diary of Private Sanford, 1876–1877."

21. Stan Roy and William Nugent said Armstrong's head found in village, and his body was buried near where he fell and was dug up during excavations May 28, 1926, Roy to Walter Camp, July 28, 1910, WMC-BYU; Nugent in *Winners of the West*, Vol. IV, No. 3, Feb. 28, 1927, 7; the *Custer Battlefield Burial Record Book* contains notation next to Armstrong's name "buried at Garry Owen," LBHB Coll, Roll 14.

22. GO 17, AGO, Mar. 15, 1869, RG 94, Entry 44, provided for reduction in the number of infantry regiments from 45 to 25. Changes included half of 37th Infantry Regiment (Companies A, C, E, F, and I) consolidated with 3rd Infantry Regiment, from August 11, 1869; Heitman, *Historical Register and Dictionary of the US Army*, Vol. 1:134.

23. GO 102, War dept AGO, Oct. 10, 1873, RG 94, Entry 44, was a presidential proclamation that all soldiers who had deserted their colors and who surrendered themselves at a military station on or before Jan. 1, 1874, would receive a full pardon, only forfeit pay and allowances due at time of desertion, and be restored to duty without trial or punishment, on condition they serve through the term of their enlistment.

24. SO 72, Hq DD, June 7, 1877, RG 393, Pt. 1, Entry 1191, was issued with regard to provisions set forth in Class 1 of GO 47, Hq Army, AGO, May 9, 1877, RG 94, Entry 44, to bring the Army strength down to the standard of 25,000 in accordance with terms of the Act of Aug. 15, 1876; Class 1 specified that soldiers whose term of service expired within four months of July 1, 1877, unless they agreed to reenlist in their companies at the date and place of their expiration of service, were to be absolutely discharged so as to get pay on final statement; all such discharges to take effect by or before June 15, 1877.

25. SO 70, Hq DD, June 4, 1877, RG 393, Pt. 1, Entry 1191, was issued in regard to the discharge of men from the 7th Cavalry coming under Class 1 of GO 47, RG 94, Entry 44, to bring the army down to the standard of 25,000 men in accordance with the terms of the Act of Aug. 15, 1876. Class 1 specified that soldiers whose term of service expired within four months of July 1, 1877, unless they agreed to reenlist in their companies at date and place of their expiration of service, were to be absolutely discharged so as to get pay on final statements; all such discharges to take effect by or before June 15, 1877.

26. A petition signed by twelve friends and relatives was submitted requesting Ascough's discharge to care for his father. His troop commander recommended his discharge, noting that his service was of little benefit to the government, being in the guard house since November 6 awaiting sentence of court-martial for prolonged absences without leave. The regimental commander added, "the man is worthless." RG 94, Entry 409, file 7974 C AGO (EB) 1881.

"Jack Ascough, the man who fell from a scaffold at the Sheridan house, is out again. Mr. Ascough leaves for Philadelphia in a few days to settle up his father's estate. He expects a handsome financial starter, and on his return to the city expects to go into the stock business." *Bismarck Tribune*, March 2, 1883.

27. See note A25 (Ascough).

B

Babcock, Elmer. Pvt co L; b. 10 June 1856 Pharsalia N.Y.; enl 21 Sep 1875 Boston Mass. for 5 yrs; age 21; farmer; brn eyes, dk hair, dk comp, 5' 6 1/2" high; join co L 29 Oct 1875 Ft Totten DT; dd superintend packing ice in ice-house 1 Dec 1875; sick hosp Ft Lincoln 18 Apr to 4 May 1876 (infl. pleura); killed with Custer column 25 June 1876.
Pension: 6 May 1885 / Mother / 326392 / 234544.

Bailey, Henry Allen. Blks co I; b. 25 Mar 1852 Foster RI; enl 24 Oct 1872 Springfield Mass. for 5 yrs; age 22; blacksmith; grey eyes, brn hair, fair comp, 5' 7 1/4" high; assd to co I as blks 5 July 1873; ds St Louis Bks awaiting transp to regt to 20 Aug 1873; ds Ft Snelling Minn. to 9 Sep 1873 when sent to join co at Ft Totten DT; killed with Custer column 25 June 1876.[1]

Bailey, Jno. A. Sad'r co B; b. 20 Sep 1845 Jo Daviess Co. Ill.; pvt & sad'r co K 1 Iowa cav 31 Aug 1862 to 15 Feb 1866; enl reg army 10 Dec 1870 Ft L'worth Kans. for 5 yrs in co B 7 cav; age 25; saddler; blue eyes, dk hair, dk comp, 5' 11 1/2" high; sad'r 1 Jan 1871; cpl 1 June 1873; pvt & sad'r 1 Nov 1873; disch 10 Dec 1875 Shreveport La. expir of serv & reenl in co B for 5 yrs; recom for medal of honor for gal cond on Reno hill when co ret from charging inds, he gave up his rifle pit to his capt, foregoing personal consid'n;[2] disch 9 Dec 1880 Ft Yates DT expir of serv a sad'r char xclt; reenl in co B 5 Jan 1881 & served continuously as co sad'r to 27 Mar 1895 when retd a sgt char xclt; died 2 June 1915 St Paul Minn.
Pension: 11 June 1915 / Wid / 1048884 / 835690.

Bailey, Wm. Jas. (alias Wm. Baker). Pvt detmt ind scouts; b. 24 Apr 1850 Alexandria Va.; drummer boy co F 152 N.Y. inf 29 Apr 1863 to 13 July 1865; enl reg army as Wm. Baker 28 Oct 1869 Winchester Va. for 5 yrs in co F 17 inf; age 21; musician; blk eyes, brn hair, dk comp, 5' 6" high; dd learning music Feb 1870; appt mus'n Oct 1870; ed qmd as ind intrpr Apr & May 1872; [co on Yellowstone Exp'n July to Oct 1872]; on furl 30 days 21 Mar 1873 Grand River Agcy; ds with Blk Hills Exp'n as ind intrpr June to Sep 1874; disch 28 Oct 1874 Ft Abercrombie DT upon expir of serv a mus'n; employed next day in post qmd as intrpr for ind scouts; hired 9 Apr 1876 at Ft Abercrombie as teamster for Sioux Exp'n; rate of pay $30 mo; tr to Lt Nowlan at Ft Lincoln 24 Apr & disch 30 Apr; enl for detmt of ind scouts 4 May by Lt Varnum for 6 mos; (Varnum said he may have used Baker as intrpr);[3] on Reno scout up Powder River 10 June says Soldier;[4] Varnum did not recall if Baker on march up Rosebud but sure not on Reno hill dur fight;[5] on str *Josephine* to Powder River 16 July;[6] carried desp from capt Snyder's wagon train near mouth of Rosebud 16 Aug to col Miles on str *Far West* at Buffalo Rapids;[7] ds Ft Lincoln 20 Oct; reenl 4 Nov at Ft lincoln by Lt Wallace for 6 mos & served continuously to 4 Nov 1877 when disch at Ft Lincoln upon expir of serv a scout char good; died 14 Oct 1933 St Cloud Fla.[8]
Pension: 11 Dec 1891 / Inv / 1077664 / 1125315. Wid / 1735774 / A-3-21-34. (XC-2,658,050).

Baker, Wm. See Bailey, Wm. Jas.

Baker, Wm. H. Pvt co E; b. 3 Dec 1848 Golconda Ill.; enl 1 Sep 1870 St Louis Mo. for 5 yrs; age 21; farmer; blue eyes, brn hair, fair comp, 5' 9" high; join co C 3 art'y 26 Sep 1870 Ft Riley Kans.; tr to co I 26 Oct 1871; ed qmd teamster Feb 1872 thro' Aug 1875; disch 1 Sep 1875 Ft Hamilton N.Y. expir of serv a pvt; reenl 1 Oct 1875 New York N.Y. for 5 yrs; join co E 7 cav 29 Oct 1875 Ft Totten DT; killed with Custer column 25 June 1876.
Pension: 23 Apr 1877 / Minor / 231009 / 180301.

Bancroft, Neil. Pvt co A; b. Oswego N.Y.; enl 20 Sep 1873 Chicago Ill. for 5 yrs; age 27 10/12; lumberman; grey eyes, fair hair, fair comp, 5' 6 3/4" high; join co A 18 Oct 1873 Ft Lincoln DT; dd co tailor Apr 1874; cpl 1

Dec 1875; pvt 20 May 1876; dd room orderly Feb 1878; dd qmd laborer Apr to July 1878; disch 20 Sep 1878 Camp J. G. Sturgis DT expir of serv a pvt char good; awarded medal of honor 5 Oct 1878 for bringing water to wounded [at LBH], but having been disch the serv & whereabouts unknown, medal returned to AGO;[9] no further attempt was made to locate him until many years later by which time he had died without knowing he had been awarded the nation's highest honor.[10]

Banks, Chas. Pvt co L; b. Dublin Ireland; enl 14 Sep 1868 New York N.Y. for 5 yrs; age 23 5/12; waiter; blue eyes, brn hair, fair comp, 5' 5 1/2" high; join co D 7 cav 10 Nov 1868 Camp Sandy Forsyth Kans.; dd co cook Apr to July 1870; disch 14 Sep 1873 Camp Terry DT expir of serv a pvt; reenl in regt 29 Sep 1873 St Paul Minn. for 5 yrs; join co L 19 Oct 1873 Ft Lincoln DT; dd qmd teamster Jan to May 1875; dd qmd with water wagon 30 Oct 1875 to 7 Mar 1876; dd regtl hq fatigue pty (morn & eve) 11 May 1876;[11] dd regtl hq orderly 6 Aug 1876; dd post hq mail carrier 30 Sep to 25 Nov 1876; dd regtl hq fatigue pty 25 Apr to 8 Oct 1877; dd regtl hq orderly June 1878; disch 29 Sep 1878 Camp J. G. Sturgis DT expir of serv a pvt char good & reenl in co L for 5 yrs; sick hosp Ft Lincoln 18 Feb to 4 May 1879 (broken l. clavicle); dd med dept nurse June 1879 to July 1880; dd co cook Aug 1880; ed post hosp nurse Dec 1880 to Sep 1881; cpl 18 Sep 1881; sgt 2 Feb 1882; pvt 10 Mar 1882; ed post hosp Apr & May 1882; dd room orderly Oct 1882; ed post hosp nurse Dec 1882 to Sep 1883; disch 27 Sep 1883 Ft Snelling Minn. expir of serv a pvt char xclt; reenl 17 Oct 1883 West Point N.Y. for 5 yrs in cav detmt USMA; cpl 3 Apr 1884; dd chg of meadows June 1884; dd chg of stables Oct 1884; dd chg of stables Oct 1885 to May 1886; dd chg of stables Apr 1887; pvt 28 Nov 1887; disch 17 Oct 1888 at West Point by expir of serv a pvt & reenl in same unit for 5 yrs; on furl 25 days; on sick report from 15 Apr 1889; sent to army & navy hosp Hot Springs Ark 3 July 1889; disch 27 Sep 1889 at West Point on surg cert dis (ac. rheum.; dis 1/2) a pvt char xclt; died 14 May 1901 West Point N.Y.

Pension: 17 Oct 1889 / Inv / 734153 / 549235. Wid / 742397 / 554903.

Barnett, Chas. Clinton. Pvt co G; b. 7 May 1857 Camden Ohio; enl 25 Mar 1876 Cincinnati Ohio for 5 yrs; age 19; carpenter; blue eyes, brn hair, fair comp, 5' 9" high; join co G 27 Apr 1876 St Paul Minn.; broke his carbine 17 May; ds camp Powder River MT 15 June 1876;[12] ds with ordn wagon 6 Aug;[13] dd regtl hq mtd msgr 26 Nov to 5 Dec 1876; dd qmd June 1878; sick 23 Aug to 30 Sep 1878 (typhoid fever); ds Ft Lincoln Oct & Nov 1878; ds qmd at Bismarck Dec 1878 thro' Jan 1879; dd bldg co stables June 1879; dd co carpenter Oct 1879 to Jan 1880; on furl 30 days 20 Feb 1881 Alkali Creek; disch 24 Mar 1881 Ft Meade DT expir of serv a pvt; died 3 Apr 1935 Anacortes Wash'n.

Pension: 13 Jan 1899 / Inv / 1216703. Ind. Surv. / 17014 / 11082. (XC-2,578,199).

Barry, Jno. Pvt co I; b. Waterford Ireland; enl 21 Sep 1875 Boston Mass. for 5 yrs; age 26; laborer; grey eyes, dk hair, ruddy comp, 5' 7 3/4" high; join co I 21 Oct 1875 Ft Lincoln DT; killed with Custer column 25 June 1876.

Pension: 17 Nov 1878 / Mother / 240342 / 255512.

Barry, Peter O. Pvt co B; b. Wash'n D.C.; enl 16 July 1867 at Wash'n for 5 yrs; age 22; farmer; brn eyes, brn hair, dk comp, 5' 9 1/4" high; join co B 14 Sep 1867 Ft Dodge Kans.; dd regtl hq Mar to May 1869; cpl 10 Aug 1871 & ds regtl hq to Nov 1871; sgt 1 Feb 1872; disch 16 July 1872 Spartanburg SC expir of serv a sgt & reenl in co B for 5 yrs; pvt 1 Sep 1872; cpl 13 Dec 1872; sgt 1 May 1873; abs sick hq Yellowstone. Exp'n 29 Aug to 10 Sep 1873; pvt 8 Oct 1873; ed subs dept laborer Nov 1873 to Sep 1874; (ds Ft Lincoln July & Aug 1874); sen gen cm 22 June 1875 forf $10 pay per mo for 6 mos & conft same period; ed subs dept laborer 13 May 1876; dd subs dept June to Sep 1876;[14] ed subs dept laborer 12 Nov 1876 to 4 Feb 1877; ed subs dept 25 Apr 1877 (with Lt Gibson); disch 16 July 1877 camp near Cedar Creek MT by expir of serv a pvt char good; reenl 21 Feb 1880 Ft Meade DT for 5 yrs; assd to co E 7 cav; dd co cook Apr to Sep 1880; dd co cook

Dec 1881; cpl 12 July 1882; sgt 1 Jan 1883; pvt 2 Jan 1884; disch 20 Feb 1885 Ft Meade DT expir of serv a pvt char xclt; reenl 11 May 1885 Wash'n D.C. for 5 yrs; disch 18 May 1885 per SO 113 AGO 1885 (by way of favor upon own appn, having been appt to city police 12 May); died 3 July 1907 Morgan Md.
Pension: 6 Apr 1897 / Inv / 1188401. (Rej on grd no ratable dis from alleged malarial poisoning, lumbago & stric.). Ind. Wid / 13489 / 8942.

Barsantee, Jas. Franklin. Pvt co B; b. 10 Feb 1853 Boston Mass.; enl in navy 10 June 1867 Portsmouth N.H. for 3 yrs as 2d cl. boy; hazel eyes, lt hair, lt comp, 4' 9 1/2" high; msgr boy on frigate *Minnesota* [on cruise to Europe]; des 3 Mar 1868 at Portsmouth; reenl 18 Apr 1872 at Boston for 3 yrs a seaman on sloop *Tuscarora* [assd to south pacific sta]; disch 29 Sep 1875 at Boston; enl in army 8 Mar 1876 at Boston for 5 yrs; age 23; sailor; hazel eyes, brn hair, fair comp, 5' 5 1/2" high; join co B 7 cav 27 Apr 1876 St Paul Minn.; des 29 Mar 1877 Ft Lincoln DT; reenl in navy 20 Jan 1883 at Boston for 3 yrs; des 11 July 1883 from str *Powhatan* [cruised Cuban waters Jan to May 1883]; enl in army as Wm. Evans 10 Oct 1883 New York N.Y. for 5 yrs; join co H 2 inf 20 Nov 1883 Ft Spokane WT; dd co baker Feb to Apr 1884; des 9 May 1884 at Ft Spokane; enl in marine corps 27 July 1893 at Boston for 5 yrs; sick (hematuria) 31 July in navy yard hosp & tr to naval hosp at Chelsea Mass. (peritonitis); disch upon report of med survey 23 Sep 1893 still in hosp; disch from hosp two days later upon own req (against advice); died 7 July 1941 Boston Mass.
Pension: 17 Aug 1910 / Inv [Navy] / 1391965. (Rej on grd no ratable dis shown). 13 Mar 1917 / Ind. Surv. / 9663. (Rej on grd clmt des 7th Cav, on which serv claim based & never recd hon disch).

Barth, Robt. Pvt co E; b. Pforzheim Germany; enl 6 Dec 1872 Albany N.Y. for 5 yrs; age 22; jeweler; grey eyes, brn hair, fair comp, 5' 10 1/2" high; join co E 13 Feb 1873 Unionville SC; dd subs dept herder Oct 1873 to Mar 1874; sick Ft Randall DT 4–28 June 1875 (pr. syph.); dd co cook Oct 1875; killed with Custer column 25 June 1876.
Pension: 24 Jan 1877 / Mother / 229668. (Abandoned).

Bates, Jos. Pvt co M; b. Providence RI; enl as Jos. C. Murphy 29 Mar 1858 Buffalo N.Y. for 5 yrs; age 22; clerk; blue eyes, brn hair, swarthy comp, 5' 9" high; assd to co F 2 drg; (redesig 2 cav Aug 1861); disch 29 Mar 1863 camp near Falmouth Va. by expir of serv a pvt; enr 27 Oct 1863 a sgt 1 Mass. cav; 1 Lt 5 Dec 1863; capt 6 Jan 1864; m.o. vol serv 26 June 1865; enl reg army as Jos. Bates 27 Mar 1866 New York N.Y. for 3 yrs; join co M 7 cav 10 Dec 1866 Ft Riley Kans.; 1sgt 13 Dec 1866; abs in arrest June 1867 Ft Hays Kans.; pvt 9 Aug 1867; dd actg sgt-maj of escort for ind peace com'n Sep & Oct 1867; dd clerk in adjt's office Nov 1867; cpl 16 Dec 1867; sgt 11 Jan 1868; dd regtl color bearer Oct 1868 to Feb 1869; awl 30 days 27 Feb 1869; disch 27 Mar 1869 Medicine Bluff Creek IT expir of serv a sgt; reenl 18 July 1870 Carlisle Pa. for 5 yrs; join co F 7 cav 31 Jan 1872 Louisville Ky.; cpl 1 Feb 1872; sgt 5 Feb 1872; des 11 May 1872 at Louisville; apph 20 Dec 1873 at Louisville; sick hosp Lebanon Ky. to 11 Jan 1874 (frac. r. arm); in conft St Louis Bks Mo. to 12 Feb 1874; in conft Ft Snelling Minn. to 20 June 1874 when restored to duty without trial (to make good time lost) & tr to regtl hq; dd with Lt Wallace & detmt ind scouts 21 Aug 1874; dd post hq Sep 1874; dd qmd teamster Dec 1874; tr to co M 4 Jan 1875; cpl 2 Aug 1875; pvt 6 Nov 1875; disch 27 Feb 1877 Ft Rice DT expir of serv a pvt; reenl same day for 5 yrs in co H; cpl 1 Apr 1877 to date 27 Feb; dd chg of horse & mule herd Oct 1877; pvt 21 Jan 1878; disch 19 Feb 1878 at Ft Rice on surg cert dis (too free use of alcoholic stimulants); hired in qmd as citizen teamster; injured 13 May 1880 when dragged on grd by mule team that became unmanageable & in hosp to 30 Aug 1880 (frac. jaw, loss of teeth & left ear); died 13 Sep 1893 Sturgis SD (suicide thro' despondency & results); never married.
Pension: 29 Apr 1891 / Inv / 1017491. (Rej, not ratably disabled under act 27 June 1890).

Bauer, Jacob. Pvt co K; b. Baden Germany; enl 4 Nov 1866 Brownsville Tex. for 5 yrs; age 24; soldier; brn eyes, blk hair, fair comp, 5' 5" high; assd to co E 4 cav; disch 4 Nov 1871 Ft Richardson Tex. by expir of serv a pvt; reenl 4 Mar 1876 McComb City Miss for 5 yrs in co K 7 cav; sick hosp Ft Lincoln DT 5–19 May 1876 (tert. intm. fever); sent with Lt Garlington on str *Josephine* 24 July to join co in field; dd co cook Aug 1876; sick hosp Ft Lincoln 7 Oct to 8 Nov 1876 (cont'n l. side, fall from horse); in conft Feb 1877; des 12 Apr 1877 at Ft Lincoln & apph two days later near Ft Rice DT; ds with detmt at Carroll MT Sep 1877; dd qmd laborer June 1880; disch 3 Mar 1881 Ft Totten DT by expir of serv a pvt char very good; reenl 23 Mar 1881 Ft L'worth Kans. for 5 yrs; assd to co C 6 cav; tr to co D; disch 22 Mar 1886 Ft Cummings NM expir of serv a pvt char xclt; reenl 9 Apr 1886 at Ft L'worth for 5 yrs; assd to co B 2 cav; tr to co D 6 cav; dishon disch 23 May 1888 Ft Stanton NM sen gen cm & conft one yr mil prison (drunk at morn inspection & used abusive language toward co comdr).

Baumbach, Conrad. Pvt band; b. Berlin Germany; enl 26 June 1875 St Louis Mo. for 5 yrs; age 35; musician; blue eyes, dk hair, ruddy comp, 5' 6" high; join 7 cav 14 Apr 1876 Ft Lincoln DT (with Lt Reily's detmt); assd to band 28 Apr; ds camp Powder River MT 14 June; ds str *Josephine* 6 Aug to Ft Lincoln with band; sick hosp 26 Dec 1876 to 2 May 1877 (frostbite both feet); sick qrs 10 June to 5 Aug 1877 (frostbite recur); des 30 June 1878 at Ft Lincoln.

Baumgartner, Louis. Pvt co A; b. Baden Germany; enl 3 Feb 1872 Cincinnati Ohio for 5 yrs; age 22; laborer; brn eyes, brn hair, fair comp, 5' 6 1/2" high; join co A 21 Feb 1872 E'town Ky.; ds Oct 1872 to Jan 1873 with detmt at Huntsville Ala; disch 3 Feb 1877 Ft Rice DT expir of serv a pvt char very good; reenl 22 Dec 1877 at Cincinnati for 5 yrs; join co A 7 Oct 1878 Ft Lincoln DT; cpl 1 Sep 1879; sgt 19 Jan 1880; 1sgt 22 July 1881; disch 21 Dec 1882 Ft Meade DT expir of serv a 1sgt & reenl in co A for 5 yrs; on furl 5 mos 22 Dec 1882 at Cincinnati; disch 21 Dec 1887 Ft Keogh MT expir of serv a 1sgt char xclt & reenl in co A for 5 yrs; on furl 22 Dec 1887 to 3 May 1888 Bristol Pa.; ds 22 June to 13 July 1888 Ft Riley Kans.; on furl 30 days 14 Jan 1890 at Cincinnati; appt comsy sgt USA 25 Mar 1891 at Ft Randall SD; disch 21 Dec 1892 Ft Pembina N.Dak. expir of serv a comsy sgt char xclt & reenl for 5 yrs; tr to Watertown Ars'l N.Y. 23 Mar 1893; tr to Ft Trumbull Conn. 17 Nov 1893; disch 4 Aug 1894 at Ft Trumbull per SO 178 AGO 1894 a comsy sgt; reenl 27 Aug 1894 New Haven Conn. for 3 yrs (auth AGO) for co I 7 cav; sick hosp Ft Riley Kans. 12 Sep 1894 (paresis); tr to hosp Wash'n D.C. 14 Oct 1894; disch 10 Nov 1894 on surg cert dis (progressive paralysis of insane, contr line of duty) a pvt char xclt; died in hosp 22 May 1895.[15]

Beck, Benj. Pvt band; b. 15 Oct 1852 Phil'a Pa.; enl 3 Jan 1876 New York N.Y. for 5 yrs; age 23; moulder; hazel eyes, lt brn hair, fair comp, 5' 5 1/4" high; join 7 cav 14 Apr 1876 Ft Lincoln DT (with Lt Reily's detmt); assd to band 28 Apr; ds camp Powder River MT 14 June 1876; ds str *Josephine* 6 Aug 1876 to Ft Lincoln with band; disch 2 Jan 1881 Ft Meade DT expir of serv a pvt char xclt; reenl 28 Jan 1881 Ft Wayne Mich. for 5 yrs; assd to band 10 inf; disch 27 Jan 1886 Ft Union NM expir of serv a pvt char xclt; reenl 16 June 1886 Detroit Mich. for 5 yrs; assd to band Jeff'n Bks Mo.; disch 15 June 1891 at Jeff'n Bks expir of serv a pvt char xclt; reenl 21 June 1891 at Jeff'n Bks for 5 yrs; assd to band 23 inf; disch 20 June 1896 Ft Clark Tex. expir of serv a prin mus'n char xclt; reenl 30 June 1896 Eagle Pass Tex. for 3 yrs in band 16 inf (auth AGO, providing his weight 200 pounds [10 pounds above max & 70 pounds above proportional weight] not interfere with performance of duty; plays bass horn & violin [all upper teeth false on rubber plate]); disch 29 June 1899 Ft Crook Neb expir of serv a sgt char xclt & reenl in same unit for 3 yrs; disch 29 June 1902 Presidio San Francisco Calif. expir of serv a sgt char xclt; reenl next day in 3d band coast art'y corps for 3 yrs; disch 29 June 1905 at Presidio by expir of serv a prin mus'n char xclt & reenl in same unit; retd 28 Sep 1906 a prin mus'n; died 30 Apr 1910 Camden NJ.[16]

Bell, Jas. Montgomery. 1Lt co D; b. 1 Oct 1837 Williamsburg Pa.; grad Wittenberg college in 1862; 1Lt 86 Ohio inf (3 mo troops)

10 June to 25 Sep 1862; capt indpt co militia cav 30 June 1863 (desig co D 13 Pa. cav); m.o. vol serv 14 July 1865 Raleigh NC; appt reg army com'n 2Lt 7 cav 24 Nov 1866 to date 28 July 1866; join regt 26 Jan 1867 Ft Riley Kans. & assd to co I; 1Lt 2 Apr 1867; recd bvt 1Lt, capt & maj Dec 1867 dated 2 Mar 1867 for gal serv in battles of Wilderness & Reams Sta Va.; rqm 1 Nov 1867; (remembered for his timely arrival with supply wagons dur action at Washita 27 Nov 1868);[17] actg aqm in field 7 Dec 1868 to 27 Apr 1869; rqm 26 Oct 1869; assd to co D 2 Jan 1871; ds rctg duty 13 Jan 1871 Pittsburgh Pa.; join co D 22 Apr 1873 Ft Snelling Minn.; actg aqm & comsy NBS May to Oct 1873; ds St Paul Minn. Mar 1874 with bd purchasing horses; ds Ft Lincoln DT 29 July 1874 chg of horses; ds Shreveport La. 7 Oct 1874 with co B; comd detmt to Vienna La. 7 Nov 1874 to aid Lt Hodgson's detmt with mob of angry citizens; comd co B at Shreveport to 31 Jan 1876; arr Ft Lincoln 11 Mar 1876 from gen Custer's snowbound train; awl 6 mos 24 Mar 1876;[18] ordered 11 July to rejoin regt; arr Ft Lincoln 25 July;[19] dep on str *Key West* 2 Aug to join co in field; ret to Ft Lincoln 13 Aug on str *Josephine* with band;[20] purchased one pub horse from qmd 17 Aug; prom capt co F 20 Aug from 26 July; dep on str *Durfee* eve 31 Aug to join co in field; ordered back from Ft Buford 7 Sep acc't low water in Yellowstone River & arr Ft Lincoln 10 Sep;[21] appt to bd of officers 23 Sep to appraise value of govt horse ridden by gen Custer & which officers of regt desired to present to Mrs. Custer; comd co F from 26 Sep & in field 17 Oct to 14 Nov disarming inds at Cheyenne Agcy & cond ind pony herd to Ft Abercrombie; awl 30 days 17 Dec 1876 (illness of father); on pvt business at St Paul 9 Jan to 21 Mar 1877; comd co F in field May to Oct 1877; ds str *General Meade* 26 Oct (mouth of Squaw Creek [Camp Hale MT] on Missouri River) enroute to Ft Abercrombie to cond tr of co prop (& move family) to new sta; awl 2 mos 1 Dec 1877 (upon death of father); post comdr Ft Totten DT Feb to July 1878; with co guarding NPRR ext'n May to Oct 1880; with co to Poplar MT Dec 1880 & cond band of Sioux inds to Ft Buford; pres at surd of Sitting Bull's band 19 July 1881 at Ft Buford;[22] with co guarding NPRR ext'n Aug to Oct 1881; [co F at Ft Buford to Aug 1887 when tr to Ft Meade DT]; bvt Lt-col 27 Feb 1890 for gal serv in action against Nez Perce inds at Canon Creek MT 13 Sep 1877; sick 18 Nov 1890 to 22 Jan 1891 Ft Sill IT & awl on surg cert to 25 Mar 1892; prom maj 1 cav 23 May 1896; gsw l. leg (frac. both bones) 24 June 1898 Las Gausima Cuba; awl to 7 Nov 1898; col 27 US vol inf 5 July 1899 & sailed with regt to Philippines; brig-gen vols 20 Jan 1900 & mil gov'r southern Luzon to Mar 1901; m.o. vol serv 20 June 1901; (Lt-col 8 cav from 10 Jan 1900 & col 24 Mar 1901); retd 1 Oct 1901 a brig-gen; died 17 Sep 1919 Hermosa Beach Calif.
[1855 ACP 1876]. Pension: 13 Oct 1919 / Wid / 1147747. (XC-2,701,065).

Bender, Henry. Sgt co L; b. Berlin Prussia; enl in co L 28 Jan 1873 New Orleans La. for 5 yrs; age 29; clerk; hazel eyes, blk hair, dk comp, 5' 9" high; cpl 26 Apr 1873; sgt 13 Apr 1874; dd actg co qm sgt Oct 1875; ds Ft Totten DT 24 Mar 1876 with wagon train for co prop; ds camp Powder River MT 10 June 1876 chg co prop; 1sgt 1 Aug 1876 to date 1 July; sgt 21 Dec 1876; in conft Feb 1877 (accused with comsy sgt Inman in theft of govt bacon & selling same to merchants at Bismarck); acquited in gen cm 21 Apr 1877 & restored to duty; ds Ft Lincoln 1 May 1877 chg co prop; disch 28 Jan 1878 at Ft Lincoln by expir of serv a sgt char xclt.

Bennett, Jas. C. Pvt co C; b. Shelby Ohio; enl 23 July 1870 Cincinnati Ohio for 5 yrs; age 22; laborer; grey eyes, dk hair, dk comp, 5' 6" high; join co C 8 cav 4 Oct 1870 Ft Bayard NM; cpl 21 Nov 1871; sgt 25 Mar 1872; dd post sgt-maj May 1872 to June 1873 Ft Selden NM; ed qmd Apr to June 1874; ds Ft Wingate NM Aug to Dec 1874; ed qmd Feb to Apr 1875; disch 23 July 1875 Ft Wingate NM expir of serv a sgt; reenl 11 Sep 1875 New York N.Y. for 5 yrs; join co C 7 cav 21 Oct 1875 Ft Lincoln DT; dd regtl hq 22 Oct 1875 to 5 May 1876; gsw chest 26 June on Reno hill (in dorsal spine, complete paralysis below seat of injury); died 5 July 1876 on str *Far West* en route to Ft Lincoln.[23]

Benteen, Fred'k Wm. Capt co H; b. 24 Aug 1834 Petersburg Va.; moved to St Louis Mo. in 1849; org vol troops dur summer 1861; appt 1Lt co C 10 Mo. cav 1 Sep 1861; capt 1 Oct 1861; maj 19 Dec 1862; Lt-col 27 Feb 1864; m.o. with regt 30 June 1865 Nashville Tenn; col 138 US col'd inf 15 July 1865; m.o. vol serv 6 Jan 1866 at Atlanta Ga.;[24] appt reg army com'n capt 7 cav 24 Nov 1866 to date 28 July 1866; join co H 29 Jan 1867 Ft Riley Kans.; bvt maj & Lt-col Sep 1867 (dated 2 Mar 1867) for gal serv in battle of Osage Mo. & chg on Columbus Ga.; bvt col May 1869 for gal cond against hostile inds at Saline River Kans. 13 Aug 1868; with co at Nashville Tenn May 1871 to Mar 1873; sick qrs 30 Apr 1873 Yankton DT; comd cos H & C at supply camp mouth of Glendive Creek July to Sep 1873 dur Yellowstone Exp'n; comd co with Blk Hills Exp'n July & Aug 1874; with co at New Orleans La. from Oct 1874; tr to Ft Randall DT May 1875 & in field ejecting miners from Blk Hills to Sep 1875; post comdr Ft Rice DT 25 Oct 1875 to 1 May 1876; comd l. wing 12 May to 22 June; comd cos H, D, & K 25 June; sick (dysentery) on str *Josephine* 6 July mouth of Big Horn River & on boat to Powder River 16 July; on str *Far West* to Rosebud 20 July;[25] ds str *Carroll* 27 Aug to Ft Buford (enroute to St Louis Bks for rctg duty by 1 Oct); arr Ft Rice 9 Sep on str *Benton*; join capt McDougall & gen Terry on train to St Paul 20 Sep; stayed at home of gen Terry & accomp him on train to Chicago 26 Sep; arr St Louis 30 Sep & assd rctg sta at Phil'a; stayed at home of maj Merrill till relieved 10 Oct upon own req; return to Ft Rice 26 Oct (with maj Tilford);[26] comd co in field from 1 May 1877 & comd cos H, G, & M from 28 July & in action with Nez Perce inds at Canon Creek MT 13 Sep;[27] comd regt 8 Oct 1877 to Ft Lincoln; ds Chicago Ill. Jan 1879 witness in Reno court of inq; prom maj 9 cav 22 Jan 1883 & join regt 20 July at Ft Riley Kans.; post comdr Ft Sill IT 21 May 1884; ds Ft Custer MT 23–30 June 1886; post comdr Ft DuChesne UT 23 Aug 1886; in arrest 18 Dec 1886 upon report of chr. drunkenness; sen gen cm 25 Feb 1887 to dismissal from serv but mitigated to suspension from rank & duty for one yr at half pay; sick qrs May & June 1888 Ft Niobrara Neb; retd 7 July 1888 for med reasons contr line of duty; bvt brig-gen 27 Feb 1890 for gal serv in action at Little Big Horn & at Canon Creek; died 22 June 1898 Atlanta Ga.[28]
[5142 ACP 1876]. Pension: 14 Oct 1898 / Wid / 684023 / 480723.

Berwald, Frank. Pvt co E; b. 3 Dec 1852 Posen Poland; enl 25 Jan 1873 Pittsburgh Pa. for 5 yrs; age 22; blacksmith; grey eyes, brn hair, florid comp, 5' 5 3/4" high; assd to co E as blks 5 July 1873; ds St Louis Bks awaiting transp to regt to 20 Aug & at Ft Snelling Minn. to 9 Sep; join co E 22 Sep 1873 Ft Lincoln DT; pvt 18 Oct 1873; blks 1 Mar 1874; pvt 23 Nov 1874; ed qmd blks Nov 1875 thro' Feb 1876; [at LBH with pack train said himself];[29] cpl 1 Oct 1876 to date 1 Sep; sgt 30 Mar 1877; disch 25 Jan 1878 at Ft Lincoln expir of serv a sgt char good; reenl 6 Feb 1878 Chicago Ill. for 5 yrs; join co K 7 inf 1 June 1878 Ft Shaw MT; dd co cook 20 June 1878; dd qmd blks Aug 1878; dd co cook Feb 1879; dd hq fatigue Apr 1879; ed qmd teamster July 1879; dd co cook Oct & Dec 1879; dd qmd herder Mar 1880; cpl 25 Oct 1880; pvt 3 Nov 1881; dd co cook Nov 1881; dd co cook May 1882; ed qmd blks Aug & Oct 1882; dd co cook Dec 1882; disch 5 Feb 1883 Ft Laramie Wyo. expir of serv a pvt char good; reenl 14 Feb 1883 Davenport Iowa for 5 yrs; join co H 3 cav 3 Mar 1883 Whipple Bks AT; dd asst co cook Apr 1883; dd co gardener Oct 1883; ed hosp nurse Feb & Apr 1884; ed hosp cook June 1884; ed hosp attdt Aug & Oct 1884; ed hosp cook Dec 1884; ed co cook Apr 1885; ed subs dept laborer June 1885; dd co cook Dec 1885; dd co cook Apr 1887; cpl 29 Sep 1887; disch 13 Feb 1888 Ft McIntosh Tex. expir of serv a cpl char xclt & reenl next day in hosp corps for 5 yrs;[30] disch 13 Feb 1893 West Point N.Y. expir of serv a pvt char xclt & reenl in hosp corps for 5 yrs; disch 13 Feb 1898 at West Point expir of serv a pvt char xclt & reenl in hosp corps for 3 yrs;[31] disch 13 Feb 1901 at West Point expir of serv a pvt char good & reenl in hosp corps for 3 yrs; on furl 5 mos 1 Oct 1902; retd 20 Feb 1903 a 1st cl. pvt (cook); died 9 Oct 1936 Highland Falls N.Y.
Pension: 17 Oct 1936 / Wid / XC-972589.

Bischoff, Chas. H. Pvt co C; b. 23 Sep 1855 Bremen Germany; enl 23 Nov 1872 Phil'a Pa. for 5 yrs; age 21; barber; blue eyes, lt hair, fair comp, 5' 4 1/2" high; join co C 12 Feb 1873 Charlotte NC; dd orderly June 1874; dd hosp attdt with Dr. Williams July & Aug 1874; dd subs dept May to Sep 1875; dd regtl hq mtd msgr 30 Apr to 3 May 1876;[32] ds camp Powder River MT 10 June 1876;[33] tr to co I 18 Sep 1876; cpl 1 Oct 1876; sgt 29 Jan 1877; ds Ft Lincoln DT 15 Oct 1877; disch 23 Nov 1877 at Ft Lincoln expir of serv a sgt char xclt; died 14 Feb 1924 Baltimore Md.
Pension: Ind. Surv. / 11292 / 7921. Ind. Wid / 16726 / 10869. (XC-2,659,415).

Bishley, Henry. Pvt co H; b. 9 Oct 1846 Chicago Ill.; pvt co C 133 Ill. inf 30 Apr 1864 to 24 Sep 1864; pvt co A 150 Ill. inf 1 Feb 1865 to 16 Jan 1866; enl reg army 2 Oct 1866 Peoria Ill. for 3 yrs; age 20; farmer; hazel eyes, auburn hair, lt comp, 5' 7" high; assd to co I 34 inf; (consol with 11 inf Apr 1869 to form 16 inf); disch 2 Oct 1869 Grenada Miss expir of serv a pvt char xclt & reenl in co I 16 inf for 5 yrs; disch 2 Oct 1874 Little Rock Ark expir of serv a pvt char xclt & reenl in same co for 5 yrs; disch 2 Oct 1875 at Little Rock on surg cert dis (chr. alcoholism) a pvt; reenl 6 Oct 1875 St Louis Bks Mo. for 5 yrs; age 34; join co H 7 cav 29 Oct 1875 Ft Rice DT; gsw r. shoulder 26 June 1876 (fl. wd. sl.); remain with co in field; in conft Dec 1876 (sleeping on gd duty); sen gen cm 27 Feb 1877 to one yr conft remitted in consid'n of his xclt char dur 9 yrs serv; dd co cook Apr 1877; dd co cook Feb 1878; dd co cook Oct 1878 to Jan 1879; in conft Feb 1879; disch 9 June 1879 Ft Lincoln DT on surg cert dis a pvt char fair to middling; (granular conjunctivitis both eyes, treated at intervals without improvement; subject to relapse at any time from alkali dust in summer & snow in winter; contr line of duty; dis 1/4); died 18 Mar 1929 vets home Napa Co. Calif.
Pension: Inv / 1354895 / 1131740. (XC-2,489,338).

Bishop, Alexander Browne. Cpl co H; b. 22 Nov 1853 Brooklyn N.Y.; enl in co H 15 Apr 1875 New Orleans La. for 5 yrs; age 22; sailor; hazel eyes, lt hair, fair comp, 5' 6" high; ed subs dept Nov 1875 to Jan 1876; clerk in adjt's office Feb to Apr 1876; cpl 1 May 1876; gsw r. forearm 26 June (fl. wd. sl.); tr on str *Far West* 3 July to hosp Ft Lincoln DT; tr in wagon to Ft Rice 16 July; duty 20 July; dd actg post sgt-maj 24 Aug; sgt 6 Oct 1876; disch 29 Oct 1876 at Ft Rice per SO 218 AGO 1876 (by way of favor, having become sole support of family) a sgt char xclt;[34] died 19 Sep 1935 Brooklyn N.Y.
Pension: 23 Nov 1876 / Inv / 227938 / 144209. Ind. Surv. / 14147 / 6868.

Bishop, Chas. Henry. Pvt co H; b. 11 May 1854 Wash'n D.C.; enl in co H 15 April 1875 New Orleans La. for 5 yrs; age 22; watchmaker; hazel eyes, lt hair, fair comp, 5' 8" high; dd comsy dept herder Oct 1875; ed qmd storekeeper Nov 1875 to Mar 1876; gsw r. shoulder 26 June (fl. wd. sl.); tr on str *Far West* 3 July to hosp Ft Lincoln DT; tr on str *Durfee* 12 July to hosp Ft Rice; duty 31 July 1876; dd subs dept herder June to Sep 1877; ds Big Horn MT 14 Sep thro' Oct 1877; cpl 1 Jan 1878; sgt 1 Nov 1878; dd qmd overseer of laborers Apr 1879; disch 14 Apr 1880 Ft Meade DT expir of serv a sgt char a good man & xclt soldier; died 4 Dec 1929 East St Louis Ill.[35]
Pension: 7 Dec 1902 / Inv / 1293915 / 1070665. Wid / 1656464. Also see Ind. Surv. Orig'l / 16184 / 9375.

Black, Henry. Pvt co H; b. Donegal Ireland; enl 23 Nov 1872 St Louis Mo. for 5 yrs; age 22; laborer; blue eyes, lt hair, fair comp, 6' 0 1/2" high; join co H 3 Dec 1872 Nashville Tenn; pres in conft June to Sep 1873; sen gen cm 2 July 1873 forf $8 pay per mo for 3 mos & conft same period; dd subs dept herder Oct 1875; dd qmd laborer Nov 1875 to May 1876; gsw r. hand (severe) 26 June 1876; tr on str *Far West* 3 July to hosp Ft Lincoln DT; tr on str *Durfee* 12 July to hosp Ft Rice; duty 8 Aug 1876; in conft at Ft Lincoln 25 Oct 1876 (chg of assaulting sgt-maj McCurry with his fist); acquited in gen cm 28 Dec; dd regtl hq fatigue pty 18 June to 11 Aug 1877; disch 23 Nov 1877 Camp Buford DT expir of serv a pvt char good when sober.

Blair, Jas. C. Pvt co K; b. 18 Dec 1850 Camden NJ; enl 29 Dec 1874 Pittsburgh Pa. for 5 yrs;

age 24; carpenter; blue eyes, lt brn hair, fair comp, 5' 8 1/4" high; join co K 9 Feb 1875 Colfax La.; dd qmd Sep & Oct 1875; ed qmd laborer Nov 1875 to Feb 1876; ds Ft Lincoln DT 17 May 1876 chg co prop & garden; sent with Lt Garlington on str *Josephine* 24 July to join co in field; dd qmd 13 Nov to 27 Dec 1876; dd co carpenter Dec 1876 to Apr 1877; dd qmd carpenter Feb to Apr 1878; dd qmd carpenter June to Oct 1879; disch 28 Dec 1879 Ft Totten DT expir of serv a pvt char good; died 25 Aug 1918 Pittsburgh Pa.
Pension: 12 Mar 1917 / Ind. Surv. / 9669 / 6656. Ind. War Wid / 14035 / 8785.

Blair, Wilbur F. Pvt co A; b. Lewisburg Pa.; pvt band 45 Pa. inf 15 Sep 1861 to 27 Sep 1862; pvt co C 201 Pa. inf 18 Aug 1864 to 21 June 1865; enl reg army 18 Sep 1872 Harrisburg Pa. for 5 yrs; age 31; printer; hazel eyes, dk hair, ruddy comp, 5' 6" high; join co A 7 Feb 1873 E'town Ky.; dd qmd teamster Feb to Apr 1874; dd qmd herder Blk Hills Exp'n 21 Aug 1874; dd co cook Oct 1874; cpl 8 Nov 1876; pvt 8 Apr 1877; disch 24 June 1877 camp on Tongue River MT per SO 70 Dept of Dak. 1877 a pvt char good;[36] died 2 Oct 1891 Lewisburg Pa.
Pension: 17 July 1890 / Inv / 846440 / 614620. Wid / 528306 / 360912.

Blake, Thos. Pvt co A; b. New York N.Y.; enl 15 Jan 1872 at New York for 5 yrs; age 21; clerk; grey eyes, dk hair, dk comp, 5' 8 1/2" high; join co A 11 Feb 1872 E'town Ky.; dd co cook Oct 1876; disch 15 Jan 1877 Ft Rice DT expir of serv a pvt char xclt; reenl 29 Jan 1877 St Louis Bks Mo. for 5 yrs in gen mtd serv; tr to co D 2 cav 4 June 1880 Ft Ellis MT; sgt 11 Jan 1881; 1sgt 15 Nov 1881; disch 28 Jan 1882 at Ft Ellis expir of serv a 1sgt char xclt & reenl in same co for 5 yrs; on furl 30 Jan 1882 Ft Custer MT; pvt 18 Feb 1882 (own req); tr to co C 2 cav 18 Mar 1882 (at Ft Custer); cpl 25 June 1882; sgt 8 Feb 1884; 1sgt 8 Jan 1885; disch 28 Jan 1887 Ft Bidwell Calif. expir of serv a 1sgt char xclt & reenl in same co for 5 yrs; disch 28 Jan 1892 Ft Wingate NM expir of serv a 1sgt char xclt & reenl next day in same co for 5 yrs; on furl 30 days 25 Jan 1896 St Louis Mo.; disch 28 Jan 1897 Ft Riley Kans. expir of serv a 1sgt char xclt & reenl in same co for 3 yrs; on furl 4 mos 25 Feb 1897 St Louis Mo.; prom sqdn sgt-maj 8 Apr 1899; disch 28 Jan 1900 Matanzas Cuba expir of serv a sqdn sgt-maj char xclt & reenl for 3 yrs; appt regtl comsy-sgt 1 July 1900; retd 15 Oct 1900 a regtl comsy-sgt char xclt; died 12 Mar 1927 New York N.Y.[37]

Blunt, Geo. Pvt co K; b. 9 Jan 1846 Baltimore Md; enl 10 Sep 1866 at Baltimore for 5 yrs; age 21; carpenter; blue eyes, dk hair, sallow comp, 5' 6 3/4" high; join co K 30 Sep 1866 Ft Riley Kans.; cpl 17 June 1867; sgt 27 Jan 1868; pvt 1 June 1868 (own req); cpl 1 Sep 1868; dd permanent gd over comsy wagon in field 15 Dec 1868; pvt 11 Jan 1869; cpl 1 Apr 1869; sgt 3 Feb 1871; disch 10 Sep 1871 Yorkville SC expir of serv a sgt & reenl in same co for 5 yrs; pvt 1 Oct 1872 (own req); ed qmd teamster Dec 1872; cpl 1 May 1873; pvt 4 Dec 1873; ed qmd laborer 15 Apr 1874; ds Ft Rice DT 20 June to 31 Aug 1874; ds Ft Rice Sep 1874 to Apr 1875 chg of qmd storehouses; dd night watchman July 1875 to Jan 1876; disch 6 Aug 1876 camp mouth of Rosebud Creek MT (in time to go down river by first boat) per GO 24 AGO 1859 a pvt char xclt;[38] arr Ft Lincoln 10 Aug on str *Durfee*; reenl 19 Oct 1876 at Baltimore for 5 yrs; join co D 2 cav 4 June 1878 Ft Custer MT; cpl 21 Oct 1878; sgt 12 Apr 1879; 1sgt 5 Jan 1880; pvt 17 Apr 1880 (own req); disch 10 Oct 1881 Ft Ellis MT per GO 24 AGO 1859 a pvt char xclt; reenl 9 Nov 1881 St Louis Mo. for 5 yrs; assd to co I 2 cav; disch 8 Nov 1886 Ft Walla Walla WT expir of serv a 1sgt char xclt; reenl for co I 2 cav 22 Nov 1886 Jeff'n Bks Mo. for 5 yrs; disch 21 Nov 1891 Ft Huachaca AT expir of serv a 1sgt char xclt; reenl 17 Dec 1891 at Baltimore for 5 yrs; assd to co M 3 cav; disch 16 Dec 1896 Jeff'n Bks Mo. expir of serv a sgt char xclt & reenl in same co for 3 yrs; retd 6 Feb 1897 at Jeff'n Bks a sgt; died 22 Nov 1905 at Baltimore (gas asphyxia, suicide).[39]

Boam, Wm. Pvt co B; b. Manchester England; enl 22 Dec 1874 Boston Mass. for 5 yrs; age 21; sailor; grey eyes, brn hair, medium comp, 5' 9" high; join co B 10 Feb 1875 Shreveport

41

La.; in conft Aug 1875; sen gen cm 27 Aug 1875 forf $10 pay per mo for 2 mos & conft same period; dd co cook Aug 1876; sick hosp Ft Lincoln DT 8 Dec 1876 to 12 Apr 1877 when disch on surg cert dis (pulmonary consumption; degree of dis 1/2) a pvt char good; res no. 36 Bowery, NYC.
Pension: 25 May 1877 / Inv / 236577 / 148756; (appv for disease of lungs; notice to clmt returned to P. A. 7 Dec 1877).

Bobo, Edwin. 1sgt co C; b. Franklin Co. Ohio; enl 23 Dec 1867 New York N.Y. for 5 yrs; age 22; clerk; hazel eyes, brn hair, fair comp, 5' 6 1/2" high; join co C 5 Feb 1868 Ft L'worth Kans.; cpl 1 Nov 1868; sgt 9 Apr 1869; 1sgt 17 Aug 1871; disch 23 Dec 1872 Charlotte NC expir of serv a 1sgt & reenl in co C for 5 yrs; killed with Custer column 25 June 1876 (near capt Keogh);[40] survived by wife & 2 ch.; (widow m. sgt Knipe 12 Apr 1877).
Pension: 14 Apr 1879 / Wid / 243853 / 184410. Minor / 236326 / 183565.

Bockerman, August. Pvt co A; b. Elberfeld Prussia; enl 12 Feb 1872 Chicago Ill. for 5 yrs; age 21; book keeper; blue eyes, lt hair, lt comp, 5' 11" high; join co A 21 Feb 1872 E'town Ky.; dd co cook Sep 1872; ds Oct 1872 to Jan 1873 with detmt at Huntsville Ala; dd pioneer 18 Apr 1873; abs sick at supply camp on Yellowstone River (Stanley's Stockade) 28 July to 8 Sep 1873; ds Ft Lincoln Sep 1874 to May 1875; dd mus'n in band 21 May 1875; ds camp Powder River MT 15 June 1876 with band; ds str *Josephine* 6 Aug 1876 to Ft Lincoln with band; ds Ft Lincoln 17 Oct to 3 Nov 1876; disch 12 Feb 1877 at Ft Lincoln expir of serv a pvt char xclt & reenl in band for 5 yrs; disch 11 Feb 1882 Ft Meade DT expir of serv a pvt char xclt, a good mus'n; died 17 Apr 1904 St Joseph Mo.
Pension: 16 Jan 1899 / Inv / 1216711 / 1078394. Wid / 805401 / 743506.

Boggs, Jas. Pvt co H; b. 10 Mar 1846 Carlisle Pa.; pvt co D 45 Ohio inf 31 July 1862 to 12 June 1865; enl reg army 18 May 1866 Cincinnati Ohio for 3 yrs; age 21; farmer; grey eyes, brn hair, lt comp, 5' 5 1/2" high; assd to co A 5 inf; disch 18 May 1869 Ft Lyons Colo. Ty expir of serv a wag; reenl 13 Jan 1870 at Cincinnati for 5 yrs; assd to co B 7 inf; disch 23 Oct 1874 Ft Shaw MT per GO 24 AGO 1859 a pvt;[41] reenl 15 Sep 1875 at Cincinnati for 5 yrs; join co H 7 cav 29 Oct 1875 Ft Rice DT; sick hosp from 17 Mar 1876; disch 15 May 1876 on surg cert dis (enlarged liver; erect posture painful & pressure of belt intolerable; no reason to believe contr line of duty); reenl 26 July 1876 Baltimore Md for 5 yrs; assd to co B 1 inf; disch 25 July 1881 near Ft Davis Tex. expir of serv a sgt char xclt & reenl in same co for 5 yrs; disch 25 July 1886 Ft Gaston Calif. expir of serv a 1sgt char xclt; reenl 17 Aug 1886 San Francisco Calif. for 5 yrs; assd to co A 9 inf; disch 16 Aug 1891 Whipple Bks AT expir of serv a 1sgt & reenl in same co for 5 yrs; retd 18 June 1892 a 1sgt; died 7 Oct 1921 Harrisburg Pa.
Pension: 13 Oct 1921 / Wid / 1180293 / 912695.

Bohner, Aloys. Trump'r co D; b. Baden Germany; enl 19 Dec 1853 Newport Ky. for 5 yrs; age 25; farmer; join co G 2 art'y 8 Apr 1854 Ft Myers Fla; tr to band 12 Nov 1856; des 9 May 1857 Ft Hamilton N.Y.; reenl 11 Aug 1857 Rochester N.Y. for 5 yrs as Louis Braun (Brown); assd to co E 3 inf; surd as des'r 20 Oct 1858 Albuquerque NM; restored to duty without trial 1 Feb 1859 & tr to co E 3 inf to make good time lost; disch 12 July 1860 Ft Defiance NM expir of serv a pvt; reenl 21 July 1860 at Albuquerque for 5 yrs; assd to co I mtd rifles; (redesig 3 cav regt Aug 1861); disch 14 Apr 1863 Keokuk Iowa on surg cert dis a pvt (secondary syph. 2 yrs standing & gen debility); enr 30 Sep 1863 Davenport Iowa as chf-trump'r 8 Iowa cav for 3 yrs; captured 30 July 1864 Newman Ga. & paroled 20 Nov 1864 Savannah Ga.; m.o. vol serv 13 Aug 1865 Macon Ga.; enl reg army 2 Jan 1866 New York N.Y. for 3 yrs; hazel eyes, brn hair, dk comp, 5' 7 3/4" high; join co I 7 cav as trump'r 29 Sep 1866 Ft Riley Kans.; appt chf-trump'r 9 Nov 1867; disch 2 Jan 1869 Ft Cobb IT expir of serv a chf-trump'r & reenl for 5 yrs; tr to co D as trump'r 29 Nov 1870; in conft Feb 1872; in conft Oct 1872; disch 22 Dec 1873 Ft Totten DT per GO 24 AGO 1859 a trump'r; reenl for co D 12 Jan 1874 St Paul Minn. for 5 yrs;

rejoin co as trump'r Feb 1874 at Ft Totten; appt chf-trump'r 23 July 1878; disch 12 Jan 1879 Ft Lincoln DT expir of serv a chf-trump'r char xclt & reenl for 5 yrs; disch 13 Dec 1879 Ft Meade DT on surg cert dis (chr. dyspepsia) a chf-trump'r char xclt; died 27 July 1887 Burlington Iowa.
Pension: 31 Mar 1880 / Inv / 354792 / 348444.

Boissen, Christian C. Sad'r co K; b. 26 May 1840 Denmark; enl in co K 25 Mar 1873 Memphis Tenn for 5 yrs; age 31; bootmaker; blue eyes, brn hair, fair comp, 5' 6" high; ds Ft Rice DT 29 Sep to 5 Oct 1874 with co prop awaiting transp to La.; sad'r 1 Dec 1874; pvt 11 Dec 1876; dd hq fatigue pty 25 Apr to 8 Oct 1877; ds in field 30 Aug 1877; ds in field (escort) 28 Sep 1877; disch 25 Mar 1878 at Ft Rice expir of serv a pvt char xclt; died 21 Jan 1923 Ft Smith Ark.
Pension: 29 July 1892 / Inv / 1124033. Ind. Surv. / 11864 / 11493. Ind. War Wid / 16282 / 10677.

Bonner, Hugh. Pvt co B; b. Boston Mass.; enl 18 Mar 1876 at Boston for 5 yrs; age 21 3/12; laborer; grey eyes, dk hair, dk comp, 5' 7 1/2" high; join co B 27 Apr St Paul Minn.; ds camp Powder River MT 10 June; des 7 July [with Littlefield & Williamson] taking two mules & one horse; apph 13 July near Ft Lincoln in starving cond'n;[42] escaped from conft at Ft Lincoln 6 Sep 1876.

Boren, Ansgarius. Pvt co B; b. Linkoben Sweden; enl 12 Feb 1872 Chicago Ill. for 5 yrs; age 22; student; blue eyes, lt hair, lt comp, 5' 5 1/4" high; join co B 26 Feb 1872 Spartanburg SC; abs sick on str *Western* 23 Apr 1873 Yankton to Ft Rice DT; ds Ft Rice June to Sep 1873 gd regtl prop; des 6 Apr 1874 Ft Lincoln DT & apph 14 Apr near Jamestown DT; sen gen cm 18 June 1874 forf all pay due & 2 yrs conft at sta of co thence to dishon disch; unexpired portion of sen rem'd 19 Dec 1874; ed hosp attdt 1 Mar to 18 Apr 1876; ds camp mouth of Rosebud Creek 8 Aug 1876 dismtd; disch 12 Feb 1877 at Ft Lincoln expir of serv a pvt char good; reenl 16 Jan 1878 Ft Wayne Mich. for 5 yrs; assd to co C 22 inf; disch 15 Jan 1883 Ft Lyon Colo. expir of serv a pvt char xclt; reenl 6 Feb 1883 Ft L'worth Kans. for 5 yrs in co H 20 inf; ed as overseer of post schools Oct 1883 to Feb 1885; ed as school teacher Apr 1885; disch 2 Dec 1885 Ft Assiniboine MT per SO 268 AGO 1885 a pvt char xclt(upon own req, having been accepted as student for the ministry by Academy of New Church at Phil'a Pa. with stipend dur term of studies).[43]

Borter, Ludwig. Pvt co A; b. DeWalle Switz; enl 4 Oct 1873 New York N.Y. for 5 yrs; age 23; farmer; grey eyes, brn hair, dk comp, 5' 5" high; join co A 18 Oct 1873 Ft Lincoln DT; ds Ft Lincoln June thro' Aug 1874; des 26 Mar 1875 Livingston Ala; apph 13 June 1876 Indianapolis Ind.; escaped from conft 10 Aug 1876 Columbus Bks Ohio.

Bott, Geo. Pvt co A; b. Ft Wayne Ind.; enl 16 Sep 1875 Cincinnati Ohio for 5 yrs; age 22; clerk; grey eyes, brn hair, fair comp, 5' 7" high; join co A 21 Oct 1875 Ft Lincoln DT; pres sick (cont'n l. side) 22 Aug 1876 Powder River MT; tr on str *Carroll* 28 Aug to Ft Buford; tr on str *Benton* 3 Sep to hosp at Ft Lincoln; duty 16 Sep 1876; ds in field 2 Sep 1877; cpl 8 Jan 1878; sgt 1 Sep 1878; pvt 13 Dec 1878; disch 15 Sep 1880 Ft Meade DT expir of serv a pvt char good; reenl 10 Feb 1882 St Louis Mo. for 5 yrs; assd to co H 7 inf; des 24 June 1882 Ft Snelling Minn.; surd 7 July 1882 Jeff'n Bks Mo.; dishon disch 4 Aug 1882 sen gen cm & 5 yrs conft mitigated to one yr conft mil prison Ft L'worth Kans.

Botzer, Edw. Sgt co G; b. Bremerhaven Germany; enl 26 Nov 1866 New York N.Y. for 5 yrs; age 24; clerk; blue eyes, brn hair, fair comp, 5' 6 1/2" high; join co G 27 Dec 1866 Ft Harker Kans.; trump'r 24 May 1867; ds Camp Supply IT Dec 1868 to Mar 1869; awl Apr 1871; pvt 1 Aug 1871; cpl 1 Nov 1871; disch 26 Nov 1871 Spartanburg SC expir of serv & reenl in co G for 5 yrs; co qm sgt 1 Jan 1872; duty sgt 1 May 1873;[44] dd chg co mess & forage June to Sep 1873; dd actg co qm sgt Oct 1873 to July 1875; actg 1sgt May & June 1876; killed dur retreat from valley fight 25 June 1876 at river crossing, on east side (near Lt. Hodgson).[45]

Bouyer, Mitch. Boyer, Michel; guide qmd; b near Ft Pierre DT ca. 1837 son of a French trader & Sioux woman; moved near Ft Laramie in 1849 where he became a protégé of Jim Bridger & selected by him to guide the celebrated English hunter Sir Geo. Gore dur his visit to the west;[46] later served as intrpr with Pierre Shane at Ft Smith on the Big Horn & at Crow Agcy on the Yellowstone; diffident & low-spoken, he uttered his words in a hesitating way as if uncertain what he was going to say; tho' he dressed like a white man he looked ind & was known for his vest of tanned buffalo-calf skin;[47] he was popular for his quiet demeanor & often employed as guide for the mil & other exploring ptys incl the Hayden exp'n in 1872 seeking a route for the NPRR along the Yellowstone; he was hired 8 Apr 1876 at Crow Agcy to guide col Gibbon's comd; rate of pay $5 per day;[48] Gibbon said Boyer was the best guide in that part of the country who could give distances accurately in miles;[49] he was loaned to gen Terry 10 June to guide maj Reno's scout up Powder River & later for gen Custer's scout up Rosebud Creek; accomp Lt Varnum to the Crow's Nest night of 24 June; killed with the Custer column 25 June;[50] survived by wife Mary (Magpie Outside) & 2 ch.[51]

Bowers, Frank. See Volkenstine, Frank.

Boyle, Jas. P. Pvt co G; b. 15 Dec 1855 Tyrone Co. Ireland; enl 7 Dec 1874 Boston Mass. for 5 yrs; age 21; laborer; hazel eyes, auburn hair, ruddy comp, 5' 6 3/8" high; join co G 10 Feb 1875 Shreveport La.; dd with pack train June 1876;[52] gsw in back 26 June (fl. wd. sl.); remained with co in field; dd 11 Aug to 18 Sep 1876; dd kit'n police Feb 1878; dd co cook Oct 1878; disch 6 Dec 1879 Ft Meade DT expir of serv a pvt char good; reenl 6 Jan 1880 at Boston for 5 yrs; join co B 7 cav Apr 1880 Ft Yates DT; cpl 21 Apr 1883; pvt 26 June 1883; awl 90 days 5 Sep 1884; in conft Dec 1884; disch 5 Jan 1885 at Ft Yates expir of serv a pvt char good, a reliable soldier in the field; died 2 Sep 1920 Bismarck N.Dak.
Pension: 4 May 1917 / Ind. Surv. / 12209. Rej on grd act of 4 Mar 1917 made no prov'n for pensioning vets of ind wars who had not reached age 62 yrs at date of filing & 1860 census shows clmt born 1855; also entire serv rendered after ind wars named in prior acts.

Boyle, Owen. Pvt co E; b. Waterford Ireland; pvt 12 Mass. art'y 9 Dec 1862 to 25 July 1865; enl reg army 15 Sep 1866 Boston Mass. for 3 yrs; age 24; hostler; grey eyes, lt hair, lt comp, 5' 6" high; join co I 36 inf Oct 1866 Ft Kearney Neb. Ty; tr to co I 7 inf 3 June 1869 upon consol'n of regts; ed qmd saw mill June to Aug 1869; disch 15 Sep 1869 Ft Fred Steele Wyo. Ty expir of serv a pvt; reenl 27 Oct 1869 at Boston for 5 yrs; join co F 22 inf Dec 1869 Ft Stevenson DT; cpl 1 Sep 1870; pvt 11 Sep 1870; in conft from June 1871; sen gen cm 29 Jan 1872 to dishon disch & conft hard labor for remainder of term wearing 30 pound ball & chain; unexecuted portion of sen rem'd 11 July 1872; disch 14 July 1874 Ft Wayne Mich. per SO 133 Mil Div of the Atlantic a pvt; reenl 19 Dec 1874 at Boston for 5 yrs; join co E 7 cav 8 Feb 1875 Opelika Ala; in conft Feb to June 1875; sen gen cm 24 Feb 1875 forf $10 pay per mo for 3 mos; killed with Custer column 25 June 1876.
Pension: 3 Apr 1877 / Father / 230716 / 185313.

Braden, Chas. 1Lt co L; b. 23 Nov 1847 Detroit Mich.; grad USMA 15 June 1869 & appt 2Lt 7 cav; join regt 29 Sep 1869 Ft L'worth Kans.; ds cond rcts to Ft Union NM 23 Nov 1869; join co L 30 Dec 1869 at Ft L'worth; actg aqm & actg adjt detmt in field 23 June 1870; actg comsy with col Dodge exp'n locating road from Ft Lyon to Ft Union Sep & Oct 1870; actg aqm post at Winnsboro SC June to Dec 1871; gsw l. thigh (comp'd frac. r. femas) 11 Aug 1873 mouth of Big Horn River MT in action with Sioux inds; carried on litter 28 days to supply camp mouth of Glendive Creek thence tr to str *Josephine* 11 Sep to Ft Lincoln DT;[53] tr to dept hq St Paul Minn. 26 Oct & med treatment at Ft Snelling; awl 6 mos 12 Mar 1874; rejoin co 9 Sep 1874 at Ft Lincoln; sick qrs 30 Sep & awl on surg cert 5 Oct 1874; 1Lt 9 Dec 1875; td rctg serv St Louis Bks Mo. 18 Aug 1876; abs sick 23 Jan 1877 awaiting action of retiring bd; retd 25 June 1878 on surg cert; engaged at pvt

school Riverdale N.Y. to June 1879 & teaching at post school West Point N.Y. to Nov 1881; engaged in manufacturing enterprise at Phil'a Pa. to Sep 1882; prof of mil academy at Cornwall N.Y. from Nov 1888; secretary of association of graduates USMA 1880 to 1900 & 1907 to 1918; assisted in preparation of volumes 3 & 4 of the gen Cullum registers & personally edited volume 5 (1910); died 15 Jan 1919 Highland Falls N.Y.
[4331 ACP 1873].

Brady, Wm. Pvt co F; b. Pittsburgh Pa.; enl 15 Sep 1875 Cincinnati Ohio for 5 yrs; age 27; plumber; blue eyes, brn hair, ruddy comp, 5' 6 1/2" high; join co F 21 Oct 1875 Ft Lincoln DT; in conft Dec 1875; in conft Feb 1876; in conft Apr 1876; killed with Custer column 25 June 1876.

Braendle, Wilhelm Friedrich. Pvt co C; b. 1 Nov 1855 Wurtemburg Germany; enl as Wm. Brandle 8 Oct 1873 St Louis Mo. for 5 yrs; age 21; laborer; hazel eyes, brn hair, fair comp, 5' 9 1/4" high; join co C 21 Oct 1873 Ft Rice DT; ed qmd Apr 1874; ed qmd Oct 1874 to Mar 1875; ed qmd Oct 1875; ds camp Powder River MT 10 June 1876; cpl 15 Oct 1876; ds with co prop to Ft Totten DT 19 Nov 1876; dd chg co cook house Feb 1877; sgt 30 Nov 1877; dd prov sgt Apr 1878; disch 8 Oct 1878 Camp J. G. Sturgis DT expir of serv a sgt; died 15 Dec 1932 Santa Rosa, Calif.
Pension: 16 May 1927 / Inv / 1581515/ A-2-10-28. Wid / 1730192.

Brainard, Geo. Pvt co B; b. Brooklyn Ohio; enl 13 Aug 1860 Cleveland Ohio for 5 yrs; age 22 5/12; farmer; grey eyes, brn hair, lt comp, 5' 7 1/2" high; join co D 1 inf 15 Jan 1861 Ft Cobb IT; cpl 1 Oct 1861; pvt 10 Aug 1862 (own req); ed qmd laborer Aug 1862; ed qmd teamster Apr to July 1863; sick St Louis Mo. July to Sep 1863 & Nashville Tenn to Nov 1863; cpl 18 Dec 1863; disch 19 July 1864 New Orleans La. upon reenlmt in co for 3 yrs; sgt 1 Sep 1865; disch 19 July 1867 Amite City La. expir of serv a sgt; reenl 22 Jan 1872 at Cleveland for 5 yrs; age 25 10/12; teamster; blue eyes, lt hair, lt comp, 5' 9 1/2" high;[54] join co B 7 cav 14 Feb 1872 Spartanburg SC; ed qmd wag Oct 1872; co wag 1 Nov 1872; ed qmd wag Nov 1872 to Mar 1873; ed qmd teamster 12–26 Apr 1873; sgt 1 May 1874; pvt 2 Mar 1875 sen gen cm & forf $10 pay per mo for 3 mos; dd qmd teamster Dec 1875 to Feb 1876; orderly dept hq in field 10 May 1876 (verbal order gen Terry);[55] ds Ft Lincoln DT 17 Oct 1876 dismtd; disch 22 Jan 1877 at Ft Lincoln by expir of serv a pvt char very good; died 20 Nov 1886 Cleveland Ohio (consumption).
Pension: 15 Aug 1890 / Wid / 429810; (duplicate appn 14 Mar 1892); pension atty made every effort to have clmt furn required evidence, says clmt very ignorant (b. Bohemia) unable to speak English language.

Brandle, Wm. See Braendle, Wilhelm Friedrich.

Brandon, Benj. Far'r co F; b. Hopkinsville Ky.; enl 21 July 1855 St Louis Mo. for 5 yrs; age 22; carpenter; grey eyes, dk hair, ruddy comp, 5' 6" high; assd to co E 2 cav at Jeff'n Bks Mo. Aug 1855; ed qmd express rider May & June 1856; ds with Capt Stoneman Nov 1856 to Jan 1857; dd co far'r Aug 1857; appt far'r 1 Sep 1857; ed qmd blks Dec 1857; pvt Aug 1858 & ed qmd blks to Feb 1859; far'r 1 Sep 1859; reenl in co 21 May 1860 at camp on Rio Grande Tex. for 5 yrs; des 4 Dec 1860 camp at Resaca de la Palma Tex. while on ds looking for suitable place to burn coals; enl in co K 9 Conn. inf 24 May 1862 Carrollton La. for 3 yrs; sgt 27 Nov 1862; 1sgt 27 Jan 1863; pvt 23 Aug 1863; reenl in regt as vet vol 9 June 1864 New Haven Conn.; tr to co D 12 Oct 1864; m.o. vol serv 3 Aug 1865 Hilton Head SC; reenl reg army 6 Sep 1865 Ft Preble Me for 3 yrs in co F 2 battn 17 inf; des 27 July 1866 Ft Gratiot Mich.; enl as Robt Nelson 10 Aug 1866 Cincinnati Ohio for 5 yrs; join co F 7 cav 10 Sep 1866 Ft Riley Kans. & appt cpl; sgt 20 Sep 1866; pvt 12 Dec 1866; blks 1 Mar 1867; far'r 1 Mar 1868; des 29 Nov 1869 Ft L'worth Kans. & surd two days later; in conft Dec 1869; acquited 20 Jan 1870; pvt 5 Apr 1870 & in conft; tr to co D as blks 20 Nov 1870; disch 10 Aug 1871 Mt Vernon Ky. expir of serv a blks; reenl in co D as blks 8 Sep 1871 at Mt

Vernon for 5 yrs; far'r & blks Aug 1872; far'r Dec 1872; in conft Feb 1873; sen gen cm 16 May 1873 forf $10 pay per mo for 4 mos; surd as des'r 16 Nov 1873 under GO 102 AGO 1873; restored to duty without trial 31 Jan 1874 & tr to co D 7 cav to serve bal of orig'l enlmt; blks 1 July 1875; disch 1 Nov 1875 Ft Lincoln DT per GO 24 AGO 1859 & reenl for 5 yrs in co F 7 cav; far'r 20 Nov 1875; killed with Custer column 25 June 1876.

Brant, Abram B. Pvt co D; b. New York N.Y.; enl 27 Sep 1875 St Louis Bks Mo. for 5 yrs; age 26; civil engineer; hazel eyes, lt hair, fair comp, 5' 5 7/8" high; join co D 21 Oct 1875 Ft Lincoln DT; dd June 1877; dd co clerk Jan 1878; dd co clerk Aug 1878; died 4 Oct 1878 camp near Bear Butte DT accdt gsw in abdomen when handing revolver to sgt Oman; (awarded medal of honor 5 Oct 1878 for bringing water to wounded at LBH while under heavy fire).[56]

Braun, Frank. Pvt co M; b. Berne Switz; enl 23 Sep 1875 Louisville Ky. for 5 yrs; age 27; laborer; hazel eyes, brn hair, fair comp, 5' 6 1/4" high; join co M 21 Oct 1875 Ft Rice DT; gsw l. hip & l. cheek 25 June 1876 on Reno hill; (nursed by pvt Gallenne);[57] tr on str *Far West* 3 July to hosp Ft Lincoln DT; operated on under ether 13 Sep, Dr. Middleton probed & enlarged wd & made counter opening from which some arterial hemorrhage; died early morn 4 Oct 1876.

Braun, Franz C. Pvt co I; b. Aixla-Chapelle Germany; enl 13 May 1873 Chicago Ill. for 5 yrs; age 28; turner; blue eyes, lt hair, fair comp, 5' 8 1/2" high; join co I 3 June 1873 Ft Snelling Minn.; ds Ft Totten DT 1 Sep 1873; in conft Feb 1875; dd regtl hq June to Aug 1876; [with band but went to LBH says Eix(enberger); with pack train says Jones; not in fight says Caddle];[58] ds str *Josephine* 6 Aug to Ft Lincoln with band; ds Ft Lincoln 16 Oct to 11 Nov 1876 with band; dd in band as laborer (tinsmith) to Apr 1877; ed qmd Dec 1877 thro' Apr 1878; disch 13 May 1878 at Ft Lincoln expir of serv a pvt char xclt.

Brennan, Jno. Pvt co C; b. Waterford Ireland; enl 24 Sep 1875 St Louis Mo. for 5 yrs; age 26; laborer; grey eyes, brn hair, lt comp, 5' 5 1/4" high; join co C 21 Oct 1875 Ft Lincoln DT; with Custer column 25 June 1876 but left behind when horse gave out;[59] in conft Nov 1876 to Mar 1877; dd co tailor Apr to June 1877; sen gen cm 12 Mar 1878 forf $6 pay per mo for 6 mos; sen gen cm 30 July 1878 to conft one mo hard labor; sen gen cm 24 Sep 1878 forf $10 pay per mo for 3 mos & conft same period; dd co cook Feb 1879; sen gen cm 6 June 1879 forf $10 pay per mo for 3 mos & conft same period; dishon disch 4 Dec 1879 Ft Meade DT per SO 265 AGO 1879 (utter worthlessness, having been in conft over 500 days dur last three yrs; no reliance could be placed on him for at every chance he would drink, whence he became a perfect beast).[60]

Bresnahan, Cornelius. Pvt co K; b. Mt Auburn Mass.; enl 3 Oct 1873 Boston Mass. for 5 yrs; age 21; laborer; hazel eyes, red hair, medium comp, 5' 9" high; join co K 20 Oct 1873 Ft Rice DT; dd co cook June 1877; dd co cook Oct 1877; in conft Apr 1878 (des his post while on mtd stable gd); dishon disch 31 May 1878 sen gen cm & conft until expir of serv; reenl in co K 22 Aug 1878 upon recom'n of co comdr & appv by AGO;[61] tr to co L 20 Nov 1878; cpl 4 Sep 1881; sgt 18 Sep 1881; pvt 20 Dec 1881; dd co cook June 1882; disch 21 Aug 1883 Ft Buford DT expir of serv a pvt char good; res 40 Reed Street, North Cambridge Mass.[62]

Brightfield, Jno. Pvt co C; b. 23 June 1853 Dearborn Co. Ind.; enl 7 Oct 1875 Cincinnati Ohio for 5 yrs; age 22; cabinet maker; brn eyes, brn hair, dk comp, 5' 9 1/4" high; join co C 21 Oct 1875 Ft Lincoln DT; dd regtl hq fatigue pty (morn & eve) from 11 May 1876; killed with Custer column 25 June 1876.
Pension: 18 Sep 1876 / Mother / 227984 / 297235.

Bringes, Jno. Far'r co A; b. Hanover Germany; enl 23 Aug 1866 Chicago Ill. for 5 yrs; age 21; laborer; blue eyes, brn hair, ruddy comp, 5' 5 3/4" high; join co A 10 Sep 1866 Ft Riley Kans.; far'r 16 May 1869; disch 23 Aug 1871 E'town Ky. expir of serv a far'r; reenl in co A 22 Sep 1871 at E'town for 5 yrs; far'r 1 Dec 1871; disch 22 Sep 1876 Ft Berthold DT expir of serv a far'r char xclt.

Brinkerhoff, Henry. Pvt co G; b. 12 Apr 1854 Gettysburg Pa.; enl 1 Dec 1874 St Louis Mo. for 5 yrs; age 22; laborer; blue eyes, lt hair, fair comp, 5' 6" high; join co G 10 Feb 1875 Shreveport La.; dd May & June 1876;[63] cpl 9 July 1876; sgt 9 Feb 1877; dd chg co kit'n Feb 1877; dd actg co qm sgt Apr 1877 to Feb 1878; on furl 4 mos 1 Apr 1878 in Illinois; dd regtl hq Aug to Oct 1878; disch 30 Nov 1879 Ft Meade DT expir of serv a sgt char xclt; died 4 Feb 1933 natl mil home Los Angeles Calif.
Pension: Ind. Surv. / 19442 / 11924. Wid / 1731411 / A-10-24-33. (XC-2,655,702).

Briody, Jno. Cpl co F; b. New York N.Y.; enl 9 Aug 1866 New York N.Y. for 5 yrs; age 20; laborer; blue eyes, brn hair, fair comp, 5' 5" high; join co F 10 Sep 1866 Ft Riley Kans.; cpl 30 Sep 1869; pvt 30 Mar 1870; on furl 30 days 10 June 1871; disch 9 Aug 1871 Meridian Miss expir of serv a pvt; reenl 13 Aug 1872 New York N.Y. for 5 yrs; join co F 1 Dec 1872 Louisville Ky.; dd actg co far'r June to Oct 1873; appt far'r 1 Nov 1873; pvt 20 Nov 1875; cpl 21 Dec 1875; dd chg co mess Apr 1876; killed with Custer column 25 June 1876.

Broadhurst, Jos. F. Pvt co I; b. Phil'a Pa.; enl 22 Sep 1873 at Phil'a for 5 yrs; age 21; weaver; brn eyes, dk hair, ruddy comp, 5' 5" high; join co I 22 Oct 1873 Ft Totten DT; in conft Dec 1875; sick qrs 18 Feb to 7 Mar 1876 (cont'n l. groin); killed with Custer column 25 June 1876.

Brogan, Jas. Pvt co E; b. Pittsburgh Pa.; enl 15 Mar 1871 at Pittsburgh for 5 yrs; age 21; teamster; hazel eyes, brn hair, ruddy comp, 5' 8 1/2" high; join co F 7 cav 10 Apr 1871 Taylor Bks (Louisville) Ky.; ds herding co horses Aug 1872; ds subs dept herding cattle Oct 1873 to Jan 1874; dd subs dept herding cattle Feb to May 1874; dd qmd teamster Aug to Oct 1874; dd co cook Feb to May 1875; dd qmd teamster Oct 1875 to 15 Mar 1876 when disch at Ft Lincoln DT by expir of serv a pvt char xclt; reenl 1 Apr 1876 Ft Seward DT for 5 yrs in co E 7 cav; killed with Custer column 25 June 1876.

Bromwell, Latrobe. Pvt co E; b. Feb 1847 Frederick Co. Md; pvt co H 2 regt eastern shore inf 2 Jan 1864; (redesig 11 Md inf); m.o. vol serv 15 June 1865; enl reg army 12 July 1870 Baltimore Md for 5 yrs; age 23 5/12; clerk; grey eyes, lt hair, lt comp, 5' 6" high; join co G 2 cav 7 Oct 1870 Ft Ellis MT; disch 12 July 1875 at Ft Ellis expir of serv a pvt; reenl 9 Aug 1875 at Baltimore for 5 yrs; join co E 7 cav 29 Oct 1875 Ft Totten DT; dd co cook Dec 1875 to May 1876; sick qrs (tert. intm. fever) 8–13 June 1876 camp Powder River MT;[64] ds with batt'y in field 16 Oct 1876; cpl 1 Dec 1876; sgt 1 Jan 1877; (m. widow of sgt Hohmeyer 25 Feb 1877); dd prov sgt Dec 1878 to Apr 1879; dd co qm sgt June 1879 to 8 Aug 1880 when disch at Ft Meade DT by expir of serv a sgt; reenl same day for 5 yrs & cont'd as co qm sgt; regtl qm-sgt 5 Sep 1883; ds Ft Snelling Minn. 29 July to 9 Sep 1885 with dept rifle comp'n; disch 8 Aug 1885 upon expir of serv a qm-sgt & reenl same day for 5 yrs; disch 11 Nov 1889 Ft Riley Kans. per SO 259 AGO 1889 (to be chf cook in new consol post mess hall) a qm-sgt char xclt; hired 12 Nov 1889 as instr in use of cooking apparatus; rate of pay $100 mo;[65] reenl 25 Jan 1892 at Ft Riley for 5 yrs (auth AGO) & appt regtl qm-sgt; sd as stew'd in post mess hall Mar 1892 to May 1895; disch 24 Jan 1897 Ft Grant AT expir of serv a qm-sgt & reenl same day for 3 yrs; retd 14 Jan 1900 Columbia Bks Cuba a regtl qm-sgt char xclt; stew'd of post canteen Ft Oglethorpe Ga. thence instr in school of bakers & cooks at Ft Riley 1905 to 1908;[66] died 29 Apr 1923 Wash'n D.C.

Brown, Alexander. Sgt co G; b. 19 Feb 1844 Aberdeen Scotland; enl 13 Dec 1866 Chicago Ill. for 5 yrs; age 21; shoemaker; hazel eyes, blk hair, dk comp, 5' 8" high; join co G 23 Mar 1867 Ft Harker Kans.; cpl 1 Dec 1867; sgt 26 Dec 1868; ds actg qm sgt detmt 7 cav Feb to May 1870; dd chg co mess Oct 1871; disch 13 Dec 1871 Spartanburg SC expir of serv a sgt & reenl in co G for 5 yrs; dd actg post sgt-maj Apr to July 1872; sick hosp 6–20 Aug 1873 (typhoid fever); dd chg co kit'n June to Aug 1874; 1sgt 19 Sep 1874; sgt 6 Aug 1875; with pack train 25 June 1876;[67] disch 13 Dec 1876 Ft Lincoln DT expir of serv a sgt; reenl same day in co G for 5 yrs & on furl 3 mos St Paul Minn.; actg sgt-maj of capt Benteen's battn Sep 1877;[68] cited by capt Benteen for conspic gal in two mtd chgs against Nez Perce inds at Canon Creek 13 Sep 1877; dd chg co mess Aug to Nov 1878; dd chg co stables Dec 1878; dd actg co qm sgt Feb to May 1881; dd actg 1sgt June to Sep 1881; dd actg co qm sgt Oct 1881; disch 12 Dec 1881 Ft L'worth Kans. expir of serv a sgt char xclt & reenl in co G for 5 yrs; sen gen cm 19 Apr 1882 forf $10 pay per mo for 4 mos; unexpired portion of sen rem'd 17 June 1882; pvt 1 Oct 1882; tr to co H 3 July 1883; sick hosp (intm. fever) 27 Aug to 23 Sep 1883; cpl 5 Sep 1883; sgt 20 Oct 1883; sick (bronc.) Oct 1883; sick hosp from Dec 1883; disch 14 Feb 1884 Ft Meade DT on surg cert dis (locomotor atoxia; partial paralysis lower extremities) a sgt char xclt; died 7 Apr 1884 at Ft Meade; not married.

Brown, Benj. Franklin. Pvt co F; b. Taylor Co. Ky.; enl in co F 12 Mar 1872 Louisville Ky. for 5 yrs; age 22; farmer; hazel eyes, lt hair, fair comp, 5' 9" high; ds herding co horses Aug 1872; dd pioneer 20 Apr 1873; dd qmd teamster Oct 1874 to May 1875; dd qmd stonecutter June to Nov 1875; dd qmd teamster Dec 1875 to May 1876; killed in action 25 June 1876; [killed on Reno hill says Rooney; killed with Custer says Gregg].[69]
Pension: 3 Dec 1877 / Mother / 234381 / 184460.

Brown, Chas. Comsy-sgt USA; b. July 1846 Bavaria Germany; enl 4 Oct 1867 Chicago Ill. for 3 yrs; age 21; laborer; hazel eyes, brn hair, ruddy comp, 5' 7 1/2" high; appt sgt & qm sgt co E 44 inf 15 Oct 1867; regtl comsy-sgt 7 Feb 1868; regtl qm sgt 13 May 1869; (regt consol with 17 inf June 1869); disch 4 Oct 1870 Ft Rice DT expir of serv a qm-sgt & reenl same day for 5 yrs; appt comsy-sgt USA 21 June 1873 assd to Ft Lincoln DT; disch 4 Oct 1875 at Ft Lincoln expir of serv a comsy-sgt; reenl same day for 5 yrs & on furl 6 mos with perm'n to go beyond the sea; assd to gen Terry's exp'n 21 Apr 1876 (report to Lt Smith for field duty);[70] ordered from Ft Buford to St Paul 9 Sep 1876 (report to Lt Thompson, actg comsy); on duty dept hq thro' Oct 1876; appn for disch 30 Oct (to tend his share farm at LeRoy Minn.) disappv as reason not sufficient to justify disch; des 21 Nov 1876 enroute to Ft Buford; res North Star Ohio in 1879 & fearing arrest he said he was going to Germany; [true name Adam Karl Reinwald].[71]

Brown, Geo. C. Cpl co E; b. Baltimore Md; enl 19 Oct 1872 Phil'a Pa. for 5 yrs; age 21; candy maker; brn eyes, brn hair, ruddy comp, 5' 5 1/2" high; join co E 10 Dec 1872 Unionville SC; cpl 3 Mar 1876; killed with Custer column 25 June 1876.[72]

Brown, Hiram Erastus (Groves). Pvt co F; b. Mt Vernon Ohio; pvt co I 2 Ohio art'y July 1863 to Aug 1865 (as Erastus G. Brown); enl reg army 8 Mar 1871 Cincinnati Ohio for 5 yrs; age 24; machinist; brn eyes, brn hair, fair comp, 5' 8 1/4" high; join co F 10 Apr 1871 Louisville Ky.; ed qmd laborer May 1872 to June 1873 & dd regtl hq to Aug 1874;[73] dd qmd teamster Oct 1874 to 8 Mar 1876 when disch at Ft Lincoln DT by expir of serv; reenl same day in co F for 5 yrs; dd qmd teamster in field June 1876;[74] ds with wagon train Aug 1876 dd qmd teamster; dd qmd 12–28 Sep 1876 at Ft Lincoln with 281 cav horses at post; ds with supply train 30 Aug 1877; cpl 29 Jan 1878; dd chg co mess Dec 1878; disch 7 Mar 1881 Ft Buford DT expir of serv a cpl char very good & reenl in co F for 5 yrs; sgt 1 Apr 1881; dd co qm sgt June 1882; ds Ft Buford July to Nov 1882 chg co garden; dd co qm sgt Dec 1882; ds chg of gd at hay camp Oct 1883 to Feb 1884; dd chg co stables Apr to Sep 1884; on furl 60 days 6 Oct 1884 New York N.Y.; dd chg co kit'n Apr to Oct 1885; disch 7 Mar 1886 at Ft Buford expir of serv a sgt char xclt & reenl in co F for 5 yrs; on furl 6 mos 8 Mar 1886 Columbus Ohio;[75] dd chg co stables Apr 1887 & Oct 1888 to Dec 1889; dd chg co mess Aug 1890; disch 7 Mar 1891 Ft Sill Okla. Ty expir of serv a sgt char xclt; reenl 26 Mar 1891 Watervliet Ars'l N.Y. for 5 yrs in ordn detmt; disch 25 Mar 1896 at Watervliet Ars'l expir of serv a sgt char xclt & reenl same day in ordn detmt; retd 8 Oct 1897 a sgt char xclt; died 20 May 1904 Watervliet N.Y.
See pension, Ira N. Haney: Inv / 1169854. Wid / 1146906 / 894343. (Widow, Celia Brown Haney died 9 Jan 1946 Schenectady N.Y.).

Brown, Jas. Pvt co B; b. Queens Co. Ireland; enl 23 Mar 1876 Baltimore Md for 5 yrs; age 22; moulder; blue eyes, blk hair, dk comp, 5' 6 1/2" high; join co B 27 Apr 1876 St Paul Minn.; ds camp Powder River MT 10 June 1876; dd qmd 23 Apr to 12 June 1877; ds enroute to Ft Lincoln with co prop Oct 1877; ed qmd Dec 1877; dd qmd Feb to Sep 1878; dd qmd Apr 1879 to May 1880; dd qmd Dec 1880; dd qmd saw mill Feb 1881; disch 22 Mar 1881 Ft Yates DT expir of serv a pvt char very good; reenl 19 Nov 1881 Ft Snelling Minn. for 5 yrs; assd to co K 7 inf; des 6 May 1882 at Ft Snelling; enl as Jas. Anderson 12 May 1882 Chicago Ill. for 5 yrs; assd to co C 4 cav; in conft from Feb 1883; (stole one razor from a comrade & sold to citizen at Central City NM); dishon disch 17 May 1883 Ft Bayard NM sen gen cm & one yr conft mil prison Ft L'worth Kans.; surd as Jas. Brown 5 Aug 1883; rel from prison 7 Mar 1884.

Brown, Jos. Pvt co K; b. Berlin Prussia; enl 20 Aug 1869 Mobile Ala. for 5 yrs; age 22; farmer; grey eyes, brn hair, fair comp, 5' 10 3/4" high; assd to co K 2 inf; disch 20 Aug 1874 Mt Vernon Ala expir of serv a pvt; reenl 27 Jan 1875 St Louis Bks Mo. for 5 yrs; age 30; carpenter; join co K 7 cav 9 Feb 1875 Colfax La.; dd qmd Feb to Mar 1875; ed qmd carpenter Oct 1875 to Mar 1876; dd qmd carpenter Dec 1876 to Apr 1877; dd qmd carpenter Feb 1878; tr to co I 21 Nov 1878; dd co carpenter Dec 1878 to Nov 1879; dd co cook house Dec 1879; disch 26 Jan 1880 Ft Lincoln DT expir of serv a pvt char very good; reenl 12 Oct 1881 Chicago Ill. for 5 yrs; age 37; assd to co E 5 cav; disch 4 May 1882 Ft Sidney Neb on surg cert dis a pvt char xclt (disease of heart; on sick report constantly from 2 Jan when thrown from horse); reenl 16 Sep 1882 Ft Omaha Neb for 5 yrs; assd to co K 4 inf; disch 15 Sep 1887 Ft Spokane WT expir of serv a sgt char good; reenl 22 Aug 1889 Ft Riley Kans. for 5 yrs in co C 7 cav; disch 9 Jan 1890 at Ft Riley on surg cert dis a wag char good (gen debility from chr. lead poisoning contr working in lead mills at Omaha, supervening upon const. syph; dis total as to mil serv; 1/2 as to his trade); res Omaha, Neb.

Brown, Nathan T. Pvt co L; b. Marion Co. Ind.; enl 24 July 1869 Indianapolis Ind. for 5 yrs; age 26; carpenter; grey eyes, blk hair, dk comp, 5' 7" high; assd to gen serv Newport Bks Ky.; dd hosp nurse Aug 1869 to Mar 1870; ed qmd teamster Oct 1870 to Jan 1872; ed qmd carpenter Apr 1872; tr to "music boys" 28 June 1872; join co H 6 inf as mus'n 30 Aug 1873 Ft Stevenson DT; disch 24 July 1874 at Ft Stevenson by expir of serv a mus'n [fifer]; reenl 11 Aug 1874 Camp Hancock (Bismarck) DT for 5 yrs in co D 17 inf; enlmt canceled 4 Sep 1874 per GO 62 AGO 1874 [reduction of army];[76] reenl 25 Nov 1874 Ft Lincoln DT for 5 yrs in co L 7 cav; ed qmd carpenter 6 Oct 1875 to 7 Mar 1876; sick qrs 10–15 Mar 1876 (severe frostbite ends all toes both feet);[77] [stayed with wagon train at Powder River June 1876 says Burkman];[78] ds Ft Lincoln 17 Oct 1876 chg co prop; dd qmd 5 Mar to 23 Apr 1877; killed 13 Sep 1877 Canon Creek MT in action with Nez Perce inds.[79]

Brown, Wm. Pvt co F; b. Hamburg Germany; enl 5 Dec 1867 New York N.Y. for 5 yrs; age 34; laborer; blue eyes, brn hair, fair comp, 5' 5" high; join co F 22 Jan 1868 Ft L'worth Kans.; dd co cook Apr to June 1868; wd (sl.) r. arm 27 Nov 1868 in action at Washita; dd co cook Dec 1868 to May 1869; ds Ft Hays Kans. June to Sep 1869; dd co cook Nov 1869; dd co cook June to Oct 1870; ed qmd teamster Dec 1870 to Feb 1871; dd co cook Mar to Sep 1871; dd co cook Nov 1871; dd co cook Jan 1872; ed qmd May & June 1872; dd co cook July 1872; dd co cook Oct 1872; disch 5 Dec 1872 Louisville Ky. by expir of serv a pvt; reenl in co F 10 Dec 1872 for 5 yrs; dd regtl hq Dec 1872; dd post hq detmt Apr to June 1873; dd co cook Feb 1874; sick Ft Lincoln DT June to Aug 1874; dd post qmd Apr 1875; killed with Custer column 25 June 1876 [body found in ind camp opposite where Custer chg down to river says Rooney].[80]

Bruce, Pat'k. Pvt co F; b. Cork Ireland; enl 29 Oct 1864 New York N.Y. for 3 yrs; age 20; laborer; blue eyes, brn hair, fair comp, 5' 7" high; assd to co C 7 inf 8 Dec 1864 Ft Schuyler N.Y.; dd co cook Apr 1866; cpl 1

July 1867; pvt 21 Sep 1867; disch 29 Oct 1867 Gainesville Fla expir of serv a pvt; reenl 11 Apr 1868 Charleston SC for 3 yrs in co B 6 inf; ed qmd teamster Aug 1869 to Mar 1870 & Aug to Nov 1870; disch 11 Apr 1871 Ft Gibson IT expir of serv a pvt & reenl in co B for 5 yrs; ed qmd teamster June to Sep 1871; ed qmd teamster Apr 1872; ed qmd laborer Oct 1872 to July 1873; dd post gardener Apr 1874; ed qmd teamster June to Sep 1874; dd med dept Feb to May 1875; dd post gardener June to Sep 1875; disch 11 Apr 1876 Ft Lincoln DT expir of serv a pvt; reenl 1 May 1876 at Ft Lincoln for 5 yrs in co F 7 cav ; killed with Custer column 25 June 1876.

Bruns, Carl August. Pvt co E; b. 23 June 1830 Brunswick Germany; enl 20 Nov 1875 New York N.Y. for 5 yrs; age 37; musician; hazel eyes, dk hair, sallow comp, 5' 8 1/2" high; join 7 cav 14 Apr 1876 Ft Lincoln DT (with Lt Reily's detmt); ds Ft Lincoln from 15 May (await result of appn for disch acc't inability to understand or speak English language); dd co garden June 1876; dd with band Aug 1876 to Nov 1880; disch 19 Nov 1880 Ft Meade DT expir of serv a pvt char xclt; died 4 Jan 1910 Mandan N.Dak.
Pension: 24 Oct 1892 / Inv /1138429 / 871169.

Bucknell, Thos. J. Trump'r co C; b. Cincinnati Ohio; enl 24 Aug 1870 at Cincinnati for 5 yrs; age 21; laborer; grey eyes, lt hair, lt comp, 5' 8 1/4" high; join co B 8 cav 18 Oct 1870 Ft Stanton NM; trump'r 16 Nov 1872; pvt 1 Dec 1873 (own req); ed qmd mech Apr 1874; cpl 15 Oct 1874; disch 24 Aug 1875 Ft Union NM expir of serv a cpl; reenl 23 Sep 1875 at Cincinnati for 5 yrs; join co C 7 cav 21 Oct 1875 Ft Lincoln DT; trump'r 22 Oct 1875; killed with Custer column 25 June 1876. (with packs till morn 25 June but assd co duties when regt divided up).[81]

Burdick, Benj. F. Pvt co A; b. 27 Apr 1852 Grafton N.Y.; enl 13 Jan 1872 Troy N.Y. for 5 yrs; age 21 8/12; cooper; blue eyes, brn hair, fair comp, 5' 8 3/4" high; join co A 11 Feb 1872 E'town Ky.; ed subs dept herder Oct 1873; in conft Dec 1873; dd co teamster Dec 1874 to May 1875; dd co teamster Oct 1875 to Jan 1876; dd co cook Apr 1876; ds camp Powder River MT 15 June 1876; ds Ft Lincoln 13 Aug 1876; dd qmd 12–28 Sep 1876 with 281 cav horses at post; disch 13 Jan 1877 Ft Rice DT expir of serv a pvt char very good & reenl in co A for 5 yrs; dd co cook June 1877; ds in field 2 Sep 1877; dd qmd teamster Apr to July 1878; dd qmd teamster Feb 1879; in conft Feb 1880; dd co teamster Dec 1880; in conft Feb 1881; ds Little Mo. River repairing tel line Mar to May 1881; ds repairing mil tel line Oct & Nov 1881; disch 12 Jan 1882 Ft Meade DT expir of serv a pvt char good; reenl 5 Sep 1883 Albany N.Y. for 5 yrs; assd to co H 15 inf; disch 12 Mar 1884 Ft Randall DT on surg cert dis (chr. rheum.; not contr line of duty; dis 1/2) a pvt; died 11 Jan 1930 hosp for incurables, Kenwood, Albany N.Y.
Pension: 19 Apr 1913 / Inv / 1409386. Rej on grd mil serv not rendered dur Rebellion. Claim appv under act 3 Mar 1927 / Ind. Surv. / A-5-9-28. (XC-2,350,213).

Burgdorf, Chas. Pvt co K; b. Hanover Germany; enl 28 Jan 1867 New York N.Y. for 3 yrs; age 21; clerk; blue eyes, fair hair, ruddy comp, 5' 5 1/2" high; assd to co E 36 inf; (regt consol with 7 inf May 1869); disch 28 Jan 1870 Ft Bridger Wyo. Ty expir of serv a pvt; reenl 14 Feb 1870 Omaha Bks Neb for 5 yrs; assd to co C 7 inf; disch 14 Feb 1875 Ft Ellis Mt expir of serv a sgt; reenl 28 Feb 1876 Chicago Ill. for 5 yrs; join co K 7 cav 27 Apr 1876 St Paul Minn.; ds camp Powder River MT 15 June 1876; cpl 31 May 1878; ds Camp J. G. Sturgis DT Aug to Nov 1878; pvt 13 June 1879; dd co clerk Aug & Dec 1879; disch 27 Feb 1881 Ft Totten DT expir of serv a pvt char very good.

Burke, Edmund H. Blks co K; b. Manchester England; cpl & sgt co C 21 Iowa inf 16 Aug 1862 to 17 July 1865; enl reg army 11 Dec 1868 Omaha Bks Neb for 3 yrs; age 24; butcher; hazel eyes, blk hair, ruddy comp, 5' 8" high; assd to co C 3 art'y; disch 11 Dec 1871 Columbia SC expir of serv a pvt; reenl 16 Dec 1871 Yorkville SC for 5 yrs in co L 7 cav; tr to co K 15 Aug 1872; in conft Aug 1872 to Feb 1873; sen gen cm 1 Oct 1872 forf $10 pay per mo for 6 mos & conft same period; blks 1 Apr

1873; ed qmd blks 28 July to 11 Sep 1873; sick hosp Ft Rice DT 3 Sep to 3 Oct 1874 (l. frac.[from Blk Hills Exp'n]); ed qmd 6 Jan to 21 Oct 1875; cpl 1 Aug 1876; sd with Lt Hare's sec. of parrott guns 8 Oct to 12 Nov 1876; disch 14 Dec 1876 Ft Lincoln DT expir of serv a cpl char good; res Sumner Iowa in 1923.
Pension: 23 Sep 1865 / Inv / 90958; (abandoned). Renewed claim April 1877; (declared no mil serv since July 1865); appvdon cert. 153982 at $4 mo. from 18 July 1865 & $18 mo. from 5 May 1877.

Burke, Jno. See Pardee, Oscar F.

Burkhardt, Chas. Pvt co K; b. Summerville Ohio; pvt co B 6 Ohio inf 8 June 1861 to 26 Aug 1866; enl reg army 7 Sep 1866 at Chicago Ill. for 5 yrs; age 25; cigarmaker; hazel eyes, brn hair, dk comp, 5' 4" high; join co K 7 cav 29 Sep 1866 Ft Riley Kans.; dd co cook Feb 1867; dd orderly detmt hq Sep 1867; dd hosp attdt Nov 1867 to Mar 1868; dd co cook Dec 1869 to Oct 1870; ds regtl hq Nov 1870 to Sep 1871; disch 7 Sep 1871 Louisville Ky. expir of serv a pvt & reenl in co K for 5 yrs; dd co cook Dec 1871 to Sep 1873; sick 5 May 1873 Yankton DT (orchitis) & tr on str *Katie P. Kountz* 8 May to Ft Rice DT;[82] dd co cook Apr 1874 to Mar 1875; dd co cook Oct 1875 to Mar 1876; (cook for Lt Godfrey May to Aug 1876);[83] disch 6 Aug 1876 camp mouth of Rosebud Creek MT (in time to go down river by first boat) per GO 24 AGO 1859 a pvt char xclt; arr Ft Lincoln 10 Aug on str *Durfee*; died about 1888 near Natchitoches La.
Pension: 27 July 1906 / Wid / 852914. (Rej on grd no evidence sol.'s fatal cancer contr in serv & line of duty).

Burkman, Jno. Pvt co L; b. 10 Jan 1839 Allegheny Pa.; enl 16 Aug 1870 Limestone Creek Kans. for 5 yrs in co A 7 cav; age 30; laborer; hazel eyes, dk hair, ruddy comp, 5' 7" high; ed qmd teamster Dec 1870 to July 1871; dd orderly to Lt-col Custer Apr 1873 to Aug 1874; dd post hq Sep 1874 to 16 Aug 1875 when disch at Ft Lincoln DT by expir of serv a pvt; reenl in co A 1 Sep 1875 at Ft Lincoln for 5 yrs; dd post hq to Mar 1876; tr to co L 1 Apr 1876; dd regtl hq Apr to July 1876; (with pack train 25 June leading gen Custer's extra horse); dd qmd teamster Dec 1876 to Mar 1877; dd qmd hostler Apr 1877; ds Ft Lincoln 15 Oct 1877; dd qmd hostler Feb to May 1878; dd regtl hq hostler June 1878; dd qmd Camp J. G. Sturgis DT July to Sep 1878; dd qmd hostler Dec 1878; sick hosp Ft Lincoln 10 Mar to 17 May 1879 when disch on surg cert dis (epilepsy) a pvt char good; died 6 Nov 1925 Billings MT.[84]
Pension: 25 Feb 1887 / Inv / 599363 / 899473.

Burlis, Edmond. Pvt band; b. 19 Mar 1848 Klingnau Switz; enl 13 Nov 1871 Chicago Ill. for 5 yrs; age 23; musician; hazel eyes, dk hair, dk comp, 5' 6" high; des 14 May 1873 St Louis Bks Mo.; surd 12 Nov 1873 at St Louis Bks under GO 102 AGO 1873; assd to 7 cav 6 Dec 1875; join regt 14 Apr 1876 Ft Lincoln DT (with Lt Reily's detmt); assd to band 28 Apr & appt lance cpl; ds camp Powder River MT 14 June 1876; ds str *Josephine* 6 Aug 1876 to Ft Lincoln with band; disch 28 May 1877 at Ft Lincoln expir of serv a pvt char good; reenl 12 Dec 1877 at St Louis for 5 yrs; assd to band 6 cav; disch 11 Dec 1882 Ft Lowell AT expir of serv a trump'r; died 22 Oct 1924 St Louis Mo.
Pension: Ind. Surv. / 12767 / 7676. Ind. Wid / 17043 / 11155. (XC-2,659,409).

Burnham, Lucian. Pvt co F; b. Conkling N.Y.; enl 9 Dec 1872 Scranton Pa. for 5 yrs; age 21; sawyer; grey eyes, red hair, ruddy comp, 5' 8 1/2" high' join co F 7 Feb 1873 Louisville Ky.; sick qrs Apr 1873 Yankton DT & tr on str *Katie P. Kountz* 8 May to Ft Rice DT;[85] ds Ft Rice June to Oct 1873 gd regtl prop; dd subs dept herding cattle Apr 1874; dd qmd teamster Feb 1875; dd co cook Oct 1875; dd qmd teamster Dec 1875 to Mar 1876; killed with Custer column 25 June 1876.[86]

Burns, Chas. Pvt co B; b. Howard Co. Md; enl 24 Oct 1870 Baltimore Md for 5 yrs; age 23; laborer; blue eyes, brn hair, florid comp, 5' 9" high; assd to co K 8 inf; disch 24 Oct 1875 Camp Apache AT expir of serv a pvt; reenl 8 Mar 1876 at Baltimore for 5 yrs; join co B 7 cav 27 Apr 1876 St Paul Minn.; ds camp Powder River MT 10 June 1876; ed qmd Nov 1876 to Jan 1877; abs conft Camp Hancock (Bismarck) DT 23 Feb 1877; in conft Tongue River MT 19 Oct & with Lt Gibson's detmt to Ft Lincoln 27 Oct; dd qmd Apr 1878 to Nov 1879; in conft Dec 1879; dd qmd Apr 1880; dd qmd Dec 1880; disch 7 Mar 1881 Ft Yates DT expir of serv a pvt char good.

Bustard, Jas. Sgt co I; b. Donegal Ireland; enl 19 Mar 1867 New York N.Y. for 3 yrs; age 21; clerk; hazel eyes, lt hair, fair comp, 5' 6 1/2" high; join co K 10 inf 9 Apr 1867 Ft L'worth Kans.; dd learning music Apr to June 1869; ed hosp attdt Oct 1869 to Mar 1870; disch 19 Mar 1870 Ft Shaw MT expir of serv a pvt; reenl 19 July 1870 Chicago Ill. for 5 yrs; join co I 7 cav 4 Aug 1870 Ft L'worth Kans.; cpl 14 Aug 1871; ds Taylor Bks Aug to Oct 1871; pvt 7 Nov 1871 (own req); sgt 4 Dec 1871; ds Louisville Ky. Nov 1872; ds St Paul Minn. 6 Apr 1874; ds Ft Snelling Minn. 29 Apr to 10 May 1874 awaiting transp to regt; disch 19 July 1875 Ft Lincoln DT expir of serv a sgt & reenl two days later in co I for 5 yrs; killed with Custer column 25 June 1876.[87]

Butler, Jas. 1sgt co L; b. Albany N.Y.; enl 3 Apr 1860 at Albany for 5 yrs; (upon consent of mother);[88] age 21; farmer; grey eyes, sandy hair, ruddy comp, 5' 5" high; join co G 2 drg 5 Sep 1860 Ft Garland NM; (regt redesig 2 cav Aug 1861); ed hosp attdt Feb to Aug 1862 Las Vegas NM; wd 9 June 1863 & in hosp Phil'a Pa. to Nov 1864; disch 3 Apr 1865 Point of Rocks Md upon expir of serv a pvt; reenl 31 May 1870 Cincinnati Ohio for 5 yrs; age 28; qm & comsy clerk; join co L 7 cav 26 June 1870 Ft L'worth Kans.; dd clerk in adjt's office Nov 1870 to May 1871; cpl 22 May 1871; sgt 27 June 1871; 1sgt 26 May 1872; sick (intm. fever) 2 May 1873; duty 3 May; sick on str *Miner* 2 June Grand River DT (unfit to travel with comd per senior med officer);[89] in hosp Ft Rice DT 11 June (cont'n sim. frac.); sgt 23 June 1873; rejoin co L 15 Oct Ft Lincoln DT; 1sgt 7 Dec 1873; disch 31 May 1875 at Ft Lincoln by expir of serv a 1sgt & reenl same day for 5 yrs; on furl 30 days 19 June 1875; (m. 7 July 1875 Brooklyn N.Y. to Mary Murray); appt comsy-sgt USA 8 July 1875 & join post Camp Sheridan Neb 18 Sep 1875; appmt revoked 21 Oct 1875; rejoin 7 cav 17 Dec 1875 at Ft Lincoln a pvt; assd to co L 31 Dec Ft Totten DT; appt 1sgt 14 Mar 1876; killed with Custer column 25 June 1876.

Pension: 9 Oct 1876 / Mother / 228303; (clmt not aware son had married). Wid / 240662 / 210533.

Butler, Jas. W. Pvt co F; b. 1 Apr 1844 Limerick Ireland;[90] pvt co C 1 Pa. art'y June 1861 to June 1864; enl reg army 26 Sep 1865 Phil'a Pa. for 3 yrs; age 21; soldier; grey eyes, red hair, ruddy comp, 5' 8" high; join co C 2 cav 30 Sep 1865 Monrovia Md; cpl 1 Nov 1865; ds Big Creek Kans. Dec 1865 guarding Butterfield-Overland Stage route; des 4 Feb 1866 while escorting mail train to Ft Ellsworth Kans.; surd 14 Aug 1866 Governor's Isl NYH under GO 43 AGO 1866;[91] assd to gen serv rcts 17 Sep 1866; tr to co K 3 battn 19 inf 25 Sep 1866 Ft Columbus NYH; (redesig 37 inf regt Dec 1866);[92] dd co cook Oct & Dec 1867; ed qmd Feb to June 1868; in conft Oct 1868 to Apr 1869; tr to co B 5 inf June 1869 (dur reorganization of inf regts);[93] disch 14 Aug 1869 Ft Wallace Kans. expir of serv a pvt; enl in 7 cav 18 Sep 1869 Fitzmeadow Colo. Ty for 5 yrs; assd to co E 3 Oct 1869; in conft Oct to Dec 1869; sen gen cm 23 Dec 1869 forf $12 pay per mo for 6 mos; in conft to Sep 1870; dd qmd teamster Oct 1870; in civil jail L'worth City Kans. Dec 1870 to June 1871; ds Louisville Ky. Sep to Nov 1871; cpl 6 July 1872; sgt 1 Sep 1873; pvt 15 Oct 1873; ed qmd teamster Dec 1873; dd qmd teamster Feb to June 1874; dd qmd herder 21 Aug 1874; disch 18 Sep 1874 Ft Lincoln DT expir of serv a pvt & reenl same day for 5 yrs in co F; dd qmd teamster Feb to Dec 1875; sick (cont'n testicle) 2 Aug to 7 Sep 1875; sick 26 Oct to 12 Nov 1875 (infl. testicle); sick hosp Ft Lincoln 4 Jan to 23 Feb & 20 Mar to 6 May 1876 (infl. testicle); dd regtl hq fatigue pty (morn & eve) from 11 May 1876;[94] sick qrs 5–12 June 1876 (orchitis); [at Powder River camp says himself];[95] sick hosp Ft Lincoln 30 Sep to 17 Oct 1876 (infl. testicle); sick hosp Ft Abercrombie DT 8–22 Dec 1876 (abscess scrotum); ed qmd teamster Jan 1877; dd qmd teamster Oct 1877;[96] dd co teamster Feb to Dec 1878; disch 17 Sep 1879 Ft Totten DT expir of serv a pvt char good; reenl 2 May 1881 Phil'a

Pa. for 5 yrs; assd to co F 20 inf; disch 1 May 1886 Ft Assiniboine MT expir of serv a pvt char good; reenl 21 Sep 1887 Camden NJ for 5 yrs; assd to co E 12 inf; disch 20 Sep 1892 Ft L'worth Kans. expir of serv a pvt char drunkard; died 8 June 1924 Phil'a Pa. Pension: 12 Sep 1905 / Inv / 1340194 / 1137051.

Notes—B

1. There are 25 letters, 1873–76, from Bailey and War Department, in possession of his niece, Mrs. Samuel Fields, of Springfield, Mass. *The Springfield (Mass.) Republican*, June 24, 1951, and Aug. 22, 1954.

2. RG 94, Entry 409, file 10818 A (EB) AGO 1878, Capt McDougall to Lt Garlington, Regimental Adjutant, Mar. 17, 1878.

3. Varnum to Walter Camp, Nov. 3rd (no year), Univ. of Maine, WMC-BYU.

4. Hammer, *Custer in '76*, 187; however, Bailey indicated otherwise, relating that, "Our wagon train was left at Powder River and from Powder River we took a pack outfit up to the Rosebud to the mouth of that river," Bailey to Walter Camp, April 19, 1910, WMC-BYU.

5. Lt. Varnum said Baker may have been absent with mail or dispatches and came up on the boat and mustered present June 30. Varnum to Walter Camp, May 14 [no year] Orono, Me., WMC-BYU; Bailey said Lt. Nowlan took him to Custer's battlefield to help identify the dead. Bailey (Baker) "Reminiscence" [SC 376], Montana Historical Society); Bailey said he and Nowlan were first to visit Custer's field, Fremont Kipp to Gen. Godfrey, Nov. 17, 1921, Bailey folder, Wm. James Ghent Papers (hereafter cited as Ghent Papers), LOC.

From his interviews with Young Hawk and Strikes Two (ca 1912), Walter Camp said he concluded Baker was not with the 'Rees at all, but was probably on the steamer all the time until June 27, perhaps from Fort Lincoln or Powder or Rosebud, WMC, interview notes, box 5, env 41, BYU; Camp later said he had good evidence Bailey was in the fight with Reno. Camp to Fremont Kipp, Nov. 19, 1921, Edward S. Godfrey Papers (hereafter cited as Godfrey Papers), LOC. Varnum said Camp interviewed Baker and he (Baker) was reticent about what happened on Reno Hill. Varnum to Gen. Godfrey, Feb. 13, 1928, Godfrey Papers.

Young Hawk said Baker was surely in the fight, had horse killed, ("I think he means Herendeen"—WMC). Young Hawk thought Baker to be Chokawo, and Billy Cross to be Ieska; said Chokawo's horse was killed and Chokawo was left in timber and got a Sioux horse, (this must have been Cross—WMC).

Strikes Two says Billy Cross joined scouts to water horses; says Choka Wo came down hill with 'Rees to water horses and were cut off from Reno by Sioux and went back to Powder River with 'Rees, (Choka Wo must therefore have been Cross—WMC). Neither Young Hawk nor Strikes Two appeared to remember Baker. Hardorff, *Camp, Custer, and the Little Big Horn*, 49–55.

Little Sioux said a half-blood scout went back to Powder River with his party Chakawo (the drummer), Chahcawo, Hammer, *Custer in '76*, 181; In his interview with Walter Camp, Oct. 8, 1910, Bailey said the 'Rees called him Chakaboo which means drummer. Said he was on the skirmish line in the valley fight and during the retreat his horse was killed on east side of river; said he and Young Hawk went with message for medicine on June 27; Young Hawk said no, it was he and Forked Horn did this, Hardorff, *Camp, Custer, and the Little Big Horn*, 69; Hammer, *Custer in '76*, 193; *The Evening Star* (Washington, DC), Nov. 10, 1921.

Varnum said Bailey's "story of having been sent after medicines by Reno is pure rot," that Reno's command had medical stores with the pack train, "or at least as good a supply as Gen. Terry . . . and had a Medical Officer." Varnum to Nelson A. Mason, Secretary to Sen. Lynn J. Frazier (N.Dak.), Nov. 9, 1927, Ghent Papers.

Young Hawk said, on June 27, he and Goose, Forked Horn, and Red-Foolish-Bear, with Gerard and Varnum, and some soldiers (one of whom the Sioux called Jack Drum Beater), went down to look for Custer's body, Libby, *Arikara Narrative*, 107.

Bailey filed claims for the loss of his horse in the battle. In Dec. 1926, Sen. Frazier introduced Bill S.4614 (69th Cong. 2nd Sess.), for the relief of William J. Bailey, alias William Baker, the sum $125 reimbursement for loss of a horse while serving as Indian Scout during Battle of Little Big Horn, Bailey folder, Ghent Papers.

Of possible significance regarding Baker's status at the time of the battle is that when applying for invalid pension in 1891, Baker claimed a large ganglion (2 3/4 by 1 1/2 inches) on his right arm near the wrist was from a gunshot wound inflicted at the Little Big Horn, June 26, 1876 (Pension File, RG 15).

6. Fred Gerard did not know how Baker came to go on the boat but thought he was striker for Moylan, Gerard to Walter Camp, May 1910, WMC-BYU.

7. Lt. Baldwin said two scouts came in [Aug. 16] with dispatches from Capt. Snyder, and Miles immediately sent two dispatches to Snyder. Miles said Baker reported seeing party of 12 or 15 men east of Rosebud, James Willert, *March of the Columns*, 380–82; Soldier said he and a party of 'Rees carried mail from Powder River to mouth of Rosebud and met Chakawo and party of 'Rees carrying messages in opposite direction, Hammer, *Custer in '76*, 190.

8. Roger Williams, "The Story of William Baker.".

9. RG 94, Entry 409, file 10818 A (EB) AGO 1878; Lt. Godfrey always understood only those who volunteered to get water were recommended for the medal, as he did. When the regiment was in Camp J. G. Sturgis, the recommendations were referred to a Board of Officers of which Maj. Merrill was president. Godfrey recalled that the board turned down all except those who made the first and perhaps second "Rush" for water, and only those then in service, Godfrey to Walter Camp, May 14, 1923, WMC-BYU.

10. Chandler, *Of Garryowen in Glory*, 397.

11. SO 39, Hq 7th Cavalry, May 11, 1876, RG 391, Entry 859. Dennis Lynch said about 120 men accompanied the packs exclusive of Company B, but about 60 of these were officer's servants and some of the headquarters fatigue, whose duties consisted in putting up and taking down the officer's tents as occasion required, were also with the pack train. Lynch to Walter Camp, Dec. 27, 1908, WMC-BYU.

John McGuire said, besides the pack detail there were headquarters details, strikers, cooks, and men leading officer's extra horses to the number of two or three to each company, Hammer, *Custer in '76*, 124 note 3.

12. Sgt. Botzer, Troop Duty Book (hereafter cited as Botzer Troop Duty Book), Museum of the American Indian, New York, indicates Barnett present on regular duty May 23 through June 17, and "DS" from June 18, see note B45 (Botzer).

13. Sgt. Alex Brown's troop duty book shows Barnett "D" August 1–5, and "DS" August 6 to Sept. 26 in Reynolds and Brown, *Journal*. The company muster roll, August 31st, shows Barnett on detached service with Ordnance Wagon, see note B67 (Brown).

14. SO 41, Hq 7th Cavalry, May 13, 1876, RG 391, Entry 859. Lt. R. E. Thompson, ACS on Gen. Terry's staff, said the men detailed to go with him went on the boat and up the Big Horn, Hammer, *Custer in '76*, 247.

15. RG 94, Entry 297, file 1871 AGO 1894.

16. RG 94, Entry 25, file 10742 PRD 1891.

17. Lt. Gibson's account in Chandler, *Of Garryowen In Glory*, 19; Utley, *Life in Custer's Cavalry*, 249; RG 92, Entry 238, report 1868/304.

18. "Major Bell of 7th Cavalry reported to Gen. Custer at Fort Lincoln, Saturday, but goes east in a few days on six months leave," *Bismarck Tribune*, Wed., March 15, 1876; Lt. Bell was a passenger on Gen. Custer's snowbound train, *St. Paul (Minn.) Dispatch*, March 21, 1876.

19. Lt. Ernest A. Garlington, who was assigned to the 7th Cavalry after graduation from West Point, June 15, 1876, relinquished the remainder of his leave, to join the regiment early. On the way he stopped at division headquarters in Chicago on July 17, where he met Lt. Bell who was also en route to join, and together they went to St. Paul. Garlington timed their departure from St. Paul to connect with the steamboat, but when Bell joined him at the station, just as the train was about to pull out, he said he could not leave that day and asked Garlington to take charge of a maid servant destined for some post on the Missouri River. Carroll, *The Lieutenant E. A. Garlington Narrative*, 4.

20. At Fort Buford the *Key West* was ordered by Col. J. W. Forsyth (of Gen. Sheridan's staff) to unload and return to Bismarck. Forsyth had just arrived on the Steamer *Carroll* from Gen. Terry's camp Aug. 4 and deemed it impractical for boats to continue up the Yellowstone because of low water. On Aug. 10, the Steamer *Josephine* came down with news that Gen. Terry's command had left the Yellowstone with 40 days' worth of supplies, and that the river was no longer navigable because of low water. Bell boarded the *Josephine* and returned to Fort Lincoln for further instructions, considering that if reinforcements were forwarded to Gen. Terry, it would be from Bismarck where his opportunities would be better than from Buford, Lt. Bell to AAG, DD, Aug. 13, 1876, (2210 DD 1876), NA, M1734, Roll 16.

Capt. Weston (commissary of subsistence), who was also on the *Key West* and *Josephine* with Bell, left Bismarck again Aug. 16 on the *Josephine* for the Yellowstone. On Aug. 27, Weston told Lt. Godfrey that Mrs. Godfrey gave mail to Bell but he stayed at Lincoln, Fort Buford Medical History, RG 94, Entry 547; *Bismarck Tribune*, Nov. 8, 1876; Godfrey, *Diary*, 42; Willert, *March of the Columns*, 451; Lt.

Wallace said "Bell let boat leave him (?) at Bismarck," Wallace to Dr. Knoblauch, Aug. 4, 1876, Westfall, *Letters From the Field*, 27.

21. SFO 43, Hq DD In the Field, Sept. 8, 1876, Fort Buford, DT, RG 94, Entry 44; Lt. Wallace said Bell shirked out of joining the regiment and he would report him absent without leave from Sept. 2 through the time he reports, Wallace to Dr. Knoblauch, Sept. 19, 1876, Westfall, *Letters From the Field*, 32; *Bismarck Tribune*, Sept. 27, 1876.

22. Capt. Bell claimed Sitting Bull's gun as his personal keepsake, a well-worn smoothbore Northwest trade gun, Hedren, "Sitting Bull's Surrender at Fort Buford."

23. Classified return of wounds and list of wounded at battle of Little Big Horn, from Dr. John Williams, chief medical officer of expedition, RG 94, Entry 624, file F464.

24. In November 1865, Benteen purchased the Haydon Plantation, 115 acres about 3 1/2 miles south of Atlanta, which he later renamed Hermitage Heights. In 1892 he purchased a town house at 39 Pavilion Street, overlooking Grant Park, Mills, *Harvest of Barren Regrets*, 123, 369.

25. In the siege on Reno hill, Benteen received a slight scratch on his right thumb from a spent bullet, which did not prevent his letter writing. It was also said that the heel of his boot was shot off, stunning his foot so that he walked lame for a few days, Carroll, *Camp Talk*, 25; Mills, *Harvest of Barren Regrets*, 271; Hardorff, *Camp, Custer, and the Little Big Horn*, 66; Hammer, *Custer in '76*, 122.

Benteen said he was put on the boat by Dr. Williams, having allowed himself to rundown from a severe two-day attack of diarrhea and doing nothing for it. He was on the boat continuously while at the camp at mouth of Big Horn River and stayed on for the trip to the supply depot at Powder River, July 16–18. There he boarded the Steamer *Far West* to accompany his two private horses and their groom, Frank Jones, an African American boy whom Benteen referred to as "Cuff," Carroll, *Camp Talk*, 44.

Jones was 16 years old when he testified at the court martial of Capt. French in January 1879 and said he came to Dakota with Company H in 1875 from New Orleans, RG 153, file QQ994; "Cuff" is mentioned by Fougera, *With Custer's Cavalry*, 146; Mills, *Harvest of Barren Regrets*, 219, 296, 314.

26. RG 94, Entry 547, Fort Buford, DT. *Bismarck Tribune*, Sept. 13 and Nov. 1, 1876; Gen. Terry and Gen. Card left St. Paul the night of Sept. 26 for Chicago to consult with Gen. Sheridan. That same day, Capt. Benteen wrote to his wife that he had seen the order [not yet issued] revoking his detail and was leaving that evening for Chicago to try for railroad passes and to see his cousins for one day before proceeding to St. Louis anyway. At Philadelphia, Oct. 6, he encountered Maj. Merrill on the grounds of the Centennial Exhibition and accepted his offer of quarters at his house, *Red River Star (Moorhead, Minn.)*, Sept. 22, 1876, *St. Paul Dispatch*, Sept. 26, 1876; Carroll, *Camp Talk*, 54–58.

27. Greene, *Nez Perce Summer 1877*, 216–18.

28. See Mills, *Harvest of Barren Regrets*, 374.

29. RG 94, Entry 25, file 452197 AGO 1902; Berwald inquired of the AGO, Feb. 24, 1910, if he was entitled to an Indian Campaign Medal, having served with Troop E, 7th Cavalry in 1873 and 1874 and in the 1876 Custer massacre (wounded). Berwald was interviewed by Walter Camp in 1911, and again Oct. 11, 1912, WMC-BYU.

30. *New York Times* (Illustrated Weekly Magazine), Nov. 28, 1897, features interview with Frank Berwald, and photo, copy in, Box 7, folder 2, WMC-BYU.

31. Berwald, a cook in the hospital mess at the military academy in 1900, was mentioned in connection with a scandal involving food purchases. Between October 1899 and February 1900, the daily cost of subsistence per cadet increased from $.82 to $1.01. Another cook, Private Louis Desmond, was convicted for transferring food bought for the cadet hospital mess to the hospital corps enlisted mess, and taking money from outside dealers with whom the system ran up abnormal bills. Hospital steward Guy Westerdahl was not believed to have been a party to the dishonorable practices of the cook or to have benefited monetarily, but he was faulted for failing to exercise proper supervision over the cadet mess and disobedience of repeated orders given him by the surgeon to give attention to the catering and rapid increase in expenses. Though his conduct justified a court-martial, he instead was given an honorable discharge, with character, in consideration of his long service (18 1/2 years). Berwald was believed to have known of the illicit practices but evidence failed to link him directly. He was recommended for transfer to a smaller post to finish his service—then having served 27 years five months—on account of his being an old and simple man and on account of his long service, to avoid compromising discipline of the men of the hospitals, RG 94, Entry 25, file 334075 AGO 1900.

32. Peter Thompson mentioned Gen. Custer's orderly, a man named Bishop, during the march to Powder River, Magnussen, *Peter Thompson's Narrative of the Little Big Horn Campaign*, 59; Thompson

also said Bishoff was orderly for Custer on day of the fight, Questionnaire from Walter Camp, to Thompson, nd, WMC-LBHB.

33. Tom Custer said Bischoff was in his [Tom's] tent fixing things now, Letter to Emma Reed, May 20, 1876, in O'Neil, ed., *Garry Owen Tid Bits*, Vol, VII; Bischoff said Tom Custer rode his horse, his [Tom's] horse having a sore back, Bischoff interview with Walter Camp, nd, WMC-BYU; John McGuire referred to Bischoff as "the prevaricator," McGuire to Walter Camp, Oct. 2, 1909, WMC-BYU.

34. On Aug. 4, 1876, Alex Bishop wrote to Prof. F. Knapp, Baltimore, Md., (father of Wm. A. Knapp, civilian clerk in post quartermaster's office at Fort Rice), requesting his influence at the War Department to help him get discharged from the army. Bishop had promise of a clerkship at a wholesale house in New York City. Lt. Gibson investigated the facts of the case and reported to the Adjutant General, Oct. 6, 1876, that he strongly recommended discharge, stating that Bishop was a bright young man who would doubtless do well in civil life.

Bishop's mother, of Brooklyn, wrote to President Grant, Dec. 6, 1876, seeking his help for her son to obtain a clerkship in the general service, he having applied but was informed no vacancy. RG 94, Entry 409, file 9513 B (EB) AGO 1876.

Alex Bishop was described as "a neat little player, sure catch, fair batter, good runner. Considering that he intends to become a minister of the gospel in the future he loves base ball as [others do] roast possum. He will be one of the best in the coming seasons." Anderson, "The Benteen Base Ball Club."

35. Charles Bishop "a boy from the capitol 'good as wheat,' plays a remarkably fine game anywhere, though needing continually the sharp eye of the captain, not being exactly lazy, but born woefully tired. He is one of the best in the nine, heavy hitter with the willow, tricky base runner and an aggravating sure catcher. Is 22, but as lazy as 86." Anderson, "The Benteen Base Ball Club."

36. See note A25 (Ascough).

37. Sgt. Thomas Blake was interred in Cypress Hills National Cemetery, sec 2 Grave 9866, in Brooklyn, NY. RG 92, Entry 1944. (At the time Blake transferred to Troop C, 2nd Cavalry, there was also serving in that troop, Edward Blake, born in New York City ca 1853).

38. See note A7 (Abrams); Blunt was entrusted Aug. 5 to carry Lt. Godfrey's letter, and diary, to Mrs. Godfrey, Godfrey, *Diary*, 31.

39. RG 94, Entry 25, file 49728 AGO 1897.

40. Walter Camp map of markers on Custer battlefield, WMC-BYU; See Taunton, *Custer's Field*, 20–21; Knipe said Bobo was a bald-headed man and was not mutilated. Knipe recognized Bobo, Finkle, and Finley because they were lying close to their horses and he recognized the horses first. Questionaire from Camp to Knipe, n.d., WMC-BYU.

Col. Homer W. Wheeler, a retired officer of the 5th Cavalry, wrote to Walter Camp that in the Cheyenne village of Dull Knife in Nov. 1876, they found the memorandum book carried by Sgt. Bobo, Company C, 7th Cavalry. The book contained the names of all of Company C, also the details made the morning of June 25, 1876. Wheeler said the book was in the collection at Governor's Island a number of years, but the whole collection of Indian relics, including the memo book, was finally sold to a French artist and the whole thing lost by the sinking of the steamer on which the Frenchman was taking to France, Camp to Daniel Knipe, Mar. 30, 1920, WMC-LBHB.

41. See note A7 (Abrams).

42. Meddaugh, Diary; Scott, *Some Memories of a Soldier*, 44–45.

43. RG 94, Entry 409, file 7898 B (EB) AGO 1885.

44. GO 61 AGO Apr. 23, 1873, RG 94, Entry 44, directed that each troop of cavalry would have one 1st Sgt. and five duty sergeants; no company quartermaster sergeant would be appointed because they were not enumerated in the act of May 15, 1872, and were not entitled to its benefit. (Thereafter one noncommissioned officer was noted on the muster roll as "acting" company quartermaster sergeant—).

45. Theodore Goldin to Albert W. Johnson, Jan. 17, 1933, Carroll, *The Benteen-Goldin Letters*, 41; Augustus Devoto to Walter Camp, Nov. 15, 1917, WMC-LBHB; Botzer's Troop Duty Book (erroneously credited to Sgt. Alex Brown), May 13 to June 24, 1876, was recovered in Dull Knife's village of Cheyennes, Nov. 25, 1876, and is currently in the collections of the Museum of the American Indian in New York City. See Powell, "High Bull's Victory Roster."

46. *Helena (Mont.) Daily Herald*, July 15, 1876. Gray, *Custer's Last Campaign*, 6–10; in his testimony at Fort Phil Kearney, July 27, 1867, before the Sanborn Commission investigating the Fetterman fight, Michael Boyer said he was then 28 years of age, and had been in the mountains since 1849, NA, M740, Roll 1.

William Garnett told Walter Camp that, "Mich Bouyer's mother was Yankton Sioux raised by my mother. Mich Bouyer's father had my mother before Lt. Garnett did and took another wife. My mother lived with Lt. Garnett until he was ordered to Mexico. Then Bouyer bought my mother back again and I lived with them and did not know until later years that Garnett was my father. Sally Bouyer was my half sister through mother [and] married Philip White. Mich was one of four including Antoine by the Yankton woman, or, perhaps, old man Bouyer had two wives—I am not certain which way the case," Walter Camp interview notes with William Garnett, Indian Scout, nd, WMC-BYU. Garnett was born about 1855 at Fort Laramie, Wyo., son of an Oglala woman and Lt. Richard B. Garnett, who was killed at Gettysburg in 1863, DeLand, *History of the Sioux Wars*, 349.

Antoine Bouyer said Mitch's father was Vital Boyer, a full-blood Frenchman of Canada killed by an Indian war party in 1863 while trapping near Fort Laramie. He was married to three Sioux; Mitch's mother was full-blood Santee. Their brother, John, was hung for murder, Interview with Walter Camp, July 13, 1912, WMC-IU. John Boyer, a half-blood, was reported hung in 1871 for double murder, "Thomas Jefferson Carr—a Frontier Sheriff," *Annals of Wyoming*, Vol. 20, No. 2, July 1948.

47. George Herendeen interview with Walter Camp in Hammer, *Custer in '76*, 222; James Sipes interview with Walter Camp, May 22, 1909, in Hammer, *Custer in '76*, 241; Gibbon, *Adventures on the Western Frontier*, 113; Gray, *Custer's Last Campaign*, 12–19.

48. RG 92, Entry 238, report, 1876/240. Gray, *Custer's Last Campaign*, 92.

49. Gibbon, *Adventures on the Western Frontier*, 150.

50. Boyer's good friend, Tom Leforge, who also scouted for Gibbon in 1876, said that several years after the battle he talked with a Sioux Indian who visited the battlefield. The Sioux told Leforge that after the command had been wiped out, the Sioux found Boyer lying near the river, still living, his back broken by a gunshot wound. Boyer told them that though they had killed these few soldiers many thousands more would come. He asked to be killed to be put out of his misery, and the warrior obliged, afterward taking Boyer's vest and throwing the body in the river. Boyer's vest made of the skin of a spotted calf was found near the river after the battle, "Statement of Thomas H. Laforge," in *The Tepee Book*, Vol. II, No. VI, June 1916, 54.

A similar story was told to the Crows by one of six Arapaho warriors who were in the hostile camp at the time of the battle. Boyer and a bugler escaped from the encirclement around Custer's men and hid in the brush on the west side of the river They were discovered by the Arapaho and some Sioux or Cheyenne companions, and Boyer, desperately wounded, begged to be killed. Both men were killed and their bodies thrown into the river. Boyer's identity was accepted by the Crows as the Arapaho said this victim claimed to be half Sioux and tribal affiliation with the Crows and was wearing a calf-skin vest, Marquis, *Custer Soldiers Not Buried*, 9.

Curley said they found Bouyer's saddle and horse in the village but not his body, Hammer, *Custer in '76*, 171. See also Hardorff, ed., *The Custer Battle Casualties*, 119–20, and Hardorff, ed., *The Custer Battle Casualties, II*, 83–85.

51. Bouyer was due $395.00 (April 8 to June 25) less $3.95 for subsistence and $26.00 board 52 days with Company H, 2nd Cavalry, RG 92, Entries 778, and 781.

Tom Leforge said Mitch Bouyer's widow accompanied the Crows when they followed Gibbon's command to Fort Ellis, Sept. 24, 1876, and received the pay that was due Mitch, Marquis, *Memoirs of a White Crow Indian*, 264.

52. Botzer Troop Duty Book lists Boyle "DD" June 9–18; June 19 is blank and rest of book incomplete. Sgt. Alex Brown's Troop Duty Book shows Boyle on daily duty Aug. 11 to Sept. 18, 1876, Reynolds and Brown, *Journal*.

William A. Falconer (early resident of Bismarck), said James Boyle of McIntosh's troop was with the pack train at the Little Big Horn, Falconer to Mrs. Custer, Aug. 9, 1916, Elizabeth Bacon Custer Collection, LBHB, (hereafter cited as EBC-LBHB), Microfilm Roll 3, frames 2458 through 2466. Falconer said he knew Boyle was with the pack train, Falconer to William J. Ghent, May 31, 1933, Ghent Papers.

53. The *Josephine* left the command Sept. 11 and expected to reach Bismarck in 4 or 5 days, but because of seasonal low water in the rivers, spent more time aground on sand bars than in motion and was delayed a full ten days, Frost, *Custer's 7th Cav*, 101; Merington, *The Custer Story*, 266.

Detailed information on the delay of the *Josephine*, with letters from the boat's captain and pilot and a report of a board of survey is found among, "Letters Received, Headquarters Dept. of Dakota, 1873," NA, M1734, Roll 14.

Braden's narrative of his final field service appeared in the *Cavalry Journal,* Oct., 1905, and republished by Carroll in, *The Yellowstone Expedition of 1873*. Included in the latter volume is an account of Braden's ordeal, "An Incident of the Yellowstone Expedition of 1873," first published in the *Cavalry Journal,* Oct., 1904.

In a letter to his wife, Sept. 7, 1873, Gen. Custer related that his cook, Mary, prepared something special nearly every day for Braden. "Think of him, with his shattered thigh, having to travel over a rough country some 300 miles. He is not carried in an ambulance, but on a long stretcher on wheels, pushed and pulled by men on foot. It requires a full company every day to transport him. . . . When the command divided I had the band take a position where he would pass, and when his escort approached they struck up Garryowen . . . He acknowledged the compliment as well as he could. . ." Merington, *The Custer Story*, 263.

The Bismarck Tribune, Sept. 24, 1873, reported, "Lieut. Barden [sic] who was so seriously wounded in the fight with Sitting Bull and who was reported as past hope, is now on the Josephine, and the General says recovering fast."

Because of his reliability and solid build, with square head and dark eyes, and he rode a thickset horse, Braden was described as "Old Gothic," Fougera, *With Custer's Cavalry*, 83.

54. The signature of George Brainard on his 1864 and 1872 enlistment papers are near identical. RG 94, Entry 91.

55. SO 38, Hq 7th Cavalry, May 10, 1876, RG 391, Entry 859; John Bailey was sure Brainard was with Gen. Terry on boat, WMC, rosters, IU.

56. Brant to Chas. Dawsey, brother of Private David Dawsey, Jan. 10, 1878, typescript copy at LBHB; Chas. King (Milwaukee, Wis.) to Col. Godfrey, Aug. 15, 1901, says Brant's medal in possession of relatives who wished to frame it with brief statement of act for which it was awarded, LBHB Coll., Roll 9, frames 0368–0369.

57. Wm. E. Morris to Wm. Slaper, Apr. 11, 1915, newspaper clipping, np, nd, in William O. Taylor, Scrapbook and Notes, "With Custer on the Little Big Horn," p. 80 (hereafter cited as Taylor Scrapbook) Beinecke Library, Yale University, New Haven, Conn.

58. WMC, rosters, LBHB; Henry P. Jones to Walter Camp, June 2, 1911, WMC-BYU; Caddle said, "F. C. Braun not in fight M[?] of Band went by boat from Powder River to Ft Lincoln," Caddle to Walter Camp, Nov. 8, 1909, (Caddle drew line through Braun's name on list of Co. "I" men at LBH), WMC-BYU.

Gustave Korn said trooper Brown wanted to end Comanche's suffering when horse found after battle, *Winners of the West*, Vol. XIII, No. 2, Jan. 30, 1936, 1; "Who Knew Gustave Korn of Troop I, 7th U.S. Cavalry in the Custer Fight," says Korn's own account made at Ft. Meade DT, May 21, 1888.

59. Peter Thompson said Brennan turned his horse to the rear about two miles beyond the lone tepee, Brown and Willard, *The Black Hills Trails*, 154; Magnussen, *Peter Thompson's Narrative*, 117; John McGuire said among C troop men it was always the opinion that Brennan and Fitzgerald fell back from Custer's command out of cowardice and they often joked about it afterward, Hammer, *Custer in '76*, 126; Sgt. Hanley said Brennan, Fitzgerald, and Thompson were not with the packs June 25 but were with their company and straggled back from Custer after the packs reached Reno hill, Hammer, *Custer in '76*, 127; The Arikara scout, Soldier, mentioned meeting two white soldiers whose horses were down, Libby, *The Arikara Narrative*, 116.

60. RG 94, Entry 409, file 13182 A (EB) 1879; John McGuire said he met Brennan in Rapid City during summer 1886, but he had no conversation with him owing to the fact he was under influence of liquor, McGuire to Walter Camp, May 13, 1909, WMC-BYU; Thompson said the last time he saw Brennan he went by the name Welch, Questionnaire to Thompson from Walter Camp, Feb. 1909, WMC-LBHB.

61. RG 393, Part I, Entry 1173.

62. WMC, rosters, LBHB; Camp said he and Gen. Godfrey met old Sgt. Harrison and Sgt. Bresnahan in 1916, and they talked over the whole matter of Weir's advance in detail, Hammer, *Custer in '76*, 125, note 6.

63. Botzer's Troop Duty Book shows Brinkerhoff "DD" May 23 through June 18; June 19 is blank; and rest of book incomplete; Brinkerhoff said he remained at Reno's headquarters after the battle and way into August when he rejoined his troop and took charge of the quartermaster's department, Brinkerhoff to Sen. Lynn Frazier, Dec. 18, 1927, Bailey folder, Ghent Papers.

64. RG 94, Entry 544, Montana T'y Prescription Book No. 54. Bromwell said he was sick at Rosebud and had to be sent back to Powder River, Bromwell interview with Walter Camp, nd, WMC-BYU. (Bromwell likely meant he was sick at camp up Powder River and when Company E went on Reno scout, he went with Custer to the Yellowstone.)

65. RG 94, Entry 409, file 9490 A 1889; RG 92, Entry 238, report, 1890/187.

66. Pride, *The History of Fort Riley*, 239; *The Fort Riley Guidon*, May 21, 1905, and, Oct. 3, 1908; It was reported that Bromwell had purchased a house in Baltimore for $7000 where he intended to take it easy; he and his wife having relatives there. They received quite a send off at the train station. The 7th Cavalry band played "The Girl I Left Behind Me," and, "Auld Lang Syne," and as the couple boarded the train, struck up the lively melody of "Garry Owen," accompanied by the cheering of a large crowd of officers with their families, enlisted men and civilian employees which gathered at the depot to bid them goodbye. While waiting for the train the band also played an old-fashioned dance tune and catching the spirit of the moment, the officers present and their wives, formed a circle about Sgt. and Mrs. Brommell and circled about them much to the merriment of everyone present, *The Fort Riley Guidon*, Oct. 31, 1908; see also, RG 94, Entry 25, file 7734 PRD 1891.

67. Walter Camp interviews with several Troop G men, also John Rafter and Roman Rutten, in Hammer, *Custer in '76,* 120. Reynolds and Brown, *Journal,* a portion published by Koury, ed., *Diaries of the Little Big Horn*, 33–37.

68. Benteen said he knew Brown for many years, that he was a good clerk and an excellent man but for the whiskey habit, Benteen to Theodore Goldin, Feb. 20, 1896, Carroll, *The Benteen-Goldin Letters*, 273–74.

69. Rooney to Walter Camp, Feb. 23, 1910, WMC-BYU; Gregg to Camp, Mar. 30, 1910 (Gregg did not recall any man of Company F killed on Reno hill), WMC-LBHB.

70. Lt. Thompson said the supplies and wagon train of both the quartermaster and commissary were left in camp at Powder River, and the commissary sergeant, it is quite certain, was left at Powder with the main supplies, Thompson to Walter Camp, Dec. 3, 1910, WMC-BYU; Lt. Hare said Brown was left at Powder River, Hammer, *Custer in '76*, 68.

Commissary-Sgt. Brown's affidavit, July 12, 1876, affirmed the correctness of Lt. Thompson's accounts of May and June for sales of subsistence stores to officers killed at Little Big Horn. (Gen. Terry and staff then at camp mouth of Big Horn).

Brown witnessed the signature ("x") of Dennis Lynch, Aug. 31 and Sept. 5, on the payroll of citizens employed in the subsistence department. Accounts and Vouchers of Lt. R. E. Thompson, 6th Inf., ACS, May to Sept. 1876, Settlement 1545, January 1877, and Settlement 1765, April 1877, RG 217, Entry 1002 (UD).

71. Anna Smyer (former fiancée of Sgt. Brown) to President Hayes, Oct. 30, 1879, RG 94, Entry 297, file 5946 ACP 1879 (filed with 3954 ACP 1875).

72. See Mangum, "The George C. Brown Story," *Research Review* (LBHA), Vol. 13, No. 2, Summer, 1999.

73. Hiram E. Brown's horse broke loose July 2 at Camp No. 2 and went back toward Fort Lincoln. Private Brown and 2 Indian scouts were ordered back to overtake the horse. Brown returned with his horse early morning July 4 and brought a letter from Mrs. Custer, Frost, ed., *With Custer in '74*, 21–22.

74. Jacob Huff said Hiram E. Brown went with Custer from Powder River in charge of one of his horses and from mouth of Rosebud went with Gen. Terry. Sgt. Tritten said "DD as teamster with" (on muster roll) would indicate at Powder River with wagon train, WMC, notes, IU.

75. In 1886, Hiram Brown visited his brother, Wm. B. Brown, (ex-mayor of Mt. Vernon, Ohio), for the first time in fifteen years. The local press reported that Hiram was at the Custer massacre and mere chance saved his life. Just before the fight, two men from each company in Custer's command were sent to the rear to establish a camp, and he was chosen as one of these and thus his life was spared, *Mount Vernon* [Ohio] *Republican*, March 20, 1886.

76. On issuance of GO 62, AGO, June 22, 1874, RG 94, Entry 44, in accord with an Army appropriation act, recruiting for the Army was discontinued until further orders to reduce the number of enlisted men to 25,000, including Indian Scouts. Noncommissioned officers and other meritorious soldiers could be reenlisted at the post where they were stationed on expiration of their present term.

77. RG 94, Entry 529; Dr. DeWolf said, "Brown [the] Carpenter[,] Caldwell & Sergt. Zimmerman are quite severely frostbitten (feet)," DeWolf to his wife, Mar. 12, 1876 in Luce, ed., "The Diary and Letters of Dr. James M. DeWolf."

Private Vetter said twenty men suffered frostbite, their feet looking blue and black, and would lose their toes, Letter from Vetter to his brother, Mar. 27, 1876. Michael Vetter Letters, 1874–1876, (hereafter cited as Vetter Letters) State Historical Society, Bismarck, N.Dak., B373; see Collin, "Dear Brother: A Soldier's Letters," *Newsletter* (LBHA), Vol. 25, No. 10, Dec., 1996.

Troops E and L left Fort Totten the morning of March 10 and reached Fort Seward at 8 P.M., on the fourth day (March 13), a distance of 83 miles, the entire march in a furious northeast snowstorm, men and animals suffering intensely. The number of men frost-bitten on the march was 41 (two severely and the rest slightly) out of a command of 125. Two men, Sgt. Zimmerman and Pvt. Colwell, were left behind the morning of March 13 at Lake Belland (35 miles from Totten and 48 miles from Seward) and came through with the mail carrier from Totten, arriving Seward the evening of the 15th. On March 28, Dr. DeWolf removed four toes (between 1st and 2nd joints) from the right foot of Sgt. Zimmerman, RG 94, Entry 547, Fort Seward, DT. Report of Capt. McDougall, March 20, 1876, to AAG, DD, St. Paul, Minn., 786 DD 1876; see also Report of Lt. Col. L. C. Hunt, Post Commander Fort Totten, March 11, 1876, to AAG, DD, 755 DD 1876, NA, M1734, Roll 15.

The Battalion Return for Companies E and L for part of March 1876, is filed with the post returns of Fort Seward, NA, M617, Roll 1153; the monthly report of sick and wounded, Companies E and L, 7th Cavalry, March 1876, LBHB Coll., Roll 9, frames 0423 through 0424.

Dr. DeWolf took every care of the men, making them tear up their blankets and capes and roll them around their hands and feet, but not withstanding his care, nearly half the command were frostbitten to one degree or another, *St. Paul Dispatch*, Mar. 21, 1876.

78. John Burkman to Walter Camp, Nov. 12, 1908, WMC-BYU; the troop muster roll, June 30, reports Brown present with troop. RG 94, Entry 53.

79. Nathan T. Brown, Company L, and Private Frank T. Goslin, Company M, (Blacksmith Edson Archer, Company L, died of his wounds Sept. 14), were buried in a trench. A witness said, "The men were literally shot to pieces, but no time was taken or effort expended in fixing or cleaning them up in any manner, but they were put into the trench with spurs, belts or other wearing apparel upon them." An officer conducted a service and a shot was fired over the graves, Greene, *Nez Perce Summer 1877*, 224.

Years later, when a flood down Canon Creek gouged out the shallow graves, John Burkman, residing in nearby Billings, built a wagon box and draped it with a U.S. flag for the purpose of removing the bodies to Custer Battlefield, but he was unable to identify the remains of his two comrades, referred to as the carpenter and the blacksmith, one of whom had been his bunk mate forty years earlier at Fort Lincoln, Wagner, *Old Neutriment*, 224; Dr. DeWolf also referred to Nathan Brown as "Carpenter," see note B77 (Nathan T. Brown).

Brown was reinterred at Custer Battlefield, May 20, 1916, Grave 1415, Custer Battlefield Burial Record Book, LBHB Coll., Roll 14.

80. James Rooney to Walter Camp, July 19, 1909, and Feb. 23, 1910, WMC-BYU. WMC, notes LBH II, IU.

81. Daniel Knipe to Walter Camp, Nov. 23, 1908, WMC-BYU.

82. RG 94, Entry 544, USA Medical Register 113; the *Katie P. Kountz* departed Yankton, May 12, 1873, Darling, *Custer's Seventh Cavalry Comes to Dakota*, 146.

83. Godfrey, *Diary*, 14.

84. Pension File, RG 15. See Wagner, *Old Neutriment* (the story of John Burkman).

85. The *Katie P. Kountz* departed Yankton, May 12, 1873, Darling, *Custer's Seventh Cavalry Comes to Dakota*, 146.

86. Lucian Burnham was the 2nd of five children, and eldest son (he and twin sister, Lucia, both age 7 on federal census, July 1860), of Calista and James W. Burnham. Lucian's youngest brother, Chas. W., was the father of Col. Lucian W. Burnham, USMC, retired 1946.

87. Lt. Edgerly, who knew Bustard well, said he was found near Capt. Keogh, Hammer, *Custer in '76*, 58; Hardy said Bustard had DeLacy's horse, which was found dead on village side of river down near the ford (but it might have been led over there captive and shot because too badly wounded—WMC), Walter Camp, notes, LBH II, IU.

88. In deposition Oct. 4, 1882, Bridget Butler, mother of Sgt. Butler, declared her son was only 17 years old when he went from school at Albany and enlisted a year before the war and did not return until after President Lincoln was shot. She described her son when last seen by the family in 1875 as about 5' 5" tall with stout muscular build, large high forehead, brown hair, mustache and full side whiskers that were lighter than his hair, sandy; no chin whiskers, light complexion, blue eyes, long Roman nose and good teeth. Pension File, RG 15.

89. SO 39, Hq 7th Cavalry, Camp on Grand River, DT, June 2, 1873, RG 391, Entry 881.

90. On enlistment, Butler said he was born in Riverton NJ, but on his pension claim he declared his birthplace as Limerick, Ireland.

91. GO 43, AGO, July 3, 1866, RG 94, Entry 44, (Presidential Proclamation), offered pardon to deserters from the regular Army who surrendered themselves voluntarily before August 15, to be returned to duty without trial or punishment, on condition they forfeit all pay and allowances for time absent. Such deserters who surrender themselves at any other place than the station of their regiment, were subject to assignment to other regiments as if they were unattached recruits.

92. GO 92, AGO, Nov. 23, 1866, RG 94, Entry 44.

93. GO 17, AGO, Mar. 15, 1869, RG 94, Entry 44, provided for reduction in the number of infantry regiments from 45 to 25; changes included half of 37th Infantry Regiment (Companies B, D, G, H, and K) consolidated with 5th Infantry Regiment, Heitman, *Historical Register*, 1: 134.

94. SO 39, Hq 7th Cavalry, May 11, 1876, RG 391, Entry 859.

95. RG 94, Entry 544, MT, Prescription Book No. 14; Walter Camp said he met Butler at the Soldier's Home in Johnson City, Tenn., and according to Butler's own statement he was guarding the wagon train at Powder River at the time of the Little Big Horn battle. Camp said he got no information of importance from him and that Butler had either forgotten or was afraid of him (Camp), Camp to John Ryan, Oct. 25, 1908, WMC-LBHB.

96. Maj. Merrill reported that, in the advance to Canon Creek, Sept. 13, 1877, Private James W. Butler, Company F, was left behind when his horse was too fatigued, but Butler followed on foot until he captured a pony, which he mounted bareback and galloped forward to the skirmish line and behaved gallantly during the fight, Greene, *Nez Perce Summer 1877*, 226.

C

Caddle, Mich'l C. Sgt co I; b. 9 June 1845 New York N.Y.; pvt co B 1 N.Y. cav 20 Sep 1864 to 6 June 1865; enl reg army 29 Sep 1873 NYC for 5 yrs; age 22; conductor; blue eyes, lt hair, fair comp, 5' 5 1/2" high; join co I 22 Oct 1873 Ft Totten DT; cpl 1 Nov 1874; sgt 10 Mar 1876; ds camp Powder River MT 10 June 1876;[1] ds with Lt Scott 20 Feb to 10 Mar 1877 cond mil convicts to Ft L'worth; dd co qm sgt Apr 1877 to May 1878; (m. widow of pvt McIlhargy 25 Dec 1877); ds Ft Lincoln DT chg co garden Aug 1878; disch 29 Sep 1878 at Ft Lincoln expir of serv a sgt char xclt; died 1 May 1919 Ft Rice N.Dak.
Pension: 10 Oct 1891 / Inv / 1066131 / 934986.

Cain, Morris (Maurice). Pvt co M; b. 29 Apr 1857 Pittsfield Mass.; enl 16 Sep 1875 Boston Mass. for 5 yrs; age 22; farmer; brn eyes, blk hair, dk comp, 5' 7" high; join co M 21 Oct 1875 Ft Rice DT; dd qmd Apr 1876; disch 4 July 1877 camp on Sunday Creek MT per SO 124 AGO 1877 a pvt char xclt (a minor);[2] died 13 Aug 1906 Colville Wash'n.
Pension: 14 Apr 1927 / Wid / 1578203. (XC-2,998,945).

Caldwell, Wm. M. Pvt co B; b. 22 Feb 1857 Curwensville Pa.; enl 23 Mar 1876 Baltimore Md for 5 yrs; age 21; laborer; blue eyes, blk hair, fair comp, 5' 7" high; join co B 27 Apr 1876 St Paul Minn.; ds camp Powder River MT 10 June 1876; abs sick on str *Far West* Aug 1876; ds Ft Lincoln DT 17 Oct 1876 dismtd; des 22 Apr 1877 at Ft Lincoln; died 30 Oct 1913 Clearfield Pa.
Pension: 24 Oct 1919 / Wid / 14747. (Rej on grd sol not honorably disch).

Calhoun, Jas. 1Lt co C; b. 24 Aug 1845 Cincinnati Ohio; grad Mt Pleasant Mil Academy Ossining N.Y. June 1860; enl 7 Jan 1865 New York N.Y. for 3 yrs; age 19; clerk; brn eyes, lt hair, fair comp, 5' 11" high; join co D 2 battn 14 inf 22 Feb 1865 Harts Isl NYH; appt 1sgt same date; with co in Virginia Mar to July 1865; dep NYC 15 Aug 1865 with co on steamer to Calif. (via Panama) thence to Ft Boise Idaho Ty; (battn redesig 23 inf regt Nov 1866 [from 21 Sep 1866]); disch 24 Oct 1867 Camp Warner Ore. to accept com'n 2Lt 32 inf;[3] join co I 28 Jan 1868 Camp Grant AT; on scouting exp'n comd by col T. L. Crittenden Apr & May 1868;[4] post adjt 25 June 1868; actg aqm & comsy 4 Jan 1869; (32 inf consol with 21 inf May 1869); awl 2 mos 17 Feb 1870 with perm'n to leave div; awl ext'd 4 mos 5 Apr 1870; awol from 17 Aug 1870;[5] unassd (to regt) 29 Oct 1870; appeared before spl exam'g bd at Wash'n D.C. dur Dec 1870 & found not unfit for the serv;[6] tr to 7 cav 2 Jan 1871 (recom'n gen Custer); join co I 1 Feb 1871 Ft Harker Kans.; 1Lt co C 22 Apr 1871 to date 9 Jan;[7] join co at Rutherfordton NC 5 July; ds hq Dept of Ariz. 20 July 1871 for bd of inq in his case;[8] rejoin regt 6 Jan 1872 E'town Ky. & appt post adjt, actg aqm & comsy; awl 20 days 1 Mar 1872;[9] adjt detmt 7 cav on Yellowstone Exp'n June to Sep 1873; post adjt Ft Lincoln DT Oct 1873 to June 1874; actg aag Blk Hills Exp'n July & Aug 1874;[10] post adjt & comd band & detmt ind scouts at Ft Lincoln Sep 1874 to Dec 1875; (actg regtl adjt 14 Sep to 27 Nov & comd co C 10 Oct to 17 Dec 1875); comd co L from 22 Mar 1876 Ft Seward (Jamestown) DT; killed with Custer column 25 June 1876; survived by wife.
[C97 CB 1870]. Pension: 9 Apr 1877 / Wid / 230796 / 177515.

Callahan, Jno. J. Cpl co K; b. 18 July 1853 Salem Mass.; enl 5 Nov 1872 Boston Mass. for 5 yrs; age 21; currier; grey eyes, dk hair, fair comp, 5' 7" high; join co K 9 Dec 1872 Yorkville SC; ds hq Yellowstone Exp'n Aug 1873 care for unserviceable horses; dd subs dept Feb 1874; dd co cook Dec 1874; cpl 15 Apr 1875; dd hosp stew'd 8 Aug 1875; hosp stew'd 3d cl. 31 Mar 1876; hosp stew'd 2d cl. 15 May 1876; actg hosp stew'd with Dr. Lord

13 June 1876; killed with Custer column 25 June 1876.
Pension: 7 Feb 1891 / Father / 499348 / 330005.

Callan, Jas. Pvt co B; b. Glasgow Scotland; enl 11 Mar 1876 Baltimore Md for 5 yrs; age 27; shoemaker; grey eyes, dk hair, fair comp, 5' 7" high; join co B 27 Apr 1876 St Paul Minn.; ds camp Powder River MT 10 June 1876; des 2 Feb 1877 Ft Lincoln DT; apph 10 Jan 1880 Detroit Mich.; dishon disch 13 Apr 1880 Ft Wayne Mich. sen gen cm & 2 yrs conft mil prison Ft L'worth Kans.

Callan, Thos. J. Pvt co B; b. 13 July 1853 Louth Ireland; enl 10 Mar 1876 Boston Mass. for 5 yrs; age 22; morocco dresser; blue eyes, dk hair, fair comp, 5' 9 1/2" high; join co B 27 Apr 1876 St Paul Minn.; dd qmd Dec 1877; dd co cook Apr to July 1878; dd qmd Aug 1878; ds cutting logs Apr to July 1879; dd qmd Oct 1879 to May 1880; dd qmd with escort NPRR Oct 1880; sick qrs Dec 1880 (frostbite l. foot); disch 9 Mar 1881 Ft Yates DT expir of serv a pvt char good; recd medal of honor 24 Oct 1896 (upon own app'n) for bringing water to wd at LBH & displaying conspic good cond in assisting to drive away the inds;[11] died 5 Mar 1908 Yonkers N.Y.
Pension: 19 Feb 1919 / Ind. War Wid / 14380 / 9043. (XC-2,658,911).

Campbell, Chas. Pvt co G; b. Feb 1857 Guthrie Iowa; enl 3 Apr 1876 St Louis Mo. for 5 yrs; age 21 2/12; carpenter; blue eyes, lt hair, ruddy comp, 5' 5 1/2" high; join co G 27 Apr 1876 St Paul Minn.; gsw r. shoulder (fl. wd.) 26 June 1876; tr on str *Far West* 3 July to hosp Ft Lincoln; duty 10 Aug; ds cond mil convicts to Ft L'worth Oct 1876; dd regtl hq msgr 24 Aug 1877; disch 2 Apr 1881 Ft Meade DT expir of serv a pvt char xclt & reenl for 5 yrs; on furl 3 mos 20 Apr 1881 Bismarck DT; tr to co L 1 Aug 1881 at Ft Lincoln; cpl 18 Sep 1881; sgt 20 Dec 1881; regt qm sgt 1 Jan 1882; sgt Apr 1882; 1sgt 3 Sep 1882; sgt 3 May 1883; dd co qm sgt Apr 1884; 1sgt 2 May 1884; disch 2 Apr 1886 Ft Buford DT expir of serv a 1sgt & reenl in co L for 5 yrs; on furl June to Dec 1888 Ft L'worth Kans.; regt qm-sgt 13 Nov 1889; gsw lower jaw 29 Dec 1890 Wounded Knee Creek SD in action with Sioux inds; (treated to 2 July 1891 [dental plate inserted in lower jaw]); disch 2 Apr 1891 Ft Riley Kans. expir of serv a qm-sgt & reenl for 5 yrs; post qm sgt USA 28 Apr 1891; disch 2 Apr 1896 Ft Omaha Neb expir of serv a post qm sgt & reenl for 3 yrs; disch 2 Apr 1899 Ft Sheridan Ill. expir of serv a post qm sgt & reenl for 3 yrs; in arrest June to Aug 1899 (chg of falsifying vouchers as to amount of oats recd); acquited in gen cm 26 July; dishon disch 23 Aug 1899 per SO 135, Hq Dept of the Lakes (breach of arrest, left qrs each day 19–22 July for city & arrested by police for drunk & disorderly); reenl for 7 cav 10 June 1902 Chicago Ill. for 3 yrs (auth AGO upon recom'n by officers of regt); join co C 14 June 1902 Camp Thomas Chicamauga Park Ga.; tr to co L 1 Sep 1902 at Camp Thomas; sgt 3 Sep 1902; in arrest Oct 1902 (insubordination [would not stop talking when ordered]); sen gen cm 1 Nov 1902 forf $10 pay per mo for 6 mos; pvt 26 Mar 1903 & tr to co G at Camp Thomas; tr to gen rctg serv 24 Apr 1903 Wheeling W.Va.; disch 5 Aug 1903 per SO 175 AGO 1903 (to enter Sol. Home) a pvt char good; reenl 4 Dec 1903 Ft Myer Va. for 3 yrs; assd to detmt a.s.m. [army service men] qmd USMA; appt post qm sgt 4 Feb 1905; ds Ft Bayard NM 18 Sep 1905 for med treatment (tuberculosis); died 2 Aug 1906 Silver City NM (Ft Bayard).
Pension: 25 Aug 1903 / Inv / 1303196 / 1069571. Dropped from roll 27 Apr 1907, failure to claim; last paid to 4 Dec 1903. (XC-1,069,571).

Campbell, Chas. A. Pvt co B; b. 3 Feb 1850 Boone Co. Ill.; enl 22 Jan 1872 Cincinnati Ohio for 5 yrs; age 21; painter; hazel eyes, lt brn hair, ruddy comp, 5' 8 1/2" high; join co B 26 Feb 1872 Spartanburg SC; in conft Oct 1872 to Mar 1873; sen gen cm 29 Nov 1872 forf $8 pay per mo for 5 mos & conft same period; cpl 28 Jan 1874; sgt 1 Mar 1875; dd chg co cook house Apr 1875; pvt 4 June 1876; dd regtl hq Oct 1876; dd post hq & qmd Dec 1876 care of pub horses [with perm'n to take co horse]; disch 22 Jan 1877 Ft Lincoln DT by expir of serv a pvt [his horse left unassd to be turned in to post qm by co comdr];[12] res

Bismarck N.Dak. (gd at penitentiary); died 25 Nov 1920 at Bismarck.[13]

Campbell, Jeremiah. Sgt co K; b. 11 Feb 1844 Sangamon Co. Ill.; pvt co E 32 Ill. inf 28 Oct 1861; gsw 21 Mar 1865 battle of Bentonville NC (ball entered behind r. ear exiting l. side of nose; 2d ball thro' front r. shoulder exiting below shoulder blade); treated in rebel hosp thence retaken by union forces & treated in regtl hosp; (totally deaf r. ear); m.o. vol serv 16 Sep 1865 Ft L'worth Kans.; enl reg army 11 Jan 1869 at Ft L'worth for 3 yrs; age 24; laborer; grey eyes, dk hair, fair comp, 5' 8" high; assd to co B 4 art'y; disch 11 Jan 1872 Ft McHenry Md expir of serv a pvt; reenl 16 Jan 1872 Cincinnati Ohio for 5 yrs; join co K 7 cav 5 Feb 1872 Yorkville SC; cpl 1 Jan 1873; dd chg co mess Apr 1873; sgt 1 Aug 1873; on furl 30 days 31 Mar 1876 to Illinois; pvt 1 Dec 1876 (sen gar cm but remitted upon recom'n of court based on sol.'s long & faithful serv & gal cond at LBH); pvt 14 Dec 1876; disch 16 Jan 1877 Ft Lincoln DT expir of serv a pvt char good; died 8 May 1884 Decatur Ill. (struck by rail car he failed to hear approach).
Pension: 31 Oct 1881 / Inv / 432383 / 233796. Mother / 316915.

Capes, Wm. Sgt co M; b. Portland Me; enl 30 Dec 1872 New York N.Y. for 5 yrs; age 25; laborer; grey eyes, blk hair, ruddy comp, 5' 9 1/2" high; join co M 9 Feb 1873 Oxford Miss; cpl 12 June 1873; sgt 15 Aug 1873; dd actg sgt-maj l. wing Blk Hills Exp'n Aug 1874; dd actg co qm sgt Oct 1874 to May 1875; dd chg co kit'n June to Nov 1875; ds camp Powder River MT 15 June 1876; dd chg co kit'n Apr to Dec 1877; cited by capt Benteen for conspic gal in two mtd chgs against Nez Perce inds at Canon Creek MT 13 Sep 1877; disch 30 Dec 1877 Ft Lincoln DT expir of serv a sgt char good in every respect; died 10 Apr 1900 Pittsburgh Pa.[14]

Carey, Jno. J. Pvt co B; b. 7 June 1853 Troy N.Y.; enl 25 Oct 1872 at Troy for 5 yrs; age 21; hostler; blue eyes, brn hair, sallow comp, 5' 5 1/2" high; join co B 9 Dec 1872 Spartanburg SC; dd co cook June 1874; dd co cook Dec 1874; ds hq distr upper Red River (Shreveport) July to Sep 1875; dd co cook Feb 1876; disch 23 July 1877 Cedar Creek MT per GO 47 AGO 1877 a pvt char good;[15] died 23 Dec 1929 Benton City Wash'n.[16]
Pension: 28 Jan 1893 / Inv / 1144517. Rej on grd serv not rendered dur Rebellion as required by act of 27 June 1890. Also see Ind. Surv. / 8776 / 7188.

Carey, Pat'k. Sgt co M; b. 14 Apr 1828 Tipperary Ireland; enl 14 Sep 1866 Troy N.Y. for 3 yrs; age 29; laborer; grey eyes, brn hair, dk comp, 5' 7 1/2" high; assd to co I 36 inf; (consol with 7 inf June 1869); disch 14 Sep 1869 Ft Fred Steele Wyo. Ty expir of serv a pvt; reenl 4 Mar 1870 Ft L'worth Kans. for 5 yrs in co M 7 cav; ed qmd teamster Aug & Sep 1870; cpl 15 Aug 1873; sgt 10 Dec 1874; disch 4 Mar 1875 Ft Rice DT expir of serv a sgt; reenl in co M (as sgt) 22 Mar 1875 for 5 yrs; left in timber dur retreat from valley fight 25 June 1876 & rejoin co on Reno hill; gsw r. hip 26 June; tr on str *Far West* 3 July to hosp Ft Lincoln; tr to Ft Rice 10 Aug; duty 11 Aug; pvt 10 Nov 1876; sgt 15 Dec 1876; pvt 26 Apr 1877; dd driving teams Aug to Nov 1877; dd qmd Dec 1877; dd room orderly Feb 1878; dd qmd hostler Apr 1878; dd qmd teamster June 1878; sgt 3 Sep 1879; in arrest Oct 1879; pvt 18 Nov 1879 sen gen cm & forf $10 pay per mo for 4 mos; disch 21 Mar 1880 Ft Meade DT expir of serv a pvt char good; reenl 19 Apr 1880 Ft Omaha Neb for 5 yrs; assd to co L 7 cav 5 May 1880; dd qmd Oct 1880; dd post hq Dec 1880; far'r 9 June 1881; pvt 1 Dec 1881; in conft Dec 1881; far'r 1 Mar 1882; pvt 12 Apr 1882; cpl 20 June 1882; sgt 5 Aug 1883; pvt 12 July 1884; disch 18 Apr 1885 Ft Buford DT expir of serv a pvt char very good & reenl for 5 yrs; assd to co E 1 cav; disch 1 July 1887 Ft Custer MT on surg cert dis (chr. rheum.) a pvt; died 3 Oct 1893 Sol. Home Wash'n D.C.
Pension: 22 July 1887 / Inv / 616898 / 372932.

Carmody, Thos. Pvt co B; b. New York N.Y.; cpl & sgt co I 107 NY inf 5 Aug 1862 to 5 June 1865; enl reg army 25 June 1866 at New York for 3 yrs; age 24; baker; blue eyes, brn hair, fair comp, 5' 3 1/2" high; assd to co M 5 cav; disch 25 June 1869 Ft McPherson Neb expir of serv a pvt; reenl 30 July 1869 Carlisle

Pa. for 5 yrs; join co A 7 cav 11 Feb 1872 E'town Ky.; ds regtl hq Taylor Bks (Louisville) Ky. Sep to Dec 1872; abs sick on str *Western* 23 Apr 1873 Yankton to Ft Rice DT; dd co cook Apr 1874; ds Ft Lincoln DT 20 June 1874; disch 30 July 1874 at Ft Lincoln expir of serv a pvt; reenl 1 Aug 1874 for 5 yrs in co B; dd post bakery June 1875; dd regtl hq Dec 1876 to June 1877; ds in field 24 Sep 1877; dd chg co stock June 1879; disch 31 July 1879 Ft Yates DT expir of serv a pvt char good; reenl 1 Oct 1879 Ft Schuyler N.Y. for 5 yrs; assd to co F 3 art'y; disch 30 Sep 1884 San Antonio Tex. expir of serv a pvt char good & reenl in same co for 5 yrs; disch 1 Oct 1889 at San Antonio expir of serv a pvt char very good & reenl in same co for 5 yrs; cpl 5 Feb 1891; retd 20 Apr 1891 a cpl; died 13 Aug 1912 New York N.Y. (cancer).

Carney, Jas. Pvt co F; b. West Meath Ireland; enl 13 Mar 1866 New York N.Y. for 3 yrs; age 23; laborer; grey eyes, blk hair, dk comp, 5' 4" high; join co E 3 battn 12 inf 31 Mar 1866 Ft Hamilton NYH; (battn redesig 30 inf regt Dec 1866); ds with detmt at Potters Sta Neb guarding railroad prop Apr 1868; ed qmd teamster Dec 1868 to Mar 1869; disch 13 Mar 1869 Ft Sanders Wyo. Ty expir of serv a pvt; reenl 9 Dec 1872 St Louis Mo. for 5 yrs; join co F 7 cav 7 Feb 1873 Louisville Ky.; dd qmd Oct 1874; in conft Dec 1874; dd qmd laborer June to Sep 1875; killed with Custer column 25 June 1876.

Carrier, Adam. See Round-Wooden-Cloud.

Carroll, Dan'l.[17] sgt co B; b. Chicago Ill.; enl 19 Nov 1866 New York N.Y. for 5 yrs; age 21; bartender; brn eyes, blk hair, fair comp, 5' 7 1/2" high; join co M 7 cav 10 Dec 1866 Ft Riley Kans.; cpl 31 May 1867; appd for disch as minor 17 Oct 1867; in arrest Apr 1868; sgt 1 Jan 1869; sen gen cm 13 Aug 1869 forf $10 pay per mo for 2 mos; in arrest Apr to June 1870; pvt 6 July 1870; disch 19 Nov 1871 Yorkville SC expir of serv a pvt; reenl 19 Dec 1871 New York N.Y. for 5 yrs; join co B 7 cav 14 Feb 1872 Spartanburg SC; dd subs dept baker Mar 1872 to May 1873; dd co cook June 1873; dd distr hq Shreveport La. as tel msgr Apr to July 1875; sgt 26 July 1875; ds Ft Lincoln DT 6 May 1876;[18] actg 1sgt post detmt June 1876; sent with Lt Garlington on str *Josephine* 24 July to join co in field; sd with Lt Hare's sec. of parrott guns 8 Oct to 12 Nov 1876; disch 19 Dec 1876 at Ft Lincoln expir of serv a sgt char very good; reenl 18 Jan 1877 Ft Hamilton N.Y. for 5 yrs; assd to co C 3 art'y; disch 19 Jan 1882 Little Rock Ark expir of serv a sgt char good & reenl next day in same co for 5 yrs; disch 28 Feb 1883 at Little Rock on surg cert dis a pvt (chr. rheum. induced by severe exposure & stric. caused by hard riding, contr line of duty); died 2 May 1910 Chicago Ill.
Pension: 21 Mar 1883 / Inv / 476788 / 322163. Minor / 948015.

Carroll, Jos. Pvt band; b. 19 Jan 1847 New York N.Y.; enl 11 June 1860 at New York for 5 yrs; (with consent of mother); blue eyes, brn hair, fair comp, 4' 8" high; assd to band 12 inf; disch 26 July 1864 Ft Hamilton NYH by reenlmt for 3 yrs a mus'n; disch 26 July 1867 Wash'n D.C. expir of serv a pvt; reenl 1 Oct 1868 Richmond Va. for 3 yrs; age 21; blue eyes, blk hair, dk comp, 5' 4" high; assd to co L 5 art'y; tr to band; des 17 May 1871; surd 18 Dec 1873 St Louis Bks Mo. under GO 102 AGO 1873; tr to depot band gen mtd serv 30 Mar 1874; disch 2 May 1874 at St Louis Bks by expir of serv a pvt; reenl 1 July 1875 at St Louis for 5 yrs; assd to 7 cav 17 Feb 1876; join regt 14 Apr 1876 Ft Lincoln DT (with Lt Reily's detmt); assd to band 28 Apr (drummer);[19] ds camp Powder River MT 14 June 1876; ds str *Josephine* 6 Aug 1876 to Ft Lincoln with band; disch 30 June 1880 Ft Meade DT expir of serv a pvt char good; died 23 Dec 1904 nat'l mil home Danville Ill.
Pension: 27 May 1892 / Inv / 1113521 / 1095550. Wid / 819270 / 592063.

Carter, Andrew. Pvt band; b. Lincoln England; enl 20 Oct 1875 Cincinnati Ohio for 5 yrs; age 24; laborer; brn eyes, brn hair, ruddy comp, 5' 6 1/4" high; join 7 cav 14 Apr 1876 Ft Lincoln DT (with Lt Reily's detmt); assd to band 28 Apr; ds camp Powder River MT 14 June 1876; ds str *Josephine* 6 Aug 1876 to Ft Lincoln with band; in conft Dec 1876 (stole three 3 rifles from band qrs & pawned same at Bismarck); dishon disch 27 Jan 1877 sen gen cm & 2 yrs conft hard labor; escaped from post guardhouse 5 Feb 1877.

Carter, Cassius R. Trump'r co G; b. Baltimore Md; enr 1 Jan 1864 Wash'n D.C. a bugler co D 1 D.C. cav for 3 yrs; (vet vol); tr to co C 4 July 1864; tr to co A 6 Mar 1865; m.o. vol serv 26 Oct 1865 Ft Monroe Va.; enl reg army 31 Oct 1865 Carlisle Pa. for 3 yrs; age 19; soldier; blk eyes, blk hair, dk comp, 5' 5 1/4" high; des 12 Nov 1865 at Carlisle Bks; surd 10 Aug 1866 under GO 43 AGO 1866;[20] assd to co E 7 cav as trump'r Sep 1866 Ft Riley Kans.; disch 10 Aug 1869 Cheyenne Wells Colo. Ty expir of serv a trump'r; reenl in co E 24 Sep 1869 Fitz Meadow Colo. Ty for 5 yrs; trump'r 8 Oct 1869; des 8 June 1871 Spartanburg SC; apph 7 Feb 1872 L'worth City Kans.; restored to duty without trial (forf all pay due & make good time lost) 11 Apr 1872 & tr to co F as trump'r; in conft Sep 1874; sen gen cm 12 Oct 1874 forf $5 pay & restored to duty;[21] disch 23 May 1875 Ft Lincoln DT expir of serv a trump'r; reenl 22 June 1875 St Louis Bks Mo. for 5 yrs; join co G as trump'r 1 Aug 1875 Shreveport La.; ds Shreveport 19 Apr to 8 June 1876 (tel auth hq Dept of the Gulf); actg chf-trump'r Ft Lincoln June 1876;[22] disch 21 June 1880 camp Box Elder Creek MT expir of serv a trump'r char good & reenl in co G for 5 yrs; tr to co E 6 Sep 1880; pvt 1 Jan 1881 & dd with band; ds with band Feb 1882 to Sep 1884; disch 21 June 1885 Ft Meade DT expir of serv a pvt char good & reenl for 5 yrs; trump'r 2 July 1885; pvt 1 July 1888; trump'r 1 Oct 1888; disch 21 June 1890 Ft Sill IT expir of serv a trump'r char xclt; reenl 1 July 1890 St Louis Mo. for 5 yrs; assd to co G 5 cav; tr to 7 cav 22 Nov 1890 & assd to co A; ds Ft Riley Kans. 28 Nov 1890 to 26 Jan 1891; tr to co F 27 Jan 1891; trump'r 1 Feb 1891; ds rctg tour with Lt Perry 22 May to 16 June 1893; ds Ft Myer Va. 14 July to 3 Aug 1894; tr to co E 6 cav as pvt 4 Oct 1894 (own req acc't short time until retirement); disch 30 June 1895 at Ft Myer expir of serv a pvt char xclt & reenl next day; retd 15 Aug 1895 a sgt; died 10 Feb 1896 Chicago Ill. (asphyxiation from inhaling illuminating gas in his room at Palmer House).[23]

Cashan, Wm. Sgt co L; b. Queens Co. Ireland; enl 7 Jan 1867 Cleveland Ohio for 3 yrs; age 21; laborer; blue eyes, brn hair, ruddy comp, 5' 9 1/2" high; join co D 34 inf 30 Jan 1867 Nashville Tenn; ed qmd teamster Oct 1868 to Apr 1869; (co consol with co D 11 inf Apr 1869 & desig co D 16 inf); disch 7 Jan 1870 Grenada Miss expir of serv & reenl in same co for 5 yrs; ed subs dept laborer Feb to Sep 1870; on furl 60 days 12 Aug 1871 at Nashville; ds Tupelo Miss Oct 1871 assist civil auth enforce federal laws; disch 3 Aug 1872 Humboldt Tenn on surg cert dis a pvt (const. syph.; on sick report 54 days in 1871 & 40 days dur 1872; lame from sores in soles of feet & unable to march nor perform severe serv in field; dis 1/2); reenl 17 Dec 1872 Boston Mass. for 5 yrs; join co L 7 cav 11 Feb 1873 New Orleans La.; cpl 3 Feb 1874; sgt 13 Oct 1874; dd prov sgt Mar to July 1875; dd post prov sgt Dec 1875; killed with Custer column 25 June 1876.

Pension: 5 Dec 1883 / Mother / 311282 / 240656.

Cassella, Jno. See James, Jno.

Cather, Armentheus D. Pvt co F; b. Shippensville Pa.; enl 8 Nov 1872 Pittsburgh Pa. for 5 yrs; age 22; pumper; grey eyes, brn hair, fair comp, 5' 8 1/2" high; join co F 1 Dec 1872 Louisville Ky.; unfit for duty with Yellowstone Exp'n 21 July 1873 & tr by boat to hosp Ft Lincoln DT (tert. intm. fever [convulsive]); duty 10 Sep 1873; ds Ft Randall DT Oct 1874; dd cook post hosp 23 Nov 1875 to 2 May 1876; dd regtl hq mtd msgr 3 May 1876; killed with Custer column 25 June 1876.

Causby, Thos. Wellesley. Qm-sgt ncs; b. 9 May 1848 Liverpool England; educ Collegiate Institute at Everton (Liverpool); came to America Mar 1869; enl 1 Jan 1872 Memphis Tenn for 5 yrs; age 25 9/12; laborer; blue eyes, lt hair, fair comp, 5' 10 3/4" high; join co B 7 cav 5 Feb 1872 Spartanburg SC; dd clerk post hq Oct 1872; dd clerk detmt hq Mar to Nov 1873; cpl 18 June 1873; pvt 1 Dec 1873 (own req); ed qmd carpenter Dec 1873 to Feb 1874; ed subs dept herder Mar to Nov 1874; (attd to band Oct 1874); ed subs dept laborer Dec 1874; dd post hq Ft Lincoln

DT Feb to Apr 1875; appt regtl qm-sgt 8 Oct 1875; sick hosp 29 Feb to 27 Apr 1876 (con-t'n l. foot); ds camp Powder River MT 14 June 1876; appd for com'n 2d Lt 29 July 1876; disch 1 Jan 1877 at Ft Lincoln expir of serv a regtl qm-sgt char xclt & reenl same day for 5 yrs; ds in field 14 Oct 1877; withdrew appn for com'n Apr 1878 & appd for appmt of comsy-sgt; disch 3 June 1879 at Ft Lincoln per SO 123 AGO 1879 a regtl qm-sgt (upon own appn, having a large family to support & fearing regt would be ordered away);[24] died 16 Oct 1906 Davenport Iowa.

Channell, Wm. Pvt co H; b. Dorchester Mass.; enl 27 Sep 1875 Boston Mass. for 5 yrs; age 26; shoemaker; brn eyes, dk hair, dk comp, 5' 6 7/8" high; join co H 29 Oct 1875 Ft Rice DT; dd qmd laborer Nov 1875 to May 1876; des 26 July camp mouth of Big Horn River MT (with pvt Nees, taking small boat & box of hardtack); passed maj Moore's comd 27 July at Big Porcupine Creek & refused to stop when ordered; apph 29 July hiding in brush near Powder River when troops from str *Carroll* went ashore to investigate small boat on bank with two army coats & captive eagle in the stern sheets; taken to camp at Rosebud & placed in irons; tr under gd on str *Durfee* 5 Aug to Ft Lincoln;[25] dishon disch 30 Nov 1876 sen gen cm & 4 yrs conft mil prison Ft L'worth Kans.; escaped from guardhouse at Ft Lincoln 14 Dec 1876.

Chapman, Wm. H. Pvt co E; b. Glastenburg Conn.; enl 10 Mar 1876 Boston Mass. for 5 yrs; age 24; farmer; grey eyes, dk hair, ruddy comp, 5' 9 1/4" high; join co B 7 cav 27 Apr 1876 St Paul Minn.; tr to co E 1 June; [not sure if at LBH says Berwald; not recall at all says Pandtle]; ds Yellowstone River gd on steamboat 24 Aug;[26] des 15 Oct 1876 enroute from Ft Totten to Ft Lincoln DT;[27] enl as Wm. H. Dutton 21 Mar 1882 Ft L'worth Kans. for 5 yrs; assd to co D 23 inf; des 11 June 1882 Ft Union NM; enl as Wm. H. Smith 27 Dec 1884 Ft Douglas UT for 5 yrs (face pitted from smallpox); assd to co B 9 inf; des 13 July 1885 Ft Bridger Wyo. Ty; apph 29 Sep 1885 Salt Lake City UT; dishon disch 4 Dec 1885 sen gen cm & 3 yrs conft mil prison Ft L'worth Kans.; surd as Wm. H. Chapman 7 July 1886; rel from prison 15 May 1888 under Regs. par 925, 165 days abatement.[28]

Charley, Vincent. Far'r co D; b. Lutzern Switz; enl 4 Mar 1871 Chicago Ill. for 5 yrs; age 22; farmer; hazel eyes, red hair, sandy comp, 5' 10 1/4" high; join co D 7 Apr 1871 Mt Vernon Ky.; far'r 12 Aug 1871; pvt 1 May 1872 & in conft to Aug 1872; sen gen cm 26 Aug 1872 forf $5 pay for one mo; far'r 1 July 1875; disch 4 Mar 1876 Ft Lincoln DT expir of serv a far'r & reenl in co D for 5 yrs; gsw thro' hips 25 June near Weir Point & left behind dismtd; body found 27 June (stick rammed down throat).[29]

Cheever, Ami. Pvt co L; b. 16 May 1851 Elizabeth Pa.; enl 30 July 1866 Pittsburgh Pa. for 3 yrs; age 18; laborer; grey eyes, brn hair, fair comp, 5' 8 1/2" high; assd to co C 3 battn 11 inf; (battn redesig 29 inf regt Dec 1866); (cos C & F consol Apr 1869 & desig co K 11 inf); disch 30 July 1869 Sulphur Springs Tex. expir of serv a pvt; reenl 21 Sep 1872 Harrisburg Pa. for 5 yrs; age 21; farmer; grey eyes, dk hair, lt comp, 5' 11 3/4" high; join co L 7 cav 9 Dec 1872 Yorkville SC; cpl 13 Oct 1874; dd chg of boats crew Apr 1875; sgt 28 July 1875; pvt 28 Jan 1876 (own req); killed with Custer column 25 June 1876.
Pension: 24 Mar 1879 / Mother / 242957 / 197161.

Chesterwood, Chas. See Creighton, Jno. Chas.

Churchill, Benj. Franklin. Citizen packer, qmd; b. Lexington Me. ca. 1848;[30] hired Apr 1876 St Paul Minn. by Lt Gibbs 6 inf actg aqm to drive teams in train of exp'n; rate of pay $30 mo & entitled to one ration per day & transp back to St Paul if hon disch; tr to Lt Nowlan at Ft Lincoln DT 17 Apr 1876 with pay to commence from that date; accomp 7 cav from Powder River as packer; disch as teamster 30 June due $60 pay from 1 May; hired as packer 1 July at $50 mo; disch 23 Sep 1876 due $138.33 pay from 1 July;[31] res near Ft Keogh MT a rancher; witness in Reno court of inq at Chicago 4 Feb 1879 (described as a garrulous young man not bad looking with a soupçon of the frontiersman in his get-up);[32] married 4 July

1880 Minneapolis Minn. to Emily Valentine;[33] lumber salesman at St Paul & partner in lumber firm with Jas. P. McGoldrick to Sep 1881.[34]

Clark, Frank. Pvt co B; b. Sheldon Vt; enl 16 Mar 1876 Boston Mass. for 5 yrs; age 21 4/12; teamster; brn eyes, blk hair, dk comp, 5' 6 1/4" high; join co B 27 Apr 1876 St Paul Minn.; dd qmd woodchopper Jan 1877; in conft Camp Hancock (Bismarck) DT 23 Feb 1877; des 29 Mar 1877 Ft Lincoln DT.

Clear, Elihue F. Pvt co K; b. Randolph Co. Ind.; enl 5 Jan 1867 Cincinnati Ohio for 5 yrs; age 23; farmer; dk blue eyes, brn hair, dk comp, 5' 6 1/2" high; join co K 1 Apr 1867 Ft Dodge Kans.; cpl 4 Feb 1868; pvt 8 Apr 1868; gsw 11 Apr 1868 camp near Ft Hays Kans.; duty 29 May 1868; dd co cook June 1868; dd co cook Feb 1869; ds orderly for regtl comdr Apr 1869; disch 4 Jan 1872 Yorkville SC expir of serv a pvt; reenl same day in co K for 5 yrs & on furl 30 days Columbia SC; cpl 1 May 1872; sgt 1 Jan 1873; dd detmt hq 4 May 1873; dd chg of pioneer detmt June to Aug 1873; dd regtl hq chg of fatigue pty Oct to Dec 1873; dd prov sgt Apr 1874; dd battn hq June to Aug 1874; pvt 13 Feb 1875 (own req); ds chg of one pub horse left behind at Cairo Ill. 20 Apr 1876; rejoin co 5 May Ft Lincoln DT; orderly for Lt Hare 25 June 1876 & killed dur retreat from valley fight (eastside of river).[35]

Clyde, Edw. See Rankin, Franklin.

Coakley, Pat'k. Pvt co K; b. Kings Co. Ireland; enl 26 Dec 1866 Chicago Ill. for 5 yrs; age 24; laborer; hazel eyes, brn hair, fair comp, 5' 7 1/2" high; join co M 7 cav 22 Jan 1867 Ft Riley Kans.; wag Dec 1867; pvt 17 Sep 1868; dd regt hq orderly Nov 1868; tr to co K 9 May 1869; dd orderly for co comdr Dec 1869; in conft Aug 1871; disch 26 Dec 1871 Yorkville SC expir of serv a pvt & reenl in co K for 5 yrs; on furl 30 days 30 Dec 1871 Hartford Conn. & ext'd 30 days; des while on furl; surd 18 Apr 1872 Yorkville SC; ret to duty without trial 2 May 1872 to forf all pay due at time of des'n & make good time lost; dd orderly for co comdr Oct 1872 to Mar 1873; dd detmt hq Yellowstone Exp'n May to Sep 1873; dd night watchman Apr 1875 to Jan 1876; dd orderly for gen Terry May to Sep 1876;[36] disch 8 Feb 1877 Ft Lincoln DT expir of serv a pvt char xclt; reenl 8 July 1878 Wash'n D.C. for 5 yrs; assd to co I 2 art'y; disch 16 June 1879 Ft Ontario N.Y. on surg cert dis (consumption, contr line of duty) a pvt; died 13 Nov 1881 Sol. Home Wash'n D.C.
Pension: 1 Aug 1879 / Inv / 301200 / 165276. Wid / 289193. Ind. Wid / 14666 / 9922.

Cody, Henry M. Cpl co M; b. Nashua N.H.; enl as Henry M. Scollin 24 Sep 1873 Boston Mass. for 5 yrs; age 22; painter; blue eyes, dk hair, medium comp, 5' 7" high; join co M 21 Oct 1873 Ft Rice DT; dd qmd painter Nov & Dec 1873; dd co cook June 1874; wag Oct 1874; pvt 14 July 1875 & ed qmd painter; cpl 2 Aug 1875; killed dur retreat from valley fight 25 June 1876; horse shot down after leaving timber & when Thorpe stopped to take him on behind on his horse, it fell; Thorpe caught an ind pony & escaped while Scollin remained & was killed; sgt Ryan tho't Scollin lay near Reynolds about half way from timber to river & about 1/4 way from McIntosh to river.[37]
Pension: 24 Feb 1891 / Father / 502829 / 327609.

Cody, Jno. Francis. Cpl co A; b. Phil'a Pa.; enl 1 Apr 1852 New York N.Y. for 5 yrs; age 22; hatter; grey eyes, fair hair, fair comp, 5' 10 1/2" high; assd to co F 2 drg; disch 1 Apr 1857 Ft Riley Kans. expir of serv a pvt; reenl 21 Apr 1857 Ft L'worth Kans. for 5 yrs; assd to co B 1 cav; des 15 May 1858; apph 4 Oct 1858; (regt redesig 4 cav Aug 1861); disch 28 Mar 1862 St Louis Mo. by reenlmt for 3 yrs in co G 4 cav a pvt; gsw r. leg spring 1863 Shelbyville Tenn; disch 28 Mar 1865 Macon Ga. expir of serv a pvt; reenl 22 June 1871 E'town Ky. for 5 yrs in co A 7 cav; cpl 17 Aug 1871; sgt 14 Jan 1872; 1sgt 1 Aug 1872; sgt 22 Oct 1872; dd actg sgt-maj 27 Apr 1873; 1sgt 13 May 1873; sgt 22 July 1873; dd chg regtl band Sep 1873 to Aug 1874; pvt 30 Nov 1874; cpl 23 Feb 1876; disch 22 June 1876 Ft Lincoln DT expir of serv a cpl char xclt;[38] reenl 22 July 1876 St Louis Bks Mo. for 5 yrs; assd to co H 4 cav; disch 25 Mar

1879 Ft Reno IT on surg cert dis (amblyopia contr line of duty; unfit for proper performance of duty past 8 mos; dis 3/4) a pvt; died 22 Apr 1910 Sol. Home Wash'n D.C.
Pension: 23 May 1879 / Inv / 287808 / 186117.

Coleman, Chas. Cpl co F; b. Terre Haute Ind.; enl 9 Sep 1873 Cincinnati Ohio for 5 yrs; age 22; laborer; blue eyes, dk hair, ruddy comp, 5' 5 1/4" high; join co F 18 Oct 1873 Ft Lincoln DT; [bunkie with Finnegan];[39] cpl 24 Nov 1875; sick 7–15 May 1876 (tert. intm. fever); killed with Custer column 25 June 1876.

Coleman, Thos. W. Pvt co B; b. 25 Dec 1850 Troy N.Y.; enl in navy 3 June 1864 a 2d cl. boy on str *Commodore Morse*; hazel eyes, brn hair, lt comp, 4' 7" high; disch 31 May 1865 Wash'n D.C. navy yard; enl in army 4 Jan 1872 Troy N.Y. for 5 yrs; age 21 1/12; carpenter; grey eyes, brn hair, fair comp, 5' 5 1/8" high; join co B 5 Feb 1872 Spartanburg SC; ed qmd Oct 1873; ed qmd carpenter Dec 1875 to Mar 1876; with water pty on Reno hill 26 June;[40] disch 4 Jan 1877 Ft Lincoln DT expir of serv a pvt char very good; died 30 Nov 1921 Sol. Home Los Angeles Calif.
Pension: 17 May 1917 / Ind. Surv. / 12787 / 7551. Also see Navy Inv. Orig'l / 52866 / 37782.

Colwell, Jno. R. Pvt co L. b. Urbana Ohio; enl 16 Sep 1875 Chicago Ill. for 5 yrs; age 30; clerk; brn eyes, brn hair, fair comp, 5' 4" high; join co L 29 Oct 1875 Ft Totten DT; suffered severe frostbite of feet dur march thro' snowstorm from Ft Totten 10–12 Mar 1876;[41] left at Lake Belland [ranch of Mr. Hays] with sgt Zimmerman & accomp mail carrier to Ft Seward 15 Mar; with co to Ft Lincoln 17 Apr & in hosp to 25 July thence ed hosp nurse to 5 Oct; cpl 4 Oct 1876; sgt 7 July 1877; ds in field 30 Aug 1877; abs sick 15 Oct [on str *Silver City*]; adm to hosp Ft Lincoln 26 Oct (frostbite); duty 30 Oct; dd prov sgt Dec 1877; dd co qm sgt Apr to Sep 1878; on furl June to Sep 1880 NPRR ext'n; disch 15 Sep 1880 at Ft Lincoln expir of serv a sgt char good; reenl 18 June 1881 Ft Meade DT for 5 yrs in co G 7 cav; cpl 7 Sep 1881; sgt 16 Jan 1882; des 7 May 1882 Ft L'worth Kans.; reenl 23 June 1883 St Louis Mo. for 5 yrs; assd to 16 inf; apph 11 Aug 1883 Ft Concho Tex.; sen gen cm Sep 1883 to 2 yrs conft mil prison Ft L'worth; escaped from gd 11 Sep 1883 at Ft Concho.

Conelly, Pat'k. See White, Pat'k C.

Conlan, Mich'l. See Personeus, Martin.

Conlan, Thos. Pvt co D; b. Ayrshire, Scotland; enl 18 Sep 1875 Boston Mass. for 5 yrs; age 21 11/12; marble cutter; blue eyes, brn hair, dk comp, 5' 6 3/4" high; join co D 21 Oct 1875 Ft Lincoln DT; ds camp Powder River MT 15 June 1876 guarding wagon train; des 16 Dec 1876 Ft Rice DT & apph five days later; dishon disch 12 Mar 1877 sen gen cm & 2 yrs conft at sta of co; escaped from post guardhouse 20 June 1877 [with pvt Sims].

Connell, Jno. Trump'r co B; b. Ogdensburg N.Y.; enl 6 Feb 1872 Erie Pa. for 5 yrs; age 21; porter; blue eyes, brn hair, lt comp, 5' 7" high; join co B 26 Feb 1872 Spartanburg SC; dd subs dept herder 19 May to 22 June 1873; trump'r 1 Mar 1876; sick qrs 29 May to 13 June 1876 (incised wd r. knee, kick by horse); sick camp Powder River MT 10 June 1876; disch 6 Feb 1877 Ft Lincoln DT expir of serv a trump'r char very good.

Connelly, Pat'k. See White, Pat'k C.

Connor, Andrew. Pvt co A; b. Limerick Ireland; enl 6 Aug 1861 Chicago Ill. for 3 yrs; age 21; ropemaker; lt blue eyes, lt brn hair, lt comp, 5' 4 3/4" high; assd to co A 1 battn 16 inf; taken pris'r 20 Sep 1863 battle of Chicamauga Ga. & exchanged 21 Mar 1864 City Pt Va.; disch 10 Aug 1864 Atlanta Ga. expir of serv a pvt; pvt co C Mass. lt art'y 3 Nov 1864 to 7 Aug 1865; reenl reg army 8 Nov 1872 Lowell Mass. for 5 yrs; age 30; moulder; blue eyes, grey hair, florid comp, 5' 4 3/4" high; join co A 7 cav 7 Feb 1873 E'town Ky.; pres in conft June thro' Oct 1873; sen gen cm 2 July 1873 forf $10 pay per mo for 4 mos & conft same period; dd hq Blk Hills Exp'n 25 June to 31 Aug 1874; ed nurse field hosp 14 Oct 1877 & arr Ft Rice DT 26 Oct; disch 8 Nov 1877 at Ft Rice expir of serv a pvt char

xclt; reenl 6 June 1878 Boston Mass. for 5 yrs; assd to co C 11 inf; disch 5 June 1883 Ft Buford DT expir of serv a pvt char fair; reenl 2 July 1883 Columbus Bks Ohio for 5 yrs; assd to co G 13 inf; disch 2 July 1888 Ft Elliott Tex. expir of serv a pvt char good & reenl in same co for 5 yrs; disch 3 Apr 1890 Camp Wade IT on surg cert dis (hearing blunted & vision much impaired) a pvt char good; died 14 May 1911 Wash'n D.C. (govt hosp for insane).
Pension: 21 Apr 1890 / Inv / 770145 / 498515.

Connor, Edw. Pvt co E; b. Clare Ireland; enl 5 Dec 1867 Boston Mass. for 5 yrs; age 21; laborer; hazel eyes, brn hair, ruddy comp, 5' 8 1/2" high; join co E 22 Jan 1868 Ft L'worth Kans.; dd co cook Sep & Oct 1870; disch 5 Dec 1872 Unionville SC expir of serv a pvt & reenl in co E for 5 yrs; dd pioneer Apr & June 1873; dd post hq Dec 1873 to May 1874; cpl 15 June 1874; pvt 24 Jan 1875; killed with Custer column 25 June 1876.[42]

Connors, Thos. Pvt co I; b. Harlem N.Y.; enl 25 July 1870 Chicago Ill. for 5 yrs; age 24; teamster; blue eyes, dk hair, fair comp, 5' 7 1/2" high; join co I 8 cav Oct 1870 Ft Selden NM; ds Brennan's saw mill Oct 1871; in conft Ft Bayard NM Aug 1873; disch 25 July 1875 Eagle Springs Tex. expir of serv a pvt; reenl 20 Aug 1875 St Louis Mo. for 5 yrs; join co I 7 cav 21 Oct 1875 Ft Lincoln DT; sick 9–14 May 1876 (tert. intm. fever); killed with Custer column 25 June 1876.

Considine, Martin. Sgt co G; b. Clare Ireland; enl 23 Aug 1865 Phil'a Pa. for 3 yrs; age 20; watchmaker; blue eyes, brn hair, ruddy comp, 5' 7 1/2" high; join co G 6 cav 8 Sep 1865 camp near Frederick Md; ds hq 5th mil distr (New Orleans La.) 6 Mar 1867; ds with gen Sheridan 5 Sep 1867 to 23 Aug 1868 when disch at Ft L'worth Kans. upon expir of serv a pvt; reenl 19 Jan 1870 at Phil'a for 5 yrs; age 22; join co B 8 cav 26 Oct 1872 Ft Union NM; cpl 22 Nov 1872; pvt 12 Dec 1873 (own req) & dd learning signaling till Mar 1874; ds Ft Lyon Colo. Ty 27 Dec 1874 verbal order co comdr; disch 19 Jan 1875 at Ft Lyon by expir of serv a pvt; reenl 28 Jan 1875 St Louis Mo. for 5 yrs; join co G 7 cav 10 Feb 1875 Shreveport La.; cpl 6 Aug 1875; sgt 3 Apr 1876 to date 13 Mar 1876; killed dur retreat from valley fight 25 June 1876.

Cooke, Wm. Winer. 1Lt & adjt; b. 29 May 1846 Mt. Pleasant Canada; recruited for 24 N.Y. cav dur summer 1863 & appt 2Lt co M 26 Jan 1864 at Rochester; recd shrapnel wd l. thigh (fl. wd.) 17 June 1864 near Petersburg Va.; in hosp 4 wks thence awl 30 days; ds subs dept Cedar Level Va. to Nov 1864; chg of comsy depot at Patrick Sta (mil railroad Army of Potomac) to Feb 1865; (1Lt co A 14 Dec 1864); rejoin regt with gen Sheridan's cav corps for Richmond campn; m.o. vol serv 24 June 1865 when regt consol with 10 N.Y. cav; appt reg army com'n 2Lt 7 cav 18 Oct 1866 to date 28 July 1866; join co D 16 Nov 1866 Ft Riley Kans.; tr to co M 10 Dec; actg adjt to Jan 1867; tr to co A 24 Feb 1867; actg rqm & comsy Apr 1867; with gen Custer's detmt from Ft Wallace 15 July; 1Lt 31 July 1867; ds Ft L'worth Kans. Aug to Oct 1867 witness in gen cm; tr to co H 25 Sep 1867; recd bvt capt, maj & Lt-col Aug 1868 dated 2 Mar 1867 for gal serv in battles of Petersburg, Dinwiddie Court House, & Sailor's Creek;[43] comd sharpshooter detmt Nov & Dec 1868; adc to gen Custer 7 Dec 1868 to 24 Mar 1869; tr to co I 8 Apr 1869 & comd co June to Nov 1869 camp near Ft Hays Kans.; awl 20 days 3 Dec 1869 (with Tom Custer) & ext'd 3 mos; actg adjt of gen Custer's detmt Apr to Oct 1870; regtl adjt 1 Jan 1871; with regtl hq at Louisville Ky. Mar 1871 to Apr 1873 & at St Paul Minn. to Oct 1874; (awl 6 mos 21 July 1873 with perm'n to cross the sea); awl 7 days 28 Apr 1875 & ext'd 5 days; awl 30 days 14 Sep 1875 (with Tom Custer) & ext'd 30 days; arr Bismarck 27 Nov (with Tom Custer) on extra stage from Fargo;[44] post adjt & comd band & detmt ind scouts to 1 May 1876; comd ncs & band May 1876; killed with Custer column 25 June 1876.
[695 ACP 1873].

Cooney, David. Pvt co I; b. Cork Ireland; enl 16 Dec 1872 Boston Mass. for 5 yrs; age 24; laborer; grey eyes, dk hair, fair comp, 5' 6" high; join co I 9 Feb 1873 Lebanon Ky.; gsw r. hip 26 June 1876; tr on str *Far West* 3 July to

Cooper, Eugene L. Cpl co I; b. 4 July 1851 Georgetown Del; enl as Geo. C. Morris 26 Oct 1872 Phil'a Pa. for 5 yrs; age 21; carriage maker; brn eyes, brn hair, fair comp, 5' 5 3/4" high; join co I 2 Dec 1872 Shelbyville Ky.; ed qmd Feb 1873; ed qmd Oct 1874 to Feb 1875; cpl 10 Mar 1876; killed with Custer column 25 June 1876.
Pension: 27 Apr 1892 / Mother / 548357 / 364863.

Cooper, Jno. Pvt co H; b. Cork Ireland; enl 27 Sep 1873 New York N.Y. for 5 yrs; age 27; laborer; blue eyes, brn hair, dk comp, 5' 5" high; join co H 20 Oct 1873 Ft Rice DT; gsw r. elbow 26 June 1876; tr on str *Far West* 3 July to hosp at Ft Lincoln DT; tr on str *Durfee* 12 July to hosp Ft Rice; duty 28 Sep 1876; dd actg co far'r Oct 1877 to Feb 1878; disch 27 Sep 1878 at Ft Lincoln expir of serv a pvt char xclt; reenl 19 Nov 1878 Baltimore Md for 5 yrs; join co E 1 cav 25 Apr 1879 Ft Simcoe WT; dd co cook Aug 1879; dd co armorer Feb to Apr 1880; dd co tailor Aug to Oct 1880; ds Boise Bks Idaho Ty escorting pub animals Dec 1881; disch 11 Aug 1882 Ft Walla Walla WT on surg cert dis a pvt char good (varicose veins l. lower extremity; contr line of duty; dis 1/2; does not desire to enter Sol. Home); died 1903 Harris Iowa.[45]

Corcoran, Jno. Pvt co C; b. Staffordshire England; enl 8 Oct 1873 Phil'a Pa. for 5 yrs; age 21; boltmaker; blue eyes, dk hair, ruddy comp, 5' 8" high; join co C 21 Oct 1873 Ft Rice DT; in conft Apr 1874; sen gen cm 2 July 1874 forf $10 pay per mo for 2 mos; sen gen cm 29 Jan 1876 forf $10 pay per mo for 6 mos & conft same period; sent with Lt Garlington on str *Josephine* 24 July to join co in field; in conft Ft Lincoln DT 17 Oct 1876 to 24 Feb 1877; dd co cook Feb 1878; sen gen cm 12 Mar 1878 forf $8 pay per mo for 3 mos; disch 8 Oct 1878 Camp J. G. Sturgis DT expir of serv a pvt char "intemperate but otherwise an excellent soldier."

Corcoran, Pat'k. Pvt co K; b. 15 Mar 1844 Leshine Canada; enl 27 July 1867 St Louis Mo. for 5 yrs; age 22; laborer; hazel eyes, brn hair, fair comp, 5' 9 1/2" high; join co K 8 Sep 1867 Ft Hays Kans.; ds orderly distr hq Camp Supply IT 23 Nov 1868 to 30 Mar 1869; dd co cook Oct 1871; in conft Dec 1871; disch 27 July 1872 Chester SC expir of serv a pvt; reenl 23 Aug 1872 Kansas City Mo. for 5 yrs; join co K 9 Dec 1872 Yorkville SC; dd battn hq June to Sep 1874; dd night watchman Feb to Apr 1875; dd regtl hq (morn & eve) 11 May 1876; gsw r. shoulder 25 June 1876 (fl. wd. severe); tr on str *Far West* 3 July to hosp Ft Lincoln DT; in post hosp to 29 Jan 1877 when disch on surg cert dis a pvt char good; died 4 Mar 1922 Sol. Home Wash'n D.C.
Pension: 27 Feb 1877 / Inv / 231682 / 146750.

Corwine, Rich'd W. Sgt co A; b. Maysville Ky.; pvt co I 41 Mo. inf 15 Aug 1864 to 11 July 1865; enl reg army 11 Aug 1865 St Louis Mo. for 3 yrs; age 20; merchant; hazel eyes, red hair, lt comp, 5' 6" high; assd to co E 6 cav; tr to co G; disch 11 Aug 1868 New Orleans La. expir of serv a pvt; reenl 29 May 1871 at St Louis for 5 yrs; age 24; clerk; join co A 7 cav 2 Dec 1872 E'town Ky.; ed with asst comsy Dec 1872 to Mar 1873; ed subs dept watchman Apr 1873; cpl 25 June 1873; dd chg co kit'n Aug 1873 to Oct 1874; ed subs dept Feb 1875; sgt 26 Mar 1875; dd chg co kit'n June 1875; dd actg co qm sgt Aug 1875; dd chg co kit'n Oct 1875 to May 1876; disch 29 May 1876 Ft Lincoln DT expir of serv a sgt char xclt & reenl in co A for 5 yrs; cpl 15 July 1876; sent with Lt Garlington on str *Josephine* 24 July to join co in field; sgt 20 Oct 1876; dd chg of cattle herd 2 May 1877; ed asst to comsy (Lt Gibson) 12 Aug Cant'mt Tongue River MT; dep for proper sta 26 Oct with pvt Murphy [in mackinaw boat to Ft Buford thence on str *Rosebud* to Ft Lincoln]; dd actg co qm sgt Dec 1877 to Nov 1878; dd chg co mess Dec 1878; in arrest Feb 1879; pvt 10 Apr 1879 sen gen cm & forf $10 pay per mo for 2 mos; cpl 17 July 1879; sgt 9 Nov 1879; regtl qm-sgt 15 Oct 1880; disch 28 May 1881 Ft Meade DT expir of serv a regtl qm-sgt char xclt & reenl for 5 yrs; sgt co L 1 Jan 1882; actg co qm sgt Feb to Nov 1882; 1sgt 3 May 1883; sgt 6 Dec 1883; pvt

Dec 1884; disch 28 May 1886 Ft Buford DT expir of serv a pvt char xclt & reenl for 5 yrs; tr to co A 11 June 1886 at Ft Meade; cpl 21 Aug 1886; sgt 11 Apr 1887; appt sgt-maj 22 July 1888; killed 29 Dec 1890 Wounded Knee Creek SD in action with Sioux inds.

Coveney, Mich'l. Pvt co A; b. Cork Ireland; enl 2 Dec 1874 Boston Mass. for 5 yrs; age 22; teamster; blue eyes, dk hair, medium comp, 5' 8 1/2" high; join co A 6 Feb 1875 Livingston Ala; des 17 May 1876 Ft Lincoln DT.

Cowley, Cornelius. Pvt co A; b. Cork Ireland; enr 16 Jan 1865 as Jno. Sullivan pvt co F 24 Mass. inf; awol 3 Aug 1865 in hosp Wash'n D.C. (sim. frac. maxilla l. side [by a blow]) & convalescent to 23 Nov 1865; (m.o. vol serv 6 Dec 1870 per SO 245 Dept of the East 1870 chg of des'n removed); enl reg army as Cornelius Cowley (his right name) 28 July 1866 Portland Me for 3 yrs; age 27; baker; blue eyes, brn hair, lt comp, 5' 10" high; join co K 17 inf 8 Oct 1866 Newport Bks Ky.; tr to co F 24 May 1869; disch 31 Oct 1869 Winchester Va. expir of serv a pvt (made good time lost); enl in navy as Jno. Sullivan 30 Nov 1869 Boston Mass. for one yr as landsman [naval rank] on str *Tallapoosa;* reenl as seaman 29 Dec 1870 at Boston on sloop *California* [cruise from New York to San Francisco & Hawaii Mar 1871 to June 1873]; disch 30 Sep 1873 at New York; reenl 7 Nov 1873 at Boston on monitor *Mahopac* [sailed to Key West Fla 21 Nov]; disch 4 Aug 1874 at Key West a 1st cl. fireman; reenl in army as Cornelius Cowley 9 Dec 1874 Boston Mass. for 5 yrs; age 28; stonemason; join co A 7 cav 6 Feb 1875 Livingston Ala; dd qmd laborer Oct 1875 to Feb 1876; sick 26 June 1876 on Reno hill (insane from thirst & had to be tied);[46] sick camp mouth of Big Horn River MT July 1876 (insane); tr on str *Josephine* 7 Aug to hosp Ft Lincoln (anemia); duty 22 Sep 1876; sick in hosp Ft Lincoln 12 Oct to 1 Nov 1876 when disch on surg cert dis (valvular disease of heart) a pvt char good; died 6 Aug 1908 Wash'n D.C. (govt hosp for insane).
Pension: 13 Jan 1877 / Inv / 229710 / 144032.

Cowley, Stephen. Pvt co D; b. Sligo Ireland; enl 14 Nov 1872 Chicago Ill. for 5 yrs; age 24; butcher; brn eyes, brn hair, florid comp, 5' 6 1/2" high; join co D 8 Dec 1872 Opelika Ala; dd detmt hq June to Sep 1873; temporary duty regtl hq 7 May 1876 chg of pub horses; ds camp Powder River MT 15 June 1876 gd to wagon train; ds qmd Tongue River MT 8 Aug 1876; furn transp by post qm Ft Buford 24 Sep to Ft Lincoln (with Gaffney & Hegner);[47] dd regtl hq in field 21 Oct to 3 Nov 1876; tr to co I 26 Nov 1876; ds Ft Lincoln 15 Oct 1877; cited by maj Merrill for good cond in action against Nez Perce inds at Canon Creek MT 13 Sep 1877; disch 14 Nov 1877 at Ft Lincoln expir of serv a pvt char xclt & reenl in co D for 5 yrs; ed ordn dept msgr Apr to June 1878; dd subs dept Aug 1878; dd ordn dept msgr Dec 1878 to Feb 1879; disch 10 Sep 1882 Ft Totten DT per Regs. par 235 [accord with GO 24 AGO 1859] a pvt char good.

Cox, Thos. Pvt co D; b. Cincinnati Ohio; enl 22 Sep 1873 Phil'a Pa. for 5 yrs; age 29; brickmaker; blue eyes, dk hair, ruddy comp, 5' 8" high; join co D 22 Oct 1873 Ft Totten DT; cpl 24 June 1877; post prov sgt Feb 1878; dd chg boats crew Apr 1878; disch 22 Sep 1878 Camp J. G. Sturgis DT expir of serv a cpl char xclt.

Crandall, Chas. A. Cpl co C; b. New Milford Pa.; pvt co A 5 N.Y. cav 1 Feb 1864 to 19 July 1865; enl reg army 9 Dec 1872 Scranton Pa. for 5 yrs; age 24; sawyer; grey eyes, brn hair, dk comp, 5' 10 1/2" high; join co C 12 Feb 1873 Charlotte NC; dd subs dept herder 24 May to 22 June 1873; dd co gardener Feb to Apr 1874; ds Ft Rice DT June to Sep 1874 gd co prop; dd co cook Feb to Apr 1875; cpl 3 June 1875; ds camp Powder River MT 10 June 1876; sgt 28 Sep 1876; in arrest Nov 1876 to Feb 1877; disch 9 Dec 1877 Ft Lincoln DT expir of serv a sgt char "a good soldier;" died 23 Apr 1885 Conklin N.Y.
Pension: 20 Dec 1879 / Inv / 327740 / 188459. Wid / 327345 / 221431.

Crawford, Wm. L. Pvt co K; b. Newfield N.Y.; enl 13 Feb 1875 St Louis Bks Mo. for 5 yrs; age 25; boat builder; grey eyes, lt hair, fair comp, 5' 9 1/2" high; join co K 27 Apr

1876 St Paul Minn.; ds camp Powder River MT 15 June 1876; sick on str *Carroll* 2 Aug to Ft Lincoln DT (typhoid fever); died 20 Aug 1876 in post hosp at Ft Lincoln.

Craycroft, Wm. Thos. 1Lt co B; b. 28 Jan 1847 Springfield Ky.; grad USMA 15 June 1869 & appt 2Lt 7 cav; join co E 18 Oct 1869 camp Fitz Meadow Colo. Ty; actg comsy 20 Mar to 12 Apr 1873 dur tr of regt from Memphis Tenn to DT;[48] sick at Yankton 4 May 1873 & was recom to be moved by boat;[49] sick on str *Miner* 16–18 May Ft Randall to Ft Thompson & 30 May to 9 June Ft Sully to Ft Rice; sick 19 June (inquinal hernia) unfit for field serv; rejoin co 8 Oct 1873 Ft Lincoln DT; sick 16 Dec 1873 (sprain r. ankle); sick qrs 24 Dec 1873 to 5 Apr 1874 thence awl on surg cert; rejoin co 2 Oct 1874 Greensboro Ala; actg aqm & comsy Opelika Ala Dec 1874 to Apr 1875; battn adjt (cos AEH) at Ft Randall DT May to July 1875; actg aqm & comsy Ft Totten DT 11 Nov 1875 to 1 Mar 1876; comd co L at Ft Totten 10 Dec 1875 to 10 Mar 1876 & at Ft Seward DT to 22 Mar; (prom 1Lt co B 2 Dec 1875); awaited action on appn for surg cert to 14 Apr then dep with capt McDougall enroute to join co;[50] ds St Paul Minn. 24 Apr with bd purchasing horses for 7 cav; arr Ft Lincoln 21 Sep 1876 with Lt Nave; appt to bd of officers 23 Sep to appraise value of govt horse ridden by gen Custer & which officers of regt desired to present to Mrs. Custer; ds Wash'n D.C. 10 Oct 1876 before retiring bd;[51] awl on surg cert to 28 June 1878 when retd for disability incident to serv; (m. sister of Lt Hare); died 31 Oct 1906 Dallas Tex.
[4849 ACP 1872].

Creighton, Jno. Chas. Pvt co K; b. 4 Mar 1850 Massilon Ohio;[52] enl as Chas. Chesterwood 6 Jan 1872 Chicago Ill. for 5 yrs; age 22; machinist; blue eyes, red hair, sandy comp, 5' 5 1/2" high; join co K 5 Feb 1872 Yorkville SC; ed qmd Oct to Dec 1873; dd regtl hq fatigue pty Aug to Oct 1876; on furl Dec 1876 Bismarck DT; disch 6 Jan 1877 Ft Lincoln DT expir of serv a pvt char good; reenl 29 Jan 1877 St Louis Bks Mo. for 5 yrs; join co E 7 cav 7 Oct 1878 at Ft Lincoln; tr to co L 11 Nov 1878; cpl 23 Jan 1879; dd actg co qm sgt Feb 1880 to Dec 1881; sgt 7 Sep 1881; disch 28 Jan 1882 at Ft Lincoln expir of serv a sgt; died 30 Jan 1935 Tacoma Wash'n.
Pension: 20 July 1892 / Inv / 1122660 / 882070.
Ind. Surv. / 11315 / 7379.

Criddle, Christopher. Pvt co C; b. 11 Oct 1845 New Canton, Va.; enl 22 Sep 1875 Cincinnati Ohio for 5 yrs; age 24; laborer; grey eyes, brn hair, dk comp, 5' 8" high; join co C 21 Oct 1875 Ft Lincoln DT; killed with Custer column 25 June 1876.
Pension: 23 June 1883 / Father / 305803 / 224217.

Crisfield, Wm. B. Pvt co L; b. Kent England; enl 21 Oct 1858 Boston Mass. for 5 yrs; age 19; farmer; grey eyes, blk hair, ruddy comp, 5' 5 1/2" high; join co F 1 cav 10 June 1859 Ft Riley Kans.; (regt redesig 4 cav Aug 1861); disch 21 Oct 1863 Maysville Ala expir of serv a pvt; sgt co G 41 Mo. inf Aug 1864 to July 1865; reenl reg army 17 Jan 1870 Ft L'worth Kans. for 5 yrs in co C 7 cav; ed qmd Dec 1872; unfit to march with regt 4 May 1873 Yankton DT; tr on str *Katie P. Kountz* 8 May to Ft Rice DT;[53] sick qrs 30 July to 23 Aug 1873 (whitlow); tr to co L 10 Dec 1873 (to benefit family, being a married man & there being no laundresses in co L while six women with co C); dd qmd corral Oct to Dec 1874; disch 17 Jan 1875 Ft Lincoln DT expir of serv a pvt; reenl in co L 11 Feb 1875 at Ft Lincoln for 5 yrs; dd qmd packing grain Sep 1875; killed with Custer column 25 June 1876; surv. by wife & 3 ch.; (widow m. pvt Personeus 23 Nov 1876).
Pension: 25 May 1878 / Minor / 237442 / 185391.
11 Aug 1879 / Wid / 249582 / 186988.

Criswell, Benj. C. Sgt co B; b. 9 Feb 1849 Cameron W.Va.; enl 31 May 1870 Cincinnati Ohio for 5 yrs; age 21; farmer; hazel eyes, blk hair, dk comp, 5' 6 1/4" high; join co B 26 June 1870 Ft L'worth Kans.; dd co cook Nov 1870 to Mar 1871; ed hosp attdt 1 Dec 1872 to 12 June 1873; (ds enroute to Ft Rice DT 1 May 1873); cpl 7 May 1873; unfit to march with comd 11 Sep 1873 (remain with Exp'n hq); sgt 28 Jan 1874; 1sgt 17 Mar 1875; disch 31 May 1875 Shreveport La. expir of serv a

1sgt; reenl in co B 1 Mar 1876 to date 23 Feb (auth AGO) at Shreveport for 5 yrs; cpl 16 Mar 1876; sgt 4 June 1876; on furl 30 days 26 Oct 1876 St Louis Bks Mo.; dd chg co kit'n Feb 1877; gd to regtl standard 7 Mar to 28 Apr 1877; on furl 3 mos 4 Sep 1877 St Paul Minn.; 1sgt 7 Dec 1877; disch 3 Apr 1878 Standing Rock Agcy DT per SO 63 AGO 1878 (upon own appn to care for his aged parents) a 1sgt char xclt;[54] awarded medal of honor 5 Oct 1878 for rescuing body of Lt Hodgson from within enemy lines [at LBH] & bringing up amm'n & encouraging the men in the most exposed positions under heavy fire; he having been disch the serv, medal filed in AGO & tho' no rec of removal, it was not found in June 1911 in exhaustive search of sol.'s personal papers wherein it might have been filed;[55] died 17 Oct 1921 Eldorado Okla. Pension: 6 Mar 1917 / Inv / 1426913 / 1178810. Also see Ind. Surv / 6487. Also see Ind. Wid / 15657.

Criswell, Harry. Pvt co B; b. Marshall W.Va.; enl 11 Apr 1876 Pittsburgh Pa. for 5 yrs; age 21; farmer; dk brn eyes, dk brn hair, fair comp, 5' 7" high; join co G 7 cav 27 Apr 1876 St Paul Minn.; tr to co B 4 May 1876; pres sick (ac. diar.) 22 Aug 1876 Powder River MT; tr on str *Carroll* 28 Aug to Ft Buford & on str *Benton* 3 Sep to hosp Ft Lincoln DT; duty 22 Sep 1876; ed qmd Nov 1876 to Jan 1877; sick qrs (ride in wagon) 29 Oct 1877 (cont'n big toe stepped on by horse); sent with co from Ft Buford to Ft Lincoln 9 Nov 1877 care of Dr. Havard; duty 21 Nov 1877; dd stable police Feb 1878; sen gar cm 5 Mar 1879 forf $5 pay; des 23 Mar 1879 Ft Yates DT.

Crittenden, Jno. Jordan. 2Lt 20 inf; b. 7 June 1854 Frankfort Ky.; cadet USMA 1 July 1871 to 26 June 1874 when disch for deficiency in philosophy; recom by pres't Grant 15 June 1875 for com'n of 2Lt; passed exam'n before army bd at St Paul Minn. (hq Dept of Dak.) 27 July 1875; appt 2Lt 20 inf 15 Oct 1875; (accepted 23 Oct while visiting his father col T. L. Crittenden, post comdr Ft Abercrombie DT); injured in hunting accdt 25 Oct when a cartridge jammed in the chamber of his shotgun & in attempt to extract it the shell exploded, sending a piece into one eye & filling the other with powder; awl on surg cert 22 Nov; left eye removed by oculist at Cincinnati 25 Nov [replaced with glass eye]; joined his regt 17 Mar 1876 at Ft Ripley Minn.; arr Ft Lincoln 25 Apr with co G 20 inf; attd to 7 cav 12 May upon instr'n of gen Terry & assd to co L; killed with Custer column 25 June 1876.[56]
[3505 ACP 1875].

Cross, Wm. (E-esk, Ieska).[57] pvt detmt ind scouts; b. DT ca. 1854;[58] (1/2 Sioux); employed Dec 1871 at Ft Rice with trading firm Durfee & Peck & accdtly wd himself with a Henry rifle;[59] intrpr for post trader at Standing Rock Agcy Mar 1875; 3d enlmt as ind scout 17 Apr 1876 at Ft Lincoln by Lt Cooke for 6 mos; age 21; brn eyes, blk hair, copper comp, 5' 6" high; (Gerard said Cross short & heavy set);[60] in valley fight & retreat to bluffs 25 June says Watokshu;[61] not with captured horses says Young Hawk & Strikes-Two; left timber before Young Hawk's pty; wore handkerchief tied on head when he passed co D on bluffs says Wylie;[62] Burkman said Cross with scouts who bro't Sioux horses to pack train two miles from Reno hill (had one stirrup shot off);[63] Cross said Sioux too many;[64] told Strikes-Two they ought to get horses farther away to make sure thing of them; Ring Cloud said Cross with his pty to Powder River; Red Bear said E-esk stayed behind to keep Sioux off;[65] Soldier said Cross rode a buckskin horse & with Watokshu & Tonhechi-Tu left pty at mouth of Rosebud & beat others to Powder River; Strikes-Two said Cross with pty all the way back;[66] at Powder River sol.'s crowded around Cross to hear what happened (he spoke good English & had some education);[67] ds in field 8 Aug [with White Cloud]; disch 17 Oct mouth of Tongue River a scout char good;[68] hired as scout for col Miles' comd 8 Oct 1876 Cant'mt Tongue River; rate of pay $50 mo;[69] with Miles' comd in action with Sioux inds at Cedar Creek 21 Oct;[70] paid $300 (job) Mar 1877 for dangerous serv going to hostile camp on Little Horn & return with important information;[71] with escort for Sioux & Cheyenne pris'rs to Ft Lincoln Dec 1877; post intrpr at Ft Keogh July 1878 to Feb 1880;[72] served as scout at

Poplar River & Ft Buford Nov 1890 to Dec 1893 & disch a sgt; died July 1894 near Culbertson MT from injuries when his wagon upset while carrying new mowing machine; surv by wife Kate (Elk) & 4 ch.[73]
Pension: 28 Apr 1920 / Ind. Wid / 14980. (Abandoned).

Crowe, Mich'l. Pvt co B; b. Cork Ireland; enl 8 July 1867 New York N.Y. for 3 yrs; age 21; pedler; grey eyes, dk brn hair, fair comp, 5' 5 1/2" high; assd to co F 34 inf 30 Aug 1867; (regt consol with 11 inf to form 16 inf Apr 1869); ed qmd Feb 1870; wag 1 Mar 1870; in conft Apr 1870; sen gen cm 9 May 1870 forf $3 pay; disch 8 July 1870 Nashville Tenn expir of serv a wag; reenl 9 July 1870 Cincinnati Ohio for 5 yrs; age 21; join co E 7 cav 5 Aug 1870 Ft L'worth Kans.; sen gen cm 23 Nov 1870 to 2 mos conft hard labor at sta of co; dd co tailor Jan to Aug 1872; in conft Feb 1875; disch 9 July 1875 White River DT expir of serv & reenl in co E for 5 yrs; tr to co B 1 June 1876; ds Ft Lincoln 16 Oct 1876 dismtd; disch 8 July 1880 Camp Houston DT expir of serv a pvt char good & reenl in co B for 5 yrs; died 8 June 1883 Ft Yates DT a pvt (heart disease).

Crowley, Jno. Pvt co L; b. 7 Feb 1849 Fitchburg Mass.; ret home from navy in 1870; enl in army as Jno. Duggan 24 Sep 1873 Boston Mass. for 5 yrs; age 24; carpenter; gray eyes, dk hair, fair comp, 5' 9 1/2" high; join co L 19 Oct 1873 Ft Lincoln DT; dd orderly for gen Custer 14 May 1876; killed with Custer column 25 June 1876.[74]
Pension: 29 Mar 1877 / Mother / 230652 / 200261.

Crowley, Pat'k. Pvt co B; b. Bangor Me; enl 14 Dec 1874 Boston Mass. for 5 yrs; age 21 11/12; butcher; grey eyes, brn hair, fair comp, 5' 6 1/4" high; join co B 10 Feb 1875 Shreveport La.; dd co cook Dec 1875; cpl 7 Mar 1877; ds Ft Lincoln DT 1 May 1877 chg co prop; des 27 Sep 1877 at Ft Lincoln; due U.S. for ordn & ordn stores $376.78 & qm stores $250.00.

Crump, Jno. Blks co B; b. Lissendorf Germany; enl 14 Apr 1876 St Louis Mo. for 5 yrs; age 22; blacksmith; grey eyes, lt hair, fair comp, 5' 7" high; join co B 12 May 1876 Ft Lincoln DT; appt blks 15 May 1876; des 29 Mar 1877 at Ft Lincoln.[75]

Crussy, Melanchton H. See Krusee, Henry M.

Culbertson, Ferdinand A. Sgt co A; b. Roxbury Pa.; pvt co I 9 Pa. cav 14 Oct 1861 to 24 Dec 1864; enl reg army 3 Jan 1868 Carlisle Pa. for 5 yrs; age 23; clerk; grey eyes, brn hair, fair comp, 5' 9 3/4" high; assd to co G 3 cav; disch 3 Jan 1873 Ft Russell Wyo. Ty expir of serv a cpl; reenl 1 Feb 1873 St Louis Mo. for 5 yrs; join co A 7 cav 6 Feb 1875 Livingston Ala; cpl 26 Mar 1875; ds 26 July to 17 Sep 1875 Ft Randall DT; sgt 23 Feb 1876; dd chg co kit'n June 1876; pvt 13 Sep 1876 [for carelessness that caused fire in camp near Wolf Pt][76] tr to co I 29 Sep 1876; cpl 1 Oct 1876; dd qmd chg of ice detail Dec 1876 to Feb 1877; cited by maj Merrill for good cond in action against Nez Perce inds at Canon Creek MT 13 Sep 1877; sgt 30 Nov 1877; disch 1 Feb 1878 Ft Lincoln DT expir of serv a sgt char xclt; reenl in regt 28 Feb 1878 at Ft Lincoln for 5 yrs; assd to co I 22 Mar 1878 & appt sgt; dd with maj Merrill June 1878; ds Chicago Ill. Jan 1879 witness in Reno court of inq;[77] dd qmd chg of water wagon Dec 1879 to Apr 1880; ds hq escort NPRR Aug to Nov 1880; dd chg of targets Apr to Sep 1881 & Apr to June 1882; dd overseer of laborers Aug to Nov 1882; disch 26 Dec 1882 Ft Totten DT per Regs. par. 235 (accord with GO 24 AGO 1859) a sgt; reenl 3 Jan 1883 Chicago Ill. for 5 yrs & attd to gen serv rctg pty at Chicago; tr to rctg pty Detroit Mich. 20 Oct 1885; disch 10 Jan 1888 at Detroit expir of serv a rct char xclt & reenl in gen serv for 5 yrs; sick hosp Ft Wayne Mich. 22 Feb 1888 (ac. tuberculosis both lungs); duty 18 Mar 1888 (improved, cure not complete); died 10 Jan 1889 at Detroit (hemorrhage lungs) a lance sgt.[78]
Pension: 9 Mar 1889 / Wid / 390717 / 256821.

Cunningham, Albert Jos. Cpl co D; b. Leeds England; enl 24 Dec 1866 Baltimore Md for 5 yrs; age 29; cloth draper; blue eyes, dk hair, fair comp, 5' 5" high; join co D 22 Jan 1867 Ft Riley Kans.; dd as baker July

1867; ds Ft Wallace Kans. Aug 1867 chg co prop; ds Ft Larned Kans. Oct 1867 with escort for peace com'n; sick camp near Ft Hays Kans. 14 June to 4 Sep 1870; dd detmt hq Oct 1870; disch 24 Dec 1871 Chester SC expir of serv a pvt; reenl in co D 20 Jan 1872 at Chester for 5 yrs; sick Ft Snelling Minn. 13 Apr to 29 May 1873 (pr. syph.); sick 30 May to 16 June 1873 (lacerated wd. upper lip & forehead sl. frac. r. frontal bone); sick hosp Ft Pembina DT 2 July to 15 Aug 1873 (const. syph.); cpl 1 Aug 1874; ds camp Powder River MT 15 June 1876 gd to wagon train; disch 20 Jan 1877 Ft Rice DT expir of serv a cpl char capable & faithful; reenl same day in co D for 5 yrs; sgt 1 Mar 1877; ds Fargo DT July to Nov 1878; witness in gen cm of capt French 23 Jan 1879 Ft Lincoln DT; disch 10 Oct 1879 Ft Yates DT on surg cert dis (chr. rheum.; contr line of duty; degree of dis 1/2) a sgt; res Wash'n D.C.

Cunningham, Chas. Cpl co B; b. Hudson N.Y.; enl 8 Dec 1874 New York N.Y. for 5 yrs; age 29; cooper; grey eyes, lt hair, fair comp, 5' 7 1/4" high; join co B 10 Feb 1875 Shreveport La.; cpl 12 Dec 1875; gsw neck (fl. wd. sl.) 25 June 1876; remain with co in field; in arrest Feb 1877; pvt 3 Mar 1877; cpl 12 Oct 1877; (awarded medal of honor 5 Oct 1878 for declining to leave the line [at LBH] when wd in neck dur heavy fire & fighting bravely all the next day); pvt 6 Mar 1879; disch 7 Dec 1879 Ft Yates DT expir of serv a pvt char good.

Curtiss, Wm. A. Sgt co F; b. Albany N.Y.; enl 28 Mar 1867 New York N.Y. for 5 yrs; age 21; boatman; brn eyes, brn hair, dk comp, 5' 6 1/4" high; assd to co F 1 cav; cpl 1 Jan 1870; pvt 15 Aug 1870; disch 28 Mar 1872 Camp Warner Ore. expir of serv a pvt; reenl 28 Aug 1872 New York N.Y. for 5 yrs; join co F 7 cav 1 Dec 1872 Louisville Ky.; cpl 10 Dec 1873; sgt 1 Mar 1874; in arrest Apr 1875; in arrest Dec 1875; chg of co pack train June 1876; 1sgt 25 Sep 1876; sick qrs (ac. rheum.) 20 Dec 1876 to 27 Jan 1877; [m. widow of pvt Kelly 25 Feb 1877]; disch 28 Aug 1877 Camp New Crow Agcy MT expir of serv a 1sgt char xclt & reenl in co F for 5 yrs; dd co qm sgt Aug 1879; disch 18 Apr 1881 Ft Buford DT per SO 75 AGO 1881 a 1sgt char xclt (to procure good home for his family of 4 ch. on claim he must settle on soon or lose near Valley City DT; [declared 18 yrs 6 mos serv]); appn to reenlist in 7 cav 14 July 1890 at Ft Buford appv pending med exam'n; (said family died some years ago).[79] Pension: 22 July 1893 / Wid / 580087; (rej on grd no title under act 27 June 1890, sol. not shown to have served dur late war of rebellion; [clmt declared husband died 27 Oct 1888 Helena MT]).

Custer, Boston. Guide qmd; b. 31 Oct 1848 New Rumley Ohio; employed for a time in drayage business of bro-in-law David Reed at Monroe Mich.; res St Louis Mo. 1871–1872; visited Tom Custer at Ft Hays Kans. in Mar 1871; met gen Custer at Topeka Kans. 22 Jan 1872 dur his return from buffalo hunt with Grand Duke Alexis of Russia;[80] arr Ft Lincoln DT spring 1874 hoping open air of plains would benefit his consumptive tendency;[81] employed as guide with Blk Hills Exp'n 12 June to 31 Aug 1874; rate of pay $100 mo; hired in post qmd from 1 Sep 1874 alternately as forage master (pay $75 mo) & storekeeper ($60 mo); hired by Lt Nowlan 3 Mar 1876 as guide for Sioux Exp'n; rate of pay $100 mo;[82] tented with bro Tom dur march to Powder River thence bunked with nephew Autie Reed; became good friends with capt Marsh of str *Far West* & almost stayed on boat 22 June upon offer of a cabin to avoid rigors of the campn but at last moment went with regt;[83] with Custer column 25 June & went back to pack-train for fresh pony;[84] rejoined bro's comd in battle & was killed in last stand on Custer hill.[85]

Custer, Geo. Armstrong. Lt-col; b. 5 Dec 1839 New Rumley Ohio & from 1850 often res at Monroe Mich.; grad USMA 24 June 1861 & appt 2Lt 2 cav;[86] awaiting orders to 29 June & in arrest to 17 July [87] join co G 21 July 1861 near Centreville Va.; (2 cav redesig 5 cav Aug 1861);[88] adc to gen Kearny (1 NJ brig) Aug 1861;[89] awl 60 days 3 Oct 1861 on surg cert (remit fever last 4 wks); rejoin co 3 Dec 1861 Camp Cliffburne D.C.;[90] pres sick 31 Jan 1862;[91] comd co 28 Feb to 8 Mar 1862;

ds engr duty with gen Smith's div 23 Apr 1862;[92] capt & addl adc on staff of gen McCellan 5 June 1862;[93] (1Lt co M 17 July 1862);[94] awl 11 Nov 1862 Monroe Mich & awaiting orders to 3 Apr 1863;[95] ds NYC 11 Apr with gen McClellan preparing reports; ordered 13 Apr to join regt, revised 16 Apr to join co at Wash'n; adc to gen Pleasonton 6 May 1863 camp near Falmouth Va.;[96] appt brig-gen vols 29 June 1863 (recom'n gen Pleasonton) & comd Mich. cav brig (2 brig 3 cav div);[97] awl 20 days 14 Sep 1863 on surg cert (leg wd [fl.wd tibial] when shell fragment killed his horse under him at Culpeper Va.);[98] awl 20 days 29 Jan 1864 to be married;[99] awl extd 10 days & rejoined comd near Stevensburg Va.;[100] awl 20 days 24 Mar 1864 Wash'n D.C. on surg cert (concussion) & extd 7 days to ensure full recovery;[101] rejoin comd 11 Apr 1864 (first meeting of gen Sheridan, new comdr of cav corps);[102] awl 20 days 11 July 1864 on surg cert (remit fever); appt comdr 3 cav div 30 Sep 1864;[103] bvt maj-gen vols 24 Oct 1864 for gal serv in battles of Winchester & Fisher's Hill;[104] awl 20 days 16 Jan 1865 Monroe Mich.;[105] at Appomattox dur surd of gen Lee 9 Apr 1865 & in field to 18 May when encamped near Wash'n; appt maj-gen vols from 24 Apr 1865 (recom'n gen Sheridan)[106] & ordered to report (with staff) to gen Sheridan at New Orleans La.;[107] assd comd of five regts vol cav at Alexandria La. 23 June; desig 2 cav div Mil Div of the Gulf 17 July;[108] marched with div to Hempstead Tex. 8–26 Aug; (recd bvts maj, Lt-col, col, & brig-gen for gal serv in battles of Gettysburg, Yellow Tavern, Winchester, & Five Forks);[109] marched with div to Austin Tex. 30 Oct & appt chf of cav Dept of Tex.;[110] m.o. vol serv 1 Feb 1866 at Austin;[111] capt 5 cav from 8 May 1864; appn to delay joining regt 60 days appv 13 Mar 1866;[112] appn to delay joining regt until further orders appv 28 Apr 1866;[113] recom for Lt-col 9 cav 3 Aug 1866;[114] bvt maj-gen from 28 July 1866 (recom'n gen Sheridan) for gal serv in campn ending in surd of insurgent army of northern Va.;[115] ordered 24 Sep to join 7 cav at Ft Riley Kans.;[116] joined regt 3 Nov 1866; ds Wash'n D.C. 26 Nov to 18 Dec 1866 before exam'g bd;[117] comd detmt with gen Hancock's exp'n against hostile inds from Mar 1867; in arrest 21 July 1867 Ft Harker Kans.;[118] sen gen cm 20 Nov 1867 to suspension from rank & comd for one yr & forf all pay same period;[119] unexpired portion of sen remitted 25 Sep 1868 upon req of gen Sheridan in need of cav officers for field serv;[120] rejoin regt 7 Oct 1868 Ft Dodge Kans. & in winter campn against hostile inds to Apr 1869; awl 15 days 11 June 1869 L'worth City;[121] with detmt at camp on Big Creek near Ft Hays Kans. to Oct 1869 & hosted buffalo hunts for visiting pty's;[122] awl 20 days 10 Nov & extd 30 days 2 Dec 1869;[123] comd detmt at Big Creek May thro' Oct 1870 hosting buffalo hunts for excursionist pty's;[124] ds Wash'n D.C. 11–30 Dec 1870 [in connection with Lts Calhoun & McIntosh before spl exam'g bd];[125] awl 30 days 11 Jan 1871 NYC & extd thro' Aug 1871; post comdr E'town Ky. from 3 Sep 1871;[126] ds Louisville Ky. (regtl & dept hq) 21 Sep 1871 with bd inspecting cav horses; awl 6 Jan 1872 to accomp gen Sheridan & staff to North Platte Neb for buffalo hunt with Grand Duke Alexis of Russia; on tour with ducal suite to Denver & Louisville to 30 Jan & to Memphis to 7 Feb; awl 20 days 8 Feb & with ducal pty at New Orleans to 19 Feb;[127] pres't of gen cm at Louisville 27 Feb to 4 May 1872; (with gen Sheridan at Detroit 9 Apr for vets convention & unveiling of monument to Mich. sol.'s); returned to E'town 22 May; at Monroe 4 July for reunion of vets of war of 1812;[128] awl 10 days 1 Sep 1872 to Louisville, Lexington & Cincinnati (expositions at first & last);[129] awl 30 days 21 Nov 1872 at New Orleans for meeting of Louisiana jockey club;[130] awl 7 days 27 Feb 1873 to Lexington Ky. & arr Louisville 3 Mar;[131] comd seven cos from Memphis Tenn to Yankton DT 11 Mar to 6 Apr 1873; sick qrs 14–15 Apr dur great blizzard at Yankton;[132] comd ten cos on march to Ft Sully 7–24 May & to Ft Rice 30 May to 9 June;[133] comd same cos & band 20 June to 22 Sep 1873 escort NPRR survey to Yellowstone River & in fight with Sioux inds 11 Aug near mouth of Big Horn River;[134] post comdr Ft Lincoln DT from 23 Sep 1873;[135] awl 30 days 9 Oct 1873;[136] return to Bismarck 16 Nov on last train of season;[137] pres't of gen cm at Ft Lincoln 3 Dec 1873 cont'd 1–28

May & 12 June 1874;[138] ds dept hq St Paul Minn. 4–10 June to review plans for summer exp'n;[139] comd ten cos & band 2 July to 30 Aug 1874 exploring Black Hills;[140] ds div hq Chicago Ill. 11 Sep to report to gen Sheridan; return to Ft Lincoln 26 Sep to revise findings of gen cm of 12 June & deliver court rec to dept hq;[141] ds div hq 2 Oct report to gen Sheridan;[142] return to Bismarck on spl train 14 Nov 1874;[143] with cos F & L to Bismarck 26 Mar 1875 to recover govt grain stolen from post qmd & arrest thieves;[144] ds dept hq 27 Apr 1875 (after opening of NPRR);[145] awl 10 days 1 May to NYC; awl ext'd 10 days 12 May & further ext'd 5 days 20 May;[146] ds div hq at Chicago 26 May; arr St Paul eve 28 May & arr Bismarck eve 2 June 1875;[147] aided *New York Herald* investigation of fraud by post traders on upper Missouri River to Sep 1875;[148] awl 30 days 24 Sep 1875 NYC & ext'd 30 days 20 Oct;[149] awl further ext'd 60 days 13 Dec 1875;[150] awl still further ext'd 10 days from 5 Feb 1876;[151] ds dept hq St Paul 15 Feb to 2 Mar awaiting first train to Bismarck;[152] arr Fargo eve 5 Mar on spl train;[153] dep morn 8 Mar & early next day train snowbound 26 miles from Bismarck; a pocket-relay found on the cars on 3d day was used to splice into the tel line & tap out a call that bro't relief within hours;[154] ds Wash'n D.C. 20 Mar upon summons from committee investigating secy of war Belknap;[155] disch by committee 29 Apr but stayed in city to 1 May (Monday) to see pres't Grant (as recom by gen Sherman); denied audience by pres't (all day) then recd auth at war dept to leave city on night train;[156] stopped over at Monroe 3 May & dep on eve train accomp by niece & nephew;[157] detained at Chicago morn 4 May upon order of gen Sherman, to await further orders;[158] proceeded on morn train 5 May (after exchange of tel's with gen Sherman) & arr St Paul morn 6 May;[159] accomp gen Terry & staff on morn train 9 May & with overnight stop at Fargo arr Bismarck eve 10 May;[160] killed with entire comd 25 June 1876 at Little Big Horn MT.[161] [1239 ACP 1871]. Pension: 9 Apr 1877 / Wid / 230802 / 178408.

Custer, Thos. Ward. Capt co C; b. 15 Mar 1845 New Rumley Ohio; enr 2 Sep 1861 a pvt co H 21 Ohio inf for 3 yrs; age 18; blue eyes, sandy hair, lt comp, 5' 7" high; ds div hq with escort to gen Negley Apr to Nov 1863 & with escort to gen Grant Dec 1863; reenl 5 Jan 1864 Chattanooga Tenn & appt cpl; on furl 15 Jan 1864; ds with escort to gen Palmer June 1864; disch 23 Oct 1864 Galesville Ala to accept com'n 2Lt 6 Mich. cav; join regt 8 Nov 1864 Cedar Creek Va. & appt addl adc to gen Custer; captured enemy flag 2 Apr 1865 action at Namozine Church Va.; gsw r. cheek (fl. wd.) 6 Apr 1865 capturing enemy flag at Sailor's Creek Va.; in hosp City Point Va. 11 Apr & at Wash'n 14 Apr; presented flags at war dept 24 Apr & awarded two medals of honor & 30 day furl [to Monroe Mich.]; rejoin comd 22 May at Wash'n;[162] adc with gen Custer to 31 Jan 1866; m.o. vol serv 24 Apr 1866 to date 24 Nov 1865 (with regt); appt reg army com'n 2Lt 1 inf dated 23 Feb 1866; join co H 10 June at Jackson Bks (New Orleans) La.;[163] appt 1Lt 7 cav 22 Sep 1866 to date 28 July 1866;[164] passed exam'n before cav bd at Wash'n 22 Oct; join regt 13 Nov 1866 Ft Riley Kans. & assd to co A; actg rqm 3 Dec 1866; sick qrs 11 Dec 1866 to 26 Mar 1867 (dengue fever); td comdg co H 31 May 1867; ds with gen Custer's detmt from Ft Wallace Kans. 15 July 1867; ds hq distr upper Ark (Ft Harker Kans.) 12 Aug 1867; ds Ft L'worth Kans. 15 Sep to 29 Oct 1867 witness in gen cm; recd bvt capt 19 Nov 1867 dated 2 Mar 1867 for gal cond in action at Waynesboro Va.; bvt maj & Lt-col Aug 1868 (recom'n gen Sheridan) to date 2 Mar 1867 for dist cond & courage at Namozine Church & Sailor's Creek;[165] comd co A 27 Nov 1868 to 17 Jan 1869; tr to co M 3 Sep 1869 (own req); awl 20 days 3 Dec 1869 (with Lt Cooke) & ext'd 3 mos; comd co M to 8 Feb 1871 Ft Hays Kans. thence awl 20 days; awl 7 days 30 Mar 1871; awl 20 days 8 Feb 1872 Jersey City NJ & ext'd 60 days;[166] awl 7 days 1 Dec 1872 & extd 30 days; comd co B July to Sep 1873 with Yellowstone Exp'n; tr to co B 1 Nov 1873; td comdg co L 8 Mar 1874; awl 30 days 7 Apr 1874 & abs to 27 May 1874; comd co L July & Aug 1874 with Blk Hills Exp'n; with capt Yates' detmt to Standing Rock Agcy 12 Dec 1874 to arrest the Sioux warrior Rain-in-the-Face;[167] awl 30

days 14 Sep 1875 (with Lt Cooke) & ext'd 30 days; arr Bismarck 27 Nov on extra stage from Fargo (with Lt Cooke);[168] prom capt co C 17 Dec 1875; not on Reno scout 10–20 June 1876;[169] killed with Custer column 25 June 1876.
[4577 ACP 1875]. Pension: 9 Apr 1877 / Mother / 230802 / 178167. Father / 289960 / 194962.

Notes—C

1. Caddle said he was detailed with three men of his troop, Fred Myers, John Rivers, and Goosebaker, to take charge of the company wagons, *The Mandan (N.Dak.) News*, Nov. 6, 1914; Grant Marsh, Capt. of the Steamer *Far West*, said Caddle was on the boat after the battle in charge of sixteen dismounted troopers from several companies who had lost their horses in the battle, Hanson, *Conquest of the Missouri*, 302; Caddle said he was on the boat as related by Marsh but about one month after the battle, Caddle to Walter Camp, Oct. 4, 1909, WMC-BYU.

2. RG 94, Entry 409, file 12285 B (EB) AGO 1876; Morris Cain was the first man to carry the mail from Bismarck to Fort Keogh, which was hard in those days, the Indians being thick and not kind to non-Indians. At Glendive, Cain built a paint shop in addition to his large wheelwright and blacksmith shops, *Mandan (N.Dak.) Pioneer*, Jan. 13, 20, 1882.

3. GO 92, AGO, Nov. 23, 1866, redesignated the three battalions of the 14th Infantry Regiment as the 14th, 23rd, and 32nd Infantry Regiments, resp., from Sept. 21, 1866, RG 94, Entry 44; see, Heitman, *Historical Register*, 1: 122.

Calhoun was recommended by his company commander, April 1, 1865, as a suitable noncommissioned officer for promotion to 2nd Lt., but on examination May 8 he was declared unqualified. He was again recommended by his company commander, Sept. 21, 1866, and successfully passed the requisite examination.

4. Also on this scout was Lt. Thos. McDougall, Company B, 32nd Infantry. Col. Thos. L. Crittenden assumed command of the 32nd Infantry in Apr. 1867 (headquarters at Camp Lowell, Tucson, Ariz., T'y) and was transferred in Sept. 1868 to division headquarters at San Francisco, where he was appointed superintendent of recruiting for the military division of the Pacific. He transferred to Dakota Territory in Sept. 1870 and commanded the posts of Fort Rice to Aug. 1873, and Fort Abercrombie to June, 1876. Col. Crittenden's son, John, was killed next to Calhoun at the Little Big Horn.

5. Calhoun visited Fort Leavenworth, Ks., where he attended a masquerade ball, Mar. 17, 1870, in company with his friend, Tom McDougall, who was at the post visiting his sister, Mrs. (Col.) Buel. Also in attendance were Gen. and Mrs. Custer, and Margaret Custer, (sister of the General), and a number of officers of the 7th Cavalry. Millbrook, ed., "Rebecca Visits Kansas and the Custers.".

While at Fort Leavenworth, May 5, 1870, Calhoun applied for transfer to the 7th Cavalry, with the recommendation of Gen. Custer, and endorsed by Col. Sturgis who forwarded the application to the adjutant general's office in Washington. Custer wrote to Gen. Sherman, May 30, that Calhoun's tastes and qualifications fit him far better for duties in the cavalry than infantry and pointed out that the regiment was short of officers (with several on staff duty, many companies had but one officer) and although Calhoun would rank all other 2nd lieutenants in the regiment, he was willing to come in at the foot of the list. If it would facilitate transfer, Calhoun would apply to be placed on the army list of unassigned officers and be transferred from that.

Sherman told the adjutant general (Townsend), if the transfer could be lawfully made he would approve it, but Townsend notified Custer, June 11, that there had been so many such applications, the secretary of war had concluded not to make them. On August 4, Calhoun, then at the home of his widowed mother in Madison, Ind., wrote to the adjutant general requesting to be placed on the "waiting orders" list, to facilitate transfer. Townsend apprised Calhoun, Sept. 9, at Monroe, Mich., that his request of Sept. 1st for further extension of leave had not been favorably considered, and would probably be three months before the question of transfer was acted on. Calhoun learned Sept. 27 that his application to be placed on duty [with the 7th Cavalry] to await decision on transfer was disapproved and he must join his regiment without delay.

The secretary of war directed that Calhoun be placed on the waiting orders unassigned list (SO 290, AGO, Oct. 29, 1870, RG 94, Entry 44), but before issuing the order, Maj. Vincent, assistant adjutant general, inquired of the adjutant general whether it was simply the unassigned list of infantry officers, or the list of supernumeraries, as sometimes the lists were confounded. Townsend penciled across the bottom of

Vincent's note, "'Supernumerary' To go out of service," and at this point in the case record, Calhoun is listed as supernumerary.

Libbie Custer wrote to cousin Rebecca Richmond, Nov. 6, 1870, that, "Autie has at last succeeded in getting him [Calhoun] on waiting orders and he may be assigned to a vacancy in the cavalry before January. His great desire was not to return to Arizona and Autie could have had him assigned to the 7th but his quartermaster papers were wrong[—]through no fault of his however. He has been a long time in Monroe." EBC-LBHB, Roll 1, frames 0188 through 0191.

6. Col. George Stoneman, commanding the 21st Infantry, submitted Calhoun's name Oct. 10, 1870, to a list of officers to be brought before a special examining board in Washington, under provisions of an Act of Congress, July 11, 1870, (published in GO 92, AGO, 1870, RG 94, Entry 44). Stoneman accused Calhoun of evident rascality [in the loss of forage] while quartermaster at Camp Grant and recommended his discharge and one years' pay withheld until he satisfactorily settled his defalcations.

The board, nicknamed "Benzine Board," convened Oct. 17, by virtue of SO 265, AGO, 1870, RG 94, Entry 44. Its purpose was to examine officers reported "unfit for the proper discharge of their duties from any cause except injuries incurred or disease contracted in the line of duty." In reality, its function was somewhere between court-martial and retiring board, the importance of its task demonstrated by its composition of two general officers and three full colonels. Johnson, "Weir and the Custers," 6.

Calhoun was ordered before the board by SO 320, AGO, Nov. 19, 1870, RG 94, Entry 44, and his case attended Dec. 5–21. He introduced a letter from quartermaster Gen. Meigs to Lt. Col. Custer in which Meigs conceded he did not think Calhoun derived any pecuniary advantage or that his integrity was called into question, and there was no indication he acted dishonestly, but he [Calhoun] could not establish facts to relieve him from the greater part of the loss. Meigs had told Custer he was at liberty to use his note for Calhoun's benefit and hoped it would aid in retaining him in the army.

In his testimony, Calhoun did not deny the statement of facts in reference to forage, as given in the brief of proceedings but did deny that he [Calhoun] was told to take as much as he wanted but only from day to day. Calhoun admitted he had never cared for corn fodder before and that this was put up in the rainy season in the fall and the rain had wet it. When asked if he desired the board to postpone the case until all depositions of witnesses to whom interrogatories had been sent were received, Calhoun preferred to close the case at once and had no objection to other evidence not yet received being attached to the record after the case concluded and the proceedings transmitted to the adjutant general. The board then closed and after mature deliberation upon the evidence adduced, announced that Lt. Calhoun was not unfit for the service. The opinion was approved by the secretary of war, Dec. 23, and Calhoun was directed to report to the adjutant general for orders.

The *Daily Morning Chronicle* (Washington, DC), Dec. 24, 1870, lists Calhoun and Gen. Custer among arrivals at Washington's National Hotel.

7. Calhoun wrote to Gen. Custer, Apr. 23, 1871, "I have just received my commission as 1st Lt in the 7th Cavalry, and it reminds me more vividly than ever how many, many times I am under obligations to you for your very great kindness to me in my troubles. I shall do my best to prove my gratitude. If the time comes you will not find me wanting." Merington, *The Custer Story*, 236.

8. GO 1, Hq DA, Jan. 12, 1871, RG 393, Part I, Entry 185, temporarily moved department headquarters to Drum Barracks, Calif., (near Los Angeles), but a few months later, (Sept.), one of the first moves of Gen. Crook on assuming command of the department, was to bring headquarters to Fort Whipple, AT, a ramshackle post one mile from the town of Prescott. Lt. Bourke, aide-de-camp to Gen. Crook, explained that Los Angeles was "some five hundred miles across the desert, to the west, and in the complete absence of railroad and telegraph facilities they might just as well have been in Alaska." Bourke, *On the Border With Crook*, 159; see also, GO 17, Hq DA, Aug. 18, 1871, RG 393, Part I, Entry 184.

Calhoun's request for a board of inquiry into circumstances leading to a 3/4 pay stoppage against him, for an alleged deficiency in his quartermaster accounts at Camp Grant, was approved by the Secretary of War, June 29, 1871, and convened at Camp Grant, Nov. 1, 1871, SO 76, Hq DA, Oct. 17, 1871.

Calhoun explained that in Oct. 1869, he had been verbally directed by the post commander, Maj. John Green, that when laying in hay for the fiscal year ending June 30, 1870, not to receive any sorghum fodder but to accept all the corn fodder offered by the ranchmen of the post. Maj. Green left the post on a scouting expedition Nov. 1st, and during his absence Calhoun estimated he accepted 50 to 75 tons of corn fodder which, although well stacked, soon spoiled because of internal heat and rain. After Green's return Dec. 3, some of the cavalry officers reported corn fodder issued by the quartermaster was not fit to feed as it was damaged, and on inquiry, Calhoun informed Green that the fodder was surplus. Green suggested a board of survey, telling Calhoun if the fodder were surplus it should be fed to the beef cattle because they would at least eat a portion and all would not be lost. The fodder was carted away and part fed to the commissary cattle as hay and part destroyed. Calhoun, believing there was enough surplus on hand to cover the loss, did not think a board necessary.

He was succeeded as quartermaster Feb. 5, 1870, by Lt. Moses Harris, 1st Cavalry, who receipted for property as invoiced. A month later, Harris transferred the property to his successor, Lt. Geo. Bacon, 1st Cavalry, when there was found to be a deficiency in the amount of hay, and a board of survey was convened on application of Lt. Harris, (Post Order No. 17, Hq Camp Grant, Mar. 10, 1870, RG 393 Part V). It was determined that Calhoun's reporting fodder as hay, a different kind of forage, was an inaccurate and improper mode of doing business and by which Calhoun rendered himself liable for a quantity deficient. Maj. Green said he instructed Calhoun not to receive more corn fodder than could be consumed each day, and on his return he found Calhoun had directly disobeyed his orders. Green could only account for the deficiency by supposing Calhoun erred in the amount of corn fodder damaged and fed to the cattle. The report of the board was submitted to Calhoun for remark, and he admitted he erred in estimating the amount of hay on hand and in not calling for a board of survey but denied Green instructed him not to receive more corn fodder than could be consumed each day.

On approval of Col. Stoneman, Aug. 19, 1870, the report was forwarded to the adjutant general's office in Washington, where it was referred to quartermaster Gen. Meigs, Sept. 15. Meigs remarked that the looseness in keeping accounts deserved some official action; the reporting of corn fodder as hay was inexcusable, and the practice of depending on surplus was wrong; regulations required surplus be accounted for as other public property. He recommended approval and returned the report to the adjutant general, Sept. 20. It was submitted to Secretary of War Belknap, Sept. 23, who approved the proceedings and ordered that 3/4 of the monthly pay of Calhoun be stopped until the money value of the hay (nearly 80 tons) was made good to the government at the contract price of $25 gold coin per ton (SO 260, AGO, Sept. 30, 1870, RG 94, Entry 44).

In an effort to remove the stoppage, Calhoun wrote to the Secretary of War, Oct. 26, repeating, in substance, the explanation previously furnished by him to the Board of Survey. The letter was referred to quartermaster Gen. Meigs, Nov. 4, who remarked to Gen. Townsend that the letter did not enable him to recommend any change in the order already made in the case. Gen. Sherman agreed, Nov. 17, and Calhoun was notified that removal of the pay stoppage was not approved by the general of the army.

One year later, (SO 88, Hq DA, Nov. 27, 1871, RG 393, Part I, Entry 184), the court of inquiry requested by Calhoun, upon investigating the circumstances of the case, concluded the stoppage of pay was unjust and that the order directing it should be countermanded. The proceedings and findings of the court were approved and submitted to the War Department for action, and the stoppage was officially removed per SO 23, AGO, Jan. 27, 1872, RG 94, Entry 44 (the quartermaster department to refund to Calhoun the amount already, removed). It was learned from Calhoun's subsistence returns that the hay deficient was consumed by animals belonging to the subsistence department, which was to make good the amount involved to the quartermaster department.

    9. Calhoun married Margaret Custer (sister of General and Tom Custer), Mar. 7, 1872 at Monroe, Mich. "Maggie" had taken a liking to Calhoun from the moment she met him on her first visit to Fort Leavenworth, Frost, *General Custer's Libbie*, 200.

    10. Frost, ed., *With Custer in '74*, 8. This is Calhoun's diary of the Black Hills Expedition.

    11. John Henley, former 1st Sergeant of Company B, said Callan really received the medal for carrying dispatches with another man to Gen. Miles at Ft Keogh during the Nez Perce campaign in 1877. Callan's horse gave out and the other man went on and left Callan. When the other man got in he made no mention of it, and after Callan got in Gen. Miles put this man in the guard house and praised Callan much, Henley interview with Walter Camp, nd, WMC-BYU; see also, Liddic and Harbaugh, *Camp On Custer*, 82–83.

    12. SO 259 & 261, Hq Fort Lincoln, Dec. 21 & 23, 1876; SO 24, Hq Fort Lincoln, Jan. 30, 1877, RG 393, Part V.

    13. WMC, rosters, IU; *Bismarck Daily Tribune*, Nov. 26, 1920; William A. Falconer, of Bismarck, said Charles Campbell of McDougal's troop was living in Bismarck and was with the pack train at the Little Big Horn. Falconer to Mrs. Custer, Aug. 9, 1916, EBC-LBHB, Roll 3, frames 2458 through 2466.

Falconer also said Campbell lived with one of the colored maids or cooks from Fort Lincoln who moved to Bismarck after the Custer battle, Manion, "Custer's Cooks and Maids," *Custer and His Times, Book II*, 177.

14. WMC, rosters, IU; John Ryan said Sgt. Capes and Private Widmayer were left at Powder River with the company teams and probably one or two other privates as company teamsters. Taylor, Scrapbook, 94 (also cited in Taylor, *With Custer on the Little Big Horn,* 179).

15. See notes A24 (Arnold) and A25 (Ascough).

16. *Winners of the West*, Vol. VII, No. 12, Nov. 30, 1930, "Taps."

17. John Ryan said Carroll was known as "Knobby Dan," Ryan to Walter Camp, Oct. 20, 1909, WMC-BYU.

18. GO 3, Hq 7th Cavalry, May 6, 1876, RG 391, Entry 859, authorized company commanders to leave behind one noncommissioned officer and two privates to guard company property and garden.

19. WMC, rosters, IU.

20. See, note B91 (Butler).

21. GCMO 69, DD, Oct. 12, 1874, RG 393, Part I, Entry 1190; Carter appropriated a sack of oats and corn (60 pounds) from the company wagon, Aug. 25, 1874, on Heart River, DT. The finding of the court was disapproved as essential elements in the record as to crime of theft were entirely wanting. Capt. Yates believed Carter's motive was pride in his horse, a new one, never ridden before, and the men deviled him he would be unable to ride him in.

22. Carter remained behind at Shreveport by authority of an official telegram from headquarters department of the Gulf, New Orleans, La., April 19, 1876, which also directed that, "he must join company at his own expense if quartermaster cannot work with [rail] roads to reserve him a ticket out of transportation provided for his company." Carter was ordered to join his company per SO 26, Hq US Troops, Shreveport, La., June 8, 1876, RG 393, Part I, Entries 1965 and 1972.

In a letter to Gen. Custer, Libbie wrote, "Carter has returned and is chief trumpeter. He really sounds the calls beautifully. But his long-drawn notes make me heartsick. I do not wish to be reminded of the Cavalry." Merington, *The Custer Story*, 299; The dating of this letter as the month of May is in error as Libbie also mentioned, "About a hundred men with John Stevenson in command have gone to the Black Hills. Nearly twenty-five teams have passed by"; The *Bismarck Tribune*, June 21, 1876, reported, "A train of upwards of seventy wagons will leave Bismarck for Crook City today; among them will be teams as follows: Don Stevenson 18, . . . About one hundred men, whose names we will try to give next week, will also accompany the train." (Sgt. Frank Lloyd of Company G was acting sergeant-major at Fort Lincoln during absence of the regiment).

23. RG 94, Entry 25, file 722 AGO 1894.

24. RG 94, Entry 297, file 453 ACP 1877; RG 94, Entry 409, file 6453 B (EB) AGO 1879; A brief biography of Causby (born 1847) in Andreas, *Andreas' Historical Atlas of Dakota*, 238; the federal census, 1900, Scotts County, Iowa, Davenport, reports Causby was born May 1848; see Russell, "Custer's Quartermaster Sergeant."; Regimental headquarters, Band, and Troops A, C, G, and H were transferred from Fort Lincoln to Fort Meade, DT, during June 1879.

25. Willert, *March of the Columns*, 208, 221.

26. WMC, notes, Misc. IX, IU; Pandtle to Walter Camp, July 14, 1919, WMC-BYU; The Company Return, Aug. 31, indicates Chapman's whereabouts from Aug. 24 were unknown, being temporarily assigned to infantry being dismounted. LBHB Coll. Rolls 12 and 15. The Regimental Return, Aug. 31, reports Chapman on Yellowstone River, Aug. 24, guard on steamer. NA, M744; Lt. Godfrey recorded Aug. 24, "Orders have been issued for all dismounted men to be sent down on boat," Godfrey, *Diary*, 40. The steamer *Carroll* was loaded [Aug. 24] with sick men from the various commands & got in readiness for a homeward trip. Miles, Journal of Notes of a trip to Montana, July to Sept. 1876 (hereafter cited as Miles Journal), Montana Historical Society.

Chapman's name does not appear on the muster and payroll of Company E, June 30, (troops were paid Aug. 2) and is the last name on the adjutant general's office copy of the muster roll—RLW. LBHB Coll. Rolls 13 and 15. RG 94, Entry 53.

27. Company returns of Company E, June through Sept., 1876, note, "Property all left at Fort Totten, D. T." LBHB Coll. Rolls 12 and 15

28. *Regulations of the Army of the United States and General Order in Force on 17th of February, 1881*, par. 925, "An abatement of five days upon each month of consecutive good conduct may be allowed to military prisoners upon each sentence to confinement for over six months. . ."

29. Hammer, *Custer in '76*, 57; Hardorff, *The Custer Battle Casualties*, 160–61; Charley's remains were reportedly unearthed in 1903 by Superintendent Andrew Grover, probably assisted by Henry Mechling who visited the battlefield during the 27th anniversary. *Mount Pleasant* (Pa.) *Journal*, July 24,

1903; also, letter from Mechling to James Braddock, Mount Pleasant, Pa., July 16, 1921, Mss. Coll., Army War College, Carlisle, Pa.

Mechling told Walter Camp where Grover found the body, and Camp noted that it was the same place several "D" troop men had informed him Charley was buried or killed, Mechling interview, nd, WMC-IU; see Hardorff, *Camp, Custer, and the Little Big Horn*, 76–78; Camp also said Edgerly gave him the location of Charley's body. Camp to Gen. Godfrey, Nov. 6, 1920, Godfrey Papers.

Camp fixed the spot as 260 paces (650 feet) from south Weir peak, and probably about opposite the ravine, on east side of bluffs, in which cedar trees are growing (now called Cedar Coulee). The coulee runs exactly east and west and all the way down to South Coulee (Medicine Tail Coulee). Camp described Weir peaks as two peaks and a narrow flat-top crescent shaped hill adjacent thereto on the east; the crescent 350 feet long around the crescent, and concave toward the west, Miscellaneous Map Data, WMC-BYU.

Sgt. Harrison said Charley was killed between the two Edgerly peaks, Hardorff, *Camp, Custer, and the Little Big Horn*, 62; elsewhere, Harrison said Charley was hit near a ravine to the left, perhaps 1/4 mile or less from the two peaks, Liddic and Harbaugh, *Camp On Custer*, 97.

William R. Logan (son of Capt. Logan, 7th Infantry), a citizen with Gibbon's command, said he "found the body of Mitch Boyer on the ridge something over half-way between where Custer fell and where Reno made his stand on the high butte. The body was lying on the east slope of the ridge, pretty well down towards the bottom of the coulee. . . south of a dry creek, and I should say something over half way between the Custer battle field and Reno's position. The body laid on the hillside, and I do not think it was ever buried as none of the burial party were anywhere near it." In the margin of this paper, Camp noted, "It was probably Vincent Charley." Logan to Walter Camp, May 17, and Aug. 28, 1909, WMC-BYU.

For a story on the identification of Charley's skeletal remains, see, Scott and Willey, "Custer's Men Took Names To Their Graves."

30. The federal census, Lexington Twp., Somerset Co., Maine, Aug. 17, 1850, lists Franklin Churchill, age 2, youngest of six children of Jesse, and Climena Churchill. The census for the same family ten years later, June 27, 1860, lists Benjamin F., age 12.

Benjamin F. Churchill married Jan. 29, 1870 at Charlestown, Mass., to Edith Walton, age 27. Reside Lowell, Mass., June 1870, as Frank Churchill, age 24, laborer, and Edith W. Churchill, age 31, works cotton mill, Federal Census, Lowell, Mass., Ward One, 1870. One child, Edith, Mar. 1872, died Aug. 1872; Benjamin deserted family in 1873; divorced Aug. 1876, Bryan, *Descendants of John Hutchins of Newbury and Haverhill Massachusetts*, 260.

The federal census of St. Paul, Minn., June 10, 1880, reports Benjamin F. Churchill, age 31, salesman, married, born in Maine. (On the same page is, Eugene B. Gibbs, quartermaster United States Army, and wife, residing at the Metropolitan Hotel.)

The City Directories of St. Paul, 1880–81, and, 1881–82, list Benjamin F. Churchill, salesman, Eugene Smith Co., and, B. Frank Churchill (Churchill and McGoldrick), respectively.

The directories were apparently published in August of the first year, as the *St. Paul Dispatch*, Sept. 3, 1883, quoted a story from the *Yellowstone* (Miles City, Mont.) *Journal*, Aug. 25, 1883, that, "The new directory of St. Paul just completed, shows 35,351 names, representing a population of 88,376."

31. Churchill testified that he was employed by Lt. Nowlan to go into the pack train as packer at Powder River and was discharged when the pack saddles were put on the boat. Nichols, *Reno Court*, 464, 474–75; Lt. Godfrey journaled Sept. 18, 1876, at Fort Buford, "We turned over our pack mules. . ." Godfrey, *Diary*, 53.

32. Utley, *The Reno Court of Inquiry*, 348.

33. Records of District Court, Hennepin County, Minn., 1880; Emily Valentine, age 35, widow, of Brockville, Canada, resided same block as Churchill, federal census of St. Paul, Minn., June 1 and June 10, 1880. [Valentine recorded as Valentino].

34. Churchill, McGoldrick, and Abner Haycock, were partners as Haycock & Company in early 1881, doing business as wood dealers in St. Paul, but by July Churchill and McGoldrick evidently formed their own lumber firm. Churchill had charge of the outside, or road business principally and was thus engaged during August and September 1881 at Omaha, Neb., receiving nineteen car-loads of lumber shipped to him for sale by McGoldrick. On returning to St. Paul, Sept. 17, he learned that the firm's books, accounts, and property had been transferred by McGoldrick to "Walker, Judd, & Veazie" of Marine, Minn.

Churchill attested in District Court, Dec. 9, 1881, that this was his first intimation the firm was insolvent, his partner having written to him at Omaha that the business was doing well and should make some money. Churchill believed the firm's total indebtedness at the time of the failure was not over $9000, while assets totaled $13000. He declared that McGoldrick informed him the transfer was necessary so as to give a preference and, Churchill believed, to prevent other creditors from securing a portion of the firm's assets.

A petition for a Receiver of the estate of Churchill & McGoldrick was filed by creditors, Nov. 29, 1881, under the insolvent laws of the state, but was later determined to be indefinite and defective and a motion to dismiss all proceedings under the petition was granted, Mar. 29, 1882.

In an apparent separate case, No. 16906, the Ramsey County Treasurer vs. B. F. Churchill, July 16, 1883, only to show cause was issued and delivered to the sheriff, and returned two months later unable to find the defendant (Churchill) within the county. A judgment in the amount of $9.56 was docketed against Churchill, Oct. 18, 1883. Execution issued to Ramsey County and delivered to the sheriff Jan. 4, 1884, was returned unsatisfied and filed, Jan. 12, 1885. Ramsey County District Court, 2nd Judicial District, Register of Civil Actions, 1858–1899, Civil Case Files, Nos. 14448, 14605, 14608, 14631, 14819, 16906. (Original file 16906 was destroyed in 1970 pursuant to state statutes, before transfer of court files to the Historical Society).

James P. McGoldrick (b. Dec. 1859) became manager of the St. Paul yard of Walker, Judd & Veasey in 1881, which was purchased three years later by Jefferson & Kasson, a large lumber manufacturer, and with whom he remained until 1900 when they closed out their interests. He then formed the McGoldrick Lumber Company and subsequently removed to Spokane, Wash. He died in August, 1939, age 79. McGoldrick, *The McGoldrick Lumber Company Story*, 6, 12, 41, 135–36.

Churchill's brother, Myron, died May 22, 1913, and it was reported, "He leaves one brother in Seattle, Wash." *Waterville* [Maine] *Morning Sentinel*, May 27, 1913. The one brother was evidently Forrest M., who died at Tacoma, Wash., Feb. 23, 1937, age 78. *Tacoma* (Wash.) *News-Tribune*, Feb. 25, 1937. Forrest, with wife and daughter, resided at Villard, Minn., ca 1882 to 1901.

35. Lt. Hare testimony, in Nichols, *Reno Court*, 278, 281.

36. Muster rolls, Company K, June 30, and Aug. 31, 1876 RG 94, Entry 53; SO 39, Hq 7th Cavalry, May 11, 1876 RG 391, Entry 859; see also, Crussy, Loyd, Lynch, and McHugh.

37. Hammer, *Custer in '76*, 131–32; Ryan to Walter Camp, April 7, 1920, WMC-LBHB.

38. Hardy said Cody went back east and told that he was in the battle. WMC, rosters, IU.

39. WMC, rosters, LBHB.

40. John A. Bailey said Coleman and Spinner were the first to go for water, Liddic and Harbaugh, *Camp on Custer*, 82; Stan Roy said Coleman was with water party June 26. Hammer, *Custer in '76*, 115; see Liddic, ed., *I Buried Custer*, 105.

41. Dr. DeWolf to wife, March 12, 1876, Luce, "The Diary and Letters of Dr. James M. DeWolf."

42. Connor was unmarried, and he allegedly acknowledged he was not 18 years old when enlisted in 1867. Endorsement of Lt. DeRudio, April 5, 1877, regarding communication from adjutant general's office, March 22, 1877, RG 391, Entry 869.

43. Cooke's brevets were evidently the result of his mother's personal intercession with President Johnson, citing three instances in which her son's bravery entitled him to three brevets, Terrell and Walton, *Faint the Trumpet Sounds*, 94–95; Arnold, "Cooke's Scrawled Note." See also Arnold and French, *Custer's Forgotten Friend*.

44. *Bismarck Tribune*, Nov. 27, 1875; Cooke and Tom Custer arrived in Bismarck by special stage. The weekly stage trip, providing mail, freight, and passenger service between Bismarck and Fargo during winter months when the Northern Pacific Railroad ceased operations took four days in each direction. Occasionally an extra, or special stage, was added, as traffic warranted. *Bismarck Tribune*, June 23, and Nov. 20, 1875.

45. Letter from Mrs. Flossefa Robertson (daughter of John Cooper), Portland, Ore., nd, to LBHB; personal conversation with Ken Hammer, Dec. 1981.

46. Roy said they became thirsty on Reno hill and chewed grass to get saliva in their mouths. Cowley went insane from thirst and had to be tied fast on June 26. He did not recover for some time, Hammer, *Custer in '76*, 114.

Lt. Varnum said an Irishman of Troop A went crazy in camp at mouth of Big Horn and had to be tied and sent to an insane asylum, Carroll, *Custer's Chief of Scouts*, 76; Cowley believed his attack of heart disease was due to over fatigue and exhaustion and the overpowering effect from vast number of corpses, both human and animal, in various stages of decomposition and putrefaction lying on the field during and after the battle. Private Cowley, declaration for pension, Jan. 8, 1877, RG 15.

47. SO 177, Hq Fort Lincoln, Sept. 24, 1876, RG 393, Part V, directed the post quartermaster furnish transportation from Fort Buford to Fort Lincoln for Sgt. Gaffney, Company I, Private Hegener, Company F, and Private Crowley, Company D, 7th Cavalry.

48. His services would have been retained on the staff for which important duty he had shown himself eminently qualified, but for the fact there was only one officer on duty with Troop E, GO 1, Hq Detmt 7th cav, April 12, 1873, Yankton, DT, RG 391, Entry 881.

49. The sick who could not move on horseback were left in Yankton, to be shipped by the quartermaster to Fort Rice, in care of Dr. Mann who accompanied them, GO 7, Hq Detmt 7th cav, May 5, 1873. Seventeen invalided soldiers of 7th Cavalry who remained at the hospital in Yankton on departure of the regiment, May 7, left that city five days later on the Steamer *Katie P. Kountz. Dakota* (Yankton) *Herald*, May 13, 1873.

On their way up river, the *Kountz* was passed May 17 by the Steamer *Miner* (carrying supplies for the 7th Cavalry, and seven wives of officers of the regiment) at Pease Island (between Forts Randall and Thompson). Two days later the *Kountz* passed the *Miner* at Thompson and ran aground about a mile above the fort, *Dakota Herald*, June 17, 1873; Darling, *Custer's Seventh Cavalry Comes to Dakota*, 146, 162, 192; E. B. Custer, *Boots and Saddles*, 80.

50. The Northern Pacific Railroad was opened (from snow blockade) Apr. 13, 1876, with trains arriving (Jamestown) from both east and west, Lt. Craycroft and Capt. McDougall departed Fort Seward the next day en route to join their company. Company B was then en route from Shreveport to St. Paul, RG 94, Entry 547, Fort Seward, DT.

51. *Bismarck Tribune*, Sept. 27, 1876; Craycroft applied to department headquarters, Oct. 5, 1876, to be relieved from the summons and allowed to accompany his regiment about to take the field, not wanting to leave in the face of such a movement. He requested the commanding general to suspend effect of the summons until return of the regiment; he (Lt. Craycroft) would assume responsibility for his condition during the campaign. Though endorsed by Maj. Reno, Gen. Terry said the application could not be favorably considered knowing that Lt. Craycroft was not fit for field service, (2974 DD 1876), NA, M1734, Roll 17.

52. Burdick, *The Army Life of Charles "Chip" Creighton*, 5; Creighton, Bresnahan, and Madden went for water for the wounded at Little Big Horn, WMC, transcript, BYU-666.

53. The *Katie P. Kountz* departed Yankton, DT, May 12, 1873; Darling, *Custer's Seventh Cavalry Comes to Dakota*, 146.

54. RG 94, Entry 409, file 3053 A (EB) AGO 1878.

55. RG 94, Entry 409, file 10818 A (EB) AGO 1878; see Caniglia, "Private Augustus L. DeVoto."

56. Lt. Crittenden was described as a handsome, manly boy, and as junior officer of his company, and having just joined, was anxious to go on the expedition. After the campaign he hoped to attend artillery school at Fortress Monroe for two years, Parmelee, "A Child's Recollections of the Summer of '76"; Farioli and Nichols, "Fort A. Lincoln, July 1876."

Crittenden's commission was apparently assisted by a letter from his mother to her sister at Louisville, Ky., asking her to remind President Grant of his promise as to her son's appointment, and as a great additional kindness that his commission might bear the same date as that of his graduating class. Mrs. A. M. Coleman to President Grant, June 12, 1875, (ACP file), RG 94, Entry 297.

Crittenden's former classmate, Harvey Ellis of Albany, NY, recalled that Crittenden was modest and shy, but showed a plucky determination to get along, and having a slight physique, the class relieved him from the harsher duties of cadet life and forbade altogether harassing him with hazing. He bore blue Kentucky blood, being the son of (Col.) "Tom" Crittenden, and grandson and namesake of the famous Senator of Kentucky, a family of as aristocratic pretensions as the Clays and Breckenridges. *Saint Paul and Minneapolis Pioneer-Press and Tribune*, July 20, 1876.

Col. Crittenden had been proposed by Gen. Terry to lead the expedition after President Grant had removed Custer. Hughes, "The Campaign against the Sioux, 1876," in Graham's, *The Story of the Little Big Horn*, 9. See also a letter from Col. Hughes to his wife, June 30, 1876, in Noyes, "Captain Robert P. Hughes and the Case against Custer," in *Newsletter* (LBHA), Vol. 33, No. 1, Feb. 1999.

Col. Crittenden accompanied Gen. Terry on the train from Fargo, May 10, and they consulted until the day before the expedition departed. *Bismarck Tribune*, May 17, 1876.

Lt. Calhoun, and Capt. McDougall, both served in the 32nd Infantry when Crittenden was colonel of that regiment. Afterward, Col. Crittenden commanded the post of Fort Rice, Sept. 1870 to Aug. 1873, thence Fort Abercrombie until June 1876.

57. Sioux (Dakota) translation for "Interpreter."

58. Mrs. John Bruguier said Cross was born in 1856, died June 1894, and was half Teton Sioux (father a white man). Walter Camp to Joseph Culbertson, sr., Chief of Police, and Official Interpreter, Poplar, MT., Oct. 29, 1909, with questionnaire directed to Mrs. Bruguier, WMC-BYU; Culbertson served several enlistments as scout at Fort Keogh, 1880–85, said Cross was half Yankton Sioux. Letter and questionnaire from Camp, Mar. 6, 1909, WMC-BYU; Sam Bruguier, brother of John, said Cross was half Minniconjou, Liddic and Harbaugh, *Camp on Custer*, 90.

The Teton Dakota, or Prairie, or Western Sioux, comprised seven bands; Brulé, Oglala, Hunkpapa, Minniconjou, Sans Arc, Two Kettles, and Blackfeet; Vestal, *Sitting Bull Champion of the Sioux*, 4, 50, 65; Milligan, *Dakota Twilight*, 3.

The Indian census, taken during June of each year 1887 to 1894, is not consistent regarding the age of Billy Cross; 33 in each of the first three years; 36 in 1890; 37 in both 1891 and 1892; 41 in 1893, and 37 in 1894; NA, M595, Roll 151, RG 75.

Cross' enlistment papers, 1890–93, are no less inconsistent, his age varying from 37 to 42. Place of birth consistent as South Dakota.

59. RG 94, Entry 547, Fort Rice, DT. Billy Cross with Bear-Come-Out, and others, was active in the liquor trade at Standing Rock Agency in 1875; Milligan, *Dakota Twilight*, 51; Gray, "Ree Scouts With Custer."

60. Notes, env 135, WMC-IU.

61. Notes, env 135, WMC-IU; Watokshu interview with Walter Camp, Aug. 2, 1910. Watokshu thought Cross went back to Powder with the 'Rees and was not among the first to arrive there. In his talks with Sam Bruguier about the Little Big Horn, Cross always told of being in the fight with Reno in the bottom, Liddic & Harbaugh, *Camp On Custer*, 90.

62. Hardorff, *Camp, Custer, and the Little Big Horn*, 49, 54; Hammer, *Custer in '76*, 129 (interview with Cpl. Wylie); Hammer, *Custer in '76*, 190 (interview with Soldier [Arikara scout]).

63. John Burkman, in Wagner, *Old Neutriment*, 158; Also, Burkman interview with Walter Camp, Feb. 5, 1911, WMC-BYU; Mrs. John Bruguier said the Sioux overtook Cross about 15 or 20 miles from the battlefield; Cross was riding a swift horse and they shot one stirrup off but did not hurt him, Questionnaire with letter to Joe Culbertson, from Walter Camp, Oct. 29, 1909, WMC-BYU.

Private Watson said he met a scout, whom he identified as Billy Jackson, on the trail on top of the hill. (This after Watson was left behind with a lame horse). Jackson was in a fearful state of mind and said Custer had shot at him, cutting away the strap that connected his stirrup to the saddle and to save his life Jackson had ridden away. Watson saw the stirrup strap was broken and he thought Jackson, without any hat and casting fearful glances around him as if in mortal terror, presented a wild appearance. Jackson suddenly put spurs to his horse and rode away, his long hair streaming in the wind and he looking right and left as if expecting the enemy to appear at any moment. The strangest part was that instead of taking the back trail, Jackson struck straight across country and as far as Watson could see him Jackson was urging his pony to its utmost speed, Magnussen, *Peter Thompson's Narrative*, 159; As Billy Jackson is known to have been left behind in the valley, the scout described by Watson was likely Billy Cross.

64. Lt. Mathey, in Nichols, *Reno Court*, 513.

65. When Herendeen's group came up the bluff from the valley, they met Billy Cross coming down leading a party of Rees, and they were all mounted, Hammer, *Custer in '76*, 185, 222, 225; Libby, *The Arikara Narrative*, 131; Hardorff, *Camp, Custer, and the Little Big Horn*, 53–54, 58.

66. Hammer, *Custer in '76*, 185, 190.

67. John H. Smith, A Soldier's Report of the Custer Massacre and the Battle of the Little Big Horn (hereafter cited as Smith A Soldier's Report), typescript copy, 2 pp, nd, LBHB Coll.

Harvey A. Fox said Cross was first to reach Powder River with one or two 'Rees. Cross could give no satisfactory account of the fighting but seemed to think all were killed, Hardorff, *Camp, Custer, and the Little Big Horn*, 39.

Dick Roberts (brother-in-law of Capt. Yates) and herder left at Powder River said Cross and two 'Ree scouts came into camp with news of the battle, and their story was substantiated by the other scouts, Roberts, *Custer's Last Battle, Reminiscences of General Custer*, 24.

Cross' statement was published in the *Chicago Tribune*, July 15, 1876; Willert, "The Billy Cross Interview."

68. Descriptive Roll of Indian Scouts, Fort A. Lincoln, DT, RG 393, Part V.

Military Register of Custer's Last Command Notes to Section C

69. RG 92, Entry 238, report, 1876/565, Lt. Randall, 5th Inf., qm, Cantonment Tongue River, MT; Gen. Terry authorized Col. Miles to employ 12 white scouts for the new post at mouth of Tongue River, to be paid by the quartermaster department. Two at the rate of $90 per month each, and the others each $50 per month with ration, Memo Orders from dept Hq, in the field, Cantonment mouth of Glendive Creek, Sept. 1, 1876 (filed with 1876/565).

On the report for Sept. 1876, Cross is the eleventh scout hired, the tenth hired Sept. 14, and the twelfth Sept. 21. However, Cross is the only one without a date of hire and rate of pay. Though not officially employed until Oct. 8, he appears to have been assured one of the twelve jobs.

Col. Miles was impressed with Cross's scouting ability and sent him on the Steamer *Far West* to Standing Rock Agency to hire eight Indian scouts for service with the 5th Infantry at Tongue River Cantonment, Willert, *March of the Columns*, 488.

70. Greene, *Yellowstone Command*, 103; Quaife, *Yellowstone Kelly*, 154, 158. Constant military activity in the field in 1876 fostered division among the nonreservation Indians. On Dec. 16, five Miniconjou chiefs on a peaceful mission, were pulled from their ponies and slain by Crow scouts as they approached the Tongue River Cantonment. Just before this, Johnny Bruguier and Billy Cross were sent out to talk with the hostile camp, to tell them if they surrendered they would not be punished. To ascertain the truth of the matter, the Sioux sent a delegation of seven men into the post to talk over the offer and told Cross to tell the commander to see that the Crow scouts made no trouble. Cross went in and did not do this, but said the Sioux would be there at a certain date (which was later than the Sioux had appointed). Thus, the Sioux came in unexpectedly and the Crows killed them, Liddic and Harbaugh, *Camp on Custer*, 88–89.

71. RG 92, Entry 238, report, 1877/319, Lt. Randall, 5th Inf., Cantonment Tongue River, MT. On the same report, Yellowstone Kelly was paid $400 "For dangerous and extraordinary services in going from Cherry Creek to Cabin Creek MT," Oct. 20–21, 1876. Kelly said Miles directed him to take some scouts and make a night march to ascertain if the Indians left their camps below on the river or were still hiding. He had four scouts besides Billy, a half-blood who was of much use in reaching the point aimed for, Quaife, *Yellowstone Kelly*, 154.

72. RG 92, Entry 238, reports, 1877/174; 1878/12; 1878/116; 1878/117; 1879/108; 1879/416; 1880/99.

73. C. B. Lohmiller (supt, Fort Peck Agency, 1905–17) to Walter Camp, Jan. 4, 1911, WMC-BYU; Lohmiller said he knew Cross and his wife personally.

The names and ages of the Cross children on the census of Fort Peck Agency, 1895, are Annie, 12; Lucy, 11; John, 8; Jennie, 6; and Helen, 5, NA, M595, Roll 151; the children moved to the Cheyenne River Reservation, SD, where an uncle lived. Cross's widow married Nimrod Davis, an Assiniboine, about 1895. She died about a year or two later, Lohmiller to Camp, Jan. 4, 1911, WMC-BYU.

The Indian census at Cannonball Agency (part of Standing Rock Reservation), May 1910, reports William Cross, age 33, born in North Dakota, member of Santee tribe; blood proportions, 3/4 Indian, and 1/4 white; Tribe of father, "Two Kettle and white," born in South Dakota; mother, Santee, born in North Dakota. NA, M595.

74. SO 42, Hq 7th Cavalry, May 14, 1876, RG 391, Entry 859. Burkman said Crowley, alias Duggan, was Custer's striker orderly (permanent) on the expedition, WMC-LBHB; In 1904 a boot with initials "J.D." and containing human bones was found in Deep Coulee, Greene, *Evidence and the Custer Enigma*, 33.

75. John Crump, 7th Infantry, mentioned in Rickey, *Forty Miles*, 336.

76. Godfrey, *Diary*, 52.

77. Culbertson was described as "a weatherbeaten sun tanned warrior," who gave his testimony in an intelligent manner, Utley, *The Reno Court of Inquiry*, 297.

78. Culbertson was alleged to have found a troop guidon beneath the body of one of Custer's soldiers on June 28, 1876, and four years later made a gift of the flag to the wife of Sgt. Charles Fowler, 1st Infantry. When Fowler died, his widow married Ordnance-Sgt. Zachary Reidel who subsequently retired and resided in Detroit. In 1895 the flag was presented to the Institute of Art by a group of prominent Detroiters, among them Don M. Dickinson, who had acquired the flag from Mrs. Reidel. "Memento of a Massacre," *Detroit Free Press*, Mar. 31, 1895; Graham, *Colors of the Seventh*, 110.

79. RG 94, Entry 25, file 9832 PRD 1890.

80. O'Neil, ed., *Letters From Boston Custer;* Frost, *General Custer's Libbie*, 199; Tom Custer was stationed at Fort Hays until May 1871.

81. Whittaker, *A Complete Life*, 603; E. B. Custer, *Boots and Saddles*, 118. Snow, "With Custer in the Black Hills"; Harrison, *The Story of the Dining Fork*, 213; *The Toledo (Ohio) Blade*, May 28, 1910. The

Northern Pacific Railroad ceased operation for the winter west of Fargo DT, Nov. 17, 1873 to Mar. 16, 1874, *Bismarck Tribune*, Nov. 19, 1873 and Apr. 15, 1874.

82. RG 92, Entry 238, reports, 1874/51; 1875/110; 1875/314; 1876/328.

83. Tom Custer to Emma Reed, May 16, 1876, in O'Neil, *GarryOwen Tidbits*, Vol. VII, 1993, Tom O'Neil, ed. Autie Reed to Emma Reed, June 21, 1876, in *Newsletter*, (LBHA), Vol. XXVIII, No. 3, April 1994. Hanson, *The Conquest of the Missouri*, 250, 264; statement of Grant Marsh in *Bismarck Tribune*, Jan. 23, 1906.

84. Whittaker, *A Complete Life*, 589; Before Reno separated from Custer, Boston told Trumpeter Hardy that he was going where the fighting would be. Hardy said Boston had two Indian ponies (says Haddon had Boston's extra pony), Hardy interview with Walter Camp, nd, WMC-IU; in response to Camp's inquiry as to the identity of Haddon, Hardy wrote that, "Haddon I would say that I do not remember to what Troop he belonged but I think that he was in I or D Troop." Camp made notation "perhaps Hardden," Hardy to Camp, Mar. 9, 1910, WMC-BYU.

Capt. McDougall said he talked with Boston Custer when he came back to the pack train, Hammer, *Custer in '76*, 69; Lt. Edgerly thought Boston had stayed back with the pack train; says Boston gave a cheery salutation as he rode his pony passed Benteen's battalion watering their horses east of the lone tepee; article written by Edgerly at Fort Clark, Texas (ca. 1892–95), copy in Ghent Papers.

Trumpeter Martin, on his way to Capt. Benteen with Gen. Custer's last message, said he met Boston Custer near where Reno fortified. He told Boston to look out, that he had just been fired on, and Boston replied that he would catch up with the command no matter what was in the way, Walter Camp to Dennis Lynch, Jan. 2, 1909, WMC-LBHB; see also Hammer, *Custer in '76*, 101, 104.

85. Boston's remains were not removed from the battlefield in July 1877, the secretary of war having authorized removal of none but the officers. However, through efforts of Lt. Fred Calhoun, 14th Infantry, (brother of Lt. James Calhoun), at Camp Robinson, Neb., and Mr. Frank D. Yates, (brother of Capt. Yates), trader at Red Cloud Agency, adjacent Camp Robinson, Mr. W. H. Brown, father-in-law of Mr. Yates, took charge of removal of the remains of Boston and his nephew, and brought them by means of transportation belonging to Mr. Yates, to Cheyenne, Wyo., Jan. 2, 1878. The next day they were shipped express to Chicago where they were met by Mr. David Reed, Autie's father, and taken charge of by Mr. George Chase, secretary to the superintendent of the Lake Shore & Michigan Southern Railroad, who accompanied them to Monroe, Mich. There, on arrival the morning of Jan. 11, a procession of friends and relatives was formed and the remains conveyed to Woodland Cemetery where appropriate burial service was had, *The Daily Leader* (Cheyenne, Wyo.), Jan. 3, 4, 1878; *Monroe* (Mich.) *Commercial*, Jan. 11, 1878.

Frank Yates was under government contract to supply hay for the military station at mouth of Little Big Horn River (Fort Custer), July 1 to Dec. 31, 1877, RG 92, Entry 778, Claim "U" 354 QMGO 1878; see also, Buecker, "Frederic S. Calhoun."

86. Custer's class was originally to have graduated in 1862, but after the surrender of Fort Sumter, April 15, 1861, President Lincoln's call for 75,000 volunteers to put down the rebellion created a need for educated officers to instruct and command the new troops, and caused Washington to abandon the five-year course at the military academy and reestablish that of four years. The decision produced in that year, two classes instead of one, with the regular class commissioned May 6, 1861, whereas the former class of 1862 was commissioned June 24, 1861.

In his "Civil War Memoirs," Custer related that, of the 34 graduates in his class, 33 graduated above him. However, Custer also wrote that, his roommate, James P. Parker, from Missouri, "while sympathizing with the South, had remained at the Academy long enough to graduate and secure a diploma." (Parker is reported to have graduated 35th.) Shortly after leaving the academy, Custer met Parker in Washington and was shown the order from the War Department dismissing Parker from the rolls of the army for having tendered his resignation (July 16) in the face of the enemy. (Parker later served in the Confederate Army). Custer also noted, "The names of two others of my classmates appeared in the same order." Clarence Derrick (4th), and Frank A. Reynolds (33rd), both of whom also served with Confederate forces, are included on lists of Custer's graduating class, whereas Parker is not.

Another often overlooked fact concerning Custer's class standing, is the resignation of 22 Southern classmates between December 1860 and April 1861, which, as Custer himself postulated, "took away from the Academy a few individuals who, had they remained, would probably have contested with me the debatable honor of bringing up the rear of the class." O'Neil, ed., *The Civil War Memoirs of General George Armstrong Custer*; Heitman, *Historical Register*, 1: 368, 770, 825; Whittaker, *A Complete Life*, 39–43, 90; Sergent, *They Lie Forgotten,* 38; Kirshner, *The Class of 1861*, 162–71; O'Neil, ed., *Custeriana One*, 17–24.

87. The day after graduation, and while awaiting orders, Custer was in hospital with a complaint of "Clavus," (a callous growth; a corn). He returned to duty June 28, and the next day detailed as officer of the guard. While walking tour near dusk, he came upon two cadets engaged in a fistfight and as he pushed his way through the gathering crowd he called out loudly, "Stand back boys let's have a fair fight." Scarcely had he said the words when the crowd dispersed at sight of two officers fast approaching, who immediately berated Custer for failing to suppress the near "riot," as they termed it, and ordered him to report next morning to the commandant. There, no explanation would satisfy the requisites of military justice, and he was placed in arrest. Within hours his class received orders to report to the adjutant general's office in Washington for assignment, except Custer, who was to remain at the academy pending resolution of his case.

Custer was arraigned before a court-martial July 5 and found guilty of neglect of duty and conduct to the prejudice of good order and military discipline. He was sentenced "to be reprimanded in orders," the court adding that leniency was due to his peculiar situation and in consideration of his general good conduct, as attested by his commander.

He remained in arrest until approval of his sentence was received from the War Department, July 15, followed two days later by telegraphic orders to report in person to the adjutant general. Custer always believed some of his classmates who preceded him to Washington had used their influential friends there to secure his release from arrest, O'Neil, ed., *Civil War Memoirs;* Sergent, *They Lie Forgotten,* 27; Millbrook, "Cadet Custer's Court-Martial," in *Custer and His Times,* 59–83; Merkel, *Unravelling the Custer Enigma,* 56–85; RG 153, File II-385 (1861).

88. GO 55, AGO, August 10, 1861, RG 94, Entry 44, abolished the three separate mounted corps (dragoons, mounted riflemen, and cavalry), and consolidated them into one corps designated cavalry; Existing regiments were then redesignated, Steffen, *The Horse Soldier,* 2: 67; Heitman, *Historical Register,* 71.

89. A few days after the action at Bull Run, Custer's company was ordered from Arlington to Alexandria, and attached August 4 to the 1st New Jersey Brigade, in camp on the grounds of Fairfax Seminary and awaiting arrival of its new commander, Brig. Gen. Philip Kearny. Kearny arrived August 7 and not having a single staff officer, inquired of Custer's company commander, First Lt. Drummond, if he could not dispense with the services of his junior lieutenant (Custer). Drummond assented and Custer was detailed as aide-de-camp on Kearny's staff. The assignment was short lived owing to the issuance of GO 57, AGO, August 15, 1861, prohibiting general officers of volunteers from selecting their aides from officers of the regular Army, O'Neil, ed., *Civil War Memoirs;* Merington, *The Custer Story,* 25; Baquet, *History of the First Brigade,* 9; Werstein, *Kearny the Magnificent,* 163. Appointment as aide-de-camp carried a pay increase of $10 dollars per month. Merington, *The Custer Story,* 29.

90. As his leave ended, Custer departed Monroe expecting to travel from Toledo to Washington without stopover, but was compelled to be all night in Cleveland until 10 o'clock next day. When he went for lodging at the Weddell House, he met one of his West Point friends who promptly invited him to a grand ball and supper just getting under way at the hotel, Custer to his sister, (Lydia) Ann Reed, Feb. 21, 1862, EBC-LBHB, Roll 1, frame 0405; The event was the 16th anniversary of St. Andrew's Society, announced to take place Monday evening, Dec. 2, 1861, at 6 o'clock, at the Weddell House. *Cleveland* (Ohio) *Leader,* Friday, Nov. 29, 1861.

91. Capt. Eagle, commanding Company G, resigned Jan. 15, 1862, and with 1st Lt. Drummond absent on leave since Dec. 31, 2nd Lt. Ash of Company H commanded Company G from Jan. 17. (Ash joined the 2nd Cavalry from civil life April 30, 1861). Regimental returns, Jan. 31, 1862, report Custer present "Sick," and on Feb. 28, "Comm'g Co'y since Febry 28/62," (Lt. Ash present with Company H), NA, M744, Roll 51; In the letter to his sister, Ann Reed, Feb. 21, 1862, Custer made no mention of illness, EBC-LBHB, Roll 1, frame 0405.

92. Custer assisted Lt. Bowen, chief topographical engineer on the staff of Gen. Wm. F. (Baldy) Smith and was assigned the planning and construction of a small rifle pit for sharpshooters near the enemy line. He was also assigned to balloon reconnaissance and made four ascents to detect enemy positions, O'Neil, ed., *Civil War Memoirs;* Custer to sister, Ann Reed, May 15, 1862, EBC-LBHB, Roll 1, frame 0445.

93. GO 131, Hq Army of the Potomac, Camp near New Bridge, Va., May 23, 1862, RG 393, Part I, Entry 3982; EBC-LBHB, Roll 1, frame 0449; The appointment resulted from an incident that occurred the night of May 22, when Custer was selected to assist Gen. Barnard, the chief engineer, locate fording points along the Chickahominy River, and when they stood alone on the swampy bank, Barnard told Custer to "jump in." Custer obeyed and, despite signals from Barnard, waded stealthily across to the other side and cautiously reconnoitered the entire enemy position along the opposite bank. For his initiative and daring, he was interviewed by Gen. McClellan who was sufficiently impressed to appoint Custer to his staff, Whittaker, *A Complete Life,* 108–15; Garst, *Custer Fighter of the Plains,* 51–52.

Recounting the incident years later, Custer said he was brought before Gen. McClellan in his dripping clothes, *Bismarck Tribune*, Dec. 15, 1875, notes from interview with Gen. Custer by Prof. William F. Phelps while a member of the scientific corps with the Yellowstone Expedition of 1873, and originally published in *The National Teacher's Monthly*.

In what may be another version of this story, it is alleged that Custer had an impatience with pomposity, and when the army halted on the banks of a small stream during the march through the swamps on the Virginia peninsula, he received one of his first assignments. "While more cerebral types on staff debated the proper way of measuring the probable depth of the water, [Custer] rode his horse into mid-stream, halted, and called back, 'it's this deep!'" Sergent, *They Lie Forgotten*, 65.

94. When cavalry regiments were raised to twelve companies, Gen. McClellan recommended Custer for an original vacancy in Company M, Whittaker, *A Complete Life*, 134.

95. Gen. McClellan was removed as commander of the Army of the Potomac, Nov. 7, 1862, at Warrenton Va., and ordered home to await further orders. The status of his staff being dependent on him, they too went home to await orders, Custer returning to Monroe, to the home of his sister, Ann Reed, and brother-in-law, David Reed, *Ibid.*, 134; *Monroe Commercial*, July 2, 1863.

Custer left Monroe, April 2, 1863, on the early morning train to Detroit, but returned in time for Sunday church three days later. Elizabeth "Libbie" Bacon, (Custer's bride-to-be), journaled in her diary that "Autie" again left Monroe on her birthday, April 8, (Wed.). On arriving in Washington (Fri. eve.), Custer said he learned from an officer of the War Department that he was needed in New York City, and he boarded the first train the following morning. He spent Saturday evening with General and Mrs. McClellan at their new home on West 31st Street, one of Manhattan's more desirable residential areas. McClellan told Custer he would have sent for him sooner had he known his whereabouts. Custer assisted McClellan prepare reports of his time as commander of the Army of the Potomac, Frost, *General Custer's Libbie*, 55, 70 note 1; Sears, *The Young Napoleon*, 343–53; Custer to Ann Reed, April 13, 1863, EBC-LBHB, Roll 1, frames 0481 through 0485; Muster rolls of Company M, 5th Cavalry, April 30, 1863, report Custer joined April 3, (he is also the mustering officer on that roll). RG 94, Entry 53.

96. SO 169, AGO, April 13, 1863, RG 94, Entry 44, (through Gen. McClellan), directed Custer to join his regiment without delay. That same day, Custer wrote to sister, Ann Reed, that the order sending all of McClellan's staff to the army had been made out and would soon be published, that when it was he would leave New York and go where he was ordered.

Also on April 13, the commanding officer of Custer's company, "M," Capt. William McLean, died at the Clarendon Hotel in Washington, leaving the company without a commissioned officer. This apparently prompted the issuance of SO 174, dated April 16, suspending SO 169, and directing Custer to join his company at Washington. RG 94, Entry 44.

A note at the bottom of Custer's copy of SO 174 reads, "Recd Tues Eve April 21/63." The next day he was issued a quantity of blankets and clothing by the military storekeeper at Washington, and on April 30 mustered Company M at Camp East of the Capitol (where the company arrived March 4 from Carlisle Barracks). The assistant quartermaster at Washington reported receiving from "Lieut. G. A. Custer," April 30, a six-mule team with wagon, harness, and accoutrements, EBC-LBHB, Roll 1, frames 0481 through 0500. Custer recalled that he joined his regiment as the battle of Chancellorsville was being fought [May 1–5], and remained with his company only on that day and the next when Gen. Pleasonton detailed him as aide-de-camp, *Bismarck Tribune*, Dec. 15, 1875, notes from interview with Gen. Custer by Prof. William F. Phelps while a member of the scientific corps with the Yellowstone Expedition of 1873, and originally published in *The National Teacher's Monthly*.

Custer wrote to Gen. McClellan from Gen. Pleasonton's headquarters, May 6, that he had command of one company of his regiment, George B. McClellan Papers (hereafter cited as McClellan Papers), Manuscript Division, LOC, Washington, D.C.; the regimental return, May 31, 1863, reports 25 men of Company M on detached service at Gen. Pleasonton's Headquarters, NA, M744, Roll 51.

A List of commissioned officers of the 5th Cavalry absent without leave, dated May 26, 1863, reports Custer absent without authority from March 31, 1863, "said to be at Gen. Pleasantan's HdQrs," RG 391, Entry 771.

Various regimental returns, 5th Cavalry, 1863–65, report Custer absent from his company from May 6, and May 16, NA, M744; see also Frost, *General Custer's Libbie*, 64–65; Whittaker, *A Complete Life*, 160; Merington, *The Custer Story*, 56.

97. After the battle of Aldie, Va., June 16, 1863, Pleasonton began a reorganization of the cavalry corps and recommended Custer and two others for promotion to Brigadier-General. Whittaker, *A Complete Life*, 160–61,166; Merington, *The Custer Story*, 57; Leckie, *Elizabeth Bacon Custer*, 29..

98. Welsh, *Medical Histories of Union Generals*, 88.

99. SO 18, Hq Army of the Potomac, Jan. 21, 1864 (with permission to apply for extension of ten days, the leave to have effect upon return of Gen. Kilpatrick), RG 393, Part I, Entry 3984.

Libbie wrote to Custer, "You'll be here a week from Monday. If it takes you three days to travel you'll start on Friday . . . The Episcopalians want to be present. As Lent starts Wednesday, Tuesday will make it right for them." Merington, *The Custer Story*, 80; Custer and Libbie were married, Tues., Feb. 9, 1864, in the Presbyterian church at Monroe. See Frost, *General Custer's Libbie*, 91–95, and *Monroe Commercial*, Feb. 11, 1864.

100. SO 41, Hq Army of the Potomac, Feb. 13, 1864, RG 393, Part I, Entry 3984; Gen. Pleasonton telegraphed Feb. 26 to Capt. Parsons, assistant adjutant general, cavalry corps, inquiring when Gen. Custer's leave expires, RG 94, Compiled Military Service Records of Gen. George A. Custer, 1856–1876, in General's Papers, Union Staff Officer's Files.

101. Custer was thrown from his carriage when it collided with a horse and rider, the impact separated the carriage from its team and threw Custer over the dashboard, rendering him insensible for some ten or twelve hours. Mrs. Custer was with him but was not injured. *Monroe Commercial*, Mar. 24, 31, 1864.

Witnesses said if the horses had not detached instantly from the wagon, Mrs. Custer should have been killed, for they ran down to the stalls, turning over an ambulance and a cow on the way. Custer was up and around five days later, though not perfectly well. He recalled nothing of the accident or his subsequent delirium, Libbie to her parents, Mar. 20, 1864, Marguerite Merington Papers (hereafter cited as Merington Papers), Manuscript Division, New York Public Library.

Custer received medical leave and he and Libbie accompanied Gen. Grant on his special train to Washington, Frost, *General Custer's Libbie*, 103–104; Leckie, *Elizabeth Bacon Custer*, 42.

102. That same month, April 1864, the Michigan Brigade was redesignated, 1st Brigade, 1st Cavalry Division. Custer said this was the post of honor in the corps. Custer to his father, April 23, 1864, EBC-LBHB, Roll 1, frame 0541.

103. Custer later said that, when he got his old brigade he would have the best division in the army, Merington, *The Custer Story*, 120; Several officers of the Michigan Brigade circulated petitions among their regiments, gathering over 300 signatures, in an unsuccessful attempt to have the brigade transferred to Custer's division, EBC-LBHB, Roll 2, frames 1030 through 1043.

104. Monday morning, Oct. 24, 1864, Custer led ten of his troopers into the War Department in Washington, bearing rebel flags captured by each of the men in the recent battle at Cedar Creek. At the conclusion of the ceremony, Secretary of War Stanton turned to the assembled veterans and announced, "To show how good generals and good men work together, I have appointed [breveted] your commander, Custer, Major-General," Merington, *The Custer Story*, 126.

105. To join the celebration of the marriage, January 12, of Libbie's friend, Nettie Humphrey, to Capt. Jacob Greene of Gen. Custer's staff, Frost, *General Custer's Libbie*, 123–24.

106. The Hon. John A. Bingham, who originally nominated Custer to West Point, wrote to Secretary of War Stanton, April 3, 1865, that he had learned of a vacancy in the regular army of the rank of Brigadier, and requested promotion for Custer, that Gen. Sheridan had recommended him for full major-general of volunteers, which rank he then held only by brevet, ACP File, RG 94, Entry 297.

Sheridan wrote to the Secretary of War, April 19, seeking Custer's promotion to major-general of volunteers, Frost, *General Custer's Libbie*, 139, note 18.

Custer was appointed April 24, to rank from April 3, for gallant and distinguished conduct during the campaign terminating in the fall of Richmond. In a letter to Secretary of War Stanton, May 18, Custer said he had been officially notified of his appointment dating from April 3, but owing to the fact that he was constantly in the field and on the march during the past six weeks, the appointment itself had failed to reach him in proper time and was believed then to be at Gen. Halleck's headquarters in Richmond. Custer requested that in consideration of these circumstances he be credited with the appointment so that his acceptance of it should be of same date with the appointment.

Stanton approved the request May 19, and the record made to appear that Custer had accepted the appointment April 3, or 21 days before it was made. He was paid as major-general from that date.

The question arose whether the request of Gen. Custer and the approval of the secretary of war did not contemplate April 24, the date of actual appointment, and not April 3, the date of rank given in it. He was nominated by the Senate for the appointment, Jan. 31, 1866, but with rank from April 15, 1865, and was so confirmed February 23, 1866. The reason for the change in date of rank was not explained, and it was judged that, as his rank from April 3 was not in conflict with the rank of any other officer of his grade, it was presumed to be clerical error. Correspondence between 2nd Auditor, and Col. John C. Kelton, AAG, April, 1886, ACP File, RG 94, Entry 297.

107. While in Washington, Gen. Sheridan asked Custer if he would like to command a division of cavalry on the Red River in Louisiana and march into Texas, with the possibility of entering Mexico, E. B. Custer, *Tenting on the Plains* (1915), 20; EBC-LBHB, Roll 2, frame 1109.

Custer was officially relieved from duty with the Army of the Potomac, May 22, 1865, and ordered to report, with his personal staff, to Gen. Sheridan at New Orleans. After marching with his division in the Grand Review parade in Washington, May 23, Custer began preparations for the long journey to Texas, Carroll, *Custer in Texas*, 6; E. B. Custer, *Tenting on the Plains* (1915), 17.

He and his staff arrived in Monroe, May 25, and during the next few days were called on by many of Monroe's citizens. On May 31, they boarded the morning train to Louisville, where they took passage on the steamboat *Ruth* for New Orleans. On arrival June 16, they registered at the St. Charles Hotel where Gen. Sheridan and his staff had taken apartments June 3, E. B. Custer, *Tenting on the Plains* (1915), 32–34; *Monroe Commercial*, June 1, 1865; *New Orleans (La.) Daily True Delta*, June 3, 17, 1865; Frost, *General Custer's Libbie*, 136; Leckie, *Elizabeth Bacon Custer*, 70.

108. SO 13, Hq Mil. Div. of the Southwest, New Orleans, La., June 18, 1865, in Carroll, *Custer in Texas*, 8; the five regiments were formed into two brigades; 5th and 12th Illinois and 7th Indiana, the first brigade and 2nd Wisconsin and 1st Iowa, the 2nd brigade. The division was gradually dissolved beginning July 21 when the 7th Indiana was consolidated to six companies; on Sept. 14 the 12th Illinois was detached to Houston; Oct 6 the 5th Illinois departed for home; and Nov. 15 the 2nd Wisconsin was mustered out at Austin. Carroll, *Custer in Texas*, 96, 247. Millbrook, "Custer's March to Texas"; Dyer, *A Compendium of the War*, Part 3.

109. A few days before reaching Hempstead, terminus of the Brenham & Houston Railroad, a staff officer brought mail out to the column. Custer received notice, "He was brevetted major, lieutenant-colonel and brigadier-general in the regular army," also a dispatch from Gen. Sheridan instructing him to halt his command near Hempstead for refitting. "Here General Sheridan and some of his staff came, by way of Galveston, and brought with them [Custer's father], whom [Custer] had sent for. . ." Custer, *Tenting on the Plains* (1915), 96; Merington, *The Custer Story*, 169; EBC-LBHB, Roll 1, frames 734 through 736.

110. Carroll, *Custer in Texas*, 138, 141; Statement from AGO, Dec. 17, 1890, as to military service of G. A. Custer, ACP File, RG 94, Entry 297; General Wesley Merritt was relieved as Chief of Cavalry, Nov. 8, 1865, and replaced by Gen. Custer, Alberts, *Brandy Station to Manila Bay*, 171; Libbie said a rumor reached them "that General Merritt is relieved and that Autie commands all the cavalry." Libbie to [cousin] Rebecca Richmond, Nov. 17, 1865, EBC-LBHB, Roll 1, frame 0007.

111. GO 168, AGO, Washington, Dec. 28, 1865, RG 94, Entry 44, directed the muster out of Generals of volunteers serving in Texas to date from Feb. 1, 1866, with leave of absence for thirty days from date of muster out.

Custer and his staff left Austin by ambulance the morning of Feb. 6, and using relays of horses, reached Brenham much quicker than their march over. The next segment was by train over worn down and loosely secured rails to Galveston, where they were detained awaiting the arrival of their steamer, a crowded former blockade-runner, built up with two stories of cabins for passengers. The quartermaster department was authorized Feb. 13 to furnish transportation by boat, and they reached New Orleans after a stormy nighttime voyage in the Gulf of Mexico.

Local newspapers reported a severe storm Sunday evening, Feb. 11, in the Attakapas country of southwest Louisiana, with violent wind and occasional showers continuing all day Monday and Monday night, when it also began to hail. The hailstones, some as large as hen's eggs, pelted many birds to death and cut twigs and branches from oak trees lining the Teche River, almost carpeting the ground. On Tuesday morning, the hailstones, still not melted, gave the appearance of cotton seed scattered along the banks. A cold wind on the Mississippi river Wednesday and Thursday rendered navigation difficult and dangerous, especially for stern-wheel steamers, *New Orleans Daily True Delta*, Feb. 17, 1866.

At New Orleans, the quartermaster department was authorized on Feb. 20 to furnish transportation for Gen. Custer, servants, and horses, to Monroe, Mich. The party boarded a riverboat for Cairo, Ill., where some members of the staff departed for home, while the remainder disbanded at Detroit. The Custers reached Monroe, March 3, *Southern Intelligencer* (Austin, Tex.) , Feb. 8, 1866; Carroll, *Custer in Texas*, 176–79; E. B. Custer, *Tenting on the Plains* (1915), 169–90; Frost, *General Custer's Libbie*, 145.

Military Register of Custer's Last Command Notes to Section C

Custer departed Monroe on March 7, having been ordered to Washington to give his report of conditions in Texas to the joint committee on Reconstruction, Frost, *General Custer's Libbie*, 146; Custer's report was published in, Carroll, *Custer in Texas*, 271–78; see also *Monroe Commercial*, April 19, 1866.

112. SO 113, AGO, March 13, 1866, RG 94, Entry 44; Custer's request for one year leave of absence, prompted by an offer for the post of adjutant general of the Mexican Liberal Army, with a salary in gold twice that of major-general in the U.S. Army, was not approved that the policy of President Johnson for strict neutrality along the Rio Grande should prevail, E. B. Custer, *Tenting on the Plains* (1915), 196–97; Merington, *The Custer Story*, 182–84; Frost, *General Custer's Libbie*, 150–52; see also, Registers of Letters Received, AGO, 1866, NA, M711.

113. SO 196, AGO, April 28, 1866, RG 94, Entry 44; Custer wrote to Libbie, April 23, from New York, that he planned to start for home within the next two days, Frost, *General Custer's Libbie*, 149.

114. Five days after passage of the Army Reorganization Act of July 28, 1866, Gen. Grant sent to the secretary of war his recommendations for appointments of field officers of colored troops, Custer to be lieutenant-colonel of the 9th Cavalry. On Aug. 3, Col. Townsend, assistant adjutant general, directed that letters of appointment be made out for officers of colored cavalry regiments, to rank from July 28. Col. Kelton, assistant adjutant general, penciled on fold of letter, "Mr McSweeney keep these appts confidential. Make out letters & send over for the Sec'y signature," NA, M1064, Roll 297, (letter, S 1096 CB 1866); see Simon, *The Papers of Ulysses S. Grant*, 16: 274–75; Whittaker, *A Complete Life*, 344.

Col. George A. "Sandy" Forsyth, of Gen. Sheridan's staff, wrote to Custer, Jan. 9, 1866, that he thought six new regiments of cavalry were to be added to the army and that Custer was "perfectly safe for a Colonelcy in any event." Forsyth said Gen. Sheridan had already recommended him "for an additional brevet, ie., to be Bvt. Major Genl. USA."

On April 6, 1866, Sheridan recommended to Secretary of War Stanton, that Custer be appointed colonel of cavalry under the reorganization of the army, "as a reward to one of the most gallant and efficient officers that ever served under me." This was endorsed by Gen. Grant (Gen. in Chief) on May 3, EBC-LBHB, Roll 2, frames 1122, and 1141.

115. In a letter to Secretary of War Stanton, Dec. 9, 1865, Gen. Sheridan recommended Custer for brevet major general, but receiving no action he wrote again, May 3, 1866, reurging Custer's appointment, EBC-LBHB, Roll 2, frames 1119, and 1144.

Sheridan's division commanders in the last campaign of the war, Custer, Thomas Devin, and Wesley Merritt, were made lieutenant-colonels and breveted brigadier and major-generals in the regular army all at the same time, on the recommendation of their chief, Whittaker, *A Complete Life*, 337–38; All three were appointed lieutenant-colonel to rank from July 28, 1866, but the actual dates of their appointments were: Custer, August 3; Devin, August 29, 8th Cavalry; Merritt, September 18, 9th Cavalry; Adjutant general to Lt.-Col. Custer, Jan. 19, 1875, in answer to his query, Dec. 27, 1874, seeking the date of appointment of each lieutenant-colonel of cavalry then in service, to that grade, ACP File, RG 94, Entry 297.

Custer spent much of the summer of 1866 in Monroe. On July 26, his name appeared in a notice calling for soldiers and sailors of Monroe County who served in the late rebellion to attend a meeting at the courthouse on Aug. 4. Custer addressed the meeting and was nominated for president of the association. Five days later he attended the National Union Party convention in Detroit and was elected a delegate to the party convention at Philadelphia. He left Detroit on Friday, Aug. 10, allowing time to visit Washington before the convention assembled Tuesday.

Having evidently learned of his pending promotion, Custer wrote directly to President Johnson, Aug. 11, regarding appointments in the reorganization of the army, trusting that he would consider his claim for the position of colonel of either cavalry or infantry, (referring to the recommendation from Gen. Sheridan).

Before leaving for Philadelphia, he wrote again to the President, Aug. 13, stating that the recommendation from Gen. Sheridan then on file in Gen. Grant's office, was under the supposition that a much larger increase of cavalry would be authorized by Congress, but as only a limited increase was provided for, he respectfully requested that while still preferring cavalry, he might be appointed colonel of one of the new infantry regiments, provided he could not be appointed colonel of cavalry. (Custer signed these letters, Bvt. Maj.Gen. USA), Andrew Johnson Papers (hereafter cited as Johnson Papers), Manuscript Division, Library of Congress, Washington D.C.; see, Bergeron, ed., *The Papers of Andrew Johnson*, 11: 68–69.

Also on Aug. 13, Capt. and brevet Maj-Gen. Custer wrote to Col. Townsend, assistant adjutant general, requesting assignment to duty in Michigan because of the death of his father-in-law. (Judge Bacon died May 18, 1866 at Monroe.) Gen. Grant's endorsement of the letter pointed out that Custer was recommended for lieutenant-colonel of a colored regiment, which, if he got, would preclude giving him the detail he was seeking, however, he (Grant) was willing to transfer his appointment to a white regiment.

Col. Kelton, assistant adjutant general, returned the letter to Grant, Aug. 18, asking recommendation for the regiment to which Custer should be transferred, noting that Capt. Merritt was proposed as lieutenant-colonel of the 7th Cavalry, and as yet no one was decided on for the 8th Cavalry. Grant replied Aug. 20 that he had no further recommendations to make in the Custer case.

However, to Secretary of War Stanton's inquiry, (undated), Grant replied that, "The regiment to which Gen. Custer has been appointed is already recruited and assembled at Jefferson Barracks, Mo. He can not therefore be of service to the Government if assigned according to his request. Further, no officers have been appointed to the 7th Cavalry as yet, except the Field officers. It is therefore very important that these officers should be on duty with it without delay. All the Field officers to the 7th Cavalry, who have received their appointments, have been ordered to join it," Simon, *The Papers of Ulysses S. Grant* 16: 276–77.

Meanwhile, Custer returned to Monroe Aug. 25, but left again three days later, having been invited to join President Johnson's "swing around the circle" tour. Along with Gen. Grant and Admiral Farragut, Custer accompanied the presidential caravan August 30 to Sept. 13, from New York City to Chicago and St. Louis, thence back east, with a dozen stops along the way. He left the tour at Steubenville, Ohio, and after escorting Libbie to Monroe, where she had joined during the westward swing, he was in Cleveland for the Soldiers and Sailors Convention, Sept. 15–18.

Custer arrived in Washington, Sept. 21, and the next day called on the Secretary of War to discuss officers appointed to the 7th Cavalry, and to seek Tom Custer's transfer to the regiment. Captains and lieutenants were to be appointed in five days as the regimental ranks were fully recruited at Jefferson Barracks. On Sept. 24, Gen. Grant notified Col. Townsend, assistant adjutant general, that in view of the 7th Cavalry being at Fort Riley, Gen. Custer may be ordered to join his regiment without delay, with authority to go to Monroe for his horses and baggage, Frost, *General Custer's Libbie*, 152–55; NA, M711, Roll 46, Custer letters, 712, 712A, 714.

116. SO 474, AGO, Sept. 24, 1866, RG 94, Entry 44; The Custers began their journey to the west Saturday night, Oct. 6, stopping over in Detroit until Monday night with their friend, Mayor Barker, who had invited them to share a special car with Mrs. Barker and a group of friends to St. Louis. The group included Barker's daughter, Caddie, and niece Josie Eaton, their friend, Miss Strong, her lover Mr. Whitbeck, and a gentleman friend of the Barkers. The latter may have been Prince Nicholas Ourossof, nephew of the Czar of Russia, who reportedly also arrived in St. Louis in the special car from Detroit, and was to accompany the General to Fort Riley. ("Count Olsonfieff" was with the hunting party of Grand Duke Alexis of Russia in Jan. 1872. See, Katz, *Custer in Photographs*, 93).

Custer's party consisted of Libbie's friend from Monroe, Anna Darrah, their servant Eliza, and an African American lad who had been their jockey in Texas and was to tend the General's horses, three of which were transported in a stock car, with one bull dog, one greyhound, and several trail hounds. The Custers spent two days touring the city, including an evening at DeBar's Opera House where they enjoyed the performance of Lawrence Barrett in the drama *Rosedale*. Custer was so impressed with the perfection of intonation and expression in Barrett's voice, that after the performance he went backstage and introduced himself, the gesture launching a lifelong friendship with the famous tragedian.

The Custers reached Leavenworth City, Kansas on the Saturday morning train, Oct. 13, and registered at the Planters' House hotel. While in town, they heeded the advice of an officer experienced in the West, and purchased an outfit of camp equipage from the local shops, including a cook stove which subsequently proved the most beneficial. They departed Tuesday morning, Oct. 16, and their westward journey by rail ended late that afternoon about ten miles from Fort Riley, in the midst of what had been a gala day. Gen. Sherman had arrived that morning from his inspection tour of frontier posts, and at the behest of railroad officials, drove the final spike of the Eastern Division of the Union Pacific road, then completed to that point. The Custers found a wagon waiting for their luggage, and an ambulance to carry them the rest of the way to the post, E. B. Custer, *Tenting on the Plains* (1915), 211–32; Whittaker, *A Complete Life*, 631–32; Frost, *General Custer's Libbie*, 155–56; Millbrook, ed., "Mrs. General Custer at Fort Riley 1866"; *St. Louis* (Mo.) *Daily Times*, Oct. 13, 1866; *Leavenworth* (Kans.) *Daily Conservative*, Oct. 14, 16, 1866; *Leavenworth* (Kans.)*Daily Bulletin*, Oct. 16, 1866; *Leavenworth* (Kans.) *Daily Times*, Oct. 16, 1866; *Junction City* (Kans.) *Union*, Oct. 20, 1866.

117. During the reorganization of the army in 1866, all appointees to new regiments were required to appear before the Army examining board in Washington. Most of the officers who had seen service before

the war, or were graduates of West Point, thought the requirement mere formality, but many of the younger inexperienced officers were found deficient and were dropped. Custer satisfactorily passed the requisite exam December 5, ACP File, RG 94, Entry 297; E. B. Custer, *Tenting on the Plains* (1915), 267.

118. Custer was accompanied by his family, and due to an outbreak of cholera at Fort Harker, he was sent to Fort Riley to await formal charges. SO 426, AGO, Aug. 27, 1867, ordered a general court martial convened at Fort Leavenworth, a larger post, offering a greater number of officers and facilities, and trial was held Sept. 15 through Oct. 11, RG 94, Entry 44.

119. Custer was charged with absenting himself from his command (July 15 at Fort Wallace) without proper authority and executing an unauthorized journey on private business, taking a portion of his command on unfit horses on a rapid march of 150 miles in 55 hours to Fort Hays.

During the march on July 17, after sending a detachment back on the trail to bring up the man leading Custer's mare, whose horse had played out, and when informed on the return of this detachment that they were attacked by Indians and left two men behind, he failed to take proper measures to pursue such Indians or recover those of his command presumed killed.

On arriving at Fort Hays, July 18, at 3 A.M., he procured two government ambulances and four mules for conveyance of himself and part of his escort, (Tom Custer, Lt. Cooke, and two troopers) to Fort Harker, where they arrived at 2 A.M., July 19. After arranging for supplies for the return trip, he awoke the post commander, Col. Smith, and allegedly received authority to proceed on the 3 A.M. train to Fort Riley where his family awaited. On arrival at Fort Riley later that morning, he received telegraphic orders from Col. Smith to return to Fort Harker on the first train.

Lt. Mathey related that the reason Custer left his command without permission and in such a hurry was that an officer of the regiment wrote an anonymous letter to a newspaper accusing Capt. Weir, who was at Fort Riley (or wherever Mrs. Custer was), of paying too much attention to Mrs. Custer. This was brought to Custer's attention and he became very impatient to get to Fort Riley. Mathey interview with Walter Camp, Oct. 19, 1910, WMC-BYU.

Custer was also charged with having ordered on July 7, the pursuit and shooting dead of supposed deserters, without trial, causing the severe wounding of three men, hauling them eighteen miles in government wagons, and all the while persistently not allowing medical treatment, causing the death of one man, Frost, *The Court Martial of General George A. Custer*; see also, Kennedy, *On the Plains with Custer and Hancock*.

Found guilty, sentence was issued in GCMO 93, AGO, Nov. 20, 1867, RG 153, File OO-2555, and published to the command at Dress Parade, the evening of Nov. 25. Though it required that Custer not wear his uniform or have anything to do during the year's suspension, he would still receive about $65 in monthly allowances. Capt. Barnitz later remarked, "Oh, that I too could be similarly suspended!" Utley, *Life in Custer's Cavalry*, 128.

Custer remained at Fort Leavenworth, but not entitled to quarters he accepted apartments proffered by Gen. Sheridan, the new commander of the Department of Missouri, (headquartered at Fort Leavenworth), and not yet arrived, Whittaker, *A Complete Life*, 411; Frost, *The Court Martial of General George A. Custer*, 256; Utley, *Life in Custer's Cavalry*, 136.

In a carryover from the court-martial, a warrant was issued by the civil court of Leavenworth City, Jan. 3, 1868, arresting Gen. Custer and Lt. Cooke on a charge of murder in connection with the shooting of deserters the previous summer. Several days of examination determined that the charge was not sustained by evidence and the defendants were released from arrest Jan. 18, Frost, *The Court Martial of General George A. Custer*, 261–65.

Custer departed Fort Leavenworth, August 12, 1868, NA, M617, Roll 611.

120. Hutton, *Phil Sheridan and His Army*, 51.

121. With brother Tom, Custer took his thoroughbred mare, *Fanchon,* to the National Horse Fair in Leavenworth City, where he was vice president of the fair association and served as judge for several events, Burkey, *Custer Come At Once*, 81.

122. *Ibid.*, 83–89; Frost, *General Custer's Libbie*, 184–85; E. B. Custer, *Following the Guidon*, 268–76.

123. Custer arrived at the Tremont House in Chicago, Nov. 12, 1869. He went to Monroe, Mich., on personal business, stopping in Detroit to visit his friend, Kirkland Barker, and was back in Chicago, Nov. 24. He met with Gen. Sheridan who was convalescing from a prolonged illness after returning from Louisville and the reunion of the Army of the Tennessee, Nov. 17–18, *Chicago* (Ill.) *Times*, Nov. 13, 18, 20, 24, 25, 1869.

Sheridan expressed enthusiasm about the upcoming reunion of the Army of the Potomac in Philadelphia next April 9, and insisted that unless Custer was engaged in active warfare he should accompany him to it, even if he had to be ordered to report to him.

Custer said he had a pleasant stay with Col. Crosby of Sheridan's staff, finding it favorable to economy, no hotel bills, etc., and that his evenings on the theater circuit with Gen. Sheridan's staff were noted in the local press. Gen. Sheridan's condition improved in early December, but not completely, and he asked Custer to go to Washington on official business, allowing time to stop at Monroe to finish his personal matters.

Custer arrived at Monroe Dec. 13, with Tom and Lt. Cooke, the latter on his way home to Hamilton, Canada, invited Gen. Custer to join him. The trio were in Detroit Dec. 15 for a visit with Kirkland Barker before Custer proceeded to Washington. After completing business at the War Department, he stopped at Philadelphia to get a pair of troop boots before going to New York City to see Gen. McClellan. He was back in Monroe in time for Christmas, and on Dec. 28, having accepted Lt. Cooke's invitation, made a quick trip to Hamilton, accompanied by Kirkland Barker, Frost, *General Custer's Libbie*, 185–87; Merington, *The Custer Story*, 229–31; Leckie, *Elizabeth Bacon Custer*, 127, note 56; Arnold and French, *Custer's Forgotten Friend*, 27; Merington Papers. (As an aside, former Secretary of War Stanton died at Washington, Dec. 24, 1869).

124. Gen. Custer decided not to go to Philadelphia in April, 1870 for the reunion of the Army of the Potomac, not wanting to be absent from his command when about to take the field. He had at first supposed there would be time to accompany the troops when they moved out early in March as intended, and return in time to go to Philadelphia as Gen. Sheridan had earnestly requested. He was going solely on Sheridan's account. Rebecca Richmond (at Fort Leavenworth) to her parents, March 21, 1870, in O'Neil, ed., *Life in Kansas with the Custers*, 64; see also, Pohanka, *A Summer on the Plains, 1870*; Burkey, *Custer Come At Once!*, 99–101; Frost, *General Custer's Libbie*, 190.

125. *Leavenworth* (Kans.) *Daily Commercial*, Dec. 11, 1870, reported, "Custar has gone to Washington to be absent a couple of weeks." On the way he spent an evening with friends at the theatre in New York City, before appearing at the Army Board in Washington, Dec. 17, on behalf of Lieut. McIntosh, ACP File, 168 ACP 1871, RG 94, Entry 297.

On Dec. 20, he met with quartermaster-Gen. Meigs regarding the case of Lt. Calhoun, Meigs providing a written statement he hoped would help keep Calhoun in the army. The same day, Calhoun requested the board notify Gen. Custer to appear as a character witness in his case. Custer's deposition was taken Dec. 21 by Maj. Goodfellow, Judge Advocate, ACP File, C97 CB 1870, RG 94, Entry 297. Custer and Calhoun were reported among arrivals at Washington's National Hotel, *Daily Morning Chronicle*, Dec. 24, 1870.

Custer managed to spend a second consecutive Christmas at Monroe, afterward visiting Kirkland Barker in Detroit, Dec. 27, and returning to Fort Leavenworth in time to greet the New Year with Libbie, Merington, *The Custer Story*, 230; Frost, *General Custer's Libbie*, 190–91; Leckie, *Elizabeth Bacon Custer*, 125–27.

126. Custer went on a thirty-day leave-of-absence to New York City, Jan. 11, 1871, with permission to apply to division headquarters in Chicago for a 30-day delay rejoining his command, which was granted Jan. 23 (SO 8, Hq MDM, as noted on 7th Cav. Returns and Muster rolls). He applied to Adjutant General Townsend, at Washington, March 5, to delay joining his command until April 1st, by reason that his presence in New York until that date would probably secure him the sum of $30,000 which he was liable to lose if called away.

Gen. Townsend replied March 9 that no action could be taken unless the approval of his department commander be submitted therewith. Gen. Pope, commanding Department of the Missouri, telegraphed Gen. Sherman (Headquarters Army), March 11, that Custer had his sanction to apply for extension of leave until April 10, when he should join his regiment in Kentucky. The extension to April 1st was approved in SO 100, AGO, Mar. 11, RG 94, Entry 44.

Three days later, March 14, Custer requested the adjutant general amend the order to grant him authority to delay joining his command until April 10, as Gen. Pope had telegraphed permission to apply for the delay and his application of March 5 to that effect was on file at the War Department. Maj. Vincent, assistant adjutant general (AGO), noted to Gen. Townsend that this was the first time he had observed department and division commanders assume to authorize and grant delays, that if the delay as started had not been cut short by the recent leave Custer now asked to be modified to a delay, he would have received thus far in 1871 nearly 1/4 of a year absence without deduction of pay, when law authorized but thirty days. Townsend replied to Custer, March 18, that delays in cases of officers absent as he then was, were no longer favorably considered, that Gen. Pope had recommended in his case an extension of leave.

Townsend also notified Gen. Sheridan, commanding the military division of Missouri, that under orders of the Secretary of War and the General of the Army, it was not competent for department or division commanders to sanction or grant such delays, that a delay in joining for duty or return from leave, amounts in most cases to a leave of absence and must be governed by laws and regulations applicable to that indulgence; exceptional cases were determined exclusively by the Secretary of War and the General of the Army.

On March 22, Custer applied to the adjutant general, through headquarters department of the Missouri, for extension of thirty days till May 11, stating that three if not four field officers of his regiment were on duty with it, and his application for extension was based on the same grounds as his current extension. However, as eight companies of the 7th Cavalry had been transferred to the Department of the South, and the remaining companies under orders for the same department, Gen. Pope made no recommendation and forwarded the matter through division headquarters to the adjutant general's office.

The application was received at division headquarters April 1st, and in absence of the lieutenant-general (Sheridan), forwarded the same day by Col. Hartsuff, assistant adjutant general, with remark that if the application was granted, Custer would be absent that year 120 days to May 11.

In separate communication to Adjutant General Townsend, March 28, Custer explained that he had applied through headquarters of department of the Missouri for extension of leave, and that his reasons, as previously stated, were wholly of a business character involving a large amount of property that he was liable to lose if called away. He had forwarded his application through Gen. Pope's headquarters as four companies of the 7th Cavalry were still in that department, and he had not been relieved from duty there. The adjutant general granted the extension of thirty days in SO 137, AGO, April 5, RG 94, Entry 44.

Ten days later, Custer applied to Gen. Townsend for further extension of thirty days, stating that his only reason for asking the indulgence was his personal attention and presence were needed in New York to conclude the transfer of a valuable piece of property, which was certain to be concluded within the limits of the time specified and but for unforeseen delays the request would not be necessary. Further extension was approved in SO 171, AGO, April 27, RG 94, Entry 44.

On June 3, Custer and wife Libbie arrived in Monroe, where they were expected to pass several weeks "rusticating." One week later, Custer successfully applied for still further extension of leave, for 60 days, for the purpose of attending to important private business, and on the supposition that he could be spared from his post and department. This further extension was authorized by the Secretary of War in, SO 244, AGO, June 21, RG 94, Entry 44.

Custer returned to New York City, July 11, and within an hour, he said, received more invitations than he could accept. The date is determined from his letter informing Libbie of his arrival "last night," and, "the 'Herald' announces the death of Col. Myers." This was Bvt. Lt.-Col. Edward Myers, Capt., 7th Cav., who died July 11, 1871, Merington, *The Custer Story*, 232–33. Heitman, *Historical Register*, I: 739.

On Friday, July 14, Custer met his friend, Kirkland Barker, at Saratoga for the much lauded 2 and 1/4-mile match race billed as the grandest ever on the continent, between *Longfellow*, owned by John Harper of Kentucky, and *Kingfisher*, pride of the stables of August Belmont, with whom Custer had recently conferred concerning certain mining stock. (Race won by *Longfellow* in 4:02 for the seventh Saratoga Cup). Hotaling, *They're Off!* 90–92; *Daily Saratogian*, July 13–19, 1871.

Custer returned to New York City on Sunday, and the following Thursday telegraphed Libbie to meet him Saturday, July 22, in Detroit for a visit with the Barkers at their Grosse Isle home.

During August, Custer was in New York promoting the sale of his mining interests, and at the end of the month, Libbie wrote to her Aunt Eliza Sabin that, "Autie has sold his mine. We go to Elizabethtown, Kentucky." Before leaving, Custer met with Gen. Sheridan late on Sept. 1st, on his return from a year-long European visit, and until 1 A.M. was regaled with every detail from beginning to end.

During March, 1871, the 7th Cavalry was transferred to various posts in the Department of the South, Custer assigned to command the small post at Elizabethtown, Ky., consisting of Company A, 7th Cavalry and Company F, 4th Infantry, Merington, *The Custer Story*, 232–40; Frost, *General Custer's Libbie*, 191–97; Leckie, *Elizabeth Bacon Custer*, 128–32; Slotkin, *The Fatal Environment*, 404–407; Hutton, *Phil Sheridan and His Army*, 206.

127. Tucker, *The Grand Duke Alexis in the U.S.A.*; Millbrook, "The Duke Comes to Kansas."; Manion, "Custer, Cody, and the Grand Duke Alexis."; Palmer, "Custer and the Grand Duke."; *The Daily Picayune* (New Orleans), Feb. 11–20, 1872; *Memphis* (Tenn.) *Press-Scimitar*, Jan. 21–22, 1972; *Commercial Appeal* (Memphis), Feb. 4, 1972, and, Nov. 20, 1997.

128. Frost, *General Custer's Libbie*, 200.

129. Letter from Libbie Custer, in Merington, *The Custer Story*, 241. Though Merington dated this letter 1871, certain statements indicate it must have been 1872, *viz.*, Libbie said they returned from a two-week visit to Louisville, Lexington, and Cincinnati, that, "poor Annie will feel better after her baby comes," (George L. Yates was born Dec. 11, 1872 at Louisville), and, "Maggie is on her way to her husband," (Maggie Custer married in March 1872).

A story datelined Sept. 2, Louisville, reported the gathering of delegates there for the Democratic Convention, and that Gen. Custer, there to attend the opening of the Exposition, was in the rotunda of the Galt House conversing with Dr. Kellar, a prominent physician of the city, when they were casually interrupted by Col. Blanton Duncan, and a sharp conversation ensued that ended with blows being exchanged between Kellar and Blanton before they could be separated, *Cincinnati* (Ohio) *Enquirer*, Sept. 3, 1872.

130. Dippie, ed., *Nomad, George A. Custer in Turf, Field and Farm*, 97–101.

131. At the request of Lt. Varnum, Custer purchased, *King Bernadotte*, a saddle horse noted for speed in hurdle races. *Courier-Journal* (Louisville), March 4, 1873; Frost, *General Custer's Thoroughbreds*, 114; "The Babe of the Regiment," EBC-LBHB, Roll 4, frames 3594 through 3616.

132. E. B. Custer, *Boots and Saddles*, 9–19.

133. See Darling, *Custer's Seventh Cavalry Comes to Dakota*.

134. See Frost, *Custer's 7th Cav and the Campaign of 1873*, and, Carroll, *The Yellowstone Expedition of 1873*.

135. "Return of the Yellowstone Expedition. Custer had arrived the night previous of course, in frontier regulation buckskin, but this had been doffed and in its place donned the well remembered plain blue pants, with their yellow stripe, the blue flannel shirt, with its wide collar and cuffs, loose at the throat, the black slouch hat, and the jingling spurs." *Bismarck Tribune*, Sept. 24, 1873.

136. SO 222, Hq DD, Oct. 7, 1873, RG 393, Part I, Entry 1191; Custer accompanied Gen. Sheridan to Toledo, Ohio for the reunion of the Army of the Tennessee, Oct. 15–18. They were joined Oct. 16 by Libbie, who came down from Monroe for the grand reception at the Toledo Opera House. President Grant and Gen. Sherman also attended. Custer and Libbie went to Monroe, Oct. 18, from where during the next two weeks, they visited friends in Kentucky and Detroit and attended the dedication of the new University Hall at Ann Arbor on Nov. 5. When they departed for Dakota they were accompanied by Libbie's friend, Agnes Bates, Custer having encouraged Libbie to interest attractive Monroe girls to come to Fort Lincoln for the winter. Frost, *General Custer's Libbie*, 206; *Monroe Commercial*, Nov. 6, 13, 1873.

137. "Gen. Custer and family returned to Bismarck on the last train which arrived Sunday evening," *Bismarck Tribune*, Wed., Nov. 19, 1873; Custer was considered absent without leave for eight days from Nov. 9, for which the pay department enacted a pay stoppage of $80. In response to a letter from the paymaster general, Feb. 21, 1874, Custer explained his delay was caused by the discontinuance of regular train service by the Northern Pacific, and his detention verbally authorized by the division and department commanders. Gen. Terry, commanding Department of Dakota, confirmed that Custer was delayed in St. Paul when the trains ceased to run regularly, and at the time his explanation to him was satisfactory. On April 25, the adjutant general's office modified Custer's status for the eight days to on leave half pay, but in a letter to department headquarters, May 14, Custer thought he should be allowed full pay as his absence was occasioned by the cessation in the running of regular trains between Fargo and Bismarck before the expiration of his leave, and when he did get through it was by arrangement with the superintendent (Northern Pacific Railroad) as a personal favor to him. On recommendation of Gen. Terry, the pay stoppage was removed May 23 and Custer allowed full pay for the eight days.

138. The court-martial of Capt. Frederick Grossmann, 17th Infantry, convened Dec 3, but adjourned the same day owing to the absence of material witnesses and the inability of the judge advocate to specify the day when the witnesses would attend, there being great danger of loss of life in crossing the region between Fargo and Bismarck during winter months. The Court reconvened May 1, 1874, RG 153, file PP4183.

139. *Bismarck Tribune*, June 3, 10, 1874; *St. Paul Pioneer-Press and Tribune*, June 5, 6, 9, 1874; *St. Paul Dispatch*, June 5, 6, 1874.

140. See Frost, *With Custer in '74;* Carroll and Frost, eds., *Private Theodore Ewert's Diary;* Krause and Olson, *Custer's Prelude to Glory*; Also of interest are the comments about Gen. Custer made by George Bird Grinnell, paleontologist with the expedition, which are noted in Reiger, ed., *The Passing of the Great West,* 105–107, 124–25.

141. Gen. Custer left Fort Lincoln Sept. 11, with Libbie, who was accompanying Agnes Bates back to Monroe. He was reported going on thirty-day leave to visit his old home in Michigan and other points.

Capt. Yates and Lt.'s Varnum and Wallace came over to Bismarck to bid them farewell. Also on the eastbound train were Capt. Moylan and wife. *Bismarck Tribune*, Sept. 16, 1874.

Custer was in Columbus, Ohio, Sept. 16, with Gen. Sheridan for the reunion of the Society of the Army of the Cumberland, of which Sheridan was president, and two days later joined Libbie at Monroe. He was at the Palmer House in Chicago, Sept. 22, enroute back to Fort Lincoln, (SO 73, Hq MDM, as noted on 7th Cav. Returns and muster rolls), the reviewing authority of the Grossmann court-martial requiring a revision of the findings and sentence. Custer departed the next morning for St. Paul, and reached Fort Lincoln, Sat., Sept. 26. The court reopened Monday morning at 9:10 A.M. and adjourned fifty minutes later, sine die. Custer delivered the court record to department headquarters at St. Paul, Oct. 2. (SO 211, Hq DD, Sept. 26, 1874, RG 393, Part I, Entry 1191); *Cincinnati* (Ohio) *Daily Times*, Sept. 16, 1874; *Cincinnati* (Ohio) *Commercial*, Sept. 17, 1874; *Chicago Times*, Sept. 17, 1874; *Chicago Tribune*, Sept. 23, 24, 1874; *Bismarck Tribune*, Sept. 30, 1874.

142. Pursuant to orders from Gen. Sheridan, Custer reported at division headquarters for further instructions. (Regimental returns report Custer absent on detached service from Oct. 2.) He was among arrivals at the Palmer House in Chicago, Oct. 5, in time for the opening that evening of Lawrence Barrett's two-week engagement at the Academy of Music, considered the dramatic event of the season. Custer and Barrett were constant companions during the greater part of the two weeks.

On Oct. 13, Custer was in Springfield for the unveiling of a monument to President Lincoln during the annual reunion of the Army of the Tennessee. President Grant and Gen. Sherman also attended, Gen. Sheridan being off on the plains was not expected. Custer returned to Chicago, Oct. 17, and three days later he and Libbie attended the gala wedding of Lt. Fred Grant of Gen. Sheridan's staff (and son of the President), Whittaker, *A Complete Life*, 634; *Chicago Evening Journal*, Oct. 3, 6, 17, 1874; *Chicago Tribune*, Oct. 14, 17, 18, 1874; *Monroe Commercial*, Oct. 22, 1874.

143. The Custers left Monroe, Nov. 7, in company with Libbie's friend, Florence Boyd; Libbie having successfully campaigned for the single officers at Fort Lincoln who had pressed her to bring back another girl, Frost, *General Custer's Libbie*, 214; *Bismarck Tribune*, Nov. 11, 18, 1874.

144. *Bismarck Tribune*, Mar. 31, 1875; Barnard, *Ten Years with Custer*, 248–49; see also, Slaughter, "The Establishment of Fort Abraham Lincoln," in, *The Record* (Fargo, N.Dak.), June 1898.

145. SO 59, Hq DD, April 12, 1875, RG 393, Part I, Entry 1191, confirmed telegraphic instructions directing Custer to report at department headquarters as soon as the Northern Pacific Railroad opened. Custer telegraphed Gen. Sheridan inquiring, "Gen. Terry has ordered me to St. Paul, can you extend it to Chicago." Sheridan, then in New Orleans, replied the next day through Col. Drum, assistant adjutant general, "Unless Colonel Custer desires to see me on important official business I do not see how I can order him," RG 393, Part I, Entry 2546.

Custer left Fort Lincoln April 27 accompanied by Florence Boyd, returning to Monroe after a winter on the frontier, Lt. Cooke, on ten days leave, Lt. Willey, 6th Infantry, and Fred Calhoun, brother of James, newly commissioned in the 14th Infantry, en route to join his regiment. The party arrived at the Metropolitan Hotel in St. Paul, April 29.

The next morning, Custer was interviewed by the *St. Paul Pioneer-Press* concerning military plans in Dakota in the summer ahead but did not feel warranted to give such information until reviewing dispatches expected from the War Department. He spent the day in consultation with Gen. Terry, presumably laying out plans for a second expedition into the Black Hills.

146. Custer left St. Paul the evening of April 30 for New York, intending to remain three days completing business that called him there, and on the return would be compelled to tarry one day at Chicago. Before leaving St. Paul he again telegraphed Gen. Sheridan saying, "As opinions might differ regarding the importance of my visit to Chicago please consider my request as never having been preferred. I regret my action in the matter," RG 393, Part I, Entry 2546; *Bismarck Tribune*, April 28, 1875; *St. Paul Dispatch*, April 30, 1875; *St. Paul Pioneer-Press*, April 30, 1875.

Custer was interviewed at his hotel in New York the evening of May 21 regarding the Black Hills and was quoted that he expected, "to start about the 1st of July with about 1200 men," (*New York Herald*, May 22, 1875). The adjutant general telegraphed Gen. Terry, May 17, that the Secretary of War was receiving many applications but had no information concerning Custer's Black Hills Expedition, and that Gen. Sheridan did not know of any expedition to go to the Black Hills under Custer, NA, M666, Roll 192, file 2530 AGO 1875; Slotkin, *The Fatal Environment*, 421.

Also on May 21, Custer learned of the death of his friend Kirkland Barker in a boating accident at Detroit. The funeral was May 23, Frost, *General Custer's Libbie*, 216; *Detroit* (Mich.) *Tribune*, May 20–21, 1875; *Detroit Free Press*, May 21–25, 1875.

147. On his return from New York, Custer was joined at Monroe by Libbie's friends Emma and Nellie Wadsworth, who were to visit Libbie at Fort Lincoln, Frost, *General Custer's Libbie*, 216; *Chicago Tribune*, May 28, 1875; *St. Paul Pioneer-Press,* May 29, 1875; *Bismarck Tribune*, June 2, 1875. Gen. Sheridan was married at Chicago, June 3, 1875, and the night before gave a grand party for his bachelor friends. *Bismarck Tribune*, June 9, 1875; Hutton, *Phil Sheridan and His Army*, 274–76.

148. The alleged activity became national news when it was rumored to involve Secretary of War Belknap, and Orville Grant, brother of President Grant. The *New York Herald* sent reporter Ralph Meeker, using the alias J. D. Thompson, to investigate, and relied on the help of a few local citizens privy to his secret; see Gray, *Centennial Campaign*, 59–71.

Also during the summer of 1875, the Northern Pacific Railroad reduced rates to attract settlers to Dakota Territory, many of the excursionists stopping at Fort Lincoln for the purpose of seeing Gen. Custer. At one point, rather than be on exhibition, Custer escaped hastily to an unroofed chicken coop still under construction, where he hid some time in the broiling sun, hatless, and afterward found ill with mild sunstroke, E. B. Custer, *Boots and Saddles*, 230–31.

The post was also visited Sept. 3 by Secretary of War Belknap and party, returning from Yellowstone Park on the Steamer *Key West,* see Strong, *A Trip to the Yellowstone National Park*, 158–60.

Gen. Terry, with Col. Barr and Maj. Hughes of his staff, were in Bismarck from August 24 awaiting Belknap's arrival, and were to depart for the east on a special train immediately afterward, *Bismarck Tribune*, Sept. 1, 1875.

149. "General Custer left for New York Thursday [Sept. 23] to be absent about thirty days when he [will] return fully prepared to go into winter quarters," *Bismarck Tribune*, Wed., Sept. 29, 1875; SO 172, Hq DD, Sept. 6, 1875; SO 108, Hq MDM, Oct. 20, 1875, RG 393, Part I, Entry 1191.

150. Having ascertained by telegram that Gen. Terry would approve a further extension, Custer made formal application Nov. 18, through department and division headquarters, to headquarters of the Army, for extension of 60 days, but presuming he already had the approval of his department commander, he failed to include reasons for desiring the extension. Gen. Sheridan disapproved the request on Dec. 1st and forwarded it to Gen. Sherman in St. Louis (where Sherman had moved headquarters army in Oct. 1874, [and removed by him back to Washington in April 1876]). Sheridan remarked that Custer had many indulgences granted him during the previous two years in the way of absences from his regiment and judging between the interests of the public service and the fair indulgences that should be granted to officers, he was reluctantly compelled to disapprove the application.

On Dec. 8, Custer received a communication dated headquarters army, Dec. 4, and headquarters military division of the Missouri, Dec. 6, informing him that without approval of the lieutenant-general (Sheridan), the general of the army [Sherman] could not grant the extension. Custer immediately renewed his application to division headquarters, stating in full the reasons impelling him to seek a further extension; that he was a party in a civil suit in the city courts for the last two months or more, and having been summoned to appear in person as an important material witness in the case, his failure to appear when the case was called for trial would result in a decision by default against him and subject him to arrest for contempt of court. In addition, his abrupt departure before the times anticipated would result in a pecuniary loss to him of several thousand dollars, and as a field officer had been assigned to duty at his post, he requested the lieutenant-general, in view of all these facts, to give his approval to his application for extension. (The suit concerned a debt of $8,578 owed a Wall Street broker for speculations in the purchase and sale of stocks on margin, totaling more than $389,000 since May 1875), Leckie, *Elizabeth Bacon Custar*, 176, 207; Slotkin, *Fatal Environment*, 424; Frost, *General Custer's Libbie*, 239.

Adding to his travail, Custer was notified Dec. 10 by the Pay-Master General that he was subject to a full pay stoppage from Nov. 23, unless he forwarded to the adjutant general authority for his absence, sufficient to effect an amendment of the record to show absent with leave to Nov. 30. Custer promptly apprised the adjutant general and again stated his reason for desiring an extension of leave, adding that he hoped to learn within a few days the action taken on his renewed application. He requested the adjutant general submit his explanation to the Pay-Master General, merely to show the steps taken to correct the record.

The next day, Dec. 11, Custer forwarded to the adjutant general a copy of an official telegram from division headquarters, informing him that Gen. Sheridan had recommended his leave be extended two months longer, and he [Custer] requested the adjutant general consider the telegram as part of his letter of the previous day in reply to the Pay-Master General. Gen. Sheridan had also telegraphed Col. Whipple, assistant adjutant general, and Aide-de-camp to Gen. Sherman, that on account of reasons given by Custer he approved his application for extension. (Further extension was approved in SO 70, Hq Army, Dec. 13, 1875, RG 94, Entry 44).

151. SO 26, AGO, Feb. 7, 1876, RG 94, Entry 44; After the holidays, Custer called at the office of the Northern Pacific Railroad in New York. A few days later, on Jan. 11, he applied to the adjutant general for still further extension of leave, to April 1st, as trains of the Northern Pacific in Dakota were suspended until that date, otherwise a journey to Fort Lincoln could only be made by wagon or sled from Fargo, and being accompanied by his family, he hoped to avoid the danger of attempting a trip across 200 miles of plains at the most inclement season of the year. Custer also stated that when he came East on his present leave he expected to return to his post within sixty days, otherwise he would have applied for a longer leave in the first place. In addition, it was extremely important to his present interests that he remain in New York until April 1st, as it would be at great pecuniary sacrifice if compelled to leave sooner. He enclosed a letter from his attorney, S. J. Storrs, dated Jan. 11, stating that the suit to which he was a party had been placed on the calendar for trial and likely to be called up at any time. As he was a necessary witness in the case, his absence would be fatal to his success therein.

Gen. Terry disapproved the application Jan. 15, as did Gen. Sheridan, Jan. 21. Three days later it was forwarded by Col. Whipple, assistant adjutant general, headquarters army (St. Louis), to the adjutant general in Washington, where, having been denied by the department and division commanders, Gen. Townsend was unable to grant the extension sought.

Custer learned of the disapproval Jan. 31 and immediately telegraphed Gen. Terry at St. Paul, expressing hope the general might reconsider his action. He reiterated the great importance that the indulgence be granted, that a suit had been decided against him owing to his absence, but which he had obtained a reopening and in doing so agreed to meet the case when brought to trial, in what would certainly be within the time mentioned. Of greatest importance was the condition of his business affairs there. If forced to leave then he would be thrown into bankruptcy with a positive loss of over $10,000, all of which could be prevented if his application were granted.

Custer also telegraphed division headquarters in Chicago, begging (as termed by Gen. Sheridan) for approval of his application, stating that if compelled to leave New York he would lose all he owned. A series of telegrams followed to Feb. 5, ending with Gen Sheridan's reluctant approval of an extension of ten days, with the proviso that no further indulgence would be authorized. (File 3948 DD 1875; NA, M1734, Roll 18.)

On Feb. 10, after signing a six-month promissory note for $8,500, with 7 percent interest, to be paid at the office of the broker, Justh & Co., Custer departed for the West. Libbie recalled the winter in New York was delightful, the early weeks in company with Tom Custer and one of their oldest friends in the regiment (Lt. Cooke) and were obliged to leave only when they had used all the money saved for the occasion; see "Emil Justh vs. Benjamin Holliday," reported by Mackey in *Reports of Cases Argued and Adjudged*, 346–60; E. B. Custer, *Boots and Saddles*, 236–39.

152. The Custers were in Monroe on Saturday, Feb. 12, stopping over one train. The next morning they arrived at Chicago and while awaiting the afternoon train, Custer was interviewed by a reporter from the *Tribune* during a brief sojourn at the Palmer House. They reached St. Paul Tuesday morning and after paying respects to Gen. Terry, Custer returned to the Metropolitan Hotel.

A reporter from the *St. Paul Dispatch*, hoping to meet Terry and Custer together, called at headquarters in the forenoon, shortly after Custer had left, and in the course of the interview, Terry said it was undecided but Custer would probably remain there several days or perhaps weeks. He instructed the quartermaster's department to furnish quarters for Custer while he was temporarily on duty in the city, until departure of the first train for Fort Lincoln, SO 26, Hq DD, Mar. 1, 1876, RG 393, Part I, Entry 1191; *Monroe Commercial*, Feb. 17, 1876; *Chicago Tribune*, Feb. 14, 1876; *St. Paul Dispatch*, Feb. 15, 1876; *St. Paul Pioneer-Press*, Feb. 15, 16, 1876.

153. *Brainerd Tribune*, Mar. 4, 11, 1876; *Bismarck Tribune*, Mar. 8, 1876; *St. Paul Pioneer-Press*, Mar. 7, 8, 1876; *Red River Star*, Mar. 11, 1876. *St. Paul Dispatch*, Mar. 8, 21, 1876.

154. The work train sent out Feb. 21 to open the road west, returned to Fargo the night of March 7, having thrown out mountains of snow and received a hero's welcome at Bismarck, March 4, for ending their three months of desolation. Preparations were immediately begun for Custer's train to depart the next morning. Just before train time at 10 A.M., a reporter for *The Red River Star* called on the general for an interview about the approaching summer campaign. Custer was pleasant and provided what information he could, until the talk was abruptly broken off by the conductor's call, "All aboard for the west."

As the train rolled slowly out of Fargo the atmosphere was damp and perfectly still, frost clinging to branches of trees and nearly an inch thick on fences. Old-timers said it looked "mighty blizzardy," but being so late in the season there was little concern.

The train, with two complete crews, was described as immense, with three enormous engines, the first equipped with a snowplow, and looming above everything was an eating house built on a flat car where were housed and fed some forty employees of the road who were taken along as shovelers. There were eight freight cars with coal and baggage, one loaded with goods for the merchants of Bismarck, also one express and three passenger coaches, one with Mayor McLean of Bismarck, Clement Lounsberry of the *Tribune*, and a party of miners for the Black Hills.

Several stock cars carried cattle for the miners, together with a pack of three foxhounds belonging to Gen. Custer, a gift from the showman P. T. Barnum during a recent visit to Connecticut. Last of all was the observation car, or paymasters car, occupied by the Custers and the officers accompanying the troops on board, (which included 27 recruits for the 17th Infantry and 24 men of the 20th Infantry to comprise a Gatling gun battery for Custer's expedition). The car also had a kitchen and a sitting room, and most importantly, a small stove.

During regular operation, the 200-mile route to Bismarck required about twelve hours including a dinner stop at Jamestown, the half-way point, but by mid-afternoon the Custer train had only passed Jamestown (where the paymaster and his clerk departed to pay troops at Forts Seward and Totten).

Forward progress slowed even more as many cuts had refilled with drifted snow, and from Crystal Springs, forty miles west of Jamestown, trouble came in quick succession, requiring sudden jolting stops and starts, each time the train men piled out and with energetic work cleared the track.

The next morning, March 9, they approached 16th Siding, (merely old box cars lifted from their wheels) 26 miles from Bismarck, where passage was effectually barred by a mountain of snow. Though the work train had come through less than a week earlier, Libbie Custer described the wall as the accumulation of the entire winter, with successive layers of ice and snow.

The cars were backed down the track some three miles and detached, allowing the engines full power, building momentum up to 50 miles per hour in a run to push the plow through, the procedure called "snow bucking," or "bucking the drifts," and managed to open four big cuts to the siding before one tremendous dash embedded the plow and engine so deeply they could not be withdrawn.

It was decided to lay up for the night (leaving the cars in the distance), when a fearful storm set in and the inspired efforts of the large work crew were unable to provide relief, the work performed mostly in blizzard conditions that finally exhausted the fuel and put out the fires in the engines.

As the blowing snow claimed the silent goliath and refilled the cuts, the men made their way back to the cars and shelter from the storm that continued until the next night without abatement. When morning dawned, clear and cold, shovel brigades were formed through the drifts to the engines. At the same time a search of the cars produced a small battery and pocket-relay, sometimes used by train men to report the position of an off schedule train, Also found was a telegraph operator, believed to have been Mark Kellogg.

Gen. Custer directed the main telegraph wire to be cut and a distress call tapped out. Within hours sleighs were at train side to transport Mayor Mclean, Clement Lounsberry, and Gen. Custer, and other notables to Bismarck, using the telegraph poles as guides across the snow covered prairie. More passengers set out on foot even as teams began hauling food and fuel out to the train. Once back at Fort Lincoln, Custer immediately dispatched a detachment of twenty men and ten six-mule teams to the job, and offered more. *Bismarck Tribune*, March 1, 8, 1876; *Red River Star*, March 4, 11, 1876; *Brainerd Tribune*, March 4, 11, 1876; *St. Paul Pioneer-Press*, March 8, 16, 1876; *St. Paul Dispatch*, March 21, 1876; "Snow Bucking in 1876," *The Record* (Fargo), Jan. 1897; E. B. Custer, *Boots and Saddles*, 240–46; Carroll, *Garlington Narrative*, 4; "Reminiscences of Sgt. Hugh A. Hynds."; Knight, "Mark Kellogg Telegraphed For Custer's Rescue." ; Letters from H. A. Towne, superintendent, to George Stark, Vice-President, Dec. 1875 through March, 1876, Northern Pacific Railroad Papers (hereafter cited as NPRR Papers), Minnesota Historical Society, St. Paul.

155. Custer departed for Washington on the Monday morning (Mar. 20) stage (sleigh), the railroad still blockaded. The stage provided regular semi-weekly mail, freight, and passenger service between Bismarck and Fargo during the winter when the Northern Pacific did not run. With sixteen teams, eight stations (advertised as comfortable and convenient stopping places) were established about twenty miles apart over the 200 mile distance, the trip requiring four days in each direction.

Also reported leaving on March 20 were Lts. Calhoun and Smith en route to join their troops at Fort Seward, and J. C. Wagoner the newly hired chief packer for the expedition who was going to St. Paul to engage assistants.

Custer's stage left Fort Seward the morning of the 22nd, and pulled up at the Headquarters Hotel (adjacent the train depot) in Fargo on Thursday.

On arrival in St. Paul on Friday he evidently called on Gen. Terry, for that day Terry renewed his request of Feb. 16 (when Custer was last in St. Paul), to Gen. Sheridan, seeking transfer of the three 7th Cavalry troops in the Department of the South, to Department of Dakota for duty with the Sioux expedition. After a square meal at Culver's hostelry (at the Metropolitan), Custer continued his journey east, spending Sunday in Monroe, and reaching Washington Tuesday night, pressed for time and sleep. He went before the committee on Wednesday, and was also summoned before the military affairs committee the following week. *Bismarck Tribune*, June 23, Nov. 13, 20, 1875, Jan. 5, Feb. 23, and March 22, 1876; Dr. DeWolf to wife, March 22, 1876, Luce, ed., "The Diary and Letters of Dr. James M. DeWolf."; *The Red River Star*, March 25, 1876; *St. Paul Dispatch*, March 25, 1876; Merington, *The Custer Story*, 281. Hughes, "The Campaign against the Sioux in 1876," 15–16; see also, Prickett, "The Malfeasance of William Worth Belknap."

156. Custer obtained authority from the adjutant general (Townsend) and the inspector general (Marcy), written and verbal, to proceed to his command, Hughes, "The Campaign against the Sioux in 1876," 9–10; It was reported that Custer was relieved from duty as commanding officer under the brevet rank and went to join his regiment simply as its lieutenant-colonel, the first time since early in the late war that he did any duty except as a general officer, and he seemed "considerably chapfallen." *The New York Times*, May 2, 1876; *Chicago Evening Journal*, May 3, 1876; Whittaker, *A Complete Life*, 552–54.

157. *Monroe Commercial*, May 4, 1876; Frost, *General Custer's Libbie*, 222.

158. Custer was on the train in Chicago just seven minutes from departure at 9:20 A.M., when Gen. Sheridan's brother came on board with orders to stop him, saying he left Washington without seeing the president or Gen. Sherman. Custer and his young party (Autie and Emma Reed) then had the pleasure of picking up their baggage and returning to the Palmer House. (Custer and the Reeds are listed among morning arrivals on May 4, and with evening arrivals on May 5). They stayed in house all morning, not knowing what they might have to do, though in the afternoon they called on Mr. Chase at the Lake Shore & Michigan Southern Railroad Depot. (Gen. Custer purchased two canary birds). They left Chicago Friday morning and were 24 hours on the train, reaching St. Paul at 7 A.M., Young Autie found it quite cold, an overcoat buttoned up not being too warm. Autie Reed to his parents, May 6, 1876, typescript copy in Lawrence A. Frost Collection at the Monroe County (Mich.) Library; *Chicago Evening Journal*, May 4, 5, 1876; see also, *Chicago Tribune*, May 9, 1876 (Special Dispatch, St. Paul, May 8).

159. For the telegrams during Custer's Chicago stopover, see, Hughes, "The Campaign Against the Sioux in 1876,"10–11, and Whittaker, *A Complete Life*, 553–60.

160. "Gen. Terry and staff will leave this morning for Fort Lincoln, a special train at Fargo awaiting their arrival at that point. Gen. Custer will accompany Gen. Terry," *St. Paul & Minneapolis Pioneer-Press and Tribune*, May 9, 1876.

At Fargo it was reported that, "Gen. Custer appeared glum and in ill-humor—out of sorts—don't like the change his too lively tongue has wrought at all." *Red River Star*, May 13, 1876; Col. T. L. Crittenden to accompany Gen. Terry from Fargo to Fort Lincoln, SFO 1, Hq DD, May 10, 1876, RG 94, Entry 44.

161. Mrs. Gen. Custer, Mrs. J. Calhoun, Mrs. G. W. Yates, two children and servant, Mrs. A. E. Smith, widowed by the Little Big Horn fight, and Miss Reed, accompanied by the latter's father, Mr. David Reed, and Mr. Roberts, brother of Mrs. Yates, arrived at St. Paul from Bismarck the morning of August 2nd on a special car furnished them by the railroad, and stopped at the Metropolitan. All left that evening for Chicago, thence to their respective homes. *Bismarck Tribune*, Aug. 2, 1876; *St. Paul Dispatch*, Aug. 2, 1876; *St. Paul & Minneapolis Pioneer-Press and Tribune*, Aug. 3, 1876; see also, Frost, *General Custer's Libbie*, 229–32.

162. Day, *Tom Custer Ride to Glory*, 75–80; Merington, *The Custer Story*, 151; Millbrook, *A Study in Valor*, 20–6.

In a letter to his sister, Ann Reed, Apr. 21, 1865, Gen. Custer said Tom's wound was serious but not dangerous. Tom, then in Washington to present flags to the War Department, and would receive two medals for his gallantry and be offered leave of absence for at least thirty days, EBC-LBHB, Roll 1, frame 0728.

Libbie Custer was in Washington at the time and attended the flag ceremony, involving 51 soldiers with flags. see E. B. Custer, "A Beau Sabreur," in Rodenbough, ed., *The Bravest Five Hundred of '61*.

Lt. Elliott M. Norton, 6th Michigan Cavalry, who also captured a Confederate flag at Sailor's Creek, mentioned in his account of events that, on turning over the captured flags to the Secretary of War, each soldier received a medal of honor and a furlough of thirty days, Rodenbough, *Uncle Sam's Medal of Honor*, 141.

Tom Custer evidently carried to Monroe, the small table used by Gen. Grant to write the surrender terms for Gen. Lee's army, and afterwards presented to Libbie Custer by Gen. Sheridan. The table was reported to be at Monroe in early May, *Monroe Commercial*, May 4, 1865.

Judge Bacon wrote to Libbie (in Washington), Sunday, May 14, 1865, that Tom was leaving the first of next week, Frost, *General Custer's Libbie*, 134.

"In his report [as Chief] of the Record and Pension Office in 1901, [Gen.] Frederick C. Ainsworth states that any second medal awarded to a soldier was awarded in error. 'It is believed that in the very few cases in which the second medal has been awarded to the same person the award was made through oversight and in ignorance of the fact that a previous award had been made to that person.' Annual Report of the War Department, 1901, p. 1094," Millbrook, *A Study in Valor*, 53 n. 2.

163. Gen. Custer was in Washington, March 10, 1866, to appear before the joint committee on Reconstruction, and afterward called on Secretary of War Stanton, who informed him that he had honored his request by appointing Tom a commission in the regular army. In a letter to Libbie, March 12, Custer boasted that the secretary told him, "I tell you Custer, there is nothing in my power to grant I would not do if you would ask me." Custer stated further that Tom was most fortunate in his appointment considering the number and rank of applicants, several of those appointed lieutenants having been major-generals of volunteers. Merington, *The Custer Story*, 177–78.

164. When in Washington in September 1866, Gen. Custer again called on the Secretary of War, and no sooner mentioned his desire to have Tom transferred to the 7th Cavalry, than Stanton sat down and wrote out directions for the order to be made out, saying, "I will not only transfer him but I will promote him to First Lieutenant." Frost, *General Custer's Libbie*, 154.

165. Tom said he received his appointment of Brevet Captain on Nov. 19, 1867 and was unexpected to him. Tom to Ann Reed, Nov. 20, 1867. O'Neil, ed., *GarryOwen Tidbits VII*. Tom's brevet of captain was originally confirmed for gallant and meritorious service at Sailors Creek but was revised on recommendation of Gen. Custer and Gen. Sheridan (at Fort Leavenworth), June 29, 1868, in conjunction with additional brevets of major and lieutenant-colonel, ACP File, RG 94, Entry 297.

166. See Day, *Tom Custer Ride to Glory*, 155.

167. Reports of the incident involving Rain-in-the-Face were consolidated with File 1224 AGO 1874 and filmed on NA, M666, Roll 147. See also, File 4228 AGO 1875, on M666, Roll 225.

168. *Bismarck Tribune*, Nov. 27, 1875; Tom Custer arrived in Bismarck by special stage. The weekly stage trip, providing mail, freight, and passenger service between Bismarck and Fargo during winter months when the Northern Pacific Railroad ceased operations took four days in each direction. Occasionally an extra, or special stage, was added, as traffic warranted. *Bismarck Tribune*, June 23, and Nov. 20, 1875.

169. Tom to Emma Reed, June 12, 1876 Yellowstone River, O'Neil, *GarryOwen Tidbits VII*. Sgt. Knipe interview with Walter Camp, Feb. 13, 1909, WMC-IU.

D

Dalious, Jas. Cpl co A; b. Sunbury Pa.; enl 5 Nov 1872 Toledo Ohio for 5 yrs; age 21; railroader; brn eyes, dk hair, ruddy comp, 5' 10 1/2" high; join co A 2 Dec 1872 E'town Ky.; dd as pioneer Aug 1873; des 26 Mar 1875 Livingston Ala; apph next day at Selma Ala; sen gen cm 27 Apr 1875 forf $10 pay per mo for 6 mos & conft same period; dd qmd teamster Feb 1876; cpl 20 May 1876; killed dur retreat from valley fight 25 June 1876 (east side of river).

Dann, Geo. Pvt co D; b. Elmira N.Y.; enl in co D 3 June 1873 Ft Snelling Minn. for 5 yrs; age 21; laborer; blue eyes, lt hair, fair comp, 5' 8 1/4" high; ed hosp nurse 18 June to 31 Aug 1874; dd regtl hq fatigue pty June 1877; des 19 Mar 1878 Bismarck DT while on ds; enl as Guy F. Arlington 30 Dec 1879 Harrisburg Pa. for 5 yrs; assd to co E 19 inf; des 14 Mar 1880 Ft Garland Colo.; apph 3 days later Alamosa Colo.; dishon disch 20 May 1880 sen gen cm & 2 yrs conft mil prison Ft L'worth Kans.; surd as Geo. Dann 19 Mar 1881 while serving sen; rel from prison 10 Jan 1882.

Darcey, Jas. Wilber. Pvt co M; b. 2 Aug 1849 Laurel Md; enl as Jas. Wilber 8 Sep 1875 Chicago Ill. for 5 yrs; age 26; laborer; hazel eyes, lt hair, fair comp, 5' 8 3/4" high; join co M 21 Oct 1875 Ft Rice DT; gsw l. leg 26 June 1876 on Reno hill (frac. tibia, severe, splints appd); tr on str *Far West* 3 July to hosp at Ft Lincoln; disch 1 Nov 1876 at Ft Lincoln on surg cert dis a pvt char good; died 13 July 1920 Sol. Home Wash'n D.C.
Pension: 19 Dec 1876 / Inv / 228917 / 145537. Ind. Surv. / 9827 / 7369. Wid / 15170 / 10153.

Darris, Jno. Pvt co E; b. Goshen N.Y.; pvt co K 1 NJ cav 27 Aug 1861; abs as des'r 2 June 1862 to 17 Apr 1863; sick hosp 18 Aug to 12 Nov 1863 (sim. frac. l. arm, accdt fall from horse); m.o. vol serv 31 May 1865; enl reg army 9 Sep 1875 Cincinnati Ohio for 5 yrs; age 29; fireman; blue eyes, brn hair, dk comp, 5' 6 1/2" high; join co E 7 cav 29 Oct 1875 Ft Totten DT; killed with Custer column 25 June 1876.[1]
Pension: 7 Nov 1877 / Minor / 234065 / 181884. 19 Apr 1916 / Wid / 1064760.

Davenport, Wm. H. Pvt co B; b. Williamsburg N.Y.; enl 15 Mar 1876 Boston Mass. for 5 yrs; age 22; policeman; blue eyes, lt brn hair, fair comp, 5' 9 1/4" high; join co B 27 Apr 1876 St Paul Minn.; sick field hosp 12–13 Aug 1876 (cont'n);[2] abs sick on str *Far West* 31 Aug 1876; ds cond mil convicts to Ft L'worth mil prison 20 Feb to 10 Mar 1877; sick on str *Far West* 17 May 1877; sick Ft Buford DT June 1877; sick (orchitis) Tongue River Cant'mt to 20 Aug when tr to Ft Lincoln DT; duty 23 Aug; sick Ft Lincoln Oct 1877 (infl. testicle); dd post hq 20 Nov 1877; sick hosp 5 Dec 1877 (infl. testicle); disch 19 Dec 1877 at Ft Lincoln on surg cert dis a pvt char good (chr. infl. l. testicle; thrown against pommel of saddle 24 June 1876; no probability of complete cure); employed as actor in theatre at Bismarck & Fargo to 1887 when he moved to Montana;[3] died 18 Dec. 1904 Missoula MT.[4]

Davern, Edw. Pvt co F; b. Limerick Ireland; enl 16 May 1864 Cleveland Ohio for 3 yrs; age 19; brass finishing; grey eyes, brn hair, ruddy comp, 5' 7 1/2" high; assd to co G 5 cav; disch 16 May 1867 Montgomery Ala expir of serv a pvt; reenl 12 Aug 1867 New York N.Y. for 5 yrs; age 21; join co F 7 cav 8 Sep 1867 Ft Hays Kans.; cpl 17 Dec 1867; pvt 21 Dec 1867; cpl 3 Jan 1868; pvt 8 Apr 1868 sen gen cm & forf $12 pay per mo for 12 mos; unexpired portion of sen rem'd 18 Aug 1868; sgt 1 Sep 1868; 1sgt Apr 1869; in arrest Oct 1869; pvt 1 Jan 1870; cpl 1 Mar 1871; pvt 20 June 1871; disch 12 Aug 1872 Louisville Ky. expir of serv & reenl in co F for 5 yrs; cpl 17 Oct 1872; pvt 27 May 1873; sgt 1 Oct 1873 & actg co qm sgt to Jan 1874; actg 1sgt Feb 1874; pvt 25 Sep 1874; in conft Oct 1874; dd co cook Aug 1875; dd orderly to comdg officer r. wing [maj Reno] 15 May

1876; dd regtl hq Aug 1876; sgt 27 Sep 1876; dd prov sgt Dec 1876 & Jan 1877; disch 12 Aug 1877 camp on Yellowstone River MT expir of serv a sgt char xclt & reenl in co F for 5 yrs; gsw l. arm (fl. wd.) 13 Sep 1877 Canon Creek MT in action with Nez Perce inds; tr in mackinaw boat 22 Sep to hosp Cant'mt Tongue River; tr to hosp Ft Lincoln DT 20 Oct & arr 30 Oct; tr to Ft Totten DT 4 Nov 1877 with detmt of co F; ed post qm sgt Feb to Sep 1878; ds Chicago Ill. Jan 1879 witness in Reno court of inq;[5] sen gen cm 18 Dec 1880 forf $10 pay per mo for 5 mos; dd chg co mess June 1881; pvt 16 Sep 1881 sen gen cm & forf $10 pay per mo for 3 mos; dd co cook Feb 1882; disch 11 Aug 1882 camp near Ft Snelling Minn. expir of serv a pvt char xclt; reenl 31 Aug 1882 at Ft Snelling for 5 yrs; join co F 6 Sep 1882 Camp Villard (near Billings) MT; dd co cook Dec 1882; dd co cook Apr 1883; dd co cook Oct 1883; dd asst co cook Dec 1884; dd co cook June 1885; cpl 1 Jan 1887; dd actg co qm sgt June 1887; disch 31 Aug 1887 Ft Meade DT expir of serv a cpl char xclt & reenl in co F for 5 yrs; acquited in gen cm 11 Feb 1888; pvt 25 Mar 1888; dd co cook Dec 1888; cpl 1 Nov 1889; pvt 4 Apr 1890; sd co tailor Aug 1891; cpl 12 Oct 1891; sgt 13 Jan 1892; pvt 10 Apr 1892; disch 30 Aug 1892 Ft Myer Va. expir of serv a pvt char good & reenl two days later in co F; retd 2 Nov 1892 Wash'n D.C. a pvt char good; died 10 Aug 1896 at Wash'n (heat stroke [asthenia]); age 52; single.[6]

Davis, Henry Harrison. Pvt co M; b. 19 Jan 1846 Fayette City Pa.; pvt co A 193 Pa. inf 13 July to 9 Nov 1864; pvt co M 4 Pa. cav 2 Feb to 1 July 1865; enl reg army 21 Dec 1866 St Louis Mo. for 5 yrs; age 21; miner; brn eyes, sandy hair, ruddy comp, 5' 6 1/2" high; join co M 7 cav 22 Jan 1867 Ft Riley Kans.; sick field hosp 16 Oct 1868 (ac. diar.); tr to hosp Ft Dodge Kans. 25 Oct 1868; duty 17 Nov 1868; far'r Dec 1869; pvt 30 Jan 1870; ed qmd laborer Oct 1870 to Jan 1871; disch 21 Dec 1871 Unionville SC expir of serv a pvt & reenl in co M for 5 yrs; dd subs dept herder Aug 1873; dd hq Yellowstone Exp'n Sep 1873; dd pioneer hq Blk Hills Exp'n June thro' Aug 1874; in conft Oct 1874; dd subs dept herder Nov 1874 to Jan 1875; dd co cook Aug 1875; dd qmd teamster Nov 1875 to May 1876; with pack train 25 June 1876;[7] cpl 1 Aug 1876; pvt 16 Oct 1876; disch 21 Dec 1876 Ft Rice DT expir of serv a pvt char xclt; reenl 4 Jan 1879 Ft Lincoln DT for 5 yrs in co H 7 cav; dd co cook Apr 1879; tr to co M 18 Aug 1879; dd co gardener Apr 1882; disch 3 Jan 1884 Ft Meade DT expir of serv a pvt char very good; reenl 7 Jan 1884 at Ft Meade for 5 yrs in co E 7 cav; ed qmd laborer Feb 1887; ed qmd teamster Oct 1887 to Jan 1889; disch 6 Jan 1889 Ft Sill IT expir of serv a pvt char xclt; died 21 May 1918 Monessen Pa.
Pension: 9 July 1890 / Inv / 800690 / 620497. Wid / 1121851 / 905064.

Davis, Wm. Pvt co E; b. Vandalia Ill.; enl 19 Dec 1874 St Louis Mo. for 5 yrs; age 23; laborer; grey eyes, brn hair, fair comp, 5' 6" high; join co E 8 Feb 1875 Opelika Ala; des 25 Feb 1875 at Opelika & apph 3 days later Loachapoka Ala; sen gen cm 24 Apr 1875 forf $10 pay per mo for 6 mos & conft same period; dd hq fatigue pty r. wing (morn & eve) 15 May 1876; killed with Custer column 25 June 1876.
Pension: 8 July 1882 / Mother / 294492 / 209142.

Dawsey, David Edw. Pvt co D; b. Belleville Ohio; enl 17 Dec 1872 Toledo Ohio for 5 yrs; age 21; farmer; grey eyes, sandy hair, sandy comp, 5' 4 1/2" high; join co D 10 Feb 1873 Opelika Ala; dd detmt hq fatigue duty Aug 1873 escort NBS; ed qmd teamster Oct 1873; in conft Dec 1873 to May 1874; sen gen cm 18 Apr 1874 forf $10 pay per mo for 3 mos; (recom by Lt Edgerly for medal of honor for conspic gal at LBH; [Edgerly not sure if Dawsey or Horn helped Holden bring up amm'n to the men thro' a galling fire without flinching]);[8] dd subs dept herder June 1877; killed 30 Sep 1877 Snake Creek MT (Bear's Paw Mtns) in action with Nez Perce inds.

Day, Clarence F. Pvt co D; b. South Asley Mass.; enl 1 Feb 1870 Cincinnati Ohio for 5 yrs; age 21; carpenter; blue eyes, lt hair, fair comp, 5' 5" high; join co D 19 Feb 1870 Ft Harker Kans.; des 19 June 1871 Mt Vernon Ky.; apph 15 Oct 1872 at Cincinnati; sen gen cm 3 Mar 1873 forf $10 pay per mo for 12 mos; tr under gd to sta of co 30 Apr 1873; in conft Ft Rice DT May to Sep 1873 & in conft Ft Lincoln DT to Dec 1873; awaiting transp to 26 June 1874 when sent to Ft Buford DT to join co on NBS; disch 19 May 1876 at Ft Lincoln by expir of serv a pvt (made good time lost by des'n).

Day, Jno. H. Pvt co H; b. Warren Co. Ind.; enl 23 Sep 1873 Chicago Ill. for 5 yrs; age 22 1/12; shoemaker; hazel eyes, auburn hair, fair comp, 5' 7" high; join co H 20 Oct 1873 Ft Rice DT; dd subs dept Feb to Apr 1874; with pack train June 1876;[9] dd co cook Oct 1877; disch 23 Sep 1878 Ft Lincoln DT expir of serv a pvt char "this man has done his duty well since being in my co;" reenl 19 Oct 1878 St Louis Bks Mo. for 5 yrs; assd to co F 4 cav; des while on furl 12 Apr 1882; apph 23 Dec 1882 San Marcia NM; dishon disch 12 Mar 1883 Ft Cummings NM sen gen cm & 3 yrs conft mil prison Ft L'worth Kans.; sen reduced & rel from prison 14 Sep 1884; died 13 June 1894 Monroe La. (murdered).
Pension: 27 Aug 1890 / Inv / 1012048; (rej, no title under act 27 June 1890, serv not dur Rebellion). Wid / 719447; (rej on grd sol.'s death by murder was not due to mil serv).

Deetline, Fred'k. Blks co D; b. Offenheim Germany; enl 21 July 1870 Baltimore Md for 5 yrs; age 24 4/12; laborer; grey eyes, brn hair, fair comp, 5' 10 3/4" high; assd to co C 22 inf; disch 21 July 1875 Ft Brady Mich. expir of serv a pvt; reenl 5 Aug 1875 at Baltimore for 5 yrs; join co D 7 cav 21 Oct 1875 Ft Lincoln DT; appt blks Dec 1875; gsw r. shoulder 30 Sep 1877 Snake Creek MT (Bear's Paw Mtns) in action with Nez Perce inds; tr to str *Silver City* 14 Oct at mouth of Squaw Creek (on Mo. River); adm to hosp Ft Rice DT 26 Oct 1877; duty 6 Jan 1878; ds Fargo DT 28 June to 26 Nov 1878; (awarded medal of honor 5 Oct 1878 for bringing water to wounded [at LBH] while under heavy fire); cpl 11 Jan 1879; dd actg co qm sgt Apr to June 1880; sgt 19 June 1880; disch 4 Aug 1880 Ft Yates DT expir of serv a sgt char xclt; reenl 21 June 1881 St Louis Mo. for 5 yrs; assd to co G 5 cav; disch 20 June 1886 Ft Reno IT expir of serv a sgt char xclt; reenl 8 Sep 1886 Ft Walla Walla WT for 5 yrs; assd to co B 2 cav; disch 7 Sep 1891 Ft Huachuca AT expir of serv a sgt char xclt; reenl 29 Sep 1891 Ft Reno IT for 5 yrs in co G 5 cav; tr to co B 2 cav; disch 28 Sep 1896 Denver Colo. expir of serv a sgt char xclt & reenl in same co for 3 yrs; disch 28 Sep 1899 Santa Clara Cuba expir of serv a qm-sgt char xclt & reenl for 3 yrs; retd 29 July 1900 a qm-sgt char xclt; died 13 Dec 1910 San Antonio Tex.[10]

Deihle, Jacob. Pvt co A; b. Wurtemburg Germany; enl 1 Oct 1875 New York N.Y. for 5 yrs; age 22; bartender; grey eyes, brn hair, ruddy comp, 5' 6 1/2" high; join co A 21 Oct 1875 Ft Lincoln DT; orderly for capt Moylan 25 June 1876; gsw l. cheek (lost 4 teeth) 26 June 1876 on Reno hill; tr on str *Far West* 3 July to hosp Ft Lincoln; duty 10 Aug 1876; dd co garden 31 Aug 1876; ds Ft Lincoln 17 Oct 1876 chg co prop; ds Ft Rice DT Apr to Nov 1877; ds Ft Lincoln July to Nov 1878; disch 30 Sep 1880 Ft Meade DT expir of serv a pvt char xclt; reenl 30 Nov 1880 Louisville Ky. for 5 yrs; assd to co C 8 cav; sick Ft Clark Tex. 20 June to 15 Aug 1882 (frac. r. forearm [horse fell]); on furl 2 mos 10 May 1884; sick 1 July to 11 Sep 1884 San Antonio Tex. when disch on surg cert dis (chr. rheum.) a sgt; died 2 Sep 1885 Sol. Home Wash'n D.C.
Pension: 24 Sep 1884 / Inv / 523046 / 294365.

DeLacy, Milton J. Sgt co I; b. Ulster Co. N.Y.; enl 13 May 1870 St Louis Mo. for 5 yrs; age 23; clerk; blue eyes, red hair, lt comp, 5' 5 3/4" high; join co I 26 June 1870 Ft L'worth Kans.; dd co clerk Apr 1871; ed qmd June to Aug 1871; cpl 27 Sep 1871; ed subs dept 29 Sep 1871; sgt 7 Nov 1871; sick hosp Shelbyville Ky. 5 Aug to 11 Sep 1872 (prim. syph.); sick hosp Lebanon Ky. 2 Jan to 23 Feb 1873 (syph.); co qm sgt June to Sep 1873 (battn qm sgt 9 June to 31 Aug 1873); disch 13 May 1875 Ft Lincoln DT expir of serv a sgt & reenl in co I for 5 yrs; with pack train 25 June 1876 (actg co qm sgt);[11] found capt Keogh's horse Comanche in ravine 28 June;[12] 1sgt 3 Aug 1876 (suspended 7 Aug); sen field court martial 22 Aug 1876 forf $10 pay (awol) but sen rem'd by maj Reno in consid'n of length of serv & faithful disch of duty; in arrest Dec 1876 & in conft thro' Apr 1877; pvt 28 Jan 1877; dishon disch 21 Apr 1877 sen gen cm & 2 yrs conft mil prison Ft L'worth Kans.; escaped from post guardhouse at Ft Lincoln 8 May 1877.[13]

Delaney, Mich'l. Pvt co K; b. Broome Co. N.Y.; enl 20 May 1875 Cincinnati Ohio for 5 yrs; age 21; clerk; blue eyes, brn hair, dk comp, 5' 8 1/4" high; join co K 27 Apr 1876 St Paul Minn.; ds camp Powder River MT 15 June 1876; gsw r. thumb 7 July & tr on str *Josephine* 19 July to hosp at Ft Lincoln DT; ed hosp nurse 12 Aug to 4 Oct 1876; dd co clerk Oct 1876; cpl 1 Aug 1877; gsw thro' lung 30 Sep 1877 Snake Creek MT (Bear's Paw Mtns) in action with Nez Perce inds; tr to str *Silver City* 14 Oct at mouth of Squaw Creek (on Mo. River); adm to hosp Ft Lincoln 26 Oct 1877; sgt 12 Nov 1877; tr to hosp Ft Rice DT 15 Jan 1878; disch 20 May 1878 at Ft Rice on surg cert dis a sgt char xclt (effects gsw thorax & r. side; dis 3/4); died 12 Feb 1884 Olney Ill.
Pension: 21 June 1878 / Inv / 257543 / 157284. Wid / 313736 / 206038. Ind. Wid / 14117. (XC-2,661,891).

Delliehausen, Eduard Gustaf. Pvt co D; b. 14 Feb 1848 Frankfurt Germany; enl 20 Dec 1866 New York N.Y. for 3 yrs; age 21; mason; brn eyes, blk hair, dk comp, 5' 8" high; join co C 33 inf Jan 1867 Macon Ga.; des 17 July 1867 Atlanta Ga.; enl as Edw. Housen 5 July 1870 Cincinnati Ohio for 5 yrs; join co D 7 cav 17 July 1870 camp near Ft Hays Kans.; dd co cook Apr 1872; des 18 June 1872 Opelika Ala; surd 5 Nov 1873 New York N.Y. under GO 102 AGO 1873; join St Louis Bks 15 Nov 1873; ds Ft Snelling Minn. 1 Jan to 14 July 1874; ds Ft Lincoln DT till 7 Aug 1874 when sent with govt horses to Ft Totten DT & await return of co from field; killed 26 June 1876 on Reno hill.[14]

Demoss, Chas. Pvt co A; b. Nelson Co. Ohio; enl 24 Aug 1866 Cincinnati Ohio for 5 yrs; age 26; farmer; blue eyes, dk hair, dk comp, 5' 9 1/2" high; join co A 10 Sep 1866 Ft Riley Kans.; in conft Dec 1866; des 20 Feb 1867 at Ft Riley; (a civilian Wm. H. Stroud [tho't to be Demoss] was apph at St Louis 17 Feb 1876 & tr to Ft Lincoln DT [with Lt Reily's detmt] where court martial failed to identify him as Demoss); surd 29 Jan 1879 at St Louis; dishon disch 14 Feb 1879 sen gen cm & 4 yrs conft hard labor (remitted).

DeRudio, Chas. [Carlo] Camillo. 1Lt co E; b. 26 Aug 1832 Belluno Venetia (a count by noble birth); cadet Austrian mil academy at Milan 1845–48; patriot in fight for Italian independence & exiled to England in 1855; arrested at Paris France 14 Jan 1858 in plot on life of Napoleon III; sen to the guillotine but upon the plea of his English wife to Empress Eugenié sen commuted to life in prison (at Fr. Guiana);[15] escaped to British Guiana in 1859 & recd passage to England; came to America Feb 1864 & app'd for com'n in union army; enr 25 Aug 1864 NYC a pvt 79 N.Y. inf; age 32; blk eyes, blk hair, dk comp, 5' 7" high; join co A 29 Sep 1864 near Petersburg Va.; disch 19 Oct 1864 to accept com'n 2Lt 2 US col'd inf; join co D 11 Nov 1864 Key West Fla; m.o. vol serv 5 Jan 1866 at Key West; appt reg army com'n 2Lt 2 inf 31 Aug 1867 but canceled 21 Sep when rej by med bd;[16] cancellation annulled 4 Nov upon reexam'n & favorable result; join co F 28 Nov 1867 Louisville Ky.; comd mtd detmt Sep 1868 to Apr 1869; unassd 17 Apr 1869 (when 16 inf consol with 2 inf); tr to 7 cav 14 July 1869 (recom'n gen Thomas); join co H 25 Aug 1869 near Ft Hays Kans.; with co in field June to Sep 1873; ds regtl hq St Paul Minn. Jan thro' June 1874 with bd purchasing horses; ds Ft Rice DT July & Aug 1874; prom 1Lt co E 15 Dec 1875; ds with co H to 1 May 1876;[17] assd td with co A 12 May; appt adjt l. wing 17 May; attd to co A 22 June;[18] left behind dur retreat from valley fight 25 June when he stopped to retrieve guidon & his horse pulled away; rejoined co night of 26 June; given horse of sgt. Pahl 27 June by capt Benteen;[19] comd co E from 30 June 1876;[20] comd co in field May to Nov 1877 (with Lt Doane 2 cav & his Crow scouts from Cant'mt Tongue River 2 Aug & rejoin 7 cav 25 Oct mouth of Squaw Creek [Camp Owen Hale] on Missouri River); ds Chicago Ill. Jan 1879 witness in Reno court of inq; capt co H 1 Feb 1883; ds

rctg duty Sep 1884 to Oct 1886 NYC; sick qrs 8 Dec 1890 & awl on surg cert 30 Dec 1890 to 30 Sep 1891; tr to co D 29 June 1893 Ft Sam Houston Tex.; ds San Diego Calif. 2 May 1896 awaiting retirement; retd 26 Aug 1896; maj on retd list 23 Apr 1904; died 1 Nov 1910 Los Angeles Calif.[21]
[2357 ACP 1872]. Pension: 8 Dec 1910 / Wid / 953863 / 716801.

DeTourriel, Louis. Pvt co B; b. Tours France; enl 3 Apr 1876 New York N.Y. for 5 yrs; age 21; farmer; blue eyes, brn hair, dk comp, 5' 5" high; join co B 27 Apr 1876 St Paul Minn.; ds camp Powder River MT 10 June 1876; des 30 Sep 1876 Ft Lincoln DT.

DeVoto, Augustus L. Pvt co B; b. 27 Feb 1851 Genoa Italy; enl 4 Oct 1873 St Louis Mo. for 5 yrs; age 22; bookbinder; hazel eyes, blk hair, dk comp, 5' 9" high; join co B 19 Oct 1873 Ft Lincoln DT; with pack train June 1876; dd qmd Dec 1877; disch 4 Oct 1878 Standing Rock Agcy DT expir of serv a pvt char good; died 3 Nov 1923 Tacoma Wash'n.[22]
Pension: 25 June 1906 / Inv / 1350037; (rej, no serv dur Rebellion). 2 June 1917 / Ind. Surv. / 13575 / 8428.

Dewey, Geo. W. Pvt co H; b. Middlebury Vt; enl in co H 13 Apr 1873 Yankton DT for 5 yrs; age 22; carpenter; grey eyes, dk hair, ruddy comp, 5' 6" high; dd co cook June to Aug 1877; disch 13 Apr 1878 Ft Rice DT expir of serv a pvt char xclt & reenl in co H for 5 yrs; dd co cook Apr to June 1878; des 11 Oct 1880 Ft Meade DT & apph 5 days later at Cheyenne River DT; dishon disch 18 Dec 1880 sen gen cm & 3 yrs conft mil prison Ft L'worth Kans.

DeWolf, Jas. Madison. Actg asst surg; b. 14 Jan 1843 Mehoopany Pa.; enr 28 May 1861 as pvt co A 1 Pa. art'y for 3 yrs; age 18; farmer; gray eyes, lt hair, lt comp, 5' 8" high; cpl 1 Aug 1861; gsw r. forearm 30 Aug 1862 in 2d battle of Bull Run; disch 29 Oct 1862 hosp Wash'n D.C. on surg cert dis (necrosis of ulna); employed as nurse in same hosp; reenl 1 Sep 1864 in former co for one yr; m.o. vol serv 13 June 1865 Richmond Va.; enl reg army 5 Oct 1865 New York N.Y. for 3 yrs; assd to co E 2 battn 14 inf; (redesig 23 inf regt Sep 1866); dd hosp attdt Jan to May 1866 when appt hosp stew'd; disch 5 Oct 1868 Camp Lyon Idaho Ty upon expir of serv a hosp stew'd & reenl for 3 yrs; disch 5 Oct 1871 Camp Warner Ore. by expir of serv a hosp stew'd & reenl for 5 yrs; tr to Watertown Ars'l Mass. 16 May 1873; grad Harvard Med School 25 June 1875 having attended one full term (Oct to June) med lectures & instr'n & one winter term (Feb to June) graduate course on regional anatomy & surgery; on furl 18 July to 30 Sep 1875; disch 5 Oct 1875 (upon own appn) at Watertown Ars'l per SO 189 AGO 1875; entered mil contr 23 Oct 1875 as actg asst surg in Dept of Dak.; arr Ft Totten eve 14 Nov (dur snow storm, having traveled by team from Fargo with wife);[23] with cos E & L 7 cav to Ft Lincoln 10 Mar 1876; delayed at Ft Seward (Jamestown) from 13 Mar awaiting removal of snow blockade on NPRR;[24] arr Bismarck 14 Apr on first train & encamped at Camp Hancock; crossed Missouri River on str *Union* 17 Apr to Ft Lincoln; joined gen Terry's exp'n 14 May assd to r. wing 7 cav (cos BCE-FIL) & scouts; on maj Reno's scout up Powder River 10–20 June; killed dur retreat from valley fight 25 June 1876 (eastside of river near hilltop); survived by wife, no ch.[25]
Pension: 14 Dec 1863 / Inv / 13335 / 21424 (temporary 18 mos). Wid / 227900 / 176398.

Diamond, Edw. Pvt co H; b. 11 June 1853 Stoughton Mass.; enl 18 Sep 1875 Boston Mass. for 5 yrs; age 22; crimper; gray eyes, dk brn hair, ruddy comp & 5' 5 3/4" high; join co H 29 Oct 1875 Ft Rice DT; dd qmd laborer 15 Mar to 4 May 1876; in conft 28 Nov 1876; sen gen cm 28 Dec 1876 forf $10 pay per mo for 3 mos; in conft Apr 1877 at Ft Rice; in conft May 1877 thro' Jan 1878 at Ft Lincoln awaiting trial; rejoin co 4 Feb 1878 at Ft Rice; dd co cook Apr 1879; dd co cook Aug 1879; disch 17 Sep 1880 Ft Meade DT expir of serv a pvt char fair; enl in marine corps 21 Dec 1880 at Boston for 5 yrs; disch 28 Dec 1885 Mare Isl Calif. upon expir of serv; reenl in army 5 Oct 1887 at Boston for 5 yrs; assd to co F 12 inf; disch 4 Jan 1891 Ft Lincoln N.Dak. per GO 80 AGO 1890 a pvt char xclt.[26]

Dohman, Anton. Pvt co F; b. Hanover Germany; enl 3 Aug 1866 Cincinnati O. for 5 yrs; age 21; barkeeper; blue eyes, brn hair, fair comp & 5' 2 1/2" high; join co F 10 Sep 1866 Ft Riley Kans.; dd co tailor Jan 1867; ds dept hq Apr 1867 chg of co prop; sick hosp Ft Hays Kans. 20 May to 8 June 1867; dd co tailor July to Nov 1867; ds June 1868; sick field hosp 25 Sep to 23 Oct 1868 (const. syph.); sent to post hosp Ft Dodge Kans. 9 Nov 1868; duty 4 Apr 1869; in conft 27 Apr 1869; ds June to Sep 1869 Ft Hays; in conft Oct & Dec 1869; ds Taylor Bks Ky. 22 July 1871; disch 3 Aug 1871 Meridian Miss by expir of serv & reenl for 5 yrs; dd co tailor Dec 1873 to May 1874; dd co tailor & awol Oct 1874; dd co tailor Dec 1874; in conft Dec 1875; in conft Feb 1876; killed with Custer column 25 June 1876.

Dolan, Jno. Pvt co M; b. 14 Apr 1843 Dublin Ireland; pvt co K 5 N.Y. cav 4 Oct 1861 to 19 July 1865; enl reg army 15 Feb 1866 Phil'a Pa. for 3 yrs; age 22; laborer; hazel eyes, dk hair, fair comp, 5' 10" high; join co H 1 cav 7 Apr 1866 Carlisle Bks Pa.; sick in hosp 14 Apr–2 July 1866 (opthalmia); cpl 20 May 1867; pvt 8 Apr 1868; cpl 20 Oct 1868; disch 15 Feb 1869 Camp Warner Ore. expir of serv a cpl; reenl 13 Mar 1869 Portland Ore. for 5 yrs in co I 1 cav; cpl 17 June 1869; sgt 1 Jan 1870; 1sgt 15 Oct 1870; des 10 June 1871 Benicia Bks Calif.; enl as Thos. Brown 1 Oct 1873 New York N.Y. for 5 yrs; join co M 7 cav 21 Oct 1873 Ft Rice DT; surd as des'r 17 Nov 1873 under GO 102 AGO 1873; restored to duty without trial 15 Apr 1874 & tr to co M to serv bal of orig'l enlmt; cpl 10 Dec 1874; sgt 2 Aug 1875; dd actg post prov sgt 8–22 Nov 1875; dd qmd chg of corral 22 Nov 1875 to 4 May 1876; pvt 14 June 1876 (recom'n co comdr);[27] ds dept hq on str *Far West* 22 June awaiting disch; disch 3 July 1876 camp mouth of Big Horn River MT expir of serv a pvt char xclt;[28] reenl 2 Aug 1876 St. Louis Bks Mo. for 5 yrs; join co B 7 cav 28 Sep 1876 at Ft Lincoln; cpl 7 Mar 1877; sgt 14 Dec 1880; dd prov sgt Feb & Apr 1881; awl 30 days 13 June 1881 Standing Rock Agcy; disch 1 Aug 1881 Ft Yates DT expir of serv a sgt char xclt; reenl 1 Jan 1882 Ft Lincoln DT in co L 7 cav for 5 yrs; cpl 2 Feb 1882; sgt 17 June 1882; dd co qm sgt Dec 1882; dd co qm sgt Oct 1883 to Mar 1884; disch 31 Dec 1886 Ft Buford DT expir of serv a sgt & reenl in co L for 5 yrs; on furl 4 mos 25 Jan 1887 Bismarck DT; ds 28 May–21 Aug 1887 at Ft Buford; pvt 27 July 1888; cpl 20 Oct 1888; sgt 4 Apr 1890; attd to co I 9 Sep 1890;[29] attd to co C 12 Dec 1890; sick qrs 27 Jan to 15 Feb 1891 (cont'n l. shoulder in train accdt enroute from Pine Ridge SD to Ft Riley Kans.); disch 31 Dec 1891 at Ft Riley expir of serv a sgt; reenl 26 Jan 1892 at Ft Riley for 5 yrs in co B 7 cav; tr to co I 7 Feb 1892; cpl 9 Mar 1892; sgt 27 July 1893; disch 10 Apr 1896 Ft Grant AT on surg cert dis (deafness both ears) a sgt char very good; died 31 Mar 1922 Ft Myer Va. Pension: 22 Apr 1896 / Inv / 1176782 / 923179.

Doll, Jacob W. Pvt co B; b. Russel England; enl 21 Mar 1876 Baltimore Md for 5 yrs; age 26; baker; brn eyes, blk hair, fair comp, 5' 7" high; join co B 27 Apr 1876 St. Paul Minn.; dd qmd teamster May 1876; ds camp Powder River MT 10 June 1876; dd teamster with wagon train Aug 1876; des 19 Nov 1877 Ft Lincoln, DT.

Donahoe, Jno. Sad'r co M; b. Galway Ireland; enl 24 Sep 1866 Boston Mass. for 5 yrs; age 23; shoemaker; hazel eyes, brn hair, lt comp, 5' 3" high; assd to co A 6 cav; disch 24 Sep 1871 Camp Lime Stone Creek Kans. expir of serv a sad'r; reenl 20 Oct 1871 Chicago Ill. for 5 yrs; join co M 7 cav as sad'r 22 Dec 1871 at Unionville SC; disch 20 Oct 1876 camp near Ft Lincoln DT expir of serv a sad'r char xclt & reenl in co M for 5 yrs; ds Ft Rice DT 22 Oct to 10 Nov 1876; in conft Dec 1877; disch 19 Oct 1881 Ft Meade DT expir of serv a sad'r char very good & reenl in co M for 5 yrs; in conft Feb 1885; in conft June 1885; disch 19 Oct 1886 at Ft Meade expir of serv a sad'r char xclt & reenl in co M for 5 yrs; tr to co G 9 Sep 1890; tr to co E 28 Oct 1890; disch 19 Oct 1891 Ft Riley Kans. expir of serv a sad'r char good & reenl in co E for 5 yrs; disch 19 Oct 1896 Ft Grant AT expir of serv a sad'r char xclt & reenl in co E; retd 11 Nov 1896 at Ft Grant a sad'r; died 16 Nov 1905 at San Francisco Calif. (heart failure).

Donahue, Jno. F. Pvt co K; b. 22 Feb 1853 Tipperary Ireland; enl 14 Dec 1874 Boston Mass. for 5 yrs; age 22; laborer; hazel eyes, dk hair, fair comp, 5' 9" high; join co K 9 Feb 1875 Colfax La.; with pack train June 1876;[30] dd asst co cook Oct 1877; (m. widow of sgt Finley 7 Feb 1878); dd orderly for gen cm Apr 1878; ds 4 July 1878 Ft Lincoln DT chg of surplus co horses; sick hosp 14 Aug to 18 Oct 1878 (typhoid fever); ds Ft Totten DT Nov 1878; dd post hq Dec 1878 to May 1879; disch 13 Dec 1879 at Ft Totten expir of serv a pvt char very good; enl 7 May 1898 Helena MT for 2 yrs in co K 1 MT inf; unfit for duty from 4 Oct 1898 acc't varicose veins both legs causing great pain performing duties (existed prior to enlmt); disch 21 Jan 1899 Manila P. I., on surg cert dis; died 3 Dec 1924 Butte MT.
Pension: 18 Apr 1917 / Ind. Surv. / 11318 / 9887; (dropped from roll 4 Aug 1923 acc't orig'l issue, act 5 June 1920 vets of war with Spain & Philippine Insurrection); Inv / 1481730 / 1230656. Wid / 1227183.

Donnelly, Timothy. Pvt co F; b. Dullington, England; enl 21 Sep 1875 Boston Mass. for 5 yrs; age 21 5/12; laborer; blue eyes, dk hair, fair comp, 5' 6" high; join 7 cav 21 Oct 1875 Ft Lincoln DT unassd rct; on duty with band Dec 1875 thro' Feb 1876; assd to co F 2 Mar; 1876; killed with Custer column 25 June 76.
Pension: 17 Mar 1877 / Mother / 230468. (Abandoned).

Dooley, Pat'k. Pvt co K; b. Queens Co Ireland; enl 4 Nov 1857 New York N.Y. for 5 yrs; age 25 8/12; laborer; blue eyes, brn hair, ruddy comp, 5' 6" high; assd to co B 2 cav; (redesig 5 cav Aug 1861); disch 4 Nov 1862 Falmouth Va. expir of serv a pvt; enr 6 Feb 1864 NYC a pvt (vet rct) co M 18 N.Y. Cav; tr to co A 22 Mar 1864; dd ambulance driver Sep to Nov 1864; dd cook regtl hosp Dec 1864 & Jan 1865; co cook May & June 1865; abs sick July to Oct 1865 hosp San Antonio Tex.; dd regtl hosp Mar & Apr 1866; m.o. vol serv 31 May 1866 Victoria Tex. a pvt; reenl reg army 11 Sep 1866 NYC for 5 yrs; join co K 7 cav 29 Sep 1866 Ft Riley Kans.; cpl 10 Oct 1866; sgt 27 Nov 1866; ds Ft Hays Kans. June 1867; pvt Feb 1868; cpl 6 Apr 1868; pvt 19 June 1868 & appt wag from 1 June 1868; far'r 1 Aug 1868; abs sick Ft Harker Kans. Oct 1868; cpl 4 Feb 1869; sgt 15 Sep 1870; disch 11 Sep 1871 Yorkville SC expir of serv a sgt; reenl same day in co K for 5 yrs & on furl 60 days NYC [see Mich'l Murphy]; pvt 16 Jan 1872; ds with detmt at Chester SC Mar 1872 to Jan 1873; dd co cook Feb & Apr 1873; abs sick (diar.) Ft Lincoln DT 15 May to 18 June 1876; disch 11 Sep 1876 at Ft Lincoln by expir of serv a pvt char xclt.

Dorman, Isaiah. Intrpr qmd; b Pa. ca. 1832;[31] his father was said to be a Jamaica negro & his mother indian;[32] he was also believed to be an escaped slave & of more than ordinary intelligence;[33] considered reliable & trustworthy he was long in the employ of officers on the frontier & recd the respect of the sol.'s in spite of his color;[34] he said he was with gen Sully in 1864–65 dur his campn against the Sioux;[35] from Nov 1865 he was often hired in the qmd at Ft Rice DT as courier & mail carrier to Ft Wadsworth;[36] also employed as woodcutter for Chas. Galpin & for the trading firm Durfee & Peck[37] at one time he had a woodyard a half-mile north of Standing Rock Agcy, the remains of dugouts he made could be seen for many years afterward;[38] (m. a Santee Sioux woman);[39] hired 9 Sep 1871 at Ft Rice as guide with the mil escort for surveyors of the NPRR to Yellowstone River;[40] upon return of the exp'n he was employed as post intrpr at Ft Rice from 19 Oct 1871;[41] rec'd contusion 1 Nov 1875 (no diag) & in hosp ten days;[42] ordered to Ft Lincoln 14 May 1876 to accomp gen Terry's exp'n as [Sioux] intrpr;[43] rate of pay $75 mo; he said he wanted to see the western country once more as he was getting old & would probably be his last campn;[44] killed dur Reno's retreat from the valley fight 25 June (on prairie dog town at end of bushes where battle began);[45] survived by wife, no ch.[46]

Dorn, Rich'd. Pvt co B; b. 12 Feb 1853 Bronson Mich.; enl 30 Jan 1872 Chicago Ill. for 5 yrs; age 21; laborer; gray eyes, dk hair, dk comp, 5' 9" high; join co B 26 Feb 1872 Spartanburg SC; in conft Oct & Dec 1872; sen gen cm 25 Nov 1872 forf $10 pay per mo

for 2 mos & conft same period; unfit to march with comd 11 Sep 1873 & tr on str *Josephine* from Ft Buford to Ft Lincoln DT; ed qmd teamster 26 Dec 1873; dd qmd teamster 1 Mar 1874; killed on Reno hill 26 June 1876 (while waking capt McDougall).[47]
Pension: 9 June 1885 / Mother / 327813 / 221284.

Dose, Henry. Trump'r co G; b. Holstein Germany; enl 4 Jan 1870 Davenport Iowa for 5 yrs; age 22; carpenter; gray eyes, brn hair, fair comp, 5' 6" high; join co I 3 inf 28 July 1870 Ft Lyon Colo. Ty; ed qmd Nov 1870 to July 1871; appt artf'r 1 Sep 1871; dd qmd Aug to Dec 1872; ed qmd Feb to July 1874; disch 4 Jan 1875 Alexandria La. expir of serv an artf'r; reenl 1 Feb 1875 Shreveport La. for 5 yrs in co G 7 cav (auth AGO); trump'r 17 June 1875; in conft Oct 1875; dd qmd carpenter Dec 1875; ed qmd carpenter Feb 1876; dd 1–19 June 1876; killed with Custer column 25 June 1876 (orderly trump'r to gen Custer); surv by wife & 2 ch; (widow m. sgt Garlick 22 Nov 1876).[48]
Pension: 24 Feb 1879 / Wid / 241901 / 195433. Minor / 241902 / 195434.

Dougherty, Jas. Cpl co B; b. 29 Feb 1856 Oxford NJ; enl 5 Dec 1872 Wilkes-Barre Pa. for 5 yrs; age 21; brakesman; gray eyes, dk hair, ruddy comp, 5' 7 3/4" high; join co B 13 Feb 1873 Spartanburg SC; in conft Dec 1873; ds Wash'n D.C. 27 Apr 1875 [escort pvt Flood to govt hosp];[49] cpl 24 July 1875; dd actg co qm sgt Aug 1875 to May 1876; sgt 9 June 1877; disch 5 Dec 1877 Standing Rock DT expir of serv a sgt char good; reenl 13 May 1878 New York N.Y. for 5 yrs; assd to co E 17 inf; disch 12 May 1883 Ft Custer MT expir of serv a sgt char good; died 6 Oct 1884 Nicholson Pa.[50]

Downing, Alexander. Pvt co F; b. New Madison Ohio; pvt co G 145 Ill. inf (100 days troops) 30 Apr to 23 Sep 1864; pvt co A 39 Ohio inf 9 Jan to 9 July 1865; enl reg army 18 Sep 1875 Cincinnati Ohio for 5 yrs; age 27; farmer; gray eyes, brn hair, dk comp, 5' 7 1/2" high; join co F 21 Oct 1875 Ft Lincoln DT; dd with band from Dec 1875; ds Ft Lincoln 13 May 1876 chg of band prop & garden; sent with Lt Garlington on str *Josephine* 24 July to join co in field; ret to post 10 Aug on str *Durfee*; blks 11 Oct 1876; pvt 22 Apr 1877; tr to co A 4 May 1877; blks 30 May 1877; disch 17 Sep 1880 Ft Meade DT expir of serv a blks char xclt; died 2 Aug 1884 Pleasant Hill Ohio.
Pension: 16 Mar 1883 / Inv / 476215 / 247516. Wid / 324618 / 246465.

Downing, Thos. P. Pvt co I; b. 6 Mar 1856 Limerick Ireland; enl in co I 12 Feb 1873 Lebanon Ky. for 5 yrs; age 21; laborer; blue eyes, sandy hair, florid comp, 5' 8 1/4" high; dd clerk hq NBS Aug 1873; ed qmd laborer Dec 1873; killed with Custer column 25 June 1876.
Pension: 14 Oct 1876 / Mother / 228360 / 180728.

Drago, Henry. Sgt co F; b. Lucas Co Ohio; pvt co K 14 Ohio inf (3 mo troops) 25 Apr to 13 Aug 1861; enr 8 Nov 1861 a pvt co K 67 Ohio inf for 3 yrs; sick hosp 28 Dec 1862 to 26 Aug 1863 when disch on surg cert dis (cardiac disease); enr 26 Dec 1863 a pvt 25 Ohio inf for 3 yrs; join from rct depot 7 Mar 1864; dd div pioneer Feb 1865; ds signal corps Apr 1865; dd mtd orderly & courier Sep 1865 to Feb 1866; des 12 Mar 1866 Columbia SC; [chg of des'n removed 14 July 1884 to complete mil rec]; enl reg army 15 Aug 1866 Toledo Ohio for 5 yrs; age 28; sailor; hazel eyes, dk hair, dk comp, 5' 7" high; join co F 7 cav 10 Sep 1866 Ft Riley Kans.; dd bldg co qrs Oct 1866; dd blks helper Dec 1866; sgt 23 Jan 1867; dd bldg stables Feb 1867; pvt 26 Feb 1868 sen gen cm & forf one mos pay; with escort for peace com'n Apr to June 1868; cpl 7 June 1868; pvt 20 Aug 1868; cpl 17 Sep 1868; sgt 20 Sep 1869; 1sgt 22 Sep 1869; sgt 1 Mar 1870; ds Taylor Bks Ky. 22 July 1871; disch 15 Aug 1871 Louisville Ky. by expir of serv a sgt & reenl for 5 yrs; 1sgt 1 Mar 1872; pvt 20 Nov 1873; dd co gardener June & Aug 1875; cpl 1 Oct 1875 & actg co qm sgt; sgt 26 Dec 1875; ds Ft Lincoln DT 13 May 1876 chg co prop & garden; disch 15 Aug 1876 at Ft Lincoln by expir of serv a sgt char xclt; reenl in co F 29 Aug 1876 at Ft Lincoln for 5 yrs; sgt 25 Sep to date 1 Sep 1876; dd qmd 12–28 Sep with 281 cav horses at post; ds Ft Lincoln 16

Oct chg co prop; (baggage & dismtd men co F tr to Ft Abercrombie 15 Nov); in arrest 12 Dec 1876; dd actg co qm sgt June 1877 to May 1880; sick hosp 23 Mar to 13 Apr 1880 (broken rib); ds Ft Totten DT May to Nov 1880 chg co prop; ds Ft Buford DT Dec 1880 chg co prop; sick hosp Ft Buford 27 Jan to 26 Mar 1881 when disch on surg cert dis (chr. rheum.) a sgt; took passage on str *General Sherman* 22 Apr 1881 to Bismarck [with pvt Schlieper];[51] died 14 July 1892 Toledo Ohio. Pension: 19 May 1881 / Inv / 422396 / 200805.

Drinan, Jas. Pvt co A; b. Cork Ireland; enl 2 Dec 1874 Boston Mass. for 5 yrs; age 21; laborer; gray eyes, lt brn hair, fair comp, 5' 7 3/8" high; join co A 6 Feb 1875 Livingston Ala; dd qmd laborer Oct 1875 to Mar 1876; killed dur retreat from valley fight 25 June 1876.[52]

Driscoll, Edw. Pvt co I; b. Waterford Ireland; enl 19 May 1873 Chicago Ill. for 5 yrs; age 22; laborer; hazel eyes, lt hair, lt comp, 5' 6" high; join co I 3 June 1873 Ft Snelling Minn.; dd fatigue duty Aug 1873 (escort NBS); in conft June & Aug 1875; sen gen cm 21 Aug 1875 forf $10 pay per mo for 6 mos & conft same period; killed with Custer column 25 June 1876.

Duggan, Jno. See Crowley, Jno.

Durselew, Otto. Pvt co A; b. Frankfurt, Germany; enl 5 Dec 1874 New York N.Y. for 5 yrs; age 24; clerk; blue eyes, lt brn hair, fair comp, 5' 9" high; join co A 6 Feb 1875 Livingston Ala; cpl 15 July 1876 to date 1 July 1876; sgt 1 Feb 1877; killed 30 Sep 1877 Snake Creek MT (Bear's Paw Mtns) in action with Nez Perce inds.[53]

Dwyer, Edmond. Pvt co G; b. Fairfax Co Va.; enl 14 Apr 1876 St Louis Mo. for 5 yrs; age 25 4/12; laborer; blue eyes, brn hair, fair comp, 5' 5 1/2" high; join co G 27 Apr 1876 St Paul Minn.; dd 5–18 June & 1 Aug to 1 Sep 1876;[54] cited by capt Benteen for conspic gal in two mtd chgs against Nez Perce inds 13 Sep 1877 Canon Creek MT; dd cooking for band Dec 1877 & Feb 1878; dd asst co cook June 1878; des 15 Aug 1878 Camp J. G. Sturgis DT; surd 8 Nov 1880 Ft L'worth Kans.; dishon disch 26 Jan 1881 sen gen cm & 2 yrs conft in mil prison.

Dye, Wm. Pvt co L; b. July 1850 Marietta Ohio; enl 23 Sep 1875 Cincinnati Ohio for 5 yrs; age 25; butcher; brn eyes, blk hair, fair comp, 5' 9 1/2" high; join co L 29 Oct 1875 Ft Totten DT; killed with Custer column 25 June 1876.

Notes—D

1. A boot with initials "J. D." containing human bones was found in Deep Coulee in 1904. Greene, *Evidence and the Custer Enigma*, 33.
2. RG 94, Entry 544, MT, Prescription Book No. 14, (missing pages Aug. 9–11, 1876); in a letter to Capt. E. W. Smith, aide-de-camp to Gen. Terry, on Aug. 15, 1876, Maj. Reno reported the number of extra horses, including one horse in Company B, the horse of a man kicked and sent in the wagon train the day the regiment left the Rosebud (Aug. 11). NA, M1734, Roll 18; see also note W50 (Wight).
3. Mentioned in numerous issues of *Bismarck Tribune* from March 1878.
4. *The Daily Missoulian* (Missoula, Mont.), Dec. 19, 1904; *The Fargo (N.Dak.) Forum*, Dec. 20, 1904. Obituary declares Will Davenport born 1852 at Boston.
5. Testified Jan. 30, 31, and Feb. 2, and described as a young trooper with an ancient Hibernian accent. Utley, *The Reno Court of Inquiry,* 279.
6. RG 94, Entry 25, file 40157 AGO 1892.
7. Walter Camp, rosters, IU; Rutten named Davis in valley fight. Sgt. Ryan said he superintended burying General and Tom Custer on June 28 and had with him Privates Harrison Davis, Frank Neely, and James Severs. Ryan to Camp, Feb. 26, 1910, WMC-LBHB.
8. RG 94, Entry 409, file 10818 A (EB) 1878.
9. In his application for pension (for hernia), John Day declared that, during the night march from Custer's battleground to the Big Horn River June 27, 1876, he was on duty with the pack train; the prairie had been on fire, stumps were burned out, leaving holes in the ground, and his horse stepped in

one, and the horse falling ruptured his (Day's) left side. He was treated in hospital in camp at mouth of Big Horn.

10. *Newsletter* (LBHA), Vol. XII, Nov. 1978, 4.

11. Utley, *The Reno Court of Inquiry,* 121; Walter Camp, rosters, LBHB; Henry Jones to Walter Camp, June 2, 1911, WMC-BYU.

12. *Bismarck Tribune*, May 10, 1878.

13. DeLacy was awol Dec. 18–19, 1876 and under the influence of intoxicating liquor in presence of men of his troop at Ft Lincoln Dec.18. The next day he ordered Sgt. Gaffney to take 12 sacks of oats from government stables at Fort Lincoln to Bismarck and exchange same for fowls and vegetables. On May 2 DeLacy applied to Capt. Nowlan to have his sentence remitted, and Nowlan recommended the reviewing authority mitigate the sentence because the offense was committed openly with evident intent of benefiting the company, with total absence of self consideration or gain, and while culpable, his mistaken zeal for the supposed interest of the company led him to the crime. Nowlan added that DeLacy had served seven years in the troop, had always been a faithful and efficient soldier, and had been recommended for distinguished gallantry at the Little Big Horn. Col. Sturgis' agreed that the case appeared to be mistaken zeal rather than criminal intent. NA, M1734, Roll 19.

14. In Sept. 1876, Housen's father applied through the U.S. Consulate in Frankfurt Germany for a death certificate, a copy of which was sent, through Lt. Harrington, *USS Juniata* at New London, Conn., to the lady formerly engaged to Housen. RG 94, Entry 409, file 11366 A (EB) AGO 1876.

15. DeRudio's wife succeeded in interesting John Walter of the *London Times*, who circulated a petition in her husband's behalf, signed by Sir Richard Main and others influential at the British Court. Queen Victoria instructed the British ambassador at Paris to make a personal appeal to the French Empress. Stone, "Things Seen."

16. The cancellation of DeRudio's appointment was understood to have resulted from his involvement in the plot against Napoleon III being called to the attention of the War Department. Magnussen, *Peter Thompson's Narrative*, 246.

17. DeRudio wrote to Gen. Sherman, April 18, 1876, requesting an order assigning him to duty with the company to which his promotion carried him. The unusual delay seemed extraordinary especially as another 1st lieutenant had been placed in command of his company, leaving him unidentified with any, and his regiment on the eve of an expedition in which he expected to participate.

After the arrival of Gen. Terry at Fort Lincoln, May 10, DeRudio requested a personal interview, stating that his present anomalous position reflected on his ten years service as an officer and tended to prejudice his character and qualifications in the eyes of his fellow officers. Maj. Reno forwarded the request with remark that he did so without entering into the personal merits of the case, as neither officer had served under him in the field, but the claim of Lt. DeRudio was based on justice; the rules of the service giving him the right to command the company and if he could not do so after ten years service than he should certainly not remain a commissioned officer of the army.

Gen. Terry informed DeRudio May 14 that he "would not answer his communication at present," and DeRudio then wrote to the adjutant general in Washington that he regarded the manner of his treatment by the present regimental commander unjust, which was sanctioned by the department commander, and he requested action may be taken on his request of last April. He stated further that 1st Lt. Smith had been assigned to command his (DeRudio's) Company "E," whereas he (DeRudio) was assigned to Company "A," to which Smith properly belonged, and hoped the general of the army would adjust his lawful claim by ordering him to assume command of his own company.

Gen. Custer explained that DeRudio was the junior 1st Lt. of the regiment, having been only recently promoted to that grade, whereas Lt. Smith had held the grade for several years and was an officer of extensive experience not only as a company commander but in service against hostile Indians. DeRudio possessed neither the experience nor ability of Smith, nor was he a fit person (in Custer's opinion) to receive not only the command of, but to be the only officer present with, a cavalry company, liable to be called on at any moment to engage hostile Indians. DeRudio was a confirmed grumbler, and according to his own confession, he was a natural conspirator, having once barely avoided the death penalty for conspiring against the life of the sovereign of the land in which he formerly resided. He is, all things considered, the inferior of every 1st lieutenant in the regiment as an efficient and subordinate officer. His transfer to "A" Company was made partially at his request and to give two officers to each company. No better commentary could probably be made on the value of Lt. DeRudio's services as a company officer than to state that the captain of the company to which he was assigned protested against having him in the company, preferring to perform the entire duty alone. Custer added that although he regarded Lt. Smith as a most excellent company commander, he was not designated by him to command Lt. DeRudio's company. 1109 DD 1876, and, 1379 DD 1876, NA, M1734, Rolls 15 and 16.

18. When DeRudio was assigned to Company A, Capt. Moylan would not take him into his mess, though it was only composed of Moylan and Varnum, and DeRudio had to trudge three times daily to Fred Gerard's shack to eat. When the Rice battalion arrived at Lincoln on May 5, Benteen found DeRudio with no horse and no mess kit, and so he mounted "the Count" on his former "H" horse, took him into his mess, and made him adjutant of the Left Wing. Benteen to David F. Barry, April 1, 1898, in Carroll, ed., *The D. F. Barry Correspondence,* 51.

DeRudio was the only man in the regiment who carried a saber on the campaign. On the morning of June 25, before going to the Crow's Nest, Lt. Cooke asked DeRudio to loan Gen. Custer his field glasses, the strongest in the regiment, made by an Austrian optician. DeRudio had reputation for being quite a storyteller; the other officers were fascinated with his piercing black eyes, witty conversation, and deep bass chuckle. He was a fearful liar and had an alleged title of "Count." Hammer, *Custer in '76,* 84, 87; Mills, *Harvest of Barren Regrets,* 194; Terrell and Walton, *Faint the Trumpet Sounds,* 95–96.

19. Hammer, *Custer in '76,* 85–86.

20. Benteen persuaded Reno to assign DeRudio to his own Company, "E." Benteen to wife, July 10, 1876, Carroll, *Camp Talk,* 32.

21. See Mills, *Charles C. DeRudio*; also, Marino, "Rudio Revisited."

22. Several letters to Walter Camp, from Devoto, 1917, WMC-LBHB; see Schoenberger, "A Trooper with Custer"; see also Caniglia, "Private Augustus L. DeVoto."

23. RG 94, Entry 547, Fort Totten, DT; Luce, ed., "The Diary and Letters of Dr. James M. DeWolf."

24. The companies were commanded by Capt. McDougall and Lt. Craycroft. Though bright and clear, the temperature was ten below zero and Dr. DeWolf took every care of the men, making them tear up their blankets and capes and roll them around their hands and feet, but notwithstanding his care, when they reached Fort Seward, three days and 81 miles later, nearly half the command of 120 men were frost bitten to some extent. *St. Paul Dispatch,* March 21, 1876.

For Capt. McDougall's report of the march, see NA, M1734, Roll 15; the battalion return for Companies E and L, March 10–31, 1876, is found with Post Returns, Fort Seward, DT, NA, M617, Roll 1153. The monthly report of sick and wounded, Companies E and L, March 1876, Fort Seward, DT, and letter from DeWolf to medical director, DD, Mar. 31, 1876, are with the papers of Dr. DeWolf, LBHB Coll., Roll 9.

25. "Mrs. J. M. DeWolf, wife of Dr. DeWolf, who was killed in the battle of the Little Big Horn, was registered at the Headquarters Hotel [Fargo] on Monday," *Red River Star,* Fri., Aug. 11, 1876.

26. GO 80, Hq Army, AGO, July 26, 1890, in accord with Section 2 of the act of Congress approved on June 16, 1890, provided for furlough and discharge of certain soldiers, who on that date had served faithfully three years or less and on their own application received furlough not to exceed three months so dated to expire with discharge not later than last day of third month following end of third year of enlistment, and not be eligible to again enlist in the Army for one year from date of discharge.

27. Wm. E. Morris said Dolan reduced account of a fistfight with Capt. French. WMC, rosters, IU.

28. Company return, June 1876, LBHB Coll., Rolls 12 and 15; Dolan evidently took advantage of the Steamer *Far West* going East on the day of his discharge. He arrived at St. Louis, July 13, and his story of the battle, in a St. Louis special to the *Chicago Times,* appeared in the *St. Paul and Minneapolis Pioneer-Press and Tribune,* July 16, 1876.

29. GO 79, AGO, July 25, 1890, skeletonized Troop's L and M, and attached noncommissieoned officers and transferred privates to other troops in the regiment, Chandler, *Of Garry Owen in Glory,* 80.

30. In a letter to the *Bismarck Tribune* in January 1888, Donahue gave his story of the battle, and intimated he was with the pack train during the march up the Rosebud; Saum, "John F. Donohue's Recollections". Another story of Donahue, with photo, is in, *The Butte* (Mont.) *Daily Post,* Aug. 27, 1921.

31. Isiah Damon (African American), age 28, is enumerated as "Domestic" in household of Capt. Alfred Sully, federal census, Fort Kearney, Nebraska T'y, June 30, 1860. John Burkman said Isaiah came to Fort Pierre with Gen. Harney in 1859, Burkman interview, Feb. 5, 1911, WMC-BYU. Sully and Harney were both at the peace council at Fort Pierre in 1856. See Gray, "The Story of Mrs. Picotte-Galpin."

32. Theo. Goldin to Albert W. Johnson, Jan. 4, 1933, Dustin Coll., LBHB, Roll 10. See also Carroll, *The Benteen-Goldin Letters,* 40–41; and Theo. Goldin to Earl A. Brininstool, Aug. 10, 1932, Earl Alonzo Brininstool Collection (hereafter cited as Brininstool Coll., BYU), Mss. 1412, Harold B. Lee Library, Brigham Young University, Provo, Utah, Box 1.

Further evidence of Dorman's parentage is intimated in an incident that occurred during the 1871 Yellowstone Expedition. The plan was to strike Heart River the day after leaving Fort Rice and follow the old Sully trail, but Isaiah called Fawn Creek, Heart River, for which error much opprobrium was cast on him. On Sept. 15, a rumor circulated that Dorman had left the column the day before, owing to the officers in charge having paid little attention to his counsel and made no provision for his comfort or mess, but he was made to shift for himself. They first disregarded him as a guide and then misled the column two or three miles themselves, rendering him no assistance in his endeavors to find a practicable route, and kept him near the train, whereas he should have been permitted to ride ahead with two or three scouts with instructions to leave them stationed at proper intervals to designate the route; all this disgusted him and he left. The story proved a fabrication of the quartermaster clerk, but the matter concerning his treatment was true nevertheless and considered sufficient justification for such a course. Capt. Javan B. Irvine, Diary and Letters (hereafter cited as Irvine Papers), South Dakota State Archives, Pierre, SD.

The guide who lost his bearings was described as a man said to be half Indian and half African American according to a member of the survey party, Patterson, "A Short Account of the Preliminary Survey," in NPRR Papers. Manuscript provided by Patterson's son, Rev. James O. Patterson, St. Luke's Church, Glenside, Pa., July 27, 1955.

33. EBC-LBHB, Roll 6, frame 5686, an undated, unsigned "Memo," in which the writer says Isaiah was believed to be an escaped slave; the handwriting of the Memo is similar to that of Lt. Godfrey and describes an incident that also points to him: In Oct. 1873 when a steamboat loaded with supplies for Fort Rice was "frozen in" (Missouri River) just below Standing Rock Agency, a sudden thaw cleared the river of ice and the steamer unloaded its cargo and went South to avoid the winter, but it was not until just before Christmas that the river again froze over so the ice was safe for (wagon) trains. Maj. Tilford, commanding Fort Rice, then sent the writer (of the memo) with a wagon train to go down and get the supplies. The muster roll of Company K, Dec. 31, 1873, shows Godfrey, "On detached service at Standing Rock for government supplies."

34. Walter Camp interview with Fred Gerard, Apr. 3, 1909, WMC-BYU. See Hammer, *Custer in '76*, 224 n. 12, and Walker, *Campaigns of General Custer*, 53.

35. Capt. Irvine to wife, Sept. 8, 1871, Irvine Papers. Several letters written by General Sully in Virginia during 1862–63, mention Isaiah who tended his horses. At Harper's Ferry, March 19, 1862, Sully, then Colonel of 1st Minn. Volunteers, wrote, "Isaiah is with me. I don't know if it is his attachment to me or Bob [a horse] or the new grey, Possum, that keeps him." On January 11, 1863, near Falmouth, Sully wrote, "Isaiah leaves me in a few days. I think he is sick of the war. He was very brave at the first part of the war but of late he manages to keep out of the way when the shells and balls are about. The late proclamation has ruined all the [African Americans]. He has become like all the rest, very impudent to some officers of my staff." General Alfred Sully, Papers (hereafter cited as Sully Papers), Beinecke Libray, Yale University, New Haven, Conn., folder 96. See also Sully, *No Tears For the General*, 142–43, 149, 155.

36. Dorman made the trip each month on foot, a distance of about 180 miles, the mail and dispatches wrapped in waterproof cloth strapped with his bedding on his back, and carried provisions sufficient for his needs. Subzero weather added to the hardship of the journey. With no settlements or roads over the untracked prairie, he would camp where night or exhaustion overcame him. The trip usually took about five days but on at least one occasion, Dec. 8, 1866, to Jan. 21, 1867, (the dates coinciding with a period of Dorman's employment) the mail courier to Fort Wadsworth was absent six weeks before he finally returned, apparently without explanation. It was thought the long delay would demand an investigation as to the cause. Crawford, *Rekindling Camp Fires*, 154; Irvine Papers, Jan. 21, 1867; see also McConnell, "Isaiah Dorman and the Custer Expedition," 344–52.

Dorman was also employed as mail carrier to James River, May 11 to June 30, 1867, where three mail carriers (selected from the best scouts at Fort Wadsworth) were stationed; two of whom arrived every Thursday at the wooded "Coolies" at the foot of the Coteau des Missouri, which was a well-defined point that could not be mistaken by carriers from either post. On several occasions the Wadsworth carriers waited at the "Coolies" from Thursday, the day the mail should arrive from Fort Rice, until Sunday, when in accordance with instructions they returned to Fort Wadsworth without it. Maj. Hayman, c.o. Fort Wadsworth, to c.o. Fort Rice, July 6, 1867, RG 393, Part V, Fort Sisseton, DT. (Fort Wadsworth was renamed Fort Sisseton in 1876.)

37. Major Charles Galpin was an early trader at Fort Pierre and was married to Eagle Woman, former wife of Honoré Picotte, the previous post trader. He served as chief guide and interpreter on the staff of Gen Sully and was appointed sutler of Fort Rice upon its construction by Sully in 1864. He later had an

independent trading post at Grand River Agency, until his death in Nov. 1869. His wife took over the operation, becoming the first woman merchant among the Sioux. Gray, "The Story of Mrs. Picotte-Galpin, a Sioux Heroine." The firm of Durfee & Peck was the largest supplier for the military on the Upper Missouri. Delo, *Peddlers and Post Traders,* 161.

After fulfilling their winter contract with the garrison, Durfee & Peck set men to work in the springtime cutting and stacking wood at convenient places along the banks of the Missouri River for summer sale to steamboats. Crawford, *Rekindling Camp Fires,* 148–53.

Traders or contractors sometimes employed men on a share basis and furnished them with tools and supplies. Other men organized into partnerships, cutting wood all winter and made their profit during the season of navigation. The river being navigable six months of the year, a woodcutter working from April to October could realize a profit of $1000 to $1200 for the season, Quaife, *Army Life in Dakota,* 19.

In Spring 1868, at a natural peculiarity named by the Sioux, "Standing Rock," Isaiah and three other woodhawks occupied buildings erected two years earlier by Durfee & Peck for a trading post but never completed, and subsequently acquired by Maj. Galpin. After cutting wood and banking it on either side of the river for the steamboats, they were required to plaster the rooms and put a roof on them. When they finished, Isaiah took up residence in the buildings and was left to sell and collect for the wood while his comrades returned to Fort Rice, Crawford, *Rekindling Camp Fires,* 153–57; see also, Standing Rock Annual Report, Sept. 1, 1875, NA, M234, Roll 846. For the dangers of operating a wood yard in those days, see Welty, "The Frontier Army on the Missouri River."

38. Vestal, *New Sources of Indian History,* 339. On Sept. 4, 1871, Capt. Irvine, 22nd Infantry, enroute with his company to Fort Rice on the Steamer *Far West,* pushed off from Grand River Agency at 8 A.M., and after a good run that day, tied up at the wood yard of Isaiah Dorman. Irvine visited Isaiah's "ranche," describing the doors of the house as very low, causing him to stoop on entering, and he was entertained with a dish of wild plums. They left next morning at daybreak, accompanied by Isaiah, and reached the Cannonball River at 11 A.M., and Fort Rice at precisely 12 o'clock. Irvine Papers.

39. Sam Bruguier, (half-blood Sioux) interpreter at Fort Rice from June 11, 1876, said Isaiah's wife's name was, "Visible." Walter Camp, Notes, Misc. IX, WMC-IU. The Sioux translation of "Visible" is "Tanin," or, Taninwin (pronounced Tah-nee-way). Female proper names often take the termination, "win," a contraction of win'yan, which translates as female, feminine. Williamson, ed., *An English-Dakota Dictionary,* vii, 255; Crawford, *Rekindling Camp Fires,* 154; Burgum, *Zezula,* 56, 184.

To become man and wife, mutual consent was all that was necessary among the people in that country. Crawford, *Rekindling Camp Fires,* 146. Col. Chas. Dimon, 1st U.S. Volunteers (galvanized Yankees), commanding Fort Rice in 1865, noted the market price of Indian women nearby was one horse and one blanket. Post Ledger Book, in, Col. Charles A. R. Dimon, Papers (hereafter cited as Dimon Papers), Beinecke Library, Yale University, New Haven, Conn.

In 1873, the Agent at Cheyenne Agency issued notice that all persons cohabiting with Indian women should have the marriage ceremony celebrated between them in legal form of the Episcopal church, including the ring, though it be of bone, stone, or brass. But after all the candidates, half-bloods, Frenchmen, ex-soldiers, and other hangers-on of the Sioux tribe had made great preparations to celebrate their nuptials in true frontier style, including large quantities of whiskey, boxes of candles to be burned, and numerous fiddles for entertainment, the Indian women objected, and the event was postponed, a dance given instead by the half-bloods on the occasion. Capt. Irvine to wife, Feb. 12, 1873, Irvine Papers.

In January 1876, Edwin H. Allison, agency interpreter at Standing Rock, negotiated to purchase an American Indian woman and pay for her with a rifle and pony—which were actually delivered but through the interposition of friends the debauching of a good virtuous Indian girl was prevented. NA, M666, Roll 225, (file 4228 AGO 1875). See Milligan, *Dakota Twilight,* 57. An article on Allison, with photos, is in the *Sioux City (Iowa) Tribune,* March 1910.

From Bismarck south to Fort Randall, white inhabitants, except as employed by some departments of the government, were found at intervals of five, ten, or fifteen miles, although in some river bottoms a few clustered cabins were observed. The occupants had generally adopted Indian custom as regards the marriage relation, and led a precarious life dependent largely for safety from attack on the influence of the women with whom they cohabited. Their occupation consisted in furnishing the wood needed by steamboats, in a slight cultivation of the soil, and in both honest and illicit traffic. Yet some were upright industrious men if measured by the approved morality and industry of that section. Report of the Annual Inspection of the Military Posts & Stations in the Dept. of Dakota, Nov. 10, 1875, Lt-Col. E. S. Otis, 22d Inf., trip from St. Paul, June 22 to Sept. 29, 1875, NA, M1734, Roll 15.

40. RG 92, Entry 238, report 1871/578, (includes expedition papers, orders, etc.). Maj. Joseph Whistler's Report of the Yellowstone Expedition, (751 MDM 1871), is found in RG 393, Part I, Entry 2546.

41. RG 92, Entry 238, report 1871/247. Isaiah's duties included issuing rations to the Indian scouts of the post. Capt. James Scully, AQM, to Post Hq, Jan. 3, 1875, RG 393, Part V, Fort Rice, DT.

Sgt. Ryan said Dorman "could talk a number of the different Indian dialects." Barnard, *Ten Years with Custer,* 184.

Linda Slaughter, who resided at Fort Rice in 1871–72, said that Isaiah, an intelligent African American man with a Sioux wife, was interpreter at the post and gave valuable information as to the meaning of certain words. Slaughter, "Leaves from Northwestern Society," 223.

Slaughter related that the interpreter's house and buildings of the post trader, including billiard rooms for officers and men, were outside the stockade with the corral, stables, and icehouses, and that the white walls of the fort showed brilliantly in sunshine. She recalled how one day in early 1872, Isaiah came into the fort with information that a young Sioux chief had fallen in love with her luxuriant hair, which she wore loosely curled about her neck, and vowed he would one day have her scalp. Burgum, *Zezula,* 56. Eastman, ed., *Fortress to Farm,* 27, 38.

Two letters signed by Isaiah Dorman to Edmond Palmer, agent at Standing Rock Agency, July 9 and Aug. 28, 1874 (requesting provisions for Indian scouts at Fort Rice), are part of a private collection. See *The Battlefield Dispatch,* Vol. 21, No. 4, Fall 2002.

Another letter, ("T.32"), is listed under Dorman's name in RG 393, Part I, Entry 1172. However, only letters with prefix H, R, and S, of this series, have been found.

Sam Bruguier said Isaiah was with Capt. Yates's detachment to Standing Rock Agency (Dec. 1874) to arrest Rain-in-the-Face and entered the store as interpreter with Tom Custer, accompanied by five soldiers. They walked up to Rain and Tom shook hands with him saying, "How Kola" and told Rain he was under arrest. Isaiah was so frightened or disconcerted that he trembled from head to foot and could not get the words out of his mouth. Rain asked what was the matter, and Johnny Bruguier (Sam's brother), clerk in the store, told Rain he was under arrest. Liddic and Harbaugh, *Camp on Custer,* 101.

Dorman is not mentioned in official reports of the incident. NA, M234, Roll 846; see also Gray, "Custer Throws a Boomerang." Sgt. Knipe did not think Isaiah was at Standing Rock for capture of Rain-in-the-Face; says Charley Reynolds was with the troop. Knipe to Walter Camp, Dec. 24, 1911, WMC-BYU.

42. RG 94, Entry 544, Dakota T'y Hospital Register No. 102.

43. RG 92, Entry 238, report 1876/328; 1876/395. SO 2, Hq Middle District, DD, Fort Abraham Lincoln, May 14, 1876; see McConnell, "Isaiah Dorman and the Custer Expedition," 351.

44. Sam Bruguier in Walter Camp, Notes, Misc. IX, WMC-IU; also, Vestal, *Sitting Bull Champion of the Sioux,* 166; Gen. Terry recorded in his diary, June 11, that, "Weir not returned determined to trust to Isaiah. Custer with one company the advance." This refers to Terry's entry June 10 that Weir was sent with his company to find a route to the mouth of Powder River. Terry continued, "Self with main body start 5.00. Halt to make road 6.15. Successive halts for road making until at 8 o'clk reached plateau. Marched on plateau 3/4 mile & halted. Advanced at 9.30. at 10.30 halted at head of ravine to determine whether to follow Custer's trail or to cross the ravine perpendicularly. Wagons started on Custer's trail without authority therefore directed column to follow. Trail led to bottom lands of Powder . . . Reached camp on Yellowstone at 1.55." The Diary of General Alfred H. Terry, Mss. Div., LOC.

The Arikara scout, Red Star, may have recalled the same march (to the Yellowstone), "Custer had ridden ahead with a scout in search of a trail. When the rest of the command reached a place where the roads forked, no one knew which way Custer had gone. Some one asked Custer's negro servant, Isa, which road to take and he chose the fork of the road in the other direction from the one taken by Custer because it was a very good road. When Custer and his scout returned he found that the whole command had not halted but had taken the other road. Red Star was at some distance scouting among the hills, but as he rode into camp he saw Isa on his knees before Custer, who was cursing him furiously, while the darky was crying and begging for mercy. The next day as a punishment Isa had to go on foot all day." Libby, *Arikara Narrative,* 195.

When the regiment (Left Wing) reached mouth of Tongue River, June 16, Red Star said they found a burial scaffold on the site of an abandoned Sioux camp. "Custer had the scaffold taken down and the negro, Isaiah, was told to take the clothing and wrappings off the body . . . Isaiah threw the body into the river, and as he was fishing there later, they suppose he used this for bait." Libby, *Arikara Narrative,* 75.

During the march up the Rosebud, Dorman assisted Lt. Varnum pack the mules carrying baggage and rations for the American Indian Scouts. Varnum to QM Gen. Dec. 26, 1876, RG 393 Part V, Fort Abraham Lincoln.

John Burkman said Isaiah and a 'Ree scout brought a message to Gen. Custer from Varnum at the Crow's Nest during breakfast the morning of June 25. Burkman to Mrs. Custer, Feb. 3, 1911, EBC-LBHB, Roll 3; Wagner, *Old Neutriment*, 148.

45. Libby, *Arikara Narrative*, 95, 110; Vestal, *Sitting Bull Champion of the Sioux*, 165; Chief Runs-the-Enemy said the Indians shot at a black man in a soldiers uniform and riddled his horse with bullets. Dixon, *The Vanishing Race*, 173; The Cheyenne warrior, Wooden Leg, said Dorman was a big man. Marquis, *A Warrior Who Fought Custer*, 261.

Herendeen said Isaiah was killed not far from Charley Reynolds who fell about 150 yards from the timber. Isaiah had pistol balls in his legs from the knees down and believed they were shot into him while alive. Hammer, *Custer in '76*, 223; Graham, *The Custer Myth*, 260; see also, Hardorff, ed., *The Custer Battle Casualties*, 148–50, and Hardorff, ed., *The Custer Battle Casualties*, II, 124–25.

A possible explanation for the pain inflicted to Isaiah's legs may be in a letter from Gen. Sully, Nov. 20, 1862, Camp near Falmouth, Va., "The mail carrier also brought the bundle. The leggings are of no use here in mud up to the horse's knees, besides I can't draw them over my heavy riding boots. I have given them to Isaiah, he has cut the feet off and says he will wear them like Indian leggings. He'll cut a figure for his legs are very crooked." Sully Papers.

An officer of the (African American) 9th Cavalry in 1866 wrote of the enlisted men in his command, "All had been slaves . . . showed signs of overwork and of malnutrition. Nearly every one had malformed hands and distorted feet." Kinevan, *Frontier Cavalryman*, 27.

46. Fort Rice, Post Return, July, 1876, NA, M617. Isaiah was due $102.50 pay from May 15 to June 25. When Isaac McNutt, an employee of the post trader's store at Fort Rice and part-time carpenter, claimed to be assignee of Dorman's pay vouchers, he was asked by the Third Auditor (General Accounting Office) to provide evidence of the assignment or anything tending to show that he cashed his pay. William A. Knapp, civilian quartermaster clerk at Fort Rice, stated that "The vouchers were sent by the QM at Fort Rice but were lost while enroute to Chief Quartermaster."

The auditor informed McNutt, May 15, 1878, that, inasmuch as duplicate vouchers purporting to be the original duplicates were then in the claim in his office, an explanatory statement was desired with affidavit showing when and where Dorman signed and delivered his vouchers to him. The claim was disallowed by the third auditor, May 23, 1879, and referred to the second comptroller, who concurred with the decision, Sept. 25, 1879. RG 217, Entry 658 (claim 42.848); see also, letters sent by the quartermaster division of the third auditor's office.

McNutt was born in Canada, ca. 1840, and was a civilian carpenter at Fort Rice during construction of the cavalry stables, Aug. to Nov. 1873. RG 92, Entry 238, report 1873/43; he was employed in the post trader's store in 1875–76 (see GO No. 1, Hq Fort Rice, Jan. 5, 1876). Sgt. Ryan said McNutt was the bartender of the enlisted men's bar room, which was connected with the post trader's, or sutler's store. Barnard, *Ten Years with Custer*, 182.

McNutt was described as an old turf man when he helped judge a horse race at Fort Rice. *Bismarck Tribune*, May 10, 31, 1878; he later became a lumber contractor at Fort Custer, MT. *Bismarck Tribune*, Jan. 25, 1884; see also Upton, *Fort Custer on the Big Horn*, 73.

Isaiah has often been mistaken for Blackhawk, a full-blood African American slave (also known as Peter Frank), who was brought up the Missouri River to Fort Clark by Francis Chardon, ca. 1837, and lived for many years among the Sioux. Newgard, Sherman, and Guerrero, *African Americans in North Dakota*, 17; statement of Dr. Samuel S. Turner, agency physician, Jan. 27, 1876, NA, M666, Roll 225.

Blackhawk had a wood yard two miles above Grand River Agency and was later employed as interpreter at Standing Rock Agency. Irvine Papers, Sept 4, 1871; he was allegedly of dubious character, the Sioux attributed much of the troubles at the agency to his introduction of liquor and believed him responsible for the killing of Little Goose on Feb. 8, 1875, after a late night whiskey party given by Blackhawk. Correspondence from Capt. Poland, 6th Inf., commanding U.S. Troops at Standing Rock agency, 1875–76, NA, M234, Roll 846, and M1734, Roll 15.

Blackhawk died at the agency and his Sioux wife and five children (four sons and one daughter) were living there in 1881 when James McLaughlin assumed charge as the new agent. By 1909 only two sons remained, Baptiste Pierre, or Blackhawk, and Peter Pierre, or Blackhawk. McLaughlin to Walter Camp, June 15 and July 1, 1909, WMC-BYU.

Frank Blackhawk and Peter Blackhawk, were students at Hampton Institute, Va., 1881-85 and 1887-90 respectively. Hultgren, "To Be Examples To . . ."

Walter Camp wrote to Mrs. George Hunt at Fort Totten, N.Dak., Dec. 13, 1919, having been told she was the widow of Isaiah Dorman when he lived at Fort Rice, but Mrs. Hunt replied that she was not born at the time of the Custer battle, being only 38 years old (in 1919) and guessed whoever told him was mistaken. WMC-BYU.

With computer technology and the availability of census records on-line, it has been learned that George Hunt was the English name of Hehakahowaste (Good Voice Elk), born 1853, and husband (1902-1909) of Visible (Taninwin or Ataninwin), born 1858. He is reported widowed on the Federal Census of 1910. He apparently married again about 1914 and thereafter, as George Hunt, Sr., resided with wife Tiyodutewin, born 1863. Nearby was the family of George Hunt, Jr., born 1883, and wife Margaret, born 1890. U.S. Indian Census, Devils Lake Agency (Fort Totten), NA, M595.

The Camp material contains an interview, May 21, 1909, with Good Voice Elk, age 56 (a Hunkpapa Sioux), relating to the Custer Fight at the ford, WMC-DPL, Folder 64.

Elsewhere, Camp wrote a reminder to inquire at Standing Rock for Sam King, believing him a stepson of Isaiah Dorman and might have a photo of him. WMC-DPL, Folder 14.

Sam King died in Sept. 1950 at Cannonball, N.Dak., where for many years he was Justice of the Peace and noted for his influence carrying friends to victory at election time. His mother was married to Isaiah Dorman and sometime after the Custer battle she married King's father. Samuel King was born about 1882 and was also known as Walking Earth (Makamani). He and his sister, Mary (Atanin), two years (or five) his elder, are listed as orphans in 1891 and afterward lived with an uncle and aunt, Crazy Dog (Sungnaskinyan), and Door (Tiyopa).

Sam King was said to be part negro, though most records report him full-blood Sioux. His marriage license in 1901 at Fort Yates, N.Dak., shows his mother's name was "Otanin," and that his father's name was unknown. *Sioux County Pioneer-Arrow*, Sept. 22, 1950. *Bismarck Tribune*, Sept. 25, 1950. U.S. Indian Census, NA, M595. Marriage Registers and Licenses, Standing Rock Agency, 1890-1922, microfilm roll 5516, South Dakota State Archives.

The passing of Sam King was learned through the courtesy of Lilah Morton Pengra, whose biography of Dorman is now in preparation. See, "My Search for Isaiah Dorman," by Dr. Lilah Morton Pengra, in the *Newsletter*, (LBHA), Vol. XLII, No. 9, Nov. 2008.

47. Hammer, *Custer in '76*, 71; the skeleton of one of General Custer's men was found in 1928 by Frank Berthune, an American Indian. It was found "near the fence enclosing the battlefield. An arrowhead still was imbedded in the spine, nearby was a time eroded rifle scabbard bearing the initials 'R. D.'" *Bangor* (Maine) *Daily News*, Oct. 19, 1928, clipping in pension file.

48. Botzer, Troop Duty Book; The son of Henry Dose, age eight, died May 6, 1876, days after arriving at Fort Lincoln from Shreveport. Dose to his wife, June 8, 1876, Doerner, "The Boys of '76."

49. SO 18, Hq US Troops, Shreveport, Apr. 27, 1875, RG 393, Part I, Entry 1972. Dougherty and Sgt. McCrea, Company K, 3rd Infantry, were ordered back to their station, per SO 79, AGO, May 1, 1875, RG 94, Entry 44; McCrea returned to Shreveport, May 11, Regimental Returns, NA, M665, Roll 34.

50. Information on headstone of James Dougherty, age 28 years, 7 months, 7 days, son of Matthew and Bridget Dougherty; courtesy of Garford F. Williams, Nicholson, Pa., 1997.

51. RG 94, Entry 547, Fort Buford. The Steamer *Eclipse* arrived at Fort Buford, April 16, 1881, the first boat of the season.

52. Stan Roy said Drinan weighed 145 to 150 pounds and was killed near the river. Roy to Walter Camp, July 28, 1910, WMC-BYU; Hardy said he found Drinan's horse wounded in the back and he had to be killed. Hardorff, *Camp, Custer, and the Little Bighorn*, 81.

53. Stan Roy said Durselew told him he had a wife and child in New York City. Roy to Walter Camp, Dec. 18, 1909, WMC-BYU; Alcott said Durselew was a Prussian Lt. in Franco-Prussian War. WMC, rosters, IU.

54. Botzer, Troop Duty Book. The regimental return, August 1876, reports Dwyer on detached service on Yellowstone River as guard on steamboat from June 15, whereas the company return reports him at Yellowstone Depot from June 15. He is not listed absent on returns of June or July. Sgt. Brown's duty book reports Dwyer, "D" August 1–30, and, "DD" August 31 to Sept. 1st, thence regular duty to Sept. 26. Reynolds and Brown, *Journal*.

E

Eades, Wm. Pvt co F; b. Dublin, Ireland; enl in co F 9 Sep 1871 Louisville Ky. for 5 yrs; age 27; clerk; gray eyes, blk hair, fair comp, 5' 7" high; ds herding co horses Aug 1872; ds subs dept herding cattle Oct 1873 to Mar 1874; dd qmd clerk June 1875; ed qmd mech Aug 1875 thro' Apr 1876; ed qmd mech with exp'n 6 May 1876; [with wagon train says Rooney; doubtful with packs says Lynch];[1] disch 4 Aug 1876 camp mouth of Rosebud Creek MT per GO 24 AGO 1859 a pvt char xclt; hired 1 Aug as packer in qmd; rate of pay $50 mo; disch 26 Sep 1876 due $93.33 pay; res Bismarck DT proprietor of saloon & café;[2] died 12 May 1887 near Dickinson DT.[3]

Eagan, Thos. P. Cpl co E; b. Ireland; enl as Thos. Hagan 12 Sep 1873 St Louis Mo. for 5 yrs; age 25; laborer; grey eyes, sandy hair, lt comp, 5' 5 1/4" high; join co E 18 Oct 1873 Ft Lincoln DT; dd co cook Oct 1873; dd room orderly Apr 1874; dd co cook Feb 1875; cpl 1 Mar 1875; killed with Custer column 25 June 1876.

Easley, Jno. Thos. Sgt co A; b. Montgomery Co Ill.; enl 7 Dec 1874 St Louis Mo. for 5 yrs; age 21; laborer; brn eyes, lt hair, fair comp, 5' 8 1/4" high; join co A 6 Feb 1875 Livingston, Ala; cpl 9 Jan 1876; sgt 4 June 1876; pvt 14 Oct 1876; des 17 Oct 1876 Ft Lincoln DT.[4]

Edgerly, Winfield Scott. 2Lt co D; b. 29 May 1846 Farmington N.H.;[5] grad USMA 15 June 1870 & appt 2Lt 7 cav; join co D 28 Sep 1870 Ft L'worth Kans.; with co on NBS June to Oct 1873 & again June to Sep 1874; [almost killed 25 June 1876 at Weir Point dur struggle to mount his frightened horse & inds swarmed near]; appt rqm 27 June 1876; 1Lt 26 July 1876; arr Bismarck 22 Sep on str *Key West* (with maj Reno & Lt Wallace); resd rqm 14 Nov 1876; td comdg co L to 3 Mar 1877; assd to co C 28 Apr 1877 Ft Totten DT; with co guarding Blk Hills stage route Aug to Dec 1877; ds Chicago Ill. Jan 1879 witness in Reno court of inq; tr to co D June 1879; ds rctg duty Jan 1883 to Nov 1884 Cincinnati Ohio; (capt co G 22 Sep 1883); comd co in action with Sioux inds 29 Dec 1890 Wounded Knee SD; instr of mil science at state college Orono Me Aug 1895 to July 1896; instr of natl gd at Concord N.H. to June 1898 when appt Lt-col of vols & inspector gen at various posts to Apr 1899; (maj 6 cav 9 July 1898 [never joined]; tr to 7 cav 5 Jan 1899); with regt in Cuba Sep 1899 to May 1902 when assd td in war dept; (Lt-col 10 cav 19 Feb 1901 [never joined]; tr to 7 cav 20 Mar 1901); joined regt at Chickamauga Park Ga. July 1902; prom col 2 cav at Ft Myer Va. 17 Feb 1903 & with regt to Philippines Dec 1903; prom brig-gen 23 June 1905 & comd Dept of Luzon; return to U.S. Jan 1907 & comd Dept of the Gulf (hq Atlanta Ga.); ds to Germany as official observer of Kaiser maneuvers dur summer 1907; comd Dept of Dak. (hq St Paul Minn.) 1908 to 1909;[6] prom'n to maj-gen & comd Dept of Calif. not appv upon med exam'n; retd 29 Dec 1909 owing to ill health; recalled to active duty 26 July 1917 & comd mobilization camp at Concord N.H. six weeks; died 10 Sep 1927 Farmington N.H.[7] [4598 ACP 1884]. Pension: 6 Dec 1927 / Wid / 1593714 / A11-14-27.

Eisemann, Geo. Pvt co C; b. 16 May 1854 Phil'a Pa.; enl 15 Jan 1872 at Phil'a for 5 yrs; age 21; brushmaker; blue eyes, dk hair, fair comp, 5' 5 1/4" high; join co C 18 Feb 1872 Rutherfordton NC; ed qmd Oct 1873 to Jan 1874; dd subs dept herder Feb to May 1874 & Oct 1874 to May 1875; dd co cook Oct 1875; dd qmd Dec 1875; dd hq fatigue party, r. wing (morn & eve) 15 May 1876; killed with Custer column 25 June 1876.
Pension: 23 Sep 1884 / Father / 319653 / 227134.

Eixenberger, Peter. Pvt band; b. 12 June 1860 Munich Bavaria Germany; enl 15 Nov 1875 New York N.Y. for 5 yrs; age 19; musician

[violinist]; dk eyes, dk hair, fair comp, 5' 5 1/2" high; assd to 7 cav 1 Mar 1876; join regt 14 Apr 1876 Ft Lincoln DT (with Lt Reily's detmt); assd to band 28 Apr 1876; ds camp Powder River MT 14 June 1876; ds str *Josephine* 6 Aug 1876 to Ft Lincoln with band; ds 1 May 1877 Ft Lincoln with band; disch 14 Nov 1880 Ft Meade DT expir of serv a pvt char xclt & reenl in band for 5 yrs; lance cpl Dec 1881; sgt band 19 July 1884; sick hosp 10 July to 25 Sep 1885 (sprain r. knee); disch 14 Nov 1885 at Ft Meade expir of serv a sgt char an xclt sol. & mus'n; died 12 Sep 1917 near Sykes MT.
Pension: 4 Aug 1919 / Ind. Wid / 14722 / 9867. (XC-2,660,258).

Eldridge, Edwin. Pvt co A; b. 2 Mar 1852 Newburgh Me; enl as Edwin Grant 8 Dec 1874 Boston Mass. for 5 yrs; age 22; machinist; hazel eyes, blk hair, dk comp, 5' 9 1/8" high; join co A 6 Feb 1875 Livingston Ala; des 26 Mar 1875 at Livingston; apph next day at Selma Ala; sen gen cm 27 Apr 1875 forf $10 pay per mo for 6 mos & conft same period; dd co cook Oct 1875; disch 8 May 1876 Ft Lincoln DT on surg cert dis (valvular disease of heart) a pvt char xclt; died 8 Mar 1916 Chicago Ill.
Pension: 17 Mar 1888 / Inv / 645333 / 484757. Wid / 1062421 / 807702. (XC-2,690,538).

Emerich, Jacob. (alias). See Huff, Jacob.

Engel, Gustav. Pvt co C; b. Wurtemburg Germany; enl 11 July 1870 Cleveland Ohio for 5 yrs; age 21; cooper; brn eyes, brn hair, fair comp, 5' 7 1/4" high; join co I 6 cav 20 Sep 1870 Ft Richardson Tex.; dd co cook Feb 1873; disch 11 July 1875 Ft Dodge Kans. expir of serv a pvt; reenl 27 Sep 1875 Cincinnati Ohio for 5 yrs; join co C 7 cav 21 Oct 1875 Ft Lincoln DT; killed with Custer column 25 June 1876.

Etzler, Wm. Pvt co L; b. Wheeling W.Va.; enl 9 Sep 1873 Cincinnati Ohio for 5 yrs; age 21; cigar maker; blue eyes, dk hair, fair comp, 5' 6 1/2" high; join co L 19 Oct 1873 Ft Lincoln DT; dd qm corral Oct 1874 to Feb 1875; sick hosp 8 Mar to 14 May 1877 (ac. rheum.) & ds Ft Lincoln to 20 Nov 1877;[8] disch 9 Sep 1878 at Ft Lincoln expir of serv a pvt char good; reenl 9 Sep 1882 Indianapolis Ind. for 5 yrs; join co H 2 cav 19 Oct 1882 Ft Assiniboine MT; des 18 June 1884 Camp Hell Gate Canyon near Missoula MT; apph 25 Aug 1884 Miles City MT; escaped 21 Sep 1884 from guardhouse Ft Keogh MT; apph 13 Oct 1884 Glendive MT; dishon disch 15 Nov 1884 at Ft Keogh sen gen cm & 4 yrs conft mil prison Ft L'worth Kans.

Notes—E

1. Rosters of Company F with remarks by Rooney and Lynch, WMC-BYU.
2. *Bismarck Tribune* (various issues), Nov. 1876 through May 1881; Eades married Mary Cottrel, Oct. 14, 1880, at Bismarck.
3. *Dickinson* (DT) *Press*, May 14, 1887.
4. William Nugent said Easley in his deportment was a perfect gentleman. *Winners of the West*, Vol. III, No. 4, June 24, 1926, 6.
5. Edgerly graduated from Phillips Exeter Academy in 1864 and was a classmate of Robert T. Lincoln, son of Abraham Lincoln. Newspaper clipping, Dec. 24, 1909, np, Taylor Scrapbook.
6. While in command at headquarters Department of Dakota in St. Paul, Gen. Edgerly had two lengthy interviews with Walter Camp during the winter. Camp to Frank M. Gibson, Feb. 12, 1909, WMC-LBHB.
7. *Annual Report of the Association of Graduates*, USMA, June 10, 1931, 93–96; G. M. Clark, *Scalp Dance*, 10; newspaper clipping, Dec. 24, 1909, np, Taylor Scrapbook.
8. Etzler married Mary Ann Hackett, Aug. 17, 1877, at Bismarck. *Bismarck Tribune*, Aug. 20, 1877.

F

Farber, Conrad. Pvt co I; b. Hungary; enl 21 July 1864 Cleveland Ohio for 3 yrs; age 27 6/12; carpenter; brn eyes, blk hair, dk comp, 5' 10" high; assd to co B 4 art'y; disch 21 July 1867 Ft Riley Kans. expir of serv a pvt; enl in co F 7 cav 14 Jan 1870 Ft L'worth Kans. for 5 yrs; ed qmd carpenter from Dec 1870; disch 18 June 1871 Taylor Bks Louisville Ky. for defective eyesight & in accord with GO 23 AGO 1871 (reduce number of enl men in army by 1 July); reenl in regt 10 July 1871 at Taylor Bks (upon recom'n of col Sturgis) for 5 yrs; assd to co I; ds regtl hq Taylor Bks (ed qmd carpenter) 14 July 1871 to 2 Apr 1873; ed regtl qmd (with band) at Camp Sturgis (Yankton) DT to 4 May 1873 when ordered to join co at St Paul Minn. (qmd to furn transp for Mrs. Farber, co laundress); ds dept hq at St Paul from 15 May 1873 (carpenter in qmd barn [corner 4th & Cedar streets]); disch 10 July 1876 at St Paul upon expir of serv & reenl in co I for 5 yrs; ds dept hq to 9 July 1881 when disch at Ft Snelling Minn. upon expir of serv a pvt char good; died 29 Sep 1896 St Louis Mo. (chr. alcoholism).[1]
Pension: 24 Oct 1881 / Inv / 432540 / 635906. 11 Nov 1896 / Minor / 644003 / 481178.

Farley, Wm. Pvt co H; b. Ireland; enl in co H 1 May 1875 New Orleans La. for 5 yrs (auth AGO); age 25; blacksmith; blue eyes, dk hair, florid comp, 5' 7" high; appt co blks 21 June 1875 (from 5 May, date previous blks disch); pvt 1 Jan 1876; in conft Feb 1876; gsw l. shoulder (fl. wd severe) 26 June 1876 on Reno hill; tr on str *Far West* 3 July to camp at Powder River;[2] tr on str *Josephine* 19 July (with Delaney, Hoyt & Kane) to hosp Ft Lincoln DT;[3] tr to hosp Ft Rice DT 12 Aug; duty 27 Sep 1876; dd bldg stable guardhouse Feb & Mar 1877; in conft Jan 1878; sen gen cm 26 Feb 1878 forf $10 pay per mo for 3 mos & conft same period; dd qmd blks Apr 1878; ds Camp J. G. Sturgis DT Aug 1878; ed qmd blks Oct 1878 to Apr 1879; ed qmd blks Aug 1879; disch 30 Apr 1880 Ft Meade DT by expir of serv a pvt char "a good blacksmith but not intended for a soldier."

Farrand, Jas. Pvt co C; b. Wash'n Co. Ill.; enl in co B 6 inf 27 Oct 1870 Ft Gibson IT for 5 yrs; age 31; carpenter; brn eyes, blk hair, ruddy comp, 5' 9" high; artf'r 11 Dec 1870; dd qmd carpenter Dec 1870 & Feb 1871; pvt 24 Apr 1871; ed qmd laborer Apr & June 1871; ed qmd mech Oct 1871; ed qmd carpenter Oct 1872 to Feb 1873; in conft Oct 1873; in conft Dec 1874; ds Ft Rice DT 23 Mar 1875 with escort for pub train & on td with co C 7 Cav Apr 1875; disch 27 Oct 1875 Ft Lincoln DT expir of serv a pvt; enl in 7 cav 10 Nov 1875 at Ft Lincoln for 5 yrs; attd to co C 26 Nov 1875; assd to co C 1 Mar 1876; dd with regtl hq fatigue party (morn & eve) 11 May 1876; killed with Custer column 25 June 1876.

Farrar, Morris. Pvt co C; b. 30 July 1846 Amesbury Mass.; pvt co A 53 Mass. inf 25 Aug 1862 to 2 Sep 1863; pvt co I 4 Mass. cav 30 Jan 1864 to 14 Nov 1865; enl reg army 23 Jan 1872 New York N.Y. for 5 yrs; age 26; grinder; brn eyes, blk hair, dk comp, 5' 8 3/4" high; join co C 7 cav 18 Feb 1872 Rutherfordton NC; ed qmd blks Dec 1872 & Feb 1873; dd post hq Dec 1873 to May 1874; ds Ft Rice DT June to Sep 1874 gd co prop; dd post hq Oct 1874 to July 1875; cpl 1 Sep 1876; sgt 9 Oct 1876; disch 23 Jan 1877 Ft Totten DT expir of serv a sgt char xclt; reenl 1 Sep 1881 Boston Mass. for 5 yrs; assd to co D 17 inf; des 21 Nov 1881 while on ds at Bismarck DT; died 9 Apr 1899 Phil'a Pa.
Pension: 25 Apr 1899 / Wid / 696927 / 494861.

Farrell, Rich'd. Pvt co E; b. Dublin Ireland; enl 29 Sep 1875 St Louis Mo. for 5 yrs; age 24; laborer; gray eyes, brn hair, fair comp, 5' 8 3/4" high; join co E 29 Oct 1875 Ft Totten DT; killed with Custer column 25 June 1876.
Pension: 6 Jan 1882 / Mother / 288888. (Rej upon failure of clmt after reasonable time & due notification to furn evidence to establish claim).

Fay, Jno. J. Pvt co D; b. Chicago Ill.; enl 8 Sep 1873 Detroit Mich. for 5 yrs; age 21; plasterer; gray eyes, brn hair, fair comp, 5' 5" high; join co D 22 Oct 1873 Ft Totten DT; ed qmd June 1875; sick qrs in field 20 June 1877 (insane); tr to hosp Cant'mt Tongue River 23 June; tr to Ft Rice DT 20 Aug; disch 15 Sep 1877 at Ft Rice on surg cert dis a pvt char very good (origin of disease believed prior to enlmt; dis 1/2); res Chicago Ill. in 1906.
Pension: 9 Aug 1906 / Inv / 1351400. (Rej on grd unable to connect alleged injury to head & resulting affection of memory with mil serv.).

Fehler, Henry. Sgt co A; b. Hanover Germany; enl 18 July 1866 Cincinnati Ohio for 3 yrs; age 31; laborer; gray eyes, lt hair, lt comp, 5' 7 1/2" high; join co A 10 Sep 1866 Ft Riley Kans.; dd post comsy Oct 1866; dd co cook Dec 1866; disch 20 July 1869 camp near Ft Hays Kans. expir of serv a pvt; reenl 24 Sep 1869 at Cincinnati for 5 yrs; join co A 16 Sep 1871 E'town Ky.; sick hosp Dec 1871; disch 8 Jan 1872 at E'town on surg cert dis a pvt (chr. infl. of testicle; not contr line of duty as far as known); reenl 14 Aug 1872 St Louis Mo. for 5 yrs (auth AGO); rejoin co A Oct 1872 at E'town; cpl 1 Feb 1873; ds Ft Rice DT June to Sep 1873 gd regtl prop; sgt 9 Apr 1874; in arrest Dec 1874; dd post prov sgt 2 Oct to 3 Nov 1876 Ft Lincoln DT; dd actg post qm sgt Feb 1877; pvt 27 May 1877; disch 24 June 1877 camp near Tongue River MT per SO 70 Dept of Dak. 1877 a pvt char fair;[4] reenl 26 Dec 1877 Chicago Ill. for 5 yrs; assd to co E 6 cav; disch 25 Dec 1882 Ft Lowell AT expir of serv a pvt char very good soldier; reenl 16 Jan 1883 at Ft Lowell for 5 yrs in co G 6 cav; disch 15 Jan 1888 Ft Union NM expir of serv a pvt & reenl for 5 yrs in co C 6 cav; tr to co G; died 15 May 1889 at Ft Union (alcoholic poisoning) a pvt.

Finckle, August. Sgt co C; b. Berlin Prussia; enl 27 Jan 1872 Chicago Ill. for 5 yrs; age 27; clerk; gray eyes, dk hair, dk comp, 6' 0 1/2" high; join 7 cav 20 Feb 1872 Louisville Ky. as unassd rct; join co C 1 Mar 1872 Rutherfordton NC; ed subs dept Sep 1872 to Jan 1873; cpl 18 Feb 1873; dd qmd Feb 1873; dd chg co kit'n Aug 1873; dd chg co kit'n Apr to Sep 1874; ed qmd Oct 1874 to May 1875; sgt 3 June 1875; dd actg sgt-maj Ft Rice DT July to Sep 1875; sick hosp Ft Lincoln DT 25 Apr to 14 May 1876 (bronc.); killed with Custer column 25 June 1876.[5]

Findeisen, Hugo. Sgt co L; b. Altenburg Germany; pvt co K 2 Md inf 5 Sep 1861 to 17 July 1865; enl reg army 11 Jan 1869 Omaha Bks Neb for 3 yrs; age 33; clerk; gray eyes, lt hair, fair comp, 5' 11" high; assd to co C 3 art'y; disch 11 Jan 1872 Charleston SC expir of serv a pvt; enl in co L 7 cav 14 Jan 1872 Yorkville SC for 5 yrs; in conft June to Nov 1872; sen gen cm 31 Aug 1872 forf $10 pay per mo for 4 mos; unexpired portion of sen remitted 5 Nov 1872; ds June to Sep 1874 Ft Lincoln DT guarding co prop; cpl 13 Oct 1874; sgt 28 July 1875; ds Ft Lincoln 17 May 1876 chg co garden; sent with Lt Garlington on str *Josephine* 24 July 1876 to join co in field; ds with art'y detmt Aug 1876; sd with Lt Hare's sec. of parrott guns 8 Oct to 12 Nov 1876; disch 14 Jan 1877 at Ft Lincoln expir of serv a sgt char xclt; reenl 6 Feb 1877 Ft Hamilton N.Y. for 5 yrs; assd to co C 3 art'y; died 21 May 1881 in post hosp Ft Hamilton a pvt (suicide, cut throat with knife or razor which was dropped into sink after committing the deed & could not be found).
Pension: 26 Aug 1890 / Wid / 472493 / 312020.

Finley, Jeremiah. Sgt co C; b. Tipperary Ireland; enl as Darby Finlay 29 Sep 1854 Kilkenny Ireland in 17th regt of foot; age 17 9/12; embarked with regt to Malta & Crimea Feb 1856; at camp Sebastopol & passage to Canada Apr to July 1856; disch 19 Aug 1865 Quebec Canada a pvt;[6] enl 18 Sep 1868 Chicago Ill. for 5 yrs; age 27; laborer; gray eyes, lt brn hair, lt comp, 5' 6" high; join co C 7 cav 10 Nov 1868 camp Sandy Forsyth Kans.; cpl 3 June 1869; sgt 17 Aug 1871; dd co tailor Feb 1873; dd chg co kit'n Aug 1873; disch 18 Sep 1873 Heart River DT expir of serv a sgt & reenl same day in co C for 5 yrs; ds June to Sep 1874 Ft Rice DT chg co prop; dd chg co kit'n Oct 1874; dd prov sgt Nov 1874 to Jan 1875; dd prov sgt Oct 1875 to May 1876; killed with Custer column 25 June 1876; survived by wife & 2 ch.; (widow m. pvt Donahue 7 Feb 1878).

Pension: 14 Sep 1877 / Wid / 233254 / 196197. Minor / 282715 / 196198.

Finnegan, Thos. Jas. Pvt co F; b. 2 Sep 1850 Hillsboro, Ohio;[7] enl 19 Aug 1873 Cincinnati Ohio for 5 yrs; age 23; farmer; grey eyes, blk hair, fair comp, 5' 10" high; join co F 18 Oct 1873 Ft Lincoln DT; ds June thro' Aug 1874 at Ft Lincoln;[8] ds dept hq St Paul Minn. 18 June to 19 July 1875; ds dept hq mtd msgr from 21 Sep 1875; (on furl 60 days 5 Jan 1876); [at LBH said himself; with packs leading capt Yates' extra horse says Lynch; with wagon train at Powder River says Rooney];[9] ds regtl hq Ft Lincoln Sep to Nov 1876; (dismtd men & baggage of co F tr to Ft Abercrombie 15 Nov); dd orderly for maj Reno 20 Jan 1877; dd orderly for comdg officer 28 Feb 1877; ds Ft Lincoln 26 Oct 1877; tr to Ft Totten DT 4 Nov 1877 with detmt co F; dd co cook June 1878; disch 19 Aug 1878 at Ft Totten by expir of serv a pvt char xclt;[10] died 4 Feb 1923 Natl Mil Home L'worth Kans.
Pension: 8 Dec 1899 / Inv / 1240558. (Abandoned). 2 Apr 1917 / Ind. Surv. / 10821 / 7046. Wid / 16301 / 11082. (XC-2,659,618).

Fischer, Chas. See Hanke, Chas.

Fisher, Chas. Pvt co H; b. Bavaria Germany; enl 3 Mar 1871 Carlisle Pa. for 5 yrs; age 22; laborer; hazel eyes, blk hair, dk comp, 5' 6 3/4" high; join co H 27 May 1871 Louisville Ky.; dd co cook Aug 1872; disch 3 Mar 1876 Ft Rice DT expir of serv a pvt; reenl 30 Mar 1876 Chicago Ill. for 5 yrs; join co K 27 Apr 1876 St Paul Minn.; dd orderly for capt Benteen 17 May; tr to co H 14 June to date 1 July 1876; ds camp Powder River MT 15 June chg of capt Benteen's pvt horses & prop;[11] ds str *Josephine* 7 Aug & arr Ft Rice 15 Aug (with pvt Walter);[12] far'r 6 Feb 1877; ds Ft Rice Apr thro' Dec 1877;[13] ds Ft Lincoln DT 15 Sep to 20 Nov 1878; disch 19 Mar 1881 Ft Meade DT expir of serv a far'r; reenl 12 Apr 1881 Ft Hamilton N.Y. for 5 yrs; assd to co M 3 art'y; tr to co I 2 art'y; disch 31 Mar 1886 Jackson Bks La. expir of serv a pvt char very good; reenl 12 Apr 1886 Jeff'n Bks Mo. for 5 yrs; assd to co B 4 cav; tr to prov gd; disch 11 Apr 1891 Ft L'worth Kans. expir of serv a pvt char xclt & reenl for 5 yrs; assd to detmt a.s.m. [army service men] qmd; disch 12 Apr 1896 West Point N.Y. expir of serv a sgt char xclt & reenl in same unit; died 5 Mar 1898 at West Point (asphxyation from inhalation of illuminating gas) a sgt.

Fitzgerald, Jno. Far'r co C; b. Staffordshire England; pvt co H 1 N.Y. inf 7 May 1861 to 25 May 1863; pvt co D 13 N.Y. art'y 7 July 1863 for 3 yrs; tr to co L 6 N.Y. art'y upon dissolution of regt 18 July 1865; m.o. vol serv 24 Aug 1865; enl reg army 8 Nov 1866 New York N.Y. for 5 yrs; age 32; teamster; blue eyes, brn hair, fair comp, 5' 4" high; assd to co M 8 cav; disch 8 Nov 1871 Ft Garland Colo. expir of serv a pvt; reenl 19 Jan 1872 New York N.Y. for 5 yrs; join co C 7 cav 18 Feb 1872 Rutherfordton NC; far'r 12 Apr 1873; dd detmt hq 23 Apr 1873 Camp Sturgis (Yankton) DT; with Custer column 25 June 1876 but left behind when horse gave out[14] ds enroute to Ft Lincoln 6 Aug 1876; dd qmd 12–28 Sep with 281 cav horses at post; ds Ft Lincoln 20 Oct 1876 dismtd; disch 19 Jan 1877 Ft Totten DT expir of serv a far'r char good; reenl 26 Dec 1877 New York N.Y. for 5 yrs; assd to co M 8 cav; disch 25 Dec 1882 Ft L'worth Kans. expir of serv a pvt char very good & reenl in same unit for 5 yrs; disch 25 Dec 1887 Ft Concho Tex. expir of serv a far'r char xclt & reenl in same unit for 5 yrs; tr to co I 8 cav; retd 22 Nov 1890 Ft Meade DT a pvt char xclt; died 7 May 1900 (12:30 a.m.) New York N.Y. (551 W. 45th St), age 70.[15]

Flanagan, Jas. Sgt co D; b. Dublin Ireland; pvt cpl & sgt co E 11 Ohio cav 22 July 1863 to 14 July 1866; enl in 7 cav 15 Nov 1871 Louisville Ky. for 5 yrs; age 35; soldier; blue eyes, brn hair, lt comp, 5' 10 1/2" high; join co D Dec 1871 Chester SC; cpl 1 Apr 1872; sgt 1 Aug 1874; disch 15 Nov 1876 Ft Rice DT expir of serv a sgt char xclt & reenl in co D for 5 yrs; dd post sgt-maj Dec 1876 to Feb 1877; (recom for medal of honor for conspic gal at LBH but omitted on revised list);[16] ds 26 Sep 1877 in field; dd co qm sgt Feb to June 1878; dd co qm sgt Apr to Oct 1879; in conft Aug 1880; awl 26 Apr to 9 July 1881; disch 14 Nov 1881 Ft Yates DT expir of serv

a sgt char xclt; died 21 Apr 1921 Mandan N.Dak.
Pension: 27 Dec 1890 / Inv / 975523 / 888851.

Flanagan, Jno. (alias). See Walsh, Thos.

Flint, Moses Eaton. Citizen packer qmd; b. 10 Oct 1819 Richford Vt; res Pleasant Grove Minn. from 1859; hired Apr 1876 St Paul Minn. by Lt Gibbs 6 inf actg aqm to pack supplies on pub animals of exp'n;[17] rate of pay $50 mo & entitled to one ration per day & transp back to St Paul if hon disch; tr to Lt Nowlan at Ft Lincoln DT 17 Apr 1876 with pay to commence from that date; drove pack mules alongside wagon train dur march to Powder River; return to Bismarck 10 Sep on boat from Yellowstone;[18] employed at Ft Lincoln 11–15 Sep by Lt Burns actg aqm as hostler for cav horses at post; rate of pay $30 mo; disch as packer 23 Sep 1876 due $138.33 pay from 1 July; died 21 Nov 1902 Vanderbilt SD.[19]

Flood, Phillip. Pvt co G; b. Meath Co Ireland; enl 3 Dec 1874 Boston Mass. for 5 yrs; age 27; laborer; brn eyes, brn hair, ruddy comp, 5' 6 3/4" high; join co G 10 Feb 1875 Shreveport La.; sent to govt hosp for insane at Wash'n D.C. 27 Apr 1875; disch 9 Sep 1878 to date 1 July 1877 per SO 140 AGO 1877 a pvt char good as far as known; died 7 Apr 1905 govt hosp for insane.[20]

Foley, Jno. Cpl co C; b. Salem Mass.; enl 18 Sep 1873 Boston Mass. for 5 yrs; age 23; shoe cutter; blue eyes, grey hair, ruddy comp, 5' 8 1/2" high; join co C 21 Oct 1873 Ft Rice DT; dd co cook June 1874; dd qmd Apr 1875; cpl 3 June 1875; dd qmd Aug 1875; killed with Custer column 25 June 1876.

Foley, Jno. Pvt co K; b. 15 Apr 1839 Dublin Ireland; pvt co F 22 Ohio inf 20 Apr 1861 to 19 Aug 1861; pvt co A 1 Ohio cav 29 Aug 1861; gsw l. leg 22 Aug 1862 action at Catlett's Sta; disch 21 Feb 1863 Baltimore Md on surg cert dis (permanent lameness l. leg); pvt co B 2 Ohio art'y 29 July 1863 to 23 Aug 1865; enl reg army 11 Aug 1866 Columbus Ohio for 5 yrs; age 27; farmer; grey eyes, blk hair, dk comp, 5' 9" high; join co K 7 cav 29 Sep 1866 Ft Riley Kans.; cpl 27 Nov 1866; in conft Feb & Apr 1867; pvt 9 Apr 1867; des 22 May 1867 camp near Ft Hays Kans. & apph 2 days later; restored to duty without trial Aug 1867 on cond'n he make good time lost; in conft Feb 1869; dd co cook Aug 1869; sen gen cm 27 Nov 1869 forf $10 pay per mo for 3 mos & conft same period; disch 11 Aug 1871 Yorkville SC expir of serv a pvt; reenl in regt 22 Aug 1871 Louisville Ky. for 5 yrs & rejoin co K at Yorkville; awol Dec 1871; awol 8 May 1873 (left camp 10 miles from Yankton, where apph 13 May); pres on parole June 1873; sen gen cm 2 July 1873 forf $10 pay per mo for 6 mos & conft 4 mos; in conft exp'n hq Aug 1873; in conft Oct 1873; dd battn hq 25 June to 31 Aug 1874; disch 6 Aug 1876 camp mouth of Rosebud Creek MT (in time to go down river by first boat) per GO 24 AGO 1859 a pvt char xclt; arr Ft Lincoln 10 Aug on str *Durfee*; reenl 2 Sep 1876 Chicago Ill. for 5 yrs & rejoin co K 1 Oct at Ft Lincoln; injured 30 Sep 1877 Snake Creek MT (Bear's Paw Mtns) when his horse fell & rolled on his r. thigh dur chg on Nez Perce inds; tr to str *Silver City* 14 Oct mouth of Squaw Creek (on Mo. River); adm to hosp Ft Lincoln 26 Oct; duty 14 Nov 1877; dd qmd teamster Apr 1878; disch 26 May 1878 Ft Rice DT on surg cert dis (incomplete paralysis whole r. extremity) a pvt char xclt; died 6 Mar 1926 Sol. Home, Wash'n D.C.
Pension: 2 Jan 1879 / Inv / 264454 / 159742.

Forbes, (Sir) Jno. Stuart Stuart. See Stuart-Forbes, Jno. Stuart

Foster, Sam'l. Pvt co A; b. Clay Co Ky.; enl in co A 9 May 1872 Manchester Ky. for 5 yrs; age 22; laborer; blk eyes, brn hair, dk comp, 5' 6 1/2" high; gsw upper r. arm (fl. wd. sl.) 25 June 1876 dur retreat from valley fight; tr on str *Far West* 3 July to hosp Ft Lincoln DT; duty 3 Aug 1876; dd qmd 15 Sep 1876 care for pub animals; disch 9 May 1877 at Ft Rice DT upon expir of serv a pvt char xclt; reenl 31 July 1877 Ft Snelling Minn. for 5 yrs; assd to co G 20 inf; disch 28 Jan 1879 Ft Brown Tex. on surg cert dis (consumption; dis total) a pvt; died 10 Nov 1883 on Red Bird near Manchester Ky.

Pension: 20 Feb 1879 / Inv / 268202 / 166693. Wid / 314141 / 210799. (XC-889,431).

Fowler, Isaac. Pvt co C; b. Dark Co Ohio; pvt & sgt co K 53 Ohio inf 21 Aug 1861 to 26 June 1865; enl 29 Sep 1873 Cincinnati Ohio for 5 yrs; age 29; farmer; brn eyes, dk hair, fair comp, 5' 7 1/4" high; join co C 21 Oct 1873 Ft Rice DT; dd qmd Feb & Apr 1874; dd room orderly Apr & June 1875; dd post hq Oct 1875; disch 29 Sep 1878 Camp J. G. Sturgis DT expir of serv a pvt char good; reenl 12 Oct 1878 Ft Lincoln DT for 5 yrs in co G 17 inf; sick qrs 31 Aug 1880 to 28 Feb 1881 (phthisis); disch 28 Apr 1881 at Ft Lincoln on surg cert dis (consumption & impaired vision) a pvt; died 5 Dec 1881 Union City Ind.
Pension: 25 June 1881 / Inv / 424725 / 197745.

Fox, Fred'k. Pvt co I; b. Wertumberg Germany; enl 22 Oct 1872 Phila Pa. for 5 yrs; age 22; machinist; brn eyes, brn hair, dk comp, 5' 7 3/4" high; join co I 2 Dec 1872 Shelbyville Ky.; dd co cook Dec 1873; ed post bakery 7 Aug 1875 to 16 Oct 1876 Ft Lincoln DT; dd co cook Apr to July 1877; disch 14 July 1877 at Tongue River MT per SO 70 Dept of Dak. 1877, a pvt char good.[21]

Fox, Harvey A. Pvt co D; b. Alexander Co NC; enl in co D 27 July 1871 Mt Vernon Ky. for 5 yrs; age 23; farmer; gray eyes, fair hair, fair comp, 5' 6" high; dd co cook Oct 1871 to May 1873; ds in field DT Sep 1873; ed qmd teamster Oct 1873; in conft Dec 1873 to Apr 1874; acquitted in gen cm & ret to duty; ds camp Powder River MT 15 June 1876 guarding wagon train;[22] disch 27 July 1876 camp mouth of Rosebud Creek MT expir of serv a pvt; employed post qmd Ft Lincoln DT 25–30 Aug 1876 as hostler for pub horses enroute to Yellowstone; rate of pay $30 mo; (m. Dec 1878 at Ft Lincoln to Amelia Monroe, mother of scouts Bob & Wm. Jackson); res Browning MT; died 28 Mar 1913.[23]
Pension: 20 Sep 1904 / Inv / 1324746. Rej 16 Oct 1908, clmt unable to prove origin of disability in serv.

Fox, Jno. Pvt co D; b. 1 Nov 1846 Buffalo N.Y.; enl 24 Sep 1875 St Louis Mo. for 5 yrs; age 28; cooper; blue eys, dk hair, dk comp, 5' 8 1/2" high; join co D 21 Oct 1875 Ft Lincoln DT; cpl 1 Oct 1877; sgt 6 Apr 1879; disch 23 Sep 1880 Ft Yates DT expir of serv a sgt char good; reenl 8 Oct 1880 St Louis Mo. for 5 yrs; assd to co E 1 inf; disch 7 Oct 1885 Whipple Bks AT expir of serv a pvt char good; reenl 30 Oct 1885 at Whipple Bks for 5 yrs; assd to co D 2 inf; disch 29 Oct 1890 Ft Omaha Neb expir of serv a sgt; reenl 1 Nov 1890 Chicago Ill. for 5 yrs; assd to co F 4 inf; disch 31 Oct 1895 Ft Sherman Idaho expir of serv a pvt char xclt & reenl in same co for 3 yrs; ed qmd mech engr Sep 1896; disch 26 May 1897 Ft Sheridan Ill. on surg cert dis (chr. rheum.) a pvt char xclt; died 26 Dec 1932 Sol. Home Wash'n D.C.
Pension: 1 June 1897 / Inv / 1191934 / 958087. Ind. Surv. / 9679 / 6479.

Frank, Wm. Pvt co B; b. Madgeburg Prussia; enl 18 June 1855 Louisville Ky. for 5 yrs in co F 2 cav; age 26; tailor; hazel eyes, lt hair, lt comp, 5' 8" high; wd (sl.) 1 Oct 1858 Wichita Village CN [IT] in action with Comanche inds; disch 18 Apr 1860 Ft Mason Tex. by reenlmt in co for 5 yrs; (2 cav redesig 5 cav Aug 1861); disch 1 July 1864 City Pt Va. by reenlmt in co for 3 yrs; disch 1 July 1867 Richmond Va. expir of serv a cpl; reenl 26 Oct 1867 Wash'n D.C. for 5 yrs; join co F 7 cav 5 Feb 1868 Ft L'worth Kans.; dd co tailor June to Sep 1868; dd regtl hq Oct 1868 to Apr 1869; in conft 27 Apr 1869; dd co tailor June 1869 to Apr 1870 & Dec 1870 to Oct 1872; disch 26 Oct 1872 Louisville Ky. expir of serv a pvt; reenl 12 Oct 1875 St Louis Mo. for 5 yrs; join co B 7 cav 11 Nov 1875 Shreveport La.; dd regtl hq fatigue pty (morn & eve) 11 May 1876; ds 17 Oct 1876 Ft Lincoln DT dismtd; dd co tailor Feb 1878 to Jan 1879; disch 28 Apr 1879 Ft Yates DT on surg cert dis (presbyopia defective vision) a pvt char xclt; died 6 Apr 1880 Baltimore Md; (age 53 yrs, 3 mos, 13 days).
Pension: 11 Dec 1879 / Inv / 328109 / 218723. Wid / 264147 / 268801.

Franklin, Jno. W. Pvt co A; b. Providence RI; enl 11 Jan 1875 St Louis Mo. for 5 yrs; age 24; hostler; gray eyes, brn hair, dk comp,

5' 9" high; join co A 6 Feb 1875 Livingston Ala; cpl 23 Aug 1875; pvt 7 Feb 1876; dd packer June & Aug 1876; tried by field cm 26 July camp mouth of Big Horn River (stole army revolver from body of citizen packer Mann);[24] sen gen cm forf $12 pay per mo for 6 mos & conft same period thence to dishon disch; (capt Moylan recom clemency in consid'n of former good char & being one of best men in co); in conft Oct 1876; awol 30 Nov 1876 (recd pass to go to Ft Lincoln to collect debt owed by chf-trump'r Hardy, which statement was false); sen gen cm forf $10 pay per mo for 5 mos & conft same period; des 2 Feb 1877 at Ft Rice; apph 11 Feb 1880 New York N.Y.; (capt Moylan recom restoration to duty with his co as sol. a very competent packer & men proficient in that line very scarce); dishon disch 15 Mar 1880 David's Isl NYH & 2 yrs conft mil prison Ft L'worth Kans.

Frederick, Andrew. Sgt co K; b. Bedford Co Pa.; enl 23 Nov 1866 Carlisle Pa. for 5 yrs; age 23; teamster; hazel eyes, dk hair, lt comp, 5' 3 1/2" high; join co M 7 cav 10 Dec 1866 Ft Riley Kans.; far'r 1 May 1867; ds with gen Custer's detmt 15 July 1867; cpl 7 Oct 1867; sgt 1 Sep 1868; disch 23 Nov 1871 Unionville SC expir of serv a qm sgt; enl in co K 7 cav 23 Apr 1872 Yorkville SC for 5 yrs; cpl 1 May 1872; sgt 1 July 1872; ds Standing Rock Agcy for govt prop Dec 1873; dd chg of fatigue pty Apr 1874; ds Ft Lincoln 16 Oct 1876 dismtd; pvt 9 Dec 1876; disch 23 Apr 1877 at Ft Lincoln expir of serv a pvt char xclt; reenl in co K 1 May 1877 at Ft Lincoln for 5 yrs; dd post hq mtd orderly 28 May 1877; ds Ft Lincoln June 1877; wag 1 Aug 1877; ed field hosp nurse 15–26 Oct 1877 on str *Silver City* to Ft Lincoln; pvt 1 Jan 1878; dd co cook Aug 1878; dd asst co cook Oct 1878; far'r 1 Feb 1879; pvt 1 Oct 1879; died 14 Jan 1881 Ft Totten DT, (pyaemia), a pvt.

French, Henry E. Cpl co C; b. Portsmouth N.H.; enl 22 Jan 1872 Brooklyn N.Y. for 5 yrs; age 22; painter; hazel eyes, brn hair, fair comp, 5' 6" high; join co C 18 Feb 1872 Rutherfordton NC; ed qmd laborer Dec 1872; ds in field 24 July to 10 Sep 1873; dd qmd Apr 1875; cpl 3 June 1875; killed with Custer column 25 June 1876.

French, Thos. Henry. Capt co M; b. 4 Mar 1843 near Baltimore Md; educ at Georgetown College & employed as clerk in state dept at Wash'n; enl in 10 inf 13 Jan 1864 Ft Lafayette NYH for 5 yrs; age 21; hazel eyes, brn hair, lt comp, 5' 8 1/2" high; appt clerk post hq [his uncle, col Martin Burke comdg post); recom for com'n & passed exam'n 21 Mar 1864; appt 2Lt 10 inf 18 May & joined regt near Petersburg Va.; 1Lt co A 23 June 1864; comd regt in battles on Weldon railroad dur Aug 1864; wd l. leg (severe) 1 Oct 1864 at Chapel House Va.; in hosp Georgetown D.C. to 24 Dec 1864 when assd to staff of col Burke at Ft Lafayette; bvt capt for gal serv in operations on Weldon railroad; actg div judge advocate NYC & Harbor July & Aug 1865; rejoined co 1 Sep 1865 at Ft Ripley Minn.; (declined prom'n to capt 44 inf [vet reserve corps] 21 Sep 1866 preferring active serv even in subordinate grade); prom capt co E 26 Mar 1868; post comdr Ft Ripley Aug & Sep 1868; comd escort for govt beef cattle from Ft Wadsworth to Ft Totten DT Oct 1868; unassd 19 May 1869 (being jr capt when 26 inf consol with 10 inf) & appt actg judge advocate mil com'n at Austin Tex.; [appd 9 July 1870 for any regt even as 2Lt]; appt capt 7 cav 1 Jan 1871 (recom by col Burke to gen Sherman); join co M 15 Feb 1871 Ft Hays Kans.; comd co on Yellowstone Exp'n June to Sep 1873 & on Blk Hills Exp'n July & Aug 1874; nearly wd on Reno hill 26 June 1876 when bullet passed thro' hat;[25] gsw l. hand [sl., damaged ring] 13 Sep 1877 Canon Creek MT in action with Nez Perce inds (cited by capt Benteen for conspic gal in two mtd chgs); in arrest 11 Nov 1878 Ft Meade DT (drunk & cavorted with laundresses); sen gen cm 15 Apr 1879 to suspension from rank on half pay for one yr;[26] appeared before retiring bd 22 Dec 1879 Ft L'worth Kans. (upon recom'n of col Sturgis); placed on retd list 5 Feb 1880 (in consid'n of his wds & serv) incapacitated due to intemperance not incident of serv; died 27 Mar 1882 L'worth City Kans.[27]
[B 113 CB 1870].

Frett, Jno. (Jr). Citizen packer qmd; b. 6 Jan 1840 Prussia Germany; enr 14 Oct 1861 Chicago Ill. a pvt co A 13 Ill. cav for 3 yrs; age 21; carpenter; gray eyes, brn hair, lt comp, 5' 9" high; cpl 1 Jan 1862; pvt 4 May 1862; injured l. shoulder Nov 1862 when thrown from horse; cpl 1 Jan 1864; injury renewed Dec 1864 when thrown from horse & in hosp to Mar 1865 Pine Bluff Ark; m.o. vol serv to date 30 Dec 1864;[28] abandoned trade due to injury & res on farm in McHenry Co. Ill.; moved to St Paul Minn. in 1867;[29] hired Apr 1876 at St Paul by Lt Gibbs actg aqm to pack supplies on pub animals of exp'n; rate of pay $50 mo & entitled to one ration per day & transp back to St Paul if hon disch; tr to Lt Nowlan at Ft Lincoln DT 17 Apr 1876 with pay to commence from that date; drove pack mules alongside wagon train dur march to Powder River;[30] horse shot eve 25 June on Reno hill & prop stolen; disch 8 July mouth of Big Horn River MT due $13.33 pay from 1 July;[31] testified in Reno court of inq at Chicago 5 Feb 1879 (described as a rough but honest looking fellow with high forehead & bald head);[32] died 14 May 1920 Sol. Home, Johnson City Tenn.[33]

Pension: 28 Jan 1876 / Inv / 213664 / 258894; (appv from 31 Dec 1864 for injury to left shoulder; dropped from roll 2 Mar 1881, disability having ceased to exist). 10 Sep 1920 / Wid / 1163183; rej acc't no title, marriage occurred after 3 Mar 1899 & clmt did not cohabit with sol. until his death. Claim appv in 1932, (XC-969,146).

Notes—F

1. Farber was married in Hungary to Elizabeth Stockhowe who died about 1878. He remarried some months later, July 1, 1879, to Jennie Jones, age 19, (his housekeeper since 1875), Pension file, RG 15.

2. Why Farley stayed at Powder River is uncertain. Perhaps when Private McWilliams came on the boat, Farley took his place at the camp that, "The camping-party [a detachment detailed to prepare camp] of a regiment [in campaign] consists of . . . a Corporal and two men per company," *United States Army Regulations,* 1863, Par.'s 498 and 500; or his experience as blacksmith may have been a factor, as Capt. Benteen expressed concern for his two private horses at the camp.

A more plausible explanation involves the death of Private George and the removal of his body from the boat to the supply camp for burial. Farley and George were enlisted on the same day at New Orleans by Capt. Benteen, and may have been good friends.

3. NA, M1734, Roll 18, frame 0558, "List of Sick Transferred from Supply Camp to Hospital at."

4. See note A25 (Ascough); Alcott said Fehler carried the company guidon at Little Big Horn and threw it away in timber at start of retreat so as not to be encumbered with it. Hardy said Fehler threw the guidon away when he came out of timber, that he had an unruly horse, and could not get staff in boot, WMC, Field Notes, IU; McVeigh said Fehler was in charge of company packs, Liddic and Harbaugh, *Camp on Custer,* 92.

William O. Taylor said in late evening June 25, he went to see Sgt. Feiler who was acting 1st sergeant as regular 1st sergeant was wounded and Feiler was then near lower end of the herded horses and pack mules. Taylor said Fehler was an elderly German of rather placid nature. Taylor to Walter Camp, Dec.12, 1909, WMC-BYU.

Lt. Varnum thought Fehler obtained a medal for leading one of the water parties on Reno Hill, Varnum to Gen. Joseph B. Doe, Asst. Secretary of War, Feb. 6, 1894, (reference to Theo. Goldin seeking a medal of honor), RG 94, Entry 25, file, 8521 PRD 1894.

Stan Roy said Sgt. Fehler and four others were sharpshooters to protect the water carriers, Hammer, *Custer in '76,* 114.

Fehler is not on Capt. Moylan's revised list, June 24, 1878. Gen. Terry had returned the lists to Col. Sturgis, Feb. 26, 1878, stating that it appeared, "from the great number of recommendations that company commanders have recommended every man in their respective companies that behaved ordinarily all during the action of the 25 June 1876. Medals of Honor are not intended for ordinarily good conduct, but for conspicuous acts of gallantry. These lists will be *revised* under the direction of the Colonel of the regiment or some suitable officer to be designated by him for the purpose and will be returned to these Headquarters with the names, only, of men who distinguished themselves in marked manner by conspicuous acts of gallantry in the action," RG 94, Entry 409, file, 10818 A (EB) 1878.

5. Knipe said Windolph told him Finckle had been a captain in the German army. Knipe interview, June 1908, WMC-IU.

6. Private Darby Finley was discharged from Company B, 1st Battalion, 17th Infantry; total service ten years six days. British military records (hereafter cited as British military records), The National Archives, formerly Public Record Office, Kew, Richmond, Surrey.

7. Finnegan's widow, Katie, born Sept. 8, 1855, said her husband, born Sept. 2nd, was two years older than she. Pension file, RG 15.

8. Capt. Yates' letter to his wife Aug. 1, 1874, from the Black Hills Expedition, mentions, "the servants and Finnegan. Tell Finnegan I hope the house all in good order and cooking well," *Research Review*, Vol. XI, June, 1977.

Katherine Gibson Fougera (daughter of Lt. Gibson) said strikers were referred to as "soldier houseman, in army parlance." Fougera, *With Custer's Cavalry*, 14.

The wife of Lt. Frank D. Baldwin, 5th Infantry, explained the term "striker" applied, "to those useful and necessary soldiers usually detailed in officer's quarters, who are an important adjunct to the comfort of those households, and always easily obtained, as their pay is increased thereby, with a satisfactory 'stipend,' and three meals daily, in warm and comfortable surroundings." Mrs. Baldwin referred to their own striker as "our family factotum," Baldwin, *Memoirs of Major General Frank D. Baldwin*, 129.

Lt. Godfrey said that when the regulation making it unlawful for officers to employ soldiers as servants was passed, Gen. Terry issued Circular Order No. 1, Jan. 6, 1876, forbidding the practice under any circumstance, and directed post commanders to report all violations. Obtaining servants suitable for the field was difficult because female servants were out of the question; but the soldier was generally pleased to have this detail because they had better living than in the company mess and were usually excused from guard duty. The company gained by the rations of the men so detailed, and the officers were better served, but most importantly, unlike citizen cooks, who could hardly be relied on in times of difficulty and were usually extravagant with the limited supplies, the soldier was available to put in the ranks in time of action. When Gen. Terry and his staff came (to Fort Lincoln in May 1876) provided with their servants, and when the expedition's departure was delayed several days by cold rains, the staff suffered various discomforts. They visited the 7th Cavalry camp and expressed surprise at the officers having cheerful fires and hot meals served at regular hours. As soon as they learned the secret of their comfort, inquiries were made of company commanders for a good man as orderly who had experience in field service, and when they were soon provided with orderlies, their servants were discharged or sent back to St. Paul. From lecture read before Military Service Institute at West Point, NY, May 12, 1881; Early Drafts re: Little Big Horn, Godfrey Papers.

Until the early 1880s, officers were waited on by soldier-servants and strikers assigned from their companies, often as cooks for their messes and sometimes for their families. The soldier received extra pay from the officer, ranging from $5 to $10 dollars a month, depending on the type and amount of work performed. Rickey, *Forty Miles,* 111.

9. The Walter Camp rosters of Companies E and F at Little Big Horn Battlefield have several statements credited to Finnegan; also a line is drawn through "In doubt," previously written after Finnegan's name, and replaced with "at L.B.H." Other Camp rosters of Company F contain remarks added after each name by Lynch and Rooney, WMC-BYU.

Finnegan's obituary stated that he "served in C. F. 7, the regiment under Reno, who was but three miles from General Custer at the time of the massacre." *Bonner Springs (Kans.) Chieftain*, Feb. 15, 1923.

Capt. Benteen, in a letter to his wife, July 18, 1876, from camp at Powder River, said, "Mrs. Yates has turned over her horses etc., which are up here—to dispose of for her." Carroll, *Camp Talk*, 42.

10. Finnegan was allegedly followed to St. Paul by Lucetta "Settie" Belle Craig (wife of Private Nick Klein, and sister of Fannie James, wife of Private John James), and they resided together until about 1886. *St. Paul Dispatch*, July 11, 1883, reported "Mary Quail and Belle Finnigan, two quarrelsome neighbors, were placed under bonds to keep the peace."

Thomas Finnegan and Lucretia Creigh were married Oct. 20, 1883, at Minneapolis. Finnegan said he wanted his son (James J., born Jan. 1881) to have a legal name. Tom Finnegan married again Jan. 26, 1893, at Cincinnati, Ohio, to Katie Sarbin; resided at St. Paul to 1896; Hillsboro, Ohio, to 1913 (operated poultry business); thence to Bonner Springs, Kans.; visited Soldier's Home at Leavenworth City from 1918, and back and forth from Aug. 1921 (after paralytic stroke). Pension file, RG 15. The Walter Camp material at Brigham Young University (Box 5, envelope 26, misc. notes, n.d.) include an envelope marked, "Interviews at Leavenworth Soldier's Home Oct. 1920."

11. The muster roll of Company K, June 30, 1876, LBHB Coll., Roll 13, includes the remark (with line drawn through) that Fisher was, "On Daily Duty Orderly Comdg Officer Left Wing 7th Cav'y," and written above is "D.S. Supply Camp on mouth of Powder River June 15, 1876." (The muster roll of Company K at the National Archives contains only the latter remark. RG 94, Entry 53.

Benteen wrote to his wife, June 14, 1876, that he would leave Fisher in charge of his horses, bedding, trunk, etc., Carroll, *Camp Talk*, 14; In another letter to his wife, July 12, 1876, Benteen said he received a note from Dr. Stein at Powder River, and also one from Fisher left there in charge of Williamsburg and mare. Both said they were doing well, and Fisher was being "very watchful of them—thinking they would be stolen, unless so." Carroll, *Camp Talk*, 34.

12. The regimental return reports Privates Fisher and Walter on detached service at Fort Rice, August 14. The Fort Rice post return reports two enlisted men arrived August 15 direct from Gen. Terry's command. Gen. Terry recorded in his diary Aug 7 that surplus company property to go down river on steamer *Josephine*. (The *Josephine* left mouth of Rosebud Creek, Aug. 9, and arrived at Fort Lincoln, Aug. 13.) *Bismarck Tribune*, Aug. 23, 1876; Regimental Returns, NA, M744. Post Returns, NA, M617.

13. In a letter to his wife, Nov. 17, 1877, Benteen said he wanted Fisher reminded not to neglect the feet of the horses and that their shoes must not remain on longer than one month, especially in the case of the mare "Coquette" who was last shod in October. Carroll, *Camp Talk*, 102.

14. Peter Thompson said Fitzgerald and Brennan turned their horses to the rear two miles beyond the lone tepee. Brown and Willard, *Black Hills Trails*, 154; Sgt. Hanley said Fitzgerald, Brennan, and Thompson straggled back from Custer after pack train reached bluffs but did not know just when they got back. McGuire said Company C men often joked that Fitzgerald and Brennan fell back from Custer out of cowardice, Hammer, *Custer in '76*, 126–27; Knipe said he thought Fitzgerald was with the packs but guessed he was where Thompson said he saw him where he dropped out of company, Knipe to Walter Camp, May 1, 1909, WMC-BYU.

15. RG 94, Entry 25, file 14947 PRD 1890.

16. Capt. Godfrey to regimental adjutant, May 7, 1877, listing men of Company D entitled to medals; the list revised by Lt. Edgerly who was on duty with Company D in June 1876, RG 94, Entry 409, file 10818 A (EB) 1878.

17. John C. Wagoner passed through Rochester Minn., Mar. 28, 1876 on his way to Pleasant Grove where he intended to visit a day or two. *The Rochester Post*, Apr. 1, 1876.

18. *Bismarck Tribune*, Sept. 13, 1876, mentions Flint as "one of Reno's packers," arriving by steamer from the Yellowstone. (Three steamboats, *Durfee*, *Key West*, and, *Yellowstone*, arrived in Bismarck Sept. 10. *Bismarck Tribune*, Nov. 8, 1876).

"Mr. Flint was in the Indian fight in which Gen. Custer and his command were massacred. He was with the part of the command under Gen. Reno. This latter command lost about forty men out of three hundred and fifty, while Custer's command were all slaughtered. Mr. Flint can relate a good many incidents of that fearful engagement." *The Rochester Post*, Dec. 23, 1881.

19. *The Pollock* (SD) *Progress*, Nov. 29, 1902; *Campbell County* (SD) *Progress*, May 24, 1990, Sec. B.

20. RG 94, Entry 25, file 69843 AGO 1905.

21. See note A25 (Ascough).

22. Fox alleged he received rupture of left side June 20, 1876, in camp at Powder River, when thrown from his mule while riding at the side of Col. Moore as acting aide-de-camp. Maj. James D. Nickerson (Lt. of 17th Infantry in 1876, and in charge of 7th Cavalry dismounted detachment at Powder River), declared he knew nothing of the case. Nickerson to Military Secretary, Dec. 3, 1904, and Nickerson to Adjutant General, June 29, 1907, pension file of Harvey A. Fox, RG 15.

23. WMC, rosters, LBHB.

24. Private William O. Taylor said that, when he and a comrade moved the body of citizen packer Mann back from the line, he (Taylor) took the revolver carried by the packer, having lost his own, Taylor, *With Custer on the Little Big Horn*, 58.

25. Hammer, *Custer in '76*, 71, 142.

26. RG 153, file QQ994.

27. Johnson, "A Captain of 'Chivalric Courage,'" *The Brand Book*, (English Westerners' Society), Vol. 25, Nos. 1 & 2, 1987/88. "Tracking a Custer Indian Fighter," by Eugene L. Meyer, *The Washington Post*, Mar. 27, 1980.

28. John Frett, Sr., also served in the 13th Illinois Cavalry, Sept. 1864 to May 1865.

29. St. Paul City Directories, 1876–86, list Frett as saloon keeper and carpenter. At the Reno Court of Inquiry he said he was proprietor of the Commercial Hotel and Billiard Room at St. Paul, Nichols, *Reno Court*, 502.

30. Narrative of Lt. Godfrey, in Graham, *The Custer Myth*, 127.

31. Frett said he applied to Gen. Terry for discharge about the 1st of July on the Yellowstone. Nichols, *Reno Court*, 506.

The command reached the Yellowstone the evening of July 2, where Lt. Godfrey said they received quite a mail of papers on July 3 and, "The letters we got yesterday." Frett received word of a family illness and may have been discharged in time to depart on the Steamer *Far West* (his discharge dated to allow travel time to St. Paul and to receive his daily ration to point of hire). Frett's story appeared in the *St. Paul Dispatch*, July 27, 1876.

During the campaign several soldiers were discharged with remark, "in time to enable them to go down the Missouri river by the first boat," See, SFO 37, Hq DD, Aug. 5, 1876, RG 94, Entry 44; Godfrey, *Diary*, 20–21; John Ryan said when a soldier was discharged he was allowed transportation by the government from place of discharge to the place he enlisted, Barnard, *Ten Years with Custer*, 183.

In reckoning the travel allowance to discharged soldiers, the distance was estimated by the shortest practicable route; computed by taking the distance in miles from place of discharge to place of residence, enlistment, or enrollment, and giving one day's pay and subsistence for every twenty miles of such distance. Rations estimated at the contract price at place of discharge, *Regs. 1863*, par. 1370; *Regs. 1881*, par. 2463.

32. Utley, *The Reno Court of Inquiry,* 366.

33. Frett moved to Washington D.C., in 1885 where he and wife Mary Catherine were divorced Feb. 10, 1887. He was awarded custody of their minor children, Louisa, Josephine, Catherine, and Karl, and in March 1891 claimed destitute circumstances as a widower with small children. He remarried April 9, 1901 at Alexandria, Va., to Ann Catherine (Kate) Herbert, age 32, and removed to Hampton, Va., where he operated a shoe repair shop. They separated in 1915 because of his drunkenness and abuse. A granddaughter, Mrs. Theresa Long (born 1891), recalled that he was a hard drinking man and got worse with age. Kate died Nov. 19, 1940. Pension file, RG 15.

G

Gaffney, Geo. Sgt co I; b. 1846 Cavan Co. Ireland; pvt co C 9 Mass. inf Aug 1862; tr to co D 32 Mass. inf May 1864; m.o. vol serv 29 June 1865; enl reg army 19 Nov 1866 Phila Pa. for 5 yrs; age 22; soldier; gray eyes, dk hair, dk comp, 5' 2" high; join co I 7 cav 22 Dec 1866 Ft Wallace Kans.; gsw r. foot 21 June 1867 in action with inds; duty 2 Aug 1867; ds with escort for col Greenwood's survey pty May to Nov 1868; dd co cook June & Aug 1869; ed post qmd Oct 1871; disch 19 Nov 1871 Shelbyville Ky. upon expir of serv & reenl in co I for 5 yrs; trump'r 9 May 1872; cpl 1 Feb 1873; sgt 22 Sep 1873; ed qmd Dec 1875 to Apr 1876; ed qmd mech with exp'n 6 May to 27 Sep 1876;[1] [with Lt Nowlan 22–24 June on str *Far West*];[2] furn transp by post qm Ft Buford 24 Sep to Ft Lincoln (with Cowley & Hegner);[3] disch 19 Nov 1876 at Ft Lincoln by expir of serv a sgt & reenl 2 days later in co I for 5 yrs; pvt 10 Feb 1877; cpl 23 July 1877; ed qmd Feb & Apr 1878; pvt 30 Sep 1878; dd co cook Dec 1878 & Feb 1879; cpl 10 June 1879; dd qmd chg of corral Aug 1879; acquited in civil trial Jan 1880 Fargo DT (chg of larceny of some of wardrobe of leading lady of theatrical troupe performing at Ft Lincoln);[4] ds Ft Lincoln chg co prop June to Nov 1880; sgt 10 July 1881; dd actg co qm sgt Aug 1881; disch 20 Nov 1881 Ft Totten DT expir of serv & reenl in co I for 5 yrs; dd actg co qm sgt Nov 1881 to Jan 1883; dd post prov sgt June 1883; dd qmd Aug 1883; dd chg of detail cutting wood Oct 1883; dd chg of targets Apr 1884; dd chg of detail cutting hay Aug 1884; dd qmd chg of teamsters Jan to May 1885; sen gen cm 7 May 1886 forf $10 pay; disch 20 Nov 1886 at Ft Totten expir of serv a sgt; reenl 24 Nov 1886 Chicago Ill. for 5 yrs; assd to co F 17 inf; disch 2 Aug 1889 Ft D. A. Russell Wyo. Ty on surg cert dis (hemoplegia, paralysis l. side from exposure & hardship in line of duty) a pvt char xclt; died 22 Nov 1916 Sol. Home Wash'n D.C.; (never married).
Pension: 9 Aug 1889 / Inv / 724272 / 460020.

Gallenne, Jean Baptiste Desiré. Pvt co M; b. 19 Feb 1849 L'Orient France; enl 30 Sep 1873 New York N.Y. for 5 yrs; age 24; student; brn eyes, blk hair, dk comp, 5' 5 1/4" high; join co M 21 Oct 1873 Ft Rice DT; dd subs dept herder Oct 1874; sick 20–22 June 1876 (pleurisy); horse holder dur valley fight 25 June; nurse in hosp on Reno hill; sick 8 July camp mouth of Big Horn River (pleurisy r. side);[5] sick on str *Carroll* 3 Aug (typhoid fever) to hosp Ft Lincoln DT; duty 21 Nov 1876; ed hosp attdt in field with Dr. Havard 1 May 1877; appt hosp stew'd 2d cl. 22 May 1877; gsw l. ankle 30 Sep 1877 Snake Creek MT (Bear's Paw Mtns) in action with Nez Perce inds;[6] lower l. leg amp'd 14 Oct on str *Silver City* at mouth of Squaw Creek (on Mo. River); adm to hosp Ft Lincoln 26 Oct; disch 27 Apr 1878 at Ft Rice on surg cert dis a pvt char good; died 12 Feb 1911 Wash'n D.C.
Pension: 16 May 1878 / Inv / 254827 / 155347. Wid / 959761 / 781016.

Galvan, Jas. J. Pvt co L; b. Liverpool England; enl 28 Sep 1875 Boston Mass. for 5 yrs; age 26; laborer; grey eyes, dk hair, dk comp, 5' 6 3/4" high; join co L 29 Oct 1875 Ft Totten DT; killed with Custer column 25 June 1876.[7]
Pension: 17 June 1895 / Father / 616278; (abandoned, clmt unable to prove identity).

Gannon, Peter. Sgt co B; b. Manchester England; enl 18 June 1867 Boston Mass. for 5 yrs; age 23; laborer; blue eyes, brn hair, lt comp, 5' 6 3/4" high; join co B 14 Sep 1867 Ft Dodge Kans.; cpl 1 July 1871; sgt 1 Sep 1871; disch 18 June 1872 Spartanburg SC expir of serv a sgt; reenl 16 July 1872 New York N.Y. for 5 yrs; assd to co B 28 Aug 1872 at Spartanburg; sgt 1 Nov 1872; des 5 May 1873 Yankton DT; apph 23 Aug 1873 Louisville Ky.; in conft to 9 Feb 1874 when restored to duty in consid'n of his xclt char; 1sgt 16 Apr 1874; sgt 17 Mar 1875; ds camp Powder River MT 10 June 1876; dd qmd Ft

Lincoln DT 20 Nov to 7 Dec 1876; disch 16 July 1877 camp near Sentinel Butte MT by expir of serv a sgt char xclt; reenl 12 Oct 1878 at Ft Lincoln for 5 yrs; assd to co C 7 cav 22 Nov 1878; cpl 25 Nov 1878; pvt 25 July 1879; lance cpl & actg qm sgt Oct 1879; cpl 6 Apr 1880; dd qmd Oct 1880 to May 1881; sgt 11 June 1881; pvt 9 Mar 1882; cpl 1 July 1882; pvt 18 June 1883; disch 11 Oct 1883 Ft Meade DT expir of serv a pvt char very good; reenl 22 Dec 1883 Ft L'worth Kans. for 5 yrs; assd to co A 20 inf; sick in hosp Apr 1886 (constip'n); died 12 June 1886 Ft Assiniboine MT (stric. transverse colon) a sgt.

Gardner, Jno. (alias Wm. Gardner). Pvt co F; b. 27 Feb 1845 Brockville Canada; enr 28 July 1862 Lowville N.Y. in co C battn Blk River art'y; (redesig co L 5 N.Y. art'y); cpl 12 Sep 1862; sgt 17 Jan 1863; m.o. vol serv 26 June 1865 Harper's Ferry Va.; enl reg army as Wm. Gardner 12 Aug 1870 New York N.Y. for 5 yrs; age 21; butcher; blue eyes, lt hair, lt comp, 5' 5 1/2" high; join co L 3 art'y 31 Jan 1871 Ft Jeff'n Fla; dd ordn dept laborer Apr 1871 to Feb 1872; cpl 14 Feb 1872; dd actg sgt-maj Oct 1872; ed qmd as cox swain in barge crew Dec 1872 to Aug 1873; sgt 4 Sep 1873; disch 12 Aug 1875 Ft Wadsworth N.Y. expir of serv a sgt; reenl 28 Aug 1875 New York N.Y. for 5 yrs; join co F 7 cav 21 Oct 1875 Ft Lincoln DT; dd co cook Dec 1875 & Feb 1876; td regtl hq 7 May 1876 chg of pub animals; killed with Custer column 25 June 1876.
Pension: 15 May 1890 / Mother / 422818 / 344693.

Gardner, Wm. See Gardner, Jno.

Garlick, Edw. 1sgt co G; b. 8 May 1846 Chertsey England; enl 3 Feb 1866 Richmond Va. for 3 yrs; age 21; laborer; blue eyes, lt hair, fair comp, 6' 2" high; assd to co G 2 battn 11 inf (battn redesig 20 inf regt Sep 1866); disch 3 Feb 1869 Baton Rouge La. expir of serv a cpl; reenl 14 Apr 1871 St Louis Bks Mo. for 5 yrs; age 24; join co G 7 cav 30 May 1871 Taylor Bks Louisville Ky.; dd co cook Aug 1871; cpl 16 Aug 1872; pvt 1 Jan 1873; dd co cook Dec 1873; cpl 20 May 1874; sgt 17 May 1875; 1sgt 6 Aug 1875; disch 14 Apr 1876 Shreveport La. expir of serv a 1sgt char unexceptionable; reenl same day in co G for 5 yrs & on furl 4 mos to London England; ds Ft Lincoln DT 14 Aug to 26 Sep 1876; (m. widow of trump'r Dose 22 Nov 1876); cited by capt Benteen for conspic gal in two mtd chgs against Nez Perce inds at Canon Creek MT 13 Sep 1877; on furl 13 Nov 1877 to Ft Lincoln;[8] disch 13 Apr 1881 Ft Meade DT expir of serv a 1sgt char xclt & reenl in co G for 5 yrs; on furl 6 mos 1 May 1881 with perm'n to cross the sea; sgt 1 Dec 1881 (resd 1sgt); disch 13 Apr 1886 Ft Keogh MT expir of serv a sgt & reenl in co G for 5 yrs; color sgt 1 Dec 1886; on furl 2 mos 26 May 1887; disch 5 Nov 1887 Ft Riley Kans. on surg cert dis (chr. diffuse nephritis accomp by emaciation & debility, contr line of duty) a sgt char xclt; died 25 Jan 1931 Sturgis SD.
Pension: 19 Nov 1887 / Inv / 629461 / 389457.

Gebhart, Jacob Henry. Pvt co M; b. 6 June 1848 Ligonier Pa.; enl as Jas. J. Tanner 18 Sep 1875 Chicago Ill. for 5 yrs; age 26; clerk; brn eyes, blk hair, dk comp, 5' 7 3/4" high;[9] join co M 21 Oct 1875 Ft Rice DT; gsw chest 26 June 1876 (ball lodging in l. lung) dur Benteen's chg to drive inds down hill away from line; died next day in field hosp; sgt Ryan said Tanner & Voigt buried in same grave down in depression where horses & mules were, with piece of hardtack box used for headboard & names written on with lead pencil.[10]
Pension: 23 June 1880 / Mother / 270187 / 434912.

Geesbacher, Gabriel. See Guessbacher, Gabriel.

Gehrmann, Fred'k Henry. Pvt co B; b. 18 Nov 1858 Baltimore Md; enl 13 Mar 1876 at Baltimore for 5 yrs; age 21; laborer; blue eyes, brn hair, ruddy comp, 5' 9 1/4" high; join co B 27 Apr 1876 St Paul Minn.; ds camp Powder River MT 10 June 1876; ed qmd Nov & Dec 1876; cpl 26 Sep 1878; sgt 11 Dec 1878; dd qmd June 1879; ed qmd Aug 1879; pvt 3 Dec 1880; dd qmd saw mill Dec 1880 & Feb 1881; disch 12 Mar 1881 Ft Yates DT expir of serv a pvt char xclt; reenl 31 Mar 1881 Wash'n D.C. for 5 yrs; assd to co C 2 art'y; disch 1 Apr 1886 Mt Vernon

Bks Ala expir of serv a sgt char xclt; died 10 Dec 1922 Wash'n D.C.
Pension: 15 Dec 1891 / Inv / 1079200 / 863348.

Geiger, Geo. Sgt co H; b. Cincinnati Ohio; pvt co A 47 Ohio inf 15 June 1861 to 11 Aug 1865; enl reg army 29 Nov 1867 St Louis Mo. for 5 yrs; age 24; teamster; grey eyes, lt hair, fair comp, 5' 4 1/2" high; join co M 7 cav 22 Jan 1868 Ft L'worth Kans.; ed qmd teamster Dec 1868 to Aug 1869; wag Oct 1869; pvt 1 July 1871; ed qmd teamster Apr to Nov 1872; disch 29 Nov 1872 Unionville SC expir of serv a pvt; reenl in 7 cav 18 Dec 1872 Louisville Ky. for 5 yrs & join co H at Nashville Tenn; dd battn hq as pioneer 18 Apr to 27 Sep 1873; dd qmd Nov 1873 to May 1874; cpl 5 Apr 1876; sgt 1 May 1876; with pack train June 1876; actg qm sgt June 1877; ds Cant'mt Tongue River MT Aug to Sep 1877; disch 18 Dec 1877 camp near Ft Buford DT expir of serv a sgt char xclt; awarded medal of honor 5 Oct 1878 for serving as sharpshooter [at LBH] in exposed position outside the line to provide cover for water carriers; (he having been disch the serv, medal filed in AGO & for'd to sol. in 1892 at address in pension file); died 23 Jan 1904 Sol. Home Dayton Ohio.
Pension: 8 Oct 1890 / Inv / 915333 / 712419.

Geist, Frank J. Pvt co G; b. 16 Feb 1856 Wurtzburg Germany; enl 14 Apr 1876 St Louis Mo. for 5 yrs; age 22 2/12; machinist; grey eyes, lt hair, fair comp, 5' 6" high; join co G 27 Apr 1876 St Paul Minn.; ds camp Powder River MT 15 June 1876 with regtl band; sick qrs Ft Lincoln DT 14–21 Oct 1876 (const. syph.); dd with band Nov 1876 to Nov 1878; disch 30 Jan 1879 at Ft Lincoln on surg cert dis (hypertrophy of heart) a pvt char good; died 20 Nov 1918 Minneapolis Minn.
Pension: 29 Sep 1879 / Inv / 312276 / 167348. Ind. War Wid / 14322; (abandoned, clmt deceased 2 Feb 1919).

George, Wm. Montell. Pvt co H; b. Lexington Ky.; enr 7 Sep 1864 a pvt 2 Mo. cav; unassd rct Oct 1864; tr to co B 27 Nov 1864; sen gen cm 24 Jan 1865 forf 2 mos pay & conft same period at St Louis;[11] m.o. vol serv 15 June 1865; enl reg army 25 Aug 1866 Cincinnati Ohio for 5 yrs; age 19; clerk; blue eyes, red hair, lt comp, 5' 9" high; join co E 7 cav Oct 1866 Ft Riley Kans.; ds with regtl train Apr 1867 Ft Dodge Kans.; wag 1 Nov 1867; pvt Apr 1868; wag Oct 1868; pvt 10 Jan 1869; ds with survey exp'n May & June 1869; dd teamster Aug 1869 to June 1870; ed qmd Oct 1870 to Feb 1871; disch 25 Aug 1871 Spartanburg SC expir of serv a pvt; enl in co H 1 May 1875 New Orleans La. for 5 yrs; ds with escort for surveyors Oct 1875; dd comsy dept herder Dec 1875 to Feb 1876; gsw l. side 26 June 1876 (ball entered back & was cut out in front, stomach perforated); tr on str *Far West* 3 July to Ft Lincoln but died same day & buried at camp mouth of Powder River; (a monument was placed on grave site by Prairie Co. [MT] Bicentennial Committee in 1976).[12]
Pension: 18 May 1892 / Mother / 551359 / 362962.

Gerard, Frederic Francois. Intrpr qmd; b. 14 Nov 1829 St Louis Mo.; educated at Xavier college & employed for a time in office of *St Louis Republican*; made first trip up Missouri River in Sep 1848 with Honoré Picotte (family friend & agent of American Fur co) & hired as co clerk at Ft Pierre DT;[13] tr to Ft Clark in spring 1849; chg of co store at Ft Berthold from 1857;[14] (m. Arikara woman [Julia]; 3 ch.); scout for gen Sully's exp'n against Sioux in 1864; acclaimed as skillful physician when he vaccinated 300 ind ch. dur smallpox epidemic in 1866; often assisted long time friend Father DeSmet of St Louis dur his missionary visits to inds in the region; became indpt fur trader in 1869 with stores at Ft Berthold & Ft Stevenson but moved entire stock to Ft Benton MT in 1870 when license revoked;[15] his trading venture ended in fall 1871 when his last wagon train of goods was captured by a Blackfeet war pty near the British line; hired 10 July 1872 as govt intrpr at Ft McKeen (Ft Lincoln) DT; also supplied post with dairy products from his ranch; hired 12 May 1876 by Lt Nowlan as intrpr for 'Ree ind scouts with gen Terry's exp'n; rate of pay $75 mo; rode own horse (blk stallion) dur campn; stayed behind at mouth of Rosebud 22 June to send 'Ree scouts to Powder River with mail; rejoined regt in camp up Rosebud eve 22 June; with gen Custer to Crow's Nest morn 25 June; accomp ind scouts with maj Reno's comd to river but rode back to tell Custer the Sioux were not running away; joined Reno's comd in valley & dismtd at edge of woods with Reynolds, Herendeen, Dr. Porter, and Bloody Knife; left behind in timber (with his horse) dur retreat; rejoined comd night of 26 June; req to accomp wd on str *Far West* to Ft Lincoln not appv by gen Terry; remained with regt in field & arr Bismarck 25 Sep with a few ind scouts; disch from exp'n 27 Sep at Ft Lincoln; testified in Reno court of inq at Chicago Jan 1879; disch as post intrpr at Ft Lincoln 1 July 1883 & opened grocery market in Mandan DT; removed to Minneapolis Minn. in 1890 & employed with Pillsbury flour mills; died 29 Jan 1913 St Cloud Minn.[16]

Gibbs, Wm. Pvt co K; b. 28 July 1852 Manchester, England; enl 15 Dec 1874 New York N.Y. for 5 yrs; age 22; butcher; blue eyes, brn hair, fair comp, 5' 7 1/4" high; join co K 9 Feb 1875 Colfax La.; ed post hosp nurse 7 June 1875 to 15 Apr 1876; ds Ft Lincoln 16 Oct 1877; disch 5 Apr 1878 Ft Rice DT on surg cert dis (chr. rheum.) a pvt char xclt; died 18 Feb 1934 Vet's Home, Napa Co. Calif.
Pension: 10 Feb 1891 / Inv / 988525 / 1019862. Ind. Surv. / 10641 / 7146.

Gibson, Francis Marion. 1Lt co H; b. 14 Dec 1847 Phil'a Pa.; employed June 1865 as clerk in army pay dept at Wash'n; appd for com'n in cav serv 3 Oct 1867 & two days later appt 2Lt 7 cav; passed exam'n before army bd 28 Oct; joined co A 6 Dec 1867 Ft L'worth Kans.; sd comdg dismtd men Apr to July 1868; ds with co F 3 Aug to 28 Nov 1868 & in action at Washita;[17] 1Lt co H 1 July 1872 Nashville Tenn; comd co 30 Apr 1873 Yankton DT; with co on Yellowstone Exp'n June to Sep 1873 & on Blk Hills Exp'n July & Aug 1874;[18] ds Wash'n D.C. 2 Sep 1874; awl 30 days 12 Sep 1874 & joined co at New Orleans La.; post adjt Ft Rice DT 8 Nov 1875 to 30 Apr 1876; rode point (with six men of co H) for capt Benteen's battn 25 June;[19] td comdg co G 27 June & care of co rec's; comd co H 26 Aug to 15 Nov 1876; post adjt 1 Jan 1877; actg comsy on staff of col Sturgis 23 Apr 1877; ds Tongue River Cant'mt 12 Aug actg aqm & comsy with gen Miles' comd; chg of wagon train to Bear's Paw Mtns 18 Sep & return to Cant'mt Tongue River 23 Oct; chg of detmt in mackinaw boat to Ft Buford 27 Oct (& guarding two Nez Perce ind pris'rs enroute to Bismarck); arr Ft Lincoln 5 Nov on str *Rosebud*; post adjt Ft Rice 8 Nov 1877 & comd detmt ind scouts; ds Ft Lincoln Aug 1878 chg of extra horses; ds rctg duty Sep 1878 to Oct 1880 NYC; capt 5 Feb 1880 & join co M 28 Nov 1880 Ft Meade DT; awl 5 mos on surg cert 12 June 1889 thence on rctg duty Wash'n D.C.; awl 4 mos on surg cert 1 Oct 1890; awl ext'd 6 mos 29 Jan 1891 with perm'n to cross the sea (for course of Carlsbad water in Bohemia); awl further ext'd 3 mos 4 June 1891; retd 3 Dec 1891 for disability (chr. gastro enteritis); appn for restoration to duty 10 Mar 1893 (his health recovered) disappv on grd it would set precedent injurious to interest of mil serv; appn for inspector gen of vols 23 Apr 1898 dur war with Spain not appv; employed as deputy com'r of streets NYC 1895 to 1912; died 17 Jan 1919 at New York. [3596 ACP 1874].

Gilbert, Jno. M. Pvt co A; b. Cork Ireland; enl 6 Oct 1875 St Louis Mo. for 5 yrs; age 21; laborer; hazel eyes, brn hair, fair comp, 5' 7" high; join co A 21 Oct 1875 Ft Lincoln DT; horse holder dur valley fight 25 June 1876; member of water party 26 June on Reno hill;[20] cpl 22 Feb 1877; des 28 Apr 1877 camp near Ft Lincoln.

Gilbert, Julius. Pvt co E; b. Belfort France; enl 11 Dec 1874 New York N.Y. for 5 yrs; age 21; farmer; hazel eyes, brn hair, fair comp, 5' 7 3/4" high; join co E 8 Feb 1875 Opelika Ala; dd qmd with post water wagon 30 Oct 1875 to 7 Mar 1876; ds Ft Lincoln 17 May 1876 chg co garden; sent with Lt Garlington on str *Josephine* 24 July 1876 to join co in field but ret to post 10 Aug on str *Durfee*; ds Ft Lincoln Apr to Nov 1877 chg co garden; testified in gen cm of capt French 28 Jan 1879; disch 10 Dec 1879 Ft Meade DT expir of serv a pvt char good & reenl in co E for 5 yrs; dd co carpenter Oct 1880 to May 1881; dd actg co blks

Dec 1881 to Feb 1882; blks 1 Mar 1882; pvt 1 July 1882; ds Nov 1883 to Jan 1884 cutting logs near Ft Meade; ds June to Sep 1884 Ft Custer MT; disch 10 Dec 1884 at Ft Meade by expir of serv a pvt char indifferent.

Gilbert, Wm. H. Cpl co L; b. 11 Nov 1851 Phil'a Pa.; enl 2 Oct 1873 New York N.Y. for 5 yrs; age 22; butcher; blue eyes, brn hair, dk comp, 5' 7 1/4" high; join co L 19 Oct 1873 Ft Lincoln DT; dd subs dept laborer Mar to July 1875; cpl 18 Mar 1876; killed with Custer column 25 June 1876.
Pension: 23 Apr 1909 / Wid / 918686. (Abandoned).

Gillette, David C. Pvt co I; b. Onandaga N.Y.; enl 1 Oct 1873 Detroit Mich. for 5 yrs; age 22; teacher; blue eyes, lt hair, fair comp, 5' 5" high; join co I 22 Oct 1873 Ft Totten DT; ed post hosp nurse 8 Nov 1875 to 1 May 1876; killed with Custer column 25 June 1876.

Glease, Geo. W. (alias). See Glenn, Geo. W.

Glenn, Geo. W. Pvt co H; b. Boston Mass.; pvt co K 12 Mass. inf 20 May 1861 to 21 Dec 1862; enl reg army 22 Dec 1862 Columbus Ohio for 3 yrs; age 21; painter; hazel eyes, brn hair, lt comp, 5' 5" high; assd to co C 3 battn 18 inf; tr to co E 2 battn 18 inf 1 Mar 1863; disch 2 Dec 1865 Ft L'worth Kans. expir of serv a pvt; reenl 5 Sep 1866 Cleveland Ohio for 5 yrs; (b. Manchester Mass.); age 21; assd to co C 8 cav; disch 5 Sep 1871 Ft Selden NM expir of serv a pvt; reenl in same co 15 Nov 1871 at Ft Selden for 5 yrs; cpl 1 Aug 1873; pvt 21 May 1874; des 21 July 1875; enl as Geo. W. Glease 3 Sep 1875 Cincinnati Ohio for 5 yrs; join co H 7 cav 29 Oct 1875 Ft Rice DT; des 15 Oct 1877 Camp Owen Hale MT; apph 26 Apr 1880 Ft Meade DT; dishon disch 31 July 1880 sen gen cm & 2 yrs conft mil prison Ft L'worth; surd as Geo. W. Glenn 14 Apr 1881; died 19 Sep 1914 Sol. Home, Hampton Va.[21]
Pension: 28 Mar 1896 / Inv / 1175771 / 933549.

Godfrey, Edw. Settle. 1Lt co K; b. 9 Oct 1843 Kalida Ohio; pvt co D 21 Ohio inf (3 mo troops) 26 Apr to 12 Aug 1861; grad USMA 17 June 1867 & appt 2Lt 7 cav; join co G 3 Oct 1867 Ft Harker Kans.; 1Lt co K 18 Aug 1868 to date 1 Feb 1868; with co in action at Washita 27 Nov 1868; with co on Yellowstone Exp'n June to Sep 1873; asst engr of Blk Hills Exp'n July & Aug 1874; comd cos K, G, & B from Shreveport La. to Ft Lincoln DT 19 Apr to 1 May 1876; [dismtd co K in skirmish line for rear gd dur retreat from Weir Point 25 June]; awl 4 mos 17 Nov 1876; capt co D from 9 Dec 1876; gsw l. side & horse shot under him 30 Sep 1877 in action with Nez Perce inds at Snake Creek MT (Bear's Paw Mtns); tr to str *Big Horn* 14 Oct & arr Ft Rice 24 Oct; duty 3 Jan 1878; ds Chicago Ill. Jan 1879 witness in Reno court of inq; ds USMA comdg cav detmt Aug 1879 to Aug 1883; ds Wash D.C. Feb 1888 on bd of tactics & at L'worth Kans. from Apr 1889; rejoin co 6 Dec 1890 (own req) & in action with Sioux inds 29 Dec 1890 Wounded Knee Creek SD; injured in wreck of troop train 27 Jan 1891 near Florence Kans.; in hosp Ft Riley Kans. to 27 Mar & abs on surg cert to 26 Oct 1891; tr to co H 29 June 1893 at Ft Riley; also comd cav & art'y school to May 1895; bvt maj May 1894 to date 27 Feb 1890 & awarded medal of honor for dist gal at Bear's Paw Mtns 30 Sep 1877; prom maj 1 cav 7 Jan 1897 (never joined) tr to 7 cav same date; comd sqdn at Ft Apache AT Mar 1897 & at Ft DuChesne Utah to Aug 1898; comd sqdn at Pinar del Rio Cuba Jan 1899; Lt-col 12 cav 2 Feb 1901 Ft Sam Houston Tex.; col 9 cav 26 June 1901; with regt in Philippines to Oct 1902 & Ft Walla Walla Wash'n to Oct 1904; brig-gen 17 Jan 1907 & comd Dept of Mo.; retd 9 Oct 1907; comd legion of valor sec. dur burial of unknown soldier in Arlington Natl Cemetery 11 Nov 1921; died 1 Apr 1932 Cookstown NJ.[22]
[6626 ACP 1876]. Pension: 24 May 1932 / Wid / 1718814.

Golden, Bernard. Pvt co M; b. Cavan Ireland; enl 8 Sep 1870 St Louis Mo. for 5 yrs; age 23; laborer; gray eyes, brn hair, ruddy comp, 5' 7" high; assd to co F 8 cav; disch 8 Sep 1875 Ft Garland Colo. Ty expir of serv a pvt; reenl 5 Oct 1875 at St Louis Bks for 5 yrs; join co M 7 cav 21 Oct 1875 Ft Rice DT;

dd battn hq Apr to June 1877; in conft field guardhouse Aug 1877; sick Ft Stevenson DT 17–30 Nov 1877; des 18 Dec 1877 Ft Lincoln DT; Rutten said Golden killed [Jim] Weeks & des after coming back to post; Morris said Barney Golden killed Weeks in fight during poker game at Montana Bill's Ranch.[23]

Golden, Pat'k. Pvt co D; b. Sligo Ireland; enl 22 Jan 1872 Boston Mass. for 5 yrs; age 22; slater; blue eyes, brn hair, fair comp, 5' 9 1/4" high; [a handsome young man of striking appearance, blk moustache, tall, straight as an arrow];[24] join co D 13 Feb 1872 Chester SC; ds Ft Lincoln DT 14 May 1874 & regtl hq St Paul Minn. June to Oct 1874; ds Ft Lincoln Oct 1874 to May 1875; orderly for maj Reno 5–14 May 1876; killed on Reno hill 26 June 1876 when north line chg inds.

Goldin, Theo. W. Pvt co G; b. 25 July 1858 Avon Wis; enl 8 Apr 1876 Chicago Ill. for 5 yrs; age 21; brakeman; blue eyes, brn hair, fair comp, 5' 7 3/4" high; join co G 27 Apr 1876 St Paul Minn.; dd 6–10 Aug, 18–31 Aug, 21–24 Sep 1876;[25] disch 13 Nov 1877 in field DT per SO 174 AGO 1877 (a minor);[26] recd medal of honor 21 Dec 1895 (upon own app'n) for dist gal at Little Big Horn;[27] died 15 Feb 1935 Vet's Home, Waupaca Wis.
Pension: 27 Mar 1927 / Ind. Surv. / 20075 / 12964. (XC-2,578,534).

Gordon, Henry. Pvt co M; b. Chatham England; enl 5 Dec 1872 Boston Mass. for 5 yrs; age 21; laborer; brn eyes, brn hair, fair comp, 5' 6" high; join co M 9 Feb 1873 at Oxford Miss; dd co cook Apr 1875; killed dur retreat from valley fight 25 June 1876 on east side of river, half way up bluff, by same volley that hit Meyer & Morris & all three horses simultaneously.[28]

Gordon, Thos. A. Pvt co K; b. 9 Dec 1853 Boston Mass.; enl 26 Sep 1873 at Boston for 5 yrs; age 22; laborer; gray eyes, blk hair, dk comp, 5' 6 1/2" high; join co K 20 Oct 1873 Ft Rice DT; dd regtl hq fatigue pty (morn & eve) 11 May 1876; dd qmd mtd msgr 22 Nov to 27 Dec 1876; ed field hosp nurse 8–26 Oct 1877; ds Ft Lincoln DT 16 Oct 1877; dd co cook June 1878; disch 26 Sep 1878 Sidney Bks Neb expir of serv a pvt char very good; reenl 25 Feb 1879 at Boston for 5 yrs; assd to co D 6 cav; des 2 Sep 1882 Camp Price AT; surd 24 Jan 1884 Ft Wingate NM; dishon disch 17 Sep 1884 sen gen cm & 3 yrs conft mil prison Ft L'worth Kans.; reenl 5 Sep 1888 New York N.Y. for 5 yrs; assd to co G 5 art'y; on furl 90 days 5 Sep 1891; disch 4 Dec 1891 Ft Monroe Va. per GO 80 AGO 1890, a pvt char very good;[29] died 21 Dec 1935 Chelsea Mass.
Pension: 4 Oct 1917 / Ind. Surv. / 15137 / 9598. (XC-2,579,624).

Gorham, Jno. Pvt co D; b. 20 Apr 1852 Hartford Conn.; enl as Jno. Quinn 19 June 1875 Boston Mass. for 5 yrs; age 23; blacksmith; blue eyes, brn hair, fair comp, 5' 7 3/4" high; join co D 21 Oct 1875 Ft Lincoln DT; in conft Dec 1875; ds camp Powder River MT 15 June 1876 guarding wagon train; cpl 1 Mar 1877; gsw l. shoulder 30 Sep 1877 Snake Creek MT (Bear's Paw Mtns) in action with Nez Perce inds; tr to str *Silver City* 14 Oct at mouth of Squaw Creek (on Mo. River); adm to hosp Ft Rice DT 26 Oct 1877; duty 12 Nov 1877; (cited for gal serv at Bear's Paw);[30] sgt 2 June 1878; sick hosp Mar to June 1879 (abcess); in arrest Apr 1880; disch 18 June 1880 Ft Yates DT expir of serv a sgt char good; reenl 17 July 1880 New York N.Y. for 5 yrs; join co F 7 cav 4 Oct 1880 Ft Buford DT; sick hosp 27 Oct 1881 to 1 Jan 1882 at Ft Buford when disch on surg cert dis (ulceration mucous membrane of nose with probable necrosis of nasal bones; dis 1/2) a pvt char good; reenl 31 Jan 1882 Ft Warren Mass. for 5 yrs in co F 4 art'y; cpl 7 Aug 1882; sgt 20 Jan 1883; 1sgt 14 June 1884; sgt 2 Mar 1885; disch 30 Jan 1887 Ft Snelling Minn. expir of serv a sgt char xclt & reenl in same co for 5 yrs as Jno. Gorham; 1sgt 6 Dec 1887; disch 30 Jan 1892 Ft Riley Kans. expir of serv a 1sgt char xclt & reenl 1 Feb 1892 in same co for 5 yrs; appt ordn sgt USA 21 Dec 1892; disch 31 Jan 1897 at Ft Riley expir of serv an ordn sgt char xclt & reenl for 3 yrs; disch 31 Jan 1900 Ft Warren Mass. expir of serv an ordn sgt & reenl for 3 yrs; disch 31 Jan 1903 at Ft Warren expir of serv an ordn sgt char xclt & reenl for

3 yrs; disch 31 Jan 1906 Ft Strong Mass. expir of serv an ordn sgt char xclt & reenl 9 Feb 1906 at Boston; retd 5 Mar 1906 an ordn sgt; died 26 Sep 1932 Brookline Mass.
Pension: 14 Mar 1917 / Ind. Surv. / 9736; (rej acc't sol. on retd list & therefore not entitled to pension under any law, being barred by act of 3 Mar 1891).

Graham, Chas. Pvt co L; b. Tyrone Co Ireland; enl 8 Feb 1854 New York N.Y. for 5 yrs; age 22; laborer; blue eyes, brn hair, fair comp, 5' 7" high; join co L 3 art'y 6 Mar 1854 at Ft Wood NYH; dd co cook Dec 1857; disch 8 Feb 1859 Ft Umpqua Ore. Ty expir of serv a pvt; reenl for same co 28 Mar 1859 San Francisco Calif. for 5 yrs; in conft Dec 1859; in conft Aug 1860; in conft Oct 1862; sen gen cm Dec 1862 forf 1/2 pay per mo for 2 mos & perform police duty with ball & chain for 30 days; disch 28 Mar 1864 Nashville Tenn expir of serv a pvt; reenl 1 July 1867 Wash'n D.C. for 5 yrs; join co B 7 cav 14 Sep 1867 Ft Dodge Kans.; tr to co L 8 Oct 1867 at Ft Reynolds Colo. Ty; dd co cook May to Oct 1870; disch 1 July 1872 Yorkville SC expir of serv & reenl in co L for 5 yrs; dd hq Blk Hills Exp'n 23 July to 31 Aug 1874; dd cook for regtl band Apr to July 1875; killed with Custer column 25 June 1876.

Graham, Thos. Pvt co G; b. Alton Ohio; enl 4 Nov 1872 Columbus Ohio for 5 yrs; age 18; laborer; gray eyes, lt hair, fair comp, 5' 6 3/4" high; join co G 10 Dec 1872 Laurenville SC; sick hosp 1 May 1873 Yankton DT (erysipelas); tr on str *Katie P. Kountz* 8 May to Ft Rice DT;[31] sick 4 Nov 1873 to 25 Jan 1874 (headache); dd hosp nurse Dec 1874 to June 1875; dd regtl hq Aug 1877; ds Ft Lincoln DT 14 Oct 1877; disch 4 Nov 1877 at Ft Lincoln expir of serv a pvt char xclt; died 15 July 1907 Sol. Home Dayton Ohio.
Pension: 14 Apr 1879 / Inv / 279386 / 170122.

Grant, Edwin. See Eldridge, Edwin.

Gray, Jno. Roscoe. Pvt co B; b. 8 Apr 1855 Aetna Me; enl 23 Mar 1876 Boston Mass. for 5 yrs; age 21; laborer; gray eyes, brn hair, fair comp, 5' 9 3/4" high; join co B 27 Apr 1876 St Paul Minn.; ds camp Powder River MT 10 June 1876; ds Apr 1878 with Lt Barry; ed subs dept Dec 1879 to Apr 1880; dd co cook Dec 1880; disch 22 Mar 1881 Ft Yates DT expir of serv a pvt char very good; died 30 Apr 1915 Worcester Mass.
Pension: 10 Apr 1893 / Inv / 1148963; (rej on grd no rec of alleged injury & clmt unable to furn competent evidence of origin in serv). Ind. Wid. / 15089 / Act 4 Mar 1917. (XC-2,659,984).

Gray, Wm. S. Pvt co G; b. New Bedford Mass.; enl 10 Apr 1876 Cincinnati Ohio for 5 yrs; age 21; farmer; hazel eyes, blk hair, dk comp, 5' 6 3/4" high; join co G 27 Apr 1876 St Paul Minn.; sick qrs 9–13 June 1876 (con-t'n l. leg, kick by horse); ds camp Powder River MT 15 June 1876; dd qmd 10 Nov 1876 care of pub horses; dd qmd Dec 1876 to Mar 1877; cited by capt Benteen for conspic gal in two mtd chgs against Nez Perce inds at Canon Creek MT 13 Sep 1877; dd qmd teamster Jan to June 1878; ds Ft Lincoln 27 July to 21 Nov 1878; ed hosp nurse 28 Sep 1878 to 23 May 1879; ds Fargo DT June 1879 witness in US distr court; ds carrying desps Dec 1879; disch 9 Apr 1881 Ft Meade DT expir of serv a pvt char xclt.

Grayson, Edw. Pvt co G; b. Providence R. I. enl as Edw. Wilson 18 Dec 1867 Boston Mass. for 5 yrs; age 30; laborer; blue eyes, brn hair, lt comp, 5' 5 3/4" high; join 7 cav 18 Jan 1868 Ft L'worth Kans.; join co C July 1868 Ft Lyon Colo. Ty; dd post comsy Feb 1872; disch 18 Dec 1872 Charlotte NC expir of serv a pvt; reenl same day in co C for 5 yrs as Edw. Grayson (auth AGO); ed qmd member of boats crew Oct 1873 Ft Rice DT; ed qmd Dec 1873 & Feb 1874; tr to co G 27 Mar 1874; (wife appd for his disch Apr 1874 & AGO directed regtl comdr inq if sol. desired disch);[32] dd qmd watchman Dec 1875 & Feb 1876; dd with regtl hq fatigue pty (morn & eve) 11 May 1876; dd 23 May to 19 June 1876;[33] in conft awaiting trial 21 Oct to 16 Dec 1876 when restored to duty; tr to co B 1 Mar 1877; disch 18 Dec 1877 at Ft Lincoln expir of serv a pvt char good; reenl 3 Apr 1879 Ft Adams R. I. for 5 yrs; assd to co E 1 art'y; died 24 Mar 1881 [Dropsy] at Ft Adams a pvt.[34]

139

Green, Jno. Pvt co D; b. Racine Wis; enl 5 Feb 1872 Chicago Ill. for 5 yrs; age 21; laborer; gray eyes, lt hair, lt comp, 5' 7" high; join co D 24 Feb 1872 Chester SC; ed qmd teamster Oct 1873; ds camp Powder River MT 15 June 1876 guarding wagon train; ds Ft Lincoln DT 8 Aug 1876 chg co prop; dd qmd with 281 cav horses at post 12 Sep 1876; disch 5 Feb 1877 Ft Rice DT expir of serv a pvt char xclt.
Pension: 4 Feb 1886 / Inv / 561169; (declared rightful name Henry Gross & adopted at age six by family named Green). Letters to clmt & affiants unclaimed & returned to Com'r of Pensions.

Green, Jos. H. Pvt co D; b. 8 Aug 1849 Leitrim Ireland; enl 22 Jan 1872 Boston Mass. for 5 yrs; age 22; millhand; blue eyes, brn hair, fair comp, 5' 5 3/4" high; join co D 13 Feb 1872 Chester SC; in conft June 1872; in conft Oct 1872; ds with engr party July & Aug 1873; disch 22 Jan 1877 Ft Rice DT expir of serv a pvt char good; died 13 Apr 1922 Sol. Home Wash'n D.C.
Pension: 17 Apr 1918 / Ind. Surv. / 15880 / 8631. Ind. War Wid / 16163.

Green, Thos. J. Pvt co K; b. Aurora Ill.; enl 10 Dec 1875 Boston Mass. for 5 yrs; age 21; laborer; blue eyes, dk hair, dk comp, 5' 6 3/4" high; join co K 27 Apr 1876 St Paul Minn.; ds camp Powder River MT 15 June 1876; ds Ft Lincoln DT 16 Oct 1876 dismtd; ds with art'y detmt as canoneer 2 July 1877; gsw l. thigh (accdt disch of pistol) 28 Aug 1877 Crow Agcy MT; tr from Ft Ellis MT 12 Nov 1877 to hosp at Ft Lincoln; tr to hosp Ft Rice DT 15 Jan 1878; on furl 26 Jan 1878; sick hosp St Louis Bks Mo. 18 Feb to 5 Mar 1878; sick hosp at Ft Rice 9 Apr to 25 Nov 1878 when tr to Ft Lincoln; sick qrs til 29 Jan 1879 when disch on surg cert dis (gsw l. thigh; dis 1/3) a pvt char good; died 28 Jan 1904 Springfield Mass.
Pension: 11 July 1888 / Inv / 663709 / 427686. Wid / 799332 / 581035.

Gregg, Wm. J. Pvt co F; b. 5 July 1847 Baltimore Md; pvt co C 13 Md inf 21 Jan to 29 May 1865; enl reg army 20 Aug 1866 at Baltimore for 5 yrs; age 19; clerk; blue eyes, brn hair, fair comp, 5' 6 3/4" high; join co F 7 cav 10 Sep 1866 Ft Riley Kans.; dd qmd clerk Nov 1866 to Mar 1867; ds chg co prop at dept hq in field Apr 1867; cpl 8 May 1867; disch 1 Dec 1867 Ft L'worth Kans. per SO 484 AGO 1867 (upon appn of mother); reenl in co F 11 Nov 1872 Louisville Ky. for 5 yrs; dd post qmd Dec 1872; dd clerk for gen cm 25 May to 2 June 1873 Ft Sully DT; dd pioneer June 1873; dd co clerk June to Dec 1874; sick hosp Ft Lincoln DT 7 Feb to 5 Mar 1876 (conjunctivitis); [at LBH said himself & Lefler; doubtful with packs says Lynch; with wagon train says Rooney];[35] sgt 27 Sep 1876; sick qrs 3–4 Dec 1876 (headache); sick qrs 29 Dec 1876 to 1 Jan 1877 (bronc.); in arrest Feb 1877 (awol & drunk); sen gen cm 23 Apr 1877 forf $10 pay; ds Ft Lincoln 14 Oct 1877 (arr post 26 Oct); disch 11 Nov 1877 at Ft Lincoln expir of serv a sgt char xclt; died 10 Dec 1913 Sol. Home Hampton Va.; (never married).
Pension: 5 Apr 1887 / Inv / 605219 / 552589.

Griesner, Julius. Pvt band; b. Neurode Germany; enl 3 Mar 1875 St Louis Mo. for 5 yrs; age 31; musician; gray eyes, lt hair, fair comp, 5' 5 3/4" high; assd to 7 cav 6 Dec 1875; join regt 14 Apr 1876 Ft Lincoln DT (with Lt Reily's detmt); assd to band 28 Apr; ds camp Powder River MT 14 June 1876; ds str *Josephine* 6 Aug 1876 to Ft Lincoln with band; disch 2 Mar 1880 Ft Meade DT expir of serv a pvt char good; reenl 13 May 1880 Sante Fe NM for 5 yrs; assd to band 15 inf; died 15 Feb 1882 Ft Lewis Colo. [softening of brain] a pvt.

Griffin, Pat'k. Pvt co C; b. Dingle Kerry Co Ireland; enl 16 Oct 1872 Toledo Ohio for 5 yrs; age 24; laborer; blk eyes, dk hair, ruddy comp, 5' 9" high; join co C 9 Dec 1872 Charlotte NC; dd co tailor Dec 1874 to Feb 1875; dd qmd Oct 1875 to Mar 1876; dd co cook Apr 1876; with pack train morn 25 June but when regt divided he was assd duties of the co;[36] killed with Custer column 25 June 1876.

Grimes, Andrew. Pvt co I; b. Allegheny Pa.; enl 24 Sep 1875 St Louis Mo. for 5 yrs; age 28; laborer; blue eyes, lt hair, fair comp, 5' 9 1/4" high; join co I 21 Oct 1875 Ft Lincoln

DT; ds 17 May 1876 at Ft Lincoln in co garden; sent with Lt Garlington on str *Josephine* 24 July to join co in field; ds Apr to Nov 1877 at Ft Lincoln as co gardener; ds Aug to Nov 1878 Ft Lincoln chg co garden; ds Ft Rice Dec 1878; dd qmd woodchopper Feb 1879; dd co gardener Apr to Sep 1879; sick hosp Oct 1879 (remit. fever); disch 3 June 1880 at Ft Lincoln on surg cert dis (chr. infl. r. lung & congestion of liver; dis total) a pvt char xclt.

Groesbeck, Jno. H. Sgt co F; b. Saratoga N.Y.; enr 23 Nov 1863 Utica N.Y. a pvt co H 14 N.Y. art'y; des 23 Apr 1864; enr as Jno. Vickory 10 May 1864 pvt co H 2 Mass. cav; m.o. vol serv 20 July 1865; enl reg army as Jno. Vickory 31 July 1866 Boston Mass. for 3 yrs; age 19; ostler; blue eyes, lt hair, lt comp, 5' 9 1/2" high; join co F 7 cav 10 Sep 1866 Ft Riley Kans.; cpl 21 Sep 1866; sgt 25 Jan 1867; pvt 24 Apr 1867; cpl 17 Dec 1867; sgt 26 Mar 1868; ds with escort for ind peace com'n May 1868; disch 31 July 1869 camp near Denver Colo. Ty expir of serv a sgt; reenl in co F 9 Sep 1869 camp on Monument Creek Colo. Ty for 5 yrs; sgt 22 Sep 1869; ds with gov'r McCook Sep & Oct 1869; 1sgt 1 Mar 1870; sgt 17 Aug 1870; pvt 1 Mar 1871; tr to co G 30 May 1871; cpl 4 Aug 1871; sgt 1 Sep 1871; 1sgt 1 Jan 1872; disch 9 Sep 1874 Ft Lincoln DT expir of serv a 1sgt & reenl for 5 yrs in co F; cpl 18 Sep 1874; sgt 20 Nov 1874; dd chg co mess Feb 1875; dd prov sgt Aug 1875; dd regtl hq standard bearer 15 May 1876;[37] killed with Custer column 25 June 1876.
Pension: 27 Sep 1881 / Father / 286324. (Rej on grd clmt unable to furn evidence showing sol. contributed to his support).

Gross, Geo. H. Pvt co I; b. Germany; enl 11 Nov 1872 Pittsburgh Pa. for 5 yrs; age 27; farmer; blue eyes, lt hair, fair comp, 5' 6 1/2" high; join co I 2 Dec 1872 Shelbyville Ky.; des 20 Apr 1873 Ft Snelling Minn.; surd 15 Nov 1873 St Louis Bks Mo. under GO 102 AGO 1873; ds Ft Snelling 1 Jan 1874 awaiting transp to regt; sent to Ft Lincoln DT 6 July 1874 (with pvt O'Bryan) thence to Ft Totten DT 7 Aug 1874 chg of govt horses; killed with Custer column 25 June 1876.

Gross, Henry. See Green, Jno.

Guessbacher, Gabriel. Pvt co I; b. Bavaria Germany; enl 6 Oct 1873 Phil'a Pa. for 5 yrs; age 27; miller; lt brn eyes, brn hair, ruddy comp, 5' 5 1/4" high; join co I 22 Oct 1873 Ft Totten DT; ds camp Powder River MT 10 June 1876;[38] dd in co cookhouse Dec 1877 & Apr 1878; disch 6 Oct 1878 Camp Ruhlen DT expir of serv a pvt char xclt & reenl in co I for 5 yrs; dd co cook Apr & June 1879; dd co cook Dec 1879; dd co cook Dec 1880; dd co cook June 1881 to Aug 1882; dd cutting ice for post Dec 1882; on furl 3 mos 24 May 1883 Phil'a Pa.; disch 6 Oct 1883 Ft Totten DT expir of serv a pvt; reenl 14 Oct 1883 Ft Snelling Minn. for 5 yrs; assd to co M 7 cav; tr to co I 3 Mar 1884; ds Aug 1885 at Ft Snelling as cook for rifle comp'n; ed qmd laborer Nov 1885; in conft Apr 1888; tr to 8 cav 12 May 1888 at Ft Meade DT [when 7 cav tr to Kans.]; assd to co B 24 Sep 1888; disch 13 Oct 1888 at Ft Meade by expir of serv a pvt char very good; died 4 Aug 1916 Warwick N.Dak.
Pension: 9 Jan 1899 / Inv / 1216141. (Abandoned).

Gunther, Julius. Pvt co K; b. Wurtemburg Germany; enl 29 Mar 1866 Phil'a Pa. for 3 yrs; age 24; furrier; hazel eyes, lt hair, fair comp, 5' 4 1/2" high; assd to co A 2 battn 18 inf; (redesig 27 inf regt Dec 1866); disch 29 Mar 1869 Omaha Bks Neb expir of serv a cpl & reenl in same co for 3 yrs; (tr to co B 9 inf June 1869 by consol'n of regts); disch 23 June 1869 Ft Sedgwick Colo. Ty per GO 15 AGO 1869 a sgt (enl after enlmts ext'd to 5 yrs [act of congress 3 Mar 1869] & could not be legally held to serv upon refusing to sign paper for 5 yrs); reenl 1 Nov 1869 Ft D. A. Russell Wyo. Ty for 5 yrs in co D 5 cav; des 9 Jan 1871 at Ft Russell; reenl 24 Aug 1872 Kansas City Mo. for 5 yrs; join co K 7 cav 9 Dec 1872 Yorkville SC; abs sick on str *Western* 23 Apr 1873 Yankton to Ft Rice DT; surd as des'r 7 Dec 1873 under GO 102 AGO 1873; attd to co K awaiting orders to 10 Nov 1874 when tr to co K to serve bal of orig'l enlmt; dd as mail carrier Feb 1875; sick hosp Colfax La. Apr to Aug 1875 (sim. frac. not gunshot); sick hosp 17–31 May 1876 Ft Lincoln DT (rheum.);

dd orderly for post comdr June 1876; sent with Lt Garlington on str *Josephine* 24 July to join co in field; ds 11 Aug 1876 camp mouth of Rosebud Creek MT; sick hosp 21 Apr to 7 June 1877 at Ft Lincoln (paralysis); ds Ft Lincoln to 29 Sep 1877 when disch upon expir of serv a pvt char good; reenl 1 Oct 1877 at Ft Lincoln for 5 yrs in co G 17 inf (auth AGO); ds 19 July 1880 in post ordn dept; disch 30 Sep 1882 at Ft Lincoln expir of serv a pvt char xclt; reenl next day in post ordn detmt as 2d cl. pvt for 5 yrs; disch 30 Sep 1887 at Ft Lincoln ordn depot by expir of serv a sgt char xclt; reenl same day in ordn detmt for 5 yrs; disch 30 Sep 1892 Rock Isl Ars'l Ill. by expir of serv a 1st cl. pvt char good & reenl for 5 yrs; disch 30 Sep 1897 at Rock Isl Ars'l by expir of serv a 1st cl. pvt & reenl for 3 yrs; retd 14 July 1899 at Rock Isl Ars'l a 1st cl. pvt; res Davenport Iowa; died 2 Jan 1902 at Rock Isl Ars'l (suicide).[39]

Notes—G

1. RG 391, Entry 859; Pay $.35 per diem as engineer building bridges and making roads, RG 393, Part I, Entry 1298.

2. WMC, rosters, IU; Gaffney said he cut tepee poles for stakes marking officer burials on June 28, each stake with a Roman numeral burned on by a heated ramrod, Liddic and Harbaugh, *Camp on Custer*, 93.

3. SO 177, Hq Fort Lincoln, DT, Sept. 24, 1876, RG 393, Part V.

4. *Bismarck Tribune*, July 19, 1879, and Jan. 9, 1880.

5. Galenne said he saw the doctor ten days too late. Letter to Father Jean B. M. Genin, (Missionary Apostolic to Dakota Territory), from Private Gallenne, July 8, 1876, Hospital on Yellowstone River. (Includes excerpt from Gallenne's journal later published in, *St. Paul & Minneapolis Pioneer Press*, Jan. 16, 1879; see Davis, *The Reno Court of Inquiry*, 41. William E. Morris said Frenchy Gallenne made himself useful nursing the wounded, particularly Braun. Morris to Wm. Slaper, Apr. 11, 1915, in newspaper clipping, n.p., n.d., in Taylor Scrapbook.

For an account of Father Genin in Dakota, see *Collections of the State Historical Society*, Vol. I, 1906, 224–92.

6. For description of the wounding of Private Gallenne, see Greene, *Nez Perce Summer 1877*, 289–90.

7. In 1895, James J. Miller claimed Galvin was really his son, Michael John Miller, born in Liverpool, Nov. 16, 1848; said Michael had blue eyes, light hair, light complexion and was 5' 9 3/4" tall; occupation, cooper. There is an obituary for John Galvin, Company E, 7th Cavalry, from Cincinnati, and served in Civil War, *New York Times*, July 5, 1876.

8. Capt. Benteen sent a letter from Fort Buford to his wife, Nov. 13, 1877, giving it to Sgt. Garlick, "who was going to Lincoln to see his sick wife, so he said, in giving him a furlough." Carroll, *Camp Talk*, 100.

9. Gebhart was also described as having curly hair and dimple in chin. He was a fireman and ran stationary engine at paper mill in 1872, and last employment just for short time was with a man named James J. Tanner selling and putting up lightning rods. Affidavit from mother, Mary A. Gebhart, Sept. 15, 1895, Pension file, RG 15.

10. John Ryan to Walter Camp, Dec. 17, 1908, and April 17, and Aug. 11, 1909, WMC-BYU; Taylor, *With Custer on the Little Big Horn,* 182; The bodies of Tanner, Voigt, Lell, and Meador were found in 1903 by Superintendent Grover, and with a fifth body of a Reno soldier found that year, they were interred in Custer National Cemetery, WMC, notes, env 75, IU; Custer Battlefield Burial Register, LBHB Coll., Roll 14.

11. See RG 393, Part IV, Records of Myrtle Street Prison, St. Louis, Mo., 1862–64.

12. Letter from Walter A. "Bub" Burleigh, Jr., clerk on Steamer *Far West*, dated June 29, 1876, with portion of boat's "Log," June 22 to July 5, 1876, in *The Dakota Herald*, July 22, 1876.

When Maj. Moore's detachment returned to Powder River, Aug. 2, George's body had been removed by the Sioux. Meddaugh, Diary; Brown, "The Yellowstone Supply Depot"; Clark, *Terry Country Then and Now.*

13. Hammer, *Custer in '76*, 228; Gerard's birth date appears controversial. The federal census at Fort Stevenson, July 1870, recorded his age 39; wife, Julia (Indian), age 26; prior to 1890, Dr. Orin G. Libby of the University of North Dakota, obtained a statement from Gerard, including his birth date of Nov. 14, 1829, and published it in *Collections of the Historical Society of North Dakota*, Vol. I, 1906, 344.

Historian Albert W. Johnson of Marine-on-St. Croix, Minn., said Dr. Libby only took down the story as it was told, and in letters to Libby, Johnson could get nothing because Libby said he had not gone beyond to investigate. Johnson's investigation was through Ms. Stella Drumm, librarian of Deperson Memorial Society in St. Louis, who found the old church register in which was recorded Gerard's birth date of Aug. 30, 1833, with baptismal name of Francois. Johnson to Earl A. Brininstool, May 15, May 22, and June 5, 1933, Earl Alonzo Brininstool Collection, Barker Texas History Center (hereafter cited as Brininstool Coll., Austin), University of Texas at Austin.

Gerard's wife told Walter Camp, Jan. 22, 1909, that he was 77 years old, but on April 3, 1909 Gerard himself told Camp he was born in fall of 1829 and would be 80 years old next fall. WMC-BYU, transcript, 505–506.

Gerard said his passion for hunting and the wonderful stories he had heard in regard to the Indians attracted him to their territory when he was barely sixteen years of age. Interview in *Chicago Times*, Jan. 19, 1879; see Utley, *The Reno Court of Inquiry,* 112; Gerard's birth date is given as Aug. 30, 1832, in Reid, ed., "Diary of Ferdinand A. Van Ostrand," 39 n. 58.

In 1933, Albert W. Johnson corresponded with Gerard's daughter, Sister Anastasia, who provided much valuable data. She was then 69 years old, an accomplished musician, retired to the College of Saint Benedict in St. Joseph, Minn., and was celebrating her Golden Jubilee of entry into the Catholic Sisterhood. She was interviewed at the convent, Feb. 25, 1958, by Fr. Vincent A. Yzermans; Library of St. Benedict Academy, St. Joseph, Minn.; Photo of Gerard's daughters, Sisters Anastasia, and Adelbert, in Pfaller, *Father DeSmet in Dakota,* 55.

14. Gerard used a novel method to learn to speak the Arikara language; first translating the sentence "what do you call it" into the 'Ree tongue, then during his leisure time at the 'Ree camp he wrote down the name of every material thing in view; verbs, adjectives, and other parts of speech he acquired by signs and gestures and soon boasted he could spell with the English alphabet any Arikara word.

15. Overholser, *Fort Benton,* 230, 280.

16. RG 92, Entry 238, reports 1876/328 and 1876/544.; Camp, "Another of Custer's Band Answers The Last Roll Call"; reprinted in *Big Horn-Yellowstone Journal*, Vol. 3, No. 1, Winter 1994, 11–19.

17. For Lt. Gibson's narrative of the fight at the Washita, see Chandler, *Of Garryowen in Glory,* 8–27.

18. On return of the regiment from the Black Hills, it is written that Lt. Gibson immediately married Kate Garrett, sister of Mrs. Lieut. McIntosh. A daughter, Katherine, born in Dakota, ca 1881, and later a newspaper journalist, compiled a narrative of her mother's early experiences in the west, (Fougera) "*With Custer's Cavalry.*"

Katy Garrett is mentioned with the Custer party hunting buffalo near Fort Hays, Kans., in, Pohanka's *A Summer on the Plains 1870,* 28–30, 35–36, 40–49, 51, 61.

Capt. Benteen mentioned "Mrs. Mc & Gibson" among wives accompanying the regiment during the transfer to Dakota Territory in 1873, Benteen to his wife, May 20, 1873, Carroll, *Camp Talk,* 7.

Lt. Larned also listed Mrs. Gibson among the ladies with the regiment at Yankton, Larned to his mother, April 12, 1873, See Darling, *Custer's Seventh Cavalry Comes to Dakota,* 29 n.16.

19. Gibson said Custer thought some Indians might try to escape up the valley and if so he wanted them intercepted and turned back toward the village. So Benteen's battalion was turned out of the column for that purpose, and to save the probability of an unnecessary march for the entire battalion, Benteen gave Gibson his field glasses and sent him ahead with a small detail of six men from his troop to see if such was the case. Gibson got some distance in advance, crossing a small stream running through a narrow valley (not the Little Big Horn), and kept on to the high divide on the other side. From the top he could plainly see up the Little Big Horn valley for a long distance with the aid of the glasses, but toward the village the view was obstructed by a sharp turn. He saw not a living thing in it, and he hurried back and reported to Benteen, who then changed course to pick up the trail of the regiment, Gibson to Godfrey, Aug. 9, 1908, Charles F. Bates, Papers (hereafter cited as Bates Papers), Beinecke Library, Yale University, New Haven, Conn.; For Gibson's account of the Little Big Horn, see *The Gibson and Edgerly Narratives*, John M. Carroll, ed.

20. Walter Camp interview with Stanislas Roy. Hammer, *Custer in '76,* 112–15.

21. In a series of letters in 1913, Glenn provided Walter Camp with a lengthy account of his experience in the campaign of 1876, WMC-LBHB.

22. See Moody, "Soldier of Valor."

23. Roman Rutten to John Ryan, Apr. 9, 1911, EBC-LBHB, Roll 3; Morris to William Slaper, Apr. 11, 1915, in newspaper clipping, np, nd, Taylor Scrapbook.

24. See Magnussen, *Peter Thompson's Narrative*, 222–24.
25. Brown, Troop Duty Book, Reynolds and Brown, *Journal*. (Handwriting on muster roll of Company G, August 1876, appears similar to that of Theodore Goldin—RLW).
26. RG 94, Entry 409, file, 8334 A (EB) 1877.
27. RG 94, Entry 25, file, 8521 PRD 1894; See Graham, *The Custer Myth*, 267–78; Much of Theodore Goldin's correspondence is found in Carroll, ed. *The Benteen-Goldin Letters*. Included are excerpts of Goldin's letters to Albert W. Johnson of Marine-On-St. Croix, Minn., an avid researcher of the Custer battle. Johnson said Goldin kept up during an eight-year period, a steady stream of 150 letters containing more than 400 typewritten pages; Johnson to Robert S. Ellison, March 5, 1935, Robert Spurrier Ellison, Papers (hereafter cited as Ellison Papers, BYU), (Mss. 782), Harold B. Lee Library, Brigham Young University, Provo, Utah.. Johnson died March 3, 1947 at St. Paul, Minn., age 81.
28. Hammer, *Custer in '76*, 131.
29. See note D26 (Diamond).
30. Greene, *Nez Perce Summer 1877*, 316.
31. RG 94, Entry 544, USA Register 113; see also, SO 18, Hq Detmt 7th Cav., Camp Sturgis, DT, May 4, 1873, RG 391, Entry 881.
32. RG 393, Part V, Fort Rice.
33. Botzer, Troop Duty Book.
34. John Hackett said at the Little Big Horn he and Mr. Wilson drew the task of burying the group of bodies clustered around Custer. Statement by Hackett to his stepson, see *Westerners Brand Book* (Chicago) Vol. 33, No. 3 (May–June 1976), 24.
35. Gregg told Walter Camp he was an eye witness to the battle, Gregg to Camp, Dec. 28, 1909, WMC-BYU. Hardy said he interviewed Meig Lefler who said Gregg was with the pack train, Hardy to Camp, May 15, 1910; Lynch to Camp, Nov. 28, 1908; Rooney to Camp, n.d., WMC-BYU.

In applying for pension, Gregg said his general health broke down from exposure and fatigue during the 1876 campaign. He was often unfit for active duty from general debility and was assigned to the company pack mules under Sgt. Curtiss. After the battle, they hunted fugitive hostiles all day and when going into camp he fell from his horse unconscious from nervous prostration. He was only able to go on with the company the next day because he could not be left behind; they had no surgeon with the command and he was compelled from the nature of things to keep up with the command; he claimed he was overcome by heat, that sunstroke was the disease, and he was never fit for full service after he fell. He continued to feel broken down until they reached Fort Abercrombie in November and he went to hospital.

Dr. DeWolf noted June 21, 1876, "We had two cases of slight sunstroke [during Major Reno's scout]," Luce, "The Diary and Letters of Dr. James M. DeWolf" (see Pvt. Lee, Co. I).

Handwriting on an original Company F muster roll, June 30, 1876, sent to the adjutant general's office, appears identical to that on Company F rolls June to December 1874 when Gregg was company clerk. See also note 5 in the Addendum.

Lt. Eckerson was assigned temporarily to Company F, July 31, 1876, SO 62, Hq 7th Cavalry, RG 391, Entry 859, and was ordered to have the muster roll made out and other company records completed; The survivors of Companies C, E, and F were consolidated into one company on Aug. 4, 1876, GO 15, Hq 7th Cavalry, RG 391, Entry 859.
36. Daniel Knipe to Walter Camp, Nov. 23, 1908, WMC-BYU.
37. Godfrey said Vickory carried the regimental standard, a yellow flag, and the national flag was not carried on the expedition, WMC, notes, env 130, IU; Burkman said Vickory was the handsomest mounted man in the regiment, Wagner, *Old Neutriment*, 152.
38. Guessbacher said they had to sleep on the damp ground without covering, and he contracted rheumatism. John Shauer, in affidavit supporting Guessbacher's claim for pension, said they camped at mouth of Powder River and for a week or more had wet weather, and not having tents they had to sleep on the wet ground. Shauer did not know Guessbacher at the time but said what few men of Company I were left were camped there without tents, Pension file, RG 15.
39. RG 94, Entry 25, file 244773 AGO 1902.

H

Haak, Chas. Louis. Pvt co I; b. Leipsic Germany; enl 29 Apr 1856 New Orleans La. for 5 yrs; age 31; musician; grey eyes, brn hair, fair comp, 5' 6 1/2" high; assd to band mtd rifles; disch 28 Feb 1861 Ft Stanton NM by reenlmt in same unit for 3 yrs; (mtd rifles redesig 3 cav Aug 1861); disch 4 Jan 1864 Huntsville Ala by reenlmt in same unit for 5 yrs; tr to post band Ft L'worth Kans. Feb 1867; disch 4 Jan 1869 at Ft L'worth upon expir of serv a pvt & reenl in same unit for 3 yrs; disch 31 Mar 1869 at Ft L'worth per GO 15 AGO 1869 (disch all bands then in serv except at USMA); reenl 24 Apr 1869 at Ft L'worth for 5 yrs in 7 cav; assd to co K 7 May 1869; ds with band from 10 May 1869; tr to band June 1870; ds Ft Rice DT June to Sep 1873 gd regtl prop; disch 24 Apr 1874 Ft Lincoln DT expir of serv a pvt & reenl in band for 5 yrs; tr to co I 28 Apr 1876; abs sick hosp at Ft Lincoln 1 May 1876 (chr. rheum.); disch 1 Aug 1876 at Ft Lincoln on surg cert dis (chr. rheum. & resulting disease of heart); died 24 Feb 1902 Sol. Home Wash'n D.C.; not married.
Pension: 19 May 1880 / Inv / 365317 / 179526.

Haack, Henry. Pvt co H; b. York Pa.; enl 17 Aug 1858 Baltimore Md for 5 yrs; age 22; shoemaker; hazel eyes, blk hair, fair comp, 5' 8" high; assd to co D 2 cav; (redesig 5 cav Aug 1861); disch 17 Aug 1863 Camp Buford Md expir of serv a pvt; reenl in co D 5 cav 31 May 1864 Wash'n D.C. for 3 yrs; disch 30 May 1867 Nashville Tenn expir of serv a pvt; reenl 4 Oct 1872 at Nashville for 5 yrs in co H 7 cav; cpl 1 Jan 1873; pvt 15 Sep 1874; cpl 2 Feb 1877; disch 24 June 1877 camp on Sunday Creek MT per SO 70 Dept of Dak. 1877 a cpl char xclt; (recom by capt Benteen for medal of honor for dist gal & soldierly qualities at LBH [but line drawn thro' name]);[1] reenl 13 Jan 1879 Ft Totten DT for 5 yrs in co K 7 cav to date 16 Dec 1878 (auth AGO); dd co gardener Apr to Oct 1879; sick Ft Stevenson DT 24 May 1881 (melancholia); died 27 July 1881 Wash'n D.C. (govt hosp for insane [ac. mania with exhaustion & cerebral congestion]).
Pension: [widow married Jno. Burri, 7th Cav.] see Wid Orig'l / 1601133.

Hackett, Jno. Pvt co G; b. 1855 Dublin Ireland; enl 14 Nov 1872 Chicago Ill. for 5 yrs; age 21 6/12; hostler; grey eyes, brn hair, fair comp, 5' 4 1/4" high; join co G 10 Dec 1872 Laurenville SC; dd 23 May to 18 June 1876; orderly for Lt Wallace 25 June 1876;[2] gsw l. forearm (fl. wd. sl.); remain with co in field; dd 1 Aug to 26 Sep 1876;[3] dd regtl hq Oct 1876 to Apr 1877; ds Ft Lincoln DT 14 Oct 1877; disch 14 Nov 1877 at Ft Lincoln expir of serv a pvt char xclt; reenl in co G 13 Dec 1877 at Ft Lincoln for 5 yrs; ds Ft Meade DT June to Aug 1881 chg co prop; sen gen cm 26 July 1882 forf $10 pay; disch 12 Dec 1882 Ft L'worth Kans. expir of serv a pvt char fair; reenl 1 Jan 1883 Ft Omaha Neb for 5 yrs; assd to co D 5 art'y; disch 31 Dec 1887 Ft Douglas Utah expir of serv a pvt & reenl next day for 7 cav for 5 yrs; join co L 17 Jan 1888 Ft Meade DT; in conft Oct 1888; sen gen cm 21 Nov 1888 forf $10 pay per mo for 2 mos; dd caring for sick horses June & Aug 1889; far'r 9 Sep 1889; pvt 1 Mar 1890; ds gen hosp Hot Springs Ark 4 Aug 1890 to 12 Jan 1891; (tr to co B 9 Sep 1890); lance cpl 17 July 1891; pvt 16 Jan 1892; tr to co K 21 Feb 1892; cpl 13 June 1892; disch 31 Dec 1892 Ft Sheridan Ill. expir of serv a cpl & reenl in co K for 5 yrs; in arrest 26 Jan 1893; in conft 10 Feb 1893; pvt 11 Feb 1893; sen gen cm 27 Feb 1893 forf $10 pay per mo for 2 mos & conft same period; on furl 6 mos 6 May 1893 Chicago Ill.; sen gen cm 23 May 1894 forf $10 pay & conft 15 days; disch 31 Dec 1897 Ft Huachuca AT expir of serv a pvt char good & reenl in co K for 3 yrs; far'r 1 June 1898; pvt 16 Aug 1899; far'r 1 Sep 1899; cpl 6 Oct 1900; sgt 1 Nov 1900; 1sgt 11 Dec 1900; disch 31 Dec 1900 Columbia Bks Cuba ex pir of serv a 1sgt & reenl in co K; retd 23 Feb

1901 a 1sgt; died 25 Feb 1904 Ft Sheridan Ill. Pension: 17 Nov 1904 / Wid / 816906 / 973839. (XC-2,718,891).

Hagan, Thos. See Eagan, Thos. P.

Hagemann, Otto. Cpl co G; b. Hanover Germany; (served 3 yrs in German army); enl 2 Oct 1873 New York N.Y. for 5 yrs; age 24; merchant; brn eyes, brn hair, fair comp, 5' 9 1/2" high; join co G 19 Oct 1873 Ft Lincoln DT; cpl 10 Apr 1875; dd chg co mess Dec 1875 & Feb 1876; killed dur retreat from valley fight 25 June 1876, east side of river near edge of water.[4]
Pension: 21 Nov 1892 / Mother / 564798. (Rej upon clmt's statement that sol. did not contribute to her support).

Hager, Jno. Pvt co D; b. Buffalo N.Y.; enl 10 Jan 1872 at Buffalo for 5 yrs; age 23; laborer; hazel eyes, lt hair, fair comp, 5' 8 1/2" high; join co D 3 Feb 1872 Chester SC; dd qmd teamster (with NBS) June to Sep 1873; dd qmd teamster Dec 1873; dd qmd teamster (with NBS) June to Sep 1874; ds 21 Oct 1876 Ft Lincoln DT dismtd; disch 10 Jan 1877 Ft Rice DT expir of serv a pvt char good; reenl 6 Nov 1878 Ft Union NM for 5 yrs; assd to co C 15 inf; disch 5 Nov 1883 Ft Randall DT expir of serv a pvt char xclt; reenl 17 Nov 1883 Ft L'worth Kans. for 5 yrs in gen serv provost gd; disch 28 Sep 1885 at Ft L'worth per SO 219 AGO 1885 (recom'n of comdg officer, for addiction to drink & continual misbehavior resulting in court martials), a pvt.[5]

Hale, Owen. Capt co K; b. 23 July 1843 Troy N.Y.; appt sgt-maj northern blk horse cav 23 Oct 1861 at Troy; (desig 2 N.Y. cav [by state auth] but desig 7 N.Y. cav at war dept); regt m.o. 31 Mar 1862 near Wash'n D.C. (never armed or mtd) when mil affairs committee tho't war nearly over; appt battn sgt-maj 7 N.Y. cav 24 July 1862; regtl sgt-maj 7 Apr 1863; 2Lt 10 May 1863; 1Lt 19 Oct 1864; m.o. vol serv 29 Nov 1865 City Point Va.; bvt capt vols 13 Mar 1865 for gal serv dur the war; appt reg army com'n 1Lt 7 cav 4 Dec 1866 to date 28 July 1866; join co M 29 Dec 1866 Ft Riley Kans.; comd co in action at Washita 27 Nov 1868; prom capt co K 29 Apr 1869; awl 30 days 30 Nov 1872 Troy N.Y. & ext'd 15 days; with co on Yellowstone Exp'n June to Sep 1873; awl 6 mos 10 Nov 1873; with co on Blk Hills Exp'n July & Aug 1874; ds rctg duty 18 Sep 1874 St Louis Mo.; cond rcts to New Orleans & Shreveport La. July 1875 & visited co K; cond rcts for 7 cav to Ft Lincoln DT 14–18 July 1876 thence ret to St Louis depot; awl 20 days 29 Sep 1876; rejoin co K 7 Dec 1876 at Ft Lincoln; killed 30 Sep 1877 Snake Creek MT (Bear's Paw Mtns) in action with Nez Perce inds.[6]
[4113 ACP 1873].

Haley, Timothy. Pvt co H; b. 25 Dec 1846 Cork Ireland; pvt co A 21 Va. cav [Confederate] 1 Apr 1863; captured 22 Sep 1864 Fisher Hill Va.; joined union army 14 Oct 1864 Pt Lookout Md a pvt co B 2 US vol inf; (redesig 4 US vol inf Mar 1865); dd co baker July 1865 to Mar 1866; m.o. vol serv 18 June 1866 Ft L'worth Kans.; enl reg army 28 Feb 1867 Boston Mass. for 3 yrs; age 22; baker; blue eyes, lt hair, lt comp, 5' 6 1/2" high; assd to co C 44 inf; (tr to co K 17 inf Apr 1869 by consol'n of regts); disch 28 Feb 1870 Camp Grant Va. expir of serv a pvt; reenl in same co 5 Mar 1870 Richmond Va. for 5 yrs; disch 16 Dec 1874 Cheyenne Agcy DT per SO 264 Dept of Dak. 1874 (under prov'n GO 24 AGO 1859);[7] reenl 15 Jan 1875 New Orleans La. for 5 yrs in co H 7 cav (auth AGO); dd post baker 11 Dec 1875 to 4 May 1876; dd post baker Nov 1876 to Mar 1877; disch 16 Apr 1879 Ft Lincoln DT on surg cert dis (chr. rheum.) a pvt; died 31 Dec 1913 Wash'n D.C. Pension: 25 Mar 1884 / Inv / 509163 / 285484.

Hall, Peter Curtis. Pvt co D; b. 31 Jan 1852 Lycoming Co Pa.; enl in 7 cav as Curtis Hall 9 Dec 1872 Louisville Ky. for 5 yrs; age 21; harness maker; hazel eyes, dk brn hair, ruddy comp, 5' 11" high; join co D 10 Feb 1873 Opelika Ala; dd with hq fatigue June to Sep 1873; ed qmd Oct 1874 to June 1875; sad'r 1 July 1877; ds Ft Rice DT 15 Oct 1877 nurse in hosp; disch 9 Dec 1877 at Ft Rice upon expir of serv a sad'r char xclt; reenl 4 days later in co D for 5 yrs & on furl at Bismarck, DT; pvt 1 Aug 1878 & dd co sad'r to Nov 1878; appt

sad'r 22 Nov 1878; sick hosp 30 Dec 1879 (frostbite toes both feet [heads of last phalange of great, 2d & 3d toes removed 21 Jan 1880]); duty 31 May 1880; on furl 60 days 7 Mar 1882 MT; disch 12 Dec 1882 Ft Yates DT expir of serv a sad'r; reenl in co D 27 May 1885 at Ft Yates for 5 yrs; cpl 1 Oct 1885; abs on pass 21 June to 2 July 1886 Ft Custer MT;[8] sick qrs 30 July to 6 Aug 1886 (tenderness of toes r. foot, old frostbite); sgt 11 Oct 1886; sick hosp 7 Jan 1887 Ft Riley Kans. (accdt gsw l. knee while cleaning pistol); disch 7 July 1887 at Ft Riley on surg cert dis a sgt char xclt; died 6 Apr 1908 Warsaw Ind.
Pension: 24 July 1888 / Inv / 665477 / 409648.

Hall, Edw. Pvt co D; b. 19 Apr 1851 Bridgewater N.Y.; enl 4 Jan 1872 Troy N.Y. for 5 yrs; age 21 8/12; teamster; blue eyes, lt brn hair, fair comp, 5' 5 1/2" high; join co D 13 Feb 1872 Chester SC; sick (bubo) hosp Ft Snelling Minn. 10 Apr to 13 Aug 1873 when sent to Ft Totten DT; ed qmd teamster Oct 1873 to May 1874; ed qmd teamster Sep 1874 (with NBS); ds 5 May 1876 Ft Lincoln DT in co garden; ds 21 Oct 1876 at Ft Lincoln dismtd; disch 4 Jan 1877 Ft Rice DT expir of serv a pvt char xclt.
Pension: 18 Nov 1912 / Inv / 1406935. (Abandoned).

Hamilton, Andrew. Blks co A; b. Port Glasgow Scotland; enl 17 Apr 1872 New York N.Y. for 5 yrs; age 23; blacksmith; gray eyes, lt hair, fair comp, 5' 6" high; join co A 27 Aug 1872 E'town Ky. & appt co blks; ds Oct 1872 thro' Jan 1873 with detmt at Huntsville Ala; disch 17 Apr 1877 Ft Rice DT expir of serv a blks char xclt.

Hamilton, Henry. Pvt co L; b. Dexter N.Y.; enl in co L 20 Jan 1873 New Orleans La. for 5 yrs; age 29; cook; blue eyes, brn hair, fair comp, 5' 6 1/4" high; cpl 20 Aug 1875; pvt 8 Apr 1876; killed with Custer column 25 June 1876.

Hammon, Geo. W. Pvt co F; b. Fulton Ohio; (bro Jno. E. Hammon); enl 9 Sep 1873 Cincinnati Ohio for 5 yrs; age 21; farmer; blue eyes, dk brn hair, florid comp, 5' 8" high; join co F 18 Oct 1873 Ft Lincoln DT; dd regtl hq Oct 1874 to Oct 1875; ed hosp nurse 17 Feb to 2 May 1876; killed with Custer column 25 June 1876.

Hammon, Jno. E. Cpl co G; b. 4 Dec 1857 Rochester Ohio; (bro Geo. W. Hammon); enl 1 Sep 1873 Cincinnati Ohio for 5 yrs; age 18; farmer; blue eyes, dk brn hair, fair comp, 5' 7 1/4" high; join co G 19 Oct 1873 Ft Lincoln DT; cpl 3 Apr 1876; dd 18–19 June 1876;[9] with pack train 25 June 1876;[10] sgt 9 July 1876; pvt 4 Jan 1877; dd qmd hostler Jan & Feb 1877; dd regtl hq fatigue pty Apr 1877; ds Wolf Rapids Aug 1877 gd pub prop; dd prov gd Ft Lincoln Feb 1878; dd qmd Mar to July 1878; cpl 11 Aug 1878; disch 1 Sep 1878 Camp J. G. Sturgis DT expir of serv a cpl char very good; reenl 25 Feb 1879 at Cincinnati for 5 yrs; assd to co H 2 cav; tr to co G 7 cav 17 July 1879; cpl 1 Jan 1880; disch 22 Oct 1880 Ft Meade DT per SO 217 AGO 1880 (appn of his elderly mother, having no means of support except from only remaining son; other son killed in Custer battle & 3rd son killed in train accdt when returning home after disch from army; husband lost in late war); employed Jan 1882 post qmd Ft Meade a trainmaster, also chf packer in chg of pack train;[11] capt co D 3 US vol cav 10 May to 8 Sep 1898 with Grigsby rough riders in Cuba & pack master until war's end; died 20 Jan 1909 Sturgis SD.
Pension: 1 Sep 1922 / Wid / 1201568 / 930505. Ind. War Wid / 13945 / 9414.

Hanke, Chas. Trump'r co M; b. Breslau Germany; enl as Chas. Hinke 9 Feb 1867 Brooklyn N.Y. for 3 yrs; age 24; hunter; brn eyes, brn hair, lt comp, 5' 2 1/2" high; assd to co G 1 art'y; disch 9 Feb 1870 Ft Monroe Va. by expir of serv a bugler & reenl in same co for 5 yrs as Chas. Hanke; des 5 Oct 1871 at Ft Monroe; surd 11 Mar 1872 Rock Isl Ars'l Ill.; sen gen cm 23 May 1872 to 2 yrs conft mil prison Ft L'worth Kans.; unexpired portion of sen rem'd 4 Jan 1873 & tr to co I 5 inf at Ft L'worth a trump'r; tr to co A 16 Aug 1873; tr to co E 2 Jan 1874; disch 15 July 1875 at Ft L'worth by expir of serv a mus'n; reenl 29 July 1875 Chicago Ill. for 5 yrs (band mus'n for 4 inf [performs on b.flat cornet]); disch 2 Aug 1875 Newport Bks Ky. on surg cert (intemperate habits & not band mus'n as represented); enl as Chas. Fischer 14 Sep 1875 St Louis Mo. for 5 yrs; join co M 7 cav as trump'r 21 Oct 1875 Ft Rice DT; in conft 16 Oct to 13 Nov 1876 Ft Lincoln DT; in conft Apr 1877; sick hosp 22 Feb to 20 Mar 1878 (chr. alcoholism); in conft Apr 1878; disch 16 June 1878 at Ft Lincoln on surg cert dis (chr. alcoholism); reenl as Chas. Hanke 1 Aug 1878 at St Louis for 5 yrs; assd to co A 6 cav; disch 1 Oct 1879 Ft Grant AT on surg cert dis (consumption) a trump'r char fair; reenl as Chas. Fischer 15 May 1880 Ft Garland Colo. for 5 yrs; assd to co K 4 cav; disch 20 Sep 1880 camp on Gunnison Colo. for fraud't enlmt (signed clothing rolls as Chas. Hanke, being partly intoxicated at the time); adm to city hosp at St Louis 10 Feb 1885 (phthisis pulmonalis); rel from hosp 16 Mar upon own req & re-adm two days later; app'n to reenl in army 28 Mar 1885 (claiming perfect health) not appv; rel from hosp 4 May 1885 upon own req & re-adm one wk later (phthisis pulmonalis); rel from hosp 19 May 1885 (own req).[12]

Pension: 31 Oct 1885 / Inv / 553169. (Rej on grd alleged disease of lungs [asthma] from exposure & constant blowing of bugle, not contr line of duty but attributed to other causes not incident to serv).

Hanley, Rich'd P. Sgt co C; b. Boston Mass.; enl 28 June 1865 Cincinnati Ohio for 3 yrs; age 22; laborer; blue eyes, lt brn hair, fair comp, 6' 0" high; assd to co C 3 cav; disch 28 June 1868 Ft Union NM expir of serv a pvt; reenl 27 Aug 1868 New York N.Y. for 5 yrs; assd to co L 2 cav; disch 27 Aug 1873 Ft Ellis MT expir of serv a sgt; reenl 18 Sep 1873 at Cincinnati for 5 yrs; join co C 7 cav 21 Oct 1873 Ft Rice DT; dd hosp attdt Aug 1874; dd member of boat crew Oct 1874; dd qmd Feb to May 1875; cpl 1 June 1875; sgt 24 Apr 1876; chg of co pack train June 1876; dd co qm sgt June 1877 & Dec 1877; disch 18 Sep 1878 Camp J. G. Sturgis DT expir of serv a sgt char xclt; reenl same day in co C for 5 yrs & on furl 3 mos at Boston; (awarded medal of honor 5 Oct 1878 for capturing singlehandedly & without orders, a stampeded pack mule loaded with amm'n [at LBH]);[13] dd actg co qm sgt Aug 1879; ds Ft Lincoln Dec 1879 verbal order comdg officer; 1sgt 1 Mar 1881; sgt 8 Aug 1882; ds Jeff'n Bks Mo. Oct 1882 to Jan 1883; chg of rcts to Ft Snelling Minn. Feb 1883; disch 17 Sep 1883 Ft Meade DT expir of serv a sgt & reenl for 5 yrs; assd to co L 2 cav; disch 17 Sep 1888 Ft Sherman Idaho Ty expir of serv a sgt char xclt; reenl 27 Sep 1888 Jeff'n Bks Mo. for 5 yrs in gen mtd serv instr'n regt; retd 20 Apr 1891 at Jeff'n Bks a sgt; died 13 Sep 1923 Boston Mass.[14]

Hardden, Wm. Pvt co D; b. New York N.Y.; enl 22 Jan 1872 Syracuse N.Y. for 5 yrs; age 21; laborer; gray eyes, sandy hair, dk comp, 5' 8" high; join co D 24 Feb 1872 Chester SC; ds regtl hq June 1873 to May 1875; chg of Bos Custer's extra pony 25 June 1876 [Bos had two ind ponies];[15] ds Ft Lincoln DT 12 Nov 1876 orderly at regtl hq; ds Ft Abercrombie DT 15 Jan 1877 (after furl he was attd to co F while awaiting disch); disch 22 Jan 1877 upon expir of serv a pvt char xclt; enl as Wm. Haidden 12 Feb 1877 Wash'n D.C. for 5 yrs; assd to co L 2 art'y; ed qmd teamster Feb to May 1881; ed cook post hosp McPherson Bks Ga. Aug to Oct 1881; dd as batt'y armorer Dec 1881; disch 11 Feb 1882 Ft McHenry Md expir of serv a pvt char "served honestly & faithfully & borne a good character throughout his enlistment;" res Jersey City NJ.

Pension: 31 Aug 1891 / Inv / 1056611. Alleged hernia when thrown against pommel of saddle on vicious horse which became unmanageable, in 1880. (Abandoned).

Hardy, Wm. G. Trump'r co A; b. 20 Dec 1849 Staten Isl N.Y.; enr as Chas. Laurse drummer boy in band 1 New Orleans inf Jan 1864 to June 1866; enl reg army as Wm. G. Hardy 15 Dec 1874 Boston Mass. for 5 yrs; age 24; trumpeter; gray eyes, lt hair, fair comp, 5' 6 3/8" high; join co A as trump'r 23 June 1875 Ft Randall DT; (held capt Moylan's horse dur valley fight 25 June 1876); dd regtl hq 6 Aug 1876; appt chf-trump'r 25 Aug 1876 to date 1 Aug; ds Ft Lincoln 16 Oct 1877 & join post 26 Oct; trump'r co A 23 July 1878; disch 14 Dec 1879 Ft Meade DT by expir of serv a trump'r char good when sober; reenl next day for 5 yrs & appt chf-trump'r same date; disch 14 Dec 1884 at Ft Meade expir of serv a chf-trump'r;

reenl same day for 5 yrs & on furl 90 days New York N.Y.; on furl 26 May to 9 July 1886 Baltimore Md; disch 14 Dec 1889 Ft Riley Kans. expir of serv a chf mus'n; reenl same day for 5 yrs & on furl 40 days Chicago Ill.; disch 14 Dec 1894 at Ft Riley expir of serv a chf-trump'r; reenl next day for 5 yrs & on furl 20 days at Chicago; disch 1 May 1896 Ft Grant AT on surg cert dis (nervous debility with partial paretic condition l. side; dis total) a chf-trump'r char xclt; reenl 4 Jan 1897 Wash'n Bks D.C. for 3 yrs in band 4 cav a drum-maj; disch 3 Jan 1900 Manila PI expir of serv a drum-maj & reenl for 3 yrs; disch 3 Jan 1903 Ft Riley Kans. expir of serv a drum-maj char xclt; reenl 22 Feb 1903 Ft Logan Colo. for 3 yrs in band 4 cav; disch 8 July 1905 Ft Walla Walla Wash'n per SO 117 Dept of Columbia (having less than 2 yrs 5 mos to serve & desiring to accomp regt to Phillipines) & reenl at once for 3 yrs; retd 17 Feb 1908 Ft Meade SD a color-sgt; died 17 Apr 1919 Presidio San Francisco Calif.[16]
Pension: 13 May 1896 / Inv / 1177265; (abandoned). Wid / 1201570 / 930508.

Hare, Luther Rector. 2Lt co K; b. 24 Aug 1851 Noblesville Ind.; moved to Belton, Tex., in 1853 & five yrs later to Mesilla, NM; settled in Sherman, Tex. in 1865; grad USMA 17 June 1874 & appt 2Lt 7 cav; join co K 22 Sep 1874 Ft Rice DT; with co on constabulary duty at Colfax La. & McComb City Miss to Apr 1876; assd to detmt ind scouts eve 24 June 1876; horse wd dur retreat from valley fight 25 June;[17] appt actg adjt on Reno hill & sent to hurry-up pack train, also with verbal order to capt Weir on "high point" to open communication with gen Custer; td comdg co L 27 June & care of co rec's; 1Lt co I 22 Aug 1876; sd with sec. of parrott guns in field 9 Oct to 13 Nov 1876; awl 29 Nov 1876 to 17 Mar 1877; actg engr officer in field 28 Apr to 8 Oct 1877; arr Ft Lincoln 26 Oct on str *Silver City* (with maj Merrill); ds Chicago Ill. Jan 1879 witness in Reno court of inq; rqm Dec 1881 to Nov 1883; regtl adjt Aug 1886 to July 1887; ds div hq Chicago Ill. Aug 1887 to Apr 1888 adc to gen Terry; actg battn adjt in field Nov 1890; sick Ft Riley Kans. 15 Dec 1890 to 3 Jan 1891; capt co K 30 Jan 1891; awl May 1898 to Jan 1899; (Lt-col 1 Tex. cav 28 Apr 1898; col 2 June 1898; m.o. vol serv 14 Nov 1898 Ft Sam Houston Tex.); with 7 cav to Havana Cuba 22 Jan 1899; col 33 US vol inf 5 July 1899 at San Antonio Tex. & with regt to Philippines 30 Sep 1899; briggen vols 1 June 1900 & comd 1st distr southern Luzon to Mar 1901; m.o. vol serv 20 June 1901 Wash'n D.C.; maj 12 cav from 2 Feb 1901 upon org'n of regt at San Antonio; retd 16 July 1903 for disability (injured wrist & hand in fall at Ft Sam Houston 27 Sep 1902, in line of duty); instr of natl gd at Austin Tex. Oct 1903 to June 1905 & May 1908 to Jan 1911; also mil adviser to gov'r Campbell; Lt-col on retd list 9 July 1916; appt prof of mil science at Univ of Tex. Feb 1918, also comd't of student army training corps at Simmons college in Abilene Oct 1918 to Feb 1919; awarded two silver star citations 15 Aug 1924 for gal serv at San Jacinto PI Nov & Dec 1899 comdg exp'n to liberate 22 Americans held pris'r; died 22 Dec 1929 Wash'n D.C.[18]
[3587 ACP 1875].

Harlfinger, Gustave. Pvt co D; b. Baden Germany; enl 8 Aug 1866 Phil'a Pa. for 5 yrs; age 24; soldier; blue eyes, brn hair; fair comp, 5' 5 1/2" high; join co D 10 Sep 1866 Ft Riley Kans.; dd orderly distr hq Oct 1866; dd co cook July 1867; dd co cook Oct & Nov 1867; dd co cook Feb & Aug 1868; ds camp near Ft Hays Kans. June 1869; ds Ft Wallace Kans. Aug 1869; dd co cook Dec 1870; disch 8 Aug 1871 Mt Vernon Ky. expir of serv a pvt; reenl in co D 7 Sep 1871 at Mt Vernon for 5 yrs; pres sick 19 June 1873; abs sick Ft Pembina DT 2 July to 15 Aug 1873 & rejoin co in field; dd 21 June 1874 with escort NBS; dd regtl hq 10 May 1876 as mtd msgr; ds camp Powder River MT 15 June 1876 guarding wagon train; disch 5 Aug 1876 camp mouth of Rosebud Creek MT (in time to go down river by first boat) per GO 24 AGO 1859 a pvt; arr Ft Lincoln DT 10 Aug on str *Durfee*.

Harrington, Henry Moore. 2Lt co C; b. 30 Apr 1849 Albion N.Y.; moved to Coldwater Mich. ca. 1856; grad USMA 14 June 1872 & appt 2Lt 7 cav; join co C 1 Oct 1872 Charlotte NC; with co on Yellowstone Exp'n June

1873 & comd co 24 July to 28 Sep 1873; actg post adjt Ft Rice DT Apr to June 1874; comd co on Blk Hills Exp'n July & Aug 1874; post adjt & comsy Ft Rice Sep 1874 to June 1875; awl six mos 10 Oct 1875 Coldwater Mich.; accomp Lt Reily's detmt from Ft Snelling Minn. 13 Mar 1876 & delayed at Ft Seward (Jamestown) DT 24 Mar awaiting removal of snow blockade on NPRR; arr Bismarck on first train 14 Apr (with cos E & L); comd co C on Reno scout up Powder River 10–20 June;[19] killed with Custer column 25 June 1876 (body not identified); survived by wife & 2 ch.[20]
[4287 ACP 1872]. Pension: 1 Dec 1876 / Wid / 228974 / 176560. Minor / 339603 / 224738.

Harrington, Weston. Pvt co L; b. 9 Feb 1855 Alton Ohio; enl 4 Nov 1872 Columbus Ohio for 5 yrs; age 21; laborer; brn eyes, brn hair, fair comp, 5' 8" high; join co L 9 Dec 1872 Yorkville SC; in hosp Ft Lincoln DT 17 June 1873 to 4 Jan 1874 (gsw l. elbow); ed hosp nurse Jan to May 1874; ed qmd teamster 28 Sep 1874; sick qrs 12 Nov 1874 to 16 Jan 1875 (sim. frac. r. elbow); ed qmd teamster Aug & Sep 1875; killed with Custer column 25 June 1876.

Harris, David W. Pvt co A; b. Indianapolis Ind.; enl 29 Sep 1873 Cincinnati Ohio for 5 yrs; age 21; laborer; blue eyes, brn hair, florid comp, 5' 6 1/4" high; join co A 18 Oct 1873 Ft Lincoln DT; dd co cook Dec 1873; dd hq Blk Hills Exp'n Aug 1874; dd qmd teamster Oct 1875 to Mar 1876; dd regtl hq fatigue pty (morn & eve) 11 May 1876; ds in field 2 Sep 1877; disch 29 Sep 1878 camp J. G. Sturgis DT expir of serv a pvt char good; awarded medal of honor 5 Oct 1878 for bringing water to wounded [at LBH], making two trips to river; (he having been disch the serv, medal filed in AGO & for'd to sol. 22 Mar 1879 at Columbus Bks Ohio);[21] reenl 6 Jan 1879 Indianapolis Ind. for 5 yrs; assd to gen serv at Columbus Bks; tr to co E 5 inf 2 Aug 1879; tr to co A 7 cav 10 Sep 1880; cpl 12 Aug 1881; sgt 1 Mar 1882; pvt 29 July 1883; disch 5 Jan 1884 Ft Meade DT expir of serv a pvt char good. res Wash'n D.C. in 1899.
Pension: 19 Jan 1897 / Inv / 1184728. Rej, no ratable disability shown upon med exam'n.

Harris, Jas. Pvt co D; b. Yarmouth Nova Scotia; enl 21 Sep 1875 Boston Mass. for 5 yrs; age 21 1/12; painter; gray eyes, dk hair, fair comp, 5' 6 1/2" high; join co D 21 Oct 1875 Ft Lincoln DT; sick 8–13 May 1876 (tert. intm. fever); disch 20 Sep 1880 Ft Yates DT expir of serv a pvt char xclt.

Harris, Leonard A. [Jr]. Pvt co F; b. Sep 1852 Cincinnati Ohio; enl 21 Dec 1872 at Cincinnati for 5 yrs; age 21 2/12; laborer; blue eyes, lt hair, florid comp, 5' 7" high; join 7 cav 1 Feb 1873 Taylor Bks Louisville Ky. unassd rct; des 19 Mar 1873 at Louisville; apph 19 Apr 1873 at Cincinnati; tr to civil custody 30 Apr 1873 on writ of habeas corpus (obtained by sol.'s mother) alleging sol. enl as minor & without consent; disch 2 May 1873 in civil court under statute barring minors from mil serv; re-arrested by mil auth 1 July 1873 at Cincinnati on grd that only U.S. Court had jurisdiction of mil; tr under gd 11 Aug 1873 from Newport Bks Ky. to Ft Lincoln DT; assd to co F 21 Sep 1873 (in conft); dishon disch 23 Dec 1873 sen gen cm & 4 yrs conft at sta of co wearing 24 pound ball attd to l. leg by chain six feet long; escaped from guardhouse 18 Feb 1874; news of his arrest by police at Cincinnati 24 May 1875 alerted mil auth; his mother obtained writ of habeas corpus from U.S. Court on grd that her son enl without consent when a minor (& intoxicated) & thus not amenable to mil law; judge dismissed writ when police explained sol. being held for larceny (theft of $240 from money-drawer of saloon); acquited in civil court 28 May thence taken in mil custody to Newport Bks; disch 7 June 1875 in U.S. Court at Cincinnati on habeas corpus under law passed in 1872 releasing any minor from oath of enlmt upon proof of age; re-arrestd by U.S. marshal before leaving court & jailed for perjury on his enlmt papers, having sworn he was of age; sen 12 Nov 1875 to 3 mos in county jail & $100 fine, the court having considered his lengthy time in conft.[22]

Harris, Wm. M. Pvt co D; b. 12 Jan 1851 Madison Co Ky.; enl in co D 25 Aug 1871 Mt Vernon Ky. for 5 yrs; age 21; farmer; gray eyes, lt hair, fair comp, 5' 10 1/2" high; ds

Yorkville SC Oct 1871; abs sick Opelika Ala Feb 1873; ds Ft Abercrombie DT Apr 1874; in conft Apr 1875; disch 5 Aug 1876 camp mouth of Rosebud Creek MT (in time to go down river by first boat) per GO 24 AGO 1859 a pvt; arr Ft Lincoln DT 10 Aug on str *Durfee*; awarded medal of honor 5 Oct 1878 for bringing water to wounded [at LBH]; he having been disch the serv, medal filed in AGO; killed 6 June 1885 Berea Ky. in gunfight.[23]

Harrison, Thos. W. Sgt co D; b. Sligo Co Ireland; enl 9 Aug 1866 New York N.Y. for 5 yrs; age 28; painter; hazel eyes, blk hair, dk comp, 5' 9 1/2" high; join co D 10 Sep 1866 Ft Riley Kans.; dd qmd Oct 1866; dd post bakery Nov 1866 to Feb 1867; dd orderly regtl hq Mar to Dec 1867;[24] cpl 11 Jan 1868; sgt 16 June 1871; disch 9 Aug 1871 Mt Vernon Ky. expir of serv & reenl in co D for 5 yrs; ds with Lt Nave Aug 1873; ds St Paul Minn. May to July 1874 with bd of officers purchasing horses; ds Ft Lincoln DT Aug 1874; in arrest Apr 1875; in arrest Dec 1875; disch 5 Aug 1876 camp mouth of Rosebud Creek MT (in time to go down river by first boat) per GO 24 AGO 1859 a sgt; arr Ft Lincoln 10 Aug on str *Durfee*; (recom by Lt Edgerly for medal of honor for staying back at Weir Point when he [Edgerly] had great difficulty mounting his horse & bullets flying thick & fast, also his bravery & coolness on Reno hill helped keep men in good heart & spirits);[25] died 25 Dec 1917 Phil'a Pa.
Pension: 17 Oct 1885 / Inv / 552190 / 666342. Ind. Surv. / 12872.

Harrison, Wm. H. Cpl co L; b. Gloucester Mass.; enl 6 Apr 1866 Boston Mass. for 3 yrs; age 21; sailor; hazel eyes, lt hair, fair comp, 5' 6 1/2" high; join co I 5 art'y 15 May 1866 Ft Jeff'n Fla; disch 6 Apr 1869 Ft Warren Mass. expir of serv a pvt; reenl 26 Sep 1870 Milwaukee Wis for 5 yrs; join co E 17 inf 10 Nov 1870 Ft Stevenson DT; ed qmd laborer Sep 1872 to Mar 1873; dd post hq clerk Apr to July 1873; ed qmd laborer May to July 1874; cpl 9 Oct 1874; actg post qm sgt Oct 1874 to May 1875; dd qmd clerk June to Aug 1875; sgt 1 Aug 1875; disch 26 Sep 1875 Standing Rock DT expir of serv a sgt; enl in co L 7 cav 9 Oct 1875 Ft Totten DT for 5 yrs; cpl 19 Feb 1876; killed with Custer column 25 June 1876.

Hathersall, Jas. Pvt co C; b. Liverpool England; enl 1 Sep 1870 Boston Mass. for 5 yrs; age 21; porter; blue eyes, lt hair, fair comp, 5' 6" high; join co E 3 cav 3 Dec 1870 Camp Verde AT; ds escort wagon to Prescott AT 25 Feb to 2 Mar 1871; dd qmd laborer Dec 1874 to July 1875; disch 1 Sep 1875 Camp Sheridan Neb expir of serv a pvt; reenl 13 Sep 1875 New York N.Y. for 5 yrs; join co C 7 cav 21 Oct 1875 Ft Lincoln DT; killed with Custer column 25 June 1876.

Haugge, Louis. Pvt co L; b. Alsace Germany; enl 6 Oct 1873 Cincinnati Ohio for 5 yrs; age 21 6/12; farmer; brn eyes, lt hair, fair comp, 5' 7" high; join co L 19 Oct 1873 Ft Lincoln DT; dd hq Blk Hills Exp'n June to Aug 1874; sick qrs 17–26 May 1876 (cont'n r. foot, kick by horse); killed with Custer column 25 June 1876.

Haverstick, Benj. Johnson. Pvt co G; b. Apr 1845 Lancaster Pa.; enl as Benj. Johnson 22 June 1875 Pittsburgh Pa. for 5 yrs; age 29; carpenter; hazel eyes, dk brn hair, dk comp, 5' 5 3/4" high; join co G 1 Aug 1875 Shreveport La.; dd qmd carpenter Dec 1875 to Mar 1876; left in timber dur retreat from valley fight 25 June 1876 & rejoin co on Reno hill; cpl 1 July 1877; dd qmd 13 Mar 1878; ds Ft Lincoln DT July to Nov 1878; dd bldg co stables June 1879; sgt 25 Sep 1879; disch 22 June 1880 Box Elder Creek MT expir of serv a sgt char xclt & reenl in co G for 5 yrs; ds qmd carpenter Oct 1880 to May 1881; dd actg co qm sgt June to Sep 1881; pvt 16 Jan 1882; ed qmd carpenter Oct 1882 to Apr 1885; tr to co I 1 cav 22 May 1885; disch 21 June 1885 Ft L'worth Kans. expir of serv a pvt char xclt; reenl 11 July 1885 San Francisco Calif. for 5 yrs; assd to co C 1 art'y; disch 10 July 1890 Ft Wadsworth N.Y. expir of serv a pvt char xclt & reenl in same co for 5 yrs; disch 10 July 1895 at Ft Wadsworth expir of serv a pvt char xclt & reenl in same co for 3 yrs; disch 10 July 1898 Sullivans Isl SC expir of serv an artf'r char xclt; reenl 14

July 1898 Moultrieville SC for 3 yrs; assd to co E 3 art'y; disch 8 Mar 1899 Ft Mason Calif. per GO 40 AGO 1898 a pvt char xclt;[26] reenl 10 Mar 1899 at Ft Mason for 3 yrs in hosp corps; disch 9 Mar 1902 San Francisco Calif. expir of serv a pvt char xclt & reenl in hosp corps for 3 yrs; disch 9 Mar 1905 Presidio San Francisco expir of serv a pvt 1st cl. char xclt & reenl in same unit; retd 7 Aug 1905 at Presidio a sgt hosp corps; died 15 Nov 1922 Lancaster Pa.[27]

Hayes, Chas. N. Pvt co H; b. Dresden N.Y.; enl as Chas. N. Hood 25 Aug 1873 Cincinnati Ohio for 5 yrs;[28] age 21 4/12; painter; lt brn eyes, brn hair, fair comp, 5' 6" high; join co H 20 Oct 1873 Ft Rice DT; sick qrs 25 Apr to 4 May 1876 (incised wd. r. foot [axe]); sick hosp Ft Lincoln to 31 May 1876; dd room orderly June 1876; sent with Lt Garlington on str *Josephine* 24 July 1876 to join co in field; cpl 1 Nov 1876; sick hosp Ft Lincoln Apr & May 1877 (comp'd frac. r. tibia, kick by horse); sick qrs June & July 1877; dd post qmd Aug & Sep 1877; sgt 1 Jan 1878; disch 25 Aug 1878 Camp J. G. Sturgis (Bear Butte) DT expir of serv a sgt char good; died 27 Sep 1892 Penn Yan N.Y.
Pension: 7 July 1893 / Wid / 579651. Rej on grd clmt not legal widow of sol.

Hayward, Geo. Sad'r co I; b. Little York Canada; enl 14 May 1873 St Louis Mo. for 5 yrs; age 22 2/12; harness maker; brn (hazel) eyes, lt hair, fair comp, 5' 7" high; join co I 3 June 1873 Ft Snelling Minn.; sad'r 5 Apr 1874; pvt 16 May 1875; sen gen cm 21 July 1875 forf $10 pay per mo for 6 mos & conft same period; sad'r 29 Jan 1876; sick hosp Ft Lincoln DT 6 Mar to 7 July 1876 (frostbite both feet when he laid on grd for one hr dur return from groggery across river [partial amp'n 3 toes]; sick hosp Ft Lincoln 16 Oct 1876; ds in field 28 Oct 1877; disch 14 May 1878 at Ft Lincoln by expir of serv a sad'r char xclt; reenl 14 Dec 1883 Detroit Mich. for 5 yrs; assd to co D 5 cav; disch 13 Dec 1888 Ft Sill IT expir of serv a sad'r char good & reenl in same co for 5 yrs; disch 13 Dec 1893 Ft McIntosh Tex. expir of serv a sad'r char xclt & reenl in same co for 5 yrs; disch 6 Dec 1897 Ft Sam Houston Tex. on surg cert dis (tuberculosis; dis total) a sad'r; died 17 Feb 1899 Sol. Home Wash'n D.C.
Pension: 15 Dec 1897 / Inv / 1202265 / 971625.

Heath, Wm. H. Far'r co L; b. Staffordshire England; enl 9 Oct 1875 Cincinnati Ohio for 5 yrs; age 27; coachman; blue eyes, brn hair, dk comp, 5' 7 1/4" high; join co L 29 Oct 1875 Ft Totten DT; far'r 3 Jan 1876; sick 25 Feb to 3 Mar 1876 (cont'n l. tibia, kicked); killed with Custer column 25 June 1876.

Hegner, Francis. Pvt co F; b. Berlin Germany; enl 24 July 1867 Detroit Mich. for 5 yrs; age 24; farmer; blue eyes, lt hair, fair comp, 5' 9" high; join co F 8 Sep 1867 Ft Hays Kans.; dd post gardener Apr to July 1868; dd co cook Sep to Nov 1868; ds with gov'r McCook Sep & Oct 1869; dd regtl hq Mar & Apr 1870; ed qmd teamster Aug 1870; ds regtl hq Louisville Ky. July to Nov 1871; disch 24 July 1872 at Louisville expir of serv & reenl in co F for 5 yrs; ds regtl hq St Paul Minn. 11 Apr 1873 to 6 Oct 1874 & dd regtl hq Ft Lincoln DT to Jan 1876; ed qmd mech Feb 1876; ed qmd laborer with exp'n 7 May 1876; dd qmd laborer June 1876; [with wagon train says Rooney; doubtful with packs says Lynch];[29] dd regtl hq Aug 1876; furn transp by post qm Ft Buford 24 Sep to Ft Lincoln (with Cowley & Gaffney);[30] ds hosp attdt Ft Lincoln 16 Oct & tr with dismtd men & baggage of co F to Ft Abercrombie DT 15 Nov 1876; ds Ft Abercrombie 12 Apr 1877 chg co prop; disch 7 June 1877 at Ft Abercrombie per SO 70 Dept of Dak. 1877 a pvt char very good; died 17 Jan 1891 Kenockee Twp. Mich.
Pension: 20 June 1881 / Inv / 423926 / 316768.

Heid, Geo. Pvt co M; b. Bavaria Germany; enl 17 June 1870 Cincinnati Ohio for 5 yrs; age 28; farmer; gray eyes, dk hair, ruddy comp, 5' 6 1/4" high; join co M 29 June 1870 Ft Hays Kans.; des 8 Feb 1872 Unionville SC; enl in marine corps as Geo. Hyed 27 Nov 1872 Phil'a Pa. for 5 yrs; surd as des'r 6 Nov 1873 Norfolk Bks Va. under GO 102 AGO 1873; tr to St Louis Bks Mo. 24 Nov 1873; ds Ft Snelling Minn. 1 Jan 1874 await opportunity to join regt; restored to duty without trial

4 Mar 1874 & tr to Ft Lincoln DT 19 May; dd qmd sawyer Nov 1874 to May 1875; dd room orderly Aug 1875; dd qmd laborer Dec 1876; disch 15 Mar 1877 Ft Rice DT expir of serv a pvt char xclt; reenl 19 Mar 1877 at Ft Lincoln for 5 yrs in co I 7 cav; ed hosp nurse 20 July to 20 Nov 1877; dd co tailor Dec 1880 to Feb 1881 & Aug to Oct 1881; disch 18 Mar 1882 Ft Totten DT expir of serv a pvt char good; reenl in co I 24 Mar 1882 at Ft Totten for 5 yrs; dd co tailor Apr to Dec 1882; dd qmd laborer Aug 1883; ds cutting wood for post Oct 1883; dd qmd stacking hay Aug 1884; died 1 Feb 1887 Ft Totten, DT (valvular disease of heart), a pvt.

Heim, Jno. Pvt co E; b. St Louis Mo.; enl 19 Jan 1875 at St Louis for 5 yrs; age 23; clerk; brn eyes, lt hair, fair comp, 5' 2" high; join co E 8 Feb 1875 Opelika Ala; killed with Custer column 25 June 1876.

Helmer, Julius. Pvt co K; b. Hanover Germany; enl 14 Mar 1867 Brooklyn N.Y. for 3 yrs; age 21; clerk; gray eyes, lt hair, lt comp, 5' 10" high; assd to co I 4 inf 22 Apr 1867 Omaha Neb; (consol with cos D & I 30 inf & desig co A 4 inf Apr 1869); ed comsy dept clerk June to Oct 1869; disch 14 Mar 1870 Ft Fetterman Wyo. Ty expir of serv a pvt & reenl in same co for 5 yrs; cpl 16 Apr 1870; sgt 10 May 1870; co qm sgt Oct 1870; in arrest Aug 1871; pvt 22 Sep 1871 sen gen cm & forf $12 pay per mo for 2 mos; in confr Oct 1871; ed hosp stew'd 3d cl. 10 Feb to 31 Dec 1872; dd co clerk June 1873 to Mar 1875; disch 14 Mar 1875 Ft Fetterman Wyo. Ty expir of serv a pvt; reenl 10 July 1875 Cincinnati Ohio for 5 yrs; join co K 7 cav 27 Apr 1876 St Paul Minn.; killed on Reno hill 25 June 1876 (gsw thro' bowels & died in great agony begging of his comrades to kill him to end his misery).[31]

Henderson, Geo. W. Pvt co G; b. Hornelsville N.Y.; enl 2 Mar 1876 Baltimore Md for 5 yrs; age 21; farmer; gray eyes, lt hair, ruddy comp, 5' 7 1/2" high; join co B 7 cav 27 Apr 1876 St Paul Minn.; tr to co G 4 May 1876; dd qmd teamster 31 May 1876; ds camp Powder River MT 15 June 1876; ds on str *Yellowstone* 28 Aug to 25 Sep 1876; des 2 Jan 1877 Ft Lincoln DT & apph two days later at Bismarck DT; escaped from confr 26 Jan 1877 at Ft Lincoln.

Henderson, Jno. Pvt co E; b. Cork Ireland; enl 22 Aug 1870 New York N.Y. for 5 yrs; age 21; farmer; gray eyes, lt hair, fair comp, 5' 7 3/4" high; join co G 3 cav 3 Dec 1870 Camp Verde AT; ed qmd laborer Apr 1872; ed qmd packer Feb & Apr 1873; ds Camp Robinson Wyo. Ty Aug to Nov 1874; disch 22 Aug 1875 Ft Sidney Neb expir of serv a pvt; reenl 22 Sep 1875 New York N.Y. for 5 yrs; join co E 7 cav 29 Oct 1875 Ft Totten DT; dd regtl hq fatigue pty (morn & eve) 11 May 1876; killed with Custer column 25 June 1876.

Henderson, Sykes. Pvt co E; b. Armstrong Co Pa.; enl in co E 3 Dec 1867 Ft L'worth Kans. for 5 yrs; age 22; laborer; brn eyes, brn hair, fair comp, 5' 8" high; dd co cook Apr 1869; disch 3 Dec 1872 Unionville SC expir of serv a pvt & reenl in co E for 5 yrs; dd co cook Dec 1872 & Feb 1873; cpl 1 Nov 1873; sgt 1 Sep 1874; pvt 13 Jan 1875; in confr Feb 1875; killed with Custer column 25 June 1876.

Herendeen, Geo. B. Scout qmd; b 28 Nov 1848 Parkman Twp Geauga Co Ohio; orphaned at age 13 he lived for a time on his uncle's farm at Green Ind;[32] in 1868 he went to Colo. & up to the mines for one season, thence to New Mexico & hired as cowboy with a cattle herd to Montana; settled near Bozeman & engaged in various work;[33] with the Hayden exp'n in 1872 seeking a route for the NPRR along Yellowstone River & in fight with Sioux inds near Pryor Creek; with the Yellowstone wagon road exp'n in 1874 prospecting for gold on Rosebud Creek & skirmished with Sioux war ptys; with maj Pease's exp'n during June 1875 building a trading post near mouth of Big Horn River; accomp Pease to Ft Buford 4 July; caught str. up Missouri River & helped with new agcy at Wolf Point till late Aug then joined a freight outfit on the Carroll wagon road to Helena in time for fair-week [27 Sep];[34] afterward took stage to Bozeman & accomp three friends in boats down the Yellowstone to spend the winter wolfing near Pryor Creek; joined maj Brisbin's comd 1

Mar 1876 enroute to Ft Pease to remove settlers to Bozeman; declined to scout for col Gibbon's comd from Ft Ellis 1 Apr; went down Yellowstone in mackinaw boat 6 May with friend Paul McCormick & vol as sutlers for Gibbon's camp at Ft Pease;[35] hired as scout for gen Custer 21 June (given horse of pvt Lynch co F);[36] rate of pay $50 mo (to incr should he carry desp to gen Terry);[37] with maj Reno's comd into valley 25 June & dismtd at edge of woods with Gerard & Reynolds; left behind dur retreat when his horse fell & ran away; led eleven dismtd sol.'s up Reno hill, passing Billy Cross & 'Rees on way down to water horses; found his horse on hilltop but it was later killed & he lay behind it on Moylan's line all next day; on str *Far West* to Yellowstone 30 June; sent to Crow camp at Pryor Creek 9 July to seek more scouts & returned with 60 Crows; disch 30 Sep due $16.66 pay from 21–30 June & $300 from 1 July when pay incr to $100 mo; (paid $100 for serv at LBH);[38] accomp capt Nowlan & co I in June 1877 from Cant'mt Tongue River to Custer battlefield;[39] testified in Reno court of inq Jan 1879; employed as guide at Yellowstone park in 1880; later worked as carpenter at Ft Belknap agcy, also justice of peace & police judge at Harlem MT; accomp Walter Camp up Rosebud in 1909 & 1910 on trail of 7 cav; died 17 June 1919 Havre MT.[40]
Pension: 14 May 1917 / Ind. Surv. / 12520. Rej on grd no title under act 4 Mar 1917, clmt a civil employé of qmd & not enlisted into mil serv.

Hetesimer, Adam. Pvt co I; b. Cincinnati Ohio; enl 6 Oct 1875 at Cincinnati for 5 yrs; age 28; barber; blk eyes, blk hair, dk comp, 5' 7 1/2" high; join co I 21 Oct 1875 Ft Lincoln DT; in conft Dec 1875; sen gen cm 20 Jan 1876 forf $10 pay per mo for 2 mos & conft same period; killed with Custer column 25 June 1876.

Hetler, Jacob. Pvt co D; b. 2 Aug 1852 Mansfield Ohio; enl 3 Feb 1872 Chicago Ill. for 5 yrs; age 21; carpenter; blue eyes, lt hair, lt comp, 5' 6" high; join co D 24 Feb 1872 Chester SC; dd co cook Oct 1872; dd qmd carpenter Dec 1872; ed qmd teamster Dec 1873; gsw l. side (fl. wd. [sl.]) & l. leg above knee (fl. wd. [sl.]) 25 June 1876; remained with co in field; excused from duty 3 wks; (recom by Lt Edgerly for medal of honor for conspic gal in battle); disch 3 Feb 1877 Ft Rice DT expir of serv a pvt char good; died 27 Feb 1944 Greenwich Ohio.
Pension: 20 May 1897 / Inv / 1191417. (Rej on grd no med evidence of alleged disease of eyes in serv or at disch). Ind. Surv. / 17733 / 10819. (XC-2,580,585).

Heyn, Wm. 1sgt co A; b. 12 July 1848 Bremen Germany; enl 28 Feb 1867 New York N.Y. for 5 yrs; age 21; merchant; blue eyes, brn hair, fair comp, 5' 7 3/4" high; assd to co G 3 cav; disch 28 Feb 1872 Benecia Bks Calif. expir of serv a pvt; reenl 6 Apr 1872 New York N.Y. for 5 yrs; join co A 7 cav 2 Dec 1872 E'town Ky.; ed qmd carpenter Dec 1872; cpl 1 Jan 1873; dd chg co kit'n Apr & June 1873; 1sgt (from cpl) 23 July 1873; gsw l. knee (severe) 25 June 1876 in valley fight (bullet passed into horse which was also shot thro' neck & root of tail & died next morn on hilltop); tr on str *Far West* 3 July to hosp Ft Lincoln; tr to hosp Ft Rice 13 Nov; tr to gen serv Wash'n D.C. a pvt 28 Nov 1876 per SO 226 AGO 1876 (reward for meritorious serv in ind campn); disch 6 Apr 1877 at Wash'n by expir of serv a pvt char very good; reenl in gen serv as clerk in AGO; sgt 16 Jan 1878; disch 2 Sep 1879 at Wash'n having been appt clerk cl. II AGO; disch 21 July 1886 a clerk cl. I AGO; died 11 June 1910 Wash'n D.C.
Pension: 7 June 1877 / Inv / 237291 149272.

Heywood, Chas. Irving. Pvt co A; b. Manchester New Brunswick; enl in navy as Irving Heywood 22 Dec 1869 at Portsmouth N.H.; seaman on frigate *Colorado* [with sqdn on Asiatic sta Feb 1870 to Mar 1873]; disch 25 Mar 1873 New York N.Y.; enl in army 7 Dec 1874 Boston Mass. for 5 yrs; age 30; sailor; blue eyes, brn hair, medium comp, 5' 8 3/4" high; join co A 6 Feb 1875 Livingston Ala; dd co cook Aug 1875; gsw thro' buttocks 4 Oct 1875 (in drunken brawl at house near Ft Rice DT); tr to hosp Ft Lincoln DT 18 Dec 1875; disch 14 May 1876 at Ft Lincoln on surg cert dis a pvt char xclt; res Pine City Minn. in 1910.
Pension: 3 Aug 1908 / Inv / 1376280. (Rej on grd no med evidence of alleged rheum. & deafness in serv & failure of clmt to furn proof to establish claim).

Hiley, Jno. S. See Stuart-Forbes, Jno. Stuart.

Hill, Jas. 1sgt co B; b. 23 Aug 1825 near Edinburgh Scotland; enl 10 Apr 1841 at Edinburgh in 71 regt (Highland) lt inf; age 16 9/12; labourer; 5' 5 1/2" high; cpl 5 July 1847; pvt 27 Nov 1847; cpl 1 July 1849; purchased disch 1 June 1850 at Montreal Canada;[41] enl 3 Oct 1856 Oswego N.Y. for 5 yrs in co H 4 art'y; age 30; laborer; blue eyes, brn hair, florid comp, 5' 10" high; (in campn against Seminole inds in Fla. dur 1857); cpl 12 Apr 1859; sgt 1 Nov 1859; pvt 24 Jan 1860; cpl 27 May 1860; sgt 3 Oct 1860; disch 3 Oct 1861 Ft Randall DT expir of serv a sgt; enr 3 Nov 1861 St Louis Mo. in co D 1 Mo. lt art'y; 1sgt Dec 1861; pvt 17 July 1862; sgt-maj 27 Sep 1862; pvt co D 21 Nov 1862; reenl as vet vol 1 Jan 1864 Scottsboro Ala & appd for com'n in any African batt'y that may be org in dept; recom for com'n for meritorious cond in battle of Shiloh; ds rctg duty at St Louis Apr 1864; cpl 12 June 1864; sgt 1 May 1865; m.o. vol serv 11 July 1865 at St Louis; reenl reg army 28 Sep 1865 at St Louis for 5 yrs; join co G 2 cav 29 Oct 1865 at St Louis; 1sgt 1 Nov 1865; pvt 15 Dec 1865 by order regtl comdr; cpl 1 July 1866; sgt 24 Oct 1866; dd qmd as builder Dec 1866; 1sgt from qm sgt Dec 1867; disch 1 July 1868 Ft Fred Steele DT per SO 140 AGO 1868 (appt supt Little Rock Natl Cemetery); reenl 24 June 1869 at Little Rock for 5 yrs in co D 19 inf; sgt 1 July 1869; pvt 20 Aug 1869; cpl 1 Mar 1870; sgt 5 Apr 1870; dd police sgt June 1870; 1sgt 1 July 1870; pvt 10 Mar 1873; sgt 1 Sep 1873; pvt Apr 1874; disch 24 June 1874 at St Louis expir of serv a pvt; enl for co B 7 cav 22 Mar 1875 New Orleans La. for 5 yrs (auth AGO); cpl 1 Apr 1875; 1sgt 1 June 1875; sick 29 Mar to 14 Apr 1876 (cont'n chin & neck, kick by horse); kept itinerary on Reno scout 10–20 June 1876;[42] (recom for medal of honor for extraordinary coolness & bravery at LBH); appt ordn sgt USA 27 Jan 1877 at Ft Wayne Mich.; disch 3 Mar 1880 Ft Sanders Wyo. per SO 43 AGO 1880 an ordn sgt char good; reenl in co B 7 cav 3 Apr 1880 Ft Yates DT for 5 yrs (auth AGO); ds July & Aug 1880 Camp Houston DT actg sgt-maj of escort on NPRR ext'n; sgt 21 Sep 1880; actg 1sgt Oct 1880; actg co qm sgt Dec 1880; pvt 15 Jan 1881; sgt 2 Aug 1881; disch 2 Apr 1885 at Ft Yates expir of serv a sgt char xclt & reenl in co B for 5 yrs; on furl 4 mos 4 Apr 1885; (m. 12 May 1885 Wooster Ohio to Nannie Lowery, age 32); appt ordn sgt USA 2 May 1885 at Ft Lowell AT; retd 12 Nov 1888 an ordn sgt; died 18 Nov 1906 Wooster Ohio.[43]

Pension: 29 July 1890 / Inv / 844045. (Rej on grd of no title, sol. on retd list & receiving pay). Wid / 859564 / 624144.

Hodgson, Benj. Hubert. 2Lt co B; b. 30 June 1848 Phil'a Pa.; grad USMA 15 June 1870 & appt 2Lt 7 cav;[44] join co B 30 Sep 1870 Hugo Sta Colo. Ty; actg aqm post at Unionville SC Apr to July 1871; post adjt Spartanburg SC Oct 1872 to Mar 1873;[45] with co on Yellowstone Exp'n June to Sep 1873; actg comsy Ft Lincoln DT Oct 1873 to Apr 1874; comd co on Blk Hills Exp'n July to Sep 1874; with co to Shreveport La. (Dept of the Gulf) 29 Sep 1874; comd detmt to Monroe La. 19 Oct 1874 as posse comitatus with U.S. Marshal to arrest suspected murderers; in civil arrest at Monroe 16 Nov (exceeded auth making arrests); in mil arrest Dec 1874 & sen gen cm to be reprimanded by the comdg gen;[46] ds at New Orleans before congressional committee 28 Jan to 23 Feb 1875; awl 6 mos 1 Apr 1875;[47] comd co B 1 Feb to 10 May 1876;[48] appt adjt r. wing 12 May 1876 (with maj Reno); killed dur retreat from valley fight 25 June 1876 (on east bank of river).

[1230 ACP 1875].

Hoehn, Max. Pvt co L; b. Berlin Prussia; enl 4 Oct 1873 St Louis Mo. for 5 yrs; age 21 6/12; clerk; gray eyes, lt hair, fair comp, 5' 6 3/4" high; join co L 19 Oct 1873 Ft Lincoln DT; (dd regtl hq clerk Apr 1874 to Oct 1878); ds Ft Lincoln Aug 1875 to Apr 1876; ds camp Powder River MT 10 June 1876 chg of regtl rec's; ds Ft Lincoln 17 Oct to 11 Nov 1876; ds Ft Lincoln 1 May to 19 Nov 1877; ds Ft Lincoln July thro' Sep 1878; disch 4 Oct 1878 at Ft Lincoln expir of serv a pvt char xclt; died 6 Jan 1910 Sturgis SD.

Pension: Ind. Wid. / 14460 / 9127. (XC-2,659,232).

Hohmeyer, Fred'k. 1sgt co E; b. Darmstadt Germany; enl 19 Mar 1867 New York N.Y. for 3 yrs; age 21 1/2; gardner; gray eyes, lt hair, dk comp, 5' 7 1/2" high; join co B 4 art'y 25 Mar 1867 camp near Ft Riley Kans.; dd co cartman Dec 1868 & Feb 1869; disch 19 Mar 1870 at Ft Riley expir of serv a pvt; reenl 9 May 1870 St Louis Mo. for 5 yrs; join co E 7 cav 26 June 1870 Ft L'worth Kans.; cpl 1 July 1871; sgt 1 Sep 1871; actg post sgt-maj Dec 1871 to Oct 1872; ed asst to comsy 16 Dec 1872 to 24 May 1873; 1sgt 10 May 1873; sgt 29 Dec 1874 (own req); dd comsy dept Dec 1874 & Feb 1875; disch 9 May 1875 Opelika Ala expir of serv a sgt & reenl in co E for 5 yrs; ds Ft Randall DT 9 June to 9 Aug 1875; dd post prov sgt Feb 1876; 1sgt 1 May 1876; killed with Custer column 25 June 1876; survived by wife & 4 ch.; (widow m. sgt Bromwell 25 Feb 1877).
Pension: 1 Nov 1878 / Wid / 240061 / 193948. Minor / 268973 / 193949.

Holcomb, Edw. P. Pvt co I; b. Granby Conn.; enl 28 Oct 1872 Cleveland Ohio for 5 yrs; age 27; clerk; blk eyes, blk hair, dk comp, 5' 6 1/2" high; join co I 2 Dec 1872 Shelbyville Ky.; dd co cook June 1873; cpl 24 Dec 1874; pvt 10 Mar 1876 (own req); killed with Custer column 25 June 1876.

Holden, Henry. Pvt co D; b. Brighton England; pvt co C 59 Mass. inf 5 Jan 1864 to 26 May 1865 when regt consol with 57 Mass. inf; m.o. vol serv 30 July 1865 at Wash'n D.C.; enl reg army 23 Nov 1865 Baltimore Md for 3 yrs; age 25; laborer; gray eyes, lt hair, lt comp, 5' 5" high; assd to co E 8 inf; disch 23 Nov 1868 Columbia SC expir of serv a pvt; reenl in same co 23 Dec 1868 at Columbia for 3 yrs; disch 23 Dec 1871 Chicago Ill. expir of serv a pvt; reenl 9 Jan 1872 at Chicago for 5 yrs; join co D 7 cav 13 Feb 1872 Chester SC; ds in field July & Aug 1873; cpl 8 July 1876; disch 9 Jan 1877 Ft Rice DT expir of serv a cpl char good; (awarded medal of honor 5 Oct 1878 for bringing up amm'n [to Benteen's line] under heavy fire [at LBH]; he having been disch, medal filed in AGO & for'd to sol. 5 Apr 1879 at Ft McHenry Md); reenl 10 July 1878 Wash'n D.C. for 5 yrs in co A 2 art'y; disch 28 Nov 1882 Wash'n Bks D.C. on surg cert dis a pvt (comp'd frac. r. tibia [kick by horse] causing considerable edema of leg & impaired gait; dis total); died 14 Dec 1905 Brighton England.
Pension: 4 Dec 1882 / Inv / 466430 / 244746. Wid / 1214491 / 951388.

Holmsted, Fred'k. Pvt co A; b. 9 Dec 1849 Vallund Denmark; enl 6 Nov 1872 New York N.Y. for 5 yrs; age 23; clerk; brn eyes, brn hair, fair comp, 5' 8 1/4" high; join co A 2 Dec 1872 E'town Ky.; ed qmd watchman Feb 1873; dd clerk adjt's office 29 Apr to 11 May 1873; dd regtl hq Oct 1873 to Oct 1875; sick hosp 4 Dec 1875 to 30 Jan 1876 (ac. rheum.); gsw r. forearm (fl. wd. sl.) 25 June 1876 dur retreat from valley fight; (left in timber & rejoined co on Reno hill); tr on str *Far West* 3 July to hosp Ft Lincoln DT; duty 17 July; dd post hq Aug 1876; dd regtl hq 29 Sep 1876; ds Ft Lincoln 17 Oct 1876; dd regtl hq clerk from 13 Nov 1876; sent on boat 11 Aug 1877 to Ft Lincoln chg of regtl rec's; disch 6 Nov 1877 at Ft Lincoln upon expir of serv a pvt char xclt; enl same day in post detmt of ind scouts for 6 mos; died 27 Mar 1880 at Ft Lincoln after protracted illness.[49]

Holohan, Andrew. Pvt co K; b. Kilkenny Ireland; enl 22 Dec 1874 St Louis Bks Mo. for 5 yrs; age 25; miner; blue eyes, brn hair, ruddy comp, 5' 7 1/4" high; join co K 27 Apr 1876 St Paul Minn.; ds camp Powder River MT 15 June 1876; dd cook in band Dec 1876 & Feb 1877; sick field hosp 10–14 June 1877; ds in field Aug 1877; cpl 1 June 1878; sgt 1 Oct 1879; disch 21 Dec 1879 Ft Totten DT expir of serv a sgt char very good.

Hood, Chas. N. (alias). See Hayes, Chas. N.

Hood, Jas. Pvt co D; b. 16 May 1850 Jessamine Co Ky.; enl as Jas. Hurd 30 Aug 1871 Mt Vernon Ky. for 5 yrs in co D;[50] age 22; farmer; blue eyes, blk hair, dk comp, 5' 6" high; dd co cook Dec 1871; ed qmd teamster Oct 1873 to Mar 1874; ed qmd teamster Sep 1874 (with NBS); ed qmd Feb 1875; disch 5 Aug 1876 camp mouth of Rosebud Creek MT (in time to go down river by first boat)

per GO 24 AGO 1859 a pvt; arr Ft Lincoln 10 Aug on str *Durfee*; reenl in co D 4 Sep 1876 at Ft Lincoln for 5 yrs; ds Ft Lincoln Oct 1876 dismtd; ds Ft Rice DT Apr 1877 to Jan 1878; dd co teamster June to Dec 1878; dd co teamster Feb to Apr 1880; dd co teamster Dec 1880 to Feb 1881; disch 3 Sep 1881 Ft Yates DT expir of serv a pvt char very good; res Harrodsburg Ky. in 1911.
Pension: 27 May 1907 / Inv / 1360418. (Rej, no title under act 6 Feb 1907, no serv dur Rebellion).

Hook, Stanton. Pvt co A; b. Coshocton Ohio; pvt co M 9 Ohio cav 25 Sep 1863 to 20 Feb 1865; enl reg army 12 Oct 1875 Cincinnati Ohio for 5 yrs; age 30; saddler; blue eyes, brn hair, fair comp, 5' 7 1/4" high; join co A 21 Oct 1875 Ft Lincoln DT; dd co cook Dec 1875; sick (typhoid fever) 28 Aug 1876 on str *Carroll* to Ft Buford DT; tr on str *Benton* 3 Sep to hosp at Ft Lincoln; duty 26 Sep; ds Ft Lincoln 17 Oct 1876; ds with art'y in field July to Dec 1877; dd co cook Dec 1877 to Aug 1878; sick Ft Lincoln 24 Sep to 20 Nov 1878 (incised wd. r. knee); dd co cook Dec 1878 to Aug 1879; sad'r 6 Dec 1879; disch 11 Oct 1880 Ft Meade DT expir of serv a sad'r char xclt; reenl 30 Oct 1880 at Cincinnati for 5 yrs; assd to co C 5 cav; disch 14 Dec 1882 Ft Sidney Neb on surg cert dis a sad'r char very good (gen debility, tumor in lower anterior mediasternum & removal of epithiloma from upper lip; suffering sores in mouth & throat for long time; origin unknown; dis total); died 8 Oct 1898 Denver Colo.
Pension: 24 July 1891 / Inv / 1044644 / 870703. Wid / 685710 / 508558.

Horn, Geo. Pvt co D; b. Andalusia Spain; enl 12 Jan 1872 Buffalo N.Y. for 5 yrs; age 28; laborer; dk eyes, dk hair, fair comp, 5' 6" high; join co D 3 Feb 1872 Chester SC; ds Ft Lincoln DT June 1874; (recom by Lt Edgerly for medal of honor for conspic gal at LBH; [Edgerly not sure if Horn or Dawsey helped Holden bring up amm'n to the men thro' a galling fire without flinching]); disch 12 Jan 1877 Ft Rice DT by expir of serv a pvt char good; reenl 12 Feb 1877 Oswego N.Y. for 5 yrs; assd to co F 3 art'y; disch 11 Feb 1882 St Augustine Fla expir of serv a pvt char a sober steady man & thoroughly reliable.

Horn, Marion E. Pvt co I; b. 26 Aug 1853 Richmond Ind.; enl 15 Nov 1872 Cincinnati Ohio for 5 yrs; age 21; laborer; hazel eyes, brn hair, florid comp, 5' 6 1/2' high; join co I 2 Dec 1872 Shelbyville Ky.; ed hosp nurse in field (with NBS) Aug & Oct 1873; killed with Custer column 25 June 1876.

Horner, Jacob. Pvt co K; b. 6 Oct 1855 New York N.Y.; enl 8 Apr 1876 St Louis Mo. for 5 yrs; age 21; butcher; blk eyes, blk hair, dk comp, 5' 6" high; join co K 27 Apr 1876 St Paul Minn.; ds camp Powder River MT 15 June 1876; ds Rosebud Creek 11 Aug 1876 with art'y; ed subs dept butcher Apr to Nov 1877 (ds with art'y 13 Aug thro' Sep); dd co cook Dec 1877; cpl 31 May 1878; ds camp J. G. Sturgis DT Aug & Oct 1878; sgt 1 Oct 1879; dd post prov sgt Dec 1880; disch 7 Apr 1881 Ft Totten DT expir of serv a sgt char fine; died 21 Sep 1951 Bismarck N.Dak.[51]
Pension: 5 May 1917 / Ind. Surv. / 11970 / 7479. (XC-2,579,501).

Hose, Geo. Cpl co K; b. 29 Apr 1850 Hessen Cassel Germany; enl 2 Nov 1865 Trenton NJ for 3 yrs; age 19; locksmith; hazel eyes, brn hair, fair comp, 5' 7" high; assd to co F 3 inf; disch 2 Nov 1868 Ft Dodge Kans. expir of serv a cpl; enl in co K 7 cav 24 Dec 1869 Ft Harker Kans. for 5 yrs; age 21; cpl 1 Oct 1872; in arrest Feb 1873; pvt 1 Mar 1873; pres in confit Apr 1873; dd pioneer June & Aug 1873; ed qmd Oct & Dec 1873; disch 24 Dec 1874 Colfax La. expir of serv a pvt; reenl in co K 1 Jan 1875 at Colfax for 5 yrs; cpl 15 Sep 1875; dd with dismtd detmt 15–21 May 1876; actg co qm sgt June to Oct 1876; sgt 12 July 1876; awol Nov 1876; sen gar cm 1 Dec 1876 to be reduced to pvt but sen remitted based on previous good char & serv at LBH; pvt 19 Feb 1877; cpl 1 Oct 1877; disch 5 Apr 1878 Ft Rice DT on surg cert dis (chr. pneumonia) a cpl char xclt; died 24 Sep 1924 Stillwater Minn.
Pension: 7 Oct 1889 / Inv / 732533 / 498814. Ind. Surv. / 11026 / 7000.

Houghtaling, Chas. H. Pvt co D; b. Hudson N.Y.; enr 16 Jan 1865 Albany N.Y. a pvt 175 N.Y. inf; age 22; farmer; hazel eyes, blk hair, dk comp, 5' 5" high; hosp attdt 24 Jan 1865; m.o. vol serv 10 May 1865 Hart Isl N.Y.H; enl reg army 27 Nov 1865 New York N.Y. for 3 yrs; assd to co D 15 inf; hosp stew'd gen serv 6 Dec 1867; disch 27 Nov 1868 Atlanta Ga. expir of serv & reenl as hosp stew'd for 3 yrs; disch 21 Aug 1871 at Atlanta per SO 317 AGO 1871 (intemperance) a hosp stew'd; reenl 8 Sep 1871 New York N.Y. for 5 yrs; age 27; druggist; join co D 7 cav 8 Dec 1872 Opelika Ala; hosp stew'd 3d cl. 28 Mar to 23 Oct 1873 (with NBS); ed hosp nurse 24 Oct 1873 to 29 May 1874; hosp stew'd 3d cl. 30 May to 14 Sep 1874 (with NBS); ds on str *Far West* 29 June 1876 attending wd; sgt 8 July 1876 to date 1 July 1876; disch 8 Sep 1876 Ft Buford DT expir of serv & reenl in co D for 5 yrs; (recom by Lt Edgerly for medal of honor for conspic gal at LBH); in jail Feb 1877 Bismarck DT; disch 30 Mar 1877 per SO 59 AGO 1877 (guilty of manslaughter in accdt shooting of sol. while in search of deserters) & sen to 4 yrs in prison at Ft Madison Iowa;[52] reenl 9 June 1880 Chicago Ill. for 5 yrs; assd to co D 13 inf; died 14 Aug 1881 Ft Lewis Colo. (ac. bronc.) a pvt.

Pension: 2 June 1883 / Minor / 305043. (Abandoned).

Housen, Edw. (alias). See Delliehausen, Eduard Gustaf.

Howard, Frank. (co E), See Thompson, Morris Hedding.

Howard, Frank. Pvt co F; b. 14 June 1851 Brooklyn N.Y.; enl as Henry Pearsal 26 June 1866 at Brooklyn for 3 yrs;[53] age 19; farmer; blue eyes, lt brn hair, fair comp, 5' 4 1/4" high; assd to co H 2 battn 15 inf ; (redesig 24 inf regt Sep 1866); tr to co A Apr 1869 (when 24 inf consol with 29 inf & desig 11 inf); disch 26 June 1869 Brenham Tex. by expir of serv a pvt; enl as Frank Howard 23 Sep 1875 Chicago Ill. for 5 yrs; age 23; farmer; blue eyes, lt hair, fair comp, 5' 7 3/4" high; join co F 7 cav 21 Oct 1875 Ft Lincoln DT; sick qrs 27 Feb to 10 Mar 1876 (cont'n r. knee); sick qrs 21-31 Mar 1876 (boil); [with pack train says Finnegan, Gregg, & Rooney; doubtful with packs says Lynch];[54] cpl 1 Nov 1876; in arrest 12 Dec 1876; pvt 12 Feb 1877 sen gen cm & forf $10 pay per mo for 2 mos; dd regtl hq fatigue May to Aug 1877; des 7 Jan 1878 near Ft Lincoln & apph 9 Jan at Fargo DT; dishon disch 30 Mar 1878 Ft Totten DT sen gen cm & 2 yrs conft mil prison Ft L'worth Kans.; reenl 13 May 1882 New York N.Y. for 5 yrs; join co F 28 Aug 1882 camp near Coulson MT; in conft Apr to June 1883; sen gen cm 19 June 1883 forf $10 pay per mo for 3 mos & conft same period; ed qmd sawyer Oct 1883 to Oct 1885; ed qmd laborer Feb to July 1886; ed qmd mech Aug 1886 to May 1887; disch 12 May 1887 Ft Buford DT expir of serv a pvt char xclt; reenl 28 July 1887 in ordn detmt Watervliet arsl N.Y. for 5 yrs; served continuously in same unit to 19 Feb 1907 when retd a sgt char xclt; died 16 Feb 1935 North Troy N.Y.

Pension: 23 Mar 1935 / Wid / XC-931,240.

Howell, Geo. Sad'r co C; b. Cold Springs N.Y.; enl 7 Feb 1868 West Point N.Y. for 3 yrs in co B battn of engrs; age 21; harness maker; grey eyes, dk hair, lt comp, 5' 5 1/2" high; disch 7 Feb 1871 at West Point upon expir of serv an artf'r; reenl 4 Dec 1872 New York N.Y. for 5 yrs; join co C 7 cav 12 Feb 1873 Charlotte NC; ds 30 July to 2 Aug 1873 on str *Josephine*; sad'r 12 Nov 1873; pvt 10 Apr 1874; dd battn hq Aug 1874; ed qmd Apr 1875; sad'r 8 June 1875; killed with Custer column 25 June 1876.

Hoyt, Walter. Pvt co K; b. Steuben N.Y.; pvt co G 107 Ind. inf 9 June to 18 July 1863; enl reg army 22 Apr 1870 Jackson Tenn for 5 yrs; age 22; farmer; blue eyes, brn hair, florid comp, 5' 6 3/4" high; assd to co K 16 inf; des 16 Sep 1870 & apph one week later; sen gen cm forf $10 pay per mo for 8 mos; wag 12 Apr 1874; disch 29 Apr 1875 Frankfort Ky. expir of serv a wag; reenl 19 May 1875 St Louis Bks Mo. for 5 yrs; join co K 7 cav 27 Apr 1876 St Paul Minn.; ds camp Powder River MT 15 June 1876; sick 14 July (dislocation fingers r. hand); tr on str *Josephine* 19 July to hosp Ft Lincoln DT; duty 8 Aug 1876; dd qmd 15 Sep 1876 care for pub animals; dd qmd teamster 12 Dec 1876 driving mail wagon to 18 Apr 1877; ds Bismarck DT Apr

1877; ed qmd June to Sep 1877; ds regtl hq in field 13 Aug to 13 Nov 1877; dd qmd teamster Feb to Apr 1878; dd actg co wag Aug & Dec 1878; dd co teamster Feb 1879 to 18 May 1880 when disch at Ft Totten DT by expir of serv a pvt char xclt; reenl 11 Aug 1880 St Louis Mo. for 5 yrs in gen mtd serv; disch 1 Mar 1881 Jeff'n Bks Mo. on surg cert dis (const. syph.; dis complete) a pvt; died 23 Mar 1893 Middleborough Ky.

Pension: 16 Apr 1894 / Wid [Sarah] / 594161; rej on grd sol.'s serv not dur late war & clmt married sol. [1 July 1891] subsequent to act 27 June 1890 thus not entitled to pension under act of that date.

Pension: 17 Apr 1917 / Wid [Mary] / 1099157; rej on grd clmt [m. sol. 25 Nov. 1882] not accepted as legal widow as sol. remarried after separation from her [1884] & unable to show sol. did not divorce her; also sol.'s serv not dur Rebellion as required for title under act 19 Apr 1908 & amended 8 Sep 1916.

Pension: 2 May 1917 / Ind. War Wid [Mary] / 12376 / 10467; rej on same grd as other appn of clmt; submitted 10 Feb 1922 under sec. 232 [contesting widows], claim sufficiently prima facie to warrant spl exam'n as to legal widowhood. Rej 16 Jan 1923 on grd stated, but upon appeal & intercession of Hon. Frank H. Funk, House of Reps., case reopened 14 Feb 1923; after review of salient facts, tho' evidence not conclusive, it was believed sol. did not divorce clmt & thus equities likely with her as lawful widow of sol.; claim appv under act 4 Mar 1917, sol. served over 30 days in Sioux campn of 1876.

Huber, Wm. Pvt co E; b. Wurtemburg Germany; enl 21 Dec 1874 Cincinnati Ohio for 5 yrs; age 21; gunsmith; grey eyes, lt brn hair, fair comp, 5' 7" high; join co E 8 Feb 1875 Opelika Ala; killed with Custer column 25 June 1876.

Huff, Jacob. Pvt band; b. 22 Oct 1850 Bavaria Germany; enl 23 Feb 1875 New Orleans La. for 5 yrs; age 24 4/12; baker; blue eyes, lt hair, fair comp, 5' 8 1/2" high; assd to co F 22 inf; des 8 Sep 1875 Ft Wayne Mich.; enl as Jacob Emerich 16 Oct 1875 Cincinnati Ohio for 5 yrs; assd to 7 cav 6 Dec 1875; join regt 14 Apr 1876 Ft Lincoln DT (with Lt Reily's detmt); assd to band 28 Apr; ds camp Powder River MT 14 June 1876; (brewed 2 barrels of beer for centennial celebration using wild hops, oats & yeast cakes he bro't along as baker);[55] surd as des'r 5 Aug 1876 camp mouth of Rosebud Creek MT; restored to duty with co F 22 inf at same camp, upon recom'n co comdr & verbal order gen Terry; disch 18 July 1877 Ft Lincoln DT per GO 47 AGO 1877 (reduction of army) a pvt char fair;[56] died 18 Aug 1929 Danville Ill.

Pension: 6 Dec 1894 / Ind. Surv. / 4979 / 7192.

Hughes, Francis Thos. Pvt co L; b. L'worth Kans.; enl in co L 22 May 1875 Ft Lincoln DT for 5 yrs; age 21; laborer; blue eyes, brn hair, fair comp, 5' 7 3/4" high; ed qmd teamster 21 Sep 1875 to 8 Jan 1876; killed with Custer column 25 June 1876; survived by wife & 3 ch; (widow m. sgt Rafter 17 Feb 1877).

Pension: 25 Oct 1877 / Wid / 233864 / 203671. Minor / 248460 / 203672.

Hughes, Jas. See Mullen, Jno.

Hughes, Robt. H. Sgt co K; b. Dublin Ireland; enl 17 Sep 1868 Cincinnati Ohio for 5 yrs; age 28; laborer; blue eyes, brn hair, fair comp, 5' 9" high; join co I 7 cav 10 Nov 1868 Camp Sandy Forsyth Kans.; dd co far'r Dec 1869 to Apr 1870; dd detmt hq May & June 1870; cpl 14 Aug 1871; sgt 27 Sep 1871; in arrest June 1872; pvt 6 July 1872; tr to co E 14 Sep 1872; dd detmt hq Aug 1873; disch 17 Sep 1873 Little Missouri River DT expir of serv a pvt; reenl 1 Oct 1873 Ft Rice DT for 5 yrs in co K 7 cav; dd as desp bearer Apr 1874; ds Ft Rice June thro' Aug 1874; ds Ft Rice Oct 1874; cpl 28 Jan 1875; sgt 15 Feb 1875; dd chg of hq fatigue pty (morn & eve) 5 May 1876; (carried gen Custer's personal hq flag); killed with Custer column 25 June 1876;[57] survived by wife & 3 ch.

Pension: 7 Aug 1877 / Wid / 231259 / 187173.

Hughes, Thos. Pvt co H; b. Mayo Ireland; pvt co G 13 N.Y. art'y & co M 6 N.Y. art'y 29 Mar 1864 to 24 Aug 1865; enl reg army 7 July 1866 New York N.Y. for 3 yrs; age 19; engraver; hazel eyes, dk hair, fair comp, 5' 5" high; assd to co C 2 inf; disch 7 July 1869 Montgomery Ala expir of serv a pvt; reenl 30 June 1870 New York N.Y. for 5 yrs; age 22

3/12; teamster; assd to co I 20 inf; des 19 May 1871; enl as Thos. Morgan 15 June 1873 Ft Rice DT for 5 yrs in co H 7 cav; surd as des'r 18 Nov 1873 under GO 102 AGO 1873; tr to co H 16 Apr 1874 to serve bal of orig'l enlmt; gsw l. foot (fl. wd. sl.) 26 June 1876; remained with co in field; cpl 6 Oct 1876 to date 1 Sep; sgt 4 Feb 1877; dd chg of bldg stable guardhouse Feb 1877; disch 30 Dec 1877 Ft Lincoln DT expir of serv a sgt char xclt; reenl 25 May 1878 New York N.Y. for 5 yrs; assd to co A 10 inf; disch 24 May 1883 Ft Wayne Mich. expir of serv a cpl char good; reenl 14 June 1883 New York N.Y. for 5 yrs; assd to co A 4 cav; disch 13 June 1888 Ft Lowell AT expir of serv a sgt char xclt; reenl 12 July 1888 Ft Wayne Mich. for 5 yrs; assd to hosp corps; disch 14 July 1893 at Ft Wayne expir of serv a pvt char very good; reenl 3 Aug 1893 Detroit Mich. for 5 yrs; assd to co E 10 inf; tr to hosp corps; retd 11 Oct 1897 a sgt; died 11 Aug 1911 Nashville Tenn.
Pension: 18 Mar 1907 / Inv / 1361723. (Rej on grd clmt on retd list & not entitled to draw pension under any law).

Hunt, Geo. Pvt co D; b. Boston Mass.; enl in co D 2 June 1873 Ft Snelling Minn. for 5 yrs; age 22; laborer; blue eyes, lt brn hair, ruddy comp, 5' 7" high; in conft Dec 1874 to July 1875; sen gen cm 6 Feb 1875 forf $10 pay per mo for 6 mos & conft same period; in conft Dec 1875; in conft Nov 1876 to Mar 1877; disch 1 June 1878 Ft Rice DT expir of serv a pvt char fair; reenl 4 May 1881 at Boston for 5 yrs; assd to co E 3 cav; des 3 Apr 1883; apph 25 Jan 1884; dishon disch 6 May 1884 Ft Craig NM sen gen cm & 3 yrs conft mil prison Ft L'worth Kans.

Hunt, Jno. Pvt co H; b. Boston Mass.; enl 25 Aug 1866 Phil'a Pa. for 5 yrs; age 31; clerk; blue eyes, auburn hair, ruddy comp, 5' 5 3/4" high; in conft Jeff'n Bks Mo. 20 Sep to 15 Nov 1866; join co H 18 Nov 1866 Ft Riley Kans.; sgt 19 Feb 1867; pvt 21 Oct 1867; cpl 4 Dec 1867; in arrest Dec 1867; pvt 2 Feb 1868; dd orderly at distr hq June 1868; ds Ft Harker Kans. actg post ordn sgt Sep 1868 to Mar 1869; dd co clerk Apr 1869; cpl 15 June 1869; in arrest Aug 1869; pvt 20 Oct 1869; cpl 18 Mar 1870; in arrest Aug 1870; pvt Oct 1870; disch 25 Aug 1871 Nashville Tenn expir of serv a pvt; reenl in co H 1 Sep 1871 at Nashville for 5 yrs; in conft Dec 1872; sen gen cm 9 Feb 1875 forf $12 pay per mo for 6 mos & conft 2 mos; dd comsy dept herder Oct 1875; disch 6 Aug 1876 mouth Rosebud Creek MT (in time to go down river by first boat) per GO 24 AGO 1859 a pvt char xclt; arr Ft Lincoln 10 Aug on str *Durfee*; reenl 2 Nov 1876 New York N.Y. for 5 yrs; assd to gen mtd serv; disch 28 May 1877 St Louis Mo. per GO 47 AGO 1877 (reduction of army) a pvt;[58] reenl 28 Oct 1878 St Louis Mo. for 5 yrs; assd to co D 19 inf; died 2 Jan 1880 Ft Dodge Kans. (phthisis pulmonalis) a pvt.

Hunter, Francis (Frank). Pvt co F; b. Mayo Ireland; pvt co G 1 Ohio lt art'y 18 Dec 1861 to 31 Aug 1865; enl reg army 17 Aug 1866 Toledo Ohio for 5 yrs; age 28; laborer; grey eyes, lt hair, fair comp, 5' 5 1/2" high; join co F 7 cav 10 Sep 1866 Ft Riley Kans.; dd bldg co qrs Oct 1866; cpl 23 Jan 1867; pvt 17 Dec 1867; ds dept hq (Ft L'worth) May 1868 to Mar 1869; ds div hq (Chicago Ill.) as mtd msgr Apr 1869; sick city hosp June to Sep 1869 (kicked in head by horse); (never a sound man afterward said gen Sheridan); cpl 15 Mar 1870; sgt 1 Mar 1871; pvt 27 May 1871; disch 17 Aug 1871 Louisville Ky. expir of serv a pvt; reenl in co F 30 Aug 1871 at Louisville for 5 yrs; cpl 20 Jan 1872; pvt 7 June 1872; dd herding co horses Aug 1872; abs sick on str *Western* 23 Apr 1873 Yankton to Ft Rice DT; duty 12 June 1873; in conft Oct 1873; sick 2 Dec 1873 to 10 Mar 1874 (frostbite, hands); cpl 10 Sep 1874; in arrest Dec 1874; dd chg co mess Apr 1875; pvt 7 June 1875 sen gen cm & forf $10 pay per mo for 3 mos; in conft Dec 1875; sick 7–18 Mar 1876 (boil); [with pack train says Finnegan, Lynch & Rooney; not sure says Gregg];[59] disch 4 Aug 1876 mouth of Rosebud Creek MT (in time to go down river by first boat) per GO 24 AGO 1859 a pvt char xclt; arr Ft Lincoln 10 Aug on str *Durfee*; reenl 4 Sep 1876 Cleveland Ohio for 5 yrs; join co E 3 cav 11 Nov 1876 Ft Laramie Wyo. Ty; ds Hat Creek Wyo. Ty 27 Apr to 4 May 1877; dd qm fatigue June to Sep 1877; dd qmd laborer Dec

1877 to Sep 1878; cpl 10 Jan 1879; gsw r. foot 29 Sep 1879 Milk River Colo. in action with Ute inds; duty 18 Nov 1879; pvt 18 Apr 1880; tr to co I 7 May 1880; in conft Apr 1881; disch 3 Sep 1881 Ft Fred Steele Wyo. Ty expir of serv a pvt char good; reenl 29 June 1883 Ft D. A. Russell Wyo. for 5 yrs in co E 9 inf; disch 24 Jan 1887 San Diego Bks Calif. on surg cert dis (rheum. & gen debility dis 1/2), a pvt; died 27 Dec 1899 Wash'n D.C. Pension: 17 Dec 1881 / Inv / 435556 / 357449; (less subsequent serv). Wid / 1100081 / 845049.

Hurd, Jas. (alias). See Hood, Jas.

Hutchinson, Rufus D. Sgt co B; b. Butlerville Ohio; enl 25 Sep 1873 Cincinnati Ohio for 5 yrs; age 23; farmer; blue eyes, lt hair, fair comp, 5' 10" high; join co B 19 Oct 1873 Ft Lincoln DT; cpl 15 Oct 1874; dd actg co qm sgt June 1875; sgt 26 July 1875; dd chg co kit'n Oct 1875 thro' Feb 1876; 1sgt 28 Jan 1877; sgt 27 Mar 1877 & dd as co qm sgt; 1sgt 5 Apr 1878; disch 25 Sep 1878 Standing Rock Agcy DT expir of serv a 1sgt char xclt; awarded medal of honor 5 Oct 1878 for guarding & carrying wounded [at LBH], bringing water for same, & posting & directing the men while under heavy fire;[60] reenl 28 Jan 1886 St Louis Mo. for 5 yrs; rejoin co B 21 Sep 1886 Ft Yates DT; cpl 27 Sep 1886; sgt 11 May 1887; ed qmd overseer July 1887 to Jan 1888; dd asst in chg of target range Ft Riley Kans. Aug 1888; pvt 26 Sep 1888; cpl 20 Dec 1888; 1sgt 17 June 1889; disch 27 Jan 1891 at Ft Riley by expir of serv a 1sgt char xclt.

Hutter, Anton. Pvt co E; b. Bavaria Germany; enl 9 Feb 1872 Rochester N.Y. for 5 yrs; age 21; laborer; hazel eyes, dk hair, fair comp, 5' 10 1/2" high; join co E 26 Feb 1872 Unionville SC; sick Wash'n D.C. govt hosp for insane 19 June 1872; dropped from co rolls 8 Feb 1877 by expir of serv a pvt char good as far as known; died 20 Mar 1910 in govt hosp.[61]

Notes—H

1. RG 94, Entry 409, file 10818 A (EB) 1878.
2. Botzer, Troop Duty Book; Chas. A. Varnum to Walter Camp, Apr. 14, 1909, WMC-BYU; Henry Brinkerhoff to General Godfrey, Aug. 27, 1926, LBHB Coll., Roll 9; Lt. Wallace felt deeply indebted to Hackett for once saving his life by bringing his horse to him under dangerous circumstances. Meketa, *Luther Rector Hare,* 46.

In a letter to his friend, Dr. Knoblauch of Shreveport, La., Nov. 17, 1876, Wallace mentioned Hackett in reference to his (Wallace) having just got a room and leaving everything to Hackett, Westfall, *Letters from the Field,* 38.

3. Brown, Troop Duty Book; Reynolds and Brown, *Journal.*
4. WMC, Notes, Map Data, IU.
5. RG 94, Entry 409, file 6924 C (EB) AGO 1885.
6. Hale's brother came out for his effects and scraped up all he could get his hands on and started off, leaving the body to be sent on when called for, Capt. Benteen to his wife, Dec. 9, 1877, from Fort Buford, Carroll, *Camp Talk,* 112.
7. See note A7 (William G. Abrams).
8. Cpl. Hall attended the tenth anniversary of the battle. See photos in Mills, *Harvest of Barren Regrets,* 338, and *Greasy Grass* Vol. 18, May 2002, 6.
9. Botzer Troop Duty Book, June 20–24, missing.
10. Hammon said he met band of 'Rees driving off Sioux ponies as pack train was going toward Reno, after Knipe brought message. Interview with Walter Camp, n.d., WMC-BYU.
11. RG 94, Entry 409, file 10764 B (EB) AGO 1880; RG 92, Entry 238, reports, 1882/126 and 1883/112.
12. Sgt Ryan said Fisher was better known as "Bounce" and from last accounts was at Bismarck working for Sterland who kept an eating house or boarding house there. Ryan, Hardy, Slaper, Sniffin, and Wilber all said Fisher was the man whose stirrup Lt. Hodgson grabbed when crossing river. Widmayer said he heard Fisher say he helped Hodgson across river in Reno retreat, Graham, *The Custer Myth,* 243; Ryan to Walter Camp, Aug. 11, 1909 and, Jan. 11, 1910, WMC-BYU; Hardorff, *Camp, Custer, and the Little Big*

Horn, 81; Brininstool, *Troopers with Custer,* 52; Frank W. Sniffin to Walter Camp, Apr.1, 1910, WMC-BYU; Hammer, *Custer in '76,* 145, 148.

Smith F. Foster, Trumpeter, 8th Cavalry, 1870–96, said Trumpeter Fisher afterward served in the 6th Cavalry and died in Arizona either killed or by accident. Foster said Capt. French had "bob-tailed" Fisher on discharge from 7th Cavalry, WMC, rosters, LBHB; Sgt. Ryan described a bob-tail discharge as a dishonorable discharge with the character (portion) cut off, Barnard, *Ten Years with Custer,* 48.

Regs. 1863, Par. 166, "The cause of the discharge will be stated in the body of the discharge, and the space at foot for character cut off, unless a recommendation is given."; see also McConnell, *Five Years A Cavalryman,* 120.

13. When regiment was corralled on Reno Hill, a pack mule loaded with two boxes of ammunition escaped from the herd and ran toward the Indians. Sgt. Hanley without orders mounted his horse and galloped after the mule; notwithstanding the volley fired at him from all directions, he returned after about twenty-minutes chase with the mule and ammunition, RG 94, Entry 25, file 305281 AGO 1900.

14. Sgt. Hanley worked some years with Lt. Gibson in the New York City street department, Walter Camp to Daniel Knipe, Feb. 27, 1909, WMC-LBHB.

15. WMC, Notes, LBH II, IU; Hardy said "Hadden" belonged to I or D troop (Camp noted above Hadden, "perhaps Hardden"), Hardy to Walter Camp, Mar. 9, 1910, WMC-BYU; Hardden signed his enlistment papers, and payroll with "X," but forms in his pension file are signed "Haidden." RG 15.

16. Correspondence from Hardy to Walter Camp. WMC-BYU; See also WMC, Notes, folder LBH II, IU.

17. Hare to Godfrey, Dec. 15, 1924, Godfrey Papers.

18. *Annual Report of the Association of Graduates* (USMA) June 10, 1931, 123–25; see also, Meketa, *Luther Rector Hare.*

19. Sergeants Hanley and Knipe said Lt. Harrington commanded Company C on Reno's scout. Hammer, *Custer in '76,* 128. Knipe interview June 1908, WMC-IU.

20. In a letter to Lt. Harrington's father, Sgt. Miller said the lieutenant's body was found in a ravine with others about four miles from the battlefield. It was supposed they were among the last killed, and finding no hope they tried to break through the Indian lines and reach Reno's command, *The Republican* (Coldwater, Mich.), July 28, 1876. Reprinted in, *The English Westerners' Tally Sheet* (London), Vol. 35, No. 2, Spring, 1989.

21. RG 94, Entry 409, file 10818 A (EB) 1878; endorsement by Capt. Bates, 1st Infantry, Columbus Barracks, Ohio, Mar. 5, 1879, that David W. Harris was identified as having served in Company A, 7th Cavalry, by John McGlone, former member of regiment.

22. *Cincinnati (Ohio) Times Chronicle,* May 2, 3, 1873; *Cincinnati Commercial,* May 2, 1873; *Cincinnati Daily Gazette,* May 3, July 3, 1873, May 27, 29, June 8, Nov. 13, 1875; *Cincinnati Daily Enquirer,* May 3, 5, July 3, 1873, May 25, 27, 28, 29, June 8, Oct. 26, November 13, 1875. Post Returns, Newport Barracks, Ky, NA, M617. RG 153, file PP 3757; Criminal Docket, No. 999, U.S. Circuit Court, Nov. 12, 1875.

The federal census of Cincinnati (Ward 18), 1870, lists Leonard A. Harris, age 17, "Huxter"; City Directories, 1875–80, report his occupation as, "car. painter"; during his court troubles in 1873 and 1875, he was often referred to in the local press as "the boy" Leonard A. Harris, and as "junior." *Note:* Between 1863 and 1867, Leonard Armstrong Harris (Col. 2nd Ohio Volunteers, 1861–62), was twice elected mayor of Cincinnati.

23. *The Central Record* (Lancaster, Ky.), Nov. 18, 1999; *Lexington* (Ky) *Daily Press,* June 10, 13, 1885; *The Kentucky Register* (Richmond), June 12, 1885.

24. Harrison mentioned as Gen. Custer's cook. Letter from Gen. Custer to Libbie, April 10, 1867, E. B. Custer, *Tenting on the Plains* (1971), 554.

25. RG 94, File 409, file 10818 A (EB) 1878. Harrison's photo, with his account of the Little Big Horn, is in the *Philadelphia Press,* Oct. 21, 1900.

26. GO 40 HQA, AGO, May 10, 1898 (Par. II), announced that men who enlisted or reenlisted in the regular army during the war, could apply for discharge if desired at the close of the war, RG 94, Entry 44.

27. *The Lancaster (Pa.) Daily Intelligencer,* Nov. 15, 1922.

28. Hayes said, while bartending for his father in Dresden, NY, in 1871, he had a row with Dan Mingo (listed as colored) in which he struck Mingo with a glass cutting his head badly and thinking the injury severe, he left town and soon enlisted in the army as Charles Hood. He said other men enlisted under assumed names and if he were killed his friends would never know what became of him. His brother and sisters said he left town with a circus in 1872 or '73, Pension file, RG 15.

29. Rosters of Company F with remarks by Rooney and Lynch, WMC-BYU.
30. SO 177, Hq Fort Lincoln, DT, Sept. 24, 1876, RG 393, Part V.
31. Lt. Hare interview with Camp in Hammer, *Custer in '76*, 67.
32. On the federal census, State of Ohio, Geauga County, Parkman Township, Sept. 11, 1850, George B. Herendeen is one year of age; On the federal census of Parkman Township, July 26, 1860, he is eleven years of age, son of Frederick L. Herendeen, age 43, cabinet maker, born in Massachusetts, and, Ann, age 37, born New York; brother of Frederick L., age 16, and Jane A., age 14, both born in Ohio.

Frederick, Jr., served in the 14th Battery Ohio Light Artillery during the war, and in 1868 applied for invalid pension (Claim No. 13728), for consumption attributed to his military service. He died March 14, 1869 and his sister, Jennie Ann Cranston, continued the claim, declaring in affidavit July 21, 1869, that her brother left neither wife nor child, nor mother and father; that only herself and a brother, George, residing in Noble County, Indiana, survived. RG 15.

The federal census of Indiana, Noble County, Town of Green, 1860, lists George A. Herendeen, farmer, age 47, born in Massachusetts, wife Delana, age 45, born New York; sons, Henry, 10; James, 7.

33. Employed for a time as laborer at the Crow Agency. *Official Register of the United States: Biennial Register, Sept. 30, 1873*, p. 323. Herendeen to Walter Camp, Nov. 15, 1910, WMC-BYU.
34. The Territorial Fair, Sixth Annual Exhibition of the Montana Agricultural, Mineral, and Mechanical Association, opened Sept. 27, 1875.

The Carroll wagon road ran from the town of Carroll, a steamboat landing on the Missouri River near the mouth of the Musselshell River, and provided a direct route overland for freights destined for Helena instead of making the "great bend" by Benton, *Helena Daily Herald*, Sept. 27, 1875.

35. McCormick left camp May 9 with the mail for Fort Ellis and to buy goods to start the canteen. At Bozeman he was given charge of a mackinaw boat built for carrying mail to Gibbon's command. *The Avant Courier* (Bozeman, Mont.), June 10, 1876; Johnson, "With Gibbon against the Sioux in 1876."

While awaiting McCormick's return, Herendeen volunteered (gratis) to take Capt. Clifford and his company in six small boats (skiffs), left over from the construction of Fort Pease, scouts down river, thus cover more ground than if by land. Herendeen reasoned the boats belonged to him as he was the only one present who helped build the fort, Noyes, *In the Land of Chinook*, 107; Gray, "Captain Clifford's Story of the Sioux War of 1876"; Gray, "Captain Clifford's Newspaper Dispatches".

36. RG 92, Entry 238, reports 1876/240 and 1876/328; Hammer, *Custer in '76*, 219–27.
37. Gibbon, *Adventures on the Western Frontier*, 131.
38. SFO 38, Hq DD, In the Field, Aug. 6, 1876, RG 94, Entry 44.
39. RG 92, Entry 238, report 1877/319; see also 1877/214, 1877/253, and 1877/614. NA, M1734, Roll 21, files 3479 DD 1877 and 3629 DD 1877; NA, M617, Post Returns, Fort Keogh, MT.
40. Noyes, *In the Land of Chinook*, 105–109; Johnson, "George Herendeen". See also, Topping, *The Chronicles of the Yellowstone*.
41. British military records (TNA).
42. Hardorff, "The Reno Scout."
43. *Wayne County* (Ohio) *Democrat*, May 13, 1885; Oct. 10, Nov. 21, 1906.
44. Hodgson's family wanted him to follow his forebears and become a naval officer, and his excuse for attending West Point instead of Annapolis was that he did not get as sick on a horse as he did on a ship, Terrell and Walton, *Faint the Trumpet Sounds*, 106.
45. At Spartanburg, Hodgson became good friends with Major Reno. *Ibid.*, 78.
46. RG 153, file PP4268; Hodgson's detachment of fifteen men was surrounded by an armed mob (members of the notorious White League), bent on rescuing the prisoners and when the mob began to telegraph to adjacent counties for reinforcements, the marshal had Hodgson cut the wires to end the communication. The sheriff later arrested Hodgson on a civil warrant, charging him with contempt of court for disregarding a writ of habeas corpus. However, being under command of the marshal, the responsibility of the alleged violation rested on that official. Hodgson was sentenced to a fine of $100 and imprisonment for ten days, the fine was paid by an attorney sent by military authorities and the remainder of the sentence revoked.

Hodgson's reprimand was dictated by Gen. Sheridan and became historic in army circles, reciting in a most complimentary manner Hodgson's numerous soldierly qualities, the enviable praise of his superior officers, and relating "the surprise of the Gen'l commanding that an officer of Lieut. Hodgson's merit should ever be found deserving of a reprimand." At a reception at the St. Charles Hotel, Gen. Sheridan publicly expressed not only approval of Hodgson's course, but also complimented him on having the good sense and temerity to accomplish what few men in his position would have dared do, Martinez, *Carpetbaggers, Cavalry, and the Ku Klux Klan*, 225–26; *The Evening Telegraph*, (Philadelphia), July 10, 1876.

47. During the summer of 1875, Hodgson reportedly had an affair with the wife of Lt. Bell and almost resigned his commission, Mills, *Harvest of Barren Regrets*, 220, 247; he withdrew his resignation in spring 1876 for the fun of just one last campaign, and was described by a contemporaryas a dapper little officer from a well-to-do family of paint manufacturers in Philadelphia. Fougera, *With Custer's Cavalry*, 68, 70; Terrell and Walton, *Faint the Trumpet Sounds*, 78.

48. Hodgson was put in arrest by Lt. McIntosh, April 24, 1876, while on the train en route to St. Paul, for rude conduct and speech toward McIntosh, the second such incident since leaving Shreveport. At St. Louis, Hodgson had used improper language and rudely pushed McIntosh when he prevented Hodgson from shooting a soldier who attempted to enter the officer's coach while on a spree (the soldier's sweetheart worked for one of the officers) and causing a near brawl, this in presence of the whole company. Maj. Reno investigated the incident, May 5, and looked on it as unimportant, McIntosh and Hodgson were seemingly good friends and willing that the matter went no further, NA, M1734, Roll 16, files 1119 DD 1876 and 1269 DD 1876.

The wayward soldier was identified as Private Pym; Mrs. Fred Klawitter, "Army Life at Fort Lincoln," (hereafter Klawitter, "Army Life at Fort Lincoln") transcript of interview in 1935, by Matt Lagerberg, (Mss. B18), North Dakota State Historical Society, Bismarck.

49. *Bismarck Tribune*, Apr. 2, 1880; see also, Ernst, "A Dane Who Survived the Little Big Horn Fight."

50. Hood said when he first enlisted the company clerk was a German who scarcely spoke English, and to whom he gave his correct name but the clerk entered it as Hurd. On advice of the Captain, of all the trouble a change would cause, Hood allowed the error to remain and reenlisted as Hurd so as to receive reenlistment pay, Pension file, RG 15.

51. Johnson, *Jacob Horner of the Seventh Cavalry*; Horner was the last surviving 7th Cavalryman who participated in the 1876 campaign.

52. *Bismarck Tribune*, Jan. 31, Feb. 7, Mar. 7, 1877.

53. Frank Howard said he aided troops in camp at the end of the (Civil) war. He joined the regular army at age 15, using assumed name because his father wanted him to stay home to work on a farm they had just bought at Hempstead, LI., Pension file, RG 15.

54. WMC, rosters, LBHB; Gregg interview with Walter Camp, nd, Rosters of Company F with remarks by Rooney and Lynch, WMC-BYU; Mrs. Howard said her husband, "fought under General Yates and Keough. In Gen. Custer's Battle, he had a horse shot under him and another horse wounded." He injured his nose in a bad fall when thrown from his horse. Later, eight different doctors said he had asthma until a doctor of Troy (NY) hospital took a light and looked up his nose and discovered the trouble at once. Using a fine saw (small as a hairpin) he cut the bone in the middle and though he bled for some time, the operation gave Howard great relief after many years of suffering and lost sleep.

Regarding a photo of Howard, taken when he was barely able to stand, Mrs. Howard said he had nine stripes on his sleeve, each a different color. (Howard served nine enlistments in three branches of the army.) Letters from Mrs. Mary Jane Howard, to E. L. Bailey, Director, Widows and Dependents Claims Service, Mar. 23 and Apr. 9, 1935; Oct. 22 and Nov. 7, 1941, Pension file, RG 15; Mrs. Howard died July 19, 1946 at Creedmore State Hospital, Long Island, NY.

55. Emerich interview with Walter Camp, n.d., WMC-BYU.

56. See note A25 (Ascough).

57. Pretty Shield (wife of Goes-ahead) said Custer, Boyer, and the blue soldier who carried his flag died in the river, Linderman, *Pretty Shield*, 287; The body of the roan horse formerly ridden by the sergeant who carried Gen. Custer's battle flag was found on the site of the Sioux camp. Hynds, "Reminiscences of Sergeant H. A. Hynds."

58. See note A25 (Ascough).

59. WMC, rosters, LBHB; Rosters of Company F with remarks by Lynch and Rooney, Gregg interview with Walter Camp, n.d., WMC-BYU, Stan Roy listed Hunter among water carriers on Reno hill. Hammer, *Custer in '76*, 112. (The pension file of Frank Hunter does not mention battle at Little Big Horn.)

60. Hutchinson reported his medal was stolen from his trunk with other personal property at a boarding house in St. Louis, July 4, 1885. He applied to the adjutant general's office for a new medal and paid a $3 fee for the expense of engraving, June 14, 1887.

61. RG 94, Entry 25, file 69843 AGO 1910.

I

Ilsley, Chas. Stilliman. Capt co E; b. 4 Aug 1836 Portland Me; pvt co C 71 N.Y. state militia (3 mo troops) Apr to July 1861; capt co D 15 Me inf 23 Dec 1861; with co thro' June 1863 Ship Isl Miss. & Pensacola Fla; ds in Maine after conscripts July to Dec 1863; actg aig staff of gen Ransom 24 Jan 1864 Brazos Santiago Tex.; rejoin co 1 Mar 1864 Franklin La.; actg aig staff of gen Seward Oct 1864 to Mar 1865; m.o. 25 Mar 1865 upon expir of serv; appt capt 5 N.Y. art'y 3 Apr 1865; on staff of gen Fessenden to June 1865 & adc to gen Emory to 19 July 1865 when m.o. vol serv; appt reg army com'n 1Lt 16 inf 23 Feb 1866; bvt capt 2 Mar 1867 for gal serv dur the war; adc to gen Pope 28 Jan 1868 (to 28 Aug 1879); unassd (to regt) 17 Apr 1869 (when 16 inf consol with 2 inf); assd to 1 cav 15 Dec 1870 (never joined); tr to 7 cav 23 Dec 1870 (ds staff of gen Pope comdg Dept of Mo. [hq Ft L'worth Kans.]); capt 11 July 1871; actg marshal of funeral procession for capts Custer & Yates & Lts Calhoun, McIntosh & Smith 3 Aug 1877 at Ft L'worth Natl Cemetery; join co E 26 Sep 1879 Ft Meade DT (own req);[1] comd battn in field Nov 1890 & in action with Sioux inds 29 Dec 1890 Wounded Knee SD; injured in wreck of troop train 27 Jan 1891 near Florence Kans.; prom maj 9 cav 30 Jan 1892; Lt-col 6 cav 29 Mar 1899 (never joined); retd 8 Apr 1899; died 17 Apr 1899 Salt Lake City Utah; (Brights disease). [792 ACP 1873]

J

Jackson, Henry. 1Lt co F; b. 31 May 1837 Canterbury England; served two yrs in British army as ensign & Lt & in siege of Sevastopol dur Crimea campn; came to America in 1863 to Radnor Ill.; enr 28 Dec 1863 Peoria Ill. a pvt co A 14 Ill. cav for 3 yrs; age 28; farmer; blue eyes, lt hair, lt comp, 5' 8" high; cpl 1 June 1864; dd co clerk July 1864; sick hosp Oct & Dec 1864 Camp Nelson Ky.; appt sgt-maj 5 U.S. col'd cav 2 Jan 1865 at Louisville Ky.; prom 2Lt & actg adjt 14 May 1865; 1Lt 28 Dec 1865; m.o. vol serv 16 Mar 1866 Helena Ark; appt reg army com'n 2Lt 7 cav 12 Nov 1866 to date 28 July 1866; join co G 4 Dec 1866 Ft Harker Kans.; ds chg of led horses & regtl train 15 Apr to 3 May 1867 camp on Pawnee Creek;[2] ds regtl hq in field June & July 1867;[3] ds Ft Wallace Kans. 12 Aug 1867; ds Ft L'worth Kans. Sep 1867 witness in gen cm; adjt of escort for ind peace com'n Oct 1867; 1Lt co F 20 Oct 1867; ds dept hq (Ft L'worth) Mar 1868 to May 1870 actg chf engr officer; ds Wash'n D.C. 9 Aug 1871 office of chf signal officer; ordered 11 July 1876 to rejoin regt; prom capt co C 20 Aug from 26 July 1876; dep Bismarck DT on str *Durfee* 31 Aug (after arrival eve train) enroute to join co in field; ordered back from Ft Buford 7 Sep acc't low water in Yellowstone River; arr Ft Lincoln 10 Sep; comd co C from 26 Sep 1876; with co guarding Deadwood stage route Aug to Nov 1877; post comdr Ft Totten DT Dec 1877; instr of musketry Ft Meade DT Mar 1883 to Apr 1886; comd co in action with Sioux inds 29 Dec 1890 Wounded Knee Creek SD; comd sqdn patroling Mexican border near Carrizo Tex. Dec 1892 to July 1893; post comdr Ft Hancock Tex. to Aug 1895; ds Boston Mass. on rctg duty Sep 1895; prom maj 3 cav 27 Aug 1896; Lt-col 5 cav 23 Jan 1900; col 3 cav 28 Apr 1901 (never joined); retd 31 May 1901; brig-gen on retd list 23 Apr 1904; died 9 Dec 1908 L'worth Kans.[4] [3550 ACP 1876].
Pension: 23 Jan 1909 / Wid / 912288; (rej upon death of clmt 9 Feb 1909).

Jackson, Robt. Pvt detmt ind scouts; b. Ft Benton MT ca. 1856; (1/4 Piegan ind);[5] 4th enlmt 25 Dec 1875 Ft Lincoln DT for 6 mos by Lt Cooke; age 21; brn eyes, blk hair, dk comp, 5' 8" high; disregarded orders for no unnecessary shooting in camp at Little Missouri River 29 May & fired his revolver at some ducks; for punishment he was made to stand all day with one foot at a time on a water keg turned upside down, then sent back to Ft Lincoln with mail;[6] disch 25 June 1876 at Ft Lincoln upon expir of serv; Young Hawk said Bob Jackson in camp at Powder River after the battle;[7] hired [25] Aug by Lt Michaelis (of gen Terry's staff) to carry desp to gen Terry up Powder River; hired as scout 17 Sep at Glendive Creek by verbal order of gen Terry; rate of pay $65 mo;[8] displayed bravery with col Otis' comd 15 Oct in action with inds at Clear Creek when he killed an ind with his revolver & rode out among them & killed another with his rifle; with gen Miles' comd to Wolf Mtns Jan 1877 against Crazy Horse;[9] reenl as scout 30 Mar 1877 camp Tongue River MT for 3 mos; with gen Miles' comd in fight with Lame Deer 7 May 1877;[10] served as scout at Ft Shaw MT July 1879 to May 1880;[11] res Big Timber MT to about 1895 when he left town with a wild west show;[12] last heard from about 1907 at Creede Colo. where he was tho't to have mining interests; died 3 Sep 1910 at Costilla NM.[13]

Jackson, Wm. Pvt detmt ind scouts; b. Ft Pembina DT ca. 1859; (1/4 Piegan ind);[14] 3d enlmt 25 Dec 1875 Ft Lincoln DT for 6 mos by Lt Cooke; age 19; brn eyes, blk hair, dk comp, 5' 6" high; disch 25 June 1876 on Little Horn MT & reenl by Lt Varnum for 6 mos; on skirmish line in valley fight & refused to carry message thro' Sioux lines; left in timber dur retreat & rejoined comd night of 26 June on Reno hill; said he carried mail from camp mouth of Rosebud to Ft Buford [30 July] & returned with mail [13 Aug] & same eve was sent up Rosebud with

Howling Wolf & mail for gen Terry;[15] ds Ft Lincoln 20 Oct; disch 25 Dec 1876 at Ft Lincoln upon expir of serv a scout char good; reenl as scout 30 Mar 1877 camp Tongue River MT for 3 mos; employed as scout & intrpr at Ft Keogh MT May 1877 thro' Apr 1879;[16] partner in trading post on Flat Willow near Snowy Mtns dur winter 1879–80 & later ran a guiding outfit for fishing parties & Mtn climbing trips; went to New York in 1896 chg of ind camp exhibit for *Forest & Stream* magazine at sportsmen's show; died 31 Dec 1899 at his ranch on Cut Bank River MT; survived by wife, Mary & 6 ch.[17]

James, Jno. (alias Jno. Cassella).[18] Pvt co E; b. Rome Italy; enl 21 Aug 1866 Phil'a Pa. for 5 yrs; age 19; laborer; brn eyes, brn hair, dk comp, 5' 5 1/4" high; join co F 7 cav 10 Sep 1866 Ft Riley Kans.; dd qmd laborer Nov 1866; dd regtl hq orderly June 1868; sick field hosp 9–30 Oct 1868 (pr. syph.); sick field hosp 10 Nov (pr. syph.); tr to hosp Camp Supply IT 7 Dec & to Ft Dodge Kans. 14 Dec 1868; duty 4 Apr 1869; dd co cook July & Aug 1869; dd co cook Oct 1869; ed qmd teamster May to Aug 1870 & Nov 1870 to Mar 1871; dd regtl hq orderly Apr 1871; ed hosp cook June 1871; ds Taylor Bks (Louisville) Ky. 22 July to 21 Aug 1871 when disch by expir of serv a pvt; reenl in co F 13 May 1872 at Louisville for 5 yrs; age 24; grey eyes, brn hair, dk comp, 5' 7 1/2" high; dd post mail carrier Oct 1872; ed qmd teamster 12–26 Apr 1873 camp Sturgis Yankton DT; dd co cook June 1873; ed qmd teamster Dec 1873 to May 1874; dd qmd teamster June 1874; dd qmd teamster Oct 1874 to Apr 1875; dd qmd laborer June & Aug 1875; sick 18 Aug to 2 Sep 1875 (back sprain, overlifting); dd qmd teamster Oct 1875 to Mar 1876; (appn for disch 28 Jan not appv by AGO);[19] tr to co E 1 May 1876; [at LBH says Berwald, Pandtle, & Rooney; at Powder River says Butler]; ds Yellowstone River gd on steamboat 5 Aug; joined Ft Lincoln detmt 10 Aug;[20] dd qmd 12–28 Sep with 281 cav horses at post; cpl 1 Oct to date 1 Sep 1876; disch 13 May 1877 at Ft Lincoln by expir of serv a cpl char good & reenl in co E for 5 yrs; ds Ft Lincoln May to Nov 1877; in arrest Feb 1878; pvt 28 Feb 1878; cpl 15 June 1878; sick hosp Ft Meade DT 13 Feb to 15 Apr 1879 (chr. stric. urethra [contr 1868]); sgt 1 Jan 1880; pvt 22 Jan 1880; dd qmd teamster June to Aug 1880; on furl 30 days 20 Aug 1880 Deadwood DT; disch 13 Oct 1880 at Ft Meade per SO 212 AGO 1880 (upon req of wife) a pvt char very good.[21]

James, Wm. B. Sgt co E; b. Pembrokeshire Wales; enl 5 Feb 1872 Chicago Ill. for 5 yrs; age 23; coachman; hazel eyes, lt hair, lt comp, 5' 9" high; join co E 26 Feb 1872 Unionville SC; dd hosp attdt Sep & Oct 1872; cpl 27 Jan 1875; dd qmd 11–16 Nov 1875 overseer chg of post stables; sgt 3 Mar 1876; killed with Custer column 25 June 1876.[22]

Jennys, Alonzo. Pvt co K; b. New York N.Y.; enl 12 July 1870 NYC for 5 yrs; age 22; teamster; grey eyes, brn hair, florid comp, 5' 7" high; join co C 22 inf 11 Aug 1870 Ft Randall DT; ed qmd teamster Dec 1870 to July 1871; tr to co B 8 July 1871; dd subs dept herder Dec 1871; ed qmd teamster Feb to Sep 1872; ed qmd laborer Oct 1872 to Apr 1873; ed qmd teamster Dec 1873 to Mar 1874; ed subs dept laborer Aug 1874; disch 12 July 1875 Ft Porter N.Y. expir of serv a pvt; enl in co K 7 cav 14 Mar 1876 McComb City Miss for 5 yrs; dd co cook Apr & Aug 1876; ed hosp nurse Oct 1876; dd co cook Dec 1876 & Feb 1877; des 18 Apr 1877 Ft Lincoln DT; res Mitchell SD in 1904.

Pension: 4 Apr 1892 / Inv / 1102424. (Rej on grd no rec of alleged serv as Jno. Folsom in co C 16 N.Y. cav, 1861–65).

Johnson, Benj. See Haverstick, Benj. Johnson.

Johnson, Francis. See Kennedy, Francis Johnson.

Johnson, Sam'l. Pvt co A; b. Troy N.Y.; enl 25 Oct 1872 at Troy for 5 yrs; age 21; engineer; brn eyes, brn hair, sallow comp, 5' 5 3/4" high; join co A 2 Dec 1872 E'town Ky.; dd subs dept herder Aug 1873; dd co cook June 1874; dd co cook Feb & Apr 1876; dd co cook Aug thro' Dec 1876; disch 24 June 1877 camp near Tongue River MT per SO 70 Dept of Dak. 1877 a pvt char good.

Jones, Henry P. Pvt co I; b. 8 Nov 1843 Lancaster Pa.; enl as Jas. Wilson 23 Oct 1869 Phil'a Pa. for 5 yrs; age 25; iron moulder; hazel eyes, brn hair, fair comp, 5' 7 1/2" high; assd to co H 3 cav; des 15 Oct 1870 while on ds at Camp Goodwin AT; enl as Jno. Bush 4 Apr 1873 Boston Mass. for 5 yrs; age 27; tinsmith; assd to co B 4 cav; des 10 Aug 1873 camp on Piedra Pinto Creek Tex.; enl as Henry P. Jones 8 Oct 1873 Phil'a Pa. for 5 yrs; age 29; plumber; join co I 7 cav 22 Oct 1873 Ft Totten DT; in conft Dec 1874 thro' June 1875; sen gen cm 26 Feb 1875 forf $8 pay per mo for 2 mos; with pack train June 1876; tr to co A 1 Oct 1876; dd qmd laborer Feb 1877; disch 8 Oct 1878 Camp Ruhlen DT expir of serv a pvt char xclt; reenl 19 Oct 1878 Baltimore Md for 5 yrs; assd to co F 1 cav; des 3 May 1879 camp near Wallula WT; enl as Jno. Ball 11 Oct 1879 Harrisburg Pa. for 5 yrs; age 34; plumber; assd to co G 23 inf; des 17 Oct 1880 Cant'mt IT; apph 7 Nov 1880 near L'worth Kans.; dishon disch 19 Dec 1880 sen gen cm & 2 yrs conft mil prison Ft L'worth; surd as Jas. Wilson & others 20 Feb 1882 while serving sen; res Rosslyn Va. in 1921.[23]

Jones, Julien D. Pvt co H; b. Boston Mass.; enl in co H 7 Sep 1871 Nashville Tenn for 5 yrs; age 22; painter; grey eyes, dk brn hair, dk comp, 5' 6 1/2" high; ds herding co horses June 1872; on furl 15 days 10 Oct 1872 Milwaukee Wis; ed qmd Oct 1873; dd qmd Dec 1873; dd qmd laborer Oct 1875; dd with hq fatigue pty l. wing 15 May 1876; killed on Reno hill 26 June 1876.

Jonson, Emil O. Pvt co A; b. Kilmar Sweden; enl in 7 cav 22 June 1874 St Paul Minn. for 5 yrs; age 21; laborer; blue eyes, lt hair, lt comp, 5' 6 1/2" high; join co A 27 June 1874 camp near Ft Lincoln DT; des 27 Jan 1875 Livingston Ala; surd 12 Apr 1875 Chattanooga Tenn; sen gen cm 17 May 1875 to dishon disch but not appv; dd co cook Oct 1875; dd qmd teamster Feb 1876; dd packer June & Aug 1876; dd battn hq orderly Oct 1876; des 24 Jan 1878 at Ft Lincoln;[24]

Jordan, Jno. Pvt co C; b. New York N.Y.; enl 28 July 1870 Cincinnati Ohio for 5 yrs; age 28; teamster; hazel eyes, blk hair, dk comp, 5' 5 1/4" high; join co C 4 Aug 1870 Ft L'worth Kans.; in conft Aug 1872; sen gen cm 31 Aug 1872 forf $10 pay; dd hq Blk Hills Exp'n 25 June to 31 Aug 1874; in conft Oct 1874 to Jan 1875; sen gen cm 25 Nov 1874 forf $10 pay per mo for 5 mos & conft same period; unexpired portion of sen rem'd 26 Jan 1875; sen gen cm 28 May 1875 forf all pay for 6 mos & conft same period; disch 28 Nov 1875 Ft Lincoln DT expir of serv a pvt & reenl in co C for 5 yrs; far'r 19 Jan 1877; disch 27 Nov 1880 Ft Meade DT expir of serv a far'r char xclt & reenl in co C for 5 yrs; pvt 6 Oct 1882; far'r 3 Oct 1883; disch 27 Nov 1885 at Ft Meade expir of serv a far'r char xclt & reenl in co C for 5 yrs; pvt 24 Apr 1886; dd actg co far'r June 1886; in conft Aug 1886; ed qmd teamster Sep 1886; in conft Oct 1886; cpl 29 May 1888; pvt 26 Sep 1888 sen gen cm & forf $10 pay per mo for 2 mos; far'r 31 Oct 1889; in conft June 1890; disch 27 Nov 1890 Pine Ridge Agcy SD expir of serv a far'r char good & reenl in co C for 5 yrs; pvt 24 Apr 1891; far'r 1 July 1891; pvt 28 Jan 1892; far'r 28 July 1893; disch 27 Nov 1895 Ft Grant AT expir of serv a far'r char xclt; reenl in co C 1 Dec 1895 for 3 yrs; cpl 1 Aug 1896; retd 16 Oct 1896 at Ft Grant a sgt char xclt; died 12 Jan 1906 Hartford Conn.

Jungesbluth, Julius C. Pvt band; b. Brunswick Germany; enl 9 Aug 1867 Brooklyn N.Y. for 3 yrs; age 24; clerk; brn eyes, brn hair, lt comp, 5' 7" high; assd to co C 4 art'y; disch 9 Aug 1870 Ft McHenry Md expir of serv a pvt; reenl 26 Jan 1871 Baltimore Md for 5 yrs; assd to co I 4 art'y; disch 26 Jan 1876 Ft Monroe Va. expir of serv a pvt; reenl 23 Feb 1876 St Louis Mo. for 5 yrs; join 7 cav 14 Apr 1876 Ft Lincoln DT (with Lt Reily's detmt); assd to band 28 Apr 1876; ds camp Powder River MT 15 June 1876; ds str *Josephine* 6 Aug 1876 to Ft Lincoln with band; tr to co A 8 Jan 1878; des 30 Mar 1878 at Ft Lincoln.

Notes—I–J

1. Capt. C. S. Ilsley of the 7th Cavalry, who has been so long a popular officer on the staff of Gen. Pope of Kansas, returned this week to Fort Meade to assume command of his company. *Bismarck Tribune*, Sept. 26, 1879; Ilsley had a blond goatee, Fougera, *With Custer's Cavalry*, 84; Benteen dubbed Ilsley, "Captain Marmalade," and viewed him with much contempt, for reasons unspecified, Mills, *Harvest of Barren Regrets*, 201.

2. Utley, *Life in Custer's Cavalry*, 36, 45; Capt. Barnitz said Lt. Jackson was much a gentleman and a thorough soldier. He had a large dog "Kioway," reared by the Kioway Indians and about two-thirds wolf. Utley, *Life in Custer's Cavalry*, 18, 27.

3. "Itinerary of the March of the Seventh U.S. Cavalry," June 1867, kept by Lt. Henry Jackson, RG 393, Part I, Entry 2601; see Broome, "Custer's Summer Indian Campaign of 1867."

4. *Leavenworth Daily Times*, Dec. 10, 1908; *Leavenworth Weekly Times*, Feb. 11, 1909; Col. Jackson married Mar. 4, 1870 at Leavenworth City to Elizabeth Calhoun, cousin of Lt. Calhoun and Mrs. Moylan. Capt. Benteen to Theodore W. Goldin, Jan. 31, 1896, Carroll, *The Benteen-Goldin Letters*, 243; Lt. Mathey interview, Oct 19, 1910, WMC-BYU. The federal census, June 9, 1880, Fort Meade, DT, reports Henry A. L. Jackson, Capt., 7th Cav., age 43, born England, and wife, Elizabeth.

5. Robert Jackson's mother said he was born in 1856 at Fort Benton. Mrs. Amelia Fox (Browning, Mont.) to Walter Camp, May 24, 1909, WMC-BYU; Billy Jackson said Robert was two years his elder, Schultz, *William Jackson Indian Scout*, 5.

6. Harvey A. Fox and John A. Bailey, WMC, notes, env 44, IU; Red Star said at Camp No. 9 two bull snakes were killed and Bob Jackson put one of them around each leg; says Jackson fired his revolver at a snake in the river, Libby, *Arikara Narrative*, 66–67.

Young Hawk told Walter Camp that before the older of the two Jackson boys fired all the shots in his revolver he exclaimed, "Look here, see what I will do when we meet the Sioux," Hardorff, *Camp, Custer, and the Little Big Horn*, 50; Young Hawk also said Bob Jackson was punished at Little Missouri River for riding through camp firing off his gun, Hammer, *Custer in '76*, 193.

Lt. Varnum said he punished both Jackson boys by making them stand for a while on a water keg for various little offenses. Varnum doubted Bob was sent back to Lincoln as the boys were not reliable and would not have been picked for a service of that kind, Varnum to Walter Camp, Dec. 3, 1909, WMC-BYU.

Camp said he visited the wife of Billy Jackson, and the mother of the Jacksons (wife of Harvey A. Fox), who said Bob carried mail to Fort Lincoln and returned to Powder River by June 25, Camp to John McGuire, Sept. 5, 1909, WMC-LBHB.

7. Hammer, *Custer in '76*, 193; Schultz, *William Jackson Indian Scout*, 158.

8. RG 92, Entry 238, reports 1876/110, 1876/303, 1877/487, and 1877/174; See Gray, *Centennial Campaign*, 234.

9. *St. Paul & Minneapolis Pioneer-Press and Tribune,* Dec. 3, 1876; Greene, *Yellowstone Command*, 85–93, 158.

10. Greene, *Yellowstone Command*, 208–10.

11. RG 92, Entry 238, reports 1879/130 and 1880/129; the federal census, Lewis and Clark County, MT, June 1880, shows Bob Jackson, age 25, laborer, residing at Saint Peter's Mission (near Fort Shaw), with wife, Mary, age 27, (born in Dakota; father born U.S.; mother born England), and son, Andrew, age two months.

In a letter to Mary Jackson, Castle MT, Dec. 4, 1894, from Robert Jackson, Big Timber, MT, apparently having learned her whereabouts and that Andre was attending school at the Sun River Mission, said he was anxious to hear about, "the balance of the children. . ." and to have Amelia with him so he could send her to school. He relates that Johnny attends school at Fort Shaw, and Eliza the sister's school at Helena, "she will make us a daughter we can be proud of and is studying music and can already play the piano and sew. . .", her tuition costing him $300 per year. Bob also wished Mary success in her pending marriage to Paddy Miles. Copy of original letter provided to this author in June 1994, by Mrs. Eileen Chandler, daughter of Julia Jackson.

The federal census of 1900 shows Thomas Miles, born March 1820, residing in Castle Mountain Township, MT, with wife, Mary, born Oct. 1854, (married five years), and stepchildren, all born in MT; Andrew Jackson, born Apr. 1879; Daniel, Feb. 1886; Millie, Oct. 1887; Adalene, Apr. 1888.

The Indian Census, M595, Blackfeet Agency, 1898, reports, Andrew, age 19; John, 17; Eliza, 15; Millie, 13; Lizzie, 11; residing with their grandmother, Amelia Fox, age 62, and son Alex, 21.

12. On the Indian Census rolls of Crow Agency, 1891 and 1892, Robert Jackson resides with wife Ellen, and children, John, age 10; Eliza, 7; and Julia, 2. (Robert is not found on subsequent rolls.) NA, M595. In an interview with Dr. Thomas B. Marquis, author of numerous works on the Custer battle, Ellen said she was born in March 1850, Newspaper clipping, np, White Sulphur Springs, MT, February 1, 1933; Census rolls 1893 through 1898 (NA, M595) are consistent with a birth year of 1852, whereas the federal census of 1900 reports Ellen Jackson, age 36, born March 1864, residing Big Timber Township with daughter Julia, born July 1889, RG 29.

According to an unpublished manuscript titled, "The Jackson Place," by Joe Medicine Crow, historian of Crow Agency, Bob Jackson married Helena (Ellen) Suce (Soos) Frost Fox and resided on Indian allotment land at Greycliff, near Big Timber, where two houses on their place were built with bridge timbers given to Bob in appreciation for his having crossed a rampaging creek and flagging an eastbound train, preventing it from running into a washed out bridge.

The Suce family and Bob Jackson's marriage to the widow of Dr. Frost are mentioned in Marquis, *Memoirs of a White Crow Indian*, 44–48.

When William Andrews Clark ran for U.S. Senator, Bob got a job driving the livery team around town (Absarokee) with a special harness provided by Clark. At the same time there was a circus in town and Bob left with it, later getting killed in a card game somewhere in Kansas. Walter Camp was told that Bob Jackson was employed at the Leavenworth prison and wrote an inquiry to the superintendent, Oct. 26, 1909, WMC-LBHB.

Julia Jackson said her father left the family when she was five and traveled with the Buffalo Bill wild west show. He wrote to her when she was 18 asking her to join him in Colorado. She thought he had found gold as he promised she would never want for anything if she moved there. He died in Amethyst, Colo. Thackeray, Article on life of Julia Jackson Schenderline, age 84 (born 1890), *Billings (Mont.) Gazette*, nd.

Jackson's mother, Amelia Fox, said she last heard from Bob he was in Colorado Springs, Letter to Walter Camp, May 24, 1909, WMC-BYU; Harvey A. Fox said Bob was at Colorado Springs about 1899 and his white wife wanted to get him away from there as he was drinking, WMC, notes, env 44, IU.

The wife of Billy Jackson said she received a letter from Bob at the time of her husband's death, from Washington D.C., Letter to Walter Camp, May 16, 1909, WMC-BYU.

13. *Albuquerque Morning Journal*, Sept. 8, 1910; an outline of Robert Jackson's service as Indian Scout with Gen. Custer appeared in the edition of Aug. 12, 1910.

Bob Jackson's son, Johnny, of Lennep, MT, wrote to Walter Camp, March 31, 1911, in answer to Camp's letter to Johnny's sister, Millie, seeking information on Bob Jackson. Johnny said he last heard from his father "eight years before last summer," from Creede, Colo., and thought he had interests in mining claims. He wrote three years ago to the post master at Creede asking if he knew anyone there who knew "R. H. Jackson," but was informed that nobody known there by that name, WMC-LBHB, No. 24.

The federal census, April 1910, Costilla, Taos Co., NM, (100 miles southeast of Creede, Colo.) lists Robert H. Jackson, age 50, occupation "Doctor;" born in Montana; father born in Virginia; mother born in Montana; residing with wife Felipa, age 24, born in NM; married five years (his 2nd, her 1st).

Billy Jackson said their father was a member of an old Virginia family, and their mother one-half Pikuni Indian, Schultz, *William Jackson Indian Scout*, 5.

14. *William Jackson Indian Scout*, 1, (from Billy Jackson's own words); Jackson's mother said Billy was born in 1860 at "Red River Portag Lapreary Canada," Amelia Fox to Walter Camp, May 24, 1909, WMC-BYU; On his enlistment papers, Billy reported he was born at Fort Pembina, DT. (The post was established on the Red River in 1870 about three miles from the Canadian line, and not far from Portage LaPrairie Canada.)

Billy's obituary in *Forest and Stream*, January 20, 1900, reports he was born in 1859 at Fort Benton, MT; On the Indian Census of Blackfeet Agency, MT, 1890–99, Billy's variable age is consistent with birth between 1856 and 1860 (NA, M 595); An interview with Billy Jackson, at Great Falls, MT, is in the *Anaconda* (Mont.) *Standard*, June 19, 1898; see also Innis, *Sagas of the Smoky-Water*, 332–34.

15. Schultz, *Many Strange Characters*, 104–108; Lt. Godfrey journaled the evening of July 30 that, "we are informed that a mail will leave in half an hour," Godfrey, *Diary;* The overland roundtrip to Fort Buford, 225 miles distant, employing strict vigilance and traveling only at night, required about two weeks; witness the arrival at Gen. Terry's camp Aug. 3 of scout Ed Begley and Private Cassidy, Company C, 6th Infantry, with two 'Ree scouts, couriers from Fort Buford. Cassidy was reported on

detached service at Buford from July 16, Willert, *March of the Columns*, 267; regimental returns, 6th Infantry, NA, M665, Roll 70.

Jackson recalled that he and one companion returned to their starting point five days after the command had marched up the Rosebud, and he was greatly fatigued after his long arduous ride of the last nine days.

16. RG 92, Entry 238, reports 1877/174, 1877/319, 1878/116, 1878/117, and 1879/108.

17. Walter Camp said Billy's young wife later married a Blackfoot Indian named Yellow Wolf, Camp to Stanislas Roy, Sept. 1, 1909, WMC-LBHB.

18. James Rooney interview with Walter Camp, n.d., WMC-BYU; see WMC, rosters, IU; John James's wife, Fannie (b. Ky. ca. 1848), was the sister of Lucetta "Settie" Belle Craig, wife of Nick Klein, and Tom Finnegan. Nancy Craig of Watauga, Ky., said her sister-in-law Settie went to Dakota with her sister, Fannie Crecilius, and there married Nicholas Cline. John R. Craig of Cumberland, Ky., said his aunt Fannie married a man with a peculiar name. Depositions, Oct. 5, 1931. In deposition Aug. 20, 1924, Nancy Craige said her sister-in-law, Fannie, went out to Dakota and married a man named James; also, Henry N. Denney said his aunt Settie went to Dakota with her sister Fannie James. Pension files of Nicholas Klein and Thomas Finnegan, RG 15.

19. RG 393, Part V, Fort A. Lincoln, DT; Capt. Yates' endorsement noted that the character of Private James was good, whereas that of Mrs. James not good.

20. Berwald interview, n.d.; Pandtle to Walter Camp, July 14, 1919, Rooney interview, n.d., WMC-BYU; (it appears Walter Camp wrote after James, "Butler says Powd" but drew line through remark, WMC, rosters, IU); the muster roll, and the company return, Aug. 31, show James, "D.S. Ft. Lincoln, Aug. 5th."; on the regimental return, Aug. 31, James is on Yellowstone River Aug. 5th guard on steamer. He joined the detachment at Fort Lincoln, Aug. 10, according to the post returns. RG 94, Entry 53; LBHB Collections, Rolls 12 and 15; NA, M617.

21. John James was discharged on the request of his wife, Fannie (laundress of Company E for seven years), based on Sec. 5, GO 37, AGO, 1878; "That hereafter women shall not be allowed to accompany troops as laundresses; Provided, That any such laundresses, being the wife of a soldier as is now allowed to accompany troops, may, in the discretion of the regimental commander, be retained until the expiration of such soldier's present term of enlistment." RG 94, Entry 44. Fannie related that, to make a living she had taken up a Homestead Claim, and her husband's pay as a soldier did not meet the needs sufficient to keep body and soul together on account of high prices for the necessities of life. She needed his help to comply with requirements of the Homestead Law in making improvements on the claim, which by law she was compelled to make to hold the Homestead, and without his assistance she could not. He was not a fit subject to be in the army because he was disabled on account of stricture, having been an inmate of the post hospital on two separate occasions.

Captain Ilsley, commanding Company E, endorsed Mrs. James's request, stating that James was unfitted for cavalry service in consequence of an operation occasioned by syphilis. Each time the troop was ordered into the field, he tried to escape going, and because he was not a suitable man to leave in charge of property, he recommended his discharge with loss of all allowances for travel expenses. Ilsley added that James's pay together with earnings of his wife as laundress enabled them to live comfortably and save sufficient money to purchase a wagon, three horses, seven or eight head of cattle, farming implements, large lot of poultry and such other articles as were necessary to establish a ranch and to employ a laborer on their homestead, RG 94, Entry 409, file 9612 A (EB) AGO 1880.

John James was employed in the quartermaster department at Fort Meade as civilian teamster (pay $30 per month) from Oct. 14, 1882 to July 31, 1883. The latter report bears the remark, "sick 9 days not to work," RG 92, Entry 238, reports 1882/126 and 1883/112.

Fannie James testified in the court martial of Capt. French at Fort Lincoln on Jan. 28, 1879, RG 153, file QQ994;Tom Finnegan, who was married for a time to Fannie's sister, Belle, told his sister, Ella, that Fannie "died many years ago and possibly somewhere up on the Yellowstone River," Deposition of Ella Butler, Mar. 7, 1924, Finnegan pension file, RG 15.

22. See Russell, "The Lone Welshman."

23. Jones said his address would always be Roslyn, Va., that he was age 76 on Nov. 8, Jones to Walter Camp, Nov. 21, 1919, WMC-LBHB; Fremont Kipp said Jones pedaled novelties through Maryland and Delaware and resided near the Arlington (Va.) post office in Dec. 1921 when he visited him, Kipp to

Walter Camp, Jan. 3, 1922, WMC-BYU; Michael Caddle said H. P. Jones was shot by order of Gen. Greeley, on expedition to North Pole, for stealing pork, Caddle to Camp, Nov. 8, 1909, WMC-BYU.

24. William D. Nugent said Johnson was nicknamed Swede and was a man as near without fear as any man he ever knew and proved it at different times. *Winners of the West*, Vol. III, No. 10, June 24, 1926.

K

Kane, Maurice. See Cain, Morris.

Kane, Wm. Pvt co C; b. Kerry Ireland; enl 2 Jan 1856 Toledo Ohio for 5 yrs; age 21; laborer; gray eyes, brn hair, fair comp, 5' 7 1/2" high; assd to co F 1 drg; disch 17 Dec 1860 Ft Crook Calif. per GO 24 AGO 1859 a cpl; reenl 12 Jan 1861 San Francisco Calif. for 3 yrs; assd to co C 1 drg; tr to co F; (regt redesig 1 cav Aug 1861); disch 12 Jan 1864 near Mitchell Sta Va. expir of serv a sgt; reenl 16 Aug 1864 New York N.Y. for 3 yrs; assd to co A 5 cav; disch 15 Aug 1867 Asheville NC expir of serv a sgt; reenl 16 Nov 1867 Wash'n D.C. for 5 yrs; assd to gen mtd serv; disch 16 Nov 1872 St Louis Mo. expir of serv a pvt; reenl 21 Nov 1872 at St Louis for 5 yrs; join co C 7 cav 12 Feb 1873 Charlotte NC; ds on str *Josephine* 30 July to 2 Aug 1873; ed subs dept herder Dec 1873; dd hostler hq Blk Hills Exp'n 30 June to 9 July 1874; ds Ft Rice DT 31 July to 1 Sep 1874; ed subs dept herder Dec 1874 to May 1875; dd post hq Oct 1875; dd qmd Dec 1875 to Mar 1876; sick qrs 6–13 June 1876 (infl. pleura) camp Powder River MT; diag 16 June with heart disease; tr on str *Josephine* 19 July to hosp Ft Lincoln DT; duty 17 Aug 1876; sick at Ft Lincoln 19–25 Oct 1876 (ac. rheum.); dd room orderly June 1877; ds Ft Totten DT Aug to Nov 1877 bldg cav stables; disch 21 Nov 1877 at Ft Totten expir of serv a pvt char xclt; reenl 18 Dec 1877 St Louis Mo. for 5 yrs; assd to gen mtd serv; disch 10 June 1879 Jeff'n Bks Mo. on surg cert dis (phthisis pulmonalis) a pvt char good; died 2 Nov 1879 Sol. Home Wash'n D.C.

Kanipe, Dan'l A. See Knipe, Dan'l Alexander.

Katzenmaier, Jacob. Pvt co G; b. Germany; enl 27 Mar 1876 Pittsburgh Pa. for 5 yrs; age 23; baker; blue eyes, lt brn hair, fair comp, 5' 8 1/4" high; assd to 7 cav as baker & joined co G 27 Apr 1876 St Paul Minn.; ds camp Powder River MT 15 June 1876; ed post bakery Nov 1876 to Feb 1877; ds Ft Lincoln 14 Oct 1877; ed post baker Dec 1877 to May 1878; dd co baker Aug 1878; ed post baker Dec 1878 to May 1879; ed post hosp cook June & Dec 1879; died 27 Jan 1880 Ft Meade DT (erysipelas) a pvt char very good.

Kavanagh, Chas. Pvt co M; b. Pittsburgh Pa.; enl 7 Aug 1867 St Louis Mo. for 5 yrs; age 26; tobacconist; gray eyes, fair hair, dk comp, 5' 8 3/4" high; join co G 7 cav 30 Sep 1867 Ft Harker Kans.; dd co cook June 1868; disch 7 Aug 1872 Spartanburg SC expir of serv a pvt; reenl 13 Sep 1875 New York N.Y. for 5 yrs; join co M 7 cav 21 Oct 1875 Ft Rice DT; tr to co E 19 Oct 1876; in conft Dec 1876; disch 12 Sep 1880 Ft Meade DT expir of serv a pvt char xclt; reenl 7 June 1881 Ft Schuyler N.Y. for 5 yrs; assd to co G 3 art'y; disch 10 Apr 1886 Ft McHenry Md on surg cert dis (consumption) a pvt char good; died 14 Feb 1887 Sol. Home Wash'n D.C. (phthisis pulmonalis).
Pension: 22 May 1886 / Inv / 574232 / 342685.

Kavanagh, Jno. Pvt co D; b. Roscommon Ireland; enl 3 Jan 1872 Jersey City NJ for 5 yrs; age 21; teamster; gray eyes, brn hair, ruddy comp, 5' 6" high; join co D 3 Feb 1872 Chester SC; ds Ft Totten DT 30 May to 14 Sep 1874 as gardener; dd qmd Dec 1876; disch 3 Jan 1877 Ft Rice DT expir of serv a pvt char xclt; reenl 22 Mar 1877 Ft Lincoln DT for 5 yrs in co B 7 cav; des 21 May 1878 Standing Rock Agcy DT; surd 12 July 1878 Omaha Bks Neb; dishon disch 9 Aug 1878 sen gen cm & 2 yrs conft mil prison.

Kavanagh, Thos. G. Pvt co L; b. Dublin Ireland; enl in co L 16 Jan 1873 Jackson Bks (New Orleans) La. for 5 yrs; age 28; farmer; gray eyes, red hair, ruddy comp, 5' 11 1/4" high; cpl 3 Feb 1874; dd post hq Mar & Apr 1874; sgt 13 Sep 1874; dd post hq Sep & Oct 1874; in arrest Apr 1875; pvt 17 May 1875 sen gen cm & forf $5 pay per mo for 6 mos & conft same period; unexpired portion of sen rem'd 9 Aug 1875; attd to band Aug 1875; in conft Apr 1876; killed with Custer column 25 June 1876.

Keefe, Jno. J. Pvt co B; b. Kerry Ireland; enl 11 Apr 1876 Boston Mass. for 5 yrs; age 22; shoemaker; blue eyes, brn hair, fair comp, 5' 5 3/4" high; join co B 27 Apr 1876 St Paul Minn.; ds camp Powder River MT 10 June 1876; ds camp mouth of Rosebud Creek Aug 1876 dismtd; sick hosp Ft Lincoln DT Dec 1876; disch 9 Feb 1877 at Ft Lincoln on surg cert dis (scrofulous diathesis & gen feebleness of const. & irritable heart; not line of duty & not entitled to pension).
Pension: 14 Mar 1877 / Inv / 232463. (Rej on grd disability not due to serv).

Keegan, Mich'l. Pvt co L; b. Wexford Ireland; enl 3 July 1855 Jeff'n Bks Mo. for 5 yrs; age 27; laborer; blue eyes, dk hair, ruddy comp, 5' 7" high; assd to co I 2 cav; disch 3 July 1860 Camp Rosario Tex. expir of serv a pvt; reenl same day in co E 2 cav at camp on Rio Grande Tex. for 5 yrs; (regt redesig 5 cav Aug 1861); disch 19 July 1864 Light House Point Va. by reenlmt in same co for 3 yrs; tr to co B; disch 19 July 1867 Nashville Tenn expir of serv a pvt; reenl 27 July 1867 Cincinnati Ohio for 5 yrs; join co C 7 cav 13 Sep 1867 Ft Lyon Colo.; cpl 5 Oct 1867; sgt 27 Dec 1867; in arrest Apr 1868; pvt 9 May 1868; cpl 19 Sep 1868; sgt 26 Dec 1868; cpl 9 Apr 1869; pvt 19 May 1869; dd comsy dept June 1869; dd co cook Aug to Oct 1869; dd co cook June 1870; dd co cook Mar to May 1871; ed post baker Aug 1871; disch 27 July 1872 Lincolnton NC expir of serv a pvt; reenl 6 Aug 1872 Yorkville SC for 5 yrs in co L 7 cav; in conft Oct 1872; sick 13–23 Apr 1873 (pr. syph.); dd hosp nurse 24 Apr 1873; dd hosp attdt on str *Katie P. Kountz* 8 May 1873 Yankton to Ft Rice DT; ed med dept May to Sep 1873; (cook for Lt Braden Aug 1873);[1] dd post bakery Oct 1873 to Mar 1874; dd post bake house Jan to Mar 1875 & Aug 1875 to Feb 1876; on sick call 9–10 June 1876 & ret to duty; ds camp Powder River MT 10 June 1876 chg co prop; sick at Ft Lincoln 24 Aug 1876; sick Ft Lincoln 17 Oct 1876; disch 15 Dec 1876 surg cert dis (chr. rheum. unfit for duty since 10 June) a pvt char good; died 24 July 1900 Chicago Ill.[2]
Pension: 9 Jan 1877 / Inv / 229579 / 151350.

Keller, Jno. J. Pvt co D; b. 11 Mar 1846 Millersville Pa.; pvt & cpl co E 195 Pa. inf 27 Feb 1865 to 31 Jan 1866; enl reg army 19 Sep 1868 Phil'a Pa. for 5 yrs; age 22; clerk; blue eyes, dk hair, ruddy comp, 5' 6 3/4" high; join co D 10 Nov 1868 Camp Sandy Forsyth Kans.; dd officer's servant Aug 1873;[3] disch 19 Sep 1873 Camp Terry MT expir of serv a pvt; reenl for co D 19 Oct 1873 St Paul Minn. for 5 yrs; ds Helena MT 5 May to 19 Oct 1878 when disch by expir of serv a pvt char a good soldier & reliable man; died 8 Feb 1913 Butte MT.
Pension: 30 Sep 1904 / Inv / 1325269 / 1146238.

Kelley, Geo. Pvt co H; b. 1 Jan 1847 New York N.Y.; drummer co A 91 N.Y. inf 15 Sep 1861; disch 18 Dec 1862 Pensacola Fla (per GO 154 AGO 1862) & enl in reg army co L 1 art'y for 3 yrs; age 21; teamster; hazel eyes, brn hair, lt comp, 5' 4" high; des 15 Sep 1863; apph 19 May 1864; disch 26 July 1866 Ft Porter (Buffalo) N.Y. by expir of serv a pvt; reenl in same co 26 Sep 1866 at Ft Porter for 3 yrs; disch 2 Oct 1869 Ft Niagara N.Y. expir of serv a pvt; reenl 3 Nov 1869 Detroit Mich. for 5 yrs; join co D 22 inf Dec 1869 Ft Randall DT; ed qmd laborer Aug & Oct 1871; wag 1 Feb 1872 & dd qmd teamster to May 1872; pvt 3 May 1872; ed qmd teamster Oct 1872 to Sep 1873; ed qmd teamster Aug 1874; disch 3 Nov 1874 New Orleans La. expir of serv a pvt; enl in co H 7 cav (auth AGO) 16 Apr 1875 at New Orleans for 5 yrs; dd qmd teamster 13 Oct 1875 to 4 May 1876; dd qmd teamster Jan & Feb 1877; dd co teamster Oct 1877 to May 1878; dd qmd teamster Aug to Nov 1878; dd co cook Dec 1878; dd bldg co qrs & stables Aug 1879; sick 9 Sep to 30 Oct 1879 (conjunctivitis); disch 15 Apr 1880 Ft Meade DT expir of serv a pvt char xclt; reenl 27 Sep 1880 New York N.Y. for 5 yrs; assd to co C 6 inf; cpl 14 Sep 1881; pvt 12 May 1882; disch 26 Sep 1885 Ft Douglas Utah expir of serv a pvt; reenl 15 May 1889 Rock Springs Wyo. Ty for 5 yrs in co A 7 inf; disch 29 Apr 1892 Ft Logan Colo. per SO 96 AGO 1892 (vet act 16 June 1890 [GO 80 AGO 1890]) a pvt;[4] died 21 Oct 1922 L'worth Kans.
Pension: 12 Dec 1895 / Inv / 1172326 / 925222.

Kellogg, Marcus Henry. Newspaper reporter; b. 31 Mar 1833 Brighton Canada; moved to LaCrosse Wis in 1851 where he was town tel operator for a number of yrs & in 1867 an unsuccessful candidate for city clerk; later employed as tel operator & dispatcher for NPRR at Brainerd Minn., also provided columns to the *St Paul Pioneer Press*; in the election of 1872 he edited a campn paper at Brainerd while at the same time a candidate for state legislature & defeated by a small majority; he came to Bismarck in May 1873 & joined the *Tribune* as it prepared for publication; in Nov 1875 he went to Aitkin Minn. for the winter, having been engaged there by a lumber firm in a clerical capacity; in Mar 1876 he was on gen Custer's train snowbound 26 miles from Bismarck & when a pocket-relay was found on the cars the 3d day, he cut into the tel wire & tapped out a call that bro't relief within hours;[5] with a com'n from the *New York Herald* & approval of gen Terry, he joined the Sioux Exp'n at Ft Lincoln 14 May;[6] tho' furn a horse by gen Custer, he was mtd on a slow mule when he rode up the Rosebud 22 June & borrowed spurs from Fred Gerard to help keep ahead with the scouts; killed with Custer column 25 June, his body the last found (29 June), identified by his oddly shaped boots; widowed in 1867 he was survived by two daughters at LaCrosse.[7]

Kelly, Edw. H. Pvt co I; b. Mayo Ireland; enl as Pat'k H. Kelly 13 Sep 1866 New York N.Y. for 5 yrs; age 25; laborer; gray eyes, sandy hair, fair comp, 5' 5" high; join co I Oct 1866 Ft Riley Kans.;[8] ds clerk for actg aig (capt Keogh) hq distr upper Ark June 1868 to Apr 1869; disch 13 Sep 1871 Bagdad Ky. expir of serv a pvt & reenl in co I for 5 yrs; (m. 25 Mar 1873 Louisville Ky. to Ellen Flynn [in presence of capt Keogh]); des 10 June 1873 Breckenridge Minn.; apph 4 days later at St Paul Minn.; sen gen cm 22 Sep 1873 to dishon disch & 3 yrs conft mil prison but sen rem'd & restored to duty; join co 19 Oct 1873 Ft Totten DT; ds Ft Seward DT May 1874; ds regtl hq at St Paul June 1874 & dept hq at St Paul July 1874; tr to regt 1 Feb 1876; dep Ft Snelling 2 Mar 1876 [probably on gen Custer's train]; killed with Custer column 25 June 1876; survived by wife & 2 ch. Pension: 20 Mar 1877 / Wid / 230546 / 180041. (Dropped from roll June 1884, failure to claim 3 yrs; last paid 4 Mar 1881).

Kelly, Jas. Pvt co H; b. Boston Mass.; enl 28 Aug 1866 Chicago Ill. for 5 yrs; age 26; soldier; blue eyes, lt hair, florid comp, 5' 4 1/4" high; join co H 17 Sep 1866 Ft Riley Kans. & appt cpl same date; sgt 18 Jan 1867;[9] des 11 Feb 1868 while on furl; surd 25 Nov 1873 at Chicago under GO 102 AGO 1873; arr St Louis Bks 29 Nov & tr to Ft Snelling Minn. 29 Dec 1873 to await transp to regt; join co H 21 May 1874 Ft Rice DT; dd qmd laborer Oct 1875; dd regtl hq fatigue pty (morn & eve) 11 May 1876; ds Ft Lincoln DT 1 May 1877; disch 3 July 1877 at Ft Lincoln upon expir of serv a pvt char good (made good time lost by des'n).

Kelly, Jas. Trump'r co B; b. Bangor Me; enl 4 Jan 1876 St Louis Bks Mo. for 5 yrs; age 23; plumber; blue eyes, brn hair, fair comp, 5' 4" high; join co B as trump'r 23 Jan 1876 Shreveport La.; sen gen cm 14 Mar 1876 forf $1.57 pay per wk for 7 wks & conft 3 mos (awol & sold, lost thro' neglect, or improperly disposed of his uniform clothing, one great coat $6.44 & one woolen blanket $4.55); ds Ft Lincoln DT 17 Oct 1876 dismtd; dishon disch 5 Jan 1877 at Ft Lincoln per SO 264 AGO 1876 (worthlessness).[10]

Kelly, Jno. Pvt co F; b. Easton Pa.; enl 3 Jan 1867 Carlisle Pa. for 5 yrs; age 20; pudler; hazel eyes, lt hair, lt comp, 5' 6" high; join co E 7 cav 29 Mar 1867 Ft Hays Kans.; trump'r June 1867; pvt 14 July 1869; cpl 1 July 1870; sgt 1 Sep 1871; disch 3 Jan 1872 Unionville SC expir of serv a sgt & reenl in co E for 5 yrs; pvt 5 June 1872; dd co cook June 1873; dd post hq mtd msgr Dec 1873 to June 1874; dd post hq mtd msgr Aug 1874; dd with band Oct 1874; dd regtl hq Sep 1875 to Apr 1876; tr to co F 1 May 1876;[11] killed with Custer column 25 June 1876; (survived by wife Kate & 3 ch; [widow m. sgt Curtiss 25 Feb 1877]). Pension: 9 Jan 1880 / Minor / 258785 / 189734. Wid / 274268. (Rej on grd claim not filed until 1880 & clmt having remarried in 1877 there was no period in which to allow pension).

175

Kelly, Pat'k H. See Kelly, Edw. H.

Kennedy, Francis Johnson. Pvt co I; b. 12 May 1854 Pacific Mo.; enl as Francis Johnson 27 Sep 1875 St Louis Mo. for 5 yrs; age 21; laborer; blue eyes, brn hair, dk comp, 5' 7 1/4" high; join co I 21 Oct 1875 Ft Lincoln DT; sick qrs 28 May to 9 June 1876 (poisoning by rattlesnake); with pack train June 1876 (says he led capt Keogh's horse Comanche);[12] dd qmd Apr 1878; in conft June 1878; ds in field June 1879; ed hosp nurse Aug 1879; disch 26 Sep 1880 Camp Houston DT expir of serv a pvt char xclt; reenl 24 Nov 1880 Ft Snelling Minn. for 5 yrs; assd to co K 7 inf; disch 23 Nov 1885 Ft Laramie Wyo. expir of serv a pvt; died 9 Jan 1924 St Paul Minn.
Pension: 9 Apr 1917 / Ind. Surv. / 10868 / 8118.

Kenney, Jno. Pvt co E; b. Kilmallock Limerick Ireland; enl 19 Nov 1851 at Limerick in 63d regt of foot; age 18 6/12; recd Crimea campn medal with clasps for Alma, Balaklava, & Inkerman; with regt to Nova Scotia in May 1856; cpl 4 June 1856; (m. 13 Dec 1858 at Halifax to Mary Jane Ryan);[13] pvt 17 Mar 1860 & conft 2 days; des 21 Apr 1860 & came to Gloucester Mass.; enr 20 May 1861 Ft Warren (Boston Harbor) Mass. a sgt co K 12 Mass. inf; age 25; gardener; hazel eyes, dk hair, dk comp, 5' 10" high; pvt 2 Dec 1861; pris'r of war 30 Aug to 16 Dec 1862; disch 8 Mar 1863 near Alexandria Va. on surg cert dis (disease of heart) a pvt; enl reg army as Jno. McKenna 19 Dec 1874 at Boston for 5 yrs; age 31 6/12; hostler; hazel eyes, blk hair, dk comp, 5' 8 3/4" high; join co E 7 cav 8 Feb 1875 Opelika Ala; sick qrs 18 May 1876 (boil); duty 19 May; [at LBH says Pandtle; not sure says Berwald];[14] far'r 1 Oct 1876 to date 1 Sep; pvt 15 Nov 1876; tr to co I 14 Dec to date 1 Jan 1877; ds with Lt Scott 20 Feb 1877 cond mil convicts to Ft L'worth; ds in field 27 July 1877 with Lt Scott to Cant'mt Tongue River; ds with co E (orderly to Lt Scott) 2 Aug to Oct 1877;[15] cpl 17 Oct 1878; sgt 28 May 1879; disch 18 Dec 1879 Ft Lincoln DT expir of serv a sgt char xclt; reenl 27 Dec 1880 Ft Totten DT to date 1 Dec (auth AGO) in co K for 5 yrs; [Lt Scott comdg co K]; cpl 1 Jan 1882; pvt 1 Mar 1883 & tr to co A; ds with Lt Scott's detmt to Powder River May 1883; on furl 20 days 1 July 1883; ed qmd teamster Oct 1883; dd qmd cutting logs May & June 1884; tr to co H 1 Nov 1884; cpl 4 Sep 1885; disch 30 Nov 1885 Ft Meade DT expir of serv a cpl char xclt; enl as Jno. Kenney 12 Dec 1885 Cincinnati Ohio for 5 yrs; join co E 3 art'y 27 Jan 1886 Columbus Ohio; tr to co K 17 Feb 1886; sick 19 Aug to 4 Nov 1887 (malarial fever); tr to co B Aug 1888; awol 6 Nov 1888 at Cincinnati; drowned in Ohio River, his body found 16 Dec 1888 near Constance Ky.; implied chg of des'n removed.[16]
Pension: 4 Aug 1890 / Wid / 456296 / 409061.

Kenney, Mich'l. 1sgt co F; b. Galway Ireland; enl 15 Jan 1867 Pittsburgh Pa. for 3 yrs; age 21; roller; gray eyes, brn hair, fair comp, 5' 7 1/4" high; join co F 5 art'y 22 Feb 1867 near Richmond Va.; cpl 3 Feb 1869; dd actg post prov sgt Dec 1869; disch 15 Jan 1870 Sedgwick Bks Wash'n D.C. expir of serv a cpl; reenl 10 Mar 1870 Yerba Buena Isl Calif. for 5 yrs in co D battn of engrs; age 21; disch 20 Feb 1871 Yerba Buena Isl per GO 122 AGO 1870 an artf'r;[17] reenl 7 Mar 1871 Ft L'worth Kans. for 5 yrs in co F 7 cav; cpl 9 June 1871; ds regtl hq Louisville Ky. July & Aug 1871; sgt 10 Jan 1872; pvt 18 Aug 1872; cpl 27 May 1873; sgt 10 Dec 1873; dd actg co qm sgt Feb to May 1874; 1sgt 1 June 1874 to date 1 Apr 1874; disch 7 Mar 1876 Ft Lincoln DT expir of serv a 1sgt char xclt & reenl in co F for 5 yrs; appd for 6 mos furl 12 Mar 1876 (upon return of exp'n) with perm'n to go beyond the sea; killed with Custer column 25 June 1876.
Pension: 17 Oct 1879 / Mother / 252960 / 204694.

Keogh, Myles Walter. Capt co I; b. 25 Mar 1842 Carlow Ireland;[18] educ at Carlow college to 1858 then travelled in Europe & six mos afterward entered mil serv of Italy as 2Lt in Papal army; resd com'n 20 Feb 1862 & came to America; recom for com'n in union army by archbishop Hughes of N.Y. & secy of state Seward; appt capt of vols & addl adc to gen Shields 9 Apr 1862; tr to staff of gen Buford 31 July 1862; tr to staff of gen Stoneman 16 Dec 1863 (upon death of gen Buford); prom maj & adc 7 Apr 1864 when Stoneman appt comdr of cav, army of the Ohio; captured with Stoneman 31 July 1864 near Macon Ga. & exchanged 30 Sep 1864 at Charleston SC; (declined prom'n to Lt-col 3 NJ cav & tr to staff of gen Custer Nov 1864);[19] on staff of gen Schofield dur Jan & Feb 1865; bvt Lt-col vols 13 Mar 1865 for gal cond dur the war; m.o. vol serv (with Stoneman) 1 Sep 1866 Nashville Tenn; appt reg army com'n 2Lt 4 cav 23 Aug 1866 (to date 4 May 1866) with perm'n to delay 60 days joining regt; (never joined); appt capt 7 cav 27 Oct 1866 (while in Wash'n) to date 28 July 1866; join co I 6 Nov 1866 Ft Riley Kans.; bvt maj & Lt-col Nov 1867 (to date 2 Mar 1867) for gal serv in battles of Gettysburg & Resaca; awl 30 days 3 Feb 1868 Auburn N.Y. (groomsman at wedding of gen Upton);[20] abs on surg cert 4 Mar to 2 May 1868 (frac. r. tibia 14 Feb); ds Ft Harker Kans. June 1868 to Apr 1869 actg aig distr upper Ark (on staff of gen Sully); ds Ft Harker June & July 1869 member of gen cm; awl 20 days 12 Aug 1869 & ext'd 6 mos to visit Europe; abs sick May 1870 Ft L'worth Kans.; ds Louisville Ky. July to Sep 1871; awl 60 days on surg cert 26 Feb 1872; ds Louisville Aug to Nov 1872; comd co with NBS Apr thro' Oct 1873; awl 7 mos 6 Apr 1874 home to Ireland; ds dept hq St Paul Minn. 26 Feb to 24 Apr 1875; sick qrs 17 July to 9 Aug 1875; awl 30 days 26 Aug 1875 Louisville Ky. & ext'd 30 days on surg cert; rejoin co 14 Oct 1875 Ft Lincoln DT; killed with Custer column 25 June 1876.[21] [K173 CB 1864].

Kerr, Denis. Pvt co A; b. Antrim Ireland; enl 4 Nov 1851 New York N.Y. for 5 yrs; age 24; laborer; blue eyes, lt hair, fair comp, 5' 7 1/4" high; assd to co E mtd rifles; disch 26 Sep 1856 Ft Craig NM by reenlmt in co A same regt for 5 yrs; tr to co K 30 June 1861; (regt redesig 3 cav Aug 1861); disch 26 Sep 1861 Camp Christobal NM expir of serv a sgt; reenl 13 Mar 1867 New York N.Y. for 5 yrs; join co A 7 cav 22 Jan 1868 Ft L'worth Kans.; cpl 31 Jan 1868; sgt 16 Aug 1868; sick hosp 21 Nov to 2 Dec 1868 (cont'n); in arrest Apr 1869; pvt 7 Oct 1869; far'r 1 Sep 1871; pvt 1 Dec 1871; disch 13 Mar 1872 E'town Ky. expir of serv a pvt & reenl in co A for 5 yrs; cpl 25 Sep 1872; sgt 9 Feb 1873; pvt 6 Mar 1873; sick qrs Apr 1873; ds Ft Rice DT June to Sep 1873 gd regtl prop; ds Ft Lincoln DT 5 May 1876 with co garden; ds Ft Lincoln DT 17 Oct 1876; disch 13 Mar 1877 at Ft Rice by expir of serv a pvt char xclt; died 21 Mar 1890 Sol. Home Wash'n D.C.
Pension: 20 May 1880 / Inv / 366605 / 174925.

Kilfoyle, Martin. Pvt co G; b. Clare Co Ireland; enl 4 Dec 1874 St Louis Mo. for 5 yrs; age 21; laborer; blue eyes, lt hair, fair comp, 5' 6" high; join co G 10 Feb 1875 Shreveport La.; dd under instr'n of regtl vet'y surg Oct 1875 to Mar 1876; dd asst to vet'y surg 8 May 1876; ds camp Powder River MT 15 June 1876; sick (remit. fever) 2 Aug 1876 on str *Carroll* to Ft Lincoln; duty 10 Aug & dd qmd care for pub animals; dd post hq 13 Nov 1876 to 4 Apr 1877; dd regtl hq fatigue pty 25 Apr to 8 Oct 1877; cited by capt Benteen for conspic gal in two mtd chgs against Nez Perce inds at Canon Creek MT 13 Sep 1877; far'r 1 Jan 1878; ds Deadwood DT Oct 1879; disch 3 Dec 1879 Ft Meade DT expir of serv a far'r char xclt; reenl 25 Mar 1881 Wash'n D.C. for 5 yrs; age 26 4/12; assd to co C 2 art'y; disch 24 Mar 1886 Mt. Vernon Bks Ala expir of serv a pvt; reenl 20 Apr 1886 Wash'n D.C. for 5 yrs; assd to co L 3 art'y; disch 7 June 1890 Ft Monroe Va. per SO 130 AGO 1890 (by way of favor upon own req) a cpl char xclt; died 9 Dec 1894 Wash'n D.C.
Pension: 24 Mar 1892 / Inv / 1099582 / 849843.

Kimm, Jno. G. Pvt co E; b. New York N.Y.; enl 17 Oct 1864 at New York for 3 yrs; age 19; laborer; brn eyes, dk hair, lt comp, 5' 5" high; assd to 16 inf; disch 7 Nov 1864 Ft Ontario N.Y. on surg cert (being under age 16 yrs); enr 22 Nov 1864 at NYC a pvt 20 indpt batt'y N.Y. lt art'y; age 18; m.o. vol serv 31 July 1865; reenl reg army 30 Sep 1865 Ft Hamilton N.Y. for 3 yrs; assd to co I 2 inf; disch 30 Sep 1868 Louisville Ky. expir of serv a pvt; reenl 19 Oct 1868 Wash'n D.C. for 3 yrs; assd to co A 12 inf; tr to co H 2 May 1871; tr to 1 cav 5 July 1871; disch 19 Oct 1871 Benicia Bks Calif. expir of serv a pvt; reenl 18 Jan 1872 Cincinnati Ohio for 5 yrs; age 24; laborer; gray eyes, blk hair, florid comp, 5' 10 1/2" high; join co E 7 cav 5 Feb

1872 Unionville SC; cpl 27 July 1872; pvt 17 Dec 1872; sick Ft Sully DT 27 May to 3 July 1873; ds Ft Rice DT July to Oct 1873; dd battn hq Black Hills Exp'n 15 July to 31 Aug 1874; dd co cook Aug 1875; ed hosp nurse Nov 1875; sick 21–30 Dec 1875 (cont'n r. knee, kick by horse); sick 2 May 1876 (cont'n), duty; [helped bury dead at LBH said himself & Berwald; not sure says Pandtle];[22] ds Ft Lincoln DT 16 Oct 1876 dismtd; disch 18 Jan 1877 at Ft Lincoln upon expir of serv a pvt char good; died 7 Feb 1909 Sol. Home Johnson City Tenn.
Pension: 2 Jan 1900 / Inv / 1242226 / 1020887. Wid / 963553 / 732844.

King, Geo. H. Cpl co A; b. Phil'a Pa.; enl 13 Sep 1869 at Phil'a for 5 yrs; age 21; laborer; hazel eyes, brn hair, fair comp, 5' 10 1/2" high; join co F 13 inf 22 Nov 1869 Ft Shaw MT; disch 13 Sep 1874 Camp Robinson Neb expir of serv a pvt; reenl 2 Oct 1875 Pittsburgh Pa. for 5 yrs; join co A 7 cav 21 Oct 1875 Ft Lincoln DT; cpl 4 June 1876; gsw l. lung 26 June on Reno hill; died 1 July 1876 on str *Far West* & buried in camp at Pease Bottom near mouth of Big Horn River; body removed June 1917 to Custer Battlefield Nat'l Cemetery.

King, Jno. Blks co C; b. Basel Switz; enl 22 Sep 1875 Cincinnati Ohio for 5 yrs; age 26; horse shoer; gray eyes, brn hair, dk comp, 5' 5 1/4" high; join co C as blks 21 Oct 1875 Ft Lincoln DT; killed with Custer column 25 June 1876.
Pension: 18 Nov 1876 / Mother / 228789 / 178193.

Kipp, Fremont. Pvt co D; b. 17 Oct 1856 Noble Co. Ohio; enl 2 Dec 1872 Columbus Ohio for 5 yrs; age 21 1/12; laborer; brn eyes, brn hair, dk comp, 5' 8 3/4" high; join co D 10 Feb 1873 Opelika Ala; sick hosp 19 June to 8 Aug 1875 (gonorrhea); ds Ft Berthold DT teamster 25 Feb to 2 Mar 1876; with pack train 25 June 1876 chg of amm'n mule; with detail to shoot wd horses 28 June; cpl 7 May 1877; sgt 1 Oct 1877; disch 2 Dec 1877 camp near Ft Buford DT expir of serv a sgt char xclt & reenl in co D for 5 yrs; on furl 30 days 3 Dec 1877 Bismarck DT; ds escort census enumerator in Blk Hills 16–28 June 1880; ed qmd Oct 1880 to Jan 1881; disch 2 Dec 1882 Ft Yates DT expir of serv a sgt char xclt; 1sgt co D 1 Ohio cav 27 Apr to 23 Oct 1898; reenl reg army 9 Dec 1898 Columbus Bks Ohio for 3 yrs; assd to co L 17 inf; appn for disch 13 Mar 1900 disappv; sgt of mtd detmt in pursuit & capture of outlaw leader Eugenio Avila Jan 1901 in Philippines; disch 21 June 1901 Camiling Luzon PI per SO 99 AGO 1901 (under par's 145 & 146, AR 1895) a sgt;[23] died 16 Jan 1938 Sol. Home Wash'n D.C.[24]
Pension: 1 Aug 1904 / Inv / 1321806 / 1166232. Ind. Surv. / 16314 / 9141.

Klawitter, Ferdinand. Pvt co B; b. 19 June 1836 Prussia Germany; enl 20 Jan 1870 Cincinnati Ohio for 5 yrs; age 23; farmer; blue eyes, lt hair fair comp, 5' 7 1/4" high; join co A 7 cav Feb 1870 Limestone Creek Kans.; ds Yorkville SC from Mar 1871 attd to co K; tr to co K 8 Feb 1873; ds Ft Rice DT Oct 1874; ds orderly at distr hq Shreveport La. Nov 1874; disch 20 Jan 1875 at Shreveport by expir of serv a pvt & reenl for 5 yrs in co B; ds orderly distr hq to Mar 1876; dd qmd to 8 May 1876; ds Ft Lincoln DT 17 May 1876 in co garden; sent with Lt Garlington on str *Josephine* 24 July to join co in field; ds Ft Lincoln 16 Oct dismtd; tr to co K 14 Dec 1876; ds Ft Lincoln May to Dec 1877; (sick 8 July to 13 Aug 1877 [infl. testicle]; sick hosp 1 Oct to 4 Dec 1877 [orchitis]); disch 3 Feb 1878 Ft Rice DT on surg cert dis (chr. epididymitis; struck l. testicle on pommel of saddle in fall from horse) a pvt char xclt; died 17 May 1924 Max N.Dak.[25]
Pension: 24 Feb 1879 / Inv / 269138 / 363016.

Klein, Gustav. Pvt co F; b. Wurtemburg Germany; enl 31 May 1866 New York N.Y. for 3 yrs; age 21; clerk; blue eyes, lt hair, fair comp, 5' 7 1/2" high; assd to co C 3 battn 19 inf; (redesig 37 inf regt Sep 1866); disch 31 May 1869 Camp Lowell AT expir of serv a pvt; reenl 15 Mar 1871 Ft L'worth Kans. for 5 yrs in co F 7 cav; age 23; cpl 1 Mar 1872; sgt 30 Aug 1872; 1sgt 22 Nov 1873; in arrest Feb & Mar 1874; pvt 31 Mar 1874; cpl Sep 1874; dd chg co mess Oct 1874 to Jan 1875; dd chg co mess June 1875; pvt 23 Sep 1875 sen gen cm; disch 16 Mar 1876 Ft Lincoln

DT expir of serv a pvt char xclt & reenl in co F for 5 yrs; killed with Custer column 25 June 1876.

Klein, Nicholas. Pvt co F; b. Bavaria Germany; enl 10 Feb 1872 Buffalo N.Y. for 5 yrs; age 22; butcher; hazel eyes, lt hair, lt comp, 5' 5 1/4" high; join co F 21 Feb 1872 Louisville Ky.; dd hosp nurse Dec 1872 to Mar 1873; abs sick Ft Rice DT June to Sep 1873; dd co cook Apr 1874; ds in field June 1874; dd co cook Aug 1874 to Jan 1875; dd co cook June 1875; ds Ft Lincoln DT 13 May 1876 chg co prop & garden; ds Ft Lincoln 17 Oct 1876; disch 10 Feb 1877 Ft Abercrombie DT expir of serv a pvt char good & reenl in co F for 5 yrs; on furl Feb 1877 St Paul Minn.; dd co cook Apr to July 1877; ed hosp cook Dec 1878 to July 1879; dd co cook June 1880; dd washing clothes June 1881; dd co cook Dec 1881; disch 9 Feb 1882 Ft Buford DT expir of serv a pvt char xclt; died 18 July 1904 Cleveland Ohio.[26]
Pension: 19 July 1930 / Wid / 1673657. (XC-2,634,118). See also, Wid / 1084957. (Settie B. Gill).

Klotzbucher, Henry. Pvt co M; b. Baden Germany; enl 4 Oct 1873 Phil'a Pa. for 5 yrs; age 25; cooper; brn eyes, brn hair, ruddy comp, 5' 6 1/2" high; join co M 21 Oct 1873 Ft Rice DT; dd post garden Apr 1874; dd co cook June & Dec 1874; ed hosp nurse July 1875 to Mar 1876; recom by capt French & Dr. Taylor for appmt of hosp stew'd Jan 1876;[27] killed dur retreat from valley fight 25 June 1876; (co clerk says sgt Ryan; striker for capt French said Slaper).[28]

Knauth, Herman. Pvt co F; b. Dammendorf Germany; enl 31 Jan 1872 Rochester N.Y. for 5 yrs; age 33; merchant; blue eyes, lt brn hair, fair comp, 5' 8" high; join co F 10 Feb 1872 Louisville Ky.; dd cook in band Mar 1872 to Apr 1873; ds with band 8 May 1873; dd co cook Oct 1873; ds Ft Lincoln DT June to Aug 1874; dd qmd laborer Oct & Dec 1874; dd qmd teamster Feb 1875; dd qmd laborer Apr 1875; dd co cook June 1875; killed with Custer column 25 June 1876.

Knecht, Anthony (Andy). Pvt co E; b. 12 Apr 1853 Cincinnati Ohio; enl 22 Sep 1873 St Louis Mo. for 5 yrs; age 21 6/12; butcher; hazel eyes, lt brn hair, lt comp, 5' 6½" high; join co E 18 Oct 1873 Ft Lincoln DT; dd co cook Feb to June 1874; in conft Dec 1874 & Feb 1875; sen gen cm Apr 1875 forf $10 pay for one mo; dd co cook Oct 1875; killed with Custer column 25 June 1876.
Pension: 14 Sep 1877 / Mother / 233259 / 247532.

Kneubuhler, Jos. Pvt band; b. Luzerne Switz; enl in band 14 Mar 1872 Louisville Ky. for 5 yrs; age 21; musician; gray eyes, brn hair, fair comp, 5' 7" high; ds Ft Lincoln DT 17 May 1876 chg of band garden; disch 14 Mar 1877 at Ft Lincoln upon expir of serv a pvt char good.[29]

Knipe, Dan'l Alexander. Sgt co C; b. 15 Apr 1853 near Marion NC; enl in co C 7 Aug 1872 Lincolnton NC for 5 yrs; age 21; farmer; hazel eyes, lt hair, fair comp, 5' 11" high; ed qmd Dec 1872; cpl 1 Aug 1874; sgt 3 June 1875; with Custer column 25 June 1876 till sent with message to pack train (passed band of 'Rees driving off Sioux ponies); gsw l. calf (accdt disch of pistol) 5 July 1876 camp mouth of Big Horn River;[30] tr on str *Carroll* 2 Aug to hosp Ft Lincoln DT; duty 23 Aug; dd post prov sgt 30 Aug 1876; dd qmd 12–28 Sep 1876 with 281 cav horses at post; (m. widow of sgt Bobo 12 Apr 1877); 1sgt 3 June 1877; disch 7 Aug 1877 Ft Totten DT expir of serv a 1sgt char xclt; reenl same day in co C for 5 yrs & on furl 3 mos to NC; sgt 10 Aug 1878; dd prov sgt Nov 1878 thro' Apr 1879; dd prov sgt Feb thro' June 1880; dd chg co kit'n Feb 1882; disch 6 Aug 1882 Ft Sisseton DT expir of serv a sgt char xclt; died 18 July 1926 Marion NC.
Pension: 26 Feb 1884 / Inv / 506984 / 1175828. Wid / 1551444.

Korn, Gustave. Pvt co I; b. Sprollow Silesia; enl 17 May 1873 St Louis Mo. for 5 yrs; age 21; clerk; hazel eyes, lt hair, lt comp, 5' 9 1/4" high; join co I 3 June 1873 Ft Snelling Minn.; ed qmd Dec 1875 to May 1876; [stories abound of his alleged experience at LBH];[31] blks 4 Aug 1876; ed qmd tinsmith 2 Oct 1876; cited by maj Merrill for good cond in action against Nez Perce inds at Canon Creek MT 13 Sep 1877; disch 17 May 1878

Ft Lincoln DT expir of serv a blks char xclt & reenl same day in co I for 5 yrs; disch 16 May 1883 Ft Totten DT expir of serv a blks char "a most excellent blacksmith an honest faithful soldier & in every respect a good thoroughly reliable man;" reenl in co I as blks 2 June 1883 Ft Keogh MT for 5 yrs; disch 1 June 1888 Ft Meade DT expir of serv a blks char xclt; reenl in co I as blks 3 June 1888 camp near Rapid City DT for 5 yrs; ed qmd mech Aug 1889; killed 29 Dec 1890 Wounded Knee SD in action with Sioux inds.

Kramer, Wm. Trump'r co C; b. Reading Pa.; enl 7 Oct 1875 Cincinnati Ohio for 5 yrs; age 27; painter; gray eyes, brn hair, ruddy comp, 5' 5 3/4"high; join co C 21 Oct 1875 Ft Lincoln DT; appt trump'r 22 Oct; killed with Custer column 25 June 1876; (survived by wife & 1 ch).
Pension: 21 Feb 1879 / Wid / 241846 / 185561.

Kretchmer, Jos. Pvt co D; b. Silesia Germany; enl 5 Sep 1866 Cincinnati Ohio for 5 yrs; age 28; farmer; blue eyes, brn hair, lt comp, 5' 4 3/4" high; join co L 7 cav 28 Sep 1866 Ft Riley Kans.; des 14 Jan 1867 Ft Morgan Colo. Ty; apph 26 Jan 1867 & ret to Ft Morgan; in conft to 4 Sep 1867 when restored to duty without trial per SO 195 Dept of Mo. 1867; dd post qmd June 1868; ed qmd teamster Oct & Dec 1869; ed qmd teamster Mar & June 1870; disch 5 Sep 1871 Winnsboro SC expir of serv a pvt; reenl 20 Sep 1872 Cincinnati Ohio for 5 yrs; join co D 7 cav 8 Dec 1872 Opelika Ala; dd in field June 1873 (with NBS); ds Ft Totten DT June to Sep 1874 in garden; tr to co F 1 Oct 1876; ds Ft Lincoln 17 Oct 1876; ds Ft Abercrombie DT 12 Apr 1877 chg co prop; disch 20 Sep 1877 at Ft Abercrombie expir of serv a pvt char good & reenl in co F for 5 yrs; on furl 6 mos 3 Dec 1877 with perm'n to go beyond the sea; dd qmd laborer June 1879 to Jan 1880; ds Ft Buford DT Dec 1880; dd actg co far'r Oct to Dec 1881; appt far'r 1 Jan 1882; pvt 30 June 1882; disch 19 Sep 1882 Camp Villard MT expir of serv a pvt char xclt; reenl same day in co F at Ft Custer MT for 5 yrs; disch 7 July 1886 Ft Buford DT on surg cert dis a pvt char good (epilepsy contr line of duty & excused from mtd drill since 1883 acc't liability of fit at any time; in hosp from 1 June 1886 dur which time he had several attacks); [striker for capt Bell said Kipp][32] reenl 13 June 1887 Jeff'n Bks Mo. for 5 yrs; assd to co C 2 cav; disch 12 June 1892 Ft Wingate NM expir of serv a pvt char xclt & reenl in same co for 5 yrs; disch 12 June 1897 Ft Riley Kans. expir of serv a pvt char xclt & reenl in same co for 3 yrs; retd 17 Sep 1898 a pvt; died 19 Apr 1928 Sol. Home Wash'n D.C.

Krusee, Henry M. Pvt co G; b. 5 Oct 1840 New York N.Y.; enl 18 Dec 1856 at New York for 5 yrs; age 16; clerk; hazel eyes, fair hair, fair comp, 5' 2 1/4" high; assd to gen serv music boys; tr to co E 4 art'y July 1859 a bugler; sgt co A 5 art'y Aug 1861 upon org'n of regt; disch 19 Oct 1861 Camp Hooker Md by reenlmt in co for 3 yrs; tr to band as prin mus'n June 1863 Ft Hamilton N.Y.H; disch 9 Feb 1864 NYC by reenlmt for 3 yrs a prin mus'n; abs sick regtl hq 22 Aug 1865; disch 11 Oct 1865 Ft Richmond NYH on surg cert dis (phthisis pulmonalis; dis total) a bugler; reenl 14 Aug 1866 New York N.Y. for 5 yrs; age 25; clerk; blue eyes, brn hair, fair comp, 5' 7" high; join co D 7 cav 10 Sep 1866 Ft Riley Kans. & appt 1sgt same date; actg sgt-maj June 1867; pvt 18 July 1867; 1sgt 24 Aug 1867; in arrest Apr 1869; disch 14 Aug 1871 Mt Vernon Ky. expir of serv a 1sgt; reenl two days later in co D for 5 yrs & appt 1sgt; in arrest Feb 1872; sen gen cm 26 Feb 1872 forf $8 pay per mo for 3 mos; on furl 20 days 20 Dec 1872 Lee Co. Ala; ds Opelika Ala Feb 1873; appt comsy-sgt USA 26 Oct 1873 assd to Ft Seward DT; in arrest Oct 1874; disch 5 Nov 1874 at Ft Seward per SO 232 AGO 1874 (intemperance & neglect of duty); recom'n by capt Weir to reenl in co D 4 June 1875 not appv by AGO;[33] enl as Melanchton H. Crussy 1 Dec 1875 St Louis Mo. for 5 yrs; ed qmd storekeeper St Louis Bks Feb & Mar 1876; join co G 7 cav 27 Apr 1876 St Paul Minn.; awol 30 Apr Ft Seward DT;[34] [dd May to Sep 1876];[35] ds camp Powder River MT 15 June 1876; cpl 9 July 1876; dd actg co qm sgt Oct 1876; dd post hq clerk Dec 1876; sgt 4 Jan 1877; tr to co H 8 Feb 1877; 1sgt 13 Feb 1877;[36] sgt 25 Jan 1878;

1sgt 22 Mar 1878; sgt 12 Dec 1878; pvt 4 Jan 1879; disch 30 Nov 1880 Ft Meade DT expir of serv a pvt & reenl in co H for 5 yrs; sgt 6 Sep 1881; pvt 13 Oct 1881; trump'r 1 Mar 1882; tr to co L 8 Aug 1882; pvt 31 Aug 1882; dd clerk adjt's office Feb 1883; cpl 7 Mar 1883; pvt 2 Aug 1883; in conft Dec 1883 to Mar 1884; sen gen cm 26 Jan 1884 forf $10 pay per mo for 6 mos; dd co clerk Aug 1884; disch 30 Nov 1885 at Ft Meade by expir of serv a pvt char xclt; died 3 June 1925 Hot Springs SD.
Pension: 24 June 1887 / Inv / 614292 / 1094897. (XC-2,507,183).

Kuehl, Jesse. Pvt co D; b. Los Angeles Calif.; enl 9 Oct 1875 St Louis Bks Mo. for 5 yrs; age 21; barber; brn eyes, brn hair, dk comp, 5' 7 1/2" high; join co D 21 Oct 1875 Ft Lincoln DT; ds camp Powder River MT 15 June 1876 guarding wagon train; des 27 Mar 1877 Ft Rice DT; apph 18 Feb 1878 at St Louis; tr to Ft Lincoln 5 Mar 1878 in conft awaiting trial; escaped 27 May 1878 & apph two days later near Cannonball River DT; dishon disch 29 June 1878 sen gen cm & 2 yrs conft mil prison; escaped from gd 17 July 1878 Ft Snelling Minn. while awaiting tr to Ft L'worth; enl as Jesse E. Williams 23 Feb 1884 Chicago Ill. for 5 yrs; assd to co H 23 inf; des 9 Apr 1885; apph 12 Nov 1885 Baltimore Md & delivered by city police to Ft McHenry; dishon disch 18 Jan 1886 sen gen cm & 4 yrs conft mil prison.[37]

Notes—K

1. Carroll, *The Yellowstone Expedition,* 59, 92.

2. Keegan's body was removed in May 1999 from Calvary Cemetery, Evanston Ill., to Fort Sheridan. *Chicago* (Ill.) *Sun-Times,* April 30, 1999.

3. NA, M1495, Roll 1, Morning Report, Escort Northern Boundary Survey, Maj. M. A. Reno, August 29, 1873, List of men on extra or daily duty and detached service.

When the 7th Cavalry camped near Hays City, Kans., 1869–70, Kellar reportedly stole cotton shirts from all the camp, in addition to handkerchiefs and shirts from a guest recently arrived from duty in the states and well supplied with new clothes contrasting to the campaigning outfits of the regiment's officers, and he seemed to have no moral idea of wrong regarding taking the shirts when Col. Weir spoke to him of it. In the first place he thought Weir would know nothing of it for the woman servant and Kellar took care of his money and bought everything for him; if he asked for money they gave just enough and withheld enough to keep him in necessary funds. They both wept when Weir remained out, fearing he was drunk. They growled about the sutler's store and followed his walking steps, ready to watch that no fall or accident happened to him. Emma came to Mrs. Custer to ask her to talk with him, E.B. Custer Coll., LBHB, Roll 4, Notes, "Kansas & Buffalo."; Emma was Captain Weir's servant; see letter of Captain Benteen to his wife, July 18, 1876, Carroll, *Camp Talk,* 42.

4. See note D26 (Diamond); GO 80, AGO, 1890, Section 4, provided that soldiers thus discharged were not entitled to travel allowances and could not reenlist for one year. RG 93, Entry 44.

5. *Brainerd Tribune,* July 15, 1876; *Bismarck Tribune,* March 22, and July 19, 1876; *New York Herald,* July 9 and 10, 1876; E. B. Custer, *Boots and Saddles,* 240–46.

6. Barnard, *I Go with Custer,* 107–109. In a letter to Whitelaw Reid of the *New York Tribune,* Feb. 26, 1876, Custer advised that if a special correspondent was sent, he should be someone accustomed to roughing it and should reach Fort Lincoln by 25th March., Cortissoz, *The Life of Whitelaw Reid,* 312.

While in New York in April, 1876, Custer visited the offices of the *Herald,* the editor recalling that it was privately arranged that Custer was in certain events to write of the expedition for the *Herald,* Clarke, *My Life and Memories,* 159.

7. Hammer, *Custer in '76,* 79, 231, 248; Barnard, *I Go with Custer,* 155–56, 161.

8. In December 1867, Capt. Keogh wrote to his brother Tom in Ireland that he had just received ten gallons of fine scotch whiskey, and Kelley was making a brew in his [Keogh's] sitting room. Keogh gave a taste of the scotch brew to his men at their troop dinner, much to the satisfaction of the Irish in it. Langellier, Cox, and Pohanka, eds., *Myles Keogh,* 129.

9. On June 10, 1867, Sgt. James Kelly packed a saddle from noon until retreat for visiting Fort McPherson without a pass after receiving permission from his 1st sergeant who was not aware of a pass

being necessary, the distance being not more than 1,000 yards. "Record of Events," Co. H Muster Roll, June 1867. RG 94, Entry 53.

10. RG 94, Entry 409, file 12027 A (EB) AGO 1876; Capt. McDougall recommended on Nov. 24, 1876 the discharge of Trumpeter Kelly for utter worthlessness, being a drawback to the company, and doing little or no service for the government.

11. Curiously, the Muster Rolls of Company F from May 1875 to Sept. 1876 do not include a trumpeter, nor explanation for the absence of such important personnel. RG 94, Entry 53. The omission especially noteworthy, given the "bandbox" reputation of the troop and its commander. However, with the regiment about to take the field, Private John Kelly, who had two years service as trumpeter, transferred to Troop F (from Troop E) May 1, 1876.

An identical situation occurred two years earlier in Troop E. Lt. McDougall, then commanding the troop, requested of the adjutant general's office on Sept. 22, 1874, for two trumpeters, stating that there was only one present and his term of service would expire shortly. In follow-up Jan. 13, 1875, McDougall wrote to Col. Sturgis, Superintendent of the General Mounted Recruiting Service at St. Louis, asking that his application for two trumpeters (approved Oct. 7) be filled as soon as possible; the discharge of the only one in the troop that morning, on expiration of service, had left the troop without a trumpeter at all, RG 393, Part V, Fort A. Lincoln.

12. Statement of Francis Johnson Kennedy, ca 1900, while a resident of St. Paul, to Olin D. Wheeler; copied in letter from Albert W. Johnson, Marine-on-St.Croix, Minn., to Theo. Goldin, May 4, 1933, Dustin Coll., (No. 435), LBHB, Roll 10.

13. Mary Jane Kenney died Sept. 29, 1909, at Philadelphia, Pa., age 69. In affidavits for pension in 1894, Mary J. Kenney said that when she married John Kenney, she was 14 years old and he was 23 years and six months. RG 15.

14. Chris Pandtle (Pendle) to Walter Camp July 14, 1919, WMC-BYU; Frank Berwald interview with Walter Camp, Oct. 11, 1912, WMC, notes, IU; Jacob Horner recalled that, during the march with the dismounted detachment from Fort Lincoln to Powder River, his two tent mates were, "Murphy and McKenny, both of whom survived the Bighorn battle, later fighting with him in the Nez Perce Campaign," Johnson, *Jacob Horner of the 7th Cavalry*, 9.

15. Lt. Hugh L. Scott transferred from Company E to Company I, Dec. 8, 1876, and commanded the troop until Feb. 10, 1877, when Capt. Nowlan returned. Lt. Scott was detached July 27 to command the escort for a wagon-train to Fort Custer. On his way back with one wagon, Aug. 6, near Porcupine Creek on the Yellowstone, Scott met Lt. DeRudio and Company E en route to Judith Gap with Lt. Doane, 2nd Cavalry, and his Crow scouts. Scott obtained permission for him and his orderly, McKenna, to join the detachment, who were maneuvering to harass advancing Nez Perce Indians, Scott, *Some Memories of a Soldier*, 44, 53–54; Bonney and Bonney, *Battle Drums and Geysers*, 71–73.

A few months later, Scott was sharing quarters with Lt. Hare at Fort Lincoln and mentioned that, "McKenna has the kitchen to sleep in . . ." Scott to his mother, Dec. 1, 1877, Gen. Hugh Lenox Scott, Papers, (hereafter cited as Scott Papers, LOC) Manuscript Division, Library of Congress, Washington, D.C.

16. William G. Hardy said McKenna was drowned while in some artillery regiment, Hardy to Walter Camp, March 9, 1910, WMC-BYU; John Kenney was interred in Evergreen Cemetery, Newport Ky., Dec. 19, 1888. Kenney's two sons (born in Gloucester, Mass.) also served in the 7th Cavalry; William J., with Companies K and A, 1881–86, later a mounted policeman in Washington D.C., (8th District) where he died Feb. 21, 1912, at age 52; and John M., with Company I, 1879–83, who served as senior noncommissioned officer with Lt. Garlington on the Greely Relief Expedition to Lady Franklin Bay, Greenland, in 1883. See Guttridge, *Ghosts of Cape Sabine,* 140.

Afterward, John M. Kenney joined the Washington police force, rising to commander of the 8th District in 1897. He died Feb. 8, 1954, at the veteran's hospital, Coatesville, Pa., age 92. Invalid pension claim 1.056.268, cert. 1.291.608 (XC-2,359,520); See also pension file for William J. Kenney; Invalid claim 1.171.875, cert. 918.942, RG 15.

A letter from Jack Kenney (formerly of I Troop, 7th Cav.), April 29, 1929, to Thomas Nesmith (Private Company B, 7th Cavalry, 1870–73), is mentioned in Meketa, *Luther Rector Hare,* 47 n.1; Kenney described his visit to Custer battle field several years earlier, when he sat down on the top of the ridge just behind the line of E Troop, and "cried like a kid" as he knelt down and said an Irish prayer for the souls of the men who died there. He had much praise for Lt. Hare, whom his father, mother, and brother loved.

17. GO 122, AGO, Dec. 23, 1870, reduced Companies A, B, C, and E of the battalion of engineers to 83 enlisted men each, and Company D to ten sergeants and ten privates; reductions made by discharging

such men as selected and by transfer from one company to another of such men who desired to remain in the service and considered suitable to it. RG 94, Entry 44.

18. ACP file, RG 94, Entry 297; in a letter to his brother Tom, Oct. 27, 1867, Keogh described Lt. Nowlan as about six years older than himself; Nowlan was born 1837, Taunton, "The Man Who Rode Comanche," 72.

19. Langellier, et al., *Myles Keogh,* 61–63, 82; Luce, *Keogh, Comanche, and Custer,* 14, 18.

20. Myles Keogh to brother Tom, March 27, 1868, Taunton, *"The Man Who Rode Comanche."*

21. See Taunton, "The Burial of Captain Myles Keogh."

22. Berwald interview with Walter Camp, n.d. Chris Pandtle to Walter Camp, July 14, 1919, WMC-BYU. In a letter to Mrs. Maria Dresser, mother of Sgt. Ogden, Nov. 27, 1876, in answer to her query, Kimm related that he buried her son near a large oak tree into which he cut his name, to be seen for fifty years, Original letter in private collection; copy at LBHB.

23. *Regulations for the Army, 1895,* par. 145, "Enlisted men who have served meritoriously twelve years or more, continuously or otherwise, will be classified as veteran soldiers. If it be for their material benefit, discharge may be granted them by the Secretary of War by way of favor as veterans. A soldier once discharged as a veteran will not be discharged again by way of favor." Par. 146: "Soldiers discharged as provided in paragraphs 144 and 145 will not receive travel allowance"; Kipp requested to be discharged at Columbus rather than in Manila or San Francisco, RG 94, Entry 25, file 322624 AGO 1900, filed with, 322041 AGO 1900.

24. Photo of Fremont Kipp in *Columbus* (Ohio) *Sunday Dispatch,* Feb. 17, 1907.

25. See Klawitter, "Army Life at Fort Lincoln."

26. Nick Klein was allegedly married Dec. 24, 1874, at Bismarck to Lucetta "Settie" Belle Craig (b. Ky., ca. 1856, sister of Fannie James, wife of John James). Settie reportedly left Klein and followed Tom Finnegan to St. Paul on his discharge in 1878. She later claimed that she and Klein separated in 1882 at Devil's Lake (Fort Totten), DT, and divorced at Bismarck. Records in St. Paul indicate proceedings were begun Mar. 28, 1883 but "Never completed." Klein remarried May 21, 1883, to Margaret Darmstadt, at Cleveland, Ohio.

Settie married in 1895 at Cromwell, Minn., to Civil War veteran, Harvey B. Gill (died 1909, Burnside, Ky.), and again about 1921 to James White at New Castle, Ind., where she died July 28, 1922 and was interred at Burnside, Ky., Pension files of Klein, Finnegan, and Gill, RG 15.

27. RG 393, Part V, Fort Rice, DT (Endorsement Book).

28. WMC, Notes, Unclassified, IU. Brininstool, *Troopers with Custer,* 51.

29. Mrs. Custer said, "There was a Swiss soldier in our regiment who had contrived to bring his zither with him. [Gen. Custer] would lie on the bear-skin rug in front of the fire and listen with delight as long as he ventured to tax the man. He played the native Tyrolese airs, which seemed to have caught in them the sound of the Alpine horn, the melody of the cascade, and the echo of mountain passes," E. B. Custer, *Boots and Saddles,* 206.

30. Three men of Knipe's troop thought the self-inflicted gunshot wound was for the purpose of getting out of the field. Reports of Capt. Jackson, July 11, Oct. 19, and Dec. 3, 1884, with affidavits of John Jordan, John Mahoney, and John McGuire, and reply from Gen. R. C. Drum, AG, USA, Knipe pension file; see also RG 94, Entry 410, file 5889.C.1884, RG 15.

31. Korn was reported in 1884 as a survivor of the Custer massacre, being in the first charge on the Indian camp when his horse was wounded in first fire, broke and ran, carrying Korn to Reno's camp before dropping dead from loss of blood, *Bismarck Tribune,* May 23, 1884; Korn's story was also in *The National Tribune* (Washington, DC), Jan. 15, 1891, typed copy in, WMC-BYU, Box 5.

Caddle said when Custer's command was about one-half mile from the Indian camp, Korn stopped to cinch up his saddle and when he caught up to the company, the horse would not stop but kept on going right through the Indians to within two or three rods of Maj. Reno's breastworks where it dropped dead from five bullet wounds. Korn did not get a scratch, Hanson, *The Conquest of the Missouri,* 381; also letter to Walter Camp from Caddle, Nov. 8, 1909, WMC-BYU.

William O. Taylor thought Caddle's story about Korn was outrageous, Taylor to Gen. Godfrey, Feb. 20, 1910, Godfrey Papers.

J. W. Burkett, a bunkie of Korn, 1876–79, said Korn's horse was a bolter or what was called a horse with a Roman nose. Korn could not keep his saddle from slipping forward and asked permission of Capt. Keogh to dismount and fix his saddle. After adjusting the saddle, the horse took the bit in his teeth and bolted to the command, where it turned around and made back tracks, Burkett to Walter Camp, July 12, 1912, WMC-DPL.

Henry Jones said when the packs ascended the hill they saw Korn coming toward them excited and his horse foaming at the mouth. Korn could hardly speak when he met his company packs. Sgt. DeLacy asked him how it was he left the troop, and Korn's voice trembled and seemed to choke when he said his horse ran away with him. DeLacy accused him of deserting the company and told him Capt. Keogh would prefer general charges against him. Korn had a fractious horse, hard mouthed and stubborn using no. 4 bit (largest size). Jones said Korn made a statement to a court at Fort Lincoln after the campaign but nothing official was ever released, Jones to Walter Camp, May 17, 1911, and June 2, 1911, WMC-BYU.

Gaffney said he never heard of Korn's statement to anyone at Lincoln after the campaign was over about escaping from Custer, Liddic and Harbaugh, *Camp on Custer*, 94. (Jones said Korn and Gaffney were warm friends. Jones to Camp, June 2, 1911).

Rooney said Korn came up after he (Rooney) got up with the packs. He asked him many questions but all he could say was "I don't know," Rooney interview with Walter Camp, nd, WMC-BYU.

Dennis Lynch said Korn's horse ran away from Custer across ford "B" and through the Uncpapa camp and up over Reno's battlefield and joined Reno on the hill. He was unhurt, thought the man's name was Herman or like name, and was nicknamed Yankee, Hammer, *Custer in '76*, 139.

Jeremiah Finley, (son of Sgt. Finley), born at Fort Lincoln Nov. 20, 1876, said Korn was called Yankee, *Fargo Forum*, Jan. 30, 1949.

William G. Hardy said "Yankee" Korn told him at the time that he rode through village past skirmish ground and up the bluffs, WMC, Notes, folder LBH II, IU.

Jacob Adams said just before the pack train came to Reno Hill, they halted back on low ground where a single horseman came toward them pretty fast; a white man about 45 years old, thick set, sandy hair with goatee and moustache; he said he thought they were fighting up ahead; said his horse ran away with him and he could not control him; he joined the pack train there, Hammer, *Custer in '76*, 121.

Four stories of Korn appeared in 1936 in *Winners of the West*, Vol. XIII, viz., No. 2, Jan. 30, 1936, 1, "Who Knew Gustave Korn of Troop I 7th US Cavalry in the Custer Fight," an account of the Custer battle printed on the back of a large photograph of Comanche signed by Korn, May 21, 1888, at Fort Meade DT; No. 3, Feb. 29, 1936, 3, "Another Custer Canard Narrative Alleged to Have Been Written by Gustave Korn, a Weird Yarn," letter from W. J. Ghent, Washington, D.C., telling many inaccuracies in the Korn story; No. 6, May 31, 1936, 1, "He knew Comrade Gustave Korn," letter from John McCollum, who was Korn's bunkie in 1873 and '74 during Northern Boundary Survey and in the same room at Fort Lincoln in 1875. He was well acquainted with his escape by his horse bolting and running, and talked with him after the fight and can say the account is correct by personal acquaintance; in the same issue, page 4, is, "'Yankee Korn' by Sergt. Geo. Lisk, Late Troop H, 5th U.S. Cavalry, 1877–1887. Lisk met Korn at Fort Riley in 1889. When Custer went into the fight June 25th, Korn was with Custer's command and was appointed orderly for Capt. Keogh.

"[Capt.] Keogh seems to have had some premoniscience of his coming fate for. . . [on] the day of the action sent a messenger back five miles to Capt. McDougall who was in charge of the pack train with the address of his sister Erin," Letter from Capt. Robert P. Hughes (of Gen. Terry's staff) to his wife, June 30, 1876, in Noyes, "A Look Back, Captain Robert P. Hughes."

Stan Roy thought Korn found Capt. Keogh's horse *Comanche* in the village opposite Custer's battlefield, but Ramsey also claimed that he did, and Roy thought Ramsey led the horse to the command June 28, but Korn was given full credit of it and was given the care of the horse until he died in 1892, Roy to Walter Camp, Nov. 10, 1909, WMC-BYU.

32. Fremont Kipp to Walter Camp, Jan. 3, 1922, WMC-BYU.

33. RG 94, Entry 467, file 1251 AGO (RB) 1875.

34. Regimental Return, April 1876. Krusee undoubtedly visited his family (wife, Mary, and children, Julia Dakota, two, and Arthur Wallace, nine mos.), at Fort Seward. In a remnant of a letter (n.d.) written by Krusee (to wife?) he refers to Lieut. Calhoun, "who you know well when he was at Fort Seward while I was at St. Louis." Harry Krusee Papers, (SC 1554), Montana Historical Society.

The train carrying Companies B, G, and K from St. Paul made a camp stop at Jamestown. (Johnson, *Jacob Horner of the 7th Cavalry*, 8). After getting out from Fargo a few miles [on NPRR] there was but one settlement until near Bismarck, and that was Jamestown, where passengers traveling each direction got dinner during regular operations. *Bismarck Tribune*, Nov. 13, 1875.

For a photo of Jamestown, 1876, with Fort Seward visible on hill, see "Licit Amusements of Enlisted Men in the Post-Civil War Army," by William A. Dobak, *Montana The Magazine of Western History*, Vol. 45, No. 2, Spring, 1995.

35. The troop duty books of (Acting 1st) Sgt. Botzer, and Sgt. Brown. Botzer did not list himself, nor Crussy, nor Northeg (sick May 2–21), in any of the Troop's four squads. Handwriting on Co. G muster roll, June, 1876, appears nearly identical to that of Krusee.

36. Capt. Benteen said he transferred Pvt. Helm to Co. G for Crussy. Benteen to wife, July 3, 1877. Carroll, *Camp Talk*, 81.

The wife of Sgt. Krusee (Crussy), was involved in a dispute with Mrs. Tapley at Fort Rice in 1877. See, Carroll, *Camp Talk*, 67, letter from Capt. Benteen, June 9, 1877.

37. RG 94, Entry 409, file 8929 B (EB) AGO 1885.

L

Laden, Jos. Pvt co G; b. Ireland; enl 18 Dec 1872 Pittsburgh Pa. for 5 yrs; age 23 4/12; pudler; gray eyes, brn hair, fair comp, 5' 8 1/2" high; join co G 12 Feb 1873 Newberry SC; sick hosp 2 May 1873 Yankton DT (tert. intm. fever); tr to str *Katie P. Kountz* 8 May 1873; sick Ft Randall DT 15 May to 27 June 1873 (typhoid fever); sent to Ft Rice DT 9 July 1873 to await return of co from Yellowstone Exp'n; dd co cook Apr 1874; dd post hosp nurse Dec 1875 to Apr 1876; sick Ft Lincoln DT 2–23 May 1876 (neuralgia); dd qmd laborer 24 May 1876; dd orderly to post comdr June 1876; sent with Lt Garlington on str *Josephine* 24 July 1876 to join co in field; ed qmd 13 Nov 1876 to 21 Apr 1877; ds Ft Lincoln 14 Oct 1877; cited by capt Benteen for conspic gal in two mtd chgs against Nez Perce inds at Canon Creek MT 13 Sep 1877; disch 18 Dec 1877 at Ft Lincoln expir of serv a pvt char very good; reenl 29 Dec 1877 Cincinnati Ohio for 5 yrs; join co A 6 inf 26 May 1878 Ft Rice DT; in conft Dec 1878; sen gen cm 27 Feb 1879 forf $10 pay per mo for 3 mos; des 25 Aug 1879 camp at edge of Bad Lands DT.

Lalor, Wm. Cpl co M; b. Jan 1839 Queens Co Ireland; enl 22 May 1866 Detroit Mich. for 3 yrs; age 26; tinsmith; blue eyes, brn hair, lt comp, 5' 9" high; join co E battn of engrs 28 May 1866 Jeff'n Bks Mo.; disch 22 May 1869 West Point N.Y. expir of serv an artf'r char xclt; reenl 29 Sep 1875 St Louis Bks Mo. for 5 yrs; age 30; laborer; join co M 7 cav 21 Oct 1875 Ft Rice DT; cpl 17 June 1876; sgt 1 Aug 1876; dd qmd chg post saw mill Dec 1876; ds with wagon train 30 Aug to 4 Sep 1877; dd actg co qm sgt Dec 1877; pvt 18 Jan 1878; dd co cook Feb 1878; dd regtl hq June 1878; dd co cook Oct 1878 thro' Feb 1879; dd laborer co garden Apr 1879; disch 28 Sep 1880 Ft Meade DT expir of serv a pvt char good; res Knockanina Montrath Queens Co Ireland in 1912.
Pension: 29 Dec 1911 / Inv / 1400729. (Rej on grd serv in engrs not dur Rebellion or Mexican War as required by act 6 Feb 1907).

Lamb, Jno. Pvt co A; b. Pulaski Ill.; enl 1 Oct 1875 St Louis Mo. for 5 yrs; age 23; laborer; blue eyes, brn hair, fair comp, 5' 7" high; join co A 21 Oct 1875 Ft Lincoln DT; sick hosp 5 Jan to 22 Mar 1876 (gsw index finger r. hand); des 15 May 1876 at Ft Lincoln.

Lambertine, Frank. Pvt co H; b. Kolin Germany; enl 27 Aug 1875 St Louis Bks Mo. for 5 yrs; age 23; musician; brn eyes, brn hair, ruddy comp, 5' 7" high; join 7 cav 21 Oct 1875 Ft Lincoln DT unassd rct attd to band; assd to co H 28 Apr 1876 & ds with band; sick at Ft Lincoln 17 May 1876 (intm. fever); dd band garden June to Aug 1876; dd with band to 26 Aug 1880 when disch at Ft Meade DT by expir of serv a pvt char fair; reenl 25 Sep 1880 Ft Sully DT for 5 yrs in band 11 inf; disch 24 Sep 1885 at Ft Sully expir of serv a pvt char xclt & reenl in same unit for 5 yrs; disch 24 Sep 1890 Madison Bks N.Y. expir of serv a pvt char good; reenl in same unit 29 Sep 1890 for 5 yrs; tr to co B 1 Mar 1895; disch 28 Sep 1895 Whipple Bks AT expir of serv a pvt; died 20 Oct 1913 Prescott Ariz.
Pension: 18 Feb 1927 / Wid / 1571180. (Rej on grd sol.'s death from cirrhosis of liver, contributory, excessive use of alcohol many yrs, not due to disability incurred in serv & line of duty).

Lamplough, Jno. Citizen packer qmd; b. England ca. 1830;[1] hired 16 May 1876 at Ft Lincoln DT by Lt Nowlan actg aqm to pack supplies on pub animals of exp'n;[2] rate of pay $50 mo; drove pack mules alongside wagon train dur march to Powder River; disch 23 Sep 1876 due $138.33 pay from 1 July; run over by freight wagon in early fall 1880 causing internal injuries & great suffering until death came to his relief 8 Feb 1881 at Brunsville MT.[3]

Lange, Henry. Pvt co E; b. 17 Dec 1851 Hanover Germany; enl 6 Jan 1872 Chicago Ill. for 5 yrs; age 21; laborer; gray eyes, lt hair, lt comp, 5' 8" high; join co E 5 Feb 1872 Unionville SC; ed qmd Nov & Dec 1872; [at

LBH in kitchen says Berwald; with pack train says O'Toole & Pandtle];[4] sen gar cm 15 Oct 1876 forf $10 pay & conft 20 days hard labor; abs in conft 16 Oct 1876 Ft Lincoln DT; ed hosp attdt 11 Nov 1876 to 6 Jan 1877 when disch at Ft Lincoln by expir of serv a pvt char good; died 1 May 1928 Chicago Ill.
Pension: 7 Sep 1909 / Inv / 1385778. (Rej on grd med exam'n found no evidence of disability of left hip). Ind. Surv. / 15464 / 8498.

Larned, Chas. Wm. 2Lt co F; b. 9 Mar 1850 New York N.Y.; grad USMA 15 June 1870 & appt 2Lt 3 cav (never joined);[5] tr to 7 cav 10 Oct 1870 & joined regt 23 Oct Ft L'worth Kans.; assd to co F 2 Nov 1870; awl on surg cert 27 June 1871 to 17 Feb 1872 (irregularity of heart & nervous prostration); actg aqm & comsy Taylor Bks (Louisville) Ky. Feb 1872 to Apr 1873; topographical engr regtl hq 4 Aug 1873 with Yellowstone Exp'n;[6] awl 7 days 27 Sep 1873 Chicago Ill.; awl ext'd 30 days 2 Oct & further ext'd 5 mos 24 Oct 1873; ds Wash'n D.C. 24 Dec 1873 sd with secy of war; appt asst prof of drawing USMA 28 Aug 1874; (prom 1Lt from 25 June 1876); appt prof of drawing USMA 25 July 1876 (revoking order to rejoin regt);[7] resd com'n in 7 cav 14 Aug 1876; appt prof & col USMA 28 June 1902 & pres't of academic bd; died 19 June 1911 Dansville N.Y.
[4714 ACP 1871].

Larock, Wm. H. Pvt co F; b. 14 Aug 1854 Rose N.Y.; enl 9 Feb 1872 Buffalo N.Y. for 5 yrs; age 21; laborer; hazel eyes, dk hair, fair comp, 5' 5 1/4" high; join co F 21 Feb 1872 Louisville Ky.; dd mail carrier Apr 1874; sick 2 Nov 1874 to 27 Apr 1875 (conjunctivitis); sick 28 May to 6 Sep 1875 (fistula lachrymalis); dd post bakery Apr to 14 May 1876; killed with Custer column 25 June 1876.
Pension: 11 June 1884 / Mother / 316528 / 220083.

Lasley, Wm. W. Pvt co K; b. 19 Nov 1842 St Louis Mo.; enl 17 Oct 1872 Kansas City Mo. for 5 yrs; age 29 11/12; farmer; blue eyes, blk hair, florid comp, 5' 9 1/2" high; join co K 9 Dec 1872 Yorkville SC; ds hq Yellowstone Exp'n 20 Aug 1873 care for unserviceable horses; ds co gardener Apr 1874; ds Ft Rice DT June to Sep 1874; ed subs dept Dec 1874 to Mar 1875; dd asst co cook June 1876; cpl 1 Aug 1876; in arrest Dec 1876; pvt 2 Jan 1877; disch 23 June 1877 camp on Sunday Creek MT per SO 70 Dept of Dak. 1877 a pvt char xclt; reenl 11 Jan 1879 at St Louis for 5 yrs; assd to co H 1 cav; disch 10 Jan 1884 Ft Walla Walla WT expir of serv a sgt char xclt; reenl in same co 21 Jan 1884 Chicago Ill. for 5 yrs; disch 20 Jan 1889 Ft Assiniboine MT expir of serv a pvt char very good; reenl 2 Feb 1889 at St Louis for 5 yrs; assd to co E 2 cav; disch 1 Feb 1894 Ft Huachuca AT expir of serv a cpl char xclt & reenl in same co for 5 yrs; disch 1 Feb 1899 Huntsville Ala expir of serv a 1sgt char xclt & reenl in same co for 3 yrs; disch 4 Nov 1899 Santa Clara Cuba by SO 251 AGO 1899 (to enter Sol. Home) a 1sgt char xclt; reenl in co E 2 cav 5 Jan 1901 Wash'n D.C. for 3 yrs; disch 4 Jan 1904 Gibraltar Spain upon expir of serv a 1sgt char xclt & reenl in same unit on US transport *Kilpatrick*; retd 3 May 1904 at Presidio San Francisco Calif. a 1sgt; died 2 July 1924 Sol. Home Wash'n D.C.
Pension: 17 Dec 1926 / Wid / 1564822. (Rej on grd clmt divorced from sol. & therefore no title to pension from his serv).

Lattman, Jno. Pvt co G; b. Zurich Switz; enl 4 Oct 1873 Phil'a Pa. for 5 yrs; age 25; laborer; gray eyes, auburn hair, ruddy comp, 5' 6 3/4" high; join co G 19 Oct 1873 Ft Lincoln DT; dd driver with art'y detmt Blk Hills Exp'n June 1874; left in timber dur retreat from valley fight 25 June 1876 & rejoin co on Reno hill; ds with ordn wagon 6 Aug to 26 Sep 1876;[8] dd qmd caring for horses at co stables 24 Sep 1876;[9] ds Ft Lincoln May to Nov 1877; ds Ft Lincoln co gardener July & Aug 1878; disch 4 Oct 1878 at Ft Lincoln expir of serv a pvt char xclt & reenl in co G for 5 yrs; ed nurse post hosp Aug 1879; dd co carpenter Apr 1880; ds Ft Meade DT co gardener June 1880; ed nurse post hosp Oct 1880 thro' Oct 1881; tr to co C 6 Nov 1881; dd co gardener Dec 1881 to Jan 1883; disch 3 Oct 1883 at Ft Meade expir of serv a pvt char xclt; died 7 Oct 1913 Rapid City SD.[10]

Lauper, Frank. Pvt co G; b. Montgomery Co Ohio; enl 7 Apr 1876 Cincinnati Ohio for 5 yrs; age 24; saddler; blue eyes, lt hair, lt comp, 5' 6 1/2" high; join co G 27 Apr 1876 St Paul Minn.; ds camp Powder River MT 15 June 1876; dd 1 Aug to 8 Sep 1876;[11] sad'r 1 Oct 1876; disch 6 Apr 1881 Ft Meade DT expir of serv a sad'r char xclt; reenl 2 May 1881 Cincinnati Ohio for 5 yrs; assd to co H 1 cav; sen gar cm 20 July 1882 forf $2.50 pay; des 26 July 1882 Ft Walla Walla WT.

Laurse, Chas. See Hardy, Wm. G.

Lawhorn, Thos. Pvt co H; b. Caldwell Co Ky.; enl in co C 7 cav 21 Apr 1870 Ft L'worth Kans. for 5 yrs; age 21; farmer; hazel eyes, dk hair, fair comp, 5' 6" high; in conft Dec 1872; dd hq Yellowstone Exp'n Sep 1873; dd qmd Feb to Apr 1874; sick hosp Ft Rice DT 13 Oct to 28 Nov 1874 (abscess); disch 21 Apr 1875 at Ft Rice expir of serv a pvt; reenl 12 May 1875 Yankton DT for 5 yrs in co H; dd qmd teamster Oct to Dec 1875;[12] dd qmd laborer Feb 1876; ed subs dept Nov & Dec 1876; des 7 Feb 1877 at Ft Rice.

Lawler, Jas. Pvt co G; b. Kildare Ireland; enl 21 Dec 1869 St Louis Mo. for 5 yrs; age 31; laborer; brn eyes, brn hair, dk comp, 5' 5 3/4" high; assd to co G 18 Feb 1870; sick Ft Harker Kans. 19 Feb to 10 July 1870 (rheum.); dd co cook Aug 1870; sick hosp Ft Lyon Colo. Ty 24 Jan 1871 (hoemoptysis); tr to qrs 13 Feb 1871; duty 5 Apr 1871; disch 21 Dec 1874 Shreveport La. expir of serv a pvt & reenl in co G for 5 yrs; ds Ft Lincoln DT 17 May 1876; dd post qmd June 1876; sent with Lt Garlington on str *Josephine* 24 July to join co in field; ds 24 Aug [to Ft Lincoln]; dd qmd 12 Sep with 281 cav horses at post; ds with gen Custer's horse 23 Sep 1876 to Monroe Mich.;[13] arr Ft Snelling Minn. 29 Sep on sd awaiting orders from dept hq; tr to co 4 Dec 1876;[14] far'r 12 Feb 1877; gsw (frac. skull) 13 Sep 1877 Canon Creek MT in action with Nez Perce inds; died 18 Sep 1877 in mackinaw boat on Yellowstone River enroute to Cant'mt Tongue River; buried at Terry's Landing (opposite mouth of Big Horn River).[15]

Lawless, Wm. Citizen packer qmd; b. Clare Ireland; enl 23 Aug 1852 Phil'a Pa. for 5 yrs; age 21; farmer; gray eyes, brn hair, ruddy comp, 5' 8 3/4" high; assd to co D 1 drg; disch 23 Aug 1857 Ft Buchanan NM expir of serv a pvt; reenl 4 Feb 1860 Ft L'worth Kans. for 5 yrs; age 27; assd to co H 2 inf; gsw l. hip 10 May 1864 battle of Spottsylvania Va.; disch 4 Feb 1865 post hosp Ft Columbus NYH upon expir of serv & gsw l. lumbar region, a pvt; (ball lodged against spine & was cut out at back bone, part of hip bone broken off; wd prevents walking long distance or lifting any weight; dis 1/2); res Wash'n D.C.; reenl 8 July 1867 Wash'n D.C. for 5 yrs; age 33; join co G 7 cav 10 Nov 1868 Camp Sandy Forsyth Kans.; in conft 22 Aug to 26 Nov 1869; in conft June 1870; disch 8 July 1872 Spartanburg SC expir of serv a pvt & reenl in co G for 5 yrs; cpl 1 Nov 1873; in arrest Dec 1873 & Feb 1874; pvt 12 Aug 1874 in conft; disch 26 Sep 1874 Ft Lincoln DT per SO 203 Dept of Dak. 1874 (for worthlessness); res St Paul Minn.; hired 1 Apr 1876 at St Paul by Lt Gibbs 6 inf actg aqm to pack supplies on pub animals of exp'n; rate of pay $50 mo & entitled to one ration per day & transp back to St Paul if hon disch; tr to Lt Nowlan at Ft Lincoln 17 Apr 1876 ;[16] drove pack mules alongside wagon train dur march to Powder River; disch 24 July due $40 pay from 1 July;[17] hired as teamster 17–21 Apr 1877 at Ft Lincoln by Lt Varnum rqm; rate of pay $30 mo; hired 1 June 1877 by Lt Varnum as teamster at $30 mo incr to $40 mo 1 Aug; disch 10 Nov 1877 due $163.33 from 1 July.

Pension: 12 Jan 1867 / Inv / 121020 / 135805. (Abandoned). App'd again 18 Nov 1874 / Inv / 197443 (consol with orig'l); deposed no mil serv since Feb 1865; med exam'n 5 May 1875 St Paul Minn. found wd interfered movement of hip & l. limb; dis 3/4; cert issued 14 Sep 1875; last paid 4 Mar 1876. Duplicate cert issued 11 Apr 1878; med exam'n 11 May 1879 Bismarck DT found disability impaired use of l. hip; last paid 4 Dec 1879; arrears 5 Feb 1865 to 17 Nov 1874 appv 20 Sep 1879 paid 6 Feb 1880; P. O. Stevensville MT.

Lee, Mark E. Pvt co I; b. Castine Me; enl 27 Sep 1875 Boston Mass. for 5 yrs; age 26; barber; gray eyes, brn hair, ruddy comp, 5' 8 1/4" high; join co I 21 Oct 1875 Ft Lincoln

DT; sick on str *Far West* 22 June 1876;[18] ed hosp attdt 1 July to 10 Aug 1876;[19] arr Ft Lincoln 6 Aug on str *Carroll*;[20] dd post hq Aug 1876; dd qmd 15 Sep 1876 care for pub animals; cpl 6 Jan 1877; sgt 23 July 1877; sick hosp Ft Ellis MT 1 Sep thro' Oct 1877 (sunstroke); sick Ft Lincoln 13 Feb to 15 Mar 1878 (abscess, effects venereal disease); dd post qmd actg intrpr for Cheyenne ind pris'rs Apr to July 1878; sick hosp 15 July 1878 (sunstroke); disch 19 Aug 1878 at Ft Lincoln on surg cert dis a sgt char good (epilepsy dating back nearly 2 yrs but paroxisms now occur almost daily; dis total; res Woburn Mass.); enl as Jas. Burk 20 Dec 1878 Ft Snelling Minn. for 5 yrs in co C 7 inf; tr to co E 20 Jan 1879; in conft 26 June 1879; sick hosp Ft Snelling 10 July 1879 & des next day; apph 9 Aug 1879 at St Paul; dishon disch 8 Sep 1879 sen gen cm & 2 yrs conft mil prison Ft L'worth Kans.; reenl as Jas. Burk 3 May 1881 St Louis Mo. for 5 yrs; assd to co M 6 cav; disch 2 Oct 1881 Camp Thomas AT on surg cert dis (epilepsy) a pvt char fair; reenl as Mark E. Lee 6 July 1882 Boston Mass. for 5 yrs; assd to gen mtd serv Jeff'n Bks Mo.; prior mil history revealed 15 Sep 1882 when he appd for instr'n as school teacher; disch 13 Oct 1882 per SO 134 AGO 1882 (fraud't enlmt).

Lefler, Meig. Pvt co F; b. 10 Mar 1846 Baden Germany; enl 2 Nov 1868 Cincinnati Ohio for 3 yrs; age 22; farmer; gray eyes, brn hair, florid comp, 5' 6 1/4" high; assd to co C 5 art'y; disch 2 Nov 1871 Ft Monroe Va. expir of serv a pvt char good; reenl 25 Nov 1871 at Cincinnati for 5 yrs; join co F 7 cav 1 Dec 1872 Louisville Ky.; dd hq Blk Hills Exp'n 25 June to 31 Aug 1874; dd co cook Apr 1876; [with pack train says himself, Gregg & Rooney; doubtful with packs says Lynch];[21] dd battn hq Aug 1876; dd regtl hq Oct 1876; disch 25 Nov 1876 Ft Abercrombie DT expir of serv a pvt char xclt; reenl 6 Dec 1876 Chicago Ill. for 5 yrs; join co A 7 cav 20 Nov 1878 Ft Lincoln DT; dd co carpenter Dec 1878 to May 1879; in conft Aug 1879; sen gen cm 14 Oct 1879 forf $10 pay per mo for 4 mos; ed qmd carpenter Dec 1879 to June 1880; dd co cook Aug 1880; ed qmd laborer Oct 1880 to Apr 1881; cpl 21 Mar 1881; sgt 8 Sep 1881; disch 5 Dec 1881 Ft Meade DT expir of serv a sgt char xclt; reenl 29 Dec 1881 Baltimore Md for 5 yrs; assd to co M 4 cav; disch 28 Dec 1886 Ft McDowell AT expir of serv a cpl char xclt; reenl 7 Jan 1887 Jeff'n Bks Mo. for 5 yrs; assd to co D 4 cav; disch 6 Jan 1892 Ft Walla Walla Wash'n expir of serv a far'r char xclt & reenl in same co for 5 yrs; disch 6 Jan 1897 at Ft Walla Walla expir of serv a pvt char xclt & reenl in same co for 3 yrs; retd 17 Mar 1899 Ft Yellowstone Wyo. a pvt; res San Francisco Calif. died 21 July 1910 army & navy hosp Hot Springs Ark.[22]

Lehman, Fred'k. Pvt co I; b. Berne Switz; enl in 7 cav 17 Oct 1871 Louisville Ky. for 5 yrs; age 23; upholsterer; blue eyes, lt hair, fair comp, 5' 7 1/2" high; assd to co I at Shelbyville Ky.; killed with Custer column 25 June 1876.

Lehmann, Henry. Pvt co I; b. Berlin Prussia; enl 11 Nov 1872 New York N.Y. for 5 yrs; age 33; confectioner; brn eyes, dk hair, fair comp, 5' 4" high; join co I 1 Dec 1872 Shelbyville Ky.; dd co cook Aug 1873; killed with Custer column 25 June 1876.

Lell, Geo. Cpl co H; b. Hamilton Co Ohio; enl 18 Sep 1873 Cincinnati Ohio for 5 yrs; age 26; gas fitter; blue eyes, dk hair, dk comp, 5' 9" high; join co H 20 Oct 1873 Ft Rice DT; cpl 9 Mar 1876; gsw abdomen 26 June 1876 on Reno hill (bullet entered l. side & exited r. side; died same day).[23]

Lepper, Fred'k. Pvt co L; b. Hamilton Co Ohio; enl 12 Nov 1872 Cincinnati Ohio for 5 yrs; age 23; carriage painter; hazel eyes, brn hair, fair comp, 5' 7 3/4" high; join co L 9 Dec 1872 Yorkville SC; dd qmd painter Sep & Oct 1874; dd qmd painter June 1875; ed qmd painter Nov 1875 to Mar 1876; sick qrs [wagon] 27 May to 13 June 1876 (abscess palm r. hand); abs sick camp Powder River MT 10 June; ds Ft Lincoln DT 17 Oct 1876 chg co prop; ds Ft Lincoln 15 Oct 1877; disch 12 Nov 1877 at Ft Lincoln expir of serv a pvt char xclt.

Lewis, David W. Pvt co B; b. St Louis Mo.; enl in co B 13 July 1875 Shreveport La. for 5

yrs; age 21 6/12; laborer; gray eyes, blk hair, florid comp, 5' 10" high; des 29 Mar 1876 at Shreveport (with pvt Abos); surd 26 Apr 1876 Ft Barancas Fla; sen gen cm 29 May 1876 to dishon disch & one yr conft mil prison, but sen disappv for informality (insufficient evidence) & ret to duty; ds St Louis Bks Mo. 22 Aug 1876 await transp to regt; rejoin co 26 Sep 1876 Ft Lincoln DT; sd with Lt Hare's sec. of parrott guns 8 Oct to 12 Nov 1876; cpl 11 Dec 1878; actg co qm sgt Feb 1879; sgt 6 May 1879; disch 12 July 1880 Camp Houston DT expir of serv a sgt char xclt; enl in marine corps 12 Aug 1880 Brooklyn N.Y. navy yard for 5 yrs; served on str *Quinnebaug*; disch 11 Aug 1885 at Brooklyn; died 30 Dec 1914 Wash'n D.C. govt hosp for insane.
Pension: 8 Nov 1893 / Inv / 1154144 / 886342.

Lewis, Jno. Pvt co C; b. Perry Co Pa.; enl 11 Dec 1867 Carlisle Pa. for 5 yrs; age 21; laborer; gray eyes, brn hair, fair comp, 5' 5" high; assd to co C 18 Jan 1868; ds Ft L'worth Kans. from 5 Feb 1868; join co C July 1868 Ft Lyon Colo. Ty; disch 11 Dec 1872 Charlotte NC expir of serv a pvt; reenl same day in co C for 5 yrs a trump'r; on furl 20 days 14 Dec 1872; pvt 10 Oct 1875; dd qmd Oct 1875; dd co cook Feb & Apr 1876; killed with Custer column 25 June 1876.

Lewis, Uriah S. Pvt co D; b. Montgomery Co Pa.; enl 18 Aug 1873 Phil'a Pa. for 5 yrs; age 21; painter; blue eyes, brn hair, fair comp, 5' 10" high; join co D 22 Oct 1873 Ft Totten DT; ds Ft Seward DT 14 May 1874; ds Ft Lincoln DT 1 July 1874 await return of co from field; sent to Ft Totten 7 Aug 1874 chg of govt horses; ed qmd Dec 1874; in conft Nov 1875 to Jan 1876; (struck 1sgt Martin with his fist); sen gen cm to dishon disch & 3 yrs conft mil prison but restored to duty when his statements neutralized a guilty plea & divested his acts of all criminality; sick 19 Mar to 2 Apr 1876 (infl. testicle); ds camp Powder River MT 15 June 1876 with band; ds str *Josephine* 6 Aug 1876 to Ft Lincoln with band; gsw r. leg 30 Sep 1877 Snake Creek MT (Bear's Paw Mtns) in action with Nez Perce inds; tr to str *Silver City* 14 Oct mouth of Squaw Creek (on Mo. River); sick hosp Ft Rice DT 26 Oct to 20 Nov 1877; disch 18 Aug 1878 Camp J. G. Sturgis DT expir of serv a pvt char xclt; res Gwynedd Pa.
Pension: 16 Jan 1900 / Inv / 1242716. (Rej on grd no ratable disability from gsw r. leg).

Liddiard, Herod T. Pvt co E; b. London England; enl 4 Dec 1872 Troy N.Y. for 5 yrs; age 21; boatman; blue eyes, lt hair, fair comp, 5' 5 1/4" high; join co E 13 Feb 1873 Unionville SC; abs sick on str *Western* 23 Apr 1873 Yankton to Ft Rice DT; abs sick May 1873; pres sick in qrs June 1873; abs conft 29 Aug 1873; dd driver with art'y detmt June 1874 Blk Hills Exp'n; in conft Feb 1875; sen gen cm Apr 1875 forf $5 pay; sick Ft Randall DT June 1875; gsw abdomen 25 June 1876 (bullet entered in front & exited near spine) while unpacking mules on Reno hill; died 27 June 1876.[24]

Lieberman, Andrew. Pvt co K; b. Wurtemburg Germany; enl 3 Nov 1875 at Cincinnati Ohio for 5 yrs; age 28; tailor; brn eyes, blk hair, dk comp, 5' 5 3/4" high; join co K 20 Dec 1875 Colfax La.; des 25 May 1876 Ft Lincoln DT.

Liemann, Werner L. Pvt co F; b. Bremen Germany; enl 30 Jan 1872 New York N.Y. for 5 yrs; age 30; painter; blue eyes, brn hair, lt comp, 5' 5" high; join co F 1 Dec 1872 Louisville Ky.; ed post qmd Dec 1872 & Feb 1873; dd co cook June 1874; killed with Custer column 25 June 1876.

Littlefield, Jno. L. Pvt co B; b. Portland Me; enl 28 Mar 1876 Boston Mass. for 5 yrs; age 24; drummer; blue eyes, brn hair, fair comp, 5' 10" high; join co B 27 Apr 1876 St Paul Minn.; ds camp Powder River MT 10 June 1876; des 7 July [with Bonner & Williamson], taking two mules & one horse; apph 13 July near Ft Lincoln DT in starving cond'n; escaped from conft 29 Oct but apph same date near Ft Rice DT; rel from conft 13 Dec 1876 by verbal order regtl hq (forf all pay due until apph) & assd to band; ds Ft Rice 2 Jan 1877 witness in court martial; des 22 Jan 1877 at Ft Lincoln.[25]

Lloyd, Edw. Wm. Pvt co I; b. Gloucester England; enl 30 Sep 1873 Pittsburgh Pa. for 5 yrs; age 21; engineer; gray eyes, lt brn hair, fair comp, 5' 6" high; join co I 22 Oct 1873 Ft Totten DT; killed with Custer column 25 June 1876.[26]

Lloyd, Frank Jno. Sgt co G; b. London England; enl 12 Feb 1872 Chicago Ill. for 5 yrs; age 23; clerk; gray eyes, brn hair, fair comp, 5' 6" high; join co G 26 Feb 1872 Spartanburg SC; cpl 27 July 1875; actg co qm sgt Apr 1876; sgt 3 May 1876; actg post sgt-maj Ft Lincoln DT 17 May to 4 Nov 1876; actg co qm sgt Dec 1876; disch 12 Feb 1877 at Ft Lincoln expir of serv a sgt char xclt; reenl 2 Mar 1877 Wash'n D.C. for 5 yrs in co L 2 art'y; disch 28 Aug 1881 McPherson Bks Ga. on surg cert dis (chr. diar; dis total) a 1sgt; died 23 Feb 1912 Liverpool England.
Pension: 24 Oct 1881 / Inv / 432875 / 218187.

Lobering, Louis. Pvt co L; b. Hanover Germany; enl 20 Apr 1867 New York N.Y. for 3 yrs; age 32 3/12; soldier; blue eyes, brn hair, ruddy comp, 5' 6 3/4" high; join co H 37 inf Aug 1867 Ft Union NM; ds regtl hq Oct 1867 to Apr 1869 when tr to co F; (co consol with 3 inf Aug 1869); ds with regtl band from 13 Oct 1869; disch 20 Apr 1870 Ft Dodge Kans. by expir of serv a pvt; reenl 19 May 1870 Ft L'worth Kans. for 5 yrs in band 7 cav; disch 19 May 1875 Ft Lincoln DT expir of serv a pvt & reenl for 5 yrs in co L; on furl 4 mos 21 May 1875 to Germany; ds Ft Lincoln with regtl band 22 Oct 1875; tr to band revoked 17 Dec 1875; killed with Custer column 25 June 1876.

Loeser, Christian. Citizen packer qmd; b. 31 Oct 1843 Phil'a Pa.; pvt co G 106 Pa. inf 14 Aug 1861 to 10 Sep 1864; (awol 1 July 1862 to 22 Jan 1864); enl reg army 31 Oct 1865 at Phil'a for 3 yrs; age 22; miller; gray eyes, lt hair, fair comp, 5' 11 1/2" high; join co M 1 cav 18 Nov 1865; disch 31 Oct 1868 Camp Lyon Idaho Ty expir of serv a pvt; reenl 13 Dec 1869 at Phil'a for 5 yrs; join co H 3 cav 30 Sep 1870; in hosp 13 Apr 1873 (struck on head with iron bar in row); disch 14 July 1873 Ft D. A. Russell Wyo. Ty on surg cert dis (constant dizziness after severe beating) a blks; reenl 29 Sep 1873 at Phil'a for 5 yrs; join co A 7 cav 14 Mar 1875 Livingston Ala; cpl 26 June 1875; disch 27 Dec 1875 Ft Lincoln DT per SO 254 AGO 1875 (upon own appn [& recom'n Hon. Sam'l Randall, House of Reps] wanting to be in Phil'a on very urgent business next spring]); hired 26 Mar 1876 at Ft Lincoln by Lt Nowlan as asst packer to pack supplies on pub animals of exp'n; rate of pay $50 mo;, drove pack mules alongside wagon train dur march to Powder River;[27] disch 24 July due $40 pay from 1 July;[28] hired 27 Oct 1876 by Lt Randall 5 inf actg aqm Cant'mt Tongue River as packer in chg of pack train; rate of pay $100 mo; asst wagon master 23 Jan to 8 Feb 1877 at $60 mo; hired as teamster 15 Apr 1877 by Lt Baldwin 5 inf actg aqm in field; rate of pay $30 mo; tr 30 Apr to Lt Randall at Cant'mt Tongue River; disch 4 May 1877 & hired next day as packer at $75 mo with pack train;[29] died 17 Apr 1921 Bridgewater Pa.
Pension: 4 Dec 1906 / Inv / 1354516 / 1133978. (XC-2,487,021).

Logue, Wm. J. Pvt co L; b. 4 July 1841 New York N.Y.; pvt co C 2 N.Y. cav 9 Aug 1861 to 23 June 1865; enl reg army 2 Dec 1867 New York N.Y. for 5 yrs; age 23; carpenter; gray eyes, lt brn hair, fair comp, 5' 10" high; join co K 7 cav 22 Jan 1868 Ft L'worth Kans.; cpl 8 Apr 1868; pvt 1 June 1868; cpl 25 Dec 1868; sgt 26 Jan 1870; in conft Dec 1870; pvt 17 Jan 1871 sen gen cm & forf $10 pay per mo for 2 mos & conft same period; in conft June 1871; sen gen cm 24 July 1871 forf $8 pay per mo for 8 mos & conft same period; in conft June & Aug 1872; disch 2 Dec 1872 Yorkville SC expir of serv a pvt; reenl 7 Apr 1873 Cairo Ill. for 5 yrs in co L 7 cav; ed qmd carpenter Oct 1873; dd qmd carpenter Sep & Oct 1874; in conft Nov & Dec 1874; sen gen cm 21 Jan 1875 forf $10 pay per mo for 4 mos & conft same period; dd post hq June 1875; with pack train 25 June 1876;[30] cpl 1 Aug 1876; sgt 28 Sep 1876; pvt 4 May 1877; ds in field 26 Oct 1877; dd prov gd Feb 1878; disch 7 Apr 1878 Ft Lincoln DT expir of serv a pvt char good; reenl in co L 4 Dec 1878 at Ft Lincoln for 5 yrs; dd qmd carpenter Feb 1879; wag 1 Apr 1879; in conft Dec 1879; pvt 15 July 1880; in conft Oct 1880; in conft Feb 1881; sen gen cm 4 Feb 1881 forf $12

pay; in conft Dec 1881; dd stable police Feb 1882; disch 3 Dec 1883 Ft Buford DT expir of serv a pvt; reenl 1 Jan 1884 at Ft Buford for 5 yrs in co H 11 inf; disch 30 Nov 1884 at Ft Buford on surg cert dis (accdt gsw r. foot & loss of great toe) a pvt; died 25 June 1919 Sol. Home Wash'n D.C.[31]
Pension: 13 May 1885 / Inv / 539919 / 304983.

Lombardy, Francesco K. Pvt band; b. 28 Oct 1848 Naples Italy; enl for 7 cav band 22 Sep 1871 Meridian Miss for 5 yrs; age 22; musician; dk eyes, blk hair, dk comp, 5' 3" high; abs sick Ft Lincoln DT 3 May to 4 June 1876 (sprain r. ankle); dd post qmd laborer 20 May 1876; dd band garden June to Aug 1876; disch 22 Sep 1876 at Ft Lincoln expir of serv a pvt char very good; reenl 17 Mar 1877 Omaha Bks Neb for 5 yrs; assd to band 11 inf; tr to gen serv Dept of the Platte 18 Apr 1879; tr to co M 5 cav 6 Sep 1879; disch 16 Mar 1882 Ft Robinson Neb a trump'r char very good; reenl 18 Mar 1884 San Francisco Calif. for 5 yrs; assd to co H 1 art'y; tr to band 1 inf 10 Jan 1887; disch 17 Mar 1889 Alcatraz Isl Calif. expir of serv a pvt char xclt; reenl 18 Mar 1889 at San Francisco for 5 yrs; assd to band 5 inf; disch 30 Jan 1891 Ft Bliss Tex. by SO 19 AGO 1891 a pvt char xclt; reenl 12 Nov 1894 at Ft Bliss for 3 yrs in band 18 inf; disch 11 Nov 1897 at Ft Bliss expir of serv a pvt char xclt & reenl in same unit for 3 yrs; disch 11 Nov 1900 Cupiz PI expir of serv a cpl char xclt & reenl in same unit for 3 yrs; tr to co A 6 inf 25 Aug 1901; tr to co C 22 Nov 1901; tr to co D 29 inf 14 May 1902; tr to co L 11 Sep 1902; retd 15 July 1903 at Ft Bliss a 1sgt char xclt; died 21 June 1917 San Diego Calif.
Pension: 27 Feb 1918 / Ind. Wid / 1116041 / 8980.

Lord, Geo. Edwin. Asst surg; b. 17 Feb 1846 Boston Mass. (son of Robt Lord a soldier lost in Mexican War); adopted with bro Thos. W., by uncle Rev. Thos. N. Lord of West Auburn Me;[32] grad Bowdoin College Brunswick Me in 1866 & Chicago Medical College in Mar 1871, serving one term as house physician & surg of Mercy Hosp; entered mil contr 28 Apr 1871 as actg asst surg in Dept of Dak.; served at Ft Ripley & Ft Randall to Nov 1873 & with escort for NBS June to Sep 1874; entered into new contr 15 Jan 1875 at Ft Snelling Minn.; ds Yellow Medicine Co in Mar 1875 with gov't relief for farmers suffering grasshopper plague; arr Ft Lincoln DT 20 May 1875 for duty with Blk Hills Exp'n but assd td at post; prom asst surg (1Lt) 26 June 1875; td asst post surg at Ft Snelling 25 July 1875; appt post surg Ft Buford DT 18 Aug 1875; accomp battn 6 inf (cos CDI) on str *Josephine* 14 May 1876 & joined gen Terry's exp'n on Yellowstone; attd to 7 cav as chf med officer 15 June mouth of Powder River & given horse & equipment of Dr. Clark;[33] killed with Custer column 25 June 1876.
[3231 ACP 1875].

Lorentz, Geo. Gustav. Pvt co M; b. 30 Sep 1851 Holstein Germany; enl 13 Nov 1872 St Louis Mo. for 5 yrs; age 21; painter; gray eyes, dk brn hair, fair comp, 5' 6 3/4" high; join co M 9 Dec 1872 Unionville SC; ed post hosp cook Oct 1874 to May 1875; killed in valley fight 25 June 1876.
Pension: 25 July 1877 / Mother / 232467 / 186080.

Lossee, Wm. A. Pvt co F; b. Brewster Sta N.Y.; enl 24 Sep 1875 New York N.Y. for 5 yrs; age 26; showman; gray eyes, lt hair, ruddy comp, 5' 5 1/2" high; join co F 21 Oct 1875 Ft Lincoln DT; killed with Custer column 25 June 1876.

Lovett, Meredith. Pvt co C; b. Delaware Co Pa.; enl 16 Aug 1873 Phil'a Pa. for 5 yrs; age 21; laborer; blue eyes, dk hair, ruddy comp, 5' 7 3/4" high; join co C 21 Oct 1873 Ft Rice DT; dd subs dept herder Oct 1874 to Mar 1875; des 14 Apr 1875 at Ft Rice; apph 7 May 1875 Fargo DT; sen gen cm 29 June 1875 to 2 yrs confi at sta of co & dishon disch; dishon disch 26 Mar 1877 Ft Totten DT.[34]

Loyd, Geo. Pvt co G; b. Tyrone Ireland; enl 17 Mar 1866 Phil'a Pa. for 3 yrs; age 23; soldier; gray eyes, lt hair, ruddy comp, 5' 9" high; assd to 6 cav 31 July 1866 & ds regtl hq Austin Tex.; join co I 13 Oct 1866 Jacksboro Tex.; ds escort for col Sturgis to San Antonio Tex. Apr 1868; cpl 1 Sep 1868; disch 20 Mar 1869 Canton Tex. expir of serv a cpl & reenl in same co for 5 yrs;

sgt 20 Apr 1869; in arrest Dec 1869; in arrest Dec 1871; sen gen cm Jan 1872 forf $5 pay per mo for 6 mos; 1sgt 1 July 1872; sgt 17 Jan 1873; pvt 8 Mar 73; disch 21 Mar 1874 Camp Supply IT expir of serv a pvt; reenl 13 Apr 1874 St Louis Mo. for 5 yrs; join co G 7 cav 27 Apr 1876 St Paul Minn.; (horse killed at LBH);[35] cpl 9 July 1876; ds dept hq in field 6 Aug to 17 Sep 1876;[36] sgt 13 Feb 1877; cited by capt Benteen for conspic gal in two mtd chgs against Nez Perce inds at Canon Creek MT 13 Sep 1877; disch 12 Apr 1879 Ft Lincoln DT expir of serv a sgt char xclt & reenl in co G for 5 yrs; on furl 25 days 14 Apr 1879 St Paul Minn.; ds repairing mil tel line Oct 1879; dd actg 1sgt Oct 1881; 1sgt 1 Dec 1881; pvt 13 Nov 1882; tr to co I 31 Jan 1883; cpl 22 Feb 1884; disch 12 Apr 1884 Ft Totten DT expir of serv a cpl char very good; reenl in co I 15 Apr 1884 for 5 yrs; cpl 26 Apr 1884; sgt 15 Jan 1885; dd post prov sgt Dec 1886; dd instr rcts Dec 1887; disch 14 Apr 1889 Ft Riley Kans. expir of serv a sgt char xclt & reenl in co I for 5 yrs; on furl 60 days 28 May 1889 NYC; gsw r. lung 29 Dec 1890 Wounded Knee Creek SD in action with Sioux inds; sick hosp Pine Ridge SD to 26 Jan 1891 & hosp Ft Riley to 8 Apr 1891; sick qrs to 31 May 1891; (awarded medal of honor 16 Apr 1891 for bravery especially after being severely wd thro' lung at battle of Wounded Knee); 1sgt 4 Aug 1891; sick hosp 12 Sep to 22 Oct 1892; died 17 Dec 1892 at Ft Riley (gsw forehead, suicide).

Lynch, Dennis. Pvt co F; b. 22 Feb 1846 Cumberland Md; enl 3 Aug 1866 Wash'n D.C. for 5 yrs; age 19; boatman; gray eyes, brn hair, dk comp, 5' 5 1/4" high; join co F 10 Sep 1866 Ft Riley Kans.; dd bldg co qrs Oct 1866; dd qmd laborer Nov 1866; with escort for ind peace com'n Apr & May 1868; dd regtl hq Apr 1869; disch 3 Aug 1871 Louisville Ky. expir of serv a pvt & reenl in co F for 5 yrs; ds herding co horses Aug 1872; ds Ft Rice DT June to Sep 1873 gd regtl prop; dd qmd teamster Dec 1873 to Apr 1874; dd qmd teamster Blk Hills Exp'n Aug 1874; dd qmd teamster Oct 1874 to Apr 1875; sick Ft Lincoln DT 13–20 Apr 1876 (boil); dd regtl hq fatigue pty (morn & eve) 11 May 1876; ds str *Far West* 22 June 1876;[37] disch 3 Aug 1876 camp mouth Rosebud Creek MT expir of serv a pvt char xclt; (hired as herder in subs dept 1 Aug to 5 Sep; rate of pay $60 mo);[38] reenl in co F 2 Sep 1876 at Ft Lincoln for 5 yrs; dd qmd 12–28 Sep 1876 with 281 cav horses at post; dd regtl hq mtd msgr 30 Oct 1876; ds on Missouri River 14 Oct 1877 gd on mackinaw boat; dd qmd teamster Apr 1878 thro' Apr 1880; disch 1 Sep 1881 Camp Biddle MT expir of serv a pvt char xclt; died 13 Oct 1933 Sol. Home Wash'n D.C.
Pension: 18 Aug 1883 / Inv / 493007 / 263334. Ind. Surv. / 15465 / 8445.

Lynch, Pat'k. Pvt co I; b. Carrigaholt Co Clare Ireland; enl 16 Oct 1872 Toledo Ohio for 5 yrs; age 21; laborer; blue eyes, auburn hair, lt comp, 5' 6 1/2" high; join co I 2 Dec 1872 Shelbyville Ky.; dd co cook Oct 1873; dd dept hq in field May to Sep 1876;[39] cpl 1 Oct 1876; ds Ft Lincoln 16 Oct 1876 chg co prop; sgt 10 Jan 1877; disch 14 July 1877 Tongue River MT per SO 70 Dept of Dak. 1877 a sgt char xclt; arrested Dec 1881 at his saloon at Point Pleasant (across river from Ft Lincoln) for buying stolen govt cigars;[40] res Douglas City Alaska in 1901.[41]

Lyons, Bernard. Pvt co F; b. Galway Ireland; enl 6 Sep 1875 Boston Mass. for 5 yrs; age 26; clerk; blue eyes, brn hair, fair comp, 5' 6 1/8" high; join co F 21 Oct 1875 Ft Lincoln DT; in conft Feb to Apr 1876 (acquited in gen cm); ed post bakery 27 Apr to 14 May 1876; [with wagon train says Rooney; with pack train said Lynch; at Ft Lincoln says Pickard];[42] dd post bakery 14 Dec 1876 to 6 Feb 1877; sen gen cm 5 Apr 1877 forf $10 pay per mo for 2 mos (conft 20 days remitted); arr Ft Lincoln 30 Dec 1877; sick hosp (alcoholism) 9 Jan to 6 Feb 1878 sent to co at Ft Totten DT; disch 30 Mar 1878 on surg cert dis (chr. alcoholism); unfit for duty 58 days last 2 mos; never has been since enlmt & never will be fit for a soldier; cannot make effective use of his carbine; utter prostration of nervous system from excessive use alcoholic stimulants; origin prior to enlmt; not entitled to pension.

Lyons, Daniel. Pvt co K; b. Brooklyn N.Y.; enl 4 Apr 1876 St Louis Bks Mo. for 5 yrs; age 23; blacksmith; hazel eyes, blk hair, fair comp, 5' 9 1/2" high; join co K 27 Apr 1876 St Paul Minn.; ds camp Powder River MT 15 June 1876; blks 1 Aug 1876; sick hosp 8 Dec 1876 to 22 Jan 1877 (ac. bronc.); sick 30 Apr 1877 (fistula [excused from riding]) tr on str *Far West* to Ft Buford DT; duty May 1877; wd r. thigh [sl.] 30 Sep 1877 Snake Creek MT (Bear's Paw Mtns) in action with Nez Perce inds; ret to duty; disch 9 Apr 1878 Ft Rice DT on surg cert dis a blks char xclt; (unhealed fistula which split up more than a yr ago; went into field last summer & returned with track of fistula still open indurated; treatment unsuccessful; dis 1/2; contr line of duty).

Notes—L

1. John Lamplough, age 40, laborer, born in England, resided Sauk Centre, Minn., with Mr. and Mrs. S. L. Winters, federal census, July 5, 1870, Stearns County, Minn.

2. Lamplough was probably hired to replace A. A. Robinson, a packer discharged May 15.

3. *Bismarck Tribune*, Mar. 18, 1881. During work on the Northern Pacific Railroad extension, the town at Cedar Creek on the Yellowstone was a thriving little place. A large general merchandise store there was run by Bruns & Co., and saloons were well represented being about twelve in number and a hotel did a thriving business. A large force of men were in the vicinity grading but in the course of a few weeks they would move further up toward Miles City when the town would be about abandoned, with the stores and saloons following the men. A large stock of drugs and medicines in the town were kept by Dr. T. J. Mailer of Saint Paul who did a good business the past summer and winter, *Yellowstone Journal*, April 9, 1881.

4. WMC, rosters, IU; Pandtle (Pendle) to Walter Camp, July 14, 1919; O'Toole to Camp, Mar. 26, 1909; Lange interview, n.d., WMC-BYU; In his declaration for pension, Lange said he suffered a bruised left hip on Reno Hill on June 26, when a bullet struck his belt and tore off three cartridges while he was leading a mule back to the skirmish line; the injury was painful but he was not laid up nor under the doctor's care. RG 15.

5. Larned was recommended for the artillery by the academic board of the U.S. military academy, and he applied for that branch, but while absent from the country on graduation leave he was assigned to cavalry. On Sept. 21, 1870, he applied for transfer to a regiment serving in a northern climate, for reasons of health: his rheumatic tendency said to temporarily require a dry cool climate for one or two years. The transfer was granted by direction of the Secretary of War on the ground, among others, that having been recommended for the artillery and having applied only for that branch, he was deprived thereby of the preference accorded to class standing in choice of regiment by being unexpectedly assigned to cavalry. He was however placed at the foot of 2nd lieutenants in the regiment in accordance with the established rule in cases of voluntary transfer. Larned later inquired whether a transfer granted by the War Department on such grounds, and at a time when transfers were being effected from different branches of service with retained rank, should deprive him of that which was legitimately acquired while a cadet at the academy. He claimed his rank was seriously affected by the position given him as it placed him below Lts. Hodgson (45) and Edgerly (50), graduates of his same class, both of whom he (28) ranked in class standing, Larned to adjutant general, Mar. 9, 1871 (1394 AGO [ACP] 1871), RG 94, Entry 297.

6. Larned said the day the Steamer *Josephine* left the command, Gen. Custer selected him to prepare notes and surveys for construction of a map of the route traversed. He was relieved from all company duty and given a detachment of men to serve as his guard, Larned to his mother, Sept. 6, 1873, Charles W. Larned, Papers, (hereafter cited as Larned Papers) Library, United States Military Academy, West Point, NY; Troop muster rolls report Larned absent from the company from Aug. 4, RG 94, Entry 53; Larned was newspaper correspondent for the *Chicago Inter-Ocean, Bismarck Tribune*, Oct. 1, 1873.

When the expedition arrived at Fort Lincoln in September, it was learned that construction of the new cavalry barracks would not be completed for another month or six weeks, and no accommodations for topographical work, nor material and instruments were available. Larned was granted leave of absence to Chicago where he executed all the mechanical work by his own hands until early December, when he was ordered to report to the Secretary of War for temporary duty, relinquishing the remainder of his leave. He drew full pay for the first month of his leave but for two months only received half-pay. His application to the adjutant general on April 20, 1874, asking that he be allowed full pay for the two months because he was continuously at work on his maps until departing for Washington, the largest completed in the War Department and a smaller incomplete still in his hand, was approved by the Secretary of War on April 27, 1874, (1601 ACP 1874), RG 94, Entry 297.

7. "Saw Genl Terry who told me that Larned had been appointed Prof. of D'g. He was mad & tho't it was an outrage as we all think him a systematic shirk," Godfrey, *Diary*, Aug. 2, 1876.

8. Muster rolls, RG 94, Entry 53; Brown Troop Duty Book. Reynolds and Brown, *Journal*.

9. SO 177, Hq Fort Lincoln DT, Sept. 24, 1876, RG 393, Part V.

10. Liddick and Harbaugh, *Camp on Custer*, 75. Lattman interview with Walter Camp, July 14, 1910, at Lead City.

11. Brown Troop Duty Book. Reynolds and Brown, *Journal*.

12. "Alkorn" was Lt. Gibson's striker in December 1875, Fougera, *With Custer's Cavalry*, 241.

13. SO 176, Hq Fort Lincoln, DT, Sept. 23, 1876, RG 393, Part V, convened a board of officers (Capt. Bell, and Lts. Craycroft and Wallace) to appraise the value of one horse the property of the United States but for which no officer was responsible, the horse desired by Mrs. Custer as the one often ridden by the late Gen. Custer, and to whom the officers of his regiment desired to present it; Lt. Burns, the quartermaster, shipped to Monroe, Mich., one horse and furnish transportation for one man to accompany the horse; commutation of rations will be furnished the man, Private Lawler, Company G, for 25 days. The regimental return, Sept. 1876, reports Lawler absent from Sept 11 at Monroe, Mich. NA, M744.

Lt. Hugh L. Scott, who joined the regiment (Company E), Sept. 30, said the officers purchased Gen. Custer's horse, Dandy, from the government, to be sent to Mrs. Custer, Scott, *Some Memories of a Soldier*, 29.

14. Private Lawler was ordered to join his company, per SO 149 Hq Dept. of Dakota, Nov. 23, 1876, RG 393, Part I, Entry 1191.

15. RG 94, Entry 96; Greene, *Nez Perce Summer 1877*, 230.

16. John Frett said there were some discharged soldiers with the pack train, Nichols, *Reno Court*, 503.

17. Lawless may have left the command July 19 on the steamer *Josephine*, allowing five days travel to point of hire; see note F31 (John Frett).

A letter to the post quartermaster at Fort Lincoln, Sept. 25, 1876, from John Stoyell, attorney at Bismarck, requested the amount due William Lawless be paid to Mr. Bassett, RG 393, Part V, Fort Lincoln; Chandler Bassett was employed at Fort Lincoln since Sept. 1874, as Wagon Master (in charge of post train) and was transferred to Lt. Burns, post quartermaster, upon departure of the expedition, RG 92, Entry 238, reports 1876/328, 1876/544, and 1877/475.

18. Company return, June 30, 1876, LBHB Coll., Roll 12; Dr. DeWolf noted June 21, 1876, "we had two cases of slight sunstroke," Luce, ed., "The Diary and Letters of Dr. James M. DeWolf."

19. Lee was assigned (with Hobart Ryder) to hospital duty by verbal order July 1st, per SFO 35, Hq Dept. of Dakota, In the Field, Aug. 2, 1876, RG 94, Entry 44; he was sent to Fort Lincoln and relieved from hospital duty August 10, by verbal order of Gen. Terry, Muster roll, field hospital, expedition against hostile Sioux Indians, June 30 to Aug. 31, 1876, RG 94, Entry 53.

20. Muster roll of noncommissioned staff and band and detachment 7th Cavalry, June 30 to Aug. 31, 1876, Lt. Ogle, 17th Infantry, commanding, RG 94, Entry 53; Post Return, Fort Lincoln, DT, August 1876, NA M617; see also RG 94, Entry 409, file 6498 A (EB) AGO 1879.

21. Lefler told Hardy he was with the pack train. Hardy said Lefler could only recall Sgt. Curtis and William Gregg with the pack train, Hardy to Walter Camp, Apr. 3, and May 15, 1910, WMC-BYU; Gregg interview, n.d., WMC-BYU; Rosters of Company F with remarks by Rooney and Lynch, WMC-BYU.

Rooney said Lefler was with the "old guard." Edward Pigford said the old guard was the troop packers and consisted of five men from each troop. *Morning Observer* (Washington, Pa.), Oct. 5, 1932; William E. Morris said the old guard consisted of ten men from each troop, Brady, *Indian Fights and Fighters*, 402.

22. RG 94, Entry 25, file 193276 AGO 1899.

23. RG 94, Entry 624, Classified Return of Wounds and Injuries Received, June 25 & 26, 1876, Dr. John W. Williams, Asst. Surg., Chief Medical Officer. Lell's body was found in June 1903 by Superintendent Grover in one grave with Meador, Tanner, and Voigt, WMC, Notes, env 75, IU; the body of a fifth "Reno soldier," (Charley), was also found by Grover in 1903, and all were interred in the Custer National Cemetery, Graves 453 through 456, and 458, Custer Battlefield Burial Register, LBHB Coll., Roll 14.

24. Frank Berwald interview with Walter Camp, n.d., WMC-BYU; RG 94, Entry 624.

25. Scott, *Some Memories of a Soldier*, 44–45; RG 393, Part V. Fort Rice; Private Littlefield wrote to Col. Sturgis on Nov. 22, seeking clemency, stating that he had enlisted as a musician, and when sent out on the summer's expedition, he walked from Fort Lincoln to Powder River where he was left behind with infantry under the command of Lt. Nickerson. When assigned duty as a private soldier he became dissatisfied at not being in the branch of service he enlisted for and took a horse and rations and returned to Fort Lincoln. He gave himself up with everything he brought with him, losing no government property, and was confined in the guard house with many drunken men though he had never drank a glass of spirits in his life, NA, M1734, Roll 18, file 3540 DD 1876.

26. On returning to Fort Lincoln, Private John Messangale, Company G, 17th Infantry, described the burials at Little Big Horn to the parents of Frank Anders (future historian of Custer's trail). Anders, whose mother was first cousin of Private Edward Lloyd, was born at Fort Lincoln, Nov. 10, 1875. Letters from Anders to W. A. Falconer, Jan. 19, 1942, Dr. Raymond A. Burnside, Feb. 10, 1948, and, E. A. Brininstool, Nov. 7, 1952, Frank L. Anders, Papers, (hereafter cited as Anders Papers) Chester Fritz Library, University, of North Dakota, Grand Forks; see also Anders' letter to R. G. Cartwright, Dec. 1, 1943, in Carroll, ed., *The Frank Anders and R. G. Cartwright Correspondence*, Vol. I., 16–20.

27. Stanislas Roy said Lozier was packer for headquarters and had mules carrying Gen. Custer's personal stuff, WMC, Misc. notes re pack train, Box 5, env 17, BYU.

28. A letter to the post quartermaster on Oct. 25, 1876, from John Stoyell, attorney at Bismarck, requested the amount due C. Lozier be paid to Mr. C. Bassett, RG 393, Part V, Fort A. Lincoln; Chandler Bassett was employed from Sept. 1874 as Wagon Master at Fort Lincoln.

29. RG 92, Entry 238, reports 1876/328, 1876/565, and 1877/319.

30. Burkman, Marshall, and Jones all told Walter Camp that Logue with packs. Creighton said Logue often told of seeing Lt. Nowlan take a note from a soldier who took it out of the hand of Lt. Cooke, WMC, notes, env 135, IU; McVeigh said Logue and McCarthy of L Troop were the two men who helped Tom Custer take Rain-in-the-Face in the store at Standing Rock, WMC, notes, env 134, IU.

31. Logue was in the Soldier's Home at Washington, Apr. 15, 1910, but when Walter Camp visited there May 7, 1910, Logue had been sent to the National Insane Asylum about five miles away, where Camp saw him in Oct. 1910, WMC, rosters, IU.

32. Newspaper clipping, np, nd, in Taylor Scrapbook.

33. Dr. E. J. Clark to assistant adjutant general, Mil. Div. of the Mo., Jan. 16, 1877, NA, M1734, Roll 18, file 22 DD 1877; see Vaughn, "Dr. George E. Lord, Regimental Surgeon"; Noyes, "Custer's Surgeon"; Noyes, "The Tragedy of Dr. George E. Lord."

34. In a letter to the assistant adjutant general, Department of Dakota, on Feb 2, 1877, Lovett requested a deduction of five days for each month from the term of his sentence, for having conducted himself in such manner as to be entitled to such deduction, NA, M1734, Roll 18, file 675 DD 1877.

35. Brown Troop Duty Book. Reynolds and Brown, *Journal*.

36. SO 39, Hq 7 Cavalry, May 11, 1876, RG 391, Entry 859, directed commanding officers of Companies of G, I, K, and L to furnish suitable men for orderly duty at department headquarters in the field; see Harry M. Krusee.

37. Patrick Corcoran of Company K, said Lynch only had a few days to serve and was one of a detail of twenty men on duty at headquarters when George Herendeen selected his horse. Corcoran was sure of this because he knew Lynch well, Corcoran to Walter Camp, Apr. 15, 1910, WMC-BYU; see also, Hardorff, *Camp, Custer, and the Little Big Horn*, 41.

When it was decided he was to go with Custer up the Rosebud, Herendeen said he had a saddle but no horse, and Custer gave him his choice of horses ridden by men of the headquarters detail. He selected the horse of Lynch whose term of enlistment was about to run out. Lynch was at first hesitant but finally consented, and Custer told him to get on the boat and look after his luggage, Hammer, *Custer in '76*, 221.

William Gregg said Lynch was not at the battle but was on a scouting trip during that time, Gregg to Walter Camp, Dec. 28, 1909; Rooney thought Lynch was with the wagon train, roster of Company F with remarks by Rooney, n.d., WMC-BYU. On his own roster of Company F, Lynch wrote that he was with the pack train, Lynch to Walter Camp, Nov. 28, 1908, WMC-BYU.

George Herendeen said that when he got to the boat after the fight, Lynch told him that his going on the boat saved his life. Walter Camp related that four men told him that Lynch was not at the battle at all, and though Lynch had told him so much about the battle, Camp suspected long ago that he had not been there, Camp to Daniel Knipe, Apr. 24, 1910, WMC-LBHB.

38. RG 217, Entry 1002 (UD); Records of the General Accounting Office, Settlement 1545, Jan. 1877, and Settlement 1765, April 1877, Abstracts and Contingencies, Pay-Rolls of Enlisted Men and Citizens employed in the Subsistence Department under Lt. Richard E. Thompson, 6th Inf., ACS, May–Sept., 1876.

39. SO 39, Hq 7th Cavalry, May 11, 1876, RG 391, Entry 859; see note L36 (G. Loyd).

40. *Bismarck Tribune*, Dec. 9, 1881.

41. RG 94, Entry 25, file 390320 AGO 1901; Certificate of service furnished July 27, 1901.

42. Rosters of Company F with remarks by Rooney and Lynch, WMC-BYU; Edwin Pickard interview with Walter Camp, Jan. 26, 1913, WMC, notes, env 129, IU.

Mc

McBratney, Henry (Harry) T. Citizen packer qmd; b. New York ca. 1840;[1] hired Apr 1876 St Paul Minn. by Lt Gibbs 6 inf actg aqm to pack supplies on pub animals of exp'n; rate of pay $50 mo & entitled to one ration per day & transp back to St Paul if hon disch; tr to Lt Nowlan at Ft Lincoln DT 17 Apr 1876 with pay to commence from that date; drove pack mules alongside wagon train dur march to Powder River; disch 23 Sep 1876 due $138.33 pay from 1 July; proprietor of saloon at Mandan DT from 1879; (m. 24 Nov 1881 to Mary Ann Butler); died 12 Oct 1892 at his ranch near Mandan; survived by wife & 4 ch.[2]

McCabe, Jno. Pvt co B; b. Cavan Ireland; enl 13 Oct 1870 Brooklyn N.Y. for 5 yrs; age 19; musician; gray eyes, brn hair, fair comp, 5' 3 3/4" high; assd to co K 8 inf; disch 13 Oct 1875 Camp Apache AT expir of serv a pvt; reenl 11 Apr 1876 New York N.Y. for 5 yrs; age 24; brn eyes, brn hair, fair comp, 5' 8 1/4" high; join co B 7 cav 27 Apr 1876 St Paul Minn.; sgt 1 Jan 1877; in conft Feb 1879; pvt 12 Apr 1879 sen gen cm & forf $10 pay for one mo & conft same period; dd qmd June to Oct 1879; in conft Dec 1879; disch 19 Oct 1880 Ft Yates DT on surg cert dis a pvt char good (comp'd comminutive frac. l. leg when thrown violently to grd while riding horse from water & run into by sol. on runaway horse; [other acc't says he was riding one horse & leading two others to water when horse he was riding began to rear & prance & in falling broke his leg in four places, at least]; dis total); res Baltimore Md & Sol. Home Wash'n D.C.
Pension: 27 Nov 1880 / Inv / 412457 / 183382. Dropped from roll 9 Feb 1892 upon death of clmt; last paid 4 Dec 1891.

McCall, Jos. Cpl co I; b. Chester Co. Pa.; enl 23 Sep 1873 Phil'a Pa. for 5 yrs; age 21; painter; blue eyes, brn hair, fair comp, 5' 6 1/2" high; join co I 22 Oct 1873 Ft Totten DT; cpl 10 Mar 1876; ds Ft Lincoln DT 5 May 1876 chg co prop & garden; sent with Lt Garlington on str *Josephine* 24 July to join co in field; sgt 3 Aug to date 1 July 1876; dd actg co qm sgt Dec 1876 to Mar 1877; ds Ft Lincoln Apr to Nov 1877 chg co prop; dd co qm sgt Dec 1877; des from arrest at Ft Lincoln 10 Feb 1878.

McCann, Pat'k. Pvt co E; b. Monahan Ireland; enl 19 Dec 1874 Boston Mass. for 5 yrs; age 21 5/12; laborer; gray eyes, brn hair, fair comp, 5' 6 1/8" high; join co E 8 Feb 1875 Opelika Ala; des 29 Mar 1876 Ft Seward DT & apph same day at Lake Eckleson DT; sen gen cm 2 May 1876 forf all pay for one yr & conft same period at sta of co; in conft Ft Lincoln DT to Mar 1877; dd regtl hq fatigue pty 25 Apr to 8 Oct 1877; cpl 1 Mar 1878; ds Ft Lincoln July to Nov 1878 chg co prop; testified in court martial of capt French 21 Jan 1879 at Ft Lincoln; sgt 1 July 1879; disch 18 Dec 1879 Ft Meade DT expir of serv a sgt char good.

McCarthy, Chas. Pvt co L; b. Phil'a Pa.; enl as Chas. McCarty 15 Aug 1865 at Phil'a for 3 yrs; age 19; laborer; blue eyes, brn hair, dk comp, 5' 6" high; join co F 6 cav 22 Aug 1865 near Frederick Md; des 13 Jan 1866 & apph 4 days later; sen gen cm 3 Mar 1866 to one yr conft; ds Ft Belknap Tex. as mail carrier Oct 1867; tr to co M Dec 1867; ds Camp Wilson Tex. to June 1868; disch 15 Aug 1868 Ft Richardson Tex. expir of serv a pvt; reenl 9 Sep 1868 New York N.Y. for 5 yrs; join co I 7 cav 10 Nov 1868 Camp Sandy Forsyth Kans.; dd co cook Dec 1868; des 14 May 1869 near Ft Hays Kans. & surd next day; sen gen cm 12 Aug 1869 forf $10 pay per mo for 6 mos & conft same period; in conft Feb 1871; cpl 4 Dec 1871; pvt 6 Mar 1872; cpl 6 July 1872; pvt 11 Nov 1872; disch 9 Sep 1873 Camp Terry DT expir of serv a pvt; reenl in regt 30 Sep 1873 St Paul Minn. & join co L 19 Oct 1873 Ft Lincoln DT; dd hq fatigue party (morn & eve) 11 May 1876; killed with Custer column 25 June 1876.[3]

McClurg, Wm. Pvt co A; b. Belfast Ireland; enl 23 Sep 1875 Cincinnati Ohio for 5 yrs; age 21; laborer; blue eyes, brn hair, ruddy comp, 5' 8" high; join co A 21 Oct 1875 Ft Lincoln DT; cpl 28 Apr 1877; pvt 1 Oct 1877 for bad cond in battle of Bear's Paw Mtns; des 22 Mar 1878 at Ft Lincoln; enl as Wm. Irvine 3 Jan 1881 Pittsburgh Pa. for 5 yrs; assd to co F 22 inf; surd as Wm. McClurg 9 Mar 1882 Ft Duncan Tex.; dishon disch 24 May 1882 sen gen cm & 2 yrs conft mil prison Ft L'worth Kans.

McConnell, Wilson. Pvt co K; b. 28 Jan 1839 New Castle Pa.; pvt co K 133 N.Y. inf 11 Jan 1865; tr to co A 90 N.Y. inf 2 June 1865; m.o. vol serv 9 Feb 1866 Hart's Island NYH a pvt; enl reg army 3 Jan 1867 Cincinnati Ohio for 5 yrs; age 27; boatman; gray eyes, lt hair, ruddy comp, 5' 9" high; join co K 7 cav 1 Apr 1867 Ft Dodge Kans.; dd co cook Aug 1867; far'r 1 Dec 1867; pvt 1 Aug 1868; far'r 1 Oct 1868; disch 3 Jan 1872 Yorkville SC expir of serv a far'r & reenl in co K for 5 yrs; pvt 1 Apr 1873; ed qmd teamster 12–26 Apr 1873; dd herder Aug 1873; ed qmd Dec 1873 to Feb 1874; dd teamster Aug 1874; abs on pass Dec 1876; disch 3 Jan 1877 Ft Lincoln DT expir of serv a pvt char good; reenl in co K 23 Jan 1877 at Ft Lincoln for 5 yrs; ed qmd teamster Feb to Apr 1877; dd qmd hostler Feb 1878; dd qmd teamster Apr 1878; dd qmd teamster Dec 1878 to Aug 1880; in conft Oct 1880; dd qmd laborer Feb 1881; disch 22 Jan 1882 Ft Totten DT expir of serv a pvt char indifferent morally but a good duty soldier & useful man; died 28 Dec 1906 vets home Waupaca Co. Wisc.
Pension: 18 Mar 1905 / Inv / 1333148 / 1115963.

McCormick, Jas. Pvt co M; b. New York N.Y.; enr 26 Aug 1861 Sacramento Calif. a pvt co E 1 Calif. inf for 3 yrs; age 19; musician; drummer Oct 1861; reenl as vet vol 28 Mar 1864 Los Pinos NM; tr to co A 8 Oct 1864; m.o. vol serv 9 Sep 1866 Ft Union NM; enl in reg army 19 Mar 1868 Ft L'worth Kans. for 5 yrs in co A 7 cav; age 22; soldier; dk eyes, dk hair, sallow comp, 5' 6 1/2" high; ds with band 1 Oct 1868; tr to band 19 Apr 1870; tr to co M 12 Aug 1870; in conft Oct 1870 to Feb 1871; cpl 25 Jan 1873; disch 19 Mar 1873 Memphis Tenn expir of serv a cpl; reenl in co M 2 Apr 1873 at Memphis for 5 yrs; ds with band 1 May 1873;[4] sgt 15 Aug 1873; pvt 22 Nov 1873; in conft Feb 1875; ds camp Powder River MT 15 June 1876 with band; ds on str *Josephine* 6 Aug 1876 to Ft Lincoln with band; ds Ft Lincoln Oct 1876 with band; ds Ft Lincoln May to Nov 1877 with band; disch 2 Apr 1878 Ft Lincoln DT expir of serv a pvt char xclt; reenl 17 Apr 1878 Ft Hamilton N.Y. for 5 yrs in band 3 art'y; des 12 July 1878 at Ft Hamilton [persecuted by band leader]; reenl 29 May 1879 Willets Point N.Y.H in co C battn engrs for 5 yrs; apph 12 June 1879 when recognized at Willets Point; dishon disch 4 Sep 1879 at Ft Hamilton sen gen cm & 2 yrs conft mil prison; unexpired portion of sen rem'd 2 July 1880.[5]

McCormick, Sam'l. Pvt co G; b. Tyrone Ireland; enl 29 Sep 1873 Phil'a Pa. for 5 yrs; age 25 10/12; morocco farmer; gray eyes, brn hair, ruddy comp, 5' 6 1/2" high; join co G 19 Oct 1873 Ft Lincoln DT; left in timber dur retreat from valley fight 25 June 1876 & rejoin co on Reno hill; dd 6–18 Sep 1876;[6] dd hosp nurse Apr to June 1878; ds Ft Lincoln July & Aug 1878; disch 29 Sep 1878 at Ft Lincoln expir of serv a pvt char good; reenl 29 Aug 1879 Baltimore Md for 5 yrs; assd to co A 4 cav; disch 28 Aug 1884 Ft Apache AT expir of serv a sgt char good; reenl 16 Jan 1885 Phil'a Pa. for 5 yrs; assd to co M 8 cav; tr to hosp corps 4 Nov 1888 & served therein continuously until 25 Apr 1905 when retd a cpl char xclt; died 10 Sep 1908 Sturgis SD.

McCreedy, Thos. Pvt co C; b. Dublin Ireland; enl 22 Oct 1872 Phil'a Pa. for 5 yrs; age 21; morocco finisher; gray eyes, brn hair, ruddy comp, 5' 7 3/4" high; join co C 9 Dec 1872 Charlotte NC; dd qmd Feb 1875; dd co cook June to Aug 1875; ds Ft Lincoln 5 May 1876 with co prop & garden; sent with Lt Garlington on str *Josephine* 24 July 1876 to join co in field; cpl 16 June 1877; disch 22 Oct 1877 Sulphur Creek DT expir of serv a cpl char xclt.

McCue, Martin. Pvt co K; b. 10 Nov 1851 at sea; enl 28 Oct 1872 Phil'a Pa. for 5 yrs; age 21; card stripper in woolen mill; gray eyes, brn

hair, ruddy comp, 5' 6 1/2" high; join co K 9 Dec 1872 Yorkville SC; in conft Apr 1873; ds 20 Aug 1873 hq Yellowstone Exp'n care for unserviceable horses; dd qmd Dec 1873; dd co cook June 1876; disch 23 June 1877 camp on Sunday Creek MT per SO 70 Dept of Dak. 1877 (under GO 47 AGO 1877; reduction of army) a pvt char xclt;[7] reenl 8 Dec 1877 St Louis Mo. for 5 yrs; assd to co L 1 cav; disch 7 Dec 1882 Ft Walla Walla WT expir of serv a pvt char good; reenl 6 Jan 1883 Presidio San Francisco Calif. for 5 yrs; assd to co B 1 cav; disch 5 Jan 1888 Ft Custer MT expir of serv a pvt char very good; reenl 4 Feb 1888 Phil'a Pa. for 5 yrs; assd to co I 2 cav; tr to co C; tr to co A; disch 3 Feb 1893 Ft Wingate NM expir of serv a pvt char good; reenl 17 Feb 1893 San Francisco Calif. for 5 yrs; assd to co B 10 inf; disch 7 July 1893 Ft Marcy NM on surg cert dis a pvt (loss of sight left eye from incised wd by broken glass dur row in café at Santa Fe NM; not line of duty); died 6 Dec 1923 Sol. Home Wash'n D.C.
Pension: 7 Aug 1893 / Inv / 1152800. Ind. Surv. / 10682 / 8312.

McCurry, Jos. J. 1sgt co H; b. Phil'a Pa.; enl 22 Jan 1872 at Phil'a for 5 yrs; age 21; coachmaker; brn eyes, dk hair, ruddy comp, 5' 7" high; join co H 12 Feb 1872 Nashville Tenn; cpl 20 Aug 1872; dd actg prov sgt Dec 1873 to Feb 1874; sgt 1 July 1874; 1sgt 20 Sep 1875; gsw l. shoulder (fl. wd. sl.) June 1876 on Reno hill; remained with co in field; sgt-maj 5 Aug 1876; 1sgt 2 Oct 1876 (resd sgt-maj for own reasons); disch 22 Jan 1877 Ft Rice DT expir of serv a 1sgt char xclt; employed June 1880 in carriage factory at Phil'a; age 27; single.[8]

McDermott, Geo. Sgt co A; b. Galway Ireland; enl 14 July 1866 New York N.Y. for 3 yrs; age 19; clerk; blue eyes, lt hair, fair comp, 5' 7" high; assd to co I 22 inf; tr to co A; disch 14 July 1869 Ft Sully DT expir of serv a pvt; reenl 21 Jan 1870 New York N.Y. for 5 yrs; assd to co I 5 art'y; des 21 July 1871 Ft Trumbull Conn.; enl as Mich'l Burke 15 Jan 1872 New York N.Y. for 5 yrs; join co A 7 cav 11 Feb 1872 E'town Ky.; surd 16 Nov 1873 under GO 102 AGO 1873; restored to duty without trial (auth AGO) 18 Mar 1874 & tr to co A to serve bal of enlmt; dd driver with art'y detmt Blk Hills Exp'n 14 June to 31 Aug 1874; cpl 26 Mar 1875; sgt 18 Sep 1875; actg 1sgt 26 June 1876; 1sgt 26 Nov 1876 (for meritorious cond on battlefield, having caught a runaway horse & helped a wd man to mount & escape);[9] disch 16 May 1877 camp near Ft Buford DT expir of serv a 1sgt char xclt (made good time lost by des'n); reenl same day in co A for 5 yrs & on furl 40 days at Ft Lincoln; rejoin co in field 28 June; killed 30 Sep 1877 Snake Creek MT (Bear's Paw Mtns) in action with Nez Perce inds.
Pension: 28 Dec 1877 / Mother / 234719 / 182108.

McDermott, Thos. Pvt co H; b. New York N.Y.; enl 12 Mar 1867 at New York for 5 yrs; age 22; laborer; grey eyes, brn hair, dk comp, 5' 6 3/4" high; assd to co I 3 cav; disch 12 Mar 1872 Ft McPherson Neb expir of serv a pvt; reenl 28 May 1872 Pittsburgh Pa. for 5 yrs; join co H 7 cav 3 Dec 1872 Nashville Tenn; dd battn hq pioneer Apr to June 1873; dd hq Yellowstone Exp'n Sep 1873; in conft Dec 1873; dd hq Blk Hills Exp'n 25 June to 31 Aug 1874; dd qmd laborer 8 Oct 1875 to 4 May 1876; cpl 6 Oct 1876; sgt 2 Feb 1877; (recom by capt Benteen for medal of honor for dist gal & soldierly qualities exhibited at LBH);[10] disch 28 May 1877 camp near Ft Buford DT expir of serv a sgt char xclt; reenl 6 Apr 1878 Chicago Ill. for 5 yrs; rejoin co H 7 Oct 1878 in field; dd co cook Feb 1879; dd bldg co stables & qrs Aug 1879; dd co cook Oct 1879; cpl 22 Nov 1879; sgt 16 Apr 1880; des 15 June 1880 Ft Meade DT; apph 12 Sep 1880 at Ft Meade; pvt 1 Nov 1880 sen gen cm & restored to duty; dd actg co wag Aug 1881; sgt 6 Sep 1881; pvt 14 Oct 1881; dd stable police Dec 1881; far'r 1 May 1882; pvt 1 July 1882; disch 2 July 1883 at Ft Meade expir of serv a pvt char good; reenl 17 July 1883 at Chicago for 5 yrs; assd to co A 4 cav; des 8 June 1884 Ft Wingate NM; surd 24 June 1884 Whipple Bks AT; des 23 Nov 1884 enroute to Ft Apache AT; surd 10 Nov 1885 at Presidio San Francisco Calif.; dishon disch 21 Jan 1886 sen gen cm & 2 yrs conft Alcatraz Isl Calif.

McDonald, Jas. Pvt co A; b. Boston Mass.; enl 29 Sep 1875 at Boston for 5 yrs; age 22;

laborer; grey eyes, brn hair, fair comp, 5' 6" high; join co A 21 Oct 1875 Ft Lincoln DT; killed dur retreat from valley fight 25 June 1876; (body not recovered).[11]
Pension: 19 Nov 1885 / Mother / 332729 / 222204.

McDonnell, Jno. Pvt co G; b. New York N.Y.; enl in co G 7 Apr 1873 Cairo Ill. for 5 yrs; age 28; wagoner; blue eyes, auburn hair, fair comp, 5' 9" high; ed hosp attdt Aug to Dec 1873; sen gen cm 20 Feb 1874 forf $5 pay per mo for 6 mos & conft same period; in conft Dec 1875; dd regtl hq fatigue pty (morn & eve) 11 May 1876;[12] dd qmd Nov 1876 to Feb 1877; dd qmd Apr to Dec 1877; ds Ft Buford DT Feb 1878 teamster transporting pub prop; disch 7 Apr 1878 Ft Lincoln DT expir of serv a pvt char good.

McDonnell, Pat'k. Pvt co D; b. Mar 1852 Kerry Ireland; enl 16 Nov 1872 Pittsburgh Pa. for 5 yrs; age 21 9/12; laborer; grey eyes, dk hair, fair comp, 5' 6" high; join co D 8 Dec 1872 Opelika Ala; gsw l. leg (fl. wd. sl.) 25 June 1876; tr on str *Far West* 3 July to hosp Ft Lincoln DT; disch 1 Mar 1877 Ft Rice DT on surg cert dis (unfit for duty 261 days, his leg having atrophied & almost useless; dis total) a pvt char xclt; died 9 Sep 1922 San Antonio Tex.
Pension: 26 Mar 1877 / Inv / 233077 / 145349.

McDonough, Jas. Pvt co G; b. Franklin Pa.; enl 15 Oct 1870 Phila Pa. for 5 yrs; age 29; shoemaker; grey eyes, brn hair, ruddy comp, 5' 5" high; assd to co K 8 inf; disch 15 Oct 1875 Camp Apache AT expir of serv a pvt; reenl 8 Apr 1876 St Louis Bks Mo. for 5 yrs; assd to co G 7 cav 5 May 1876; tr to regt 14 July with capt Hale's detmt of rcts; join co G 2 Aug camp mouth of Rosebud Creek MT; ds gd on str *Far West* 4 Aug 1876; in conft Feb 1878; sen gen cm 21 Mar 1878 forf $10 pay per mo for 3 mos; sick (insane) June 1880 Ft Meade DT; dd regtl hq Aug to Oct 1880; disch 7 Apr 1881 at Ft Meade expir of serv a pvt char "fair when sober."

McDougall, Thos. Mower. Capt co B; b. 21 May 1845 Ft Crawford (Prairie duChien) Wis; (son of maj surg Chas. McDougall); vol adc Oct 1863 with gen J. P. Hawkins comdg distr northeast La.; appt 2Lt 10 La. vols of African descent 18 Feb 1864; (redesig 48 U.S. col'd inf 11 Mar 1864); ds with gen Hawkins comdg 1 div U.S. col'd troops & in siege of Mobile; m.o. 2 June 1865 to accept prom'n to capt 5 U.S. vol inf; join co B 9 June St Louis Mo. & marched to Ft Riley Kans., thence to Denver Colo. for qm duty; prov marshal & asst comsy of musters on staff of gen Upton 16 Oct 1865; ordered to Ft Columbus NYH 19 June 1866; m.o. vol serv 10 Aug to accept reg army com'n 2Lt 3d battn 14 inf; (redesig 32 inf regt Sep 1866);[13] cond rcts on steamer to Calif. (via Panama) 30 Sep 1866; attd to co D 8 cav 26 Oct at Angel Isl (San Francisco harbor) & dep on steamer to Ft Walla Walla WT; prom 1Lt 5 Nov 1866; bvt capt 2 Mar 1867 for meritorious serv dur the war; tr to Drum Bks [Wilmington] Calif. Apr 1867; with detmt to Prescott AT 29 July 1867; join co B 32 inf 30 Oct 1867 Camp Grant AT; on scouting exp'n comd by col T. L. Crittenden Apr & May 1868; ds with co I Mar 1869; cond pris'rs to San Francisco Calif. Apr 1869; (32 inf consol with 21 inf Aug 1869 [from 12 May 1869]); ds Ft Vancouver WT to Nov 1869; unassd awaiting orders 21 Oct 1869; on rctg duty St Louis Mo. Apr 1870 & cond rcts to various posts; assd to 7 cav 31 Dec 1870 Ft L'worth Kans.; comd co E July 1871 to 22 Mar 1876; (capt co B 15 Dec 1875); dep Ft Seward DT 14 Apr 1876 (with Lt Craycroft) enroute to join co; arr Ft Lincoln DT 10 May (with gen Custer & gen Terry & staff) & join co B;[14] comd escort for pack train 25 June; awl 18 Sep (verbal order in field); arr Bismarck 20 Sep on str *Chambers* (with gen Terry & staff) & accomp capt Benteen on eve train to St Paul;[15] rejoin co 15 Nov 1876 at Ft Lincoln; comd co in field May to Nov 1877; attd to maj Lazelle's inf comd 13 June to 30 July & to maj Brisbin's battn 2 cav thro' Aug; at Cant'mt Tongue River 1 Sep to 19 Oct & rejoined regt 25 Oct mouth of Squaw Creek [Camp Owen Hale] on Missouri River; ds Chicago Ill. Jan 1879 witness in Reno court of inq; retd 22 July 1890 for disability contr line of duty (chr. enlargement of liver from malarial fever); maj on retd list 23 Apr 1904; res Wellsville N.Y.; died 3 July 1909 Brandon Vt.[16] [2901 ACP 1872]. Pension: 22 Sep 1909 / Wid / 927756 / 694160.

McEgan, Jno. Pvt co G; b. Kerry Co Ireland; enl 6 Feb 1872 Cincinnati Ohio for 5 yrs; age 24 4/12; laborer; grey eyes, brn hair, ruddy comp, 5' 8 3/4" high; join co G 26 Feb 1872 Spartanburg SC; ed qmd teamster Feb 1873; ed qmd teamster 12–26 Apr 1873; dd co cook Aug 1873; ed qmd Oct to Dec 1873; dd co teamster Feb to Apr 1874; dd qmd teamster (Blk Hills Exp'n) Aug 1874; dd co cook Dec 1874; dd actg co wag Aug to Oct 1875; dd co cook Feb to Apr 1876; dd 13 May to 19 Sep 1876; (lost carbine 24 June while on duty with pack train);[17] far'r 1 Oct 1876; disch 6 Feb 1877 Ft Lincoln DT expir of serv a far'r char xclt.

McElroy, Jas. Trump'r co D; b. Cavan Co Ireland; enl 24 Aug 1875 Baltimore Md for 5 yrs; age 24; laborer; grey eyes, brn hair, fair comp, 5' 6 1/2" high; join co D 21 Oct 1875 Ft Lincoln DT a trump'r; sick hosp 10 Jan to 8 May 1876 when disch on surg cert dis (hypertrophy of heart).

McElroy, Thos. Trump'r co E; b. Neagh Ireland; enl 24 May 1870 New York N.Y. for 5 yrs; age 25; laborer; blue eyes, dk hair, ruddy comp, 5' 5 1/2" high; join co G 1 inf 25 Aug 1870 Ft Porter N.Y.; fifer Dec 1870; des 11 July 1871 at Ft Porter; apph 18 Aug 1871 Buffalo N.Y.; sen gen cm 16 Sep 1871 forf $8 pay per mo for 8 mos & conft same period; disch 2 July 1875 Ft Randall DT expir of serv a mus'n; reenl 3 July 1875 at Ft Randall for 5 yrs in co E 7 cav a trump'r; killed with Custer column 25 June 1876; (survived by wife & 1 ch.).
Pension: 1 Nov 1878 / Wid / 240065 / 191055. Minor / 268659 / 191056.

McGinnis, Jno. Pvt co I; b. Longford Ireland; enl 5 Aug 1868 New York N.Y. for 5 yrs; age 35; clerk; blue eyes, brn hair, ruddy comp, 5' 8 1/2" high; assd to 5 cav; tr to 7 cav 3 Mar 1869; assd to co I 6 Apr 1869 camp near Ft Hays Kans.; dd co tailor Apr 1869 to Aug 1873; disch 5 Aug 1873 Camp Terry DT upon expir of serv a pvt & reenl in co I for 5 yrs; dd co tailor to Jan 1874; sick (infl. lungs) 6 Dec 1875 to 5 Jan 1876; sick (catarrh) 13–22 Apr 1876; sick (chr. rheum.) 16 May to 17 Oct 1876 Ft Lincoln DT;[18] ds Ft Lincoln with band to 13 Nov 1876; dd co tailor Dec 1876 to Feb 1877; ds Ft Lincoln May to Nov 1877; in conft Dec 1877; dd co tailor Feb to Aug 1878; disch 5 Aug 1878 Camp J. G. Sturgis DT expir of serv a pvt char good; reenl 8 Oct 1878 St Louis Mo. for 5 yrs; assd to co B 1 cav; disch 7 Oct 1883 Ft Coeur d'Alene Idaho Ty expir of serv a pvt; reenl for co A 7 cav 3 Dec 1883 Ft Snelling Minn. for 5 yrs; disch 2 Dec 1888 Ft Riley Kans. expir of serv a pvt char xclt.
Pension: 3 Aug 1889 / Inv / 722198 / 463469. Dropped from roll 24 July 1900, failure to claim; last paid to 4 Mar 1897. (P. A., Wash'n D.C.).

McGinnis, Jno. J. Pvt co G; b. Boston Mass.; enl 2 Dec 1874 at Boston for 5 yrs; age 25; lithographer; grey eyes, sandy hair, florid comp, 5' 7 7/8" high; join co G 10 Feb 1875 Shreveport La.; in civil jail at Shreveport 12–17 Aug 1875 (violated city ordinance); sen gar cm 28 Aug 1875 forf $8 pay & conft 5 days; killed dur retreat from valley fight 25 June 1876; (body not recovered).[19]

McGlone, Jno. Sgt co M; b. Sligo Ireland; enl 18 Dec 1872 Phila Pa. for 5 yrs; age 28; laborer; brn eyes, dk hair, ruddy comp, 5' 9 1/2" high; join co M 9 Feb 1873 Oxford Miss; cpl 10 Feb 1875; dd actg co qm sgt June to Nov 1875; sgt 17 June 1876; (lost co guidon in crossing river 25 June);[20] disch 18 Dec 1877 Ft Lincoln DT expir of serv a sgt char xclt; reenl 27 Dec 1877 Columbus Ohio for 5 yrs; assd to co F 5 inf; disch 26 Dec 1882 Ft Keogh MT expir of serv a sgt char xclt; reenl 1 May 1883 New York N.Y. for 5 yrs; assd to co C 12 inf; des 5 Sep 1883 enroute from Madison Bks N.Y. to Creedmore Long Island N.Y.; surd 9 Mar 1885 Memphis Tenn; dishon disch 19 Apr 1885 Little Rock Ark sen gen cm & 3 yrs conft mil prison Ft L'worth Kans.

McGonigal, Hugh. Pvt co G; b. 12 Feb 1836 in Ireland; enl 12 Feb 1858 Phil'a Pa. for 5 yrs; age 22; laborer; brn eyes, blk hair, dk comp, 5' 10" high; assd to co H 2 drg; (redesig 2 cav Aug 1861); disch 12 Feb 1863 Falmouth Va. expir of serv a pvt; reenl 27 June 1865 at Phil'a for 3 yrs in gen serv; tr to co F 7 cav 10 Sep 1866 Ft Riley Kans.; sgt 17

Sep 1866; 1sgt 1 May 1867; sgt 20 July 1867 (own req); dd post prov sgt Jan & Feb 1868; pvt 15 Mar 1868; dd co cook Apr 1868; disch 27 June 1868 Ft L'worth Kans. expir of serv a pvt; reenl 22 July 1872 at Phil'a for 5 yrs; join co G 10 Dec 1872 Laurenville SC; cpl 1 Jan 1873; ds hq Yellowstone Exp'n Aug 1873; pvt 8 Oct 1873; in conft Oct 1873; dd co cook Apr 1874; dd hq Blk Hills Exp'n July & Aug 1874; left in timber dur retreat from valley fight 25 June 1876 & rejoin co on Reno hill;[21] ds with ordn wagon 6 Aug to 26 Sep 1876;[22] disch 25 June 1877 camp on Sunday Creek MT per SO 70 Dept of Dak. 1877 (under GO 47 AGO 1877) a pvt char xclt;[23] died 16 Nov 1914 Sol. Home Wash'n D.C.
Pension: 25 May 1885 / Inv / 540713 / 516714.

McGucker, Jno. Trump'r co I; b. Albany N.Y.; enl 5 Aug 1850 Jeff'n Bks Mo. for 5 yrs in co F 7 inf a drummer; age 18; musician; hazel eyes, blk hair, dk comp, 5' 0 1/2" high; (declared age true & had neither parent, guardian nor master; rctg officer made diligent inq in neighborhood); sen gen cm 3 June 1853 forf $8 pay per mo for 8 mos & conft same period; disch 11 June 1855 Ft Gibson IT by reenlmt in same co for 5 yrs; in conft Apr to June 1857; disch 11 June 1860 near Ft Bridger UT expir of serv a mus'n; reenl 18 Nov 1868 Ft L'worth Kans. for 3 yrs in co B 4 art'y; age 35 3/12; soldier; hazel eyes, blk hair, ruddy comp, 5' 5" high; bugler 23 Sep 1869; in conft June to Sep 1870; sen gen cm 13 July 1870 forf $10 pay per mo for 3 mos & conft same period; disch 22 Nov 1871 Ft McHenry Md expir of serv a bugler; reenl 27 Nov 1871 St Louis Mo. for 5 yrs; join cav detmt USMA Feb 1872 a trump'r; in conft June 1872; in conft Dec 1874; tr to St Louis Depot Mo. 7 Apr 1875; assd to co I 7 cav as trump'r 14 May 1875; at Ft Randall DT 22 June to 19 July 1875 awaiting transp to co at Ft Lincoln DT; killed with Custer column 25 June 1876.

McGue, Peter. Pvt co L; b. Port Henry N.Y.; enl 23 Dec 1872 Troy N.Y. for 5 yrs; age 25 5/12; laborer; brn eyes, blk hair, dk comp, 5' 4" high; join co L 11 Feb 1873 New Orleans La.; killed with Custer column 25 June 1876.

McGuire, Jno. B. (Jr.). Pvt co C; b. 18 July 1854 Livermore Pa.; enl 4 Oct 1875 Pittsburgh Pa. for 5 yrs; age 21; farmer; brn eyes, brn hair, florid comp, 5' 8" high; join co C 21 Oct 1875 Ft Lincoln DT; with pack train 25 June 1876 (horse became lame dur march up Rosebud & Lt Harrington let him ride extra horse);[24] gsw r. arm (fl. wd. sl.) 26 June on Reno hill; tr on str *Far West* 3 July to hosp Ft Lincoln; duty 29 Aug 1876; ds Ft Totten DT 19 Nov 1876 with co baggage; ed nurse post hosp 28 Dec 1877 to 22 June 1878; disch 3 Oct 1880 Ft Meade DT expir of serv a pvt char very good & reenl in co C for 5 yrs; dd stable police Dec 1881 to Feb 1882; cpl 14 Feb 1885; pvt 8 Oct 1885 sen gen cm & 6 mos conft (retained in serv to serve sen); disch 7 Apr 1886 at Ft Meade a pvt char good prior to com'n of offense for which held; enl in co K 7 cav 21 Dec 1886 at Ft Meade for 5 yrs; tr to hosp corps 28 Oct 1887; disch 24 Apr 1889 at Ft Meade on surg cert dis (intestinal dyspepsia & anemia) a pvt;[25] died 12 Feb 1932 Saltsburg Pa.
Pension: 28 June 1889 / Inv / 713921 / 453379. Wid / 1712542.

McGurn, Bernard J. Pvt co B; b. Newton Mass.; enl 23 Mar 1876 Boston Mass. for 5 yrs; age 24; plumber; blue eyes, brn hair, ruddy comp, 5' 7 7/8" high; join co B 27 Apr 1876 St Paul Minn.; ds camp Powder River MT 10 June 1876; ds camp mouth of Rosebud Creek Aug 1876 dismtd; ed qmd Dec 1877; dd qmd June to Aug 1878; dd co cook Feb to Apr 1880; dd co cook Oct 1880; disch 22 Mar 1881 Ft Yates DT expir of serv a pvt char very good; res Roxbury Mass.[26]

McHugh, Philip. Pvt co L; b. Donegal Ireland; enl 6 Nov 1857 Harrisburg Pa. for 5 yrs; age 22; laborer; hazel eyes, blk hair, fair comp, 5' 6" high; join co H 2 cav 18 Jan 1858 Camp Cooper Tex.; lost part of r. ear from arrow wd dur campn against Comanche inds; ds Wash'n D.C. June & July 1861; (regt redesig 5 cav Aug 1861); awol Aug 1862; disch 6 Nov 1862 camp near Falmouth Va. expir of serv a pvt; enr 25 May 1863 Wash'n D.C. as 1sgt co A 1 D.C. cav; comsy sgt Oct 1863; 1sgt 1 Mar 1864; co qm sgt May & June 1865; ds chg of mtd orderlies at gen hq Norfolk Va. Aug &

Sep 1865; m.o. vol serv 26 Oct 1865 Ft Monroe Va. a sgt; reenl reg army 2 Nov 1865 Wash'n D.C. for 3 yrs in co L 5 cav; cpl 7 Mar 1866; in conft Apr 1866; sgt 1 Oct 1866; disch 2 Nov 1868 Beaver Creek Kans. expir of serv a sgt; enl in 7 cav 1 June 1869 Ft L'worth Kans. for 5 yrs; join co L in field 19 June 1869; cpl 20 June 1869; pvt 26 Sep 1869; in conft Oct & Dec 1869; cpl 11 Nov 1870; pvt 2 July 1871 (own req); cpl 28 Sep 1872; sgt 3 Feb 1873; ed qmd Nov & Dec 1873; on furl 30 days 21 May 1874 St Paul Minn.; disch 1 June 1874 by expir of serv a sgt; reenl in co L 4 June 1874 at St Paul (regtl hq) for 5 yrs; pvt 28 Sep 1874 & dd qmd plasterer to Nov 1874; dd with post boat crew Apr 1875; dd qmd plasterer May & June 1875; cpl 20 Aug 1875; pvt 8 Apr 1876; ds dept hq in field 11 May 1876;[27] cpl 4 Oct 1876; in arrest Dec 1876; pvt 23 Feb 1877 sen gen cm & forf $10 pay per mo for 2 mos (sen rem'd upon recom'n of court in consid'n of his many yrs faithful serv); sgt 4 May 1877; cited by maj Merrill for good cond in action against Nez Perce inds at Canon Creek MT 13 Sep 1877; pvt 19 July 1878; dd qmd plasterer Apr 1879; disch 4 June 1879 Ft Lincoln DT expir of serv a pvt char good; reenl 7 June 1879 St Louis Mo. for 5 yrs; join co I 8 cav 15 Mar 1881 Ft Brown Tex.; ds May 1881 to May 1883 Santa Maria Tex. patroling country along river to prevent marauding; ed nurse post hosp Aug 1883 to June 1884; disch 6 June 1884 at Ft Brown by expir of serv a pvt char xclt; reenl in same co 10 June 1884 for 5 yrs; cpl 1 July 1884; pvt 29 May 1885; ds Ft Meade DT 20 July to 3 Sep 1888;[28] cpl 8 Sep 1888; sgt 14 Feb 1889; retd 1 Mar 1889 a sgt char xclt; died 1 Apr 1910 Allentown Pa.

McIlhargey, Archibald. Pvt co I; b. Antrim Ireland; enl 19 Nov 1867 New York N.Y. for 5 yrs; age 22; laborer; brn eyes, blk hair, dk comp, 5' 5" high; join co I 22 Jan 1868 Ft L'worth Kans.; ds Camp Wichita IT Mar & Apr 1869; (lost in Wichita Mtns 9 Mar 1869 while hunting stray cattle & rejoined regt 21 Apr at Medicine Bluff Creek);[29] dd co cook June to Dec 1869; ed comsy dept June to Aug 1870; dd co cook Sep 1870 to Feb 1871; ed qm dept June 1871; dd co cook Dec 1871 to Nov 1872; disch 19 Nov 1872 Shelbyville Ky. expir of serv a pvt & reenl in co I for 5 yrs; dd co cook Nov 1872 to May 1873; dd co cook Oct 1873; ds Ft Totten DT June to Sep 1874 with co garden; dd cook for maj Reno 25 June 1876 & sent to advise gen Custer the inds were coming up valley in force; killed with Custer column; survived by wife & 2 ch.; (widow m. sgt Caddle 25 Dec 1877).
Pension: 25 Oct 1877 / Wid / 233865 / 184654. Minor / 249539 / 189031.

McIntosh, Donald. 1Lt co G; b. 4 Sep 1838 near Montreal Canada.; his father an officer of the Hudson's Bay co & mother Chippewa ind; res at various co posts in Canada to 1846 thence moved to Pacfic coast; Ft Vancouver WT to 1851; Oregon City to 1853 & Portland Ore. in 1854; clerk in qm dept Ft Dalles & Ft Steilacoom from 1855; removed to Wash'n D.C. June 1861 & employed as chf clerk in qm depot; appd for asst qm of vols 17 Feb 1863; appd for mil storekeeper 12 May 1866 but withdrew appn & appd for com'n in cav serv; appt 2Lt 7 cav 17 Aug 1867; join regt 14 Oct 1867 Ft Harker Kans. & assd to co M; post adjt Feb & Mar 1868; comd escort for UPRR surveyors May 1868; sick at Ft Harker 4 June (severe infl. r. eye from sand while with escort); sick qrs to Oct 1868; convalescent duty with rcts Nov & Dec 1868; post adjt Jan 1869; actg chf qm distr upper Ark Feb 1869; post adjt Apr 1869; rejoin co 7 May 1869 camp at Big Creek near Ft Hays Kans.; in arrest 29 Mar to 4 June 1870 (verbal order col Sturgis); prom 1Lt co G 16 July 1870; ds Wash'n D.C. Dec 1870 before spl exam'g bd (upon recom'n col Sturgis) & found not unfit for the serv;[30] comd co G Feb 1871 to June 1876; (with Yellowstone Exp'n June to Sep 1873 & Blk Hills Exp'n July & Aug 1874); appd for appmt of capt & asst qm 6 July 1875; killed dur retreat from valley fight 25 June 1876; survived by wife.[31]
[168 ACP 1871]. Pension: 9 Aug 1876 / Wid / 227472 / 174882.

McKay, Edw. J. Pvt co G; b. Galway Ireland; enl 12 Apr 1876 Cincinnati Ohio for 5 yrs; age 22; laborer; blue eyes, blk hair, ruddy comp, 5' 5" high; join co G 27 Apr 1876 St Paul Minn.; dd regtl hq fatigue pty 18 June to

24 Aug 1877; ed subs dept laborer Oct 1880 to Mar 1881; disch 11 Apr 1881 Ft Meade DT expir of serv a pvt char xclt; reenl 2 May 1881 Phil'a Pa. for 5 yrs; assd to co I 20 inf; tr to co G 7 cav 26 June 1884; in conft 25 Apr 1886; disch 1 May 1886 Ft Keogh MT expir of serv a pvt char fair.

McKee, Jno. Pvt co G; b. Meigs Co. Ohio; enl 4 Apr 1876 St Louis Mo. for 5 yrs; age 23; cooper; hazel eyes, lt hair, fair comp, 5' 10" high; join co G 27 Apr 1876 St Paul Minn.; ds camp Powder River MT 15 June 1876; cited by capt Benteen for conspic gal in two mtd chgs against Nez Perce inds at Canon Creek MT 13 Sep 1877; dd qmd Jan 1878; dd qmd teamster Apr to June 1878; disch 3 Apr 1881 Ft Meade DT expir of serv a pvt char xclt.

McKenna, Jno. (alias). See Kenney, Jno.

McLaughlin, Terence. Pvt co B; b. Harrisburg Pa.; enl 13 Mar 1876 New York N.Y. for 5 yrs; age 24; polisher; hazel eyes, brn hair, fair comp, 5' 6 3/4" high; join co B 27 Apr 1876 St Paul Minn.; sgt 8 Jan 1878; dd co qm sgt Dec 1878 to Apr 1880; disch 12 Mar 1881 Ft Yates DT expir of serv a sgt char xclt; reenl 17 Aug 1883 New York N.Y. for 5 yrs; assd to co C 6 cav; disch 16 Aug 1888 Ft Wingate NM expir of serv a sgt.

McLaughlin, Thos. F. Sgt co H; b. Phil'a Pa.; enl 6 Aug 1866 Carlisle Pa. for 5 yrs; age 24; varnisher; blue eyes, lt hair, fair comp, 5' 4 1/2" high; sick (cont'n) Ft L'worth Kans. 25 Aug to 20 Oct 1866; join co A 7 cav 23 Oct 1866 Ft Riley Kans.; cpl 1 Nov 1866; in conft Oct 1867; pvt 16 Nov 1867; disch 6 Aug 1871 E'town Ky. upon expir of serv a pvt; reenl in regt same day at Louisville Ky. for 5 yrs; assd to co H 29 Aug 1871; ds regtl hq at Louisville to Apr 1872 then joined co H at Nashville Tenn; abs sick (ac. bronc.) Mar to June 1873 at Louisville; sick (frostbite ears) 12 Dec 1873 to 11 Jan 1874 Ft Rice DT; ed qmd Feb to Apr 1874; cpl 1 Nov 1874; ed qmd painter Oct 1875; sgt 13 Mar 1876; gsw l. forearm 26 June 1876 (fl. wd. sl.); remain with co in field; disch 6 Aug 1876 camp mouth of Rosebud Creek MT expir of serv a sgt char xclt;[32] arr Ft Lincoln DT 10 Aug on str *Durfee*; reenl in regt 4 Sep 1876 at Ft Lincoln & join co E 28 Sep 1876; ed qmd laborer Nov 1876 to Feb 1877; dd regtl hq orderly 7 May 1877; ds in field 2 Aug thro' Sep 1877; ds Ft Lincoln Oct 1877; dd regtl hq Feb to Oct 1878; (tr to co G 29 Aug 1878); dd qmd painter Dec 1878 to Apr 1879; tr to co I 2 June 1879; dd qmd painter Aug 1879 to Apr 1880; ds Ft Lincoln June to Oct 1880; dd qmd painter Apr to Sep 1881; disch 3 Sep 1881 Ft Totten DT expir of serv a pvt char good; died 3 Mar 1886 Jamestown DT (gen. paresis).[33]

Pension: 3 June 1889 / Wid / 396958. (Rej, clmt unable to furn competent proof sol. died from effects of injury recd in Custer fight).

McMasters, Wm. Pvt co B; b. Glasgow Scotland; enl 14 Dec 1874 Boston Mass. for 5 yrs; age 29; brickmason; grey eyes, brn hair, ruddy comp, 5' 6 1/2" high; join co B 10 Feb 1875 Shreveport La.; dd qmd Dec 1875; dd qmd Feb 1878 to Dec 1879; disch 13 Dec 1879 Ft Yates DT expir of serv a pvt char good; reenl 12 Jan 1880 Chicago Ill. for 5 yrs; assd to co G 14 inf; disch 11 Jan 1885 Vancouver Bks WT expir of serv a pvt char very good; reenl in same co 11 Feb 1885 for 5 yrs; disch 12 Mar 1890 at Vancouver Bks upon expir of serv a pvt (made good time lost by des'n).

McNally, Jas. P. Pvt co I; b. Kildare Ireland; enl 12 Nov 1872 Troy N.Y. for 5 yrs; age 25; laborer; grey eyes, dk hair, ruddy comp, 6' 0 1/2" high; join co I 2 Dec 1872 Shelbyville Ky.; sick (carbine blow on head) 30 Dec 1872 to 12 Jan 1873; sick (ac. diar.) 23 Oct 1873 to 7 Jan 1874 Ft Totten DT; with pack train June 1876;[34] sgt 3 Aug 1876 to date 1 July 1876; in arrest Dec 1876; pvt 29 Dec 1876; dd regtl hq fatigue pty 25 Apr to 8 Oct 1877; ds Ft Lincoln DT 15 Oct 1877; disch 12 Nov 1877 at Ft Lincoln by expir of serv a pvt char xclt.

McNamara, Jas. Pvt co H; b. 1848 Roscommon Ireland; enl 12 Nov 1872 Troy N.Y. for 5 yrs; age 24 4/12; laborer; blue eyes, lt hair, lt comp, 5' 5" high; join co H 3 Dec 1872 Nashville Tenn; dd qmd laborer 8 Oct 1875 to 4 May 1876; dd regtl hq 25 Apr to 8 Oct

1877; disch 12 Nov 1877 Ft Buford DT by expir of serv a pvt char xclt; died 24 Jan 1932 Pittsfield Mass.
Pension: 13 Jan 1914 / Inv / 1412996. (No claim). 10 Apr 1920 / Ind. Surv. / 17222 / 10651.

McPeake, Alexander. Pvt co L; b. Canonsburg Pa.; enl 15 Mar 1871 Pittsburgh Pa. for 5 yrs; age 21 7/12; teamster; grey eyes, lt hair, fair comp, 5' 7 3/4" high; join co E 7 cav 16 Apr 1871 Spartanburg SC; cpl 1 Sep 1871; pvt 13 Nov 1871; des 11 Apr 1872 Unionville SC; enl as Jno. Bailey 20 May 1872 Baltimore Md for 5 yrs; assd to co F 9 inf; surd 10 Nov 1873 Omaha Bks Neb under GO 102 AGO 1873; ds Ft Randall DT 20 Dec 1873; rejoin co E 22 May 1874 Ft Lincoln DT; in conft Dec 1874 to Feb 1875; (recom for dishon disch 28 Dec 1874 for constant abs from roll calls & neglecting duty in everyway);[35] dd co cook Aug 1875; ed qmd teamster 13 Nov 1875 to 7 Mar 1876; tr to co L 1 Mar 1876; ds camp Powder River MT 10 June 1876 chg co prop; disch 24 June 1877 camp on Sunday Creek MT expir of serv a pvt char good; reenl 19 Apr 1878 St Louis Mo. for 5 yrs; join co D 17 inf 23 June 1878 Ft Lincoln DT; dd co cook Aug 1878; dd qmd laborer Oct 1879; cpl 1 Oct 1881; pvt 20 Jan 1882; disch 18 Apr 1883 Ft Yates DT expir of serv a pvt char very good; reenl 7 May 1883 Pittsburgh Pa. for 5 yrs; join co C 6 inf 8 Dec 1883 Ft Douglas UT; in conft July thro' Dec 1884; sen gen cm 22 Nov 1884 forf $10 pay per mo for 6 mos & conft 3 mos (court leniency acc't good char & long conft); unexpired portion of sen rem'd 5 Jan 1885 upon recom'n co comdr; des 13 Apr 1885 at Ft Douglas.

McShane, Jno. Pvt co I; b. Montreal Canada; enl 20 Sep 1875 Boston mass for 5 yrs; age 26; cooper; grey eyes, blk hair, dk comp, 5' 6" high; join co I 21 Oct 1875 Ft Lincoln DT; in conft Dec 1876; awol 26 Jan 1877; in conft Feb 1877; sen gen cm Mar 1877 forf $12 pay per mo for 6 mos & conft same period; died 13 Apr 1877 from pistol shot wd dur attempt to escape from post guardhouse.[36]

McVay, Jno. Pvt co G; b. Ireland; enl 21 Nov 1872 Pittsburgh Pa. for 5 yrs; age 24; laborer; grey eyes, dk hair, dk comp, 5' 8 3/4" high; join co G 10 Dec 1872 Laurenville SC; dd post mail carrier Aug 1875 to Mar 1876; dd regtl hq mtd msgr 9 May 1876;[37] gsw r. hip 25 June 1876 on Reno hill (fl. wd. severe); tr on str *Far West* 3 July to hosp Ft Lincoln DT; duty 13 Sep & dd qmd with 281 cav horses at post to 28 Sep; dd post mail carrier Dec 1876 to Mar 1877; ds Ft Lincoln 14 Oct 1877; disch 21 Nov 1877 at Ft Lincoln expir of serv a pvt char very good.

McVeigh, David. Trump'r co A; b. Phil'a Pa.; enl 29 Oct 1872 at Phil'a for 5 yrs; age 21; musician; blue eyes, lt brn hair, fair comp, 5' 7" high; join co A 2 Dec 1872 E'town Ky.; unfit to march with comd 4 May 1873 Yankton DT & tr to str *Katie P. Kountz* to Ft Rice DT; dd qmd teamster Feb 1874; dd post hq Apr 1874; dd hq Blk Hills Exp'n Aug 1874; dd regtl hq Sep 1874 to Oct 1875; dd qmd teamster Dec 1875; trump'r 1 Apr 1876; (held Lt DeRudio's horse in valley fight 25 June); dd orderly dept hq in field Aug 1876; disch 24 June 1877 camp on Tongue River MT per SO 70 Dept of Dak. 1877 a trump'r char xclt; res Phil'a Pa. in 1911.[38]

McWilliams, David. Pvt co H; b. Edinburgh Scotland; enl 14 Aug 1866 New York N.Y. for 5 yrs; age 22; teamster; blue eyes, brn hair, fair comp, 5' 5 1/2" high; join co A 7 cav 10 Sep 1866 Ft Riley Kans.; cpl 6 Mar 1867; abs sick Ft Hays Kans. June 1867; pvt 19 Aug 1867; in conft Aug 1868; dd with detmt sharpshooters Nov 1868; in conft Apr 1869; dd co cook Aug 1869; disch 14 Aug 1871 E'town Ky. expir of serv a pvt; reenl in regt 29 Aug 1871 Louisville Ky. for 5 yrs; assd to co H 29 Dec 1871; ds regtl hq at Louisville to May 1872 thence joined co H at Nashville Tenn; cpl 20 Oct 1873; pvt 26 Dec 1874; on furl 30 days 5 May 1875 New Orleans La.;[39] ed qmd painter Jan to May 1876; dd with hq fatigue pty l. wing 15 May 1876; accdt pistol shot wd r. calf while mounting horse 6 June 1876; abs sick camp Powder River MT 15 June 1876;[40] tr on str *Far West* 4 July 1876 to hosp Ft Lincoln DT;[41] tr by wagon to hosp Ft Rice DT 16 July; disch 29 Aug 1876 [hosp] Ft Rice by expir of serv a pvt (wd not healed);

enl in co A 19 Oct 1877 at Ft Lincoln for 5 yrs (auth AGO); dd qmd Dec 1877 to Feb 1878; ds Ft Lincoln June to Nov 1878; dd qmd painter Dec 1878 to Feb 1879; witness in court martial of capt French 28 Jan 1879 at Ft Lincoln;[42] in conft Aug 1880; sen gen cm 7 Sep 1880 forf $10 pay per mo for 2 mos & conft 10 days; (sen as to forf of pay rem'd 15 Sep); dd co blks Dec 1880; tr to co H 14 Feb 1881; far'r 20 Mar 1881; pvt 1 Dec 1881; sick qrs Feb 1882; disch 11 Mar 1882 Ft Meade DT on surg cert dis (old gsw lower r. leg contr line of duty; dis 1/2) a pvt char good;[43] hired in post qmd as citizen teamster 21 Apr 1882;[44] died 19 Sep 1882 at Ft Meade (laudanum overdose [suicide]).[45]

Notes—Mc

1. Federal census of Burleigh County, Dakota, June 1880, lists Harry McBratney, age 39, born in New York; however, his gravestone shows birth year "1844." Mandan Union Cemetery, Plot No. 100.

2. *Bismarck Tribune*, April 26, 1879, Nov. 25, 1881, Oct. 13, 1892; *Mandan Pioneer*, Oct. 14, 1892; Mary McBratney died August 31, 1938 at her farm near Mandan. *Mandan Daily Pioneer*, Aug. 31, 1938; see also *Mandan Pioneer*, July 2, 1897, and July 1, 1898; Peterson, *Morton Prairie Roots*, 651, 804; Fristad, *Historic Mandan and Morton County*, 14.

Although McBratney was apparently the popular proprietor of "Harry's Place," and his name often in the local newspapers, his service with the Custer expedition of 1876 was not mentioned.

3. McVeigh said McCarthy and Logue of L Troop were the two men who helped Tom Custer take Rain-in-the-Face into custody in the store at Standing Rock, WMC, Notes, env 134, IU.

4. Felix Vinatieri told Gen. Custer that McCormick would be a great acquisition for the band, Darling, *Custer's Seventh Cavalry Comes to Dakota*, 148; Frank Lombard said McCormick was a drummer in the band and was the kitchen police, Lombard to Walter Camp, Dec. 31, 1910, WMC-BYU.

5. RG 94, Entry 409, file 7212 B (EB) AGO 1879; in Feb. 1880, the Hon. S. J. Randall, Speaker of the House of Representatives, applied to Judge Advocate Gen. Dunn for remittance of a portion of James McCormick's sentence, based on his long service in the army, but Adjutant General Townsend stated that his length of service only aggravated the crime. McCormick's application May 13, 1880, to be restored to duty was also disapproved, he having been dishonorably discharged by court-martial.

In June 1880, the post surgeon recommended clemency in the belief that longer confinement would irretrievably ruin his health, noting that McCormick was on sick report 101 days during the previous six months and was pale, weak, and greatly depressed in spirits. The post commander endorsed the recommendation, and the adjutant general mitigated the unexecuted portion of the sentence. SO 46, AGO, July 2, 1880, RG 94, Entry 44.

6. Brown Troop Duty Book, Reynolds and Brown *Journal*; McCormick reportedly gave his horse to Lt. McIntosh on June 25 at the edge of the timber, during the retreat from the valley fight, and later came out with Herendeen, Hammer, *Custer in '76*, 107; Hardorff, *Camp, Custer, and the Little Big Horn*, 74; John Lattman, (Piedmont SD), to Max Hoehn, Aug. 10, 1909, WMC-BYU; Theo. Goldin to Albert W. Johnson, Feb. 16, 1933, in Carroll, ed., *The Benteen-Goldin Letters*, 41–42.

7. See note A24 (Arnold).

8. Federal census, 1880, Philadelphia, Pa. John Ryan told Walter Camp that he understood McCurry was a mounted police officer in Philadelphia, residing at 4820 Oliver Street in that city. However, Ryan later told Camp that a young man from West Newton (Mass.), called at that number but failed to see McCurry. Ryan wrote several letters to the address and never got a reply but did receive a postal card from a comrade, whose name he forgot, who told him this was not the McCurry who was in the 7th Cavalry. Ryan to Camp, Dec. 17, 1908, and, Oct. 20, 1909, WMC-BYU.

Ryan's manuscript for his articles published in the *Hardin* (Mont.) *Tribune*, June 22, 1923 and *Billings Gazette*, June 25, 1923, contain a list of 7th Cavalry First Sergeants in 1876, in which Ryan shows McCurry, "Died." LBHB Coll., Roll 10.

McCurry was captain and star pitcher of the Benteen Baseball Club from 1873 to 1876, and was actor and treasurer of the Fort Rice Minstrels theatrical group, which also performed at Fort Lincoln and Bismarck. Anderson, "The Benteen Base Ball Club."

McCurry has been suspected as the author of the Reno petition, because of a perceived similarity of his handwriting with that of several of the alleged signatures. Charles G. duBois, *Kick the Dead Lion*, 52.

9. McDermott to his sister, Margaret, Dec. 4, 1876, Pension file, RG 15.
10. RG 94, Entry 409, file 10818 A (EB) 1877; Lt. Gibson said McDermott filled canteens with water three times, Fougera, *With Custer's Cavalry*, 278.
11. RG 94, Entry 96.
12. SO 39, Hq 7th Cavalry, May 11, 1876, RG 391, Entry 859; Troop Duty Books of Sgt. Botzer and Sgt. Brown (missing pages) show McDonnell on daily duty May 13–31, June 1–5, Aug. 11 to Sept. 26, Reynolds and Brown, *Journal*; Boyle said McDonnell was a good scout. WMC, rosters, LBHB.
13. Brown, *The Galvanized Yankees*, 138; GO 92, AGO, Nov. 23, 1866, RG 94, Entry 44, redesignated the three battalions of the 14th Infantry Regiment as the 14th, 23rd and 32nd Infantry Regiments, respectively, from Sept. 21, 1866; see, Heitman, *Historical Register*, 1: 131.
14. Luce, ed., "The Diary and Letters of Dr. James M. DeWolf." RG 94, Entry 547, Fort Seward; See also note C50 (Craycroft).
15. McDougall received notice of the dangerous illness of his father and caught the steamboat and left the command. Carroll, *Garlington Narrative*, 22; Lt. Godfrey said McDougall's mother and sister died on the same day. Godfrey, *Diary*, Sept. 17; RG 94, Entry 547, Fort Buford; *Bismarck Tribune*, Sept. 27, 1876; *Red River Star*, Sept. 22, 1876.
16. Walter Camp said he spent the whole day of June 26, 1909, with McDougall, and he was in jolly mood and seemed quite vigorous, but said his heart had been troubling him for some time. McDougall sent Camp some photographs July 1 before starting on a fishing trip in Vermont the next day. Camp to Fred Gerard, July 14, 1909, WMC-LBHB.
17. Troop Duty Books of Sgt. Botzer and Sgt. Brown (missing pages) show McEgan on daily duty May 13 through' June 5, and, Aug. 1st to Sept. 19. Reynolds and Brown, *Journal*.
18. Hardy said Comanche belonged to McGuiness, and Keogh took him as an extra horse. Hardorff, *Camp, Custer, and the Little Big Horn*, 81.
19. RG 94, Entry 96.
20. Sgt. Ryan in Taylor Scrapbook, 69; Morris said Lance Cpl. Sniffin cut the colors from the staff and put them inside his shirt. William E. Morris to Robert Bruce, May 23, 1928, LBHB Coll., Roll 11.
21. McGonigle interview with Walter Camp, Oct. 1908, in Hammer, *Custer in '76*, 152; John Lattman to Max Hoehn, Aug. 10, 1909, WMC-BYU.
22. McGonigal's horse was shot June 29. Brown Troop Duty Book, Reynolds and Brown, *Journal*; Sgt. Ryan said the horses were examined thoroughly and any of the wounded they knew would not survive were killed. Barnard, *Ten Years with Custer*, 302; Lt. Edgerly said about fifty horses were killed on Reno Hill. Hammer, *Custer in '76*, 58; the "remains of forty-six horses killed at the picket line," were found in 1877, about 100 yards down the slope on Reno Hill. *Bismarck Tribune*, Nov. 8, 1877.
23. See note A25 (Ascough).
24. McGuire to Walter Camp, Dec. 4, 1908, WMC-BYU; John Mahoney said McGuire, Thompson, and Watson had horses play out while with Custer somewhere down river and came back to Reno, Mahoney interview with Walter Camp, n.d., WMC-BYU.
25. RG 94, Entry 25, file 305281 AGO 1900; McGuire applied for a medal of honor, Jan. 12, 1900, alleging he assisted with the capture of a mule carrying two boxes of carbine ammunition running toward the Indians in an open field on June 25, 1876. Sgt. Hanley rode to the left while he (McGuire) ran on foot to the right and captured the mule while under heavy fire from the Indians. Also, the next day he volunteered on request of Capt. Benteen to help drive Indians from the Company H line and was wounded in the right arm.

The application was not favorably considered when the adjutant general found no record of McGuire ever having been recommended for a medal. The Secretary of War cited GO 42, AGO, 1897 (RG 94, Entry 44), that recommendation must be made by someone other than the proposed recipient or application by claimant in the form of a deposition only.

On Dec. 2, 1902, McGuire applied directly to President Roosevelt to examine the case, and one week later McGuire was informed by the adjutant general that on full investigation, his claim was not favorably considered on the ground the incident was not mentioned in the report of the board of officers appointed June 23, 1878, to examine the recommendations of company commanders for medals of honor, and as the board acted shortly after the battle, it was presumed it provided for all cases justly entitled to medals and its action should not be revised.
26. WMC, rosters, LBHB.
27. SO 39, Hq 7th Cavalry, May 11, 1876, RG 391, Entry 859, ordered the commanding officers of Companies G, I, K, and L to furnish suitable men for orderly duty at department headquarters; see also, Crussy, Loyd, Lynch, and Coakley.

On May 27, 1876, General Terry journaled, "Sent Capt. Michaelis with 15 men & Pvt. McCue as guide to the south to find Stanley's Trail. McCue comes to the conclusion that he had been mistaken," Koury, *The Field Diary of General Alfred H. Terry*. (McCue is likely Terry's spelling for McHugh.)

The regimental return and company return, August 1876, report McHugh on orderly duty at department headquarters from Aug. 1st. However, the returns have many examples of a soldier reported absent only from the first day of the month for which the return was prepared, even though his absence actually began in a prior month, in some cases several months prior. NA, M744; LBHB Coll., Roll 12.

"During his life Sergeant McHugh described the never-to-be-forgotten scene of the [arrival of Gen. Terry's forces on Reno hill] as one of the most pathetic he ever witnessed. Old and battle-scarred veterans, bronzed by the hardships of years of constant and dangerous service, men of iron nerves and lion hearts, in the exuberance of their joy for their timely rescue from the horrible fate which had befallen their unfortunate comrades, embraced their rescuers and cried like such men only can cry, whilst many a silent, abject, heartfelt prayer ascended heavenwards for their timely and happy deliverance." *The Allentown* (Pa.) *Morning Call*, April 1, 1910.

28. See William Grant Wilkinson, "Four Months in the Saddle; The Cross-Country March of the 8th Cavalry from the Mexican to the Canadian Border." (hereafter cited as Wilkinson Four Months in the Saddle) Mss., n.d., Fort Meade, SD. Museum; (the regiment as a whole marched about 1700 miles); see also RG 94, Entry 25, file 9853 AGO 1890.

29. Gen. Custer tells a similar story of a lost trooper, in *My Life on the Plains*, 527.

30. Mrs. Custer believed the board was an "excellent thing," but that McIntosh was entirely harmless and of good habits, and that Col. Sturgis was motivated by his personal dislike of McIntosh, Mrs. Custer to Rebecca Richmond, Nov. 6, 1870, EBC-LBHB, Roll 1; McIntosh was ordered to join his station without delay, (SO 9, AGO, Jan. 9, 1871 [RG 94, Entry 44]), but permitted to delay thirty days to be with his wife when she took sacrament of confirmation at the Church of the Epiphany in Washington. Also so that he could remove the remains of a younger brother, who had recently died, from the cemetery at the Asylum in the District, to another cemetery. ACP file, RG 94, Entry 297.

31. A transcript of a small notebook kept by Lt. McIntosh from Aug. 1872 to June 1876, is among the collections of Little Big Horn Battlefield. The original, with bullet hole, was stolen from the museum in Feb. 1992 and subsequently destroyed by the culprit. *Newsletter* (LBHA), Vol. XXVI, March 1992, and Vol. XXIV, May 1995.

McIntosh's older brother, Archibald, was a military scout in the Pacific Northwest, and in Arizona Territory with Gen. Crook. See Lyon, "Archie McIntosh, the Scottish Indian Scout," and Lyon, "Donald McIntosh, First Lieutenant 7th US Cavalry," in *Clann Chatain*; Archie received several mentions by Bourke in *On the Border with Crook*.

32. "Sergt. McLaughlin's time is out tomorrow . . . he will have to remain until a boat goes down." Capt. Benteen to wife, July 30, 1876, Carroll, *Camp Talk*, 46.

33. After the 1876 campaign, McLaughlin was not the same man either in body or mind. On one occasion he struck his wife across the forehead with his saber scabbard, blackening both eyes. He was much troubled with nervousness, all the time talking about Gen. Custer and Indians and would ask do you not see them, there they are. He used to carry the book "A Life of General Custer." When he saw Custer's picture he would seem to get excited and talk incoherently, nearly going into spasms over it. His constant talk was about the fight at Little Big Horn, and he would point out on the prairie at some rocks and say there the Indians are, do you not see them. He was sent to the Jamestown Hospital for the Insane in April 1885. From statements in various affidavits in pension file, RG 15.

34. Henry Jones said McNally was a packer at Little Big Horn and the last he heard of him he was living at Bismarck. Jones to Walter Camp, May 5, 1913, WMC-DPL; Stan Roy said McNally had a saloon across the river from Fort Lincoln in 1878. Roy to Walter Camp, Nov. 22, 1909, WMC-BYU.

35. RG 391, Entry 869, Letters Sent by Troop E, 1873–1878; see Forrest, "Fighting With Custer," by Earle R. Forrest, in *The Morning Observer* (Washington, Pa.), Oct. 20, 1932.

36. *Bismarck Tribune*, April 14, 1877; Scott, *Some Memories of a Soldier*, 41.

37. Sgt. Botzer Troop Duty Book shows McVay on regular duty with the troop from May 13.

38. McVeigh was interviewed by Walter Camp, June 11, 1911. Liddic and Harbaugh, *Camp on Custer*, 91–92.

39. McWilliams wife, Annie, gave birth to their son James in May 1875 at New Orleans. Federal census, 1900, Meade County, SD.

40. Regimental and company returns, 7th Cavalry; muster roll, Company H; muster roll, hospital dept., Camp on Yellowstone River, MT, June 30, 1876. NA, M744; LBHB Coll, Roll 12; RG 94, Entry 53.

41. McWilliams apparently exchanged places with Private Farley on the Steamer *Far West* to Fort Lincoln. It was reported that his wound was sustained in the battle. *Bismarck Tribune*, July 6, 1876.

42. Court-martial of Captain French, RG 153, file QQ994.

43. McWilliams was reported lame from gunshot wound received in action at Little Big Horn, June 25, 1876. RG 94, Entry 409, file, 3873 C (EB) AGO 1882.

44. RG 92, Entry 238, report 1882/126.

45. Egge, *Old Post Cemetery*, 36; Annie McWilliams died Jan. 22, 1915 at Sturgis, SD, at the home of her son, Egge, *Old Post Cemetery*, 40; James died Jan. 29, 1925, in Sturgis and was interred in the Bear Butte Cemetery.

M

Madden, Mich'l Peter. Pvt co K; b. Galway Ireland; pvt co A 77 Mo. militia 30 Apr to 19 Dec 1864 (awol); enr 28 Mar 1865 Kansas City Mo. a pvt co A 52 Mo. inf for 1 yr; age 25; saddler; gray eyes, blk hair, lt comp, 6' 2" high; tr to co E 51 Mo. inf 1 May 1865 consol'n of regts; m.o. vol serv 31 Aug 1865 Benton Bks Mo.; enl reg army 10 Aug 1866 Cincinnati Ohio for 5 yrs; join co H 7 cav 7 Dec 1866 Ft Riley Kans.; appt co sad'r 13 Dec 1866; regtl sad-sgt 1 Mar 1867; pvt co D 19 Oct 1867; appt co sad'r 25 Oct 1867; ed qmd sad'r Aug to Nov 1870; disch 10 Aug 1871 Mt Vernon Ky. expir of serv a sad'r; reenl 28 Aug 1871 Louisville Ky. for 5 yrs in co K 7 cav; ed qmd sad'r Sep to Nov 1871; appt co sad'r 1 Apr 1872; pres sick 30 Apr 1873; ds Ft Rice DT June to Sep 1873 gd regtl prop; ed qmd Oct 1873 & Jan 1874; dd qmd Apr 1874; in conft Oct 1874; pvt 1 Dec 1874; in conft Apr 1876; gsw r. leg 26 June 1876 (frac. both bones, leg amp'd below knee);[1] tr on str *Far West* 3 July to hosp Ft Lincoln DT; sgt 12 July 1876 for dist bravery in battle;[2] disch 28 Aug 1876 hosp Ft Lincoln by expir of serv a sgt char xclt; (left hosp 13 Sep having made good recovery, stump completely healed); employed as ostler in qmd stables St Paul Minn. Sep 1876 to Apr 1877; rate of pay $30 mo;[3] res Sol. Home Wash'n D.C. June to Nov 1877;[4] appn for incr of pension 5 Sep 1877 rej on grd sol. in receipt of pension to which entitled under existing regulations.
Pension: 16 Oct 1876 / Inv / 226658 / 143683. Dropped from roll 19 Feb 1887 (failure to claim); last paid 7 Dec 1883; P. O. 318 Chestnut Street, St Louis, Mo. Note: Failure of any pensioner to claim his pension for three years was deemed presumptive evidence of his death, remarriage, recovery from disability, or otherwise, and his name stricken from the list, subject to restoration upon new application. (Sec. 4719, R. S.).

Madsen, Christian. Pvt co F; b. Kjerteminde Denmark; enl 24 Aug 1872 Cleveland Ohio for 5 yrs; age 24 11/12; tanner; blue eyes, lt hair, fair comp, 5' 11" high; join co F 1 Dec 1872 Louisville Ky.; sick hosp Yellowstone Exp'n 6 Aug 1873 (ac. dysentery); tr to str *Josephine* 13 Sep camp Glendive Creek MT to hosp Ft Lincoln DT; duty 29 Oct 1873; sick hosp Ft Lincoln 12 Apr to 7 Sep 1874 (cont'n r. knee); dd qmd laborer June to Sep 1875; killed with Custer column 25 June 1876.

Mahoney, Bartholomew. Pvt co L; b. Cork Ireland; enl 29 Oct 1872 Boston Mass. for 5 yrs; age 26; teamster; hazel eyes, dk hair, sallow comp, 5' 10" high; join co L 9 Dec 1872 Yorkville SC; dd pioneer Apr 1873; awol 29 Mar 1876; sen gar cm 6 Apr 1876 forf $10 pay; killed with Custer column 25 June 1876.

Mahoney, Dan'l. Pvt co M; b. Cork Ireland; enl 28 Sep 1875 Boston Mass. for 5 yrs; age 23; laborer; gray eyes, brn hair, fair comp, 5' 9 1/4" high; join co M 21 Oct 1875 Ft Rice DT; abs sick at Ft Rice 19 Apr to 25 Nov 1877; disch 14 Apr 1878 Ft Lincoln DT on surg cert dis a pvt char good (r. inquinal hernia requiring constant use of truss; ruptured r. testicle when thrown upon saddle horn dur retreat from valley fight 25 June 1876; dis 1/2); died 7 Aug 1885 Sol. Home Wash'n D.C.
Pension: 25 May 1880 / Inv / 367834 / 219345. Mother / 566020.

Mahoney, Jno. Pvt co C; b. Cork Ireland; enl 24 Sep 1875 St Louis Mo. for 5 yrs; age 27; laborer; blue eyes, dk hair, dk comp, 5' 7" high; join co C 21 Oct 1875 Ft Lincoln DT; appt co wag 1 Nov 1876; pvt 10 July 1877; dd co cook Dec 1877; dd regtl hq July to Oct 1878; dd qmd carpenter July & Aug 1879; disch 23 Sep 1880 Ft Meade DT expir of serv a pvt char xclt; reenl next day in co C for 5 yrs & on furl 60 days Sturgis City DT; dd qmd teamster Apr & June 1882; ds escort duty with Prof Scott of Princeton College on geological exp'n from Ft Custer MT June thro' Oct 1884; disch 23 Sep 1885 at Ft Meade expir of serv a pvt char xclt; died 27 July 1918 Sturgis SD.
Pension: 10 Nov 1902 / Inv / 1292657 / 1127214.

Mann, Frank C. Citizen packer qmd; b. New York N.Y.; enl 17 Sep 1870 Vallejo Calif. for 5 yrs; age 23; blacksmith; gray eyes, lt hair, fair comp, 5' 6 1/2" high; join co M 1 cav 3 Jan 1871 Camp Thomas AT; blks 1 July 1872; tr to co F 5 cav 2 Aug 1873 Camp Grant AT; far'r 12 Feb 1875; ed qmd blks to Apr 1875; disch 17 Sep 1875 Ft Dodge Kans. upon expir of serv a far'r; hired Apr 1876 St Paul Minn. by Lt Gibbs 6 inf actg aqm to pack supplies on public animals of exp'n; rate of pay $50 mo & entitled to one ration per day & transp back to St Paul if hon disch; tr to Lt Nowlan at Ft Lincoln DT 17 Apr 1876 with pay to commence from that date;[5] drove pack mules alongside wagon train dur march to Powder River;[6] killed 26 June 1876 on Reno hill (on line of co A).[7]

Manning, David. Pvt co D; b. Dublin Ireland; enl 1 Oct 1873 Boston Mass. for 5 yrs; age 26 2/12; shoemaker; gray eyes, sandy hair, florid comp, 5' 8 1/4" high; join co D 22 Oct 1873 Ft Totten DT; dd June 1874; dd regtl hq fatigue pty 25 Apr to 8 Oct 1877; ds Ft Rice DT 27 Oct 1877; dd boats crew Apr 1878; disch 1 Oct 1878 Camp J. G. Sturgis DT expir of serv a pvt char xclt; reenl 28 Oct 1878 Boston Mass. for 5 yrs; assd to co G 3 cav; disch 27 Oct 1883 San Carlos AT expir of serv a pvt char xclt; reenl 14 Nov 1883 at Boston for 5 yrs; assd to co M 3 cav; disch 13 Nov 1888 Ft Clark Tex. expir of serv a pvt char xclt; reenl 10 Dec 1888 at Boston for 5 yrs; assd to co F 7 inf; disch 11 Dec 1893 Ft Logan Colo. expir of serv a pvt char xclt; reenl 22 Dec 1893 New York N.Y. for 5 yrs; assd to co F 9 inf; disch 22 Dec 1898 Madison Bks N.Y. expir of serv a pvt char fair; reenl 11 Jan 1899 at Madison Bks for 3 yrs in co K 9 inf; disch 10 Jan 1902 Oras Samar PI expir of serv a cpl char xclt & reenl in same co for 3 yrs; retd 23 June 1902 San Francisco Calif. a sgt; died 25 Oct 1910 New York N.Y.

Manning, Jas. (Jee) Rial. Blks co F; b. Houston Co Ga.; enl 25 Jan 1873 Louisville Ky. for 5 yrs; age 29; blacksmith; hazel eyes, blk hair, dk comp, 5' 8 1/2" high; join co I 7 cav 3 June 1873 Ft Snelling Minn.; dd qmd blks Oct 1873; ed qmd laborer Dec 1873; ed qmd blks (NBS) 29 June to 3 Sep 1874; ed qmd Oct 1875; tr to co F 1 Mar 1876 & appt blks; killed with Custer column 25 June 1876.
Pension: 26 May 1883 / Wid / 304783 / 215931.

Maroney, Mathew. Sgt co H; b. Co Clare Ireland; pvt co B 6 N.Y. hy art'y 22 Aug 1862 to 1 Aug 1865; enl reg army 4 Jan 1867 Cincinnati Ohio for 5 yrs; age 21; teamster; blue eyes, brn hair, lt comp, 5' 7 1/2" high; assd to co L 7 cav 10 Feb 1867; join regt 13 June 1867 Ft Riley Kans.; ds regtl hq to 10 Sep 1867 when tr to co H at Ft Wallace Kans.; cpl 21 Oct 1867; sgt 21 Jan 1868; pvt 15 June 1869; ds carrying desp to Ft Larned Kans. Oct 1869; cpl 25 July 1870; sgt 2 Jan 1871; disch 4 Jan 1872 Huntsville Ala expir of serv a sgt & reenl in co H for 5 yrs; in arrest Apr 1873; pvt 14 Sep 1874; cpl 2 Nov 1875; ed subs dept chg of cattle herd Nov 1875 to Mar 1876; sgt 5 Apr 1876; disch 4 Jan 1877 Ft Rice DT expir of serv a sgt char xclt; reenl in co H 5 Mar 1877 at Ft Rice for 5 yrs; cpl 1 Jan 1878; dd actg prov sgt Apr 1878; sgt 1 July 1878; sick hosp Ft Lincoln DT from 26 Sep 1878 (intm. fever); disch 16 May 1879 at Ft Lincoln on surg cert dis (gen paralysis [atoxic]; unable to speak or cause muscular action of upper body & slightly of lower extremities; movement of arms little under control; disease occurred dur attack of Mtn fever in line of duty); died 14 Dec 1880 Sol. Home Wash'n D.C.
Pension: 13 Dec 1879 / Inv / 325532. (Abandoned).

Marshall, Jasper Rudolph. Pvt co L; b. 26 Apr 1852 Warren Co Ohio; enl 22 Sep 1875 Cincinnati Ohio for 5 yrs; age 22; farmer; gray eyes, blk hair, dk comp, 5' 5 1/2" high; join co L 29 Oct 1875 Ft Totten DT; gsw l. ankle & l. foot 26 June 1876 on Reno hill; tr on str *Far West* 3 July to hosp Ft Lincoln; disch 9 Feb 1877 Ft Lincoln DT on surg cert dis a pvt char good; died 10 May 1920 Pleasant Hill Ohio.
Pension: 19 Mar 1877 / Inv / 232655 / 145158. Ind. Surv. / 17193 / 10378.

Marshall, Jno. M. Far'r co H; b. Scarbrough England; enl 6 Feb 1872 Cincinnati Ohio for 5 yrs; age 32 3/12; laborer; blue eyes, lt hair, fair comp, 5' 6" high; join co H 23 Feb 1872 Nashville Tenn; ds herding co horses June 1872; far'r 1 Sep 1872; ds Ft Rice 20 June to 1 Sep 1874; dd subs dept butcher 4 May 1876; ds Ft Rice 5 May 1876 chg co prop & garden;[8] disch 6 Feb 1877 at Ft Rice expir of serv a far'r char good; reenl in co H 3 Jan 1878 at Ft Rice for 5 yrs; ds Ft Rice June to Nov 1878; des 10 May 1879 Ft Lincoln DT.

Marshall, Manuel. See Russell, Thos.

Marshall, Wm. August. Pvt co D; b. Prussia Germany; enl 25 Sep 1875 Chicago Ill. for 5 yrs; age 24 2/12; teamster; gray eyes, lt brn hair, fair comp, 5' 7" high; join co D 21 Oct 1875 Ft Lincoln DT; dd regtl hq fatigue pty (morn & eve) 11 May 1876; dd hosp attdt 17 Oct 1876; dd orderly for gen cm Dec 1876 to Mar 1877; cpl 3 Feb 1878; dd actg co qm sgt Aug 1878 thro' Feb 1879; dd chg co garden Apr 1879; sgt 11 Oct 1879; ds escort for census enumerator to Ft Bennett DT June 1880; disch 24 Sep 1880 Ft Yates DT expir of serv a sgt char xclt; reenl 16 Sep 1881 at Chicago for 5 yrs; assd to co K 13 inf; disch 15 Sep 1886 Ft L'worth Kans. expir of serv a sgt; reenl 25 July 1887 Columbus Bks Ohio for 5 yrs; assd to gen serv; disch 2 Nov 1891 at Columbus Bks on surg cert dis (phthisis pulmonalis, contr line of duty, dis total) a pvt char xclt; died 24 Aug 1892 Sol. Home Wash'n D.C.
Pension: 29 Feb 1892 / Inv / 1095044 / 793668. Wid / 563442 / 358275.

Martin, Jas. Cpl co G; b. Kildare Co Ireland; enl 6 Feb 1872 Chicago Ill. for 5 yrs; age 24; laborer; gray eyes, brn hair, fair comp, 5' 5" high; join co G 26 Feb 1872 Spartanburg SC; cpl 3 Feb 1875; dd chg co kit'n Aug to Nov 1875; dd 8–14 June 1876; killed dur retreat from valley fight 25 June 1876.

Martin, Jno. Trump'r co H; b. 28 Jan 1853 Sala Conzalina Italy; enl 1 June 1874 New York N.Y. for 5 yrs; age 22; musician; hazel eyes, dk hair, dk comp, 5' 6" high; join 7 cav 20 July 1874 Ft Lincoln DT & await ret of regt from field; join co H as trump'r 17 Sep 1874 Ft Rice DT; orderly trump'r to gen Custer 25 June 1876 & carried message to capt Benteen; sick qrs 12–13 Aug 1876 (ac. diar.); on str *Carroll* 28 Aug to Ft Buford & on str *Benton* 3 Sep to Ft Lincoln; arr Ft Rice 10 Sep [with pvt Ricketts]; rejoin co 4 Oct 1876 camp near Ft Lincoln; ds Chicago Ill. 9 Jan 1879 witness in Reno court of inq; disch 31 May 1879 at Ft Lincoln by expir of serv a trump'r char xclt; reenl 24 June 1879 Ft Schuyler N.Y. for 5 yrs in co G 3 art'y; disch 23 June 1884 St Augustine Fla by expir of serv a mus'n char xclt & reenl in same co for 5 yrs; disch 23 June 1889 Ft McHenry Md by expir of serv a mus'n char xclt & reenl in same co for 5 yrs; tr to co D 22 Dec 1892; tr to co L 4 art'y 14 Apr 1893 at Ft McHenry (when 3 art'y tr to Ft McPherson Ga. & he having large family of 5 minor ch. at school in Baltimore); tr to co D 21 Nov 1893; disch 23 June 1894 at Ft McHenry by expir of serv a mus'n char very good & reenl in same co for 5 yrs; disch 23 Sep 1897 at Ft McHenry per GO 80 AGO 1890 a mus'n char xclt;[9] reenl in same co 30 Sep 1897 at Ft McHenry for 3 yrs (period of exclusion waived); disch 29 Sep 1900 at Ft McHenry by expir of serv a mus'n char xclt; reenl next day for co H 7 cav for 3 yrs & on furl 60 days; joined co H 28 Nov 1900 Columbia Bks Cuba; trump'r 1 Dec; sick hosp 5 Mar to 19 May 1901 (chr. gastric catarrh); recom by post surg for tr to post hosp corps (fill vacancy for mus'n) but disappv under Regs. par. 1403 forbidding such tr of mus'ns; pvt 13 Apr 1901 but app'n for tr disappv under Regs. par. 1404 forbidding tr of married men; app'd for tr at own expense to 39th co coast art'y (formerly co D 4 art'y) at Ft McHenry, claiming to be too old for mtd serv; on furl 30 days 24 May at Baltimore when tr appv 10 June 1901; appn for tr to 90th co coast art'y at Ft McHenry (as mus'n) appv 11 July 1901; disch 29 Sep 1903 at Ft McHenry by expir of serv a cpl char xclt & reenl for 3 yrs; awl 60 days 10 Nov 1903; retd 7 Jan 1904 a sgt char xclt; died 24 Dec 1922 Brooklyn N.Y.
Pension: 29 Mar 1923 / Wid / 1203353 / 938645.

Martin, Mich'l. 1sgt co D; b. Dublin Ireland; enl in co D 6 Dec 1867 Ft L'worth Kans. for 5 yrs; age 30; soldier; gray eyes, lt hair, fair comp, 5' 6" high; ed qmd teamster Feb 1871; cpl 7 Aug 1871; sgt 1 Apr 1872; disch 6 Dec

213

1872 Opelika Ala expir of serv a sgt & reenl in co D for 5 yrs; 1sgt 1 Aug 1874; (recom by Lt Edgerly for medal of honor for conspic gal at LBH, but omitted on revised list);[10] killed 30 Sep 1877 Snake Creek MT (Bear's Paw Mtns) in action with Nez Perce inds; survived by wife & 4 ch.
Pension: 3 May 1878 / Wid / 237001 / 185371. Minor / 292301 / 250816.

Martin, Wm. Pvt co B; b. London England; enl 4 Sep 1873 St Louis Mo. for 5 yrs; age 23; laborer; blue eyes, brn hair, fair comp, 5' 5 1/4" high; join co B 19 Oct 1873 Ft Lincoln DT; dd co cook Feb & Apr 1874; in conft Oct 1874 to Mar 1875; sen gen cm 23 Jan 1875 forf $10 pay per mo for 6 mos & conft same period; unexpired portion of sen rem'd 29 Mar 1875; dd co tailor Aug 1875; in conft Oct 1875; in conft Feb 1876; ds Ft Lincoln 17 Oct 1876 dismtd; dd co tailor Dec 1876 to Feb 1877; in conft Feb 1878; in conft June 1878; disch 4 Sep 1878 Standing Rock DT expir of serv a pvt char good; reenl 9 Sep 1878 at Standing Rock for 5 yrs in co K 17 inf; ds regtl hq with band as tailor Sep 1878 to May 1883; disch 24 July 1883 Ft Yates DT on surg cert dis (deafness both ears, progressing about 2 yrs; contr line of duty) a pvt char xclt; died 13 Jan 1900 Ft McPherson Ga.
Pension: 7 Aug 1883 / Inv / 491466 / 280469.

Martini, Giovanni. See Martin, Jno.

Mask, Geo. Brown. pvt co B; b. Pittsburgh Pa.; enl 15 Nov 1872 at Pittsburgh for 5 yrs; age 22 11/12; moulder; gray eyes, brn hair, fair comp, 5' 4" high; join co B 9 Dec 1872 Spartanburg SC; unfit for duty with Yellowstone Exp'n 21 July 1873 (const. syph.) & tr by boat to hosp Ft Lincoln DT; duty 23 Sep 1873; ds Ft Lincoln 20 June to 30 Aug 1874; dd co cook Sep 1874; dd mail carrier Apr to July 1875; killed 25 June 1876; body not recovered.[11]
Pension: 1 Aug 1876 / Mother / 227375 / 179211.

Mason, Henry S. Cpl co E; b. Brownsville Ind.; enl 11 July 1870 St Louis Mo. for 5 yrs; age 23; brakeman; gray eyes, sandy hair, fair comp, 5' 11 1/4" high; join co F 7 cav 17 July 1870 camp near Ft Hays Kans.; dd orderly dept hq Jan to June 1872; sick July to Nov 1872 (ac. dysentery); dd msgr dept hq Dec 1872; dd post mail carrier Feb 1873; cpl 27 May 1873; sick 21 July 1873 (typhoid fever) & tr by boat from Yellowstone Exp'n to Ft Lincoln DT; duty 10 Sep 1873; sgt Mar 1874; pvt July 1874; dd regtl hq Dec 1874; dd msgr regtl hq Apr to July 1875; disch 11 July 1875 at Ft Lincoln expir of serv a pvt; reenl 4 Aug 1875 Louisville Ky. for 5 yrs; join co E 29 Oct 1875 Ft Totten DT; cpl 1 Nov 1875; dd chg of hq fatigue party r. wing 15 May 1876; killed in action 25 June 1876; [killed in valley fight says Finnegan; killed on Reno hill says Lange].[12]

Mathey, Edw. Gustave. 1Lt co M; b. 27 Oct 1837 Besancon France; came to America in 1845 to Corydon Ind.; enr 31 May 1861 in co C 17 Ind. inf; age 23; blk eyes, blk hair, dk comp, 5' 9 1/2" high; 1sgt 12 June 1861; 2Lt 30 Apr 1862; resd com'n 10 Aug 1862; appt 2Lt 81 Ind. inf 1 Sep 1862 upon org'n of regt; 1Lt 21 Jan 1863; capt 8 Nov 1863; maj 12 Sep 1864; m.o. vol serv 13 June 1865; appt reg army com'n 2Lt 7 cav 24 Sep 1867; join co I 19 Dec 1867 Ft Wallace Kans.; sick 27 Nov 1868 (snow blind) with wagon train dur fight at Washita; 1Lt 10 May 1870; tr to co B 21 July 1870; ds Wash'n D.C. 1 Nov 1870 before spl exam'g bd (upon recom'n col Sturgis) & found not unfit for the serv;[13] actg aqm & comsy Spartanburg SC May 1872 to Jan 1873; ds Ft Sully DT 27 Apr 1873 purchase hay for regt (verbal instr'n gen Custer); comd co B 7 May 1873; attd to co M 21 July 1873 with Yellowstone Exp'n; tr to co M 1 Nov 1873; with co on Blk Hills Exp'n July & Aug 1874; post adjt Ft Rice DT 8 July 1875 & comsy & signal officer 1 Nov 1875 to 1 Mar 1876; comd dismtd detmt 17 May to 14 June 1876;[14] comd pack train 22 June 1876; td comd co C & care of co rec's 27 June 1876;[15] awl one mo 25 Oct & ext'd 6 mos 20 Nov 1876; ds Ft Rice 24 May 1877; on str *General Sherman* 17 Aug enroute to join co in field; attd to co B 18 Sep Cant'mt Tongue River MT; with supply train to gen Miles comd & rejoin co M 25 Oct camp on Missouri River; ds str *General Meade* 26 Oct to Ft Rice; (capt co K from 13 Oct 1877); ds Chicago Ill. Jan 1879 witness in Reno court of inq; tr to co L Aug 1890; ds rctg duty Sep

1890 to Sep 1892 at Chicago; awl on surg cert 7 Oct 1892 to 5 Dec 1893; sick qrs to 13 Jan 1894 thence awl 6 mos; comd co E from 1 May 1895 Ft Grant AT; ds Presidio Calif. 16 Apr 1896 for exam'n for prom'n; awl 29 Oct 1896 Denver Colo. awaiting retirement; retd as maj 11 Dec 1896 for disability incident to serv; prof of mil science at Baylor Univ Aug 1901 to June 1903; Lt-col on retd list 23 Apr 1904; died 17 July 1915 Denver Colo.
[82 ACP 1871]. Pension: 10 Aug 1915 / Wid / 1051695 / 800119.

Maxwell, Thos. E. Pvt co L; b. Allegheny Pa.; enl 27 Dec 1872 St Louis Mo. for 5 yrs; age 22; laborer; blue eyes, brn hair, ruddy comp, 5' 5 1/2" high; join co L 11 Feb 1873 New Orleans La.; dd hq Blk Hills Exp'n 25 June to 31 Aug 1874; sick in hosp 22 Nov 1875 to 8 Jan 1876 (ac. dysentery); sick 11 Jan to 10 Feb 1876 (chr. dysentery); killed with Custer column 25 June 1876.

May, Frank. (alias). See Voit, Otto.

Meador, Thos. E. Pvt co H; b. 1851 Bedford Co Va.; enl 19 Jan 1872 Lexington Ky. for 5 yrs; age 23; farmer; brn eyes, brn hair, ruddy comp, 5' 5 1/4" high; join co H 12 Feb 1872 Nashville Tenn; ds herding co horses June 1872; ds with detmt at Breaux Bridge La. Oct to Dec 1874; ds with detmt at St Martinsville La. Feb to Apr 1875; killed 26 June 1876 on Reno hill.[16]
Pension: 29 June 1882 / Wid / 294246 / 227675.

Meadville, Jno. R. Pvt co D; b. 14 Dec 1855 Buster Co Pa.; enl as Jno. Meadwell 13 Sep 1875 Pittsburgh Pa. for 5 yrs; age 21; miner; brn eyes, brn hair, fair comp, 5' 7 1/2" high; join co D 21 Oct 1875 Ft Lincoln DT; dd regtl hq fatigue party (morn & eve) 11 May 1876; disch 26 July 1876 camp mouth of Rosebud Creek MT per SO 127 AGO 1876 (upon app'n of father, having enl as minor without consent).[17]

Meadwell, Jno. (alias). See Meadville, Jno. R.

Mechling, Henry Wm. Bigler. Blks co H; b. 14 Oct 1851 Mt Pleasant Pa.; enl 5 Aug 1875 Pittsburgh Pa. for 5 yrs; age 23; blacksmith; gray eyes, dk brn hair, fair comp, 5' 9 3/4" high; join co H 29 Oct 1875 Ft Rice DT; blks 1 Jan 1876; awarded medal of honor 5 Oct 1878 for serving as sharpshooter [at LBH] in exposed position outside the line to provide cover for water carriers; ed qmd blks Oct 1878 thro' Apr 1879; disch 4 Aug 1880 Ft Meade DT expir of serv a blks char xclt; visited Custer Battlefield June 1903;[18] died 10 Apr 1926 Sol. Home Wash'n D.C.
Pension: 25 Apr 1892 / Inv / 1108936 / 868191.

Meier, Fred'k. Pvt co C; b. Delmanhort Germany; enl 24 Dec 1875 St Louis Bks Mo. for 5 yrs; age 21; tailor; hazel eyes, brn hair, fair, comp, 5' 6 1/2" high; join co C 18 Apr 1876 Ft Lincoln DT; killed with Custer column 25 June 1876.

Meier, Jno. H. Pvt co M; b. Hanover Germany; enl 3 Sep 1873 Boston Mass. for 5 yrs; age 26; varnisher; blue eyes, red hair, lt comp, 5' 5" high; join co M 21 Oct 1873 Ft Rice DT; dd subs dept herder Nov & Dec 1875; gsw in neck (fl. wd. sl.) 25 June 1876; tr on str *Far West* 3 July to hosp Ft Lincoln DT; tr to hosp at Ft Rice 16 July; duty 17 July; rejoin co 5 Oct 1876; in conft Apr 1878; disch 3 Sep 1878 Camp Ruhlen DT expir of serv a pvt char xclt; reenl in co M 17 Sep 1878 at Camp Ruhlen for 5 yrs; cpl 9 Aug 1883; disch 16 Sep 1883 Ft Meade DT expir of serv a cpl char good & reenl in co M for 5 yrs; in arrest Dec 1886; pvt 17 Feb 1887 sen gen cm & forf $10 pay per mo for 3 mos & conft same period; cpl 1 Dec 1887; sgt 10 Apr 1888; disch 16 Sep 1888 Ft Riley Kans. expir of serv a sgt char xclt & reenl in co M for 5 yrs; dd drilling rcts Jan & Feb 1889; pvt 20 June 1889; sen gen cm 26 Aug 1889 to conft one mo hard labor; cpl 2 Apr 1890; pvt 25 Aug 1890 sen gen cm; tr to co A 10 Sep 1890 (cos L & M skeletonized); cpl 1 June 1891; sgt 1 Nov 1891; in arrest Aug 1893; pvt 16 Sep 1893 sen gen cm & disch same day at Ft Riley by expir of serv a pvt char barring weakness for drink an xclt sol.; reenl 23 Sep 1893 at Ft Riley for 5 yrs in co I 7 cav; cpl 6 July 1894; sgt 29 Aug 1896; disch 22 Dec 1896 Ft Huachuca AT per GO 80

AGO 1890 a sgt char xclt;[19] reenl 16 Mar 1897 New York N.Y. for 3 yrs; assd to co C 5 art'y; died 22 Feb 1899 Ft Hancock NJ (frac. skull) a pvt.[20]

Meineke, Ernst. Pvt co F; b. Bamburg Germany; enl 25 Sep 1875 New York N.Y. for 5 yrs; age 30; gardner; blue eyes, brn hair, fair comp, 5' 6 1/2" high; join co F 21 Oct 1875 Ft Lincoln DT; ds Ft Lincoln 13 May 1876 chg co prop & garden; ed hosp cook 3–16 Aug 1876; dd co gardener 31 Aug 1876; dd co gardener Apr to Sep 1878; dd co gardener Apr to Sep 1879; dd co gardener Apr 1880; ds Ft Totten DT chg co garden 3 May to 24 Sep 1880 when disch by expir of serv a pvt char xclt; reenl 11 Oct 1880 New York N.Y. for 5 yrs; assd to co H 8 cav; disch 10 Oct 1885 camp at Malone NM expir of serv a pvt; reenl for same co 26 Oct 1885 San Antonio Tex. for 5 yrs; disch 25 Oct 1890 camp Tongue River MT expir of serv a pvt char 1st cl.; reenl 5 Nov 1890 Chicago Ill. for 5 yrs; assd to mtd serv detmt at Jeff'n Bks Mo.; tr to co B 3 cav 20 Oct 1894; tr to co K 2 Feb 1895; disch 4 Nov 1895 at Jeff'n Bks by expir of serv a pvt char xclt; reenl in same co 6 Nov 1895 for 3 yrs; disch 28 Dec 1896 at Jeff'n Bks on surg cert dis a pvt (gen debility & old age; degree of dis 3/4; claimed to be nine yrs older than rec's show & looks older than 60 yrs); died 24 July 1907 Sol. Home Wash'n D.C. (age 79).
Pension: 5 Jan 1897 / Inv / 1183650 / 934041.

Merrill, Lewis. Major; b. 28 Oct 1834 New Berlin Pa.; grad USMA 1 July 1855 & appt bvt 2Lt 1 drg; 2Lt 2 drg 13 Dec 1855; (redesig 2 cav Aug 1861); 1Lt 24 Apr 1861 & org vol troops in Mo.; appt col & chf of cav on staff of gen Fremont Aug 1861; col 2 Mo. cav (Merrill's Horse) 23 Aug 1861 & org regt thro' Sep 1861; in Fremont's campn to Springfield Mo. to Nov 1861; comd mil distr of St Louis Jan 1862; attd to distr of southeast Mo. June 1863 & exp'n to remove rebel forces from Ark; at Little Rock to Mar 1864 when tr to St Louis for six mos; tr to army of Cumberland Jan 1865 & in exp'n against Mobile & Ohio railroad thence to Chattanooga & escort duty for trains to Atlanta; m.o. vol serv 14 Dec 1865; capt 2 cav to date 1 Oct 1861; join co G 1 Feb 1866 Ft L'worth Kans.; bvt maj for gal serv against rebel forces in north Mo.; bvt Lt-col for gal serv in capture of Little Rock; bvt col for gal serv against rebel forces in northwest Ga. & surd of rebel gen Wofford; bvt brig-gen vols for gal serv dur the war; ds Omaha Neb actg aig Dept of the Platte Sep 1866 to Sep 1868 & judge advocate to Mar 1869; prom maj 7 cav 14 Dec 1868 to date 27 Nov 1868; join regt 22 Apr 1869 camp near Ft Hays Kans.; ds Santa Fe NM Aug to Nov 1869 as judge advocate; post comdr Yorkville SC Mar 1871 to Mar 1873; ds Charlotte NC Apr & May 1873; awl one yr on surg cert 4 June 1873 & extd 40 days; post comdr Ft Rice DT 6 Aug to 3 Sep 1874; comd battn at New Orleans & Shreveport La. (distr upper Red River) Oct 1874 to Feb 1876; ds Phil'a Pa. Mar to Nov 1876 with centennial exposition;[21] (summoned before mil affairs committee at Wash'n 3 Apr 1876);[22] join regt 29 Dec 1876 Ft Lincoln DT; comd battn (cos FIL) in field 2 May to 8 Oct 1877; ds chg of hosp on str *Silver City* 16 Oct & arr Ft Lincoln 26 Oct 1877;[23] appt to bd of officers 23 June 1878 to revise medal of honor list for LBH; post comdr Ft Yates DT Apr 1879 thro' May 1880; comd escort for NPRR ext'n June to Dec 1880 & again July to Nov 1881; ds dept hq St Paul Minn. Dec 1881 thro' April 1882; comd troops with NPRR ext'n May to Nov 1882; awl 4 mos Dec 1882; awl 6 mos May 1883 on surg cert & ext'd to 21 May 1886 when retd for disability in line of duty; bvt brig-gen 27 Feb 1890 for gal serv in action at Canon Creek MT 13 Sep 1877; appt Lt-col of cav 21 Jan 1891 to rank from 9 Jan 1886 (act 27 Sep 1890);[24] died 27 Feb 1896 Phil'a Pa.
[M103 CB 1863].

Merritt, Geo. Anson. Pvt band; b. 10 Oct 1840 Stonington Conn.; pvt & cpl co C 3 Wis cav 15 Dec 1861 to 29 July 1865; enl reg army 27 Nov 1866 Chicago Ill. for 3 yrs; age 24; sailmaker; gray eyes, sandy hair, fair comp, 5' 8 3/4" high; assd to gen serv "music boys" Newport Bks Ky.; disch 27 Nov 1869 at Newport Bks by expir of serv a trump'r; reenl for same unit 3 Dec 1869 Cincinnati Ohio for 5 yrs; disch 3 Dec 1874 at Newport

Bks by expir of serv a pvt; reenl 22 Jan 1875 at Cincinnati for 5 yrs; assd to co B 7 cav 28 Jan 1875 a trump'r; ds Ft Snelling Minn. 13 Mar 1875 awaiting transp to regt (snow blockade on NPRR);[25] tr to Ft Lincoln DT 19 Apr 1875 (with Voss); tr to band 25 Apr 1875; ds Ft Lincoln 5 May 1876 [lance sgt] chg of prop;[26] pvt 2 May 1877; tr to co I 26 May 1879;[27] awl 3 mos 1 Aug 1879 Fargo DT; disch 21 Jan 1880 at Ft Lincoln expir of serv a pvt char xclt; died 24 Apr 1918 Chicago Ill. Pension: 31 Aug 1894 / Inv / 1160427 / 912512.

Methfessel, Christian. Pvt co K; b. Muhlhausen Germany; enl as Fred'k Smith 27 Nov 1867 New York N.Y. for 3 yrs; age 22; locksmith; hazel eyes, brn hair, florid comp, 5' 9 3/4" high; assd to co A 11 inf; (consol with 34 inf Apr 1869 & desig 16 inf); disch 18 Aug 1870 Louisville Ky. (a supernumerary) a cpl char xclt; reenl 22 Feb 1871 St Louis Ars'l Mo. for 5 yrs; assd to co D 3 cav ; disch 22 Feb 1876 Ft D. A. Russell Wyo. Ty expir of serv a pvt char xclt; reenl 7 Mar 1876 St Louis Bks Mo. for 5 yrs; join co K 7 cav 27 Apr 1876 St Paul Minn.; ds camp Powder River MT 15 June 1876; cpl 21 Oct 1877; sgt 31 May 1878; ds Ft Rice DT June to Oct 1878; 1sgt 1 Dec 1878; sick hosp (frac. r. leg) Aug to Oct 1879; disch 6 Mar 1881 Ft Totten DT expir of serv a 1sgt char xclt & reenl in co K for 5 yrs; sgt 17 Oct 1882; dd actg co qm sgt Dec 1882; pvt 12 May 1883; ds msgr dept hq Ft Snelling Minn. May to Nov 1883; 1sgt 9 Nov 1883; disch 6 Mar 1886 Ft Meade DT expir of serv a 1sgt char xclt & reenl in co K for 5 yrs; sgt 1 Nov 1886; pvt 24 Apr 1887; ds ordn depot Ft Lincoln DT Apr 1887 to May 1888; tr to co I 21 July 1888; cpl 4 Oct 1888; sen gen cm June 1889 forf $10 pay per mo for 2 mos; sgt 16 May 1890; ds Ft Riley Kans. 27 Sep 1890 to 26 Jan 1891 chg co prop; disch 6 Mar 1891 at Ft Riley expir of serv a sgt char xclt & reenl in co I for 5 yrs; on furl 3 mos 21 Apr 1891 Waterloo Iowa; sd chg co stables Jan 1892 to June 1893; actg 1sgt Jan to Apr 1895; disch 6 Mar 1896 Ft Grant AT expir of serv a sgt char xclt & reenl in co I for 3 yrs; sd qmd overseer Sep 1897 to Aug 1898; retd 11 Aug 1898 Ft Huachuca AT a sgt; res Reinbeck Iowa to 1901; died 18 Aug 1905 Muhlhausen Germany.[28]

Meyer, Albert H. Cpl co E; b. Prussia Germany; enl 27 Sep 1873 New York N.Y. for 5 yrs; age 21; bartender; blue eyes, lt hair, fair comp, 5' 8" high; join co E 18 Oct 1873 Ft Lincoln DT; dd co cook Dec 1874; cpl 3 Mar 1876; killed with Custer column 25 June 1876.

Meyer, August. Pvt co C; b. Hanover Germany; enl 11 Oct 1875 Cincinnati Ohio for 5 yrs; age 28; teamster; blue eyes, brn hair, dk comp, 5' 6" high; join co C 21 Oct 1875 Ft Lincoln DT; killed with Custer column 25 June 1876.

Meyer, Wm. D. Pvt co M; b. Pittsburgh Pa.; enl 16 Dec 1872 at Pittsburgh for 5 yrs; age 22 4/12; laborer; blue eyes, lt hair, fair comp, 5' 9 1/2" high; join co M 9 Feb 1873 Oxford Miss; unfit to march with regt 4 May 1873 & tr to str *Katie P. Kountz* 8 May Yankton DT; sick Ft Randall DT 15 May 1873 (ac. rheum.); duty 27 May & sent by limber to Ft Rice DT; ds Ft Rice June to Sep 1873 gd regtl prop; ed qmd tinner Oct 1873 to May 1874; dd qmd tinner Sep & Oct 1874; ed qmd tinner Feb 1875 to May 1876; killed dur retreat from valley fight 25 June 1876.

Meyers, Frank. Pvt co F; b. Quebec Canada; enl 8 Oct 1875 Cincinnati Ohio for 5 yrs; age 21; farmer; gray eyes, brn hair, dk comp, 5' 8 1/4" high; join co F 21 Oct 1875 Ft Lincoln DT; [at LBH says Finnegan & Pickard; not sure says Rooney].[29] awol six hrs 28 Nov 1876 while on fatigue duty; sen gar cm 1 Dec 1876 forf $5 pay; des 14 Dec 1876 Ft Abercrombie DT; (reported in error as apph at Portage Wis 23 Jan 1877).

Meyers, Jno. Sad'r co D; b. Wurtemberg Germany; enl 26 Dec 1866 Buffalo N.Y. for 5 yrs; age 30; brewer; hazel eyes, blk hair, dk comp, 5' 7 1/2" high; join co D 10 Feb 1867 Ft Riley Kans.; dd co cook June 1867; ds with escort for gen Custer 16 July 1867; cpl 19 Oct 1867; sgt 24 July 1869; in arrest Mar & Apr 1870; in arrest Jan & Feb 1871; pvt 15 Feb 1871 sen gen cm & forf $5 pay per mo for 4 mos; appt co sad'r 10 Aug 1871; disch 26 Dec 1871 Chester SC expir of serv a sad'r; reenl in co D as sad'r 1 Jan 1872 for 5 yrs;

sick qrs Oct & Dec 1872; sick Ft Lincoln DT 17 Oct to 9 Nov 1876 (tert. intm. fever); disch 1 Jan 1877 Ft Rice DT expir of serv a sad'r char good; enl in co K 7 cav as sad'r 13 Mar 1877 at Ft Lincoln for 5 yrs; gsw l. arm 30 Sep 1877 Snake Creek MT (Bear's Paw Mtns) in action with Nez Perce inds; tr to str *Silver City* 14 Oct mouth of Squaw Creek (on Mo. River); sick hosp Ft Lincoln 26 Oct; died 26 Dec 1877 hosp Ft Lincoln (consumption).

Mielke, Maximilian. Pvt co K; b. Frankfurt Germany; pvt 15 N.Y. art'y 27 Jan 1864 Arlington Va.; des 22 May 1864; enl reg army 27 Mar 1866 New York N.Y. for 3 yrs; age 21; soldier; blue eyes, brn hair, fair comp, 5' 9" high; assd to co H 3 battn 17 inf; (battn redesig 35 inf regt Nov 1866); disch 27 Mar 1869 Ft Mason Tex. expir of serv a sgt; reenl 9 Apr 1870 New York N.Y. for 5 yrs; assd to co G 10 inf; disch 9 Apr 1875 Ft Clark Tex. expir of serv a 1sgt; reenl 24 Mar 1876 McComb City Miss for 5 yrs in co K 7 cav; age 30 11/12; gsw l. foot (fl. wd. sl.) 26 June 1876 on Reno hill; tr on str *Far West* 3 July to hosp Ft Lincoln DT; ed nurse post hosp 8 Aug to 19 Nov 1876; ed subs dept 23 Nov 1876; dd co clerk Dec 1876; cpl 2 Jan 1877; sgt 21 Jan 1877; gd regtl standard 20 Feb to 28 Apr 1877; killed 30 Sep 1877 Snake Creek MT (Bear's Paw Mtns) in action with Nez Perce inds.
Pension: 11 Oct 1878 / Wid / 239645 / 184028.

Miles, Jas. Pvt co M; b. Oppelyn Germany; enl 28 Aug 1873 Chicago Ill. for 5 yrs; age 21; clerk; brn eyes, brn hair, fair comp, 5' 9" high; join co M 21 Oct 1873 Ft Rice DT; dd clerk in adjt's office Nov 1873 to Jan 1874; des 26 Jan 1874 while on ds at Bismarck DT; enl as Edw. Hamilton 6 July 1875 at Chicago for 5 yrs; assd to co G 2 cav; surd as Jas. Miles 4 July 1876 camp mouth of Big Horn River MT; [name on Reno petition]; enlmt canceled & restored to duty with co M 1 Aug upon recom'n capt French;[30] des 2 Nov 1876 camp near Cheyenne Agcy DT.

Miller, Chas. See Schutte, Fred'k.

Miller, Edwin. Sgt co C; b. Hanover Prussia; enl 30 Nov 1867 Cincinnati Ohio for 5 yrs; age 22; clerk; gray eyes, brn hair, fair comp, 5' 8" high; join co E 7 cav 22 Jan 1868 Ft L'worth Kans.; des 13 June 1868 camp Alfred Gibbs Kans.; enl as Hubert Herman 8 July 1868 at Cincinnati & apph same day as des'r; in conft Ft Harker Kans. 8 Oct 1868 to 24 Mar 1869; sen gen cm 1 Mar 1869 forf all pay for 6 mos & conft same period; tr to co C 12 Oct 1869 camp near Ft Hays; cpl 8 Apr 1870; co qm sgt 17 Aug 1871; disch 30 Nov 1872 Charlotte NC expir of serv a sgt; reenl same day in co C for 5 yrs & cont'd as co qm sgt; age 23; hazel eyes, dk hair, dk comp, 5' 10" high; ed qmd laborer Feb 1873; on furl 4 mos 1 July 1874 to Europe; ds Ft Lincoln DT 5 May 1876 chg co prop; dd qmd 12–28 Sep 1876 with 281 cav horses at post;[31] ds Ft Lincoln 20 Oct 1876 dismtd; ds Ft Totten DT 19 Nov 1876 chg of co baggage; actg co qm sgt Dec 1876; in conft (on parole & dd post hq) Ft Lincoln Feb to Nov 1877 awaiting trial;[32] rel from conft 1 Nov auth dept hq; disch 30 Nov 1877 at Ft Lincoln by expir of serv a sgt char good.

Miller, Henry. See Miller, Wm. Henry.

Miller, Jno. Pvt co L; b. Phil'a Pa.; enl 4 Aug 1870 Cincinnati Ohio for 5 yrs; age 21; laborer; hazel eyes, brn hair, dk comp, 5' 6" high; join co F 8 cav 2 Nov 1870 Ft Union NM; sen gen cm 21 Apr 1871 forf $10 pay per mo for 6 mos & conft same period; in conft Dec 1872 to Apr 1873; sen gen cm 26 Apr 1873 forf $10 pay per mo for 4 mos & conft same period; ds June 1873 with escort for surveyors; ed qmd laborer Feb 1874; ed qmd watchman Apr 1875; disch 4 Aug 1875 Ft Garland Colo. Ty expir of serv a pvt; reenl 4 Oct 1875 St Louis Mo. for 5 yrs; join co L 7 cav 29 Oct 1875 Ft Totten DT; killed with Custer column 25 June 1876.

Miller, Wm. E. Pvt co I; b. Exeter N.H.; enl 19 Oct 1871 Boston Mass. for 5 yrs; age 26; saddler; brn eyes, brn hair, dk comp, 5' 6 1/2" high; join co I as sad'r 9 Feb 1873 Lebanon Ky.; sick hosp 4 Dec 1873 (frostbite r. foot); duty 4 Apr 1874; pvt 5 Apr 1874; sad'r 16 May 1875; pvt 17 Sep 1875; sick hosp 4 May to 5 June 1876 Ft Lincoln DT (infl. testicle); dd qmd 8–10 Aug 1876 Ft Lincoln care for pub animals; ed in co garden 31 Aug 1876; disch 19 Oct 1876 at Ft Lincoln expir of serv a pvt.

Miller, Wm. Henry. Blks co E; b. 4 Mar 1837 Howard's Point Ill.;[33] enr as Henry Miller 27 Aug 1862 Chillicothe Ohio a pvt co B 73 Ohio inf for 3 yrs; (b. New Orleans La.); age 19 8/12; blacksmith; gray eyes, brn hair, lt comp, 5' 8" high;[34] des 30 Jan 1863 Falmouth Va.; enr as Wm. H. Miller 26 Oct 1863 Annapolis Md a pvt co I 3 Md cav for 3 yrs; (b. Fayette Co Ill.). Age 21; sailor; blue eyes, blk hair, lt comp, 5' 9" high; tr to navy 24 July 1864 at New Orleans (upon own appn) a coal heaver on str *Octorara*[35] [vessel recd 17 hits in battle of Mobile Bay 5 Aug 1864]; disch 8 Aug 1865 Brooklyn N.Y. navy yard by expir of serv;[36] enl reg army as Henry Miller 13 Nov 1871 Memphis Tenn for 5 yrs; (b. Baltimore Md); age 27 11/12; blacksmith; blue eyes, brn hair, lt comp, 5' 9" high; join co E 7 cav 5 Feb 1872 Unionville SC; blks 1 Sep 1872; pvt 1 Mar 1874; blks 23 Nov 1874; [at LBH said himself; not sure says Berwald & Pandtle];[37] sick 29 Sep to 11 Oct 1876 (ac. diar.); ds Ft Lincoln DT 16 Oct dismtd; disch 13 Nov 1876 at Ft Lincoln by expir of serv a blks; reenl 18 Sep 1878 Chicago Ill. for 5 yrs; assd to co E 8 cav a blks; disch 17 Sep 1883 Ft Clark Tex. expir of serv a blks char xclt & reenl in same co for 5 yrs; disch 17 Sep 1888 Big Beaver Creek DT expir of serv a blks char xclt & reenl in same co for 5 yrs; disch 26 Aug 1892 Ft Meade DT on surg cert dis (chr. rheum. & defective vision contr in serv) a blks char xclt;[38] died 30 Dec 1914 San Antonio Tex.
Pension: 7 Oct 1892 / Inv / 1138302; (rej on grd no ratable dis shown from alleged rheum.). 6 Sep 1897 / Inv [Navy] / 42748 / 27756. Wid / 1039827; (rej on grd sol. not hon disch from all contracts entered into dur the war). Claim for pension accruing on sailor's cert 27756 rej on grd no such pension due, being erroneously pensioned, having concealed prior serv. (See also, Inv. cert 79979 [Conrad Rull], & Wid cert 797645).

Millton, Jos. Pvt co F; b. Glasgow Scotland; enl 28 Dec 1867 New York N.Y. for 5 yrs; age 23 1/12; photographer; brn eyes, brn hair, fair comp, 5' 6 1/4" high; join co F 5 Feb 1868 Ft L'worth Kans.; dd co cook July & Aug 1868; dd with sharpshooter detmt Nov 1868; dd co cook Jan to June 1869; dd in signal dept Jan to Mar 1870; dd co cook Apr 1870; dd co cook Dec 1870 & Jan 1871; dd co cook Apr to Sep 1871; dd co cook Nov 1871; dd co cook Jan & Feb 1872; ed hosp cook May to Sep 1872; disch 28 Dec 1872 Louisville Ky. expir of serv a pvt; reenl in co F 1 Jan 1873 for 5 yrs; (blue eyes, brn hair, fair comp, 5' 6 1/2" high); ed hosp cook Feb 1873; abs sick 8 May 1873 on str *Katie P. Kountz* Yankton to Ft Rice DT; duty 10 June; ds hq Yellowstone Exp'n Aug & Sep 1873 nurse in hosp; dd chg co mess room Feb 1874; dd co cook June 1874; dd co cook Oct to Dec 1874; dd regtl hq June to Aug 1875; dd co cook Oct to Dec 1875; dd regtl band cook Mar thro' June 1876; ds Ft Lincoln 17 Oct 1876 with band; dd co cook Dec 1876 to Feb 1877; disch 1 Jan 1878 at Ft Lincoln expir of serv a pvt char xclt; reenl in co F 4 Jan 1878 for 5 yrs; cpl 29 Jan 1878; dd chg co kitchen Feb to June 1878; pvt 30 Dec 1880; dd co cook Feb 1881; cpl 15 June 1881; ds Ft Buford DT Aug & Sep 1881 chg co prop; sgt 18 Oct 1881 & dd actg co qm sgt; dd actg co qm sgt Aug to Oct 1882; disch 3 Jan 1883 at Ft Buford expir of serv a sgt char xclt & reenl in co F for 5 yrs; dd post police sgt Apr 1883; dd chg co stables Oct 1883; in arrest Oct 1884; pvt 4 Nov 1884; dd co cook Feb 1885; dd co gardener Aug to Oct 1885; dd co cook Feb 1886 to Dec 1887; disch 3 Jan 1888 Ft Meade DT expir of serv a pvt; reenl in co F 8 Jan 1888 for 5 yrs; dd co cook June 1889 to Jan 1890; cpl 13 Feb 1890; sgt 8 May 1891; pvt 10 Apr 1892; sd cook in gen mess July to Nov 1892; sd stable orderly Dec 1892; disch 7 Jan 1893 Ft Myer Va. expir of serv a pvt char very good & reenl in co F for 5 yrs; on furl 6 mos 8 Jan 1893 Glasgow Scotland; sd stable orderly July 1893; sd co tailor Aug 1893 to July 1894; sd co tailor May to Oct 1895; sd co stable orderly Oct 1895; sd co tailor Dec 1895 to Sep 1896; sd post librarian Jan 1897; cpl 26 Aug 1897; sgt 8 Oct 1897; sd chg co stables Dec 1897 to Feb 1898; disch 7 Jan 1898 Ft Grant AT expir of serv a sgt char xclt & reenl in co F for 3 yrs; retd 9 Feb 1898 at Ft Grant a sgt char xclt honest & faithful; died 1 Oct 1904 Tillsonburg, Ont. Canada.[39]

Milton, Francis E. Pvt co F; b. Hillsdale Mich.; enl 15 Aug 1866 Detroit Mich. for 5 yrs; age 18; farmer; blue eyes, lt hair, lt comp, 5' 7 1/4" high; join co F 10 Sep 1866 Ft Riley Kans.; dd qmd laborer Nov 1866; dd co cook Oct 1869; dd co cook Feb & Mar 1870; ed qmd teamster July & Aug 1870; dd co cook Oct 1870; ds Louisville Ky. 22 July 1871; disch 15 Aug 1871 at Louisville by expir of serv a pvt & reenl in co F for 5 yrs; ds at Louisville Oct 1871; dd co cook Dec 1871; dd co cook Apr 1873; ed qmd laborer 15 May to 21 July 1873; dd co cook June 1874; dd regtl hq Aug 1875 to Jan 1876; killed with Custer column 25 June 1876.

Mitchell, Jno. E. Pvt co I; b. Galway Ireland; enl 14 Sep 1866 New York N.Y. for 5 yrs; age 24; boatman; blue eyes, brn hair, ruddy comp, 5' 6 1/4" high; join co I 29 Sep 1866 Ft Riley Kans.; cpl 1 Dec 1866; pvt 8 Aug 1867; cpl 14 Aug 1868; ds with escort for gen Sully Sep & Oct 1868; pvt 29 Apr 1869; ed qmd teamster June to Aug 1869; cpl 7 July 1870; sgt 14 Aug 1871; disch 14 Sep 1871 Bagdad Ky. expir of serv a sgt & reenl in co I for 5 yrs; pvt 6 Mar 1872; dd servant for Lt Porter Aug 1873;[40] dd regtl hq fatigue pty (morn & eve) 11 May 1876;[41] killed with Custer column 25 June 1876; (survived by wife & 2 ch).
Pension: 25 Oct 1877 / Wid / 233866 / 194737. Minor / 306143 / 209400. (XC-936,600).

Moller, Jan. Pvt co H; b. 15 Sep 1849 Orsle Denmark; enl 15 Jan 1872 Chicago Ill. for 5 yrs; age 22; laborer; gray eyes, lt hair, sandy comp, 5' 8" high; join co H 12 Feb 1872 Nashville Tenn; dd bldg co gd room Dec 1873; dd co cook Aug 1875; dd subs dept herder Dec 1875 to Mar 1876; gsw r. thigh (fl. wd. severe) 26 June 1876 on Reno hill; tr on str *Far West* 3 July to hosp Ft Lincoln DT; tr to hosp Ft Rice DT 16 July; duty 31 July; cpl 4 Jan 1877; disch 15 Jan 1877 at Ft Rice expir of serv a cpl char xclt; died 23 Feb 1928 Deadwood SD.[42]
Pension: 7 Dec 1881 / Inv / 434632 / 222275. Ind. Surv. / 18110 / 11044.

Monroe, Jos. Pvt co F; b. Lorraine France; enl 14 Sep 1875 Cincinnati Ohio for 5 yrs; age 24; laborer; brn eyes, blk hair, dk comp, 5' 6 1/2" high; join co F 21 Oct 1875 Ft Lincoln DT; in conft Dec 1875 to Apr 1876 (sen gen cm 20 Jan 1876 forf $10 pay per mo for 4 mos & conft same period); killed with Custer column 25 June 1876.

Moody, Wm. Pvt co A; b. Edinburgh Scotland; enl 15 Dec 1874 New York N.Y. for 5 yrs; age 33; coachman; gray eyes, brn hair, florid comp, 5' 8" high; join co A 6 Feb 1875 Livingston Ala; dd qmd teamster Oct & Dec 1875; killed dur retreat from valley fight 25 June 1876.[43]

Moonie, Geo. A. Trump'r co E; b. Boston Mass.; enl 18 Mar 1875 at Boston for 5 yrs; age 20 3/12; clerk; hazel eyes, dk hair, fair comp, 5' 6 3/8" high; join co E as trump'r 1 July 1875 in field DT; killed with Custer column 25 June 1876.

Moore, Andrew J. Pvt co G; b. Camden NJ; enl 23 Jan 1872 Phil'a Pa. for 5 yrs; age 21; carpenter; blue eyes, dk hair, fair comp, 5' 8" high; join co G 26 Feb 1872 Spartanburg SC; ed qmd Oct to Dec 1873; dd qmd carpenter Feb 1874; dd qmd teamster Apr 1874; dd qmd carpenter Aug 1874; dd carpenter at hq distr upper Red River, Shreveport La. June to Aug 1875; dd qmd carpenter Dec 1875 to Feb 1876; left in timber dur retreat from valley fight 25 June & rejoin co on Reno hill; gsw in spine 26 June & died same day.
Pension: 20 June 1877 / Mother / 231966 / 180197.

Moore, Edw. L. Citizen packer qmd; b. Mar 1844 Green Co N.Y.;[44] enl 6 Apr 1871 St Louis Ars'l Mo. for 5 yrs; age 29; farmer; hazel eyes, brn hair, florid comp, 5' 7 1/2" high; join 7 cav 19 Apr 1871 Taylor Bks Ky. unassd rct; assd to co G 30 May 1871 at Louisville Ky.; trump'r 1 Mar 1872; cpl 1 Jan 1873; sgt 25 Nov 1873; pvt 29 Dec 1874; dd qmd Feb 1875 with post blks; dd co armorer Oct 1875 to Jan 1876; dd co cook Feb 1876; disch 6 Apr 1876 Shreveport La. expir of serv a pvt char good, temperate in habits; hired 2

May 1876 Ft Lincoln DT by Lt Nowlan to pack supplies on pub animals of exp'n;[45] rate of pay $50 mo; drove pack mules alongside wagon train dur march to Powder River; disch 23 Sep 1876 due $138.33 pay from 1 July; settled near mouth of Little Muddy River in 20 May 1893;[46] com'r of Williams Co in 1895 & partner with Gus Metzger (merchant & postmaster) running cattle on east fork of Little Muddy; sold homestead in 1900 to Stoney Creek Stock & Dairy co & became pres't of co;[47] when he retired, Wm. H. Denny (banker) paid his fare to Idaho & he was never heard of after that.[48]

Moore, Hugh N. Pvt co M; b. Dorchester Co Md; enl 24 Aug 1872 Louisville Ky. for 5 yrs; age 29 10/12; sailmaker; gray eyes, brn hair, fair comp, 5' 7 1/2" high; join co M 1 Sep 1872 Unionville SC; dd co cook June 1875; dd subs dept herder Feb 1876; cpl 1 Aug 1876; sgt 1 Dec 1876; disch 24 Aug 1877 camp Yellowstone River MT by expir of serv a sgt char "brave trustworthy & faithful soldier;" reenl same day in co M for 5 yrs; actg co qm sgt Oct 1877; in arrest Dec 1877 to Feb 1878; pvt 24 June 1879; dd co cook Oct 1879; cpl 10 May 1881; sgt 25 Oct 1881; pvt 28 Dec 1881 sen gen cm & forf $10 pay per mo for 6 mos; unexpired portion of sen rem'd 25 Feb 1882; disch 23 Aug 1882 camp Lower Guyser Natl Park MT by expir of serv a pvt; reenl same day in co M for 5 yrs; cpl 14 Feb 1883; pvt 23 Sep 1883; sen gen cm 6 Oct 1883 forf $10 pay per mo for 2 mos; ed ordn dept target repairer Apr to Aug 1884; dd asst post librarian Oct 1884 to May 1885; cpl 16 May 1885; sgt 14 Feb 1887; pvt 18 July 1887; disch 23 Aug 1887 Ft Meade DT expir of serv a pvt & reenl in regt for 5 yrs; assd to co K 7 Sep 1887; tr to co F 27 Sep 1887; in conft Nov 1887 to Feb 1888; sen gen cm 26 Dec 1887 forf $10 pay per mo for 2 mos & conft same period; dd asst librarian Feb & Mar 1888; ed subs dept laborer Feb 1889; disch 19 Aug 1889 Ft Sill IT on surg cert dis a pvt char good when sober (chr. alcoholism, not a case for pension); died 3 Sep 1900 Sol. Home Wash'n D.C.
Pension: 6 May 1890 & 13 July 1897 / Inv / 773601; (rej on grd no pensionable dis shown from alleged rheum. & injury to l. knee).

Moore, Jas. E. Far'r co B; b. 6 May 1849 Hebron Ohio; enl 9 Aug 1866 Indianapolis Ind. for 5 yrs; age 19; farmer; blue eyes, brn hair, fair comp, 5' 10" high; join co B 10 Sep 1866 Ft Riley Kans.; ds stone quarry Aug 1867; co wag Dec 1867 to May 1868; ds camp near Ft Hays Kans. June to Oct 1869; ds Ft L'worth Kans. witness in gen cm Mar & Apr 1870; ds hq detmt 7 cav near Solomon Kans. Oct 1870; disch 9 Aug 1871 Unionville SC expir of serv a pvt; reenl in co B 28 Aug 1871 for 5 yrs; far'r 1 Nov 1872; pvt June 1873; ds Ft Rice DT June to Sep 1873 gd regtl prop; far'r 15 Oct 1873; on furl 30 days 8 Apr 1874 Peru Ind.; pvt 1 May 1874; sick Ft Lincoln DT 21–30 June 1874 (chr. syph.); ds Ft Lincoln July & Aug 1874; far'r 1 July 1875; disch 6 Aug 1876 camp mouth of Rosebud Creek MT (in time to go down river by first boat) per GO 24 AGO 1859 a far'r char xclt; arr Ft Lincoln 10 Aug on str *Durfee*; died 1 Nov 1894 Union SC (consumption).[49]
Pension: 18 Apr 1887 / Inv / 607132; (rej, no rec of alleged gsw r. shoulder 24 June 1876; same shown recd long prior thereto & not line of duty). Wid / 690803 / 537423.

Moore, Lansing A. Pvt co L; b. 12 Sep 1855 Hoboken NJ; enl 27 Sep 1875 New York N.Y. for 5 yrs; age 21; carpenter; blue eyes, brn hair, ruddy comp, 5' 8" high; join co L 29 Oct 1875 Ft Totten DT; ed qmd teamster 8 Jan to 7 Mar 1876; with pack train 25 June 1876;[50] awol Feb 1877; in conft Apr 1877; sen gen cm 1 May 1877 forf $8 pay per mo for 3 mos; ds Ft Lincoln DT May to Nov 1877; dd learning music Feb 1878; trump'r 1 Mar 1878; pvt 1 Apr 1880; ed qmd tel line repairer Apr 1880; ds Grinnell's ranch as tel operator June to Sep 1880; disch 26 Sep 1880 at Ft Lincoln expir of serv a pvt char xclt; died 27 July 1931 Rawlins Wyo.[51]
Pension: 25 Oct 1926 / Inv / 1560233. (XC-2,310,668).

Morris, Geo. C. (alias). See Cooper, Eugene L.

Morris, Wm. Ephraim. Pvt co M; b. 1 May 1858 Boston Mass.; enl 22 Sep 1875 at Boston for 5 yrs; age 21 4/12; salesman; brn eyes, auburn hair, fair comp, 5' 7 1/2" high;

join co M 21 Oct 1875 Ft Rice DT; (with pack train June 1876);⁵² gsw l. breast (fl. wd. [sl.]) 25 June; tr on str *Far West* 3 July to hosp Ft Lincoln DT; duty 31 July 1876; frac. l. forearm 24 Aug 1877 camp on Yellowstone River (in drunken quarrel when Jim Weeks was killed by Barney Golden in poker game at Montana Bill's ranch); sick hosp Crow Agcy at Stillwater River to Nov 1877;⁵³ disch 11 Dec 1877 at Ft Lincoln on surg cert dis a pvt char worthless (frac. badly united, arm curved toward radial side & shortened half inch causing muscular debility of arm & almost entire lap of rotation of hand); died 26 Nov 1933 New York N.Y.
Pension: 3 June 1888 / Inv / 368124 / 174090. Ind. Surv. / 19492 / 11878.

Morrison, Jno. Pvt co G; b. Zanesville Ohio; enr 14 Oct 1861 a pvt co F 68 Ohio inf for 3 yrs; age 21; boatman; gray eyes, brn hair, lt comp, 5' 10" high; reenl 10 Dec 1863 Vicksburg Miss a vet vol; ds regtl teamster June 1864 to May 1865; m.o. vol serv 10 July 1865 Louisville Ky.; enl reg army 1 Mar 1866 Columbus Ars'l Ohio for 3 yrs; age 25; soldier; blue eyes, brn hair, lt comp, 5' 8 1/2" high; disch 1 Mar 1869 at Columbus Ars'l expir of serv a 2d cl. pvt of ordn; reenl in same unit 6 Mar 1869 for 3 yrs; disch 12 July 1869 at Columbus Ars'l per GO 15 AGO 1869 (reorganization of army) a 2d cl. pvt; reenl 29 Jan 1870 Columbus Ohio for 5 yrs; assd to co B 11 inf; tr to co I 16 Apr 1870; dd co cook Oct 1870; ed qmd teamster Dec 1870; wag 9 Jan 1871; pvt 6 Apr 1871; dd co cook June 1871; ed qmd teamster July 1871; ds as teamster with train Dec 1871; ds driving ambulance to Sherman Tex. Feb 1872; ds driving team with escort for paymaster Apr 1872; dd lance cpl Aug to Dec 1872; ds driving team with escort for surveyors Feb to June 1874; ed qmd teamster Oct 1874; dd co cook Dec 1874; disch 29 Jan 1875 Ft Richardson Tex. expir of serv a pvt; enl in co G 7 cav 21 May 1875 Shreveport La. (auth AGO) for 5 yrs; dd co cook Dec 1875; dd co cook Apr 1876; dd 13 May to 18 Sep 1876;⁵⁴ gsw r. thumb (fl. wd.) 26 June on Reno hill (remained with co in field); ds Feb 1878 teamster for pub prop to Ft Buford DT; dd qmd Apr 1878; dd co teamster June to Dec 1878; dd co gardener Apr 1879; ds Ft Lincoln DT 1 June to 17 July 1879; dd co gardener Oct 1879; dd co cook Dec 1879; disch 20 May 1880 Ft Meade DT expir of serv a pvt char good; res Lovell Wyo.
Pension: 18 Mar 1896 / Inv / 1175434. (Abandoned).

Morrow, Wm. E. Pvt co B; b. Boston Mass.; enl 24 Mar 1876 at Boston for 5 yrs; age 21 5/12; barber; hazel eyes, dk hair, fair comp, 5' 6 1/4" high; join co B 27 Apr 1876 St Paul Minn.; ds camp Powder River MT 10 June 1876; ds Ft Lincoln DT 17 Oct 1876 dismtd; des 12 Apr 1877 at Ft Lincoln.

Mortensen, Frederik Holmsted. See Holmsted, Fred'k.

Morton, Thos. (alias). See Rush, Thos. H.

Moylan, Myles. Capt co A; b. 17 Dec 1838 Amesbury Mass.; enl 8 June 1857 Boston Mass. for 5 yrs; age 20; shoemaker; gray eyes, blk hair, ruddy comp, 5' 9 1/2" high; join co C 2 drg 15 July 1857; cpl 1 Oct 1858; sgt 1 Oct 1860; 1sgt 17 May 1861; (regt redesig 2 cav Aug 1861); disch 1 Apr 1862 Pittsburg Tenn by reenlmt in co for 3 yrs; disch 28 Mar 1863 Memphis Tenn to accept com'n 2Lt 5 cav; dismissed from serv 20 Oct 1863 for being in Wash'n without proper auth & failing to report at hq as ordered; enr 2 Dec 1863 (as Chas. E. Thomas) a pvt co A 4 Mass. cav; sgt 26 Dec 1863; 1Lt 25 Jan 1864; ds regtl hq 10 Nov 1864; capt 1 Dec 1864 on staff of gen Gibbon to Aug 1865; bvt maj vols 9 Apr 1865 for gal serv dur campn in Va.; m.o. vol serv 14 Nov 1865; enl reg army (as Chas. E. Thomas) 25 Jan 1866 at Boston for 3 yrs; assd to gen mtd serv Carlisle Bks Pa.; cpl 10 Mar 1866; tr to 7 cav at Ft Riley Kans. 20 Aug 1866 a pvt; appt sgt-maj 10 Sep 1866; disch 16 Dec 1866 at Ft Riley by appmt to 1Lt (appn of gen Custer) but failed exam'n before cav bd at Wash'n; reenl 1 Jan 1867 Carlisle Pa. for 5 yrs; rejoin 7 cav 12 Jan 1867 & appt sgt-maj; prom 1Lt 3 Feb 1867 to date 28 July 1866 (under correct name);⁵⁵ regtl adjt 21 Feb 1867 thro' Dec 1870; (with regt in fight at Washita 27 Nov 1868); ds rctg duty Jan 1871 to Jan 1873

Cincinnati Ohio; (capt co A 1 July 1872); join co 12 Jan 1873 E'town Ky.; comd co on Yellowstone Exp'n June to Sep 1873 & on Blk Hills Exp'n July & Aug 1874; with co on str *Josephine* 16 July 1876 to camp at Powder River & escort wagon train to Rosebud; awl 3 mos 14 Nov 1876; gsw r. thigh 30 Sep 1877 Snake Creek MT (Bear's Paw Mtns) in action with Nez Perce inds; tr to str *Big Horn* 14 Oct & arr Ft Rice DT 24 Oct; tr to hosp Ft Lincoln DT 26 Nov; duty 11 Jan 1878; appt to bd of officers 23 June 1878 to revise medal of honor list for LBH; awl 16 Dec 1878 to 5 Mar 1879 (witness in Reno court of inq); bvt maj 27 Feb 1890 for gal serv at Bear's Paw Mtns 30 Sep 1877; comd co in action with Sioux inds 29 Dec 1890 Wounded Knee SD; prom maj 10 cav 8 Apr 1892 & join regt 4 June at Ft Assiniboine MT; retd 15 Apr 1893 for disability in line of duty; awarded medal of honor 27 Nov 1894 for dist gal in action at Bear's Paw Mtns in leading his comd until severely wd; died 11 Dec 1909 San Diego Calif.
[2090 ACP 1873]. Pension: 24 Jan 1910 / Wid / 934623 / 698596.

Mueller, Wm. Pvt co D; b. Altenburg Germany; enl 6 Oct 1875 St Louis Bks Mo. for 5 yrs; age 34; laborer; blue eyes, brn hair, dk comp, 5' 7 1/8" high; join co D 21 Oct 1875 Ft Lincoln DT; ds Ft Lincoln 5 May 1876 chg co prop; dd co gardener 30 June 1876; sent with Lt Garlington on str *Josephine* 24 July 1876 to join co in field; dd Feb 1877; ed hosp attdt Feb to May 1878; ds hosp attdt Ft Lincoln June to Nov 1878; ed hosp nurse Apr 1879 to Oct 1880; disch 5 Oct 1880 Ft Yates DT expir of serv a pvt char xclt; reenl 4 Apr 1881 Vancouver Bks WT for 5 yrs; assd to co B 1 cav; disch 3 Apr 1886 Ft Custer MT expir of serv a pvt char very good; reenl 22 Apr 1886 Presidio San Francisco Calif. for 5 yrs in co M 1 art'y; ed qmd laborer Aug to Dec 1886; dd co cook Feb 1887; des 23 Mar 1887 at Ft Mason (San Francisco).

Muering, Jno. Sad'r co A; b. St Louis Mo.; enl 11 June 1869 at St Louis for 5 yrs; age 21; saddler; gray eyes, sandy hair, fair comp, 5' 10 1/2" high; assd to co K 6 cav; disch 11 June 1874 Camp Supply IT expir of serv a sad'r; reenl 5 Dec 1874 at St Louis for 5 yrs; join co A 7 cav 6 Feb 1875 Livingston Ala; appt sad'r 10 Feb 1875; disch 4 Dec 1879 Ft Meade DT expir of serv a sad'r char xclt; reenl 23 May 1884 Ft D. A. Russell Wyo. Ty for 5 yrs; assd to co K 14 inf; disch 22 May 1889 Ft Klamath Ore. expir of serv a pvt char xclt & reenl in same co for 5 yrs; age 40 6/12; tr to co E; disch 24 May 1894 Seattle Wash'n expir of serv a pvt char very good & reenl in same co for 5 yrs; disch 24 May 1899 Manila PI expir of serv a pvt char good & reenl in same co for 3 yrs; died 15 Feb 1902 Ft Wayne Mich.

Mullen, Jno. Sgt co L; b. Pittsburgh Pa.; enl 29 June 1870 Cincinnati Ohio for 5 yrs; age 21; soldier; blue eyes, fair hair, fair comp, 5' 5 3/4" high; assd to co K 1 art'y; des 7 Apr 1871 Ft Riley Kans.; enl in 7 cav as Jas. Hughes 24 Apr 1871 Ft Wallace Kans. for 5 yrs; assd to co L 30 Apr 1871; surd as Jno. Mullen 27 Nov 1873 under GO 102 AGO 1873; restored to duty without trial 21 Apr 1874 & tr to co L to serve bal of orig'l enlmt; cpl 29 Dec 1874; sgt 19 Feb 1876; dd post prov sgt 29 Feb to 7 Mar 1876; with pack train 25 June 1876; 1sgt 21 Dec 1876; cited by maj Merrill for good cond in action against Nez Perce inds at Canon Creek MT 13 Sep 1877; disch 20 Feb 1878 Ft Lincoln DT expir of serv a 1sgt char xclt (made good time lost by des'n);[56] reenl 8 Mar 1878 at Cincinnati for 5 yrs; rejoin co L 20 Nov 1878 at Ft Lincoln & appt 1sgt; sgt 22 Feb 1880; dd chg co cookhouse Apr 1880; 1sgt 1 Sep 1881; sgt 11 Dec 1881; on furl Apr 1882 St Paul Minn.; dd prov sgt Dec 1882; disch 7 Mar 1883 Ft Buford DT expir of serv a sgt; reenl 1 June 1883 at Cincinnati for 5 yrs; assd to co A 2 cav; disch 31 May 1888 Presidio San Francisco Calif. expir of serv a sgt; reenl for same co 29 June 1888 at Cincinnati for 5 yrs; died 29 Aug 1888 at the Presidio a pvt; (failure of respiration, contr line of duty).
Pension: 7 Sep 1891 / Mother / 526344 / 324047. Sister / 897437.

Muller, Jno. Pvt co H; b. Hamburg Germany; enl in co H 13 Mar 1870 Ft Hays Kans. for 5 yrs; age 28; teamster; blue eyes, brn hair, fair comp, 5' 5" high; des 16 July 1870 camp at River Bend Colo. Ty; apph 22

Dec 1875 Columbus Ohio; sen gen cm to 3 yrs conft hard labor, rem'd to dishon disch 27 Nov 1876 at Columbus Bks.

Mullin, Martin. Pvt co C; b. Cork Ireland; enl 3 Jan 1873 Pittsburgh Pa. for 5 yrs; age 25 2/12; laborer; blue eyes, brn hair, fair comp, 5' 5" high; des 23 Jan 1873 St Louis Mo.; apph 27 Jan at Pittsburgh; sen gen cm 11 Apr 1873 forf $10 pay per mo for 6 mos & conft same period; join co C 21 Oct 1873 Ft Rice DT; dd qmd Oct 1875; sen gen cm 2 May 1876 forf $10 pay for one mo; abs conft Ft Lincoln DT Oct 1876; dd qmd Feb 1877; disch 3 Jan 1878 Ft Totten DT upon expir of serv a pvt [no char].

Murphy, Jos. C. See Bates, Jos.

Murphy, Lawrence. Sgt co E; b. Kerry Ireland; enl 30 Dec 1871 Boston Mass. for 5 yrs; age 22; laborer; blue eyes, brn hair, fair comp, 5' 5 3/4" high; join co E 5 Feb 1872 Unionville SC; in conft Aug 1872; cpl 1 June 1875; sgt 1 Nov 1875; ds camp Powder River MT 10 June 1876 chg co prop;[57] ds Ft Lincoln DT 16 Oct 1876 dismtd; disch 30 Dec 1876 at Ft Lincoln by expir of serv a sgt; reenl same day for 5 yrs in co B; cpl 9 June 1877; sgt 16 July 1877; disch 29 Dec 1881 Ft Yates DT expir of serv a sgt char very good; reenl 12 Jan 1882 Chicago Ill. for 5 yrs; assd to co K 2 cav; sick hosp (infl. larynx) 12 Nov 1885 Presidio San Francisco Calif.; disch 19 July 1886 at Presidio on surg cert dis a pvt char very good (constriction of larynx [probably syph. origin]; laryngotomy performed 13 Nov 1885 & since has worn tracheotomy tube & unable to articulate; dis total); died 13 Jan 1888 Sol. Home Wash'n D.C.
Pension: 3 Sep 1886 / Inv / 584303; (rej on grd disease not incident to serv). Mother / 380996; (rej on grd cause of son's death not connected to mil serv).

Murphy, Mich'l. Pvt co K; b. Cork Ireland; enl 10 Sep 1866 Potsville Pa. for 5 yrs; age 28; laborer; blue eyes, blk hair, fair comp, 5' 3 1/2" high; join co K 29 Sep 1866 Ft Riley Kans.; in conft Feb to June 1867; ds Ft Hays Kans. chg co prop Aug 1867; disch 10 Sep 1871 Yorkville SC expir of serv a pvt & reenl in co K for 5 yrs; on furl 60 days 11 Sep 1871 NYC [see Dooley]; in conft Dec 1871; in conft June 1872; ed qmd laborer 18 May to 21 July 1873; dd subs dept Jan to Apr 1874; dd leading mules June 1876; disch 6 Aug 1876 camp mouth of Rosebud Creek MT (in time to go down river by first boat) per GO 24 AGO 1859 a pvt char xclt; arr Ft Lincoln 10 Aug on str *Durfee*; reenl in co K 12 Aug 1876 at Ft Lincoln for 5 yrs; on furl 20 days 14 Aug 1876 St Paul Minn. & ext'd 30 days; gsw thorax & abdomen 30 Sep 1877 Snake Creek MT (Bear's Paw Mtns) in action with Nez Perce inds; tr to str *Silver City* 14 Oct mouth of Squaw Creek (on Mo. River); arr hosp Ft Lincoln 26 Oct; disch 26 May 1878 at Ft Lincoln on surg cert dis (gsw thro' chest entering l. side & exiting r. side; dis total) a pvt; died 12 June 1904 Sol. Home Wash'n D.C.
Pension: 10 June 1878 / Inv / 256400 / 156539.

Murphy, Robt. L. Sgt co I; b. Stanford N.Y.; enl 24 Jan 1872 Jersey City NJ for 5 yrs; age 21; fireman; brn eyes, brn hair, fair comp, 5' 8 3/4" high; join co I 10 Feb 1872 Shelbyville Ky.; cpl 1 Jan 1873; sgt 31 July 1875; dd dept hq in field chg of orderlies 11 May 1876; disch 24 Jan 1877 Ft Lincoln DT expir of serv a sgt char very good; reenl same day in co I for 5 yrs; 1sgt 28 Jan 1877; cited by maj Merrill for good cond in action against Nez Perce inds at Canon Creek MT 13 Sep 1877; sgt 30 Dec 1878 & actg co qm sgt to Oct 1879; des 12 Oct 1879 at Ft Lincoln; locomotive engr NPRR at Minneapolis Minn. & killed in yards there about 1900.[58]

Murphy, Thos. Pvt co K; b. Cork Ireland; enl 18 Dec 1874 Boston Mass. for 5 yrs; age 21 8/12; shoemaker; gray eyes, dk hair, fair comp, 5' 9 3/4" high; join co K 9 Feb 1875 Colfax La.; des 20 Mar 1875 at Colfax & apph 22 Mar at Alexandria La.; in conft Jackson Bks La. Apr 1875; sen gen cm 20 May 1875 to conft 4 mos at sta of co; ed subs dept with Lt Gibson May & June 1877 on str *Far West*; ds in field July & Aug 1877; ed subs dept laborer 24 Sep Cant'mt Tongue River MT; dep for proper sta 26 Oct with sgt Corwine [in mackinaw boat to Ft Buford thence on str *Rosebud* to Ft Lincoln]; dd asst co sad'r Apr 1878; disch 29 June 1878 Ft Rice DT on surg cert dis a pvt char good (partial paralysis r. side & developing r. hemiplegia; injured l. side of head in fall from horse dur campn in 1876); alias Thos. Reardon, 19 Hunting Street, Cambridgeport Mass.[59]

Murray, Henry. Cpl co K; b. Boston Mass.; enl 12 July 1866 at Boston for 3 yrs; age 21; wood carver; hazel eyes, dk hair, fair comp, 5' 9 1/2" high; join co F 4 cav 17 Sep 1866 Camp Sheridan Tex.; dd co clerk Oct 1867 to June 1868; ed clerk post comsy dept July 1868; ds hq 5th mil distr Austin Tex. 11 Nov 1868 to 12 July 1869 when disch by expir of serv a pvt; reenl 4 Nov 1869 Galveston Tex. for 5 yrs; assd to 11 inf as comsy sgt 20 Nov 1869; disch 10 Sep 1870 Ft Concho Tex. per GO 96 AGO 1870 (supernumerary non-commissioned officer) a comsy sgt; reenl 21 Nov 1870 San Antonio Tex. for 5 yrs; assd to gen mtd serv; tr to co B 11 inf 11 Sep 1872; appt sgt-maj 10 Aug 1873; tr to co B as pvt 12 Oct 1873; disch 21 Nov 1875 Ft Richardson Tex. expir of serv a cpl; reenl 4 Dec 1875 St Louis Mo. for 5 yrs; join co K 7 cav 20 Dec 1875 Colfax La.; ed subs dept laborer Feb 1876; cpl 14 June 1876; ds camp Powder River MT 15 June 1876; appt sgt-maj 12 Oct 1876; arr Ft Lincoln 22 Oct 1877 on str *Big Horn* (with col Sturgis & Lts Hare & Garlington); appt comsy sgt USA 12 June 1879; disch 12 Oct 1880 Ft Benton MT expir of serv a comsy sgt char xclt; (qm clerk 1 Nov 1880 to 15 Apr 1888); reenl 6 Nov 1888 Ft Omaha Neb for 5 yrs; assd to co D 2 inf; tr to co L 7 cav 1 Apr 1889; disch 11 Aug 1890 Ft Riley Kans. (by way of favor; under GO 81 AGO 1890) a sgt;[60] 1Lt & rqm 1 SD inf 4 May 1898; resd 16 Feb 1899; died 16 Aug 1908 San Francisco Calif.
Pension: 22 Oct 1890 / Inv / 869045 / 726319.

Murray, Thos. Sgt co B; b. Monaghan Ireland; pvt co K 37 N.Y. inf 25 May 1861; cpl 17 Oct 1861; gsw l. hand 4 May 1862 Williamsburg Va.; duty 22 July 1862; sgt 31 July 1862; m.o. with co 22 June 1863; pvt co B 13 N.Y. art'y 29 July 1863; cpl 26 May 1864; m.o. vol serv 24 Aug 1865; enl reg army 17 Aug 1866 New York N.Y. for 5 yrs; age 30 10/12; laborer; blue eyes, brn hair, ruddy comp, 5' 8" high; join co B 7 cav 10 Sep 1866 Ft Riley Kans.; cpl 17 Sep 1866; sgt 26 Sep 1866; 1sgt 19 Nov 1867; co qm sgt Mar 1868; ds camp near Ft Hays Kans. June to Oct 1869; sgt 19 Feb 1871; disch 17 Aug 1871 Unionville SC expir of serv a sgt & reenl in co B for 5 yrs; dd police sgt Apr 1872; co qm sgt May 1872; sgt 17 Dec 1872; on furl 15 days 23 Dec 1872 Spartanburg SC; pvt 2 Dec 1873; sgt 1 Jan 1874; actg 1sgt Feb 1874; pvt 20 Apr 1874; cpl 22 July 1875; actg co qm sgt Aug 1875; sgt 12 Dec 1875; actg co qm sgt June to Aug 1876; disch 17 Aug 1876 mouth of Powder River MT expir of serv a sgt char xclt & reenl in co B for 5 yrs; actg co qm sgt to Feb 1877; pvt 12 Mar 1877; cpl 12 Oct 1877; sgt 5 Dec 1877; dd chg co kit'n Dec 1877 to Feb 1878; co qm sgt Apr to Oct 1878; (awarded medal of honor 5 Oct 1878 for bringing up pack train [at LBH] & on 2nd day the rations while under heavy fire); pvt 11 Dec 1878; far'r 15 Dec 1879; disch 16 Aug 1881 Ft Yates DT expir of serv a far'r & reenl in co B for 5 yrs; disch 16 Aug 1886 at Ft Yates expir of serv a far'r & reenl two days later in co B for 5 yrs; sick hosp 19 Feb to 30 Mar 1888 & sick qrs to 14 Apr 1888 (ac. orchitis); disch 10 June 1888 Ft Meade DT on surg cert dis a far'r char xclt (debility from long serv complicated with chr. bronc. & bruised l. testicle contr line of duty; dis total); died 4 Aug 1888 Sol. Home Wash'n D.C. (phthisis pulmonalis).
Pension: 6 July 1888 / Inv / 663826; (abandoned).

Myers, Fred'k Wm. Pvt co I; b. Brunswick Germany; enl 17 May 1873 St Louis Bks Mo. for 5 yrs; age 25; laborer; hazel eyes, dk hair, dk comp, 5' 9 1/4" high; join co I 3 June 1873 Ft Snelling Minn.; dd qmd teamster June 1873 (with NBS); ed driving ambulance Aug 1873 (with NBS); ed qmd teamster Oct 1873 to Feb 1874; ds camp Powder River MT 10 June 1876; dd qmd Ft Lincoln DT 12 Sep 1876 with 281 cav horses at post; dd co garden 21 Sep 1876; ds Ft Lincoln 16 Oct 1876 qmd teamster; ds Ft Lincoln Apr to Nov 1877 co gardener; dd qmd Dec 1877 to Feb 1878; dd co gardener Apr 1878; disch 17 May 1878 at Ft Lincoln expir of serv a pvt char very good; reenl 4 Sep 1878 Baltimore Md for 5 yrs; rejoin co I 20 Nov 1878 at Ft Lincoln; dd qmd teamster Dec 1878 to June 1879; dd co cook Oct 1879; dd qmd teamster Dec 1880 to June 1881; dd qmd overseer Aug 1881 to Feb 1882; appt regtl qm sgt 22 Apr 1882; disch 3 Sep 1883 Ft Meade DT expir of serv a qm sgt; reenl 20 Nov 1883 at Baltimore for 5 yrs; assd to co K 6 cav; cpl 1 May 1884; sgt 16 Jan 1886; disch 19 Nov 1888 Ft Wingate NM expir of serv a sgt & reenl in same co for 5 yrs; (awarded medal of honor 4 Feb 1891 for dist bravery & coolness dur action with Sioux inds at White River SD 1 Jan 1891); pvt 17 Dec 1891 (own req); cpl 8 June 1892; pvt 17 Nov 1892 (own req); sgt 15 Nov 1893; disch 20 Nov 1893 Ft Niobrara Neb upon expir of serv a sgt; died 5 May 1900 Wash'n D.C. Pension: 5 Mar 1896 / Inv / 1175009 / 914501. Wid / 747812 / 755575.

Notes—M (except for Mc)

1. Lt. Hare said Madden was an intemperate fellow whom no one had much respect for and when he volunteered to go for water everyone was much surprised, Hammer, *Custer in '76*, 67; Stan Roy said when the water party got to the foot of the ravine the river was still 20 yards away. Madden was a big heavy man and his wound was painful, and he was carried up some time after dark. Hammer, *Custer in '76*, 114.

2. A letter from camp on the Yellowstone, Aug. 9, 1876, reported that some surprise had been expressed by officers of the command that no orders had been issued thanking men like Porter, Weir, Hare, and the soldier Madden, for their distinguished gallantry in the field. Those who saw these men in action say they fairly won the commendations of their general, and they ought not only to be mentioned in the papers, but even to receive brevet rank as marks of appreciation, *New York Herald*, Aug. 13, 1876; *St. Paul Dispatch*, Sept. 4, 5, 6, 1876.

Walter Camp inquired of Gen. Godfrey why Madden was not awarded a medal for going for water, and Godfrey said he recommended him but no medal was awarded, Hardorff, *Camp, Custer, and the Little Big Horn*, 65 n.3.

Recommendations by company commanders for medals for men of their companies was forwarded by Col. Sturgis to department headquarters, May 12, 1877. However, because it appeared from the number of names that commanders had recommended every man in their respective companies who behaved ordinarily all during the battle, Gen. Terry returned the list to Col. Sturgis, Feb. 26, 1878, for revision and more careful scrutiny, thence to be returned to department headquarters with the names only of men who distinguished themselves in a marked manner by conspicuous acts of gallantry. A board of officers was designated for the purpose, their report submitted July 29, 1878, and in accordance therewith medals were awarded, RG 94, Entry 409, file 10818 A [EB] 1878; additional letters relevant to the awarding of the medals are found in, RG 94, Entry 25, file 8521 PRD 1894.

Gen. Godfrey had an indistinct recollection that the Board considered only those men who made the first and perhaps second "Rush" for water, and were still in service at the time recommendations were made, in 1878. Godfrey to Walter Camp, May 14, 1923, WMC-BYU.

3. RG 92, Entry 238, reports 1876/182 and 1877/140.

4. RG 231, Entry 13, U.S. Soldier's Home Register of Inmates, 1852–1908. See Douglas D. Scott, "An agreeable sort when sober."

5. John Frett said there were some discharged soldiers with the pack train. Nichols, *Reno Court*, 503. No positive link has been found connecting Frank C. Mann, 1st Cav., with Custer's packer of same name.

6. Lieut. Godfrey narrative, in Graham, *The Custer Myth*, 127.

7. Walter Camp said he found the place where Mann was buried at right of Moylan's line. (WMC, Notes on Reno hill, Box 5, env 85, BYU). Mann's army revolver, issued by Lieut. Nowlan, was stolen from his body by Pvt. Franklin. (GCMO 47, DD, Oct. 18, 1876). Mann was due $91.66 pay, which was apparently paid through the office of the 3rd Auditor, 2nd Comptroller, (General Accounting Office) as part of Claim 42.848, "Retd Feby 23. 1877. Paid Sett 2368." RG 217, Entry 658, Docket Book of Miscellaneous Claims, Vol. 18, 414, 668. Settled accounts and claims of 3rd Auditor, 1851–1877, were not retained.

John C. Wagoner said Mann was formerly from Maine and was a member of the Odd Fellows Lodge at Leavenworth, Kans. *Bismarck Tribune*, Sept. 27, 1876.

8. Marshall was in charge, to assign work to both Tapley and Pitet. Capt. Benteen expected a big garden from Marshall and his assistants and said things must go right or there would be trouble when he

returned. Benteen was concerned his mare and colts receive good care. Benteen letters to wife, July 9, 10, 13, 1876. Carroll, *Camp Talk*, 28–35.

9. See note D26 (Diamond).

10. RG 94, Entry 409, file, 10818 A (EB) 1878.

11. RG 94, Entry 96; Augustus Devoto said Mask was orderly to Lt. Hodgson on June 25 and was the only man not accounted for after the fight. They surmised he might have been shot while crossing the river and fell and was carried down stream, Devoto to Walter Camp, July 24, and, Oct. 1, 1917, WMC-LBHB; John Bailey said Mask was with Custer as headquarters police; WMC, rosters, IU.

Camp said there was an aggregate of four men from Companies B, G, and K killed with Custer, and three men from Companiess E and L killed with Reno, Camp to Gen. Godfrey, Jan. 14, 1921, Godfrey Papers.

See also "A Baltimorean Who Died With Custer," *Baltimore Gazette*, July 15, 1876; *St. Paul and Minneapolis Pioneer-Press and Tribune*, July 20, 1876.

12. WMC, rosters, LBHB; on hearing the content of a letter received at Gen. Sheridan's headquarters, in which Maj. Walsh of the Canadian Northwest Mounted Police described a gray horse with the "US" brand he recently acquired at a Sioux camp, Maj. Reno wondered if it was the same gray horse the regiment lost two days after the battle. Reno recalled a corporal of Company C (E?) who had charge of headquarter detail and rode a high-spirited dark dapple-gray horse with white mane and tail. The corporal was killed early in the fight and in the retreat to the hill the old gray followed Reno's horse, the two animals having been together almost constantly during the campaign. Near the river the gray was shot in the hip and disabled to such extent he could only walk with great difficulty. During the march to the Yellowstone after the battle, they urged the old gray along with the other animals but in the confusion of crossing the river, he was somehow overlooked and was never seen again by the command. Utley, *The Reno Court of Inquiry*, 409.

13. Mathey carried on his own defense and convinced the board that the charges of Col. Sturgis were without foundation, Terrell and Walton, *Faint the Trumpet Sounds*, 107.

14. Lt. Godfrey said that, on the march from Fort Lincoln, Mathey was in command of the dismounted men, "over 100 I'm quite sure." Godfrey to Chas. F. Bates, n.d., Bates Papers, Box 3, folder 31.

15. Maj. Reno formed the remnants of Companies C, E, F, I, and L into a company under Lt. Mathey, he having been relieved from the pack train by Lt. Nowlan. Mathey interview, Jan. 19, 1910, in Hardorff, *Camp, Custer, and the Little Big Horn*, 43.

Sgt. Ryan said the only sword he knew of at Little Big Horn belonged to Lt. Mathey, and it was rolled up in a bundle of blankets on a pack mule, Ryan to Mrs. Custer, Mar. 17, 1908, EBC-LBHB, Roll 3; Lt. Garlington said Mathey retained his saber and on more than one occasion he found it useful in killing rattlesnakes of which there were a great number in Montana, Carroll, ed., *Garlington Narrative*, 23.

Benteen said Mathey was a small-boned average looking officer with a neat moustache and was dubbed "Bible Thumper" by the other officers for his colorful profanity, Mills, *Harvest of Barren Regrets*, 214; see Schneider, *Behind Custer at the Little Big Horn*.

16. Meador's body was found in June 1903 by Superintendent Grover, at same time as those of Lell, Tanner, and Voigt, WMC, Notes, env 75, IU; All four, together with that of a 5th Reno soldier (Charley) also found by Grover that year, were reinterred in the Custer National Cemetery, Graves 453 through 456 and 458. See Custer Battlefield Burial Register, LBHB Coll., Roll 14.

17. RG 94, Entry 409, file 5302 A (EB) AGO 1876.

18. *Mount Pleasant* (Pa.) *Journal*, July 24, 1903; while visiting his brother in Garrison, Nebraska, "Hennie" also visited the battlefield on the 27th anniversary of the battle, spending three days with Superintendent Andrew Grover. Mechling provided his account of the fight in a letter to James Braddock of Mount Pleasant, July 16, 1921, and reproduced in a family book of Mechling genealogy. Mechling was interviewed by Walter Camp, WMC, Notes, env 75, IU; An interview with Mechling's daughter, Minnie, age 89, is found in "Interview with Minnie Grace Carey," *Tribune-Review* (Pittsburgh), Oct. 13, 1996.

19. See note D26 (Diamond).

20. John Ryan said Meier fell down a cellar-way in the barracks, Ryan to Walter Camp, Mar. 21, 1909, WMC-BYU.

21. Merrill reportedly arranged through family or professional connections, to Secretary of War Belknap, for assignment to the staff of the president of the U.S. Centennial Commission, Joseph R. Hawley, with the International Exhibition, a six-month event in Philadelphia's Fairmount Park, May 10 to Nov. 10, 1876, Martinez, *Carpetbaggers, Cavalry, and the Ku Klux Klan*, 226–27.

22. Merrill was summoned to Washington to answer questions regarding charges he accepted a fee of $20,000 for prosecuting members of the Ku Klux Klan while stationed in South Carolina, and allegedly received a bribe while judge advocate of a court-martial in New Mexico in 1869, Johnson, "Custer, Reno, Merrill and the Lauffer Case."

23. Capt. Benteen said Col. Sturgis asked Gen. Howard to send Merrill home so that command of the regiment might devolve on him (Benteen), but Howard did not wish to interfere in a department in which he had no control, feeling he already exceeded his prerogatives in giving Sturgis "a leave." Sturgis then got Miles to send Merrill to Lincoln in charge of sick and wounded (from Camp Hale, MT, mouth of Squaw Creek on the Missouri River), Carroll, *The Benteen-Goldin Letters*, 204, 221, 231.

24. When Merrill appeared before a retiring board in November 1885, he was senior major of cavalry and would have been promoted Lieut.-Colonel the following January when a vacancy would be caused by retirement. However, officially, regulations prohibited promotion of an officer known to be disabled. See Martinez, *Carpetbaggers, Cavalry, and the Ku Klux Klan*, 230–37.

25. *Bismarck Tribune*, Wed., Apr. 21, 1875, reported the arrival of the first train Friday (April 16) after an interval of five months.

26. "By direction of the Dept. Commander, Sergeant Merritt in charge of 7th Cavalry Band will report for duty with his Regiment at mouth of Big Horn River, taking advantage of Str. *Far West* for transportation on return trip up Yellowstone. He will bring the Regimental Desk placed in charge of Private Hoehn, clerk at Regimental Headquarters, and superintend shipment of the Company Desks," SO 58, Hq 7th Cavalry, Camp on Yellowstone River, July 12, 1876, RG 391, Entry 859; Merritt's wife gave birth to their fourth child June 5, 1876, at Fort Lincoln. Pension file, RG 15.

27. "The soldier millionaire, George A. Merritt, has been transferred to Company A, Sixth Infantry, and will still be stationed at Fort Lincoln," *Bismarck Tribune*, June 7, 1879; a week earlier it was reported that the band and noncommissioned staff would accompany Troops C and G to Fort Meade. *Bismarck Tribune*, May 31, 1879.

Troops A and H also changed station to Fort Meade in June 1879. Troop I remained at Lincoln for another year, regimental returns. At that time, Merritt was the father of five children, at Lincoln, all under nine years of age. See Scott, "Playing Music on the Plains."

28. Report from U.S. Consulate at Brunswick Germany to the Assistant Secretary of State, Wash. DC, April 26, 1906, and to the Secretary of War, May 24, 1906, with certificate of death and statement of Smith's sister, Mrs. Schilling, that her brother, Christian Methfessel, was called Frederick Smith during his sojourn in America. RG 94, Entry 25, file 101757 AGO 1902.

29. WMC, rosters, LBHB; Pickard interview with Walter Camp, Jan. 26, 1913, WMC, Notes, env 129, IU; Remark by Rooney on roster of Company F, n.d., WMC-BYU; Dennis Lynch thought Meyers belonged to Company I, with pack train, and not a member of Company F, Lynch to Walter Camp, Nov. 28, 1908, WMC-BYU.

30. NA, M1734, Roll 17, letter 2860 DD 1876; James Miles was officially restored to duty per SO 127, Hq DD, Oct. 7, 1876. Also on a second recommendation by Capt. French, Oct. 3, 1876.

31. Sgt. Miller wrote to the father of Lt. Harrington, that the body of the lieutenant was found in a ravine with others about four miles from the battlefield. It was supposed they were among the last killed, finding no hope they tried to break through the American Indian lines and reach Reno's command, *The Republican* (Coldwater, Michigan) July 28, 1876, reprinted in a brief notice, "Henry Moore Harrington," by Walt Boyson, *The English Westerners' Tally Sheet* (London), Vol. 35, No.2, Spring, 1989.

32. On January 29, 1877, Col. Sturgis wrote to Gen. Terry that there was a gang of men in vicinity of the post (Fort Lincoln) who live on what they can get soldiers to steal and sell them, and there was little doubt that Sgt. Miller (then at Fort Totten) was deeply implicated in the villainy. Sturgis suggested the propriety of Miller being secured before he gets information that may tempt him to escape. Sturgis said Sgt. Inman could give evidence that would lead to arrest and conviction of the members, and thought it to best interest of government that Inman turn states evidence rather than he alone should suffer, NA, M1734, Roll 18.

33. Howard's Point was a small settlement in Fayette County, Ill., about 19 miles east of Vandalia, from about 1830 to 1869 when its post office and merchants moved their business to St. Elmo, a thriving new settlement 500 yards to the northeast and where plans called for construction of an East-West railroad, Hanabarger, "Howard's Point, Town Serves as Example of Rise and Fall of Communities," *The Leader-Union* (Vandalia, *Ill.*), April 16, 1997; Hanabarger also edited "Fayette Facts," quarterly publication of the Fayette County Historical Society.

34. Miller arrived in Ross County, Ohio in August 1862, with two other men, all believed to be army deserters, (possibly rebels), from a western city, thought to be St. Louis. He joined the 73rd Ohio, but the other two men would not join the Union army. Miller boasted of having "jumped" two or three or four bounties. Bounty jumpers were not uncommon, enlisting under assumed names to obtain bonuses and then deserting to enlist elsewhere under another name.

There is evidence Henry Miller served in Company H, 9th Illinois Infantry (three-month troops), April to July 1861, and as William H. Miller in Company C, 9th Illinois Infantry (three-year troops), August 1861 to August 1862. He married Sept. 25, 1862 at Chillicothe to Eliza Drake, after a courtship of only a few days, and they lived briefly at Athens, Ohio, "until the army came and took him back." Pension File, RG 15.

35. Transferred to the Navy per GO 91, War Dept., Mar. 4, 1864, RG 94, Entry 44, to increase naval forces; The certificate of the mustering officer shows Miller mustered for discharge at New Orleans July 24, by virtue of SOs 194 and 195, Dept. of Gulf, July 22 and 23, 1864, RG 393, Part I, Entry 1767; he is also shown transferred to the navy June 25, 1864, at Morganza, La., by reason of his application through his company commander. Also taken up on the rolls of the "Octorara," July 1, 1864. Pension File, RG 15.

36. After the war, Miller returned to his wife and worked several years on a farm at Kingston, Ohio, having two sons. His eldest son, William Henry, Jr., stated that he was born March 11, 1864, that his father left the family when he was 4 1/2 years old, after two brothers-in-law threatened to kill him. (Eliza married Conrad Rull in Oct. 1869.) William, Jr. said his father was born and raised in New Orleans, where his father (William, Jr.'s grandfather), surname Miller, owned a large store that was lost in the war. William, Sr., seemed well educated, talked much about New Orleans, where he said his name was William McCarter before changing to Miller, and claimed to have been married before arriving in Ohio. Others said his name was Henry Carter and had deserted the rebel army and joined the 73rd Ohio as Henry Miller. Pension File, RG 15.

37. Mrs. Miller's brother-in-law, George Oertel, served with Miller in the 8th Cavalry, said they were best friends; says Miller told him he served in the 7th Cavalry under Gen. Custer and was with the pack train in 1875–76 as blacksmith, Oertel affidavit, February 8, 1915, in Mrs. Miller's pension claim. RG 15.

Smith F. Foster, who also served with Miller in the 8th Cavalry, said Miller often told him of having been with the packs under Reno; he had to fall out to shoe a horse and in this way got with the packs, WMC, rosters, LBHB; Berwald interviews, 1911 and 1912, WMC-IU; Pandtle (Pendle) to Walter Camp, July 14, 1919, WMC-BYU.

38. Applied for invalid pension Oct. 7, 1892 as Henry Miller, 7th and 8th Cavalry, (deposed no other military service), for rheumatism contracted from exposure at Fort Buford, DT, in 1888, but was rejected Jan. 2, 1896, when no ratable disability was shown.

Applied again Sept. 6, 1897 as William H. Miller, 3rd Maryland Cavalry, and U.S. Navy, (deposed no other military service), and approved at $8 per month for neuralgia and old age. In 1916, the special examiner working on Mrs. Miller's case, remarked in his report to the commissioner of pensions that, "[Miller] was a man of very bad reputation and a crook in every way. . ." Pension file, RG 15.

39. On learning that Timothy Sullivan had been awarded a certificate of merit for carrying dispatches during the Nez Perce campaign in 1877, Joseph Millton wrote from Fort Grant, AT, Oct. 23, 1895, to Capt. Ezra Fuller, 7th Cavalry, who commanded the five-man detachment of which Millton and Sullivan were members in 1877, stating his belief that he, too, should be entitled to a certificate. Fuller then (1895) recommended Millton for certificate, but he failed to specify any distinguished service and because Millton was not mentioned in the endorsements of Gen. Miles or Col. Sturgis, the application was not favorably considered by the Assistant Secretary of War, who remarked that the case was entirely different from that of Sullivan, who had made three separate and distinct trips alone. RG 94, Entry 25, file 16105 AGO 1890.

40. Morning report, escort northern boundary survey commission, Maj. M. A. Reno, Aug. 29, 1873, NA, M1495, Roll 1.

41. Mitchell was striker for Maj. Reno June 25 and was the second messenger sent to advise Custer the Indians were attacking in force. Reno said Mitchell was with him as cook. Nichols, *Reno Court*, 561.

42. Ernst, "A Dane Who Survived."

43. Alcott said Moody an old English dragoon, WMC, rosters, LBHB.

44. Federal census, 1900, Williams County, North Dakota; enlistment paper of Private Edward L. Moore, Company G, 7th Cavalry, RG 94, Entry 91.

45. Troop G departed Shreveport by rail, April 19, 1876, and arrived Fort Lincoln, May 1st. John Frett said there were some discharged soldiers with the pack train. Nichols, *Reno Court*, 503.

46. In fall 1877, Ed Moore and W. S. Dunn of Fort Buford helped Robert Mathews build his ranch house on Stony Creek, two miles east of Williston. (Mathews was partner of George W. Grinnell in 1883 on a large buffalo hunt outfitted by Jordan & Leighton, traders at Fort Buford). Libby, ed., *Collections of the State Historical Society*, 101–104.

Walter Camp noted on his roster of packers that Moore, "Lives near Grinnells mouth of Big Muddy so someone says," WMC-LBHB; "Grinnells" (with two lines drawn through) is written above "near." The Camp rosters at Indiana University omit "Grinnells" and "so someone says."

George W. Grinnell and family operated a combination post office, roadhouse, saloon, and wood yard about 30 miles east of Williston, and was an overnight stop on the government road from Fort Berthold to Fort Buford. It also had a reputation as a hangout for outlaws and rustlers. See Innis, *Sagas of the Smoky Water*, 356–68.

Godfrey mentioned Grinnell Point, a wood yard (between Buford and Knife River), Sept. 20, 1876. Godfrey, *Diary*, 54; Big Muddy Creek is located in northeast Montana, near Culbertson on the Missouri River, whereas Little Muddy is in northwest North Dakota and flows into the Missouri River at Williston.

47. Joseph W. Jackson (Mayor of Williston in 1912) recalled that "Captain" Moore lived for a time with the Luke Rowell family, about two miles east of Williston, on what later became the Burdick farm. Luke's brother, Duffy, was one of the organizers of the Stoney Creek Dairy Company that supplied Williston with milk.

Jackson says, "old 'Cap' Moore" was said to have been one of Custer's scouts and looked the part, being small in stature with greying beard and whiskers. He may have been a civilian employee at old Fort Buford. He was usually quiet and soft spoken, and though reticent to speak of his past, he often had nightmares during which he would stand up in bed waving his arms shouting orders at the top of his voice so blood curdling that Jackson wondered when the shooting would start, "Recollections of Williston," by Jos. W. Jackson, in *Word and Picture Story of Williston*, 34–43..

See also *The Wonder of Williams; Tales of Mighty Mountraille;* Breeling, ed., *When the Trail was New in Mountraille*, 28–29.

E. L. Moore recorded his livestock brand Sept. 23, 1897. *Records of Brands*, Book A, p. 72; Williams County Treasurer/Recorder, Williston, N.Dak.. Edward L. Moore a "single man," age 56, was involved in sales of a tract of land, May 1900 and Feb. 1902, with the Stoney Creek Stock and Dairy Company (of which he was president); he settled the land in 1893 under the Homestead Act of 1862 (Deed Book B, 194–96, 318–20; and Patent Book 209, 215), Williams County Treasurer/Recorder, Williston, N.Dak.. Moore's signature is near identical to that on the enlistment paper of Private Edward L. Moore, 7th Cavalry. RG 94, Entry 91.

Moore arranged the funeral of his friend, Winfield S. Dunn (Register of Deeds), in Dec 1904. Riverview Cemetery, Funeral Record Book No. 1, p. 91. *Williston (N.Dak.) Graphic*, Dec. 8, 1904.

Moore is mentioned in several issues of the *Graphic*, including: July 9, 1895; June 24, 1898; April 26, June 21, Sept. 20, and Dec. 6, 1900; April 11 and Nov. 7, 1901; and Jan. 9, 1902.

48. Denny was elected first mayor of Williston in 1904. Innis, *Sagas of the Smoky Water*, 346, 372; see also Shemorry, "The Best Little Stories of the 20th Century," early reminiscence of D'Arcy A. "Shorty" Burgess, one of Williston's first settlers (1887), who recalled that E. L. Moore "was with Reno at the time of the Custer battle on the Little Big Horn. He was a teamster or quartermaster corral boss during the engagement." *Williston Daily Herald*, Jan. 12, 1999. Shemorry spent his entire life (born 1914) in and around Williston, and researched extensively to write numerous books and articles on the early history of the area.

DeLand in the *The Sioux Wars*, 527, mentions "the statement of one Moore, one of the Reno packers"; that this refers to Private Moore, Co. L. is determined from a letter to DeLand, July 12, 1926, from Dr. Raymond A. Burnside of Des Moines, Iowa, relating that during the fiftieth anniversary celebration at Custer Battlefield, he met, "F. J. Moore from Rawlings, Wyoming, who had been with Reno's pack train," and who agreed with DeLand "that Reno has been unnecessarily and foolishly criticized," Excerpt from Burnside letter as related to RLW by the late Dr. Lawrence A. Frost during telephone conversation, Feb. 14, 1989.

49. James E. Moore is referred to as Larry Moore in the deposition of his wife, Mary Jane "Mollie" Moore, Apr. 21, 1904, Union, SC, Pension file of William G. Abrams, RG 15.

50. Lansing Moore was attached to the pack train just before the battle began, *Rawlins* (Wyo.) *Republican*, July 28, 1931.

John Burkman also said Moore was with the packs, Roster of Company L to Burkman from Walter Camp, Nov. 20, 1908, LBHB Coll., Roll 9.

51. L. A. Moore, 72, of Rawlings, Wyo., a visitor at the battlefield's fiftieth anniversary. *Winners of the West,* Vol. III, No. 12, Aug. 30, 1926, 5; also, "The Custer Semi-Centennial Ceremonies," EBC-LBHB, Roll 7. During the event, Moore was interviewed by Dr. Raymond A. Burnside of Des Moines, Iowa, as to whether or not firing from Custer hill could be heard on Reno hill.

52. In his early account of the battle, William E. Morris said each company was provided with six or eight mules which the Old Guard, of which he was one, was compelled to lead, and when he attempted to sleep during the short halt at 3 A.M., on June 25, he hitched his horse to the strap of one boot leg and his mule to the other, Morris to Walter Camp, Dec. 24, 1909, WMC-BYU, includes newspaper clipping, np, nd, with letter from Morris to the editor of *The Record*, March 11, 1892.

53. Morris to William Slaper, Apr. 11, 1915, in newspaper clipping, np, nd, Taylor Scrapbook.

54. Botzer Troop Duty Book; Brown Troop Duty Book. Reynolds and Brown, *Journal.*

55. Mrs. Custer mentions the sergeant-major, though not by name, and gives insight into his activity between Oct. 1866 and Feb. 1867, E. B.Custer, *Tenting on the Plains* (1915), 263–65; Moylan married Charlotte Calhoun, sister of Lt. Calhoun, Oct. 22, 1872.

56. "Company L Seventh cavalry give a complimentary ball next Wednesday evening to first Sergeant John Mullen," *Bismarck Tribune*, Sat., Feb. 16, 1878.

57. Sgt. Murphy's mother said her son was formerly of Gen. Custer's own gallant greys and, "escaped the fate of his commander by being Troop QM Sgt. at the time and left in charge of baggage and Troop property some miles from the historic scene." Anne Murphy, Newmarket on Fergus, County Clare, Ireland, to Commissioner of Pensions, and to 2nd auditor of treasury, June 11, and, Sept. 5, 1888, Pension file, RG 15. Able Spencer said Sgt. Murphy was not at the battle, WMC rosters, LBHB; Frank Berwald said Murphy was at the battle, Berwald interviews, 1911 and 1912, WMC-IU; Chris Pandtle not sure, Pendle to Walter Camp, July 14, 1919, WMC-BYU.

58. Frank Geist attended some of Murphy's legal matters, WMC, rosters, IU; Michael Caddle to Walter Camp, Nov. 8, 1909, WMC-BYU.

59. WMC, rosters, LBHB.

60. GO 81, Hq Army, AGO, July 26, 1890, RG 94, Entry 44, directed that enlisted men who had served ten years or more, continuously or otherwise, shall be classified as veteran soldiers, and discharge granted thereto from the War Department by way of favor, so far as the interests of the service will admit, or the merits of each case justify. The purpose being to extend all possible indulgence to meritorious men, especially in cases where a discharge would obviously be for the material benefit of the soldier.

N

Nave, Andrew Humes. 2Lt co I; b. 23 Feb 1846 near Knoxville Tenn; grad USMA 12 June 1871 & appt 2Lt 7 cav; join co I 10 Oct 1871 Shelbyville Ky.; sick 28 Apr to 17 July 1873 Ft Snelling Minn. (sim. frac. r. clavicle [fall from horse]); rejoin co 17 Aug 1873 with NBS; chg of supply train to Ft Stevenson DT 27 Aug; sick in post hosp (frac. collarbone) to 20 Oct & rejoined co enroute to Ft Totten DT; duty 22 Nov; awl 30 days on surg cert 15 July 1874 (from NBS); awl ext'd thro' 23 mos; prom 1Lt co A 26 July 1876 & ordered to report for lt duty at Ft Lincoln DT; ds dept hq St Paul Minn. 17 Aug with bd purchasing horses; arr Ft Lincoln 21 Sep (with Lt Craycroft); ds Ft Lincoln 17 Oct comdg dismtd men; comd co A 14 Nov 1876 to 18 Feb 1877 Ft Rice DT; ds Ft Lincoln 4 Apr 1877 actg ordn officer (unfit for field serv acc't injury to collarbone); post adjt & comd band & detmt ind scouts May to Dec 1877;[1] tr to co M 28 Aug 1878; awl on surg cert 18 Aug 1880; never returned to duty (prom capt co L 6 Mar 1884); retd 23 Sept 1885 for disability contr line of duty;[2] prof of mil science univ of Tenn 1898 to 1907, also col Tenn natl gd 1899 to 1901; died 7 Dec 1924 Knoxville Tenn.
[3377 ACP 1874]. Pension: 9 Mar 1925 / Wid / 1230535. Ind. Wid. / 17188 / 11368.

Nealon, Dan'l. Cpl co H; b. Newport R. I. enl 9 Feb 1872 Buffalo N.Y. for 5 yrs; age 22; clerk; grey eyes, brn hair, fair comp, 5' 7" high; join co H 23 Feb 1872 Nashville Tenn; dd qmd herder 21–31 Aug 1874; cpl 12 Apr 1876; sgt 6 Oct 1876; disch 9 Feb 1877 Ft Rice DT expir of serv a sgt char good. res Gilt Edge MT in 1910.[3]

Neely, Frank. Pvt co M; b. Collinsville Ohio; enl 8 Apr 1871 Cincinnati Ohio for 5 yrs; age 21 1/12; painter; grey eyes, lt hair, lt comp, 5' 10" high; join 7 cav as unassd rct 19 Apr 1871 Taylor Bks Ky.; join co M 30 May 1871 at Louisville; des 20 June 1873 Ft Rice DT; surd 20 Nov 1873 regtl hq St Paul Minn. under GO 102 AGO 1873; restored to duty without trial 5 Jan 1874 & ds Ft Snelling Minn. to 17 May awaiting transp to regt; dd qmd herder 21–31 Aug 1874; dd co cook Feb 1875; dd qmd with boat crew July to Nov 1875; cpl 1 Aug 1876; disch 9 Sep 1876 camp on Yellowstone River MT expir of serv a cpl char xclt & reenl in co M for 5 yrs; pvt 16 Oct 1876; dd co cook Aug 1877; ds member of mackinaw boat crew on Missouri River 28 Oct to 19 Nov 1877; dd co cook Dec 1877; dd co cook Aug to Oct 1878; dd qmd June 1879; dd co cook Aug 1879; dd subs dept laborer Dec 1879 to Feb 1880; dd co cook Apr 1880; dd co gardener June to Nov 1880; dd co gardener Apr to Sep 1881; disch 8 Sep 1881 Ft Meade DT expir of serv a pvt; reenl 20 Mar 1882 Milwaukee Wis for 5 yrs; join co K 6 cav 24 May 1882 Ft Lowell AT; cpl 17 Apr 1883; sgt 20 Apr 1884; pvt 9 Jan 1886; tr to co D 9 Apr 1886; disch 19 Mar 1887 Ft Stanton NM expir of serv a pvt; reenl in same co 28 Mar 1887 for 5 yrs; cpl 27 Aug 1888; sgt 6 Feb 1890; pvt 29 Apr 1890; disch 23 Sep 1890 at Ft Stanton per SO 215 AGO 1890 (under prov'n GO 81 AGO 1890) a pvt.[4]
Pension: 27 Nov 1896 / Inv / 1182965. (Abandoned).

Nees, Edler. Pvt co H; b. Quierhessen Germany; enl 7 Sep 1875 New York N.Y. for 5 yrs; age 22; clerk; blue eyes, brn hair, ruddy comp, 5' 7 1/2" high; join co H 21 Oct 1875 Ft Rice DT; dd qmd laborer 15 Mar to 4 May 1876; des 26 July 1876 camp mouth of Big Horn River MT (with pvt Channell, taking a small boat & box of hardtack); passed maj Moore's comd 27 July at Big Porcupine Creek & refused to stop when ordered; apph 29 July hiding in brush near Powder River when troops from str *Carroll* went ashore to investigate small boat on bank with two army coats & captive eagle in the stern sheets; taken to camp at Rosebud & placed in irons; tr under gd on str *Durfee* 5 Aug to Ft Lincoln;[5] dishon disch 30 Nov 1876 sen gen cm & 4 yrs conft mil prison Ft L'worth Kans.

Nelson, Robert. (alias). See Brandon, Benj.

Newell, Dan'l. Pvt co M; b. 17 Mar 1848 Ballinlough Roscommon Ireland; enl 8 Oct 1873 Phil'a Pa. for 5 yrs; age 25; blacksmith; grey eyes, brn hair, dk comp, 5' 7 1/2" high; join co M 21 Oct 1873 Ft Rice DT; blks 15 Dec 1873; pvt 24 June 1875; dd qmd blks July 1875 to Feb 1876; gsw l. thigh (fl. wd. sl.) 25 June 1876 in valley fight; tr on str *Far West* 3 July to hosp Ft Lincoln; tr to hosp Ft Rice 30 July; rejoin co M 10 Nov 1876; (appt co blks 1 July 1876); ed qmd blks Dec 1876; pvt 18 Mar 1878; ds qmd blks camp J. G. Sturgis DT Aug 1878; disch 8 Oct 1878 Camp Ruhlen DT expir of serv a pvt char good; died 22 Sep 1933 Hot Springs SD.[6]
Pension: 15 May 1879 / Inv / 286456 / 299909. Ind. War Surv / 11599 / 6741. Wid / 1736913.

Nicholas, Joshua S. Pvt co H; b. London England; enl 2 Feb 1872 Chicago Ill. for 5 yrs; age 21; carpenter; blue eyes, lt hair, lt comp, 5' 6" high; join co H 23 Feb 1872 Nashville Tenn; ds herding co horses June 1872; in conft Apr 1874; in conft Feb 1875; dd qmd laborer Oct 1875 to Jan 1876; cpl 6 Oct 1876 to date 1 Sep; sgt 4 Jan 1877; disch 2 Feb 1877 Ft Rice DT expir of serv a sgt char xclt & reenl in co H as pvt for 5 yrs; cpl 1 July 1877; ds post no. 2 Big Horn (Ft Custer) 14 Sep thro' Oct 1877; sgt 1 Jan 1878; in arrest Jan 1878; (felonious assault with murderous weapon of unknown description); dishon disch 14 Apr 1878 at Ft Rice sen gen cm & 4 yrs conft mil prison Ft L'worth Kans.; reenl 11 Mar 1883 Ft Omaha Neb for 5 yrs in co D 4 inf; sen gar cm 10 May 1883 forf $2 pay & conft 5 days; des 25 June 1883 at Ft Omaha.

Nitsche, Ottocar. Pvt co C; b. Prussia Germany; enl 6 Dec 1872 New York N.Y. for 5 yrs; age 22; merchant; blue eyes, lt hair, fair comp, 5' 5 1/4" high; join co C 12 Feb 1873 Charlotte NC; ds July 1873 on str *Josephine*; dd asst post librarian Feb to Apr 1874; ed qmd Apr to Aug 1875; ds Ft Rice DT 9 Oct to 18 Nov 1875 verbal order comdg officer; ed subs dept Dec 1875 to May 1876; ds subs dept laborer 22 June 1876 on str *Far West*;[7] dd clerk post hq Ft Lincoln 27 Sep to 12 Nov 1876; ds Ft Totten DT chg co prop Aug to Dec 1877; cpl 26 Sep 1877; disch 6 Dec 1877 at Ft Totten expir of serv a cpl char xclt & reenl in co C for 5 yrs; dd chg co cook house Dec 1877; dd actg co qm sgt Feb to Apr 1878; (m. 3 Mar 1878 at Ft Totten to Molly Jacobs [step-daughter of hosp stew'd]). sgt 3 Apr 1878; ds Ft Totten June to Oct 1878 chg co prop; dd actg co qm sgt Dec 1878 to June 1879; dd post hq Oct 1880 to Feb 1882; ds Ft Meade DT Apr to June 1882; dd regtl hq July to Dec 1882; disch 5 Dec 1882 at Ft Meade expir of serv a sgt char xclt & reenl in co C for 5 yrs; dd regtl hq thro' June 1883; on furl 3 mos 1 July 1883 to Europe; des while on furl.

Niver, Garrett H. Pvt co C; b. 1 Feb 1846 Bethlehem N.Y.; enl as Garrett Van Allen 2 Oct 1873 New York N.Y. for 5 yrs; age 27; farmer; blue eyes, brn hair, dk comp, 5' 7" high; join co C 21 Oct 1873 Ft Rice DT; dd qmd Nov 1874 to Feb 1875; dd co cook June 1875; dd qmd Oct 1875 to 5 May 1876; dd exp'n qmd 6 May to 10 June 1876 when relieved to report to co for duty; killed with Custer column 25 June 1876.
Pension: 18 Apr 1892 / Mother / 548585. (Rej on grd clmt's husband owned prop which furn comfortable support & clmt not dependent as contemplated by law).

Nolan, Jno. Cpl co K; b. Tipperary Ireland; enl 4 Dec 1874 New York N.Y. for 5 yrs; age 26; groom; blue eyes, brn hair, fair comp, 5' 7 1/4" high; join co K 9 Feb 1875 Colfax La.; ed subs dept May to Oct 1875; cpl 1 Feb 1876; dd actg co qm sgt Apr to July 1876; ds camp Powder River MT 15 June 1876; sgt 19 Oct 1876; ed subs dept Apr to Aug 1877; (on str *Far West* June 1877); gsw above l. hip 30 Sep 1877 Snake Creek MT (Bear's Paw Mtns) in action with Nez Perce inds; tr to str *Silver City* 14 Oct mouth of Squaw Creek (on Missouri River) & arr hosp Ft Lincoln 26 Oct; duty 4 Dec 1877; disch 1 Feb 1878 Ft Rice DT on surg cert dis (gsw entered near spine in small of back r. side, passing obliquely downward emerging in gluteal region l. side) a sgt char xclt; died 17 July 1893 Newburgh N.Y.[8]
Pension: 20 Feb 1878 / Inv / 249082 / 153624. Minor / 584489.

Noonan, Jno. See Nunan, Jno.

Northeg, Olans H. Sgt co G; b. Nannestad Norway; enl 21 Mar 1867 St Louis Mo. for 5 yrs; age 25; clerk; grey eyes, fair hair, fair comp, 5' 9 1/2" high; assd to gen mtd serv; disch 21 Mar 1872 at St Louis Bks by expir of serv a sgt; reenl same day in same unit for 5 yrs; sen gen cm 31 Jan 1875 forf $10 pay per mo for 3 mos; join co G 7 cav 10 Feb 1875 Shreveport La.; cpl 17 May 1875; sgt 27 July 1875; sick hosp 2–14 May 1876 (ac. rheum.); sick qrs in field 15–21 May; dd actg sgt-maj Nov 1876; regtl standard bearer 20 Feb to 7 Mar 1877; disch 21 Mar 1877 Ft Lincoln DT expir of serv a sgt char very good; reenl in co G 24 Mar 1877 for 5 yrs; dd qmd Apr 1878; in conft Aug 1879 (used fraud't order to purchase merchandise from post trader); dishon disch 24 Sep 1879 Ft Meade DT sen gen cm & 3 yrs conft at sta of co; sen appv except conft longer than one yr; died 5 Nov 1882 at Ft Meade (suicide).

Noshang, Jacob. Pvt co I; b. Hamilton Ohio; enl 23 Jan 1872 Louisville Ky. for 5 yrs; age 21; laborer; hazel eyes, brn hair, dk comp, 5' 5 3/4" high; join co I 10 Feb 1872 Shelbyville Ky.; dd hq detmt June 1873; in conft Feb 1876; killed with Custer column 25 June 1876. Pension: 7 July 1877 / Father / 232249 / 227349.

Nowlan, Henry Jas. 1Lt & rqm; b. 18 June 1837 Corfu Ionian Isles [British garrison];[9] grad Sandhurst royal mil college 31 July 1854 earning first com'n free as ensign 41st regt of foot; Lt 8 Dec 1854; in Crimea campn Jan to June 1855 & recd medal & clasp for Sevastopol & Turkish war medal; sold com'n 27 May 1862 (having been senior Lt for 3 yrs & superceded twice for prom'n [not having means for purchase]) & came to America; appt 1Lt 14 N.Y. cav 17 Jan 1863; captured 15 June 1863 Port Hudson La.; escaped 2 Feb 1865 at Columbia SC & made way to gen Sherman's army marching thro' state; sent to AGO in Wash'n 21 Mar 1865 & granted 30 day delay rejoining regt; tr to 18 N.Y. cav 12 June 1865 (consol'n of regts); prom capt 24 Jan 1866; gsw l. breast 8 Mar 1866 arresting citizens at Yorktown Tex.; duty 14 May 1866; m.o. vol serv 31 May 1866 Victoria Tex.; appt reg army com'n 2Lt 7 cav 31 Oct 1866 to date 28 July 1866; join co F 12 Dec 1866 Ft Harker Kans.; 1Lt 13 Aug 1867 to date 3 Dec 1866; regtl comsy 1 Nov 1867; actg comsy Camp Supply IT 18 Nov 1868 to 29 Mar 1869; actg adjt 23 July 1869; actg rqm 20 Aug 1869; post comsy Ft L'worth Kans. Oct 1869 to Nov 1870; tr to co L 17 Dec 1870 & comd co from 17 Jan 1871; appt rqm 18 Mar 1872; actg aqm & comsy Taylor Bks (Louisville) Ky. Apr 1872 to Feb 1873; ds with detmt to Yankton DT to May 1873; with regtl hq St Paul Minn. 26 June 1873 & actg adjt July 1873 thro' Jan 1874; tr with regtl hq to Ft Lincoln DT 6 Oct 1874; post qm Apr 1875 to Apr 1876; actg aqm gen Terry's exp'n 14 May to 30 Sep 1876;[10] (capt co I 26 July 1876); join co I 19 Oct at Ft Lincoln; ds dept hq St Paul 6 Dec 1876 to 10 Feb 1877; comd co in field May to Nov 1877; [escort for capt Sheridan 20 June to 7 July to Custer battlefield]; awl 12 mos 28 Feb 1878 with perm'n to cross the sea; ds rctg duty Chicago Ill. Sep 1888 to Oct 1890; bvt maj 27 Feb 1890 for gal serv in action with Nez Perce inds at Canon Creek MT 13 Sep 1877; comd co in action with Sioux inds 29 Dec 1890 Wounded Knee SD; actg aig Dept of the East Dec 1891 to July 1894; awl on surg cert to Sep 1894; prom maj 17 July 1895; sick qrs Aug to Sep 1895 Ft Grant AT thence awl 4 mos; ds Ft Sheridan Ill. Jan to Apr 1896; post comdr Ft Huachuca AT 11 June 1896; awl on surg cert 27 Oct 1898; died 10 Nov 1898 army & navy hosp Hot Springs Ark; (chr. disease of heart). [3714 ACP 1876].

Nugent, Wm. David. Pvt co A; b. 5 Nov 1852 Litchfield Ky.; enl in co A 5 Aug 1872 E'town Ky. for 5 yrs; age 21; farmer; brn eyes, brn hair, dk comp, 5' 8 1/2" high; ed med dept nurse June 1873; ds Ft Rice DT 21 Apr 1877; disch 5 Aug 1877 at Ft Rice upon expir of serv a pvt & reenl in co A for 5 yrs; ds Ft Rice to Dec 1877; cpl 1 Nov 1877; sgt 1 Apr 1878; sick hosp Apr 1878 (consumption); disch 1 May 1878 Ft Lincoln DT on surg cert dis (phthisis pulmonalis) a sgt; died 15 Nov 1934 Independence Kans.[11]
Pension: 27 Aug 1885 / Inv / 548136. (Rej on grd no ratable dis shown). Ind. Surv. / 13837 / 7845.

Nunan, Jno. Cpl co L; b. Ft Wayne Ind.; enl 17 Nov 1865 at Ft Wayne for 3 yrs; age 21; farmer; blue eyes, dk hair, dk comp, 5' 5" high; assd to co A 18 inf; des 24 July 1866; apph 31 July 1866; disch 21 Nov 1868 Ft D. A. Russell Wyo. Ty expir of serv a pvt; reenl 17 Dec 1868 Omaha Bks Neb for 3 yrs; assd to co C 3 art'y; cpl 1 May 1869; sgt 5 July 1869; pvt 23 Oct 1869; disch 17 Dec 1871 Charleston SC expir of serv a pvt; enl in co L 7 cav 14 Jan 1872 Yorkville SC for 5 yrs; cpl 28 Sep 1872; pvt 25 Oct 1872; in conft Oct 1872; cpl 20 Jan 1873; pvt 20 Nov 1873; dd post hq Mar & Apr 1874; (orderly to Lt Custer); dd hq Blk Hills Exp'n 25 June to 31 Aug 1874; cpl 8 Apr 1876; ds camp Powder River MT 10 June 1876 chg of gd to cattle herd; sgt 1 Aug 1876 to date 1 July; abs sick (catarrh) 24 Aug 1876; arr Ft Lincoln 6 Sep on str *Benton*; duty 13 Sep & dd qmd to 28 Sep with 281 cav horses at post; disch 14 Jan 1877 at Ft Lincoln expir of serv a sgt char xclt & reenl in co L for 5 yrs; ds Ft Lincoln 1 May to 19 Nov 1877; pvt 12 Feb 1878; dd co cook Aug 1878; cpl 4 Sep 1878; died 30 Nov 1878 at Ft Lincoln (suicide).[12]

Nursey, Fred'k Wilkinson. Sgt co F; b. 5 Dec 1848 Bungay, Suffolk England;[13] enl 23 Mar 1871 Pittsburgh Pa. for 5 yrs; age 22 1/4; clerk; blue eyes, lt hair, fair comp, 5' 5 1/2" high; join 7 cav 19 Apr 1871 Taylor Bks Ky. unassd rct; join co F 27 May 1871 at Louisville; dd co clerk July 1871 to July 1872; cpl July 1872; sgt Oct 1872; dd co clerk Dec 1872; actg co qm sgt Feb 1873; dd co clerk June 1873 to Feb 1874; ds Ft Lincoln DT June & July 1874; actg co qm sgt Aug to Oct 1874; disch 23 Mar 1876 at Ft Lincoln expir of serv a sgt char xclt & reenl in co F for 5 yrs; killed with Custer column 25 June 1876.

Notes—N

1. *Bismarck Tribune*, Sept. 27, 1876; Col. Sturgis called for Lt. Nave to take charge of post ordnance stores. NA, M1734, Roll 19, letter 1354 DD 1877; Also much on Nave during August and Sept. 1877, in NA, M1734, Roll 21, letter 3543 DD 1877.

2. Col. Tilford sent Nave to Dr. Sayre, a famous bone and joint specialist, but efforts were unsuccessful and he continued unable to mount a horse or walk without a crutch. Years later, Nave was treated by an English bone setter in New York, who found a bone out of place in his instep and reset his ankle, enabling him to walk without the aid of crutches. *Annual Report of the Association of Graduates* (USMA), June 10, 1931, 111.

3. Dan Neally of H troop known as "Cracker Box Dan" because he kept hid behind a cracker box on Reno hill, Notes from interviews with John Burkman, in I. D. O'Donnell, Papers (John Burkman), Little Big Horn Battlefield, Crow Agency, MT (hereafter cited as O'Donnell Papers); see Wagner, *Old Neutriment*, 164.

4. See note M60 (Murray).

5. Willert, *March of the Columns*, 208, 221.

6. See Everett, "Bullets, Boots, and Saddles"; also, EBC-LBHB, Roll 6.

7. SFO 17, Hq DD, June 22, 1876, RG 94, Entry 44; Lt. Thompson, ACS, said the men detailed to go with him went on the boat and up the Big Horn. Hammer, *Custer in '76*, 247.

8. WMC, rosters, LBHB.

9. In June, 1837, Nowlan's father, John, was Colour Sgt. of the 11th Regiment of Foot, also acting sgt.-major. He was appointed to the medical staff in 1848, British military records (TNA).

10. Nowlan accompanied Gen. Terry and staff on the steamer *Josephine*, July 16, from camp on Big Horn to Powder River to oversee the transfer of the supply depot. He took all animals of the pack train unfit for service to be replaced with serviceable animals from the depot, which would then accompany the regiment's wagon train to the new depot at mouth of Rosebud Creek. On Sept. 6, he was directed to transfer quartermaster property to his successors at Powder River and Glendive Creek, thence report to Gen. Terry at Fort Buford. He was ordered by Gen. Terry, Sept. 17, to proceed to St. Paul to consult with the chief quartermaster. He reached Bismarck Sept. 23, the *Tribune* reporting his arrival and that he would take command of his company after closing his quartermaster work. *Bismarck Tribune*, Sept. 27,

1876; RG 92, Entry 238, reports 1876/328 and 1876/110; RG 94, Entry 44, Field Orders, DD, 1876; Koury, *The Field Diary of General Alfred H. Terry*, 29.

11. Photos of Nugent in *Greasy Grass,* vol. 3, May 1987, and vol. 7, May 1991; "Thrilling Experiences of Comrade William D. Nugent, Troop A, 7th U.S. Cavalry, near the Custer Battlefield," *Winners of the West*, Vol. III, No. 10, June 24, 1926; Vol. IV, No. 3, Feb. 28, 1927; Vol. IX, No. 7, June 30, 1932. Statement of William D. Nugent, May 13–14, 1933, "From Memory's Store," (hereafter cited as Nugent, From Memory's Store) biographical file, Little Big Horn Battlefield, Crow Agency, MT; McClure, *Two Centuries in Elizabethtown*.

12. Nunan's "wife," a laundress of Company L, died Oct. 30, 1878 at Fort Lincoln and when being dressed for burial was discovered to be a man, confirmed in examination by the post surgeon who reported the body a fully developed male in all respects, "without any abnormal condition that could cause doubt on the subject." Nunan swore his wife was a woman, and he cared nothing for post mortem examinations to the contrary, *Bismarck Tribune*, Nov. 4, 11 and Dec. 2, 30, 1878; Nunan's company commander applied for his discharge for the good of the service, as he was, "looked upon by the members of his company with repugnance and detestation." Col. Sturgis suggested that any law by which Nunan could be sent to the penitentiary be called into requisition. Gen. Terry recommended Nunan receive dishonorable discharge and instructed Col. Sturgis to bring the case to the attention of the U.S. District Attorney, RG 94, Entry 409, file, 14908 A (EB) 1878; see Schneider, *An Enigma Named Noonan*.

13. Russell, "From Bungay to the Little Bighorn," *The Crow's Nest*, Summer/Autumn 2002, Vol. 2, No. 2.

O

O'Brien, Thos. Pvt co B; b. Limerick Ireland; enl 31 Mar 1876 Boston Mass. for 5 yrs; age 22; currier; blue eyes, lt hair, fair comp, 5' 5 1/2" high; join co B 27 Apr 1876 St Paul Minn.; ds camp Powder River MT 10 June 1876; ds camp mouth of Rosebud Creek 7 Aug dismtd; abs sick (typhoid fever) 24 Aug on str *Carroll*; died 15 Sep 1876 Ft Buford DT still delirious.

O'Bryan, Jno. Pvt co I; b. Phil'a Pa.; enl in co I 8 June 1873 Breckenridge Minn. for 5 yrs; age 22; laborer; blk eyes, dk brn hair, lt comp, 5' 6 1/2" high; ds Winona Minn. 10 Oct to 18 Nov 1873 (witness in murder trial); ds Ft Snelling Minn. from 29 Nov 1873; sent to Ft Lincoln DT 6 July 1874 (with pvt Gross) thence to Ft Totten DT 7 Aug 1874 chg of govt horses; killed with Custer column 25 June 1876.[1]
Pension: 13 Oct 1881 / Mother / 286678 / 231858.

O'Connell, David J. Pvt co L; b. Cork Ireland; enl 20 Apr 1865 Baltimore Md for 3 yrs; age 22; laborer; brn eyes, dk hair, ruddy comp, 5' 7 1/2" high; join co E 4 cav 17 June 1865 Macon Ga.; sick hosp 6 June to 18 Sep 1867 (syph.); disch 20 Apr 1868 Monroe La. expir of serv a pvt; enl in 7 cav 19 May 1869 Ft L'worth Kans. for 5 yrs; assd to co L 28 May 1869; in conft Oct to Dec 1872; disch 19 May 1874 Ft Lincoln DT expir of serv a pvt & reenl in co L for 5 yrs; on furl 30 days 21 May to Ft L'worth [see sgt Smith & pvt Andrews]; dd qmd plasterer Oct 1874; dd qmd herder Mar & Apr 1875; appd for furl of 60 days 19 Feb 1876 (from 1 June) remainder of furl promised upon reenlmt; killed with Custer column 25 June 1876.

O'Connor, Pat'k Edw. Pvt co E; b. Longford Ireland; enl 18 Sep 1873 New York N.Y. for 5 yrs; age 21; shoemaker; blue eyes, lt hair, fair comp, 5' 5 1/2" high; join co E 18 Oct 1873 Ft Lincoln DT; dd co cook Feb 1876; killed with Custer column 25 June 1876.
Pension: 10 June 1889 / Mother / 397708 / 261136.

Ogden, Jno. S. Sgt co E; b. 25 Oct 1849 Newberry Mass.; enl 6 Aug 1866 Boston Mass. for 5 yrs; age 21; farmer; grey eyes, lt hair, lt comp, 5' 7 1/2" high; join co E 10 Sep 1866 Ft Riley Kans.; ds with detmt protecting Holladay stage line Nov 1866; ds camp near Ft Wallace Kans. Aug 1867 chg co prop; ds with survey exp'n May & June 1869; ed qmd Nov 1870 to Feb 1871; disch 6 Aug 1871 Spartanburg SC expir of serv a pvt; reenl in co E 15 Nov 1872 Unionville SC for 5 yrs; cpl 17 Dec 1872; pvt 1 May 1873; dd post hq Sep 1873 to Apr 1874; cpl 15 June 1874; sgt 1 Mar 1875; killed with Custer column 25 June 1876; [buried near river, a large oak tree at head with name cut in, says Kimm].[2]

O'Hara, Miles F. Sgt co M; b. Alton Ohio; enl 30 Oct 1872 Columbus Ohio for 5 yrs; age 21 1/12; laborer; grey eyes, lt hair, ruddy comp, 5' 8 1/4" high; join co M 9 Dec 1872 Unionville SC; cpl 1 Dec 1873; sgt 2 Aug 1875; killed in valley fight 25 June 1876 (on skirmish line).[3]

Oman, Wm. R. Pvt co D; b. 31 Dec 1843 Hamilton Co. Ind.; pvt 25 batt'y Ind. art'y 3 Nov 1864 to 20 July 1865; enl reg army 20 Aug 1875 Indianapolis Ind. for 5 yrs; age 29; laborer; brn eyes, brn hair, dk comp, 5' 8 1/2" high; assd to gen serv; disch 11 Oct 1875 Newport Bks Ky. on surg cert dis (for theft & gen worthlessness); reenl 12 Oct 1875 Cincinnati Ohio for 5 yrs; join co D 7 cav 21 Oct 1875 Ft Lincoln DT; in conft Feb 1876; cpl 20 Nov 1876; (recom by Lt Edgerly for medal of honor for conspic gal at LBH); sgt 7 May 1877; ds Carroll MT 9 Sep 1877; ds Ft Lincoln 28 Oct 1877 with boat crew; pvt 11 Jan 1879; dd co cook Apr 1879; dd qmd saw mill June to Aug 1879; dd qmd teamster Oct 1879 to Oct 1880; disch 11 Oct 1880 Ft Yates DT expir of serv a pvt char good; died 26 Apr 1901 Fargo N.Dak.

Pension: 24 Feb 1896 / Inv / 1174489 / 910330. Wid / 750114.

Omling, Sebastian. Pvt co F; b. Windouter Bavaria; enl in co F 21 Dec 1871 Taylor Bks Louisville Ky. for 5 yrs; age 33; blacksmith; hazel eyes, lt hair, fair comp, 5' 5 1/4" high; dd co cook Jan & Feb 1872; dd co cook June to Sep 1872; in conft Dec 1872; dd co cook Feb 1873; dd actg co blks June to Oct 1873; appt co blks 1 Dec 1873; pvt 16 Mar 1876; td regtl hq with rqm 11 May 1876; killed with Custer column 25 June 1876.

O'Neill, Bernard. Pvt band; b. Kilfurboy Ireland; enl 24 Sep 1868 New York N.Y. for 3 yrs; age 27; musician; hazel eyes, brn hair, dk comp, 5' 6" high; assd to band 30 inf; (consol with 4 inf Mar 1869); disch 3 Nov 1871 Frankfort Ky. expir of serv a pvt; enl in band 7 cav 28 Nov 1871 Louisville Ky. for 5 yrs; abs sick on str *Western* 23 Apr 1873 Yankton to Ft Rice DT; ds camp Powder River MT 15 June 1876; ds str *Josephine* 6 Aug 1876 to Ft Lincoln with band; disch 28 Nov 1876 at Ft Lincoln expir of serv a pvt char xclt; reenl 5 Apr 1877 Ft Snelling Minn. for 5 yrs in band 20 inf; became deranged of mind 10 Apr 1878 at Ft Brown Tex.; tr to govt hosp Wash'n D.C. 22 May 1878; disch 8 June 1878 on surg cert dis (insane; dis total); rel from hosp 10 Dec 1878 recovered; adm to hosp 15 Aug 1879 upon relapse & failing to sustain himself outside; rel 1 Nov 1880 but fearing another relapse he preferred to remain at hosp; actg janitor dur day (pay $12 mo) & rendered musical serv at night as required; died 27 Oct 1896 at Wash'n. Pension: 9 June 1881 / Inv / 424301 / 203758.

O'Neill, Jas. Pvt co B; b. Liverpool England; enl 8 Nov 1872 Cincinnati Ohio for 5 yrs; age 21; laborer; blue eyes, brn hair, florid comp, 5' 4 1/4" high; join co B 9 Dec 1872 Spartanburg SC; sick hosp Ft Lincoln DT 2 May to 30 June 1876 (ac. bronc.); sick hosp Ft Lincoln 21 Aug 1876 (ac. bronc.); disch 18 Sep 1876 at Ft Lincoln on surg cert dis (chr. bronc. & incipient tuberculosis originated last winter in La. & incr by tr to DT; unfit for field serv & on sick report ever since with no prospect of recovery within reasonable time; dis 1/3); res Lexington Ky.

O'Neill, Jno. Pvt co B; b. Tipperary Ireland; enl 8 Jan 1872 New York N.Y. for 5 yrs; age 23; cooper; brn eyes, blk hair, dk comp, 5' 6" high; join co B 5 Feb 1872 Spartanburg SC; sick hosp 8 July to 6 Sep 1872 (ulcer); dd co cook Oct to Dec 1873; dd co cook Dec 1874; sick hosp 18 Feb to 3 Mar & 2 Apr to 4 May 1875 (pr. syph.); dd hosp dept 10 Oct to 14 Nov 1876; disch 8 Jan 1877 Ft Lincoln DT expir of serv a pvt char xclt; reenl in co B 10 Jan 1877 for 5 yrs; ds in field 24 Sep 1877; ed nurse post hosp Dec 1877 to Aug 1878; dd co gardener Apr to Oct 1880; disch 9 Jan 1882 Ft Yates DT expir of serv a pvt; reenl 6 Feb 1884 at Ft Lincoln for 5 yrs in co K; disch 15 Sep 1887 Ft Meade DT on surg cert dis (chr. bronc. complicated by chr. ozoena & very offensive breath of long standing & incurable; dis total) a pvt char xclt; died 2 Mar 1888 Sol. Home Wash'n D.C.
Pension; 26 Oct 1887 / Inv / 627370. (Rej upon death of clmt & neither widow nor ch. came for'd to complete claim).

O'Neill, Thos. F. Pvt co G; b. 14 Jan 1846 Dublin Ireland; pvt co F 12 N.Y. state militia (3 mo troops) 31 May to 8 Oct 1862; pvt co L 16 N.Y. cav 22 Aug 1863; tr to co F 10 N.Y. inf 17 June 1864; sick hosp (chr. diar) Dec 1864 to May 1865; m.o. vol serv 30 June 1865; enl reg army 29 Nov 1865 New York N.Y. for 3 yrs; age 21; laborer; blue eyes, dk hair, fair comp, 5' 8 1/2" high; assd to co I 1 art'y; disch 29 Nov 1868 Brownsville Tex. expir of serv a pvt; reenl 21 Dec 1868 Jackson Bks La. for 3 yrs; assd to co F 1 inf; cpl 1 July 1871; pvt 1 Nov 1871; disch 21 Dec 1871 Ft Wayne Mich. expir of serv a pvt; reenl 1 Jan 1872 Chicago Ill. for 5 yrs; join co G 7 cav 5 Feb 1872 Spartanburg SC; des 18 June 1872 at Spartanburg; enl as Thos. Dean 15 July 1872 Cincinnati Ohio for 5 yrs; assd to 18 inf; surd 2 Dec 1872 Newberry SC & turned over to co G 7 cav; sen gen cm 8 Feb 1873 to one yr conft at sta of co & forf $10 pay per mo same period; sen of conft remitted 25 June 1873; dd co cook Dec 1875; dd 13 May to 26 Sep 1876;[4] left behind when horse killed under him dur retreat from valley fight 25 June; rejoin co night of 26 June on Reno hill; dd regtl band Dec 1876; cpl 12 Feb 1877; disch 19 June

1877 Ft Lincoln DT expir of serv a cpl char good; reenl 15 July 1877 at Ft Lincoln for 5 yrs in co E; cpl 5 Dec 1877; sgt 17 Jan 1878; dd co qm sgt June to Oct 1878; dd post sgt-maj Dec 1878 to Mar 1879; dd prov sgt Apr to Oct 1879; 1sgt 10 Aug 1880; disch 14 July 1882 Ft Snelling Minn. expir of serv a 1sgt; reenl 15 Nov 1883 New York N.Y. for 5 yrs; rejoin co E 13 Apr 1884 Ft Meade DT; cpl 21 Sep 1884; sgt 7 June 1886; actg 1sgt Aug to Oct 1888; disch 14 Nov 1888 Ft Sill IT expir of serv a sgt; reenl 13 Dec 1888 Cincinnati Ohio for 5 yrs; assd to gen mtd serv at Jeff'n Bks Mo.; cpl 22 Dec 1888; sgt 19 Jan 1889; pvt 18 Dec 1889; disch 27 Jan 1890 at Jeff'n Bks on surg cert dis (piles aggravated by over indulgence in alcoholic liquors; dis total) a pvt; died 22 Mar 1914 Riverdale Md.
Pension: 11 Feb 1890 / Inv / 754564 / 429121. Wid / 1026165 / 783096.

Orr, Chas. M. Pvt co C; b. Parris Canada. Enl 24 Sep 1875 St Louis Mo. for 5 yrs; age 28; painter; blue eyes, brn hair, fair comp, 5' 9 3/4" high; join co C 21 Oct 1875 Ft Lincoln DT; dd qmd Oct 1875; dd regtl band Feb 1876 to Sep 1880; ds camp Powder River MT 10 June 1876 with band; ds str *Josephine* 6 Aug 1876 to Ft Lincoln with band; disch 23 Sep 1880 Ft Meade DT expir of serv a pvt char very good.

O'Ryan, Wm. Pvt co H; b. Limerick Ireland; enl 2 Oct 1875 New York N.Y. for 5 yrs; age 21; clerk; blue eyes, sandy hair, ruddy comp, 5' 7 3/4" high; join co H 29 Oct 1875 Ft Rice DT; des 1 Feb 1877 at Ft Rice.

Osborne, Augustus. Pvt co A; b. New York N.Y.; enl 25 July 1870 at New York for 5 yrs; age 23; baker; grey eyes, lt hair, sallow comp, 5' 6" high; assd to co K 8 cav; disch 25 July 1875 Ft Wingate NM expir of serv a pvt; reenl 24 Aug 1875 at New York for 5 yrs; join co A 7 cav 21 Oct 1875 Ft Lincoln DT; sick post hosp from 6 Dec 1875 (ac. rheum.); disch 22 Apr 1876 on surg cert dis (const. syph.) a pvt char fair.

O'Toole, Francis. Pvt co E; b. Co Mayo Ireland; enl 25 Sep 1860 New York N.Y. for 5 yrs; age 26; plumber; hazel eyes, brn hair, ruddy comp, 5' 9 1/2" high; join co C 2 cav 2 Dec 1860 Ft Inge Tex.; (regt redesig 5 cav Aug 1861); cpl 11 Oct 1861; pvt 9 Jan 1862; ds orderly for gen Stoneman Jan 1863; ds hq cav corps June 1863; ds orderly hq cav bureau Wash'n D.C. Aug 1863 to July 1864; disch 21 July 1864 Light House Point Va. by reenlmt in co C for 3 yrs; cpl 1 Dec 1864; ds div hq Mar 1865; sgt 1 June 1865; pvt 18 Oct 1865; ds hq Dept of Wash'n Nov 1865 to Sep 1868; (tr to co K 20 Apr 1867); disch 11 July 1867 Wash'n D.C. & reenl in co K for 5 yrs; (retained position given to certain enl men of co K on duty at the Dept of State & the executive mansion 30 Apr 1867); tr to co H 1 Sep 1867 & ds distr hq Charleston SC to Sep 1868; in conft Feb 1869; disch 11 July 1872 Camp McDowell AT expir of serv a pvt; reenl 5 Dec 1872 New York N.Y. for 5 yrs; join co E 7 cav 18 Oct 1873 Ft Lincoln DT; dd hq Blk Hills Exp'n as hostler 30 June to 9 July 1874; dd hq Blk Hills Exp'n 27 July to 31 Aug 1874 with gen Custer;[5] sen gen cm Apr 1875 forf $5 pay per mo for 2 mos; dd asst post baker Oct 1875 to Feb 1876; dd orderly dept hq in field 14 May 1876;[6] sgt 1 Oct to date 1 Sep 1876; dd prov sgt Dec 1876 to Feb 1877; dd regtl hq chg of fatigue pty 25 Apr 1877; ds in field 2 Aug thro' Sep 1877; ds Ft Lincoln Oct 1877; disch 5 Dec 1877 at Ft Lincoln expir of serv a sgt char good; reenl 25 Sep 1879 Wash'n D.C. for 5 yrs; join co E 7 cav 1 Dec 1881 Ft Meade DT; tr to co H 27 May 1883; cpl 10 Jan 1884; sgt 15 Feb 1884; disch 24 Sep 1884 at Ft Meade expir of serv a sgt char very good; reenl 9 Oct 1884 Jeff'n Bks Mo. for 5 yrs; assd to co K 2 cav; disch 8 Oct 1889 Presidio San Francisco Calif. expir of serv a pvt char good; reenl 18 Oct 1889 Jeff'n Bks Mo. for 5 yrs; join co H 7 cav 21 June 1890 Ft Sill IT; sd co clerk June 1891; cpl 6 Nov 1891; sgt 9 Dec 1891; retd 9 Feb 1892 a sgt char xclt; died 20 Feb 1914 Wash'n D.C.[7]

Owens, Eugene. Pvt co I; b. Kildare Ireland; enl 15 Mar 1875 Boston Mass. for 5 yrs; age 26; carpenter; blue eyes, brn hair, fair comp, 5' 7 3/4" high; join co I 21 Oct 1875 Ft Lincoln DT; with pack train 25 June 1876;[8] sd with Lt Hare's sec. of parrott guns 8 Oct to 12

Nov 1876; ed qmd carpenter 27 Nov to 1 Dec 1876; dd co wag Dec 1876; dd canoneer with art'y detmt 29 Aug 1877; dd qmd Dec 1877; dd qmd carpenter Oct 1879 to Feb 1880; disch 14 Mar 1880 at Ft Lincoln expir of serv a pvt char very good; reenl 12 Apr 1880 St Louis Mo. for 5 yrs; join co H 3 cav 20 Apr 1881 Ft Washakie Wyo.; dd qmd carpenter May 1881 to May 1882; des 23 May 1882 Phoenix AT while enroute to Whipple Bks AT.

Notes—O

1. "John O'Brien of Jones County was one of the victims of the Custer massacre," *The Vinton* (Iowa) *Eagle*, Aug. 2, 1876. His family moved from Prairieburg, Iowa, in 1879, to Ness County, Kansas. See, *Greasy Grass*, vol. 4, May 1988.

2. John G. Kimm to Mrs. Maria Dresser, (mother of Sgt. Ogden), Nov. 27, 1876; see note K22 (Kimm); (Letter previously believed written by John Quinn.) See *Greasy Grass,* vol. 3, May 1987.

3. Sgt. Ryan in Graham, *The Custer Myth*, 242; Roman Rutten in Hammer, *Custer in '76*, 118.

4. Troop Duty Books of Sgts. Botzer and Brown. Reynolds and Brown, *Journal;* Capt. Benteen said O'Neill was cook for Lt. McIntosh. Benteen to wife, July 4, 1876, Carroll, *Camp Talk*, 24.

5. Stanislas Roy said O'Toole was Gen. Custer's permanent mounted orderly for a long time. Roy to Walter Camp, March 12, 1909, WMC-BYU.

6. O'Toole said he missed the battle by being at Gen. Terry's headquarters as orderly. O'Toole to George M. Williams, July 8, 1876, (Williams discharged from Company E in March, 1876), published in *Pittsburg (Pa.) Leader*, July 28, 1876. Reprinted in *That Fatal Day, Eight More With Custer: First-Hand Accounts of the Battle of the Little Big Horn,* by James W. Wengert and E. Elden Davis, eds.; letter also in *Big Horn Yellowstone Journal*, vol. I, no. 1, Winter, 1992, 8–9.

7. RG 94, Entry 25, file 21784 PRD 1890.

8. Henry Jones to Walter Camp, June 2, 1911, WMC-BYU.

P

Pahl, Jno. Sgt co H; b. Bavaria Germany; enl 4 Nov 1872 New York N.Y. for 5 yrs; age 26; teamster; brn eyes, brn hair, fair comp, 5' 6 1/4" high; join co H 3 Dec 1872 Nashville Tenn; cpl 6 Apr 1875; sgt 11 Oct 1875; gsw r. side of back near spine & lodging near l. hip (fl. wd. severe) 26 June 1876; tr on str *Far West* 3 July to hosp Ft Lincoln DT; tr to hosp Ft Rice DT 12 Aug; duty 10 Dec 1876; abs sick (old gsw) 26 Oct 1877 on str *General Meade* & arr Ft Rice 4 Nov; disch 4 Jan 1878 at Ft Rice by expir of serv a sgt char xclt (retained in serv acc't co in field); reenl 2 Feb 1878 Cincinnati Ohio for 5 yrs; join 7 cav 7 Oct 1878 Ft Lincoln DT; join co H 20 Nov 1878 upon ret of co from field; disch 23 Aug 1879 Ft Meade DT on surg cert dis (old gsw of back; dis total) a pvt char hard working xclt soldier; (ball removed [spring 1880] on l. side sacrum six inches from point of entry); res Cincinnati Ohio.
Pension: 12 Sep 1879 / Inv / 303710 / 167323. Dropped from roll 17 Oct 1895 upon death of pens'r; last paid to 4 Sep 1895.

Pandtle, Christopher. See Pendle, Christopher.

Pardee, Oscar F. Pvt co L; b. Eaton N.Y.; enl in marine corps 29 Aug 1873 New York N.Y. for 5 yrs; age 21;[1] blacksmith; hazel eyes, dk hair, dk comp, 5' 8 1/4" high; des 28 Sep 1873 from marine bks Brooklyn N.Y.; enl in army as Jno. Burke 29 Sep 1873 New York N.Y. for 5 yrs; join co L 19 Oct 1873 Ft Lincoln DT; dd qmd saw mill Sep 1874 to Mar 1875; dd post woodcutter Ft Totten DT 3 Feb to 7 Mar 1876; killed in action 25 June 1876; [killed on Reno hill says Burkman].[2]
Pension: 15 Apr 1880 / Mother / 263311 / 204283.

Parker, Jno. Pvt co I; b. Birmingham England; enl 3 Feb 1872 Chicago Ill. for 5 yrs; age 22; gunsmith; grey eyes, lt hair, lt comp, 5' 7" high; join co I 10 Feb 1872 Shelbyville Ky.; awol Dec 1872; dd hq detmt June 1873; dd co cook Aug 1873; sen gen cm 2 Feb 1875 forf $10 pay per mo for 2 mos; in conft Dec 1875; killed with Custer column 25 June 1876.

Patton, Jno. W. Trump'r co I; b. Phil'a Pa.; enl 21 Oct 1872 at Phil'a for 5 yrs; age 21; clerk; brn eyes, brn hair, ruddy comp, 5' 3 1/2" high; join co I as trump'r 20 Feb 1873 Lebanon Ky.; killed with Custer column 25 June 1876.

Pearsal, Henry. (alias). See Howard, Frank (co F).

Pendle, Christopher. Pvt co E; b. 15 June 1849 Bavaria Germany; enl as Christopher Pandtle 28 Oct 1872 Pittsburgh Pa. for 5 yrs; age 23; sawyer; brn eyes, lt hair, fair comp, 5' 4 1/2" high; join co E 10 Dec 1872 Unionville SC; ed qmd teamster Nov 1873 to Feb 1874; ed nurse post hosp Feb to May 1875; ed nurse post hosp Nov 1875 to Mar 1876; ed hosp attdt in field 14 May 1876 (with Dr. Williams); hosp nurse on str *Far West* 22 June 1876;[3] ed nurse post hosp Ft Lincoln DT 1 Oct 1876; sick in hosp 20 Apr to 24 May 1877 (ac. rheum.); disch 10 June 1877 at Ft Lincoln per SO 70 Dept of Dak. 1877 (under prov'n GO 47 Hq army 1877 [reduction of army]) a pvt char good;[4] died 4 June 1923 Tacoma Wash'n.
Pension: 28 Nov 1917 / Ind. Surv. / 15439 / 7942. Ind. Wid. / 16505 / 10758.

Penwell, Geo. B. Trump'r co K; b. Feb 1849 Phil'a Pa.; enl 1 Mar 1866 Carlisle Pa. for 3 yrs; age 18; printer; grey eyes, brn hair, fair comp, 5' 3" high; join co B 7 cav as bugler 10 Sep 1866 Ft Riley Kans.; disch 1 Mar 1869 camp Medicine Bluff Creek IT upon expir of serv a bugler; reenl 22 June 1869 at Phil'a for 5 yrs; join co L 5 cav 22 Oct 1869 a bugler; des 30 July 1870 Ft McPherson Neb; enl in co K 7 cav 16 Jan 1871 Ft L'worth Kans. for 5 yrs; appt trump'r 13 Feb 1871; surd as des'r 14 Nov 1873 under GO 102 AGO 1873; restored to duty without trial 24 Mar 1874 & tr to co K to serve bal of orig'l enlmt; orderly with Lt

Godfrey 25 June 1876; pvt 12 Apr 1877; disch 23 June 1877 camp on Sunday Creek MT per SO 70 Dept of Dak. 1877 (reduction of army) a pvt char xclt; reenl 23 May 1882 at Phil'a for 5 yrs; join co B 1 cav as trump'r 4 Apr 1884 Ft Coeur d'Alene Idaho Ty; (co tr to Ft Custer MT June 1885);[5] disch 22 May 1887 at Ft Custer by expir of serv a trump'r char xclt; reenl 28 Mar 1888 at Phil'a for 5 yrs; join co D 15 inf as mus'n 24 May 1889 Ft Randall DT; disch 17 Oct 1890 Jackson Bks La. per SO 239 AGO 1890 (by way of favor [under vet act] having served more than 12 yrs) a mus'n char xclt;[6] reenl 26 Oct 1891 Camden NJ for 5 yrs; join co C 5 inf as mus'n 12 Dec 1891 Mt Vernon Bks Ala; disch 25 Jan 1895 Ft McPherson Ga. per GO 80 AGO 1890 a mus'n char good;[7] reenl 2 Apr 1895 at Phil'a for 3 yrs; join co H 18 inf as mus'n 21 Apr 1895 Ft Bliss Tex.; disch 1 Apr 1898 at Ft Bliss expir of serv a mus'n char xclt; died 17 Dec 1905 Wash'n D.C. Pension: 13 Apr 1898 / Inv / 1206428 / 989769. Wid / 849219.

Perkins, Chas. Sad'r co L; b. York Co. Me; enl 18 Aug 1875 St Louis Mo. for 5 yrs; age 27; shoemaker; blk eyes, dk hair, dk comp, 5' 10" high; join co L 29 Oct 1875 Ft Totten DT; appt sad'r 30 Mar 1876; killed with Custer column 25 June 1876.

Personeus, Martin. Pvt co L; b. Rondout N.Y.; pvt co D 20 N.Y. state militia (80 N.Y. inf) 5 Sep 1861 for 3 yrs; sick 1 July 1863 Gettysburg Pa. (sunstroke causing brain trouble); sick hosp Phil'a Pa. 7 July 1863; tr to invalid corps 22 Dec 1863 (aphonia); reenl 29 Apr 1864 Cliffburne Bks D.C. in co D 11 regt vet reserve corps (rheum. & aphonia); des 23 Jan 1866 Alexandria Va.; enl reg army as Mich'l Conlan 19 Nov 1866 Wash'n D.C. for 5 yrs; age 22; farmer; hazel eyes, lt brn hair, dk comp, 5' 7" high; join co L 7 cav 18 Feb 1867 Ft Morgan Colo. Ty; dd co cook July 1870; ed nurse post hosp Sep 1870 to Feb 1871; dd cook post hosp Mar & Apr 1871; disch 19 Nov 1871 Yorkville SC expir of serv a pvt; reenl in co L 13 Apr 1872 at Yorkville for 5 yrs; ed qmd laborer Nov & Dec 1873; dd chg co garden June to Aug 1875; dd co cook Oct 1875; ds Ft Lincoln DT 17 May 1876 in co garden; sen gen cm 25 Sep 1876 forf $10 pay per mo for 2 mos & conft one mo; ds Ft Lincoln 17 Oct 1876 dismtd; (m. widow of pvt Crisfield 23 Nov 1876); disch 13 Apr 1877 at Ft Lincoln expir of serv a pvt char very good; (chg of des'n 23 Jan 1866 removed for error, to complete mil rec under act 5 July 1884); died 24 Dec 1889 (inanition) Jacksonville Ill. hosp for insane.
Pension: 18 Oct 1887 / Inv / 626307; (inmate hosp for insane from 16 Sep 1887). Wid / 480421. Minor / 500899.

Petring, Henry. Pvt co G; b. 29 Nov 1853 Prussia Germany; enl 9 Dec 1874 New York N.Y. for 5 yrs; age 21; cabinet maker; grey eyes, brn hair, florid comp, 5' 6 3/4" high; join co G 10 Feb 1875 Shreveport La.; dd cook post hosp 23 Mar to 18 Apr 1876; left in timber dur retreat from valley fight 25 June 1876 & rejoin co on Reno hill; ds Ft Lincoln 21 Oct 1876 chg co prop; ed qmd laborer June 1878 to Feb 1879 (ds Ft Lincoln to Nov 1878); dd co carpenter June to Aug 1879; disch 8 Dec 1879 Ft Meade DT expir of serv a pvt char good; died 7 Oct 1917 Brooklyn N.Y.[8]
Pension: 3 June 1885 / Inv / 541411 / 1168928. Wid / 1110071. Ind. Wid. / 14030 / 8581.

Phillips, Edgar. Pvt co C; b. Lynn Mass.; enl 24 Sep 1875 Chicago Ill. for 5 yrs; age 22; farmer; blue eyes, lt hair, fair comp, 5' 5 1/4" high; join co C 21 Oct 1875 Ft Lincoln DT; killed with Custer column 25 June 1876.

Phillips, Jno. Pvt co H; b. Allegheny Pa.; enl 12 Sep 1873 Pittsburgh Pa. for 5 yrs; age 21; packer; blue eyes, lt hair, fair comp, 5' 5" high; join co H 20 Oct 1873 Ft Rice DT; dd with hq fatigue party l. wing 15 May 1876; gsw l. jaw (loss of 4 teeth) 26 June 1876 & gsw r. hand & thro' tip l. thumb & l. middle finger which was then amp'd); tr on str *Far West* 3 July to hosp Ft Lincoln DT; disch 2 Nov 1876 at Ft Lincoln on surg cert dis a pvt char good; res Boston Pa.; died 23 July 1896.
Pension: 22 Jan 1877 / Inv / 230111 / 149251.

Pickard, Edwin Henry. Pvt co F; b. 27 Jan 1854 Boston Mass.; enl 6 Sep 1875 at Boston for 5 yrs; age 23; clerk; blue eyes, lt hair, fair

comp, 5' 8" high; join co F 21 Oct 1875 Ft Lincoln DT; sick hosp 16 Feb to 18 Mar 1876 (cont'n l. knee); [with pack train says Rooney; doubtful with packs says Lynch];[9] sick hosp Ft Lincoln 15 Oct 1876 (frac. r. elbow while moving co prop); tr to hosp Ft Abercrombie DT 12 Nov 1876; duty 3 Feb 1877; ds battn hq June to Aug 1877; disch 18 Jan 1878 at Ft Lincoln on surg cert dis (frac. r. arm tho' united, materially interfered use of arm) a pvt char good; died 30 Jan 1928 Portland Ore.
Pension: 21 June 1890 / Inv / 783635 / 669410. Wid / 1604421. (XC-6,322,338).

Pickering, Rufus C. Pvt co A; b. Nashua N.H.; enl 15 Sep 1875 Boston Mass. for 5 yrs; age 21 4/12; laborer; blue eyes, brn hair, dk comp, 5' 9" high; join co A 21 Oct 1875 Ft Lincoln DT; awol night of 24 Dec 1875 (visited Bismarck & on way home was overcome by frost & lost his way in blinding storm; wandered around til morn when he reached co stables & was sent to hosp; treated for 23 weeks for frostbite of hands & feet [amp'd r. foot at instep, large toe l. foot & ends of all fingers l. hand]); disch 12 May 1876 at Ft Lincoln on surg cert dis (not entitled to pension) a pvt char good; res Worcester Mass. 1903.
Pension: 22 Jan 1880 / Inv / 335925; (rej on grd dis contr while abs from co without proper auth).

Pigford, Edw. Pvt co M; b. 11 June 1856 Allegheny Pa.; enl 13 Sep 1875 Pittsburgh Pa. for 5 yrs; age 21; miner; grey eyes, auburn hair, lt comp, 5' 6 3/4" high; join co M 21 Oct 1875 Ft Rice DT; dd qmd laborer Feb 1876; disch 15 Oct 1876 Ft Lincoln DT per SO 180 AGO 1876 (appn of father, having enl as minor without consent) a pvt char xclt; died 16 Dec 1932 Lock No. 3, Pa.[10]
Pension: 28 Mar 1903 / Inv / 1298248; (rej on grd no ratable dis shown). Ind. Surv. / 9979 / 8637.

Pilcher, Albert Pvt co F; b. Parkersburg W.Va.;[11] enl 26 Sep 1871 Wheeling W.Va. for 5 yrs; age 23; boilermaker; blue eyes, dk brn hair, fair comp, 5' 7" high; join co D 13 inf 18 Oct 1871 Camp Douglas UT; ds July to Dec 1872 with escort for Lt Wheeler's survey exp'n west of 100' meridian; des 14 Apr 1873 at Camp Douglas; enl as Henry Barton 12 Sep 1873 Pittsburgh Pa. for 5 yrs; join co F 7 cav 18 Oct 1873 Ft Lincoln DT; surd as des'r 24 Dec 1873 under GO 102 AGO 1873; dd qmd teamster Apr 1874; restored to duty without trial 9 June 1874 & tr to co F to serve bal of orig'l enlmt; dd qmd teamster Sep 1874; in conft Oct 1874; dd qmd teamster Dec 1874; acquited in gen cm 29 Jan 1875 (neglected govt prop [panel doors] permitting damage by gnawing of mules or other animals); dd qmd teamster Apr 1875; sick qrs 19 June to 11 July 1875 (chr. rheum.); dd qmd teamster Oct 1875 to Mar 1876; sick 1–10 Feb 1876 (ac. rheum.); sick 18–22 Mar & 29 Mar to 3 Apr 1876 (ac. rheum.); sick qrs 29 Apr to 2 May 1876 (catarrh); dd dept hq in field June & Aug 1876; ed qmd teamster 17 Nov 1876 to 5 Jan 1877; sick qrs 19 Dec 1876 to 25 Jan 1877 (headache); ds Ft Abercrombie DT 10 Apr 1877 dismtd;[12] disch 5 June 1877 at Ft Abercrombie by expir of serv a pvt char fair.[13]

Pinkston, Jno. S. Pvt co H; b. St Clair Co. Mich.; enl in co H 1 Mar 1872 Nashville Tenn for 5 yrs; age 21 9/12; laborer; grey eyes, dk hair, fair comp, 5' 7" high; ds herding co horses June 1872; des 26 Sep 1872 at Nashville; apph 27 Jan 1873 at Nashville; sen gen cm 21 Feb 1873 forf $10 pay per mo for one yr & conft same period at sta of co; des 24 Apr 1873 Yankton DT; surd 5 Nov 1874 Ft Snelling Minn.; sen as promulgated in 1873 & remaining unexecuted, remitted 13 Apr 1875; tr to regt at Ft Lincoln DT 9 May 1875; attd to co F for duty 31 July 1875; join co H 12 Oct 1875 Ft Rice DT; dd qmd teamster 16 Jan to 4 May 1876; des 22 May 1877 camp near Ft Buford DT.

Pitter, Felix Jas. Pvt co I; b. Alesford England; enl 4 Sep 1873 St Louis Mo. for 5 yrs; age 23 6/12; grocer; hazel eyes, dk brn hair, fair comp, 5' 6 1/4" high; join co I 22 Oct 1873 Ft Totten DT; ed qmd Dec 1874; killed with Custer column 25 June 1876.

Pittet, Francis. Pvt co H; b. Freibourg Switz; enl in co H 20 Jan 1873 Nashville Tenn for 5 yrs; age 34; carpenter; grey eyes, blk hair, dk comp, 5' 9" high; abs sick hosp New Orleans La. May to Aug 1875; ds Ft Rice DT 5 May

1876 in co garden; ds Ft Rice chg co prop 21 Apr 1877 to 2 Jan 1878; disch 20 Jan 1878 at Ft Rice expir of serv a pvt char xclt; reenl 20 Mar 1878 Charleston SC for 5 yrs; assd to co E 5 art'y; disch 19 Mar 1883 Ft Schuyler N.Y.H expir of serv a pvt char xclt; reenl in same co 31 Mar 1883 for 5 yrs; disch 23 Apr 1888 Ft Hamilton N.Y. expir of serv (made good time lost awol) a pvt char good but unreliable acc't intemperate habits; reenl 25 Apr 1888 Ft Wadsworth N.Y.H for 5 yrs in co B 5 art'y; in conft June 1888; ed qmd mech July 1888; disch 26 Aug 1888 at Ft Wadsworth per SO 194 AGO 1888 (utter worthlessness from excess use of intoxicants; known to be a drinking man when enl but was valuable mech & carpenter until liquor habit increased last 2 yrs; discipline no effect).[14]

Porter, Henry Rinaldo. Actg asst surg; b. 13 Feb 1848 Lee Centre N.Y.; educated at Whitestone seminary; began med study with his father in 1868 & attended univ of Mich. med dept to 1870; grad Georgetown college med dept in 1872;[15] entered mil contr 26 June 1872 as actg asst surg in Dept of Ariz.; cited for gal in action in Superstition Mtns 16 Jan 1873 & in closing campn against Tonto Apaches in Feb & Mar 1873; appt post surg Camp Hancock (Bismarck) DT 16 Oct 1873; contr for serv with gen Terry's exp'n 15 May 1876 (with hq & batt'y [gatling guns] & co B 6 inf); accomp maj Reno's scout up Powder River 10–19 June; with Reno into valley fight 25 June & dismtd near edge of woods & looked for his orderly who had med box;[16] attended wd sol. (gsw l. breast) then joined retreat, letting his horse run full gallop thro' inds to river; ds with wd on str *Far West* 30 June to Yellowstone & to Ft Lincoln 3 July; returned to exp'n, on *Far West*, 17 July camp at Powder River; with gen Terry on *Far West* 21 July to camp at Big Horn & with Dr. Williams on *Far West* 27 July to Rosebud Creek; accomp maj Moore on *Far West* 2 Aug & in action with inds at Powder River;[17] rejoin regt 4 Aug camp mouth of Rosebud; horse stolen by inds 21 Aug near mouth of Powder River;[18] arr Bismarck on steamer from Yellowstone 10 Sep;[19] contr with exp'n canceled 30 Sep his serv no longer required; contr at Camp Hancock annulled 28 Feb 1877 (own req) & entered pvt practice at Bismarck; went to Big Horn country in June 1877 to view scenes of last summer's campn & returned 9 July on str *Fletcher* (boat carried remains of officers exhumed from Custer battlefield); testified in Reno court of inq at Chicago in Jan 1879; employed many yrs as physician for NPRR, also supt of county bd of health & pres't of state med society; died 3 Mar 1903 at Agra India while on world tour.[20]

Porter, Jas. Ezekiel. 1Lt co I; b. 12 Jan 1847 Strong Me; first candidate in New England & 2d in U.S. to enter West Point by competitive exam'n; grad USMA 15 June 1869 & appt 2Lt 7 cav; join co C 30 Sep 1869 Ft L'worth Kans.; 1Lt co I 1 July 1872; adjt of escort for NBS June to Sep 1873; comd co I Apr to Nov 1874 & adjt of escort for NBS May to Sep 1874; actg aqm & comsy Ft Totten DT Sep 1874 to Apr 1875; comd co I July to Oct 1875; killed with Custer column 25 June 1876; (body not identified); survived by wife & 2 ch.[21]
[890 ACP 1876]. Pension: 5 May 1877 / Wid / 231236 / 178027.

Porter, Jno. Pvt co I; b. Conn.; enl 15 Mar 1871 Cleveland Ohio for 5 yrs; age 21; cooper; blue eyes, lt hair, lt comp, 5' 10 1/2" high; join co I 6 Apr 1871 Bagdad Ky.; ds regtl hq 20 Apr to 31 May 1873 St Paul Minn.; des 5 June 1873 Minneapolis Minn.; apph 29 Sep 1875 at Cleveland; dishon disch 29 Nov 1876 Columbus Bks Ohio per gen cm (sen 3 yrs conft reduced to one yr).

Post, Geo. Pvt co I; b. Adrian Mich.; enl 17 July 1866 Detroit Mich. for 3 yrs; age 19; shoemaker; blue eyes, lt hair, ruddy comp, 5' 7" high; join co M 4 cav 16 Sep 1866 Camp Sheridan Tex.; sad'r 1 Aug 1867; pvt 11 Jan 1868; ed post qmd Dec 1868 to Feb 1869; cpl 3 July 1869; disch 17 July 1869 Austin Tex. expir of serv a cpl; reenl 28 June 1875 Chicago Ill. for 5 yrs; join co I 7 cav 29 July 1875 Ft Lincoln DT; sad'r 17 Sep 1875; pvt 29 Jan 1876; killed with Custer column 25 June 1876.
Pension: 18 Aug 1877 / Wid / 232822 / 178837.

Proctor, Geo. W. Pvt co A; b. Manchester N.H.; enl 15 July 1872 New York N.Y. for 5 yrs; age 22; teamster; grey eyes, brn hair, dk comp, 5' 10 1/4" high; join co A 2 Dec 1872 E'town Ky.; dd qmd teamster Feb 1873; ed qmd teamster 12–26 Apr 1873; dd pioneer Aug 1873; appt co wag 1 Nov 1873; ed qmd teamster Dec 1873 to Feb 1875; (dd qmd teamster Blk Hills Exp'n Aug 1874); pvt 23 July 1875; dd qmd laborer Feb to May 1876; disch 24 June 1877 camp on Tongue River MT per SO 70 Dept of Dak. 1877 a pvt char xclt.

Pym, Jas. Pvt co B; b. Oxfordshire England; enl 11 Dec 1874 Boston Mass. for 5 yrs; age 22; laborer; blue eyes, lt hair, fair comp, 5' 7" high; join co B 10 Feb 1875 Shreveport La.; dd co cook June 1875 to Apr 1876;[22] dd co cook Oct 1876 to Feb 1877; dd co cook Dec 1877 to Dec 1878; (awarded medal of honor 5 Oct 1878 for bringing water to wounded [at LBH] while under heavy fire in sight of the enemy); dd chg co stock Aug 1879; disch 10 Dec 1879 Ft Yates DT expir of serv a pvt char good; killed 29 Nov 1893 Miles City MT by a cowboy.[23]
Pension: 21 Oct 1891 / Inv / 1066405. (Abandoned).

Notes—P

1. Affidavits of Pardee family allege Oscar was about 19 years old when enlisted. Pension file, RG 15.
2. Letter to Walter Camp from John Burkman, (I. D. O'Donnell), Nov. 12, 1908, WMC-BYU; also LBHB Coll., Roll 9.
3. Hospital steward Alfred W. Dale (executive steward) with Dr. Williams and the hospital on the steamer *Far West*, said Pandle was detailed as nurse under Dr. Porter (as orderly to take care of his horse). However, Pendle said he was not in the battle proper but was hospital nurse on the *Far West* during the fight and did not know who was orderly for Dr. Porter, Letter to Walter Camp from Dale, Jan. 15, 1911, WMC-BYU; and from Pendle, July 14, 1919, WMC-BYU. (Perhaps Pandle was with Dr. Porter only on Major Reno's scout.)
Dale and Pandle are listed present on the muster rolls of the hospital department, June 30, 1876, camp on Little Big Horn River. RG 94, Entry 53; see Pvt. Robinson, Co. M; see also, Gray, *Centennial Campaign*, 270–75; Hospital steward Joseph Rhinehart was at Powder River.
4. See note A24 (Arnold).
5. Penwell attended the tenth anniversary of the battle. Photo in Mills, *Harvest of Barren Regrets*, 338
6. See note M60 (Murray).
7. See note D26 (Diamond).
8. Petring claimed he was injured in his left cheek on Reno Hill, June 26, when a gunshot splintered a nearby rock. He also claimed a tent pin struck his left cheek in May 1877, causing his eye to fall out on his cheek and he instantly replaced it. Lt. Wallace was positive Petring was not injured at Little Big Horn and knew nothing of his injury in 1877. Statement to adjutant general's office, from Wallace, Oct. 9, 1885, Pension file, RG 15; Petring interview with Walter Camp, in Hammer, *Custer in '76*, 133–34.
9. Rosters of Company F with remarks by Rooney and Lynch, WMC-BYU; Pickard said he was detailed the morning of June 25 to take charge of Capt. Yates' private horses when Custer ordered all extra animals taken to the pack train. He said he carelessly tried to rejoin his company "on his own hook" and had a wild ride of over three miles with 40 or 50 Sioux in hot pursuit until he reached the bluffs where Reno had fallen back. Letter from Pickard to his parents, Aug. 1, 1876, in *The Whig and Courier* (Bangor, Me.), Aug. 16, 1876.
In a later story, Pickard reiterated he was appointed orderly for Capt. Yates the morning of June 25, but he was not ordered to the pack train with the captain's extra horse until he was noticed by Gen. Custer, after the command had reached the river. On his way back along the bluffs he stopped to watch Reno's fight in the valley and was joined on the hill by the retreating troopers. He related that only he and two other men of "F" Troop survived the battle. *Oregon Sunday Journal* (Portland), Jan. 14, 1912, (includes photos of Pickard in full-dress uniform); *Portland Journal*, July 31 through Aug. 4, 1923.
Pickard's stories, edited by Edgar I. Stewart, also appeared as, "I Rode With Custer," in *Montana The Magazine of Western History*, vol. 4, no. 3, Summer, 1954.
Walter Camp interviewed Pickard in 1911, and formed the opinion that Pickard tried to make him believe he was with his company packs, but after hearing his story, Camp thought it clear enough he

must have been left back at Powder River; that Pickard evidently heard survivors tell of the fight and had a story he could tell smoothly enough, but got badly mixed up when Camp asked him questions. Camp to Daniel Knipe, March 27, 1911, WMC-LBHB.

Camp later changed his mind and, on his separate list of Companies E and F, moved Pickard (and Finnegan) from the column "At Powder River," to the column, "At Little Big Horn." WMC rosters, LBHB.

10. RG 94, Entry 409, file 5641 B (EB) AGO 1876. "Fighting With Custer," by Earle R. Forrest, in *The Morning Observer* (Washington, Pa.), Oct. 3–19, 1932, is an article on Pigford.

11. The federal census, Wood County, W. Va., 1860, shows Albert W. Pilcher, age 9, youngest of five children of Alex and Melinda Pilcher; Albert Pilcher married Julia Miles, Aug. 8, 1870. Washington County, Ohio, Marriages, 1789–1918.

12. On May 15, 1877, Camp 13, Stone Creek, D.T, Capt. Bell requested Pilcher to join his troop in the field, bringing the troop horse formerly in possession of Maj. Reno, which was much needed to replace an unserviceable one. NA, M1734, Roll 20, letter 2231 DD 1877; in another letter (2303 DD 1877), May 22, 1877, Pilcher was still on detached service at Fort Abercrombie.

13. Albert Pilcher, 23, married Sept. 19, 1877 in Wood County, W. Va., to Mary Palmer, 21; *Wood County Marriage Book II, 1877;* the federal census, June 1880, Belpre Township, Washington County, Ohio, shows Albert Pilcher, age 25, boilermaker; wife, Mary, age 17.

14. RG 94, Entry 409, file 7435 C (EB) AGO 1888 (filed with 37991 AGO 1896).

15. Dr. L. G. Walker, Jr., *Dr. Henry R. Porter,* 6–8.

16. Dr. Porter wore a linen duster and carried no weapon. He rode with Maj. Reno and Lt. Hodgson at head of the column during charge down valley to attack village and declined Reno's offer of his rifle (Reno having difficulty managing his fiery horse). Taylor, "Lonesome Charley"; Utley, *The Reno Court of Inquiry,* 189; Nichols, *Reno Court,* 202.

17. Lt. Godfrey recorded July 26, camp at Big Horn, that Gen. Terry arrived on steamer *Far West.* Godfrey, *Diary*; Dr. Paulding recorded July 27 that Dr. Williams took Dr. Porter and the coffee coolers down on the *Far West* (the command began the move to Rosebud Creek) the sick in hospital were put on the boat the night before, Johnson, ed., "Dr. Paulding and His Remarkable Diary"; Maj. Orlando Moore, Report, Aug 4, 1876, *Annual Report of the Secretary of War, 1876,* 44th Cong., 2d Sess., 1876, Ex. Doc. 1, Part 2.

18. In June, 1878, Dr. Porter received $125 for the loss of his private horse stolen during the 1876 campaign, 3625 DD 1876; it was determined that as an acting assistant surgeon, he was entitled to keep a private horse, to be fed by the quartermaster deparment, while on duty requiring him to be mounted, and the department commander considered Dr. Porter to be on such at the time his horse was stolen, RG 92, Entry 778, Vol. 2: 520.

19. SFO 46, Hq DD, Sept. 11, 1876, RG 94, Entry 44; *Bismarck Tribune,* Wed., Sept. 13, 1876, reported the steamer *Benton* arrived Saturday, the *Yellowstone* on Sunday, and the *Silver Lake* on Monday.

20. *Bismarck Tribune,* June 20 and July 27, 1877; *Minneapolis Tribune,* May 16, 1897; *Bismarck Tribune,* March 5, 1903; a scrapbook once owned by Dr. Porter is in the collections of the State Historical Society at Bismarck.

21. Butler, *A History of Farmington,* 556–57; *Annual Reunion* (USMA), June 14, 1877.

22. Mrs. Klawitter said Pym was company cook for many years. She recalled an incident when a drunk Pym attempted to enter the officer's coach on the train at St. Louis, during the trip from Shreveport to Fort Lincoln in April 1876. Klawitter "Army Life at Fort Lincoln."

23. At the time of the shooting Pym had been working as cook. Previously he was city marshal at Lake City, Minn., and at one time was engaged in the restaurant business. He was shot by his wife's paramour, Ralph Tilton, age 22, a cowboy considered belonging to that class of cowboys who wanted to be bad; Tilton was larger than Pym, not less than 5' 11" tall; his carriage and walk was like most cow punchers, his expression dull and his face not giving evidence to anything that would class him among the intellectual. He was sentenced to six years for manslaughter. *Yellowstone Journal,* Dec. 2, 9, 1893, Feb. 14, 15, 16, 21, 1894.

Q

Quinn, Jas. Pvt co I; b. Watkins NJ; enl 13 Feb 1872 Buffalo N.Y. for 5 yrs; age 21; boatman; blue eyes, red hair, lt comp, 5' 6" high; join co I 21 Feb 1872 Shelbyville Ky.; sick (prim.syph.) 21 Mar 1873 Taylor Bks (Louisville) Ky.; enroute to DT 2 Apr 1873; ds Ft Pembina DT 16 July 1873; ed qmd teamster Sep 1874 to Feb 1875; killed with Custer column 25 June 1876.

Quinn, Jno. (alias). See Gorham, Jno.

R

Rafter, Jno. Sgt co K; b. 20 Jan 1851 Lansingburg N.Y.; enl 20 Jan 1872 Troy N.Y. for 5 yrs; age 21; brushmaker; blue eyes, brn hair, ruddy comp, 5' 9 1/4" high; join co K 15 Feb 1872 Yorkville SC; in conft Feb 1873; ed qmd Oct 1873; cpl 28 Jan 1874; pvt 13 Feb 1875 (own req); cpl 1 May 1875; sgt 15 Sep 1875; with pack train 25 June 1876;[1] dd regtl hq fatigue Aug 1876; dd prov sgt Oct to Dec 1876; abs on pass Dec 1876; disch 20 Jan 1877 Ft Lincoln DT expir of serv a sgt char good; reenl 26 Jan 1877 at Ft Lincoln for 5 yrs in co L; (m. widow of pvt Hughes 17 Feb 1877); cpl 4 May 1877; abs sick (rheum.) Tongue River MT 16 Aug 1877; ds Ft Lincoln 22 Aug 1877; sgt 1 Apr 1878; dd actg co qm sgt Oct 1878; dd actg prov sgt June 1879; dd post qm sgt Aug 1879; pvt 20 Dec 1881; dd co cook Dec 1881; disch 25 Jan 1882 at Ft Lincoln expir of serv a pvt; died 16 Jan 1927 Leavenworth Kans.
Pension: Ind. Surv. / 12617 / 8244.

Ragan, Mich'l. See Reagan, Mich'l.

Ragsdale Jno. S. Pvt co A; b. 9 Dec 1850 near Elizabethown Ky.; enl in co A 23 July 1872 at E'town for 5 yrs; age 22; farmer; blue eyes, lt hair, fair comp, 5' 7" high; dd co cook Oct 1872; ed cook post hosp Dec 1872; ed med dept nurse Feb 1873; dd qmd teamster Apr 1874; des 21 May 1875 Centralia Ill.; apph 26 July 1875 St Louis Mo.; tr under gd to Ft Snelling Minn. 1 Nov 1875; tr to Ft Lincoln DT 2 Dec (with sgt Varden); acquited in gen cm 20 Jan 1876 (chg of des'n reduced to awol occasioned by accdt without fault of sol. & no criminality attd thereto); dd co cook Feb 1876; ds camp Powder River MT 15 June 1876;[2] abs sick 6 Aug 1876 to Ft Lincoln;[3] dd qmd 12–28 Sep 1876 with 281 cav horses at post; dd qmd laborer Feb 1877; disch 24 June 1877 camp on Tongue River MT per SO 70 Dept of Dak. 1877 a pvt char good; died 4 Dec 1942 Dayton Ohio.
Pension: 9 June 1886 / Inv / 576278 / 501742. Ind. Surv. / 9761 / 6505. (XC-2,581,737).

Raichel, Henry W. Pvt co K; b. Hamilton Ohio; enl 21 Feb 1869 Austin Tex. for 5 yrs; age 22; baker; blue eyes, brn hair, florid comp, 5' 8 1/2" high; assd to co M 4 cav; des 25 May 1870 & apph next day; disch 21 Feb 1874 Ft Duncan Tex. expir of serv a pvt; reenl 8 May 1875 Cincinnati Ohio for 5 yrs; assd to co K 7 cav 14 May 1875; ds St Louis Bks Mo. June 1875; join co K July 1875 Colfax La.; dd qmd Dec 1875; dd with pack train June & Aug 1876; cpl 1 Sep 1876; sgt 28 Feb 1877; killed 30 Sep 1877 Snake Creek MT (Bear's Paw Mtns) in action with Nez Perce inds.

Ramell, Wm. (alias). See Wright, Jas.

Ramsey, Chas. Pvt co I; b. Mason Mich.; enl 26 Jan 1872 Chicago Ill. for 5 yrs; age 21; laborer; grey eyes, brn hair, dk comp, 5' 7" high; join co I 21 Feb 1872 Shelbyville Ky.; awol June 1873; des 1 July 1873 Ft Pembina DT; surd 17 Nov 1873 regtl hq St Paul Minn. under GO 102 AGO 1873; dd co cook Dec 1873; ed qmd teamster July & Aug 1874 (with NBS); in conft Dec 1874; sen gen cm 2 Feb 1875 forf $10 pay; with pack train 25 June 1876;[4] tr to co C 18 Sep 1876; ds regtl hq 20 Oct 1876; ds Ft Lincoln DT 19 Nov 1876 to 11 June 1877 when disch upon expir of serv a pvt char good; reenl 24 Feb 1878 at Ft Lincoln for 5 yrs in co A; dd co teamster Dec 1878 & Apr 1879; des 3 June 1879 at Ft Lincoln.

Randall, Geo. F. Pvt co B; b. Northfield Vt; enl 15 Dec 1874 Boston Mass. for 5 yrs; age 21; farmer; blue eyes, lt hair, fair comp, 5' 7 1/8" high; join co B 10 Feb 1875 Shreveport La.; dd co cook June 1876; dd actg co far'r Oct 1876; appt far'r 1 Nov 1876; disch 14 Dec 1879 Ft Yates DT expir of serv a far'r char good.

Randall, Wm. J. Pvt co D; b. Pittsburgh Pa.; enl 15 Sep 1875 Cincinnati Ohio for 5 yrs; age 25; carpenter; brn eyes, brn hair, dk comp, 5' 7 1/4" high; join co D 21 Oct 1875 Ft Lincoln DT; dd qmd Nov 1876 to Jan 1877; killed

30 Sep 1877 Snake Creek MT (Bear's Paw Mtns) in action with Nez Perce inds.
Pension: 25 Aug 1879 / Mother / 250338. Rej on grd clmt (Susan Woolslayer) not mother of sol.; foster mothers not within meaning of the law; congress alone having power to afford relief in premises.

Rankin, Franklin. Cpl co F; b. Waukesha Wis; enl 15 Oct 1866 Madison Wis for 3 yrs; age 18 9/12; farmer; blue eyes, auburn hair, fair comp, 5' 8 1/2" high; assd to co I 15 inf; disch 5 Feb 1867 Mobile Ala per SO 29 AGO 1867 (a minor); enl as Edw. Clyde 11 Nov 1867 Ft Snelling Minn. for 3 yrs; age 21; farmer; blue eyes, red hair, ruddy comp, 5' 10" high; assd to co A 10 inf; disch 11 Nov 1870 Ft Brown Tex. expir of serv a sgt; reenl 2 Dec 1870 New Orleans La. for 5 yrs; assd to co C 19 inf; des 1 Apr 1871 Jackson Bks (New Orleans); enl as Frank Rankin 17 Apr 1871 St Louis Ars'l Mo. for 5 yrs; join co F 7 cav 27 May 1871 Taylor Bks (Louisville) Ky.; cpl 23 Feb 1872; sgt 20 Aug 1872; abs sick on str *Western* 23 Apr 1873 Yankton to Ft Rice DT; duty 12 June 1873; pvt 1 Aug 1873; surd as des'r 19 Nov 1873 under GO 102 AGO 1873; restored to duty without trial 2 Apr 1874 & tr to co F (as Edw. Clyde) to serve bal of orig'l enlmt; ed qmd carpenter Sep 1874 to Nov 1875; ed qmd mech Dec 1875 to Mar 1876; cpl 11 Mar 1876; non-commissioned officer with dismtd detmt 15 May 1876; [with wagon train says Rooney; pretty sure at Powder River says Lynch];[5] sgt 27 Sep 1876; dd chg co mess Feb 1877; dd prov sgt 24 June 1878; disch 20 July 1878 Ft Totten DT expir of serv a sgt char xclt; reenl same day in co F for 5 yrs & on furl 3 mos St Paul Minn.; dd actg co qm sgt June 1880; ds Cant'mt Bad Lands DT Aug 1880 chg qm prop; in arrest June 1881 (awol while on duty as sgt of stable gd & rode his horse inside bks at Ft Buford); ds Camp Terry MT Aug 1881; sen gen cm 6 Sep 1881 forf $10 pay per mo for 2 mos (leniency acc't xclt char given him by co officers); 1sgt 1 Oct 1881; ds Ft Snelling Minn. in rifle comp'n Aug 1882; disch 19 July 1883 Ft Buford DT expir of serv a 1sgt char most xclt & reenl in co F for 5 yrs; on furl 5 mos 6 Aug 1883 Chicago Ill.; ds Ft L'worth Kans. 1 Aug to 18 Sep 1884 div rifle team comp'n; ds Ft Snelling 28 July to 15 Sep 1885 rifle team comp'n; disch 19 July 1888 Ft Riley Kans. expir of serv a 1sgt char xclt & reenl in co F for 5 yrs (as Frank Rankin his proper name); ds Ft L'worth 17 Aug to 6 Sep 1889 in cav contest; ds competing for carbine team 5 Aug to 8 Oct 1891; on furl 3 mos 10 June 1892 Oxford Neb; disch 19 July 1893 Ft Myer Va. expir of serv a 1sgt char xclt & reenl in co F for 5 yrs; sick qrs 23 Sep 1893 (sprain l. knee) & hosp 1–19 Nov; duty 27 Feb 1894; sgt 2 Mar 1894; sick hosp 10–14 Mar 1894 (ac. alcoholism); pvt 1 Apr 1894 sen summary court martial & forf 1 mos pay (awol 3 days); on furl 30 days 3 Apr 1894 Laurel Md (for treatment upon advice of capt Bell); tr to gen serv Columbus Bks Ohio 2 June 1894 (own req & expense, to serve better where he was not 1sgt for 13 yrs & reduced to ranks for his liquor habit, now entirely cured); tr to co D 17 inf 4 Oct 1894 (own req); died 3 Jan 1895 at Columbus Bks (gsw to head, suicide); survived by wife Mary & 2 sons.[6]

Rapp, Jno. Pvt co G; b. Wertumburg Germany; enl 29 Sep 1873 Phil'a Pa. for 5 yrs; age 25; farmer; blue eyes, dk hair, fair comp, 5' 5 1/4" high; join co G 19 Oct 1873 Ft Lincoln DT; dd co cook Aug to Oct 1875; dd 13 May to 25 June 1876 (orderly for Lt McIntosh); killed dur retreat from valley fight 25 June; (body not recovered).[7]

Rauter, Jno. Pvt co C; b. Tyrol Switz; enl 4 Oct 1873 Phil'a Pa. for 5 yrs; age 27; butcher; blue eyes, dk hair, dk comp, 5' 9 3/4" high; join co C 21 Oct 1873 Ft Rice DT; dd qmd Dec 1873 to Apr 1874; dd as trump'r Dec 1874 to Apr 1875; sick qrs 2–21 Aug 1875 (jaundice); dd in band Oct 1875; ed post bakery 27 Apr to 14 May 1876; killed with Custer column 25 June 1876.

Reagan, Mich'l. Pvt co K; b. 19 Oct 1845 Queenstown Ireland; enr as Jno. Desmond 17 Oct 1864 Augusta Me a pvt co M 31 Me inf; (used false name acc't under age & swore parents not living); m.o. vol serv 15 July 1865; enl reg army 8 Nov 1872 Boston Mass. for 5 yrs; age 27; shoemaker; grey eyes, dk hair, fair comp, 5' 7" high; join co K 7 cav 9

Dec 1872 Yorkville SC; dd mail carrier Nov 1874 to Jan 1875; ds camp Powder River MT 15 June 1876;[8] sick hosp Ft Lincoln DT 16 Oct 1876 (infl. pleura); dd regtl hq fatigue pty 18 June 1877; ds Ft Lincoln 9 Sep 1877; disch 8 Nov 1877 at Ft Lincoln expir of serv a pvt char good; reenl in co K 26 Dec 1877 Ft Rice DT for 5 yrs; dd co cook Feb 1879; dd qmd teamster Dec 1879 & Feb 1880; ed qmd teamster Oct 1880; cpl 12 Aug 1881; sgt 15 Mar 1882; dd post prov sgt Apr 1882; ds chg of work party on tel line between Ft Totten & Larimore DT Aug 1882; pvt 16 Oct 1882; disch 25 Dec 1882 Ft Meade DT expir of serv a pvt char good.
Pension: 22 June 1906 / Inv / 1344584 / 1171224. Dropped from roll 4 Sep 1920, failure to claim 3 yrs; last paid 4 June 1917, P. O. Columbia Falls MT.

Reardon, Thos. See Murphy, Thos.

Redican, Pat'k. See Coakley, Pat'k.

Reed, Henry Armstrong. b. 27 Apr 1858 Monroe Mich.; (nephew of gen Custer); left school early & with sister Emma, accomp gen Custer from Monroe 3 May 1876 for a summer on the plains;[9] hired at Ft Lincoln DT 10 May as asst herder in subs dept of gen Terry's exp'n; rate of pay $60 mo;[10] tent-mate with Dick Roberts (bro-in-law of capt Yates) dur march to Powder River;[11] amused everyone dur scout up Little Missouri River 30 May when his pony mired suddenly in quicksand while crossing river & the abrupt stop hurled him over pony's head & into mud knee-deep;[12] tho' beef herd stayed with wagon train at camp on Powder River 15 June, he was put on str *Far West* with ten steers to watch over whenever boat landed;[13] accomp regt up Rosebud 22 June & was killed in last stand on Custer hill 25 June 1876.[14]

Reed, Jno. A. Pvt co G; b. Chester Co. Pa.; enl 6 Apr 1871 Pittsburgh Pa. for 5 yrs; age 25 3/12; laborer; grey eyes, brn hair, fair comp, 5' 7" high; join 7 cav as unassd rct 19 Apr 1871 Taylor Bks (Louisville) Ky.; assd to co G 30 May 1871; cpl 20 Apr 1873; sgt 1 Dec 1873; dd qmd chg of herders Blk Hills Exp'n 21 Aug 1874; pvt 27 July 1875; dd actg co wag Dec 1875 to Feb 1876; disch 6 Apr 1876 Shreveport La. expir of serv a pvt char good; reenl 18 Apr 1876 St Louis Mo. for 5 yrs; rejoin co G 27 Apr at St Paul Minn.; dd 13 May to 22 June 1876;[15] ds Yellowstone depot July 1876; ds Yellowstone River gd on boat Aug 1876;[16] ds 1 Aug to 18 Sep 1876;[17] cpl 4 Jan 1877; ds in field 17 Nov 1877; sgt 23 Jan 1878; dd prov sgt Feb to June 1878; pvt 24 July 1878; dd co teamster Feb 1879; dd co cook June to Aug 1879; dd co cook June 1880; dd regtl hq Sep & Oct 1880; far'r 1 Nov 1880; disch 17 Apr 1881 Ft Meade DT expir of serv a far'r char xclt; enl in co A 7 cav 12 Feb 1885 at Ft Meade for 5 yrs; des 24 May 1885 at Ft Meade; apph 7 Dec 1889 Crow Agcy MT; dishon disch 18 Jan 1890 Ft Custer MT sen gen cm & 4 yrs conft mil prison Ft L'worth Kans. but mitigated to 2 yrs upon recom'n of court; unexecuted part of sen remitted 12 May 1890 upon recom'n of prison comd't (having exposed daring escape plan & faced retribution of inmates); died 21 July 1897, body interred at Custer Battlefield Nat'l Cemetery.[18]

Reed, Wm. Pvt co I; b. Baltimore Md; enl 2 Jan 1867 Cincinnati Ohio for 5 yrs; age 23; laborer; grey eyes, lt hair, lt comp, 5' 9 3/4" high; join co I 10 Feb 1867 Ft Riley Kans.; ds with escort for gen Sully Oct 1868; disch 2 Jan 1872 Shelbyville Ky. expir of serv a pvt & reenl in co I for 5 yrs; ds Ft Seward (Jamestown) DT 28 May 1874; sick Ft Snelling Minn. 21 June 1874; tr to Ft Lincoln DT 12 July 1874 to await return of co from field; sent to Ft Totten DT 7 Aug 1874 chg of govt horses; killed with Custer column 25 June 1876.

Rees, Wm. Henry. Pvt co E; b. Wash'n Pa.; enl 5 Dec 1872 St Louis Mo. for 5 yrs; age 24; laborer; grey eyes, sandy hair, fair comp, 6' 1" high; join co E 13 Feb 1873 Unionville SC; killed with Custer column 25 June 1876.
Pension: 17 Oct 1883 / Mother / 309704 / 249115. Father / 396468 / 265524.

Reese, Wm. Pvt co E; b. Phil'a Pa.; enl 27 Sep 1873 at Phil'a for 5 yrs; age 23; brushmaker; blue eyes, lt brn hair, fair comp, 5' 10" high; join co E 18 Oct 1873 Ft Lincoln

DT; dd qmd teamster Apr 1874; ed qmd teamster 6 Nov 1875 to 8 Mar 1876; [with Custer says Pandtle; left at Powder River says Berwald & Bromwell];[19] ds co teamster 11 Aug 1876 (with wagon train to Yellowstone);[20] dd qmd Ft Lincoln 12 Sep 1876 with 281 cav horses at post; ed qmd 13 Sep; ed qmd teamster 14 Nov 1876 to 3 Jan 1877; far'r 17 Mar 1878; ds Ft Lincoln July & Aug 1878 chg of co horses; disch 27 Sep 1878 at Ft Lincoln upon expir of serv a far'r char good.

Reeves, Francis M. Pvt co A; b. Bluffton Ind.; pvt co D 7 Ill. inf 25 July 1861 to 9 July 1865; enl reg army 4 May 1868 St Louis Mo. for 5 yrs; age 26; farmer; grey eyes, lt hair, florid comp, 5' 5 1/2" high; assd to co L 8 cav; disch 4 May 1873 Ft Union NM expir of serv a wag; reenl 7 Oct 1875 at St Louis for 5 yrs; age 28; teamster; join co A 21 Oct 1875 Ft Lincoln DT; dd co teamster Dec 1875 to Apr 1876; gsw l. side (fl. wd. severe) & l. thigh (fl. wd.) 25 June 1876 dur retreat from valley fight;[21] tr on str *Far West* 3 July to hosp Ft Lincoln; ed nurse post hosp 8 Aug to 10 Nov 1876; dd qmd teamster Feb 1877; sick hosp Apr 1877 (infl. bladder); ds Ft Lincoln 21 Apr to 30 Dec 1877; co wag 1 Jan 1878; pvt 1 July 1878; disch 20 Dec 1878 at Ft Lincoln on surg cert dis (chr. rheum. back & legs contr line of duty; dis 1/4) a pvt char xclt; res Bismarck DT; adm to state hosp Jamestown N.Dak. in 1898.
Pension: 20 Mar 1879 / Inv / 273978 / 164801. (Dropped from roll 9 Nov 1903 upon death of pens'r; last paid 4 Sep 1902).

Reibold, Christian. Pvt co L; b. Buffalo N.Y.; enl 1 Aug 1871 Chicago Ill. for 5 yrs; age 21; shoemaker; grey eyes, lt hair, lt comp, 5' 6" high; join co L 21 Dec 1871 Yorkville SC; dd learning music Dec 1871; trump'r Feb 1872; pvt 27 Apr 1872; des 30 Apr 1872 at Yorkville; apph 29 Apr 1874 at Buffalo; tr under gd to Omaha Bks Neb 21 May 1874; tr to Ft Lincoln DT Sep 1874 in conft; restored to duty without trial 20 Nov 1874 upon recom'n co comdr (to make good time lost & expense for apph); appt co sad'r 1 Dec 1874; pvt 30 Mar 1876; killed with Custer column 25 June 1876.

Reid, Elwyn S. Pvt co D; b. Green Co. N.Y.; enl 26 Oct 1872 Albany N.Y. for 5 yrs; age 27 5/12; carpenter; hazel eyes, brn hair, dk comp, 5' 10" high; join co D 8 Dec 1872 Opelika Ala; dd co cook June 1873; ds with engr party (NBS) July & Aug 1873; ed qmd Feb 1876; disch 23 June 1877 camp on Tongue River MT per SO 70 Dept of Dak. 1877 a pvt char xclt; reenl in co D 21 Jan 1878 Ft Rice DT for 5 yrs; dd co cook June 1878; dd co carpenter Feb to Apr 1879; dd qmd carpenter June 1879 thro' Oct 1880; awl Apr 1881 Cannonball DT; on furl 30 days 12 Dec 1882 Bismarck DT; disch 20 Jan 1883 Ft Yates DT expir of serv a pvt char very good; reenl 12 Aug 1885 at Ft Yates for 5 yrs in co B 17 inf; disch 17 Aug 1890 Ft D. A. Russell Wyo. expir of serv a pvt char good (retained in serv); reenl in same co 25 Aug 1890 at Ft Russell for 5 yrs; died 20 Aug 1895 at Ft Russell (heart failure) an artf'r.

Reiley, Mich'l. Pvt co F; b. Dunmore Pa.; enl 6 Nov 1872 Wilkes Barre Pa. for 5 yrs; age 21; miner; grey eyes, lt brn hair, fair comp, 5' 8 7/8" high; join co F 1 Dec 1872 Louisville Ky.; dd co cook June 1873; unfit for duty with Yellowstone Exp'n 21 July 1873 (remit fever) & tr by boat to hosp Ft Lincoln DT; duty 16 Aug 1873; in conft Oct 1873 to May 1874; sen gen cm 20 Feb 1874 forf $5 pay per mo for 3 mos & conft same period; dd qmd herder 21–31 Aug 1874; dd qmd Apr 1875; in conft Apr 1876; gsw r. heel 21 May 1876 accdt disch of carbine while mounting; sick qrs 10 June 1876 (upon exam'n chf med officer) camp Powder River MT; [at Powder River says Finnegan; with pack train says Rooney & Lynch];[22] dd co cook Apr 1877; dd as packer Aug 1877; ds Ft Lincoln 14 Oct 1877 (arr post 26 Oct); disch 6 Nov 1877 at Ft Lincoln by expir of serv a pvt char good; res Steubenville Ohio in 1897.[23]

Reilly, Jas. T. Sgt co E; b. Baltimore Md; pvt & cpl co F Purnell legion Md vols 5 Sep 1861 to 24 Oct 1864; enl reg army 10 Aug 1866 at Baltimore for 5 yrs; age 21; laborer; blue eyes, brn hair, fair comp, 5' 9 1/4" high; join co A 7 cav 10 Sep 1866 Ft Riley Kans.; tr to co E 30 Sep 1866; cpl 28 July 1869; pvt

24 Dec 1869 sen gen cm & forf $10 pay per mo for 6 mos & conft same period; dd teamster Dec 1870; co wag 16 Jan 1871; disch 10 Aug 1871 Spartanburg SC expir of serv a wag & reenl in co E for 5 yrs; cpl 11 Aug 1871; sgt 1 Sep 1871; 1sgt 17 Jan 1872; sgt 1 May 1873; actg 1sgt Dec 1873; dd chg co kit'n Apr 1874; actg co qm sgt June 1874; 1sgt 29 Dec 1874; on furl 30 Apr 1875 Baltimore Md; sgt 11 May 1875; actg co qm sgt Aug 1875 to June 1876; gsw thro' buttocks & l. thigh (fl. wd. sl.) 26 June 1876 on Reno hill; tr on str *Far West* 3 July to hosp Ft Lincoln (suffering severe pain in wd & in great sciatic nerve to sole of foot); disch 11 Aug 1876 upon expir of serv a sgt char xclt; would have been disch on surg cert had not his term of serv expired while under treatment; disch from hosp 11 Sep 1876; (atrophy of thigh); died 21 Nov 1880 Baltimore Md.
Pension: 8 Dec 1876 / Inv / 228507 / 143780.

Reilly, Mich'l. Pvt co K; b. Longford Ireland; enl 12 May 1870 New York N.Y. for 5 yrs; age 21; framemaker; hazel eyes, dk hair, dk comp, 5' 6 1/4" high; assd to co F 10 inf; disch 12 May 1875 Ft McKavett Tex. expir of serv a pvt char xclt; reenl 8 June 1875 St Louis Bks Mo. for 5 yrs; age 23; join co K 7 cav 27 Apr 1876 St Paul Minn.; dd qmd teamster 31 May 1876; ds camp Powder River MT 15 June 1876; dd hq fatigue pty Apr to June 1877; cpl 1 Oct 1877; sgt 31 May 1878; disch 5 June 1879 Ft Totten DT per SO 124 AGO 1879 (upon own appn to care for widowed sister & assist family support) a sgt char xclt; enl as Morgan Robinson 25 Oct 1880 New York N.Y. for 5 yrs; assd to co E 3 cav; disch 24 Oct 1885 Ft Davis Tex. expir of serv a sgt char xclt; reenl next day for co D 10 inf for 5 yrs; (said to have served two enlmts as Mich'l Reilly in 7 cav & 10 inf); disch 24 Oct 1890 Ft Marcy NM by expir of serv a sgt char xclt & reenl in same co for 5 yrs; tr to prov gd 24 Jan 1893; disch 10 Oct 1894 Ft L'worth Kans. per SO 233 AGO 1894 (under prov'n GO 81 AGO 1890 [to engage in business to better his cond'n before too old]) a pvt char xclt.[24]

Reily, Wm. Van Wyck. 2Lt co F; b. 12 Dec 1853 Wash'n D.C.; educ at Georgetown College & two yrs at school in Germany; cadet USNA 24 Sep 1870 to 17 Oct 1872 (resd after failing math exam'n two yrs in row & each time turned back to next class); with survey exp'n in Nicaragua Dec 1872 to July 1873 thence employed in Wash'n navy yard superintending scrapping of old monitors; recom by pres't Grant 13 May 1875 for com'n of 2Lt;[25] passed exam'n before army bd 13 Sep; appt 2Lt 10 cav 15 Oct 1875 & accepted 23 Oct (to report in 30 days); joined cav depot St Louis Bks Mo. 22 Nov; retained at depot (upon req of col Sturgis) his serv needed & to await detmt of rcts for his regt, also as new civil appmt should remain awhile at depots for instr'n; comd two cos unassd rcts Dec 1875 thro' Feb 1876; tr to 7 cav 26 Jan 1876 (upon order secretary of war);[26] left depot 3 Mar chg of eleven mus'ns for 7 cav; delayed at Ft Seward (Jamestown) DT 24 Mar awaiting removal of snow blockade on NPRR; arr Bismarck on first train 14 Apr (with cos E & L) & encamped at Camp Hancock; crossed Missouri River on str *Union* 17 Apr & joined regt at Ft Lincoln; attd to co F 18 Apr; sick qrs 20 Apr to 6 May (ac. rheum.); killed with Custer column 25 June 1876.
[4087 ACP 1875]. Pension: 7 Jan 1878 / Mother / 234881. (Abandoned).

Reinwald, Adam Karl. See Brown, Chas.

Reno, Marcus Albert. Major; b. Dec 1834 Carrollton Ill.;[27] grad USMA 1 July 1857 & appt bvt 2Lt 1 drg;[28] join regt 1 Oct 1857 Carlisle Bks Pa.; tr to Ft Walla Walla WT Mar 1858; 2Lt 14 June 1858; 1Lt 25 Apr 1861; (regt redesig 1 cav Aug 1861); capt 12 Nov 1861 & tr to defenses of Wash'n D.C.; comd co in Peninsula campn Mar to Aug 1862; comd battn with gen Pleasonton's div Sep 1862 & escort art'y in battle of Antietam; ds Harrisburg Pa. to procure horses Oct & Nov 1862; awl 30 days on surg cert 18 Mar 1863 (hernia when horse shot under him in action at Kelly's Ford); on rctg duty at Harrisburg & superintend purchase of horses to Aug 1863; rejoin co 8 Oct 1863 Camp Buford Md; asst in cav bureau to May 1864; actg aig with cav corps to Aug 1864 & chf of staff to gen Torbert to Dec 1864; col 12 Pa. cav 1 Jan 1865 &

in skirmish with Mosby's guerrillas at Harmony Va. dur Mar 1865; m.o. vol serv 20 July 1865; bvt maj & Lt-col for gal serv at Kelly's Ford & Cedar Creek;[29] bvt col for gal serv dur the war & bvt brig-gen vols for gal serv dur the rebellion; asst instr at USMA to Oct 1865; judge advocate mil com'n New Orleans La. to Dec 1865 & prov marshal of freedmen's bureau at New Orleans to Aug 1866; appn for prom'n to pay dept Oct 1866 not appv as line officer's not eligible for paymaster; awl at Harrisburg to Feb 1867 thence cond detmt of rcts on steamer from New York to Calif. (via Panama); rejoin 1 cav 6 May 1867 Ft Vancouver WT; actg aig Dept of Columbia June 1867; prom maj 7 cav 18 June 1869 (from 26 Dec 1868); ds Santa Fe NM court martial duty to Nov 1869; join 7 cav 18 Dec 1869 Ft Hays Kans.; post comdr Spartanburg SC July 1871 to Mar 1873; in field comdg escort for NBS May to Oct 1873; awl on surg cert (ankle sprain) at Harrisburg to 10 Feb 1874; ds dept hq St Paul Minn. to 20 May 1874 & in field comdg escort for NBS to Sep 1874; (req for leave 15 July upon death of wife denied by gen Terry);[30] awl 30 days 14 Sep 1874 Harrisburg Pa.; awl ext'd 8 mos with perm'n to visit Europe; awl further ext'd 3 mos 24 Mar 1875; post comdr Ft Lincoln DT 1 Nov 1875 to 12 Mar 1876 & 20 Mar to 10 May 1876; comd r. wing 12 May to 22 June & comd regt from 25 June;[31] arr Bismarck 22 Sep on str *Key West* (with Lts Edgerly & Wallace);[32] comd battn in field 21 Oct to 3 Nov 1876 disarming inds at Standing Rock Agcy; awl 20 days 17 Nov 1876; post comdr Ft Abercrombie DT 20 Dec 1876; in arrest 28 Feb 1877 & ordered to dept hq at St Paul; sen gen cm 20 Mar 1877 to dismissal from serv but mitigated to suspension from rank & pay for 2 yrs from 1 May 1877; at Chicago Ill. Jan & Feb 1879 for court of inq (upon own app'n);[33] post comdr Ft Meade DT 22 May to 17 July 1879; in arrest 28 Oct 1879; sen gen cm 8 Dec 1879 to dismissal from serv (confirmed by pres't Hayes from 1 Apr 1880);[34] died 30 Mar 1889 Wash'n D.C. [R 314 CB 1865].

Reynolds, Chas. Alexander. Guide qmd; b. 20 Mar 1842 near Monmouth Ill.; removed to Stevensburg Ky. in 1844 & two yrs later to Abingdon Ill.; educ at Abingdon college to 1859 when family settled in Pardee Kans.; enr 16 July 1861 in capt Quigg's co of Kans. vols for 3 yrs; (redesig co B 10 Kans. inf Apr 1862); ds with escort for govt horses to Ft Union NM Sep 1863; m.o. vol serv 19 Aug 1864 L'worth City Kans. a pvt; on trading venture to Santa Fe NM in 1865 thence joined buffalo hunters in western Kansas & Nebraska; after a shooting affray at Ft McPherson in 1869 he went up to DT where his reputation as hunter & trapper earned him regular employment with the army; also employed for a time as salesman in the trader's store at Grand River Agcy; rec'd acclaim in 1873 when he carried desps from the Yellowstone Exp'n to Ft Benton MT & again in 1874 when he carried desps alone over 150 miles from the Blk Hills Exp'n to Ft Laramie Wyo.;[35] accomp capt Yates' detmt to Standing Rock Agcy 12 Dec 1874 for the arrest of Rain-in-the-Face; employed as guide for capt Ludlow's reconnaissance exp'n thro' Yellowstone Park July to Sep 1875;[36] hired 3 Mar 1876 at Ft Lincoln by Lt Nowlan as guide for the Sioux Exp'n; rate of pay $100 mo; developed painful felon on r. hand dur march to Rosebud (Dr. Porter unable to cure) but declined to stay on str *Far West* 22 June; accomp Lt Varnum to Crow's Nest night of 24 June;[37] killed dur retreat from valley fight 25 June 1876 (near Isaiah).[38]

Reynolds, Chas. H. See Brinkerhoff, Henry.

Ricketts, Jos. K. Wag co M; b. near Morrow Ohio; enl 16 Jan 1873 Cincinnati Ohio for 5 yrs; age 23 11/12; farmer; blue eyes, blk hair, ruddy comp, 5' 9" high; join co M 9 Feb 1873 Oxford Miss; appt far'r 15 May 1873; pvt 1 Aug 1873; dd qmd teamster Dec 1873; co wag 1 Mar 1874; pvt 20 June 1874; wag 1 Sep 1874; pvt 1 Oct 1874; dd qmd sawyer Oct 1874; dd qmd teamster Dec 1874 to Apr 1875; wag 14 July 1875; ds camp Powder River MT chg of mule team 15 June 1876;[39] ds with wagon train 11 Aug 1876; arr Ft Rice DT 10 Sep (with trump'r Martin); rejoin co 5 Oct 1876 camp near Ft Lincoln DT; far'r 11 Jan 1877; disch 16 Jan 1878 Ft Lincoln DT expir of serv a far'r char good; reenl 7 Feb 1878 at Ft Rice for 5 yrs in co H; dd co teamster June

to Aug 1878; dd co wag Dec 1878; dd co teamster Feb 1879; dd post hosp Aug & Oct 1881; far'r 1 Dec 1881; pvt 1 May 1882; abs sick 17 May to 14 Dec 1882 (broken l. leg, kick of horse, not line of duty); disch 6 Feb 1883 Ft Meade DT expir of serv a pvt char good; died 26 Feb 1909 Dayton Ohio.
Pension: 29 Sep 1897 / Inv / 1198656. (Rej on grd no ratable dis shown). Ind. Wid. / 11899 / 8434.

Rivers, Jno. Far'r co I; b. Westchester N.Y.; enl 10 Sep 1866 New York N.Y. for 5 yrs; age 32; sailor; grey eyes, dk hair, dk comp, 5' 7" high; join co I 29 Sep 1866 Ft Riley Kans.; cpl 1 May 1867; wd 26 June 1867 near Ft Wallace Kans. in action with inds; pvt 1 Feb 1868; dd comsy dept herdsman Aug 1868; ds with escort for gen Sully 15 Sep 1868; wag 5 Dec 1868; pvt Apr 1869; dd co far'r Oct 1869; appt far'r 1 May 1870; disch 10 Sep 1871 Bagdad Ky. expir of serv a far'r & reenl in co I for 5 yrs; far'r 1 Oct 1871; sick 24 Oct to 1 Nov 1875 (kick of horse l. leg); ds camp Powder River MT 10 June 1876; disch 7 Aug 1876 camp mouth of Rosebud Creek MT (in time to go down river by first boat) per GO 24 AGO 1859 a far'r char good; arr Ft Lincoln 10 Aug on str *Durfee*;[40] reenl in co I 17 Aug 1876 at Ft Lincoln for 5 yrs & on furl 40 days St Paul Minn.; duty with Lt Nave 12 Oct 1876 with rcts; wd (sl.) 13 Sep 1877 Canon Creek MT in action with Nez Perce inds;[41] sick hosp Ft Lincoln 10 May to 24 June 1880 (frac. r. scapula; fall from wagon); sick hosp Ft Totten DT 11–23 May 1881 (cystitis); sick hosp (chr. cystitis) 16 July to 16 Aug 1881 when disch by expir of serv a far'r char xclt; desired to reenl but unable to pass med exam'n (disease from injury recd summer 1880 in line of duty; dis 3/4).

Rix, Edw. Pvt co C; b. Lowell Mass.; enl 1 Oct 1873 Chicago Ill. for 5 yrs; age 23; railroader; grey eyes, lt brn hair, fair comp, 5' 9 3/4" high; join co C 21 Oct 1873 Ft Rice DT; ed qmd Nov 1874 to Apr 1875; dd co cook Aug 1875; sick (whitlow) 23 Nov 1875 to 24 Feb 1876; killed with Custer column 25 June 1876.

Robb, Eldorado J. Pvt co G; b. Warren Co. Ky.; enl 8 Jan 1872 Louisville Ky. for 5 yrs; age 21; laborer; hazel eyes, brn hair, ruddy comp, 5' 9 3/4" high; join co G 5 Feb 1872 Spartanburg SC; ds hq Yellowstone Exp'n Aug 1873; dd qmd teamster Apr thro' Aug 1874; in conft Dec 1875 to Feb 1876; horse shot in l. hind leg & made lame dur valley fight 25 June;[42] ed qmd 13 Nov 1876 to 8 Jan 1877 when disch at Ft Lincoln DT upon expir of serv a pvt char good.

Robers, Jonathan. Pvt co K; b. Surry Co. NC; enl in co K 4 Dec 1872 Yorkville SC for 5 yrs; age 21; farmer; blue eyes, brn hair, fair comp, 5' 8" high; dd pioneer 18 Apr 1873; sick qrs 25 Apr & hosp 1 May 1873 Yankton DT (catarrh); tr to str *Katie P. Kountz* 8 May 1873 to Ft Rice DT;[43] ed subs dept Oct 1873 to Apr 1874; dd with pack train June 1876; ds in field 13 Aug 1877; ds in field with escort 28 Sep 1877; disch 4 Dec 1877 Ft Buford DT expir of serv a pvt char xclt; reenl in co K 17 Dec 1877 at Ft Rice for 5 yrs; dd co wag Feb to June 1878; dd qmd teamster Dec 1878 to Oct 1880; disch 16 Dec 1882 Ft Meade DT expir of serv a pvt; res Ft Custer MT in 1893.
Pension: 28 Dec 1889 / Inv / 746274. (Rej on grd no dis from causes alleged).

Roberts, Henry. Pvt co L; b. London, England; enl 11 Nov 1872 Toledo Ohio for 5 yrs; age 22 9/12; laborer; blue eyes, lt hair, lt comp, 5' 9" high; join co L 9 Dec 1872 Yorkville SC; dd co cook Oct 1875; killed with Custer column 25 June 1876.

Robinson, Morgan. See Reilly, Mich'l (co K).

Robinson, Wm. Pvt co M; b. 12 Apr 1842 Co. Down Ireland; enl 30 Sep 1873 Phil'a Pa. for 5 yrs; age 31; cloth finisher; blue eyes, dk brn hair, fair comp, 5' 9" high; join co M 21 Oct 1873 Ft Rice DT; dd qmd laborer Apr 1874; dd subs dept herder Sep & Oct 1874; dd co cook Apr to June 1875; ed nurse post hosp 13 Nov 1875 to 4 May 1876; ed hosp attdt in field 16 May 1876 with Dr. Clark; [likely with Dr. Lord 15 June & Dr. Porter 22 June];[44] dd regtl hq with Dr. Taylor 4 Aug 1876;[45] ds field hosp Canon Creek MT 14 Sep 1877; arr Ft Lincoln 30 Oct (with pvt Wiedman); ed hosp attdt Dec 1877; ed cook post hosp Apr 1878;

ed nurse post hosp June 1878; ed cook field hosp July & Aug 1878; disch 30 Sep 1878 Camp Ruhlen DT expir of serv a pvt char xclt; died 4 Feb 1928 Seattle Wash'n.
Pension: 17 Dec 1895 / Inv / 1172513. (Rej on grd no ratable dis shown). Ind. Surv. / 13654 / 6990.

Rogers, Benj. F. Pvt co G; b. Madison Co. Ky.; enl 5 Jan 1872 Louisville Ky. for 5 yrs; age 24; farmer; blue eyes, lt hair, ruddy comp, 5' 10" high; join co G 5 Feb 1872 Spartanburg SC; sen gen cm 29 Nov 1872 forf $8 pay per mo for 4 mos & conft same period; ed hosp attdt Yellowstone Exp'n 24 Aug 1873; sen gen cm 25 Feb 1876 forf $10 pay per mo for 3 mos & conft same period; dd 20–27 May 1876;[46] killed dur retreat from valley fight 25 June 1876.

Rogers, Walter B. Pvt co L; b. Wash'n Pa.; enl 6 June 1873 Boston Mass. for 5 yrs; age 26; clerk; brn eyes, dk hair, medium comp, 5' 8 1/4" high; des 3 Sep 1873 from rct rendevous; apph 12 Sep 1873; join co L 19 Oct 1873 Ft Lincoln DT; dd asst post baker 31 Jan to 7 Mar 1876; killed with Custer column 25 June 1876.
Pension: 19 Apr 1878 / Wid / 236717 / 181848.

Rollins, Rich'd. Pvt co A; b. Breckenridge Co. Ky.; enl in co A 26 Nov 1872 Elizabethtown Ky. for 5 yrs; age 23; farmer; blue eyes, brn hair, fair comp, 5' 10 3/4" high; (co barber);[47] dd orderly at gar cm Feb 1876; killed dur retreat from valley fight 25 June 1876.

Rood, Edw. R. Pvt co E; b. 14 Nov 1847 Tioga Co. N.Y.; enl 19 Sep 1873 New York N.Y. for 5 yrs; age 25; fireman; hazel eyes, blk hair, dk comp, 5' 7" high; join co E 18 Oct 1873 Ft Lincoln DT; sen gen cm 24 Feb 1875 forf $10 pay per mo for 3 mos & conft same period; killed with Custer column 25 June 1876.
Pension: 14 July 1877 / Father / 232354 / 181103. Dropped 1 Dec 1880 upon evidence sol. left legal widow & no divorce had taken place, facts which pens'r admits as correct.

Rooney, Jas. M. Pvt co F; b. New York N.Y.; enl 3 Dec 1867 New York N.Y. for 5 yrs; age 22; gas fitter; blue eyes, brn hair, dk comp, 5' 8 1/4" high; join co F 22 Jan 1868 Ft L'worth Kans.; dd co cook Sep & Nov 1869; dd detmt hq May 1870; dd co cook July to Sep 1870; dd co cook Jan 1871; ds regtl hq Louisville Ky. June 1871; ds Taylor Bks (Louisville) 22 July 1871; dd cook regtl band Dec 1871 thro' Nov 1872; disch 3 Dec 1872 Louisville Ky. expir of serv a pvt & reenl in co F for 5 yrs; cpl 1 Mar 1874; dd actg co qm sgt June to Dec 1874; pvt 16 June 1875; [with pack train says himself, Lynch, & Gregg];[48] cpl 3 Oct 1876; sgt 10 Nov 1876; dd chg co mess Dec 1876; disch 3 Dec 1877 camp near Ft Buford DT expir of serv a sgt char xclt; reenl same day but rej upon med exam'n (const. syph.);[49] died 5 Aug 1918 Yankton SD.
Pension: 2 July 1891 / Inv / 1036429. (Rej on grd alleged dis [catarrh] result of disease treated in serv & not contr line of duty; syph. a factor which could not be eliminated).

Rose, Peter E. Pvt co L; b. Rockford Ill.; enl 28 Sep 1875 Chicago Ill. for 5 yrs; age 23; cooper; brn eyes, blk hair, dk comp, 5' 9" high; join co L 29 Oct 1875 Ft Totten DT; with pack train June 1876;[50] ds Ft Lincoln DT 17 Oct 1876 dismtd; cited by maj Merrill for good cond in action against Nez Perce inds at Canon Creek MT 13 Sep 1877; sen gar cm 28 Feb 1878 forf $3 pay; des 19 Mar 1878 at Ft Lincoln.

Rossbury, Jno. W. Pvt co I; b. Rochester N.Y.; enl 26 Jan 1872 at Rochester for 5 yrs; age 22; salesman; hazel eyes, dk hair, fair comp, 5' 6 1/2" high; join co I 21 Feb 1872 Shelbyville Ky.; ed qmd NBS July & Aug 1874; sick 8–15 May 1876 (gonorrhea); dd with hq fatigue pty r. wing 15 May; killed with Custer column 25 June 1876.

Roth, Francis. Pvt co K; b. Frankfurt Germany; enl 29 Mar 1871 New York N.Y. for 5 yrs; age 24; brass founder; grey eyes, brn hair, fair comp, 5' 7" high; assd to gen mtd serv; tr from permanent co Carlisle Bks Pa. to St Louis Bks Mo. Aug 1871; lance cpl Dec 1871; in arrest Apr 1872; lance sgt Oct 1872; on rctg serv Boston Mass. Dec 1872 to Oct 1873; cpl 1 Feb 1875; in arrest June 1875; pvt 1 July 1875 sen gen cm & forf $10 pay per mo for 3 mos; lance sgt Oct 1875; disch 29 Mar 1876 at St Louis Bks by expir of serv a pvt & reenl for 5 yrs; join co K 7 cav 27 Apr 1876 St Paul Minn.; ds camp Powder River MT 15 June 1876; cpl 2 Oct 1876; pvt 16 May 1877; killed 30 Sep 1877 Snake Creek MT (Bear's Paw Mtns) in action with Nez Perce inds; survived by wife at Ft Lincoln.[51]

Rott, Louis.[52] Sgt co K; b. Bavaria Germany; enl 17 Jan 1870 Cincinnati Ohio for 5 yrs; age 21; cabinet maker; hazel eyes, dk brn hair, dk comp, 5' 9" high; join co K 19 Feb 1870 Ft Harker Kans.; dd co cook Dec 1871; cpl 1 Jan 1872; sgt 1 July 1872; 1sgt 1 Jan 1873; sgt 1 May 1873; ds Ft Rice DT Oct 1874; 1sgt 1 Dec 1874; disch 17 Jan 1875 Colfax La. expir of serv a 1sgt & reenl in co K for 5 yrs; sgt 15 Sep 1875 & ed subs dept to 1 Feb 1876; actg 1sgt 1 Sep 1876; appt 1sgt 19 Oct 1876 to date 2 Oct; sgt 14 Dec 1876; dd actg co qm sgt Aug 1877; 1sgt 20 Oct 1877; disch 26 May 1878 at Ft Rice on surg cert dis a 1sgt char xclt (broke r. arm yrs ago [out of serv] causing noticeable deformity of elbow & unable to use arm without pain especially in wet weather; dis 1/4; not contr line of duty).

Rowland, Robt. Pvt co G; b. Warsaw Poland; enl 7 Apr 1876 St Louis Mo. for 5 yrs; age 32; baker; brn eyes, brn hair, ruddy comp, 5' 8" high; join co G 27 Apr 1876 St Paul Minn.; ds camp Powder River MT 15 June 1876; sd with Lt Hare's sec. of parrott guns 8 Oct to 12 Nov 1876; dd regtl band Dec 1876 to Feb 1877; ds in field with art'y detmt 2 July to 21 Sep 1877; dd asst co cook Oct 1877; cpl 23 Jan 1878; in arrest 1 Jan 1879 Bismarck DT for murder of citizen dur brawl in saloon; released when inquest found no evidence he fired shot & upon testimony he was of exemplary habits; des 10 Apr 1879 (in skiff) having learned his arrest was imminent; body found near mouth of Cannonball River 15 Apr 1879, gsw in head indicating suicide, dead 3 or 4 days;[53] chg of des'n not removed.

Roy, Stanislas. Cpl co A; b. France; enl 20 Dec 1869 Cincinnati Ohio for 5 yrs; age 23 1/12; teamster; brn eyes, brn hair, lt comp, 5' 5 1/4" high; join co H 7 cav 13 Feb 1870 Ft Hays Kans.; ds hosp nurse Ft Sully DT May to Sep 1873; abs sick June to Sep 1874 Ft Rice DT; disch 20 Dec 1874 New Orleans La. expir of serv a pvt; reenl 19 Jan 1875 at Cincinnati for 5 yrs; join co A 6 Feb 1875 Livingston Ala; cpl 28 Feb 1876; sgt 1 Oct 1876; actg co qm sgt Sep 1877 & with wagon train to Bear's Paw Mtns; (awarded medal of honor 5 Oct 1878 for bringing water to wounded [at LBH] while under heavy fire, made two trips to river);[54] disch 18 Jan 1880 Ft Meade DT expir of serv a sgt char xclt; reenl 13 Feb 1880 New York N.Y. for 5 yrs; rejoin co A 29 Sep 1881 at Ft Meade; cpl 1 Oct 1881; ed subs dept Oct 1881; sgt 6 Dec 1881 & co qm sgt to Dec 1882; ds Ft Snelling Minn. Aug 1884 with dept rifle comp'n; on furl 30 days 24 Aug 1884 at St Paul; disch 12 Feb 1885 at Ft Meade expir of serv a sgt char xclt & reenl in co A for 5 yrs; on furl 6 mos 17 Feb 1885 Piqua Ohio; disch 12 Feb 1890 Ft Riley Kans. expir of serv a sgt char xclt & reenl in co A for 5 yrs; on furl 6 mos 14 Mar 1890 Piqua Ohio; ds Ft Riley chg of prop 27 Sep to 4 Oct 1890; disch 15 Apr 1891 at Ft Riley per GO 81 AGO 1890 a sgt char xclt;[55] reenl 17 Dec 1894 at Cincinnati for 3 yrs; join co E 7 cav 29 Dec 1894 at Ft Riley; cpl 25 May 1895; sgt 20 Jan 1897; disch 16 Dec 1897 Ft Grant AT expir of serv a sgt char xclt & reenl in co E for 3 yrs; dd prov sgt Feb thro' July 1900; sd chg post bakery Aug 1900; disch 16 Dec 1900 Columbia Bks Cuba expir of serv a sgt char xclt & reenl in co E for 3 yrs; color-sgt 18 Feb 1901; retd 30 June 1901 a color-sgt char xclt; died 10 Feb 1913 Columbus Bks Ohio.[56]

Rudden, Pat'k. Pvt co F; b. Newark NJ; enl 24 Sep 1875 St Louis Mo. for 5 yrs; age 22; hatter; blue eyes, brn hair, dk comp, 5' 5 7/8" high; join co F 21 Oct 1875 Ft Lincoln DT; killed with Custer column 25 June 1876.

Rudolph, Geo. A. Pvt band; b. 24 Feb 1854 Meuterheim Germany; enl for band 21 Sep 1871 Meridien Miss for 5 yrs; age 18; musician; blue eyes, brn hair, fair comp, 5' 4 1/2" high; ds camp Powder River MT 15 June 1876; ds str *Josephine* 6 Aug 1876 to Ft Lincoln DT

with band; disch 21 Sep 1876 at Ft Lincoln expir of serv a pvt char very good; reenl 16 Aug 1877 Ft Columbus N.Y. for 5 yrs; assd to gen serv as band mus'n; disch 15 Aug 1882 David's Isl N.Y.H expir of serv a pvt char xclt; died 4 Dec 1924 Eddyville N.Y.
Pension: 9 Oct 1918 / Ind. Surv. / 16287 / 9087. Ind. Wid. / 17101 / 11444.

Rush, Thos. H. Sgt co D; b. 19 Nov 1841 Greenville Ohio; enl 21 Apr 1858 St Louis Mo. for 5 yrs; age 21; laborer; hazel eyes, lt hair, fair comp, 5' 8 1/4" high; assd to co I 5 inf; disch 9 Apr 1861 Ft Stanton NM by order secretary of war (a minor) a pvt; enr 15 Sep 1861 at St Louis a cpl co D Birge's sharpshooters for 3 yrs; sgt 12 Mar 1862; (redesig co C western sharpshooters 14 Mo. inf Apr 1862); 1sgt 1 May 1862; (regt redesig 66 Ill. inf Nov 1862); pvt 4 July 1863; reenl as vet vol 25 Dec 1863 Pulaski Tenn; sgt 20 Mar 1864; wd (sl.) 22 July & 30 Aug 1864 near Atlanta Ga.; capt 30 Mar 1865 to date 9 Sep 1864; m.o. vol serv 7 July 1865 Springfield Ill.; reenl reg army 17 Nov 1866 at St Louis for 5 yrs as Thos. Morton;[57] join co D 7 cav 18 Dec 1866 Ft Riley Kans.; cpl 27 Apr 1867; sgt 15 Jan 1868; in arrest June 1871; disch 17 Nov 1871 Yorkville SC expir of serv a sgt; reenl next day in co D for 5 yrs; in arrest Dec 1872; ds qmd Apr 1873 Yankton DT; on furl 90 days 3 Nov 1873 St Paul Minn.; sick hosp Ft Lincoln DT 17 Mar to 18 June 1876 (infl. lungs);[58] dd chg co prop 30 June 1876; sent with Lt Garlington on str *Josephine* 24 July 1876 to join co in field; ds Ft Lincoln 21 Oct 1876 dismtd; disch 18 Nov 1876 at Ft Lincoln expir of serv a sgt char good; reenl 17 Aug 1878 at St Louis for 5 yrs; rejoin co D 20 Nov 1878 at Ft Lincoln; 1sgt 6 Dec 1878; ds Ft Snelling Minn. 24 Sep to 15 Oct 1881 with rifle team comp'n; ds Ft Snelling 27 July to 11 Oct 1882; disch 16 Aug 1883 Ft Yates DT expir of serv a 1sgt char xclt; died 13 Nov 1905 Elmhurst, Alameda Co. Calif.
Pension: 12 Sep 1890 / Inv / 947069 / 748641.

Russell, Jas. Henry. Pvt co C; b. Corpus Christi Tex.; enl 11 Sep 1873 Boston Mass. for 5 yrs; age 21 8/12; school teacher; grey eyes, brn hair, fair comp, 5' 5" high; join co C 21 Oct 1873 Ft Rice DT; dd subs dept herder Oct 1874 to Apr 1875; dd co baker June to Aug 1875; dd post hq Oct 1875; dd qmd Nov 1875 to Feb 1876; killed with Custer column 25 June 1876.

Russell, Thos. Sgt co D; b. Oxford Ind.; enl as Manuel Marshal 11 Dec 1866 Lafayette Ind. for 3 yrs; age 21; shoemaker; brn eyes, dk hair, olive comp, 5' 3" high; assd to co F 24 inf; (consol with 29 inf & desig 11 inf Mar 1869); disch 11 Dec 1869 Austin Tex. by expir of serv a sgt; enl as Thos. Russell 5 Aug 1872 Chicago Ill. for 5 yrs; age 24; laborer; brn eyes, blk hair, dk comp, 5' 4" high; join co D 7 cav 8 Dec 1872 Opelika Ala; cpl 16 Nov 1873; sgt 13 May 1876; disch 23 June 1877 camp Tongue River MT per SO 70 Dept of Dak. 1877 a sgt char xclt; reenl 25 Apr 1878 St Louis Mo. for 5 yrs; age 34; assd to co C 17 inf; disch 24 Apr 1883 Ft Totten DT expir of serv a sgt char good; reenl 2 May 1883 Chicago Ill. for 5 yrs; assd to co E 3 cav; disch 1 May 1888 Ft Clark Tex. expir of serv a cpl char xclt; reenl 10 May 1888 San Antonio Tex. for 5 yrs; assd to co B 16 inf; disch 9 May 1893 Ft Douglas UT expir of serv a sgt char xclt & reenl in same co for 5 yrs; disch 9 Aug 1896 at Ft Douglas per GO 80 AGO 1890 a 1sgt char xclt;[59] reenl 21 Aug 1896 Chicago Ill. for 3 yrs; assd to co H 21 inf; sailed on USAT *Hancock* from San Francisco Calif. 18 Apr 1899 & arr Manila PI 11 May 1899; disch 20 Aug 1899 Los Barros PI expir of serv a sgt char xclt & reenl in same co for 3 yrs; ds gd on USAT *Thomas* to San Francisco 14 Apr 1900; retd 14 July 1900 Presidio San Francisco a sgt char xclt (single); died 28 May 1926 Lettermen Hosp at Presidio.[60]

Rutten, Roman. Pvt co M; b. 13 Aug 1846 Baden Germany; enl 7 Nov 1866 Phil'a Pa. for 5 yrs; age 20; tailor; hazel eyes, lt hair, fair comp, 5' 6 3/4" high; assd to co M 8 cav; disch 7 Nov 1871 Ft Garland Colo. Ty expir of serv a pvt; reenl 17 July 1872 at Phil'a for 5 yrs; join co M 7 cav 1 Sep 1872 Unionville SC; abs sick on str *Western* 23 Apr 1873 Yankton to Ft Rice DT; duty 9 June 1873; dd co tailor Apr 1874; dd co tailor Oct 1874 to

Aug 1875; gsw r. shoulder 26 June 1876 (fl. wd. severe) on Reno hill; tr on str *Far West* 3 July to hosp Ft Lincoln DT; duty 10 Nov 1876; ds Ft Rice Apr to Nov 1877 with co garden; disch 17 July 1877 upon expir of serv a pvt char very good & reenl in co M for 5 yrs; dd co tailor Dec 1877 to Apr 1878; ds Ft Lincoln Aug 1878 in co garden; dd co tailor Feb to Aug 1879; dd co tailor Aug 1880 to Feb 1881; dd co tailor Feb to Apr 1882; disch 16 July 1882 Ft Meade DT expir of serv a pvt & reenl in co M for 5 yrs; dd co tailor Dec 1882; dd co tailor Sep 1886 to May 1887; disch 16 July 1887 at Ft Meade expir of serv a pvt; reenl in co M 1 Nov 1887 Ft Riley Kans. for 5 yrs; tr to co B 9 Sep 1890;[61] disch 21 Sep 1890 at Ft Riley on surg cert dis (gen debility from wds, exposure & long serv) a pvt char xclt; died 16 Apr 1925 Leavenworth Kans.
Pension: 20 Oct 1890 / Inv / 869105 / 671181. Wid / 1233192 / 968969.

Ryan, Dan'l. Cpl co C; b. Syracuse N.Y.; enl 18 Dec 1872 New York N.Y. for 5 yrs; age 21; laborer; grey eyes, dk hair, fair comp, 5' 7 1/4" high; join 7 cav 1 Feb 1873 Louisville Ky. unassd rct; ed qmd detmt hq Apr 1873 Yankton DT; join co C 21 May 1873 Ft Thomson DT; dd co baker Aug 1873; dd co cook Oct 1874 to Apr 1875; cpl 25 Apr 1876; killed with Custer column 25 June 1876.[62]

Ryan, Jno. 1sgt co M; b. 25 Aug 1845 Newton Mass.; pvt co C 28 Mass. inf 1 Jan 1862; des 2 July 1863 Gettysburg Pa.; pvt co I 59 Pa. militia (3 mo troops) 4 Aug 1863; m.o. with co 9 Sep 1863 (never called to duty); rejoined co C 28 Mass. inf June 1864 near Petersburg Va.; gsw l. thigh & l. neck 25 Aug 1864 Ream's Sta Va.; sent home from hosp 13 Dec 1864 for m.o.; pvt co K 61 Mass. inf 30 Jan to 16 July 1865; enl reg army 23 Nov 1866 Boston Mass. for 5 yrs; age 21; carpenter; grey eyes, auburn hair, ruddy comp, 5' 6 1/2" high; join co M 7 cav 10 Dec 1866 Ft Riley Kans.; cpl 1 Feb 1867; des 20 June 1867 camp Platte River Colo. Ty; surd 22 Aug 1867 Ft Kearney Neb; acquited of des'n per gen cm 7 Feb 1868 & ret to duty a pvt; cpl 1 Sep 1868; sgt 1 Jan 1869; 1sgt 3 Feb 1870; sgt 4 Apr 1870; disch 23 Nov 1871 Unionville SC expir of serv a sgt char xclt; reenl in co M 21 Dec 1871 at Unionville for 5 yrs & appt sgt; actg co qm sgt June to Aug 1873; 1sgt 1 Nov 1873; on furl 60 days 15 Nov 1873 Boston Mass.; pvt 16 Apr 1876; 1sgt 9 May 1876; disch 21 Dec 1876 Ft Rice DT expir of serv a 1sgt char xclt; died 14 Oct 1926 West Newton Mass.[63]
Pension: 30 July 1877 / Inv / 239825 / 155938.

Ryan, Stephen L. Pvt co B; b. Tipperary Ireland; enl 17 Nov 1865 New York N.Y. for 3 yrs; age 26 1/2; laborer; blue eyes, brn hair, ruddy comp, 5' 5 1/4" high; assd to co F 3 inf; disch 17 Nov 1868 Ft Dodge Kans. expir of serv a pvt; reenl 8 Dec 1868 St Louis Ars'l Mo. for 3 yrs; assd to ordn detmt; disch 23 Apr 1869 at St Louis Ars'l per GO 27 AGO 1869 (reduce number of enl men in ordn detmt) a 2d cl. pvt; reenl 26 Nov 1869 at St Louis for 5 yrs; join co C 7 cav 17 Dec 1869 Ft L'worth Kans.; tr to co B 12 Feb 1870; in conft Oct & Nov 1872 (asleep on gd duty); sen gen cm 29 Nov 1872 forf $10 pay per mo for 8 mos & conft same period (but sen remitted in consid'n of previous good char); dd co cook Apr 1873; dd hq Blk Hills Exp'n 25 June to 31 Aug 1874; disch 26 Nov 1874 Shreveport La. expir of serv a pvt; reenl in co B 1 Dec 1874 for 5 yrs; dd qmd carpenter Dec 1875 to Feb 1876; dd regtl hq fatigue pty (morn & eve) 11 May 1876; ds Ft Lincoln DT 17 Oct 1876 dismtd; (recom for medal of honor for good cond & securing body of Lt Hodgson at LBH);[64] dd regtl hq fatigue pty 25 Apr 1877; in conft Tongue River MT 19 Oct & with Lt Gibson's detmt to Ft Lincoln 27 Oct 1877; dd co carpenter Feb to Aug 1878; dd qmd Dec 1878 to Nov 1879; disch 30 Nov 1879 Ft Yates DT expir of serv a pvt char good & reenl in co B for 5 yrs; dd qmd Dec 1879 to Apr 1880; ds Green River DT June 1880 guarding prop of troops on NPRR ext'n; injured 29 Aug 1880 when thrown onto withers of his horse; sick hosp Ft Yates DT 19 Sep 1880 to 15 Mar 1881 when disch on surg cert dis (hypertrophy of prostate gland; dis 3/4) a pvt; died 8 Apr 1885 Bismarck DT.
Pension: 9 May 1881 / Inv / 421874 / 197859. Wid / 333153 / 240117. Minor / 554819 / 348260.

Ryder, Hobart. Pvt co M; b. New York N.Y.; enl 15 Sep 1873 Chicago Ill. for 5 yrs; age 27; broker; grey eyes, brn hair, fair comp, 5' 7 1/4" high; join co M 21 Oct 1873 Ft Rice DT; dd co cook Oct 1874; dd subs dept herder Oct 1875; in conft Nov 1875 to Apr 1876; sen gen cm 20 Jan 1876 forf $10 pay per mo for 3 mos & conft same period; ed field hosp nurse 1 July to 14 Sep 1876;[65] arr Ft Rice 21 Sep with Dr. Williams & hosp stew'd Dale; rejoin co 4 Oct 1876 camp near Ft Lincoln; cpl 1 Mar 1877; pvt 25 May 1877; cpl 21 Jan 1878; disch 15 Sep 1878 Camp Ruhlen DT expir of serv a cpl char xclt & reenl in co M for 5 yrs; on furl to Nov 1878 Deadwood DT; witness in gen cm of capt French 27 Jan 1879 at Ft Lincoln;[66] in arrest Aug 1879; sen gen cm 10 Sep 1879 forf $10 pay; sgt 6 Oct 1879; 1sgt 1 Jan 1881; disch 14 Sep 1883 Ft Meade DT expir of serv a 1sgt char xclt & reenl in co M for 5 yrs; ds Ft Snelling Minn. 21 Sep 1883; on furl 6 mos 1 Oct 1883 with perm'n to go to Europe;[67] ds Ft Snelling 26 June to 10 July 1884 witness in gen cm; on furl 20 days 19 July 1888 Ft L'worth Kans.; disch 14 Sep 1888 Ft Riley Kans. expir of serv a 1sgt char xclt & reenl in co M for 5 yrs; awl 15 days 20 Aug 1889 Denver Colo.; attd to co C 9 Sep 1890;[68] sick hosp Hot Springs Ark 4 Oct 1890 to 5 Jan 1891 (dyspepsia & neuralgia); ds rctg duty 5 Jan 1891 Wheeling W.Va.; sgt 31 May 1892 (own req); tr to rctg duty Knoxville Tenn 15 May 1893; ds Greenville Tenn 28 June to 18 Aug 1893; disch 14 Sep 1893 at Knoxville by expir of serv a sgt char xclt; died Wheeling W.Va., suicide says Rutten.[69]

Rye, Wm. W. Pvt co M; b. Pike Co. Ga.; enl 9 Oct 1875 St Louis Bks Mo. for 5 yrs; age 26; farmer; grey eyes, brn hair, fair comp, 5' 8 1/2" high; join co M 21 Oct 1875 Ft Rice DT; des 20 Oct 1876 camp near Bismarck DT; apph 8 June 1877 at Bismarck; escaped from conft 14 Sep 1877 Ft Lincoln DT.

Notes—R

1. Rafter was company quartermaster sergeant, WMC, rosters, LBHB; Rafter told Rutten he was with packs. WMC, rosters, IU; John Foley said he, Rafter and Rott went for water. Hammer, *Custer in '76*, 147; Walter Camp said he met Rafter at Leavenworth. Camp to Godfrey, Oct. 15, 1918, Godfrey Papers.

2. Stanislas Roy said Ragsdale was tall and slim and not a strong constitutioned man for he was always sick or something the matter with him, and was surprised to learn he was still alive in 1909. Roy to Walter Camp, Nov. 6, 1909, WMC-BYU.

3. Ragsdale said he was treated in July or August 1876 for lung disease produced by measles at Livingston, Ala., during winter 1874 and spring 1875. Pension file, RG 15.

4. Francis Johnson Kennedy said he and Ramsey rode down into valley and over to Custer battlefield June 27. Kennedy statement to Olin D. Wheeler, ca. 1900; copied in letter from Albert W. Johnson to Theodore Goldin, May 4, 1933, and typescript copy in Dustin Coll., (No. 435), LBHB.
Korn said Ramsey washed Comanche's wounds in the river, *Winners of the West*, vol. 13, no.2, Jan. 30, 1936; John Mahoney and Peter Eixenberger said Ramsey found Comanche down at river, WMC, transcript, BYU-251; Geo. Albright (alias Charles Smith, Company I, 1876–81), said Ramsey rescued Comanche by carrying water to him in his hat and begged to carry him on the boat and Benteen agreed; Ramsey told Albright this, WMC, Notes, topics A–L, file LBH III, IU.

5. Rosters of Company F with remarks by Rooney and Lynch, WMC-BYU; GO 8, Hq 7th Cavalry, May 12, 1876, organized the regiment into four battalions: (1st), Companies B, C, and I with Capt. Keogh commanding; (2nd), Companies E, F, and L with Capt. Yates commanding; (3rd), Companies A, D, and H with Capt. Weir commanding; (4th), Companies G, K, and M with Capt. French commanding. 1st and 2nd Battalions to constitute the Right Wing, commanded by Maj. Reno, and 3rd and 4th Battalions the Left Wing, under command of Capt. Benteen.
GO 10, Hq 7th Cavalry, May 15, 1876, directed that the dismounted men of each battalion would be placed under the command of a corporal (mounted) detailed from the company having the greatest number of dismounted men; the entire detachment of dismounted men to be under command of a sergeant from the company of the regiment having the greatest number of dismounted men; " Companies B, D, F, and K will each furnish one (1) Corporal and K Company one (1) Sergeant (Mounted) for duty with the dismounted detachment, the detail will be made from these Headquarters." RG 391, Entry 859.

Gen. Custer annulled wing and battalion organizations June 22 on the Yellowstone. Maj. Reno's official report, July 4, 1876, in Nichols, *Reno Court*, 640; "Godfrey Narrative," in Graham, *The Custer Myth*, 130.

6. *Columbus Dispatch*, Jan. 3, 1895; *Columbus Press Post*, Jan. 3, 1895; see also, RG 94, Entry 25, files 32237 PRD 1892, 11059 PRD 1893, and 12509 PRD 1893.

7. Botzer Troop Duty Book. RG 94, Entry 96; RG 94, Entry 409, file 11686 A (EB) 1876; Lt. McIntosh said he found Rapp invaluable and considered himself in better fix than he ever was on an expedition. McIntosh to wife, May 20, 1876. *Newsletter* (LBHA), vol. 24, May 1995; Theo. Goldin said Rapp was McIntosh's striker and was one of the horse holders and was killed with the horses. Goldin to Albert W. Johnson, Feb. 16, 1933, Dustin Coll., (No. 124), LBHB; Thomas O'Neill said Rapp was last man out of timber leading McIntosh's horse. Hammer, *Custer in '76*, 107.

8. Jacob Horner said Charles Schmidt of Company L secured the horse of Michael Ragan on June 22. Burdick and Hart, *Jacob Horner*, 14.

9. *Monroe Commercial*, May 4, 1876; Scheduled departure time of the evening Chicago Express train was 8:20 P.M., and arrived Chicago 6:00 A.M. Gen. Custer and the Reeds are listed among morning arrivals at Chicago's Palmer House, May 4, and with evening arrivals May 5. *Chicago Evening Journal*, May 4, 5, 1876; Autie Reed's letter to his parents, May 6, 1876, from St. Paul, describes events during the trip (typescript copy at Monroe County [Mich.] Library), Lawrence A. Frost Collection.

In a letter to his parents, June 21, 1876, Autie Reed inquired, "school was out by this time is it not." *Newsletter* (LBHA), vol. 28, no. 3, April 1994. Issue includes letter from Autie to his sister, Emma, May 31, 1876.

10. Pay-Roll of citizens employed in Subsistence Department by Lt. R. E. Thompson, 6th Inf., ACS, May to September 1876. Abstract of Contingencies, Settlement 1545, January 1877, and Settlement 1765, April 1877, RG 217, Entry 1002 (UD).

Willis W. Carland, son of Lt. John Carland, Company B, 6th Infantry, also employed as herder, said the quartermaster furnished his horse, and in addition to wages the herders were issued regular rations and had their own mess. Carland to William J. Ghent, Feb. 19, and, Apr. 9, 1934, Ghent Papers.

Gen. Custer detailed enlisted men to guard the cattle at night, thus the young herders had nothing to do but drive them along. Tom Custer to Emma Reed, May 20, 1876, in O'Neil, *Garry Owen Tidbits* VII, 27; Lt. Godfrey said that during the march to Powder River, herders drove the beef herd alongside the wagon train. Godfrey, "Narrative," in Graham, *The Custer Myth*, 127.

11. Roberts was hired as herder by Lt. Smith and was to furnish his own mount. SO 84, Hq Fort Lincoln, May 4, 1876, RG 393, Part V; his pony was completely used up by June 15, and as no other horse could be procured, Roberts was left behind at the supply camp at Powder River. Later, on advice from Gen. Terry relayed by Capt. Hughes (of Terry's staff), who came down on the steamer *Far West* with the wounded July 4, Roberts got on the boat and returned to Fort Lincoln. Roberts, *Custer's Last Battle*, 24–25.

12. Tom Custer to Emma Reed, May 30, 1876, O'Neil, *Garry Owen Tidbits, VII,* 29. Gen. Custer wrote to Libbie, May 30, that many of the horses tumbled their riders into the water, but everyone laughed at everyone else's mishaps. E. B. Custer, *Boots and Saddles*, 297.

13. Autie Reed to his parents, June 21, 1876, *Newsletter* (LBHA), vol. 28, no. 3, April 1994; Willis W. Carland, (son of Lt. Carland, Company B, 6th Infantry on steamer *Far West*), who was also employed as herder in the subsistence department, related that from Powder River several head of meat cattle were put on the boat and after the battle the two or three steers yet remaining were taken off and left at the camp at mouth of Big Horn. *Winners of the West*, vol. 7, no. 10, Sept. 30, 1930, 8.

Elsewhere, Carland said five or six steers were put on the boat at Powder River and he had charge of them. Said George W. Morgan, another herder, was also on the boat and delighted in shocking Carland with language he had never heard before. Carland to William J. Ghent, Mar. 22, 1934, Ghent Papers.

James Coleman, trader on the boat, said George Morgan translated Curley's signs and speech when he came on the boat June 28. Morgan had a Crow wife and had a wood yard near the Muddy River, east of Fort Buford on the Missouri River. Libby, *Arikara Narrative*, 208.

Morgan arrived at camp mouth of Big Horn River, July 9, with dispatches from Powder River, and returned to Powder River with mail July 14. Willert, *March of the Columns*, 104, 129; he was discharged as herder July 31, and hired as a scout at $100 per month. RG 92, Entry 238, report 1876/328; Morgan was born about 1850 in Huntington Co., Pa., and served with the detachment of Indian Scouts at Fort Buford, 1870–71.

14. Lt. Edgerly said Reed accompanied the regiment eager to see the fighting if any. Edgerly interview, n.d., with Walter Camp, WMC-BYU; Autie Reed's father, David, on learning of the tragedy, departed Monroe on the evening train, July 7. He left St. Paul the evening of July 11 for Fort Lincoln to accompany Mrs. Custer and Mrs. Calhoun to the home of their parents. Frost, *General Custer's Libbie*, 229; *St. Paul Dispatch*, July 11, 1876.

Autie's remains were not removed from the battlefield until Dec. 1877, the Secretary of War having authorized exhumation of none but officers in July 1877. Through efforts of Lt. Fred Calhoun, 14th Infantry (brother of Lt. James Calhoun), at Camp Robinson Neb., and Frank D. Yates (brother of Capt. Yates), trader at Red Cloud Agency (adjacent Camp Robinson), Mr. W. H. Brown, father-in-law of Mr. Yates, took charge of the removal of the remains of Autie and his uncle Bos.

Frank Yates was under government contract to supply hay to Fort Custer, at mouth of the Little Big Horn River, RG 92, Entry 778, Claim "U" 354 QMGO 1878; Lt. Col. Buell, 11th Inf., post commander, Fort Custer, to AAG, Dept. of Dakota, Oct 28, 1877, (4591 DD 1877), NA, M1734, Roll 22.

They were located in Oct. 1877 by Mr. Kittrell, agent for Mr. Yates, and brought by means of transportation belonging to Mr. Yates, to Cheyenne, Wyo., Jan. 2, 1878. The next day they were shipped express to Chicago where they were met by Autie's father, thence taken charge of by Mr. George Chase, Secretary to the Superintendent of Lake Shore & Michigan Southern Railway. (Gen. Custer, with his niece and nephew in tow, had visited Chase at the train depot in Chicago in early May 1876.)

Upon arrival at Monroe the morning of Jan 11, a procession was formed by friends and relatives to Woodland Cemetery and appropriate burial service held, *The Daily Leader* (Cheyenne, Wyo.), Jan. 3, 4, 1878; *Monroe Commercial*, Jan. 11, 1878.

Emma Reed married Fred Calhoun in 1879. She died Dec. 11, 1949, at Back Bay, Mass. See Buecker, "Frederic S. Calhoun."

15. Botzer Troop Duty Book (missing pages) shows Reed on daily duty May 13 to June 8 and June 19–20, 22; Lt. McIntosh recorded the number of Company "G" men left at Powder River (17); present (42); and at bottom of page, "Add to 'Present' Pvt. Reed joined." Donald McIntosh, Notebook, 1876 (hereafter cited as McIntosh Notebook), Little Big Horn Battlefield Collections, Crow Agency, MT.

16. Company "G" returns, July and August, show Reed on detached service at Yellowstone Depot from June 15, whereas the regimental returns show Reed on detached service on Yellowstone River as Guard on steamer from June 15. He is absent on the Muster Roll, Aug. 31, without remark. (Reed is not absent on the muster roll, or returns of June 1876.) RG 94, Entry 53; LBHB Coll., Roll 12; NA, M744.

17. Brown Troop Duty Book. Reynolds and Brown, *Journal*.

18. RG 153, file RR 3884; Burial Record Book, Custer Battlefield National Monument, LBHB Coll., Roll 14.

19. Pandtle (Pendle) to Walter Camp, July 14, 1919, WMC-BYU; WMC, rosters, IU.

20. The company return, Aug. 1876, report Reese as company teamster. After the columns of Gen. Terry and Gen. Crook united on the Rosebud, August 10, Terry was much impressed with Crook's train of pack mules. He promptly ordered one organized by selection from his wagon teams, and the next day sent all wagons back to the supply camp on the Yellowstone. Willert, *March of the Columns*, 343; Finerty, *War-Path and Bivouac*, 165.

21. Blake said Reeves was severely wounded in the timber before the retreat started. Hardorff, *On the Little Big Horn with Walter Camp,* 181; Hardy said Reeves was shot through the body and knocked off his horse before Hardy mounted, but got on again and rode out of the bottom. WMC, notes, file LBH II, Topics A–L, IU.

22. RG 94, Entry 544, MT, Prescription Book No. 54; Dr. DeWolf to wife, May 22, 1876, Luce, ed., "The Diary and Letters of Dr. James M. DeWolf"; WMC, rosters, LBHB; Rosters of Company F with remarks by Rooney and Lynch, WMC-BYU.

23. RG 94, Entry 25, file 52574 AGO 1897.

24. See note M60 (Murray).

25. Lt. Reily's mother applied to President Grant, May 5, 1875, for an appointment for her son as lieutenant in the cavalry service, stating that his father was an officer in the U.S. Navy and was lost with the Brig. *Porpoise*. ACP file, RG 94, Entry 297.

The *Porpoise* was a ten-gun brigantine that put out to sea June 11, 1853, from Hampton Roads, Va., as part of an exploring squadron, and after rounding the Cape of Good Hope and charting many Pacific islands, arrived in China in March 1854. *Porpoise* left the other vessels Sept. 21, 1854, between Formosa and China, and was never heard from again, presumed to have foundered in a heavy typhoon which occurred a few days later. Mooney, ed., *Dictionary of American Naval Fighting Ships*, vol. 5, 353–54.

26. Reily was reportedly transferred "at Doctor's request," his mother having agitated for his transfer to a white regiment. Pohanka, "Profile: Lieut. William Van Wyck Reily"; see also Viola, *Little Big Horn Remembered*, 182–85.

27. Uncertainty exists regarding Maj. Reno's birth date. The federal census of 1840 recorded only the name of head of household, and the number of males and females, in age groups of five-year increments, within the household, but the next federal census, Nov. 27, 1850, at Carrollton Ill., lists Marcus A. Reno, age 15 years.

In the Descriptive List of New Cadets for the Year 1851 (USMA), Reno's entry August 25, 1851, in the age column, ("Yrs/Mos," topped by "Age the 1st July"), he is 16 years 9 months, but the 9 is crossed out and 10 written above it, but apparently erased. His "Engagement for Service and Oath of Allegiance," dated September 1, 1851, gives his age as sixteen years nine months, and the "Cadets Admitted Book" for the years 1846–1912 indicates under "Candidates for 1851" that Reno was admitted September 1, 1851, age 16 years 9 months. (Records and Manuscripts, USMA Archives); see also Alfield, "Major Reno and His Family in Illinois.".

28. Reno received a commission of brevet 2nd lieutenant, until a regular opening occurred at that grade, the number of cavalry officers having been fixed by Congress., Nichols, *In Custer's Shadow*, 21.

29. Henry C. Reno, (born Carrollton, Ill.), age 25, enlisted in Company I, 1st U.S. Cavalry, Sept. 18, 1864, at Berryville, Va. He was wounded at Cedar Creek in Oct. 1864 and subsequently discharged from Hicks General Hospital in Baltimore in Feb. 1866, a sergeant. He became a successful physician and surgeon and died at Spokane, Wash., Sept. 16, 1893. His pension file (XC-2,667,018), RG 15, and newspaper obituary, mention no family names.

30. Reno received news July 13, 1874, of the death of his wife three days earlier in Harrisburg, but his request for leave of absence was denied by Gen. Terry. Nichols, *In Custer's Shadow*, 134.

31. For a discussion on the number of men in Reno's battalion, June 25, 1876, see Stewart, "Variations on a Minor Theme."

Lt. Baldwin, 5th Infantry, said he had a long talk with Maj. Reno in camp at the mouth of the Rosebud, Aug. 7, 1876, and Reno related that when he first charged on June 25, he had 112 men. Willert, *March of the Columns*, 309.

Reno testified that, before crossing at the ford, during his advance to the attack, he sent word to his company commanders to report the number of men they had in the saddle. Nichols, *Reno Court*, 591.

32. See note W8 (Wallace).

33. See Nichols, *Reno Court of Inquiry*; Utley, *The Reno Court of Inquiry*.

34. Johnson, *Case of Marcus A. Reno*, 25..

35. The country traversed was thick with roving bands of hostile Indians and Gen. Custer gave Reynolds his choice of government horses for a suitable mount, which Reynolds then had equipped to his own specifications. The farrier took the horses shoes off and pared his hoofs neatly. The saddler made a set of leather shoes to fit the horse's feet so as to buckle around the fetlocks. Reynolds said they were a little dodge of his to fool the Indians, they make no trail, *Bismarck Tribune*, Aug. 23, 1876.

Private Dennis Lynch said Schlieper of "F" Troop sat up all night making leather shoes for Reynold's horse, which he used after getting out of the mountains so horse's hooves would not cut the grass and make it possible for Indians to track him. Reynolds delivered the dispatches and returned to Fort Lincoln by rail. When the regiment returned and marched in to the music of the band, Reynolds was sitting on the fence watching and all the men gave him a big cheering. WMC, transcript, BYU-200; Libby, *Arikara Narrative*, 170.

Sgt. John Henley (Company B, 1870–75) said John Bailey made the boots for Reynolds' horse when Reynolds went to Laramie. Liddic and Harbaugh, *Camp On Custer*, 61.

36. The party included George Bird Grinnell and Philetus W. Norris, future superintendent of Yellowstone Park. Best, "A Life of Mystery"; Remsburg and Remsburg, *Charley Reynolds*; see also Reiger, ed., *The Passing of the Great West*, 108–21.

37. Lt. Varnum said he took Charley Reynolds to the Crow's Nest for someone "to talk to," and in case of trouble he would be the only person he could depend on, as the Indians would all scatter on their own account. Carroll, *Custer's Chief of Scouts*, 61–62, 87.

38. RG 92, Entry 238, reports 1872/146, 1873/36, 1873/177, 1874/51, 1875/314, and 1876/328; Hanson, *The Conquest of the Missouri*, 249, 263; Hammer, *Custer in '76*, 223; Gray, "Last Rites for Lonesome Charley Reynolds.".

39. Sgt. Ryan said Sgt. Capes and Private Widdemeyer of M Troop were left at Powder River with the company teams and probably one or two other privates as company teamsters. Taylor Scrapbook, 94; see also Taylor, *With Custer on the Little Big Horn*, 179.

40. Farrier Rivers was one of sixteen 7th Cavalrymen discharged by SFO 37, Hq DD, Aug. 5, 1876, RG 94, Entry 44, to enable them to go down river by the first boat; Capt. Keogh's horse, Comanche, was also transported on the steamer *Durfee*. See Gray, "Veterinary Service on Custer's Last Campaign."

"John Rivers of Company I will conscientiously observe that he [Comanche] is never required to endure any more work. His stall will be the cleanest and warmest at the fort, and his forage the best the army affords." *Bismarck Tribune*, May 10, 1878.

41. Report of Maj. Merrill, Sept. 18, 1877, includes casualties in his battalion. NA, M1734, Roll 23 (4989 DD 1877); see also Greene, *Nez Perce Summer 1877*, 367.

42. Liddic and Harbaugh, *Camp On Custer*, 77.

43. Darling, *Custer's Seventh Cavalry Comes to Dakota*, 146.

44. SO 44, Hq 7th Cavalry, Fort Lincoln, DT, May 16, 1876, RG 391, Entry 859. Dr. Elbert J. Clark attended the Left Wing (Companies A, D, G, H, K, and M) during the march from Fort Lincoln to Powder River, where he was placed in charge of the field hospital, and gave his horse and equipment to Dr. Lord, June 15.

Robinson evidently continued as hospital attendant with the left wing, accompanying Dr. Lord to the Rosebud, where, presumably, he was assigned to Dr. Porter. (Robinson was reported present "On Extra duty in Medical Dept," on the Company M muster roll June 30, mouth of Little Big Horn River.) RG 94, Entry 53; see Pvt. Pendle, Co. E.

45. Dr. Blair Taylor was post surgeon at Fort Rice, Oct. 8, 1875 to July 22, 1876, when ordered to report to Gen. Terry for field duty, and joined the expedition on the Yellowstone, Aug. 2. Private Robinson was detailed with Dr. Taylor per SO 65, Hq 7th Cavalry, Camp mouth of Rosebud, MT, Aug. 4, 1876, RG 391, Entry 859; Private Sweeney, Company F, was detailed with Dr. Porter per SFO 38, Hq DD, Aug. 6, 1876, RG 94, Entry 44.

46. Botzer Troop Duty Book.

47. WMC, rosters, IU.

48. Rosters of Company F with remarks by Rooney and Lynch, WMC-BYU; Gregg interview with Walter Camp, n.d., WMC-BYU.

49. RG 94, Entry 544, USA Medical Register No. 9.

50. Roster of Company L from Walter Camp, Nov. 20, 1908, to John Burkman, with remarks added by Burkman, LBHB Coll., Roll 9.

51. *Bismarck Tribune*, Oct. 10, 1877.

52. Louis Rott name pronounced "Raught," WMC, rosters, IU; John Foley said he, Rott and Rafter went for water at Little Big Horn. Hammer, *Custer in '76*, 147.

53. *Bismarck Tribune*, January 6, 13, April 19, 26, 1879; RG 94, Entry 409, file 8548 A (EB) 1879.

54. Roy to Walter Camp, Dec. 18, 1909, WMC-BYU; Roy said the medals were given to the men on Christmas Day by Col. Sturgis at Fort Lincoln. Roy to Camp, Mar. 4, 1909, with answers to Camp's questionnaire. WMC-BYU.

55. See note M60 (Murray).

56. Roy's story appeared in the *Piqua* (Ohio) *Daily Call*, July 4, 1907, and is included in, *Pioneer History of Kansas*, by Adolph Roenigk; see also, *Indianapolis* (Ind.) *Star*, April 21, 1907.

57. Having been a captain in the volunteer service, Rush reenlisted in the regular army as Thomas Morton because he did not want his friends to know he had accepted a lower rank. Statement in deposition of former neighbor, John McCrory, Nov. 3, 1904, Rush, pension file, RG 15.

58. Morton (Rush) said he caught a bad cold during the severe winter of 1875–76, the barracks being poor at Fort Lincoln. When taken with fever, typhoid pneumonia, he was in hospital about four months and on release was still suffering effects, hardly able to walk. Shortly before his discharge, Troop D was ordered to Standing Rock Agency, and the doctor did not allow him to go, so he was left in charge of a lot of dismounted and disabled men, Deposition, Dec. 5, 1903, in pension file, RG 15.

59. See note D26 (Diamond).

60. RG 94, Entry 25, file 17043 PRD 1890; RG 94, Entry 91.

61. GO 79, AGO, July 25, 1890, RG 94, Entry 44, skeletonized Troops L and M and the privates transferred to other troops within the regiment. Chandler, *Of Garryowen in Glory*, 80.

62. Cpl. Martin Ryan was rumored to have been captured in the fight and held prisoner in Sitting Bull's camp near Fort Walsh, Canada, in 1877. The story was given little credence at the time because of

its improbability, though numerous reports appeared in various newspapers, including the *Bismarck Tribune*, Nov. 26, 1877 and Jan. 3, 17, 1878, and the *Deseret News* (Salt Lake City, Utah), Jan. 9, 1878; the tale was officially dented by Sir Edward Farrington of the Dominion government, on whose insistence the camp was searched, and the alleged facts in the case found to have no foundation whatever. *Bismarck Tribune*, May 17, 1878; see also Manzione, *I Am Looking to the North for My Life*, 112–13.

63. See Barnard, *Custer's First Sergeant John Ryan*; Barnard, *Ten Years with Custer*.

64. "Private Stephen Ryan not only behaved well during the battle of June 25th and 26th but when his company changed its position on the evening of the 26th to the banks of the river, he volunteered to secure the body of Lieut. Benjamin Hodgson which was a quarter of a mile away which he succeeded in doing, carrying the body all this distance over a rough unbroken country, after which he dug a grave and buried the body, for which kind, as well as arduous duty I recommend Private Stephen Ryan for a medal of honor." Capt. McDougall to Lt. E. A. Garlington, adjutant, Mar. 17, 1878, RG 94, Entry 409, file 10818 A (EB) 1878.

65. Hobart Ryder and Mark E. Lee were assigned to hospital duty July 1st by verbal order (per SFO 35, Hq DD, Aug. 2, 1876, RG 94, Entry 44); Lee was reported sick on the Steamer *Far West* from June 22 (Company Return, Co. I, LBHB Coll., Roll 12). The boat, with Gen. Terry, his staff, and the wounded, arrived at Col. Gibbon's supply camp at mouth of Big Horn River, June 30, whereas the 7th Cavalry did not reach that point until the evening of July 2. Walter Camp noted that if Ryder and Lee "had been on boat they would have been already on detail." WMC, box 2, folder 10, IU.

Hospital steward Dale, who was with Dr. Williams on the *Far West*, did not know whether Ryder and Lee were on the boat June 22 to 30, but did recall that Ryder had "Kaiser" the trick horse of the 7th Cavalry and he (Dale) rode him a good deal. WMC, notes, Topics A–L, folder LBH II, IU.

Dale thought Ryder was detailed as nurse or surgeon's orderly at Powder River on the way out and went with Custer's command. He went down with the wounded on the boat. Liddic and Harbaugh, *Camp on Custer*, 105–106.

66. RG 153, file QQ994. In his testimony, Ryder described his experience in Reno's valley fight.

67. Also on furlough to Europe, Sept. 28, 1883, was Private William Schmidt (born in Krumpel, Germany), a member of Company M since December, 1878.

68. GO 79, AGO, 1890, skeletonized Troops L and M and attached noncommissioned officers to other troops of the regiment. Chandler, *Of Garryowen in Glory*, 80.

69. WMC, rosters, IU. Walter Camp interviewed Roman Rutten in Feb. 1910. Camp to Stanislas Roy, Mar. 2, 1910, WMC-LBHB.

S

Saas, Wm. Pvt co I; b. Strasburg Germany; enl 2 Jan 1872 Cincinnati Ohio for 5 yrs; age 23; cigar maker; blue eyes, lt hair, fair comp, 5' 7" high; join co I 1 Feb 1872 Shelbyville Ky.; dd co cook Oct to Dec 1872; dd detmt hq June 1873; ds Ft Lincoln DT 17 May 1876 in co garden; ds Ft Lincoln 16 Oct 1876 chg co prop; disch 2 Jan 1877 at Ft Lincoln expir of serv a pvt char good; enl in marine corps 23 Mar 1877 Wash'n D.C. for 5 yrs; des 7 Jan 1878 while on liberty; reenl in army 9 Jan 1878 Baltimore Md for 5 yrs; join co M 6 cav 12 Mar 1878 Ft Huachuca AT; cpl 25 Nov 1878; sgt 23 Nov 1879; (recom for cert of merit for bravery in action with Apache inds at Huachuca Mtns 28 Apr 1882 when he rode amidst a shower of bullets & rescued two comrades left behind dismtd in range of the enemy);[1] disch 8 Jan 1883 Ft Bowie AT expir of serv a sgt char xclt; reenl 5 Feb 1883 at Cincinnati for 5 yrs; surd as des'r 19 Feb 1883 at Cincinnati & dropped from rolls of army per Regs. par. 224; supt rctg serv recom pardon for des'n from marine corps.

Sadler, Wm. Pvt co D; b. 10 Feb 1855 Frankfurt Germany; enl 9 Aug 1875 New York N.Y. for 5 yrs; age 21; saddler; grey eyes, lt hair, fair comp, 5' 7" high; join co D 21 Oct 1875 Ft Lincoln DT; ds camp Powder River MT 15 June 1876 guarding wagon train; dd qmd Dec 1876; ds Carroll MT Sep 1877; dd repairing horse equipment Apr 1878; dd actg co sad'r Feb 1880; disch 8 Aug 1880 Ft Yates DT expir of serv a pvt char xclt; died 12 Nov 1921 Linton N.Dak.
Pension: 17 Apr 1917 / Ind. Surv. / 11622 / 7324.

Sager, Hiram W. Pvt co B; b. 27 Nov 1850 Westport N.Y.; enl 26 Oct 1872 Troy N.Y. for 5 yrs; age 21; farmer; blue eyes, brn hair, ruddy comp. 5' 10" high; join co B 9 Dec 1872 Spartanburg SC; dd co cook Aug 1873; des 6 Apr 1874 Ft Lincoln DT; apph 14 Apr near Jamestown DT; sen gen cm 18 June 1874 to 2 yrs confnt at sta of co thence to dishon disch; unexpired portion of sen remitted 19 Dec 1874; dd co cook Feb 1875; dd hosp attdt July 1875 to Mar 1876; dd co cook Apr 1877; disch 23 July 1877 Cedar Creek MT per GO 47 AGO 1877 a pvt char good;[2] reenl in co B 9 Apr 1878 Standing Rock DT for 5 yrs; dd cook post hosp June to Aug 1878; dd co kit'n Oct 1878; dd co cook Feb to Apr 1879; dd co cook Feb 1880; ds Camp Houston DT Oct 1880 with escort for NPRR ext'n; cpl 1 Feb 1881; sgt 1 Jan 1882; disch 8 Apr 1883 Ft Yates DT expir of serv a sgt; died 21 Dec 1907 Spokane Wash'n.
Pension: 27 Mar 1917 / Ind. Wid. / 12118 / 9559.

St. John, Ludwick. Pvt co C; b. 3 Mar 1848 Columbia Mo.; enl in co C 15 Dec 1869 Ft L'worth Kans. for 5 yrs; age 25; farmer; grey eyes, brn hair, fair comp, 5' 9" high; cpl 17 Aug 1871; pvt 20 Feb 1872; cpl 15 Oct 1872; disch 15 Dec 1874 Ft Rice DT expir of serv a cpl & reenl in co C for 5 yrs; des 8 May 1875 at Ft Rice; surd 25 June 1875 Rock Isl. Ars'l Ill.; sen gen cm 20 Nov 1875 to 2 yrs confnt mil prison but mitigated to 8 mos confnt at sta of co; appd to regtl hq 29 Feb 1876 to join his co, feeling it a disgrace to be left behind when co went into the field; unexpired portion of sen remitted 28 Apr 1876 acc't prior good char & promise of future good cond; killed with Custer column 25 June 1876.
Pension: 6 May 1887 / Father / 769337 / 570128. Mother / 354672 / 245680.

Sanders, Chas. Pvt co D; b. 8 May 1842 Altenburg Germany; enl 23 May 1861 Chicago Ill. for 3 yrs; age 21; laborer; blue eyes, lt hair, fair comp, 5' 7" high; assd to co M 2 art'y; disch 1 Feb 1864 Brandy Sta Va. by reenlmt in co for 3 yrs; disch 2 Feb 1867 Presidio San Francisco Calif. by expir of serv a pvt; reenl 16 May 1867 New York N.Y. for 3 yrs; assd to gen serv inf; des 11 Dec 1867 at rct rendevouz NYC; reenl 26 Jan 1872 Chicago Ill. for 5 yrs; join co D 7 cav 24 Feb 1872 Chester SC; orderly for Lt Edgerly 25

265

June 1876; (recom for medal of honor for conspic gal);³ dd orderly regtl hq 12 Nov 1876; disch 26 Jan 1877 Ft Lincoln DT expir of serv a pvt char xclt; enl in marine corps 14 Feb 1877 Brooklyn N.Y. for 5 yrs; des 22 Jan 1878; reenl in army 24 Jan 1878 New York N.Y. for 5 yrs; join co H 6 cav 18 Mar 1878 Camp Bowie AT; dropped from rolls of army 7 May 1878 (auth AGO) a des'r from marine corps; reenl co H 6 cav 4 June 1878 (to date 7 May) at Camp Bowie; in arrest 8 July 1879 when recognized as des'r from gen serv; restored to duty per SO 204 AGO 4 Sep 1879 with co H 6 cav to serve bal of orig'l enlmt; disch 8 Feb 1882 Ft Verde AT expir of serv a pvt char xclt; reenl 28 Sep 1886 Ft Grant AT for 5 yrs; assd to co B 8 inf; disch 27 Sep 1891 Ft Niobrara Neb expir of serv a pvt char very good; reenl in same co 1 Oct 1891 at Ft Niobrara for 5 yrs; tr to band 17 Aug 1896; disch 30 Sep 1896 Ft Russell Wyo. expir of serv a pvt char xclt; reenl in band 2 Oct 1896 at Ft Russell; tr to co F 13 Oct 1896; on furl 6 mos 26 Apr 1897 to Germany; prom sgt 11 Oct 1897; retd 25 Oct 1897 a sgt char xclt; died 29 Aug 1915 Lincoln Neb.

Saunders, Rich'd. Pvt co F; b. Yarmouth Nova Scotia; enl 16 Aug 1875 Boston Mass. for 5 yrs; age 22; stonemason; blue eyes, brn hair, dk comp, 5' 9 3/8" high; join co F 21 Oct 1875 Ft Lincoln DT; dd co cook Apr 1876; killed with Custer column 25 June 1876.

Schele, Henry. Pvt co E; b. Hanover Germany; enl 5 Dec 1867 New York N.Y. for 5 yrs; age 24; laborer; blue eyes, lt hair, fair comp, 5' 6" high; join co E 22 Jan 1868 Ft L'worth Kans.; ds with survey exp'n May to Oct 1869; dd co cook Dec 1871 to Sep 1872; disch 5 Dec 1872 Unionville SC expir of serv a pvt; reenl in co E 19 Dec 1872 at Unionville for 5 yrs; ed hosp attdt Jan to Sep 1873; ds Ft Lincoln DT June to Aug 1874; ed subs dept Feb to Apr 1875; dd co cook Aug 1875; killed with Custer column 25 June 1876.

Schlafer, Christian. Trump'r co K; b. Cincinnati Ohio; pvt co K 192 Ohio inf 30 Jan to 1 Sep 1865; enl reg army 2 Oct 1868 at Cincinnati for 5 yrs; age 21; gas fitter; grey eyes, lt hair, fair comp, 5' 6" high; assd to co A 5 cav; disch 2 Oct 1873 Camp Verde AT expir of serv a trump'r; reenl 24 Mar 1875 at Cincinnati for 5 yrs; assd to co K 7 cav 14 May 1875 a trump'r; ds St Louis Bks Mo. June 1875; sick 17 Nov to 24 Dec 1875 (const. syph.); sick 23 Feb to 3 Mar 1876 (const. syph.); sick qrs camp at Ft Buford DT 14 Nov 1877 (cont'n face from blow); duty 29 Nov 1877; disch 23 Mar 1880 Ft Totten DT expir of serv a trump'r char good; reenl 6 Oct 1881 at Cincinnati for 5 yrs; join co A 7 cav 3 Nov 1881 Ft Meade DT a trump'r; cpl 4 Sep 1883; sgt 11 May 1884; disch 5 Oct 1886 at Ft Meade expir of serv a sgt char xclt; reenl 18 Oct 1886 at Cincinnati for 5 yrs; rejoin co A 1 May 1887 Ft Keogh MT; cpl 6 May 1887; sgt 21 Sep 1888; disch 8 Aug 1890 Ft Riley Kans. per SO 179 AGO 1890 (by way of favor upon own appn) a sgt char xclt; reenl for co A 14 Sep 1892 at Cincinnati for 5 yrs; join co 20 Sep at Ft Riley; sd cook post mess hall June to Oct 1893; tr to co C 6 inf 16 Oct 1893; disch 13 Dec 1895 Ft Thomas Ky. under sec. 2 act of congress appv 16 June 1890;⁴ reenl 3 Mar 1896 at Cincinnati for 3 yrs; join co K 7 cav 12 Apr 1896 Ft Huachuca AT; cpl 7 Sep 1896; sgt 1 Feb 1897; disch 30 July 1897 at Ft Huachuca per SO 170 AGO 1897 (upon own app'n to enter Sol. Home) a sgt; died 11 Feb 1905 at Cincinnati.
Pension: 7 Aug 1891 / Inv / 1050402 / 735922. Dropped from rolls 4 Dec 1896 failure to claim 3 yrs. (Erroneously paid while in serv 14 Sep 1892 to 3 Sep 1893). Appv for renewal 28 Nov 1899.

Schleiffarth, Paul. Pvt co F; b. Berlin Prussia; pvt cos A & C 1 Mo. cav 1 Aug 1861 to 1 Sep 1865; enl reg army 15 Dec 1866 St Louis Mo. for 5 yrs; age 27; butcher; grey eyes, brn hair, fair comp, 5' 6 1/2" high; join co F 23 Mar 1867 Ft Harker Kans.; sen gen cm 12 May 1868 forf $13 pay per mo for 6 mos; (unexpired portion of sen rem'd 22 June 1868); dd co cook July 1868; ed butcher comsy dept Oct 1868; dd regtl hq Dec 1868 to Apr 1869 cook for ncs; ds butcher comsy dept May to Aug 1869; ed comsy dept May to Oct 1870; dd co cook Nov 1870; dd co cook Jan 1871; dd regtl hq Apr 1871; ds Taylor Bks Ky. 22 July 1871;

dd co cook Oct 1871; dd cook for band Nov 1871; disch 15 Dec 1871 Taylor Bks Ky. expir of serv a pvt & reenl in co F for 5 yrs; dd regtl hq June to Sep 1872; dd dept hq Oct & Nov 1872; ed subs dept butcher Apr to July 1873; ds exp'n hq butcher Aug 1873; ed subs dept butcher 29 Sep 1873; ed subs dept butcher June to Aug 1874; ed subs dept butcher with exp'n 6 May 1876; [with wagon train says Rooney; doubtful with packs says Lynch];[5] ed subs dept June & Aug 1876; cpl 3 Oct 1876 & dd chg co mess; disch 15 Dec 1876 Ft Abercrombie DT expir of serv a cpl char xclt; reenl same day in co F for 5 yrs & on furl 15 days; dd actg co qm sgt Feb 1877; ds Ft Abercrombie 12 Apr 1877 chg co garden; arr Ft Lincoln 28 Oct 1877 enroute to proper sta; tr to Ft Totten DT 4 Nov with detmt co F; pvt 29 Jan 1878; dd co teamster June 1878; (due US $116.66 for one cav horse & halter lost thro' carelessness Oct 1881); dd co cook Oct 1881; disch 14 Dec 1881 Ft Buford DT expir of serv a pvt char very good; reenl 13 Jan 1882 Ft Lincoln DT for 5 yrs in co I 7 cav; cpl 1 July 1882; ed qmd overseer of teamsters Dec 1882 to Apr 1883; pvt 1 July 1884 (own req); ed cook post hosp June 1886; disch 12 Jan 1887 at Ft Totten expir of serv a pvt char xclt; reenl 21 Jan 1887 Jeff'n Bks Mo. for 5 yrs; join co F 7 cav 5 Dec 1887 Ft Meade DT; sick hosp 2–18 Apr 1888 (cont'n r. leg while drunk); dd co cook Aug & Oct 1888; dd co cook Apr 1889; dd co gardener Dec 1889; retd 10 Dec 1890 a pvt char xclt; died 19 Nov 1896 Ft Thomas Ky. (chr. dysentery).[6]

Schlieper, Claus. Sad'r co F; b. Wipperode Hesse Cassel Germany; enr 16 Dec 1861 New York N.Y. a pvt co I 41 N.Y. inf for 3 yrs; wag 1 Jan 1863; pvt Aug 1863; disch 3 Jan 1864 Folly Isl SC by reenlmt in co as vet vol; age 28 6/12; shoemaker; brn eyes, brn hair, healthy comp, 5' 7" high; on furl Feb & Mar 1864 New York; ds Wash'n D.C. Apr 1864; cpl 1 Nov 1864; sgt 1 Nov 1865; m.o. vol serv 9 Dec 1865; enl reg army 17 Dec 1866 Cincinnati Ohio for 5 yrs; age 29; shoemaker; brn eyes, dk hair, lt comp, 5' 9 3/4" high; join co F 7 cav 23 Mar 1867 Ft Harker Kans.; ds Ft Hays Kans. chg co prop June 1867; sen gen cm 19 Mar 1868 forf $12 pay per mo for 2 mos; dd co cook Sep 1869; appt sad'r 18 Mar 1870; disch 17 Dec 1871 Louisville Ky. expir of serv a sad'r & reenl in co F for 5 yrs; sick qrs (ac. diar.) 4–13 Mar 1876; sick hosp (ac. diar.) 1–8 May 1876; [sick at wagon train says Rooney; left at Powder River says Lynch; not sure says Gregg];[7] sick hosp (chr. diar.) 15 Nov to 4 Dec 1876; disch 17 Dec 1876 Ft Abercrombie DT expir of serv a sad'r char xclt; reenl same day in co F for 5 yrs & on furl 30 days; awl 15–29 Jan 1877 St Paul Minn.; abs sick (ac. diar) 26 Oct 1877 enroute to Ft Lincoln DT; tr to Ft Totten DT 4 Nov with detmt co F; sick hosp (chr. diar.) Ft Lincoln 2 June 1880; tr to Ft Totten 6 Aug 1880; duty Oct 1880; sick hosp from 4 Jan 1881; pvt 1 Mar 1881; disch 26 Mar 1881 Ft Buford DT on surg cert dis a pvt char xclt (chr. diar. contr line of duty; dis total; entitled to every consid'n for his faithful serv); took passage on str *General Sherman* 22 Apr 1881 to Bismarck [with sgt Drago];[8] res 72 Watts St, N.Y. City.
Pension: 7 Apr 1881 / Inv / 420917; (appd thro' capt Bell who req claim be adjusted speedily as sol. much in need of assistance, being entirely disabled to support himself by labor tho' not so helpless as to require an attdt); failed to appear for med exam'n Mar 1883 at N.Y. City; appn rej 15 Nov 1888 clmt not heard from since date of filing.

Schmidt, Chas. Pvt co L; b. Wertumburg Germany; enl 14 Nov 1872 New York N.Y. for 5 yrs; age 23; laborer; brn eyes, brn hair, fair comp, 5' 8 1/2" high; join co L 9 Dec 1872 Yorkville SC; [secured the horse of pvt Ragan in June 1876 says Horner];[9] killed with Custer column 25 June 1876.

Schutte, Fred'k. Pvt co F; b. Rohden Prussia: enl 10 Sep 1867 Cincinnati Ohio for 5 yrs; age 21; laborer; blue eyes, lt hair, fair comp, 5' 5 1/2" high; assd to co D 2 cav; des 2 Aug 1868 Ft Steele Wyo. Ty; enl as Chas. Miller 27 Mar 1871 Pittsburgh Pa. for 5 yrs; join co F 7 cav 27 May 1871 Taylor Bks (Louisville) Ky.; dd post mail carrier June to Aug 1872; in conft Feb 1873; unfit for duty with Yellowstone Exp'n 21 July 1873 (remit fever) & tr by boat to hosp Ft Lincoln DT; duty 13 Oct 1873; ed nurse post hosp Oct

1873; surd as des'r 20 Nov 1873 under GO 102 AGO 1873; restored to duty without trial 18 Mar 1874 & tr to co F to serve bal of orig'l enlmt; dd co cook Aug 1874; dd qmd teamster Apr 1875; ed qmd teamster Oct 1875 to Feb 1876; [with wagon train June 1876 says Rooney; with pack train says Gregg, Lynch, & Finnegan];[10] ed qmd teamster 17 Nov 1876 to 28 Jan 1877; dd as packer Aug 1877; disch 28 Dec 1877 Mercer's Ranche DT expir of serv a pvt char a good soldier.

Schwerer, Jno. Pvt co K; b. 14 Jan 1836 Prussia Germany; pvt co H 7 NJ inf 23 June 1864; tr to co A 1 Oct 1864; m.o. vol serv 17 July 1865; enl reg army 2 Nov 1872 New York N.Y. for 5 yrs; age 31; hatmaker; brn eyes, dk hair, fair comp, 5' 5 3/4" high; join co K 7 cav 9 Dec 1872 Yorkville SC; dd qmd July to Dec 1875; in conft Feb 1876; dd qmd Feb to Apr 1877; gsw l. ankle 30 Sep 1877 Snake Creek MT (Bear's Paw Mtns) in action with Nez Perce inds; tr to str *Silver City* 14 Oct at mouth of Squaw Creek (on Missouri River); adm to hosp Ft Lincoln DT 26 Oct; disch 2 Nov 1877 at Ft Lincoln by expir of serv a pvt char good [treated in post hosp to 22 Jan 1878]; died 17 Dec 1913 Natl Sol. Home Milwaukee Wis.
Pension: 30 Mar 1878 / Inv / 251320 / 156096.

Scollin, Henry M. (alias). See Cody, Henry M.

Scott, Chas. Pvt co L; b. Scotland; enl in co L 20 Nov 1873 Ft Lincoln DT for 5 yrs; age 22; cook; blue eyes, brn hair, fair comp, 5' 9" high; dd qmd teamster Feb 1874; dd qmd herder 21–31 Aug 1874; dd qmd teamster Sep 1874 to Apr 1875; dd post hq laborer June 1875; ed qmd teamster 16–17 Aug 1875; sick in hosp Aug 1875 (sim. frac. l. humurus); duty 18 Oct 1875; killed with Custer column 25 June 1876.
Pension: 28 Apr 1881 / Mother / 282394. Rej on grd no evidence sol. contributed to support of clmt for 3 yrs prior to his death.

Scott, Geo. Pvt co D; b. Lancaster Co. Ky.; enl in co D 7 Sep 1871 Mt Vernon Ky. for 5 yrs; age 21; farmer; blue eyes, brn hair, fair comp, 5' 8" high; ds with engr pty in field July to Sep 1873; disch 5 Aug 1876 camp mouth of Rosebud Creek MT (in time to go down river by first boat) per GO 24 AGO 1859 a pvt; arr Ft Lincoln DT 10 Aug on str *Durfee*; awarded medal of honor 5 Oct 1878 for bringing water to wounded [at LBH] while under heavy fire; he having been disch the serv, medal filed in AGO; it was found in Feb 1891 in the office of a Wash'n atty (who knew not how it came there) & for'd to the war dept to be restored to its owner or heirs; no rec sol. reenl & no address; memo filed June 1911.[11]

Seafferman, Henry. Pvt co G; b. Strasburg Germany; enl 11 Aug 1860 Louisville Ky. for 5 yrs; age 21; tailor; hazel eyes, blk hair, ruddy comp, 5' 7 1/2" high; join co K 2 cav 4 Feb 1861 Camp Wood Tex.; (redesig 5 cav Aug 1861); ds Aquia Creek Va. Apr 1863; disch 1 July 1864 City Point Va. by reenlmt in same co for 3 yrs; disch 1 July 1867 Wash'n D.C. expir of serv a pvt; reenl 5 July 1867 at Wash'n for 5 yrs; join co H 7 cav 24 Sep 1867 Ft Hays Kans.; ds with band 19 Oct 1867; tr to band 19 May 1870; tr to co G 11 Sep 1871; dd co tailor Oct 1871 to July 1872; disch 5 July 1872 Yorkville SC expir of serv a pvt; reenl in co G 11 July 1872 Spartanburg SC for 5 yrs; dd co tailor to Dec 1872; in conft Feb 1873; in conft Apr 1874; in conft Apr 1875; dd co tailor Oct 1875 to Feb 1876; killed dur retreat from valley fight 25 June 1876.
Pension: 22 Oct 1890 / Mother / 501760 / 323841.

Seamans, Jno. Pvt co M; b. New London N.H.; enl 21 Sep 1875 Boston Mass. for 5 yrs; age 21 8/12; clerk; blue eyes, brn hair, fair comp, 5' 9" high; join co M 21 Oct 1875 Ft Rice DT; ed subs dept Dec 1876; sick 1 Feb to 21 Apr 1877 (pneumonia); ed post comsy dept 3 May 1877; des at Ft Rice 12 May 1877.

Seayers, Thos. Pvt co A; b. Pikesville Canada; enl 6 Sep 1875 Cincinnati Ohio for 5 yrs; age 21; baker; brn eyes, brn hair, dk comp, 5' 5 3/4" high; join co A 21 Oct 1875 Ft Lincoln DT; sick (anemia) 23 Nov to 27 Dec 1875; ed post bakery Feb to May 1876; sick (ac. diar.) 28 Aug on str *Carroll* to Ft Buford DT; tr on str *Benton* 3 Sep to hosp at Ft Lincoln; duty 9 Sep 1876; dd qmd 12–28

Sep with 281 cav horses at post; dd post bakery 29 Sep to 10 Nov 1876; dd qmd laborer Feb 1877; in conft 21 Apr 1877 awaiting trial; rel from conft 10 Nov 1877 per instr'n from dept hq; des 4 June 1878 at Ft Lincoln; surd 28 Sep 1878 at Ft Lincoln; dishon disch 5 Feb 1879 sen gen cm & one yr conft mil prison Ft L'worth Kans.

Seibelder, Anton. Pvt co A; b. 31 Oct 1828 Lichtenvoorde Germany; pvt co F 9 Ohio inf 22 Apr 1861; ed brig hq teamster Feb to Apr 1862; ds div hq carpenter June 1863 to Apr 1864; m.o. vol serv 7 June 1864 a pvt; enl reg army 2 Apr 1867 Cincinnati Ohio for 5 yrs; age 36; carpenter; grey eyes, brn hair, fair comp, 5' 9" high; join co A 7 cav 10 Nov 1868 Camp Sandy Forsyth Kans.; dd co cook Mar 1869; ed qmd June 1869; ed qmd teamster July & Oct 1870; ed qmd carpenter Dec 1870 to Aug 1871; wag 1 Dec 1871; disch 2 Apr 1872 E'town Ky. expir of serv a pvt & reenl in co A for 5 yrs; ed qmd carpenter Apr to Aug 1872; dd co cook Aug 1873; dd co cook June to Aug 1874; dd qmd carpenter Dec 1874 to Apr 1875; dd co cook Aug 1875; dd co cook June to Oct 1876; dd qmd laborer Feb 1877; disch 2 Apr 1877 Ft Rice DT expir of serv a pvt char xclt; reenl in co A 27 Dec 1877 Ft Lincoln DT for 5 yrs; ds Ft Lincoln July & Aug 1878; dd qmd carpenter Feb 1879; dd co cook Apr 1879; dd carpenter finishing qrs & stables Oct 1879 to Apr 1880; dd co carpenter Aug 1880 to Feb 1881; ed qmd Aug 1881 to Feb 1882; disch 26 Dec 1882 Ft Meade DT expir of serv a pvt & reenl in co A for 5 yrs; ed qmd carpenter Oct 1883; disch 26 Dec 1887 Ft Keogh MT expir of serv a pvt & reenl next day in co A for 5 yrs; disch 13 Nov 1888 Ft Riley Kans. on surg cert dis (rheum. & debility incident to long serv) a pvt char good; died 18 Oct 1913 Sol. Home Wash'n D.C.
Pension: 28 Nov 1888 / Inv / 680160 / 429080.

Seiler, Jno. Cpl co L; b. Bavaria Germany; enl 12 Feb 1872 Buffalo N.Y. for 5 yrs; age 21; laborer; grey eyes, lt hair, fair comp, 5' 8" high; join co L 26 Feb 1872 Yorkville SC; cpl 8 Apr 1876 to date 16 Mar; killed with Custer column 25 June 1876.

Selby, Crawford. Sad'r co G; b. 5 June 1845 Ashland Co. Ohio; enl 21 June 1875 Chicago Ill. for 5 yrs; age 30; saddler; grey eyes, lt brn hair, fair comp, 5' 5 1/2" high; join co G as sad'r 1 Aug 1875 Shreveport La.; dd 23 May to 19 June 1876;[12] killed dur retreat from valley fight 25 June 1876.
Pension: 16 Nov 1929 / Wid / 1654982. Rej on grd clmt not lawful widow of sol. at his death acc't marriage dissolved in divorce 30 Dec 1874.

Senn, Robt. Pvt co M; b. Zurich Switz; enl 23 Sep 1875 Louisville Ky. for 5 yrs; age 27; farmer; blue eyes, brn hair, fair comp, 5' 7 1/4" high; join co M 21 Oct 1875 Ft Rice DT; dd clerk adjt's office Dec 1875; dd post librarian Feb 1876; dd post school teacher Dec 1876 to Mar 1877; dd co clerk Dec 1877; cpl 1 Jan 1878; sgt 21 Jan 1878; actg co qm sgt Apr 1878; dd chg co kit'n June 1878; acquited in gen cm 28 July 1878 (chg of aiding by his advice the des'n of a comrade); dd co clerk & chg co kit'n Aug 1878 to June 1879; pvt 24 July 1879; dd co cook Aug 1879; ds repairing tel line Sep to Dec 1879; dd clerk post hq Feb to June 1880; disch 22 Sep 1880 Ft Meade DT expir of serv a pvt char fair.

Severs, Jas. W. Pvt co M; b. Lyons N.Y.; enl 12 Nov 1872 Chicago Ill. for 5 yrs; age 21 1/12; teamster; blue eyes, lt brn hair, fair comp, 5' 5 3/4" high; join co M 9 Dec 1872 Unionville SC; ed qmd teamster Nov 1873 to Apr 1874; wag 20 June 1874; pvt 12 July 1874; dd qmd teamster Sep to Nov 1874; dd subs dept teamster Dec 1874; dd qmd teamster Jan to May 1875; dd post hq Aug 1875; dd qmd teamster Oct 1875 to May 1876; dd regtl hq fatigue pty (morn & eve) 11 May 1876;[13] dd qmd teamster Feb 1877; ds str *Silver City* 15 Oct 1877 to Ft Lincoln DT; disch 12 Nov 1877 Ft Rice DT expir of serv a pvt char xclt & reenl in co M for 5 yrs; dd driving teams Dec 1877; far'r 18 Jan 1878; pvt 1 Jan 1879; ds Ft Lincoln June 1879; ds repairing tel line Oct 1879; dd qmd laborer Dec 1879; ed qmd carpenter June 1880 to Oct 1881; ed qmd carpenter Feb 1882; dd co stable police Apr & Oct 1882; disch 11 Nov 1882 Ft Meade DT expir of serv a pvt char very valuable man; (sen to Wyo. state prison Dec 1896 for grand larceny but granted full pardon 17 Apr 1903 & restored to citizenship); died 1912 state hosp Rock Springs Wyo.[14]

Pension: 18 Apr 1887 / Inv / 606687 / 430444. Dropped from roll 28 June 1900 failure to claim 3 yrs. Restored to roll 10 Mar 1904. Dropped from roll 11 Dec 1912 acc't death of pens'r; (date not given); last paid to 4 June 1912.

Severs, Sam'l. Pvt co H; b. St Louis Mo.; enl in co H 16 Feb 1875 New Orleans La. for 5 yrs; age 21; laborer; blk eyes, blk hair, dk comp, 5' 6" high; dd qmd sad'r Apr 1876; dd hq l. wing fatigue pty 15 May 1876; gsw l. hip (fl. wd. severe) 26 June 1876 on Reno hill; tr on str *Far West* 3 July to hosp Ft Lincoln DT; ed nurse post hosp 8 Aug; tr to Ft Rice 11 Aug; disch 22 Sep 1876 at Ft Rice on surg cert dis a pvt; died 5 Sep 1919 Eldorado Okla. Pension: 19 Sep 1898 / Inv / 1209973 / 985768. Wid / 1183006. (XC-2,719,723).

Shade, Sam'l S. Pvt co C; b. Jamestown Pa.; enl 3 Aug 1875 Baltimore Md for 5 yrs; age 28; school teacher; blue eyes, lt hair, fair comp, 5' 8 3/4" high; join co C 21 Oct 1875 Ft Lincoln DT; dd post school teacher 9 Jan to 1 May 1876; killed with Custer column 25 June 1876.

Shanahan, Jno. Pvt co G; b. Youghal Ireland; enl 9 Dec 1874 Boston Mass. for 5 yrs; age 21 5/12; laborer; blue eyes, brn hair, fair comp, 5' 7" high; join co G 10 Feb 1875 Shreveport La.; ds camp Powder River MT 15 June 1876; ds with co wagon Aug 1876; ds 11 Aug to 26 Sep 1876;[15] dd qmd 12–28 Sep 1876 Ft Lincoln DT with 281 cav horses at post; in conft Dec 1877 to Mar 1878; sen gen cm 21 Mar 1878 forf $10 pay per mo for 2 mos & conft 40 days but sen remitted by same order; dd regtl hq June to Aug 1878; ed hosp attdt in field Sep to Nov 1878; dd repairing mil tel line Oct 1879; disch 8 Dec 1879 Ft Meade DT expir of serv a pvt char good; reenl 7 Jan 1880 Ft Hamilton N.Y. for 5 yrs in co C 3 art'y; in conft Dec 1880; disch 3 June 1881 at Ft Hamilton on surg cert dis (chr. rheum.; contr line of duty; dis 1/3); a pvt char poor.

Sharrow, Wm. Hunter. Sgt-maj ncs; b. 2 Mar 1845 York England;[16] enl 21 Mar 1865 New York N.Y. for 3 yrs; age 21; clerk; blue eyes, lt hair, lt comp, 5' 8" high; join co C 2 cav 24 Apr 1865 Winchester Va.; dd clerk regtl qmd May 1865 to Feb 1866; (tr to co E 8 Nov 1865); cpl 1 Apr 1866; ds Ft Riley Kans. Mar to Aug 1866; ds dept hq (Omaha Neb) Sep 1866 to 21 Mar 1868 when disch by expir of serv a cpl; (clerk for maj Clarke [paymaster] to Aug 1869);[17] reenl 12 Aug 1869 rct depot Ft L'worth Kans. for 5 yrs; age 24 5/12; assd to permanent co gen rctg serv 18 Sep 1869; dd post hq to Mar 1870; tr to 7 cav 26 Feb 1870 (at Ft L'worth); assd to co B 10 Mar 1870; ds clerk regtl hq 15 Mar 1870 to 17 Apr 1872 when appt regtl sgt-maj; with regtl hq St Paul Minn. 11 Apr 1873 to 12 Aug 1874 when disch upon expir of serv a sgt-maj; reenl in regt 10 Sep 1874 at St Paul for 5 yrs & cont'd as sgt-maj; killed with Custer column 25 June 1876.

Shauer, Jno. Pvt co K; b. 26 May 1852 Bavaria Germany; enl 21 Nov 1872 Pittsburgh Pa. for 5 yrs; age 21; laborer; grey eyes, dk hair, sallow comp, 5' 8" high; join co K 9 Dec 1872 Yorkville SC; ds exp'n hq Aug 1873 care for unserviceable horses; ed subs dept Oct 1873 to Feb 1874; dd desp bearer Apr 1874; dd battn hq Aug 1874; dd packer in pack train Aug 1876; gsw l. heel 30 Sep 1877 Snake Creek MT (Bear's Paw Mtns) in action with Nez Perce inds; tr to str *Silver City* 14 Oct at mouth of Squaw Creek (on Missouri River); adm to hosp Ft Lincoln DT 26 Oct; disch 21 Nov 1877 at Ft Lincoln by expir of serv a pvt char good; reenl in co K 17 Dec 1877 Ft Rice DT for 5 yrs; sick qrs Feb 1878 (l. foot); dd co cook Apr 1878; dd qmd teamster Dec 1878 to Apr 1881; dd co teamster in field June 1881; dd qmd teamster Aug 1881 to Apr 1882; ds hauling tel poles between Ft Totten & Larimore DT June 1882; dd co cook Aug 1882; dd teamster Oct 1882; disch 16 Dec 1882 Ft Meade DT by expir of serv a pvt char very good; died 7 July 1924 Seattle Wash'n.

Pension: 24 Dec 1888 / Inv / 682763 / 443587. Ind. Surv. / 10721 / 6693. Ind. Wid. / 16945 / 11059.

Shea, Dan'l. Pvt co B; b. Cork Co. Ireland; enl 11 Dec 1874 New York N.Y. for 5 yrs; age 22; laborer; blue eyes, brn hair, fair comp, 5' 7 1/4" high; join co B 10 Feb 1875 Shreveport La.; ds Ft Lincoln DT 17 Oct 1876 dismtd; dd co cook June 1879; disch 10 Dec 1879 Ft Yates DT expir of serv a pvt char good; reenl 5 Jan 1880 Ft Hamilton N.Y. for 5 yrs; assd to co C 3 art'y; died 24 July 1882 Little Rock Ark (typhoid fever) a pvt.

Shea, Jeremiah. Pvt co C; b. London England; enl 6 Sep 1875 Boston Mass. for 5 yrs; age 21 6/12; hostler; grey eyes, brn hair, ruddy comp, 5' 6 1/4" high; join co C 21 Oct 1875 Ft Lincoln DT; killed with Custer column 25 June 1876.
Pension: 21 Dec 1885 / Mother / 333658 / 231119.

Sherborne, Thos. Pvt band; b. Hampshire England; enl 30 Jan 1866 New York N.Y. for 3 yrs; age 24; musician; hazel eyes, brn hair, dk comp, 5' 7" high; assd to co G 10 inf;[18] sick 25 Dec 1866 to 3 Feb 1867 (frac. l. arm); disch 27 June 1867 Ft Snelling Minn. per SO 275 AGO 1867 a pvt; reenl 9 Feb 1870 at Ft Snelling for 5 yrs in band 20 inf; des 3 Nov 1871 at Ft Snelling; enl as Chas. Answorth 11 Jan 1873 Chicago Ill. for 5 yrs; assd to band gen mtd serv St Louis Bks Mo.; surd as des'r 7 Nov 1873 under GO 102 AGO 1873; restored to duty with band gen mtd serv to serve bal of orig'l enlmt; tr to band 7 cav 1 Mar 1876 (with Lt Reily's detmt) & joined regt 14 Apr 1876 Ft Lincoln DT; ds camp Powder River MT 14 June 1876; ds str *Josephine* 6 Aug 1876 to Ft Lincoln with band; disch 13 Feb 1877 at Ft Lincoln by expir of serv a pvt char xclt (made good time lost by des'n); reenl in band 15 Feb 1877 for 5 yrs; lance cpl Dec 1881; lance sgt Feb 1882; disch 14 Feb 1882 Ft Meade DT expir of serv a pvt char xclt (a good mus'n addicted to strong drink); reenl in band same day for 5 yrs; tr to co D 21 Aug 1882 but cont'd dd with band; tr to co M 6 Aug 1883 but cont'd dd with band; tr to band 9 Sep 1884; disch 14 Feb 1887 at Ft Meade by expir of serv a pvt char good; reenl next day for 5 yrs & assd to band 1 art'y; sick hosp 10 Apr to 21 July 1888 (cont'n r. shoulder & arm); sick hosp 28 July 1888 (colles frac. r. radius); tr to co L 23 Aug 1888; disch 12 June 1889 Ft Mason Calif. on surg cert dis (colles frac. r. radius not incident to serv; old age & gen debility contr line of duty; dis 1/2) a pvt; died 19 Aug 1910 Sol. Home Wash'n D.C., (age 79).
Pension: 29 July 1889 / Inv / 719372 / 455529.

Sheridan, Mich'l Vincent. Capt co L; b. 24 May 1842 Somerset Ohio; vol adc to gen Sheridan 1 July 1862;[19] appt 1Lt 2 Mo. inf 9 Aug 1863; ds div hq (with gen Sheridan) 10 Sep 1863; appt adc & capt of vols on staff of gen Sheridan 3 July 1864; bvt maj of vols 13 Mar 1865 for gal serv; m.o. vol serv 1 Aug 1866 New Orleans La.; appt reg army com'n 2Lt 5 cav from 23 Feb 1866; (never joined); ds div hq at New Orleans with gen Sheridan; appt capt 7 cav 23 Oct 1866 to date 28 July 1866; join co L 9 Nov 1866 Ft Riley Kans.; bvt maj & Lt-col 2 Mar 1867 for gal serv in battles of Opequan (Winchester) & Fisher's Hill Va.; ds adc to gen Sheridan 23 May 1867 to 5 Aug 1888;[20] actg aag mil div of Mo. (Chicago Ill.) 16 Apr 1869; Lt-col adc 1 Aug 1870; chg of detmt to Custer battlefield June 1877 to exhume remains of officers;[21] Lt-col mil secy 9 Apr 1878; maj aag 7 June 1883; (resd com'n in 7 cav 16 Jan 1884); col adc 1 June 1888; Lt-col aag 9 July 1892; col aag 25 Jan 1897; brig-gen vols 27 May 1898 to 12 May 1899; retd as brig-gen 16 Apr 1902; died 21 Feb 1918 Wash'n D.C.
[4432 ACP 1878].

Shields, Wm. Sad'r co E; b. Vincennes Ind.; enl 1 Aug 1866 Indianapolis Ind. for 3 yrs; age 28; harness maker; grey eyes, lt hair, fair comp, 5' 8" high; join co F 7 cav 10 Sep 1866 Ft Riley Kans.; sad'r Feb 1867; ds with escort for ind peace com'n May 1868; disch 1 Aug 1869 camp near Denver Colo. Ty expir of serv a sad'r; enl in co E 29 Sep 1869 Fitz Meadows Colo. Ty for 5 yrs; dd co sad'r Dec 1869 to Feb 1870; ed qmd Nov 1870 to Feb 1871; cpl 1 Sep 1871; pvt 11 Oct 1871; cpl 1 Jan 1872; in arrest Feb to June 1872; pvt 11 June 1872 sen gen cm & forf $10 pay per mo for 4 mos; cpl 1 May 1873; sgt 1 Sep 1873; pvt 24 Apr 1874 (own req) but disappv by regtl comdr & restored to sgt; pvt 19 May 1874 sen gar cm; disch 29 Sep 1874 Ft Lincoln DT expir of serv a pvt & reenl in co E for 5 yrs; in conft Feb 1875; sad'r 1 Mar 1875; [at LBH says Spencer, O'Toole & Pandtle; wd in buttock says Lange (others said same); at Powder River says Berwald];[22] cpl 1

Oct 1876 to date 1 Sep 1876; sgt 15 Jan 1877; pvt 22 Apr 1877; ed med dept Apr to June 1878; dd mail carrier Aug to Oct 1878; cpl 1 Jan 1879; disch 28 Sep 1879 Ft Meade DT expir of serv a cpl char xclt & reenl in co E for 5 yrs; sgt 24 Jan 1880; pvt 7 June 1880; cpl 10 July 1881; pvt 26 Nov 1881; dd mtd orderly June 1882; cpl 3 June 1883; 1sgt 25 July 1883; pvt 9 Oct 1883 (own req); ed qmd sad'r Apr to Aug 1884; disch 28 Sep 1884 at Ft Meade expir of serv a pvt char very good & reenl in co E for 5 yrs; on furl 40 days 30 Sep 1884 New York N.Y.; dd qmd sad'r Dec 1884 to Aug 1886; in conft Feb 1888; sen gen cm 11 Feb 1888 forf $10 pay per mo for 2 mos & conft same period; died 6 Sep 1888 post hosp Ft Sill IT (heart disease) a pvt.

Short, Nathan. Pvt co C; b. Lehigh Co. Pa.; enl 9 Oct 1875 St Louis Bks Mo. for 5 yrs; age 21; laborer; grey eyes, brn hair, fair comp, 5' 7" high; join co C 21 Oct 1875 Ft Lincoln DT; killed with Custer column 25 June 1876.[23]

Sicafoos (Sicafuse), Francis. See Sicfous, Francis W.

Sicfous, Francis W. Pvt co F; b. Clarion Co. Pa.; enl 4 Oct 1875 Pittsburgh Pa. for 5 yrs; age 23; painter; grey eyes, lt hair, fair comp, 5' 5" high; join co F 21 Oct 1875 Ft Lincoln DT; dd qmd teamster Oct to Dec 1875; sick qrs 7 Feb to 9 Mar 1876 (catarrh); killed with Custer column 25 June 1876.

Siefert, August B. Pvt co K; b. 26 July 1850 Darmstadt Germany; enl 5 Oct 1866 Harrisburg Pa. for 3 yrs; age 19; baker; grey eyes, lt hair, lt comp, 5' 3" high; assd to co G 16 inf; (consol with 2 inf Apr 1869); disch 5 Oct 1869 Montgomery Ala expir of serv a pvt; reenl 17 Dec 1869 St Louis Mo. for 5 yrs; assd to co C 19 inf; disch 17 Dec 1874 Ft Dodge Kans. expir of serv a pvt; reenl 16 Jan 1875 Colfax La. for 5 yrs in co K 7 cav; ed post baker Feb to Dec 1875; ds Ft Lincoln DT 16 Oct 1876 dismtd; ed post baker Nov 1876 to Feb 1877; dd co cook June 1877; ed post baker Feb to Apr 1878; ed post baker Dec 1878 to 15 Jan 1880 when disch at Ft Totten DT by expir of serv a pvt char xclt; reenl next day in co K for 5 yrs & appt cpl; sgt 8 Apr 1881; ds Ft Totten as chf baker May & June 1881; dd chg post bakery Oct 1881; dd chf baker Dec 1881; on furl 4 mos 1 June 1882; actg 1sgt Oct 1882; 1sgt 1 Nov 1882; sgt 12 Oct 1883; disch 15 Jan 1885 Ft Meade DT expir of serv a sgt char xclt & reenl in co K for 5 yrs; 1sgt 1 Nov 1886; sgt 1 Sep 1887; disch 15 Jan 1890 Ft Sill IT expir of serv a sgt char xclt & reenl in co K for 5 yrs; on furl 6 mos 17 Sep 1890 Darmstadt Germany; sd chg of stable police Apr 1891 to June 1893; actg 1sgt June & July 1893; ds Ft Sheridan Ill. July 1894; sd chg of extra horses from 6 cav Oct 1894; disch 15 Jan 1895 at Ft Sheridan by expir of serv a sgt char xclt & reenl in co K for 3 yrs; retd 26 Jan 1897 Ft Huachuca AT a sgt char xclt; died 20 Jan 1921 Highwood Ill.

Siemon, Chas. Blks co L; b. Copenhagen Denmark; enl 18 July 1867 Cincinnati Ohio for 5 yrs; age 23; blacksmith; grey eyes, brn hair, dk comp, 5' 7 1/2" high; join co L 2 Oct 1867 Ft Reynolds Colo. Ty; ed blks Oct to Dec 1867; ed qmd mech Feb 1868; ed qmd artf'r Apr to June 1868; artf'r 1 Nov 1868; blks June 1869; ed qmd blks July to Oct 1870; disch 18 July 1872 Yorkville SC expir of serv a blks & reenl in co L for 5 yrs; ed qmd June 1873 to Feb 1874; dd exp'n hq June 1874; killed with Custer column 25 June 1876.

Simenson, Bent. Pvt co L; b. Milwaukee Wis; enl 6 Feb 1872 Chicago Ill. for 5 yrs; age 21 3/12; laborer; blue eyes, lt hair, lt comp, 5' 5 1/2" high; join co L 26 Feb 1872 Yorkville SC; dd qmd with boat crew Apr 1875; dd post hq as stonecutter June 1875; trump'r 1 Nov 1875; pvt 28 Feb 1876; killed with Custer column 25 June 1876.

Simons, Pat'k. Pvt co B; b. Sligo Ireland; enl 14 Mar 1876 Baltimore Md for 5 yrs; age 21; laborer; grey eyes, brn hair, ruddy comp, 5' 7 1/4" high; join co B 27 Apr 1876 St Paul Minn.; ds camp Powder River MT 10 June 1876; des 29 June 1877 camp on Little Missouri River MT; rel from serv upon own appn 15 Feb 1892 in accord with GO 55 AGO 1890 (& act of congress appv 11 Apr 1890);[24] res Highland Park Ill.

Sims, Jno. J. Pvt co D; b. Johnson Co. Ill.; enl 1 Oct 1875 St Louis Bks Mo. for 5 yrs; age 23; painter; blue eyes, brn hair, dk comp, 5' 7 3/4" high; join co D 21 Oct 1875 Ft Lincoln DT; ds camp Powder River MT 15 June 1876 guarding wagon train; des 20 Jan 1877 Ft Rice DT; surd 25 Feb 1877 Standing Rock DT; dishon disch 10 May 1877 sen gen cm & 2 yrs conft mil prison Ft L'worth Kans.; escaped from post guardhouse at Ft Rice 20 June 1877 (with Conlan).

Sivertsen, Jno. Pvt co M; b. 10 Dec 1841 Frondorm Norway; enl in co M 19 June 1873 Ft Rice DT for 5 yrs; age 31; blacksmith; blue eyes, sandy hair, lt comp, 5' 10" high; dd qmd Nov 1874 to Apr 1875 care for pub animals; ed qmd chg of saw mill Oct 1875 to Apr 1876; left in timber dur retreat from valley fight 25 June 1876 & rejoin co on Reno hill; dd regtl hq fatigue pty June to Sep 1877; dd co blks Feb to Apr 1878; disch 19 June 1878 Ft Lincoln DT expir of serv a pvt char xclt; reenl 25 June 1878 Ft McHenry Md for 5 yrs; assd to co D 2 art'y; disch 24 June 1883 Camp Wash'n, Gaithersburg Md by expir of serv a pvt char xclt; died 30 Aug 1925 Sol. Home Wash'n D.C.
Pension: 10 June 1889 / Inv / 709825 / 540869.

Slaper, Wm. Clemens. Pvt co M; b. 23 Nov 1854 Cincinnati Ohio; enl 10 Sep 1875 at Cincinnati for 5 yrs; age 21; safe maker; blue eyes, brn hair, fair comp, 5' 8 1/2" high; join co M 21 Oct 1875 Ft Rice DT; ed qmd laborer Feb 1877; ed hosp cook Dec 1878 to Feb 1879; dd co cook Apr 1879; ed subs dept laborer June to Oct 1879; cpl 29 Oct 1879; actg co qm sgt Dec 1879 to Apr 1880; disch 9 Sep 1880 Ft Meade DT expir of serv a cpl char good; died 13 Nov 1931 Sol. Home Los Angeles Calif.[25]
Pension: 12 Apr 1917 / Ind. Surv. / 11636 / 7490.

Small, Jno. R. Pvt co G; b. Baltimore Md; enl in navy 7 Jan 1867 Phil'a Pa. for 3 yrs; age 21; tinsmith; grey eyes, brn hair, fair comp, 5' 7 1/4" high; serv on frigate *Sabine* (training ship for landsmen at New London Conn.) May 1867; str *Guard* (supply ship for European fleet) Oct 1868; str *Swatara* (cruise to Colombia Nov 1869 to Jan 1870); disch 21 Jan 1870 at New York; reenl in navy 7 Feb 1870 at Phil'a for 3 yrs; enl in army 5 Mar 1873 at Phil'a for 5 yrs; join co G 7 cav 19 Oct 1873 Ft Lincoln DT; dd co cook Aug to Oct 1875; in conft Feb to Apr 1876; dd co cook June 1876; gsw l. arm while cleaning carbine 5 Feb 1877 at Ft Lincoln; l. arm amp'd at shoulder; disch 25 May 1877 at Ft Lincoln on surg cert dis a pvt char good; died 13 May 1883 Baltimore Md.
Pension: 29 June 1877 / Inv / 238431 / 150398.

Smallwood, Wm. Pvt co E; b. Jonesville Ind.; enl 18 Dec 1874 Cincinnati Ohio for 5 yrs; age 22; farmer; brn eyes, brn hair, dk comp, 5' 8 1/2" high; join co E 8 Feb 1875 Opelika Ala; killed with Custer column 25 June 1876.

Smith, Albert A. Pvt co E; b. Queens Co. N.Y.; enl 18 Dec 1867 New York N.Y. for 5 yrs; age 29; carpenter; grey eyes, brn hair, fair comp, 5' 5 3/4" high; join co E 22 Jan 1868 Ft L'worth Kans.; dd qmd carpenter Apr 1869; ds with survey exp'n May to Aug 1869; sen gen cm 24 Dec 1869 forf $10 pay per mo for 5 mos & conft same period; dd co carpenter Feb to Aug 1871; in conft Apr to June 1872; sen gen cm 25 June 1872 forf $8 pay per mo for 2 mos; dd co carpenter Aug 1872; disch 18 Dec 1872 Unionville SC expir of serv a pvt; reenl in co E 1 Jan 1873 at Unionville for 5 yrs; dd co carpenter Feb 1873; cpl 1 May 1873; dd chg co cook house June 1873; ed qmd carpenter Oct 1873 to Apr 1874; sgt 15 June 1874; dd chg co kit'n Aug 1874; pvt 1 Oct 1874; dd co carpenter Dec 1875; ed qmd carpenter Jan & Feb 1876; killed with Custer column 25 June 1876.

Smith, Algernon Emory. 1Lt co A; b. 17 Sep 1842 Newport N.Y.; left his studies at Hamilton College & enl 10 Feb 1862 at Utica N.Y. by capt Pease for his co K 7 inf;[26] appt orderly sgt with Pease on rctg duty; disch 10 Aug 1862 Rome N.Y. to accept com'n 2Lt 117 N.Y. inf (upon req of col Pease comdg regt) & rct co G; adc to gen Ames Oct 1863; (1Lt 26 Apr 1864); ds brig hq May 1864; tr to staff of gen Foster Sep 1864; (capt 12 Oct 1864); tr to

staff of gen Terry Dec 1864; gsw l. lung & l. shoulder (fl. wd) 15 Jan 1865 in assault on Ft Fisher NC; sick hosp to 5 May 1865 thence awl on surg cert; m.o. vol serv 7 June 1865 to date 15 May 1865; bvt maj vols 13 Mar 1865 for gal serv in action at Ft Fisher; appt reg army com'n 2Lt 9 Aug 1867; passed exam'n before cav bd 23 Sep [with capt Yates] & found competent to perform duties of cav officer tho' disability to raise l. arm at r. angle to body impeded management of fiery horse & mounting tall horse; join co E 7 cav 2 Nov 1867 Ft L'worth Kans.; bvt 1Lt & capt Apr 1868 (from 9 Aug 1867) for gal serv in battle of Drury's Farm & capture of Ft Fisher; actg adjt 8 Apr to 11 Oct 1868 & actg comsy in field thro' Apr 1869; 1Lt 29 Apr 1869 & rqm to 21 Aug 1869; tr to co A 1 Oct 1869; ds post adjt Ft Scott Kans. Apr 1870; ds Wash'n D.C. Dec 1870 before spl exam'g bd (upon recom'n col Sturgis) & found not unfit for the serv; post adjt, qm & comsy E'town Ky. June 1871 to Mar 1873; comsy of detmt to DT Apr 1873 & with Yellowstone Exp'n to Sep 1873; awl 6 mos 7 Oct 1873; post comsy Ft Lincoln DT 12 Apr 1874; actg aqm & comsy Blk Hills Exp'n June thro' Aug 1874; post comsy Ft Lincoln 29 Sep 1874 to 17 Mar 1876; ds Ft Seward DT 20 Mar to comd co E; post comsy Ft Lincoln 16 Apr to 17 May thence comd co E in field; killed with Custer column 25 June 1876;[27] survived by wife.
[3152 ACP 1871]. Pension: 19 June 1865 / Inv / 73047 / 49620; (resd). Wid / 233489 / 179648.

Smith, Fred'k. See Methfessel, Christian.

Smith, Geo. Emerson. Pvt co M; b. Kennebunk Me; enl 6 Sep 1875 Boston Mass. for 5 yrs; age 25; shoemaker; grey eyes, brn hair, fair comp, 5' 6 1/2" high; join co M 21 Oct 1875 Ft Rice DT; killed in valley fight 25 June 1876.[28]
Pension: 11 Jan 1883 / Mother / 300191 / 246696.

Smith, Henry G. Pvt co D; b. Lake Co. Ind.; enl 8 Sep 1875 Chicago Ill. for 5 yrs; age 26; butcher; grey eyes, brn hair, dk comp, 5' 9" high; join co D 21 Oct 1875 Ft Lincoln DT; far'r 1 Aug 1876; des 19 Feb 1877 while on furl.

Smith. Jas. [1st]. Pvt co E; b. Tipperary Ireland; enl 25 Jan 1866 Charleston SC for 3 yrs in co L 5 cav; age 24; soldier; hazel eyes, brn hair, ruddy comp, 5' 9" high; disch 25 Jan 1869 San Francisco Creek Tex. expir of serv a pvt; reenl 20 May 1869 Ft L'worth Kans. for 5 yrs in co L 7 cav; sick hosp Ft L'worth Apr to June 1870; dd co cook Dec 1870; cpl 27 June 1871; sgt 1 Sep 1871; pvt 27 Dec 1871; in conft Dec 1871; sgt 23 July 1872; dd prov sgt Dec 1873 to May 1874; (overseer of pris'rs Jan & Feb 1874); disch 20 May 1874 Ft Lincoln DT expir of serv a sgt; reenl same day in co L for 5 yrs & on furl 30 days at Ft L'worth (see Andrews & O'Connell); sick Ft Lincoln July to Sep 1874 (chr. rheum.); dd actg prov sgt Oct 1874; pvt 22 Dec 1874; sen gen cm 21 Jan 1875 forf $10 pay per mo for 6 mos; dd post hq laborer June 1875; ed hosp nurse 25 Nov 1875 to 7 Mar 1876; tr to co E 1 Mar 1876; killed with Custer column 25 June 1876.

Smith, Jas. [2nd]. Pvt co E; b. Lynn Mass.; enl 1 Dec 1874 St Louis Mo. for 5 yrs; age 27; shoemaker; hazel eyes, blk hair, dk comp, 5' 4 1/2" high; join co E 8 Feb 1875 Opelika Ala; in conft Dec 1875; killed with Custer column 25 June 1876.

Smith, Wm. E. Pvt co D; b. 3 Aug 1853 Rouses Pt N.Y.; enl 13 Sep 1875 Boston Mass. for 5 yrs; age 22; farmer; grey eyes, dk hair, dk comp, 5' 5 1/4" high; join co D 21 Oct 1875 Ft Lincoln DT; des 28 Mar 1877 Ft Rice DT & apph same day; in conft Ft Lincoln to 27 Dec 1877 when restored to duty under Regs. pars. 1358 & 1359;[29] dd report to maj Merrill for instr'n June 1879 to May 1880; ds with maj Merrill at NPRR ext'n 6 June 1880; disch 12 Sep 1880 Camp Houston DT expir of serv a pvt char xclt; died 10 May 1918 Deerfield Mass.
Pension: 12 Sep 1903 / Inv / 1303845. Rej on grd no ratable disability found. (XC-2,658,883).

Smith, Wm. M. Cpl co B; b. Trenton NJ; enl 11 July 1872 Phil'a Pa. for 5 yrs; age 21; blacksmith; lt blue eyes, dk hair, ruddy comp, 5' 5 1/2" high; join co B 1 Nov 1872 Spartanburg SC; blks 1 Mar 1873; cpl 1 Jan 1874; sgt

21 Mar 1875; pvt 22 July 1875 sen gen cm & forf $10 pay per mo for 2 mos; blks 10 Sep 1875; pvt 1 Feb 1876; cpl 15 May 1876; gsw r. arm above elbow (frac. bone severe) 26 June 1876; tr on str *Far West* 3 July to hosp Ft Lincoln; (ball lodged but bones of elbow not injured; resected elbow joint 29 Aug rendering arm useless); in hosp to 9 Feb 1877 when disch on surg cert a cpl char xclt; died 4 Jan 1921 Woodbury NJ.
Pension: 5 Mar 1877 / Inv / 231669 / 144404.

Sniffin, Frank W. Pvt co M; b. 12 Sep 1857 New York N.Y.; enl 1 Sep 1875 St Louis Bks Mo. for 5 yrs; age 22; laborer; blue eyes, lt hair, fair comp, 5' 7" high; join co M 21 Oct 1875 Ft Rice DT; cpl 26 Apr 1877; pvt 10 Mar 1878; in conft Apr 1878; dd co cook June 1878; in conft June 1879; ds repairing tel line Sep & Oct 1879; disch 31 Aug 1880 Ft Meade DT expir of serv a pvt char good; reenl for co M 21 Sep 1880 St Louis Mo. for 5 yrs; cpl 10 May 1881; in arrest Aug 1881; sen gen cm 17 Sep 1881 forf $10 pay; sgt 1 Feb 1882; pvt 28 May 1882; sen gen cm 12 June 1882 forf $10 pay per mo for 3 mos; cpl 1 Nov 1882; sgt 9 Aug 1883; disch 21 Sep 1885 Ft Meade DT expir of serv a sgt char xclt & reenl in co M for 5 yrs; on furl 3 mos 20 Jan 1886 Pierre DT; disch 26 Apr 1887 at Ft Meade per SO 88 AGO 1887 (by way of favor) a sgt char xclt;[30] reenl in co M 4 Aug 1890 Ft Riley Kans. for 5 yrs; ed qmd plumber Aug 1892; tr to co E 20 Dec 1892; cpl 20 Jan 1893; sgt 20 Mar 1893; pvt 2 Mar 1895 (own req); ed qmd mech Apr 1895; ed qmd laborer May 1895; disch 3 Aug 1895 Ft Grant AT expir of serv a pvt char xclt & reenl in co E for 3 yrs; sd co clerk July 1896 to Jan 1898; cpl 26 Jan 1898; disch 3 Aug 1898 at Ft Grant expir of serv a cpl char xclt & reenl in co E for 3 yrs; sgt 12 Aug 1898; ds dept hq clerk Apr 1899; disch 23 Apr 1899 Pimar del Rio Cuba per GO 40 AGO 1898 a sgt char xclt;[31] reenl 19 May 1899 Camp Columbia Cuba for 3 yrs in co M; disch 18 May 1902 at Columbia Bks expir of serv a 1sgt char xclt & reenl in co M for 3 yrs; disch 15 Mar 1905 Ft Oglethorpe Ga. per GO 31 Hq DG 1904 a 1sgt & reenl in co M;[32] retd 24 Oct 1905 a 1sgt char xclt; died 17 Apr 1931 Ft Oglethorpe Ga.

Pension: 8 May 1931 / Wid / 1693595. (XC-2,641,636).

Snow, Andrew. Pvt co L; b. Surrell Canada; enl 24 Sep 1875 Boston Mass. for 5 yrs; age 22; hostler; hazel eyes, blk hair, ruddy comp, 5' 5 1/8" high; join co L 29 Oct 1875 Ft Totten DT; killed with Custer column 25 June 1876.

Spencer, Able Bennett. Far'r co E; b. 11 July 1844 Plaisville Wis; enl 8 Jan 1872 Chicago Ill. for 5 yrs; age 27; farmer; hazel eyes, dk hair, dk comp, 5' 7 3/4" high; join co E 5 Feb 1872 Unionville SC; ed qmd teamster Dec 1872 to Feb 1873; ed qmd teamster 12–26 Apr 1873; dd co cook Apr 1873; dd co cook Aug 1873; cpl 1 Nov 1873; pvt 31 May 1874; dd hq Blk Hills Exp'n 25 June to 31 Aug 1874; dd co cook Dec 1874; far'r 1 Jan 1875; [at LBH says Berwald, Lange, & Pandtle];[33] pvt 1 Oct 1876; ds Ft Lincoln 16 Oct 1876 chg co prop; disch 8 Jan 1877 at Ft Lincoln expir of serv a pvt char good; died 1 Feb 1922 Chicago Ill.

Spinner, Philip. Pvt co B; b. Baden Germany; enl 23 July 1867 New York N.Y. for 3 yrs; age 21; shoemaker; grey eyes, lt hair, fair comp, 5' 3 1/2" high; assd to co I 37 inf; (co consol with 3 inf Aug 1869); disch 23 July 1870 Ft Lyon Colo. Ty expir of serv a pvt; reenl 12 Dec 1870 Ft L'worth Kans. for 5 yrs in co B 7 cav; age 24 4/12; grey eyes, lt hair, fair comp, 5' 6 1/2" high; dd co cook June 1873; cpl 5 Mar 1875; sgt 26 July 1875; disch 12 Dec 1875 Shreveport La. expir of serv a sgt; reenl same day in co B for 5 yrs & appt cpl; pvt 20 Mar 1876; dd co cook June 1876; [Bailey said Spinner & Coleman were first to go for water];[34] dd with band 25 Nov to 5 Dec 1876; in conft Feb 1877; dd co cook Oct 1877 to Feb 1878; dd co stables Apr to Dec 1878; ds cutting logs Apr to June 1879; dd co cook Aug to Dec 1879; dd co cook June 1880; disch 11 Dec 1880 Ft Yates DT expir of serv a pvt char good; reenl for co B 4 Jan 1881 St Louis Mo. for 5 yrs; dd co cook Apr 1881; cpl 9 Sep 1883; pvt 14 Oct 1884 sen gen cm & forf $10 pay per mo for 2 mos; on furl 3 mos 10 July 1885 Ft Snelling Minn. & Bismarck DT; disch 3 Jan 1886 Ft Yates DT expir of serv a pvt char very good; reenl

25 Jan 1886 Ft L'worth Kans. for 5 yrs; assd to co B 3 cav; tr to co B 7 cav 17 Mar 1888; dd post mess hall Dec 1889 to Mar 1890; dd co baker Dec 1890; disch 24 Jan 1891 Rushville Neb expir of serv a pvt char xclt & reenl in co B for 5 yrs; on furl 2 mos 29 Jan 1891 L'worth Kans.; sd cook post mess hall May 1891; ed qmd sad'r May & June 1892; sd co cook June & July 1892; in conft Apr to June 1893; sen gen cm 12 June 1893 forf $10 pay & conft 15 days; sd cook post exchange July 1893; on furl 3 mos 2 Nov 1893 Chicago Ill.; sd co cook Aug 1894; dd co sad'r 11 Mar to 9 Apr 1895; died 12 Aug 1895 Camp Douglas Wis (gsw to chest, self inflicted) a pvt.

Sprague, Otto. Pvt co L; b. Mineral Point Wis; enl 27 Aug 1875 Chicago Ill. for 5 yrs; age 21; machinist; grey eyes, lt brn hair, dk comp, 5' 7 3/4" high; join co L 29 Oct 1875 Ft Totten DT; ds Ft Lincoln DT 17 May 1876 in co garden;[35] sent with Lt Garlington on str *Josephine* 24 July to join co in field; with art'y detmt Aug 1876; ds subs dept Aug 1877; dd co cook Apr to June 1878; ds Ft Lincoln July to Oct 1878; ds Ft Rice DT Dec 1878; ds with escort for engrs NPRR June 1879; ed qmd Apr 1880; disch 26 Aug 1880 at Ft Lincoln by expir of serv a pvt char very good.

Stafford, Benj. Pvt co E; b. Boston Mass.; enl 8 Oct 1873 at Boston for 5 yrs; age 27; currier; brn eyes, blk hair, fair comp, 5' 5 1/4" high; join co L 18 Oct 1873 Ft Lincoln DT; killed with Custer column 25 June 1876.

Stanley, Edw. Pvt co G; b. Boston Mass.; enl 22 Nov 1875 at Boston for 5 yrs; age 25; clerk; blue eyes, brn hair, fair comp, 5' 9 3/8" high; join co G 27 Apr 1876 St Paul Minn.; killed dur retreat from valley fight 25 June 1876 (body not recovered).[36]

Staples, Sam'l Fred'k. Cpl co I; b. Worcester Mass.; enl 9 Jan 1872 New York N.Y. for 5 yrs; age 22; painter; brn eyes, dk hair, dk comp, 5' 6 1/2" high; join co I 1 Feb 1872 Shelbyville Ky.; dd co cook June 1873; ds in field July 1873; cpl 22 Sep 1873; ds Ft Rice DT Sep 1873; pvt 19 Dec 1874; sick 25 Feb to 22 Apr & 5 May to 14 June 1875 (whitlow, little finger r. hand); cpl 10 Mar 1876; killed with Custer column 25 June 1876.[37]
Pension: 16 Jan 1879 / Wid / 241067 / 185227.

Stark, Frank. Wag co C; b. Bavaria Germany; pvt co H 40 Mo. inf 17 Aug 1864 to 8 Aug 1865; enl reg army 26 Jan 1870 St Louis Mo. for 5 yrs; age 21; teamster; hazel eyes, brn hair, fair comp, 5' 7 1/2" high; join co H 7 cav 13 Feb 1870 Ft Hays Kans.; ed qmd laborer Dec 1870; ed qmd teamster June 1871 to June 1872; wag 30 July 1872; ed qmd 7–29 May 1873; ed qmd teamster June 1873; ed qmd laborer Oct 1873; pvt 15 Nov 1873; dd qmd Apr 1874; dd qmd teamster 30 June to 31 Aug 1874; disch 26 Jan 1875 New Orleans La. expir of serv a pvt; reenl 7 Sep 1875 at St Louis for 5 yrs; join co C 7 cav 21 Oct 1875 Ft Lincoln DT; wag 1 Jan 1876; ds camp Powder River MT 10 June 1876; ds enroute to Ft Lincoln 6 Aug 1876; dd qmd 12–28 Sep with 281 cav horses at post; pvt 1 Nov 1876; ed qmd Dec 1876 to Apr 1877; dd teamster Aug 1877; ds North Moreau River DT Sep & Oct 1877; ed qmd Apr 1878; ds Ft Rice DT Dec 1878 & Apr 1879 driving teams; disch 6 Sep 1880 Belle Fourche DT expir of serv a pvt char good; reenl 4 Oct 1880 at St Louis for 5 yrs; assd to co M 8 cav; disch 4 Oct 1885 Ft Brown Tex. expir of serv a pvt char xclt; reenl 3 Nov 1885 Ft L'worth Kans. for 5 yrs in gen serv (prov gd mil prison); tr to co C 7 cav 26 May 1889; disch 2 Nov 1890 Ft Riley Kans. expir of serv a pvt char good; reenl 28 Nov 1890 at St Louis for 5 yrs; assd to ordn detmt; disch 28 Nov 1895 Rock Isl Ars'l Ill. expir of serv a pvt char good & reenl in same unit for 3 yrs; disch 2 Dec 1898 at Rock Isl Ars'l expir of serv a 1st cl. pvt char very good & reenl in same unit; retd 4 Feb 1899; died 13 May 1907 St Louis Mo.[38]

Steck, Chas. A. Pvt co C; b. Phil'a Pa.; enl 15 Sep 1873 at Phil'a for 5 yrs; age 24; broom maker; blue eyes, brn hair, fair comp, 5' 6 1/4" high; join co C 21 Oct 1873 Ft Rice DT; ed qmd laborer Oct 1873 to Feb 1874; des 6 Apr 1874 at Ft Rice & apph 10 Apr at Jamestown DT; sen gen cm 2 July 1874 forf all pay due & 2 yrs conft at sta of co thence to dishon disch; dishon disch 10 May 1876 Ft Lincoln DT.

Stein, Chas. A. Vet'y surg ; b. Prussia Germany ca. 1838; grad mil vet'y college at Berlin & served as vet'y surg in Prussian army; grad Merchants Vet'y College at Phil'a Pa. 1 Mar 1872; employed as inspector for Louisiana live stock insurance co at New Orleans; appd for appmt as vet'y surg 7 cav 26 Feb 1875 (upon recom'n capt Benteen); passed exam'n before army bd 22 Apr 1875; appt jr vet'y surg 7 July 1875 & attd to co B at Shreveport La.; rate of pay $75 mo; appt senior vet'y surg 1 Oct 1875; pay $100 mo; order to join regtl hq at Ft Lincoln DT 20 Dec 1875 suspended until spring, he having a large family of small ch. who would suffer severely enroute & being too poor to leave them behind; arr Ft Lincoln 21 Apr 1876;[39] ds camp Powder River MT 15 June 1876; (made 4th of July speech at camp);[40] submitted resignation 31 July effective 1 Sep but maj Reno recom it take effect at once because since joining regt he was so frequently under influence of liquor as to impair his efficiency; arr Ft Lincoln 6 Aug on str *Carroll*;[41] hired as vet'y surg in post qmd to attend sick horses 1–5 Sep; rate of pay $4 day; vet'y surg qmd St Paul Minn. 9 Sep to 20 Oct 1876 treating pub horses enroute to 7 cav; rate of pay $3.50 day;[42] served as coroner of Ramsey Co. Minn. 1878 to 1880 thence vet'y surg in St Paul until his death 19 Oct 1891; survived by wife & 5 ch.[43] [5453 ACP 1875].

Steintker, Jno. R. Far'r co K; b. Hanover Germany; enl 21 Nov 1867 Cincinnati Ohio for 5 yrs; age 32; soldier; brn eyes, dk hair, ruddy comp, 5' 11 1/2" high; join co M 7 cav 22 Jan 1868 Ft L'worth Kans.; sick field hosp 23 Nov to 2 Dec 1868 (cont'n); dd co cook Dec 1869; far'r 1 June 1870; disch 21 Nov 1872 Unionville SC expir of serv a far'r; reenl in regt 30 Nov 1872 Louisville Ky. for 5 yrs & assd to co K; ds regtl hq (Louisville) to Mar 1873; far'r 1 Apr 1873; pvt 1 June 1875; in conft Oct 1875; far'r 1 Nov 1875; in conft Apr 1876; pvt 1 Aug 1876; dd packer in pack train Aug 1876; died 28 Nov 1876 Ft Lincoln DT (found in bed in co qrs, an empty vial of laudanum in his pocket & presented appearance of poisoning by opium; he had been drinking for about 2 wks).

Stella, Alexander.[44] Pvt co E; b. Athens Greece; enl 1 Dec 1874 St Louis Mo. for 5 yrs; age 21; cook; brn eyes, blk hair, dk comp, 5' 6" high; join co E 8 Feb 1875 Opelika Ala; killed with Custer column 25 June 1876.

Stephens, Geo. W. Pvt co G; b. Madison Ind.; enl 4 Apr 1876 St Louis Bks Mo. for 5 yrs; age 23; cooper; brn eyes, blk hair, dk comp, 5' 8 1/2" high; join co G 27 Apr 1876 St Paul Minn.; ds camp Powder River MT 15 June 1876; dd regtl hq fatigue pty June 1877; dd battn hq Oct 1877; dd qmd Jan to June 1878; dd qmd laborer June to Aug 1879; ds qmd cutting logs Oct 1879; ds post hosp nurse May & June 1880; in conft Feb 1881; disch 3 Apr 1881 Ft Meade DT expir of serv a pvt char good; died 19 Mar 1887 Knox City Mo.
Pension: 20 June 1887 / Wid / 356794 / 974038. (XC-2,718,983).

Sterland, Walter Scott. Pvt co M; b. 16 Apr 1851 Sheffield England; enl 18 Nov 1872 Pittsburgh Pa. for 5 yrs; age 21; teamster; blue eyes, lt hair, fair comp, 5' 5 1/2" high; join co M 9 Dec 1872 Unionville SC; dd subs dept herder Dec 1873 to Apr 1874; dd co cook Oct to Dec 1874; dd subs dept herder Feb to Apr 1875; ed subs dept butcher Aug 1875 to May 1876; ed subs dept butcher with exp'n 13 May 1876; ds dept hq in field mouth of Big Horn River 30 June;[45] ds with wagon train 6 Aug; rejoin co 5 Sep 1876; cpl 18 Oct 1876; actg co qm sgt Apr to Aug 1877; ds str *Silver City* 15 Oct to Ft Lincoln; disch 18 Nov 1877 Ft Rice DT expir of serv a cpl char good; died 27 Aug 1922 Dickinson N.Dak.[46]
Pension: Ind. Surv. / 10938 / 7456. Ind. Wid. / 16049 / 10455.

Stevenson, Thos. J.[47] Pvt co G; b. Fermanagh Ireland; enl 27 June 1870 Chicago Ill. for 5 yrs; age 22; laborer; blue eyes, red hair, ruddy comp, 5' 5 3/4" high; assd to co E 7 inf; disch 27 June 1875 Camp Baker MT expir of serv a pvt; reenl 19 July 1875 at Chicago for 5 yrs; join co G 7 cav 27 Apr 1876 St Paul Minn.;

abs sick (gsw) on str *Carroll* 2 Aug 1876 to Ft Lincoln DT; duty 23 Aug; dd qmd 15 Sep 1876 care for pub animals; cpl 1 July 1877; actg co qm sgt Apr to June 1878; ds Ft Lincoln July to Nov 1878; pvt 12 Mar 1879; tr to co K 1 May 1879; cpl 15 June 1879; sgt 6 June 1880; disch 18 July 1880 Ft Totten DT expir of serv a sgt char good; reenl 22 July 1880 Ft Snelling Minn. for 5 yrs; assd to co H 7 inf; tr to co M 2 cav; disch 21 July 1885 Ft Couer d'Alene Idaho expir of serv a pvt char very good; reenl 29 July 1885 Chicago Ill. for 5 yrs; assd to co C 1 cav; tr to co C 8 cav; disch 12 July 1887 army & navy hosp Hot Springs Ark on surg cert dis (chr. rheum.) a pvt char good; died 29 Jan 1898 Minneapolis Minn.
Pension: 26 Sep 1887 / Inv / 624007 / 385051. Wid / 678631 / 474861. Minor / 883650 / 638564.

Stivers, Thos. W. Pvt co D; b. 15 July 1850 Madison Co. Ky.; enl in co D 16 Sep 1871 Mt Vernon Ky. for 5 yrs; age 21 2/12; clerk; blue eyes, dk brn hair, fair comp, 5' 5" high; in conft Apr 1872; in conft Aug 1872; ds Ft Seward DT 14 May to 29 June 1874; ds Ft Lincoln DT 1 July 1874 await return of co from NBS; sent to Ft Totten DT 7 Aug 1874 chg of govt horses; disch 5 Aug 1876 camp mouth of Rosebud Creek MT (in time to go down river by first boat) per GO 24 AGO 1859 a pvt; arr Ft Lincoln 10 Aug on str *Durfee*; awarded medal of honor 5 Oct 1878 for bringing water to the wounded (at LBH) while under heavy fire; he having been disch the serv, medal filed in AGO; killed 28 June 1877 near Richmond Ky. in gunfight.[48]

Stoffel, Henry. Pvt co L; b. Phil'a Pa.; enl 22 Jan 1872 at Phil'a for 5 yrs; age 21; farmer; blue eyes, lt hair, fair comp, 5' 9" high; join co L 26 Feb 1872 Yorkville SC; in conft June to Dec 1872; sen gen cm 31 Aug 1872 forf $10 pay per mo for 4 mos & conft same period; des 6 July 1873 Ft Lincoln DT; surd 2 Nov 1874 Camp Hancock (Bismarck) DT; sen gen cm 21 Jan 1875 to 2 yrs conft at sta of co thence to dishon disch;[49] unexpired portion of sen remitted 23 Oct 1875; dd wood sawyer 1 Nov 1875 to 7 Mar 1876; dd post hq woodchopper Apr 1878; disch 18 May 1878 Ft Lincoln DT expir of serv a pvt char xclt & reenl in co L for 5 yrs; cpl 2 Aug 1878; pvt 4 Sep 1879; dd qmd sawyer Dec 1879 to Feb 1880; dd post hq orderly Apr to June 1881; dd qmd Feb to Apr 1882; sick 3 June to 3 July 1882 (rheum. & lumbago); ed post sawyer Oct to Dec 1882; disch 17 May 1883 Ft Buford DT expir of serv a pvt char good.

Stout, Edw. Pvt co B; b. Calhoun Mo.; enl in co B 25 Jan 1870 Ft Lyon Colo. Ty for 5 yrs; age 28; farmer; brn eyes, brn hair, lt comp, 5' 11" high; appt wag 1 May 1872; dd qmd May to Aug 1872; pvt 1 Nov 1872; in conft Aug 1874; disch 25 Jan 1875 Shreveport La. expir of serv a pvt & reenl in co B for 5 yrs; in conft Oct 1875; sen gen cm 29 Oct 1875 forf $10 pay per mo for 2 mos; ds constructing tel line Aug 1879; disch 24 Jan 1880 Ft Yates DT expir of serv a pvt char good & reenl in co B for 5 yrs; dd qmd with water wagon Dec 1880 to Apr 1881; on furl 90 days 20 Jan 1883 Chicago Ill.; des 26 May 1883 Ft Yates DT.

Stowers, Thos. J. Pvt co B; b. 3 Dec 1848 Nashville Tenn; pvt co D 199 Pa. inf 3 Sep 1864 to 28 June 1865; enl reg army as Jas. Thomas 1 Dec 1874 Chicago Ill. for 5 yrs; age 26; laborer; hazel eyes, sandy hair, fair comp, 5' 7" high; join co B 10 Feb 1875 Shreveport La.; dd qmd Dec 1876 to Apr 1877; ds Wolf Rapids of Yellowstone River 1 Oct 1877; cpl 1 Mar 1879; dd chg co garden Apr to June 1879; disch 30 Nov 1879 Ft Yates DT expir of serv a cpl char xclt; died 26 July 1933 Baxter Tenn.
Pension: 13 July 1897 / Inv / 1194474 / 965430.

Stratton, Frank. Pvt co M; b. Nottingham Co. England; enl 18 Sep 1875 St Louis Bks Mo. for 5 yrs; age 27; printer; hazel eyes, brn hair, fair comp, 5' 5 1/2" high; join co M 21 Oct 1875 Ft Rice DT; in conft Oct 1876 to May 1877; (awol with his co horse & maliciously shot & killed said horse); sen gen cm 27 Feb 1877 forf $10 pay per mo for 4 mos & conft same period; (capt French recom remission of sen, that apart from offense of which convicted his char was always xclt); ds Ft Lincoln DT 2 May 1877 (dd post hq); des 28 July 1877 at Ft Lincoln.

Streing, Fred'k. (alias). See Stressinger, Fred'k.

Stressinger, Fred'k. Cpl co M; b. Ripley Co. Ind.; enl as Fred'k Streing 19 Oct 1872 Louisville Ky. for 5 yrs; age 21; laborer; grey eyes, lt hair, fair comp, 5' 5 1/4" high; join co M 9 Dec 1872 Unionville SC; abs sick (ac. bronc.) on str *Western* 23 Apr 1873 Yankton to Ft Rice DT; duty 9 June 1873; dd co cook Aug 1873; dd co cook Aug 1874; dd co cook Feb 1875; dd co carpenter Apr to June 1875; blks 1 July 1875; cpl 17 June 1876; killed dur retreat from valley fight 25 June 1876.
Pension: 3 Mar 1887 / Mother / 351261 / 270697.

Strode, Elijah T. Pvt co A; b. 9 Feb 1852 Monroe Co. Ky.; enl in co A 15 Oct 1872 Elizabethtown Ky. for 5 yrs; age 21 7/12; farmer; brn eyes, brn hair, fair comp, 5' 9 3/4" high; dd co cook Feb 1875; orderly for Lt Varnum June 1876; gsw r. leg (severe) 25 June dur retreat from valley fight; tr on str *Far West* 3 July to hosp Ft Lincoln; duty 25 Aug 1876; dd qmd 15 Sep 1876 care for pub animals; disch 24 June 1877 camp near Tongue River MT per SO 70 Dept of Dak. 1877 a pvt char good; reenl 4 Mar 1878 Ft Rice DT for 5 yrs in co H 7 cav; cpl 4 Jan 1879; sgt 1 Oct 1879; pvt 7 Dec 1879; dd co cook June 1880; in conft Dec 1880; killed 14 Feb 1881 Sturgis City DT (pistol shot from pvt Whalen co H).[50]
Pension: 27 Aug 1885 / Father / 330236. Rej on grd fatal cause of sol's death not in line of duty & when awol from his post.

Stroud, Wm. H. See Demoss, Chas.

Stuart, Alpheus. Pvt co C; b. New York N.Y.; enl 24 Aug 1870 Chicago Ill. for 5 yrs; age 28; laborer; grey eyes, dk hair, fair comp, 5' 10 1/2" high; join co M 8 cav 18 Oct 1870 Ft Garland Colo. Ty; cpl 1 Apr 1871; pvt 5 June 1872; ed qmd teamster July & Aug 1872; cpl 24 Apr 1873; sgt 3 Oct 1873; ds repairing tel line Feb 1874; ds as tel operator San Jose NM Jan to Apr 1875; disch 24 Aug 1875 Ft Davis Tex. expir of serv a sgt; reenl 20 Sep 1875 Cincinnati Ohio for 5 yrs; join co C 7 cav 21 Oct 1875 Ft Lincoln DT; dd orderly at gar cm Dec 1875 to Feb 1876; killed with Custer column 25 June 1876.[51]

Stuart-Forbes, Jno. Stuart. Pvt co E; b. 28 May 1849 Rugby England; enl as Jno. S. Hiley 20 Jan 1872 New York N.Y. for 5 yrs; age 23; clerk; hazel eyes, lt brn hair, fair comp, 6' 0" high; join co E 15 Feb 1872 Unionville SC; sick qrs Apr 1873; killed with Custer column 25 June 1876.[52]

Stungewitz, Ignatz. Pvt co C; b. Kovno Russia; enl 15 Sep 1873 New York N.Y. for 5 yrs; age 26; clerk; blue eyes, lt hair, fair comp, 5' 8 1/2" high; join co C 21 Oct 1873 Ft Rice DT; killed with Custer column 25 June 1876.

Sturgis, Jas. Garland. (son of col Sturgis). 2Lt co M; b. 24 Jan 1854 Albuquerque NM; grad USMA 16 June 1875 & appt 2Lt 7 cav; appn for td at St Louis Bks not appv; joined depot 15 Aug (auth AGO upon req of col Sturgis) to cond 100 rcts to San Antonio Tex.; ret to depot for balance of graduation leave; assd court martial duty 7 Sep (req of col Sturgis); start to regt delayed until 15 Oct (auth AGO) to accomp capt Thompson 7 cav with 150 rcts to Ft Lincoln DT; join co M 29 Oct Ft Rice DT; post signal officer 1 Mar to 2 May 1876; attd to co E 12 May; kept notes dur maj Reno's scout up Powder River 10–20 June; killed with Custer column 25 June 1876; body not identified.[53]
[3012 ACP 1875].

Sturgis, Sam'l Davis. Colonel; b. 11 June 1822 Shippensburg Pa.; grad USMA 1 July 1846 & appt bvt 2Lt 2 drg; 2Lt 1 drg 16 Feb 1847; captured dur Mexican war 20 Feb 1847 while on scout before battle of Buena Vista & released after battle; rqm Apr 1851 to Mar 1852; 1Lt 15 July 1853; his decisive victory against inds at Cienega NM 6 Apr 1854 & near Santa Fe NM 16 Jan 1855 elicited resolution gratitude of state legislature & req to pres't Pierce for his prom'n; capt 1 cav 3 Mar 1855 (upon org'n of regt); in campns against hostile inds in Kansas & IT to Oct 1860 then at Ft Smith Ark dur difficulty with Cherokee inds on neutral lands; removed govt stores from Ft Smith to Ft L'worth in Apr 1861 upon resignation of southern officers; prom maj 3 May 1861; (regt redesig 4 cav Aug 1861); in action with rebels at Wilson's Creek Mo. 10 Aug

1861 & took comd of troops upon death of gen Lyon; appt brig-gen vols same date; comd defenses of Wash'n D.C. May to Aug 1862; chf of staff to gen Hunter & comd reserve at 2d battle of Bull Run 29 Aug 1862; comd div in battle of Antietam 16 Sep 1862 & at Fredericksburg 13 Dec 1862; tr back to western armies Apr 1863 & chf of cav Dept of Ohio to Apr 1864 & org militia at Cincinnati dur Morgan's raid; m.o. vol serv 24 Aug 1865; bvt Lt-col & col for gal serv at Wilson's Creek & Bull Run; bvt brig-gen for gal serv at South Mtn; bvt maj-gen for gal serv at Fredericksburg; prom Lt-col 6 cav (to date 27 Oct 1863) & joined regt 14 Oct 1865 near Frederick Md; comd regt on str *Herman Livingston* 19 Oct to 2 Nov 1865 from New York to New Orleans; (threw horses overboard dur severe storm 23 Oct);[54] post comdr Austin Tex. 29 Nov 1865; awl May to Dec 1866; post comdr Ft Belknap Tex. June 1867 & Camp Wilson (Ft Griffin) Tex. Aug 1867; awl until further orders 20 Apr 1868; ds Wash'n D.C. on bd of tactics July 1868; prom col 7 cav 6 May 1869; comd regt & post Ft L'worth Kans. 6 June 1869 to 18 Mar 1871;[55] with regtl hq Taylor Bks (Louisville) Ky. to 2 Apr 1873; comd detmt at Yankton DT 1–6 May 1873;[56] with regtl hq St Paul Minn. 8 May 1873 thro' Sep 1874; ds supt gen mtd rctg serv St Louis Bks Mo. 1 Oct 1874; rejoin regt 18 Oct 1876 Ft Lincoln DT & in field disarming agcy inds to 11 Nov 1876; comd regt in field 1 May to 8 Oct 1877 & in action with Nez Perce inds 13 Sep at Canon Creek MT; arr Ft Lincoln 22 Oct on str *Big Horn* (with regtl hq); awl one mo 24 Oct at St Louis;[57] abs sick on own cert 24 Nov 1877 to 28 Feb 1878; post comdr Ft Meade DT 17 July 1879; ds Wash'n D.C. 16 June 1881 gov'r of Sol. Home; post comdr Ft Meade June to Nov 1885 thence awl 5 mos; retd 11 June 1886; died 28 Sep 1889 St Paul Minn. [1398 ACP 1881]. Pension: 3 Apr 1891 / Wid / 509833 / 315785.

Sullivan, Dan'l. Pvt co G; b. 27 Jan 1851 Cork Ireland; enl 8 Dec 1874 Boston Mass. for 5 yrs; age 22; laborer; blue eyes, dk hair, medium comp, 5' 8" high; join co G 10 Feb 1875 Shreveport La.; dd asst baker Oct 1875 to Feb 1876; ds camp Powder River MT 15 June 1876; disch 7 Dec 1879 Ft Meade DT expir of serv a pvt char good; reenl 30 Dec 1879 Boston Mass. for 5 yrs; assd to co C 16 inf; disch 29 Dec 1884 Ft Concho Tex. expir of serv a pvt & reenl in same co for 5 yrs; disch 29 Dec 1889 Ft DuChesne Utah expir of serv a pvt; reenl 25 Jan 1890 Presidio San Francisco Calif. for 5 yrs; assd to co H 19 inf; disch 24 Jan 1895 Ft Wayne Mich. expir of serv a pvt & reenl in same co for 3 yrs; disch 24 Jan 1898 Ft Brady Mich. expir of serv a pvt & reenl 26 Jan in same co for 3 yrs; tr to co K 23 June 1898; (serv in Porto Rico Aug 1898 to June 1899); disch 19 June 1899 Camp Meade Pa. per instr'n from AGO (his serv no longer required; [rheum. & resulting disease of heart]) a pvt; died 25 June 1934 Ardagilla Skibbereen Cork Ireland.
Pension: 27 June 1899 / Inv / 1230759 / 1025504. (XC-2,550,021).

Sullivan, Jno. Pvt co A; b. Dublin Ireland; enl 7 Dec 1874 Boston Mass. for 5 yrs; age 23; laborer; grey eyes, brn hair, medium comp, 5' 6 1/8" high; join co A 6 Feb 1875 Livingston Ala; in conft Dec 1875 to Mar 1876; sen gen cm 29 Jan 1876 forf $10 pay per mo for 3 mos & conft same period; killed dur retreat from valley fight 25 June 1876 (body not recovered).[58]

Sullivan, Timothy. Pvt co L; b. Chelsea Mass.; enr 11 May 1861 a pvt co K 2 Mass inf for 3 yrs; enl reg army 25 Oct 1862 Knoxville Md in co C 3 art'y for 18 mos 27 days (bal of vol enlmt); age 22; shoemaker; grey eyes, brn hair, ruddy comp, 5' 4" high; in conft Oct 1863; disch 16 Feb 1864 Stevensburg Va. by reenlmt in same co for 3 yrs; age 21; des 26 July 1865 Camp Bailey Md; reenl 6 Feb 1866 Boston Mass. for 3 yrs; join co G 1 cav 6 June 1866 camp on upper San Pedro AT; in conft Oct 1866 to Feb 1867; ds picket post San Pedro Crossing June 1867; abs scouting against hostile inds Aug 1867; on campn against hostile inds Aug 1868; dd co artf'r Oct 1868 & ds with escort for paymr; sad'r 1 Dec 1868; disch 6 Feb 1869 Camp Lowell (Tucson) AT expir of serv a sad'r; reenl 11 June 1870 Boston Mass. for 5 yrs; age 26; join co

G 5 cav 11 July 1870 camp near Sherman Wyo. Ty; cpl 1 Nov 1870; pvt June 1871; surd as des'r 15 Nov 1873 under GO 102 AGO 1873; restored to duty without trial 8 June 1874 & tr to co G 5 cav to serve bal of orig'l enlmt; ed comsy dept Aug 1874; dd stable orderly Oct 1874 to May 1875; disch 5 June 1875 Ft Whipple AT expir of serv a pvt; reenl 17 Sep 1875 Chicago Ill. for 5 yrs; join co L 7 cav 29 Oct 1875 Ft Totten DT; dd hq fatigue pty r. wing (morn & eve) 15 May 1876; dd regtl hq orderly 6 Aug 1876; ds in field 13 Sep 1877; dd qmd hostler Apr 1878; dd regtl hq orderly June 1878; dd qmd msgr Dec 1878 to Apr 1879; far'r 1 Sep 1879; pvt Apr 1880 & dd qmd hostler to June 1880; disch 16 Sep 1880 Ft Lincoln DT expir of serv a pvt char good & reenl in co L for 5 yrs; on furl 3 mos 1 Dec 1880 Bismarck DT; wag 10 Sep 1881; in conft Dec 1881; sen gen cm Jan 1882 forf all pay & conft one yr Ft Snelling Minn. thence to dishon disch; unexpired portion of sen remitted 13 Nov 1882 & restored to duty; in conft Dec 1883; ds cutting wood Apr 1884; disch 16 Sep 1885 Ft Buford DT expir of serv a pvt char a good soldier; reenl 23 Sep 1885 Chicago Ill. for 5 yrs; assd to co C 5 cav; tr to co D; disch 22 Sep 1890 Ft Sill IT expir of serv a pvt char xclt; reenl same day at Ft Sill in co H 7 cav for 5 yrs; on furl 4 mos 25 Sep 1890 St Louis Mo.; dd co tailor Nov 1891 to June 1893; far'r 1 Sep 1893; on furl 25 days 31 Oct 1893 L'worth Kans.; pvt 23 May 1894; far'r 7 June 1894; (awarded cert of merit 22 Mar 1895 for dist serv in Nez Perce campn 17 Sep 1877 [due $2 per mo for cert of merit Sep 1877 to Apr 1895);[59] disch 22 Sep 1895 Ft Grant AT expir of serv a far'r char xclt & reenl same day in co H; sgt 24 Sep 1895; retd 5 Dec 1895 a sgt char xclt (sober, industrious & trustworthy); died 10 Jan 1903 Brightwood (Wash'n) D.C.

Summers, David. Pvt co M; b. Pettis Co. Mo.; enl 24 Apr 1871 Garlington Kans. for 5 yrs; age 22; farmer; blue eyes, sandy hair, ruddy comp, 5' 8 1/2" high; join co I 6 inf camp on Drywood Creek Kans.; dd qmd teamster Oct to Dec 1871; ed qmd teamster Aug 1873 to Feb 1874; ed qmd teamster with escort for NBS June to Aug 1874; ds with co C Oct 1874; dd qmd laborer Dec 1874 to Feb 1875; dd asst co cook Apr 1875; dd subs dept herder June 1875; ed qmd teamster Aug to Dec 1875; disch 24 Apr 1876 Ft Lincoln DT by expir of serv a pvt; reenl 13 May 1876 camp near Ft Lincoln for 5 yrs in co M 7 cav; sick qrs 22 May (sore throat) & sick hosp 23–24 May; sick qrs (ride) 25 May to 12 June; duty 13 June; killed dur retreat from valley fight 25 June 1876 near edge of timber.[60]

Sweeney, Jno. Wm. Pvt co F; b. Marion Co. Mo.; enl 30 Dec 1868 Louisville Ky. for 3 yrs; age 22; carpenter; grey eyes, lt hair, fair comp, 5' 8 1/2" high; assd to co A 2 inf; disch 30 Dec 1871 Atlanta Ga. expir of serv a pvt; reenl 4 Jan 1872 at Louisville for 5 yrs in co F 7 cav; dd post mail carrier Dec 1872; dd dept hq (Louisville) Feb 1873; gsw r. thigh (fl. wd.) 11 Aug 1873 Big Horn River MT in action with Sioux inds; in field hosp to 11 Sep when tr to str *Josephine* to hosp Ft Lincoln DT; duty 19 Oct 1873; cpl Mar 1874; sgt July 1874; actg co qm sgt Feb to Aug 1875; in arrest Oct 1875; pvt 26 Dec 1875; sen gen cm 11 Jan 1876 forf $10 pay per mo for 3 mos; sick qrs 18 Mar to 4 May 1876 (frostbite great toe r. foot); rel from conft & restored to duty 26 Apr 1876; [with pack train says Finnegan & Lynch; with wagon train says Rooney];[61] on mtd duty dept hq in field 6 Aug 1876 (with Dr. Porter);[62] ed post qmd 17 Nov to 5 Dec 1876; disch 4 Jan 1877 Ft Abercrombie DT expir of serv a pvt char xclt; died 14 Apr 1884 near Graefensburg Ky.
Pension: 12 July 1878 / Inv / 258260 / 169173. Wid / 321193 / 226789. Minor / 849756 / 619139. (XC-2,662,260).

Sweeney, Wm. Pvt co F; b. Newark NJ; enl 7 Sep 1875 St Louis Mo. for 5 yrs; age 21; teamster; grey eyes, brn hair, fair comp, 5' 5 1/2" high; join co F 21 Oct 1875 Ft Lincoln DT; sick 22–27 Nov (cont'n r. eye, fighting); sick 27 Dec to 4 Jan (sprain l. shoulder, fall on ice); abs in civil jail Bismarck DT 23 Jan 1876 awaiting trial for theft; escaped in Apr 1876 but apph by sheriff;[63] des 26 Sep 1876 while in conft at Bismarck.

Sweetser, Thos. P. Pvt co A; b. Reading Mass.;

enl 8 Sep 1875 Boston Mass. for 5 yrs; age 25; carpenter; blue eyes, brn hair, dk comp, 5' 7 3/4" high; join co A 21 Oct 1875 Ft Lincoln DT; dd qmd carpenter to 19 Apr 1876 when relieved upon req of capt Moylan to receive training in duties of a sol. & made available for field serv; killed dur retreat from valley fight 25 June 1876; (body never found, says Alcott). Pension: 30 Jan 1888 / Mother / 367201. (Abandoned).

Symms, Darwin L. Pvt co I; b. Montreal Canada; enl 25 Aug 1875 Chicago Ill. for 5 yrs; age 23; clerk; blue eyes, lt hair, fair comp, 5' 9" high; join co I 21 Oct 1875 Ft Lincoln DT; killed with Custer column 25 June 1876.
Pension: 10 May 1878 / Wid / 237167 / 182943.

Notes—S

1. Certificates of merit were awarded for acts of extraordinary gallantry in presence of the enemy and entitled the soldier to extra pay of $2 per month while remaining continuously in service. *Regulations of the Army*, 1881, Par. 248–53. Though none but private soldiers were eligible under the law, the recommendation for Sgt. Saas was approved and forwarded through military channels with a view to correct the defect in the law. RG 94, Entry 409, file 4884 C 1882.

2. See notes A24 (Arnold) and A25 (Ascough).

3. RG 94, Entry 409, file, 10818 A (EB) 1878; Lt. Edgerly said Private "Saunders" was his orderly on the high point June 25, and when he (Edgerly) was having difficulty mounting his frightened horse, he handed his carbine to Saunders who was smiling broadly, although they were in a perfect shower of bullets. When asked the next day, Saunders replied, "I was laughing to see what poor shots those Indians were; they were shooting too low and their bullets were spattering dust like drops of rain." Edgerly said he never saw a cooler man under fire than Saunders. Article written by Edgerly at Fort Clark, Texas, ca. 1892–95, copy in Ghent Papers.

Elsewhere, Edgerly said Sanders accompanied Capt. Weir as orderly from Reno Hill to the high point June 25. Edgerly to Gen. Godfrey, Jan. 17, 1886, Godfrey Papers. For Sander's full military service, see RG 94, Entry 25, file 63114 AGO 1915.

4. GO 80, AGO, July 26, 1890, RG 94, Entry 44; see note D26 (Diamond).

5. Rosters of Company F with remarks by Rooney and Lynch, WMC-BYU; Sterland said Schleiffarth was with him as butcher and from mouth of Rosebud went up on the boat with Gen. Terry and was not at Little Big Horn. WMC, notes, IU; Lt. Thompson, ACS, said the men detailed to go with him went on the boat and up the Big Horn. Hammer, *Custer in '76*, 247.

6. RG 94, Entry 25, file 14721 PRD 1890.

7. Rosters of Company F with remarks by Rooney and Lynch, Gregg interview, n.d., WMC-BYU; Schlieper is not found in the two medical registers (prescription books) for the two wings of the 7th Cavalry in 1876. RG 94, Entry 544, MT, No. 14, April 19 to June 13, and, No. 54, May 15 to June 10.

Lynch said that when Charley Reynolds carried dispatches from the Black Hills to Fort Laramie in August 1874, Schlieper sat up all night making leather shoes for Reynolds' horse to prevent the hoofs cutting the grass that would allow Indians to track him, WMC, transcript, BYU-200; also statement of Charley Reynolds in the *New York Graphic,* clipping sent to Walter Camp in 1910 by W. T. Reynolds, WMC, box 5, env 123, BYU; see also Frost, *With Custer in '74*, 61–62.

8. The steamer *Eclipse* was the first boat of the season, arriving at Fort Buford, April 16, 1881. RG 94, Entry 547.

9. Burdick and Hart, *Jacob Horner*, 14.

10. Rosters of Company F with remarks by Rooney and Lynch, Gregg interview, n.d., WMC-BYU; WMC, rosters, LBHB.

11. RG 94, Entry 409, file 10818 A (EB) 1878. A memorial marker for Scott was dedicated Nov. 11, 1999, in the Lancaster (Ky.) Cemetery. *The Central Record* (Lancaster, Ky), Nov. 18, 1999; *The Garrard County* (Ky.) *News*, Nov. 18, 1999.

12. Botzer Troop Duty Book.

13. "Crazy Jim" Severs prevented a runaway pack mule from reaching the Indians on Reno Hill June 25, a similar deed for which Sgt. Hanley received the medal of honor. Story of Dan Newell in Carroll, ed., *The Sunshine Magazine Articles*; Mulford, *Fighting Indians in the Seventh Cavalry*, 109; Charles Windolph in Hunt and Hunt, *I Fought With Custer*, 105.

Sgt. Ryan said he superintended burying general and Tom Custer on June 28 and had with him Privates James Severs, Harrison Davis, and Frank Neely. Ryan to Walter Camp, Feb. 26, 1910, WMC-LBHB.

Lt. Garlington, who joined Company G, Aug. 2, recalled that the doctor attached to the regiment was a great hunter and had an orderly whom the soldiers called "Crazy Jim." Carroll, *Garlington Narrative*, 18.

14. Statement of postmaster of Saratoga, Wyo., to inquiry from the Bureau of Pensions, Nov. 25, 1912, Pension file, RG 15; William O. Taylor said Severs died in 1912 at Saratoga, Wyo. Taylor Scrapbook, 103.

15. Brown Troop Duty Book. Reynolds and Brown, *Journal*. The muster roll shows Shanahan on detached service with the company wagon. Gen. Terry sent all wagons back to the camp on the Yellowstone Aug. 11.

16. On his first enlistment, Sharrow reported he was born at York England, but on two subsequent enlistments said he was born, "At Sea." Also, on his second enlistment paper, August 1869, he recorded his age as 24 years and five months, which was confirmed in Parish registers at Borthwick Institute of Historical Research at Yorkshire. See, Russell, "Custer's Sergeant Major, 8.

17. Sharrow was accused of absconding in disgrace, "a fugitive from justice," having abused his position to contract debts upon false pretences. Maj. Robt. D. Clarke, Paymaster, USA, Omaha Neb., to Gen. Benj. W. Brice, Paymaster General, Aug. 11, 1869, RG 99, Entry 7, Letters Received, (No. 731), 1869.

18. Thomas Sherborn, age 24, and Frank Sherborn, age 26, both musicians born in London, England, enlisted the same day at New York City; Frank was assigned to field and staff, 10th Infantry, and deserted July 16, 1866.

19. Gen. Sheridan was appointed brigadier general of Volunteers, July 1, 1862 (from Capt., 13th Infantry, [and Col., 2nd Michigan Cavalry]).

20. Capt. Sheridan was the officer who intercepted Gen. Custer on the train at Chicago the morning of May 4, 1876. Custer's young nephew wrote that, "General Sheridan's brother heard that Gen. Custer was in the city [Chicago] and he came down to the train and informed the Gen. that Sheridan had orders from Washington to stop him in Chicago on the ground that he had not called on the President and leaving Washington without orders." Autie Reed to his parents, May 6, 1876, Typescript copy in Frost Coll., Monroe County (Mich.) Library.

21. For an excellent account of Capt. Sheridan's detail in 1877 to retrieve the remains of officers killed at the Little Big Horn, see Gray, "Photos, Femurs, and Fallacies": also *The Avant Courier* (Bozeman, MT), July 19, 1877; Gen. Sheridan died at his seaside cottage in Nonquitt, Mass., Aug. 5, 1888. Hutton, *Phil Sheridan and His Army*, 372.

22. WMC, roster, LBHB; WMC, roster IU; Pandtle (Pendle) to Walter Camp, July 14, 1919, WMC-BYU; Henry Lange interview, nd, WMC-BYU; O'Toole to Camp, Mar. 26, 1909, WMC-BYU; Rooney said he dug a rifle pit with Shields, Murphy, and Spencer, WMC, transcript, BYU-255.

23. Nathan Short has been linked to a dead cavalry horse found in early August 1876, near mouth of Rosebud Creek, and though speculation abounds regarding the identity of the rider, the story, mostly from the works of Walter Camp, has been elaborated on in Ellison, "Mystery along Rosebud Creek" and Doran, "The Man Who Got to the Rosebud."

24. Fifty-first Cong., Sess. I, Chap. 78. Amending Article of War 103, R. S., Sec. 1342. "No person shall be tried or punished by a court-martial for desertion in time of peace and not in the face of an enemy, committed more than two years before the arraignment of such person for such offense, unless he shall meanwhile have absented himself from the United States, in which case the time of his absence shall be excluded in computing the period of the limitation: *Provided*, That said limitation shall not begin until the end of the term for which said person was mustered into the service." See also, RG 94, Entry 25, file 24273 PRD 1892.

25. Slaper said that, through the kindness of Sgt. Ryan, he had a copy of the Company M roll call made on Reno Hill the morning of June 27, 1876. Brininstool, *Troopers with Custer*, 60.

26. Early newspaper stories reporting the histories of the slain officers, said that Lt. Smith, "left his studies at Hamilton College to enter the volunteer service. . ." *Chicago* (Ill.) *Inter-Ocean*, July 7, 1876; *New York Herald*, July 10, 1876; *Army & Navy Journal*, July 15, 1876.

27. Tribute for Lt. Smith from Gen. William R. Pease to the editor of the *Utica Morning Herald*, n.d., clipping in scrapbook compiled by Nettie Bowen Smith, wife of Lt. Smith, in LBHB Coll., Roll 18.

28. William Slaper said that, when the command halted to form the dismounted skirmish line, Smith's horse became unmanageable and ran away with him straight into the Indians. Brininstool, *Troopers With Custer*, 48.

"In the Custer massacre, the attack by Reno had at first caused a panic among women and children, and some of the warriors, who started to flee, but 'Crazy Horse,' throwing away his rifle, brained one of the incoming soldiers with his stone war-club and jumped upon his horse." Bourke, *On the Border with Crook*, 415.

29. *United States Army Regulations, 1863*, Par. 1358. Every deserter shall forfeit all pay and allowances due at time of desertion. Stoppages and fines shall be paid from his future earnings, if he is apprehended and continued in services and if they are adjudged by a court-martial; otherwise, from his arrears of pay. (Par. 1359), No deserter shall receive pay before trial, or till restored to duty without trial by the authority competent to order the trial.

Private Smith wrote to Capt. Godfrey, Nov. 2, 1877, appealing for clemency, and promising that if restored to duty he would, "serve honestly and faithfully to the end." NA, M1734, Roll 23, letter 5296 DD 1877.

30. Sniffin applied for discharge March 1, 1887, to avail himself of a promising business of sheep raising in Colorado with a cousin. Being a married man with a family, he would thereby learn a trade and enable his children a proper education. RG 94, Entry 25, file 3730 C (EB) 1887, (filed with, 10211 PRD 1890).

31. GO 40, AGO, May 10, 1898, RG 94, Entry 44, entitled men who enlisted during the war to be discharged, if desired, on their own application at the close of the war.

32. GO 31, Hq DG, Dec. 27, 1904, RG 393, Part I, Entry 2048, in compliance with GO 176, War Dept., 1904, RG 94, Entry 44, to prepare 2nd and 3rd squadrons, 7th Cavalry, for service in Philippine Islands and for filling ranks with men, who on date of sailing, had at least 2 years and 3 months to serve. . . All men of 3rd squadron, who on Mar. 15, 1905, had less than 2 years 6 months and 15 days to serve, and who desired to re-enlist immediately in the squadron, to be discharged on that date for convenience of the government. Men so discharged to be at once re-enlisted.

33. WMC, rosters, IU; Henry Lange interview, n.d., WMC-BYU; Pandtle (Pendle) to Walter Camp, July 14, 1919, WMC-BYU; James Rooney said he dug a rifle pit with Spencer. WMC, transcript, BYU-255.

Walter Camp said he found Spencer living in Chicago and his discharge paper had the endorsement of Lt. DeRudio, stating that he (Spencer) was in the battle of Little Big Horn. Camp said Spencer lived in Chicago thirty years, his memory was rather poor and could recall only three or four of Company E who were at Little Big Horn. Camp to Daniel Knipe, Mar. 27, 1911, WMC-LBHB.

34. Liddic and Harbaugh, *Camp on Custer*, 82.

35. "Tell sister Lilly that it is well with her friend Sprague was left at Lincoln or he would in all probability have gone with his company which was with Gen. C." Capt. Hughes (of Gen. Terry's staff), to his wife, June 30, 1876. Noyes, "Captain Robert P. Hughes and the Case Against Custer."

36. RG 94, Entry 96.

37. Mr. S. E. Staples, Worcester, Mass., wrote to the Hon. W. W. Rice, Nov. 9, 1877, hoping to learn if possible to have the body of his son sent home for proper burial. NA, M666, Roll 273, letter 2023 AGO 1878, (filed with 3770 AGO 1876).

38. RG 94, Entry 25, file 202221 PRD 1891.

39. The first scheduled train of the season, after opening the road from winter snow blockades, arrived at Bismarck on Monday, April 17. During the season trains were scheduled to arrive Monday, Wednesday, and Friday, and depart the next morning. *Bismarck Tribune*, April 19, 1876; *The Red River Star*, July 3, 1875.

Dr. DeWolf recorded his first impression of Dr. Stein, "the Vet not so very nice but tolerable . . . he imagines he knows something about medicine it seems so ridiculous to hear him talk mixed Latin German & English it would make you laugh." DeWolf to wife, May 8, 1876, Luce, ed., "The Diary and Letters of Dr. James M. DeWolf."

40. Lt. Hare said he remembered particularly about Stein being left at Powder River but did not recall the reason why. Hammer, *Custer in '76*, 68; WMC, rosters, IU.

41. Stein personal file; Lt. Wallace said Stein resigned and left on the boat after getting insulted when he (Wallace) made him tent near the Band. Said the steamer *Carroll* left on the 2nd (Aug.) for supplies. Wallace to Dr. Chas. F. Knoblauch, Shreveport, La., Aug. 4, 1876, in Westfall, *Letters from the field*, 27–29; it was also reported that Stein tendered his resignation because of inadequate salary after Congress refused to raise the pay and rank of veterinary surgeons. *Bismarck Tribune*, Aug. 9, 1876.

Maj Reno wrote to Libbie Custer, Aug. 2, that he was shipping Gen. Custer's horse Dandy that day to Fort Lincoln. Frost, *General Custer's Thoroughbreds*, 151; the steamer *Carroll* arrived at Fort Lincoln, Aug. 6. RG 94, Entry 547, Fort Lincoln.

42. RG 92, Entry 238, reports 1876/544 and 1876/182; see Gray, "Veterinary Service on Custer's Last Campaign." Dr. Stein recalled that he was favorably assisted at Fort Lincoln by Lt. Burns, post quartermaster, in extracting thirteen bullets from Capt. Keogh's horse, "Comanche." *Bismarck Tribune*, April 26, 1878.

43. Two notices of Dr. Stein's death, in the same newspaper, reported his age 52, and 53. *St. Paul Pioneer-Press*, Oct. 21, 1891; the federal census of St. Paul, June 3, 1880, lists Stein as 38 years old; Dr. Stein was also reported as the author of a work on the disease of horses. *St. Paul and Minneapolis Pioneer-Press and Tribune*, Sept. 10, 1876.

44. Alias Stern says Geist went to school with him in Germany. WMC rosters, IU.

45. Sterland said he drove six head of cattle and was detailed as butcher on Reno's scout from Powder River to the Rosebud. He also said he butchered some beef at Pease Bottom camp (mouth of Big Horn River) in July 1876. WMC, notes, env 64, IU; Lt. Thompson, ACS, said the men detailed to go with him went on the boat and up the Big Horn. Hammer, *Custer in '76*, 24.

Willis W. Carland, (son of Lt. Carland, Company B, 6th Infantry), employed as herder in the subsistence department, related that from Powder River several head of meat cattle were put on board the steamer *Far West*, and after the battle the two or three steers yet remaining were taken off and left at the camp at mouth of Big Horn. *Winners of the West*, vol. 7, no. 10, 8.

46. Sterland was proprietor of a confectionery and news depot at Bismarck in 1882. His large pet Newfoundland dog bit a little girl and was ordered shot, the family experiencing great sorrow. *Bismarck Tribune*, Nov. 17, 1882.

47. Private Geant, 7th Infantry, (with Gibbon's command), recorded that the first man who came down from Reno Hill June 27, 1876, was "Reddy" Stevenson who had served in the 7th Infantry and was well acquainted with the boys. Journal of Pvt. Eugene Geant, Company H, 7th Infantry, WMC-BYU.

48. *Lexington Daily Press*, July 3, 1877; *The Central Record*, Nov. 18, 1999 (copies courtesy of John Trowbridge, Kentucky Military History Museum).

49. John Burkman said that while Stoffel was in the guard house he was shackled to Rain-in-the-Face. WMC, notes, Misc. I, IU; Rain-in-the-Face escaped from the guard house during the night of April 18, 1875. RG 393, Pt. V, Fort A. Lincoln; Capt. Poland, 6th Inf., to Post Adjutant, April 30, 1875.

50. As the shooting occurred off the military reservation, trial was in the territorial district court at Deadwood. Whalen was found guilty of 2nd degree manslaughter and sentenced to 18 months in the house of correction at Detroit, Michigan. *Black Hills Weekly Times*, Feb., Mar., Aug., Sept. 1881, and Feb. 1882.

Whalen was discharged from the army by SO 64, HQA, Washington, DC, Mar. 20, 1882. RG 94, Entry 409, files 2655 A (EB) 1881, and, 2664 C (EB) 1882).

51. Smith F. Foster, (Trumpeter, Company L, 8th Cavalry, 1870–88) said Stuart was reported to have been an officer in the Confederate army, his right name to be Lightfoot. WMC, rosters, LBHB.

52. In response to inquiry from the adjutant general relating to a request from Mrs. Stuart-Forbes, Lt. DeRudio advised that the letters and carte de viste of John Stuart Forbes of E Troop were sent by mail to the address of Mrs. Jemima R. Stuart-Forbes, London, England, and that the effects of the soldier were sold at public auction in December last, and the paymaster's receipts for proceeds of sales of effects of deceased soldiers forwarded to the adjutant general. DeRudio to adjutant general, Apr 18, 1877, RG 391, Entry 869.

Hodgson, "The British Custer Trail"; Foster, *The Peerage, Baronetage, and Knightage* 237–38. (Hiley was surname of brother-in-law.)

53. Personal file. NA, M565, Roll 45; *St. Louis Republican*, July 7, 1876. *St. Louis Daily Times*, July 7, 1876; *The Cleveland Leader*, Sept. 11, 1878, mentions Mrs. Sturgis and daughter accompanied Gen. Miles from Fort Keogh to Custer battlefield; see also Van West, ed., "Roughing It Up the Yellowstone to Wonderland."

54. Carter, *From Yorktown to Santiago*, 134; NA, M744 Roll 61, Regimental Returns, 6th U.S. Cavalry. It was also reported that the steamer *Quaker City*, en route from New York to Charleston with a full compliment of passengers, encountered a severe gale off Charleston Bar the evening of Oct. 23, and rather than endanger the lives of its passengers by attempting to come up to the city, the vessel proceeded seaward a distance of one hundred miles. "During the gale [lasting 36 hours duration] the sea carried away the bowsprit, stove in the paddle boxes and caused some slight damage to the light upper work. Five horses were thrown overboard." In a signed testimonial released for publication, the passengers unanimously expressed their sincere and humble thanks for the preservation of their lives, and praised the gallant conduct of the boat's captain and the true seamanship of the officers under him. *Charleston* (S.C.) *Daily Courier*, Oct. 27, 1865; similar incidents are described by E. B. Custer in *Tenting on the Plains* (1915), 174.

The steamer *Republic*, a side paddle-wheeler, with 59 passengers and a cargo of twenty thousand gold coins from New York to New Orleans, was lost in a hurricane off Savannah, Ga., Oct. 25, 1865. The passengers were all saved but the gold went down with the ship. The wreck was discovered in August 2003 in 1700 feet of water. *New York Times*, Aug. 17, 2003.

55. Col. Sturgis and family arrived Leavenworth City, Kans., June 4, 1869. Sturgis joined with Custer to host a buffalo hunt for the benefit of two visiting English Lords in Sept. 1869, from the 7th Cavalry camp on Big Creek, near Fort Hays. Burkey, *Custer, Come at Once*, 81–88.

56. Col. Sturgis was sent to Yankton by Gen. Terry on the urging of Maj. Greene, assistant adjutant general of the department of Dakota, to report on the situation at that place and to start the regiment for Fort Rice. This after an exchange of telegrams between Greene and Gen. Custer, described by Greene to Gen. Terry as principally fault-finding. Custer was concerned about conditions en route, news of bad roads, ravines full of drifted snow, swollen creeks, etc., also the transportation of regimental baggage, for which he requested additional wagons and ambulances. Sturgis telegraphed Maj. Greene, May 6, that he did not share Custer's apprehension of conditions (Sturgis stated May 2 that he did not think it necessary he [Sturgis] accompany the command, nor did he care to).

Custer had also notified Greene, April 23, that 79 horses were required to mount the command, and on May 2 Sturgis advised Greene that they would not get horses to make up the deficiency. Sturgis asked Greene to suggest to Gen. Terry that the horses of the band be used for the march and the expedition, and the band brought to St. Paul or Fort Snelling. Greene directed Sturgis, on instruction of Gen. Terry, to dismount the band and turn the horses over to the companies, the men to Fort Snelling, and after seeing the command properly en route, he (Sturgis) was to return to St. Paul.

Sturgis reported to Greene May 6 that Custer had that morning reported a greater number of horses (614) than men (604) and the additional number in the band would actually be an inconvenience. Sturgis said he was indifferent as to the disposition of the band, but Custer's desire to have it was great. Greene replied that he had issued all the orders Gen. Terry had authorized in regard to the band and movements of the command. He could do no more and could not reach Gen. Terry by telegraph for further instructions as he was then en route to St. Paul. Sturgis was to proceed with instructions already given.

On May 8, from Bon Homme, twenty miles west of Yankton, Custer telegraphed to Maj. Greene requesting that the band, then at Yankton, be ordered to accompany the command, that they would be a source of great pleasure to the officers and men during the summer, their instruments having been purchased by private subscription of the officers. NA, M1495, Roll 1.

The band rejoined the regiment June 11 at Fort Rice, per SO 103, Hq DD, May 17, 1873, RG 393, Part I, Entry 1191; Muster roll of band, June 30, 1873, RG 94, Entry 53. The tracks of the Northern Pacific Railroad reached Bismarck June 3, and Gen. Terry, with Maj. Greene, assistant adjutant general; Maj. Lewis, inspector general; Maj. Rodney Smith, Paymaster (and clerk, John Graham), passed through Fargo June 9 en route to Fort Rice. *Red River Star*, June 14, 1873.

57. *Bismarck Tribune*, Oct. 26, 1877; Capt. Benteen said Sturgis besought Gen. Howard to give him orders to proceed to Lincoln in person (to prepare for coming in of the regiment), which Howard did, and Sturgis took with him Lts. "Garlington, Hare, the Sergt-Major [Murray] of the regiment, and every scrap of paper, leaving nothing behind but the 12 troops of the regiment, with a captain in command." Carroll, ed., *The Benteen-Goldin Letters*, 204, 221, 231;. regimental headquarters, and field &staff, were ordered to Fort Lincoln, Oct. 8th, per SFO 69, Hq Dept. of the Columbia, 1877, RG 393, Part I, Entry 755.

58. RG 94, Entry 96; Alcott said Sullivan was killed in the river. WMC, notes, env 130, IU; Burkman also said Sullivan's body was in the river. Burkman interview with Walter Camp, Feb. 5, 1911, WMC-BYU.

Stan Roy said Sullivan was found midway in the bottom in a wash ending in the river and was not mutilated; he was recognized by the number of his carbine and pistol and so naturally the Indians did not get his clothing. Roy to Walter Camp, July 28, 1910, WMC-BYU.

59. On August 11, 1877, during the Nez Perce campaign, Sullivan was a member of a five-man detachment commanded by Lt. Fuller, which left camp at mouth of Tongue River, MT, en route to Fort Ellis. Upon reaching upper Clark's Fork, the detachment learned of Col. Gibbon's fight at Big Hole and the direction of the Indians. Timothy Sullivan was sent alone with a dispatch to Col. Sturgis conveying the important information.

On the morning of September 13, Sturgis said he selected one of his most reliable men (Private Sullivan), well known for his courage, nerve and prairie craft, to carry a dispatch to Gen. Miles at Fort Keogh, notifying him of Chief Joseph's escape. Sullivan left camp alone, about one hour before the action of that day commenced, on a ride of 250 miles through an almost unknown country infested by hostile Indians, being in constant danger of attack during the trip; an extremely hazardous and gallant action, the dispatches being of great value to the service. Sullivan reached Fort Keogh on Sept. 17. He made a third trip when sent elsewhere by Gen. Miles. RG 94, Entry 25, file, 16105 AGO 1895; the incident is mentioned in the reports of Col. Sturgis and Maj. Merrill. NA, M1734, Roll 23; See note S1 (Saas).

60. William E. Morris, in Brady, *Indian Fights and Fighters*, 403; Hammer, *Custer in '76*, 131.

61. Rosters of Company F with remarks by Lynch and Rooney, WMC-BYU; WMC, rosters, LBHB.

62. SFO 38, Hq DD, Aug. 6, 1876, RG 94, Entry 44; see also, Pvt. William Robinson.

63. "William Sweeney and Paddy Hall didn't like their quarters at their present stopping place or the prospects, perhaps, and undertook to defeat justice by a short cut to the states. Deputy U. S. Marshal Ben Ash gobbled one and Sheriff Alex McKenzie the other, and now they ponder over those sad words 'It might have been.' Hall was crooked in the sale of whiskey and Sweeney is in for larceny." *Bismarck Tribune*, April 26, 1876.

T

Tanner, Jas. J. (alias). See Gebhart, Jacob Henry.

Tapley, David. Pvt co H; b. Dublin Ireland; enl 10 May 1868 Madison Ark for 3 yrs; age 30; tailor; grey eyes, brn hair, fair comp, 5' 10 3/4" high; assd to co C 19 inf; disch 10 May 1871 Jackson Bks La. upon expir of serv a pvt; reenl 1 May 1875 New Orleans La. for 5 yrs in co H 7 cav; dd co tailor Aug 1875; sick qrs Ft Rice DT 17 Apr to 18 May 1876 (chills); ds Ft Rice 19 May 1876 in co garden;[1] ds Ft Rice 21 Apr 1877 cultivating co garden; dd co tailor Apr 1878; disch 25 Nov 1878 Ft Lincoln DT per SO 250 AGO 1878 (upon recom'n capt Benteen as a malingerer & troublemaker).[2]

Tarbox, Byron. Pvt co L; b. Brooksville Me; [half-bro Wm. E. Morris]; enl 22 Sep 1875 Boston Mass. for 5 yrs; age 23; shoemaker; grey eyes, dk hair, fair comp, 5' 6 1/4" high; join co L 29 Oct 1875 Ft Totten DT; killed with Custer column 25 June 1876.
Pension: 21 July 1885 / Mother / 329153 / 236293.

Taube, Emil. Pvt co K; b. 19 Nov 1847 Damerau Germany; enl 21 Mar 1876 St Louis Bks Mo. for 5 yrs; age 28; laborer; hazel eyes, blk hair, dk comp, 5' 5 1/2" high; join co K 27 Apr 1876 St Paul Minn.; ds camp Powder River MT 15 June 1876; ds Rosebud Creek with art'y 11 Aug 1876; gsw scalp 30 Sep 1877 Snake Creek MT (Bear's Paw Mtns) in action with Nez Perce inds; tr to str *Silver City* 14 Oct mouth of Squaw Creek (on Missouri River); adm to hosp Ft Lincoln DT 26 Oct; duty 14 Nov 1877; dd cook post hosp Feb to Apr 1878; sick June 1878 to 20 Jan 1879 when disch at Ft Lincoln on surg cert dis a pvt char xclt (chr. infl. r. parotid gland & swelling r. jaw from irritation by scalp wd recd line of duty); died 12 Feb 1917 Eddy Tex.
Pension: 8 Apr 1880 / Inv / 356822 / 173434. Ind. Wid. / 14078 / 12004.

Taylor, Walter Oliver. Blks co G; b. 6 July 1855 Scituate RI; enl 22 Nov 1875 Boston Mass. for 5 yrs; age 21 4/12; horseshoer; grey eyes, lt hair, fair comp, 5' 6 3/4" high; join co G as blks 23 Jan 1876 Shreveport La.; dd 1–18 June 1876; left in timber dur retreat from valley fight 25 June & rejoin co on Reno hill;[3] dd 1–28 Aug 1876; horse lame 25 Aug & abandoned with equipment for want of transp, pack mules having 16 days rations & no wagon train along;[4] dd 2–13 Sep 1876; ds Ft Lincoln DT 28 Oct 1880 (nurse for pvt Hayes to Lawrenceburg Ind.);[5] disch 21 Nov 1880 Newport Bks Ky. expir of serv a blks char good; died 26 Jan 1931 Rockland Mass.
Pension: 14 Jan 1905 / Inv / 1330173. Wid / 1687644. Ind. Surv. / 11819 / 9263. (XC-2,639,341).

Taylor, Wm. Othniel. Pvt co A; b. 18 Feb 1855 Canandaigua N.Y.; enl 17 Jan 1872 Troy N.Y. for 5 yrs; age 21; cutler; hazel eyes, brn hair, fair comp, 5' 5 1/4" high; join co M 7 cav 14 Feb 1872 Unionville SC; tr to co A 1 Mar 1876;[6] ds on str *Durfee* 6 Aug 1876 to Ft Lincoln; disch 17 Jan 1877 Ft Rice DT expir of serv a pvt char poor soldier; died 19 Feb 1923 Orange Mass.
Pension: 14 Mar 1917 / Ind. Surv. / 9770 / 7202. Ind. War Wid / 16276 / 10660. (XC-2,659,276).

Teeman, Wm. Cpl co F; b. Denmark Germany; enl 30 Sep 1867 Pittsburgh Pa. for 3 yrs; age 21; puddler; grey eyes, lt hair, fair comp, 5' 9" high; join co B 4 art'y Oct 1867 Ft Harker Kans.; disch 30 Sep 1870 Ft Riley Kans. expir of serv a pvt & reenl in same co for 5 yrs; on furl 2 wks 18 Dec 1870; cpl 9 Jan 1871; sgt 12 Aug 1871; des 8 Sep 1871 Ft McHenry Md; enl as Wm. A. Adams 27 Aug 1872 Cincinnati Ohio for 5 yrs; join co F 7 cav 1 Dec 1872 Louisville Ky.; surd as des'r 19 Nov 1873 under prov'n GO 102 AGO 1873; restored to duty without trial 18 Mar 1874 & tr to co F to serve bal of enlmt; dd co cook Apr 1875; cpl 1 Nov 1875; killed with Custer column 25 June 1876.[7]

Tessier, Edmond D. Pvt co L; b. Montreal Canada; enl 26 Nov 1866 Detroit Mich. for 5 yrs; age 22; clerk; dk eyes, dk hair, fair comp, 5' 7" high; join co L 24 Feb 1867 Ft Morgan Colo. Ty; cpl 1 May 1867; pvt Aug 1867; dd subs dept Feb 1868; dd with aqm Apr to June 1868; dd co clerk Dec 1869 to Feb 1870; dd clerk regtl hq Mar & Apr 1870; dd co clerk May 1870 to June 1871; ed hosp stew'd 3d cl. July to Nov 1871; disch 26 Nov 1871 Yorkville SC expir of serv a pvt & reenl in co L for 5 yrs; age 24; sgt 13 Jan 1872; pvt 25 Apr 1872; ed asst to actg aqm Oct & Dec 1872; killed with Custer column 25 June 1876.

Thadus, Jno. Pvt co C; b. Guilford Co. NC; enl 17 Aug 1875 Baltimore Md for 5 yrs; age 21; farmer; blk eyes, dk hair, dk comp, 5' 6 3/4" high; join co C 21 Oct 1875 Ft Lincoln DT; killed with Custer column 25 June 1876.

Thomas, Herbert P. Pvt co I; b. So. Wales England; enl 5 May 1873 Pittsburgh Pa. for 5 yrs; age 22; miner; blue eyes, lt hair, fair comp, 5' 6 1/4" high; join co I 3 June 1873 Ft Snelling Minn.; ed mech qmd Ft Lincoln DT 8 Mar 1876 to 5 May 1878 when disch by expir of serv a pvt char xclt; reenl 25 Sep 1884 Ft Omaha Neb for 5 yrs; assd to co E 4 inf; des 25 May 1885 at Ft Omaha; apph 20 Aug 1885 Council Bluffs Iowa; dishon disch 6 Nov 1885 sen gen cm & 3 yrs conft mil prison.

Thomas, Jas. (alias). See Stowers, Thos. J.

Thompson, Morris Hedding. Pvt co E; b. 10 May 1852 Waukegan Ill.; enl as Frank Howard 8 Feb 1872 Chicago Ill. for 5 yrs; age 22; farmer; brn eyes, blk hair, dk comp, 5' 8" high; join co E 26 Feb 1872 Unionville SC; sad'r 1 May 1873; pvt 1 Mar 1875; (appd to regtl hq 19 Apr 1876 that his proper name appear on co roll, having used assumed name to avoid parental objection to enlmt);[8] dd co cook Apr 1876; ds Ft Lincoln DT 17 May 1876 chg co garden; sent with Lt Garlington on str *Josephine* 24 July 1876 to join co in field; ret to post 10 Aug on str *Durfee*; sad'r 1 Oct 1876 to date 1 Sep 1876; ds Ft Lincoln 16 Oct 1876 dismtd; pvt 15 Nov 1876; disch 2 Feb 1877 at Ft Lincoln expir of serv a pvt char good; died 27 Nov 1911 Cloverdale Calif.
Pension: Ind. Wid. / 14221 / 9403. (XC-2,659,016).

Thompson, Peter. Pvt co C; b. 28 Dec 1856 Fifeshire Scotland; enl 21 Sep 1875 Pittsburgh Pa. for 5 yrs; age 21; miner; brn eyes, brn hair, ruddy comp, 5' 8 3/4" high; join co C 21 Oct 1875 Ft Lincoln DT; dd qmd Oct 1875; with Custer column 25 June 1876 but left behind when horse gave out;[9] gsw r. hand (fl. wd. sl.) 26 June on Reno hill; tr on str *Far West* 3 July to hosp Ft Lincoln; duty 1 Aug 1876; ds Ft Totten DT 14 Aug to 26 Dec 1877; (awarded medal of honor 5 Oct 1878 for bringing water to wounded [at LBH] while under heavy fire, in which effort he was shot thro' hand, but made two more trips, not withstanding remonstrances of his sgt); dd qmd teamster Dec 1878 to Apr 1879; ed qmd laborer June to Aug 1879; ds repairing mil tel line Sep & Oct 1879; on furl 60 days 24 Nov 1879 Redwater DT; dd qmd Feb to Sep 1880; disch 20 Sep 1880 Ft Meade DT expir of serv a pvt char xclt; died 4 Dec 1928 Hot Springs SD.
Pension: 7 June 1915 / Inv / 1419941 / 1178401. Ind. Surv. /13667 / 8456. Wid / 1632460. (XC-3,023,451).

Thornberry, Levi. Pvt co M; b. 3 Feb 1853 Marietta Ohio; enl 20 Sep 1875 Cincinnati Ohio for 5 yrs; age 22; teamster; blue eyes, brn hair, dk comp, 5' 6 1/4" high; join co M 21 Oct 1875 Ft Rice DT; dd qmd laborer Nov 1875 to Apr 1876; wag 11 Jan 1877; pvt 25 Feb 1878; des 7 June 1878 Ft Lincoln DT [with Varner]; died 27 May 1902 Watertown Ohio.[10]

Thorp, Mich'l. Pvt co F; b. Somerset Ohio; enl 16 June 1870 Louisville Ky. for 5 yrs; age 21; laborer; hazel eyes, lt brn hair, fair comp, 5' 10 1/4" high; join co F 29 June 1870 Ft Hays Kans.; dd co cook Feb 1871; ds regtl hq Taylor Bks (Louisville) Ky. Sep & Oct 1871; ed post qmd Apr to Dec 1872; dd qmd teamster 12–26 Apr 1873; dd subs dept herder 24 May to 22 June 1873; dd post qmd Oct & Dec 1873; dd regtl band Feb 1875; in conft Apr 1875; disch 16 June 1875 Ft Lincoln DT expir of serv a pvt; reenl next day with band for 5 yrs; tr to co F 28 Apr 1876; ds Ft Lincoln 13 May 1876 chg band prop & garden; dd with band Aug 1876; ds with band Oct 1876; sick qrs 29 Nov to 20 Dec 1876 (dislocation l. clavicle); disch 5 Apr 1877 Ft Abercrombie DT on surg cert dis a pvt (chr. dislocation l. clavicle with partial loss of motion of arm; injured while riding in horse race at Ft Lincoln 4 July 1876; not line of duty).[11]

Thorpe, Rollins L. Pvt co M; b. 6 Nov 1859 New York N.Y.; enl 7 Sep 1875 Chicago Ill. for 5 yrs; age 21; hostler; grey eyes, dk brn hair, dk comp, 5' 7 1/2" high; join co M 21 Oct 1875 Ft Rice DT; disch 7 July 1876 camp mouth of Big Horn River MT per SO 101 AGO 1876 (a minor) a pvt char good; sick field hosp thro' July & left camp 5 Aug on str *Durfee* to Bismarck DT.[12]

Tilford, Jos. Green. Major; b. 26 Nov 1828 Georgetown Ky.; grad USMA 1 July 1851 & appt bvt 2Lt mtd rifles; 2Lt 27 Jan 1853; 1Lt 14 June 1858; capt 31 July 1861; (regt redesig 3 cav Aug 1861); bvt maj for gal serv at battle of Valverde NM 21 Feb 1862; bvt Lt-col 13 Mar 1865 for meritorious serv dur the war; assd rctg duty Nov 1865 Carlisle Pa. but tr to his regt at Ft Selden NM upon own req; prom maj 7 cav 16 Sep 1868 (from 14 Nov 1867); ds comdg Ft Reynolds Colo. Ty to 29 Sep 1868; awl to Apr 1869 thence cond rcts for 3 cav to New Mexico; join 7 cav 13 July 1869 camp near Ft Hays Kans.; post comdr Chester SC Mar 1871 & Mt Vernon Ky. Apr 1871 & Crab Orchard Ky. Oct 1871; ds Jackson Bks La. Dec 1872 to Mar 1873; chg of invalids on str *Western* 23 Apr to 10 May 1873 Yankton to Ft Rice DT;[13] awl 30 days on surg cert 12 June 1873 Geneva Lake Wis; awl ext'd 3 mos; post comdr Ft Rice Nov 1873 to Apr 1877; ds in field with Blk Hills Exp'n June thro' Aug 1874; awl one yr 25 Oct 1875 (visit Europe);[14] rejoin post 26 Oct 1876 (arr with capt Benteen); post comdr Ft Lincoln DT May 1877 to Feb 1878; on bd of officers 23 June 1878 to revise medal of honor list for LBH; Lt-col 22 Sep 1883; comd regt & post Ft Meade DT Nov 1883 to June 1885; post comdr Ft Meade July 1887 to June 1888; post comdr Ft Sill IT from Aug 1888; col 9 cav 11 Apr 1889; retd 1 July 1891 upon own appn; brig-gen on retd list 23 Apr 1904; died 24 Feb 1911 Wash'n D.C.
[1754 ACP 1883]. Pension: 4 Mar 1911 / Wid / 959882 / 722063.

Tinkham, Henry L. Pvt co B; b. Montpelier Vt; enl 30 Mar 1876 Boston Mass. for 5 yrs; age 21 4/12; farmer; blue eyes, brn hair, fair comp, 5' 8 3/4" high; join co B 27 Apr 1876 St Paul Minn.; ds camp Powder River MT 10 June 1876; des 22 Apr 1877 Ft Lincoln DT.

Tolan, Frank. Pvt co D; b. Malone N.Y.; enl 31 Aug 1875 Boston Mass. for 5 yrs; age 21 3/12; farmer; grey eyes, brn hair, fair comp, 5' 8 1/2" high; join co D 21 Oct 1875 Ft Lincoln DT; dd co cook June 1877; dd qmd teamster Feb 1878; sick qrs Feb & Apr 1878; (awarded medal of honor 5 Oct 1878 for bringing water to wounded [at LBH] while under heavy fire); dd as teamster Oct 1878; disch 30 Aug 1880 Ft Yates DT expir of serv a pvt char fair.[15]

Torrey, Wm. A. Pvt co E; b. Weymouth Mass.; enl 12 Nov 1872 Boston Mass. for 5 yrs; age 22 4/12; bootmaker; grey eyes, lt hair, fair comp, 5' 4 1/2" high; join co E 10 Dec 1872 Unionville SC; dd woodchopper 18 Nov 1875 to 7 Mar 1876; dd regtl hq fatigue pty (morn & eve) 11 May 1876; killed with Custer column 25 June 1876.
Pension: 5 Jan 1877 / Mother / 229429 / 176660.

Tourtellotte, Jno. Eaton. Capt co G; b. 3 July 1833 Thompson Conn.; grad Brown univ June 1856; formed law partnership at Mankato Minn. in 1857; recruited "valley sharpshooters" Sep 1861 (desig co H 4 Minn. inf) & elected capt 13 Dec 1861; Lt-col 1 Sep 1862; col 5 Oct 1864; comd regt in assault on Vicksburg & comd brig dur gen Sherman's campn thro' Carolina; bvt brig-gen vols 13 Mar 1865 for gal serv dur the war; m.o. vol serv 21 June 1865; appt reg army com'n capt 28 inf 11 Oct 1866 to date 28 July 1866 (recom'n of gen Sherman); join regt 13 Nov 1866 & comd post of Camden Ark; bvt maj, Lt-col, & col 2 Mar 1867 for gal serv in siege of Vicksburg & battles of Allatoona Ga. & Bentonville NC;

actg aig 4th mil distr Feb to July 1868; unassd (to regt) 15 Mar 1869 when regt consol with 19 inf; assd to 7 cav 15 Dec 1870 (never joined); ds adc & col on staff of gen Sherman from 1 Jan 1871; escort for Marquis of Lorne (gov'r-gen of Canada) & Princess Louise dur their visit to U.S. in 1883;[16] prom maj 22 Sep 1883; awl one yr 8 Feb 1884 (upon retirement of gen Sherman); retd 20 Mar 1885 for disability; died 22 July 1891 LaCrosse Wis.[17] [5381 ACP 1882].

Tritten, Jno. Godfried. Sad-sgt ncs; b. 8 Oct 1846 Berne Switz; enl 6 Aug 1866 Cincinnati Ohio for 5 yrs; age 20; saddler; blue eyes, lt hair, lt comp, 5' 7" high; join co A 7 cav 10 Sep 1866 Ft Riley Kans.; co sad'r Feb to Apr 1867; in conft June & Aug 1867; sad'r 1 Sep 1867; pvt 1 Dec 1867; dd regtl qmd sad'r Mar 1868 to Feb 1869; appt regtl sad-sgt 1 Mar 1869; disch 6 Aug 1871 Taylor Bks (Louisville) Ky. expir of serv a sad-sgt; reenl 22 Dec 1873 at Cincinnati for 5 yrs; assd to co L 7 cav as sad'r 1 July 1874; ds regtl hq (St Paul Minn.) 16 July 1874; appt regtl sad-sgt 18 Nov 1874; ds camp Powder River MT 14 June 1876;[18] ds Ft Lincoln DT Oct 1876; ds str *Big Horn* 15 Oct 1877 to Ft Lincoln; ds Camp Ruhlen DT Oct 1878; disch 22 Dec 1878 at Ft Lincoln by expir of serv a sad-sgt char an xclt & faithful workman, an industrious & sober man; died 12 Dec 1918 Dayton Ohio.
Pension: 24 Sep 1903 / Inv / 1304165. Ind. Surv. / 9656 / 6883. Ind. Wid. 14323 / 8888.

Troy, Jas. E. Pvt co I; b. Richmond Mass.; enl 30 Dec 1871 Boston Mass. for 5 yrs; age 22; shoemaker; grey eyes, brn hair, dk comp, 5' 5 1/4" high; join co I 1 Feb 1872 Shelbyville Ky.; sen gen cm 3 June 1872 forf $10 pay per mo for 4 mos & conft same period; in conft Dec 1872 to June 1873; sen gen cm 11 Feb 1873 forf pay for 2 mos; in conft Dec 1875 to May 1876; sen gen cm 2 Mar 1876 forf pay for 3 mos & conft same period thence to dishon disch; sen appv except dishon disch & forf of pay beyond period of conft; killed with Custer column 25 June 1876.

Trumble, Wm. Pvt co B; b. Iowa; enl 9 Sep 1873 Cincinnati Ohio for 5 yrs; age 21; laborer; grey eyes, brn hair, florid comp, 5' 8" high; join co B 19 Oct 1873 Ft Lincoln DT; dd driver with art'y detmt Blk Hills Exp'n June 1874; dd co cook June 1875; dd orderly for Lt Hodgson 25 June 1876;[19] ds Ft Lincoln DT May to Oct 1877 gd co prop; disch 9 Sep 1878 Standing Rock DT expir of serv a pvt char good; reenl 21 Sep 1878 St Louis Mo. for 5 yrs; join co M 7 cav 9 Nov 1878 Camp Ruhlen DT; ed subs dept laborer Apr 1880 to Aug 1881; dd actg co sad'r Oct 1881; dd co cook Apr 1882; dd co cook Aug 1882; on furl 3 mos 1 Apr 1883 Chicago Ill.; disch 20 Sep 1883 Ft Meade DT expir of serv a pvt char a good & trusty man; reenl 22 Sep 1883 at Ft Meade for 5 yrs in co E 7 cav; ed hosp cook Oct 1883; on furl Apr to July 1884; in conft Apr 1885; in conft Feb 1886; sen gen cm 15 May 1886 forf $10 pay per mo for 6 mos & conft same period; ed qmd laborer Feb 1887; des 21 July 1888 camp near Ft Riley Kans.; surd 11 Oct 1888 Ft L'worth Kans.; restored to duty without trial 19 Nov 1888 (upon recom'n capt Ilsley);[20] disch 19 Jan 1889 Ft Sill IT expir of serv a pvt char xclt & reenl next day for 5 yrs; assd to co C 8 cav; des 3 May 1889 at Ft Meade; apph 13 Oct 1889 Omaha Neb; dishon disch 21 Dec 1889 at Ft Omaha sen gen cm & 3 yrs conft mil prison.

Tulo, Jos. Pvt co G; b. Rand France; enl 7 Mar 1876 St Louis Mo. for 5 yrs; age 23; laborer; grey eyes, brn hair, fair comp, 5' 8 1/2" high; join co G 27 Apr 1876 St Paul Minn.; ds camp Powder River MT 15 June 1876; ds Ft Lincoln DT 21 Oct 1876; des 2 Sep 1877 camp on Clarks Fork MT.

Turley, Henry. Pvt co M; b. Troy N.Y.; enl 29 Oct 1872 at Troy for 5 yrs; age 21 4/12; laborer; brn eyes, blk hair, dk comp, 5' 4 1/8" high; join co M 9 Dec 1872 Unionville SC; sick qrs Ft Rice DT 9–25 Apr 1874 (cont'n l. foot stepped on by horse); sick post hosp 23 May to 20 July 1874 (gsw); ds Ft Rice Aug 1874; dd subs dept herder Oct 1874 to Apr 1875; killed in valley fight 25 June 1876; sgt Ryan said Turley lost control of his horse & was carried toward ind camp;[21] Morris said Turley killed near Lt Hodgson on east bank of river.[22]

Tweed, Thos. S. Pvt co L; b. North Liberty Ohio; enl 1 Sep 1875 Cincinnati Ohio for 5 yrs; age 22; printer; grey eyes, brn hair, fair comp, 5' 5 1/4" high; join co L 29 Oct 1875 Ft Totten DT; killed with Custer column 25 June 1876.

Notes—T

1. Benteen said Tapley and Pitet were under Marshall's orders, who assigns them work, whatever it might be. Benteen letters to wife, July 9, 13, 1876, Carroll, *Camp Talk*, 29, 35.

2. Benteen related that Tapley and his family, wife and four children, were the cause of much trouble at every post Company H had been stationed. Benteen to Post Adjutant, Oct. 29, 1878. Tapley was examined by the post surgeon to see if he was a fit subject for discharge on certificate of disability, but was found able-bodied and healthy, though he had a depressed cicatrix on the front part of his head, the result of a blow received during the New Orleans riots in 1874. RG 94, Entry 409, file 14572 A (EB) AGO 1878.

In 1877, Sgt. Crussy accused Tapley of abusing his (Crussy's) wife and Benteen said he would have Mrs. Benteen look into the matter. Benteen believed Tapley desired to obtain the Crussy quarters, that the Tapleys were scheming and troublesome people. Benteen to his wife, June 9, 1877, Carroll, *Camp Talk*, 67.

Benteen met Tapley in 1888 at Fort Niobrara, Neb., where the old fellow found occasional work and lived nearby with his family of eight children. Visiting Tapley's house, Benteen judged he was not in good circumstances. Carroll, *Camp Talk*,, 147.

Tapley was caretaker of Fort Rice after its abandonment. His widow, in 1905, was said to reside with a son, Joe Tapley, at the Presidio San Francisco. J. Schmidt, special examiner, to commissioner of pensions, March 13, 1905, pension file of William G. Abrams, RG15.

3. John Lattman to Max Hoehn, Aug. 10, 1909, WMC-BYU.

4. Brown Troop Duty Book. Reynolds and Brown, *Journal*.

5. Private Joseph E. Hayes, Company G, sick (congestion of spine) in hospital at Fort Lincoln to Oct. 29, 1880, thence on furlough to Lawrenceburg, Ind., about 25 miles from Newport, Ky.

6. Taylor transferred to Company "A" to be with his brother-in-law, Samuel Alcott, that they might go home together when discharged, having enlisted at the same time. William O. Taylor to Gen. Godfrey, Feb. 20, 1910, Godfrey Papers.

Taylor's scrapbooks and notes for his proposed book, "With Custer on the Little Big Horn," are in the Bienecke Library, Yale University, New Haven, Conn.

7. Rooney said Tieman was neither scalped nor mutilated in any way. His blouse was taken off and his face covered, which was probably done by Rain-in-Face as he had great liking for Tieman because he always gave him tobacco and sweet things. Rooney to Walter Camp, April 25, 1909, WMC-BYU.

Burkman said Teeman lay with his blouse over his face. He was a prisoner in the guard house with Rain-in-Face at Fort Lincoln. Cpl. Klein was in charge of the guard when Rain first tried to get through a hole he could not pull through, having too many blankets on he got stuck. They pulled him back and he took off his clothes and then got through. He shook hands when he left. Burkman interview, Feb. 5, 1911, WMC-BYU.

Fremont Kipp said when the regiment got back to Fort Lincoln in fall 1876, there was a good deal of talk about burials on Custer battlefield, that Teeman lay in the group badly mutilated near the general, but Teeman had his blouse over his face and was not mutilated, etc. It was then recalled that while Rain was in the guard house at Lincoln, Teeman was a fellow prisoner for getting drunk and how he shared his rations with Rain and other Indians while they were prisoners. As these facts were talked over, the story was taken up by outsiders (civilians) and naturally grew. Kipp interview, n.d., WMC-IU; WMC-DPL, env "Kipp."

Bischoff said, "The sergeant or corporal who was chained to Rain-in-Face at Lincoln in 1874 was killed with Custer & was the one at first put into Custer's box by mistake when we took remains of officers away in 1877." Bischoff interview, n.d., WMC-BYU.

8. RG 393, Part V, Fort A. Lincoln, DT.

9. The Arikara scout, Soldier, told of finding a white soldier on the bluffs above the river trying to get his horse up, cursing and swearing, pounding his horse's head with his fists and kicking him under the belly. A little further along the ridge the scouts found another white soldier with his horse down. This soldier signed that he belonged to Custer's command. Libby, *Arikara Narrative*, 116.

Peter Thompson said the last set of fours in Company C were himself, Watson, Fitzgerald, and Brennan, but neither reached Custer's battlefield. Questionnaire from Walter Camp to Thompson, n.d., WMC-LBHB;

Fitzgerald and Brennan took the back trail to the pack train, while Thompson and Watson left their horses and followed Custer's trail on foot, sometimes running. Fremont Kipp to Walter Camp, Nov. 14, 20, and, Dec. 1, 1921, WMC-BYU; Camp believed Thompson and Watson were left behind somewhere between Reno Hill and where Custer was killed. Walter Camp to Kipp, Nov. 19, 1921, Godfrey Papers. Camp said he was on the battlefield in person with Knipe and Thompson in 1910, and he explained his whole story in detail while they walked over the ground, Camp debating several matters with him. Knipe told Camp privately, right there, that certain things in Thompson's story were unbelievable, though the two were bosom friends. Knipe said Thompson was with the troop when he (Knipe) was sent back with the message to the pack train, and when he next saw Thompson he was coming up from the river leading his horse, alone, about the time Troop K was holding off the Indians and falling back. Watson was not with him. Walter Camp to Gen. Godfrey, May 28, 1923, Hardorff, *On the Little Big Horn with Walter Camp*, 164–70.

Earl A. Brininstool said he met Thompson at the 50th anniversary of the battle, where Thompson was ostracized by other former 7th Cavalrymen and nearly got into a fist fight with Bill Slaper who branded his story as absolutely false. Typed statement signed by Brininstool and attached to a copy of a letter from Walter Camp to J. S. Smith, Mgr. *Belle Fourche Bee* , March 24, 1914. In this letter Camp related details of his quest to locate Thompson. Brininstool Coll., BYU.

Theodore Goldin heard of the altercation that Thompson and his wife nearly came to blows with Slaper who told Thompson to his face that he did not believe a word of his story. Mrs. Thompson being more of a scrapper than her husband. Goldin said Anthony Baron (Company E, 1879–84), intervened to prevent a physical encounter. Albert W. Johnson to Robert S. Ellison, March 5, 1935 (quoting two letters from Goldin to Johnson, Dec. 16, 1928, and, Mar. 16, 1930). Johnson also attached a letter from Fremont Kipp, May 3, 1928, concerning the Thompson story, Ellison Coll., BYU.

See also Magnussen, ed., *Peter Thompson's Narrative*.

10. *Marietta* (Ohio) *Times*, Sept. 8, 1998. Article on Washington County soldiers in the Custer battle, and seeking information on William Dye. Includes photo of Levi Thornberry.

11. "The soldiers had a celebration. Lt. Ogle read the declaration of Independence—various amusements then took place among them a hurdle race, in which two men were thrown, one fracturing the acremion [?] process & clavicle, the other receiving a sprain & contusion of ankle." Post Medical History, Fort Lincoln, July 4, 1876, RG 94, Entry 547.

12. Capt. French to the adjutant general, Aug. 10, 1876. Thorpe was discharged on application of his father, the order not received until after the battle. RG 94, Entry 409, file 3391 A (EB) AGO 1876; The *Bismarck Tribune*, Friday, Dec. 19, 1879, reported that, "Rolls L. Thorpe and Annie E. Smith were married by Justice Glas on Sunday last."

13. The detachment comprised of 29 enlisted men and 38 laundresses. See Darling, *Custer's Seventh Cavalry Comes to Dakota*, 112.

14. *Bismarck Tribune*, Oct. 27, 1875, Nov. 1, 1876.

15. Frank Tolan, nurse at pest house. *Bismarck Tribune*, Apr. 14, 1882.

16. The Marquis of Lorne (John Douglas Sutherland Campbell), English statesman and author, and ninth Duke of Argyll. Governor-General of Canada, 1878–83. Married Princess Louise Alberta, fourth daughter of Queen Victoria, for whom the province of Alberta was named. *The World Book Encyclopedia*, vol. A: 380.

17. *Mankato, Its First Fifty Years*, 317–19. A biographical file of John E. Tourtellotte is also at the library of Brown University, Providence, RI.

18. Tritten said he was put in charge of the band until they rejoined the regiment at mouth of Rosebud; he had charge of regimental records and one clerk; says Band horses were not taken by Custer at Powder River; the horses were taken from the band at mouth of Rosebud and the band sent to Fort Lincoln, Tritten staying with the regiment. The horses were turned over to company trumpeters, they being white horses and all 7th Cavalry trumpeters had white or gray horses. Tritten to Walter Camp, March 2, 5, 1914, WMC-DPL; Lt. Garlington said the saddler-sergeant of the regiment rode a handsome white horse. Carroll, ed., *Garlington Narrative*, 19.

Tritten said the camp was on a sagebrush flat on the Yellowstone 1/4 mile below mouth of Powder. Maj. Moore (camp commander) had pitch pine on Sheridan Butte; also on butte two miles back on south side; said he was going to light up the Yellowstone in celebration of the centennial anniversary. The celebration came off the night of July 3rd, the eve of the anniversary. WMC, transcript, BYU-535.

James Sipes, barber on the steamer *Far West*, says on the way down with the wounded, the camp at Powder River was passed July 4th; soldiers there had piled up wood for a big bonfire to celebrate but when they heard the news they gave up the idea. Hammer, *Custer in '76*, 240–41.

19. Capt. McDougall recommended Trumble for a medal of honor, stating that Trumble was orderly for Lt. Hodgson and during the charge became unhorsed and fought on foot gallantly until he secured a horse and fought his way through the Indians to the command. McDougall to regimental adjutant, Mar. 17, 1878, RG 94, Entry 409, file 10818 A (EB) 1878.

John A. Bailey also said Trumble was orderly for Lt. Hodgson and was the second man to get to the top of the bluffs in the retreat, Reno being first. Liddic and Harbaugh, *Camp on Custer*, 82.

20. Capt. Ilsley said Trumble had served fifteen years in the regiment, lacking two months, and his character was always regarded as excellent. He was well known to all the officers of the regiment and his desertion was a great surprise as his enlistment had nearly expired. He was always regarded as a man "non compos mentis" and . . . the cause of his desertion was due to his being an inveterate gambler and met with heavy losses at the time he deserted and knew he would be unable to pay his debts. His mind was affected thereby and so he left under a fit of insanity. He had several times done the same thing for other causes but did not remain absent more than two days. He was a very ignorant man and could neither read nor write . . . recommend he be restored to duty without trial and ordered to join his troop to make good the time lost . . . did not recommend any leniency other than his being restored to duty. RG 391, Entry 869, Letters Sent, Troop E. Ilsley to post commander, Nov. 13, 1888.

21. Graham, *The Custer Myth*, 242; Ryan to Walter Camp, Dec. 17, 1908, WMC-BYU; "In the Custer massacre, the attack by Reno had first caused a panic among women and children, and some of the warriors, who started to flee, but 'Crazy Horse,' throwing away his rifle, brained one of the incoming soldiers with his stone war-club and jumped upon his horse." Bourke, *On the Border with Crook*, 415.

22. Hammer, *Custer in '76*, 131; Brady, *Indian Fights and Fighters*, 403.

V

Vahlert, Jacob. Pvt co C; b. Hessen-Nassau Germany; enl 9 Sep 1875 New York N.Y. for 5 yrs; age 21; butcher; hazel eyes, lt hair, fair comp, 5' 11 3/4" high; join co C 21 Oct 1875 Ft Lincoln DT; sick hosp at Ft Lincoln from 7 Apr 1876 (infl. cardium); ed nurse post hosp 25 July to 3 Aug; disch 25 Aug 1876 on surg cert dis (hypertrophy of heart; severe palpitation which resists all treatment) a pvt char good; res Phil'a Pa.

Van Allen, Garrett H. (alias). See Niver, Garrett H.

Van Pelt, Wm. E. Pvt co K; b. New York N.Y.; enl 13 Mar 1876 St Louis Bks Mo. for 5 yrs; age 27 4/12; clerk; blue eyes, brn hair, fair comp, 5' 7" high; join co K 27 Apr 1876 St Paul Minn.; ds camp Powder River MT 15 June 1876; ds with art'y detmt 11 Aug 1876 Rosebud Creek MT; dd qmd clerk 22 Nov 1876; ed qmd laborer Dec 1876 to Apr 1877; ds qmd on str *Far West* May & June 1877; ds in field July 1877; ds chg of ordn stores at camp Tongue River MT 12 Aug 1877; ds Ft Buford DT 16 Sep 1877 chg regtl prop; on str *Big Horn* 19 Oct [with pvt Abbotts] to Ft Lincoln DT; dd with regtl qm Jan 1878; cpl 2 Feb 1878 & tr to Ft Rice; dd post hq clerk Feb to Apr 1878; sgt 1 Mar 1878; ds Camp J. G. Sturgis DT Aug to Nov 1878 & at Ft Lincoln thro' June 1879; appt regtl qm-sgt 9 July 1879; disch 16 Jan 1880 Ft Meade DT per SO 12 AGO 1880 a qm-sgt char xclt; reenl 25 July 1880 Buffalo N.Y. for 5 yrs; assd to co F 10 inf; disch 24 July 1885 Ft McDowell AT expir of serv a post qm-sgt char xclt & reenl same day for 5 yrs; disch 24 July 1890 Ft Wadsworth N.Y. expir of serv a post qm-sgt & reenl for 5 yrs; disch 24 July 1895 at Ft Wadsworth expir of serv a post qm-sgt & reenl for 3 yrs; died 20 Nov 1895 at Stapleton (Staten Isl.) N.Y.

Van Sant, Cornelius. Pvt co E; b. Cincinnati Ohio; enl 5 Sep 1872 at Cincinnati for 5 yrs; age 22 4/12; clerk; blue eyes, brn hair, fair comp, 5' 7 1/4" high; join co E 13 Feb 1873 Unionville SC; dd clerk post hq Oct 1873 to May 1874; dd hq June 1874; dd clerk post hq Aug to Oct 1874; killed with Custer column 25 June 1876.

Varden, Frank E. 1sgt co I; b. Yarmouth Me; enr as Frank E. Noyes 7 Nov 1861 a pvt co A 11 Me inf for 3 yrs; age 18; m.o. vol serv 18 Nov 1864 Augusta Me; enl reg army as Frank E. Varden 15 Dec 1866 Boston Mass. for 5 yrs; age 21; machinist; blue eyes, brn hair, lt comp, 5' 10" high; join co I 22 Jan 1867 Ft Riley Kans.; cpl 13 July 1867; sgt 3 Oct 1868; cpl 4 Jan 1869; sgt 18 Nov 1870; des 7 Aug 1871 Bagdad Ky.; enl as Frank E. Noyes 23 Nov 1871 Boston Mass. for 5 yrs; apph as des'r 11 Jan 1872 Omaha Bks Neb; restored to duty without trial 26 Mar 1872 (upon recom'n capt Keogh) forf all pay due & make good time lost; disch 26 May 1872 Shelbyville Ky. by expir of serv a pvt; reenl same day in co I for 5 yrs & appt sgt; 1sgt 1 June 1872; on furl 3 mos 1 Dec 1873; on furl Oct 1875 Boston Mass.; ds Ft Snelling Minn. 27 Nov 1875; tr to Ft Lincoln DT 2 Dec 1875 (with pvt Ragsdale); killed with Custer column 25 June 1876.

Varner, Thos. B. Pvt co M; b. Franklin Co. Mo.; enl 24 Aug 1875 Louisville Ky. for 5 yrs; age 22; farmer; blue eyes, brn hair, fair comp, 5' 8 1/4" high; join co M 21 Oct 1875 Ft Rice DT; gsw l. ear 26 June 1876 (fl. wd. sl.); tr on str *Far West* 3 July to hosp Ft Lincoln DT; duty 20 July & tr by wagon to Ft Rice; rejoin co 4 Oct at Ft Lincoln; dd qmd laborer Feb 1877; dd co cook Oct 1877; in conft Dec 1877; ds with wagon train to Ft Keogh MT Feb 1878; dd qmd teamster Apr 1878; des 7 June 1878 at Ft Lincoln [with Thornberry].

Varnum, Chas. Albert. 2Lt co A; b. 21 June 1849 Troy N.Y. & two yrs later removed to Dracut Mass.; moved to Pensacola Fla in 1866; (father with state legislature in 1870 &

adjt-gen to 1877, also mayor of Gainesville in 1882); grad USMA 14 June 1872 & appt 2Lt 7 cav; join co A 1 Oct 1872 E'town Ky.; with co on Yellowstone Exp'n June to Sep 1873 & on Blk Hills Exp'n July & Aug 1874; post qm Livingston Ala Oct 1874 to Feb 1875; awl six mos 3 Nov 1875 (dep Bismarck on last train till spring); comd detmt of ind scouts from 2 May 1876 (order of gen Custer);[1] sent with pty of scouts to Crow's Nest night of 24 June; gsw l. calf (fl. wd.) & 2d ball tore yellow stripe from r. trouser leg 26 June; assd care of co I rec's 27 June; mustered co I & ind scouts 30 June mouth of Little Horn River; sent on str *Josephine* 16 July to org detmt 7 cav at Powder River & march with wagon train to Rosebud Creek;[2] prom 1Lt 26 July 1876; comd provisional co of survivors of cos CEF 4 Aug;[3] comd co I 16 Oct to 11 Nov 1876 with exp'n disarming inds at Cheyenne Agcy; rqm 14 Nov 1876 thro' Oct 1879; actg aqm on staff of col Sturgis 1 May 1877, also actg comsy from 15 Aug; (cited by col Sturgis for skilled management of supply train dur Nez Perce campn); ds Chicago Ill. Jan 1879 witness in Reno court of inq; post adjt Ft Lincoln DT Nov 1879 to Apr 1880 when assd to co H; capt co B 22 July 1890; recd silver star citation for gal cond against Sioux inds at Wounded Knee SD 29 Dec 1890; awarded medal of honor for dist gal against Sioux inds at White Clay Creek SD 30 Dec 1890; ds Ft Sheridan Ill. Oct 1892 for opening of world's fair at Chicago; prof of mil science at univ of Wyo. Sep 1895; asst chf qm purchasing horses at Denver Colo. July & Aug 1898; with regt to Marianas Cuba Jan 1899; ds May 1899 cond shipload of disch sol.'s to New York; sick Ft McPherson Ga. 9 June to 24 Oct 1899 (typhoid fever) & on med leave to 9 May 1900; prom maj 2 Feb 1901; aag Dept of Colo. (Denver) to May 1903 thence rejoin regt at Chicamauga Park Ga.; tr to 9 cav Sep 1904 Ft Walla Walla WT; Lt-col 4 cav 10 Apr 1905 at Ft Walla Walla & with regt in Philippines Sep 1905 to June 1907; retd 31 Oct 1907 for disability but remained on active status upon own req; instr of natl gd Boise Idaho to Oct 1909; prof of mil science univ of Maine at Orono to June 1912; on rctg duty Portland Ore. to Feb 1917 & Kansas City Mo. to Sep 1918 when draft precluded further rctg; col (retd) 1 Oct 1918; finance officer Ft Mason (Presidio) San Francisco Calif. to 8 Apr 1919 when relieved from active duty;[4] died 26 Feb 1936 at the Presidio. [2260 ACP 1876].

Vetter, Johann Mich'l. Pvt co L; b. 23 Dec 1853 Hessen Germany; enl 4 Oct 1875 Pittsburgh Pa. for 5 yrs; age 23; carpenter; blue eyes, lt hair, fair comp, 5' 9 1/4" high; join co L 29 Oct 1875 Ft Totten DT; killed with Custer column 25 June 1876.[5]
Pension: 25 May 1880 / Mother / 266166 / 218652.

Vickory, Jno. (alias). See Groesbeck, Jno. H.

Vinatieri, Felix Villiet. Chf mus'n ncs; b. 1834 Turin Italy; enr as Felix Williet 5 Aug 1861 Cambridge Mass. in band 16 Mass. inf for 3 yrs; appt band leader 1 Sep 1861; req for disch on surg cert (for debility) not appv 20 July 1862; disch by order of comdg gen 3d corps 22 July 1862 camp near Harrison Landing Va.; enl reg army 26 Dec 1867 Ft Columbus NYH for 3 yrs; age 33; musician; grey eyes, brn hair, fair comp, 5' 2 1/2" high; appt band leader 22 inf 1 Feb 1868; join regt 6 June 1868 Ft Sully DT; ds with band 15 July to 1 Oct 1868 Ft Rice DT; appt chf mus'n 11 Mar 1869; on furl 40 days 26 Aug 1869 NYC; disch 26 Dec 1870 at Ft Sully by expir of serv a chf mus'n; enl in 7 cav as chf mus'n [upon req of gen Custer] 23 May 1873 St Paul Minn. for 5 yrs;[6] joined regt 11 June at Ft Rice (with band) & accomp Yellowstone Exp'n to Sep 1873; accomp Blk Hills Exp'n July thro' Aug 1874 with band;[7] ds camp Powder River MT 14 June 1876 with band; ds str *Josephine* 6 Aug 1876 to Ft Lincoln with band; relieved as chf mus'n 19 Oct 1876; on furl 17 days 1 Dec 1876; disch (resd) 18 Dec 1876 at Ft Lincoln per SO 251 AGO 1876 (recom'n of col Sturgis, his serv no longer required) a pvt char very good;[8] returned to Yankton with wife & 2 ch. & agreed to take chg of city cornet band;[9] died 5 Dec 1891 at Yankton.

Voigt, Henry Carl. Pvt co M; b. 24 June 1855 Hanover Germany; enl 1 Oct 1873 Phil'a Pa.

for 5 yrs; age 18; baker; blue eyes, brn hair, fair comp, 5' 5 1/2" high; join co M 21 Oct 1873 Ft Rice DT; dd post baker Dec 1873; sick hosp 4 June to 27 July 1874 (const. syph.); ds Ft Rice Aug 1874; dd post baker Dec 1874 to Aug 1875; killed 26 June 1876 on Reno hill, gsw to head while leading capt French's wd horse away from corral near field hosp.[10]

Pension: 4 June 1880 / Father / 266928. (Rej on grd clmt not dependent on sol. for support).

Voit, Otto. Sad'r co H; b. Baden Germany; enl 1 Dec 1864 Louisville Ky. for 3 yrs; age 18 10/12; harness maker; brn eyes, dk hair, fair comp, 5' 1 1/4" high; assd to co D 13 inf; des 21 Feb 1866 Ft Riley Kans.; enl as Frank May 21 Dec 1866 St Louis Mo. for 5 yrs; join co H 7 cav 16 Jan 1867 at Ft Riley; sad'r 1 Mar 1867; disch 21 Dec 1871 Nashville Tenn expir of serv a sad'r & reenl in co H for 5 yrs; surd as des'r 15 Dec 1873 under GO 102 AGO 1873; restored to duty without trial 11 July 1874 & tr to co H to serve bal of enlmt; disch 24 Sep 1875 Ft Randall DT expir of serv a sad'r; reenl 9 Oct 1875 St Louis Mo. for 5 yrs; age 30; hazel eyes, dk hair, dk comp, 5' 3 3/4" high; rejoin co H 29 Oct 1875 Ft Rice DT; sad'r Nov 1875; gsw l. leg 26 June 1876 (fl. wd. sl.); remained with co in field; pvt 1 Mar 1878 & ed ordn dept to June 1878; sad'r 25 June 1878; ds Ft Lincoln DT Sep & Oct 1878; awarded medal of honor 5 Oct 1878 for serving as sharpshooter (at LBH) in exposed position outside the line to provide cover for water carriers; regtl sad-sgt Feb 1879; disch 8 Oct 1880 Ft Meade DT expir of serv a sad-sgt char xclt & reenl for 5 yrs; disch 8 Oct 1885 at Ft Meade expir of serv a sad-sgt char xclt & reenl for 5 yrs; on furl 10 days 10 Oct 1885 Deadwood DT; disch 8 Oct 1890 Topeka Kans. expir of serv a sad-sgt & reenl for 5 yrs; on furl 30 days 15 Oct 1890 Louisville Ky.; disch 8 Oct 1895 Ft Grant AT expir of serv a sad-sgt char xclt & reenl for 3 yrs; on furl 25 days 9 Oct 1895 San Francisco Calif.; retd 19 Apr 1898 a sad-sgt char xclt; died 1 June 1906 Louisville Ky.

Volkenstine, Frank. Pvt co M; b. 15 Nov 1844 Birmingham Mich.; enr 18 Jan 1864 Detroit Mich. a pvt co K 16 Mich. inf for 3 yrs; shell wd l. shoulder 27 July 1864 near Petersburg Va.; in hosp to 15 June 1865 when m.o. vol serv at Detroit; enl reg army 1 Nov 1865 at Detroit for 3 yrs; age 21; shoemaker; brn eyes, brn hair, ruddy comp, 5' 11" high; join co A 1 battn 18 inf Dec 1865 Jeffn Bks Mo.; des 27 May 1866 Booneville Colo. Ty; apph 31 May near Colo. City; in conft to 4 Dec 1866 Ft Laramie DT; sen gen cm forf all pay due at time of des'n & rejoined co at Ft Caspar DT; disch 4 Nov 1868 Ft Russell Wyo. Ty expir of serv a pvt; enl as Frank Bowers 4 Jan 1870 Ft L'worth Kans. for 5 yrs in co M 7 cav; cpl 4 Feb 1870; des 28 Apr 1870 at Ft L'worth; surd 1 Dec 1873 Ft Wayne Mich. under GO 102 AGO 1873; restored to duty without trial & tr to co D 1 inf (at Ft Wayne) to serve bal of enlmt, but des 11 Mar 1874 before order issued; apph 14 Feb 1876 in Detroit; suffered spell of lunacy while awaiting trial at Ft Wayne; (it was learned he was arrested by Detroit police in Aug 1874 as an insane man); examined by post surg 6 May 1876 to determine if he should be disch the serv or sent to govt hosp for insane sol.'s; post comdr recom disch without trial in interest of the serv as sol. not sufficiently responsible for his acts to properly subject him to penalty for des'n; dishon disch 31 May 1876 at Ft Wayne per SO 104 AGO 1876 (periodical insanity); arrested 6 Oct 1881 for making false affidavit & sen to 18 mos hard labor in Detroit House of Correction;[11] died 3 Dec 1919 at Detroit.

Pension: 27 June 1865 / Inv / 74642 / 116551; cert issued 25 Apr 1872 (arrears paid from 16 June 1865 less Nov 1865 to Nov 1868); dropped from roll 3 Sep 1874 failure to claim; last paid 3 Sep 1873. Restored 2 June 1880 (arrears paid from 4 Sep 1873); last paid 4 Sep 1881. Payment suspended 8 May 1882 by order com'r of pensions until amount overpaid dur subsequent serv Jan 1870 thro' May 1876 should be reimbursed to govt. App'd for restoration 12 June 1889 & sum of overpayment deducted 19 Sep 1889.

Von Arnim, Julius. Pvt co C; b. Prussia Germany; enl 16 Aug 1866 New York N.Y. for 5 yrs; age 33; machinist; brn eyes, dk hair, dk comp, 5' 3 1/4" high; join co C 10 Sep 1866 Ft Riley Kans.; dd co cook June to Nov 1867; dd co cook Feb 1868; dd hosp attdt Oct 1868; dd co cook Dec 1868 & Jan 1869; dd co cook

Apr to Oct 1869; ds with band from 24 Jan 1870; disch 16 Aug 1871 Taylor Bks (Louisville) Ky. by expir of serv a pvt & reenl same day in band for 5 yrs; attd to co F July to Sep 1873 in field;[12] attd to co L Dec 1874 to Apr 1875; tr to co C 28 Apr 1876 & dd with band from same date; ds camp Powder River MT 10 June 1876 with band; ds str *Josephine* 6 Aug 1876 to Ft Lincoln with band; disch 16 Aug 1876 at Ft Lincoln expir of serv a pvt char good.

Von Bramer, Chas. Pvt co I; b. Canterbury N.Y.; enl 3 Jan 1872 Chicago Ill. for 5 yrs; age 21; laborer; grey eyes, dk hair, dk comp, 5' 9 1/2" high; join co I 1 Feb 1872 Shelbyville Ky.; sick hosp 31 Dec 1872 to 4 Mar 1873 (syph.); dd with detmt hq June 1873; sick 25 Aug to 14 Sep 1875 (cont'n l. thumb, knife); killed with Custer column 25 June 1876.

Voss, Henry. Chf-trump'r ncs; b. Hanover Germany; enl in co G 5 cav 1 June 1866 Wash'n D.C. for 3 yrs; age 17;[13] laborer; blue eyes, lt hair, ruddy comp, 5' 3 3/4" high; trump'r 13 July 1866; disch 21 May 1869 Omaha Neb by expir of serv a trump'r & reenl in same co for 5 yrs; tr to co H 17 May 1871; sick hosp 5–9 Aug 1873 Camp Lowell (Tucson) AT (cont'n l. arm, thrown from horse while enroute with co from San Carlos); disch 21 May 1874 at Camp Lowell upon expir of serv a trump'r; reenl 18 Jan 1875 New York N.Y. for 5 yrs; age 25; blue eyes, lt hair, fair comp, 5' 8 3/4" high; assd to 7 cav as trump'r 8 Mar 1875; ds Ft Snelling Minn. 13 Mar 1875 awaiting transp to regt [snow blockade on NPRR]; tr to Ft Lincoln DT 19 Apr 1875 (with pvt Merritt);[14] appt chf-trump'r 24 Apr 1875; in arrest July & Aug 1875 (struck sad-sgt Tritten without provocation); sen gen cm 21 Aug 1875 forf $8 pay per mo for 4 mos; pvt 19 Nov 1875 sen gar cm (awol) but commuted to forf $5 pay (in consid'n of extenuating circumstances); pvt co E 16 Jan 1876 (own req); appt chf-trump'r 8 May 1876; killed with Custer column 25 June 1876.

Notes—V

1. Carroll, *Custer's Chief of Scouts*, 55–56; Lt. Hugh L. Scott, who joined the regiment in Sept. 1876, later observed that command of the scouts was a position sought after by the more adventurous lieutenants, "The position was analogous to that of an aviator of to-day [1928]; one could always be ahead of the command, away from the routine that was irksome, and sure to have a part in all the excitement." Scott, *Some Memories of a Soldier*, 32.

Varnum said Custer was absent in Washington but left orders that he (Varnum) was to organize and command the Indian scouts on the campaign; said he had one soldier as a sort of personal orderly. Carroll, ed., *Custer's Chief of Scouts*, 56–57; Running Wolf said Varnum had one orderly and a cook. Libby, *Arikara Narrative*, 136.

Lt. Nickerson, 17th Infantry, had charge of the Indian Scouts from about July 17 to Sept. 6, 1876, as Varnum was commanding a company. Major Reno to assistant adjutant general, Dept. of Dakota, Oct. 8, 1876, in answer to communication asking for reports of Scouts for July and August. NA, M1734, Roll 17, letter 2990 DD 1876.

2. Capt. Moylan and Company "A" were also sent on the steamer *Josephine* to escort the wagon train from Powder River to the Rosebud; the band attached to Company "A" for the march. SFO 29, Hq DD, July 16, 1876; SFO 31, Hq DD, July 19, 1876. RG 94, Entry 44. On arrival at the Rosebud, the men of Varnum's detachment rejoined their companies.

3. Varnum said Troop C was formed temporarily from the remnants of three of the troops which were with Custer. Some of the men had been with the pack train and some with the wagon train, and a batch of recruits had been left at Powder River dismounted. Horses for these had arrived and thirty of this detachment made a fair troop. Carroll, *Custer's Chief of Scouts*, 77.

GO 15, Hq 7th Cavalry, Aug. 4, 1876, directed that for purposes of detail, march, and encamping, the regiment would be divided into eight companies: A and I; B; C, E, and F; D; H and L; K; and M. (Company G is not listed but is presumed to be the eighth company.) GO 17, Hq 7th Cavalry, Aug. 6, 1876, RG 391, Entry 859, directed that the regiment would be organized into two battalions; 1st battalion, Capt. Benteen, Companies H, G, C, and M; 2nd battalion, Capt. Weir, Companies A, B, K, and D.

4. See, Carroll, *Custer's Chief of Scouts*, 99–104.

5. Michael Vetter Papers, 1874–76; (file B373) 9 items, State Historical Society, Bismarck, N.Dak. Letters published as *The Cowboy Soldier*, Rex Moore, ed.; see also *Newsletter*, (LBHA), vol. 25, no. 10, Dec. 1996, 7, "Dear Brother: A Soldier's Letters," by Rick Collin.

6. A complimentary reception ball, April 24, 1873, welcomed the 7th Cavalry to Yankton, DT; music provided by Prof. Vinatieri, long time leader of the Yankton Brass Band, who led a group of 29 musicians assembled for the occasion, and added much interest to the entertainment by his skill as a violinist, in rendering the "mocking bird." It was rumored that Prof. Vinatieri had connected himself with the band of the 7th Cavalry. *Dakota Herald*, April 29, 1873; *The Yankton Press*, April 30, 1873; Darling, *Custer's Seventh Cavalry Comes to Dakota*, 123–24, 143.

7. Krause and Olson, *Prelude to Glory*, 143–44, contains a brief account of the Black Hills Expedition by Vinatieri.

8. RG 94, Entry 409, file, 11684 A (EB) AGO 1876.

9. *Dakota Herald*, Jan. 20, 27, 1877.

10. John Ryan to Walter Camp, Dec. 17, 1908, WMC-BYU; William E. Morris to William Slaper, Apr. 11, 1915, in newspaper clipping, np, nd, Taylor Scrapbook; Voigt's body, with Tanner, Lell, and Meador, was found in June 1903 by Superintendent Grover. WMC, notes, env 75, IU; These four bodies, and a fifth body of a Reno soldier, were interred in Custer National Cemetery. Custer Battlefield Burial Register, LBHB Coll., Roll 14. John Ryan said Voight and Tanner were buried in one grave down in the depression where the mules and horses were. Taylor, *With Custer on the Little Bighorn*, 182.

11. Volkenstine was indicted but not tried, though a willing victim in a conspiracy of fraudulent pension schemes unearthed in 1882. Report of F. A. Woodall, Special Examiner, Apr. 27, 1882. (Pension file). See also, RG 94, Entry 409, file 11047 A (EB) AGO 1873.

12. Felix Vinatieri wrote to Gen. Custer, April 28, 1873, that two men in the band (Von Arnim and Langer) were not and never would be of any account as musicians to it. Darling, *Custer's Seventh Cavalry Comes to Dakota*, 143–44.

13. Army regulations provided for the enlistment of minors. *Regs.* 1863, Par. 927: "If minors present themselves, they are to be treated with great candor; the names and residences of their parents or guardians, if they have any, must be ascertained, and these will be informed of the minor's wish to enlist, that they may make their objections or give their consent."

Par. 929; "Any free white male person above the age of eighteen and under thirty-five years, being at least five feet three inches high, effective, able-bodied, sober, free from disease, of good character and habits, and with a competent knowledge of the English language, may be enlisted. This regulation, so far as respects the height and age of the recruit, shall not extend to musicians or to soldiers who may "re-enlist," or have served honestly and faithfully a previous enlistment in the army."

Par. 968; "The general superintendent will cause such of the recruits as are found to possess a natural talent for music, to be instructed (besides the drill of the soldier) on the fife, bugle, and drum, and other military instruments; and boys of twelve years of age, and upward, may, under his direction, be enlisted for this purpose. But as recruits under eighteen years of age and under size must be discharged, if they are not capable of learning music, care should be taken to enlist those only who have a natural talent for music, and, if practicable, they should be taken on trial for some time before being enlisted." *Revised United States Army Regulations of 1861.* (Michael Reagan and Morris Cain also enlisted underage, having sworn they had no parents living.) Statements in pension files, RG 15.

Hercules H. Price, who served with Voss in Company G, 5th Cavalry, said Voss was a native of Gestemunde, Holland, and interpreted for the doctor who treated Indians wounded in the Battle of Summit Springs, Kans., in July, 1869. Roenigk, *Pioneer History of Kansas*, 244.

14. "The cars have once more commenced running to Bismarck after an interval of just five months . . . the first train through arriving here Friday." *Bismarck Tribune*, Wed., April 21, 1875.

W

Wagoner, Jno. C. Chf packer qmd; b. Newark Twp, Tioga Co. N.Y. ca. 1835;[1] asst wagon master Blk Hills Exp'n 10 June to 31 Aug 1874; rate of pay $45 mo;[2] blks qmd Ft Lincoln DT July & Aug 1875; rate of pay $65 mo; hired by Lt Nowlan 18 Mar 1876 (to date 1 Mar) to take chg of pack train of exp'n; rate of pay $100 mo; sent to St Paul Minn. 20 Mar to hire assistants;[3] gsw forehead (by spent bullet) eve 25 June on Reno hill (fell from his horse unconscious till next day); treated in field hosp (bullet not removed) & remained with exp'n in field;[4] disch 23 Sep 1876 due $276.66 pay from 1 July;[5] died 6 May 1899 Stillwater Minn.[6]
Pension: 16 July 1888 / Inv / 664252 / 409324; appv by spl act of congress upon bill introduced by Hon. Edmund Rice of Minn.

Walker, Geo. (alias). See Weldon, Geo. P.

Walker, Robt. Pvt co C; b. Boston Mass.; enl 20 Aug 1875 at Boston for 5 yrs; age 22; safemaker; brn eyes, blk hair, dk comp, 5' 7 1/4" high; join co C 21 Oct 1875 Ft Lincoln DT; ds camp Powder River MT 10 June 1876 in qmd; dd qmd laborer Sep 1876; tr to co A 5 Oct 1876; in conft Dec 1876; des 2 Feb 1877 Ft Rice DT; apph 21 May 1878 at Boston; dishon disch 15 June 1878 sen gen cm & 3 yrs conft mil prison Ft L'worth Kans.[7]

Wallace, Geo. Dan'l. 2Lt co G; b. 29 June 1849 Yorkville SC; grad USMA 14 June 1872 & appt 2Lt 7 cav; awl on surg cert 30 Sep 1872; join co G 31 Oct 1872 Laurenville SC; with co on Yellowstone Exp'n June to Sep 1873; comd detmt ind scouts with Blk Hills Exp'n May to Sep 1874; actg aag hq distr upper Red River (Shreveport La.) 20 Oct 1874 to 4 Mar 1876; actg engr officer 22 June 1876; accomp Lt Varnum into valley fight 25 June & comd co G dur retreat; appt actg adjt 27 June & comd co F & care of co rec's; 1Lt & adjt 26 July 1876; arr Ft Lincoln 22 Sep on str *Key West* with maj Reno & Lt Edgerly;[8] appt to bd of officers 23 Sep to appraise value of govt horse ridden by gen Custer & which officers of regt desired to present to Mrs. Custer; post adjt & comd band 24 Sep & comd detmt ind scouts 29 Sep 1876; resd adjt 6 June 1877 & assd comd of co G;[9] cited by capt Benteen for gal in two mtd chgs against Nez Perce inds at Canon Creek MT 13 Sep 1877; ds Chicago Ill. Jan 1879 witness in Reno court of inq; awl on surg cert 29 Aug 1880 to 21 May 1881 (chr. rheum. & malarial fever); ds with div rifle team 29 Aug to 15 Sep 1884; capt co L 23 Sep 1885; sd range officer with dept rifle comp'n 21 Aug to 2 Oct 1886; ds 26 Aug to 10 Sep 1887 at div rifle comp'n; ds range officer with dept comp'n 26 July to 13 Aug 1888; tr to co K 19 Aug 1890; killed 29 Dec 1890 Wounded Knee SD in action with Sioux inds.[10]
[27 ACP 1887]. Pension: 24 Jan 1891 / Wid / 499240 / 291468.

Wallace, Jno. W. Pvt co G; b. Salem Ind.; enl 1 Nov 1872 Kansas City Mo. for 5 yrs; age 22 10/12; farmer; blue eyes, auburn hair, florid comp, 5' 9" high; join co G 10 Dec 1872 Laurenville SC; ed qmd Oct 1873; ds herding cattle Dec 1873 to Apr 1874; cpl 19 Aug 1874; pvt 13 July 1875 sen gen cm & forf $10 pay per mo for 2 mos; dd qmd carpenter Dec 1875 to Feb 1876; cpl 9 July 1876; disch 25 June 1877 camp on Sunday Creek MT per SO 70 Dept of Dak. 1877 a cpl char xclt;[11] reenl 22 June 1881 St Louis Mo. for 5 yrs; assd to co I 1 cav; disch 21 June 1886 Ft L'worth Kans. expir of serv a sgt char xclt; reenl 22 Sep 1886 at St Louis for 5 yrs; join co E 1 cav 14 Nov 1886; sick hosp Ft Custer MT 26 Nov 1886 to 2 Feb 1887 when disch on surg cert dis (chr. rheum. contr line of duty; dis total) a pvt char xclt.
Pension: 12 Apr 1887 / Inv / 606258. (Abandoned, mail to clmt at Omaha Neb stamped "Returned to Writer").

Wallace, Rich'd A. Pvt co B; b. Boston Mass.; enl 7 Dec 1874 at Boston for 5 yrs; age 22;

teamster; grey eyes, dk hair, sallow comp, 5' 7 1/2" high; join co B 10 Feb 1875 Shreveport La.; dd co cook Dec 1875; drowned morn 25 July 1876 near mouth Big Horn River MT (upon returning from brkft a ravine that earlier had 3 ft of water had risen to 10 ft & swift & he was thrown from his horse & could not swim);[12] body not recovered.[13]

Walsh, Fred'k. Trump'r co L; b. Carlisle Pa.; enl in 7 cav as trump'r 1 Dec 1872 Louisville Ky. for 5 yrs; age 21; laborer; hazel eyes, brn hair, dk comp, 5' 7" high; attd to band Apr 1873 unassd pvt; assd to co L as trump'r 11 May 1873 camp near Choteau Creek DT; excused from trumpeting 23 May 1876 (cerulo simplex on lip);[14] killed with Custer column 25 June 1876.

Walsh, Mich'l Jos. Pvt co H; b. Balandien Ireland; enl 29 Aug 1854 St Louis Mo. for 5 yrs; age 21; machinist; blue eyes, brn hair, fair comp, 5' 4 1/2" high; assd to co A 6 inf; des 13 Mar 1857 Lawrence Kans.; enl in co H 7 cav 15 June 1873 camp near Ft Rice DT; (b. Mayo Ireland); age 34; barber; blue eyes, brn hair, florid comp, 5' 5 1/4" high; surd 18 Nov 1873 under GO 102 AGO 1873 a des'r from co A 13 inf (old org'n); being impossible to glean information from AGO or regt he stated he des from, he was tr to co H Apr 1874;[15] sen gen cm 26 Dec 1874 forf $10 pay per mo for 3 mos & conft same period; des 6 Apr 1875 New Orleans La.; surd 10 May 1876 Jackson Bks La.; sen gen cm 29 July 1876 Holly Springs Miss to dishon disch & one yr conft mil prison Ft L'worth Kans.

Walsh, Thos. Pvt co F; b. Boile Roscommon Co. Ireland; enl in co G 6 cav 18 July 1866 New Orleans La. for 3 yrs; [co at gen Sheridan's hq];[16] age 26 2/12; laborer; brn eyes, brn hair, dk comp 5' 4" high; cpl 15 Aug 1866; des 20 Sep 1866 at New Orleans; surd 26 Feb 1867 at New Orleans; return to duty without trial 6 Mar 1867 a pvt (forf all pay due & make good time lost); cpl 1 Dec 1867; pvt 18 Jan 1868; des 27 May 1868 at New Orleans; enl in co F 7 cav as Jno. Flanagan 21 July 1868 Ft L'worth Kans. for 5 yrs; in conft June to Aug 1869; sen gen cm 12 Dec 1869 forf $10 pay per mo for 6 mos & conft same period; in conft Feb 1871; ds herding co horses Aug 1872; in conft May & June 1873; acquited in gen cm 2 July 1873 chg of drunk on gd duty; disch 21 July 1873 Ft Rice DT by expir of serv a pvt; reenl in co F 9 Aug 1873 at Ft Rice for 5 yrs; surd as des'r 24 Dec 1873 Ft Lincoln DT under GO 102 AGO 1873; restored to duty without trial 9 June 1874 & tr to co F to serve bal of orig'l enlmt; dd battn hq Blk Hills Exp'n 25 June to 31 Aug 1874; sick 3 Sep to 7 Oct 1874 (ac. diar.); in conft Dec 1874; sick 11–22 July 1875 (cont'n l. testicle struck jumping on horseback); disch 21 July 1875 at Ft Lincoln by expir of serv a pvt (made good time lost); reenl 21 Sep 1875 St Louis Bks Mo. for 5 yrs; rejoin co F 21 Oct 1875 at Ft Lincoln; sick qrs 4–10 Apr & sick hosp 11–19 Apr 1876 (headache); [with wagon train (June 1876) says Rooney; doubtful with packs says Lynch];[17] ds Yellowstone River 5 Aug 1876 gd on steamboat & arr Ft Lincoln 10 Aug on str *Durfee*; sick hosp 12 Aug to 3 Sep 1876 (ac. rheum.); sick hosp 15–25 Nov 1876 (infl. testes); sen gen cm 23 Apr 1877 forf $10 pay per mo for 6 mos & conft 4 mos (at Ft Lincoln); sick hosp 20 May to 3 July (tonsilitis); tr with detmt co F to Ft Totten DT 4 Nov 1877; sick hosp 12 Sep to 24 Oct 1878 (neuralgia); in conft Feb & Apr 1879; sen gen cm 8 Apr 1879 forf one mos pay & conft same period; sick hosp 1–24 Sep & 31 Oct to 22 Nov 1879 (rheum.); sick hosp 3 Feb to 12 Apr 1880 when disch at Ft Totten on surg cert dis a pvt char good (gen debility incident to long serv; treated in hosp on nine separate occasions dur last 2 yrs & recovered but slowly from any affection however slight; appears entirely broken down & utterly unfit for serv; dis 3/4; res Wash'n D.C.). Butler said Walsh died in Wash'n D.C.[18]

Walter, Aloyse Louis. Pvt co H; b. Willer France; enl 25 July 1851 Newport Ky. for 5 yrs; age 24; butcher; hazel eyes, brn hair, fair comp, 5' 7" high; join co H 5 inf 10 Dec 1851 Ft Belknap Tex.; dd comsy dept herding cattle to June 1852; ed qmd Aug 1852 to Apr 1853; cpl 1 Aug 1853; sgt 1 Mar 1854; ed comsy dept Aug 1854 to Feb 1856; disch 25 July 1856 Ft McIntosh Tex. expir of serv a

sgt; reenl 29 Sep 1856 St Louis Mo. for 5 yrs; assd to 6 inf; tr to co A 1 cav 2 May 1857 Ft L'worth Kans.; cpl 4 May 1857; sgt 1 Dec 1857; pvt 14 May 1859 (own req); des 18 Sep 1859 Ft Smith Ark; reenl 26 May 1860 at Ft L'worth for 5 yrs; assd to co A 2 art'y; recognized as des'r 2 Nov 1860 & ret to co A 1 cav; (redesig 4 cav Aug 1861); disch 25 Jan 1862 Wash'n D.C. by reenlmt in co for 3 yrs; cpl 1 Nov 1862; sgt 1 Mar 1863; pvt 22 June 1863; sgt 1 Sep 1863; sick hosp Apr 1864 Columbia Tenn whence disch 15 Nov 1864 by expir of serv a sgt; reenl 13 Oct 1865 St Louis Mo. for 3 yrs; rejoin co A 4 cav 6 Dec 1865; cpl 1 Feb 1866; sgt 25 Feb 1866; 1sgt 16 Mar 1866; sgt 29 May 1866; pvt 1 July 1866; ds clerk dept hq July to Oct 1866; dd co clerk Feb to June 1867; dd co clerk 15 Jan to 13 Oct 1868 when disch at Ft McKavett Tex. by expir of serv a pvt; reenl in same co 6 Jan 1869 Ft Concho Tex. for 5 yrs; cpl 14 Jan 1869; sgt 23 Jan 1869; pvt 1 Mar 1869 (prom'n disappv by regtl comdr); ed qmd Apr 1869 to Feb 1870; cpl 18 Feb 1870; pvt 19 June 1870; dd co clerk Feb 1871 to Feb 1872; dd co clerk Oct to Dec 1872; sick (chr. alcoholism) 4–18 Feb 1873; dd co clerk Apr 1873; sen gen cm 23 June 1873 forf $10 pay per mo for 3 mos & conft same period; dd clerk post hq Dec 1873; disch 6 Jan 1874 Ft Clark Tex. expir of serv a pvt; enl in co H 7 cav 1 Mar 1875 New Orleans La. for 5 yrs; ds camp Powder River MT 16 June 1876 chg co prop; ds str *Josephine* 7 Aug & arr Ft Rice 15 Aug (with pvt Fisher);[19] rejoin co 28 Sep camp near Ft Lincoln; disch 5 Mar 1877 at Ft Rice on surg cert dis a pvt char xclt (unfit for anything but clerical duty; an old man over 50 yrs of age with chr. rheumatic affection partly the result of tomahawk wd of knee recd before the war; also short of breath from emphysema; dis total); adm to Sol. Home Wash'n D.C. 12 June 1878; dropped from roll of Sol. Home 14 Apr 1881 (awol).[20]
Pension: 25 Mar 1880 / Inv / 354289 / 184849. Dropped from roll 30 June 1886; last paid 5 Mar 1883.

Warner, Oscar T. Pvt co C; b. Berne N.Y.; enr 22 Oct 1861 a pvt co H 3 N.Y. inf for 3 yrs; dd co carpenter Feb & Nov 1862 to Jan 1863; dd co cook Apr to July 1863; ds div hq teamster Aug 1863 to Apr 1864; abs wd July 1864 (concussion from shell); disch 17 Nov 1864 gen hosp Buffalo N.Y. upon expir of serv & surg cert (disability none, having recovered entirely from wd) a pvt; enl reg army 8 Oct 1875 St Louis Bks Mo. for 5 yrs; age 35; carpenter; blue eyes, brn hair, fair comp, 5' 5 3/4" high; join co C 21 Oct 1875 Ft Lincoln DT; killed with Custer column 25 June 1876.[21]
Pension: 12 June 1877 / Wid / 231867 / 178154.

Warren, Amos B. Sgt co L; b. Brooklyn N.Y.; enl 13 Sep 1873 at Brooklyn for 5 yrs; age 24 3/12; cooper; hazel eyes, brn hair, dk comp, 5' 10" high; join co L 19 Oct 1873 Ft Lincoln DT; dd qmd carpenter Dec 1874 to July 1875; cpl 8 July 1875; dd chg co kit'n Oct 1875; sgt 8 Apr 1876; killed with Custer column 25 June 1876.

Warren, Geo. Pvt co F; b. Gibson Co. Ind.; enl 7 Sep 1875 St Louis Mo. for 5 yrs; age 35; carpenter; hazel eyes, brn hair, fair comp, 5' 9 1/2" high; join co F 21 Oct 1875 Ft Lincoln DT; dd qmd carpenter Oct 1875; ed qmd mech Feb to Apr 1876; killed with Custer column 25 June 1876.

Wasmus, Ernest Emil. Pvt co K; b. Brunswick Germany; enl 17 Dec 1874 New York N.Y. for 5 yrs; age 27 11/12; book keeper; brn eyes, brn hair, fair comp, 5' 8 3/4" high; join co K 27 Apr 1876 St Paul Minn.; dd clerk post hq 12 Nov 1876 to 31 Jan 1877; dd co clerk Feb 1877; cpl 1 Aug 1877; sgt 2 Feb 1878; actg co qm sgt to Apr 1878; actg co qm sgt Dec 1878 thro' Nov 1879; disch 16 Dec 1879 Ft Totten DT by expir of serv a sgt char xclt & reenl in co K for 5 yrs; on furl 4 mos 13 Jan 1880 to Germany; actg co qm sgt June 1880 to Sep 1881; pvt 14 Oct 1881 & ds Ft Snelling Minn. as msgr dept hq; tr to gen serv at dept hq 30 Dec 1881; cpl 29 Aug 1882; sgt 1 Oct 1883; disch 16 Dec 1884 at Ft Snelling by expir of serv a sgt & reenl in gen serv for 5 yrs; disch 30 June 1886 at Ft Snelling to reenlist as gen serv clerk (cl. 3) at dept hq; mysteriously disappeared 31 Mar 1890; disch 29 Apr 1890 to date 1 Apr 1890 in consequence of awol same date, char xclt (a sober industrious man,

a good clerk, competent & of a high degree of intelligence & attainments).
Pension: 4 Feb 1899 / Wid / 691468; (no claim). 7 Mar 1923 / Ind. Wid. / 16261 / 10856. (XC-2,659,411).

Watson, Jas. Pvt co C; b. Hudson N.Y.; enl 10 Sep 1875 Cincinnati Ohio for 5 yrs; age 25; laborer; blue eyes, brn hair, fair comp, 5' 6 1/2" high; join co C 21 Oct 1875 Ft Lincoln DT; sick qrs 12 June 1876 (cont'n) camp Powder River MT; duty 13 June;[22] with Custer column 25 June but left behind when horse gave out;[23] ds wood camp near Ft Totten DT Feb 1877; dd co cook June to Aug 1877; ds Ft Lincoln 16 Nov 1877; ds Ft Totten June to Oct 1878 chg co prop & garden; dd chg co kit'n June 1879; dd co cook Dec 1879; disch 9 Sep 1880 Ft Meade DT expir of serv a pvt char very good.[24]

Way, Thos. N. Pvt co F; b. Chester Co. Pa.; enr 14 Sep 1861 a pvt co I 1 Ohio inf for 3 yrs; disch 24 Oct 1861 on surg cert dis (no diag); reenl same co 19 Dec 1861 Camp Wood Ky. for 3 yrs; ds ordn dept clerk Feb 1862; ds pioneer corps Nov 1862 to Apr 1863; wd & captured 19 Sep 1863 battle of Chickamauga Ga.; escaped 24 Dec 1864; m.o. vol serv 17 Apr 1865 Columbus Ohio; enl reg army 5 June 1866 Pittsburgh Pa. for 3 yrs; age 22; carpenter; hazel eyes, dk hair, dk comp, 5' 7" high; join co M 5 cav 9 July 1866 Nashville Tenn; cpl 1 July 1867; in arrest Dec 1867 to June 1868; pvt 5 Aug 1868 sen gen cm & forf $10 pay per mo for 3 mos; sick Sep 1868 to Mar 1869 (sim. frac. l. leg); disch 5 June 1869 Ft McPherson Neb expir of serv a pvt; reenl 13 Nov 1869 Allegheny Ars'l Pa. for 5 yrs in ordn dept; disch 21 June 1871 at Allegheny Ars'l per SO 237 AGO 1871 a 2d cl. pvt; reenl 11 July 1872 Chicago Ill. for 5 yrs; join co F 7 cav 1 Dec 1872 Louisville Ky.; dd regtl hq Feb to Apr 1874; ds Ft Lincoln June to Aug 1874 & dd qmd carpenter to Aug 1875; in conft Feb 1876; sen gen cm 2 Mar 1876 forf $10 pay per mo for 4 mos; killed with Custer column 25 June 1876; (survived by wife).
Pension: 24 Aug 1878 / Wid / 238975 / 196492. Father / 372700.

Weaver, Geo.[25] Pvt co M; b. Lancaster Pa.; enl 15 Mar 1871 Harrisburg Pa. for 5 yrs; age 28 5/12; railroader; blue eyes, brn hair, florid comp, 5' 7" high; join co M 30 May 1871 Louisville Ky.; ds Yankton DT Oct 1874 witness in civil court; ds regtl hq Ft Lincoln DT 10 Feb to 24 Mar 1875; disch 15 Mar 1876 Ft Rice DT expir of serv a pvt char xclt; reenl same day in co M for 5 yrs & on furl 20 days Bismarck DT; far'r 1 Jan 1879; disch 14 Mar 1881 Ft Meade DT expir of serv a far'r char xclt & reenl in co M for 5 yrs; ds Ft Meade 3 June to 8 Oct 1882; disch 14 Mar 1886 at Ft Meade expir of serv a far'r char xclt & reenl in co M for 5 yrs; died 14 Oct 1886 at Ft Meade (peritonitis) a far'r.

Weaver, Henry C. Trump'r co M; b. Phil'a Pa.; enl 11 Aug 1869 at Phil'a for 5 yrs; age 27; hat finisher; grey eyes, dk hair, ruddy comp, 5' 5" high; assd to G 7 inf; disch 11 Aug 1874 Ft Shaw MT expir of serv a pvt; reenl 1 May 1875 Pittsburgh Pa. for 5 yrs; join co M 7 cav as trump'r 21 Oct 1875 Ft Rice DT; pvt 14 Nov 1876; dd co cook Aug 1877; in conft Feb to June 1878; sen gen cm 9 May 1878 forf $10 pay per mo for 2 mos; ds Camp Ruhlen DT Oct 1878; in conft Nov 1878; (awol twice from stable duty until forcibly bro't back each time, & struck 1sgt White in face with his fist); dishon disch 4 Feb 1879 Ft Meade DT per sen gen cm & forf all pay due.

Weaver, Howard H. Pvt co A; b. Willimantic Conn.; enl 4 Nov 1872 Springfield Mass. for 5 yrs; age 21 10/12; machinist; grey eyes, auburn hair, ruddy comp, 5' 5 3/4" high; join co A 2 Dec 1872 E'town Ky.; ed subs dept herder Dec 1873 to Apr 1874; dd co cook Dec 1875; gsw r. arm 30 Sep 1877 Snake Creek MT (Bear's Paw Mtns) in action with Nez Perce inds; tr to str *Silver City* 14 Oct at mouth of Squaw Creek (on Missouri River); adm to hosp Ft Rice DT 26 Oct; disch 4 Nov 1877 at Ft Rice by expir of serv a pvt char xclt; died 2 Dec 1884 Scotland Conn.[26]
Pension: 24 May 1878 / Inv / 255471 / 157488.

Weeks, Jas. Pvt co M; b. Halifax Nova Scotia; enl 23 Aug 1875 Boston Mass. for 5 yrs; age 21 2/12; laborer; blue eyes, brn hair, fair comp, 5' 9 7/8" high; join co M 21 Oct 1875 Ft Rice DT; dd qmd laborer Dec 1875 to Apr 1876; des 3 Feb 1877 at Ft Rice; apph 20 Feb at Bismarck; in conft Feb 1877; dd regtl hq fatigue pty Apr 1877; dd subs dept herder June 1877; died 26 Aug 1877 Crow Agcy MT from pistol shot wd l. hip recd 24 Aug in quarrel at camp on Yellowtone River.[27]

Weihe, Henry Chas. Sgt co M; b. 16 Sep 1847 Saxony Germany; enl as Chas. White 6 Nov 1867 Phil'a Pa. for 3 yrs;[28] age 21; farmer; grey eyes, lt brn hair, swarthy comp, 5' 3 3/4" high; assd to co D 17 inf at Houston Tex.; disch 6 Nov 1870 Ft Rice DT expir of serv a sgt char very good; reenl 8 Mar 1871 at Phil'a for 5 yrs; join co M 7 cav 30 May 1871 Louisville Ky.; cpl 25 Jan 1873; dd chg co kit'n Apr 1873; sick 19 June 1873 (sim. frac. r. thigh) & sent to hosp Ft Lincoln DT; tr to Ft Rice DT 29 Sep 1873; sgt 1 Dec 1873; actg co qm sgt June 1874; ed subs dept chg of cattle herd Oct 1874 to Feb 1875; ed qmd chg of corral July to Oct 1875; disch 8 Mar 1876 at Ft Rice expir of serv a sgt char xclt & reenl in co M for 5 yrs; gsw r. arm 25 June 1876 & left in timber dur retreat from valley fight; rejoin co on Reno hill;[29] tr on str *Far West* 3 July to hosp at Ft Lincoln; tr by wagon to Ft Rice 15 July; duty 20 July; ds Ft Rice 6 Oct 1876 chg co prop; 1sgt 1 Jan 1877; sick hosp Tongue River MT 10 Aug 1877 (intm. fever); tr to Ft Lincoln 16 Aug & tr to hosp Ft Rice 22 Aug (ac. bronc.); duty 29 Oct 1877; sgt 9 Jan 1879; on furl 60 days 4 May 1879; in arrest Aug 1879; dishon disch 5 Oct 1879 Ft Meade DT sen gen cm & 6 mos conft post guardhouse; unexecuted portion of sen remitted 6 Nov 1879;[30] reenl 16 Mar 1881 at Ft Meade (auth AGO) for 5 yrs in co H; dd co gardener June to Aug 1881; cpl 12 Sep 1881; sgt 14 Oct 1881; pvt 28 Apr 1883; tr to co K 1 May 1883; cpl 18 Sep 1883; dd chg post garden Apr to Nov 1884; dd chg post garden Mar 1885 to Jan 1886; sgt 16 Sep 1885; on furl 30 days 29 Jan 1886; disch 15 Mar 1886 at Ft Meade expir of serv a sgt char xclt & reenl in co K for 5 yrs; dd chg post garden Mar to Nov 1886; sick qrs 6 Nov 1886 to 28 Jan 1887 (abscess); dd chg post garden Mar to July 1887; pvt 13 Aug 1887 sen gen cm & forf $10 pay per mo for 3 mos; on furl 30 days 26 Aug 1887 to visit his farm in Lawrence Co DT; disch 15 Nov 1887 at Ft Meade per SO 260 AGO 1887 a pvt char xclt (recom'n capt Mathey for being physically broken down; chr. rheum. from repeated exposure in field serv & while wd 25 June 1876 was compelled to run a mile & in a lather of sweat to swim across river); died 29 Oct 1906 Ft Meade SD. Pension: 17 July 1888 / Inv / 664644 / 413146. Wid / 860504 / 635717.

Weir, Thos. Benton. Capt co D; b. 28 Nov 1838 Nashville Ohio; moved to Shiawassee Mich. in 1842 & to Albion Mich. in 1852; grad univ of Mich. June 1861; enr 27 Aug 1861 a pvt co B 3 Mich. cav; gray eyes, brn hair, lt comp, 6' 0" high; appt 2Lt from 1sgt 2 Nov 1861; 1Lt 19 June 1862; captured on picket near Booneville Miss 26 June 1862; paroled 8 Jan 1863 Aiken's Landing Ga.; capt co C 26 Feb 1863 (from 1 Nov 1862); actg aag with col Mizner comdg distr of Jackson Tenn to Apr 1864; maj 18 Jan 1865; actg aig 1 cav div mil distr west Miss. May 1865; actg aig 1 cav div mil div of the Gulf July & Aug 1865 & at San Antonio Tex. Oct 1865; Lt-col 6 Nov 1865; actg aig on staff of gen Custer 22 Dec 1865; m.o. vol serv 12 Feb 1866 at San Antonio; appt reg army com'n 1Lt 7 cav 23 Nov 1866 to date 28 July 1866; join regt 19 Feb 1867 Ft Riley Kans.; regtl comsy 24 Feb 1867; actg aag on staff of col Smith [7 cav] comdg distr upper Ark (hq Ft Harker Kans.) 26 Mar 1867; prom capt 31 July 1867 & bvt maj & Lt-col for gal serv in battle of Farmington Tenn & engagement with gen Forrest at Ripley Miss.; witness in gen cm Oct 1867 Ft L'worth Kans.; asst judge advocate Dept of Mo. (Ft L'worth) 3 Nov 1867 to 4 Sep 1868; join co D 28 Sep 1868 camp Bluff Creek Kans.; comd co in action at Washita 27 Nov 1868; in arrest 30 Mar to 4 Apr 1869 (verbal order gen Custer);[31] recom by col Sturgis 18 Aug 1870 to go before spl exam'g bd at Wash'n but name withdrawn upon recom'n of gen Sherman;[32] comd co with NBS June to Oct 1873 & again June to Sep 1874; (led co D toward sound of guns 25 June 1876 till turned back at high point by large force of inds); comd regt 17–26 Sep 1876 dur march from Ft Buford to Ft Lincoln DT;[33] ds rctg duty 30 Sep 1876 NYC;³⁴ died 9 Dec 1876 at New York (congestion of brain).³⁵ [P 325 CB 1870].

Weiss, Jno. Pvt co A; b. 16 Mar 1849 Cincinnati Ohio; enl 17 June 1870 at Cincinnati for 5 yrs; age 21; farmer; blue eyes, brn hair, lt comp, 5' 9" high; join co A 26 June 1870 Ft L'worth Kans.; dd co cook Feb 1871; des 5 Oct 1872 E'town Ky.; surd 8 Dec 1873 at Cincinnati under GO 102 AGO 1873; restored to duty without trial & tr to Ft Snelling Minn. 29 Dec 1873; rejoin co A 13 June 1874 Ft Lincoln DT; dd co cook Dec 1874; dd co gardener Feb to Apr 1875; dd co teamster Oct 1875; ds Ft Lincoln 5 May 1876 in co garden; disch 20 Aug 1876 at Ft Lincoln by expir of serv a pvt char xclt; reenl 30 Nov 1876 at Ft Lincoln for 5 yrs in co L 7 cav; ds Ft Lincoln May to Nov 1877 chg co garden; wag 20 Nov 1877; dd qmd June 1878; pvt 1 Dec 1878; dd co teamster Dec 1878 to Feb 1879; dd co gardener Apr to Aug 1880; dd co cook Dec 1880 to Feb 1881; dd co gardener Apr to Aug 1881; disch 29 Nov 1881 at Ft Lincoln by expir of serv a pvt; reenl 27 Feb 1882 at Cincinnati for 5 yrs; join co F 3 cav 13 July 1883; disch 26 Feb 1887 Ft Davis Tex. expir of serv a pvt char very good; reenl 10 Mar 1887 at Cincinnati for 5 yrs in gen mtd serv; tr to hosp corps 22 Oct 1887; disch 9 Mar 1892 Jeff'n Bks Mo. by expir of serv a pvt char good & reenl in same unit for 5 yrs; tr to army & navy hosp Hot Springs Ark 14 Nov 1894; disch 9 Mar 1897 at Hot Springs on surg cert dis (chr. articular rheum. & deafness both ears from exposure & long serv; dis total) a pvt; died 18 July 1927 Durango Colo.
Pension: 16 Mar 1897 / Inv / 1187649 / 946277.

Weiss, Markus. Pvt co G; b. Czabocz Hungary; enl 17 Aug 1866 Detroit Mich. for 3 yrs; age 20; laborer; grey eyes, brn hair, fair comp, 5' 8" high; join co G 17 Sep 1866 Ft Riley Kans.; des 26 Mar 1867 Ft Harker Kans.; surd 27 May 1867 Cincinnati Ohio; sen gen cm June 1867 to 4 mos conft & forf all pay; join co G 4 Nov 1867 at Ft Harker; des 20 May 1869 camp near Ft Hays Kans.; surd 31 Oct 1873 St Louis Bks Mo. under GO 102 AGO 1873; restored to duty without trial & tr to Ft Snelling Minn. 29 Dec 1873; rejoin co G 13 June 1874 Ft Lincoln DT; in conft June 1875; disch 27 Jan 1876 Shreveport La. by expir of serv a pvt char very good; reenl in co G 27 Feb 1876 at Shreveport for 5 yrs; dd 9–19 June 1876;³⁶ left in timber dur retreat from valley fight 25 June & rejoin co on Reno hill;³⁷ died 15 Nov 1879 Ft Meade DT when bank of earth fell on him while at work constructing stable guardhouse.
Pension: 9 Dec 1893 / Father / 587121 / 485445.

Welch, Chas. H. Pvt co D; b. New York N.Y.; enl in co D 3 June 1873 Ft Snelling Minn. for 5 yrs; age 23; laborer; grey eyes, brn hair, fair comp, 5' 7 3/4" high; cpl 8 July 1876; ds in field with batt'y 21 Oct 1876; sgt 15 Nov 1876; dd post qm sgt Dec 1876; gsw r. hip & l. knee 30 Sep 1877 Snake Creek MT (Bear's Paw Mtns) in action with Nez Perce inds; tr on str *Silver City* 14 Oct mouth of Squaw Creek (on Missouri River) to hosp Ft Buford DT; tr to Ft Rice DT 10 May 1878;³⁸ disch 2 June 1878 at Ft Rice on surg cert dis (gsw frac. base r. thigh causing shortening of limb; dis 3/4) a sgt char xclt; awarded medal of honor 5 Oct 1878 for bringing water to wounded [at LBH] while under heavy fire; (he having been disch the serv, medal filed in AGO); died 22 June 1915 LaSalle Colo.
Pension: 4 Feb 1879 / Inv / 266185 / 166391. Wid / 1050874 / 821734. (XC-2,695,215).

Weldon, Geo. P. Pvt co E. b. Providence RI; enl as Geo. Walker 12 Dec 1874 New York N.Y. for 5 yrs; age 22; hostler; grey eyes, brn hair, florid comp, 5' 6 1/2" high; join co E 8 Feb 1875 Opelika Ala; killed with Custer column 25 June 1876.³⁹
Pension: 4 Oct 1887 / Mother / 361700 / 260992.

Wells, Benj. Far'r co G; b. Sangamon Co. Ill.; enl 28 Nov 1866 Springfield Ill. for 5 yrs; age 23; laborer; blue eyes, fair hair, fair comp, 5' 6 1/2' high; join co G 23 Mar 1867 Ft Harker Kans.; far'r 28 May 1867; des 21 Nov 1867 Ft L'worth Kans. but returned 30 Nov; pvt 1 Dec 1867; far'r 10 Apr 1868; disch 28 Nov 1871 Louisville Ky. expir of serv a far'r; reenl in co G 5 Dec 1871 at

Louisville for 5 yrs & appt far'r; awl 10 days 28 Sep 1873 Ft Rice DT; dd 23 May–19 June 1876;⁴⁰ killed dur retreat from valley fight 25 June 1876.⁴¹ (survived by wife & 1 ch.).
Pension: 11 Apr 1884 / Wid / 314710 / 209677. Minor / 324158 / 213884. Mother / 347212.

Wells, Jno. S. Sgt co E; b. Ross Co. Ohio; sgt co F 22 Ohio inf (3 mo troops) 20 Apr to 19 Aug 1861; pvt co C 54 Ohio inf 12 Sep to 2 Nov 1861; 2Lt 14 Jan 1862; 1Lt & actg capt 20 Mar 1863; capt 3 June 1863; m.o. vol serv 10 Nov 1864 Vining Sta Ga. by expir of serv & worthlessness to the comd;⁴² enl reg army 11 Jan 1867 Cincinnati Ohio for 5 yrs; age 34; miller; blue eyes, lt hair, lt comp, 5' 9 3/4" high; join co E 7 cav 29 Mar 1867 Ft Hays Kans.; cpl 25 Feb 1868; sgt 1 Jan 1869; disch 11 Jan 1872 Unionville SC expir of serv a sgt & reenl in co E for 5 yrs; actg co qm sgt June 1873 to Apr 1875; 1sgt 8 June 1875; sgt 1 May 1876 (own req); ds Ft Lincoln DT 17 May 1876 chg co prop; on furl 5 June to 18 Aug 1876 by spl auth from div hq with perm'n to visit Phil'a [centennial exposition]; dd qmd 12–28 Sep 1876 with 281 cav horses at post; ds Ft Lincoln 16 Oct 1876 chg co prop; disch 11 Jan 1877 at Ft Lincoln by expir of serv a sgt char very good; hired Feb 1879 Ft Meade DT in qmd as wagon master for wagon train to Ft Assiniboine MT; rate of pay $60 mo; enl in co F 3 inf 29 July 1880 Ft Shaw MT (auth AGO) for 5 yrs; age 35; disch 23 Mar 1881 at Ft Shaw on surg cert dis (valvular disease of heart & epilepsy) a cpl; enl as Jas. Blanchard 17 Oct 1881 Ft Point (San Jose) Calif. for 5 yrs in co A 4 art'y; disch 11 May 1882 Ft Trumbull Conn. on surg cert dis a pvt char xclt (paralysis of obscure origin, had pronounced hemiplegia, recovered motion in face & upper extremities, l. leg useless, sight of l. eye destroyed, aphonia continues); reenl as Jas. Blanchard 21 Dec 1882 Springfield Ill. for 5 yrs; recognized as Jno. Wells at Columbus Bks Ohio but recom'n for disch for fraud't enlmt not appv by AGO 6 Jan 1883; assd to co F 13 inf at Ft Wingate NM;⁴³ tr to co G 22 inf at Ft Lewis Colo. 22 Aug 1883 (own req);⁴⁴ on furl 2 mos 21 Sep 1885; des 19 Nov 1885 enroute from Jeff'n Bks Mo.; died 27 Aug 1893 Bismarck N.Dak. (never married).⁴⁵

Pension: 23 Aug 1890 / Inv / 899332. (Rej on grd no ratable disability shown. If clmt & Jas. Blanchard are same person, clmt is a deserter since 19 Nov 1885).

Wetzel, Adam. Cpl co B; b. 9 Oct 1846 St Louis Mo.; pvt co D 9 Mo. cav 16 Sep 1862; (regt consol with 10 Mo. cav Dec 1862); m.o. vol serv 20 June 1865; enl reg army 17 June 1867 at St Louis for 5 yrs; age 21; tinner; blue eyes, sandy hair, fair comp, 5' 7" high; join co M 7 cav 8 Sep 1867 Ft Harker Kans.; cpl 11 Dec 1868; pvt June 1869; dd co cook Nov 1869 to June 1870; ed qmd laborer Dec 1870; disch 28 June 1872 Unionville SC expir of serv a pvt; reenl 5 July 1872 Spartanburg SC for 5 yrs in co B 7 cav; dd co cook Oct 1872 to Feb 1873; dd co cook Feb to Apr 1874; cpl 1 Oct 1874; pvt 16 Jan 1875; ed hosp cook Apr 1875 to Mar 1876; cpl 4 June 1876; dd chg co kit'n June 1876 to Jan 1877; in arrest Feb 1877; pvt 2 Mar 1877; disch 5 July 1877 camp on Little Missouri River MT by expir of serv a pvt char good; res Salesville MT.
Pension: 5 Nov 1908 / Inv / 1378654 / 1153953; (dropped from roll 28 Apr 1909 upon death of pens'r, date unknown).

Whaley, Wm. B. Pvt co I; b. Harrison Co. Ky.; enl 24 Sep 1873 Cincinnati Ohio for 5 yrs; age 24; farmer; brn eyes, dk hair, florid comp, 5' 6" high; join co I 22 Oct 1873 Ft Totten DT; killed with Custer column 25 June 1876.
Pension: 9 Oct 1890 / Father / 466356. (Abandoned).

Whisten, Jno. Valentine. Pvt co M; b. 14 Feb 1852 New York N.Y.; enl 22 Sep 1873 at New York for 5 yrs; age 21; laborer; blue eyes, lt hair, fair comp, 5' 5 1/2" high; join co M 21 Oct 1873 Ft Rice DT; ed qmd laborer Oct 1873; in conft Dec 1876 to Feb 1877; sen gen cm 28 Dec 1876 forf $10 pay per mo for 4 mos; dd battn hq Apr 1877; in conft Feb 1878; disch 22 Sep 1878 Camp Ruhlen DT expir of serv a pvt char xclt; reenl 19 July 1879 Ft Hamilton N.Y. for 5 yrs in co D 3 art'y; disch 18 July 1884 St Augustine Fla expir of serv a pvt char xclt & reenl in same co for 5 yrs; disch 18 July 1889 Ft Monroe Va. expir of serv a pvt char good & reenl in same co for 5 yrs; tr to co D 11 inf 25 May

1890; disch 23 July 1894 San Carlos AT expir of serv a pvt char good (made good time lost awol); reenl 30 July 1894 Ft McPherson Ga. for 5 yrs in co H 3 art'y; disch 29 July 1899 Calumpit PI expir of serv a pvt char good; reenl 8 Sep 1899 San Francisco Calif. for 3 yrs in co O 3 art'y; tr to co E 23 July 1900; (redesig 28th co coast art'y Feb 1901 dur reorganization of art'y corps); disch 19 Sep 1902 at Presidio San Francisco by expir of serv a pvt (made good time lost awol) & reenl in same co; tr to 70th co coast art'y 2 May 1903; retd 23 Sep 1903 a sgt; died 20 Nov 1912 Oakland Calif.
Pension: 7 Dec 1912 / Wid / 998335. Also see Ind. War Wid / 13595 / 8632.

White, Chas. (alias). See Weihe, Henry Chas.

White, Pat'k C. (Pat'k Conelly).[46] sgt co H; b. 22 Mar 1845 Tipperary Ireland; pvt co A 40 Mo. inf 22 Aug 1864 to 8 Aug 1865; enl reg army 28 Aug 1865 St Louis Mo. for 3 yrs; age 21; soldier; blue eyes, brn hair, ruddy comp, 5' 7" high; assd to co G 6 cav; disch 28 Aug 1868 New Orleans La. expir of serv a pvt; reenl 11 Sep 1868 at St Louis for 5 yrs; join co H 7 cav 10 Nov 1868 Camp Sandy Forsyth Kans.; cpl 27 July 1869; sgt 29 Sep 1870; ds Ft Rice DT 28 July to 11 Sep 1873 when disch by expir of serv a sgt; reenl in co H 5 Oct 1873 at Ft Rice for 5 yrs; dd chg hq fatigue pty l. wing 15 May 1876; gsw l. shoulder (fl. wd. sl.) 26 June on Reno hill; remain with co in field; des 2 Oct 1876 Ft Lincoln DT; surd 26 Jan 1878 St Louis Mo.; restored to duty without trial 7 Mar 1878 upon recom'n comdg officer (forf all pay due & make good time lost); cpl 1 Nov 1878; pvt 22 Apr 1879; dd bldg co stables & finishing co qrs Aug 1879; disch 31 Jan 1880 Ft Meade DT expir of serv a pvt char xclt; died 28 Sep 1909 Minneapolis Minn.
Pension: 14 May 1887 / Inv / 609864 / 575006. Wid / 928226 / 743636.

Whitaker, Alfred. Pvt co C; b. New Orleans La.; enl 26 Sep 1873 Phil'a Pa. for 5 yrs; age 26; blacksmith; blue eyes, dk hair, fair comp, 5' 6" high; join co C 21 Oct 1873 Ft Rice DT; dd qmd Sep & Oct 1874; dd qmd Feb to Apr 1875; dd qmd Oct to Dec 1875; gsw r. elbow (fl. wd. sl.) 26 June 1876 on Reno hill; tr on str *Far West* 3 July to hosp Ft Lincoln DT; duty 25 Aug; sick hosp Ft Seward DT 24 Nov 1876 to 4 Jan 1877 (burn r. ankle); dd qmd Ft Totten DT Feb 1877; ds Ft Seward Apr 1877 verbal order comdg officer; dd qmd May & June 1877; cpl 30 Nov 1877; dd chg co cook house Feb 1878; actg co qm sgt June 1878; pvt 28 July 1878; disch 26 Sep 1878 Camp J. G. Sturgis DT expir of serv a pvt char very good; reenl 7 Oct 1878 at Ft Totten for 5 yrs in co C 17 inf; cpl 23 Dec 1878; sick hosp Feb 1879 (bronc.); sgt 29 May 1880; dd prov sgt June 1880; sick hosp Feb 1881 (bronc.); sick hosp Feb & Apr 1882 (bronc.); pvt 1 June 1882 & appt hosp stew'd 3d cl.; appt hosp stew'd 1st cl. 19 May 1883 & tr to med dept; disch 6 Oct 1883 Ft Totten DT expir of serv a hosp stew'd char xclt & reenl same day for 5 yrs; died 10 Feb 1887 Kansas City Mo. (tuberculosis).

Whitlow, Wm. Pvt co K; b. Cavendish Vt; enl by capt Hale for co K 10 Dec 1872 Troy N.Y. for 5 yrs; age 27; barber; blk eyes, blk hair, dk comp, 5' 5" high; join co 15 Dec 1872 Yorkville SC; dd hq Blk Hills Exp'n 30 June to 23 July 1874; dd qmd Dec 1875; killed 30 Sep 1877 Snake Creek MT (Bear's Paw Mtns) in action with Nez Perce inds.

Whytefield, Albert. Wag co K; b. Sandusky Ohio; enl 10 Sep 1866 Detroit Mich. for 5 yrs; age 20; painter; blue eyes, lt hair, fair comp, 5' 4 1/2" high; join co K Oct 1866 Ft Riley Kans.; ed qmd teamster Dec 1866; des 20 May 1867 camp near Ft Hays Kans.; apph 7 July 1873 at Sandusky; in conft Newport Bks Ky. to 11 Aug 1873 when tr under gd to Ft Lincoln DT; tr to co K at Ft Rice DT 4 Feb 1874 in conft; sen gen cm 1 May 1874 to 3 yrs conft thence to dishon disch; restored to duty 20 June 1874 (auth gen Custer) to accomp Blk Hills Exp'n;[47] unexpired portion of sen remitted 14 Oct 1874; ed qmd teamster Nov & Dec 1874; appt co wag 1 Dec 1874; ed qmd teamster Dec 1875 to Feb 1876; ds camp Powder River MT 15 June 1876; ds camp mouth of Rosebud Creek 11 Aug 1876; ds Ft Buford DT driving teams 31 Aug 1876; dd qmd Ft Lincoln 12–28 Sep 1876 with 281 cav horses at post; ds Ft Lincoln 16 Oct 1876 dismtd; dd qmd teamster 17 Oct to 18 Nov; disch 23 June 1877 camp on Sunday Creek MT per SO 70 Dept of Dak. 1877 a wag char xclt. [Siefert tho't Whytefield killed in row].[48]

Widmayer, Ferdinand. Pvt co M; b. 18 Feb 1849 Wertumburg Germany; enl 26 Sep 1873 Phil'a Pa. for 5 yrs; age 24; dyer; blue eyes, brn hair, fair comp, 5' 5" high; join co M 21 Oct 1873 Ft Rice DT; ed qmd laborer Oct 1873; dd qmd laborer Apr 1874; dd qmd teamster Sep to Dec 1874; dd subs dept teamster Jan to Apr 1875; dd qmd laborer July 1875 thro' Apr 1876; ds camp Powder River MT 15 June 1876 chg of 6-mule team; dd co cook Apr 1877; dd co cook Oct 1877; dd qmd teamster Apr to June 1878; disch 26 Sep 1878 Camp Ruhlen DT expir of serv a pvt char xclt & reenl in co M for 5 yrs; wag 1 Nov 1878; pvt 1 Jan 1879; dd co wag Apr to June 1879; dd co cook Oct to Dec 1879; dd co cook Oct 1880; ed qmd teamster June 1881; ed hosp cook Aug 1881; dd actg co wag Oct 1881; dd co cook Dec 1881; dd co cook Aug to Oct 1882; ed qmd teamster Dec 1882; disch 25 Sep 1883 Ft Meade DT expir of serv a pvt & reenl for 5 yrs in co E 7 cav; ed qmd teamster Dec 1884 to Feb 1885; ed hosp nurse June 1885 to June 1886; tr to hosp corps 8 Oct 1887; disch 25 Sep 1888 Ft Yates DT expir of serv a pvt char very good & reenl next day for 5 yrs; assd to co A 2 cav; disch 25 Sep 1893 Ft Wingate NM expir of serv a pvt & reenl in same co for 5 yrs; tr to co A 7 cav 28 Apr 1895; sd co cook May to Oct 1895; sd co cook Feb to July 1896; on furl 25 July to 15 Dec 1896 Bonita AT (near Ft Grant); sd co cook Dec 1896 to Apr 1897; ds on topographical survey July & Aug 1897; dd co cook Dec 1897 to Aug 1898; appt cook with rank of cpl 9 Aug 1898; disch 25 Sep 1898 Ft Du Chesne Utah expir of serv a pvt & reenl two days later for 3 yrs; assd to co K 5 cav; disch 13 Apr 1899 Manati Porto Rico per GO 40 AGO 1898 a pvt & reenl in same co for 3 yrs;[49] disch 13 Apr 1902 Pasig Rizal PI expir of serv a cpl & reenl in same co; tr to ncs 30 July 1902; retd 4 Nov 1902 a color-sgt; died 18 Sep 1913 Palmyra NJ.
Pension: 25 Apr 1914 / Wid / 1026741 / 888733.

Wiedman, Chas. Theodore. Pvt co M; b. 28 May 1856 Boston Mass.; enl 23 Sep 1875 at Boston for 5 yrs; age 21 4/12; machinist; grey eyes, brn hair, dk comp, 5' 9 1/4" high; join co M 21 Oct 1875 Ft Rice DT; gsw l. thigh (fl. wd. sl.) 26 June 1876 on Reno hill; remain with co in field; ed hosp cook Dec 1876 to Feb 1877; sick hosp Tongue River MT 11 Aug 1877 (gonorrhea); sick hosp Ft Lincoln DT 30 Oct 1877; duty 19 Nov 1877; sick hosp Ft Lincoln 28 Jan to 20 Mar 1878 when disch on surg cert dis (const. syph. resulting in chr. infl. joints of extremities; unable to walk rapidly or perform labor requiring muscular exertion; not contr line of duty; dis 1/2); died 15 May 1921 Oatman Ariz.
Pension: 14 Nov 1918 / Inv / 1430812. Ind. Surv. /16360 / 9935. Ind. Wid. / 15806 / 10616.

Wight, Edwin B. Pvt co B; b. 25 Dec 1851 Casco Me; enl 29 Mar 1876 Boston Mass. for 5 yrs; age 24; stonemason; blue eyes, brn hair, ruddy comp, 5' 8 1/2" high; join co B 27 Apr 1876 St Paul Minn.; ds camp Powder River MT 10 June 1876; sick qrs 12–13 Aug 1876 (cont'n);[50] abs on str *Far West* 31 Aug 1876; sick 6–18 Sep 1876 (quotidian intm. fever); dd co cook Dec 1876; ed qmd carpenter Mar & Apr 1877; dd qmd to June 1877; ed qmd Dec 1877; dd qmd June 1878; dd qmd Feb 1879; dd co wag Apr 1879; dd qmd Aug 1879; disch 28 Mar 1881 Ft Yates DT expir of serv a pvt char very good; died 19 Mar 1917 Sol. Home Togus Me.[51]
Pension: 23 June 1892 / Inv / 1118251. Rej on grd no evidence of alleged gsw at Little Big Horn & no ratable disease found. Renewed claim 28 May 1915 & rej on grd no rec of alleged gsw & Brights disease nor evidence of origin in serv or at disch.

Wilber, Jas. See Darcey, Jas. Wilber.

Wild, Jno. Cpl co I; b. Buffalo N.Y.; enl 21 May 1873 Chicago Ill. for 5 yrs; age 23 5/12; printer; hazel eyes, brn hair, fair comp, 5' 9 1/4" high; join co I 3 June 1873 Ft Snelling Minn.; cpl 24 Dec 1874; killed with Custer column 25 June 1876 (near capt Keogh).[52]
Pension: 17 Sep 1881 / Mother / 286211. Rej on grd clmt not dependent nor supported by sol. & income of clmt's husband such that she was well

taken care of in 1876; clmt's husband died 1880 leaving her a small income.

Wilkison, Jno. K. Sgt co F; b. Salem N.Y.; enl 5 Jan 1872 Troy N.Y. for 5 yrs; age 24 5/12; farmer; grey eyes, dk brn hair, florid comp, 5' 7 3/4" high; join co M 7 cav 5 Feb 1872 Unionville SC; cpl 22 Nov 1872; sgt 25 Jan 1873; actg co qm sgt Aug 1874; pvt 26 Sep 1874; tr to co F 4 Jan 1875;[53] dd co cook Aug 1875; cpl 1 Sep 1875; dd chg co mess Oct 1875; sgt 8 Nov 1875; dd chg co mess Dec 1875 to Feb 1876; killed with Custer column 25 June 1876; survived by wife.
Pension: 27 Nov 1877 / Wid / 234337 / 195739.

Williams, Chas. Pvt co M; b. Delaware Co. Pa.; enl 15 July 1870 Phil'a Pa. for 5 yrs; age 21; farmer; blue eyes, brn hair, fair comp, 5' 5" high; assd to co C 22 inf; disch 15 July 1875 Ft Brady Mich. expir of serv a pvt; reenl 3 Aug 1875 Baltimore Md for 5 yrs; join co M 7 cav 21 Oct 1875 Ft Rice DT; cpl 25 May 1877; dd chg co kit'n Dec 1877; pvt 18 Jan 1878; in conft Feb 1878; dd qmd teamster June 1878; dd co cook Aug 1878; in conft June 1879; disch 2 Aug 1880 Ft Meade DT expir of serv a pvt char good; reenl in 7 cav 29 May 1881 at Ft Meade for 5 yrs; assd to co G 13 June 1881; dd co gardener Oct 1881; ed qmd carpenter June to Aug 1884; dd qmd storekeeper Dec 1884 to Apr 1885; disch 28 May 1886 Ft Keogh MT expir of serv a pvt char xclt; reenl 10 June 1886 in prov gd (mil prison) Ft L'worth Kans. for 5 yrs; disch 7 Sep 1890 at Ft L'worth per SO 205 AGO 1890 (without char & forf retained pay under AR par. 1503) upon recom'n comdg officer, his serv being no longer desirable; res L'worth City Kans.[54]
Pension: 8 Apr 1898 / Inv / 1206283; (declared no mil serv since May 1886). Abandoned.

Williams, Jesse E. (alias). See Kuehl, Jesse.

Williams, Wm. C. Pvt co H; b. 28 Mar 1856 Wheeling Va.; enl 27 Sep 1873 Cincinnati Ohio for 5 yrs; age 21; farmer; grey eyes, lt hair, fair comp, 5' 10" high; join co H 20 Oct 1873 Ft Rice DT; dd post baker Apr 1874; ds with escort for surveyors Oct 1875; in conft Apr 1876; dd regtl hq fatigue pty (morn & eve) 19 May 1876; gsw l. hip 26 June 1876 on Reno hill (fl. wd. sl.); remain with co in field; cpl 15 Jan 1877; sgt 1 July 1877; actg co qm sgt Feb 1878; disch 27 Sep 1878 Ft Lincoln DT expir of serv a sgt char xclt; reenl 10 Aug 1880 at Cincinnati for 5 yrs; join co C 1 cav 1 Sep 1880 Ft Bidwell Calif.; des 24 Jan 1881 at Ft Bidwell; died 23 May 1919 Norfolk Va.
Pension: 5 Apr 1920 / Ind. Wid. / 14934 / 9796. (XC-2,658,947).

Williamson, Pasavan. Pvt co G; b. Petersburg Ohio; enl 1 Apr 1876 Pittsburgh Pa. for 5 yrs; age 28; harness maker; blue eyes, brn hair, lt comp, 5' 9 1/4" high; join co G 27 Apr 1876 St Paul Minn.; lost his pistol on Beaver Creek 4 June;[55] ds camp Powder River MT 15 June 1876; des 7 July [with Bonner & Littlefield] taking two mules & one horse;[56] apph 13 July near Ft Lincoln DT in starving cond'n; escaped from conft at Ft Lincoln 4 Dec 1876; arrested at Bismarck 9 Dec 1876; dishon disch 10 Feb 1877 sen gen cm & 4 yrs conft mil prison Ft L'worth Kans.; tr to Kansas penitentiary 9 Apr 1877.[57]

Wilson, Edw. See Grayson, Edw.

Wilson, Geo. A. Pvt co K; b. Madison Co. Ohio; enl 6 Sep 1866 Columbus Ohio for 5 yrs; age 27; blacksmith; blk eyes, blk hair, dk comp, 5' 6 1/2" high; join co L 7 cav 28 Sep 1866 Ft Riley Kans.; cpl 1 Aug 1868; pvt 26 Sep 1869; tr to band 18 Apr 1870; tr to co K 14 Nov 1870; dd co cook Dec 1870 to Feb 1871; dd hosp attdt July to Sep 1871; disch 6 Sep 1871 Yorkville SC expir of serv a pvt; reenl for co K 2 Oct 1871 Louisville Ky. for 5 yrs; cpl 1 July 1872; sgt 1 Feb 1873; pvt 1 Aug 1874; in conft Aug 1875; ds camp Powder River MT 15 June 1876; dd packer in pack train Aug 1876; disch 2 Oct 1876 Ft Lincoln DT expir of serv a pvt char xclt.

Windolph, Chas. Pvt co H; b. 9 Dec 1851 Bergen Germany; enl 21 Nov 1871 Brooklyn N.Y. for 5 yrs; age 21; shoemaker; brn eyes, dk hair, ruddy comp, 5' 6 1/2" high; assd to co A 2 inf; des 18 July 1872 Atlanta Ga.; enl in co H 7 cav as Chas. Wrangel 23 July 1872

Nashville Tenn for 5 yrs; surd as des'r 18 Nov 1873 under GO 102 AGO 1873; restored to duty without trial 16 Apr 1874 & tr to co H to serve bal of enlmt; dd orderly to comdg officer l. wing [capt Benteen] 15 May 1876; cpl 6 Oct 1876 to date 1 Sep 1876; sgt 1 Nov 1876; dd battn hq June 1877; actg co qm sgt Aug to Dec 1877; actg 1sgt 25 Jan 1878; disch 22 Mar 1878 Ft Rice DT expir of serv a sgt char xclt & reenl in co H for 5 yrs; actg co qm sgt Apr to June 1878; ds Ft Lincoln DT July to Oct 1878; (awarded medal of honor 5 Oct 1878 for serving as sharpshooter [at LBH] in exposed position outside the line to provide cover for water carriers); in arrest Apr 1879; pvt 1 May 1879; cpl 1 Dec 1880; 1sgt 4 Sep 1881; sgt 10 Oct 1882; on furl 2 mos 4 Jan 1883 Hot Springs DT; disch 21 Mar 1883 Ft Meade DT expir of serv a sgt char xclt; died 11 Mar 1950 Lead SD.[58]
Pension: 11 July 1901 / Inv / 1271870 / 1178971. Ind. Surv. / 11453 / 6744.

Winney, DeWitt. 1sgt co K; b. Saratoga N.Y.; enl 5 Nov 1872 New York N.Y. for 5 yrs; age 27; laborer; grey eyes, brn hair, dk comp, 5' 4 1/2" high; join co K 9 Dec 1872 Yorkville SC; cpl 1 May 1873; dd chg co mess June 1873; sgt 1 Nov 1874; ed subs dept Apr to Aug 1875; 1sgt 15 Sep 1875; killed on Reno hill eve 25 June 1876.

Witt, Henry Nicholaus Peter. Pvt co K; b. 10 Dec 1852 Heide Denmark; enl 9 Dec 1875 Cincinnati Ohio for 5 yrs; age 23; piano maker; blue eyes, brn hair, fair comp, 5' 9" high; ed hosp nurse St Louis Bks Mo. 1 Mar to 5 Apr 1876; join co K 27 Apr 1876 St Paul Minn.; ed qmd Jan & Feb 1877; cpl 28 Feb 1877; sgt 21 Oct 1877; with battn qm closing papers Jan 1878 at Ft Lincoln; actg post sgt-maj Feb to Apr 1878; 1sgt 1 May 1878; sgt 1 Dec 1878; actg 1sgt Aug to Oct 1879; dd post prov sgt Feb 1880; disch 8 Dec 1880 Ft Totten DT expir of serv a sgt char xclt; died 5 Aug 1929 Santa Monica Calif.
Pension: 22 Dec 1917 / Ind. Surv. / 15518 / 8457. Ind. Wid. / 1650339. (XC-2,622,572).

Wood, Wm. Melvin. Far'r co M; b. Grafton N.Y.; enl 11 Jan 1872 Troy N.Y. for 5 yrs; age 23 2/12; farmer; blue eyes, red hair, fair comp, 5' 10 1/4" high; join co M 14 Feb 1872 Unionville SC; ed qmd teamster Feb 1873; appt far'r 1 Aug 1873; ds Ft Rice DT 5 May 1876 chg co prop; disch 11 Jan 1877 at Ft Rice by expir of serv a far'r char xclt; reenl 12 Nov 1881 Albany N.Y. for 5 yrs; assd to co E 15 inf; des 28 May 1882 Ft Lewis Colo.; res Chicago Ill. as Jas. White employed as teamster for coal dealer & killed accdtly Dec 1885.
Pension: see, Invalid claim 359557, Albert H. Campbell (2nd husband of Mrs. Wood).

Woodruff, Jerry. Pvt co E; b. Mount Joy Pa.; enl 20 Jan 1866 Harrisburg Pa. for 3 yrs; age 18; laborer; blue eyes, lt hair, fair comp, 5' 4 1/2" high; assd to co D 3 battn 13 inf; (redesig 31 inf regt Sep 1866); disch 6 Nov 1868 Ft Totten DT per GO 24 AGO 1859 a pvt; reenl 8 Nov 1870 at Harrisburg for 5 yrs; age 22; musician; grey eyes, brn hair, florid comp, 5' 6 1/2" high; assd to gen serv cav; join co E 7 cav 13 Feb 1873 Unionville SC; dd post hq Ft Lincoln DT Feb to May 1874; ds Ft Lincoln 30 Sep 1874 to 14 Apr 1876 with band; (disch 8 Nov 1875 by expir of serv & reenl for 5 yrs); ds Ft Lincoln 16 May 1876 in co garden;[59] in conft Dec 1876; dd with band June 1878 to Nov 1880; disch 7 Nov 1880 Ft Meade DT expir of serv a pvt char fair; reenl in regt 10 Nov 1880 at Ft Meade for 5 yrs & assd to band; in conft Dec 1880; tr to co E 1 Oct 1884; in conft Dec 1884 & Feb 1885; disch 11 Nov 1885 at Ft Meade by expir of serv a pvt char good.

Woods, Aaron. Pvt co B; b. 25 Sep 1854 Phil'a Pa.; enl 2 Sep 1873 at Phil'a for 5 yrs; age 21; laborer; brn eyes, dk hair, ruddy comp, 5' 7 1/2" high; join co B 19 Oct 1873 Ft Lincoln DT; ds distr hq Shreveport La. Oct 1875 to Mar 1876; dd co cook Aug 1876; ds regtl hq in field 13 June thro' Oct 1877 (orderly for maj Merrill); dd stable police Feb 1878; disch 2 Sep 1878 Standing Rock Agcy DT expir of serv a pvt char good; died 26 Mar 1902 Phil'a Pa.
Pension: 8 Nov 1901 / Inv / 1277387. Wid / 760384. (XC-2,658,792).

Woolslayer, Wm. J. See Randall, Wm. J.

Wrangel, Chas. (alias). See Windolph, Chas.

Wright, Jas. (jr). Trump'r co H; b. 25 Dec 1851 Staten Isl N.Y.; enl as mus'n 25 Jan 1868 New York N.Y. for 3 yrs (with consent of father); age 16 1/12; hazel eyes, brn hair, fair comp, 4' 6" high; assd to co A 4 inf; disch 25 Jan 1871 Ft Fetterman Wyo. Ty expir of serv a mus'n; reenl as mus'n 5 Jan 1874 Jersey City NJ for 5 yrs; age 21; tinsmith; hazel eyes, brn hair, fair comp, 5' 3 1/2" high; assd to gen serv "music boys;" des 22 May 1874 Ft Columbus N.Y.H; enl as Wm. Ramell 1 June 1874 Phil'a Pa. for 5 yrs; join 7 cav 20 July 1874 Ft Lincoln DT; join co H as trump'r 17 Sep 1874 Ft Rice DT; gsw face (fl. wd. sl.) 26 June 1876 on Reno hill; remain with co in field; des 1 Feb 1877 at Ft Rice; enl as Jas. Pierce 25 Oct 1878 New York N.Y. for 5 yrs; assd to co L 8 cav; des 6 July 1879; enl as Jas. Wright 29 Jan 1881 St Louis Mo. for 5 yrs; assd to co H 7 inf; des 6 May 1881; enl as Jno. Colter 28 Sep 1881 Baltimore Md for 5 yrs; assd to co I 4 cav; surd as Jas. Wright 14 Mar 1882 Ft Stanton NM; dishon disch 30 May 1882 sen gen cm & 2 yrs conft mil prison Ft L'worth Kans.; rel 9 Dec 1883 for good cond; enl as Jas. Lee 11 Feb 1884 Chicago Ill. for 5 yrs; assd to co I 1 cav as trump'r; in conft July 1884; recom for disch as disgrace to uniform & object of dislike to men of co;[60] disch 16 Aug 1884 Ft Custer MT per SO 192 AGO 1884 (under par. 2464 AR [fraud't enlmt]);[61] died 21 July 1924 Bayonne NJ.
Pension: 12 Dec 1922 / Ind. Surv. / 18905; [declared only serv in 4th inf]; rej on grd clmt rendered no ind war serv. 14 Mar 1927 / Wid / 1574650; rej on grd sol. rendered less than 30 days serv in zone of active ind hostilities.

Wright, Willis B. Pvt co C; b. 7 June 1859 Oskaloosa Iowa; enl 25 Aug 1875 Cincinnati Ohio for 5 yrs; age 21; laborer; blue eyes, brn hair, ruddy comp, 5' 6 1/2" high; join co C 21 Oct 1875 Ft Lincoln DT; killed with Custer column 25 June 1876.[62]

Wylie, Geo. Washington. Cpl co D; b. 28 Feb 1848 New Orleans La.; enl 16 Oct 1867 Cincinnati Ohio for 5 yrs; age 21; striker; blue eyes, lt hair, fair comp, 5' 8" high; assd to co E 6 cav Jan 1868; cpl 1 Feb 1870; awl 60 days 8 Feb 1870 at Cincinnati; disch 15 July 1870 Ft Richardson Tex. per SO 145 AGO 1870 a cpl; reenl 17 Mar 1873 Memphis Tenn for 5 yrs in co D 7 cav; ds with supply train to Ft Stevenson DT Aug 1873; cpl 7 Jan 1875; sick qrs 31 Jan to 15 Mar 1876 (cont'n r. leg); carried co guidon 25 June 1876 till staff shot off by inds at Weir Pt; also recd ball thro' canteen);[63] sgt 15 Nov 1876; sick 26 Jan to 14 Feb 1877 (cont'n r. leg, kick by horse); pvt 7 May 1877; sick on str *Far West* 24 May 1877 (old cont'n r. leg broke open again); sick hosp Ft Lincoln DT 5–18 June & hosp Ft Rice DT to 11 July 1877; ds Ft Rice thro' Dec 1877; disch 17 Mar 1878 at Ft Rice by expir of serv a pvt char good; reenl 22 Mar 1878 Cincinnati Ohio for 5 yrs; rejoin 7 cav 7 Oct 1878 at Ft Lincoln & join co K 20 Nov upon return of co from field; dd qmd engr June to Dec 1879; dd co cook Apr 1880; dd qmd engr June to Oct 1880; cpl 8 May 1881; ds qmd as marine engr May to Aug 1881; sgt 21 Aug 1881; actg post prov sgt Dec 1881; disch 21 Mar 1883 Ft Meade DT by expir of serv a sgt char very good; reenl 4 May 1883 Jeff'n Bks Mo. for 5 yrs; assd to co E 4 cav; des 9 Mar 1884 Ft Craig NM; surd 16 Sep 1884 at Cincinnati; dishon disch 14 Nov 1884 sen gen cm & 2 yrs conft mil prison Ft L'worth Kans.;[64] reenl 1 Oct 1889 Ft Riley Kans. for 5 yrs in co A 7 cav; disch 1 Oct 1894 at Ft Riley by expir of serv a pvt & reenl in co A for 3 yrs; disch 18 Sep 1896 Ft Grant AT per SO 213 AGO 1896 (under par's 145 & 146, AR 1895) a pvt char xclt barring occasional sprees;[65] reenl 9 Oct 1898 at Ft Riley for 3 yrs; assd to co B 1 cav; disch 25 Feb 1899 Ft Robinson Neb (instr'n from AGO) a pvt char good;[66] reenl 2 Mar 1899 at Ft Riley for 3 yrs; assd to co E 6 cav; disch 21 Mar 1902 Angel Isl Calif. by expir of serv a pvt char xclt (retained in serv per instr'n from war dept); reenl 3 Apr 1902 at Ft Riley for 3 yrs; assd to co B 4 cav; disch 2 Apr 1905 Ft Walla Walla Wash'n by expir of serv a sgt char xclt & reenl in same co; tr to co C 4 cav; retd 22 Oct 1906 a 1sgt; died 13 Mar 1931 Kansas City Mo.
Pension: 31 Mar 1931 / Wid / 1690729. (XC-2,640,818).

Wyman, Henry. Pvt co C; b. Woburn Mass.; served in union navy 1861–65; master's mate on frigate *Cumberland* when rebels controlled Potomac River (entire crew merited commendation of admiral Radford);[67] masters mate on gunboat *Tioga* on James River dur Peninsula campn in 1862; with str *Vanderbilt* to Rio Janeiro in 1863 (on year long hunt for rebel raider *Alabama*); resd Apr 1865 & employed by navy dept as chf mate on transport running from New Orleans to Mobile; employed as clerk in qm dept at Mobile in May 1865 & promised appmt as asst supt of dock yards; enl in army 2 Aug 1873 Boston Mass. for 5 yrs; age 33; machinist; brn eyes, dk hair, dk comp, 5' 6 1/4" high; join co C 21 Oct 1873 Ft Rice DT; dd qmd Feb 1874; dd qmd (verbal order post comdr) Oct 1874 to Apr 1875; dd qmd Dec 1875 to Mar 1876; killed with Custer column 25 June 1876.
Pension: 12 Sep 1878 / Mother / 239209 / 183877.

Wynn, Jas. Pvt co D; b. Dublin Ireland; enr 11 Sep 1861 Central City Colo. Ty a pvt co K 1 Colo. cav for 3 yrs; ds hosp attdt Ft Union NM Apr to June 1862; dd co tailor July 1862; reenl as vet vol 1 Jan 1864 Ft Lyon Colo. Ty; tr to co A Jan 1865; m.o. vol serv 26 Oct 1865 at Denver Colo.; enl in co D 7 cav 1 Mar 1868 Ft L'worth Kans. for 5 yrs; age 32; tailor; grey eyes, brn hair, fair comp, 5' 5" high; dd co tailor Oct 1868; dd co tailor Aug 1869 to Aug 1870; dd co tailor Feb to July 1871; dd co tailor Nov 1871; dd co tailor Apr 1872 to Feb 1873; disch 1 Mar 1873 Opelika Ala expir of serv a pvt; reenl in co D 12 Mar 1873 Livingston Ala for 5 yrs; dd co tailor Apr to June 1873; dd co tailor Oct 1873; (amused men of his co 25 June 1876 at Weir Pt when the instant he mounted his horse [old & blind in one eye] it ran away with him at full speed, he pulling at reins with both hands, his carbine dangling by his side, & not stopping until at Reno hill);[68] ds Ft Lincoln DT 21 Oct 1876 dismtd; ds Ft Rice DT Apr thro' Dec 1877; dd co tailor Feb to Mar 1878; disch 12 Mar 1878 at Ft Rice expir of serv a pvt char xclt; reenl in co D 19 Mar 1878 at Ft Rice for 5 yrs; on furl June to Nov 1878 Standing Rock DT; dd co tailor Dec 1878 to Oct 1879; dd co tailor Feb to Aug 1880; dd co tailor Feb 1881; disch 28 Mar 1883 Ft Yates DT on surg cert dis a pvt char xclt (retained in serv ten days pending action on surg cert); effects of premature old age, seeming much older than 47 yrs owing to stiffness of joints & being somewhat fat & unable to stoop without great congestion of head; cannot properly groom or mount his horse, drill or perform fatigue; eyesight defective; dis 2/3); res Ft Yates N.Dak.; (froze to death on ice of Missouri River at Standing Rock says Fox).[69]
Pension: 10 Dec 1889 / Inv / 742878 / 593341; (last paid to 4 July 1892).

Notes—W

1. Son of Smith Wagoner, listed on federal census of Newark Township, Tioga County, New York, 1830, 1840, and 1860; the federal census of Aztalan Township, Jefferson County, Wis., 1850, lists Smith Wagoner, age 52, born in New York, residing with Daniel and Ann Caswell, and William Wagoner, age 10, and Smith Wagoner, age 3. Nearby is Julia A. (Wagoner) Caswell, age 20, born in New York, residing with husband Oscar Caswell, and Charles Wagoner, age 6, born in New York. In close proximity between the two Caswell residences, is John Wagoner, age 22, teamster, born in New York.

At the same time, residing together in Salem, Wis., fifty miles southeast of Aztalan, are John C. Wagoner, age 19, and J. Bolivar Wagoner, age 24, farmers born in New York.

Abram Wagoner, born 1823 in Albany, New York, moved to Aztalan in 1844 and during the Civil War served in the 29th Wis. Infantry. Invalid pension claim 572.767, cert. 362.327, RG 15.

The age of John C. Wagoner is controversial. Papers in his pension file indicate he was 39 years old in Sept. 1888, and 47 in 1896. At the time of his death, the coroner recorded his age as 64, whereas the death certificate and cemetery register show age 63, the information likely provided by Wagoner's brother, Charles F., who apparently handled the final arrangements. Though most newspapers reported he was 58 years old, the *St. Paul Dispatch*, May 6, 1899, listed his age as 68.

2. RG 92, Entry 238, report 1874/51; John Wagoner, from Pleasant Grove, Minn., was described as one of the most experienced, practical, and useful men on the (Black Hills) expedition, having traveled extensively in every state and territory west of the Mississippi, and bore recommendations from the Hon. Edmund Rice of St. Paul. He was familiar with life on the plains, in the mountains, and among the Indians, and knew all about freighting, by wagons and by pack trains. Krause and Olson, *Custer's Prelude to Glory*, 75.

White-Man-Runs-Him said that, when he first met Gen. Custer in June 1876 at the mouth of Powder River, there was a packer there who talked a little Crow. *The Tepee Book*, vol. 2: 53.

3. RG 92, Entry 238, reports 1875/314 and 1876/328; *Bismarck Tribune*, Mar. 22, 1876, reported Wagoner left Bismarck on Monday morning (likely on the stage with Gen. Custer, who was returning to Washington, and Lts. Calhoun and Smith, en route to join Companiess E and L at Fort Seward, DT).

Wagoner passed through Rochester, Minn., March 28, on his way to visit a day or two at nearby Pleasant Grove. *Rochester Post*, April 1, 1876; he was married there in Nov. 1870, (and divorced Oct. 1, 1877, for desertion about 1874). His sister, Eliza Higbee (Higby), also resided at Pleasant Grove (federal census, 1860); Wagoner may have been accompanied to St. Paul by Moses Flint, a resident of Pleasant Grove, 1859–1902.

4. Dr. Porter certified under date of Oct. 22, 1885, that the ball struck Wagoner on the forehead above the nose, and when he treated the wound he thought it would prove fatal, as the ball passed through the skull and into the brain. House Report No. 2049, 50th Cong., 1st Sess., To accompany Bill H. R. 2530.

5. During the winter of 1876–77, Wagoner was involved in a much publicized imbroglio. He was apparently hired as chief herder at Fort Lincoln about Nov. 8 by Lt. John Carland, 6th Infantry, and authorized to employ up to thirty assistants to conduct a herd of 884 ponies seized from the Sioux at Standing Rock Agency to St. Paul for sale in public auction. Originally they were to be escorted by companies C and G of the 7th Cavalry, commanded by Capt. Jackson (SO 217, Hq Fort Lincoln, Nov. 6, 1876), but changed the next day (SO 218) per instructions from department headquarters, and Lt. Carland given charge of the herd. (He is shown on detached service from his company from Nov. 12 until June, 1877, in connection with the ponies.) RG 393, Part V, Fort A. Lincoln.

The herd reached Fort Abercrombie on the Red River (separating Dakota and Minnesota) Nov. 26, where another 500 ponies seized from Cheyenne Agency were added. The whole were said to be principally "squaw" ponies—used for transporting tepees and the old and sick when the Indians were on the move—the old and broken down animals, unfit for use by the warriors when on the war path. The huge herd started overland the morning of Nov. 30, moving slowly, and passed the frontier settlements of Minnesota, where Wagoner allegedly sold several ponies to various interested citizens, and for which activity he was discharged Dec. 12 by Lt. Carland at the town of Melrose.

Carland was three days going from Melrose to St. Cloud, having been arrested for responsibility when some of the ponies died within the corporate limits of Sauk Centre, in violation of village sanitary regulations. His appeal was met with the court, "instructing the jury that the civil was superior to the military in time of peace, and that if it had been General Grant or Queen Victoria they would be equally responsible," whereupon the jury found Carland guilty and sentenced him to pay the fine of $10 and costs, or in default, imprisonment in the county jail for thirty days.

A resident of Sauk Centre stated that at least 75 head broke down completely between that place and St. Cloud and had to be shot, and that of some 25 left at Sauk Centre as unable to travel, all but one died within the next 38 hours.

Wagoner was arrested Dec. 16 by the U.S. Marshal at St. Paul, charged by Lt. Carland with three counts of stealing government property, though in the final verdict, June 6, 1877, at Winona, he was found guilty on only one count and fined $300. Special agents who went back over the trail, accounted for all but one pony, which Wagoner had given to a pretty school teacher who admired it as the train passed the school house. He reportedly lassoed the pony and left it tied to a tree nearby. For this act of gallantry he was acquitted of any criminal intent, but was jailed when unable to pay his fine. He was released July 7, 1877, on his own application, citing a provision of an act of Congress approved June 1, 1872, and proof that he had no property, real or personal, exceeding $20 in value except such as by law was exempt from levy and sale on execution for debt. *St. Paul Dispatch* and *St. Paul and Minneapolis Pioneer-Press*, various issues Dec. 12, 1876, through Jan 4, 1877, and June 1877; *Winona (Minn.) Republican*, June 7, 1877; *Winona (Minn.) Herald,* June 8, 1877; Records of U. S. Commissioner's Court, District of Minnesota, 1876–1877. Minnesota Historical Society.

"John C. Wagoner was found guilty of stealing Indian ponies, five of them, and was fined three hundred dollars. A light penalty we should think." *Bismarck Tribune*, June 8, 1877.

Wagoner was entitled to a voucher from Lt. Carland for about one month's service, and transportation from St. Paul to Bismarck, the courts having dealt with his offense and in the law all was settled. John B. Sanborn, (Wagoner's attorney), to Gen. Terry, Aug. 23, 1877. NA, M1734, Roll 21, letter, 3338 DD 1877.

Wagoner was considered a gentleman of unimpeachable character, and well known to a number of St. Paul's prominent citizens who did not believe in his guilt. He was formerly in the employ of the firm of Hill & Acker, the latter, together with Col. Allen of the Merchant's Hotel, acted as bondsmen for Wagoner's release from jail. Acker declared he had never known Wagoner to do a crooked thing and was confident there was some mistake about the matter. *St. Paul and Minneapolis Pioneer-Press*, Dec. 17, 1876.

Lt. Carland's son said his father never fully recovered from the freezing endured on the 500-mile trek. Correspondence from Willis W. Carland to William J. Ghent, 1934, Ghent Papers.

6. Wagoner was survived by four brothers, Charles. F., and James B., of Eagle Lake, Minn.; Abram, of Ashland, Wis.; William, from near Reno, Nev., and two sisters, Mrs. Julia Caswell, Castle Rock, Wash.; and Mrs. Eliza Higbee, Wasioja, Minn. *Stillwater* (Minn.) *Gazette*, May 10, 1899; *Eagle Lake* (Minn.) *News*, May 12, 1899.

John Wagoner was reportedly raised from age seven by Edmund Rice of St. Paul, who secured passage of the Act granting Wagoner's special pension, one of only a few cases in which a man drew a pension though never having enlisted as a soldier. When Wagoner was 21 years old, he went south and was a cowboy in Texas and Mexico until the beginning of the Civil War, when he entered the Confederate army and attached to a corps that planned and built the defenses at Mobile, Ala. He deserted after becoming a fireman on the Mobile & Ohio railroad and came north and turned over to Gen. Grant the plans and maps of the Mobile defenses. After the war he returned to St. Paul and remained a year or two before going to the Pacific coast, where he prospected for gold and for several years drove a pack train between Los Angeles, Calif., and Tucson, Ariz., a trip that required three months. *Stillwater Gazette*, May 10, 1899.

Wagoner's brother, Charles F., after discharge from the Union army, toured California and Arizona before settling in Eagle Lake, Minn., in 1874. *Mankato Free Press*, Aug. 21, 1910.

Charles Wagoner said he was born in 1844 in Broome County, New York (next to Tioga County), and during the war served in the 3rd Minnesota Infantry, and as Lt. in the 57th U.S. Colored Infantry. Upon discharge in Dec. 1866, he resided in Trenton, Minn., until May 1867; Gallatin, MT, 1868; Utah 1869; Arizona (Turkey Bay) [Turkey Flat? east of Fort Grant], Dec. 1871; San Francisco, Feb. 1873; finally Eagle Lake, Minn., in 1873 (where he died, Aug. 20, 1910). Invalid pension claim, 567.786, Cert. 352.823; widow claim, 948.757, Cert. 714.580; (XC-2,683,333). NA, T288. RG 15.

Confederate military records (RG 109), contain service papers of Private John C. Wagoner, Company G, 3rd Texas Cavalry; (born St. Louis, Mo.); enlisted June 13, 1861 at Dallas, Texas for one year; age 26; occupation railroader; blue eyes, dark hair, light complexion, 5' 9 1/4" high; discharged Aug. 17, 1862 at Saltillo, Miss., on surgeons certificate of disability; severe stab penetrating right lung, followed by abscess and loss of muscular tissue, greatly impairing strength and usefulness of right arm; the lung weak and irritable causing severe fit of coughing upon any undue exertion; also inguinal hernia of left side difficult to retain with a truss.

The signature of Private Wagoner is remarkably similar to that of Custer's chief packer; and Saltillo, Miss., was directly on the line of the Mobile & Ohio Railroad. However, medical examinations of the chief packer (height 5' 9") in 1888 and 1896, do not mention scars on the upper body, though it was noted that he wore a double truss to retain a double inguinal hernia, larger on left side.

7. Walker's story, told while a convict at Governor's Island, New York, awaiting transfer to Fort Leavenworth, appeared in, *The Indianapolis* (Ind.) *Daily Sentinel*, August 17, 1878.

8. Lt. Wallace to Dr. Charles F. Knoblauch, Sept. 19, 1876, on board the "Steamer Key West on the wild Missouri," in Westfall, *Letters from the Field*; the Fort Buford Medical History, Sept. 18, reported that Reno, Edgerly, and Wallace, were to go down river on the steamer *Josephine*. RG 94, Entry 547; both boats reached Bismarck on Sept. 22. *Bismarck Tribune*, Sept. 27, Nov. 8, 1876.

9. "In connection with the '77 campaign, Wallace will never know now the premeditated meanness Sturgis intended him when he relieved him as Adjutant, and appointed Lieut. Garlington in his stead. . ." Capt. Benteen to Theo. Goldin, Nov. 17, 1891, Carroll, ed., *The Benteen-Goldin Letters*, 205.

10. See Mackintosh, *Custer's Southern Officer*, and Mackintosh, "Lakota bullet ends Wallace's life." Also, Westfall, *Letters from the Field*.

Lt. Wallace was the son of U.S. Congressman Alexander S. Wallace, an anti-Klan crusader who received the nickname "Buttermilk" following an incident in the summer of 1871, at Yorkville, when an opponent attempted to douse him with a pitcher of cream as he dined with Maj. Merrill and members of a Republican subcommittee. Martinez, *Carpetbaggers, Cavalry, and the Ku Klux Klan*, 142, 174.

11. See note A25 (Ascough).

12. Godfrey, *Diary*, 27.

13. RG 94, Entry 96; John A. Bailey said Wallace's body was never found; his horse got to other bank and was not drowned. Liddic and Harbaugh, *Camp on Custer*, 84.

14. RG 94, Entry 544, MT, Prescription Book, No. 14.

15. The 13th Infantry regiment was discharged in 1848 and not reorganized until 1861. Heitman, *Historical Register*, 106; "Old organization," refers to army prior to 1861.

16. Carter, *From Yorktown to Santiago*, 136.

17. Rosters of Company F with remarks by Rooney and Lynch, WMC-BYU; Muster Roll, Company Return, and Regimental Returns, August, 1876, RG 94, Entry 53; LBHB Coll., Roll 12; NA, M744. Muster Roll of Detachment 7th Cavalry, Fort A. Lincoln, DT, Lt. Ogle, 17th Infantry, commanding, Aug. 31, 1876. Willert, *March of the Columns*, 284; *Bismarck Tribune*, Nov. 8, 1876.

18. WMC, rosters, IU.

19. The regimental return reports Privates Walter and Fisher on detached service at Fort Rice, August 14. The Fort Rice post return reports two enlisted men arrived August 15 direct from Gen. Terry's command. Gen. Terry recorded in his diary Aug. 7 that surplus company property to go down river on steamer *Josephine*. (The *Josephine* arrived Fort Lincoln Aug. 13.) NA, M744; NA, M617.

20. RG 231, Entry 13; RG 15, Entry 2; Capt. Benteen said Walter had neither disease of lungs nor rheumatism, but from long service he was entitled to go to the Soldier's Home, which was the pretext on which his discharge was given, though not deserving of any other bounty from the government. Pension file, RG 15.

Sometimes an officer would arrange a pensionable discharge for a faithful old soldier who had served several enlistments and was no longer able to perform the required duties, rather than have him be refused reenlistment at the end of his current term and thrust out without a disability pension. Rickey, *Forty Miles a Day*, 53.

A death certificate is on file (Office of Vital Records, District of Columbia), for Albert L. Walter, age 59, ex-soldier, single, born in France, resident of D.C. 7 months, died April 14, 1883 of typhoid fever at Freedmen's Hospital and interred three days later in Potters Field at the hospital.

21. Before Walter Camp had a chance to bring up the subject, Frank Sniffin told him that the dead soldier found near the Rosebud in August 1876 was identified as Oscar T. Warner of Company C; said his name was in his hat and the matter was well discussed among the enlisted men that night. Sniffin did not see the remains but recalled that the man was wounded and had a dead horse. Liddic and Harbaugh, *Camp On Custer*, 86–87; see also Ellison, "Mystery Along Rosebud Creek."

22. RG 94, Entry 544, MT, Prescription Book, No. 14.

23. Brininstool, *Troopers with Custer*, 54; Watson met William Slaper on the hill and told him that his horse played out and he dropped back to the rear guard and was there all the time. Brininstool to General Godfrey, April 1, 1923. Godfrey Papers.

Watson and Slaper enlisted together and were good friends. Slaper remembered distinctly that Watson came in with rear guard evening of June 25 leading his horse, and explained that his horse had played out some distance back toward the Rosebud, and he joined the rear guard when it came along and walked with it leading his played out horse. Walter Camp to Daniel Knipe, April 4, 1923, in Hardorff, *On the Little Big Horn with Walter Camp*, 165.

John Martin told Walter Camp, May 4, 1910, that on his way to Benteen with the message, he met first Boston Custer on the bluffs, and farther along on the bluffs, two enlisted men who were together and inquired for Custer's command. WMC, notes, env. 130, IU.

John McGuire said Watson was the first man to tell him the story about he and Thompson going together to join Custer; says Watson and Thompson came up out of the valley just a few minutes after the mule capturing episode. McGuire described Watson as a rather small man, about 5' 7" tall, weight 135 to 140 pounds, clean shaven. McGuire to Walter Camp, May 13 and Oct. 12, 1909, WMC-BYU.

The Arikara scout, Soldier, told of finding a white soldier on the bluffs above the river trying to get his horse up, cursing and swearing, pounding his horse's head with his fists and kicking him under the belly. A little farther along the ridge the scouts found another white soldier with his horse down, this soldier signed that he belonged to Custer's command. Libby, *Arikara Narrative*, 116.

24. Watson returned to Cincinnati with Slaper after discharge in 1880. Theo. Goldin to Fred Dustin, Feb. 22, 1934, Carroll, ed., *The Benteen-Goldin Letters*, 111.

25. Sniffin and Widmayer said George Weaver was called "Cully" for a nickname. Liddic and Harbaugh, *Camp on Custer*, 85; Hammer, *Custer in '76*, 145.

26. WMC, rosters, LBHB; Nugent said Howard Weaver was their historian and encyclopedian and all disputes were referred to him for decision. *Winners of the West*, vol. 3, no. 10, June 24, 1926.

27. RG 94, Entry 544, USA Medical Register No. 117; William E. Morris said Jim Weeks was killed by Barney Golden in a poker game at Montana Bill's Ranch. Morris to William Slaper, April 11, 1915, in newspaper clipping, np, nd, in Taylor Scrapbook.

28. Weihe gave his correct name when he enlisted in 1867, but the clerk not being versed enough to spell it, wrote the name Charles White, and he (White) could not explain to him how it was spelled, not being able to read or write it proper at that time. Affidavit before Max Hoehn (Notary Public), Meade County, SD, Dec. 16, 1905. Pension file, RG 15.

29. White said he was wounded as soon as he took his place on the skirmish line. Testimony in court-martial of Capt. French, Jan. 27–28, 1879, RG 153, file QQ 994; Sgt. Ryan said White and Carey were left dismounted in the bottom and stood in water up to their neck under the embankment to keep out of sight of the Indians. Ryan to Walter Camp, Aug. 11, 1909, WMC-BYU; an extract of Sgt. Weihe's diary, written up by him contemporaneously, was loaned to Walter Camp in 1909. (Copies are in the Camp material at Denver Public Library and Brigham Young University.) Mrs. Jennie Weihe to Walter Camp, Nov. 30, 1909, WMC-BYU.

30. Sgt. White was discharged for aiding by his advice, the desertion of a fellow soldier. On his apprehension the charge against the soldier was changed to absent without proper authority and he was restored to duty. RG 94, Entry 409, file 5620 B (EB) AGO 1879.

31. Custer started from Camp Supply at daybreak, leaving Captains Weir and Robbins, and Lt. Custer, and Dr. Renick drunk in camp, they being sent to the next camp in a post ambulance the same afternoon. Capt. Benteen to Theo. Goldin, Feb. 14, 1896, Carroll, ed., *The Benteen-Goldin Letters*, 258.

32. The purpose of the board, also called the "Benzine Board," was to rid the army of supposed unqualified officers. Gen. Pope originally recommended that Capt. Weir not be required to appear before the board, but after Col. Sturgis respectfully protested the withdrawal of Weir's name, Pope worded his final endorsement to include a technicality that, rather than approving Col. Sturgis' recommendation, he (Pope) merely, "interpose[d] no further objection to his [Weir] being brought before the Board." Gen. Sherman advised Secretary of War Belknap that Pope's submission did not meet the requirements of the law and Weir's name was withdrawn. Johnson, "Weir and the Custers."

Gen. Custer allegedly had a private conversation with Gen. Pope before the latter's recommending against Weir's dismissal. Terrell and Walton, *Faint the Trumpet Sounds*, 71.

33. Weir is credited with having said, "As the Sioux have failed to find us, we are going home." *St. Paul Dispatch*, Sept. 18, 1876.

34. Capt. Weir was interviewed at his quarters on Hudson Street in Nov. 1876 by Frederick Whittaker, Gen. Custer's first biographer. According to Charles Braden, who was a guest at Weir's hotel, Weir complained of Whittaker constantly pestering him to sign a paper that Reno failed to assist Custer. Graham, *The Custer Myth*, 330; Frost, *General Custer's Libbie*, 236; Leckie, *Making of a Myth*, 210–11.

35. Weir's physician, Dr. Orten, in answer to Libbie Custer's request for details, said Weir's death was as a result of melancholia. Frost, *General Custer's Libbie*, 236; Lt. Baldwin (of Gen. Miles' staff) on meeting 7th Cavalry officers in Aug. 1876, said, "Col. Weir is very much broken from the use of liquor & it will not be strange if he soon goes under." Willert, *March of the Columns*, 306.

Another contemporary described Weir as, "very well read, and social in his disposition." Capt. Albert Barnitz to his wife, Sept. 27, 1868. Utley, *Life in Custer's Cavalry*, 196.

Lt. Garlington said Weir was a highly educated gentleman and always carried his shoulders high; he wore a little narrow brimmed hat, much like a small boy's hat from which the band had been lost giving it a sugarloaf shape. Carroll, *Garlington Narrative*, 15, 23.

Dr. DeWolf in a letter to his wife, Apr. 19, 1876, said he liked Capt. Weir very much. Luce, ed., "The Diary and Letters of Dr. James M. DeWolf."

36. Botzer Troop Duty Book.

37. John Lattman to Max Hoehn, Aug. 10, 1909, WMC-BYU.

38. "Sergeant C. W. Welsh, Co. D, 7th Cavalry, now lying at Fort Buford, is not expected to live." *Bismarck Tribune*, Oct. 26, 1877; Twenty-nine wounded from Gen. Miles' fight, with the bodies of Capt. Hale and Lt. Biddle, arrived the same date on the Steamer *Silver City*.

39. Weldon's brother, Thomas J., 187 Bowery St., New York City, on April 20, 1877, requested his brother's personal effects be sent to him. Lt. DeRudio replied that the box was the only one remaining unsold, and that it would probably be necessary to prepay the expressage as its contents were unknown to the express company. RG 391, Entry 869.

John G. Kimm said he was present when Weldon, otherwise Walker, was with others buried. Affidavit from Kimm, Aug. 29, 1889, New York City. Weldon pension file, RG 15.

40. Botzer Troop Duty Book.

41. A marker for Wells should be at bend of river directly north of Lt. McIntosh. WMC, Notes, Map Data, IU; James Boyle told Walter Camp, Feb. 5, 1913, that Wells's body was found in the river about due north or northwest of where McIntosh lay. He was in the water face down with his arms spread out and no Indians had found him apparently as his clothes were still on his body. WMC, Notes, env 129, IU.

42. Circular No. 75, AGO, 1863, RG 94, Entry 44; it was noted on Wells's muster out record, "To receive no final Payment until he has satisfied the Pay Dept that he is not indebted to the Govt as he has failed to produce any evidence that his Quarterly Returns of Quartermaster's Property have ever been rec'd by the proper Bureaus at Washington." By direction of Commanding General, 15th Corps, NA, M552.

43. Blanchard was recognized by the post surgeon at Columbus Barracks and was brought before a board of inspectors (for certificates of disability), Dec. 27, 1882, and recommended for discharge for fraudulent enlistment. The proceedings of the board were transmitted to the adjutant general's office for approval but were returned Jan. 6, 1883, with remark that recruits not physically disqualified should not be brought before a board of inspectors, which has no power to decide that a man is unfit for duty by reason of fraudulent enlistment, but reported to the adjutant general's office by the commanding officer for discharge by order. The adjutant general disapproved discharge and directed that Blanchard be held to the service, noting his previous discharge on certificate of disability and reason therefore.

44. Capt. Waterbury, commanding Company F, 13th Infantry, on learning of Wells's prior service and discharge, and that after said discharge he had stolen a horse and buggy and served a term in prison, made application Apr. 13, 1883, for his discharge without character, a disgrace to the service, and a dangerous individual. The application, though approved by regimental and district commanders, was disapproved by the adjutant general and returned to Fort Wingate ordering Wells's examination by the post surgeon. When no traces of disease were found, Capt. Waterbury added that physically Wells was all right, but morally all wrong and again urged discharge.

The adjutant general deduced that in view of the disapproval of Wells's discharge in Jan. 1883 for fraudulent enlistment, and he held to service when his fraudulent enlistment was known, he could not then be discharged for fraudulent enlistment. If discharged otherwise, by order, he would be entitled to travel pay. On June 8, the adjutant general decided that Wells, "will be held to service & the defects in character corrected by discipline."

With the prejudicial feeling against him, Wells applied July 1st for transfer to Company G, 22nd Infantry, at Fort Lewis, Colo., wanting to remain in the army and not wishing to desert, but he could not serve where he had not the confidence and good will of his superiors. He added that, as the distance between the two stations was so short he was willing to bear the expense of his transportation. On approval of the respective commanders, transfer was approved. RG 94, Entry 409, file 452 C (EB) AGO 1883.

In August 1890, Wells, residing at Bismarck, N.Dak., applied for invalid pension based on his service in the Civil War, alleging chronic rheumatism, kidney complaint, and general debility. A medical examination in May 1891 reported he was entitled to a rating for rheumatism, but further investigation disclosed his service in the 7th Cavalry, and in affidavit under oath in May 1892, Wells denied having any military service since Jan. 11, 1877.

45. "John S. Wells, familiarly known as 'Dad' Wells, died at the hospital Sunday of Bright's disease." *Bismarck Daily Tribune*, August 29, 1893; Henry Lange said "Dad" Wells was left at Fort Lincoln (in 1876). Lange interview with Walter Camp, n.d., WMC-BYU.

46. Patrick Connelly was president of the Benteen Baseball Club. Anderson, "The Benteen Base Ball Club."

47. Endorsement, June 19, 1874, on letter from Gen. Custer directing that all dismounted men, and men in confinement whom their company commanders desire to be sent with the four companies leaving June 20. Also, letter from Maj. Tilford, Sept. 28, 1874, in answer to query from department headquarters to ascertain by whose authority certain men were released from guard house and restored to duty to accompany the Black Hills Expedition. RG 393, Part V, Fort Rice, DT.

48. WMC, rosters, IU.

49. GO 40, Hq Army, AGO, May 10, 1898, Par. II, "By direction of the Secretary of War, it is announced that men enlisted or reenlisted in the Regular Army during the war may be informed that they will be granted their discharges, if desired at the close of the war, upon their individual applications." RG 94, Entry 44.

50. RG 94, Entry 544, MT, Prescription Book, No. 14 (missing pages Aug. 9–11, 1876); in a letter to Capt. E. W. Smith, aide-de-camp to Gen. Terry, Aug. 15, 1876, Maj. Reno reported the number of extra horses, including one horse in Company B, the horse of a man kicked and sent in the wagon train the day the regiment left the Rosebud (Aug. 11). NA, M1734, Roll 18; see also note D2 (Davenport).

51. WMC, rosters, LBHB; Wight claimed he was detailed to carry an order to Maj. Reno as the fight began. *Lewiston* (Maine) *Journal*, July 23, 1910.

52. The headboard for Cpl. Wild is visible in the Stanley Morrow photos of Capt. Keogh's marker (1879) appearing in numerous publications, including Graham, *The Custer Myth*, 368; *Montana The Magazine of Western History* (Special Custer Edition), vol. 16, no. 2, Spring, 1966, 38–39; Scott, Fox, Jr., Connor, and Harmon, *Archaeological Perspectives*, 67.

53. Wilkison transferred from Company M after being remonstrated by Sgt. Ryan for being chummy with the Indian Scouts of Fort Rice and bringing them into the barracks and allowing them to sit on the bunks of the soldiers. Barnard, *Ten Years with Custer*, 214.

54. *Regulations for the Army of the United States, 1889*, Par. 1503. "The retained pay provided for in sections 1281 and 1282, Revised Statutes, is forfeited for the following causes:

1st. Dishonorable discharge by sentence of general court-martial on expiration of term of service or after completion of imprisonment extending beyond term of service. 2d. Imprisonment by sentence of general court-martial continuing until the end of or beyond the term of service. The retained pay does not accrue to the soldiers under the law: 1st. When discharged before end of term of service under sentence of general court-martial. 2d. When discharged for minority or other cause involving fraud on his part in enlistment. 3d. When discharged because of imprisonment by civil authority or for disability caused by his misconduct. The cause of forfeiture of retained pay must be stated on the muster and pay-rolls and on the final statements of the soldier."

"Williams was here when I came. He was driving for a banker across the street from my house. He left here in '98 as a teamster in the Q.M. for Cuba. I have not heard anything of him since." Roman Rutten (Leavenworth City) to John Ryan, Mar. 26, 1911, EBC-LBHB, Roll 3.

55. Botzer Troop Duty Book.

56. Meddaugh Diary.

57. A batch of ten military prisoners under charge of Lt. Hugh L. Scott, 7th Cavalry, left Fort Lincoln, Feb. 19, 1877, en route to Fort Leavenworth, "One man in particular, named Williamson, seemed to have a mania for cutting people, having tried to cut Lieutenant McIntosh on the Yellowstone, and having succeeded in cutting a wagon-master on Powder River. After that episode he had deserted with several others, but eventually they had all been picked up near Fort Lincoln in a starving condition . . ." He later "cut a companion with a shoe-knife in the [prison] shoe shop and was then put in the Federal Prison at Leavenworth, where he committed suicide. . ." Scott, *Some Memories of a Soldier*, 44–45.

58. Windolph was the last surviving 7th Cavalryman who participated in the battle of the Little Big Horn. Story in Hunt and Hunt, *I Fought With Custer*, and Everett, "Bullets, Boots, and Saddles."

59. General Custer told Capt. McCaskey, 20th Infantry, post commander during summer 1876, to apply a little discipline to Private Woodruff. Custer to McCaskey, May 31, 1876; McCaskey noted that Woodruff took care of horses and was generally worthless on account of rum. Farioli and Nichols, "Fort A. Lincoln, July 1876."

60. RG 94, Entry 409, file 5234 C (EB) AGO 1882.

61. *Regs.* 1881, Par. 2464, "Every enlisted man discharged as a minor, or for disease which existed prior to enlistment, or for other cause involving fraud on his part in the enlistment, shall forfeit all pay and allowances, including traveling allowances, due at the time of discharge, and shall not receive final statements."

62. Willis Wright's name was originally on the monument as "W. B. Right," but was corrected on order from the quartermaster general's office, June 15, 1912. Custer Battlefield Burial Register, LBHB Coll., Roll 14.

63. Wylie interview with Walter Camp, Oct. 16, 1910. Hammer, *Custer in '76*, 129–30.

64. RG 153, File RR576. Wylie related that, before his desertion he was sick in quarters with a severe case of stricture, and was told by Dr. Whitney he would have to be discharged. He received a signed certificate of disability from his company commander, Lt. Hatfield, with orders to give it to the doctor. Three days later the Lt. and the surgeon concluded to keep him until fall and he was marked for duty. Within two weeks the stricture ulcerated, causing stoppage of urine and severe pain, and when told by the doctor he was able to do duty, he left the post intending to consult a physician when he arrived home.

He was taken sick from the train at Big Spring, Texas, by a Dr. Wilson, a fellow passenger and placed in a tub of hot water until the stricture dilated, allowing passage of urine, and there he remained two days under the doctor's care. He proceeded to Cincinnati and on feeling able to do duty, surrendered himself to Capt. Edgerly, hoping to be shown leniency. (Edgerly then on recruiting duty at Cincinnati.)

65. See note K23 (Kipp).

66. Wylie was one of 45 men of his troop, and over 500 in the regiment, who were discharged per telegraphic instructions of the adjutant general's office, Feb. 20, 1899 (under GO 40 AGO 1898). See note S31 (Sniffin).

67. Endorsement of Rear Admiral William Radford, July 10, 1872, on letter of Joseph Whitehurst requesting recommendation for honorable discharge. NA, T1099.

68. Incident described by Lt. Edgerly in an article written by Edgerly at Fort Clark, Texas, ca 1892–95, copy in Ghent Papers.

69. WMC, rosters, LBHB. This was either Harvey A. Fox whom Camp interviewed in 1909, or John Fox, a resident of the Soldier's Home in Washington from 1897, and where Camp visited several times after 1907. Both men served in Co. D, 7th Cavalry in 1876.

Y-Z

Yates, Geo. Wilhelmus. Capt co F; b. 26 Feb 1843 Albany N.Y.; visited Texas in 1860 intent on moving there but the election of pres't Lincoln caused such bitterness thro' the state that he returned north; enr 20 June 1861 Adrian Mich. a pvt co A 4 Mich. inf for 3 yrs; age 22; qm sgt 1 Nov 1861; 1Lt & adjt 26 Sep 1862; ds actg aag on staff of col Swietzer (comdg brig) Nov 1862 near Falmouth Va; ds on staff of gen Pleasonton 7 June 1863 (recom by Lt Custer);[1] tr to Dept of Mo. (hq St. Louis) Apr 1864 (with gen Pleasonton); m.o. with regt 28 June 1864 by expir of serv & recom by gen Pleasonton for com'n in 13 Mo. cav (lest he lose him as adc unless he found another com'n); appt 1Lt 45 Mo. inf 13 Aug 1864 (never joined); resd adc 22 Sep 1864 to accept com'n of capt 13 Mo. cav; org co G at Benton Bks to Oct 1864 (never joined); ds with gen Pleasonton 23 Oct 1864 at St Louis; bvt maj vols 13 Mar 1865 for gal serv dur the war & Lt-col vols for conspic gal at Fredericksburg, Beverly Ford & Gettysburg; m.o. vol serv 11 Jan 1866 at St. Louis; appt clerk in state dept Wash'n D.C. (recom by gen Custer) but preferred mil serv & appt com'n 2Lt 2 cav 26 Mar 1866 (upon recom'n gen Custer);[2] join co A 3 July 1866 Ft McPherson Neb; post qm & comsy 23 July 1866; rqm 15 May 1867; ds Ft Sedgwick Colo. Ty July 1867 receiving pub horses; prom capt 7 cav 21 Aug 1867; passed exam'n before cav bd at Wash'n 23 Sep [with Lt Smith]; joined co F 19 Nov 1867 Ft L'worth Kans.; ds with escort for ind peace com'n Apr to June 1868; awl 30 days 11 Jan 1871; awl 10 days 5 Feb 1872; comd detmt to Standing Rock Agcy 12 Dec 1874 to arrest the Sioux warrior Rain-in-the-Face;[3] ds Louisville Ky. 28 May to 22 July 1875 with bd purchasing horses;[4] killed with Custer column 25 June 1876;[5] survived by wife & 3 ch.[6] [485 ACP 1875].
Pension: 30 Apr 1877 / Wid / 231149 /178886.

Zametzer, Jno. Pvt co M; b. Bavaria Germany; enl 12 Aug 1867 New York N.Y. for 5 yrs; age 32; laborer; grey eyes, brn hair, fair comp, 5' 9 3/4" high; join co M 8 Sep 1867 Ft Harker Kans.; cpl 14 Feb 1870; sgt 1 Aug 1871; pvt 18 Oct 1871; disch 12 Aug 1872 Unionville SC expir of serv a pvt; reenl 23 Dec 1874 Boston Mass. for 5 yrs; join co A 7 cav 6 Feb 1875 Livingston Ala; tr to co M 1 Mar 1876; sick hosp Ft Rice DT 22 Apr to 20 July 1876 (infl. lungs); join co M 5 Oct 1876 camp near Ft Lincoln; cpl 18 Oct 1876; sick hosp Ft Rice 26 Feb to 19 Aug 1877 when disch on surg cert dis (pulmonary consumption, contr line of duty; dis total) a cpl char xclt; died 24 Sep 1877 Sol. Home Wash'n D.C.

Notes—Y–Z

1. In a letter to a friend, May 26, 1863, Lt. Custer said he induced Gen. Pleasonton to appoint Lt. Yates to his staff. Whittaker, *A Complete Life*, 151.
2. Merington, *The Custer Story*, 179.
3. See note C167 (Tom Custer).
4. Three car loads of horses purchased for 7th Cavalry by Capt. Yates in Kentucky arrived at Bismarck on Friday. *Bismarck Tribune*, July 28, 1875.
5. Lt. Gibbs, of Gen. Terry's staff, said 32 men of Yates' company were found on Custer Hill. Gibbs, personal notes on Little Big Horn fight. Gibbs' description was apparently used by Frederick Whittaker in *A Complete Life*, 594, 601.
6. Yates and Capt. Benteen had been good friends, and at the camp on Powder River, July 18, Benteen received a letter from Mrs. Yates, who, "turned over her horses, etc., which are up here—to dispose of for her." Two weeks later, Benteen wrote, "I have sold Capt. Yates' horse to Lieut. Jacobs, 7th Infty—for

$655.00 (a fair good price) and wrote to her informing of same." Benteen to his wife, July 18, Aug. 1, 1876, Carroll, ed., *Camp Talk*, 41–42, 46.

Lt. Jacobs had asked Annie Gibson Roberts (Yates) to be his wife in January 1870. Pohanka, *A Summer on the Plains*, 19; see, A. G. R. Yates, "Colonel George W. Yates"; also Pohanka, "George Yates, Captain of the Band Box Troop."

Indian Scouts

Barking Wolf (Si-ti-wa-na), Schiri-Tiwana, Schiri-Tirchiwa;[1] Pvt detmt ind scouts; b. DT; enl 9 May 1876 at Ft Lincoln for 6 mos by Lt Varnum; age 21; blk eyes, blk hair, copper comp, 5' 7" high; ds carrying desps in field 22 June (one of four 'Rees sent with mail from Rosebud & arr Powder River camp morn 24 June); (str *Josephine* arr same day); one of seven 'Rees sent with mail to gen Terry eve 24 June; (incl desp from gen Sheridan warning of large incr in number of hostiles); arr camp mouth of Big Horn River 28 June 4 P.M.; sent across Yellowstone with Running Wolf (morn 30 June) to look for steamboat coming down Big Horn; stayed with Curly Head in camp 5 July when gen Terry sent 'Rees down Yellowstone to hunt for Sioux crossing; ds in field 30 Aug;[2] disch 11 Nov 1876 at Ft Lincoln upon expir of serv a scout char good. See, Howling Wolf.

Bear (Coonough), Foolish-Angry-Bear, Foolish Bear, Gunuhc Sahckuny. Pvt detmt ind scouts; b. DT; 3d enlmt 9 May 1876 at Ft Lincoln for 6 mos by Lt Varnum; age 29; blk eyes, blk hair, dk comp, 5' 6" high; ds carrying desps in field 22 June (chg of 'Rees sent with mail from Rosebud & arr Powder River camp morn 24 June); when scouts arr 5 July with report of gen Crook's fight, Foolish Bear & White Cloud were picked to carry desp to gen Terry & given two best horses; arr camp mouth of Big Horn River 9 July; after a time (night of 12 July) they were sent back & (15 July) called Strikes-Two & Bull-in-the-Water to cross over & carry mail on to Ft Buford; Foolish Bear & White Cloud then crossed river & joined other scouts;[3] ds Ft Lincoln 20 Oct; disch 11 Nov 1876 at Ft Lincoln upon expir of serv.

Bear-Come-Out (Mato-e-nam-pa), Matokianapa, Comes the Bear,[4] Old Caddoo.[5] Pvt detmt ind scouts; b. DT (Blackfeet); active in liquor trade at Standing Rock Agcy in 1875;[6] 10th enlmt 3 Feb 1876 at Ft Lincoln for 6 mos by Lt Cooke; age 49; blk eyes, dk hair, dk comp, 5' 9" high; with Reno scout up Powder River 10 June; Strikes-Two said Caroo crossed river with Reno's comd 25 June & skirmished with Sioux as troops dismtd; says Karu with scouts watering horses when Sioux corralled Reno on hill;[7] Red Bear said Caroo started for Rosebud with rear-guard; arr Powder River camp 28 June 2 P.M.; disch 3 Aug camp on Yellowstone River & reenl by Lt Varnum for 6 mos; ds with gen Crook 26 Aug (carry desps between comds); carried mail with Running Wolf & Young Hawk (6 Sep) from head of Heart River to Ft Lincoln;[8] disch 3 Feb 1877 at Ft Lincoln upon expir of serv a scout char good; killed 8 June 1878 at Ft Lincoln in personal affray with squaw.[9]

Bear-Running-in-the-Timber (Mato-chunway-a-ga-mun), (Mato-chan-ekna-inyanka),[10] Ptä-ä'-tê (Buffalo Ancestor, Buffalo Body),[11] Tonhechi-Tu (Whole Buffalo).[12] Pvt detmt ind scouts; b. DT (Yanktonai); 2d enlmt 11 May 1876 at Ft Lincoln for 6 mos by Lt Varnum; age 40; blk eyes, blk hair, copper comp, 5' 8" high; horse lost race in camp 27 May against one owned by Stabbed;[13] with Reno scout up Powder River 10 June; at Crow's Nest morn 25 June says One Feather; Strikes-Two saw Whole Buffalo & One Feather come from rear as Reno's comd began to fire; Little Sioux said Whole Buffalo (Tonhechi-Tu) with scouts after big bunch of Sioux horses opposite timber; says Tonhechi-Tu & One Feather took after two horses;[14] One Feather said he spoke to Whole Buffalo in woods;[15] Red Star said Pta-a-te & One Feather had bunch near ford but were retaken by Sioux; Red Bear said Pta-a-te started back with captured horses; says Whole Buffalo knew the way & scouts followed him & reached Rosebud about midnight; Soldier said Whole Buffalo with pty who bro't captured horses; says Tonhechi-Tu, Watoksha, & Billy Cross left pty at mouth of Rosebud & beat others to Powder River;[16] One Feather said Whole Buffalo had two horses when they got to Powder River;[17] disch 11

323

Nov 1876 at Ft Lincoln by expir of serv a scout char good. Bear-Running-in-the-Woods (Matocan-wekna-iyanka) listed in Standing Rock Agcy census as late as June 1895, age 64.

Bears Eyes (Coonough-chee-ruk), Gunuhc Chiriku, Wolf-Stands-in-the-Cold, Wolf-in-the-Blizzard. Pvt detmt ind scouts; b. DT; 7th enlmt 1 Apr 1876 at Ft Lincoln for 6 mos by Lt Cooke; age 31; dk eyes, blk hair, dk comp, 5' 5" high; ds Ft Lincoln 17 May; Young Hawk said Bears Eyes, Owl, & Black Porcupine went back with messages from Powder River; courier to gen Terry's exp'n night of 26 June;[18] disch 1 Oct 1876 at Ft Lincoln by expir of serv a scout char good;[19] (married to sister of Red Bear); died Oct 1887 Ft Berthold Agcy DT.
Pension: 23 Apr 1921 / Minor / 1173332.

Bear Waiting (Ma-tok-sha). See Round-Wooden-Cloud.

Big Belly. See Half-Yellow-Face.

Black Calf (Hunni-ca-til), Hani-katil, Anikadil, Boy Chief. Pvt detmt ind scouts; b. DT; enl 26 Apr 1876 at Ft Lincoln for 6 mos by Lt Cooke; age 19; blk eyes, blk hair, copper comp, 5' 6" high; (tho't med examiner would throw him out as he was very young); crossed river with Reno's comd 25 June & with Red Star & Strikes-Two took after big bunch of Sioux horses opposite timber; drove 28 horses across flat on eastside of river & up bluffs; sol.'s at rear of column [Custer] passing on hilltop fired at scouts wd'g Boy Chief's horse in jaw; drove captured horses back to pack train & took fresh horse (the one Red Star promised Soldier); rode back to hilltop as Reno's men straggled up; Boy Chief rode down among Sioux to look for his brother Red Bear but was driven back; started for Rosebud with scouts detailed to keep Sioux back & arr Powder River camp 28 June 2 p.m.; Running Wolf said Boy Chief with scouts sent with desp to gen Crook (25 Aug) & attd to scout for his comd; says Boy Chief one of four 'Rees sent with mail from Beaver Creek (to gen Terry 2 Sep);[20] disch 11 Nov 1876 at Ft Lincoln by expir of serv a scout char good (final statement dated 26 Oct); died 4 June 1922 Armstrong, N.Dak.
Pension: Ind. Surv. / 17814. Ind. Wid. / 17020 / 11284.

Black Fox (Chi-wa-koo-ca-til), Chewaku-ca-teet. Pvt detmt ind scouts; b. DT;[21] 3d enlmt 9 May 1876 at Ft Lincoln for 6 mos by Lt Varnum; age 29; blk eyes, blk hair, copper comp, 5' 7" high; vol with Forked Horn to cook & scouts chose them for that work; (cooks were not to go on scout);[22] Custer said if Black Fox repeated his trick of last time & took his wife along he would be well punished;[23] with Lt Varnum to Crow's Nest night of 24 June; (activity 25 June uncertain);[24] Goes Ahead & Red Star say Black Fox & Curley were with Custer when he stood above where Hodgson's stone stands; Pretty Face said when he joined scouts he saw 'Ree with a white cloth on his head & only Black Fox wore this; Red Star said Black Fox met Curley near Reno ford & they went back to where sol.'s left some hardtack whence Curley said he was going home; Soldier said Black Fox led a horse when he overtook scouts at mouth of Rosebud morn 27 June; Strikes-Two said Black Fox had a mare & colt & came from the front, having started back ahead with Crows who told him way to mouth of Rosebud; at gen Terry's camp dur July a Crow who wore belt of buffalo hide taken from chin of buffalo where hair longest, (Goes-Ahead) told Young Hawk that after the fight the Crows chased a 'Ree who wore two rabbit ears (Black Fox) & they gave him a blk horse; Young Hawk said this is the blk horse Black Fox rode when he overtook scouts at mouth of Rosebud; Running Wolf said Black Fox with scouts sent with desp to gen Crook (25 Aug) & attd to scout for his comd; says Black Fox one of four 'Rees sent with mail from Beaver Creek (to gen Terry 2 Sep);[25] ds Ft Lincoln 20 Oct; disch 11 Nov 1876 at Ft Lincoln upon expir of serv a scout char good; listed on Ft Berthold Agcy census, July 1896, age 53.[26]

Black Porcupine (Sa-nu-ca-til), Sunu katil. Pvt detmt ind scouts; b. DT; enl 9 May 1876 at Ft Lincoln for 6 mos by Lt Varnum; age 21; blk eyes, blk hair, copper comp, 5' 8" high; ds Ft Lincoln 17 May; pres at Ft Lincoln 31 May; (courier to gen Terry's exp'n dur June); Red Star said Black Porcupine stayed at camp on Powder River; Young Hawk said Black Porcupine, Bear's Eyes, & Owl went back with messages from Powder River;[27] disch 11 Nov 1876 at Ft Lincoln upon expir of serv a scout char good.

Bloody Knife (Nes-i-ri-pat), Netsiri-paat. Guide qmd; b. DT ca. 1840; father Hunkpapa Sioux & mother Arikara; courier with gen Sully's nw ind exp'n Aug 1865; rate of pay $5 day;[28] served ten enlmts as ind scout May 1868 to Nov 1874; became gen Custer's favorite ind scout for his valuable serv in the Yellowstone Exp'n of 1873 & Blk Hills Exp'n of 1874; spent summer 1875 at Ft Lincoln often in long talks with gen Custer, seated on the grass, the general's dogs laying nearby;[29] hired in qmd 3 Mar 1876 by Lt Nowlan as guide for exp'n; rate of pay $50 mo; blk eyes, blk hair (slightly grey), dk comp, 5' 8" high; used own rifle (a repeater) & only scout with govt saddle horse;[30] with Reno scout up Powder River 10 June;[31] Gerard found Bloody Knife under influence of whiskey eve 22 June in camp on Rosebud; Red Star said Bloody Knife was drunk somewhere & joined scouts at brkft 23 June;[32] rode at head of column with gen Custer dur night march 24 June; with Custer to Crow's Nest morn 25 June; crossed river ahead of Reno's comd & reached timber before sol.'s; drove three Sioux horses out of woods & gave to scouts on skirmish line;[33] killed next to maj Reno at edge of timber by gsw to head, the shock blamed for Reno starting retreat from valley.[34]
Pension: 16 Nov 1899 / Minor / 708602. Rej on grd no title, clmt's father being a civil employee & not an appt or enlisted man in U.S. serv.

Bobtailed Bull (Ho-cus-ta-rix), Hukos-tarix. (Sgt) detmt ind scouts; b. DT; leader of Grass Dance Society & member of police; enl 26 Apr 1876 at Ft Lincoln for 6 mos by Lt Cooke; age 45; blk eyes, blk hair, copper comp, 5' 11" high; appt leader of ind scouts by gen Custer 16 May & issued coat with three stripes on sleeve;[35] horse had curbed bit with fancy trimmings & ind saddle with wooden frame covered with rawhide; led pty of scouts on back-trail morn 29 May with fresh horse & brkft for Red Bear;[36] with gen Custer to Crow's Nest morn 25 June; crossed river with Reno's comd; Young Hawk said Bobtail Bull was farthest left on skirmish line & joined Young Hawk's pty following Reno's line of retreat; scouts crossed river lower down than Reno & were headed off by Sioux on eastside who chased Bobtail Bull into river; his horse ran past Red Bear on east bank, the saddle bloody in front & blood marks down legs & on hoofs; a sol. rode him to hilltop where Strikes-Two tied him among pack mules; after battle Young Hawk found where Bobtail Bull was chased over river bank & saw four leafy branches of willow sticking up in the shallow water;[37] survived by wife, Bear Woman (She Bear) & 3 ch.; (widow died July 1876).
Pension: 24 May 1879 / Minor / 245944 / 191294.

Boy Chief. See Black Calf.

Broken Penis (Cha-gon-hur-pa), Chagoo-Hurpa. Pvt detmt ind scouts; b. DT [Sioux]; enl 13 Nov 1875 at Ft Lincoln for 6 mos by Lt Calhoun; age 40; brn eyes, blk hair, copper comp, 5' 9" high; disch 13 May 1876 at Ft Lincoln upon expir of serv. Gerard said there were two Sioux scouts with the command, Ca-don, & Penis; Penis killed Cardon in a drunken brawl at Ft Lincoln; no notice was taken by the authorities & he absconded that night.[38] (See Bear Come Out).

Brush. See Bush.

Buffalo Ancestor, **Buffalo Body**. See Bear-Running-in-the- Timber.

Bull (Ho-cus), Hukos. Pvt detmt ind scouts; b. DT; 2d enlmt 9 May 1876 at Ft Lincoln for 6 mos by Lt Varnum; age 19; blk eyes, blk hair, copper comp, 5' 8" high; with Lt Varnum to Crow's Nest night of 24 June & with Red Star carried note to gen Custer at dawn 25 June; rode to the charge with Reno's comd but being poorly mtd he was left behind & did not cross river; joined Soldier, Stabbed, & White Eagle along Custer's trail on ridge;

325

met scouts driving off Sioux horses & helped drive herd back to pack train; Strikes-Two saw Bull & Skare' (they were not in the fight) each leading a pack mule; Red Bear said Bull came to Reno hill with herd of captured horses (about 40); with rear-guard scouts to Rosebud & sent ahead by Strikes-Two to tell scouts with horses to go faster; stayed with herd & arr Powder River camp eve 28 June; disch 11 Nov 1876 at Ft Lincoln upon expir of serv a scout char good.[39]
Pension: 19 Aug 1933 / Soldier / 1734805. (XC-2,605,257).

Bull-in-the-Water (Ho-cus-ty-arit), Bull-Stands-in-the-Water, Hukos Tihahrt. Pvt detmt ind scouts; b. DT; (leader of Da-roch'-pa Society, members had crescent moon shaved on back of head); 3d enlmt 9 May 1876 at Ft Lincoln for 6 mos by Lt Varnum; age 29; blk eyes, blk hair, copper comp, 5' 11" high; Red Star said Bull-in-Water & Red Bear had chg of one mule & made brkft 25 June; says Bull-in-Water rode to the charge with Reno's comd but did not cross river; Strikes-Two said Bull-in-Water pursued horses captured by Bloody Knife when they stampeded across river & drove whole bunch over ridge & back some distance; Red Bear & Soldier said Bull-in-Water took fresh horse & rode back to ridge; Red Star said Bull-in-Water with younger scouts to water horses & started for Rosebud when Sioux corralled Reno; Red Bear said Bull-in-Water & Red Wolf rode ahead of herd after sundown & upon hearing shots fired ahead, tho't Sioux coming & took fresh horses & escaped; arr Powder River camp 28 June; when Foolish Bear & White Cloud bro't mail from Big Horn (15 July) Bull-in-the-Water & Strikes-Two took mail on to Ft Buford;[40] disch 11 Nov 1876 at Ft Lincoln upon expir of serv a scout char good; listed on Ft Berthold Agcy census July 1893, age 40.

Bush (Na-pa-ran-ough), Brush, Naparanuhc, Red Brush, Red Wolf (The Bush).[41] Pvt detmt ind scouts; b. DT; (bro. of Little Sioux); 6th enlmt 26 Apr 1876 at Ft Lincoln for 6 mos by Lt Cooke; age 27; blk eyes, blk hair, copper comp, 5' 6" high; with Bobtail Bull's pty 29 May bringing fresh horse to Red Bear; rode to the charge with Reno's comd 25 June but left behind & did not cross river; Soldier said he met Red Wolf & Strikes-the-Lodge where Sioux horses came up & drove herd back to pack train; Red Bear said Red Wolf came to Reno hill with captured horses (about 40); Red Star said Red Wolf with younger scouts to water horses & started for Rosebud when Sioux corralled Reno; Red Bear said Red Wolf & Bull-in-Water rode ahead of herd after sundown & upon hearing shots fired ahead, tho't Sioux coming & took fresh horses & escaped; arr Powder River camp 28 June;[42] disch 11 Nov 1876 at Ft Lincoln upon expir of serv a scout char good; (final statement dated 26 Oct); died about 1916.[43]

Cards (Ca-soo). Pvt detmt ind scouts; b. DT (Sioux); enl 13 Nov 1875 at Ft Lincoln for 6 mos by Lt Calhoun; age 21; brn eyes, blk hair, copper comp, 6' 0" high; disch 13 May 1876 at Ft Lincoln by expir of serv.

Ca-roo. See Bear Come Out.

Carrier. See Round-Wooden-Cloud.

Cha-ra'-ta (Wolf). See Howling Wolf.

Charging Bull. See Rushing Bull.

Charging Up the Hill. See Climbs the Bluff.

Choka Wo. See Baker, Wm.

Climbs the Bluff (Te-ru-chitt-ho-nochs), Tiranchit Hunohc, Charging-up-the-Hill, Scabby Wolf.[44] Pvt detmt ind scouts; b. DT; 8th enlmt 1 May 1876 at Ft Lincoln for 6 mos by Lt Cooke; age 30; blk eyes, blk hair, copper comp, 5' 9" high; with Bobtail Bull's pty 29 May bringing fresh horse to Red Bear; ds carrying desp's in field 1 June; Running Wolf said Charging-up-the-Hill & Wagon (who were left at Ft Lincoln) rode out from Powder River camp at sunrise 24 June to greet 'Rees bringing mail from Custer; (str *Josephine* arr same day); one of seven 'Rees sent with mail to gen Terry eve 24 June; (incl desp from gen Sheridan warning of large incr in number of hostiles); arr camp mouth of Big Horn 28 June 4 P.M.;⁴⁵ sent with Running Wolf (29 June) to look for steamboat coming down Big Horn; with 'Rees sent down Yellowstone by gen Terry 5 July to look for Sioux crossing; Running Wolf said Charging-up-the-Hill sent with desp to gen Crook (25 Aug) & attd to scout for his comd; one of four 'Rees sent with mail from Beaver Creek (to gen Terry 2 Sep); disch 11 Nov 1876 at Ft Lincoln upon expir of serv a scout char good; died 9 Mar 1880 at Ft Lincoln (infl. of lungs).⁴⁶

Crooked Horn. See Forked Horn.

Curley (Shuh-shee-ahsh), Shi-shi'-esh. b. MT ca. 1859;⁴⁷ enl 10 Apr 1876 Crow Agcy MT by Lt Bradley till disch; attd to 7 cav 22 June; with Lt Varnum to Crow's Nest night of 24 June; says he & Mitch Boyer left Crow scouts near Edgerly peaks & rode down to meet Custer in coulee near river; says Boyer sent him back early in fight;⁴⁸ Red Star said Black Fox met Curley near Reno ford & went back to where sol.'s lost some hardtack whence Curley said he was going home;⁴⁹ Curley said he went to Tullock Creek & down Sarpy Creek to Yellowstone then up south bank to Big Horn where he had sign talk with Tom Leforge on north bank; followed Gibbon's trail up Big Horn & met boat at mouth of Little Horn (morn 28 June);⁵⁰ sent with desp to battlefield (saw dead not all buried) then carried desp to boat; camped with Half-Yellow-Face after boat left with wd 30 June; accomp troops down Big Horn & was first to be ferried with his horse across Yellowstone;⁵¹ left camp 4 July with Half-Yellow-Face & Leforge & went home to Crow camp at Pryor Creek.⁵² rejoined gen Terry's camp 15 July; Crows disch 20 Aug mouth of Powder River, wanting to go home to prepare for coming winter for families & as troops unable to catch Sioux; when Gibbon comd passed Crow Agcy (24 Sep) whole band followed to Ft Ellis & scouts paid 30 Sep; Leforge said Crows with their women went to Bozeman & purchased supplies till money used up; in June 1877 Curley & Half-Yellow-Face accomp capt Sheridan's detail to Custer battlefield;⁵³ died 22 May 1923 at Crow Agency.

Pension: 12 May 1922 / Ind. Surv. / 18533 / 11344. Ind. Wid. / 16468 / 10689.

Curly Head (Pich-ga-ri-wee), Curly Hair, Pahc Kariwi. Pvt detmt ind scouts; b. DT; enl 27 Apr 1876 at Ft Lincoln for 6 mos by Lt Cooke; age 19; blk eyes, blk hair, copper comp, 5' 6" high; ds carrying desps in field 22 June (one of four 'Rees sent with mail from Rosebud & arr Powder River camp morn 24 June); (str *Josephine* arr same day); one of seven 'Rees sent with mail to gen Terry eve 24 June; (incl desp from gen Sheridan warning of large incr in number of hostiles); arr camp mouth of Big Horn River 28 June 4 p.m.; stayed with Howling Wolf in camp 5 July when gen Terry sent 'Rees down Yellowstone to hunt for Sioux crossing; disch 11 Nov 1876 at Ft Lincoln upon expir of serv a scout char good; (final statement dated 27 Oct); listed on Ft Berthold Agcy census, June 1900, age 43.

E-esk, or **(Ieska)**. See Cross, Wm.

Foolish-Angry-Bear. See Bear.

Foolish Bear (Coonough-sen-quagh), Red-Foolish-Bear, (Foolish) Red Bear, Gunuhc-Sanhiwaat. Pvt detmt ind scouts; b. DT; 6th enlmt 9 May 1876 at Ft Lincoln for 6 mos by Lt Varnum; age 28; blk eyes, blk hair, copper comp, 5' 8" high; carried mail to Ft Lincoln 20 May (with One Horn); bro't large mail out to exp'n 26 May; with Lt Varnum to Crow's Nest night of 24 June; on skirmish line in valley fight & with Young Hawk's pty dur retreat; led wd Goose on his (Red-Foolish-Bear's) horse up to Reno's camp as Sioux swarmed back from Custer; fixed travois to carry Goose to boat 29 June; with 'Rees sent down Yellowstone by gen Terry 5 July to look for Sioux crossing; disch 11 Nov 1876 at Ft Lincoln upon expir of serv a scout char good.⁵⁴

Forked Horn (Arri-chitt), Crooked Horn, Ari-chit. Pvt detmt ind scouts; b. DT; leader of New Dog Society (oldest men in it); 9th enlmt 27 Apr 1876 at Ft Lincoln for 6 mos by Lt Cooke; age 36; blk eyes, blk hair, copper comp, 5' 10" high; vol with Black Fox to cook

& scouts chose them for that work; (cooks were not to go on scout); on Reno scout up Powder River 10 June; with Lt Varnum to Crow's Nest night of 24 June; on skirmish line in valley fight & with Young Hawk's pty dur retreat; sent with Young Hawk morn 27 June to meet troops (Terry & Gibbon) on site of Sioux camp; with 'Rees sent down Yellowstone by gen Terry 5 July to look for Sioux crossing; disch 11 Nov 1876 at Ft Lincoln upon expir of serv a scout char good; (final statement dated 27 Oct); died 1894.[55]

Goes Ahead (Bah-suk-usk), One Ahead (Bahsukush), Comes Leading (Man-With-Fur-Belt). b. MT 1852 near Platte River where timber very big; enl 10 Apr 1876 Crow Agcy MT by Lt Bradley till disch; attd to 7 cav 22 June; with Lt Varnum to Crow's Nest night of 24 June; says four Crows & one 'Ree with Custer after Reno separated; Curley & Black Fox went with 'Rees driving off Sioux horses;[56] three Crows with Mitch Boyer rode to bluff beyond where Custer turned down coulee to right; Crows dismtd at end of high ridge & fired into Sioux camp, then rode back along ridge & met 'Rees & the blk horse riders (co D);[57] says Crows helped fight awhile then after dark took to pine hills over east & before daylight swam across Big Horn to west side; yelled back to Gibbon's Crows that Custer wiped out; says scouts recd perm'n to go home;[58] joined gen Terry's camp mouth of Big Horn 15 July;[59] Crows disch 20 Aug mouth of Powder River, wanting to go home to prepare for coming winter for families & as troops unable to catch Sioux;[60] when Gibbon comd passed Crow Agcy (24 Sep) whole band followed to Ft Ellis & scouts paid 30 Sep; Leforge said Crows with their women went to Bozeman & purchased supplies till money used up; in 1878 Goes Ahead & wife Pretty Shield & her uncle Half-Yellow-Face, visited battlefield, showing where Custer fell into river;[61] died 29 May 1919 at Crow Agency.
Pension: 25 Mar 1924 / Ind. Wid / 16770 / 11239. (XC-2,659,520).

Good Elk (Wah-nee), Handsome Elk, Red Bear. Pvt detmt ind scouts; b. Sep 1853 Ft Clark DT; (bro. of Boy Chief); 3d enlmt 13 May 1876 at Ft Lincoln for 6 mos by Lt Varnum; age 20; blk eyes, blk hair, copper comp, 5' 5" high; (wore green colored goggles acc't opacity of r. eye injured pitching hay in 1872); Custer told Red Bear, Owl, & Wagon (thro' Gerard) they were last to enlist & must remain at post; Red Bear said he was left at Ft Lincoln because his mare was heavy with foal;[62] accomp Foolish Bear 26 May with large mail for exp'n; his mare gave out beyond Heart River & Foolish Bear cont'd on to camp; next morn Bobtail-Bull bro't fresh horse & brkft to Red Bear; Running Wolf said Strikes-Two loaned Red Bear his spare horse;[63] Red Star said Red Bear & Bull-in-Water had chg of one mule & made brkft 25 June; on skirmish line in valley fight & thrown from his horse dur retreat but caught him in river; dismtd on eastside to seize rope of Sioux horse but let go when horse jumped about thro' rosebushes, taring Red Bear's bare feet (his moccasins lost in river); Soldier said Red Bear straggled up shoeless & the boys pulled prickly-pear prongs out of his feet;[64] Red Bear picked up two horses on hilltop then joined White Cloud leading one horse up from valley & started for place scouts took horses; met four Crow scouts looking for other two Crows; said they would come back & Red Bear & White Cloud waited a long time before rejoining Reno as 'Rees came on fresh horses;[65] started for Rosebud near sundown with herd of captured horses; arr Powder River camp 28 June & found pty led by Strikes-Two; disch 11 Nov 1876 at Ft Lincoln upon expir of serv a scout char good; died 7 May 1934 Nishu, N.Dak.
Pension: 28 Nov 1904 / Inv / 1328131 / 1167258. (XC-896,806).

Good Face (Sca-ri'), Pretty Face, Skare'. Pvt detmt ind scouts; b. DT; enl 9 May 1876 at Ft Lincoln for 6 mos by Lt Varnum; age 21; blk eyes, blk hair, copper comp, 5' 4" high; chg of five mules carrying supplies for ind scouts 25 June; rejoined scouts as they picked fresh mounts from captured Sioux horses; started for Rosebud eve 25 June with herd of horses & arr Powder River camp eve 28 June; disch 11 Nov 1876 at Ft Lincoln upon expir of serv a scout char good.[66]

Goose (Co-st), Gauht, Gaht, Goht, Gohc.[67] Pvt detmt ind scouts; b. DT; 5th enlmt 26 Apr 1876 at Ft Lincoln for 6 mos by Lt Cooke; age 19; blk eyes, blk hair, copper comp, 5' 8" high; (Custer recalled Goose from Blk Hills Exp'n); earned $128 selling game to sol.'s dur march to Powder River; courier with Stab to Yellowstone night of 7 June & next morn bro't mail to Custer's camp up Powder River;[68] with Reno scout up Powder River 10 June; detailed with mail pty 22 June but retained by gen Custer;[69] on skirmish line in valley fight 25 June & with Young Hawk's pty dur retreat; gsw r. hand & his horse killed on eastside of river in grove of trees; put on Red-Foolish-Bear's horse & led up to Reno's camp as Sioux swarmed back from Custer; Young Hawk dressed his wd hand & bro't food & water dur fight on hilltop; Red-Foolish-Bear fixed travois to carry Goose & Young Hawk led pony to boat 29 June; they put Goose at rear of deck near wheel; at Yellowstone (30 June) Running Wolf saw Goose near engine room with blanket over his shoulders & his wd hand wrapped up; Horns-in-Front helped Goose off boat & unwrapped & washed his badly swollen hand; Goose said he recd no care on boat;[70] put back on boat morn 3 July & went down river to Ft Berthold;[71] disch 11 Nov 1876 at Ft Lincoln upon expir of serv a scout char good; (final statement dated 26 Oct).

Hairy Moccasin (Sah-pee-wish-ush). b. MT ca. 1853; enl 10 Apr 1876 Crow Agcy MT by Lt Bradley till disch; attd to 7 cav 22 June; with Lt Varnum to Crow's Nest night of 24 June; says four Crow scouts with Mitch Boyer ahead of Custer column after Reno separated; Custer sent Crows to high point then took comd down coulee toward river; says Crows chg'd north to where Custer headed; (Curley left them at Weir peaks);[72] three Crows stopped to fire into Sioux camp then rode back & met Benteen near Reno Creek; Crows started to join 'Rees up creek (with Sioux horses) but Benteen said to stay; three Crows got away after sundown circling east to tributary to mouth of Little Horn & before daylight swam across Big Horn; called back to Gibbon's Crows that Custer comd all killed, then cont'd to main Crow camp two sleeps away on Pryor Creek; joined gen Terry's camp mouth of Big Horn 15 July; Crows disch 20 Aug mouth of Powder River, wanting to go home to prepare for coming winter for families & as troops unable to catch Sioux; when Gibbon's comd passed Crow Agcy (24 Sep) whole band followed to Ft Ellis & scouts paid 30 Sep; Leforge said Crows with their women went to Bozeman & purchased supplies till money used up; died 9 Oct 1922 Lodge Grass MT.[73]
Pension: 10 Mar 1922 / Ind. Surv. / 18388 / 12736. Ind. Wid. / 17367 / 11565.

Half-Yellow-Face (Iss-too-sah-shee-dah), Big Belly. b. MT ca. 1835;[74] enl 10 Apr 1876 Crow Agcy MT by Lt Bradley till disch; leader of Crow scouts attd to 7 cav 22 June; (a large jolly looking handsome ind popular with the troops);[75] scouted ahead of regt 24 June till after 9 p.m.; rode at head of column with gen Custer dur night march;[76] told gen Custer morn 25 June his plan to wait until dark was bad & should attack at once; near Little Horn Custer told Half-Yellow-Face & White Swan to go on ridge to see if Sioux running away but they instead joined Reno's scouts as they moved for'd;[77] took captured Sioux horse proffered by Young Hawk on skirmish line & let own horse go, it being a poor one; with Young Hawk's pty dur retreat & dragged wd White Swan into brush, saving him from Sioux; led White Swan on his horse up to Reno's camp;[78] made travois to carry White Swan & led pony to boat 29 June, many sol.'s commented on his ingenuity; camped with Curley after boat left with wd 30 June & marched with troops to Yellowstone; left camp 4 July with Curley & Leforge & went home to Crow camp at Pryor Creek;[79] rejoined gen Terry's camp 15 July; Crows disch 20 Aug mouth of Powder River, wanting to go home to prepare for coming winter for families & as troops unable to catch Sioux; when Gibbon comd passed Crow Agcy (24 Sep) whole band followed to Ft Ellis & scouts paid 30 Sep; Leforge said Crows with their women went to Bozeman & purchased supplies till money used up; in June 1877 Half-Yellow-Face & Curley accomp capt Sheridan's detail to Custer battlefield;⁸⁰ went there again in 1878 with Goes-Ahead & wife Pretty Shield, showing hole in hill where scouts hid dur retreat from valley fight;⁸¹ died in 1879.⁸²

Handsome Elk. See Good Elk.

High Bear. See Long Bear.

Horn-in-Front (Arrin-quis-coo), Horns-in-Front, Arin-quisk. Pvt detmt ind scouts; b. DT; 6th enlmt 9 May 1876 at Ft Lincoln for 6 mos by Lt Varnum; age 42; blk eyes, blk hair, copper comp, 5' 10" high; courier to gen Terry's exp'n dur May;⁸³ ds Yellowstone depot 15 June;⁸⁴ one of seven 'Rees sent with mail to gen Terry eve 24 June; (incl desp from gen Sheridan warning of large incr in number of hostiles); arr camp mouth of Big Horn 28 June 4 P.M.; helped Goose off boat eve 30 June & washed his wd hand; Goose told Horns-in-front his son (Young Hawk) with troops coming down Big Horn; when troops came along (2 July) he was very glad to see his son alive & embraced him as when he was little;⁸⁵ with 'Rees sent down Yellowstone by gen Terry 5 July to look for Sioux crossing; disch 11 Nov 1876 at Ft Lincoln upon expir of serv.

Howling Wolf (Schi-ri-ti-wa-na), Iche-re-ti-wa-na, Wolf (Cha-ra'-ta [Hcarotc] Mandan name).⁸⁶ Pvt detmt ind scouts; b. DT; 2d enlmt 26 Apr 1876 at Ft Lincoln for 6 mos by Lt Cooke; age 20; blk eyes, blk hair, copper comp, 5' 6" high; ds Yellowstone depot 15 June; Red Star said Cha-ra-ta was left at Powder River because he had only a colt to ride; Running Wolf said Cha-ra-ta was left sick in care of Tall Bear; Billy Jackson said Howling Wolf accomp him up Rosebud (eve 13 Aug) with mail for gen Terry but fled back to Yellowstone same night dur encounter with Sioux war pty in midst of thunderstorm;⁸⁷ disch 11 Nov 1876 at Ft Lincoln upon expir of serv a scout char good; (final statement dated 26 Oct); listed on Ft Berthold Agcy census, Apr 1910, age 53.

Laying Down (Si-ti-wa-ra), Ti-sha, Ticha, Disha. Pvt detmt ind scouts; b. DT; enl 9 May 1876 at Ft Lincoln for 6 mos by Lt Varnum; age 18; blk eyes, blk hair, copper comp, 5' 2" high; ds Ft Lincoln from 17 May; (a couple scouts were kept out from morn till dk lying flat on knoll & if someone approached were to ride back zig-zag to signal alarm);⁸⁸ ds Ft Lincoln 20 Oct; disch 11 Nov 1876 at Ft Lincoln upon expir of serv a scout char good.

Left Hand (Quigh), Left Handed. Pvt detmt ind scouts; b. DT; 9th enlmt 9 Dec 1875 at Ft Lincoln for 6 mos by Lt Cooke; age 45; blk eyes, blk hair, copper comp, 5' 8" high; Red Star & Red Bear said Left Hand & Scabby Wolf were sent back with mail to Ft Lincoln in the snowstorm (1st June);⁸⁹ disch 9 June at Ft Lincoln upon expir of serv a scout char xclt & reenl next day for 6 mos by Lt Ogle; (pres on post return from June); ds Ft Lincoln 20 Oct; disch 10 Dec 1876 at Ft Lincoln by expir of serv. See also Climbs-the-Bluff.

Little Brave (Naha-cus-chu-re-posch), Nahukoc-Chiripas. Pvt detmt ind scouts; b. DT; 5th enlmt 9 May 1876 at Ft Lincoln for 6 mos by Lt Varnum; age 27; blk eyes, blk hair, copper comp, 5' 7" high; with gen Custer to Crow's Nest morn 25 June; on skirmish line in valley fight; dur retreat Red Bear saw Little Brave on eastside of river riding slowly toward ridge, blood running down his white shirt from wd under r. shoulder; Soldier said Little Brave's spotted pony came up on hill & Strikes-Two tied him among pack-mules; Young Hawk found Little Brave's body to left of Reno's line of retreat (farther on from Isaiah) where trees chopped down near river, a willow branch thrust into his chest the leafy part outside; Young Hawk led Little Brave's spotted pinto pony to Yellowstone.⁹⁰

Little Crow. See Rushing Bull.

Little Sioux. See Sioux.

Long Bear (Coonough-ti-ku-chees), Tall Bear, High Bear, Gunuhc-Tiwichess. Pvt detmt ind scouts; b. DT; 7th enlmt 9 May 1876 at Ft Lincoln for 6 mos by Lt Varnum; age 45; blk eyes, blk hair, copper comp, 5' 7" high; (High Bear at Ft Lincoln 31 May);⁹¹ ds Yellowstone depot 15 June; at Powder River maj Reno told High Bear he could not go on with others because his horse was badly galled; High Bear disputed him & grew very angry whereupon Reno threatened to shoot High Bear who then started for Reno with his knife; Bloody Knife sprang between them & urged Reno to let him go & Reno consented; Running Wolf said Tall Bear was left behind to care for the sick Horns-in-front & Cha-ra-ta;[92] one of seven 'Rees sent with mail to gen Terry eve 24 June; (incl desp from gen Sheridan warning of large incr in number of hostiles); arr camp mouth of Big Horn 28 June 4 p.m.; with 'Rees sent down Yellowstone by gen Terry 5 July to look for Sioux crossing; disch 11 Nov 1876 at Ft Lincoln upon expir of serv a scout char good; listed on Ft Berthold Agcy census, June 1899, age 67.

Ma-tok-sha (Bear Waiting). See Round-Wooden-Cloud.

One Feather (Ha-cui-tu), Hahe-Hitu, Ahc Hitu. Pvt detmt ind scouts; b. spring 1832 in land of the Pawnee; 2d enlmt 9 May 1876 at Ft Lincoln for 6 mos by Lt Varnum; age 45; blk eyes, blk hair, copper comp, 5' 7" high; with Reno scout up Powder River 10 June; with Lt Varnum to Crow's Nest night of 24 June; Red Bear said One Feather ate food found inside lone tepee 25 June; crossed river ahead of Reno's comd & did not take three Sioux horses driven from timber by Bloody Knife; scolded Gerard for going back with sol.'s leaving scouts without an intrpr to give orders; joined Strikes-Two driving off Sioux horses then started after two other horses; met Whole Buffalo in woods, telling him he should help get horses away; Little Sioux said One Feather & Tonhechi-Tu took after two horses; Red Star saw One Feather & Pta-a-te with bunch near ford but these were retaken by Sioux who fired at scouts, wd'g One Feather's horse in foot; the wd swelled on way back to Rosebud & he had to leave him; got extra horse from Foolish Bear (some scouts had extra horses on trip back); at Powder River camp Rushing Bull gave One Feather a horse & he paid him $10;[93] ds Ft Lincoln 20 Oct; disch 11 Nov 1876 at Ft Lincoln by expir of serv a scout char good; listed on Ft Berthold Agcy census as late as June 1914, age 91.

One Horn (Ach-no-arri-cas), Ach-co-Arricoe, Hckorik. Pvt detmt ind scouts; b. DT; 8th enlmt 26 Apr 1876 at Ft Lincoln for 6 mos by Lt Cooke; age 24; blk eyes, blk hair, copper comp, 5' 9" high; ds Ft Lincoln May to Sep; Red Bear & Running Wolf said One Horn & Red-Foolish-Bear were sent back to Ft Lincoln with mail at sunset 20 May; Red Bear said One Horn stayed at Ft Lincoln when his horse gave out;[94] disch 11 Nov 1876 at Ft Lincoln upon expir of serv a scout char good; (final statement dated 26 Oct); listed on Ft Berthold Agcy census, June 1901, age 51.

Owl (Ho-ru), Whuru. Pvt detmt ind scouts; b. DT; enl 13 May 1876 at Ft Lincoln for 6 mos by Lt Varnum; age 19; blk eyes, blk hair, copper comp, 5' 5" high; Custer told Owl, Red Bear & Wagon (thro' Gerard) they were last to enlist & must remain at the post; ds Ft Lincoln 17 May; pres at Ft Lincoln 31 May; (courier to gen Terry's exp'n dur June);[95] Young Hawk said Owl, Black Porcupine, & Bears Eyes went back with messages from Powder River;[96] disch 13 Nov 1876 at Ft Lincoln upon expir of serv a scout char good.

Pretty Face. See Good Face.

Pta-a-te. See Bear-Running-in-the-Timber.

Red Bear. See Good Elk.

Red Brush. See Bush.

Red-Foolish-Bear. See Foolish Bear.

Red Star. See Strike Bear.

Red Wolf. See Bush.

Round-Wooden-Cloud (Mach-pa-ya-chun-ga-lash-ca), Ring Cloud, Watokshu (Carrier), (English name, Adam Carrier).[97] (bro. of Bear-Come-Out).[98] Pvt detmt ind scouts; b. DT (Blackfeet); 3d enlmt 31 Mar 1876 at Ft Lincoln for 6 mos by Lt Cooke; age 40; brn eyes, blk hair, copper comp, 5' 11" high; with Reno

331

scout up Powder River 10 June;⁹⁹ with Varnum on divide early 25 June & could see Sioux ponies; told Custer too many Sioux; Strikes-Two said Watokshu & another Sioux crossed river with Reno's comd & made rush for Sioux horses;¹⁰⁰ Carrier said when troops broke he got away by getting into creek bottom & keeping in timber;¹⁰¹ Strikes-Two said Watokshu & Good Elk came from timber same time as Herendeen pty; Carrier said when packs came up he went to river to drink & while gone Sioux corralled Reno & cut off scouts who went back on trail;¹⁰² says captured horses driven ahead at first but when under good motion his pty passed them & they followed; Red Bear said Matoksha joined rear-guard scouts when herd had not gone far;¹⁰³ Ring Cloud said he slept twice on way back & nearly starved, getting nothing to eat until Powder River;¹⁰⁴ Soldier said they had moldy crackers at mouth of Rosebud & Watoksha, Cross, & Tonhechi-Tu left pty & beat others to Powder River;¹⁰⁵ disch 30 Sep 1876 at Ft Lincoln upon expir of serv a scout char good; listed on Standing Rock Agcy census to 1914, age 75.¹⁰⁶

Running Wolf. See Wolf Runs.

Rushing Bull (Ho-cus-na-quin), Charging Bull, Hukos-Tunawinhc, (Little Crow).¹⁰⁷ Pvt detmt ind scouts; b. DT; 2d enlmt 9 May 1876 at Ft Lincoln for 6 mos by Lt Varnum; age 45; blk eyes, blk hair, copper comp, 5' 6" high; rode to the charge with Reno's comd 25 June but did not cross river;¹⁰⁸ Red Bear said Charging Bull bro't herd of captured horses to Reno hill; Red Star said Little Crow with younger scouts watering horses & escaped when Sioux corralled Reno;¹⁰⁹ One Feather said scouts were very hungry on way back & begged Rushing Bull to let them kill his colt & he consented (he had a mare & colt); arr Powder River camp eve 28 June;¹¹⁰ Rushing Bull gave One Feather a horse for $10; ds with gen Crook 26 Aug (carry desps between comds); disch 11 Nov 1876 at Ft Lincoln upon expir of serv a scout char good.

Scabby Wolf. See Climbs-the-Bluff.

Sioux (Sen-nen-net), Little Sioux, Sananat Pichiripost; (1/4 Sioux & 3/4 Arikara);¹¹¹ Pvt detmt ind scouts; b. 1857 Ft Clark DT; 2d enlmt 3 Feb 1876 at Ft Lincoln for 6 mos by Lt Cooke; age 20; dk eyes, blk hair, copper comp, 5' 7" high;¹¹² courier to gen Terry's exp'n dur May;¹¹³ crossed river with Reno's comd 25 June & with Boy Chief, Red Star, & Strikes-Two took after bunch of Sioux horses opposite timber; (rode farther ahead than skirmish line); ran horses back across flat & up bluff curving in front of them, not altering course; his horse played out on hillside (the one he rode from the first) & he mtd a blk Sioux horse; sol.'s at rear of column (Custer) passing on hilltop fired at scouts by mistake; met scouts who had not crossed river & drove horses back from ridge; returned to hilltop as sol.'s straggled up; helped round up captured horses when packs fortified & started for Rosebud; got nothing to eat until moldy crackers found at old camp on Yellowstone;¹¹⁴ arr Powder River camp 28 June just as bugles blew for dinner;¹¹⁵ disch 3 Aug camp on Yellowstone River & reenl by Lt Varnum for 6 mos; ds with gen Crook 26 Aug (carry desps between comds); disch 3 Feb 1877 at Ft Lincoln upon expir of serv a scout char good; died 31 Aug 1933 Nishu, N.Dak.
Pension: 28 Feb 1921 / Ind. Surv. / 17793 / 12434. (XC-922,970).

Skare'. See Good Face.

Soldier, (Kunanch), Hoo-nanch, Hcunatch, Hcunahc. (Cpl) detmt ind scouts; b. late fall 1831 in village near mouth of Grand River; leader of New Dog Society (oldest men in it);¹¹⁶ 13th enlmt 26 Apr 1876 at Ft Lincoln for 6 mos by Lt Cooke; age 45; blk eyes, blk hair, copper comp, 5' 6" high; appt 2d leader of ind scouts by gen Custer 16 May & issued coat with two stripes on sleeve;¹¹⁷ rode to the charge with Reno's comd 25 June but having a lazy horse he was left far behind & did not cross river; (always regretted not firing a shot in the fight); joined White Eagle, Bull, & Stab along Custer's trail on ridge; (passed sol. with horse down, then 2d sol. with horse down); met scouts driving off Sioux horses & offered big spotted horse by Strikes-Two while Red Star offered a mouse-colored horse because it was strong & he was heavy; followed herd back to pack train & took fresh horse & returned to

ridge; proposed scouts water horses & while doing so Reno besieged by Sioux who pressed scouts back beyond lone tepee; struck Rosebud before dark with rear gd; stopped once next day to shoot & cook sage hens, only time horses grazed until at Yellowstone; arr Powder River camp 28 June 2 P.M.; his eyes went bad at this camp but improved after applying lump of alum given him by Stab; carried mail to Rosebud & found 'Rees there in rags, also many Crows with their women; ds with gen Crook 26 Aug (carry desps between comds); one of four 'Rees sent with mail from Beaver Creek (to gen Terry 2 Sep);[118] disch 26 Oct 1876 at Ft Lincoln by expir of serv a scout char good; died 7 May 1921 Elbowoods, N.Dak.
Pension: 1 Mar 1921 / Ind. Surv. / 17797. Rej upon death of clmt & leaving no widow or minor ch. surviving entitled to complete claim.

Stab (Ca-wars), Stabbed, Kawashc. Pvt detmt ind scouts; b. DT; (uncle of Little Sioux); enl 9 May 1876 at Ft Lincoln for 6 mos by Lt Varnum; age 45; blk eyes, blk hair, dk comp, 5' 6" high; (carried own Winchester & lots of cartridges in feed bag);[119] horse won race in camp 27 May against one owned by Pta-a-te;[120] courier with Goose to Yellowstone night of 7 June & next morn bro't mail to Custer's camp up Powder River;[121] when Custer came down from Crow's Nest morn 25 June Stab prayed & exhorted young men & rubbed clay carried for the purpose on their chests for good medicine;[122] rode to the chg with Reno's comd but was left behind & did not cross river; joined Soldier, White Eagle, & Bull along Custer's trail on ridge; Little Sioux saw Stab at rear of column of sol.'s on hilltop wave his hat to stop sol.'s firing at scouts coming up with Sioux horses; Strikes-Two said Stab helped drive herd back to pack train & proposed scouts water horses; Red Bear said Stab proposed scouts go to Powder River as Custer told them; Stab put own horse in herd & rode captured mule & accomp rear gd says Soldier; arr Powder River camp 28 June 2 p.m.; disch 11 Nov 1876 at Ft Lincoln by expir of serv a scout char good; (final statement dated 9 Nov); killed in 1882 while hunting in Missouri River Bad Lands when he went out after dark to look after horses & was shot by Sioux who ran off all the horses.[123]

Sticking Out (Bo-ho-e-na-ge), Boin-e-naga, Titkawehrt. Pvt detmt ind scouts; b. DT; enl 11 Nov 1875 at Ft Lincoln for 6 mos by Lt Calhoun; age 22; blk eyes, blk hair, copper comp, 5' 9" high; disch 11 May 1876 at Ft Lincoln by expir of serv.

Strike Bear (Coonough-to-cha), Strikes-the-Bear, Gunuhc-Tiche, White Calf, Red Star, alias Saha-Tipaat (seven stars in dipper).[124] Pvt detmt ind scouts; b. spring 1858 Ft Clark DT; enl 9 May 1876 at Ft Lincoln for 6 mos by Lt Varnum; age 21; blk eyes, blk hair, dk comp, 5' 3" high; with Lt Varnum to Crow's Nest night of 24 June & with Bull carried note to gen Custer at dawn 25 June; crossed river with Reno's comd & joined Boy Chief & Strikes-Two after big bunch of Sioux horses opposite timber; drove 28 horses across flat & up thro' hills into ravine; took fresh horse (the big one Strikes-Two offered Soldier) & returned to ridge above river; saw pack mules unharnessed in hollow by their drivers; went with younger scouts to water horses & escaped when Sioux attacked Reno & chased older scouts on back trail;[125] Red Bear & Soldier said Red Star with herd of captured horses; arr Powder River camp 28 June 2 p.m.; ds with gen Crook 26 Aug (carry desps between comds); ds Ft Lincoln 20 Oct; disch 11 Nov 1876 at Ft Lincoln upon expir of serv a scout char good; died 7 June 1929 Ree N.Dak.
Pension: 29 July 1929 / Wid / 1647925. See Ind. Surv. / 17788 / 12432.

Strikes Enemy. See White Swan.

Strikes-the-Lodge (Tay-ku-che), Tekche. Pvt detmt ind scouts; b. DT; leader of Daroch'-pa Society (members had crescent moon shaved on back of head); 3d enlmt 9 May 1876 at Ft Lincoln for 6 mos by Lt Varnum; age 29; blk eyes, blk hair, copper comp, 5' 9" high; with Lt Varnum to Crow's Nest night of 24 June; rode to the chg with Reno's comd but was left behind & did not cross river; Soldier said he met Strikes-the-Lodge

& Red Wolf where Sioux horses came up; Strikes-Two said Strikes-the-Lodge & Assiniboine (nickname for unidentified scout) helped drive Sioux horses back to pack train; Strikes-the-Lodge took fresh horse & returned to hilltop says Soldier & Red Bear; helped round up captured horses & start for Rosebud when packs fortified says Little Sioux; Red Bear tho't Strikes-the-Lodge with scouts detailed to keep Sioux back;[126] arr Powder River camp 28 June; ds with gen Crook 26 Aug (carry desps between comds); disch 11 Nov 1876 at Ft Lincoln upon expir of serv a scout char good.

Strikes-Two (Ti-ta-ra-wi-cha), Ta-ta-ree-we-chi. Pvt detmt ind scouts; b. 1844 Ft Clark DT; 4th enlmt 9 May 1876 at Ft Lincoln for 6 mos by Lt Varnum; age 29; blk eyes, blk hair, copper comp, 5' 9" high;[127] earned $200 selling game to sol.'s dur march to Powder River; found two Sioux horses on Rosebud 24 June; first scout to reach lone tepee 25 June striking it with his whip;[128] crossed river with Reno's comd & joined Boy Chief & Red Star after big bunch of Sioux horses; drove 29 head up bluffs as Custer column passed on hilltop; scouts waved their hats to stop sol.'s firing at them by mistake; met scouts who had not crossed river & drove horses back to pack train; left horses with holders & returned to bluffs; took horses to water then stopped to smoke; saw Reno corralled by Sioux & at sundown (could see flash of guns) started for Rosebud with rear-guard; passed scouts detailed to carry off horses (the Sioux had chased them & retook horses); camped to rest at mouth of Rosebud where moldy hardtack found;[129] arr Powder River camp 28 June; when Foolish Bear & White Cloud bro't mail from Big Horn (15 July) Strikes-Two & Bull-in-the-Water took mail on to Ft Buford; disch 11 Nov 1876 at Ft Lincoln upon expir of serv a scout char good; died 8 Sep 1922 Elbowoods, N.Dak.
Pension: 22 Oct 1904 / Inv / 1326420. Ind. Surv. / 17796. Ind. Wid. / 16608 / 10933.

Tall Bear. See Long Bear.

The Shield (Wa-ha-chun-ca), Waha-Chayka. Pvt detmt ind scouts; b. DT (Sioux); enl 11 Nov 1875 at Ft Lincoln for 6 mos by Lt Calhoun; age 27; blk eyes, blk hair, copper comp, 5' 9 1/2" high; disch 11 May 1876 at Ft Lincoln upon expir of serv; died 17 July 1919 Missouri River.
Pension: 5 Dec 1929 / Wid / 1655942.

Wagon (Saparano), Sap-pa-ran-nee-wa, Sapireniwohc. Pvt detmt ind scouts; b. DT; enl 13 May 1876 at Ft Lincoln for 6 mos by Lt Varnum; age 20; blk eyes, blk hair, copper comp, 5' 6" high; Custer told Wagon, Owl & Red Bear (thro' Gerard) they were last to enlist & must remain at post; ds Ft Lincoln 17 May; courier to gen Terry's exp'n before 31 May;[130] Running Wolf said Wagon & Charging-up-the-Hill rode out from Powder River camp at sunrise 24 June to greet 'Rees bringing mail from Custer; (str *Josephine* arr same day); one of seven 'Rees sent with mail to gen Terry eve 24 June; (incl desp from gen Sheridan warning of large incr in number of hostiles); arr camp mouth of Big Horn 28 June 4 p.m.; with 'Rees sent down Yellowstone by gen Terry 5 July to look for Sioux crossing;[131] ds Ft Lincoln 20 Oct; disch 13 Nov 1876 at Ft Lincoln upon expir of serv a scout char good.

Watokshu, Watoksha. See Round-Wooden-Cloud.

White Calf. See Strike Bear.

White Cloud (Mach-pa-a-ska), Mahc-pē'-aska. Pvt detmt ind scouts; b. DT (Yanktonai); 2d enlmt 14 May 1876 at Ft Lincoln for 6 mos by Lt Varnum; age 21; blk eyes, blk hair, copper comp, 5' 8" high; with Reno scout up Powder River 10 June; Strikes-Two said Mahpiya-ska crossed river with Reno's comd & skirmished with Sioux as sol.'s dismtd;[132] Carrier said White Cloud stayed until troops broke then got away by having a fresh swift horse & swimming the river;[133] led one horse up from valley & met Red Bear leading two horses on ridge & started for place scouts took horses; met four Crow scouts looking for other two Crows, said they would come back & White Cloud & Red Bear waited a long time before rejoining Reno as 'Rees came on fresh horses;[134] with Strikes-Two pty watering horses when Sioux corraled Reno & pressed scouts hard back beyond lone tepee; with rearguard & caught a blk Sioux horse near Rosebud, an intelligent horse, smelled of the ground often & followed back-trail well;[135] arr Powder River camp 28 June 2 p.m.; when scouts arr 5 July with report of gen Crook's fight, White Cloud & Foolish Bear were picked to carry desp to gen Terry & given two best horses; arr camp mouth of Big Horn River 9 July; after a time (night of 12 July) they were sent back & (15 July) called Strikes-Two & Bull-in-the-Water to cross over & carry mail on to Ft Buford; White Cloud & Foolish Bear then crossed river & joined other scouts;[136] ds in field 8 Aug (with Billy Cross); disch 14 Nov 1876 at Ft Lincoln upon expir of serv a scout char good; listed on Standing Rock Agcy census, July 1885, age 31.

White Eagle (Na-ta-sta-ca), Natakos Taka. Pvt detmt ind scouts; b. DT; enl 9 May 1876 at Ft Lincoln for 6 mos by Lt Varnum; age 27; blk eyes, blk hair, copper comp, 5' 4" high; rode to the chg with Reno's comd 25 June but having a very small horse (not much larger than a dog) he was left behind & did not cross river; joined Soldier, Stabbed, & Bull along Custer's trail on ridge; helped drive captured horses back to pack train; Red Bear said White Eagle came to Reno hill with herd of captured horses (about 40); Red Star said White Eagle with younger scouts watering horses & left them when Sioux corraled Reno; Soldier said White Eagle started for Rosebud with captured horses; arr Powder River camp 28 June; disch 11 Nov 1876 at Ft Lincoln upon expir of serv a scout char good;[137] listed on Ft Berthold Agcy census, June 1890, age 39.

White-Man-Runs-Him (Mahr-stah-shee-dah-ku-rosh), Crow-Who-Talks-Gros Ventre. b. MT ca. 1854; enl 10 Apr 1876 Crow Agcy MT by Lt Bradley till disch; attd to 7 cav 22 June; guided Lt Varnum's pty to Crow's Nest night of 24 June;[138] says four Crow scouts with Custer after Reno separated 25 June; Curley joined 'Rees running off big band of Sioux horses;[139] when Custer took comd down coulee, Crows went on high ridge & fired into Sioux camp before starting back to pack train as Boyer told them; met Benteen's comd & had talk with sol. who spoke a little Crow; after sundown three Crows slipped thro' Sioux lines & rode all night thro' rainstorm to mouth of Little Horn & before daylight swam across Big Horn; yelled back to Gibbon's Crows about Custer's fight; said their horses worn out & going home to get fresh horses;[140] joined gen Terry's camp mouth of Big Horn 15 July; Crows disch 20 Aug mouth of Powder River, wanting to go home to prepare for coming winter for families & as troops unable to catch Sioux; when Gibbon comd passed Crow Agcy (24 Sep) whole band followed to Ft Ellis & scouts paid 30 Sep; Leforge said Crows with their women went to Bozeman & purchased supplies till money used up;[141] died 2 June 1929 Lodge Grass MT.[142]
Pension: 23 July 1929 / Wid / 1647276. Ind. Surv. / 18404 / 11785.

White Swan (Mee-nah-tsee-us), Strikes Enemy. b. MT ca. 1852; enl 10 Apr 1876 Crow Agcy MT by Lt Bradley till disch; age 24; blk eyes, blk hair, copper comp, 5' 6 1/2" high; attd to 7 cav 22 June; with Lt Varnum to Crow's Nest night of 24 June; near Little Horn Custer told White Swan & Half-Yellow-Face to go on ridge to see if Sioux running away but they instead joined Reno's scouts as they moved for'd;[143] on skirmish line in valley fight & with Young Hawk's pty dur retreat; gsw r. wrist (frac. hand) & horse shot three times; saved from Sioux when dragged into brush by Half-Yellow-Face & Young Hawk;[144] put on horse led by Half-Yellow-Face up to Reno's camp; gsw r. thigh while in hosp on hilltop; carried on travois fixed by Half-Yellow-Face who led pony to boat 29 June; Running Wolf saw Strikes-Enemy on prow of boat at Yellowstone; in hosp at camp mouth of Big Horn till 8 July when he went home;[145] when Gibbon comd passed Crow Agcy (24 Sep) whole band followed to Ft Ellis & scouts paid 30 Sep; Leforge said Crows with their women went to Bozeman & purchased supplies till money used up; died 11 Aug 1904 at Crow Agency.
Pension: 19 Jan 1897 / Inv / 1184464 / 956271.

Whole Buffalo. See Bear-Running-in-the-Timber.

Wolf (Cha-ra-ta). See Howling Wolf.

Wolf Runs (Schi-ri-tu-nuch), Running Wolf, (Ses-che-ree-do-nakh). Pvt detmt ind scouts; b. Dec 1855 Ft Berthold DT; enl 9 May 1876 at Ft Lincoln for 6 mos by Lt Varnum; age 21; blk eyes, blk hair, copper comp, 5' 3" high; ds carrying desps in field 22 June (one of four 'Rees sent with mail from Rosebud & arr Powder River camp morn 24 June); (str *Josephine* arr same day); one of seven 'Rees sent with mail to gen Terry eve 24 June;[146] (incl desp from gen Sheridan warning of large incr in number of hostiles); saw pty of inds tho't to be Sioux near mouth of Rosebud; (this was pty of Strikes-Two); arr camp mouth of Big Horn 28 June 4 P.M.; given field-glasses (29 June) & sent across Yellowstone with Charging-up-the-Hill to look for steamboat coming down Big Horn; sent on same duty next morn with Howling Wolf; with 'Rees sent down Yellowstone by gen Terry 5 July to look for Sioux crossing & upon return found gen Terry's camp moved to Rosebud; one of seven scouts sent with desp to gen Crook (25 Aug) & attd to scout for his comd; carried mail with Young Hawk & Caroo (6 Sep) from Heart River to Ft Lincoln; disch 11 Nov 1876 at Ft Lincoln upon expir of serv a scout char good; died 13 Mar 1936 Elbowoods, N.Dak.[147]
Pension: 28 Feb 1921 / Ind. Surv. / 17790 / 12496. (XC-2,577,474).

Young Hawk (Ach-ta-wi-si-humne), Nekutawihsu-Hani. Pvt detmt ind scouts; b. spring 1859 DT; 4th enlmt 9 May 1876 at Ft Lincoln for 6 mos by Lt Varnum; age 20; blk eyes, blk hair, dk comp, 5' 6" high; (Custer recalled Young Hawk from Blk Hills Exp'n); with Reno scout up Powder River 10 June; detailed with mail pty 22 June but retained by gen Custer;[148] captured Sioux horse on skirmish line in valley fight 25 June & gave to Half-Yellow-Face; followed Reno's line of retreat from timber but crossed river lower down & took refuge in thick grove of trees (below Edgerly peaks); helped Half-Yellow-Face drag White Swan into brush to save him from Sioux; saw U.S. flag (Benteens) on highest point; tied white handkerchief to stick as flag & led scouts up to Reno's camp, running on foot last few rods when horse shot down by Sioux swarming back from Custer;[149] cared for Goose dur siege on hill, dressing his wd hand & bro't him food & water; led pony with travois carrying Goose to boat 29 June; rode blk Sioux pony & led Little Brave's pinto pony to Yellowstone & there [2 July] placed bridle of Sioux pony into hand of his father (Horns-in-front) as a gift; with 'Rees sent down Yellowstone by gen Terry 5 July to look for Sioux crossing; ds with gen Crook 26 Aug (carry desp's between comds); carried mail with Running Wolf & Caroo (6 Sep) from Heart River to Ft Lincoln;[150] disch 11 Nov 1876 at Ft Lincoln upon expir of serv a scout char good; died 16 Jan 1915 Elbowoods, N.Dak.
Pension: 1 Mar 1921 / Ind. Wid. / 15367 / 10858.

Notes—Indian Scouts

1. Red Star and Running Wolf apparently referred to Barking Wolf as Howling Wolf. Red Star identified Howling Wolf in the group with whom he enlisted (May 9), whereas it was Barking Wolf who enlisted on that date; and Red Star and Running Wolf place Howling Wolf with scouts sent back with mail June 22, whereas Lieut. Varnum's muster roll reports Barking Wolf carried despatches June 22. Also, Red Star and Running Wolf each related that Wolf, Cha-ra'-ta (Mandan name) was left at Powder River, and the muster roll reports Howling Wolf detached at the Yellowstone depot (Powder River) June 15. Libby, *Arikara Narrative*, 53, 74, 85, 139–40, 197.

(The confusion may be attributed to the similarity of names, and if correct, *The Narrative* and Muster Roll are in agreement.) Walter Camp noted that Barking Wolf's right name was Wolf Standing in the Cold (Schiri-Tipsikahrt). WMC, Notes, Box 5, env 65, BYU. However, Young Hawk stated that the second name of Bear's Eye was Wolf-Stands-in-the-Cold. Libby, *Arikara Narrative*, 50. See note 86 (Howling Wolf).

The Walter Camp material contains several lists of Indian scout names and translations. WMC-BYU, Box 5, envs. 65 and 119; also WMC-DPL, folder FF17. One list is credited to Boy Chief, and another headed, "Official List Scouts Revised 8/10/11." (This is the date of Camp's interview with One Feather.) See Liddic and Harbaugh, *Camp on Custer,* 127–32.

2. Barking Wolf may have been detailed to carry mail. Lieut. English, 7th Inf., (Col. Gibbon's comd), journaled Aug. 30, "Marched across to the Head of Deer Creek. Mail went down to the River" (Yellowstone, 13 miles distant). Johnson, "With Gibbon against the Sioux in 1876."

Also Lieut. Baldwin, adjutant 5th Inf., left Gen. Terry's camp at 9 p.m., Aug. 30, enroute to Bismarck, and said he took "three men well mounted" down Deer Creek to its mouth where he reached the camp of Lieut. Rice, 5th Inf., about three hours later. Baldwin said the ride was very fatiguing owing to the rough route. Baldwin, Diary; see also, Willert, *March of the Columns,* 470.

That Baldwin's party included an Indian scout is surmised from similar situations recorded at about the same time. On Aug. 27, Lieut. Rice reported he furnished one Indian guide to a party of seven soldiers carrying despatches to Gen. Terry. And in a despatch to Terry, Aug. 29, Rice requested that the Indian Scouts he (Rice) had sent with despatches from time to time, be ordered to report to him (Rice), that he had used soldiers but they could not find their way any distance from the river. Willert, *March of the Columns,* 453, 462.

Barking Wolf evidently was still absent early the next morning, Aug. 31, when the detachment of Indian scouts and the whole of the 7th Cavalry were sent on a scout down the Yellowstone, and that evening, after marching 20 miles, mustered near the mouth of Fox Creek.

3. Libby, *Arikara Narrative,* 134, 140; Gray, "Arikara Scouts With Custer," 468; Gray, *Centennial Campaign,* 203. Foolish Bear and White Cloud were evidently accompanied by scout George W. Morgan. Strikes-Two and Bull-in-the-Water were apparently accompanied to Fort Buford by scout Vic Smith and two soldiers of 6th Inf., Pvts. Cassidy, Co. C, and Smith, Co. I. Cassidy with two Indian scouts and white scout Ed Begley returned to camp with mail from Buford, Aug. 3. Willert, *March of the Columns,* 104, 129, 132, 267; Godfrey, *Diary,* 22.

4. Letters to Walter Camp from Edwin A. Lindsay, Wakpala, SD, Oct. 30, and, Nov. 9, 1909, concerning conversations with Adam Carrier (brother, [or cousin] of Bear-Come-Out). WMC-BYU.

5. Lieut. Varnum said Bear Comes Out was called Old Caddoo. Note from Varnum about four Sioux scouts in his command, in Taylor, notes (p. 38) for, "With Custer on the Little Big Horn."

6. Bear Come Out and Billy Cross were among six scouts engaged in illicit liquor activity. Milligan, *Dakota Twilight,* 51.

7. Edwin A. Lindsay to Walter Camp, Nov. 9, 1909, WMC-BYU; Hammer, *Custer in '76,* 185.

8. Running Wolf identified Caroó among seven scouts selected by Col. Gibbon to carry a letter to Gen. Crook, who, upon receipt of same, told the scouts they were to stay and scout for him. Libby, *Arikara Narrative,* 147–49. Lieut. Bourke, aide to Gen. Crook, journaled that Gen. Terry loaned five 'Rees to Gen. Crook, and proved of great service. Two carried despatch's to Gen. Terry on Sept. 2, while the others were sent to Fort Lincoln the morning of Sept. 6 with an important despatch for Gen. Sheridan. Bourke, *On the Border With Crook,* 361, 365–66; Willert, *Bourke's Diary,* 173.

9. Muster Roll of Indian Scouts, Fort A. Lincoln, DT, June 30, 1878. (RG 94, Entry 53). Fred Gerard said Ca-don (or Cardon), was killed by a Sioux scout named Penis in a drunken brawl at Fort Lincoln; no notice was taken by authorities and he absconded that night. Gerard to Walter Camp, July 19, 1909, WMC-BYU. Gerard says Cardu was brother-in-law of Mrs. Galpin. Gerard interview, 1909, WMC, Misc. notes, BYU.

10. Note from Lieut. Varnum about four Sioux scouts in his command lists Bear remaining in the timber. Taylor, notes (p. 38) for, "With Custer on the Little Big Horn."

11. Libby, *Arikara Narrative,* 59, 139.

12. Libby, *Arikara Narrative,* 133; Hammer, *Custer in '76,* 180, 190; Liddic and Harbaugh, *Camp on Custer,* 127–130. Tonhechi-Tu pronounced Ton-hā-chee'-Tu, the Arikara translation of Whole Buffalo. (Author telephone conversation with language instructor at White Shield School, N.Dak.)

13. Libby, *Arikara Narrative,* 66.

14. Libby, *Arikara Narrative,* 139; Liddic and Harbaugh, *Camp on Custer,* 128; Edwin A. Lindsay to Walter Camp, Nov. 9, 1909, WMC-BYU.

15. Hammer, *Custer in '76,* 180–81, 184; Liddic and Harbaugh, *Camp on Custer,* 129.

16. Libby, *Arikara Narrative,* 118, 131–33; Hammer, *Custer in '76,* 184, 190.

17. Liddic and Harbaugh, *Camp on Custer,* 130.

18. Libby, *Arikara Narrative,* 50; Hardorff, *Camp, Custer, and the Little Big Horn,* 49. The three scouts are on the Post Returns of Fort Lincoln, May 31, but not June 30. (NA, M617). Bears Eyes, Horn

in Front, and Sioux, are listed absent as couriers to Gen. Terry's Expedition on the Muster Roll of Indian Scouts, Fort A. Lincoln, Lieut. J. M. Burns, 17th Inf., commanding, June 30, 1876. RG 94, Entry 53.

Capt. McCaskey, temporary post commander, in a letter to his wife, June 27, 1876, mentioned Bear Eyes as one of the scouts sent with mail. Farioli and Nichols, "Fort A. Lincoln July 1876."; Gray, "Arikara Scouts with Custer," 468.

The scouts having no suitable horses at the post, the QM Dept. furnished them with two mules to carry despatches to Gen. Terry's Expedition. SO 115, Hq Fort A. Lincoln, DT, June 28, 1876, RG 393, Part V.

19. "'Bear's Eyes,' an old pioneer Indian, was in town yesterday from Fort Berthold. He has had a varied experience in the Indian wars, and bears many scars received in his fights with the early settlers." *Mandan Pioneer,* Feb. 15, 1884.

20. Libby, *Arikara Narrative,* 55, 119, 147–49; Gray, *Centennial Campaign,* 240–41; Willert, *March of the Columns,* 492; Hammer, *Custer in '76,* 180, 184.

21. Black Fox visited Washington in 1875 with a group of Arikara and Mandans led by Bad Gun (Rushing-After-the-Eagle), and interpreters Charles Packineau and Peter Beauchamp. *Collections of the State Historical Society of North Dakota,* Vol. II, Part I, 1908, 466. A photo of Black Fox in, Gray, "Arikara Scouts with Custer," 446.

22. Libby, *Arikara Narrative,* 198.

23. Libby, *Arikara Narrative,* 58.

24. Red Bear said Black Fox crossed the river with Reno's command and went with Boy Chief, Red Star, Strikes-Two, and Little Sioux after Sioux horses by the timber. Little Sioux saw Black Fox in front of the soldiers when Reno formed the skirmish line. Goes Ahead said one Arikara and four Crows were with Custer when he left Reno's trail, and when Custer took the command to the right down the draw toward the river, the three Crows rode to the left along the ridge above the river. This is when Black Fox and Curley disappeared. Libby, *Arikara Narrative,* 122, 150, 159–60.

25. Libby, *Arikara Narrative,* 119, 122, 147–49, 155; Hammer, *Custer in '76,* 185, 190, 192; Gray, *Custer's Last Campaign,* 329–32.

26. Walter Camp's official list of Indian Scouts revised 8/10/11, shows Black Fox "Dead." See, Liddic and Harbaugh, *Camp on Custer,* 131.

27. Libby, *Arikara Narrative,* 85; Hardorff, *Camp, Custer, and the Little Big Horn,* 49. Black Porcupine is present on the Post Returns of Fort Lincoln, May 31, but is not found on the Return for June (NA, M617), nor is he mentioned on Lieut. Burns's muster roll June 30. He is present on Lieut. Varnum's muster roll Aug. 31. RG 94, Entry 53.

28. RG 92, Entry 238, report 1865/1733 (Lieut. F. O. Udall, qm), lists Bloody Knife as messenger, August 1–12, 1865.

29. Libby, *Arikara Narrative,* 58 n.9; Gray, "Bloody Knife."

30. RG 92, Entry 238, report 1876/328. Libby, *Arikara Narrative,* 96, 127; Hammer, *Custer in '76,* 184.

31. (McDougall told Walter Camp), Camp to Mrs. Custer, Aug. 24, 1919, EBC-LBHB, Roll 3. Ferdinand Widmayer also said Bloody Knife went on Reno's scout; he recalled it well because after Reno had gone the boys said they did not see how Custer could go anywhere without Bloody Knife. Hammer, *Custer in '76,* 145.

32. Gray, *Custer's Last Campaign,* 206; Libby, *Arikara Narrative,* 77–78.

33. Red Bear and Little Sioux, in Libby, *Arikara Narrative,* 122, 150; Strikes-Two, in Hammer, *Custer in '76,* 184; One Feather in, Liddic and Harbaugh, *Camp on Custer,* 128.

34. Various testimony at Reno Court of Inquiry. Gray, "Bloody Knife." Bloody Knife's wife, Yellow Calf (San-een-a-kata), died in Spring, 1877; they reportedly lived together as man and wife according to Indian custom for about fifteen years, and had a son, Milton Fowler, of Fort Berthold, N. Dak., born March 1864.

Another Arikara woman, Owl Woman, appeared before the agent at Fort Berthold, April 4, 1879, claiming to have been married to Bloody Knife for ten years, her eldest child being nine years old, and she was the sole and only legal representative of Bloody Knife. She apparently received his pay $91.66 due him when he was killed. (Claim 42.848), "Retd May 22, 1879, . . . Paid Sett. 5465," RG 217, Entry 658, Docket Book of Miscellaneous Claims, Vol. 18, 414, 668. See also, Innis, *Bloody Knife,* 162.

35. Libby, *Arikara Narrative,* 56–59, 136; Lieut. Varnum referred to Bobtailed Bull as, "My Indian 1st Sergt." Carroll, *Custer's Chief of Scouts,* 68.

36. Libby, *Arikara Narrative,* 65, 137.

37. Libby, *Arikara Narrative*, 95–98, 112, 127; Hammer, *Custer in '76*, 185, 189, 192.
38. Gerard to Walter Camp, July 19, 1909, WMC-BYU.
39. Libby, *Arikara Narrative*, 130, 132; Hammer, *Custer in '76*, 184, 188.
40. Libby, *Arikara Narrative*, 59, 83, 85, 118–20, 131–32, 135; Hammer, *Custer in '76*, 184, 190.
41. Affidavit from Red Wolf (The Bush), May 27, 1907, in pension file of Strikes-Two. Also numerous papers in pension file of Little Sioux. RG 15.
42. Libby, *Arikara Narrative*, 65, 85, 117–20, 130-132; Hammer, *Custer in '76*, 181, 190.
43. Affidavit of Little Sioux, Oct. 11, 1924, in pension file. RG 15.
44. The matching of Climbs-the-Bluff with Scabby Wolf is based upon the statements of Red Star and Red Bear that Scabby Wolf and Left Handed were sent back to Fort Lincoln with mail in the snowstorm, (Libby, *Arikara Narrative*, 67; Hammer, *Custer in '76*, 194), and that Climbs-the-Bluff is the only scout on Lieut. Varnum's muster roll shown on detached service from June 1st (the day the regiment awoke in falling snow). Godfrey, *Diary*, 4. Left Hand was discharged at Fort Lincoln on June 9.

Also, Walter Camp's official list of Indian Scouts revised 8/10/11, notes after the name of Climbs-the-Bluff, "This man's name was Wolf." Liddic and Harbaugh, *Camp on Custer*, 131; see note 86 below.

45. Libby, *Arikara Narrative*, 141; Gray, "Arikara Scouts With Custer," 464–65.
46. NA, M233, Roll 71, Registers of Enlistments, Indian Scouts.
47. Curley was born near what was then called by the Indians, Rosebud Creek, a main stream now known as Stillwater River, into which (near town of Absaroka) flows an east branch once called Stillwater Fork, where Crow Agency was moved, but by 1876 the nomenclature of the two streams was completely reversed. Stewart, *The March of the Montana Column*, 39; Marquis, *Memoirs of a White Crow Indian*, 110.

Curley said he was 16 or 17 years old at the time of the battle. *The Tepee Book*, Vol. II, No. VI, June 1916, 56. Tom Leforge said Curley was 17 years old. Marquis, *Memoirs of a White Crow Indian*, 248. Col. Gibbon remarked that Curley "was quite a young man." Gibbon, *Adventures on the Western Frontier*, 116. Dixon, *The Vanishing Race*, 140.

48. Hammer, *Custer in '76*, 155–73. Graham, *The Custer Myth*, 7–19. Curley said to Walter Camp in 1910 that he always told the same story but there were different interpreters. Hammer, *Custer in '76*, 170.

Tom Leforge, who knew Curley from early boyhood, maintained that Curley always declared he did nothing wonderful, that he was not in the fight. When the action opened he was behind with the other Crows, and he hurried away to a distance of about a mile before pausing to look back briefly at the conflict. When farther away he stopped on a hill to look again, and seeing some horses running loose over the hills he captured two of them, but later released them when they were an impediment to his progress getting away from the Sioux. Leforge, who was in hospital at Gibbon's supply camp at Pease bottom, said Curley arrived Monday morning on the south bank of the Yellowstone and they had a sign talk. Curley made no mention of a fight. Marquis, *Memoirs of a White Crow Indian*, 247–51.

Curley also admitted to Gen. Woodruff in 1908 that he was not in the Custer fight and only saw it from a distance. Hutchins, *The Papers of Edward S. Curtis*, 105.

49. Libby, *Arikara Narrative*, 120. John Burkman said when the pack train was on Reno Creek about two miles from Reno hill, Curley & Billy Cross & other scouts came along with about 80 Sioux horses, & he saw Curley try to catch a white faced buckskin bronco out of the herd; this occurred when first shots were heard from Custer hill, proof Curley left Custer before the fight began. Wagner, *Old Neutriment*, 159. Hutchins, *The Papers of Edward S. Curtis*, 105.

50. Curley reached the steamer *Far West* at 9 A.M., June 28, according to the boat's log kept by clerk, Walter "Bub" Burleigh, Jr., a portion published in *The Dakota Herald* (Yankton), July 22, 1876.

James Sipes, citizen barber on the boat, told Walter Camp that Curley had three ponies and a red Sioux blanket when he first appeared and held up his gun, a carbine or Winchester, and made the peace sign. Sipes also noticed Curley had taken down his hair (pompadour). Curley told Camp he had only one horse when he arrived at the boat. Hammer, *Custer in '76*, 173, 241.

Grant Marsh, skipper of the *Far West*, described the scout as of magnificent physique and stark naked save for a breech clout when he burst through the thicket on his sweating pony, and was recognized as a Crow by his erect scalp-lock. He had captured two horses. Hanson, *The Conquest of the Missouri*, 274; Hammer, *Custer in '76*, 169.

James Coleman, clerk for John Smith, trader for the expedition on the *Far West*, said Curley wore a cloth about his head, a black shirt, a breech clout, and moccasins. Libby, *Arikara Narrative*, 208.

51. Hammer, *Custer in '76*, 170. Dixon, *The Vanishing Race*, 164.

52. RG 94, Entry 544, MT, Prescription Book No. 53, reports Laforge on 14 days furlough from night of July 4. Lieut. Freeman, 7th Inf., recorded July 4th, "2 of the Indians started home tonight." Schneider, ed., *The Freeman Journal,* 66; Marquis, *Memoirs of a White Crow Indian,* 254, 264; Gray, *Custer's Last Campaign,* 382.

53. Curley showed Sheridan his route and where he hid during the fight, and described through a good interpreter the time and place he deserted Custer. Sheridan was fully convinced Curley had run away before the fight really began and the greater part of his tale was untrustworthy. Graham, *The Custer Myth,* 374.

54. Libby, *Arikara Narrative,* 63, 85, 95–96, 102, 113, 122, 137, 145.

55. Libby, *Arikara Narrative,* 59, 85, 95–96, 122, 145, 193–94, 198; Hammer, *Custer in '76,* 182.

56. Hammer, *Custer in '76,* 174; Libby, *Arikara Narrative,* 159–60, 205.

57. Goes Ahead said it was sunset when Crows got to the black horse riders at Reno's entrenchment. *The Tepee Book,* Vol. 2, No. 6, June 1916, 57–58, and Vol. 2, No. 11, Nov. 1916, 16–21; Dixon, *The Vanishing Race,* 167–68.

Goes-Ahead told Walter Camp the three Crows did not see Custer after he turned down the coulee to the right; they turned back too early to see beginning or any part of Custer fight or whether he went to the river. Hammer, *Custer in '76,* 175; see also, Hutchins, *The Papers of Edward S. Curtis,* 170–71, 178.

Pretty Shield (wife of Goes-Ahead), said the three Crows met the packers who formed the pack train into a circle. They helped the packers dig pits and beside these holes the dead mules stopped many bullets. When the Crows left, they told the chief packer they were going to get water and each was given a flat canvas bottle to fill and bring back. Linderman, *Pretty Shield,* 237–42.

58. Libby, *Arikara Narrative,* 160; Hammer, *Custer in '76,* 175. Col. Gibbon said the three Crows were at first sight mistaken for Sioux and chased by his Crows across the Big Horn River. When each group identified the other, the three Crows told a story of the Custer fight and afterwards positively refused to rejoin Gibbon's command, declaring they and their horses too exhausted to cross the river again. Gibbon, *Adventures on the Western Frontier,* 133–34.

59. Willert, *March of the Columns,* 128.

60. Gibbon, *Adventures on the Western Frontier,* 164; Willert, *March of the Columns,* 409.

61. Marquis, *Memoirs of a White Crow Indian,* 264; Linderman, *Pretty Shield,* 236, 246.

62. Libby, *Arikara Narrative,* 53, 63; Hammer, *Custer in '76,* 194.

63. Libby, *Arikara Narrative,* 137. Red Bear said in camp Strikes-Two loaned him a big black horse to ride. Libby, *Arikara Narrative,* 66. Red Bear said he arrived at camp three days before the snowstorm (June 1st). Hammer, *Custer in '76,* 194.

64. Hammer, *Custer in '76,* 189; Libby, *Arikara Narrative,* 125–28.

65. Libby, *Arikara Narrative,* 129–30. Strikes-Two said Good Elk & Watokshu escaped from the timber same time as Herendeen party. Hammer, *Custer in '76,* 184.

66. Libby, *Arikara Narrative,* 77, 85, 118, 131.

67. On his roster of Indian scouts, Walter Camp noted after the name of Goose, "Gauht better Gaht or Goht." WMC-LBHB. (Arikara word for Goose is Ko-ut, or Goht, Go-hc. WMC-DPL, folders FF13, and FF17).

68. Libby, *Arikara Narrative,* 61, 72, 141; Gray, *Custer's Last Campaign,* 172–74. See, Jackson, *Custer's Gold,* 42, 58 and Krause & Olson, *Prelude to Glory,* 105, 155, 160, 200.

69. Custer was very fond of Goose and Young Hawk because they were jolly young fellows, reckless and full of life, and he retained them because they had found traces of the Sioux. Libby, *Arikara Narrative,* 140. Goose may have been the eighth Indian scout sent with Major Reno's reconnaissance up Powder River June 10. Gray, "Arikara Scouts With Custer," 462; Gray, *Custer's Last Campaign,* 184.

70. Libby, *Arikara Narrative,* 113–14, 144.

71. Libby, *Arikara Narrative,* 145. The clerk of the steamer *Far West,* Walter "Bub" Burleigh, Jr., logged July 5, "We passed Fort Stevenson at 2 P.M. and Fort Berthold an hour previous, where we left a Ree Indian—one of General Custer's scouts who had been wounded in the fight." Letter from Burleigh to ex-Governor Faulk, extracts published in *The Dakota Herald* (Yankton), July 22, 1876.

On July 26, Capt. McCaskey, temporary post commander at Fort Lincoln, queried the commanding officer at Fort Stevenson that if the wounded scout "Goose" was convalescent and able to travel, he should be sent to Fort Lincoln. RG 393, Part V, Fort A. Lincoln.

72. Hammer, *Custer in '76,* 177. In an interview July 17, 1910, Hairy Moccasin told Walter Camp that Curley left before Custer and Reno separated. Hardorff, *Camp, Custer, and the Little Big Horn,* 59.

73. *The Tepee Book,* Vol. 2, No. 6, June, 1916, 54–55; Gibbon, *Adventures on the Western Frontier,* 164; Marquis, *Memoirs of a White Crow Indian,* 264. Hairy Moccasin said that after the Crows left Custer and rode back along the bluffs, a dismounted soldier came up the bluffs (a little north of the DeWolf marker) and went with them to the pack train. Hammer, *Custer in '76,* 176–77.

74. Pretty Shield said Half-Yellow-Face was the brother of her father, Crazy-sister-in-law. The census of Crow Agency, 1891–98 (M595, Roll 79), lists Pretty Shield and her father as next-door neighbors, and their ages consistent during this period indicate Pretty Shield was born about 1856, and her father about 1828. (Presumably, Half-Yellow-Face was a younger brother.)

75. Gibbon, *Adventures on the Western Frontier,* 116. Tom Leforge, in Gray, "Captain Clifford's Story of the Sioux War of 1876"; Taylor, notes for "With Custer on the Little Big Horn."

Tom Leforge said Half-Yellow-Face was a man of quietude and wisdom and had a strong influence over his companions. Marquis, *Memoirs of a White Crow Indian,* 236.

76. Gerard in Nichols, *Reno Court,* 85; Hammer, *Custer in '76,* 60, 176. Lieut. Varnum said he took to the Crow's Nest, five Crows, about a dozen Rees for messengers, and Boyer, also Charley Reynolds. Carroll, *Custer's Chief of Scouts,* 62, 87.

77. Libby, *Arikara Narrative,* 92. Pretty Shield (wife of Goes-Ahead), said Half-Yellow-Face and White Swan had not understood and went with Reno by mistake. Linderman, *Pretty Shield,* 244.

78. Libby, *Arikara Narrative,* 99; Liddic and Harbaugh, *Camp on Custer,* 118. Among the spoils found on the Sioux campsite June 27 was a fine elk robe, which from the totems and marks on it, was thought to belong to Sitting Bull. A number of scouts were examined to determine the truth of the rumor that Sitting Bull was among the slain, and Half-Yellow-Face provided the most accurate description of Sitting Bull's physical peculiarities, having known the renowned Sioux medicine man from his youth when he wandered around the boundary of the Crow reservation looking for stray ponies. *The Daily Pioneer Press* (St. Paul), July 21, 1881.

79. When they arrived at the Crow camp, the wife of Half-Yellow-Face ran up to him crying for joy as she put her arms around his neck(he having been reported slain). Half-Yellow-Face caught his breath a number of times but managed to walk along as though unconcerned. Gray, "Captain Clifford's Story of the Sioux War of 1876"; Marquis, *Memoirs of a White Crow Indian,* 254.

80. Marquis, *Memoirs of a White Crow Indian,* 264; Gibbon, *Adventures on the Western Frontier,* 164. Sheridan remarked that Half-Yellow-Face was of no more account than Curley and gave up the idea of obtaining the Indian story of the battle. Graham, *The Custer Myth,* 374.

81. Linderman, *Pretty Shield,* 107, 237–45. Goes-Ahead also showed Pretty Shield where Boyer, Custer, and the "blue horse-soldier that carried his flag" fell into the river.

82. Col. Chas. A. Booth to Walter Camp, March 13, 1911, WMC-BYU. (In June 1876, Booth was Lieutenant in Co. B, 7th Inf., guarding Gibbon's supply camp at mouth of Big Horn River.) Curley told Walter Camp that Half-Yellow-Face died soon after the fight. Hammer, *Custer in '76,* 166.

83. Lieut. Burns' muster roll of Indian Scouts, Fort Lincoln, DT, April 30–June 30, 1876. RG 94, Entry 53. Horns-in-Front is not listed with Indian Scouts on the Post Returns of Fort Lincoln, May 31 and June 30, 1876. NA, M617.

84. Lieut. Varnum's muster roll, June 30, 1876. RG 94, Entry 53. Soldier, Red Star, and Running Wolf said Horns-in-Front was left sick at the base camp. Hammer, *Custer in '76,* 187; Libby, *Arikara Narrative,* 74, 139.

85. Libby, *Arikara Narrative,* 114–15. Little Sioux found Horns-in-Front in camp at Powder River when his group arrived June 28. Ibid., 156.

86. Walter Camp's official list of Indian Scouts revised 8/10/11, WMC-DPL, folder FF17; WMC, rosters, LBHB. Red Star and Running Wolf recalled Howling Wolf was sent back with mail from Rosebud June 22, while Lieut. Varnum reported Howling Wolf detached at Powder River since June 15, and Barking Wolf was mail carrier June 22.

As Red Bear, Red Star, and Running Wolf each declared that Wolf (Cha-ra'-ta [Mandan name]) was retained at the base camp at Powder River, it is presumed Howling Wolf in *The Arikara Narrative* may be Barking Wolf on the muster roll. While the latter is not mentioned in any scout interview, Howling Wolf and Cha-ra-ta are referred to as separate individuals, and if three different scouts put Cha-ra-ta at Powder River, he may be Howling Wolf on the muster roll. Furthermore, with the similarity of names, it seems either scout could be alluded to without the interpreter being aware which one was meant. Thus, it is speculated herein that one was referred to by a Mandan name (see note 44 above).

87. Libby, *Arikara Narrative,* 73–74, 85, 139, 156; Schultz, *Many Strange Characters,* 106–108.

88. Farioli and Nichols, "Fort A. Lincoln July 1876." Lt. Varnum's muster roll June 30 (RG 94, Entry 53), translates Laying Down as "Si-ti-wa-ra," while the Register of Enlistments (NA, M233) shows the translation "Ti-sha," as recorded on his enlistment paper (RG 94, Entry 92).

89. Libby, *Arikara Narrative,* 67. Hammer, *Custer in '76,* 194.

90. Libby, *Arikara Narrative,* 90, 103, 110, 145; Hammer, *Custer in '76,* 185, 192; Hardorff, *Camp, Custer, and the Little Big Horn,* 49. Little Brave was omitted from the initial list of casualties, which reported "Stab" among the Indian scouts killed. Graham, *The Reno Court of Inquiry,* 290; Utley, *The Reno Court of Inquiry,* 27; Nichols, *Reno Court,* 653.

During preparation for inscriptions on the monument planned for Custer Battlefield, Little Brave's name appeared in a list from the Adjutant General's Office, dated Nov. 1, 1878, and marked, "For office use: Has been compared with Official List; with Muster Rolls, and with Final Statements." The names of the three Indian Scouts killed include a side note, "Heyn says these were with Reno." RG 94, Entry 632, Misc. File No. 299.

The AGO furnished their list (endorsed Nov. 2, 1878), of all personnel killed at the Little Big Horn, to General Meigs, Quartermaster General of the Army, who, under date of Feb 8, 1879, inquired of General Terry at Dept. of Dakota headquarters as to certain Indian scouts on the list. Terry referred the inquiry to Col. Sturgis at Fort Lincoln, who returned the letter Feb. 23 with the statement of Fred Gerard, "Bobtailed Bull was an Arickaree, Bloody Knife, half Sioux—half Arickaree, Stab was not killed, but Little Soldier who was, was also an Arickaree."

Terry forwarded the information to Gen. Meigs, March 1st, adding the proposal to substitute the name of Little Soldier for that of Stab. Meigs returned the list to the Adjutant General, March 8, enclosing a copy of Gen. Terry's letter relative to the Indian scouts killed, and noted that the reported death of Stab appeared to be a mistake, "and the name of Little Soldier, who, it seems, was killed in the action referred to, is not included in the list furnished by your office." NA, M666, Roll 273 (file 1517 AGO 1879, filed with 3770 AGO 1876).

Actually, Little Soldier (Whenoch-Chree-pus), though a veteran Arikara scout, was not a member of Lieut. Varnum's detachment, having enlisted in May 1876 at Fort Stevenson, and where he was discharged six months later. NA, M233.

91. Post Returns, Fort Lincoln. NA, M617.

92. Libby, *Arikara Narrative,* 73 n.38, 139, 141, 145.

93. One Feather interview with Walter Camp, Aug. 10, 1911, in Liddic and Harbaugh, *Camp on Custer,* 127–30; and with Orin G. Libby, Aug. 1912, in Libby, *Arikara Narrative,* 203–204.

94. Lieut. Varnum muster roll, June 30. Post Returns, Fort Lincoln, and Lieut. Burns muster roll, report One Horn present from May 19. NA, M617; RG 94, Entry 53; Libby, *Arikara Narrative,* 63, 137; Hammer, *Custer in '76,* 194.

95. Libby, *Arikara Narrative,* 53. Lieut. Varnum muster roll, June 30. Owl not on Post Returns after May 31, and not on Lieut. Burns muster roll, June 30. He is present on Lieut. Varnum's muster roll, August 31. RG 94, Entry 53; NA, M617.

96. Hardorff, *Camp, Custer, and the Little Big Horn,* 49.

97. Watoksu is the Sioux translation of Carrier, but his only and real Indian name is Mahpiya Changleska. Edwin A. Lindsay to Walter Camp, Oct. 30, 1909, WMC-BYU. Curiously, Libby's interview with the Arikara scout Red Bear (Libby, *Arikara Narrative,* 131), refers to one of the Sioux scouts as "Bear-Waiting (Matōksha)," the translation being Sioux for Red Bear.

98. Carrier interview with Walter Camp, May, 1909, WMC-BYU; Hardorff, *Camp, Custer, and the Little Big Horn,* 56–58.

99. Libby, *Arikara Narrative,* 139.

100. Hammer, *Custer in '76,* 183; Hardorff, *Camp, Custer, and the Little Big Horn,* 53, 56–58.

101. Hardorff, *Camp, Custer, and the Little Big Horn,* 58. Lindsay to Walter Camp, Nov. 9, 1909 (Lindsay talked to Carrier same day), WMC-BYU.

102. Hammer, *Custer in '76,* 184–85; Carrier interview, see note 98 above.

103. Libby, *Arikara Narrative,* 131.

104. Carrier interview, *Loc. cit.*

105. Hammer, *Custer in '76,* 190. Watokshu thought Cross went back to Powder River with 'Rees and was not among the first to arrive. WMC-IU, notes, env 135 (Watokshu interview, Aug. 2, 1910 [George Baine, interpreter]).

106. WMC, rosters, LBHB; U.S. Indian Census, NA, M595.

107. One Feather mentioned "Little Crow (Rushing Bull)," and Walter Camp noted on his official list of Indian Scouts revised 8/10/11, "Rushing Bull (dead) (Little Crow—name changed)." Liddic and Harbaugh, *Camp on Custer,* 131.

Camp's list from Boy Chief translates Little Crow (Kapa Ciripas). WMC-BYU, Box 5, env 119. Red Star and Strikes-Two also mentioned Little Crow. Libby, *Arikara Narrative,* 120; Hardorff, *Camp, Custer, and the Little Big Horn,* 53.

108. Libby, *Arikara Narrative,* 85, 130–31.

109. Libby, *Arikara Narrative,* 120. Red Star and Boy Chief said they captured 28 Sioux horses while Strikes Two put the number at 29, including one suckling colt. Libby, *Arikara Narrative,* 119; Hammer, *Custer in '76,* 184. Red Bear said the captured herd numbered about forty. Libby, *Arikara Narrative,* 130.

110. Liddic and Harbaugh, *Camp on Custer,* 129–30.

111. Little Sioux said his brother was Red Wolf (Red Brush), and Bloody Knife and Stabbed were his uncles. Libby, *Arikara Narrative,* 150, 191, 193. Pension file, affidavit of Robert Paint to Stephen Janus, July 11, 1924. RG 15.

112. Hammer, *Custer in '76,* 181, 184. Little Sioux said Custer issued army saddles to scouts who had no saddles.

113. Sioux is listed as a courier to Gen. Terry's expedition on Lieut. Burns muster roll, June 30 (RG 94, Entry 53). Sioux not on Post Returns May through August (NA, M617). Little Sioux did not mention his courier service. Libby, *Arikara Narrative,* 149–56. Hammer, *Custer in '76,* 180–82.

114. Hammer, *Custer in '76,* 180–81, 184, 188–89; Libby, *Arikara Narrative,* 150–54.

115. Libby, *Arikara Narrative,* 155–56.

116. Libby, *Arikara Narrative,* 59, 181.

117. Libby, *Arikara Narrative,* 55–56. Hammer, *Custer in '76,* 188.

118. Libby, *Arikara Narrative,* 116–17, 131, 147–48; Hammer, *Custer in '76,* 185, 190.

119. Hammer, *Custer in '76,* 184, 188.

120. Libby, *Arikara Narrative,* 66.

121. Libby, *Arikara Narrative,* 72–73. Godfrey, *Diary,* 6; Willert, *Little Big Horn Diary,* 99, 105.

122. Libby, *Arikara Narrative,* 84.

123. Libby, *Arikara Narrative,* 118, 130–31, 193; Hammer, *Custer in '76,* 180–85, 189.

124. WMC, rosters, LBHB.

125. Libby, *Arikara Narrative,* 86–93, 119–20.

126. Hammer, *Custer in '76,* 181, 184. Libby, *Arikara Narrative,* 117, 130–31.

127. Strikes-Two said scouts all had infantry rifles with two bands, except Stabbed who had his own gun—a repeater. Hammer, *Custer in '76,* 184.

128. Libby, *Arikara Narrative,* 72, 78, 94.

129. Hardorff, *Camp, Custer, and the Little Big Horn,* 52–53; Hammer, *Custer in '76,* 183–86; Libby, *Arikara Narrative,* 142.

130. Libby, *Arikara Narrative,* 53; Lieut. Varnum muster roll, June 30. Wagon not on Post Returns, May 31 through Aug. 31, and not on Lieut. Burns muster roll, June 30. He is present on Lieut. Varnum's muster roll Aug. 31. RG 94, Entry 53; NA, M617.

131. Libby, *Arikara Narrative,* 141, 145.

132. Hammer, *Custer in '76,* 183.

133. Edwin A. Lindsay to Walter Camp, Nov. 9, 1909. WMC-BYU.

134. Libby, *Arikara Narrative,* 129–30.

135. Hammer, *Custer in '76,* 185, 189–90.

136. See note 3 (Bear).

137. Libby, *Arikara Narrative,* 85, 116–17, 120, 130; Hammer, *Custer in '76,* 188, 190.

138. Graham, *The Custer Myth,* 21.

139. Graham, *The Custer Myth,* 16, 24. White-Man-Runs-Him said that when the 'Ree scouts drove the Sioux horses up on the heights where Custer was, Curley joined them and they saw him no more. Hutchins, *The Papers of Edward S. Curtis,* 52.

In an interview with Gen. Hugh L. Scott in 1919, White-Man-Runs-Him said Curley left the other Crows on Reno Creek.Graham, *The Custer Myth,* 17.

Gen. Woodruff (Lieut., 7th Inf. in 1876 with Gibbon) spent two days in 1908 in the company of the Crow scouts on the field, and with a most capable interpreter, was told that when Curley saw the 'Rees running away, he joined them and went back to Reno Creek. Hutchins, *The Papers of Edward S. Curtis,* 105.

140. Dixon, *The Vanishing Race,* 156–57. Before leaving Reno hill, White-Man-Runs-Him signed to the chief packer they were going to get water and each was given a flat canvas bottle to fill and bring back. Linderman, *Pretty Shield,* 239; White-Man-Runs-Him told Walter Camp that Half-Yellow-Face and White Swan had not come out of the valley when he and Goes Ahead and Hairy Moccasin left Reno. Hammer, *Custer in '76,* 178–79; George Herendeen said Half-Yellow-Face and White Swan were already on Reno hill when he got there. Hammer, *Custer in '76,* 226.

141. *The Tepee Book,* Vol. 2, No. 6, June 1916; Gibbon, *Adventures on the Western Frontier,* 164; Marquis, *Memoirs of a White Crow Indian,* 264.

142. Graham, *The Custer Myth,* 13–24;see Harcey & Croone, *White-Man-Runs-Him.*

143. Pretty Shield, wife of Goes-Ahead, said Half-Yellow-Face and White Swan had not understood and went with Reno by mistake. Linderman, *Pretty Shield,* 244; in "Recollections of a Famous Fight," told by White Swan through an interpreter, "He says that morning when they were galloping out there toward the camp to make the charge he and another Indian were on one side and just as they were there to where two Sioux come from other side and they run right into each other and they run one way and the Sioux the other and the Sioux were hollering and waked the Sioux up and soon as they woke up they got their horses, and they went back to General Custer." *The Tepee Book,* Vol. 1, No. 10, Nov.–Dec. 1915, pp. 26–29.

White Swan told a similar story in an interview in 1894 (J. G. Burgess interpreter). WMC-LBHB, Sec. 79. The last page of White Swan's story was found by Mrs. Burgess and sent to Walter Camp (n.d.). WMC-BYU, Box 2, folder 16.

144. Libby, *Arikara Narrative,* 99; Hammer, *Custer in '76,* 192. Pvt. Seifert said he saw White Swan near the river on the west side standing beside his horse and firing at a half dozen Sioux. He would not mount up to try to get away, but stood and fought. When some men ran down the bluff and fired, the Sioux withdrew. Afterward Half-Yellow-Face helped Seifert get White Swan out of the valley. Liddic and Harbaugh, *Camp On Custer,* 71–72.

145. RG 94, Entry 544, MT, Prescription Book No. 53, reported on July 8 that White Swan "Gone and left us!" Lieut. Bradley left at daylight (July 8) with two men for the Crow camp, and Fort Ellis. Willert, *March of the Columns,* 100; Curley said White Swan stayed at Pease Bottom until his folks came after him. Hammer, *Custer in '76,* 171; General Terry recorded July 7 that, "A party of seven Crows came into camp to-day searching for information of friends who were in the action." Koury, *The Field Diary of General Alfred H. Terry,* 29; Marquis, *Memoirs of a White Crow Indian,* 264.

Pvt. Geant, 7th Inf., wrote July 7, "Two Crow squaws came into camp to look after their bucks in the hospital." Journal of Pvt. Eugene Geant, Co. H, 7th Inf. WMC-BYU.

146. Running Wolf said a white soldier went with this party of scouts, Libby, *Arikara Narrative,* 141. The "soldier" is identified as Wesley Brockmeyer, a scout whom Gen. Terry ordered July 1 to be paid $100 for bringing dispatches from Powder River to Dept. Headquarters at mouth of Big Horn River. SFO 19, Hq DD, July 1, 1876, RG 94, Entry 44. See Gray, "Arikara Scouts with Custer," 465.

147. Gray, "Arikara Scouts With Custer," 464; Libby, *Arikara Narrative,* 135–49. Running Wolf told Walter Camp there were three wolves among the scouts; Red Wolf—Schiri Tipaht; Howling Wolf—Schiri Tiwahua; Running Wolf—Schiri Dunhc. Interview Feb. 6, 1913 (WMC-IU, env. 64).

Red Bear said it was customary for Indians, as with the English, to use two names; Running Wolf was customarily addressed by the 'Rees as simply, Wolf (Ses-che-ree-do-nakh [Running Wolf]). Deposition of Red Bear, June 17, 1925, in pension file of Running Wolf. RG 15.

148. Libby, *Arikara Narrative,* 61, 140. Gen. Custer was very fond of Young Hawk and Goose because they were jolly young fellows, reckless and full of life, and retained them because they had found traces of the Sioux, also he knew Young hawk could shoot well. Walter Camp's interview notes with Young Hawk are found in Hardorff, *Camp, Custer, and the Little Big Horn,* 49–51, 54–56; also in Hammer, *Custer in '76,* 192–94, partly with Camp's interview with Red Bear, a portion of which appears as the first two paragraphs of Camp's interview with Soldier, ibid., 187. See WMC, interview notes, Group 3, Box 4, BYU.

149. Libby, *Arikara Narrative,* 96–102; Hammer, *Custer in '76,* 192. Young Hawk related that, while in the brush, "On the ridge above me on the highest point I saw a United States flag." Capt. Benteen described how he left the guidon of Co. H standing on the highest point for Custer to see. Nichols, *Reno Court,* 423, 428; Graham, *The Custer Myth,* 195.

150. Libby, *Arikara Narrative,* 113–15, 145, 149.

Addendum

Ashton, Isaiah H. Actg asst surg; b. 13 Nov 1848 Byberry (Phil'a) Pa; entered mil contr 22 Mar 1876 as actg asst surg in dept of Dakota; arr Ft Lincoln 27 Apr for duty with gen Terry's exp'n; assd to inf battn [cos C & G 17 inf] 14 May; accomp sick men to Yellowstone River 8 June & assd to field hosp at camp mouth of Powder River; accomp Dr. Porter with wd on str *Far West* 3 July to Ft Lincoln; returned to Powder River camp 17 July on *Far West*; chg of sick sol.'s on str *Carroll* 2 Aug to Ft Lincoln; contr annulled 16 Aug his serv no longer required (char good, efficiency not satisfactory); died 16 Feb 1889 Dobbs Ferry NY.

Clark, Elbert Judson. Actg asst surg; b. 6 Sep 1847 Java NY; moved to Pecatonica Ill ca. 1856; pvt co C 146 Ill inf July 1864 to June 1865; began med study with hometown doctor in spring 1868 & that fall attended med lectures in Chicago; grad Chicago Medical College in June 1871; entered mil contr 11 July 1871 as actg asst surg in dept of Dakota; post surg Grand River Agcy to 15 Oct 1872 when contr annulled upon own req; entered new contr 23 Mar 1874 as actg asst surg at Cheyenne Agcy DT; arr Ft Lincoln 13 Apr 1876 for duty with gen Terry's exp'n; assd to left wing 7 cav (cos ADGHKM) 5 May; chg of field hosp at camp mouth of Powder River 15 June to 21 July; chg of hosp at camp mouth of Rosebud Creek 8 Aug & removed to Powder River 21 Aug & to Glendive Creek 6 Sep; sick in field hosp 11–26 Sep; with escort for wagon train to Tongue River Cant'mt to 28 Oct when ordered to rejoin Cheyenne Agcy; contr annulled 15 June 1877 upon own req; died 7 May 1921 Cleveland Ohio.[1]

Dale, Alfred W. Hosp stew'd USA; b. 26 May 1849 Lehighton Pa; enl as Alfred Dormitzer 21 Oct 1869 New York NY for 5 yrs; age 22; clerk; brn eyes, blk hair, dk comp, 5' 7" high; assd to co B 22 inf; sen gen cm 25 Jan 1872 to dishon disch & 2 yrs conft in prison Stillwater Minn (embezzled subs stores); sen remitted 6 Dec 1872 upon appn of family & friends & recom'n of co comdr; enl as Alfred W. Dale 13 Dec 1872 Ft Snelling Minn for 5 yrs; assd to co G 20 inf; appt hosp stew'd 14 Feb 1876 Ft Ripley Minn; arr Ft Lincoln 20 Mar for duty with gen Terry's exp'n; with dept hq as exec stew'd with Dr. Williams 14 May to 9 Sep; (on str *Far West* 22 June to 3 July); arr Ft Rice DT 21 Sep with Dr. Williams & pvt Ryder; disch 13 Dec 1877 Lower Brulé Agcy upon expir of serv a hosp stew'd char very good & reenl for 5 yrs; disch 12 Dec 1882 Ft Hale DT by expir of serv a hosp stew'd char xclt (his efficiency of the highest order); died 6 May 1926 Sioux City Ia.[2]
Pension: 12 July 1921 / Ind. Surv. / 17992 / 12066.

Rhinehart, Jos. H. Hosp stew'd USA; b. 1 Nov 1849 Cincinnati Ohio; enl 23 Feb 1867 at Cincinnati for 3 yrs; age 18; clerk; blue eyes, lt hair, fair comp, 5' 6 1/2" high; assd to co I 22 inf; tr to co A; disch 23 Feb 1870 Ft Sully DT by expir of serv a mus'n; attended Miami Medical College at Cincinnati & tr to Starling Medical College at Columbus; grad Ohio Medical College at Cincinnati in 1873; reenl in army 24 Mar 1874 at Ft Snelling Minn for 5 yrs; blue eyes, chestnut hair, fair comp, 5' 10" high; assd to co G 20 inf; appt hosp stew'd 16 Feb 1876 Ft Ripley Minn; arr Ft Lincoln 20 Mar for duty with gen Terry's exp'n; assd to field hosp at camp mouth of Powder River 15 June; return to Ft Lincoln 20 Sep; assd to Ft Custer MT 17 Apr 1877 & in field with battn 11 inf May 1877; disch 24 Mar 1879 at Ft Custer by expir of serv a hosp stew'd & reenl for 5 yrs; on furl 6 mos 20 Sep 1879 at Cincinnati to attend med lectures; disch 24 Mar 1884 Columbus Bks Ohio by expir of serv a hosp stew'd char xclt;

entered pvt med practice at Billings MT; also coroner, supt of schools, & mayor; died 31 Dec 1908.³

Stone, Henry A. Pvt co E; b. Brooklyn N.Y.; enl 5 July 1876 Chicago Ill for 5 yrs; age 28; bookkeeper; grey eyes, blk hair, dk comp, 5' 8 1/2" high; join co E 3 Aug 1876 mouth of Rosebud Creek MT; ds chg co prop 11 Aug Yellowstone River [with Reese];⁴ ds Ft Lincoln DT 16 Oct chg co prop; cpl 15 Feb 1877; ds Ft Lincoln chg co prop Apr thro' Dec 1877; (sgt June 1877); in arrest Feb 1878; restored to duty 21 Mar 1878 sen gen cm; dd adjts office Apr 1878; tr to gen serv 5 June 1878; disch 15 June 1878 St Paul Minn (serv no longer required), a pvt char xclt.

Sturla, Sam'l R. Pvt co F; b. London England; enl 4 Sep 1876 Detroit Mich for 5 yrs; age 25; salesman; brn eyes, brn hair, fair comp, 5' 6 1/4" high; join co F 28 Sep 1876 Ft Lincoln DT; dd co clerk Dec 1876 & Feb 1877; dd co clerk Apr 1881 to 3 Sep 1881 when disch at Camp Biddle MT by expir of serv a pvt char xclt.⁵

Williams, Jno. Winfield. Capt & asst surg; b. 8 Dec 1839 Wash'n DC later removed to Gainesville Miss; grad Natl Medical College (Wash'n DC) 20 Feb 1861; entered mil serv as 1Lt & asst surg 11 July 1862; chg of Trinity hosp at Wash'n Oct to Nov 1862 & with co I 1 art to May 1863; with 1 cav gen Buford's div to Aug 1863; bvt capt 18 Aug 1863 for gal serv at Berryville Va; with 2 cav thro' Aug 1864; surg in chf 1 cav div 3 Sep 1864; bvt maj 13 Mar 1865 for meritorious serv dur the war; on duty at Jarvis hosp Baltimore Md Mar to July 1865 & Ft McHenry to Sep 1865; with 8 inf at Charleston SC May 1866; chg of post hosp & smallpox quarantine at Hilton Head SC June 1866; capt & asst surg 28 July 1866; chg of post hosp Raleigh NC Jan 1868; post surg McPherson Bks (Atlanta) Ga Aug 1868; post surg Charleston SC Nov 1869; post surg Ft Sullivan (Eastport) Me June 1870; post surg Ft Rice DT from 23 Oct 1872; chf med officer Blk Hills Exp'n June to Sep 1874; awl 4 mos 26 Oct 1875 & at Ft Columbus NYH to 3 May 1876; arr Ft Lincoln DT with gen Terry & staff 10 May; chf med officer of gen Terry's exp'n 14 May to 9 Sep 1876; (return to Ft Rice 21 Sep with hosp stew'd Dale & pvt Ryder); at Wash'n DC ars'l 30 Oct 1876; maj & surg 8 Nov 1877; post surg Ft Sill IT June 1878; post surg Ft Couer d'Alene Ida Ty Oct 1882; post surg Ft Walla Walla WT Mar 1883; awl 6 mos on surg cert 1 Nov 1883; post surg Vancouver Bks WT Mar 1886; post surg Jackson Bks (New Orleans) La Dec 1886; died 15 Apr 1889 at Jackson Bks.
Pension: 28 June 1889 / Wid / 398856 / 262702.

Notes—Addendum

1. *Rockford Register-Gazette,* May 9, 1921; *Pecatonica News,* May 13, 1921. See also, Church, *Historical Encyclopedia of Illinois and History of Winnebago County,* vol. 2, 1023.

2. Dale declared that he left home at age thirteen and lived some years with a family named Dale. He said his middle initial "W" was used as ornament only. Dale to Commissioner of Pensions, June 16, 1924. Pension file RG 15. See, "Sketches of the Frontier," by Lee Noyes, *The Battlefield Dispatch,* (Custer Battlefield Historical & Museum Association), vol. 20, no. 2, Spring 2001.

3. See, *Medicine in the Making of Montana,* written by Paul C. Phillips from his own researches and The Pioneer Manuscripts of Llewellyn L. Callaway.

4. It is odd that responsibility for company property was given a new man just joined, rather than someone longer with the troop or who had been with the company property at Powder River during June and July.

5. Handwriting on the muster rolls of Company F, August 1876, and December 1876 through August 1881, appears to be in the distinctive backward slant style of Pvt. Sturla. See also note G35 (Gregg).

Appendices

TABLE A.1.
Tabulation (Approximate) of Enlisted Men

	Present and Absent May 17	Total absent on May 17	Left at Powder River June 15	Present at Rosebud June 22	Killed on June 25–26	Wounded on June 25–26	Present on Reno Hill June 27	Names on Reno Petition July 4
NCS	5	—	3	2	2	—	—	—
Band	16	3	13	—	—	—	—	—
Co. A	58	7	4	47	8	7	39	27
B	71	5	19	47	2	2	43	38
C	66	6	9	51	36	4	14	7
D	65	4	11	50	3	2	47	41
E	61	7	?e	?e	37	1	?e	6
F	68	7	?e	?e	36	—	?e	7
G	65	6	16	43	13	5	29	3
H	55	8	3a	45	3	19	42	31
I	65	11	4	50	36	1	10	3
K	68	6	20a	41	5	3	35	33
L	67	4	6	57	44	1	11	5
M	64	3	4	57	12	10	43	34
Total	**794**	**77**	**130**b	**587**c	**237**	**55**d	**329**	**235**f

a Pvt. Charles Fisher transferred from Co. K to Co. H June 14, effective July 1.
b Dr. Elbert J. Clark, in charge of the field hospital at Powder River, reported the detachment of 7th Cavalry at the camp numbered about 130. Monthly Report, July 1876, RG 94, Entry 561.
c Approximately twenty troopers were detached June 22 to Gen. Terry and the steamer *Far West*.
d The Classified Return of Wounds, prepared by Dr. Williams, chief medical officer, lists 59 wounded enlisted men, including Herod T. Liddiard, Andrew J. Moore, Geo. Lell, and Jas. J. Tanner, who died of their wounds on Reno Hill. RG 94, Entry 624.
e Records of Cos. E & F are incomplete, not showing any men detached at the supply camp on Powder River, though it is known all companies left at least a few men to guard company property. In addition, Co. F is known to have had a number of dismounted men.
f Five troopers on the petition did not participate in the battle: Pvts. Fisher & Walter, Co. H; Pvt. Coakley, Co. K; Pvts. Miles & Sterland, Co. M.

Appendix A

Rosters of the 7th Cavalry, June 1876

An asterisk (*) before a name indicates the soldier probably did not participate in the battle. A raised sword (†) after a name denotes the soldier's signature appears on the Reno Petition (see Introduction and notes 1 and 2).

Field, Staff, and Band

Col	*Sam'l D. Sturgis
Maj	*Jos. G. Tilford
"	*Lewis Merrill
"	Marcus A. Reno
1st Lt & RQM	*Henry J. Nowlan
Attached Actg Asst Surg	Henry R. Porter

Killed in Action

Lt-Col	Geo. A. Custer
1st Lt & Adjt	Wm. W. Cooke
Attached 2d Lt (20th Inf)	Jno. J. Crittenden
" Asst Surg (1st Lt)	Geo. E. Lord
" Actg Asst Surg	Jas. M. DeWolf

Noncommissioned Staff and Band

QM Sgt	*Thos. W. Causby
Saddler Sgt	*Jno. G. Tritten
Chief Mus'n	*Felix Vinatieri
Attached Comsy Sgt	*Chas. Brown

Appendix A

Band

Pvt *Arndt, Otto
" *Baumbach, Conrad
" *Beck, Benj.
" *Burlis, Edm.
" *Carroll, Jos.
" *Carter, Andrew
" *Eixenberger, Peter
" *Emerich, Jacob

Pvt *Griesner, Julius
" *Jungesbluth, Julius C.
" *Kneubuhler, Jos.
" *Lombard, Frank
" *Merritt, Geo. A.
" *O'Neill, Bernard
" *Rudolph, Geo.
" *Sherborne, Thos.

Vet'y Surg *Chas. A. Stein

Killed in Action

Sgt-Maj   Wm. H. Sharrow
Chief Trump'r   Henry Voss

Appendix A

Company A

Capt	Moylan, Myles	Pvt	Conner, Andrew†
2d Lt	Varnum, Chas. A.	"	*Coveney, Mich'l
1st Sgt	Heyn, Wm.	"	Cowley, Cornelius
Sgt	Fehler, Henry†	"	Deihle, Jacob
"	*Alcott, Sam'l	"	Durselew, Otto†
"	*Corwine, Rich'd	"	Foster, Sam'l
"	McDermott, Geo.†	"	Franklin, Jno. W.†
"	Culbertson, Ferd. A.†	"	Gilbert, Jno. M.†
"	Easley, Jno. T.†	"	Harris, David
Cpl	*Cody, Jno. F.	"	Holmsted, Fred'k
"	Roy, Stanislas†	"	Hook, Stanton†
"	King, Geo. H.	"	Johnson, Sam'l†
Trump'r	Hardy, Wm. G.†	"	Jonson, Emil O.†
"	McVeigh, David†	"	*Kerr, Denis
Farrier	Bringes, Jno.†	"	*Lamb, Jno.
Blks	Hamilton, Andrew†	"	McClurg, Wm.†
Saddler	Muering, Jno.	"	Nugent, Wm. D.†
Pvt	Aller, Chas.†	"	Proctor, Geo. W.†
"	Bancroft, Neil†	"	*Ragsdale, Jno. S.
"	Baumgartner, Louis†	"	Reeves, Francis M.
"	Blair, Wilbur F.†	"	Seayers, Thos.†
"	Blake, Thos.†	"	Seibelder, Anton†
"	*Bockerman, August	"	Strode, Elijah T.
"	*Borter, Ludwig	"	Taylor, Wm. O.†
"	Bott, Geo.	"	Weaver, Howard H.
"	*Burdick, Benj. F.	"	*Weis, Jno.

Killed in Action

1st Lt	Algernon E. Smith	Pvt	Wm. Moody
Cpl	Jas. Dalious	"	Rich'd Rollins
Pvt	Jno. E. Armstrong	"	Jno. Sullivan
"	Jas. Drinan	"	Thos. P. Sweetser
"	Jas. McDonald		

Appendix A

Company B

Capt	McDougall, Thos. M.	Pvt	Crowley, Pat'k†
1st Lt.	*Craycroft, Wm. T.	"	Davenport, Wm. H.†
1st Sgt	Hill, Jas.†	"	*Detourriel, Louis
Sgt	*Gannon, Peter	"	Devoto, Augustus L.†
"	Hutchinson, Rufus D.†	"	*Doll, Jacob W.
"	*Carroll, Dan'l	"	Frank, Wm.†
"	Murray, Thos.†	"	*Gehrmann, Fred'k
"	Criswell, Benj. C.†	"	*Gray, Jno. R.
Cpl	Dougherty, Jas.†	"	*Keefe, Jno. J.
"	Cunningham, Chas.†	"	*Klawitter, Ferd.
"	Smith, Wm. M.	"	*Lewis, David W.
"	Wetzel, Adam†	"	*Littlefield, Jno. L.
Trump'r	*Connell, Jno.	"	Martin, Wm.†
"	Kelly, Jas.	"	McCabe, Jno.†
Farrier	Moore, Jas. E.†	"	*McGurn, Bernard
Blks	Crump, Jno.†	"	McLaughlin, Terence†
Saddler	Bailey, Jno. A.†	"	McMasters, Wm.†
Pvt	*Abos. Jas. A.	"	*Morrow, Wm. E.
"	*Barry, Peter O.	"	*O'Brien, Thos.
"	Barsantee, Jas. F.	"	*O'Neill, Jas.
"	Boam, Wm.	"	O'Neill, Jno.†
"	*Bonner, Hugh	"	Pym, Jas.†
"	Boren, Ansgarius†	"	Randall, Geo. F.†
"	*Brainard, Geo.	"	Ryan, Stephen L.†
"	*Brown, Jas.	"	Sager, Hiram W.†
"	*Burns, Chas.	"	Shea, Dan'l†
"	*Caldwell, Wm.	"	*Simons, Pat'k
"	*Callan, Jas.	"	Spinner, Phillip†
"	Callan, Thos. J.	"	Stout, Edw.†
"	Campbell, Chas. A.†	"	Thomas, Jas.†
"	Carmody, Thos.†	"	*Tinkham, Henry L.
"	Carey, Jno. J.†	"	Trumble, Wm.†
"	Clark, Frank†	"	Wallace, Rich'd A.†
"	Coleman, Thos. W.†	"	*Wight, Edwin B.
"	Criswell, Harry†	"	Woods, Aaron†
"	Crowe, Mich'l†		

Killed in Action

2d Lt	Benj. H. Hodgson
Pvt	Rich'd Dorn
"	Geo. B. Mask

352

Appendix A

Company C

Sgt	*Miller, Edwin	Pvt	Jordan, Jno.†
"	Knipe, Dan'l†	"	*Kane, Wm.
"	Hanley, Rich'd P.	"	*Lovett, Meredith
Cpl	*Crandall, Chas. A.	"	Mahoney, Jno.†
Farrier	Fitzgerald, Jno.	"	*McCreedy, Thos.
Wagoner	*Stark, Frank	"	McGuire, Jno.
Pvt	*Anderson, Chas. L.	"	Mullin, Martin†
"	*Arnold, Herbert	"	*Nitsche, Ottocar
"	Bennett, Jas. C.	"	*Orr, Chas. M.
"	*Bischoff, Chas. C.	"	Thompson, Peter
"	*Brandal, Wm.	"	*Vahlert, Jacob
"	Brennan, Jno.†	"	*Von Arnim, Julius
"	*Corcoran, Jno.	"	*Walker, Jno.
"	Farrer, Morris†	"	Watson, Jas.
"	Fowler, Isaac†	"	Whittaker, Alfred

Killed in Action

Capt	Thos. W. Custer	Pvt	Jas. Hathersall
1st Lt	Jas. Calhoun	"	Jno. Lewis
2d Lt	Henry M. Harrington	"	Fred'k Meier
1st Sgt	Edwin Bobo	"	August Meyer
Sgt	Jeremiah Finley	"	Edgar Phillips
"	August Finckle	"	Jno. Rauter
Cpl	Henry E. French	"	Edw. Rix
"	Jno. Foley	"	Jas. H. Russell
"	Dan'l Ryan	"	Sam'l S. Shade
Trump'r	Thos. J. Bucknell	"	Jeremiah Shea
"	Wm. Kramer	"	Nathan Short
Blks	Jno. King	"	Ludwick St. John
Saddler	Geo. Howell	"	Alpheus Stuart
Pvt	Fred E. Allan	"	Ignatz Stungewitz
"	Jno. Brightfield	"	Jno. Thadus
"	Christopher Criddle	"	Garret Van Allen
"	Geo. Eisemann	"	Oscar Warner
"	Gustave Engel	"	Willis B. Wright
"	Jas. Farrand	"	Henry Wyman
"	Pat'k Griffin		

Appendix A

Company D

Capt	Weir, Thos. B.	Pvt	Harris, Wm. M.†
1st Lt	*Bell, Jas. M.	"	Hetler, Jacob
2d Lt	Edgerly, Winfield S.	"	Holden, Henry†
1st Sgt	Martin, Mich'l†	"	Horn, Geo.†
Sgt	*Morton, Thos.	"	Houghtaling, Chas. H.†
"	Harrison, Thos. W.†	"	Hunt, Geo.†
"	Flanagan, Jas.†	"	Hurd, Jas.†
"	Russell, Thos.†	"	Kavanagh, Jno.
Cpl	*Cunningham, Albert J.	"	Keller, Jno.†
"	Wylie, Geo. W.†	"	Kipp, Fremont†
Trump'r	Bohner, Aloys†	"	Kretchmer, Jos.†
Blks	Deetline, Fred'k†	"	*Kuehl, Jesse
Saddler	Meyers, Jno.†	"	*Lewis, Uriah S.
Pvt	Alberts, Jas. H.†	"	Manning, David†
"	Ascough, Jno. B.†	"	Marshall, Wm. A.†
"	Brant, Abram B.†	"	McDonnell, Pat'k
"	*Conlan, Thos.	"	Meadwell, Jno.
"	*Cowley, Stephen	"	*Mueller, Wm.
"	Cox, Thos.	"	Oman, Wm.†
"	Dann, Geo.†	"	*Quinn, Jno.
"	Dawsey, David E.	"	Randall, Wm. J.†
"	*Day, Clarence F.	"	Reid, Elwyn S.†
"	Fay, Jno. J.†	"	*Sadler, Wm.
"	*Fox, Harvey A.	"	Sanders, Chas.†
"	Fox, Jno.†	"	Scott, Geo.†
"	*Green, Jno.	"	*Sims, Jno. J.
"	Green, Jos. H.†	"	Smith, Henry G.†
"	Hager, Jno.†	"	Smith, Wm. E.†
"	Hall, Curtis†	"	Stivers, Thos. W.†
"	*Hall, Edw.	"	Tolan, Frank†
"	Hardden, Wm.†	"	Welch, Chas. H.†
"	*Harlfinger, Gustave	"	Wynn, Jas.†
"	Harris, Jas.†		

Killed in Action

Farrier	Vincent Charley
Pvt	Pat'k Golden
"	Edw. Housen

Appendix A

Company E

Capt	*Ilsley, Chas. S.	Pvt	*Chapman, Wm. H.
1st Lt	DeRudio, Chas. C.	"	*Gilbert, Julius
Sgt	*Wells, Jno. S.	"	*Howard, Frank
"	Riley, Jas. T.	"	*Hutter, Anton
"	*Murphy, Lawrence	"	James, Jno.
Farrier	Spencer, Abel B.†	"	Kimm, Jno. G.
Blks	Miller, Henry†	"	Lange, Henry†
Saddler	Shields, Wm.†	"	*McCann, Pat'k
Pvt	Abbotts, Harry	"	McKenna, Jno.
"	*Ackison, David	"	*O'Toole, Francis
"	Berwald, Frank†	"	*Pandtle, Christopher
"	*Bromwell, Latrobe	"	Reese, Wm.†
"	*Bruns, August	"	*Woodruff, Jerry

Killed in Action

1st Sgt	Fred'k Hohmeyer	Pvt	Sykes Henderson
Sgt	Jno. S. Ogden	"	Jno. S. Hiley
"	Wm. B. James	"	Wm. Huber
Cpl	Thos. Hagan	"	Andy Knecht
"	Henry S. Mason	"	Herod T. Liddiard
"	George C. Brown	"	Pat'k O'Connor
"	Albert H. Meyer	"	Wm. H. Rees
Trump'r	Thos. McElroy	"	Edw. Rood
"	Geo. A. Moonie	"	Henry Schele
Pvt	Wm. H. Baker	"	Wm. Smallwood
"	Robt. Barth	"	Albert A. Smith
"	Owen Boyle	"	Jas. Smith [1st]
"	Jas. Brogan	"	Jas. Smith [2d]
"	Edw. Connor	"	Benj. Stafford
"	Jno. Darris	"	Alexander Stella
"	Wm. Davis	"	Wm. A. Torrey
"	Rich'd Farrell	"	Cornelius Van Sant
"	Jno. Heim	"	Geo. Walker
"	Jno. Henderson		

Appendix A

Company F

1st Lt	*Jackson, Henry	Pvt	*Klein, Nicholas
2d Lt	*Larned, Chas. W.	"	Lefler, Meig†
Sgt	Curtiss, Wm. A.†	"	*Lynch, Dennis
"	*Drago, Henry	"	Lyons, Bernard†
Cpl	*Clyde, Edw.	"	*Meinike, Ernst
Saddler	Schlieper, Claus	"	*Millton, Jos.
Pvt	*Brown, Hiram E.	"	Meyers, Frank
"	*Butler, Jas. W.	"	Pickard, Edwin H.†
"	Davern, Edw.	"	*Pilcher, Albert
"	*Downing, Alexander	"	*Reiley, Mich'l
"	*Eades, Wm.	"	Rooney, Jas. M.†
"	Finnegan, Thos. J.	"	*Schleiffarth, Paul
"	Gregg, Wm. J.	"	Schutte, Fred'k†
"	*Harris, Leonard A.	"	Sweeney, Jno. W.†
"	*Hegner, Francis	"	*Sweeney, Wm.
"	Howard, Frank	"	*Thorp, Mich'l
"	Hunter, Frank	"	Walsh, Thos.

Killed in Action

Capt	Geo. W. Yates	Pvt	Anton Dohman
2d Lt	Wm. Van W. Reily	"	Timothy Donnelly
1st Sgt	Mich'l Kenney	"	Wm. Gardner
Sgt	Fred'k Nursey	"	Geo. W. Hammon
"	Jno. Vickory	"	Jno. Kelly
"	Jno. K. Wilkison	"	Gustave Klein
Cpl	Chas. Coleman	"	Herman Knauth
"	Wm. Teeman	"	Wm. A. Lossee
"	Jno. Briody	"	Wm. H. LaRock
Farrier	Benj. Brandon	"	Werner L. Liemann
Blks	Jas. R. Manning	"	Christian Madsen
Pvt	Thos. Atchison	"	Francis E. Milton
"	Wm. Brady	"	Jos. Monroe
"	Pat'k Bruce	"	Sebastian Omling
"	Benj. F. Brown	"	Pat'k Rudden
"	Wm. Brown	"	Rich'd Saunders
"	Lucian Burnham	"	Francis W. Sicfous
"	Jas. Carney	"	Geo. Warren
"	Armantheus Cather	"	Thos. N. Way

Appendix A

Company G

Capt	*Tourtellotte, Jno. E.	Pvt	*Laden, Jos.
2d Lt	Wallace, Geo. D.	"	Lattman, Jno.
1st Sgt	*Garlick, Edw.	"	*Lauper, Frank
Sgt	Brown, Alexander	"	*Lawler, Jas.
"	Northeg, Olans H.†	"	Loyd, Geo.
"	*Lloyd, Frank	"	McCormick, Sam'l
Cpl	Hammon, Jno. E.	"	McDonnell, Jno.
"	Akers, Jas.	"	McEagan, Jno.
Trump'r	*Carter, Cassius R.	"	McGonigal, Hugh
Blks	Taylor, Walter O.	"	*McKay, Edw. J.
Pvt	*Barnett, Chas.	"	*McKee, Jno.
"	Boyle, Jas. P.	"	McVay, Jno.
"	Brinkerhoff, Henry	"	Morrison, Jno.
"	Campbell, Chas.	"	O'Neill, Thos. F.
"	*Crussy, Melanchton H.	"	Petring, Henry
"	Dwyer, Edm.	"	Reed, Jno. A.
"	*Flood, Phillip	"	Robb, Eldorado J.
"	*Geist, Frank G.	"	*Rowland, Robt.
"	Goldin, Theo. W.†	"	*Shanahan, Jno.
"	Graham, Thos.	"	Small, Jno. R.
"	*Gray, Wm. S.	"	*Stephens, Geo. W.
"	Grayson, Edw.	"	Stevenson, Thos.
"	Hackett, Jno.	"	*Sullivan, Dan'l
"	*Henderson, Geo. W.	"	*Tulo, Jos.
"	Johnson, Benj.	"	Wallace, Jno. W.†
"	*Katzenmaier, Jacob	"	Weiss, Markus
"	*Kilfoyle, Martin	"	*Williamson, Pasavan

Killed in Action

1st Lt	Donald McIntosh	Saddler	Crawford Selby
Sgt	Edw. Botzer	Pvt	Jno. J. McGinnis
"	Martin Considine	"	Andrew J. Moore
Cpl	Jas. Martin	"	Jno. Rapp
"	Otto Hagemann	"	Benj. F. Rogers
Trump'r	Henry C. Dose	"	Henry Seafferman
Farrier	Benj. Wells	"	Edw. Stanley

357

Appendix A

Company H

Capt	Benteen, Fred'k W.	Pvt	Glease, Geo. W.†
1st Lt	Gibson, Frank M.	"	Haack, Henry†
1st Sgt	McCurry, Jos.†	"	Haley, Timothy†
Sgt	Conelly, Pat'k†	"	*Hood, Chas. N.
"	Pahl, Jno.	"	Hughes, Thos.†
"	McLaughlin, Thos.†	"	Hunt, Jno.†
"	Maroney, Mathew†	"	Kelley, Geo.
"	Geiger, Geo.†	"	Kelly, Jas.†
Cpl	Nealon, Dan'l†	"	*Lambertin, Frank
"	Bishop, Alex. B.	"	Lawhorn, Thos.†
Trump'r	Martin, Jno.†	"	McDermott, Thos.†
"	Ramell, Wm.†	"	McNamara, Jas.†
Farrier	*Marshall, Jno. M.	"	*McWilliams, David
Blks	Mechlin, Henry W. B.†	"	Moller, Jan
Saddler	Voit, Otto†	"	*Muller, Jno.
Pvt	Adams, Jacob†	"	Nees, Edler†
"	*Avery, Chas. E.	"	Nicholas, Joshua S.†
"	Bishley, Henry†	"	O'Ryan, Wm.†
"	Bishop, Chas. H.	"	Phillips, Jno.
"	Black, Henry	"	Pinkston, Jno. S.
"	Channell, Wm.†	"	*Pittet, Francis
"	Cooper, Jno.	"	Severs, Sam'l
"	Day, Jno.†	"	*Taply, David
"	Dewey, Geo. W.†	"	*Walsh, Mich'l J.
"	Diamond, Edw.†	"	*Walter, Aloyse L.†
"	Farley, Wm.	"	Williams, Wm. C.†
"	George, Wm.	"	Windolph, Chas.†

Killed in Action

Cpl	Geo. Lell
Pvt	Julien D. Jones
"	Thos. E. Meador

Appendix A

Company I

2d Lt	*Nave, Andrew H.	Pvt	Johnson, Francis†
Sgt	DeLacy, Milton J.†	"	Jones, Henry P.
"	*Gaffney, Geo.	"	Korn, Gustave
"	*Murphy, Robt. L.	"	*Lee, Mark E.
"	*Caddle, Mich'l C.	"	*Lynch, Pat'k
Cpl	*McCall, Jos.	"	*McGinnis, Jno.
Farrier	*Rivers, Jno.	"	McNally, Jas. P.
Saddler	*Hayward, Geo.	"	McShane, Jno.†
Pvt	Braun, Franz C.	"	*Miller, Wm. E.
"	Cooney, David	"	*Myers, Fred
"	*Farber, Conrad	"	Owens, Eugene
"	*Fox, Fred'k	"	*Porter, Jno.
"	*Geesbacher, Gabriel	"	Ramsey, Chas.
"	*Grimes, Andrew	"	*Saas, Wm.
"	*Haack, Chas. L.	"	*Thomas, Herbert P.

Killed in Action

Capt	Myles W. Keogh	Pvt	Marion E. Horn
1st Lt	Jas. E. Porter	"	Pat'k H. Kelly
1st Sgt	Frank E. Varden	"	Fred'k Lehman
Sgt	Jas. Bustard	"	Henry Lehmann
Cpl	Jno. Wild	"	Edw. W. Lloyd
"	Geo. C. Morris	"	Arch'd McIlhargey
"	Sam'l F. Staples	"	Jno. E. Mitchell
Trump'r	Jno. McGucker	"	Jacob Noshang
"	Jno. W. Patton	"	Jno. O'Bryan
Blks	Henry A. Bailey	"	Jno. Parker
Pvt	Jno. Barry	"	Felix J. Pitter
"	Jos. F. Broadhurst	"	Geo. Post
"	Thos. Connors	"	Jas. Quinn
"	Thos. P. Downing	"	Wm. Reed
"	Edw. Driscoll	"	Jno. W. Rossbury
"	David C. Gillette	"	Darwin L. Symms
"	Geo. H. Gross	"	Jas. E. Troy
"	Adam Hetesimer	"	Chas. Von Bramer
"	Edw. P. Holcomb	"	Wm. B. Whaley

Appendix A

Company K

Rank	Name	Rank	Name
Capt	*Hale, Owen	Pvt	Foley, Jno.†
1st Lt	Godfrey, Edw. S.	"	Gibbs, Wm.†
2d Lt	Hare, Luther R.	"	Gordon, Thos. A.†
Sgt	Rott, Louis†	"	*Green, Thos.
"	Frederick, Andrew†	"	*Gunther, Julius
"	Campbell, Jeremiah†	"	*Holohan, Andrew
"	Rafter, Jno.†	"	*Horner, Jacob
Cpl	Hose, Geo.†	"	*Hoyt, Walter
"	*Nolan, Jno.	"	Jennys, Alonzo†
"	*Murray, Henry	"	Lasley, Wm. W.†
Trump'r	Penwell, Geo. B.†	"	*Lieberman, Andrew
"	Schlafer, Christian†	"	*Lyons, Dan'l
Farrier	Steintker, Jno.†	"	Madden, Mich'l P.
Blks	Burke, Edm. H.†	"	McConnell, Wilson†
Saddler	Boissen, Christian†	"	McCue, Martin†
Wagoner	*Whytefield, Albert	"	Mielke, Max
Pvt	*Ackerman, Chas.	"	Murphy, Mich'l†
"	*Anderson, Geo.	"	Murphy, Thos.†
"	*Bauer, Jacob	"	*Ragan, Mich'l
"	*Blair, Jas. C.	"	Raichel, Henry W.†
"	Blunt, Geo.†	"	*Reilly, Mich'l
"	Bresnahan, Cornelius†	"	Robers, Jonathan†
"	Brown, Jos.†	"	*Roth, Francis
"	*Burgdorf, Chas.	"	Schwerer, Jno.†
"	Burkhardt, Chas.†	"	Siefert, August†
"	Chesterwood, Chas.†	"	Shauer, Jno.†
"	*Coakley, Pat'k	"	*Smith, Fred'k
"	Corcoran, Pat'k	"	*Taube, Emil
"	*Crawford, Wm. L.	"	*Van Pelt, Wm. E.
"	*Delaney, Mich'l	"	Wasmus, Ernst†
"	Donahue, Jno.†	"	Whitlow, Wm.†
"	*Dooley, Pat'k	"	*Wilson, Geo. A.
"	*Fisher, Chas.†	"	*Witt, Henry

Killed in Action

Rank	Name
1st Sgt	DeWitt Winney
Sgt	Robt. H. Hughes
Cpl	Jno. J. Callahan
Pvt	Elihue F. Clear
"	Julius Helmer

Appendix A

Company L

Capt	*Sheridan, Mich'l V.	Pvt	*Hoehn, Max
1st Lt	*Braden, Chas.	"	*Keegan, Mich'l
Sgt	*Bender, Henry	"	*Lepper, Fred'k
"	*Findeisen, Hugo	"	Logue, Wm. J.
"	Mullen, Jno.	"	Marshall, Jasper
Cpl	*Nunan, Jno.	"	*McHugh, Phillip
Pvt	Abrams, Wm. G.†	"	*McPeake, Alexander
"	Banks, Chas.†	"	Moore, Lansing A.
"	Brown, Nathan T.	"	Rose, Peter E.†
"	Burkman, Jno.	"	*Sprague, Otto
"	*Colwell, Jno. R.	"	Stoffel, Henry†
"	*Conlan, Mich'l	"	Sullivan, Timothy
"	Etzler, Wm.†		

Killed in Action

1st Sgt	Jas. Butler	Pvt	Weston Harrington
Sgt	Wm. Cashan	"	Louis Haugge
"	Amos B. Warren	"	Francis T. Hughes
Cpl	Wm. Harrison	"	Thos. G. Kavanagh
"	Jno. Seiler	"	Louis Lobering
"	Wm. H. Gilbert	"	Bartholomew Mahoney
Trump'r	Fred'k Walsh	"	Thos. E. Maxwell
Farrier	Wm. H. Heath	"	Chas. McCarthy
Blks	Chas. Siemon	"	Peter McGue
Saddler	Chas. Perkins	"	Jno. Miller
Pvt	Geo. E. Adams	"	David J. O'Connell
"	Wm. Andrews	"	Christian Reibold
"	Antony Assadaly	"	Henry Roberts
"	Elmer Babcock	"	Walter B. Rogers
"	Jno. Burke	"	Chas. Schmidt
"	Ami Cheever	"	Chas. Scott
"	Wm. B. Crisfield	"	Bent Simenson
"	Jno. Duggan	"	Andrew Snow
"	Wm. Dye	"	Byron Tarbox
"	Jas. J. Galvan	"	Edm. D. Tessier
"	Chas. Graham	"	Thos. S. Tweed
"	Henry Hamilton	"	Mich'l Vetter

Appendix A

Company M

Capt	French, Thos. H.	Pvt	Morris, Wm. E.
1st Lt	Mathey, Edw. G.	"	Neely, Frank†
1st Sgt	Ryan, Jno.†	"	Newell, Dan'l
Sgt	*Capes, Wm.	"	Pigford, Edw.†
"	White, Chas.	"	Robinson, Wm.
"	Carey, Pat'k	"	Rutten, Roman
"	McGlone, Jno.†	"	Ryder, Hobart
Cpl	Lalor, Wm.†	"	Rye, Wm. W.†
Trump'r	Fischer, Chas.†	"	Seamans, Jno.†
"	Weaver, Henry C.†	"	Senn, Robt.†
Farrier	*Wood, Wm. M.	"	Severs, Jas.†
Saddler	Donahoe, Jno.†	"	Sivertsen, Jno.†
Wagoner	*Ricketts, Jos. K.	"	Slaper, Wm. C.†
Pvt	Bates, Jos.†	"	Sniffin, Frank†
"	*Bowers, Frank	"	*Sterland, Walter S.†
"	Braun, Frank	"	Stratton, Frank†
"	Cain, Morris†	"	Thornberry, Levi†
"	Davis, Harrison†	"	Thorpe, Rollins L.†
"	*Dolan, Jno.	"	Varner, Thos. B.
"	Gallenne, Jean B. D.†	"	Weaver, Geo.†
"	Golden, Bernard†	"	Weeks, Jas.†
"	Heid, Geo.†	"	Whisten, Jno.†
"	Kavanagh, Chas.†	"	*Widmayer, Ferd.
"	Mahoney, Dan'l†	"	Wiedman, Chas. T.†
"	*McCormick, Jas.	"	Wilber, Jas.
"	Meier, Jno. H.	"	Williams, Chas.†
"	Moore, Hugh N.†	"	*Zametzer, Jno.

Killed in Action

2d Lt	Jas. G. Sturgis	Pvt	Wm. D. Meyer
Sgt	Miles F. O'Hara	"	Geo. E. Smith
Cpl	Henry M. Scollin	"	David Summers
"	Fred'k Streing	"	Jas. J. Tanner
Pvt	Henry Gordon	"	Henry Turley
"	Henry Klotzbucher	"	Henry C. Voigt
"	Geo. Lorentz		

Appendix A

Lt. Varnum's Detachment of Indian Scouts

In addition to scouting for the troops, the Indian scouts were the vital line of communication during the campaign, a responsibility requiring great vigilance and bravery as they carried important dispatches and mail through a hostile country infested by enemy war parties.

Lieut. Varnum said that the Crow scouts (Curley, Goes Ahead, Hairy Moccassin, Half-Yellow-Face, White-Man-Runs-Him, and White Swan) acted under the direct supervision of Gen. Custer and that Varnum saw little of them till the night of June 24, when he went to the Crow's Nest. Carroll, *Custer's Chief of Scouts,* 85.

*Baker, Wm.
*Barking Wolf (Si-ti-wa-ra)
*Bear (Coonough)
  Bear Come Out (Mato-e-nam-pa)
  Bear Running in the Timber
    (Mato-chun-way-a-ga-mun)
*Bears Eyes (Coonough-chee-ruk)
  Black Calf (Hunni-ca-til)
  Black Fox (Che-wa-koo-ca-til)
*Black Porcupine (Sa-nu-ca-til)
*Broken Penis (Cha-gon-hur-pa)
  Bull (Ho-cus)
  Bull-in-the-Water (Ho-cus-ty-arit)
  Bush (Napa-ran-ough)
*Cards (Ca-soo)
*Climbs the Bluff (Te-ru-chitt-ho-nochs)
  Cross, Wm. (E-esk)
*Curly Head (Pich-ga-ri-wee)
  Foolish Bear (Coonough-sen-quagh)
  Forked Horn (Arri-chitt)
  Good Elk (Wah-nee)
  Good Face (Sca-ri)
  Goose (Co-st)
*Horn-in-Front (Arrin-quis-coo)
*Howling Wolf (Schi-ri-ti-wa-no)

*Jackson, Robt.
 Jackson, Wm.
*Laying Down (Si-ti-wa-ra)
*Left Hand (Quigh)
*Long Bear (Coonough-ti-ku-chees)
 One Feather (Ha-cui-tis)
*One Horn (Ach-ko-arri-cas)
*Owl (Ho-ru)
 Round Wooden Cloud
   (Mach-paya-chunga-lash-ca)
 Rushing Bull (Ho-cus-na-quin)
 Sioux (Sen-nen-net)
 Soldier (Kunanch)
 Stab (Ca-wars)
*Sticking Out (Bo-ho-e-na-ge)
 Strike Bear (Coonough-to-cha)
 Strikes-the-Lodge (Tay-ku-che)
 Strikes-Two (Ti-ta-ra-wi-cha)
*The Shield (Wa-ha-chun-ca)
*Wagon (Saparano)
 White Cloud (Mach-pa-a-ska)
 White Eagle (Na-ta-sta-ca)
*Wolf Runs (Schi-ri-tu-nuch)
 Young Hawk (Ach-ta-wi-si-humne)

Killed in Action

Bloody Knife (Nes-i-ri-pat)[a]
Bobtailed Bull (Ho-cus-ta-rix)
Little Brave (Naha-cus-chu-re-posch)

---

[a] Bloody Knife was an employee of the qm dept.

Appendix A

Letter of Lt. Varnum, February 4, 1877

Office of the A.A.Q.M.
Fort A. Lincoln, D.T.
Feb. 4, 1877

Adjutant General, U.S. Army
Washington, D.C.
 Sir,
In reply to your communication of the 25th, ult., directing that I forward Muster Rolls of Detachment of Indian Scouts, for the months of May and June 1876. I have the honor to state the Muster Rolls were made out when the command under General Terry was in camp at Mouth of Rosebud Creek, MT., in July last. I furnished the two copies for the Paymaster in time to have the Detachment paid,* and finished the Roll for the AGO just before the command left camp Aug. 9, 1876. Having no opportunity for sending off the Roll I put it with my retained copy in my valise and took it with me. When the command under General Terry joined that under General Crook, we left the wagon train and having only Pack Mules for transportation I was obliged to leave my valise in the Wagon, and when I found it again it had been robbed of its contents and both Rolls were lost. I cannot replace them unless I can get access to the two Rolls delivered to the Paymaster, Maj. William Smith, USA. As at the time just after the Battle of June 25 and 26 I could keep no memorandum from which to make a [—] one.
[signed] Chas. A. Varnum
1st Lt., RQM, 7th Cavalry
A.A.Q.M.

Source: RG 393, Part V, Fort A. Lincoln, D.T., Entry 19, Letters Sent, Volume 2.
* Detachment payroll (Voucher No. 75), filed in RG 217 (UD) Entry 530.

Appendix A

Wounded June 25–26, 1876

	Rank	Co.		Rank	Co.
Heyn, Wm.	1st Sgt	A	Bishop, Chas. H.	Pvt	H
King, Geo. H.	Cpl	A	Black, Henry	"	H
Deihle, Jacob	Pvt	A	Cooper, Jno.	"	H
Foster, Sam'l	"	A	Farley, Wm.	"	H
Holmsted, Fred'k	"	A	George, Wm.	"	H
Reeves, Francis M.	"	A	Hughes, Thos.	"	H
Strode, Elijah T.	"	A	Moller, Jno.	"	H
Cunningham, Chas.	Cpl	B	Phillips, Jno.	"	H
Smith, Wm. M.	"	B	Severs, Sam'l	"	H
Bennett, Jas. C.	Pvt	C	Williams, Wm. C.	"	H
McGuire, Jno.	"	C	Windolph, Chas.	"	H
Thompson, Peter	"	C	Cooney, David	"	I
Whittaker, Alfred	"	C	Corcoran, Pat'k	"	K
Hetler, Jacob	"	D	Madden, Mich'l P.	"	K
McDonnell, Pat'k	"	D	Mielke, Max	"	K
Riley, Jas. T.	Sgt	E	Marshall, Jasper	"	L
Boyle, Jas. P.	Pvt	G	Carey, Pat'k	Sgt	M
Campbell, Chas.	"	G	White, Chas.	"	M
Hackett, Jno.	"	G	Braun, Frank	Pvt	M
McVay, Jno.	"	G	Meier, Jno. H.	"	M
Morrison, Jno.	"	G	Morris, Wm. E.	"	M
McCurry, Jos.	1st Sgt	H	Newell, Dan'l	"	M
Connelly, Pat'k	Sgt	H	Rutten, Roman	"	M
McLaughlin, Thos.	"	H	Varner, Thos. B.	"	M
Pahl, Jno.	"	H	Wiedman, Chas.	"	M
Bishop, Alex B.	Cpl	H	Wilber, Jas.	"	M
Ramell, Wm.	Trump'r	H	Goose	'Ree Scout	
Voit, Otto	Saddler	H	White Swan	Crow Scout	
Bishley, Henry	Pvt	H	Wagoner, Jno. C.	Chief Packer	

Note: The field hospital on Reno hill was improvised by Dr. Porter and Lt. Mathey in the shallow depression, or swale, of the saucerlike hilltop (with one side out), in an open space among the horses and mules corralled in a circle with their reins tied together and tied to a picket line secured to the legs of fallen animals. A breastwork of boxes and packsaddles separated the hospital from the corral and afforded added protection from the Indians' fire. Nichols, *Reno Court*, passim.

White Swan said: "[T]hey took all the mules and fixed a kind of fence round and that morning they were laying there where there couldn't any bullets get to them." *The Tepee Book,* Vol. 1, No. 10 (Nov.–Dec. 1915), 28.

Goes Ahead said the packers formed the pack train into a circle, and the three Crow scouts helped the packers dig pits and beside these holes the dead mules stopped many bullets. Linderman, *Pretty Shield: Medicine Woman of the Crows,* 237.

Appendix A

Civilians

Frederic F. Gerard	Interpreter
Geo. B. Herendeen	Scout (Job)
Jno. C. Wagoner	Chief Packer
Wm. Alexander	Packer
B. F. Churchill	"
Moses E. Flint	"
Jno. Frett	"
Jno. Lamplough	"
Wm. Lawless	"
Christian Loeser	"
Harry McBratney	"
E. L. Moore	"

Killed in Action

Mitch Bouyer	Guide
Boston Custer	Guide
Isaiah Dorman	Interpreter
Mark H. Kellogg	Newspaper reporter
Frank C. Mann	Packer
Henry A. Reed	Herder
Charley Reynolds	Guide

Appendix B

Recapitulations of Enlisted Men and Horses, compiled from monthly Regimental Returns, and Company Returns, and Bimonthly Muster Rolls*

Each table is followed by notes relative to that unit.

TABLE B.1
Non-commissioned Staff & Band

	Jan	Feb	Mar	Apr	May	Jun	Jul	Aug
Present								
For duty	13	13	13	20	18	—	16	4
On extra or daily duty	—	—	—	—	—	—	—	—
Sick	—	—	—	—	—	—	—	—
Under arrest or in confinement	—	—	—	—	—	—	—	—
Total	**13**	**13**	**13**	**20**	**18**	**—**	**16**	**4**
Absent								
On detached service	—	—	—	—	2	18	2	3
With leave	—	—	—	—	—	—	—	1
Without leave	—	—	—	—	—	—	—	—
Sick	—	—	—	—	1	1	1	—
Under arrest or in confinement	—	—	—	—	—	—	—	—
Total	**—**	**—**	**—**	**—**	**3**	**19**	**3**	**4**
Horses								
Serviceable	22	22	22	22	22	18	18	16
Unserviceable	2	2	2	2	2	2	2	2
Lost in action, died, abandoned, or transferred	—	—	—	—	—	4	—	2

*Numbers in brackets appear on the muster rolls and differ from numbers on the returns in that category.

"When it is desired to have bands of music for regiments, there will be allowed for each, sixteen privates to act as musicians, in addition to the chief musicians authorized by law, provided the total number of privates in the regiment, including the band, does not exceed the legal standard. When a regiment occupies several stations, the band will be kept at the headquarters, provided troops (one or more companies) be serving there." *Regs.* 1863, Pars. 81 & 83.

Sgt. John Ryan said the band and noncommissioned staff and all trumpeters in the regiment had gray horses. Barnard, *Ten Years with Custer*, 68. Pvt. Windolph recalled that the band rode white horses; also buglers, so they could be picked out quickly. Hunt, *I Fought with Custer*, 56, 76.

Pvt. Lombard said Lt. Cooke took his horse, Peet, a good walker. Lombard to Walter Camp, Dec. 6, 1910, WMC-BYU.

Capt. Benteen tried to induce Lt. Cooke to leave his thoroughbred mare, Malita, at Powder River. She was killed in the battle. Cooke left horse Piggy back at Powder River. Benteen letter to his wife, July 12, 1876. Carroll, *Camp Talk*, 34.

Appendix B

Richard A. Roberts (brother-in-law of Capt. Yates) said Lt. Cooke rode a white horse. Roberts, *Custer's Last Battle*, 42. Lt. Godfrey said Cooke rode an almost white horse. Graham, *The Custer Myth*, 346; Stewart, *Custer's Luck*, 474.

Capt. Benteen found a white horse on June 28, a little below the middle ford "B," wounded, lying in a pool of mud and water. He killed this horse to end its misery. Nichols, *Reno Court*, 419.

James J. O'Kelly (newspaper correspondent for *NY Herald*) bought a large, handsome black horse that had belonged to the adjutant of the regiment, Colonel Cooke. Carroll, *Garlington Narrative*, 11.

Lt. Ernest Garlington, fresh from West Point when he joined the regiment at Rosebud Creek, Aug. 2, said Capt. Benteen detailed him battalion adjutant and he was given one of the band's horses, the band having been dismounted and about to be sent back to Fort Lincoln. It was a good horse too—pure white, without a mark of any kind. Says the saddler-sergeant of the regiment rode a very handsome white horse; during a lively buffalo chase Aug. 29 the sergeant shot a buffalo and when he got down to cut out its tongue, the horse pulled loose from him and disappeared over a hill with the herd, never to be seen again. Carroll, *Garlington Narrative*, 8.

Matthew Carroll (Gibbon's wagon master) said that during the buffalo hunt some horses went away with the buffalo and could not be recovered. Sgt. Alex Brown said that one band horse was injured and had to be abandoned. Willert, *March of the Columns*, 460.

Sgt. Tritten said the band horses were not taken by Custer at Powder River. The horses were taken from the band at mouth of the Rosebud and the band sent to Fort Lincoln. The horses were turned over to company trumpeters, they being white horses, and all 7th Cavalry trumpeters had white or gray horses. Tritten to Walter Camp, Mar. 2, and Mar. 5, 1914, WMC-DPL.

Pvt. Geist said, when they got into the badlands, the band boys got tired of playing and pretended to have got sand in their instruments, so on occasion Custer put them at pick and shovel with the pioneer corps. The band was mounted and remained at Powder River with their horses. Hardorff, *Camp, Custer, and the Little Big Horn*, 37.

Lt. Varnum said Wallace, having been appointed adjutant, made the muster rolls of the Field & Staff, June 30. Varnum to Col. Chas. F. Bates, May 3, 1932, Bates Papers, Yale Univ.

In April 1873, during the regiment's transfer to Dakota Territory, twenty-eight horses of the band were lost en route, most by epidemic at Memphis. After the regiment experienced a furious late-season snowstorm at Yankton, Gen. Custer telegraphed to department headquarters at St. Paul that seventy-nine horses were needed to remount the command. A board of officers was appointed to purchase suitable horses from the Yankton area, but by May 1 only three had been accepted. Col. Sturgis was sent from the regiment's new headquarters at St. Paul to assess the situation and to start the command for Fort Rice. Two days after reaching Yankton, Sturgis notified department headquarters (May 2) that horses were not being found to make up the deficiency. He suggested the band be dismounted, their horses (about thirty) utilized for the march, and the band brought to St. Paul. Gen. Terry approved the move May 4, the horses to be turned over to the companies and the men sent to Fort Snelling.

However, the next day, Sturgis questioned the wisdom of dismounting the band, the disparity between the number of men and number of horses having diminished with the desertion of twenty men since paid and with the planned transporting of seventeen sick men on the steamboat *Miner*. When Gen. Custer reported the morning of May 6 a greater number of horses (614) than men (604), adding that the horses of the band would actually be an inconvenience, Sturgis relayed the information to St. Paul, stating that he was indifferent as to the disposition of the band, but the desire of Col. Custer to have it was very great.

With orders unchanged, Custer departed Yankton with the regiment on May 7, and the next day, from Bon Homme, about twenty miles distant, telegraphed department headquarters requesting that the band, presumed still at Yankton, be ordered to accompany the command, that they would be a source of great pleasure to the officers and men during the summer, the

Appendix B

more just by the fact the band's instruments were originally purchased by private subscription of the officers. RG 391, Entries 880, 881, 882. (With completion of the NPRR to Bismarck, June 5, the band rejoined the regiment at Fort Rice and accompanied the expedition to the Yellowstone).

Appendix B

TABLE B.2
Company A

	Jan	Feb	Mar	Apr	May	Jun	Jul	Aug
Present								
For duty	40	36	42	43	42	28	26	25
On extra or daily duty	16	18	15	9	9	4	7	6
Sick	8	10	4	8	—	—	2	—
In arrest or confinement	1	1	1	1	—	—	1	—
Total	**65**	**65**	**62**	**61**	**51**	**32**	**36**	**31**
Absent								
On detached service	—	—	—	—	3	6	3	2[5]
With leave	—	—	—	—	—	—	—	—
Without leave	—	—	—	—	—	—	—	—
Sick	—	—	—	—	—	7	6	—[13]
In arrest or confinement	—	—	—	—	—	—	1	—
Total	—	—	—	—	**3**	**13**	**10**	**2**
Horses								
Serviceable	52	52	52	52	52	38	38	37
Unserviceable	8	—	—	—	—	—	—	—
Lost in action, died, abandoned, or transferred	—	—	—	—	—	14	—	1

Capt. Moylan said he took thirty-eight men into the (valley) fight. Nichols, *Reno Court*, 230.

Sgt. Alcott said the guidon lost in the timber when Reno started retreat belonged to Co. A, and says Sgt. Fehler threw it away so as not to be encumbered with it (Alcott interview, n.d., WMC-IU). Trumpeter Hardy said Fehler had an unruly horse and could not get guidon in foot, and threw it away when he came out of the timber. DeRudio rode over and dismounted and tried to get it, when his horse jerked away from him. Hardy interview, n.d., WMC-IU.

Trump'r Hardy said Drinan's horse was found wounded in the back and had to be killed. Hardorff, *Camp, Custer, and the Little Big Horn*, 81.

Pvt. Taylor said one noncom and six men with pack train and each company had eleven pack mules; says also that each company had one spade brought along by the company cook to cut trenches for his fires. *Springfield* (Mass.) *Sunday Republican*, Dec. 19, 1920. Taylor, *With Custer on the Little Big Horn*, 74.

Appendix B

TABLE B.3
Company B

	Jan	Feb	Mar	Apr	May	Jun	Jul	Aug
Present								
For duty	25	30	27	62	55	60[36]	58	58[47]
On extra or daily duty	14	10	7	4	10	4	4	4
Sick	4	—	8	—	1	—	—	—
In arrest or confinement	2	3	1	2	—	—	—	—
Total	**45**	**43**	**43**	**68**	**66**	**64**	**62**	**62**
Absent								
On detached service	2	2	—	—	—	2[24]	2	2[7]
With leave	—	—	—	—	—	—	—	—
Without leave	—	—	—	—	—	—	—	—
Sick	—	—	—	—	1	1[3]	2	—[6]
In arrest or confinement	—	—	—	1	2	2	2	—[4]
Total	**2**	**2**	—	**1**	**3**	**5**	**6**	**2**
Horses								
Serviceable	49	52	52	49	52	40[52]	40	51
Unserviceable	12	9	9	—	—	3[1]	3	—
Lost in action, died, abandoned, or transferred	—	—	—	1	—	9*	—	7

*Company return shows 8 horses lost in action and 44 serviceable.

Capt. McDougall said his company [at LBH] was composed of about forty-five men. Nichols, *Reno Court*, 528.

Pvt. Devoto said each troop detailed ten men to the packs, and B Troop mules were placed at front of the pack train. Devoto to Walter Camp, July 1917, WMC-LBHB.

Appendix B

TABLE B.4
Company C

	Jan	Feb	Mar	Apr	May	Jun	Jul	Aug
Present								
For duty	42	43	45	43	47	15[10]	14	15[14]
On extra or daily duty	19	17	14	15	12	5[1]	4	—[1]
Sick	3	3	—	3	—	4	1	—
In arrest or confinement	6	7	7	6	1	—	—	—
Total	**70**	**70**	**66**	**67**	**60**	**24**	**19**	**15**
Absent								
On detached service	—	—	—	—	3	3[10]	3	2[29]
With leave	1	—	—	—	—	—	—	—
Without leave	—	—	—	—	—	—	—	—
Sick	—	—	—	—	1	1[6]	4	—[5]
In arrest or confinement	—	—	—	—	2	2	2	—[1]
Total	**1**	**—**	**—**	**—**	**6**	**6**	**9**	**2**
Horses								
Serviceable	58	58	57	56	56*	10	10	10
Unserviceable	—	—	1	2	—	2	2	2
Lost in action, died, abandoned, or transferred	—	—	—	—	—	46	—	—

*The numbers shown here for Co. C horses in May reflect the Regimental Return. The Company Return for May has a corrected total of 59 serviceable horses (the larger and darker "9" imposed over a "6" originally written. Also, the top half of a "2" appears in the unserviceable column [adjudged by comparing numbers on same page]).

    Pvt. Bischoff said Tom Custer rode his horse, Custer's own horse having a sore back. Bischoff interview, n.d., WMC-BYU.
    Pvt. McGuire said he was ordered to the pack train when his horse became very lame during the march up the Rosebud; Lt. Harrington let him ride his extra horse. McGuire to Walter Camp, Dec. 4, 1908, WMC-BYU.
    Capt. Benteen said very few C Co. horses were found. Benteen letter to his wife, July 4, 1876; Carroll, *Camp Talk*, 24.
    Lt. DeRudio and Capt. Benteen said five or six sorrel horses of Co. C lay on top of Custer Hill and appeared as if they had been led there (in an arc) and were shot down for a barricade, as empty shells lay behind them. Hammer, *Custer in '76*, 87; Nichols, *Reno Court*, 437.
    Pvt. Goldin said that on and around the knoll where Custer made his final stand were perhaps a half dozen dead cavalry horses, shot for breastworks. Carroll, *Custer in Periodicals*, 116.
    Capt. Jackson said there were fourteen men of Co. C with Major Reno's command, five of whom were wounded and one died of his wounds. Jackson to Lt. Garlington, Regimental Adjutant, Mar. 10, 1878, RG 94, Entry 409, file 10818 A (EB) 1878.
    A temporary troop was formed from the remnants of Cos. C, E, and F. Some of the men had been with the pack train and some with the wagon train, and a batch of recruits had been left at Powder River without horses. Horses for these arrived, and thirty of the detachment made a fair troop, commanded by Lt. Varnum. (GO 15, Hq 7th Cavalry, Aug. 4, 1876). Carroll, *Custer's Chief of Scouts*, 77.

Appendix B

TABLE B.5
Company D

	Jan	Feb	Mar	Apr	May	Jun	Jul	Aug
Present								
For duty	41	44	43	47	44	45	41	49
On extra or daily duty	16	20	19	14	17	—	12	—
Sick	7	2	5	5	—	—	2	—
In arrest or confinement	5	1	—	—	—	—	—	—
Total	69	67	67	66	61	45	55	49
Absent								
On detached service	—	1	—	—	2	14	2	1[4]
With leave	—	—	—	—	—	—	—	—
Without leave	—	—	—	—	—	—	—	—
Sick	—	—	—	—	1	2	2	—[1]
In arrest or confinement	1	—	—	—	—	—	—	—
Total	**1**	**1**	**—**	**—**	**3**	**16**	**4**	**1**
Horses								
Serviceable	52	52	52	52	53	47	49	49
Unserviceable	1	1	1	1	2	2	—	5
Lost in action, died, abandoned, or transferred	—	—	—	—	—	6	—	2

Capt. Weir rode a very handsome black horse named Jake and known all through the regiment as "Old Jake." Carroll, *Garlington Narrative*, 23.

Pvt. Kipp said Co. D was one of the strongest of the regiment (in numbers) and, when Gen. Custer divided the regiment on the divide (Davis Creek), he had taken D as one of his five companies. When Benteen, who wanted D Co. because of its strength, protested, Custer said rather impatiently, "Well, damn it to hell, take D Co." Hardorff, *On the Little Big Horn with Walter Camp*, 184.

Major Reno said Co. D was the strongest company they had (on the hill). Nichols, *Reno Court*, 568.

Lt. Godfrey said Capt. Weir became impatient at the water hole while Benteen's battalion was watering its horses and started off with his troop, taking the advance, whereas his place in column was second. *The Sunday Star* (Washington, DC), Nov. 13, 1921.

Goes-Ahead said when the Crows left Custer and rode back along the bluffs, they "got to the black horse riders at the pack-mule entrenchments." *The Tepee Book*, Vol. 2, No. 11, Nov. 1916.

Appendix B

TABLE B.6
Company E

	Jan	Feb	Mar	Apr	May	Jun	Jul	Aug
Present								
For duty	51	51	49	54	43	13[11]	13	15
On extra or daily duty	9	10	6	5	11	2[3]*	2	1
Sick	2	1	—	1	—	—	—	—
In arrest or confinement	1	—	1	1	—	—	—	—
Total	63	62	56	61	54	15	15	16
Absent								
On detached service	2	3	3	—	5	4	4	1[34]
With leave	—	—	—	—	—	1	1	1
Without leave	—	—	—	—	—	—	—	—
Sick	1	1	1	1	1	3	3	—[2]
In arrest or confinement	—	—	—	—	1	1	1	—[1]
Total	**3**	**4**	**4**	**1**	**7**	**9**	**9**	**2**
Horses								
Serviceable	61	61	55	55	55	11	11	11
Unserviceable	4	4	—	—	—	—	—	—
Lost in action, died, abandoned, or transferred	—	—	—	—	—	44	—	—

*The collection of 7th Cavalry records at Little Big Horn Battlefield include two copies of the Company E Muster Roll, June 30, 1876. One, ragged and torn (and unsigned), reports *four* privates on extra or daily duty, while the other, neatly prepared and signed by Lt. DeRudio, reports *three* privates on extra or daily duty. The AGO copy at the National Archives, also signed by Lt. DeRudio, reflects the signed copy at the battlefield. See, RG 94, Entry 409, file 4218 B AGO (EB) 1877.

SO 75, Hq Fort A. Lincoln, DT, April 24, 1876, directed the commanding officer of Co. E to turn over to the post quartermaster one gray horse that Lt. A. E. Smith desired to purchase for his private use, provided that said horse was not the mount of a trooper.

Lt. Edgerly said one of E Troop's gray horses was found wounded at the river near Custer's battlefield and appeared to be much frightened and very shy, but followed the troops at a distance all the way to the crossing of the Yellowstone. Hammer, *Custer in '76*, 58.

Fred Gerard testified that, when they went to bury Custer's troops, he found a wounded gray horse standing in the river (where the letter "L" is in "Little Big Horn" on the map of Lt. Maguire). Nichols, *Reno Court*, 99, 637.

Hardy said the gray horse found on the battlefield was taken to Fort Lincoln and the children used to ride him. His name was Nap. Hardorff, *Camp, Custer, and the Little Big Horn*, 81.

Lt. DeRudio "saw a heap of men in a gully and says the dead horses nearest the river were gray ones belonging to Company E." Hammer, *Custer in '76*, 87.

Pvt. Goldin estimated there were a dozen or fifteen dead gray horses in the ravine leading from Custer hill down toward the river. Carroll, *Custer in Periodicals*, 116.

SO 54, Hq 7th Cavalry, June 27, 1876, temporarily attached the men of Cos. C, F, I, and L, whose permanent commanders were killed in battle, to Co. E for rations.

A temporary troop was formed from the remnants of Cos. C, E, and F. Some of the men had been with the pack train and others with the wagon train, and a batch of recruits had been left at Powder river without horses. Horses for these arrived, and thirty of the detachment made a

Appendix B

fair troop, commanded by Lt. Varnum. (GO 15, Hq 7th Cavalry, Aug. 4, 1876.) Carroll, *Custer's Chief of Scouts*, 77.

Pvt. Pendle said that, after the battle, "there was only 5 or 6 of us came back except what was with the wagon train." Pendle to Walter Camp, July 14, 1919, WMC-BYU.

Pvt. O'Toole recalled that Sgt. Riley was in charge of his troop pack mules; also Lang, Bill Shields, and possibly the man who rode Duche were with the pack train. (Duche was wounded on Reno hill.) O'Toole to Walter Camp, Mar. 26, 1909, WMC-BYU.

Note: The Battalion Return for Cos. E and L, March 1876, is filed with Post Returns, Fort Seward, DT, NA, M617, Roll 1153.

Appendix B

TABLE B.7
Company F

	Jan	Feb	Mar	Apr	May	Jun	Jul	Aug
Present								
For duty	40	36	39	42	45	11[15]	11	12
On extra or daily duty	21	19	16	17	15	13[10]	13	13
Sick	2	4	5	4	1	1	1	1
In arrest or confinement	3	5	3	2	—	—	—	—
Total	**66**	**64**	**63**	**65**	**61**	**25**	**25**	**26**
Absent								
On detached service	1	1	1	—	5	5	5	2[22]
With leave	—	—	—	—	—	—	—	—
Without leave	—	—	—	—	—	—	—	1
Sick	—	—	—	—	—	—	—	—
In arrest or confinement	3	2	2	2	2	2	2	—[2]
Total	**4**	**3**	**3**	**2**	**7**	**7**	**7**	**3**
Horses								
Serviceable	59	59	57	55	57	12[19]	12	21[22]
Unserviceable	—	—	2	2	—	3[2]	3	3[—]
Lost in action, died, abandoned, or transferred	—	—	—	—	—	42	—	—

SO 75, Hq Fort A. Lincoln, DT, April 24, 1876, directed Capt. Yates to turn over to the post quartermaster two horses that Major Reno desired to purchase for his private use, provided that said horses were not the mounts of troopers.

Major Reno said he lost both his horses (in the battle). Nichols, *Reno Court*, 646.

Lt. Reily, upon returning from Major Reno's scout up Powder River, wrote to his mother, June 21, 1876: "Our horses are almost played out, we lost two inroute." Viola, *Little Big Horn Remembered*, 185.

Pvt. Lynch, Co. F, gave his horse to George Herendeen, June 22, at mouth of Rosebud Creek. (Herendeen said this horse was killed on Reno hill.) Hammer, *Custer in '76*, 221, 225.

Lt. Godfrey said the horse of Pvt. Davern (Co. F) was killed in the valley, and Davern then caught an Indian pony and rode to the command on Reno hill. Graham, *The Custer Myth*, 140. Davern implied that he rode his horse to the command. Nichols, *Reno Court*, 364.

Stan Roy supposed that, on June 28, the remnant of the seven troops averaged about thirty able-bodied men per troop, and the detachment from Custer's five troops that were with the pack train numbered about six men to a troop. Hardorff, *On the Little Big Horn with Walter Camp*, 40.

Dennis Lynch identified ten men of Co. F with the pack train. Lynch to Walter Camp, Nov. 28, 1908, with roster of Co. F and remarks by Lynch after each name. WMC-BYU. Lynch also said his company had 14 pack mules. Hammer, *Custer in '76*, 138.

James Rooney identified eight men of Co. F with the pack train. Roster of Co. F from Walter Camp to Rooney, n.d., with remarks added by Rooney after each name. WMC-BYU.

Lt. Eugene B. Gibbs, of Gen. Terry's staff, said thirty-two men of Yates's company were found on (Custer) hill, which seemed to have been held by Yates's company (Gibbs's Ms. [SC 33], Montana Historical Society).

Appendix B

Richard A. Roberts (brother-in-law of Capt. Yates), who spoke with Captains Smith and Hughes of Gen. Terry's staff related that where Gen. Custer made his last stand, he was surrounded by Co. F. Roberts, *Custer's Last Battle: Reminiscences*, 46.

In a letter to his wife, July 18, 1876 (from Powder River), Capt. Benteen said Mrs. Yates "had turned over her horses, etc., which are up here—to dispose of for her." Benteen sold Capt. Yates's horse to Lt. Jacobs, 7th Inf., of Col. Gibbon's command, for $655. Benteen letter to his wife, Aug. 1, 1876; Carroll, *Camp Talk*, 42, 46.

SO 62, Hq 7th Cavalry, July 31, 1876, assigned newly joined Lt. Edwin Eckerson temporary duty commanding Co. F, and to have the muster rolls made out, company records completed, and the company equipped for the field as quickly as possible.

GO 15, Hq 7th Cavalry, Aug. 4, 1876, formed a temporary troop from the remnants of Cos. C, E, and F. "Some of the men had been with the pack train & some with the wagon train, and a batch of recruits had been left at Powder River without horses. Horses for these had arrived and thirty of this detachment made a fair troop. I [Lt. Varnum] was placed in command in addition to my other duties." Carroll, *Custer's Chief of Scouts*, 77.

On Aug. 2, the 7th Cavalry received about sixty horses. Co. F reported nine more horses in August than in July. Cos. C and E reported no change. Koury, *The Field Diary of General Terry*; Company, and Regimental, Returns, Aug. 1876.

When Major Reno notified Dept. HQ, Feb. 9, 1876, the number of horses required to mount the cavalry companies at Fort Lincoln, he stated that Co. F needed eleven horses. RG 393, Part V, Fort Lincoln, DT.

Muster Rolls of Co. F between May 1875 and Sept. 1876 do not report a trumpeter with the troop, nor any remarks to explain the absence of these important personnel. *Note:* Pvt. John Kelly, who had two years service as trumpeter, transferred to Co. F, May 1, 1876.

For comparison, an identical situation occurred two years earlier in Co. E, when Lt. McDougall, commanding the company, wrote to the AGO, Sept. 22, 1874, requesting that two trumpeters be assigned to his company, as there was only one present with the company and his term of service was expiring shortly. Following up Jan. 13, 1875, McDougall wrote to Col. Sturgis, Supt. of the Mounted Recruiting Service at St. Louis, requesting that his application for two trumpeters (approved Oct. 7) be filled as soon as possible; and saying that the discharge of the only one in the company that morning, on expiration of service, had left the company without a trumpeter at all. RG 393, Part V, Fort A. Lincoln.

The *Bismarck Tribune*, Dec. 4, 1875, reported, "The post garden at Fort Lincoln embraces fifteen acres. The ground was broken in 1874 and a light crop raised. This year was the first of thorough cultivation. It is divided into five lots, or tracts, and apportioned to the several companies. Company F, 7th Cavalry, commanded by Capt. Yates, produced on their three acres 600 bushels of potatoes, 100 bushels of oats, 300 heads of cabbage, 18 bushels of onions, 75 bushels of turnips, 5 barrels of tomatoes, and radishes, lettuce, etc., etc., in almost unlimited quantities."

Note: For authorship of the Co. F muster rolls during the campaign of 1876, see note G35 (Gregg), and, note 5 in the Addendum.

Appendix B

TABLE B.8
Company G

	Jan	Feb	Mar	Apr	May	Jun	Jul	Aug
Present								
For duty	26	26	25	55	50	28[27]	17	26
On extra or daily duty	18	16	13	3	7	1	9	10
Sick	3	3	7	1	—	2	1	—
In arrest or confinement	2	4	3	2	2	—	—	—
Total	49	49	48	61	59	31	27	36
Absent								
On detached service	—	—	—	1	4	20	23	2[13]
With leave	—	—	—	1	1	1	1	—
Without leave	1	—	—	1	—	—	—	—
Sick	1	1	1	1	2	1	2	—[5]
In arrest or confinement	2	1	—	—	—	—	—	—
Total	**4**	**2**	**1**	**4**	**7**	**22**	**26**	**2**
Horses								
Serviceable	47	46	46	45	50	25	25	37
Unserviceable	9	10	9	—	—	—	—	—
Lost in action, died, abandoned, or transferred	1	—	1	1	—	25	—	—

The notebook of Lt. McIntosh (transcribed copy at LBHB) provides statistics of Co. G after June 15, 1876: On furlough & ds 7; left at Powder River 17; present 42; horses 50; men 66; horses left at Powder River 4; present 47; add to "present" Pvt. Reed joined.

Sgt. Alex Brown's troop duty book, pp. 53–54, "Lists of horses killed in Battle, 23; horses left 25, Total 48."

Major Reno supposed there were forty men in Co. G (in valley fight). Nichols, *Reno Court*, 562. Lt. Wallace said Reno had three companies averaging thirty-five to forty men each, and after the valley fight he could find only seven men of Co. G. Wallace also said each company had ten men with the packs. Ibid., 22–23, 35, 59.

Pvt. Boyle said that on Reno hill, G Co. men were on the line with K Co. (Boyle interview, n.d., WMC-BYU).

Upon arriving at Fort Lincoln the last week of September, Lt. Garlington could find no man in the troop (G) who had knowledge of company papers, nor one who could write a respectable hand. The first sergeant and the company clerk were both absent abroad, on furlough—one an Englishman, the other an Irishman. No returns had been made out for months, so he took up the work himself, with no guide except the retained papers and the property on hand. He made out the original copy of each return and the required report, including the muster roll. Carroll, *Garlington Narrative*, 24–25.

Note: Handwriting on Co. G muster rolls of June 1876 appears nearly identical to that of Pvt. Crussy (Krusee).

Appendix B

Table B.9
Company H

	Jan	Feb	Mar	Apr	May	Jun	Jul	Aug
Present								
For duty	50	47	42	37	37	34[33]	34	31
On extra or daily duty	16	15	17	12	11	—	2	—
Sick	—	3	1	2	—	—	—	—
In arrest or confinement	—	1	—	2	—	—	—	—
Total	**66**	**66**	**60**	**53**	**48**	**34**	**36**	**31**
Absent								
On detached service	—	—	—	—	—	1*	—	1[3]
With leave	—	—	—	—	—	—	—	1
Without leave	—	—	—	—	—	—	—	—
Sick	—	—	—	—	4	14[15]	13	—[13]
In arrest or confinement	1	1	1	1	3	3	3	—[4]
Total	**1**	**1**	**1**	**1**	**7**	**18**	**16**	**2**
Horses								
Serviceable	64	64	63	61	50	44	44	44
Unserviceable	—	—	1	3	—	—	—	—
Lost in action, died, abandoned, or transferred	—	—	—	—	—	6	—	—

*Omitted from the tally of absent on detached service June 30 were Pvt. Fisher, whose transfer to Co. H was not official until July 1, and Pvt. McWilliams, listed with absent sick.

In a telegram to Gen. Custer, Feb. 7, 1876, Capt. Benteen said his company would lose twelve men between March 7 and April 14, and if not filled up, six horses for battery. RG 393, Part V, Fort Rice.

When the Fort Rice battalion (Cos. H and M) arrived at Fort Lincoln, May 5, 1876, Benteen found Lt. DeRudio with no horse and no mess kit, and so he mounted "the Count" on his former H Co. horse, took him into his mess, and made him adjutant of the left wing. Benteen to David F. Barry, April 1, 1898. Carroll, *D. F. Barry Correspondence at the Custer Battlefield.*

Capt. Benteen said both his horses (U.S. horses) were wounded. Benteen to his wife, July 4, 1876, in Carroll, *The Benteen-Goldin Letters*, 156.

Benteen left his two private horses, Williamsburg and a mare, at Powder River in charge of Pvt. Fisher, along with their groom, Frank Jones, or "Cuff," a "negro" boy age thirteen. Benteen letters to his wife, July 12, 18, and 24, 1876, in Carroll, *Camp Talk*, 34, 42, 44. Cuff is mentioned as a "small negro waif" to whom someone had once fed a decent meal and who was fond of Lt. Gibson because his name was also Frank. Fougera, *With Custer's Cavalry*, 146. (*Note:* Cuff testified in the court martial of Capt. French in Jan. 1879.)

Pvt. Windolph said that (on Reno hill) H Co.'s men were behind a horseshoe facing south and toward the river. The men behind the horseshoe facing toward Custer and on the line facing east were from the pack train details. WMC transcript, BYU-197. Sgt. Knipe also said Benteen had part of the packers detail. WMC transcript, BYU-40.

Windolph said each troop had twelve pack mules. Hunt, *I Fought with Custer*, 66. Windolph also related that the first party to visit Custer battlefield after the battle was the remains of Co. H, with fourteen men left in the saddle, three of whom were wounded. Windolph to Walter Camp, May 10, 1909, WMC-BYU.

Appendix B

Pvt. Glenn (alias Glease) said, "Many of the men left at the Powder River camp were fellows who played up sick. The officers inquired of the sergeants who were not able to go and such as were thought not to be well and rugged enough were left behind. In each company there was a detail, but there were others who did not want to go, and they pretended to be unwell. In Company H there were none of these, and that is why so few of our company were left there." Hammer, *Custer in '76*, 135.

Appendix B

TABLE B.10
Company I

	Jan	Feb	Mar	Apr	May	Jun	Jul	Aug
Present								
For duty	39	39	36	42	40	12[7]	12	34
On extra or daily duty	20	19	18	16	13	—	—	4[—]
Sick	3	4	6	5	1	—	—	—
In arrest or confinement	5	4	3	1	—	—	—	—
Total	**67**	**66**	**63**	**64**	**54**	**12**	**12**	**38**
Absent								
On detached service	2	2	—	1	6	10[14]	10	1[9]
With leave	—	1	1	—	—	—	—	—
Without leave	—	—	—	—	—	—	—	—
Sick	—	—	—	—	4	6	6	—[4]
In arrest or confinement	2	1	1	1	1	1[2]	1	—[2]
Total	**4**	**4**	**2**	**2**	**11**	**17**	**17**	**1**
Horses								
Serviceable	59	59	59	59	56	15	15	16
Unserviceable	—	—	—	—	3	—	—	—
Lost in action, died, abandoned, or transferred	—	—	—	—	—	44	—	—

Sgt. Caddle said he was detailed with three men of his troop, Fred Myers, John Rivers, and Goosebaker, to take charge of the company wagons. *Mandan News*, Nov. 6, 1914.

Pvt. Francis Johnson said that he was detailed to the pack train with four others of Co. I June 22, and that he led Capt. Keogh's horse, *Comanche*. Statement of Francis Johnson Kennedy, ca. 1900. Letter from Albert W. Johnson, Marine-on-St.-Croix, Minn., to Theo. Goldin, May 4, 1933, Dustin Coll., LBHB.

Lt. Hugh L. Scott said Keogh rode the government horse *Paddy* up to the fight when he changed to *Comanche*. Keogh and Nowlan were close friends, and Nowlan loved Paddy and rode him in 1877. Scott, *Some Memories of a Soldier*, 47.

Hardy said *Comanche* was not Keogh's regular horse, but one belonging to Pvt. McGuinness, and Keogh had him as an extra horse. McGuinness was left sick at Lincoln. Hardorff, *Camp, Custer, and the Little Big Horn*, 81.

Lt. Mathey never heard that Keogh had bought *Comanche* and believed he was a government horse. DeRudio also said *Comanche* was a troop horse and did not belong to Keogh. Hardorff, *Camp, Custer, and the Little Big Horn*, 46.

For accounts of the finding of *Comanche* after the battle, see the sketches of Pvts. Franz C. Braun, Gustave Korn, and Charles Ramsey, this volume. See also Lawrence, *His Very Silence Speaks*, 74–81.

Comanche was transported about August 5 on the steamer *Durfee* from camp at mouth of Rosebud Creek to Fort Lincoln. *Chicago Times*, Aug. 20, 1876. See Gray, "Veterinary Service on Custer's Last Campaign."

"The Steamer *Durfee* had on board Capt. Keogh's horse *Comanche*, which was suffering from seven bullet wounds received in the battle." Newspaper clipping, n.d., in scrapbook of Mrs. Nettie Bowen Smith (wife of Lt. Smith).

Appendix B

Note: Farrier Rivers was discharged Aug. 5 at mouth of Rosebud Creek (and may have cared for *Comanche* during the trip to Fort Lincoln). Steamboat movements in early August were as follows: *Carroll* left Rosebud Aug. 2, arrived Fort Buford Aug. 4, and Fort Lincoln Aug. 6; *Durfee* left Rosebud Aug. 6, arrived Buford Aug. 8, and Lincoln Aug. 10; *Josephine* left Rosebud Aug. 9, arrived Buford Aug. 11, and Lincoln Aug. 13. Fort Buford Medical History (RG 94, Entry 547); Fort Lincoln Post Returns (NA, M617). See also, *Vinton* [Iowa] *Eagle*, Aug. 30, 1876.

Dr. Stein recalled that he was favorably assisted at Fort Lincoln by Lt. Burns, post quartermaster, in extracting thirteen bullets from *Comanche*. *Bismarck Tribune*, April 26, 1878.

Hardy said Bustard had DeLacy's horse, which was found dead on the village side of the river near the ford. Hardorff, *Camp, Custer, and the Little Big Horn*, 82.

"Keogh seems to have had some premoniscience of his coming fate for . . . [on] the day of the action sent a messenger back five miles to Capt. McDougall who was in charge of the pack train with the address of his sister Erin." Capt. Robert P. Hughes (of Gen. Terry's staff) to his wife, June 30, 1876, cited in C. Lee Noyes, "A Look Back: Captain Robert P. Hughes and the Case against Custer: An Early Perspective of the Little Big Horn," *Newsletter*, LBHA, Vol. 33, Feb. 1999.

Keogh had with him a picture of McDougall's sister, which was recovered from Indians years after the battle with a spot of blood on it. Hammer, *Custer in '76*, 72.

GO 15, Hq 7th Cavalry, Aug. 4, 1876, mouth of Rosebud Creek, temporarily consolidated the remnant of Co. I with Co. A.

Appendix B

TABLE B.11
Company K

	Jan	Feb	Mar	Apr	May	Jun	Jul	Aug
Present								
For duty	47	42	28	62	49	25	43	38
On extra or daily duty	5	8	6	2	12	8	8	8
Sick	1	1	1	—	1	—	—	—
In arrest or confinement	—	1	2	2	—	—	—	—
Total	**53**	**52**	**37**	**66**	**62**	**33**	**51**	**46**
Absent								
On detached service	—	—	15	1	3	24	3	1[7]
With leave	—	—	—	1	—	—	—	—[1]
Without leave	—	—	—	—	—	—	—	—
Sick	—	—	—	1	3	6	8	—[5]
In arrest or confinement	—	—	—	—	—	—	—	—
Total	**—**	**—**	**15**	**3**	**6**	**30**	**11**	**1**
Horses								
Serviceable	44	41	42	41	41	27	34	56
Unserviceable	12	15	14	—	4	7	7	—
Lost in action, died, abandoned, or transferred	—	—	—	—	—	11	—	—

Lt. Godfrey requested authority to transfer fourteen condemned horses to the QM Dept., the chief QM to investigate if these horses could be sold advantageously at McComb City. Godfrey to Hq Dept. of the Gulf, April 12, 1876, RG 393, Part I, Entries 1968 and 1969.

Godfrey said, "My troop 'K' had only two recruits (selected) to take the places of one Non-Com and one man left with the property at Supply Camp, together with the other recruits. I think the presence of recruits with the command is overworked." Godfrey to Col. Charles F. Bates, n.d., Bates Papers, Yale Univ.

Godfrey said, "The total strength of the company [K] after leaving the supply camp on the Yellowstone was forty-two, and these were disposed on June 25 as follows : with the pack-train, 7; with General Custer as flag-bearer, 1; hospital steward, 1; orderly to Dr. DeWolf, 1; total detached, 10. In action, 32, of whom 10 were detailed as horse-holders, leaving a fighting strength of 22." Graham, *The Story of the Little Big Horn*, 118.

Lt. Hare testified that six men of Co. K, a non-commissioned officer and five men, were with the pack train. The other companies may have had more. Nichols, *Reno Court*, 290.

Lt. Hare's extra horse, and Lt. Godfrey's too, was with the pack train (June 25, 1876). Hare to Godfrey, Dec. 15, 1924, Godfrey Papers, LOC.

Godfrey recorded, August 4, 1876, "We also got some horses but many have the distemper and will probably give it to many of the old horses." Three days later Godfrey wrote, "We had mounted inspection at 8am. I have 44 men in ranks; 1 teamster, 2 at Reg't Hdqars, 5 at Dept. Hdquars, Artillery & ordnance detachments –8 absent –47 serviceable horses present, 3 unserviceable; 3 on details." Godfrey, *Diary*, 31–32.

Appendix B

TABLE B.12
Company L

	Jan	Feb	Mar	Apr	May	Jun	Jul	Aug
Present								
For duty	46	60	52	63	50	11	11	17[19]
On extra or daily duty	10	4	3	1	12	1	7	2[3]
Sick	1	3	3	2	1	—	—	—
In arrest or confinement	1	—	7	1	—	—	—	—
Total	**68**	**67**	**65**	**67**	**63**	**12**	**18**	**19**
Absent								
On detached service	2	2	2	—	3	8	3	2[30]
With leave	—	—	—	—	—	—	—	1
Without leave	—	—	—	—	—	—	—	—
Sick	—	—	—	—	1	3	2	—[4]
In arrest or confinement	—	—	—	—	—	—	—	—
Total	**2**	**2**	**2**	**2**	**4**	**11**	**5**	**3**
Horses								
Serviceable	59	59	64	64	62	13	13	15
Unserviceable	1	—	—	—	—	—	—	—
Lost in action, died, abandoned, or transferred	—	—	—	—	—	49	—	—

Lt. Calhoun rode a white horse. Roberts, *Custer's Last Battle*, 42. See also Stewart, *Custer's Luck*, 474.

Capt. Benteen testified that Calhoun's position had the only approach to a line on the field, five or six horses at equal distances like skirmishers; and ahead of those were five or six men at about the same distances, showing that the horses were killed and the riders jumped off and were all heading to get where Gen. Custer was. Nichols, *Reno Court*, 417–18.

GO 15, Hq 7th Cavalry, Aug. 4, 1876, mouth of Rosebud Creek, temporarily consolidated the remnant of Co. L with Co. H.

Note: The Battalion Return for Cos. E and L, March, 1876, is filed with Post Returns, Fort Seward, DT, NA, M617, Roll 1153.

Appendix B

TABLE B.13
Company M

	Jan	Feb	Mar	Apr	May	Jun	Jul	Aug
Present								
For duty	46	47	38	49	53	27[28]	23	28
On extra or daily duty	17	18	18	10	7	6	15	8
Sick	3	2	2	2	1	10	1	—
In arrest or confinement	2	—	2	—	—	—	—	—
Total	**68**	**67**	**60**	**61**	**61**	**43**	**39**	**36**
Absent								
On detached service	1	1	1	1	1	7	1	—[4]
With leave	—	—	1	—	—	—	—	1
Without leave	—	—	—	—	—	—	—	—
Sick	—	—	—	—	1	1	10	—[12]
In arrest or confinement	1	2	2	1	1	1	—	—
Total	**2**	**3**	**4**	**2**	**3**	**9**	**11**	**1**
Horses								
Serviceable	62	62	62	62	64	37[45]	45	42
Unserviceable	1	—	—	—	—	8[0]	—	—
Lost in action, died, abandoned, or transferred	—	1	—	—	1	19	—	3

One horse was shot at Fort Lincoln, May 10, 1876, on account of an incurable broken leg (Company, and Regimental, Return, May 1876).

Capt. French said his troop of forty-five men lost thirteen killed and nine wounded. French to Mrs. Augusta Cooke (mother of Lt. Cooke), Aug. 6, 1880, Godfrey Papers, LOC.

Sgt. Ryan said M Troop went into the battle numbering forty-five men and forty-five horses, and all the horses were killed but nine. Ryan to Walter Camp, Nov. 29, 1908, WMC-BYU.

Note: The muster roll of Co. M, June 30, 1876, shows forty-three enlisted men present (excluding Pvts. Dolan and Sterland and forty-five horses.

Pvt. Gallenne recorded that, when Reno galloped to the charge, his company "counted thirty-five men." Portion of Gallenne's journal included in his letter, July 8, 1876, to Rev. Father Genin of Duluth, and published in the *Saint Paul and Minneapolis Pioneer Press*, Jan. 16, 1879.

Pvt. Slaper said that, through the kindness of Sgt. Ryan, he had a copy of the Co. M roll call made on Reno hill the morning of June 27. Brininstool, *Troopers with Custer*, 60.

George W. Glenn offered Walter Camp a copy of the roll of Co. M at the time of the battle. Glenn to Camp, Sept. 23, 1913, WMC-LBHB.

Sgt. Ryan believed his troop had about six men with the pack train. Ryan to Walter Camp, Nov. 29 and Dec. 17, 1908; also Camp to Ryan, Dec. 6, 1908, WMC-BYU.

Sgt. Ryan said twelve pack mules were assigned to each company of the Left Wing when they departed from Powder River. For the scout up the Rosebud each company was issued about twelve or fifteen pack mules, and one Arapahora. Graham, *The Custer Myth*, 240.

Pvt. Morris related that the old guard of ten men from each troop was compelled to lead the pack mules. Brady, *Indian Fights and Fighters*, 402.

Morris said each company was provided with six or eight mules. (See note M52 [Morris] in sketches.)

Appendix B

Pvt. Pigford said the old guard was the troop packers and consisted of five men from each troop. *Morning Observer* (Washington, Pa.), Oct. 5, 1932.

Sgt. Ryan said Sgt. Capes and Pvt. Widdemeyer were left at Powder River with the company teams and probably one or two other privates as company teamsters. Taylor, *With Custer on the Little Big Horn*, 179.

With regard to the Medal of Honor for men of Co. M who distinguished themselves at Little Big Horn, Roman Rutten said he "always understood that French [Co. commander] gave [recommended] all the men who were in the battle and he furthermore made the remark 'All or none.'" Rutten to John Ryan, April 9, 1911, EBC-LBHB, Roll 3.

Appendix C

Research Notes and Minutiae

Dismounted Detachment

GO 8, Hq 7th Cavalry, Fort A. Lincoln, DT, May 12, 1876, organized the regiment into four battalions of three companies each: 1st Battalion, Cos. B, C, I, commanded by Capt. Keogh; 2d Battalion, Cos. E, F, L, commanded by Capt. Yates; 3d Battalion, Cos. A, D, H, commanded by Capt. Weir; 4th Battalion, Cos. G, K, M, commanded by Capt. French. Battalion commanders to detail one noncommissioned officer as acting battalion Sgt-Major. 1st and 2d Battalions constitute the Right Wing commanded by Major Reno; 3d and 4th Battalions the Left Wing commanded by Capt. Benteen.

GO 10, Hq 7th Cavalry, Fort A. Lincoln, DT, May 15, 1876, designated the dismounted men of each battalion to be under the command of a corporal (mounted) detailed from the company having the greatest number of dismounted men, and the entire detachment of dismounted men to be under the command of a sergeant from the company of the regiment having the greatest number of dismounted men.

The dismounted men to be armed with carbines only and carry fifty rounds of ammunition on their persons and march in rear of and act as guard to the wagon train. Company commanders not to authorize the dismounted men of their commands to ride in wagons or march elsewhere than as required by this order. While in camp the dismounted men were under the authority of their company commander and subject to details for guard, fatigue, and stable duty.

"Under the foregoing order Companies B, D, F and K will each furnish one (1) Corporal and K Company one (1) Sergeant (Mounted) for duty with the dismounted detachment," the detail to be made from Regimental Headquarters.

Lt. Godfrey said, "We were short of horses and on the march from Fort Lincoln, Lt. Mathey was in command of the dismounted men; over 100 I'm quite sure." Godfrey to Col. Charles F. Bates, n.d., Bates Papers, Box 3, folder 31, Yale Univ.

Harvey A. Fox said, "Lieutenant Nickerson was in command of the Detachment guarding the wagon train but am not certain of the regiment he was in think it was 6th or 20th Infantry." Fox to John W. Morris, Attorney at Law, Washington, DC, Oct. 17, 1904 (pension file). RG 15.

Lt. James D. Nickerson, 17th Inf., wrote, "I was at the camp at the mouth of the Powder river, Montana, from the early part of June 1876, to about the end of July 1876, and had command of nearly a hundred men of the 7th U. S. Cavalry, who had been left there with the regimental and company property. Men of every company in the regiment were there. I believe I did scouting and outpost work for the camp for about six weeks with these men." Nickerson to Military Secretary, Dec. 3, 1904 (pension file of Harvey A. Fox). RG 15.

A dispatch dated, June 24, Camp on Yellowstone, reported: "We are not entirely destitute of cavalry, having a large company, known as the 'Long-eared Cavalry," doing picket duty. This company is composed of cavalry that was left in charge of the company property and partly of dismounted men who were unable to procure horses; these are mounted on picked mules, and are encamped about a mile to the right of the main camp. . . . A few days ago a large detachment of the 'Long-Ears' was sent on a scout. After reconnoitering pretty thoroughly on the prairie and neighboring bluffs they struck a good size Indian trail not more than thirty six hours old leading in a diagonal direction from Powder river to a point on the Yellowstone ten miles below here, where the remains of their camp was found." *New York Sun*, July 11, 1876, reproduced in *Big Horn Yellowstone Journal*, Vol. 1, No. 2, Spring 1992.

Appendix C

Pvt. Littlefield, Co. B, said he was left behind with the infantry and did duty as a private soldier under Lt. Nickerson of 6th or 17th Infantry. (3540 DD 1876.) NA, M1734, Roll 18.

"On July 4, the 7th's band was to play in celebration of Independence day. Horner and others were in formation, under command of Lt. William Nicholson of the 17th infantry, ready to fire a three-volley salute." Johnson, *Jacob Horner of the Seventh Cavalry*, 10. (*Note:* Horner evidently confused Lt. Nickerson, 17th Inf., with Lt. William Nicholson, who was appointed to the 7th Cavalry, Aug. 15, 1876.)

Saddler-Sgt. Tritten said the supply camp on the Yellowstone was on a sagebrush flat below the mouth of Powder River. Major Moore (camp commander) had pitch pine on Sheridan Butte; also on butte two miles back on south side; said he was going to light up the Yellowstone in celebration of the centennial anniversary. WMC, transcript, BYU-535.

Photos of Sheridan Butte are in Heski, "Camp Powell: The Powder River Supply Depot."

James Sipes (barber on steamer *Far West*) said the camp at Powder River was passed on July 4, and soldiers there had piled up wood for a big bonfire to celebrate. Hammer, *Custer in '76*, 241.

Dr. Elbert J. Clark, in charge of the field hospital at Powder River, said he "was assigned as Medical Officer in charge of the command, consisting of five companies of infantry, and about one hundred and thirty cavalrymen (detachment of the 7th Cavalry) and a wagon train consisting of one hundred and fifty wagons." Monthly Return of Dr. Clark, July 31, 1876, NA, RG 94, Entry 561.

Capt. Walter Clifford, 7th Inf. (with Col. Gibbon's command), estimated there were ninety dismounted 7th Cavalrymen at Powder River. Gray, "Captain Clifford's Newspaper Dispatches."

"The camping-party of a regiment consists of the regimental Quartermaster and Quartermaster-Sergeant and a Corporal and two men per company." *Regs.*, 1863, Article XXXVI (Troops in Campaign), Par. 500 (unchanged in *Regs.*, 1881, Par. 1035).

Also, "A camp is the place where troops are established in tents, in huts, or in bivouac.... The camping-party is a detachment detailed to prepare a camp." *Regs.* 1863, Par. 498 [and *Regs.* 1881, Par. 1033].

GO 3, Hq 7th Cavalry, May 6, 1876, authorized company commanders to leave behind (at Fort Lincoln) one noncommissioned officer and two privates to guard company property and garden. NA, RG 391, Entry 859.

For further comparison: Circular No. 77, Hq Battalion 7th Cavalry, Camp on Yellowstone River, MT, Aug. 8, 1873: "Two men and one noncommissioned officer from each troop may be left with the wagons provided that number of disabled horses or men are in each troop." NA, RG 391, Entry 881.

On July 16, 1876, Lt. Varnum said he was taken along with (his) troop, A, on the steamer *Josephine* to the camp at Powder River, he having been detailed to take charge of the detachment of 7th Cavalrymen (Co. A excepted) left in charge of their company property, together with all other dismounted men of the regiment, and organize them into a company. SFO 30, Hq DD, July 18, 1876. Carroll, *Custer's Chief of Scouts*, 77.

The band of the 7th Cavalry was attached to Capt. Moylan's company for the march to the camp at mouth of Big Horn River. SFO 31, Hq DD, July 19, 1876.

Upon arrival at the new camp, established at the mouth of Rosebud Creek, the men of Lt. Varnum's detachment were ordered to report to their respective companies for duty. SO 62, Hq 7th Cavalry, July 31, 1876.

Horses

In Nov. 1868 Gen. Custer followed the cavalry tradition of "coloring the horses" each troop having all the same color, (all buglers on gray or white).

Appendix C

Band & N.C.S.	gray or white;	Co. G	chestnut sorrels
Co. A	dark bay or brown	Co. H	blood bays
Co. B	light bays	Co. I	bays
Co. C	sorrels or light sorrels	Co. K	sorrels
Co. D	black	Co. L	bays or light bays
Co. E	gray	Co. M	"brindles" (mixed colors)*
Co. F	bays or light bays		

*Sgt. Ryan said Co. M originally had mostly bays but when a number of these played out in the winter campaign of 1868, they were replaced with mostly roan horses. While in the southern states they received as many as 45 black horses, giving them three different colors in the troop. Custer, *My Life on the Plains*, 269-270. Utley, *Life in Custer's Cavalry*, 204. Barnard, *Ten Years with Custer*, 68, 140. Hunt, *I Fought with Custer*, 56. Graham, *The Custer Myth*, 346. Carroll, *Garlington Narrative*, 24.

On Feb. 9, 1876 Major Reno telegraphed department headquarters, reporting the number of horses required for the cavalry companies then at Fort Lincoln: Co. A 18; Co. C 12; Co. D 18; Co. F 11; Co. I 11. RG 393, Part V, Fort Lincoln, DT

Companies reporting fewer horses in May than April: Co. C 2; Co. H 14; Co. L 2.

Companies reporting more horses in May than April: Co. B 3; Co. D 2; Co. G 5; Co. K 4; Co. M 3. Company, and Regimental, Returns, April 30 and May 31; Muster Rolls, April 30 and June 30.

Dr. DeWolf said horses for the medical officers were provided by the quartermaster. DeWolf to wife, May 8, 1876, in Luce, "The Diary and Letters of Dr. James M. DeWolf."

On June 15, Dr. Lord received the horse and equipment of Dr. E. J. Clark at Powder River. Dr. Clark to AAG, Military Division of the Missouri, Jan. 16, 1877, NA, M1734, Roll 18 (22 DD 1877).

Dr. Porter rode a powerful black horse. Hanson, *The Conquest of the Missouri*, 293–94. Dr. Porter's private horse was stolen by Indians, Aug. 21, 1876, near mouth of Powder River, MT. RG 92, Entry 778, Vol. 2.

Captain Marsh (of steamer *Far West*) left Bismarck on 9th of July with a cargo of supplies and sixty cavalry horses, ordered up by General Terry to partially remount the 7th Cavalry, which had been reorganized into a regiment of eight troops under Major Reno. Hanson, *Conquest of the Missouri*, 317; *Bismarck Tribune*, July 19, 1876.

Steamer *Durfee* arrived at 2 o'clock with Gen. Miles six companies of 5th Inf. and 150 cavalry recruits. At the same time, the *Josephine* arrived with supplies and guns and sixty-four horses. Koury, *The Field Diary of General Terry*, Aug. 2, 1876 (camp mouth of Rosebud).

Companies reporting more horses in August than July: Co. B 15; Co. D 7; Co. F 9; Co. G 12; Co. I 1; Co. K 15; Co. L 2. Company, and Regimental, Returns.

Major Reno wrote to Libbie Custer, Aug. 2, 1876, that he was shipping "Dandy" by boat that same day to Lt. Burns at Fort Lincoln. Frost, *General Custer's Thoroughbreds*, 151.

Lt. Godfrey noted Aug. 2, "[the steamer] Carroll pulled out for Lincoln." Godfrey, *Diary*, 30.

The *Carroll* arrived at Fort Buford Aug. 4, bound for Lincoln. RG 94, Entry 547, Fort Buford Medical History.

"The *Carroll* returned Sunday morning [Aug. 6]. Dr. C. A. Stein, Veterinary Surgeon, 7th Cavalry, has tendered his resignation, and has returned to his family at Fort Lincoln." *Bismarck Tribune*, Aug. 9, 1876.

Lt. Burns wrote to Libbie Custer, Aug. 19, that "Dandy" had arrived on the last steamer from the Yellowstone and he would wait to hear from her before sending him. Frost, *General Custer's Libbie*, 237.

Steamer *Durfee* arrived Fort Buford Aug. 8, on way to Yankton. Steamer *Josephine* arrived Buford Aug. 11 and left for Bismarck. RG 94, Entry 547, Fort Buford Medical History.

Appendix C

SO 176, Hq Fort A. Lincoln, DT, Sept. 23, 1876: "Subject to the approval of the Department Commander, a Board of Officers is hereby convened to appraise the value of one horse the property of the United States but for which no officer is responsible, the horse is desired by Mrs. General Geo. A. Custer as the one often ridden by the late General Custer, Lt. Col., 7th Cavalry, and to whom the officers of his regiment desire to present it.

"The A.A.Q.M. will take up on his papers the horse and receipt for the amount paid for him as per appraisement and account to the United States Treasury therefore.

"1st Lt. J. M. Burns, 17th Inftry, A.A.Q.M. will ship to Maine [sic] Mich. one horse and furnish transportation for one man to accompany the horse. Commutation of rations will be furnished the man, Private Lawler, Co. 'G' 7th Cavy for 25 days. By Order of Major M. A. Reno."

Lt. Hugh L. Scott, who joined the 7th Cavalry in Sept. 1876, said he was asked by the officers of the regiment to participate in the purchase from the government of Custer's horse, Dandy, to be sent to Mrs. Custer. Scott, *Some Memories of a Soldier*, 29.

Capt. Bell, Co. F, in a letter dated April 23, 1877, to Capt. Van Horne, post commander at Fort Abercrombie, claimed that from all he was able to learn from officers who had duty in the QM Dept., the two horses then at Fort Abercrombie in possession of Major Reno were public horses. The one known as the "blooded horse" was ridden by Gen. Custer and was a public horse, and after the battle, Reno took possession of him, saying that he intended to keep him as his private horse in place of his private horse killed in the fight. The other horse, Bell said, belonged to his company (F) and was not a private horse, unless purchased by Reno from Lt. Burns after the return of the expedition last October at Fort Lincoln. Bell requested that the horses be sent to him (at Fort Lincoln) unless it appeared from Lt. Burns's papers that they were purchased by Reno.

Capt. Van Horne's endorsement April 29 states that Major Reno had sent an order to the post trader to send one of the horses to St. Paul, that the one ordered sent, Van Horne believed, was the one claimed by Capt. Bell as a company horse, and that Lt. Burns might be able to throw some light on the subject.

General Terry replied on May 1 that the records of the chief QM at Dept. HQ showed that Maj. Reno purchased one horse from the government last November. Lt. Burns, the QM making the sale thought that was the horse ridden by Gen. Custer. There was no record of Maj. Reno having purchased any other horse from the government since June 25, 1876. RG 393, Part V, Fort Abercrombie, DT.

In May 1877, Capt. Bell, Co. F, requested that Pvt. Pilcher join the company in the field, with the company horse formerly in possession of Major Reno and much needed to replace an unserviceable one. Letter from Captain Bell, May 15, 1877, Stone Creek, DT, NA, M1734, Roll 20 (2231 DD 1877).

Regs. 1863, Par. 1123. "Forage shall be issued to officers only for the horses actually kept by them in service, not exceeding in number as follows . . . in time of peace, general and field officers, three horses; officers below the rank of field officers, two horses.

Regs. 1863, Par. 1143. "In the field, on the frontier, or in active service, the commanding officer may authorize a mounted officer to take from the public stables one or two horses at a price one-third greater than the average cost of the lot from which he selects, or at the actual cost of the horse when that can be ascertained; providing he shall not take the horse of any trooper. A horse so taken shall not be exchanged or returned. Horses of mounted officers shall be shod by the public farrier or blacksmith."

GO 13, Hq Dept. of Dakota, St. Paul, Minn., June 12, 1876. Letter of instruction from the General of the Army [Gen. Sherman], June 6, 1876, to the Commanding General, Dept. of Dakota, St. Paul, Minn: "It is reported to the General of the Army that mounted officers keep in service public horses, and at same time draw forage for private horses. This cannot be allowed, nor must they use public animals, except as authorized by Army Regulations." NA, M1734, Roll 16.

Appendix C

SO 79, Hq 7th Cavalry, Fort A. Lincoln, DT, Oct. 1, 1876. "In accordance with GO 13, Dept. of Dakota, Officers of the Regiment will provide themselves with a mount as is intended by the greater allowance of pay they receive and not expect to ride Government horses. They are under this order allowed to purchase from the Government and if they desire to do so will make immediate application. If an officer should be dismounted from any cause in the field it is authorized for him to use a Government horse, but under such circumstances he will not draw private forage and the horse will be foraged with the company."

GO 11, Hq Fort Lincoln, Jan. 30, 1877. Reference to GO 13, Hq DD, June 12, 1876, and SO 79, Hq 7th Cavalry, Oct. 1, 1876. "The use of Company horses for any purpose other than that for which they were assigned to the troopers (except in cases especially authorized from these Headquarters) is strictly prohibited, and officers desiring to avail themselves of the privilege granted in the foregoing orders will do so in the manner therein prescribed."

Capt. Albert Barnitz, upon joining his troop, G, March 23, 1867, related that he then had two excellent horses for himself. Utley, *Life in Custer's Cavalry*, 18.

Trumpeter Mulford, Co. M, on the march in May 1877, wrote, ". . . we take no extra horses along for the men. Each officer has two for his own use . . ." Mulford, *Fighting Indians*, 74.

John Ryan said all government horses were branded with both the company and regimental mark. The officer's private horses that they rode had no mark on them. Barnard, *Ten Years with Custer*, 34. See Hutchins, *Boots and Saddles at the Little Big Horn*, 56.

In April 1873, for the march from Yankton to Fort Rice, "Custer . . . issued an order which will prevent the use of troop horses for private purposes, except that perhaps those officers who are not mounted will be allowed the privilege of riding a govt. horse until they can suit themselves." Lt. Larned to his mother, April 25, 1873, Charles W. Larned Papers, USMA.

"When this command moves from this post there will be no led horses authorized with the respective troops except one led horse to such officer who owns and keeps in service at least one horse. All serviceable horses will be required to mount the command, horses with sore backs will not be considered as unserviceable but will be lead in rear of the troop to which they belong, the rider to accompany the command dismounted until his horse is in fit condition for service. No horses will be transferred from one troop to another except under orders from this Headqrs." Circular No. 67, Hq Detach't 7th Cavalry, Camp near Fort Rice, DT, June 14, 1873, NA, RG 391, Entry 881.

"Each officer of the 7th Cavalry is permitted to ride one public horse in addition to his private horses, this is in accordance with a decision of a former Dept. Commander (Major General Hancock, then commanding Dept. of the Missouri)." Excerpt from letter of Gen. Custer to the acting assistant adjutant general, Yellowstone Expedition, July 9, 1873, in Carroll, *Yellowstone Expedition of 1873*, p. 33.

Dr. Lawrence A. Frost defined a public horse as "one that was assigned to every officer and enlisted man in the cavalry corps but was government property. It was common practice for officers to purchase an additional horse, usually a thoroughbred, to use as an alternate while in the field so that a fresh and rested mount was always available." Frost, *Custer's 7th Cav and the Campaign of 1873*, 61.

On June 24, when Lt. Hare was assigned to the Detachment of Indian Scouts, Lt. Varnum said he (Varnum) changed horses and went back with some of his 'Rees to examine an Indian trail that had been reported to Gen. Custer by Lt. Godfrey. Varnum to Walter Camp, April 14, 1909, in Hammer, *Custer in '76*, p. 59 n2.

Before starting to the Crow's Nest the night of June 24, Lt. Varnum said he changed to his horse Sioux and left his thoroughbred King Bernadette, which Gen. Custer had bought for him at his request in Kentucky two years before. "The Babe of the Regiment," EBC-LBHB, Roll 4:3594–3616.

Dennis Lynch said there were but few extra horses among Benteen's command, and they were the personal property of the troop commanders. Lynch to Walter Camp, Jan. 17, 1908.

Appendix C

John McGuire said he was ordered to the pack train when his horse became very lame during the march up the Rosebud and Lt. Harrington let him ride his extra horse. McGuire to Walter Camp, Dec. 4, 1908, WMC-BYU.

When Major Reno detailed Lt. Hare to ride back to hurry up the packs, Hare said he traded horses with Lt. Godfrey because his extra horse, and Godfrey's too, were with the pack train. Hare to Godfrey, Dec. 15, 1924, Godfrey Papers, LOC.

Lt. Mathey said that, about an hour after Benteen's command left on their scout, he (Mathey) had a horse that was very warm and he changed him for another one and went to the head of the (pack) train. Nichols, *Reno Court*, 512.

Regs. 1881, Par. 293 [GO 17, 1876]. Specifications for purchase of cavalry horses: "To be geldings, of hardy colors, sound in all particulars, in good condition, well broken to the saddle, from fifteen to sixteen hands high, not less than five nor more than nine years old, and suitable in every respect for Cavalry service."

Regs. 1881, Par. 297. "A descriptive book of public animals will be kept at the headquarters of every regiment of Cavalry . . . wherein will be recorded the descriptive list accompanying each animal transferred. . . . Purchasing officers and others, transferring animals, are required to see that they are marked plainly, and to specify such marks on the descriptive list, for the purpose of ready identification."

Regs. 1881, Par. 298. "At the headquarters of every regiment of Cavalry, with every company of Cavalry . . . and with the records of every officer in immediate charge of public animals, a descriptive list of horses and mules shall be kept, showing the name, age, size, color, and other peculiarities of each animal, how and when acquired, his fitness for service, how long he has been in service, the name of his rider or driver, and the particular use to which he is or was applied."

Regs. 1881, Par. 300. "After an animal has been assigned, his rider or driver shall not exchange or surrender him to the use of any other person without the written permission of the Captain of his company or of the officer responsible for him."

"It often happens that a trooper retains the same animal through his entire enlistment, and it comes to be his most intimate friend. There is nothing he will not do to provide him with food; if the forage runs low or the grazing is insufficient, stealing for his horse is reckoned a virtue among soldiers. [See Cassius Carter, note C21.] Imagine then, the anxiety, the real suffering, with which a soldier watches his faithful beast growing weaker day by day, from exhaustion or partial starvation. He walks beside him to spare his strength, and finally, when it is no longer possible to keep up with the column, and the soldier knows how fatal the least delay may be in an Indian country, it is more pitiful than almost any sight I recall, the sadness of his departure from the skeleton, whose eyes follow his master in wondering affection, as he walks away with the saddle and accoutrements. It is the most merciful farewell if a bullet is lodged in the brain of the famished or exhausted beast, but some one else than his sorrowing master has to do the trying deed." Custer, *Tenting on the Plains*, 230.

"[C]avalrymen grew very fond of their horses and spent a great deal of time caring for them. The name of each horse was inscribed over his stall. The owners delighted in foraging for special treats for their animals. Each horse appeared to have a personality of its own. Some were difficult to handle. Among these were horses which would nip the hand that was pouring oats into the feed bin, or kick as the man was leaving the stall. Horner said he had one horse which caused him considerable grief. The animal had a habit of taking on a dancing, prancing gait when traveling with other horses in formation. When it was traveling alone with its rider it behaved normally. On a march to Fort Totten on one occasion, Horner was so badly shook up, he obtained permission to ride by himself. He was glad when an officer at that post ordered it condemned. Shortly thereafter a new supply of horses arrived at Fort Totten and he was permitted to select a fine sorrel pacer. It had a comfortable single-step gait and riding it was like being in a rocking chair. Women at the fort fell in love with the horse and often asked their officer husbands if they might ride it. Horner was not happy over this situation and after a time

Appendix C

he discovered the horse suffered from the too gentle handling. He faintly complained and the practice was stopped." Johnson, *Jacob Horner of the Seventh Cavalry*, 26–27.

For additional information on the relationship between a cavalryman and his horse, see Lawrence, *His Very Silence Speaks*, 291–318. See also the narrative of Gen. Godfrey in Graham, *The Custer Myth*, 125–149, and Chandler, *Of Garry Owen in Glory*, 51–69.

Capt. Benteen counted seventy dead cavalry horses on Custer's battlefield. Nichols, *Reno Court*, 419.

Lt. Godfrey said there were thirty-nine dead horses (and forty-two bodies) on Custer hill. Graham, *The Custer Myth*, 377.

Stan Roy said he was detailed on June 28 to help shoot about twenty wounded horses scattered down the side of the bluffs, which had been left during Reno's retreat, and wounded horses that had strayed out from Reno hill during the two days' fight, some of which had been turned loose after being wounded. Hammer, *Custer in '76*, 116.

Lt. Edgerly thought there must have been as many as fifty dead horses on Reno hill. On the morning of the 27th, the horses were very thirsty and were taken directly down the bluffs to water. They would sit on their haunches and slide at the steepest places. Their rush for the river when they got near to it was very pathetic. Ibid., 58. Stan Roy said it was a pitiful sight to see the poor animals plunge their heads into the water up to their eyes and drink. Ibid., 116.

Col. Gibbon spent two hours on Reno hill June 27, conversing with the officers, and thought he counted forty-eight dead horses in one little valley, an exposed place. Nichols, *Reno Court*, 557.

"On the hill where Reno made his stand, the numerous rifle pits and breast works show what his men did for their defense. Down the hill about a hundred yards lie the remains of forty-six horses, killed at the picket line." *Bismarck Tribune*, Nov. 8, 1877.

"Pack-Train"

Pack transportation was a new experience for the officers and men of the 7th Cavalry, and the mules too, which were taken from the six-mule wagon teams, the swings and leaders but not the wheelers (those closest to the wheels).* The leaders tended to be smaller than the swings while the wheelers were good heavy mules. Chandler, *Of GarryOwen*, 54. *Custer in 76*, 138. Barnard, *Ten Years with Custer*, 22. See, Custer, *Tenting on the Plains*, 222-226.

Twelve of the biggest strongest mules, with the Spanish leather aparejos, carried 24 boxes of carbine ammunition; each troop assigned one mule with two boxes of 1000 rounds each. Hunt, *I Fought with Custer*, 64-66. Hammer, *Custer in '76*, 68.

Mules were allowed to each company in a ratio to its number of men, the average being 13 mules per company. *New York Sun*, July 11, 1876, dispatch from camp on Yellowstone, "Closing on the Indians."

General Terry's journal contains two pages of numbers presumed to be a distribution of pack-mules: "Cos 7 Cav 152; Medical 2; Custer 2; Reno 1; N.C.Staff 1; Packer 1; Scouts inc Officer 5; Guides & Ints 1; Co. Officers 13." The Diary of General Alfred H. Terry, Mss. Div., LOC. See also, Koury, *The Field Diary of General Terry*, 35-36.

For comparison: Gen. Crook's command also used two mules to carry medical supplies, instruments, dressings, medicines, 24 blankets, a rubber bed cover, and several bottles of brandy. Gillette, "United States Army Surgeons and the Big Horn-Yellowstone Expedition of 1876."

Pvt. Davern testified that, on Reno hill, Major Reno told him to go to *his* pack-mule and get his bedding. Nichols, *Reno Court*, 356.

---

*For more information on the nature of pack trains, see, Essen, "Notes and Documents: Mules, Packs, and Packtrains;" also, Bourke, *On the Border With Crook*, 151-155.

Appendix C

Lt. Varnum said *his* pack-mule was lost and he had no baggage. Brininstool, *Troopers with Custer*, 151.

Lt. Mathey testified he had about 160 mules in the pack train. B. F. Churchill estimated 175 mules. Nichols, *Reno Court*, 465, 512.

A dispatch dated Custer's Battle Field, June 28, reported 185 pack mules went up the Rosebud with the 7th Cavalry. *New York Herald*, July 8, 1876.

On June 8, Lt. Godfrey received eleven pack mules and saddles (in preparation for an eight day's scout) and had considerable amusement with the raw mules. Godfrey, *Diary*, 6. Godfrey said each troop detailed a non-commissioned officer and four men as packers. Chandler, *Of Garryowen in Glory*, 54.

A few civilian packers with the expedition gave instructions, especially how to tie the "diamond hitch". Chandler, *Of GarryOwen*, 54. Pvt. Kipp said it was some little trouble to teach a man to pack a mule using the Diamond Hitch, and an officer required a good reason to substitute a learned man with a green man, especially after a four day trip and just going into battle. Kipp to Walter Camp, Dec. 1, 1921, WMC-BYU.

B. F. Churchill thought there were 6 or 7 citizen packers. John Frett and Capt. McDougall each estimated 5 or 6 altogether. Lt. Mathey judged there were 4 or 5. Nichols, *Reno Court*, 465, 509, 512, 528.

Pvt. Thompson related that he found the five citizen packers in the ravine on Reno hill. However, Thompson also noted five citizen packers with Reno's scout June 10. Magnussen, *Peter Thompson's Narrative*, 63, 235. [Presumably other packers accompanied the mules with Gen. Custer and the Left Wing from Powder River on June 15 – RLW]. Sgt. Ryan said 12 pack mules were assigned to each company of the Left Wing when they departed from Powder River. In addition, Gen. Terry had Custer take 25 extra mules to replace any that may have broken down on Reno's scout. (Reno had a hundred mules). Graham, *The Custer Myth*, 240. Koury, *The Field Diary of General Terry*, 22. Willert, *The Terry Letters*, 19.

For the march up the Rosebud, Sgt. Ryan said the mules were laden with rations for 15 days, and one-half forage for the horses. Graham, *The Custer Myth*, 240.

Lt. Godfrey said the regiment transported 15 days' rations of hard bread, coffee, and sugar, and 12 days' rations of bacon. Chandler, *Of Garryowen in Glory*, 55.

Running Wolf said the steamboat landed boxes of hardtack crackers, at mouth of the Rosebud, June 22, and when the bugle blew, they all rode to where the crackers were and each one took rations enough to fill his leather saddle bags. Libby, *The Arikara Narrative*, 140.

The daily ration is defined as: sixteen ounces of hard bread; twelve ounces of bacon; to every one hundred rations, eight pounds of coffee; fifteen pounds of sugar. *Regs.* 1863, Par. 1190, (unchanged in *Regs.* 1881, Par. 2150). For horses, daily portions of forage were twelve pounds oats, corn or barley, and for mules, nine pounds. *Regs.* 1863, Par. 1121, and, *Regs.* 1881, Par. 1886. See John S. Gray, "The Pack Train of George A. Custer's Last Campaign."

Also among the packs were boxes of canned fruit and vegetables (their juices later used to satisfy thirst on Reno hill), and some ginger ale. George W. Glenn to Walter Camp, n.d., [1913], WMC-LBHB. Hardorff, *On the Little Big Horn With Walter Camp*, 185. Marquis, *Custer, Cavalry & Crows*, 81.

Dennis Lynch said each mule was loaded with about 300 pounds, says bacon sacks were placed between two boxes of hardtack. Hammer, *Custer in '76*, 139.

Pvt. Glenn recalled the pack train was heavily loaded, not less than 300 [pounds] weight on every mule. Glenn to Walter camp, nd, [1913], WMC-LBHB.

Appendix C

In Gen. Crook's pack trains the net average weight carried by each mule was 320 pounds, though a government pamphlet said the weight should not exceed 175 pounds. The aparejo varied between 55 and 65 pounds. Bourke, *On the Border With Crook*, 151, 154.

Major Reno said, due to the limited capacity, the men carried four days' rations on their person, and the remaining eleven days were on the pack-mules. Nichols, *Reno Court*, 579, 589.

To further relieve the pack-mules, the troopers overloaded themselves with ammunition, each man carrying 100 rounds for his carbine, his cartridge belt full and the rest in his saddle-bags; his pistol was loaded and enough to load twice more. Nichols, *Reno Court*, 45-46, 230, 282. Saddle pockets contained two extra horseshoes (one front and one hind), nails, currycomb and brush, and cartridges. Hammer, *Custer in '76*, 135. Taylor, *With Custer*, 156.

Lt. Godfrey and Pvt. Windolph said each man carried a twelve-pound bag of oats tied to his saddle. They let their horses graze as much as they could and with two or three pounds of oats a day the mounts did fairly well. Chandler, *Of Garryowen in Glory*, 55. Hunt, *I Fought with Custer*, 73.

Pvt. Goldin said most of the men carried a small sack containing twelve quarts of oats, which were later emptied out in front of their steed, the sack then rounded out with their spare clothing. See, Carroll, *Custer in Periodicals*, 96-118.

Sgt. Knipe told of small sacks of oats taken along as precaution against running short of feed; though not compelled, each man who wanted to did so, carrying perhaps two gallons apiece in small sacks. Hammer, *Custer in '76*, 92.

When the regiment left the Yellowstone, June 22, cargo on the pack-mules began falling off before the column was even out of camp, and the mules straggled badly all that day. Graham, *The Custer Myth*, 134.

Pvt. Kipp said most of the mules carrying commissary stores were equipped with the sawbuck packs which gave great distress to the mules, causing the loads to frequently fall off and have to be repacked. Deposition (nd), Box 18, folder 256, Charles F. Bates Papers.

During the night march June 24, Co. F lost a pack of hard bread and the detail, led by Sgt. Curtiss, sent back to recover it, found the boxes being opened by an Indian who immediately galloped away into the hills. Graham, *The Custer Myth*, 137-138.

Pvt. Taylor, Co. A, recalled the loss of a sack of frying pans on the Rosebud. Taylor to Godfrey, Mar. 31, 1912, Godfrey Papers, LOC.

Pvt. Devoto, Co. B, said it was so dark during the night march June 24 he could scarcely see the man riding in front of him and had to follow the noise of camp kettles hitting against the pack-saddle of his mule. Devoto's "Description of Reno's Fight", nd, WMC-LBHB.

Pvt. Morris, Co. M, during the short halt about 3 a.m., June 25, hitched his horse to the strap of one boot and his mule to the other. Morris to editor of *The Record*, Mar. 11, 1892; newspaper clipping, nd, sent with letter from Morris to Walter Camp, Dec. 24, 1909, WMC-BYU.

Pvt. Kipp, Co. K, said he had charge of one ammunition mule, which were all picked mules furnished with aparejos to keep their backs in good condition. Deposition (nd), Box 18, folder 256, Charles F. Bates Papers.

Before crossing the divide June 25, Custer instructed the officers that only one non-commissioned officer and six men of each troop should remain with the packs, confirming an order issued on the Yellowstone. Carroll, *The Benteen-Goldin Letters*, 153, 181. Godfrey, *Diary*, 11.

Godfrey said each private led two mules and the non-com assisted in adjusting the packs. Godfrey to Col. Charles F. Bates, Feb. 9, 1928, Bates Papers, Yale Univ.

Appendix C

Dennis Lynch said about 120 men accompanied the packs (exclusive of Troop B), however, only about half that number were regular "packers," the others were officer's servants and some of the headquarters fatigue, whose duties consisted in putting up and taking down the officer's tents as occasion required. Lynch to Walter Camp, Dec. 27, 1908, WMC-BYU.

John McGuire said there were strikers, cooks, headquarters details, and men leading officer's extra horses, to the number of two or three to each troop, with the pack train. Hammer, *Custer in '76*, 124, n. 3.

Lt. Nowlan reported July 6 that only about fifty mules were fit for service in the 7th Cavalry. Koury, *The Field Diary of General Terry*, 27.

The Dakota column's inexperience with pack transportation was again displayed in August 1876, when Gen. Terry distributed mules and pack-saddles to the several regiments and battalions of his command, in proportion to their strength, and sent his wagons back to the Yellowstone. GFO 8, Hq DD, Aug. 10, 1876.

Lt. Bourke, aide to Gen. Crook, whose pack train was a marvel of system, the mules in continuous training since the preceding December and moved along with clockwork precision, described Gen. Terry's train as a sad burlesque, a string of mules of all sizes, each led by one soldier and beaten and driven along by another – attendants often rivaling animals in dumbness. On the first day's march [Aug. 11] Terry's train dropped, lost, or damaged more stores than had Crook's command since the campaign began. Lt. Godfrey said some of the packs did not get out of camp for over an hour. Bourke, *On the Border with Crook*, 353. Godfrey, *Diary*, 34.

Appendix D

Rates of Pay in the U.S. Cavalry Service, 1876

Commissioned officers were entitled to the annual amounts listed below, paid in monthly installments by the paymaster:

Colonel	$3,500
Lieutenant Colonel	3,000
Major	2,500
Captain	2,000
Regimental Adjutant	1,800
Regimental Quartermaster	1,800
First Lieutenant	1,600
Second Lieutenant	1,500

Commissioned officers below the rank of brigadier-general were paid 10 percent of their current yearly pay for each term of five years of service, the total amount of such increase not to exceed 40 percent. The pay of a colonel was not to exceed $4,500 a year, and the pay of a lieutenant-colonel not to exceed $4,000 a year. The salaries "shall be in full of all commutation of quarters, fuel, forage, servants' wages and clothing . . ." (Brevets conferred did not entitle an officer to any increase of pay.)

Each officer received allowances for quarters (number of rooms according to rank) and fuel (cords of wood per month based on season). In addition, each regimental grade was allowed forage for two horses, with increased allowance from September to April, depending on whether north or south of the 43d degree north latitude.

Monthly pay of enlisted men during first term of enlistment:

Sergeant Major	$23.00
Quartermaster Sergeant	23.00
Saddler-Sergeant	22.00
Chief Trumpeter	22.00
Chief Musician	60.00
First Sergeant	22.00
Sergeant	17.00
Corporal	15.00
Blacksmith	15.00
Farrier	15.00
Saddler	15.00
Wagoner	14.00
Trumpeter	13.00
Private	13.00

With the exception of chief musicians, whose pay remained constant, all other grades received one dollar per month for the third year, one dollar more for the fourth year, and one dollar more per month for the fifth year. The increases were considered as retained pay, and not paid to the soldier until his discharge from the service, and forfeited unless he served honestly and faithfully until the date of discharge.

Appendix D

Enlisted men honorably discharged who reenlisted within one month, after five years' service, including their first enlistment, were paid at the rate allowed to those serving in the fifth year of their first enlistment: Provided, that one dollar per month be retained from the pay of the reenlisted man, of whatever grade, during the whole period of his reenlistment, to be paid to the soldier at discharge, but forfeited unless he served honestly and faithfully to the date of discharge.

Thus, every soldier honorably discharged who re-enlisted within one month thereafter was further entitled, after five years' service, including his first enlistment, to receive, for the period of five years next thereafter, two dollars per month in addition to the ordinary pay of his grade; and for each successive period of five years of service, so long as he remained continuously in the army, a further sum of one dollar per month.

These allowances were indicated on the bimonthly troop muster rolls with the remark: "$2 per mo. for five years' continuous service"; "$3 per mo. for ten years' continuous service"; and so forth. Men serving subsequent enlistments but who had not reenlisted continuously were indicated with the remark: "Entitled to re-enlistment pay." From the pay of all enlisted men, the paymaster deducted twelve and a half cents per month for support of the "Soldiers' Home."

Also of note: Privates on extra duty as laborers of not less than ten days' duration received compensation of twenty cents per day.

Enlisted men employed continuously in hospitals as cooks and nurses for a period exceeding ten days were paid for extra duty at twenty cents per day.

Company cooks were detailed in turn from the privates of each company at the rate of one cook for each company numbering thirty men, and two cooks for each company numbering more than thirty men; and were to serve on each detail ten days.

(Soldiers on "pioneer" duty were members of work-parties mending roads and removing obstacles to the march.)

Official Army Register for January, 1876, AGO, Washington, DC, Jan. 1, 1876. *The Revised Statutes of the United States*, 2d ed., 1878; Laws Relating to the Military Service, Chap. 1 and Chap. 3. *Regulations of the Army of the United States on the 17th of February, 1881*; Pars. 1225, 2299, 2450–56. See also, Rickey, *Forty Miles a Day on Beans and Hay*, passim.

Indian scouts received the pay and allowances of a private soldier and in addition were entitled to forty cents per day "Use & Risk" pay when furnishing their own horse and equipment. Muster and Pay Roll of Lt. Varnum's detachment of Indian scouts, June 30, 1876. RG 217, (UD) Entry 530.

Bibliography

The terms "entry" and "series" are synonymous.

Archival Sources

National Archives and Records Administration (Principal records consulted for this work)

Record Group 15. Preliminary Inventory of Pension Case Files of the Bureau of Pensions and the Veterans Administration, 1861–1942. (NM-17). 1963.
    Entries 1–7: Indian Wars Pension Files, 1892–1926
    Entries 14–27: Civil War and Later Pension Files, 1861–1942

Record Group 15. Financial Records and Pension Control Registers of the Bureau of Pensions and the Veterans Administration, 1805–1933. (NM-21). 1964.
    Entry 2: Pension Agency Payment Books, 1805–1909

Record Group 29. Records of the Bureau of Census. Federal Population Decennial Census Schedules.

Record Group 75. U.S. Indian Census Schedules, 1884–1940. Microfilm Publications M595.

Record Group 92. Part I: Textual Records of the Office of the Quartermaster General. (NM-81). 1967.
    Entry 38: General and Miscellaneous Letters Sent, 1871–1883
    Entry 42: Registers of Letters Received (general), 1871–1883
    Entry 43: Miscellaneous Letters and Reports Received, 1871–83
    Entry 225: Consolidated Correspondence File, 1794–1890
    Entry 228: Reporting Officer Index to Part (1861–94) of Series 238
    Entry 229: Station Indexes to Part (1861–67) of Series 238.
    Entry 232: Card Index to Names of Scouts Mentioned in Series 238
    Entry 238: Reports of Persons and Articles Hired, 1818–1905
    Entry 751: Letters Sent Relating to Claims, 1871–89
    Entry 755: Registers of Claims Letters Received, 1871–89
    Entry 778: Letters Sent Relating to Miscellaneous Claims, 1875–89
    Entry 781: Registers of Miscellaneous Claims Letters Received, 1875–89
    Entry 891: List of Miscellaneous Claims, Under the Act of March 3, 1849; Referred to the Third Auditor for Settlement, 1876–80.
    Entry 893: List of Claims Allowed, of Claims Not Allowed, and of Claims Allowed in Part, July 1878–Nov. 1880
    Entry 894: List of Miscellaneous Claims Referred to the Third Auditor, 1880–1892
    Entry 1105. Annual, Personal, and Special Reports of Quartermaster Officers, 1872–78
    Entry 1138: Register of Assignments of Quartermaster Officers (station books), 1861–94
    Entry 1944: Interment Reports from National Cemeteries

Record Group 94. Records of the Adjutant General's Office. Preliminary Inventory No. 17. Washington: 1949. National Archives Publications Nos. 49–21. 1981.
    Entry 1: Letters Sent, 1800–1889

Bibliography

Entry 2: Letters Sent, 1874–1887
Entry 6: Endorsements, 1850–1889
Entry 7: Endorsements, 1864–1867
Entry 12: Letters Received, 1805–1889
Entry 25: Document File, 1890–1917 (see M698)
Entry 27: Indexes to Document File, 1890–1917
Entry 44: Orders and Circulars, 1797–1910
Entry 53: Muster Rolls of Regular Army Organizations, 1784–1912
Entry 57: Muster Rolls of Volunteer Organizations: Civil War, and Other Wars, 1836–65
Entry 61: Returns of Departments, 1818–1916
Entry 62: Returns of Territorial Divisions, Departments, and Districts, 1809–1916
Entry 63: Returns of Military Posts, early 1800s–1916
Entry 66: Returns of Military Organizations, early 1800s–1916
Entry 67: Returns of "Expeditions, 1806–1916
Entry 89: Registers of Enlistments, 1798–1914
Entry 91: Enlistment Papers, 1798–1912
Entry 92: Enlistment Papers, Indian Scouts, 1866–1914
Entry 93: Index to Enlistment Papers, Indian Scouts, 1866–1914
Entry 94: Personal Papers," 1812–1912. Includes certificates of disability, discharges, final statements, medical papers, and burial records, relating to personnel of the regular Army
Entry 95: Surgeons Certificates of Disability, 1812–99
Entry 96: Final Statements," 1862–99 (Incomplete)
Entry 98: Registers of Discharges, 1872–83
Entry 243: Application Papers of Cadets (USMA), 1814–66
Entry 271: Record of Admissions to the Insane Asylum, 1862–1917 (St. Elizabeth since 1916)
Entry 272: Register of Insane Soldiers, 1853–1919
Entry 273: Index to Register of Insane Soldiers, 1853–1919

Appointment, Commission, and Personal Branch, 1783–1917

Entry 287: "Miscellaneous File." Early 1800s–1917. Original Documents relating to many subjects. Indexed in "General Information Index" (Entry 289)
Entry 297: Letters Received, 1863–94; Letters, Reports, and Related Papers Received by the Commission Branch, 1863–70; and by the Appointment, Commission, and Personal Branch, 1871–94. Index in Entry 299.

Enlisted Branch, 1848–89

Entry 406: Letters Sent, 1863–1889 (copies of letters sent in response to inquiries relating to recruitment, discharges, furloughs, and other matters concerning enlisted men of Regular Army and volunteer forces). Index in Entry 407.
Entry 408: Endorsements and Memoranda, 1863–1870. Index in each volume.
Entry 409: Letters Received, 1862–1889. Index in Entry 411.
Entry 410: Registers of Letters Received, 1863–1889. Index in Entry 411.
Entry 413: Indexes to Special Orders Relating to Enlisted Men, 1864–1865, 1875–1889. Recruiting Division.
Entry 467: Letters Sent, 1825–82

Correspondence and Related Papers of the Record and Pension Office, 1889–1904

Entry 501: Document File, 1889–1904. Consists chiefly of correspondence relating to service of Volunteer soldiers. Index in Entry 503.

Bibliography

Carded Medical Records, 1812–1912

>   Entry 529: Carded Medical Records, Regular Army, 1821–1884
>   Entry 530: Carded Medical Records, Regular Army, 1894–1912
>   Entry 531: List of Uncarded Medical Registers, nd.
>   Entry 534: Carded Medical Records, Volunteers of Mexican and Civil War
>   Entry 538: Carded Medical Records of Hospital Stewards, Noncommissioned Staff Officers, and Musicians, 1821–84

Medical Records, 1814–1919

>   Entry 544: Field Records of Hospitals, 1821–1912. Arranged under four headings: States and Territories; Army Corps; Departments; US Army Regimental.
>   Entry 547: Medical Histories of Posts, 1868–1913
>   Entry 561: Personal Papers, Medical Officers and Physicians prior to 1912. Personal reports showing station and duty.
>   Entry 565: Monthly Returns of Medical Officers, 1859–1886
>   Entry 585: Miscellaneous Medical Record Books, 1861–1903
>   Entry 593: Papers Relating to Hospital Stewards, 1862–1893
>   Entry 600: Returns of Hospital Stewards, 1865–1887

Reports on Diseases and Individual Cases, 1841–1893

>   Entry 622: "File B" 1860s–1870s. Reports on methods of transportation of wounded
>   Entry 624: "File F" 1861–1889. Lists of casualties in various engagements
>   Entry 627: "SSD Files" 1861–1888. Reports of Army surgeons, mainly from posts and expeditions in the West and general medical reports of campaigns
>   Entry 629: Special Scientific and Historical Reports, 1860s–1880s. Reports on diseases, wounds, deaths, medical operations, etc.
>   Entry 632: Miscellaneous Reports, 1870s–early 1900s. Reports on various subjects including reports of surgeons accompanying expeditions
>   Entry 641: "B Books" 1860s–ca. 1919. Registers of patients in hospitals, usually monthly. Index in Entry 676.
>   Entry 643: Registers of Deaths, Regular Army, 1860–89
>   Entry 644: Registers of Discharges, Regular Army, 1861–86
>   Entry 675: "F Books," 1860s–ca 1914. Miscellaneous hospital records, including records of hospital stewards, and prescription books, etc.
>   Entry 676: Index to "B Medical Cards and "B, E, F, G, and H Books"
>   Entry 681: Monthly Reports of Posts and Stations, 1869–1872, 1874–1876, 1878, 1880–1887
>   Entry 688. Record of Missing Reports of Medical Officers, 1850–1880

Record Group 99. Records of the Office of the Paymaster General. Preliminary Inventory 9. 1948.
>   Entry 1: Letters Sent, 1808–89
>   Entry 7: Letters Received, 1799–1894
>   Entry 9: Indexes to Letters Received, 1799–1894
>   Entry 54: Registers of Payments to Troops, 1841–1913
>   Entry 55: Registers of Payments to Enlisted Men, Retired, 1885–1913
>   Entry 56: Index to Registers of Payments to Enlisted Men, Retired, 1885–1907
>   Entry 101: List of Civilian Employees, 1861–1911
> Supplement to Preliminary Inventory No. 9. (NM-34). 1964.
>   Entry 8: Registers of Letters Received, 1799–1894

Bibliography

    Entry 12A: Unregistered Letters Received, 1869–1906
    Entry 46: Record of Paymasters' Accounts, 1871–1912
Record Group 111. Records of the Office of the Chief Signal Officer. Supplement to Preliminary Inventory 155. (NM-77). 1967.
    Entry 40U: Press Copies of Receipts ("Line Receipts") for Supplies Sent and Received ("Letters") and ("Vouchers"), ca. 1881–1882. The volume marked vouchers also contains letters sent and received in 1896 by Capt. R. E. Thompson, Signal Corps, relating to "Custer's Last Stand"
Record Group 112. Records of the Office of the Surgeon General. (NM-20). 1964.
    Entry 94: Station Books of Medical Officers, 1857–1902. Two volumes. One for officers at permanent posts, the other at temporary camps and stations. (Volume 2 lists Dr. E. J. Clark, AAS, Camp on Yellowstone River, June to August 1876. Dr. Henry R. Porter, AAS, May 14, 1876 to January 2, 1877, with Gen. Terry's Command on Sioux Campaign. Dr. Isaiah C. Ashton, AAS, April 21 to August 16, 1876, with Gen. Terry's Expedition.)
Record Group 217. *Records of the Accounting Officers of the Department of the Treasury.* Inventory 14 (Revised). Compiled by William F. Sherman with addition and index by Craig R. Scott. Lovettsville, Va.: Willow Bend Books, 1997.
    Entry 209: Registers of Quartermaster Accounts and Miscellaneous Claims Reported on by the Third Auditor, 1878–1894
    Entry 621: Letters Sent by the Claims Division, 1876–1894
    Entry 657: Index to Docket Books of Miscellaneous Claims, 1847–1897
    Entry 658: Docket Books of Miscellaneous Claims, 1847–1913
    Entry 712: Settled Accounts and Claims, 1847–1850; 1878–1897
    Entry 715: Certificates of Settlements, 1817–1894
    Entry 730: Quartermaster Abstracts, 1854–80. See also Entry 730A.
  Undescribed Materials (UD)
    Entry 530 (UD). Paymaster Accounts of Maj. William Smith, Department of Dakota, 1876–1877
    Entry 1002 (UD): Army Subsistence Accounts Third Auditor, 1865–1877
Record Group 231. Records of the United States Soldiers Home. (NM-61). 1965.
    Entry 12: Register of Men Admitted and of Inmates at the Military Asylum and at the Soldiers' Home in Washington, D.C., May 1851–Feb. 1881
    Entry 13: Registers of Inmates, 1852–1908
    Entry 17: Consolidated Morning Reports of Inmates, 1857–1927
    Entry 22: Monthly Returns Relating to Inmates, Jan. 1879–Dec. 1908
    Entry 24: Daily Lists of Men Admitted, Suspended, Readmitted, Dismissed, Transferred and Deceased, 1886–87; 1898–1912
    Entry 32: Registers of Inmates Reported Sick, 1881–1908
    Entry 35: Register of Deaths, 1852–1942
    Entry 36: Certificates of Deaths, 1876–89; 1913–29
    Entry 37: Statements of Service and Descriptions of Deceased Inmates, 1880–1942
    Entry 38: Discharges and Other Personal Papers of Inmates, 1869–1922
Record Group 391. Records of United States Regular Army Mobil Units 1821–1942. (NM-93). Washington, D.C.: 1970.
  Regimental Records 5th Cavalry (and 2nd Cavalry), 1855–1920.
    Entry 771: Letters, Orders, and Reports Received from or Relating to Members of the 5th Cavalry ("Name File"), 1861–1866
  Regimental Records 7th Cavalry, 1866–1917
    Entry 858: General and Special Orders and Circulars Issued, 1867–1870
    Entry 859: General and Special Orders, and Circulars, 1874–1877
    Entry 860: General Orders Issued, 1878–1881
    Entry 862: Special Orders Issued, 1878–1881

Bibliography

Entry 864: Miscellaneous Records, 1867–1916
Entry 869: Letters Sent by Troop E, 1873–1878, 1885–1891
Entry 870: Name Indexes to Part (1885–1888 and 1897–1906) of Series 871
Entry 871: Register of Letters Received by Troop E. 1885–1888 and 1892–1906
Entry 875: History of Troop K, 1867–1917
Entry 877: Letters Sent by a Detachment of the 7th Cavalry (General Orders and Circulars issued by the detachment in 1868 are also included), April–May 1867
Entry 878: Letters Sent by the Surgeon of a Detachment in Kansas and Arizona, 1868 and under General Custer, 1870
Entry 880: Letters Received by General Custer's Detachment, 1873
Entry 881: General and Special Orders and Circulars Issued by General Custer's Detachment, April 1873–Sept. 1874
Entry 882: Letters Received by a Detachment on the Yellowstone Expedition, 1873–75

Record Group 393. Part I: Records of United States Army Continental Commands, 1821–1920. Volume I: Geographical Divisions and Departments and Military (Reconstruction) Districts. Preliminary Inventory 172 (72-8) 1973.

Department of Arizona
Entry 183: General Orders, Circulars, and Court-Martial Orders, 1870–1893
Entry 184: Special Orders, 1870–1893
Entry 185: General and Special Orders and other orders issued and received, 1866–1889

Department of the Columbia
Entry 754: Special Orders, 1868–1911
Entry 755: General and Special Orders Issued by Headquarters in the Field (Howard's Expedition), July–Oct. 1877

Department of Dakota
Entry 1167: Headquarters, Letters Sent, 1866–71, 1874–75
Entry 1172: Name and Subject Indexes to Series 1173 and 1174
Entry 1173: Registers of Letters Received, 1866–96
Entry 1175: Letters and Reports Received, 1866–1904
Entry 1190: General Orders and Circulars, 1867–1911, and Court-Martial Orders, 1869–1894
Entry 1191: Special Orders, 1866–1911
Entry 1201: Special Orders Received from Headquarters Escort, Northern Boundary Survey Commission in the Field, May–Sept. 1874
Entry 1297: Reports of Persons and Articles Hired, 1872–1900
Entry 1298: Rolls of Enlisted Men Employed on Extra Duty, 1873–1876;

Yellowstone Expedition, 1872–1873
Entry 1333: Letters Sent, Register of Letters Received, Endorsements, Orders and Circulars Issued, Mar.–Sept. 1873
Entry 1334: Letters and Telegrams Received, July 1872–Oct. 1873
Entry 1336: Circulars Issued, June–Aug. 1873

Northern Boundary Survey Commission Escort, 1873–1876
Entry 1337: Letters Sent, 1873–1874
Entry 1338: Endorsements Sent, 1873–1874
Entry 1339: Special Orders Issued, 1873–1874
Entry 1340: General Correspondence Book of a Detachment of Indian Scouts, 1874–1876

Black Hills Expedition, 1874
Entry 1341: General and Special Orders Issued, June–Aug. 1874

Big Horn and Yellowstone Expedition, 1876
Entry 1342: Letters, Telegrams, and Endorsements Sent, May–Oct. 1876
Entry 1343: Orders and Circulars Issued by the Infantry Battalion Headquarters, July–Oct. 1876

Bibliography

Department of the East

    Entry 1409: Headquarters. Special Orders, 1865–1868

Department of the Gulf

    Entry 1767: Special Orders, 1861–1866
    Entry 1962: Letters Sent, 1871–1878
    Entry 1964: Endorsements Sent, Nov. 1871–June 1876
    Entry 1965: Telegrams Sent, 1871–1878
    Entry 1967: Name and Subject Indexes to Series 1968
    Entry 1968: Registers of Letters Received, 1871–1878
    Entry 1969: Letters Received, 1873–1877
    Entry 1972: Special Orders Issued, 1873–1877
    Entry 2048: General Orders and Circulars, 1904–1911

Department of the Lakes

    Entry 2274: General Orders, Circulars, and Special Orders, 1898–1910

Military Division of the Missouri

    Entry 2538: Letters Sent, 1868–91
    Entry 2545: Registers of Letters Received, 1871–1891
    Entry 2546: Letters Received, 1866–1867 and 1871–1891
    Entry 2547: Special File of Letters Received, 1863–1885

Department of the Missouri

    Entry 2593: Letters Received, 1861–1867
    Entry 2594: Unentered Letters Received, 1861–1867
    Entry 2595: Miscellaneous Letters and Reports Received, 1861–1867
    Entry 2601: Letters Received, 1868–1898
    Entry 2625: Special Orders, 1861–1870

Division and Department and Army of the Potomac

    Entry 3982: General Orders Issued, 1861–1865
    Entry 3984: Special Orders and Circulars Issued, 1861–1865

Department of the South

    Entry 4131: Special Orders, Aug. 1868–Mar. 1871, 1872, and 1874

Record Group 393. Part III: Records of United States Army Continental Commands, 1821–1920. Preliminary Inventory 172. Vol. III: Geographical Districts and Subdistricts

District of Yellowstone and Yellowstone Command, 1876–1881

    Entry 902: General Orders, Special Orders, and Circulars Issued, Oct. 1876–Sept. 1877
    Entry 903: General Orders and Circulars Issued, Sept. 1877–June 1881
    Entry 904: Special Orders Issued, June 1877–Mar. 1881

Bibliography

Record Group 393. Part IV: Records of United States Army Continental Commands, 1821–1920. Preliminary Inventory 172. Vol. IV: Military Installations, 1821–1881 (records that could not be separated from those of departments, divisions, and districts)

Fort Ridgely, Minn., 1859–1867

    Entry 1068: Letters Sent, Oct. 1862–May 1867
    Entry 1070: General and Special Orders, Oct. 1861–Mar. 1863, and Nov. 1864–May 1867
    Entry 1071: General and Special Orders, Mar. 1863–Nov. 1864

Fort Wadsworth, DT, 1864–66

    Entry 1321: Letters Sent, Aug. 1864–Sept. 1866
    Entry 1322: Letters Received From the District of Minnesota, July 1864–Dec. 1865

Record Group 393. Part V: Records of United States Army Continental Commands, 1821–1920. Preliminary Inventory 172. Vol. V: Military Installations (records separated from those of departments, divisions, and districts)

    Fort Abercrombie, DT
    Fort Abraham Lincoln, DT
    Fort Buford, DT
    Fort (Camp) Grant, AT
    Fort Meade, DT
    Fort Myer, Va.
    Newport Barracks, Ky.
    Fort Rice, DT
    Fort Ridgely, Minn.
    Fort Seward, DT
    Post of Shreveport, La.
    Fort Sisseton (Wadsworth), DT
    Fort Snelling, Minn.
    Fort Totten, DT

British Military Records

The National Archives (TNA), formerly the Public Record Office (PRO), Kew, Richmond, Surrey.
Royal Military Academy Sandhurst, Camberley, Surrey.

Manuscript Collections

Allison, Edwin Henry. Manuscript. William L. Clements Library, University of Michigan, Ann Arbor. Allison's autobiography, ca. 1882, "The Surrender of Sitting Bull."

Anders, Frank L. Papers. Chester Fritz Library, University of North Dakota, Grand Forks. Born at Fort Lincoln in 1875 and prominent resident of North Dakota until his death in 1966, Anders pursued a life-long interest in the Custer battle.

Bailey (Baker), William J. "Reminiscence." (SC 376). Montana Historical Society, Helena.

Baldwin, Frank D. Diary, 1876. Huntington Library, San Marino, Calif.

Bates, Charles Francis. Papers. Beinecke Library, Yale University, New Haven, Conn. Contains pertinent letters from Col. Varnum, Gen. Godfrey, and Richard A. Roberts; also copies of letters to Godfrey from Walter Camp and several battle participants.

Bond, Fred. G. Writings. (SC 1535). Montana Historical Society, Helena.

Botzer, Edward. Troop Duty Book (High Bull's Double Trophy Roster). Museum of the American Indian, Heye Foundation, New York.

Bibliography

Bowman, Daniel H. Manuscript Collection. (SC 454). Montana Historical Society, Helena. Contains correspondence from Walter M. Camp, 1920–1925.
Brininstool, Earl Alonzo. Manuscript Collection. Barker Texas History Center, University of Texas at Austin.
Brininstool, Earl Alonzo. Manuscript 1412. Harold B. Lee Library, Brigham Young University, Provo, Utah.
Brown, Alexander, and Charley Reynolds. Journal of 1876. Minnesota Historical Society, St. Paul.
Brown, Edwin M. Papers from Sioux Campaign, 1876–77. (SC 476). Montana Historical Society, Helena.
Brown, William Carey. Papers. Norlin Library, University of Colorado, Boulder. Includes Walter Camp material, and photos.
Camp, Walter Mason. Field Notes and Maps. Lilly Library, University of Indiana, Bloomington.
Camp, Walter Mason. Notes and Correspondence. Little Big Horn Battlefield Collections, Crow Agency, Mont..
Camp, Walter Mason. Notes and Correspondence. (Mss. 57), Harold B. Lee Library, Brigham Young University, Provo, Utah.
Capron, Thaddeus H. Diary 1876. American Heritage Center, University of Wyoming, Laramie.
Cincinnati, Ohio, City Directories, 1850–1880. Cincinnati Historical Society. Also in the Public Library of Cincinnati, History Dept.
Cincinnati, Ohio, Records of U.S. Circuit Court, Southern District of Ohio, 1875. RG 21. NA regional facility, Chicago, Ill.
Coon, Homer L. "The Outbreak of Chief Joseph." Beinecke Library, Yale University, New Haven, Conn.
Crow, Joe Medicine. "The Jackson Place" (Part I). Typescript copy, 5 pp, original in private collection.
Custer, Elizabeth Bacon. Manuscript Collection. Little Big Horn Battlefield, Crow Agency, Mont.
Custer, George Armstrong, and Elizabeth Bacon Custer. Papers. Beinecke Library, Yale University, New Haven, Conn.
Dimon, Charles A. R. Papers. Beinecke Library, Yale University, New Haven, Conn. Includes register of visitors at Fort Rice.
Dustin, Fred. Dustin Collection. Little Big Horn Battlefield, Crow Agency, Mont.
Ellison, Robert Spurrier. Papers. Lilly Library, University of Indiana, Bloomington.
Ellison, Robert Spurrier. Manuscript 782. Harold B. Lee Library, Brigham Young University, Provo, Utah.
Ellison, Robert Spurrier, and Walter M. Camp. Papers. Western History Department, Public Library, Denver, Colo.
Frost, Lawrence A. Collection of Custeriana, Monroe County Library, Monroe, Mich.
Geant, Eugene. Journal of, March 17 to Oct. 6, 1876. Copy in Walter M. Camp Papers, Harold B. Lee Library, Brigham Young University, Utah.
Ghent, William James. Papers. Manuscript Division, Library of Congress, Washington, D.C.
Gibbs, Eugene B. Manuscript of personal notes and observations on Battle of Little Big Horn. (SC 33). Montana Historical Society, Helena.
Godfrey, Edward S. Papers. Manuscript Division, Library of Congress, Washington, D.C.
Godfrey, Edward S. Family Papers. U.S. Army Military History Institute, Army War College, Carlisle, Pa.
Hagner, Francis R. Collection. Manuscript Division, New York City Public Library.
Harper, James W. Collection. Texas Tech University, Lubbock. Contains some correspondence of Gen. Hugh L. Scott.
Hennepin County Minn., Records of District Court, 1880–1885. Minnesota Historical Society, St. Paul.
Irvine, Javan B. Diary and Letters. State Archives, South Dakota, Pierre.
Johnson, Andrew. Papers. Manuscript Division, Library of Congress, Washington, D.C.
Klawitter, Mrs. Fred. Manucript (B18), "Army Life at Fort Lincoln." State Historical Society, Bismarck, N. Dak. Transcript of interview in 1935 by Matt Lagerberg,
Krusee, Harry M. (aka Melanchton H. Crussy) Papers. (SC 1554). Montana Historical Society, Helena.
Larned, Charles W. Papers. Library, United States Military Academy, West Point, N.Y.
Libby, Orin G. Papers (A85). State Historical Society, Bismarck, N. Dak.
Marquis, Thomas B. "From Newspaper Clipping, White Sulphur Springs, Mont., dated 1 Feb. 1933." Interview with Mrs. Helena Jackson, age 83, former wife of Custer scout, Robert Jackson.
McClellan, George B. Papers. Manuscript Division, Library of Congress, Washington, D.C.

Bibliography

McIntosh, Donald. Notebook, 1876. Little Big Horn Battlefield Collections, Crow Agency, Mont.

McLaughlin, James. Papers. Assumption College, Richardton, N. Dak.

Mechling, Henry. Letter to James Braddock, Mt. Pleasant, Pa., July 16, 1921. Manuscript collection, U.S. Army Military History Institute (Army War College), Carlisle, Pa. Account of his experience at the Battle of the Little Big Horn with Capt. Benteen.

Meddaugh, Samuel L. Diary, May 14– Sept. 15, 1876. Newberry Library, Chicago, Ill.

Merington, Marguerite. Papers. Manuscript Division, New York City Public Library.

Miles, George M. (nephew of Gen. Miles). Journal of Notes of a trip to Montana, July to Dec., 1876. (SC 318). Montana Historical Society, Helena.

Minneapolis, Minn., City Directories, 1875–1885. Minnesota Historical Society, St. Paul.

Minnesota, District of. Records of U.S. Commissioners Court, 1876–1877. Minnesota Historical Society, St. Paul.

Northern Pacific Railroad. Papers. Minnesota Historical Society, St. Paul.

Noyes, Alva J. Papers. (SC16). Montana Historical Society, Helena. Contains undated typescript of interview with George B. Herendeen.

Nugent, William D. "From Memory's Store." Biographical File, Little Big Horn Battlefield, Crow Agency, Mont.

O'Donnell, I. D. Papers. Little Big Horn Battlefield, Crow Agency, Mont. Friend and interviewer of John Burkman.

Patterson, Robert Maskell. A Short Account of the Preliminary Survey of the Northern Pacific Railway in 1871 by a member of the survey party on the Expedition. Northern Pacific Railroad Papers. Minnesota Historical Society, St. Paul.

Porter, Henry R. Papers and scrapbook (B291). State Historical Society, Bismarck, N. Dak.

Ramsey County, Minn. Records of District Court, 2nd Judicial District, 1874–1885. Minnesota Historical Society, St. Paul.

Reynolds, Charley, and Alexander Brown. Journal of, 1876. Minnesota Historical Society, St. Paul. (Entries made by Brown, July 1 to Sept. 10, 1876. Entries by Reynolds, May 17 to June 22, 1876.)

Saint Paul, Minn. City Directories, 1875–1906. Minnesota Historical Society, St. Paul.

Sanford, Wilmot P. Diary, 1876. Beinecke Library, Yale University, New Haven, Conn.

Scott, Gen. Hugh Lenox. Papers. Manuscript Division, Library of Congress, Washington, D.C.

Scott, Hugh Lenox. Papers. Library, U.S. Military Academy, West Point, N.Y.

Scott, Hugh Lenox Papers. Rosenbach Museum and Library, Philadelphia, Pa.

Slaughter, Benjamin F., and Linda Warfel. Papers (A3). State Historical Society, Bismarck, N. Dak.

Smith, John Henry A Soldier's Report of the Custer Massacre. Little Big Horn Battlefield Collections, Crow Agency, Mont.

Smith, Nettie Bowen (wife of Lieut. A. E. Smith). Scrapbook. Bancroft Library, University of California, Berkeley. Also on Little Big Horn Battlefield Collections, microfilm roll 18.

Sully, Alfred. Papers. Beinecke Library, Yale University, New Haven, Conn.

Taylor, William O. Scrapbook, and Notes for "With Custer on the Little Big Horn." Beinecke Library, Yale University, New Haven, Conn.

Terry, Alfred H. Field Diary, May 17 to Aug. 22, 1876. Manuscript Division, Library of Congress, Washington, D.C.

Vetter, Michael. Papers, 1874–1876 (B373). State Historical Society, Bismarck, N. Dak.

Wilkinson, William Grant, A. R. "Four Months in the Saddle; the Cross-country March of the 8th Cavalry from the Mexican to the Canadian Border." Manuscript at Old Fort Meade Museum, S. Dak.

Yzermans, Fr. Vincent A. Interview with Sister Anastasia, daughter of Fred Gerard, Feb. 25, 1958. Library of St. Benedict Academy, St. Joseph, Minn.

Government Publications

Annual Report of the Secretary of War, 1876. 44th Cong., 2nd Sess., House E. Doc. 1, Part 2.

Annual Report of the Secretary of War, 1877. 45th Cong., 2nd Sess., Vol. III, Part 2.

Bibliography

Executive Documents of the House of Representatives for the First Session of the Fifty-Second Congress, 1891–92. Washington, D.C.: Government Printing Office, 1892.

Laws of the United States Governing the Granting of Army and Navy Pensions; Together with Regulations and Instructions Relating Thereto In Effect November 1, 1923. Washington, D.C.: Government Printing Office, 1923.

Official Army Register for January, 1876. Washington, D.C.: Adjutant General's Office, 1876.

Official Army Register for January, 1877. Washington, D.C.: Adjutant General's Office, 1877.

Official Army Register for January, 1881. Washington, D.C.: Adjutant General's Office, 1881.

Official Register of the United States: Biennial Register, Sept. 30, 1873, List of Officers and Employees in the Civil, Military, and Naval Services, 1861–1905. Washington, D.C.: Government Printing Office.

Outline Description of the Posts in the Military Division of the Missouri Commanded by Lieutenant General Philip H. Sheridan. Chicago, Ill., Military Division of the Missouri, 1876. Facsimile edition, The Old Army Press, Fort Collins, Colo., 1972.

Regulations of the Army of the United States and General Orders in Force on the 17th of February, 1881. Washington, D.C.: Government Printing Office 1881.

Regulations for the Army of the United States, 1889. Washington, D.C.: Government Printing Office, 1889.

Regulations for the Army of the United States, 1895. Washington, D.C.: Government Printing Office, 1895.

Regulations for the Army of the United States 1901. Washington, D.C.: Government Printing Office, 1901.

Statutes At Large of the United States of America, From December 1889, to March 1891. Vol. 26. Washington, D.C.: Government Printing Office, 1891.

United States Army Regulations of 1861. Revised. Washington, D.C.: Government Printing Office, 1863.

VA History in Brief. What it is, was, and does. VA Pamphlet No. 06-83-1. Washington, D.C.: Government Printing Office, 1986.

Microfilm

Selections from *Microfilm Resources for Research, A Comprehensive Catalog*, National Archives, 1986

Compiled service records of volunteer Union soldiers, 1861–1865, Name index by state and territory. RG 94.

Compiled service records of Confederate soldiers, 1861–1865. Name index by state and territory. Consolidated index in microfilm publication M253. RG 109.

M6: Letters Sent by the Secretary of War Relating to Military Affairs, 1800–1889, RG 107

M22: Registers of Letters Received by the Office of Secretary of War, Main Series, 1800–1870, RG 107

M221: Letters Received by the Secretary of War, Registered Series, 1801–1870, RG 107

M233: Register of Enlistments in U.S. Army, 1798–1914, RG 94

M234: Letters Received by the Office of Indian Affairs, 1824–1881, RG 75

M565: Letters Sent by the Office of the Adjutant General (Main Series), 1800–1890, RG 94

M592: Proceedings of a Court of Inquiry Concerning Conduct of Major Marcus A. Reno at the Battle of the Little Big Horn, June 25–26, 1876, two rolls

M595: Indian Census Rolls, 1884–1940, RG 75.

M617: Returns from U.S. Military Posts, 1800–1916, RG 94

M619: Letters Received by the Office of the Adjutant General (Main Series), 1861–1870, RG 94

M665: Returns from Regular Army Infantry Regiments, 1821–1916, RG 94

M666: Letters Received by the Office of the Adjutant General (Main Series), 1871–1880, RG 94

M686: Index to General Correspondence of the Record and Pension Office, 1889–1920, RG 94

M690: Returns from Regular Army Engineer Battalions, 1846–1916, RG 94

M691: Returns from Regular Army Coast Artillery Corps Companies, 1901–1916, RG 94

M698: Index to General Correspondence of the Office of the Adjutant General, 1890–1917, RG 94

M711: Registers of Letters Received, Office of the Adjutant General, 1812–1889, RG 94

M725: Indexes to Letters Received by the Office of the Adjutant General (Main Series), 1846, 1861–1889, RG 94

M727: Returns from Regular Army Artillery Regiments, 1821–1901, RG 94

Bibliography

M740: Records Relating to Investigations of the Fort Philip Kearney (or Fetterman) Massacre, 1866–1867
M744: Returns from Regular Army Cavalry Regiments, 1833–1916, RG 94 and RG 391
M745: Letters Sent by the Office of the Quartermaster General, Main Series, 1818–70, RG 92
M850: Veterans Administration Pension Payment Cards, 1907–33, RG 15
M857: Letters Sent by the Headquarters of the Army (Main Series), 1828–1903, RG 108
M903: Descriptive Commentaries from the Medical Histories of Posts, RG 94 and RG 393
M1064: Letters Received by the Commission Branch of the Adjutant General's Office, 1863–70, RG 94
M1105: Registers of the Records of Proceedings of the U.S. Army General Courts–Martial, 1809–1890, RG 153
M1495: Special Files of Headquarters, Military Division of the Missouri, Relating to Military Operations and Administration, 1863–1885, RG 393
M1635: Letters Received by the Headquarters of the Army, 1827–1903, RG 108
M1734: Letters Received by Headquarters, Department of Dakota, 1866–77, RG 94
T288: General Index to Pension Files, 1861–1934, RG 15
T289: Organization (Regimental) Index to Pension Files of Veterans Who Served between 1861 and 1900, RG 15
T1103: General Court Martial of Gen. Geo. A. Custer, 1867
T1118: Muster Rolls of US Marine Corps, 1798–1860, 1866–92, RG 127

Little Big Horn Battlefield Microfilm Collection (Rolls 1 through 8 comprise the Elizabeth Bacon Custer Collection). Rolls 1 through 18 were filmed ca. 1971–73.

Roll 1: Correspondence and Memorabilia (frames 0001–1024)
Roll 2: Correspondence, Orders, and Miscellaneous Documents (frames 1025–1843)
Roll 3: Other Correspondence, Orders, and Miscellaneous Documents (frames 1848–2882)
Roll 4: Other Correspondence, Orders, and Misc. Documents (frames 2887–3235); E. B. Custer Library Manuscripts and Notes (frames 3241–4021)
Roll 5: Literary Manuscripts and Notes of E. B. Custer (frames 4026–5244)
Roll 6: Broadsides & Clippings/ Memorabilia, (5251–6446)
Roll 7: Broadsides-Clippings/Memorabilia (frames 6452–6566); Pamphlets (frames 6572–7309)
Roll 8: Pamphlets (frames 7314–7986)
Roll 9: (frames 0001–1405), Sections M and N of Battlefield Study Collection; Correspondence and Manuscripts of other collections (e.g., Godfrey, Gibson, DeWolf, Snyder, O'Donnell (Burkman), Bowen, Barry)
Roll 10: (frames 1406–2746), Sections "O, P, Q, R, S, T, U, V, W" of Battlefield Study Collection (O, Broadsides; P, Covers; Q, Memorabilia; R, Miscellaneous; S , Clippings; T, Fred Dustin Correspondence; U, Dustin Miscellaneous and Notes; V, Dustin Pamphlets; W, Dustin Research Collections in Dustin's order number)
Roll 11: (frames 2747–3986), Section W of Battlefield Study Collection.
Roll 12: (frames 3987–5306), Section W and X of Battlefield Study Collection; Section X is 7th Cavalry Collection, (monthly returns for Companies A through M, 1876).
Roll 13: (frames 5307–5939), 7th Cavalry Muster Rolls, oversize newspapers and magazines, oversize certification and miscellaneous.
Roll 14: (frames 5942–6107), Journal of Letters, Reports and Comments by George A. Custer, and original Custer National Cemetery Burial Registers.
Roll 15: 7th Cavalry Muster Rolls (Companies A, C, E, K, and M), 1876, and all Company Returns, 1876 (except April).
Roll 16: Reno Court of Inquiry Transcripts by Col. W. A. Graham and Mrs. E. S. Luce
Roll 17: Cemeterial File, Custer Battlefield, from Records of the War Department, Office of the Quartermaster General Records. Reservation File; Medical; Special Reports; Scientific and Historical File; Letters; Telegrams; Indian Interviews
Roll 18: Scrapbook of Mrs. Nettie Bowen Smith; 7th Cavalry Regimental History-Fort Bliss,1866–1942; Custer Items from Eli S. Ricker Collection; Transcript "The Battle of Prairie Dog Creek—1867" by Capt. A. J. Pliley; Winners of the West

Bibliography

Newspapers

Albuquerque (NM) *Morning Journal*
Allegany County (N.Y.) *Democrat*
The Allentown (Pa.) *Morning Call*
The American Lumberman (Chicago, Ill.)
Anaconda Standard (MT)
The Avant Courier (Bozeman, MT)
Baltimore (Md.) *Gazette*
Bangor (Maine) *Daily News*
Billings (MT) *Gazette*
Bismarck (N. Dak.) *Tribune*
Black Hills (S. Dak.) *Weekly Times*
Bonner Springs (Kans.) *Chieftain*
Bonner Springs (Kans.) *Herald.*
Bozeman (MT) *Times*
Brainerd (Minn.) *Tribune*
The Butte (MT) *Daily Post*
Campbell County (S. Dak.) *Progress*
The Central Record (Lancaster, Ky.)
Charleston (S.C.) *Daily Courier*
Chicago (Ill.) *Evening Journal*
Chicago (Ill.) *Inter-Ocean*
Chicago (Ill.) *Sun-Times*
Chicago (Ill.) *Times*
Chicago (Ill.) *Tribune*
Cincinnati (Ohio) *Commercial*
Cincinnati (Ohio) *Daily Gazette*
Cincinnati (Ohio) *Daily Times*
Cincinnati (Ohio) *Daily Enquirer*
Cincinnati (Ohio) *Times Chronicle*
The Cleveland (Ohio) *Leader*
Columbus (Ohio) *Dispatch*
Columbus (Ohio) *Sunday Dispatch*
Columbus (Ohio) *Press Post*
Commercial Appeal (Memphis, Tenn.)
Courier-Journal (Louisville, Ky.)
The Daily Leader (Cheyenne, Wyo.)
The Daily Missoulian (Missoula, MT)
Daily Morning Chronicle (Washington, D.C.)
The Daily Patriot (Harrisburg, Pa.)
The Daily Picayune (New Orleans, La.).
The Daily Saratogian (Saratoga, N.Y.)
Dakota Herald (Yankton)
Deseret News (Salt Lake City, Utah)
Detroit (Mich.) *Free Press*
Detroit (Mich.) *Tribune*
Dickinson Press (DT)
Dupuyer Acantha (MT)
Eagle Lake (Minn.) *News*
The Evening Star (Washington, D.C.)
The Evening Telegraph (Philadelphia, Pa.)

Bibliography

The Fargo (N. Dak.) *Forum*
The Fort Riley (Kans.) *Guidon*
Frontier Scout (Fort Rice, DT)
Galveston (Tex.) *News*
The Garrard County (Ky.) *News*
Hardin Tribune (MT)
Harlem News (MT)
Helena (MT) *Daily Herald*
Helena (MT) *Independent*
Hillsboro (Ohio) *Dispatch*
Hillsboro (Ohio) *Gazette*
Hillsboro (Ohio) *News-Herald*
Hillsboro (Ohio) Highland Weekly News
The Indianapolis (Ind.) *Daily Sentinel*
Indianapolis (Ind.) *Star*
Junction City (Kans.) *Union*
The Kentucky Register (Richmond)
The Lancaster (Pa.) *Daily Intelligencer*
The Leader-Union (Vandalia, Ill.).
Leavenworth (Kans.) *Daily Bulletin*
Leavenworth (Kans.) *Daily Commercial*
Leavenworth (Kans.) *Daily Conservative*
Leavenworth (Kans.) *Daily Times*
Leavenworth (Kans.) *Weekly Times*
Lewiston (Maine) *Journal*
Lexington (Ky.) *Daily Press*
The Mandan (N.Dak.) *News*
Mandan (N.Dak.) *Pioneer*
Mankato (Minn.) *Free Press*
Marrietta (Ohio) *Times*
Memphis (Tenn.) *Press-Scimitar*
Minneapolis (Minn.) *Tribune*
The Monroe (Mich.) *Commercial*
The Morning Observer (Washington, Pa.)
Mount Pleasant (Pa.) *Journal*
Mount Vernon (Ohio) *Republican*
The National Tribune (Washington, D.C.)
New Orleans (La.) *Daily True Delta*
New York Graphic
New York Herald
The New York Times
Oregon Sunday Journal
Pecatonica News (Ill.)
Philadelphia (Pa.) *Press*
Piqua Daily Call (Ohio)
The Pittsburg (Pa.) *Leader*
The Pollock Progress (S.Dak.)
Portland (Ore.) *Journal*
Rawlins Republican (Wyo.)
The Record (Fargo, N.Dak.)
The Red River Star (Moorhead, Minn.)

Bibliography

The Republican (Coldwater, Mich.)
Rochester (Minn.) *Post*
The Rockford (Ill.) *Register-Gazette*
St. Louis (Mo.) *Republican*
St. Louis (Mo.) *Daily Times*
Saint Paul (Minn.) *Dispatch*
Saint Paul (Minn.) *Daily Pioneer*
Saint Paul (Minn.) *Pioneer Press*
Saint Paul (Minn.) *Daily Press*
Saint Paul and Minneapolis Pioneer-Press and Tribune
Sauk Centre Herald (Minn.)
Sing Sing Republican (N.Y.)
Sioux City (Iowa) *Tribune*
Sioux County (S.Dak.) *Pioneer-Arrow*
Southern Intelligencer (Austin, Tex.)
The Springfield (Mass.) *Republican*
Stillwater (Minn.) *Gazette*
Tacoma (Wash.) *News-Tribune*
The Times News (Pa.)
The Toledo (Ohio) *Blade*
Toronto (Can.) *Daily Star*
Tribune-Review (Pittsburgh, Pa.)
The Vinton (Iowa) *Eagle*
The Washington Post
Waterville (Maine) *Morning Sentinel*
The Wayne County (Ohio) *Democrat*
Whig and Courier (Bangor, Me.)
Williston (N.Dak.) *Daily Herald*
Williston (N.Dak.) *Graphic*
Winona (Minn.) *Herald*
Winona (Minn.) *Republican*
Yellowstone Journal (Miles City, MT)

Periodicals

America's Civil War Magazine
Annals of Wyoming
Annual Report of the Association of Graduates of the United States Military Academy, 1870–1916
Annual Report of the Association of Graduates of the United States Military Academy, 1917–1941
Army and Navy Journal
The Battlefield Dispatch, Custer Battlefield Historical & Museum Association, (CBHMA)
Big-Horn Yellowstone Journal: The History of a Military Expedition (Howell, Mich.)
By Valor & Arms
Civil War Times Illustrated
Clann Chatain (Edinburgh, Scotland)
Collier's, The National Weekly
The Crow's Nest (Custer Association of Great Britain)
The English Westerners' Tally Sheet (London)
Forest and Stream
Greasy Grass, Custer Battlefield Historical & Museum Association, (CBHMA)
The Guidon (Journal of British Custeriana)

Bibliography

The Journal of Arizona History
The Journal of Negro History
Journal of the United States Cavalry Association
The Kansas Historical Quarterly
Mercator's World
Military Images Magazine
Missouri Historical Review
Montana The Magazine of Western History
Nebraska History
Negro Digest
Newsletter (Little Big Horn Associates)
North Dakota Historical Quarterly
North Dakota History
The Prairie Scout (Kansas Corral of the Westerners')
Research Review (Journal of the Little Big Horn Associates)
South Dakota State Historical Collections
South Dakota History
South Western Historical Quarterly
The Sunshine Magazine:Advancing the Resources of the Northwest (The Sunshine Magazine Co., Sioux Falls, S. Dak.)
The Tepee Book (Sheridan, Wyo.)
The Westerners' Brand Book (Chicago)
The Westerners' Brand Book (Kansas City)
The Westerners' New York Posse Brand Book
Winners of the West (St. Joseph, Mo.)

Books and Pamphlets

Alberts, Donald E. *Brandy Station to Manila Bay: A Biography of General Wesley Merritt.* Presidial Press, Austin, Tex., 1980.
Allison, Edwin H. *The Surrender of Sitting Bull.* Walker Litho. & Printing Co., Dayton, Ohio, 1891.
Andreas, Alfred T. *Andreas' Historical Atlas of Dakota.* Lakeside Press, Chicago, 1884.
Armes, George A. *Ups and Downs of an Army Officer.* Np, Washington, D.C., 1900.
Arnold, Steve, and Tim French. *Custer's Forgotten Friend: The Life of W. W. Cooke.* Powder River Press, Howell, Mich., 1993.
Ashburn, P. M. *A History of the Medical Department of the United States Army.* Houghton Mifflin Co., Boston, 1929.
Baldwin, Alice Blackwood. *Memoirs of Major General Frank D. Baldwin.* Wetzel Publishing Co., Los Angeles, 1929.
Baquet, Camille. *History of the First Brigade, New Jersey Volunteers from 1861 to 1865.* Np, Trenton, N.J., 1910.
Barnard, Sandy. *I Go with Custer: The Life and Death of Reporter Mark Kellogg.* The Bismarck Tribune, Bismarck, N. Dak., 1996.
———. *Custer's First Sergeant John Ryan.* AST Press, Terre Haute, Ind., 1996.
———. *Ten Years with Custer: A 7th Cavalryman's Memoirs.* AST Press, Terre Haute, Ind., 2001.
Bates, Charles F., and Charles F. Roe. *Custer Engages the Hostiles.* Old Army Press, Fort Collins, Colo., 1973.
Bergeron, Paul H., ed. *The Papers of Andrew Johnson.* Vol. 11, *August 1866–January 1867.* University of Tennessee Press, Knoxville, 1994.
Billings, John D. *Hard Tack and Coffee: or, The Unwritten Story of Army Life.* G. M. Smith, Boston, 1888.
Black, David. *The King of Fifth Avenue: The Fortunes of August Belmont.* Dial Press, New York, 1981.

Bibliography

Bond, Fred G. *Flatboating on the Yellowstone, 1877.* Reprint of 1925 edition. Ward Hill Press, Staten Island, N.Y., 1998.
Bonney, Orrin H., and Lorraine Bonney. *Battle Drums and Geysers: The Life and Journals of Lt. Gustavus Cheyney Doane, Soldier and Explorer of the Yellowstone and Snake River Regions.* The Swallow Press, Chicago, 1970.
Bourke, John G. *On the Border with Crook.* University of Nebraska Press, Lincoln, 1971.
Boyes, William. *Custer's Black White Man.* South Capitol Press, Washington, D.C., 1972.
Brady, Cyrus Townsend. *Indian Fights and Fighters.* McClure, Phillips & Company, New York, 1904.
Breeling, Lutie Taylor. *When the Trail Was New in Mountraille.* Np, Ross, N. Dak., 1956.
Brininstool, Earl A. *Troopers with Custer.* Stackpole Co., Harrisburg, Pa., 1952.
———, ed. *Campaigning with Custer 1868–69.* Edited by David L. Spotts. University of Nebraska Press, Lincoln, 1988.
Brown, Bill A. *Fort Seward, Territory of Dakota.* Np, Jamestown, N. Dak., 1987.
Brown, D. Alexander. *The Galvanized Yankees.* University of Illinois Press, Urbana, 1963.
Brown, Jesse, and A. M. Willard. *Black Hills Trails.* Journal Publishing Co., Rapid City, S. Dak., 1924.
Brown, Mark H., and W. R. Felton. *The Frontier Years: L. A. Huffman, Photographer of the Plains.* New York: Henry Holt & Company, 1955.
Brown, Mark H. *The Plainsman of the Yellowstone: A History of the Yellowstone Basin.* University of Nebraska Press, Lincoln, 1969.
Bryan, Edwin Colby. *Descendants of John Hutchins of Newbury and Haverhill Massachusetts.* Edited by Jack Randolph Hutchins. Goetz Press, Washington, D.C., 1975.
Burdick, Usher L. *The Army Life of Charles "Chip" Creighton.* National Reform Associates, Paris, Md., 1937.
———. *Some of the Old-Time Cow Men of the Great West.* Baltimore, Md., 1957.
———, and Eugene D. Hart. *Jacob Horner and the Indian Campaigns of 1876 and 1877.* Wirth Bros., Baltimore, Md., 1942.
Burgum, Mrs. Jessamine Slaughter. *Zezula, or Pioneer Days in the Smoky Water Country.* Getchell and Nielsen. Valley City, N. Dak., 1937.
Burkey, Blaine. *Custer, Come At Once! The Custer Years of Fort Hays 1867–1870.* Society of Friends of Historic Fort Hays, Hays, Kans., 1991.
Butler, Francis Gould. *A History of Farmington County, Maine, from the Earliest Explorations to the Present Time, 1776–1885.* Np, Farmington, 1885.
Carroll, John M., ed. *The Benteen-Goldin Letters on Custer and His Last Battle.* J. M. Carroll Company, Mattituck, N.Y., 1974.
———. *Camp Talk: The Very Private Letters of Frederick W. Benteen to His Wife 1871 to 1888.* J. M. Carroll Company, Mattituck, N.Y., 1983.
———. *Custer in Periodicals: A Bibliographic Check List.* Old Army Press, Fort Collins, Colo., 1975.
———. *Custer in Texas: An Interrupted Narrative.* Sol. Lewis Books, New York, 1975.
———. *Custer's Chief of Scouts: The Reminiscences of Charles A. Varnum.* University of Nebraska Press, Lincoln, 1982.
———. *The D. F. Barry Correspondence at the Custer Battlefield* (1888–1932). Privately printed, Bryan, Tex., 1980.
———. *The Frank Anders and R. G. Cartwright Correspondence* (1939–1956), 3 vols. Privately printed, Bryan, Tex., 1982.
———. *The Gibson and Edgerly Narratives.* Privately printed, Bryan, Tex., nd.
———. *The Lieutenant E. A. Garlington Narrative.* Privately printed, Bryan, Tex., 1978.
———. *They Rode with Custer: A Biographical Directory of the Men that Rode with General George A. Custer.* J. M. Carroll Company, Mattituck, N.Y., 1987.
———. *The Sunshine Magazine Articles.* Privately printed, Bryan, Tex., 1979.
———. *The Tepee Book.* Sol. Lewis Books, New York, 1974.
———. *Who Was This Man Ricker and What Are His Tablets That Everyone is Talking About.* Privately printed, Bryan, Tex., 1979.

Bibliography

———. *The Yellowstone Expedition of 1873: Cavalry Bits, One of Seven Volumes*. J. M. Carroll Company, Mattituck, N.Y., 1986.

Carroll, John M., and Lawrence A. Frost, eds. *Private Theodore Ewert's Diary of the Black Hills Expedition of 1874*. CRI Books, Piscataway, N.J., 1976.

Carter, William H. *From Yorktown to Santiago with the Sixth U.S. Cavalry*. State House Press, Austin, Tex., 1989.

Chandler, Melbourne C. *Of GarryOwen in Glory: The History of the Seventh United States Cavalry Regiment*. Turnpike Press, Annandale, Va., 1960.

Church, Charles A. *Historical Encyclopedia of Illinois and History of Winnebago County*. 2 vols. Munsell Publishing Company, Chicago, 1916.

Clark, George. M. *Scalp Dance: The Edgerly Papers on the Battle of the Little Big Horn*. Heritage Press, Oswego, N.Y., 1985.

Clark, W. P. *The Indian Sign Language*. L. R. Hamersly & Co., 1885. Reprint by Bison Books, , University of Nebraska Press, Lincoln, 1982.

Clarke, Joseph I. C. *My Life and Memories*. Dodd Mead and Co., New York, 1925.

Clarke, Norm. *Terry Country Then and Now*. Terry, Mont., THS Class of 1960.

Clarke, W. P. *Dusting off the Old Ones*. Np, Miles City, Mont., 1961.

Cogley, Thomas S. *History of the Seventh Indiana Cavalry Volunteers*. Morningside House, Dayton, Ohio, 1991.

Cortissoz, Royal. *The Life of Whitelaw Reid*. 2 vols. Charles Scribner's Sons, New York, 1921.

Cox, John E. *Five Years in the United States Army*. Sol Lewis Books, New York, 1973.

Crawford, Lewis F. *Rekindling Camp Fires*. Capital Book Company, Bismarck, N. Dak., 1926.

Cullum, George W. *Biographical Register of the Officers and Graduates of the United States Military Academy*. Ten vols., 1850–1950. United States Military Academy, West Point, N.Y.

Custer, Elizabeth Bacon. *Boots and Saddles*. Harper & Brothers, New York, 1913.

———. *Tenting on the Plains*. Harper & Brothers, New York, 1915.

———. *Tenting on the Plains*. With introduction by Jane R. Stewart. University of Oklahoma Press, Norman, 1971.

———. *Following the Guidon*. University of Oklahoma Press, Norman, 1966.

Custer, George A. *My Life on the Plains*. University of Nebraska Press, Lincoln, 1971.

Darling, Roger. *Custer's Seventh Cavalry Comes to Dakota*. Potomac-Western Press, Vienna, Va., 1988.

———. *Custer's Seventh Cavalry Comes to Dakota*. Upton & Sons, El Segundo, Calif., 1989.

———. *A Sad and Terrible Blunder: Generals Terry and Custer at the Little Big Horn: New Discoveries*. Potomac-Western Press, Vienna, Va., 1990.

Davis, E. Elden, ed. *The Reno Court of Inquiry: Articles and Editorials from the Pioneer Press, St. Paul and Minneapolis, 1878–1879*. Powder River Press, Howell, Mich., 1993.

———. *The Indian Campaign of 1876, A Pittsburg Perspective: Articles from* The Pittsburg Leader. Powder River Press, Howell, Mich., 1991.

Day, Carl F. *Tom Custer Ride to Glory*. Frontier Military Series, 22. Arthur H. Clark Company, Spokane, Wash., 2002.

DeLand, Charles E. *History of the Sioux Wars*. South Dakota Historical Collections, Vol. 15, Pierre, S. Dak., 1930.

———. *History of the Sioux Wars*. South Dakota Historical Collections, Vol. 17, Pierre, S. Dak., 1934.

Delo, David Michael. *Peddlers and Post Traders: The Army Sutler on the Frontier*. University of Utah Press, Salt Lake City, 1992.

Dictionary of American Naval Fighting Ships. 8 vols. Naval Historical Center, Washington, D.C., 1958–1981.

Dippie, Brian W. *Nomad: George A. Custer in Turf, Field and Farm*. University of Texas Press, Austin, 1980.

Dixon, Joseph K. *The Vanishing Race—The Last Great Indian Council*. Doubleday, Page and Co., Garden City, N.Y., 1913.

Drips, J. H.. *Three Years among the Indians of Dakota*. With a new introduction by John M. Carroll. Sol. Lewis Books, New York, 1974.

Bibliography

duBois, Charles G. *Kick The Dead Lion: A Casebook of the Custer Battle.* Upton and Sons, El Segundo, Calif., 1987.
Dyer, Frederick H. *A Compendium of the War of the Rebellion.* 3 vols. Thomas Yoseloff, Publisher, Sagamore Press, New York, 1959.
Eastman, Hazel, ed. *Fortress to Farm: or, Twenty-three Years on the Frontier.* Exposition Press, New York, 1969.
Eberhart, Perry. *Guide to the Colorado Ghost Towns and Mining Camps,* 4th rev. ed. Swallow Press, Athens, Ohio, 1969.
Egge, Phyllis Bridges, ed. *Old Post Cemetery: Fort Meade, S.D., 1878–1943.* Old Fort Meade Museum and Historic Research Association, Fort Meade, S. Dak., 1989.
Finerty, John F. *War-Path and Bivoua: Or, the Conquest of the Sioux.* University of Oklahoma Press, Norman, 1967.
Forest, Earle R. *Witnesses at the Battle of the Little Big Horn.* Introduction by John M. Carroll. Monroe County Library System, Monroe, Mich., 1986.
Foster, Joseph. *The Peerage, Baronetage, and Knightage of the British Empire: for 1883.* Np, London, England, 1883.
Fougera, Katherine Gibson. *With Custer's Cavalry: From memoirs of Mrs. Katherine Gibson, widow of Captain Frank M. Gibson, 7th Cavalry.* University of Nebraska Press, Lincoln, 1968.
Franklin, John Hope, and Loren Schweninger. *Runaway Slaves: Rebels on the Plantation.* Oxford University Press, New York and Oxford, 1999.
Frederick, J. V. *Ben Holladay: The Stagecoach King.* University of Nebraska Press, Lincoln, 1989.
Fristad, Palma. *Historic Mandan and Morton County: Early Days to 1970.* Np, Mandan, N. Dak., 1970.
Frost, Lawrence A. *General Custer's Libbie.* Superior Publishing Company, Seattle, Wash., 1976.
———, ed. *With Custer in '74: James Calhoun's Diary of the Black Hills Expedition.* Brigham Young University Press, Provo, Utah, 1979.
———. *Custer Legends.* Bowling Green University Popular Press, Bowling Green, Ohio, 1981.
———. *Custer's 7th Cav and the Campaign of 1873.* Upton and Sons, El Segundo, Calif., 1986.
———. *General Custer's Thoroughbreds: Racing, Riding, Hunting and Fighting.* J. M. Carroll Company, Mattituck, N.Y., 1986.
———. *The Court-Martial of General George Armstrong Custer.* University of Oklahoma Press, Norman, 1987.
Garst, Shannon. *Custer, Fighter of the Plains.* Illustrated by Harve Stein. Julian Messner, Inc., New York, 1948.
Gibbon, Major-General John. *Adventures on the Western Frontier.* Edited by Alan Gaff and Maureen Gaff. Indiana University Press, Bloomington, 1994.
Gillette, Mary C. *The Army Medical Department, 1866–1917.* Government Printing Office, Washington, D.C., 1995.
Godfrey, Edward S. *Diary of the Little Big Horn: The Field Diary of Lt. Edward Settle Godfrey, 7th Cavalry.* Edited with an Introduction and Notes by Edgar I. Stewart and Jane R. Stewart. Champoeg Press, Portland, Oreg., 1957.
Graham, William A. *The Story of the Little Big Horn.* Stackpole Co., Harrisburg, Pa., 1926.
———. *The Colors of the Seventh at the Little Big Horn: Custer's Battle Flags.* Pacific Palisades, Calif., 1952.
———. *The Reno Court of Inquiry: Abstract of the Official Record of Proceedings.* Stackpole Co., Harrisburg, Pa., 1954.
———. *The Custer Myth: A Source Book of Custeriana.* Stackpole Co., Harrisburg, Pa., 1957.
Gray, John S. *Centennial Campaign: The Sioux War of 1876.* Old Army Press, Fort Collins, Colo., 1976.
———. *Custer's Last Campaign: Mitch Boyer and the Little Big Horn Reconstructed.* University of Nebraska Press, Lincoln, 1991.
Greene, Jerome A. *Evidence and the Custer Enigma: A Reconstruction of Indian-Military History.* Kansas City Posse of the Westerners, Kansas City, Mo., 1973.

———. *Indian Wars Veteran Organizations.* The Guidon Monograph Series, J. M. Carroll Company, Mattituck, N.Y., 1985.
———. *Slim Buttes, 1876: An Episode of the Great Sioux War.* University of Oklahoma Press, Norman, 1990.
———. *Yellowstone Command: Colonel Nelson A. Miles and the Great Sioux War, 1876–1877.* University of Nebraska Press, Lincoln, 1991.
———. *Frontier Soldier: An Enlisted Man's Journal of the Sioux and Nez Perce Campaigns 1877.* Montana Historical Society Press, Helena, 1998.
———. *Nez Perce Summer 1877: The U.S. Army and the Nee-Me-Poo Crisis.* Montana Historical Society Press, Helena, 2000.
Guttridge, Leonard F. *Ghosts of Cape Sabine: The Harrowing True Story of the Greely Expedition.* Putnam and Sons, New York, 2000.
Hammer, Kenneth. *Men with Custer: Biographies of the 7th Cavalry, 25th June, 1876.* Old Army Press, Fort Collins, Colo., 1972.
———, ed. *Custer in '76: Walter Camp's Notes on the Custer Fight.* Brigham Young University Press, Provo, Utah, 1976.
———. *Men with Custer: Biographies of the 7th Cavalry.* Edited by Ronald H. Nichols. Custer Battlefield Historical and Museum Association, Hardin, Mont., 1995.
Hampton, Bruce. *Children of Grace: The Nez Perce War of 1877.* Henry Holt & Company, New York, 1994.
Hanson, Joseph Mills. *The Conquest of the Missouri: Being the Story of the Life and Exploits of Captain Grant Marsh.* Murray Hill Books, Inc., New York, 1946.
Harcey, Dennis W., and Brian R. Croone, with Joe Medicine Crow. *White-Man-Runs-Him, Crow Scout with Custer.* Evanston Publishing, Inc., Evanston, Ill., 1995.
Hardorff, Richard G., ed. *The Custer Battle Casualties: Burials, Exhumations, and Reinterments.* Upton and Sons, El Segundo, Calif., 1989.
———. *Camp, Custer, and the Little Big Horn: A Collection of Walter Mason Camp's Research Papers on General Custer's Last Fight.* Upton and Sons, El Segundo, Calif. 1997.
———. *The Custer Battle Casualties, II: The Dead, the Missing, and a Few Survivors.* Upton and Sons, El Segundo, Calif., 1999.
———. *On the Little Big Horn with Walter Camp: A Collection of Walter Mason Camp's Letters, Notes and Opinions on Custer's Last Fight.* Upton and Sons, El Segundo, Calif., 2002.
———. *Walter M. Camp's Little Big Horn Rosters.* Arthur H. Clark Company, Spokane, Wash., 2002.
Harrison, Joseph T. *The Story of the Dining Fork: The Dining Fork Valley, Turkey-Foot Road, Carroll and Harrison Counties, Ohio.* C. J. Krehbiel Company, Cincinnati, Ohio, 1927.
Hart, John P. *Custer and His Times, Book Four.* Little Big Horn Associates, Printed by Thomson-Short, Inc., Dexter, Mich., 2001.
Hasskarl, Robert A., Jr. *Brenham Texas 1844–1958.* Banner Press Company. Brenham, Tex., 1958.
Hassrick, Royal B. *The Sioux: Life and Customs of a Warrior Society.* University of Oklahoma Press, Norman, 1964.
Hedren, Paul L., ed. *The Great Sioux War 1876–77: The Best from* Montana the Magazine of Western History. Montana Historical Society Press, Helena, 1991.
Heitman, Francis B. *Historical Register and Dictionary of the United States Army.* 2 vols. Olde Soldiers Books, Inc., Gaithersburg, Md., 1988.
Hoig, Stan. *The Battle of the Washita: The Sheridan-Custer Indian Campaign of 1867–69.* University of Nebraska Press, Lincoln, 1979.
Horn, W. Donald. *Portrait of a General: George Armstrong Custer and the Battle of the Little Big Horn.* Don Horn Publications, West Orange, N.J., 1998.
Hotaling, Edward. *They're Off! Horse Racing at Saratoga.* Syracuse University Press, Syracuse, N.Y., 1995.
Howard, Hamilton Gay. *Civil-War Echoes: Character Sketches and State Secrets. A United States Senator's Son and Secretary.* Howard Publishing Company, Washington, D.C., 1907.
Hunt, Frazier, and Robert Hunt. *I Fought with Custer: The Story of Sergeant Windolph the Last Survivor of the Battle of the Little Big Horn.* Charles Scribner's Sons, New York, 1947.

Bibliography

Hutchins, James S., ed. *Boots & Saddles at the Little Big Horn.* Old Army Press, Fort Collins, Colo., 1976.
———. *The Papers of Edward S. Curtis Relating to Custer's Last Battle.* Upton and Sons, El Segundo, Calif., 2000.
———. *The Army and Navy Journal on the Battle of the Little Big Horn and Related Matters 1876–1881.* Upton and Sons, El Segundo, Calif., 2003.
Hutton, Paul A. *Custer and His Times.* Little Big Horn Associates, El Paso, Tex., 1981.
———. *Phil Sheridan and His Army.* University of Nebraska Press, Lincoln, 1989.
Innis, Ben. *Bloody Knife! Custer's Favorite Scout.* Old Army Press, Fort Collins, Colo., 1973.
———. *Wide, Wild, Wonderful Williams!* Williams County Historical Society, Williston, N. Dak., 1976.
———. *Sagas of the Smoky Water: True Stories Reflecting Historical Aspects of the Missouri-Yellowstone Confluence Region 1805–1910.* Centennial Press, Williston, N. Dak., 1985.
———. *Bloody Knife: Custer's Favorite Scout.* Edited by Richard E. Collin. Smoky Water Press, Bismarck, N. Dak., 1994.
Jackson, Donald. *Custer's Gold: The United States Cavalry Expedition of 1874.* University of Nebraska Press, Lincoln, 1972.
Jensen, Richard E., R. Eli Paul, and John E. Carter. *Eyewitness at Wounded Knee.* University of Nebraska Press, Lincoln, 1991.
Johnson, Barry C. *Case of Marcus A. Reno.* The English Westerners' Society, Special Publication No. 3. London, 1969.
———. *Heitman and the "Old Army."* The English Westerners' Society, Publication No. 193. London, 1973.
———. *Baronet in an Earth Lodge. The Life of Sir St. George Gore and His Singular Adventures in the Great West.* The English Westerners' Society, Special Publication 8B. London, 1997.
Johnson, Barry C., and Francis B. Taunton, ed. *More Sidelights of the Sioux Wars.* The English Westerners' Society, Special Publication No. 10, London, 2004.
Johnson, Roy P. *Jacob Horner of the Seventh Cavalry.* State Historical Society of North Dakota, Bismarck, nd.
Katz, D. Mark. *Custer in Photographs.* Bonanza Books, New York, 1985.
Katz, Irving. *August Belmont: A Political Biography.* Columbia University Press, New York, 1968.
Kaufman, Fred S. *Custer Passed Our Way.* North Plains Press, Aberdeen, S. Dak., 1971.
Kearny, Thomas. *General Philip Kearny: Battle Soldier of Five Wars.* G. P. Putnam's Sons. New York, 1937.
Keim, De B. Randolph. *Sheridan's Troopers on the Borders: A Winter Campaign on the Plains.* University of Nebraska Press, Lincoln, 1985.
Kennedy, W. J. D. *On the Plains with Custer and Hancock: The Journal of Isaac Coates, Army Surgeon.* Johnson Books, Boulder, Colo., 1997.
Kenner, Charles L. *Buffalo Soldiers and Officers of the Ninth Cavalry 1867–1898.* University of Oklahoma Press, Norman, 1999.
Kinevan, Marcos. *Frontier Cavalryman: Lieutenant John Bigelow with the Buffalo Soldiers in Texas.* Texas Western Press, El Paso, 1998.
Kinsley, D. A. *Custer Favor the Bold: A Soldier's Story.* Promontory Press, New York, 1988.
Kirshner, Ralph. *The Class of 1861: Custer, Ames, and Their Classmates after West Point.* Southern Illinois University Press, Carbondale, 1999.
Knight, Oliver. *Following the Indian Wars: The Story of the Newspaper Correspondents Among the Indian Campaigners.* University of Oklahoma Press, Norman, 1993.
Koury, Michael J., ed. *Diaries of the Little Big Horn.* Old Army Press, Fort Collins, Colo., 1968.
———. *The Field Diary of General Alfred H. Terry: The Yellowstone Expedition, 1876.* Old Army Press, Bellevue, Neb., 1970.
Krause, Herbert, and Gary D. Olson. *Prelude to Glory: A Newspaper Accounting of Custer's 1874 Expedition to the Black Hills.* Brevet Press, Sioux Falls, S. Dak., 1974.
Langellier, John P., Kurt Hamilton Cox, and Brian C. Pohanka, eds. *Myles Keogh: The Life and Legend of an "Irish Dragoon" in the Seventh Cavalry.* Upton and Sons, El Segundo, Calif., 1991.

Bibliography

Lawrence, Elizabeth Atwood. *His Very Silence Speaks: Comanche—The Horse Who Survived Custer's Last Stand.* Wayne State University Press, Detroit, Mich., 1989.
Leckie, Shirley A. *Elizabeth Bacon Custer and the Making of a Myth.* University of Oklahoma Press, Norman, 1993.
Lee, Robert. *Fort Meade and the Black Hills.* University of Nebraska Press, Lincoln, 1991.
Libby, Orin G., ed. *Collections of the State Historical Society of North Dakota*, Vol. 1. Bismarck, N. Dak., 1906.
———. *The Arikara Narrative of the Campaign against the Hostile Dakotas June, 1876.* Vol. 6. North Dakota Historical Collections, Bismarck, N. Dak., 1920.
———. *Collections of the State Historical Society of North Dakota*, Vol. 7, Grand Forks, N. Dak., 1925.
———. *The Arikara Narrative of the Campaign against the Hostile Dakotas June, 1876.* Custeriana Series. Sol. Lewis Books, New York, 1973.
Liddic, Bruce R., ed. *I Buried Custer: The Diary of Pvt. Thomas W. Coleman, 7th U.S. Cavalry.* Creative Publishing Company, College Station, Tex., 1979.
Liddic, Bruce R., and Paul Harbaugh, eds. *Camp on Custer: Transcribing the Custer Myth.* Arthur H. Clark Company, Spokane, Wash., 1995.
Linderman, Frank B. *Pretty Shield; Medicine Woman of the Crows.* University of Nebraska Press, Lincoln, 1974.
Logan, Rayford W., and Michael R. Winston, eds. *Dictionary of American Negro Biography.* W. W. Norton Co., New York, 1982.
Luce, Edward S. *Keogh, Comanche and Custer.* John S. Swift Co., St. Louis, Mo., 1939.
Mackey Franklin H., reported by. *Reports of Cases Argued and Adjudged in The Supreme Court of the District of Columbia, General Term, May 25, 1882, to October 29, 1883.* "Emil Justh vs. Benjamin Holliday," 346–60. Printed by John L. Ginck, Washington, D.C., 1884.
Mackintosh, John D. *Custer's Southern Officer: Captain George D. Wallace.* Cloud Peak Press, Lexington, S.C., 2002.
Magnussen, Daniel O., ed. *Peter Thompson's Narrative of the Little Big Horn Campaign 1876.* Arthur H. Clark Company, Glendale, Calif., 1974.
Manion, John S. *General Terry's Last Statement to Custer.* Monroe County Library System, Monroe, Mich., 1983.
Mankato, Its First Fifty Years: Prepared for the Fiftieth Anniversary of the Settlement of Mankato, 1852–1902. Free Press Printing, Mankato, Minn., 1903.
Manzione, Joseph. *I Am Looking to the North for My Life.* University of Utah Press, Salt Lake City, 1991.
Marino, Cesare. *Dal Piave al Little Bighorn: La straordinaria storia del Conte Carlo Camillo diRudio.* Belluno, Italy, 1996.
Marquis, Thomas B. *Memoirs of a White Crow Indian. (Thomas H. LeForge).* Century Company, New York, 1928.
———. *Custer Soldiers Not Buried.* Privately printed, Hardin, Mont., 1933.
———. *Wooden Leg: A Warrior Who Fought Custer.* University of Nebraska Press, Lincoln, 1963.
———. *Custer, Cavalry, & Crows.* Old Army Press, Fort Collins, Col., 1975.
Marszalek, John F. *Sherman: A Soldier's Passion for Order.* The Free Press, New York, 1993.
Martinez, J. Michael. *Carpetbaggers, Cavalry, and the Ku Klux Klan: Exposing the Invisible Empire during Reconstruction.* Rowman & Littlefield Publishers, Lanham, Md., 2007.
McClernand, Edward J. *On Time for Disaster: The Rescue of Custer's Command.* University of Nebraska Press, Lincoln, 1989.
McClure, Daniel E., Jr. *Two Centuries in Elizabethtown and Hardin County, Kentucky.* County Historical Society, Elizabethtown, Ky., 1979.
McConnell, H. H. *Five Years a Cavalryman: Or, Sketches of Regular Army Life on the Texas Frontier, 1866–1871.* University of Oklahoma Press, Norman, 1996.
McGoldrick, Jim. *The McGoldrick Lumber Company Story, 1900–1952.* Tornado Creek Publications, Spokane, Wash., 2004.

Bibliography

McJimsey, George. *Genteel Partisan: Mantan Marble*. Iowa State University Press, Ames, 1971.
McVey, Everett E. *The Crow Scout Who Killed Custer*. Reporter Printing Company, Billings, Mont., 1952.
Meketa, Ray. *Luther Rector Hare, a Texan with Custer: A Biography of an American Hero*. J. M. Carroll Company, Mattituck, N.Y., 1983.
Merington, Marguerite, ed. *The Custer Story: The Life and Intimate Letters of General Custer and His Wife Elizabeth*. Devin-Adair Company, New York, 1950.
Merkel, Charles E., Jr.. *Unravelling the Custer Enigma*. Merkel Press, Enterprise, Ala., 1977.
Meyer, Roy W. *History of the Santee Sioux: United States Indian Policy on Trial*. University of Nebraska Press, Lincoln, 1967.
———. *The Village Indians of the Upper Missouri: The Mandans, Hidatsas, and Arikaras*. University of Nebraska Press, Lincoln, 1977.
Miles, General Nelson A. *Personal Recollections & Observations of General Nelson A. Miles*. 2 vols. University of Nebraska Press, Lincoln, 1992.
Millbrook, Minnie Dubbs. *A Study in Valor: Michigan Medal of Honor Winners in the Civil War*. Michigan Civil War Centennial Observance Commission, Lansing, Mich., 1966.
Miller, David, James Shanley, Dennis J. Smith, Joseph R. McGeshick, and Caleb Shields. *The History of the Assiniboine and Sioux Tribes of the Fort Peck Indian Reservation, Montana, 1800–2000*. Montana Historical Society, Helena, 2008.
Miller, David Humphreys. *Custer's Fall: The Indian Side of the Story*. Duell, Sloan and Pearce, New York, 1957.
Milligan, Edward A. *Dakota Twilight: The Standing Rock Sioux, 1874–1890*. Exposition Press, Hicksville, N.Y., 1976.
Mills, Charles K. *Charles C. DeRudio*. J. M. Carroll Company, Mattituck, N.Y., 1983.
———. *Harvest of Barren Regrets: The Army Career of Frederick William Benteen 1834–1898*. Arthur H. Clark Company, Glendale, Calif., 1985.
Milner, Joe E., and Earle R. Forrest. *California Joe: Noted Scout and Indian Fighter*. University of Nebraska Press, Lincoln, 1987.
Monaghan, Jay. *Custer: The Life of General George Armstrong Custer*. University of Nebraska Press, Lincoln, 1971.
Mountrail County, N. Dak. A History of *Tales of Mighty Mountrail*. Vol. I. Mountrail County Historical Society, 1979.
Mulford, Ami Frank. *Fighting Indians in the 7th United States Cavalry*. Paul Lindsley Mulford, Corning, N.Y., 1879.
Newgard, Thomas P., William C. Sherman, and John Guerrero. *African-Americans in North Dakota: Sources and Assessments*. University of Mary Press, Bismarck, N. Dak., 1994.
Nichols, Ronald H., ed. *Reno Court of Inquiry: Proceedings of a Court of Inquiry in the Case of Major Marcus A. Reno*. Custer Battlefield Historical & Museum Association, Crow Agency, Mont., 1992.
———. *In Custer's Shadow: Major Marcus Reno*. Old Army Press, Fort Collins Colo., 1999.
———. *Men with Custer: Biographies of the 7th Cavalry*. Custer Battlefield Historical & Museum Association, Hardin, Mont., 2000.
Noyes, Alva J. *In the Land of Chinook, or the Story of Blaine County*. State Publishing Co., Helena, Mont., 1917.
O'Neil, Alice Tomlinson. *Life in Kansas with the Custers: The Diary and Correspondence of Rebecca Richmond*. Arrow and Trooper, Brooklyn, N.Y., 1995.
O'Neil, Tom, ed. *The Civil War Memoirs of General George Armstrong Custer*. Arrow and Trooper, Brooklyn, N.Y., 1991.
———. *GarryOwen Tidbits VII*. Arrow and Trooper Publishing, Brooklyn, N.Y., 1993.
———. *Letters from Boston Custer*. Arrow and Trooper, Brooklyn, N.Y., 1993.
———. *Custeriana One*. Arrow and Trooper, Brooklyn, N.Y., 1999.
Overholser, Joel. *Fort Benton: World's Innermost Port*. Fort Benton, Mont., 1987.

Bibliography

Parsons, John E. *West on the 49th Parallel: Red River to the Rockies, 1872–1876.* William Morrow & Co., New York, 1963.

Peterson, Marion Plath, ed. *Morton Prairie Roots: Bicentennial Heritage Project 1776–1976.* Morton County Historical Society, Mandan, N. Dak., ca. 1975.

Pfaller, Louis L, O.S.B. *Father De Smet in Dakota.* Assumption Abbey Press, Richardton, N. Dak., 1962.

Phillips, Paul C., and Llewellyn L. Callaway. *Medicine in the Making of Montana.* Montana Medical Association. Montana State University Press, Missoula, 1962.

Pohanka, Brian. *A Summer on the Plains, 1870.* J. M. Carroll Company, Mattituck, N.Y., 1983.

Powell, William H. *Records of Living Officers of the U.S. Army.* L. R. Hamersly Company, Philadelphia, Pa., 1884, 1890, 1900.

Powell, William H., and Edward Shippen. *Officers of the Army and Navy (Regular) Who Served in the Civil War.* L. R. Hamersly Company, Philadelphia, Pa., 1892.

Price, Sir Rose Lambart. *The Two Americas; An Account of Sport and Travel.* London: Sampson Low, Marston, Searle, and Rivington, 1877.

Pride, Woodbury F. *The History of Fort Riley.* Fort Riley, Kans., 1926.

Quaife, Milo M., ed. *Army Life in Dakota.* Lakeside Press, Chicago, Ill., 1941.

———. *Yellowstone Kelly: The Memoirs of Luther S. Kelly.* University of Nebraska Press, Lincoln, 1973.

Rand McNally's Pioneer Atlas of the American West. Rand McNally & Company, 1969.

Reedstrom, E. Lisle. *Custer's 7th Cavalry: From Fort Riley to the Little Big Horn.* Sterling Publishing Company, New York, 1992.

Reiger, John F., ed. *The Passing of the Great West: Selected Papers of George Bird Grinnell.* Winchester Press, New York, 1972.

Remsburg, John E., and George J. *Charley Reynolds: Soldier, Hunter, Scout, and Guide.* Edited by John M. Carroll with a Historical Introduction by John S. Gray. J. M. Carroll Company, Mattituck, N.Y., 1978.

Reno, Ottie W. *Reno and Apsaalooka Survive Custer.* Cornwall Books, Cranbury, N.J., 1997.

Rickey, Don, Jr. *Forty Miles a Day on Beans and Hay.* University of Oklahoma Press, Norman, 1989.

Riggs, Stephen R. *Mary and I: Forty Years With the Sioux.* W. G. Holmes, Chicago, 1880.

Roberts, Richard A. *Custer's Last Battle: Reminiscences of General Custer.* Preface and notes by Lawrence A. Frost. Custeriana Monograph Series No. 4 (Frost Collection). Monroe County Library System, Monroe, Mich., 1978.

Rodenbough, Theo. F., ed. *Uncle Sam's Medal of Honor: Some of the Noble Deeds for Which the Medal Has Been Awarded, Described by Those Who Have Won It, 1861–1886.* G. P. Putnam, New York, 1886.

———. *The Bravest Five Hundred of '61: Their Noble Deeds Described by Themselves . . .* G. W. Dillingham, New York, 1891.

Roenigk, Adolph. *Pioneer History of Kansas.* A. Roenigk, Lincoln, Kansas, 1933. Reprinted by the Lincoln County Historical Society, Lincoln, Kans., 1973.

Ronsheim, Milton. *The Life of General Custer.* Custeriana Monograph Series No. 1. Lawrence A. Frost Collection. Monroe County Library System, Monroe, Mich., 1978.

Schneider, George A., ed. *The Freeman Journal: The Infantry in the Sioux Campaign of 1876.* Presidio Press, San Rafael, Calif., 1977.

Schneider, James V. *An Enigma Named Noonan.* Privately printed, Fort Wayne, Ind., 1988.

———. *Behind Custer at the Little Big Horn: The Story of Lieutenant Edward Mathey and the Pack Train.* Privately printed, Fort Wayne, Ind., nd.

Schuler, Harold H. *A Bridge Apart: History of Early Pierre and Fort Pierre. A Centennial Publication.* State Publishing Company, Pierre, S. Dak., 1987.

———. *Fort Pierre Chouteau.* University of South Dakota Press, Vermillion, 1990.

———. *Fort Sully, Guns at Sunset.* University of South Dakota Press, Vermillion, 1992.

———. *Fort Sisseton.* The Center for Western Studies, Sioux Falls, S. Dak., 1996.

Schultz, James Willard. *William Jackson, Indian Scout.* William K. Cavanagh, Springfield, Ill., 1976.

———. *Many Strange Characters: Montana Frontier Tales.* University of Oklahoma Press, Norman, 1982.

Bibliography

Scott, Douglas D., Richard A. Fox, Jr., Melissa A. Connor, and Dick Harmon. *Archaeological Perspectives on the Battle of the Little Big Horn*. University of Oklahoma Press, Norman, 1989.

Scott, Hugh Lenox. *Some Memories of a Soldier*. Century Company, New York, 1928.

Sears, Stephen W. *The Young Napoleon: General George B. McClellan*. Ticknor and Fields, New Haven, Conn., 1988.

Sergent, Mary Elizabeth. *They Lie Forgotten: The United States Military Academy 1856–1861, Together With a Class Album for the Class of May, 1861*. Prior King Press, Middletown, N.Y., 1986.

Simon, John Y. *The Papers of Ulysses S. Grant*. Vol. 16 of 22. 1866. Southern Illinois Univ. Press, Carbondale, 1988.

Slaughter, Linda W. *Fortress to Farm: or Twenty-three Years on the Frontier*. Edited by Hazel Eastman. Exposition Press, New York, 1969.

Slotkin, Richard. *The Fatal Environment: The Myth of the Frontier in the Age of Industrialization, 1800–1890*. University of Oklahoma Press, Norman, 1998.

Smith, Sherry L. *Sagebrush Soldier: Private William Earl Smith's View of the Sioux War of 1876*. University of Oklahoma Press, Norman, 1989.

Smith, Victor Grant. *The Champion Buffalo Hunter: The Frontier Memoirs of Yellowstone Vic Smith*. Edited by Jeanette Prodgers. TwoDot, Guilford, Conn., 2009.

Spotts, David L. *Campaigning With Custer, 1868–69*. Edited by Earl A. Brininstool. University of Nebraska Press, Lincoln, 1988.

Stanley, David S. *Personal Memoirs of Major-General David S. Stanley, U.S.A.* Reprint. Olde Soldier Books, Gaithersburg, Md., 1987.

Steffen, Randy. *The Horse Soldier 1776–1943: The United States Cavalryman*. Vol. II, *The Frontier, the Mexican War, the Civil War, the Indian Wars, 1851–1880*. University of Oklahoma Press, Norman, 1992.

Stewart, Edgar I. *Custer's Luck*. University of Oklahoma Press, Norman, 1955.

———, ed. *The March of the Montana Column: Journal of Lieut. James H. Bradley, 7th Inf., March 17 to June 27, 1876*. University of Oklahoma Press, Norman, 1991.

Strong, General W. E. *A Trip to the Yellowstone National Park in July, August, and September, 1875*. University of Oklahoma Press, Norman, 1968.

Sully, Langdon. *No Tears for the General: The Life of Alfred Sully, 1821–1879*. American West Publishing Company, Palo Alto, Calif., 1974.

Taunton, Francis B., ed. *Sidelights of the Sioux Wars*. The English Westerners' Society, London, 1967.

———, in collaboration with Brian C. Pohanka. *Custer's Field: "A Scene of Sickening Ghastly Horror."* Johnson-Taunton Military Press, London, England, 1986.

———, ed. *No Pride in the Little Big Horn*. The English Westerners' Society, Special Publication, No. 7, London, 1987.

Taylor, Joseph Henry. *Frontier and Indian Life and Kaleidoscopic Lives*. Washburn Fiftieth Anniversary Committee, Washburn, N. Dak., 1932.

Taylor, William O. *With Custer on the Little Big Horn: A Newly Discovered First Person Account*. With a Foreword by Greg Martin. Viking Books, New York, 1996.

Terrell, John Upton, and Colonel George Walton. *Faint the Trumpet Sounds: The Life and Trial of Major Reno*. David McKay Company, New York, 1966.

Topping, E. S. *The Chronicles of the Yellowstone: An Accurate, Comprehensive History*. Ross & Haines, Inc., Minneapolis, Minn., 1968.

Tucker, William Warren. *The Grand Duke Alexis in the U.S.A. Newspaper Accounts*. Sol. Lewis Books, New York, 1972.

Upton, Richard. *Fort Custer on the Big Horn, 1877–1898*. Arthur H. Clark Company, Glendale, Calif., 1973.

Urwin, Gregory J. W., and Roberta E. Fagan, eds. *Custer and His Times Book Three*. Little Big Horn Associates, University of Central Arkansas Press, 1987.

Utley, Robert M. *The Reno Court of Inquiry: The Chicago Times Account*. Old Army Press, Fort Collins, Colo., 1972.

Bibliography

———. *Life in Custer's Cavalry: Diaries and Letters of Albert and Jennie Barnitz, 1867–1868.* Yale University Press, New Haven, Conn., 1977.
———. *Frontier Regulars: The United States Army and the Indian, 1866–1891.* University of Nebraska Press, Lincoln, 1984.
Van de Water, Frederic F. *Glory-Hunter: A Life of General Custer.* University of Nebraska Press, Lincoln, 1988.
Vestal, Stanley. *New Sources of Indian History, 1850–1891: The Ghost Dance, the Prairie Sioux—a Miscellany.* University of Oklahoma Press, Norman, 1934.
———. *Sitting Bull, Champion of the Sioux.* University of Oklahoma Press, Norman, 1957.
Vetter, Michael. *The Cowboy Soldier.* Edited by Rex Moore. Devil's Lake Sioux Manufacturing Corp., Fort Totten, N. Dak., ca. 1979.
Viola, Herman J. *Little Big Horn Remembered: The Untold Indian Story of Custer's Last Stand.* Times Books, New York, 1999.
Wagner, Glendolin Damon. *Old Neutriment.* Sol. Lewis Books, New York, 1973.
Walker, Judson Elliott. *Campaigns of General Custer in the Northwest and the Surrender of Sitting Bull.* Promontory Press, New York, 1966.
Walker, L. G., Jr. *Dr. Henry R. Porter: The Surgeon Who Survived Little Bighorn.* McFarland & Co., Jefferson, N.C., 2008.
Washington County, Ohio. *Birth Records, 1876–1887.* Washington County Public Library, Marietta, Ohio.
Washington County, Ohio. *Marriages, 1789–1918.* Wes Cochran, Parkersburg, W. Va., 1986. Mahn Center, Alden Library, Ohio University, Athens, Ohio.
Welsh, Jack D. *Medical Histories of Union Generals.* Kent State University Press, Kent, Ohio, 1996.
Wengert, James W. *The Custer Despatches: The Words of the New York Herald Correspondents in the Little Big Horn Campaign of 1876.* 2 vols. Sunflower University Press, Manhattan, Kans., 1987.
Wengert, James W., and E. Elden Davis, eds. *That Fatal Day: Eight More with Custer—First Hand Accounts of the Battle of the Little Big Horn.* The Powder River Press, Howell, Mich., 1992.
Werstein, Irving. *Kearny the Magnificent: The Story of General Philip Kearny.* John Day Company, New York, 1962.
Westfall, Douglas Paul. *Letters from the Field: Wallace at the Little Big Horn.* Edited by James Willert. Paragon Agency, Orange, Calif., 1997.
Wheeler, Homer W. *Buffalo Days: The Personal Narrative of a Cattleman, Indian Fighter & Army Officer.* Reprint of 1925 edition. University of Nebraska Press, Lincoln, 1990.
Whittaker, Frederick. *A Complete Life of General George A. Custer.* 2 vols. University of Nebraska Press, Lincoln, 1993.
Willert, James. *The Terry Letters: The Letters of General Alfred Howe Terry to His Sisters during the Indian War of 1876.* James Willert, Publisher, La Mirada, Calif., 1980.
———. *The Cuthbert Mills Letters to New York Times during the Indian War of 1876.* James Willert Publisher, La Mirada, Calif., 1984.
———. *Bourke's Diary: From Journals of 1st Lt. John Gregory Bourke, June 27–Sept. 15, 1876.* James Willert, Publisher, La Mirada, Calif., 1985.
———. *March of the Columns: Chronicle of the 1876 Indian War June 27–September 16, 1876.* Upton and Sons, El Segundo, Calif., 1994.
———. *Little Big Horn Diary: Chronicle of the 1876 Indian War.* Upton and Sons, El Segundo, Calif., 1997.
———. *To The Edge of Darkness: A Chronicle of the 1876 Indian War.* Upton and Sons, El Segundo, Calif., 1998.
The Wonder of Williams: A History of Williams County, North Dakota. 2vols. Williams County Historical Society, Williston, N. Dak., 1975.
Williamson, John P., ed. *An English-Dakota Dictionary: Wasicun Ka Dakota; Ieska Wowapi.* Ross & Haines, Minneapolis, Minn., 1970.
Wolle, Muriel Sibell. *Stampede to Timberline: The Ghost Towns and Mining Camps of Colorado.* Sage Press, Denver, Colo., 1962.

Bibliography

Wood County, W. Va. *Marriage Book II, 1877.* Compiled and published by Wes Cochran. Washington County, Ohio, Library, Marrietta, Ohio.
Wooster, Robert. *Nelson A. Miles & the Twilight of the Frontier Army.* University of Nebraska Press, Lincoln, 1993.
Word and Picture Story of Williston and Area since 1887: 75th Anniversary Diamond Jubilee, August 8–11, 1962. Williams County Historical Society, Williams County, N. Dak., 1962.
The World Book Encyclopedia. 18 vols. The Quarrie Corp., Chicago, 1946.

Articles

Alfield, Philip L. "Major Reno and His Family in Illinois," *The English Westerners' Brand Book* (London) Vol. 13, No. 4, July 1971.
Anderson, Harry H. "The Benteen Base Ball Club: Sports Enthusiasts of the Seventh Cavalry," *Montana the Magazine of Western History,* Vol. 20, No. 3, Summer 1970.
Arnold, Steve. "Cooke's Scrawled Note," *Greasy Grass,* Vol. 14, May, 1998.
Beckley, Gilbert W. "Marcus Albert Reno 1835–1889," *New Cumberland Frontier,* 1973.
Bell, James M. "Reminiscences," *Journal of the United States Cavalry Association,* Vol. 10, No. 39, Dec., 1897.
Best, Thomas. "A Life of Mystery: Lonesome Charley Reynolds," *Newsletter* (LBHA), Vol. 27, Nos. 1, 2, 3, Feb. Mar. Apr., 1998.
Boyson, Walt. "Henry Moore Harrington," *The English Westerners' Tally Sheet,* Vol. 35, No. 2, Spring 1989.
Brigham, Earl K. "Custer's Meeting with Secretary of War Belknap at Fort Abraham Lincoln," *North Dakota History,* Vol. 19, No. 2, April 1952.
Broome, Jeff. "Custer's Summer Indian Campaign of 1867," *Research Review,* Vol. 20, No. 2, Summer 2006.
Brown, Lisle G. "The Yellowstone Supply Depot," *North Dakota History,* Vol. 40, No. 1, Winter 1973.
Buecker, Tom. "Frederic S. Calhoun," *Greasy Grass,* Vol. 10, May, 1994.
Cabaniss, A. A. "Troop and Company Pack Trains," *Journal of the U. S. Cavalry Association,* Vol. 3, 1890.
Caniglia, Salvatore A. "Private Augustus L. DeVoto, Unsung Hero at the Battle of the Little Big Horn," *Research Review,* Vol. 16, No. 2, Summer 2002.
Carlile, Richard. "The First D. C. Cavalry," *Military Images Magazine,* Vol. 3, No. 2, Sept. Oct., 1986.
"Thomas Jefferson Carr—a Frontier Sheriff" (compiled from C. G. Coutant's notes made in 1884–1885, *Annals of Wyoming,* Vol. 20, No. 2, July, 1948.
Carroll, John M. "Anheuser Busch and Custer's Last Stand." *Greasy Grass,* Vol. 3, May 1987.
Carroll, Matthew. "Diary of, kept while Master in Charge of Transportation for Col. Gibbon's Expedition against the Sioux, 1876." *Contributions to the Historical Society of Montana,* Vol. 2, 1896.
Clow, Richmond L. "General Philip Sheridan's Legacy: The Pony Campaign of 1876," *Nebraska History,* Vol. 57, No. 4, Winter 1976.
Coburn, Wallace D. "The Battle of the Little Big Horn," *Montana The Magazine of Western History,* Vol. 6, No. 3, July 1956.
Collin, Rick. "Dear Brother: A Soldier's Letters," *Newsletter* (LBHA), Vol. 25, No. 10, Dec. 1996.
Cox, John E. "Soldiering in Dakota Territory in the Seventies: A Communication," *North Dakota Historical Quarterly,* Vol. 6, No. 1, Oct. 1931.
Crofford, Mrs. H. E. "Pioneer Days in North Dakota," *North Dakota Historical Quarterly,* Vol. 2, No. 2, Jan. 1928.
Danker, Donald F. "The Eli Ricker Tablets," *The Prairie Scout,* Vol. 1, The Kansas Corral of the Westerners, Abilene, Kans., 1973.
Dobak, William A. "Licit Amusements of Enlisted Men in the Post-Civil War Army," *Montana The Magazine of Western History,* Vol. 45, No. 2, Spring 1995.

Bibliography

Doerner, John A. "The Boys of '76," *True West Magazine* (Collector's Edition), Vol. 48, No. 4, May/June 2001.

Doran, Robert E. "The Man Who Got to the Rosebud," *Research Review,* Vol. 16, No. 1, Winter 2002.

duBois, Charles G. "The Edgerly Narrative," *Research Review,* Vol. 3, No. 3, Sept. 2006.

Ege, Robert J. "Custer's Negro Interpreter," *Negro Digest,* Vol. 14, No. 4, Feb. 1965.

———. "Legend Was a Man Named Keogh," *Montana The Magazine of Western History* (Special Custer Edition), Vol. 16, No. 2, Spring 1966.

———. "Braves of All Colors," *Montana The Magazine of Western History,* Vol. 16, No. 1, Winter 1966.

———. "Dorman, Isaiah," In *Dictionary of American Negro Biography*. Edited by Rayford W. Logan and Michael R. Winston. Norton Company, New York, 1982.

Ellison, Douglas W. "Mystery along Rosebud Creek," *Greasy Grass,* Vol. 17, May, 2001.

"Emil Justh vs. Benjamin Holliday." In *Reports of Cases Argued and Adjudged in The Supreme Court of the District of Columbia, General Term, May 25, 1882, to October 29, 1883*. Washington, D.C.: John L. Ginck, 1884.

Ernst, Leif Rudi. "A Dane Who Survived the Little Big Horn Fight," *The Crow's Nest,* Spring/Summer 2005, Vol. 5, No. 1.

Essin, Emmett M. "Mules, Packs, and Packtrains," *Southwestern Historical Quarterly,* Vol. 74, July 1970.

———. "Army Mule," *Montana The Magazine of Western History,* Vol. 44, No. 2, Spring 1994.

Everett, John P. "Bullets, Boots, and Saddles," *Sunshine Magazine,* Vol. 11, No. 1, Sept. 1930.

Farioli, Dennis, and Ron Nichols. "Fort A. Lincoln, July 1876," *Greasy Grass,* Vol. 17, May 2001.

Gerber, Max E. "The Custer Expedition of 1874: A New Look," *North Dakota History,* Vol. 40, No. 1, Winter 1973.

Gillette, Mary C. "United States Army Surgeons and the Big Horn-Yellowstone Expedition of 1876," *Montana The Magazine of Western History,* Vol. 39, No. 1, Winter 1989.

Gray, John S. "Bloody Knife Ree Scout For Custer," *The Westerners Brand Book* (Chicago), Vol. 17, No. 12, Feb. 1961.

———. "Custer Throws a Boomerang," *Montana The Magazine of Western History,* Vol. 11, No. 2, April 1961.

———. "Last Rites for Lonesome Charley Reynolds," *Montana The Magazine of Western History,* Vol. 13, No. 3, Summer 1963.

———. "Photos, Femurs, and Fallacies," *The Westerners Brand Book* (Chicago), Vol. 20, Nos. 6 and 7, Aug. and Sept. 1963.

———. "Ree Scouts With Custer," *The Westerners Brand Book* (Chicago), Vol. 20, No. 12, Feb. 1964.

———. "The Reno Petition," *The Westerners Brand Book* (Chicago), Vol. 24, No. 6, August 1967.

———. "Medical Service on the Little Big Horn Campaign," *The Westerners Brand Book* (Chicago), Vol. 24, No. 11, Jan. 1968.

———. "Arikara Scouts with Custer," *North Dakota History,* Vol. 35, No. 2, Spring 1968.

———. "Captain Clifford's Story of the Sioux War of 1876," *The Westerners Brand Book* (Chicago), Vol. 26, Nos. 10 and 11, Dec. 1969 and Jan. 1970; and Vol. 29, No. 6, Aug. 1972.

———. "Captain Clifford's Newspaper Dispatches," *Montana The Magazine of Western History,* Vol. 27, No. 11, Jan. 1971.

———. "Nightmares to Daydreams," *By Valor & Arms,* Vol. 1, No. 4, Summer 1975.

———. "The Pack Train on George A. Custer's Last Campaign," *Nebraska History,* Vol. 57, No. 1, Spring 1976.

———. "Veterinary Service on Custer's Last Campaign," *The Kansas Historical Quarterly,* Vol. 43, No. 3, Autumn 1977.

———. "Couriers of Disaster," *Research Review,* Vol. 17, No. 12, Dec. 1983.

———. "The Story of Mrs. Picotte-Galpin, a Sioux Heroine," *Montana The Magazine of Western History,* Vol. 36, Nos. 2 and 3, Spring and Summer, 1986.

Gwyther, Annie R. "Pioneer Days on Fort Rice Military Reserve," *North Dakota History,* Vol. 26, No. 3, Summer 1959.

Bibliography

Hammer, Kenneth M. "Frontier Doctor," *The Westerners New York Posse Brand Book,* Vol. 7, No. 3, 1960.
———. "Marcus Albert Reno," *The Westerners New York Posse Brand Book,* Vol. 8, No. 3, 1961.
———. "Territorial Towns and the Railroad," *North Dakota History,* Vol. 36, No. 4, Fall 1969.
Hardorff, R. "Dutch." "The Reno Scout, the Itinerary of Sergeant James Hill," *Research Review*, Vol. 11, No. 12, Dec. 1977.
Hardorff, Richard G. "Packs, Packers, and Pack Details: Logistics and Custer's Pack Train." In *Custer and His Times, Book Three*, edited by Gregory J. W. Urwin and Roberta E. Fagan. University of Central Arkansas Press, 1987.
Hart, George. "Henry Seafferman, 7th Cavalry," *Military Images Magazine,* Vol. 3, No. 2, Sept. Oct. 1986.
Hedren, Paul. "Sitting Bull's Surrender at Fort Buford," *North Dakota History,* Vol. 62, No. 4, Fall 1995.
———. "On Duty at Fort Ridgely, Minnesota: 1853–1867," *South Dakota History,* Vol. 7, No. 2, Spring 1977.
Heski, Thomas S. "Camp Powell: The Powder River Supply Depot," *Research Review,* Vol. 17, No. 1, Winter 2003.
Hill, Michael D., and Ben Innis, eds. "The Fort Buford Diary of Private Sanford, 1876–1877," *North Dakota History,* Vol. 52, No. 3, Summer 1985.
Hixon, John C. "Custer's 'Mysterious' Mr. Kellogg," *North Dakota History,* Vol. 17, No. 3, July 1950.
Hodgson, Leslie. "John Stuart Stuart Forbes, A. K. A. Trooper John S. Hiley," *Newsletter* (LBHA), Vol. 33, Feb. 1999.
———. "The British Custer Trail," *The Guidon: Journal of British Custeriana,* Vol. 1, No. 1, Oct. 1997.
Hoyt, William D., Jr. "Rosser's Journal, Northern Pacific Railroad Survey, September, 1871," *North Dakota Historical Quarterly,* Vol. 10, No. 1, Jan. 1943.
Hughes, Robert P. "The Campaign against the Sioux in 1876," *Journal of the Military Service Institute of the United States*, Vol. 18, No. 79, Jan. 1896.
Hultgren, Mary Lou. "To Be Examples to . . . Their People: Standing Rock Sioux Students at Hampton Institute, 1878–1923 (Part Two)," *North Dakota History,* Vol. 68, No. 3, 2001.
Hynds, Sgt. H. A. "Reminiscences of," *Research Review,* Vol. 6, No. 4, Winter 1972.
Innis, Ben, ed. "The Fort Buford Diary of Private Wilmot P. Sanford," *North Dakota History*, Vol. 33, No. 4, Fall 1966.
Johnson, Barry C. "George Herendeen: Montana Scout," *The English Westerners' Brand Book* (London), Vol. 2, Nos. 3 and 4, April and July 1960.
———. "With Gibbon against the Sioux in 1876: The Field Diary of Lt. William L. English (7th Inf.)," *The English Westerners' Brand Book* (London), Vol. 8, No. 4, July 1966, and Vol. 9, No. 1, Oct. 1966.
———. "Dr. Paulding and His Remarkable Diary: *Sidelights of the Sioux Wars,*" The English Westerners' Society, London, 1967.
———. "Custer, Reno, Merrill and the Lauffer Case," *The English Westerners' Brand Book* (London), Vol. 12, No. 4, July 1970, and Vol. 13, No. 1, Oct. 1970.
———. "Reno as Escort Commander: The Northern Boundary Survey Party of 1873 and 1874," *The Westerners Brand Book* (Chicago), Vol. 29, No. 7, Sept. 1972.
———. "Weir and the Custers." In *No Pride in the Little Big Horn*, edited by Francis B. Taunton. The English Westerners' Society, London, 1987.
———. "A Captain of 'Chivalric Courage,' Captain Thomas H. French, 7th Cavalry," *The Brand Book,* Vol. 25, Nos. 1 and 2, 1987/88. The English Westerners' Society, London, 1989.
Kimball, James P. "Fort Buford," *North Dakota Historical Quarterly*, Vol. 4, No. 2, Jan. 1930.
Knight, Oliver. "Mark Kellogg Telegraphed for Custer's Rescue," *North Dakota History,* Vol. 27, No. 2, Spring 1960.
Korn, Gustave. Stories of, in *Winners of the West,* Vol. 13, No. 2, Jan. 30, 1936, 1, "Who Knew Gustave Korn of Troop I 7th U.S. Cavalry in the Custer Fight"; No. 3, Feb. 29, 1936, 3, "Another Custer Canard"; No. 6. May 31, 1936, 1, "He Knew Comrade Gustave Korn"; No. 6, May 31, 1936, 4, "'Yankee Korn,' by Sergt. Geo. Lisk Late Troop H, 5th U.S. Cavalry, 1877–1887."
LaForge, Thomas. "Statement of Thomas H. LaForge," in *The Tepee Book*, Vol. 2, No. 6, June 1916.

Bibliography

Larson, Andre P. "Custer's Last Band . . . Vinatieri's Music Will Be Played." *Newsletter,: America's Shrine to Music Museum,* Vol. 28, No. 2, May 2001.

Larson, Arthur J. "The Northwestern Express and Transportation Company," *North Dakota Historical Quarterly,* Vol. 6, No. 1, Oct. 1931.

Longacre, Edward G. "Alfred Pleasonton, 'The Knight of Romance,'" *Civil War Times Illustrated,* Dec. 1974.

Luce, Edward S., ed. "The Diary and Letters of Dr. James M. DeWolf," *North Dakota History,* Vol. 25, Nos. 2 and 3, April and July, 1958.

Lyon, Juana Fraser. "Archie McIntosh, the Scottish Indian Scout," *The Journal of Arizona History,* Vol. 7, No. 3, Autumn 1966.

———. "Donald McIntosh, First Lieutenant, 7th US Cavalry," *Clann Chatain,* Vol. 5, No. 2, 1965, Edinburgh, Scotland.

Mackintosh, James. "Lakota bullet ends Wallace's life—14 years after Little Big Horn," *Greasy Grass,* Vol. 16, May 2000.

Mangum, Neil C. "The George C. Brown Story," *Research Review,* Vol. 13, No. 2, Summer 1999.

Manion, John S. "Custer's Cooks and Maids," in *Custer and His Times, Book II,* Little Big Horn Associates, El Paso, Tex., 1984.

———. "Custer, Cody, and the Grand Duke Alexis," *Research Review,* Vol. 4, No. 1, Jan. 1990.

Marino, Cesare. "Rudio Revisited, Searching for the Man Beyond the Stereotype," *Research Review,* Vol. 18, No. 1, Winter 2004.

Mattison, Ray H. "Old Fort Stevenson," *North Dakota History,* Vol. 18, Nos. 2 and 3, April and July, 1951.

———. "Diary of Surgeon Washington Matthews, Fort Rice, D. T.," *North Dakota History,* Vol. 21, No. 1–2, Jan.–April 1954.

McConnell, Roland C. "Isaiah Dorman and the Custer Expedition," *The Journal of Negro History,* Vol. 33, No. 3, July 1948.

McDermott, Paul D. "Plotting Custer's Last Stand," *Mercator's World, The Magazine of Maps, Exploration, and Discovery,* Vol. 3, No. 1, Jan/Feb 1998.

Millbrook, Minnie Dubbs, ed. "The West Breaks in General Custer," *The Kansas Historical Quarterly,* Vol. 36, No. 2, Summer 1970.

———. "The Duke Comes to Kansas," *The Westerners' Brand Book* (Chicago), Vol. 24, No. 10, Dec. 1972.

———. "Custer's March to Texas," in *The Prairie Scout,* Vol. I, *The Kansas Corral of the Westerners,* Abilene, Kans., 1973.

———. "Mrs. General Custer at Fort Riley 1866," *The Kansas Historical Quarterly,* Vol. 40, No. 1, Spring 1974.

———. "Big Game Hunting With the Custers, 1869–1870," *The Kansas Historical Quarterly,* Vol. 41, No. 4, Winter 1975.

———. "Rebecca Visits Kansas and the Custers: The Diary of Rebecca Richmond," *The Kansas Historical Quarterly,* Vol. 42, No. 4, Winter 1976.

———. "Cadet Custer's Court Martial," in *Custer and His Times.* Little Big Horn Associates, El Paso, Tex., 1981.

Moody, Judge William E., with Joseph E. Moody, "Soldier of Valor," *Research Review,* Vol. 15, No. 1, Winter 2001.

Moyne, Ernest J. "Fred Snow's Account of the Custer Expedition of 1874," *North Dakota History,* Vol. 27, Nos. 3 & 4, Summer and Fall 1960.

Nichols, Ronald H. "Capt. Owen J. Sweet reports on marble markers at Battlefield," *Greasy Grass,* Vol. 19, May 2003.

Noyes, C. Lee. "An Officer's Perception of the Little Big Horn and a Centennial Expose," *The Brand Book,* Vol. 30, 1992–1993, English Westerners' Society, London.

———. "Captain Robert P. Hughes and the Case Against Custer: An Early Perspective of the Little Big Horn," *Newsletter* (LBHA), Vol. 33, No. 1, Feb 1999.

Bibliography

———. "The Guns 'Long Hair' Left Behind," *The Brand Book,* Vol. 3, No. 2, Summer 1999. English Westerners' Society, London.

———. "Custer's Surgeon," *Greasy Grass,* Vol. 16, May 2000.

———. "The Tragedy of Dr. George E. Lord," *Newsletter* (LBHA), Vol. 34, July 2000.

———. "Sketches of the Frontier," *The Battlefield Dispatch,* Vol. 20, No. 2, Spring 2001.

O'Brien, Francis A. "The Great Rebel Beefsteak Raid," *America's Civil War,* July 1996.

Palmer, Robert G. "Custer & the Grand Duke: Hunting Buffalo with Royalty," *Greasy Grass,* Vol. 19, May 2003.

Parmelee, Mary Manley. "A Child's Recollections of the Summer of '76," in *The Tepee Book,* Vol. 1, No. 6, June 1915.

Pengra, Lilah Morton. "My Search for Isaiah Dorman," *Newsletter* (LBHA), Vol. 42, No. 9, Nov. 2008.

Petersen, Edward S. "Surgeons of the Little Big Horn," *The Westerners Brand Book* (Chicago), Vol. 31, No. 6, Aug. 1974.

Pfaller, Louis. "The Fort Keogh to Bismarck Stage Route," *North Dakota History,* Vol. 21, No. 3, July 1954.

———. "Roy P. Johnson," *North Dakota History,* Vol. 30, No. 1, Jan. 1963.

———. "Sully's Expedition of 1864," *North Dakota History,* Vol. 31, No. 1, Jan. 1964.

Pohanka, Brian C. "Profile: Lieut. William Van Wyck Reily, 7th US Cavalry," *Greasy Grass,* Vol. 2, May 1986.

———. "Myles Keogh," *Military Images Magazine,* Vol. 3, No. 2, Sept./Oct. 1986.

———. "George Yates; Captain of the Band Box Troop," *Greasy Grass,* Vol. 8, May 1992.

Powell, Father Peter J. "High Bull's Victory Roster," *Montana The Magazine of Western History,* Vol. 25, No. 1, Winter 1975.

Powers, Ramon, and Gene Younger. "Cholera on the Plains: The Epidemic of 1867 in Kansas," *The Kansas Historical Quarterly,* Vol. 37, No. 4, Winter 1971.

Prickett, Robert C. "The Malfeasance of William Worth Belknap," *North Dakota History,* Vol. 17, Nos. 1 and 2, Jan. and Apr. 1950.

Reid, Russell. "Diary of Ferdinand A. Van Ostrand," *North Dakota Historical Quarterly,* Vol. 9, No. 4, July 1942, and Vol. 10, Nos. 1 and 2, Jan. and Apr. 1943.

Rose, Margaret, compiler. "Manuscript Collections of State Historical Society," *North Dakota History,* Vol. 30, No. 1, Jan. 1963.

Russell, Don. "906 Custer's Last Fight Pictures," *Westerners Brand Book* (Chicago), Vol. 25, No. 2, April 1968.

Russell, Peter. "From Bungay to the Little Bighorn," *The Crow's Nest,* Vol. 2, No. 2, Summer/Autumn 2002.

———. "Custer's Sergeant Major," *The Crow's Nest,* Vol. 3, No. 1, Winter/Spring 2003.

———. "The Lone Welshman," *The Crow's Nest,* Vol. 4, No. 1, Spring/Summer 2004.

———. "Custer's Quartermaster Sergeant," *The Crow's Nest,* Vol. 4, No. 2, Autumn/Winter 2004.

Saum, Lewis O. "John F. Donohue's Recollections on the Little Big Horn," *Montana The Magazine of Western History,* Vol. 50, No. 4, Winter 2000.

Schneider, James V. "Rations, Forage, and Ammunition," *Research Review,* Vol. 5, No. 2, June 1991.

Schoenberger, Dale. "Custer's Scouts," *Montana The Magazine of Western History,* Vol. 16, No. 2, Spring 1966 (Special Custer Edition).

———. "A Trooper With Custer: Augustus DeVoto's Account," *Montana The Magazine of Western History,* Vol. 40, No. 1, Winter 1990.

Scott, Douglas D. "'An Agreeable Sort When Sober': The Myth of Michael Madden," *Greasy Grass,* Vol. 25, May 2009.

———. "Playing Music on the Plains—7th Cavalry Band Member George A. Merritt," *Greasy Grass,* Vol. 20, May 2004.

Scott, Douglas D., and P. Willey. "Custer's Men Took Names to Their Graves," *Greasy Grass,* Vol. 12, May 1996.

Bibliography

Shields, L. R. "Reminiscences of a Railroad Builder." *North Dakota Historical Quarterly,* Vol. 1, No. 3, April 1927.
Slaughter, B. F. "Portions of the Diary of Dr. B. F. Slaughter, Dakota Territory," *North Dakota Historical Quarterly,* Vol. 1, No. 2, Jan. 1927.
Slaughter, Linda W. "Leaves from Northwestern History," in *Collections of the State Historical Society of North Dakota,* Vol. 1, 1906
Snow, Antelope Fred. "With Custer in the Black Hills," *North Dakota History,* Vol. 27, No. 4, Fall 1960.
Stewart, Edgar I. "Variations on a Minor Theme." *Montana Magazine of Western History,* Vol. 1, No. 3, July 1951.
Stone, Melville E. "Things Seen," *Colliers, The National Weekly* May 15, 1920.
Taunton, Francis B. "The Burial of Captain Myles Keogh," *The English Westerners' Brand Book* (London), Vol. 7, No. 3, April 1965.
———. "The Man Who Rode Comanche," *Sidelights of the Sioux Wars.* The English Westerners' Society (London), 1967.
———. "The Mystery of Miss Adams," *The Brand Book,* Vol. 28, No. 2, Summer 1991. English Westerners' Society, London.
Taylor, Joseph Henry. "Fort Berthold Agency in 1869," *North Dakota Historical Quarterly,* Vol. 4, No. 4, July 1930.
———. "Lonesome Charley," *North Dakota Historical Quarterly,* Vol. 4, No. 4, July 1930.
———. "Fort Totten Trail," *North Dakota Historical Quarterly,* Vol. 4, No. 4, July 1930.
Unrau, William E. "The Story of Fort Larned," *The Kansas Historical Quarterly,* Vol. 23, No. 3, Autumn 1957.
Van West, Carroll, ed. "Roughing It Up the Yellowstone to Wonderland: An Account of a Trip Through the Yellowstone Valley in 1878, by Colgate Hoyt." *Montana The Magazine of Western History,* Vol. 36, No. 2, Spring 1986.
Vaughn, J. W. "The Mark H. Kellogg Story," *The Westerners New York Posse Brand Book,* Vol. 7, No. 4, 1961.
———. "Dr. George E. Lord, Regimental Surgeon," *The Westerners New York Posse Brand Book,* Vol. 9, No. 2, 1962.
Watson, Elmo Scott. "Orlando Scott Goff, Pioneer Dakota Photographer," *North Dakota History,* Vol. 29, Nos. 1 and 2, Jan.–April 1962.
Welty, Raymond L. "The Frontier Army on the Missouri River, 1860–1870," *North Dakota Historical Quarterly,* Vol. 2, No. 2, Jan. 1928.
Will, George F. "Arikara Ceremonials," *North Dakota Historical Quarterly,* Vol. 4, No. 4, July 1930.
Willert, James. "The Billy Cross Interview," *Research Review,* Vol. 16, Dec. 1982.
Williams, Roger L. "The Story of William Baker," *Research Review,* Vol. 10, No. 2, June 1996.
Wright, Dana. "Military Trails in North Dakota," *North Dakota History,* Vol. 18, Nos. 2 and 3, April and July 1951.
Yates, Mrs. Annie Gibson Roberts. "Colonel George W. Yates," with notes by Brian C. Pohanka, *Research Review,* Vol. 15, No. 9, Sept. 1981.

www.ingramcontent.com/pod-product-compliance
Lightning Source LLC
Chambersburg PA
CBHW081756300426
44116CB00014B/2132